POETRY

INDEX

1912 - 1997

POETRY
INDEX

1912-1997

Compiled and with an Introduction by

Jayne Marek

CHICAGO

POETRY PRESS

A PUBLICATION OF
POETRY
THE MODERN POETRY ASSOCIATION

ISBN 1-881505-09-X

Publication of this book was made possible by a grant from
Lannan Foundation

DESIGNED BY CHAD GAYLE AND DREW SWINGER

CONTENTS

INTRODUCTION

I. Historical Perspectives

*"The history of poetry in America and of POETRY in America
are almost interchangeable, certainly inseparable."*
—*A. R. Ammons*

When the first issue of *Poetry, a Magazine of Verse* appeared in October 1912, there were few other outlets for poetry, and none that would offer financial and intellectual support for experimental work. At that time, journals seldom published longer poems or poetry in translation, let alone informed critical discussions about poetic craft, significant books, political and social issues affecting the art, and the relative merits of literary customs—especially those that would soon be challenged in the new magazine's pages.

The decision to include these topics in her journal arose directly from the founding editor's own experience. Despite a relatively high degree of success for her time, Harriet Monroe could find few markets for her poems. Traditional in training but unconventional in outlook, Monroe was an experienced writer and reviewer who had taught herself about current trends and voices in poetry. (She had also learned the value of active engagement on behalf of poets' rights when she won a lawsuit against the New York *World* for printing without permission her "Columbian Ode," written for the World's Columbian Exposition held in Chicago in 1892.) During a trip around the world in 1910, Monroe, an avid traveler, took time to meet with writers and purchased Ezra Pound's books *Personae* and *Exultations* from Elkin Mathews in London, and read them while riding the train across Siberia toward Beijing. When she returned to Chicago, the idea came to her to start a magazine specifically for poets.

The breadth of her own experience intensified Monroe's awareness that poetry was the least appreciated of the fine arts. She felt the irony of this situation particularly because she lived in a city that boasted a lively theater scene, superb architecture, an impressive Art Institute, and a world-class orchestra and opera company. Even serious fiction had gained attention through the Chicago *Dial* and the *Friday Literary Review* of the *Chicago Evening Post*, a paper for which Monroe occasionally wrote. She decided to create a forum in which poetry enjoyed the same status, the same kinds of social and financial support, as other arts. Poets were writing, but what they needed was an energetic, empathetic editor who was listening and who could reach—indeed, create—the right audience. She would be that editor.

From the beginning, Monroe also understood the necessity of blending financial and public support from "powerful citizens" with a populist agenda that would address the needs of poets and readers alike. With the encouragement of influential friends such as Hobart Chatfield-Taylor, she started her twofold campaign to raise money to underwrite a magazine of "the new verse" and to solicit manuscripts from writers of many styles. She knew that, to make a lasting difference for the condition of poetry and to attract the best efforts of many kinds of poets, her magazine would need to be dependable—and remunerative. The Editor soon had over a hundred Guarantors, who pledged support for the first five years, while poets at home and abroad responded enthusiastically to her circular announcing the new publication. Through her knowledge, determination, and devotion, Harriet Monroe had created the first real showcase for modern poetry in English, an achievement all the more impressive because of the magazine's persistence to this day.

Poetry's deliberate eclecticism encouraged the kinds of innovations that were once inconceivable but have become the hallmarks of twentieth-century poetry. Since *Poetry*'s debut, it has held preeminence among the countless other publications that its own success helped make possible, not least because of Monroe's democratic policy, announced in Volume I:

> The Open Door will be the policy of this magazine—may the great poet we are looking for never find it shut, or half-shut, against his ample genius! To this end the editors hope to keep free of entangling alliances with any single class or school. They desire to print the best English verse which is being written today, regardless of where, by whom, or under what theory of art it is written. Nor will the magazine promise to limit its editorial comments to one set of opinions.

As even the poet and gadfly Ezra Pound eventually admitted, *Poetry*'s eclecticism was an important factor in the magazine's survival. A more restrictive policy—as evidenced in many post-*Poetry* publications that boasted radical agendas, lived fast, and died young—would not have provided sufficient flexibility or wide audience appeal. *Poetry*'s catholicity has been a major factor in its continuation and a crucial aspect of its enshrinement as an "American Institution," to borrow T. S. Eliot's phrase. By printing writers as idiosyncratic as E. E. Cummings, Dylan Thomas, Louis Zukofsky, Diane Wakoski, and Charles Olson along with traditionalists and formalists such as Richard Wilbur, John Hollander, James Merrill, and Alfred Corn; by representing "Objectivists" as well as "Confessional" poets; and even by including the parodies of the "Spectrists" (albeit innocent of the imposters' purpose), *Poetry* embodied a diversity that ranges from the

wildflowers to the topiary of modern poetic craft. Yet in a sense the magazine's strongest achievement rests on its own longevity, and not simply in terms of its fiscal perseverance. Over time, in its pages *Poetry* has helped scores of excellent poets to develop and mature.

Throughout *Poetry*'s history, the goal, if not always the actuality, has been to publish "the best new work," especially poems "of more intimate and serious character than other magazines can afford to use" as part of "a public-spirited effort to gather together and enlarge a poet's public and increase his earnings," as Monroe stated in the circular she sent to prospective poet-contributors in 1911. "We promise to refuse nothing because it is too good, whatever be the nature of its excellence. We shall read with special interest poems of modern significance, but the most classic subject will not be declined if it reaches a high standard of quality."

Monroe's idealistic words notwithstanding, it is true that much of what was published in *Poetry* serves more as background, as evocation of particular cultural moments, than it does as demonstration of genius. Genius is here, certainly, in abundance; virtually every major figure of modern poetry in English is represented, some to great extent. But any high expectations that every page should shimmer with gold could not be met. Monroe herself understood the limitations of her eclecticism and "open door" policy, which admitted multifarious types of work, not all of which she personally liked but which she saw as vital to maintaining dialogue and development within the art. Monroe's standards provided grounds for criticism no matter from which direction the critical winds blew. In later decades, *Poetry*'s presentation of "classic subjects" at a time when formalism was under fire brought the magazine as much criticism as had its earlier support for imagism and free verse. Yet there is no doubt that *Poetry* in the aggregate provides a map of the art's twentieth-century terrain, including the lesser foothills from which arose the mighty mountains around which the rest of modern poetic literature orients itself.

In this way, the staggering amount of work that *Poetry* has published in 1,020 issues over eighty-five years reflects broader tendencies at work in English-language poetry. Most of the contributors listed in this Index are obscure. But, as Daryl Hine pointed out in his introduction to *The POETRY Anthology, 1912-1977*, many figures whose works seem dull or formulaic now were well-known among their contemporaries; whereas the ability to comprehend the surpassing quality of a Wallace Stevens, a Marianne Moore, or a John Ashbery requires the benefit of hindsight. But the magazine may justly pride itself that so many of its editors' gambles paid off, while the general level of craftmanship has remained consistently high. Indeed, one of the magazine's great strengths, as Carolyn Kizer has remarked, is that "*Poetry* has never lost sight of its standards."

One of *Poetry*'s notable contributions to modern letters is its institution of special issues, which have included numbers devoted to individual authors, issues on war or anti-war poetry, a number focused on university writing workshops, miscellanies of translations, and issues on foreign-language poetry and poetics. "First Appearances" issues, which began with one such issue in 1961, eventually became a regular feature that continued until 1984. Since then, between a quarter and a third of the poets published in *Poetry* during the course of a year have been new to its pages; often their contributions mark their first appearances in print anywhere. The revolution in awareness encouraged by *Poetry*'s special issues on foreign poetry remains as profound (and pragmatic) as was Monroe's determination to pay real money for poems. If, before 1912, publishing poetry was a chancy venture that few cared to risk, publishing foreign poetry was worse—with the possible exception of classics, which might find a home in university courses and a few private libraries. At first, by offering in its pages selections by Rabindranath Tagore (thanks to the assiduity of Ezra Pound as "Foreign Correspondent") and occasional poems from the French, Spanish, and Chinese, and later by providing special issues with informative survey articles on poetry from many nations and languages and on the politics and aesthetics of translation, *Poetry* cultivated ground of immense significance: poets have often been more influenced by international developments than by work in English.

Over the decades, *Poetry* has offered an unparalleled introduction to the world's wealth of modern poetic art, printing work from Central and South America, Belgium, Canada, China, Finland, France, Germany, India, Japan, Korea, Russia, and Ukraine. The roster of illustrious foreign poets who have appeared in this little magazine that was once scorned by East Coast critics as "provincial" includes Nobel Prize winners Tagore, St.-John Perse, W. B. Yeats, Juan Ramón Jiménez, Pablo Neruda, Gabriela Mistral, Salvatore Quasimodo, Jorge Luis Borges, George Seferis, Eugenio Montale, Odysseus Elytis, and Seamus Heaney. Given a special boost under the editorship of Karl Shapiro in the early 1950s, the tradition of publishing foreign poets has continued to be a fundamental aspect of *Poetry*'s importance, with recent decades featuring special issues or sections on contemporary poetry from Greece, Italy, Great Britain, Ireland, and Australia.

Monroe's encompassing vision for her magazine included using well-informed critical exchange as a means of addressing directly, if not educating, the "great audiences" she expected to reach. From the earliest years, when Monroe and her first co-editor, Alice Corbin Henderson, dissected the poetry that came in over the transom, *Poetry* provided book reviews and essays examining poetic traditions and individual accomplishments with sharp yet sympathetic eyes. (And they did not hesitate to print pieces that

took issue with *Poetry*'s contents.) Monroe's initial intention of providing a limited, if regular, prose forum to accompany the poems gradually changed to accommodate lengthier comments, both in formal articles and in reviews. A partial listing of prose contributors indicates the quality and diversity of the criticism *Poetry* has presented over the decades: W. H. Auden, John Berryman, R. P. Blackmur, Kenneth Burke, Malcolm Cowley, T. S. Eliot, William Empson, Dudley Fitts, Robert Fitzgerald, Ford Madox Ford, Wallace Fowlie, Sandra M. Gilbert, John Hollander, Richard Howard, Hugh Kenner, Archibald MacLeish, J. D. McClatchy, Robert Pinsky, Ezra Pound, John Crowe Ransom, M. L. Rosenthal, Delmore Schwartz, Stephen Spender, Allen Tate, Mona Van Duyn, Helen Vendler, Robert Penn Warren, Richard Wilbur, and Yvor Winters.

Under the editorships of Morton Dauwen Zabel and George Dillon, the "News Notes" at the back of the magazine took on a life of their own. The heyday of prose in *Poetry* was reached in the late 1940s, when the poetry was sometimes dwarfed by pages upon pages of articles and reviews that, even so, were not enough: the editorial staff, led by Dillon and Hayden Carruth, went so far as to publish separate pamphlets as "critical supplements." One such spinoff (William Elton's *A Glossary of the New Criticism*) achieved notable success, while the pamphlet addressing Ezra Pound's receipt of the 1949 Bollingen Prize achieved what might better be termed notoriety. This prose proliferation, not surprisingly, coincided with the ascendance of the New Criticism, so that in a sense *Poetry* embodied the spirit of this academic movement as it increased critical attention on a canon of closely-read texts.

To appreciate the magazine's achievement, it is also important to understand *Poetry*'s frequent financial struggles. After the relative security of the first five years, which Monroe had ensured by obtaining the pledges of local guarantors, the magazine faced continual crises. At several points during Monroe's editorship, it seemed that the magazine might fold. Monroe herself thought *Poetry* would be unable to continue without her. When she died in 1936—at age 75, while climbing in the Andes to Machu Picchu—and it was announced that the magazine would close down, *Poetry*'s readers and supporters protested, and contributed enough money to enable the publication to continue. In 1941, the Modern Poetry Association was formed as a not-for-profit organization to provide consistent support for the magazine.

The difficulties of blending idealistic visions with pragmatic results, as is clear to readers of *Poetry*'s history, offer all the more reason to applaud the magazine's persistence through the lean years. In the 1950s and '60s, Editor

Henry Rago exercised his considerable skills in raising funds for the magazine, as Joseph Parisi recounted in his article, "The Care and Funding of Pegasus" (*TriQuarterly*, Fall 1978). In the twenty years since that essay appeared, the magazine's fiscal condition, while never completely secure, has stabilized. Grants providing for allied educational projects have always been a feature of the magazine's history, and under Parisi these have grown to include symposia and public programs in addition to the prestigious Poetry Day reading series, inaugurated by Robert Frost in 1955. *Poetry*-The Modern Poetry Association also produced the "Poets in Person" audio series, broadcast on public radio and used in library discussion groups throughout the country.

In accord with Monroe's original aim to recognize poets, like other artists, with monetary rewards, several prizes were established for work appearing in the magazine, beginning with the Levinson Prize in 1914. Other prizes have been added over the years, including the Ruth Lilly Poetry Prize, one of the major awards to poets in the United States, and two annual Lilly Fellowships, offered to undergraduate and graduate student poets. The number of awards and the richness of *Poetry*'s educational efforts seem natural outgrowths of Monroe's fundamental intentions, as well as of the particular strengths and interests of her successors.

Responding to the ever-evolving conditions of poetry, and to aesthetic and cultural changes generally, later editors have maintained the tradition of excellence Monroe established, while placing the stamp of their individual judgments and tastes upon the magazine. In their efforts, they have had the support of many hands, as the lists of *Poetry* personnel below indicate. Several staff members and advisors served for decades, often with little or no pay. The editors and their assistants also emulated the founder's example by offering authors, well known and aspiring alike, individual attention through notes of encouragement and letters of detailed, practical advice, as the *Poetry* correspondence files amply attest. Such personal concern is another reason the magazine has not only earned respect but elicited remarkable loyalty and, for an "Institution," extraordinary affection, as well.

II: Format of the Index

This Index is intended to be a tool that is attractive as well as useful, providing easy and thorough guidance into the heart of the most important little magazine of all. Serious readers and scholars alike have long known about the riches included in the pages of *Poetry*, which during the magazine's eighty-five years of continuous publication have included virtually the entire range of achievement and critical exchange in twentieth-century poetry. However, gaining access to that wealth often presented problems. The semiannual indexes were cumbersome to use and sometimes suffered from errors or omissions, as did the earlier cumulative indexes. Further, the indexing formats used for individual issues and volumes changed over time, and often could not meet the requirements of *Poetry*'s extensive audience of readers and researchers. Finding information about translators, editors of books reviewed, discussions of influential figures not cited in article titles, and significant addenda on misprints and source notes required readers to spend hours scanning prose sections and back matter. While there is much to be said for the serendipitous discoveries such a hunt may provide—anecdotes, complaints, gems of wit, and tidbits of gossip that bring the subjects alive—researchers need a tool that works efficiently while indicating the many pleasures of the texts.

This Index is intended to provide numerous access points not only to the poetry but also to the prose sections of the magazine, as well as to correct omissions from earlier compilations and semiannual indexes. The basic structure of the 1963 index volume has been retained, wherein the author's name is followed by entries categorized under six rubrics:

Poems
Translations
Articles
Reviews (the author's reviews of others' books)
Books Reviewed (reviews written about the author's books)
Articles About

Volume and page numbers appear at the end of the first full item of each entry. Some items require extra lines in order to accommodate all pertinent information (including bracketed cross-references) before the volume and page numbers are given. The first line of an entry may simply provide the title or first line in a set of poems or books reviewed. Users of this book should refer to the *Key to Issues* at the end of the Index, to identify individual numbers in volumes by year and month of publication.

Over the years, changes in *Poetry*'s house style have led to discrepancies that required a more regularized format. At the head of the list is the prob-

lem of alphabetizing authors' names—not as straightforward a question as it may seem. For example, Chinese and Japanese names appearing in past decades might or might not have been alphabetized under the presumption that the final element of the name is a surname. Transliterations of names from non-Roman alphabets might be spelled in any of several ways over a number of years. Authors with double surnames might appear alphabetized under the first surname in one instance, the second surname in another. Given such inconsistencies, the conventions of naming in this Index represent a compromise:

Chinese names (such as Su Shih) are alphabetized without inversion—in this case "Su" being placed as the equivalent to an Anglophone surname—and with a cross-reference provided for readers looking under "Sh."

Japanese names, on the other hand, are alphabetized in the same way as Anglophone names, with the final element being treated as a surname.

Spanish names and some other **doubled surnames** are alphabetized according to the first surname in the sequence—Jose Santos Chocano appears under "Sa," for instance, and T. Sturge Moore under "St," again with cross-references provided. The cross-references should accommodate most cases where the order of a poet's names might create confusion. In some cases, distinctions between given names and surnames could not be determined, so an entry will appear under the letter of the surname as deduced from the form in which the name was originally or most often printed, as is the case with Japanese names.

Writers who published under more than one name are listed under the name used most commonly, with appropriate cross-references. Women who published under both their maiden and married names, for instance, will have their works consolidated, as in the case of Alice Corbin Henderson. Henderson continued to publish her poetry under the name "Alice Corbin" and her prose under "Alice Corbin Henderson," a practice which some other writers have followed. In this Index, all entries by "Alice Corbin," "Alice Corbin Henderson," and "A. C. H." appear under "Henderson, Alice Corbin."

Pseudonyms are included in brackets and are cross-referenced. Persons who use pseudonyms for some of their writings, or whose names have changed substantially during the course of their writing lives (as in the case of those taking religious orders), will have two sets of entries, in part to preserve any distinctions the poet may have intended to make between the two "identities." On ocassion, when a note of attribution or other information

clarifies the gender of an ambiguous name, gender has been indicated. Some hyphenated names (M. D. Herter-Norton) appeared in both hyphenated and non-hyphenated forms over many years, and generally this Index will follow the most frequent usage. **Anonymous** here as elsewhere offers a home for entries which would otherwise have none.

Misspellings, variant spellings, and errors in names or titles have been corrected and noted whenever possible. The use of **initials**, however, presented a different problem. Often the authorship of a piece printed under initials could be deduced from the volume's masthead or from contributors' notes, but there are exceptions which readers should bear in mind. For instance, both Amy Lowell and Agnes Lee wrote reviews for the magazine during the same general time period, and many pieces appeared under the initials "A. L." Thus the questionable reviews are listed under "A. L.," with a "See also" cross-reference after Lowell's and Lee's names. Another example involves a review under the initials "P. D." which appeared years before Peter De Vries began to write regularly for the journal. In this case, the review has been indexed under "P. D.," while other reviews under those initials which appeared during De Vries's years of association with the magazine have been put in De Vries's entry. A third type of problem occurs when "K. M. B." reviews a book in an issue in which "Kate Meldram Buss" has correspondence—Buss as reviewer can be assumed but cannot be verified, for one thing because "Meldram" is a misprint of "Neldram." The possibility of such confusion has resulted in some entries being made solely under initials. *Readers may therefore want to check whether any entries have been made under the initials of their targeted authors, bearing in mind that safe assumptions have been made, but not all assumptions are equally safe.*

Simple titles like "Poem" and "Song" are followed by the poem's opening words or a bracketed note. In the case of untitled pieces, as with many by Rabindranath Tagore or E. E. Cummings, first lines are included in parentheses. Prize poems, which were sometimes reprinted in the issues announcing the awards, are not listed separately, although a few inadvertent duplications may exist. **Group titles or subtitles** may or may not be used. If all subtitles in a complete set could be inferred from the main title (as in the apocryphal example "The House," which might have subtitles such as "The Door," "The Window," "The Front Bedroom," etc.), the subtitles are not included. Group titles are generally omitted if the group title is also the title of an individual poem in the set. In some cases for which an issue's table of contents lists only a group title, individual poem titles are given in this Index in order to distinguish between sets with similar titles.

Books reviewed as a group are all listed according to the first page of the review, although the discussion of a particular item may occur several pages later. The same situation holds true for some translations of longer poems, where the poem appears first in its original language and subsequently in its English version. Consecutive reviews by the same reviewer that have separate titles or that are interrupted by other reviews are generally listed separately. Some essays and articles are treated as book reviews, if all the publishing information appropriate to a review has been included.

This particular Index offers an unprecedented spectrum of opportunities for browsers and scholars alike. The most notable change is the vast expansion of entries under the rubric "Articles About." Earlier indexes to *Poetry* were not fully reliable, since they had not been checked against the actual pages of the issues. Therefore, occasional mistakes, multiplied over the course of decades and abetted by changes in house styles and in editorial preferences, mandated both formal regularization and exhaustive cross-checking. The wealth of information—biographical, anecdotal, and critical—contained in the articles and book reviews lay largely unmapped; unless a subject's name appeared in a title, even an in-depth discussion would not be referenced to her or his name. This Index allows readers and researchers quickly to discover scores of new entries that trace the arcs and parabolas of influence in the prose comments in *Poetry*. Such entries are crucial to any consideration of the significance of figures such as W. H. Auden and T. S. Eliot, who published relatively few poems in *Poetry* but whose names are continually invoked in articles and reviews. "Articles About" entries document aspects of literary reputation and critical response that would go wholly undetected if one consulted only "Poems" or "Books Reviewed."

Cross-references as "Articles About" have been made when there is a statement or context of more than two sentences that offers information about a subject's biography, oeuvre, or critical reputation. Names that have been dropped merely for epigrammatic, rather than analytic, purposes, or names of persons who are quoted only for a sentence or two and who are not being analyzed or characterized with background information, are not included. Long or significant quotations are cross-referenced to their authors or subjects. I have erred on the side of inclusion, perhaps to the frustration of some searchers who prefer not to have to read additional paragraphs. However, for many authors the rubric "Articles About" provides the only way to gain access to information that can help determine these authors' relative importance within discussions of poetry and critical theory.

There are very few cross-references according to subject matter; readers will need to use authors' names. There is no way to cross-reference items

like *The Sacco-Vanzetti Anthology of Verse*, *The Grub Street Book of Verse*, or the anthology *The Spirit of St. Louis* (32:96), since there are no editors listed, or the persons or objects mentioned in the books' titles may have had nothing to do with the poetry therein. In general, the Index omits the names of writers of forewords and introductions of books reviewed, unless there is no author or editor listed.

Articles discussing general topics, such as "poetic drama," are not cross-referenced for all the individuals who may be mentioned in passing. For articles treating, say, a national poetry, a cross-reference will be made even if the mention is brief. For example, in volume 61, F. C. Weiskopf's article on "Serbian Poetry" does not include any extended discussion of poets, but does mention two names (V. S. Karadjich and P. P. Nyegosh) which are cross-referenced, to help lead students of Serbian poetry to the article.

Readers of the magazine are encouraged to consult the "News Notes" and contributors' notes at the end of most issues of *Poetry*. These sections contain a miscellany of information about poets, poems, reviewers and critics, errata and misprints, authors' comments about terminology and sources, and prizes and awards, not to mention arguments and clarifications, all of which add to *Poetry*'s historic value as a forum for discussing modern poetics. Reading the contributors' notes in the magazine's earlier decades along with the numbers may slightly blur one's focus, since a contributor's note sometimes appeared in the issue *before* the contribution, very likely as the result of having the item (usually a single poem) bumped by page make-up at the last moment. Notices of misprints are included in this Index (under "Articles About") only when significant portions of a work were omitted, altered, or transposed. Readers should check the first and last pages of several issues subsequent to the one in which a misprint is suspected.

A few final notes about this Index and *Poetry* itself deserve mention. Readers interested in the history of "little magazines" in particular should consult the detailed discussions of "Recent Magazines" written by Harriet Monroe, Morton Dauwen Zabel, and William Van O'Connor. In these discussions—too minutely particular to bear exhaustive cross-referencing—are summarized editorials, editors' policies, trends, and opinions. Scholars suspicious that *Poetry* may have doffed its hat to, or taken a swipe at, any particular target should scan the appropriate years' offerings.

Considerable changes in format and contents have occurred since Monroe's tenure, and some of the magazine's innovations, such as use of photographs in the late 1940s, have been laid aside. Most notable in terms of indexing are the changes in typography and design that took place during the late 1940s and early 1950s, as the delicate fonts and hanging indents

of *Poetry*'s original indexing format turned into blocks of boldface text squeezed tightly into double columns that are as unnecessarily hard to read as some of the prose sections printed in that time period. During the late 1950s, Henry Rago provided an exponential improvement in readability through the introduction of the elegant typography of Greer Allen that continues in use, with further refinements, to this day.

The massive redundancy of this Index has proven to be a necessary adjunct to its completeness. The immense amounts of time required to make entries, check, and recheck them were sometimes ameliorated by the appearance of long articles that were not in fact about anyone and thus required no cross-references. However, the time factor was more often increased by some reviewers' habits of including twenty or more books for review (necessitating entries and cross-checks for authors, editors, translators, and poets under discussion) while the prose spent most of its time on polemic, passing off the books with a sentence or so apiece. Finer pleasures were to be found in reading the poems and prose themselves.

The scores of histories and critical surveys that have been written about *Poetry* often indicate the magazine's importance to modern literature by pointing to the same well-known selections: H. D.'s "Hermes of the Ways," as graceful and mysterious as when it first appeared. Ezra Pound's "To Whistler, American," with its famous epithet. Carl Sandburg's "Chicago," the opening lines of which every school child used to know. And, of course, T. S. Eliot's "The Love Song of J. Alfred Prufrock," perhaps the most influential poem of the twentieth century. Or Joyce Kilmer's "Trees," a poem equally enduring in the public consciousness, but for different reasons.

There is more, much more. Harriet Monroe's astonishingly ambitious vision has been fulfilled, one hundred and seventy times over. The poet Billy Collins provides a fitting postscript:

> As we approach the strangely rounded year of 2000, the deep history of *Poetry* begins to take on new significance. If we mark the true beginning of the twentieth century at the outbreak of the first World War, then *Poetry* can be said to have virtually covered the century and thus the beginnings and the full development of modernist and even post-modernist poetry. A complete index of the magazine provides us with not only a valuable research tool but with a kind of flip-book in which we can observe the dramatic shape-shiftings of twentieth-century poetry. More than a magazine, *Poetry* is a log of the good ship Poetry, a way of recording its amazing voyage.

—JAYNE MAREK

EDITORSHIPS

HARRIET MONROE
October 1912–September 1936

Editorial Staff: Emanuel Carnevali, George H. Dillon, Alice Corbin Henderson, Helen Hoyt, Jessica Nelson North, Ezra Pound, Marion Strobel, Eunice Tietjens, Morton Dauwen Zabel

Support Staff: Mila Straub, Margery Swett, Geraldine Udell, Marianna Von Moltke

Advisors: William T. Abbott, Aksel K. Bodholdt, Percy H. Boynton, H. C. Chatfield-Taylor, George Dillon, Henry B. Fuller, Charles H. Hamill, Arthur T. Leonard, Robert Morss Lovett, Jessica Nelson North, Lew Sarett, Marion Strobel, Eunice Tietjens, Thornton Wilder, Edith Wyatt

MORTON DAUWEN ZABEL
October 1936–October 1937

Editorial Staff: Jessica Nelson North

Support Staff: Geraldine Udell

Advisors: Percy H. Boynton, George Dillon, Charles H. Hamill, Arthur T. Leonard, Robert Morss Lovett, Lew Sarett, Eunice Tietjens, Thornton Wilder

GEORGE DILLON
November 1937–August 1942

Editorial Staff: Peter De Vries, Jessica Nelson North

Support Staff: Amy Bonner, Margedant Peters, Geraldine Udell

Advisors: Percy H. Boynton, Charles H. Hamill, Arthur T. Leonard, Robert Morss Lovett, Jessica Nelson North, Lew Sarett, Eunice Tietjens, Thornton Wilder

GROUP EDITORSHIP
September 1942–April 1949

Editors: Peter De Vries, George Dillon, John Frederick Nims, Jessica Nelson North, Margedant Peters, Marion Strobel

Editorial Staff: Hayden Carruth, Katinka Loeser, John Frederick Nims, Margedant Peters, Marion Strobel

Support Staff: Rufus Beyle, Amy Bonner, Vladimir Dupré, J. M. Eichelberger, Marlys Johnston, Herbert Kalk, John Nerber, Margedant Peters, Julia Siebel, Geraldine Udell

Advisors: Amy Bonner, Julia Bowe, Percy H. Boynton, J. V. Cunningham, Peter De Vries, George Dillon, Thomas C. Lea, Arthur T. Leonard, Katinka Loeser, Robert Morss Lovett, William S. Monroe, John Frederick Nims, Jessica Nelson North, Margedant Peters, Lew Sarett, Marion Strobel, Eunice Tietjens, Thornton Wilder

HAYDEN CARRUTH
May 1949–January 1950

Support Staff: J. M. Eichelberger, Marlys Johnston, Herbert Kalk, John Nerber, Julia Siebel, Geraldine Udell

Advisors: Amy Bonner, Julia Bowe, J. V. Cunningham, George Dillon, Thomas C. Lea, Arthur T. Leonard, Robert Morss Lovett, William S. Monroe, John Frederick Nims, Jessica Nelson North, Margedant Peters, Lew Sarett, Marion Strobel, Thornton Wilder

KARL SHAPIRO
March 1950–September 1955

Editorial Staff: Isabella Gardner, Nicholas Joost, Robert Mueller, Henry Rago, Joseph Wiley

Support Staff: Jane Broeksmit, Gleah Brown, Margaret Cunningham, Margaret Danner, Harold E. Donohue, J. M. Eichelberger, Joan Farwell, Barbara Harris, Marlys Johnston, Nicholas Joost, Herbert Kalk, Madeleine Kilpatrick, Bertha Mayer, Patricia McEnerney, Cornelia McNamara, Charlotte Miller, Robert Mueller, Sue Neil, John Nerber, Evalyn Shapiro, Julia Siebel, Geraldine Udell, Joseph Wiley, Harry Yates

Advisors: Amy Bonner, Julia Bowe, J. V. Cunningham, George Dillon, Wallace Fowlie, Hugh Kenner, Thomas C. Lea, Arthur T. Leonard, Robert Morss Lovett, William S. Monroe, John Frederick Nims, Jessica Nelson North, Margedant Peters, Lew Sarett, Marion Strobel, Thornton Wilder

HENRY RAGO
October 1955–June 1969

Editorial Staff: Frederick Bock, Margaret Danner, Daryl Hine, Robert Mueller, John Frederick Nims, Joseph Wiley

Support Staff: Grace Carone, Flora Grippo, Helen Lothrop, Patricia McEnerney, Julie McLauchlin, Donald H. Merwin, Elizabeth Wright

Advisors: George Dillon, Wallace Fowlie, Hugh Kenner, Jessica Nelson North, Marion Strobel

DARYL HINE
July 1969–December 1977

Editorial Staff: Michael Mesic, Joseph Parisi, Joseph Wiley

Support Staff: Rob Colby [Allen], Nadine Cummings, Helen Lothrop Klaviter

Advisors: Virgil Burnett, Wallace Fowlie, Hugh Kenner, Sally Spector, R. Williams

JOHN FREDERICK NIMS
January 1978–August 1983

Editorial Staff: Joseph Parisi

Support Staff: Nadine Cummings, Helen Lothrop Klaviter

JOSEPH PARISI
September 1983–

Editorial staff: Jim Elledge, Davis McCombs, Drew Swinger, Stephen Young

Support Staff: Nadine Cummings, William D. Falloon, Chad Gayle, Helen Lothrop Klaviter, Michael Blaise Kong, Allison Lemieux, Davis McCombs, Douglas Milam, Drew Swinger, Rex Wilder, Stephen Young

WITH TITLES AND DATES OF SERVICE

This list is drawn from the title pages of each volume of the magazine. Staff whose names were not included on a semi-annual index masthead are not listed here. Dates of service may not accurately reflect involvement with day-to-day operations, since criteria for credit on the masthead have varied; several staff members served for months or years before being listed. Guest editors for special issues are not included.

Abbott, William T. Administration/Administrative Committee, 1912-1922

Allen [see Colby]

Beyle, Rufus Research, 1948-1949

Bock, Frederick Assistant Editor, 1955-1960

Bodholdt, Aksel K. Administrative Committee, 1922-1930

Bonner, Amy Eastern Business Representative, 1938-1948; Advisory Committee, 1948-1950

Bowe, Julia Administrative Committee, 1947-1950

Boynton, Percy H. Associate Committee of The University of Chicago, 1935-1939; Associate Committee, 1939-1946

Broeksmit, Jane Secretary, 1950-1951

Brown, Gleah Editorial Assistant, 1953-1955

Burnett, Virgil Art Director, 1969-1974

Carnevali, Emanuel Associate Editor, 1919-1920

Carone, Grace Staff Assistant, 1965-1969

Carruth, Hayden Associate Editor, 1948-1949; Editor, 1949-1950

Chatfield-Taylor, H. C. Advisory Committee, 1912-1920

Colby, Rob Assistant Editor, 1972-1973

Cummings, Nadine Circulation Manager, 1970-1989

Cunningham, J. V. Editorial Board, 1949-1950

Cunningham, Margaret [see Danner]

Danner, Margaret Editorial Assistant, 1952-1955; Assistant Editor, 1955-1956

De Vries, Peter Associate Editor, 1938-1942; Editor, 1942-1946; Contributing Editor, 1946-1947

Dillon, George [H.] Associate Editor, 1925-1927; Advisory Committee, 1928-1937; Editor, 1937-1942; Advisory Committee, 1942-1946; Editor, 1946-1949; Advisory Committee Chairman, 1949-1950; Advisory Editor, 1953-1954; Advisory Committee, 1954-1962

Donohue, Harold E. Business Manager, 1952

Dupré, Vladimir Advertising, 1947-1949

Eichelberger, J. M. Advertising, 1949-1950

Elledge, Jim Assistant Editor, 1984-1988

Falloon, William D. Editorial Assistant, 1989-1996

Farwell, Joan Editorial Assistant, 1951; Secretary, 1951-1952; Editorial Assistant, 1953-1954

Fowlie, Wallace Advisory Editor, 1950-1954; Contributing Editor, 1954-1955; Foreign Editor, 1955-1969

Fuller, Henry B. Advisory Committee, 1912-1929

Gardner, Isabella Assistant Editor, 1952-1953; Associate Editor, 1953-1955

Gayle, Chad Assistant Editor, 1996-1997

Grippo, Flora Staff Assistant, 1965-1968

Hamill, Charles H. Administration/Administrative Committee, 1912-1941

Harris, Barbara Editorial Assistant, 1951

Henderson, Alice Corbin Associate Editor, 1913-1922

Hine, Daryl Visiting Editor, 1968-1969; Editor, 1969-1977

Hoyt, Helen Associate Editor, 1918-1919

Johnston, Marlys Subscription Manager, 1948-1950

Joost, Nicholas Editorial Assistant, 1952; Assistant Editor, 1952-1953; Associate Editor, 1953; Acting Editor, 1953-1954; Associate Editor, 1954

Kalk, Herbert Circulation, 1948-1950

Kenner, Hugh Contributing Editor, 1954-1969

Kilpatrick, Madeleine Editorial Assistant, 1951

Klaviter, Helen Lothrop Managing Editor, 1968-1969, 1976-1996; Business and Projects Manager, 1996-

Kong, Michael Blaise Editorial Assistant, 1992-1994

Lea, Thomas C. Administrative Committee, 1947-1950

Lemieux, Allison Editorial Assistant, 1997-

Leonard, Arthur T. Administrative Committee, 1930-1941; Administrative Chairman, 1941-1946; Administrative Committee, 1947-1950

Loeser, Katinka Associate Editor, 1943-1946; Contributing Editor, 1946-1947

Lothrop [see Klaviter]

Lovett, Robert Morss Associate Committee of The University of Chicago, 1935-1939; Associate Committee, 1939-1947; Advisory Committee, 1947-1950

Mayer, Bertha Secretary, 1952-1953

McCombs, Davis Editorial Assistant, 1995-1996

McEnerney, Patricia Secretary, 1955-1956

McLauchlin, Julie Assistant to the Editor, 1965-1966

McNamara, Cornelia Editorial Assistant, 1951-1952

Merwin, Donald H. Business Manager, 1965-1966

Mesic, Michael Associate Editor, 1970-1976

Milam, Douglas Editorial Assistant, 1997-

Miller, Charlotte Secretary, 1954-1955

Monroe, Harriet Editor, 1912-1936

Monroe, William S. Associate/Administrative Committee, 1947-1950

Mueller, Robert Editorial Assistant, 1952-1953; Assistant Editor, 1953-1960; Associate Editor, 1960-1965

Neil, Sue Editorial Assistant, 1953; Secretary, 1953-1954

Nerber, John New York Representative, 1949-1950

Nims, John Frederick Editor, 1946-1948; Editor of Supplement, 1948; Advisory Committee, 1948-1949; Editorial Board, 1949-1950; Visiting Editor, 1960-1961; Editor, 1978-1983

North, Jessica Nelson Associate Editor, 1927-1929; Editor, 1929; Advisory Committee, 1929-1936; Associate Editor, 1936-1938; Advisory Committee, 1938-1942; Editor, 1942-1943; Advisory Committee, 1943-1946; Contributing Editor, 1946-1947; Advisory Committee, 1947-1950; Advisory Editor, 1953-1954; Advisory Committee, 1954-1962

Parisi, Joseph Associate Editor, 1976-1983; Acting Editor, 1983-1985; Editor, 1985-

Peters, Margedant Subscription Manager, 1940-1943; Associate Editor, 1943-1946; Editor, 1946-1947; Contributing Editor, 1947; Advisory Committee, 1947-1950

Pound, Ezra Foreign Correspondent, 1912-1919

Rago, Henry Acting Editor, 1955; Editor, 1955-1969

Sarett, Lew Advisory Committee, 1921-1946; Associate Committee, 1946-1947; Advisory Committee, 1947-1950

Shapiro, Evalyn Managing Editor, 1950-1952

Shapiro, Karl Editor, 1950-1955

Siebel, Julia Editorial Assistant, 1948-1950

Spector, Sally Art Director, 1975-1976

Straub, Mila Business Manager, 1920-1922

Strobel, Marion Associate Editor, 1920-1925; Advisory Committee, 1926-1927; Associate Editor, 1942-1943; Editor, 1943-1949; Editorial Board, 1949-1950; Advisory Editor, 1953-1954; Advisory Committee, 1954-1962

Swett, Margery Business Manager, 1922-1925

Swinger, Drew [Andrew] Editorial Assistant, 1994; Assistant Editor, 1994-1995, 1996-1997

Tietjens, Eunice Associate Editor, 1916-1917; Advisory Committee, 1919-1944

Udell, Geraldine Business Manager, 1925-1929, 1930-1950

Von Moltke, Marianna Business Manager, 1929-1930

Wilder, Rex Editorial Assistant, 1988-1994

Wilder, Thornton Associate Committee of The University of Chicago, 1935-1939; Associate Committee, 1939-1947; Advisory Committee, 1947-1950

Wiley, Joseph Editorial Assistant, 1952-1953; Assistant Editor, 1953-1960; Associate Editor, 1960-1975

Williams, R. [Robert] Art Director, 1973-1975

Wright, Elizabeth Research Assistant/Editor, 1955-1966

Wyatt, Edith Advisory Committee, 1912-1919

Yates, Harry Advertising Manager, 1955

Young, Stephen Editorial Assistant, 1988; Assistant Editor, 1988-1989; Associate Editor, 1989-1996; Senior Editor, 1996-

Zabel, Morton Dauwen Associate Editor, 1929-1936; Editor, 1934-1935; Editor, 1936-1937

—Compiled by Helen Lothrop Klaviter

INDEX

"A. B."
ARTICLES
Correspondence:
Modern Poetry at the U. of C.   17   56

"A. C. H."
[See HENDERSON, ALICE CORBIN]

"A. D. F."
[See FICKE, ARTHUR DAVISON]

"AE"
[Pseud. of RUSSELL,
GEORGE WILLIAM]
BOOKS REVIEWED
Collected Poems   7   154
Vale and Other Poems   38   276
Song and Its Fountains   42   177
Selected Poems   48   290

ARTICLES ABOUT
[Note]   32   116
A Letter from Ireland,
by Joseph M. Hone   45   332
AE, by Jessica Nelson North   46   334
Correspondence from Charlotte Arthur   47   174

"A. F."
[See LEE, AGNES
(AGNES LEE FREER)]

"A. K."
[See KREYMBORG, ALFRED]

"A. L."
[See also LEE, AGNES,
or LOWELL, AMY]
REVIEWS
The Lonely Dancer, and Other Poems,
by Richard Le Gallienne   4   30
Merchants from Cathay,
by William Rose Benét
The Sister of the Wind,
by Grace Fallow Norton   5   87
Six French Poets, by Amy Lowell   7   202

"A. L. F."
[See LEE, AGNES
(AGNES LEE FREER)]

"A. N."
POEMS
Out of the Dark   16   135

"A. Y. W."
REVIEWS
The Solitary,
by James Oppenheim   16   49

AAEN, PAUL
POEMS
All Gargoyle   81   242

AARON, DANIEL
BOOKS REVIEWED
Emerson: A Modern Anthology
(Ed. with Alfred Kazin)   96   382

Shelburne Essays on American Literature,
by Paul Elmer More (Ed.)   104   369

AARON, JONATHAN
POEMS
Warsaw to Paris   104   234
Essential Company   122   67
The Blindfold

BOOKS REVIEWED
Second Sight   143   163

ABBE, GEORGE
POEMS
Never Follow   49   16
Departure
Open High Windows
Alder Red   59   136
Little We Knew
Seagull City
New York Subway   63   72
The Black Panther After Every War
Line-Plunger   84   204

I

The Passer
Half-Back in the Open
The Bridge — 88 372

BOOKS REVIEWED
Wait for These Things — 57 332
Letter Home — 65 154
Bird in the Mulberry — 88 52
Collected Poems — 100 404

ABBOTT, CHARLES DAVID
ARTICLES
Poetry in the Making
[Stephen Spender] — 55 258
Rev. of *Poets at Work*,
by W. H. Auden, Karl Shapiro,
Rudolf Arnheim, and
Donald A. Stauffer — 72 311

ABBOTT, CLAUDE COLLEER
BOOKS REVIEWED
*Further Letters
of Gerard Manley Hopkins* (Ed.) — 53 150
Poems and Plays,
by Gordon Bottomley (Ed.) — 86 363
*Further Letters
of Gerard Manley Hopkins*,
2nd ed. (Ed.) — 92 113

ARTICLES ABOUT
Hopkins in His Letters,
by M. D. Zabel — 46 210

ABEL, DARREL
REVIEWS
Domination of June,
by David Cornel De Jong — 66 45
Flight into Darkness,
by Ralph Gustafson — 66 100

ABEL, LIONEL
POEMS
The Midwives of History — 56 76
Sign
Death at Lenin's Tomb

REVIEWS
The Man Coming Toward You,
by Oscar Williams — 56 214

BOOKS REVIEWED
Some Poems of Rimbaud (Tr.) — 56 95
Playbook: Five Plays for a New Theater
(With Robert Hivnor, Junjo Kinoshita,
James Merrill, and I. A. Richards) — 89 253

ABER, LOUREINE
POEMS
From Laurel Wreaths — 14 189
The Fallen
The Soldier to Helen
My Friend
Farewell
From City Lanes — 19 10
City Wed
If
Elevator Man
Bereft
Old Man
Girl
Death
Trees — 23 302
Listen to the Years Flying
Kinship
Your Arms
Stars on a Night
Death

BOOKS REVIEWED
We, the Musk Chasers — 20 96

ABERCROMBIE, LASCELLES
BOOKS REVIEWED
The Theory of Poetry — 28 169
The Theory of Poetry — 28 227
The Poems of... — 40 47

ARTICLES ABOUT
Drinkwater on Abercrombie,
by Harriet Monroe — 18 30

ABERG, W. M.
POEMS
Cymbeline — 139 285

ABRAHAM, SUSAN
POEMS
Dear God — 160 92

ABRAHAMS, WILLIAM
POEMS
Poem ("It is the formless I...") — 59 188
Meditation as Epitaph — 63 119
Poem in Time of War
The Labyrinth — 65 308
A Meditation for This Time — 66 186
Rimbaud
Prides Crossing — 72 66
Postcard from Boston
Winter Sonnet
Sargasso
Eclogue in Central Park — 73 260
A Wake for Hart Crane — 81 106
Tapestry Figures — 88 307
Nobody Here But Us

REVIEWS
  Program of Entertainment   74   118
    Stranger at Coney Island,
      by Kenneth Fearing
    Poems, by David Ignatow

ARTICLES ABOUT
  Henry James and the Poets,
    by Leon Edel   62   328

ABRAMS, DOUG
POEMS
  The Marshes   130   131
  Freezes
  Credences the Saplings Know

ABRAMS, IRWIN BURBANK
BOOKS REVIEWED
  Another Challenge   77   215

ABRAMSON, GLENDA
TRANSLATIONS
  Poems by Yehuda Amichai
    (Tr. with Tudor Parfitt)   138   137

BOOKS REVIEWED
  Great Tranquillity: Questions and Answers,
    by Yehuda Amichai
    (Tr. with Tudor Parfitt)   145   99

ABRIL, XAVIER
BOOKS REVIEWED
  Vallejo   105   196

ABSE, DANNIE
POEMS
  Near the Border of Insanities   69   309
  Delilah   73   322
  Photograph and Yellow Tulips   81   105
  The Frontier   81   238
  The Meeting
  Anniversary   86   317
  Poem and Message
  On Hearing the Monologue of a Deaf Poet   89   279
  Progress of a Marriage   95   204
  Chalk
  The Bereaved   120   158
  Explanation of a News Item
  Forgotten
  An Old Commitment
  Ghosts   124   66
  Angels
  Last Words   133   261
  X Ray
  The Power of Prayer
  Pantomime Diseases
  Quests   142   328
  Bloody Horse   146   225
  Of Two Languages   151   1

  Smiling Through   151   469
  Musical Moments   156   278
  Between 3 and 4 A.M.   161   70
  Shmelke
  How I Won the Raffle
  A Doctor's Register
  Talking to Blake   165   87
  Chocolate Box
  In the Villa Borghese
  Two Photographs

BOOKS REVIEWED
  After Every Green Thing   75   102
  Mavericks
    (Ed. with Howard Sergeant)   91   124
  Poems, Golders Green   102   193
  Selected Poems   118   102
  Funland and Other Poems   123   353
  Collected Poems 1948-1976   132   230
  One-Legged on Ice   145   161

ABSHER, TOM
POEMS
  Fish   144   331

ABY, ROBERT-PETER
POEMS
  Étude II   74   29

**A CHEAVASA, MOIREEN FOX
[MOIREEN FOX]**
POEMS
  Liadain to Curithir   5   262
  Love   10   85
  Foreboding
  In Absence
  Deirdre   17   188
  Silence
  Disillusion

ACKERMAN, BARBARA
POEMS
  Shifting Colors   26   250
  Discoveries   29   256
    Change
    Aspiration
    The White Sun
    Strong

ACKERMAN, DIANE
POEMS
  St. Louis Botanical Gardens   150   29
  Gramercy Park
  Lament of the Banyan Tree
  We Are Listening   151   346
  Letter of Retainer   152   32
  Beija-Flor   152   200
  Natural Wonders   164   334
  City of Dreams

ACKLAND, VALENTINE
BOOKS REVIEWED
Whether a Dove or Seagull
(With Sylvia Townsend Warner)　44　165

ACKROYD, PETER
BOOKS REVIEWED
The Diversions of Purley　154　29

ACORN, MILTON
BOOKS REVIEWED
Jawbreakers　104　385

ACTON, ELLEN
POEMS
Bus Trip in Cornwall　54　13

ACTON, HAROLD
TRANSLATIONS
Poems by Hsu Tse-Mo,
Ho Chi-Fang, and Lin Keng　46　14

ARTICLES
Contemporary Chinese Poetry
[Hu Shih, Kuo Mo-Jo, Hsu Tse-Mo]　46　39

BOOKS REVIEWED
Oxford Poetry: 1924
(Ed. with Peter Quennell)　26　47
An Indian Ass　28　112

ADAM, HELEN DOUGLAS
BOOKS REVIEWED
*The Elfin Pedlar
and Tales Told by Pixy Pool*　24　279

ADAMS, FRANKLIN P. ["F. P. A."]
BOOKS REVIEWED
Something Else Again　17　100
*The Melancholy Lute;
Selected Songs of Thirty Years*　50　210

ARTICLES ABOUT
Cattle in the Garden,
by M. D. Zabel　38　268

ADAMS, HAZARD
POEMS
A Wreath of Elegies　109　310

REVIEWS
The Rescued Year,
by William Stafford　110　42

BOOKS REVIEWED
*William Blake:
A Reading of the Shorter Poems*　107　65

ADAMS, J. DONALD
ARTICLES
The Arraignment　68　262

ARTICLES ABOUT
The Hazards of Criticism,
by Francis C. Golffing　68　265
Speaking of Bookishness,
by Herbert J. Muller　68　283

ADAMS, J. J.
POEMS
The Sirens　39　256

ARTICLES ABOUT
English Poetry Today,
by Basil Bunting　39　264

ADAMS, JOHN
ARTICLES ABOUT
John Adams' Prophecy,
by Harriet Monroe　18　327

ADAMS, JOHN QUINCY
ARTICLES ABOUT
Poets and Politicians,
by Coleman Rosenberger
[Bennett Champ Clark]　65　322

ADAMS, KAYWYNNE
POEMS
Semantikos/Rejectementa　116　96

ADAMS, LÉONIE
POEMS
The Mysterious Thing　29　295
The Gift
Twilit Revelation
Counsel to Unreason
The Lament of Quarry
Certainly Beauty
The Moon and Spectator

REVIEWS
Pastures and Other Poems,
by Lizette Woodworth Reese　44　40
End and Beginning,
by John Masefield　44　106
Contrast and Collaboration　44　165
Opus 7, by Sylvia Townsend Warner
Whether a Dove or Seagull,
by Sylvia Townsend Warner
and Valentine Ackland
The White Threshold, by W. S. Graham　82　272
So Many Daughters,
by Eda Lou Walton　85　114
Collected Poems, 1923-53,
by Louise Bogan　85　165

BOOKS REVIEWED
   Those Not Elect   27   275
   High Falcon   35   332
   Poems: A Selection   87   45

ARTICLES ABOUT
   Allen Tate: A Poet on Poetry, 1924-1944,
      by Ashley Brown   135   103

ADAMS, TERRY
POEMS
   The Touching   157   264
   Pietà   158   315

ADAMS, WALTER R.
BOOKS REVIEWED
   The Dead Lie Down   46   53

ADAMSON, ROBERT
ARTICLES ABOUT
   Towards a Contemporary
   Australian Poetics,
      by John Kinsella   169   94

ADCOCK, FLEUR
BOOKS REVIEWED
   High Tide in the Garden   122   47
   The Scenic Route   127   164

ADDISON, MEDORA C.
POEMS
   Motherhood   19   261

BOOKS REVIEWED
   Dreams and a Sword   22   168

ADLER, LUCILE
POEMS
   Sisterly   88   376
   The Hunter
   When the People Are Avenues   97   170
   Maria Over Winter
   Feast
   Anita with White Lilac
   Desert Almanach   102   12
   A Whisper for K.
   While You Sleep
   The Women Looking Out

ADLER, MORTIMER J.
POEMS
   The Fearless   17   197

ADOFF, ARNOLD
BOOKS REVIEWED
   I Am the Darker Brother:
     An Anthology of Modern Poems
     by Negro Americans   113   262

ADRIANSEN, ROLF
POEMS
   Ends for Silences   50   249
   Poem ("He that thinks...")
   Foray
   Decor
   Desert Night

AESCHYLUS
BOOKS REVIEWED
   Oresteia
     (Tr. by Richmond Lattimore)   84   112
   The Oresteia of...
     (Tr. by Robert Lowell)   137   220

ARTICLES ABOUT
   Rev. of *The Poetry of Greek Tragedy*,
     by Richmond Lattimore   95   190

AGAR, HERBERT
BOOKS REVIEWED
   The Garment of Praise:
     The Necessity for Poetry
     (With Eleanor Carroll Chilton)   34   161

AGEE, JAMES
BOOKS REVIEWED
   Permit Me Voyage   46   48
   The Collected Poems of James Agee
     (Ed. by Robert Fitzgerald)   114   409
   The Collected Short Prose of James Agee
     (Ed. by Robert Fitzgerald)   114   411

AGGELER, WILLIAM
BOOKS REVIEWED
   The Flowers of Evil,
     by Charles Baudelaire (Tr.)   85   55

AGOOS, JULIE
BOOKS REVIEWED
   Above the Land   151   419

AGUERO, KATHLEEN
POEMS
   Captain Colette   160   78

AHMAD, AIJAZ
TRANSLATIONS
   Poems by Ghalib
     (Tr. with W. S. Merwin)   116   335

AI [FLORENCE ANTHONY]
POEMS
   Winter in Another Country   135   336
   The Psychiatrist
   Kristallnacht
   Interview with a Policeman   151   2

BOOKS REVIEWED
   Killing Floor   139   35
   Sin   149 231
   Fate   159 101
   Greed   164 285

AIKEN, CONRAD
POEMS
   Discordants   6 287
   Many Evenings   14 233
     Prelude
     Melody in a Restaurant
     Illicit
     Haunted Chambers
     Counterpoint: Two Rooms
     Multitudes Turn in Darkness
   King Borborigmi   26 321
   ("Broad on the sunburnt hill...")   30 179
   ("What music's devious voice...")
   ("Think, love, how when a starry...")
   ("My love, I have betrayed you...")
   ("*Imprimis*: I forgot...")
   ("What lunacy is this...")
   Ballad ("Into the wood...")   36 304
   Prelude   38 147
   Blues for Ruby Matrix   45 179
   Spanish Easter 1926   55 289
   The Cyclads   81   1
   The Ego   81 237
   Love's Grammarians   101   1

ARTICLES
   Correspondence:
     Mr. Aiken and the Essential Industry   13 230
   Correspondence
     [James Dickey]   103 402

REVIEWS
   The Charnel Rose, by Conrad Aiken   14 152
   Body and Raiment and *Profiles from China*,
     by Eunice Tietjens   15 272
   Active Anthology
     (Ed. by Ezra Pound)   44 276
   The Rock: A Pageant Play and
     After Strange Gods, by T. S. Eliot   45 161
   The World I Breathe, by Dylan Thomas   56 159

BOOKS REVIEWED
   Turns and Movies and Other Tales in Verse   9 98
   The Jig of Forslin   10 162
   Nocturne of Remembered Spring
     and Other Poems   13 102
   The Charnel Rose   14 152
   Scepticisms   15 283
   The House of Dust   17 220

   Punch, the Immortal Liar   18 160
   Modern American Poets (Ed.)   22 53
   Selected Poems   37 221
   John Deth and Other Poems   38 107
   The Coming Forth by Day of Osiris Jones   40 39
   Preludes for Memnon
   Landscape West of Eden   46 162
   Time in the Rock: Preludes to Definition   50 103
   And in the Human Heart:
     A Sonnet Sequence   60 149
   The Soldier   66 159
   An Anthology of Famous English
     and American Poetry
     (Ed. with William Rose Benét)   68 106
   The Kid   72 224
   The Divine Pilgrim   76 162
   Skylight One
   Ushant, an Autobiographical Narrative   81 313
   A Letter from Li Po and Other Poems   88 175
   A Letter from Li Po and Other Poems   88 179
   Mr. Arcularis   91 333
   Sheepfold Hill   94 41
   A Reviewer's ABC:
     Collected Criticism of Conrad Aiken
     from 1916 to the Present
     (Ed. by Rufus A. Blanshard)   96 318
   Selected Poems   99 309
   The Morning Song of Lord Zero   103 187
   Collected Poems 1916-1970   118 287

ARTICLES ABOUT
   Its Inner Meaning,
     by Harriet Monroe
     [Imagism]   6 302
   Poetry an Essential Industry,
     by Harriet Monroe   13 96
   Correspondence from Elizabeth Pollet
     [Edward Dahlberg]   82 176

AIKEN, WILLIAM
POEMS
   Fractals   165 19
   Draper Mountain, Pulaski   166 8

AISEN, MAURICE
TRANSLATIONS
   Poem by George Cosbuc
     and other poems from Roumanian   4 146

ARTICLES
   Doina   4 162

AISENBERG, NADYA
POEMS
   Measures   168 125

AITKEN, ADAM
POEMS
From *Crossing Lake Toba: A Guide*   169   1
Graves
Easy Riders
Symbiosis
I Met a Man Going to a Funeral
Boatman Song 2

AIVAZ, DAVID
POEMS
Who Turn the Tables   77   20

AKHMATOVA, ANNA
[ANNA ANDREYEVNA GORENKO]
POEMS
Snow
(Tr. by Babette Deutsch)   70   253
La Muse
(Tr. by Sophie Laffitte)   98   376
The Muse   98   376
From *The White Flight*
(Tr. by Stanley Burnshaw)
The Muse   122   96
Epigram
The Death of Sophocles
Lot's Wife
(Tr. by Stanley Kunitz
with Max Hayward)

BOOKS REVIEWED
Poems of...
(Tr. by Stanley Kunitz
with Max Hayward)   124   232

ARTICLES ABOUT
Rev. of *Three Poets of Modern Russia*,
by Leonid I. Strakhovsky   76   112
A Note on the Poetry
of Anna Akhmatova,
by Vera Sandomirsky   76   114

AKINS, ZOË
POEMS
Conquered   5   163
The Wanderer
Driftwood Burning   12   316

BOOKS REVIEWED
Interpretations   1   97
The Hills Grow Smaller   51   223

ARTICLES ABOUT
[Note]   5   248
Down East, by Harriet Monroe   8   85
Mr. Yeats and the Poetic Drama,
by Harriet Monroe   16   32

AKKAMAHADEVI
POEMS
The Lord as Lover
(Tr. by A. K. Ramanujan)   98   382

ALBERT, WALTER
BOOKS REVIEWED
Selected Writings,
by Blaise Cendrars (Ed.)   111   124

ALBERTI, RAFAEL
BOOKS REVIEWED
Selected Poems
(Tr. by Lloyd Mallan)   67   166
Selected Poems
(Ed. and tr. by Ben Belitt)   111   46
The Owl's Insomnia
(Ed. and tr. by Mark Strand)   124   280

ALBERTUS, ALEXANDER
POEMS
Bit of an Elegy   139   157
Now and Again

ALCOSSER, SANDRA
POEMS
Each Bone a Prayer   138   102
The Entomologist's Landscape
Ruddy Glow Against a Black Background
Learning the Gleaner's Song   144   13
But This Is Not the Yucatan   151   275

BOOKS REVIEWED
A Fish To Feed All Hunger   149   231

ALDAN, DAISY
POEMS
Women at Windows   104   232
Frozen Frames of a Last Meeting   108   243
A Dance Without Touch
The Sky Is Moving Farther Back, Opaque
Vertical Is Our New Sight   111   150
Your Letter
The Cometary Script
Everywhere in Constancy,
He Is Intoning, Look! Look!
I Awake in These Hills   116   147
He Has Entered Midnight
Stones: Avesbury   120   18
Glaciers
Mutilated Fire
The Little Mermaid
Under the Marble Arches   131   325
The Bay

REVIEWS
The Words of the Tribe   118   35
Adam's Dream, by Julia Randall

Word Rain, by Madeline Gins
Ordinary, Moving, by Phyllis Gotlieb
Cold Turkey, by Mac Hammond
The Republic of Many Voices,
    by Paul Zimmer

BOOKS REVIEWED
   The Destruction of Cathedrals   103   324

ARTICLES ABOUT
   French Chronicle: Recent Publications,
    by Wallace Fowlie   88   408

ALDEN, ADA
POEMS
   Rigors   28   249
    The Mills of the Gods
    Charm

ALDEN, RAYMOND M.
BOOKS REVIEWED
   The Sonnets of Shakespeare:
    Variorum Edition (Ed.)   9   156

ARTICLES ABOUT
   Our Contemporaries,
    by Alice Corbin Henderson   6   259

ALDINGTON, RICHARD ["R. A."]
POEMS
   Χορικοσ   1   39
   To a Greek Marble
   Au Vieux Jardin
   ("I have drifted along this river...")   3   133
   Lesbia
   Argyria
   The Poplar
   Glaucopis
   War Yawp   5   78
   Dancers   5   221
    Palace Music Hall
    Interlude
   Images   7   23
   Prayers and Fantasies   13   67
   In France (1916-1918)   14   175
    Insouciance
    Two Impressions
    Compensation
    Loss
    Beauty Unpraised
   Madrigal   22   117
   La Rochelle   38   80
   Dilemma   43   188

TRANSLATIONS
   Article by Remy de Gourmont   4   154
   Article by Remy de Gourmont   5   184

ARTICLES
   Correspondence: Death of a French Poet
    [Charles Péguy]   5   144
   The Poetry of the Future   14   266
   Correspondence: A London Letter
    [John Masefield, Arthur Waley]   15   226
   Campion's "Observations"   15   267
   English and American   16   94

   The Disciples of Gertrude Stein
    [Guillaume Apollinaire,
    Blaise Cendrars, Jean Cocteau,
    M. G. Ribemont-Dessaignes]   17   35
   The Poet and Modern Life   18   99

REVIEWS
   Recent French Poetry   15   42
    Europe, by Jules Romains
    Le Secret, by André Spire
    La Vierge et les Sonnets,
     by Francis Jammes
    Les Enchanteurs; Barbe Bleue,
     Jeanne d'Arc et Mes Amours; and
     Chansons à la Gauloise,
     by Paul Fort
    De Stéphane Mallarmé au prophète Ezéchiel,
     by Edouard Dujardin   16   164
    Quia Pauper Amavi, by Ezra Pound   16   213
   Flint and Rodker   17   44
    Otherworld, by F. S. Flint
    Hymns, by John Rodker
   The Poetry of the Sitwells   17   161
    Argonaut and Juggernaut,
     by Osbert Sitwell
    The People's Palace,
     by Sacheverell Sitwell
    Clowns' Houses, by Edith Sitwell
   The Sacred Wood, by T. S. Eliot   17   345
   Terra Italicà, by Edward Storer   18   103

BOOKS REVIEWED
   Some Imagist Poets—An Anthology   6   150
   Images Old and New   8   49
   Some Imagist Poets, 1917   11   339
   Reverie: A Little Book of Poems for H.D.   12   44
   Some Imagist Poets   14   281
   War and Love   14   338
   Images (New ed.)   15   162
   Medallions in Clay (Tr.)   18   284
   The Poets' Translation Series: Second Set
   Collected Poems   34   42
   Imagist Anthology 1930
    (With John Cournos,
    H. D., John Gould Fletcher,
    F. S. Flint, Ford Madox Ford,
    James Joyce, D. H. Lawrence,
    and William Carlos Williams)   36   213

Last Poems,
  by D. H. Lawrence
  (Ed. with Giuseppe Orioli)   42   163
The Poems of...   45   47
The Crystal World   52   160
The Viking Book of Poetry
  of the English-Speaking World (Ed.)   59   346
A Wreath for San Gemignano (Ed. and tr.)   68   293

ARTICLES ABOUT
  Review of Des Imagistes: An Anthology   5   38
  Our Contemporaries:
    Autumn Leaves from England   7   99
  Correspondence
    from Maxwell Bodenheim
    [John Rodker]   17   170
  [Resignation]   18   176
  The Editor in England,
    by Harriet Monroe   23   32

ALDIS, ARTHUR T.
ARTICLES
  Correspondence:
    Concerning Awards   18   347

ALDIS, DOROTHY (KEELEY)
POEMS
  On the Wing   19   193
  Clover Tops   24   236
    Intangible
    Grapes
    Morning
    Evening
    Sleep
    April
    Brides
    Sonnet ("Lovers, stir not...")
  Tumble-Weed   28   9
    The Reason
    Insight
    Tongues
    Intruders
    Vegetables
    Unheralded
    Spring Puddle
  Stones to Skip   30   24
    The Choice
    Inanimates
    Let the Grass Grow Long
    The Secret
    High Morning
  Spring   32   18
  Flowers at Night
  Words
  Any Spring   36   235
  Maine Shore
  Bare Feet
  His Daughter

Panic
Boy and Girl
Emily Dickinson

REVIEWS
  Three Younger Poets   24   280
    Hidden Waters,
      by Bernard Raymund
    Last Lutanist,
      by Dean B. Lyman, Jr.
    Silver Wands, by Marion Boyd

BOOKS REVIEWED
  Here, There and Everywhere   33   162
  Everything and Anything
  Any Spring   43   346
  Before Things Happen   55   221

ALDIS, MARY
POEMS
  The World Cry   6   76
  A Little Girl   8   78
  Thrones   13   18
  O Bitter Day
  Embarcation
  Go from Me
  To One Who Asks   17   190
  The Happening   21   201
  The Other One Comes to Her
  The Wandering One
  She Remembers
  She Thinks of the Faithful One
  The Wandering One Makes Music
  They Meet Again
  Search   23   183

REVIEWS
  The Writing and Reading of Verse,
    by Lt. C. E. Andrews   16   113

BOOKS REVIEWED
  Flashlights   8   318

ALDIS, OWEN F.
POEMS
  To a Mocking Bird   3   13

ALEGRIA, FERNANDO
BOOKS REVIEWED
  Instructions for Undressing the Human Race
    (Tr. by Matthew Zion
    and Lennart Bruce)   115   440

ALEIXANDRE, VICENTE
BOOKS REVIEWED
  A Longing for the Light: Selected Poems of...
    (Tr. by Lewis Hyde)   136   40

ALESHIRE, JOAN
POEMS
Mourning Doves: Maryland   142   63
Slipping
Perpetual Motion   145   151
Persephone
Nausikaa   147   147
Orion
Images from the Floating World
Engrams   152   279
Healing
Top of the World   158   330

ALEXANDER, ELIZABETH
POEMS
Stravinsky in L.A.   160   18
Apollo
Cough Medicine
Equinox   162   313
Manhattan Elegy
L.A. by Night   163   276
At the Beach

BOOKS REVIEWED
The Venus Hottentot   158   214

ALEXANDER, HARTLEY (BURR)
BOOKS REVIEWED
Odes and Lyrics   21   158
Manito Masks   28   53
God's Drum   31   286

ARTICLES ABOUT
In the Aboriginal Mode,
   by Harriet Monroe   42   332

ALEXANDER, LEWIS
ARTICLES ABOUT
Racial Bias and Negro Poetry,
   by Edward Bland   63   328

ALEXANDER, MICHAEL
BOOKS REVIEWED
The Earliest English Poems (Tr.)   111   395

ALEXANDER, PAMELA
POEMS
*"That Excellent & By All Physitians
   Approved Chinean Drink"*   123   195
Table of Elements   153   144
Six   153   201
Safe

BOOKS REVIEWED
Navigable Waterways   147   102

ALEXANDER, PAUL
POEMS
The Swimmers   148   223

ALEXANDER, SHEILA
POEMS
Love, My Dangerous Pet   70   306
Lions and Lovers
The Good Wife's Song
Work Chant

ALEXANDER, SIDNEY
BOOKS REVIEWED
The Man on the Queue   59   220
The Marine Cemetery,
   by Paul Valéry (Tr.)   76   172
Tightrope in the Dark   77   215

**ALEXANDHROU, ARIS
[Pseud. of VASILIADHIS,
ARISTOTLE]**
POEMS
Perturbation   139   87
No Man's Land
Flavius Marcus to Himself
The Knife
   (Tr. by Kimon Friar)

ARTICLES ABOUT
Post-War Greek Poets,
   by Kimon Friar   139   99

ALFORD, JOHN
POEMS
The Seringa   4   216

ALGREN, NELSON
POEMS
Home and Goodnight   55   74
Travelog
Local South   58   308
How Long Blues
Epitaph: The Man with the Golden Arm   70   316

REVIEWS
Collected Poems, by Robert Graves   55   157
The Red Kite, by Lloyd Frankenberg   56   46
Poems, by William Pillin   57   278
We Thank You with Reservations   59   220
   I Went into the Country,
      by Harry Roskolenko
   The Man on the Queue,
      by Sidney Alexander
   We Thank You All the Time,
      by Norman Macleod
For My People, by Margaret Walker   61   634
Varying Viewpoints   62   50
   Blind Dawn,
      by Stanley Kidder Wilson
   Fence of Fire,
      by Reitza Dine Wirtschafter

Rind of Earth,
   by August Derleth
Magic and Melancholy   63   52
   Lines for the Canonization
     of Pedro Domecq,
     by George Smedley Smith
   The Masculine Dead
     and *Ten War Elegies,*
     by William Everson
Coal Dust on the Fiddle,
   by George Korson   63   106
Three Against the World   65   51
   Flight Above Cloud,
     by John Pudney
   Sailing or Drowning,
     by Allen Curnow
   The Second Man,
     by Julian Symons

ALHASHMI, RAHM ALI
TRANSLATIONS
   Poem by Jigar Morabadi
     (Tr. with Tambimuttu)   93   235

ALI, AGHA SHAHID
POEMS
   At the Museum   156   34

ALIGER, MARGARITA
ARTICLES ABOUT
   Rev. of *Back to Life*
     (Ed. by Robert Conquest)   97   192

ALIGHIERI, DANTE
   [See DANTE]

ALI-SHAH, OMAR
BOOKS REVIEWED
   The Original Rubaiyyat of Omar Khayaam,
   A New Translation
   with Critical Commentaries
     (Tr. with Robert Graves)   113   262

ALLAMAND, JACQUES
ARTICLES
   The Genealogy of Lettrism
     (Tr. by Julia Bowe)   71   141

ALLBERY, DEBRA
POEMS
   Walking Below Zero You Tell Yourself 147 313
   Forgiveness
   Children's Story   150   275
   Offering
   Lapse

ALLEN, BETH
POEMS
   Psyche   55   68

ALLEN, BEVERLY
TRANSLATIONS
   Poem by Andrea Zanzotto   155   57
   Poems by Maria Luisa Spaziani 155   67
   Poems by Amelia Rosselli   155   85
   Poems by Marica Larocchi   155   115

ALLEN, CHARLES
BOOKS REVIEWED
   The Little Magazine:
     A History and a Bibliography
     (With Frederick J. Hoffman
     and Carolyn F. Ulrich)   70   274

ARTICLES ABOUT
   [Note]   51   289

ALLEN, DICK
POEMS
   Theory of the Alternate Universe 115 219
   To the S-F Woman
   Escape Velocity
   Poster Poem
   Oh Rousseau, Rousseau   117 376
   The New Medievalist
   Notes Toward a Credo
   The Day After June   123 197
   Durations
   Poem for My 36th Birthday   129   12
   The Afterlife
   Small Hotel   134 125
   The Persistence
   Sunshower
   Green Pastures
   A Winter Morning   138   20
   Janes Avenue   140 284
   Grandfather's Jigsaw Puzzle
   Dignity
   The Poet at Eighteen   145 147
   Notes After Ether   150   6
   Barge Lights on the Hudson
   The Commuter
   Another Knowledge   151   4
   The Narrow Mind   154 324
   Outside Elements   160   15
   The Same River, Twice
   Still Waters
   Time To Hear Ourselves Think 168 275

REVIEWS
   Holding Your Eight Hands:
     An Anthology of Science Fiction Verse
     (Ed. by Edward Lucie-Smith) 117 115
   The Contemporary American Poets:
     American Poetry Since 1940
     (Ed. by Mark Strand)   119 109
   Shifts   120 235
     Messages, by Sidney Goldfarb

Upstate, by Dugan Gilman
Heaved from the Earth,
   by Besmilr Brigham
Power Politics,
   by Margaret Atwood
The Tattooed Desert,
   by Richard Shelton
Pili's Wall, by Philip Levine
Homespun of Oatmeal Gray,
   by Paul Goodman
To the End of West,
   by Henry Chapin
The Donner Party,
   by George Keithley   122   173
The Gift To Be Simple   124   103
   The Lady in Kicking Horse Reservoir,
     by Richard Hugo
   The Country of Marriage,
     by Wendell Berry
   From Snow and Rock, from Chaos,
     by Hayden Carruth
   Impossible Buildings,
     by Judith Johnson Sherwin
   Moly and *My Sad Captains*,
     by Thom Gunn
To the Wall   130   342
   Keeping Watch, by Robert Pack
   Hush, by David St. John
   The Private Life, by Lisel Mueller
   Climbing Down, by Carl Dennis
   Come the Sweet By and By,
     by Eleanor Lerman
   A Rain of Rites and *A Father's House*,
     by Jayanta Mahapatra

BOOKS REVIEWED
Anon and Various Time Machine Poems   121   303
Regions with No Proper Names   132   288
Overnight in the Guest House of the Mystic 145   348
Flight and Pursuit   153   106

ALLEN, DON CAMERON
BOOKS REVIEWED
Four Poets on Poetry:
   Essays by R. P. Blackmur,
   Yvor Winters, Marianne Moore,
   and Mark Van Doren (Ed.)   96   382
Image and Meaning:
   Metaphoric Traditions in
   Renaissance Poetry   99   187
The Moment of Poetry (Ed.)   102   198

ALLEN, DONALD (M.)
BOOKS REVIEWED
The Selected Poems of García Lorca
   (Ed. with Francisco García Lorca)   87   303
The New American Poetry: 1945–1960 (Ed.)   98   242

A Quick Graph:
   Collected Notes and Essays,
     by Robert Creeley (Ed.)   119   99
The Collected Poems
   of Frank O'Hara (Ed.)   122   40

ALLEN, EFFIE ALGER
POEMS
   The Phantom Steamer   21   245
   The First Red Man
   Two Sad Songs   32   316
   Bereavement
   Song of the Hearse

ALLEN, GAY WILSON
BOOKS REVIEWED
   The Solitary Singer   87   183
   Walt Whitman Abroad (Ed.)
   American Poetry
     (Ed. with Walter B. Rideout
     and James K. Robinson)   109   345

ALLEN, GEORGE
POEMS
   Sky   48   193

ALLEN, HARBOR
POEMS
   A Grace in Death   30   312

ALLEN, HEATHER
POEMS
   The Country of Childhood   158   69
   Dream Cycle   162   279

ALLEN, HERVEY ["H. A."]
POEMS
   The Sea-Islands   20   6
     Shadows
     Sunshine
     Macabre in Macaws
     Hag-Hollerin' Time
     Upstairs Downstairs
     Palmetto Town
   Northern Earth Mood   25   312
     In the Beginning
     Geological
     Prehistoric
     Lyric Interlude Astronomical
     Bronze and Iron
     Minoan into Greek
     Carthaginian
     Roman

ARTICLES
   Poetry South
     (With Hervey Allen)
     [Edgar Allan Poe, Sidney Lanier]   20   35
   Poe in South Carolina   20   48

BOOKS REVIEWED
The Bride of Huitzil   21   226
Wampum and Old Gold
Carolina Chansons:
    Legends of the Low Country
    (With DuBose Heyward)   22   89
Earth Moods and Other Poems   27   96
Israfel
    [Edgar Allan Poe]   29   266
New Legends   35   342

ALLEN, PHILIP SCHUYLER
BOOKS REVIEWED
The Romanesque Lyric:
    Studies in its Background and Development
    from Petronius to the Cambridge Songs
    (With trs. by Howard Mumford Jones)   33   227

ALLEN, SARA VAN ALSTYNE
POEMS
Vine in Early Spring   58   67

ALLEN, VIOLA
ARTICLES ABOUT
Poetry on Records,
    by Harry T. Moore   57   338

ALLING, KENNETH SLADE
POEMS
Gulls on a Rowboat   34   145
Gull   38   320
Hummingbird   40   202
Going On   41   308
    Clocks
    Water Snake
    Portrait of a Toad
    Cemetery Brook
Noon   43   79
Dark Song   45   81
Within Be Fed   50   23
Mown Hay   51   16
Room   55   133
Portrait
Iron Urn
Wooden Statue   57   136
Pumpkins
Clock
Visitor
Briareus   58   126
Old Leaves   62   194
Ploughed Field
Turtle
"A Sun Dyall in a Grave"
Autumn out of Summer   63   254
Winter Frost
Music
Skeleton   65   124

Identification
Old Man
Killdeer   66   78
Moth
Crow
Batdom
Locusts, etc.
Woodpecker
Yellow Bird
Amazing Minute   70   247
Car Top
Jack-in-the-Pulpit   72   134
Dead Wasp
First World War   74   23
Onion Skin in Barn   74   258
Dr. Donne   75   87
Mind   77   6
On the Park Bench
Letter
Pariah
Monsoon
The Toad   84   274
Oak
Doves
Quatrain

BOOKS REVIEWED
Core of Fire   58   226
Kingdom of Diagonals   86   287

ALLISON, JOHN
POEMS
Night Animal   131   88

ALLMAN, JOHN
POEMS
Into   127   20
Away & Towards
Return
The Token   145   14
Croton Dam

BOOKS REVIEWED
Walking Four Ways in the Wind   140   35

ALLOTT, KENNETH
POEMS
Calenture   50   75
Cheshire Cat   70   241

ALONDRA, A.
POEMS
The Trenches   13   21

ALPERS, PAUL
TRANSLATIONS
Poem by Virgil   128   143

ALQUIT-BLUM, B.
POEMS
  Three Poems
     (Tr. by Etta Blum)   104   88
     ("I drew you out...")
     ("Is there a darkness...")
     ("Since I scarcely know...")

ALTERMAN, NATHAN
POEMS
  From Nude Fire
     (Tr. by Ruth Finer Mintz)   92   235
  From The Ten Plagues of Egypt
     (Tr. by Robert Friend)

ALTHAUS, KEITH
POEMS
  Poem ("The terror of new...")   117   24
  Toy Soldiers
  Traveling in Europe   123   200

ALTOUNYAN, E. H. R.
BOOKS REVIEWED
  Ornament of Honor
     [T. E. Lawrence]   50   285

ALTROCCHI, JULIA COOLEY
[See COOLEY, JULIA]

ALTROCCHI, RUDOLPH
POEMS
  Summons to Youth   10   191

ALVAREZ, A(LFRED)
POEMS
  The Survivor   97   375
  Love Affair
  Waking
  The Gate
  Autumn Marriage
  Lost   102   228
  The Hunt
  Spring Fever

BOOKS REVIEWED
  Stewards of Excellence   95   122
  The School of Donne   99   261

ARTICLES ABOUT
  Contemporary British Poetry:
    A Romantic Persistence?
    by John Bayley   146   227

ALVAREZ, JULIA
POEMS
  Heroics   140   87
  New Clothes

BOOKS REVIEWED
  The Other Side/El Otro Lado   168   281

ALVER, BETTI
ARTICLES ABOUT
  Rev. of *Anthology of Modern Estonian Poetry*
    (Ed. and tr. by W. K. Matthews)   84   236

ALVORD, JAMES CHURCH
POEMS
  Easter Evening   10   23
  The Carpenter   12   240

ALYEA, DOROTHY (COLLINS)
POEMS
  From One Transplanted   34   26
    Oregon
    Ride, Cowhorse!
    First Love
    The Housewife
    You Are My Friend
    Here Is a Face
  Passing on Her Way   47   256
  Silver Thaw   50   147
  No Beauty
  Long Live the Queen
  Test of Love
  Galatea
  There's Margaret   67   81
  The Teacher   68   304
  Hard Rain   70   183

AMABILE, GEORGE
POEMS
  Honeymoon: Lake Washburn, Minn.   101   331

AMBLER, ERIC
ARTICLES ABOUT
  Dagger of the Mind,
    by James Sandoe   68   146

AMES, ALFRED C.
REVIEWS
  From Left to Right   67   282
    Ballad of the Bones and Other Poems,
      by Byron Herbert Reece
    Here and Now, by Irving Layton
    The Task, by Robert Bhain Campbell
    Fearful Symmetry:
      A Study of William Blake,
      by Northrop Frye   71   101
    A House in Chicago,
      by Olivia Howard Dunbar
      [Harriet Moody]   71   277
    Poets and Pundits: A Collection of Essays,
      by Hugh l'Anson Fausset   72   329

AMES, LUCILE PERRY
POEMS
Nocturne   26   185
Old Lady Wobblecane

AMES, WESLEY
POEMS
Pointed Leaves   38   303
  Lament for the Sun-Bright Lover
  Exultation
  Song Against Ease
  A Goodfellow
  Paganini

AMICHAI, YEHUDA
[YEHUDA AMIHAI]
POEMS
Sonnet ("My father fought...")
  (Tr. by Robert Friend)   92   254
The Mediators, the Peace-Makers
  (Tr. by Margalit Benaya)
Poem ("His thoughts came slowly...")
  (Tr. by Meir Mindlin)
Things That Have Been Lost   138   137
A Meeting with My Father
Rain in a Foreign Land
  (Tr. by Tudor Parfitt
  and Glenda Abramson)

BOOKS REVIEWED
Poems
  (Tr. by Assia Gutmann)   116   120
Great Tranquillity:
  Questions and Answers
  (Tr. by Glenda Abramson
  and Tudor Parfitt)   145   99
The Selected Poetry
  (Ed. and tr. by Chana Bloch
  and Stephen Mitchell)   150   286
Even a Fist Was
  Once an Open Palm with Fingers
  (Tr. by Barbara and
  Benjamin Harshav)   159   157

ARTICLES ABOUT
[Note]   93   56

AMIS, KINGSLEY
BOOKS REVIEWED
A Case of Samples   91   45
A Look Round the Estate:
  Poems 1957-1967   114   266
Collected Poems 1944-1979   138   107

ARTICLES ABOUT
Rev. of Poets of the 1950's:
  An Anthology of New English Verse
  (Ed. by D. J. Enright)   89   260

AMMA, BALAMANI
POEMS
The Housewife   93   258

AMMONS, A. R.
POEMS
Joshua Tree   93   371
Close-Up
Grassy Sound
Gravelly Run   97   94
Epiphany
Mansion
Expressions of Sea Level   102   169
Catalyst
Street Song   104   352
Connection
Dark Song
World
Halfway   106   270
Landscape with Figures
Ithaca, N. Y.
Composing
Love Song ("Like the hills under...") 110   153
Love Song (2) ("Rings of birch...")
Mission
Treaties   113   410
This Bright Day
If Anything Will Level With You
  Water Will   115   297
Conserving the Magnitude of Uselessness
The Unifying Principle
Spiel
Transaction
Cut the Grass
Runoff
Pluralist
September Drift   117   7
Mountain Talk
Here & Now
Square
Admission
Cougar
Project
Reversal
Dominion
Countering
Working Still
Then One
Play
Bonus   124   322
Persistences   132   88
The Brook Has Worked Out
  the Prominences of a Bend   133   80
Strolls
Easter Morning   134   1
Singling and Doubling Together   141   1
Meeting Place
Yadkin Picnic

Coming Clearing	153	1
Anxiety's Prosody		
The Surprise of an Ending		
All's All		
An Improvisation		
for the Pieties of Modernism	159	1
An Improvisation		
for Angular Momentum		
An Improvisation for Soot and Suet		
Prey	167	206
A Sense of Now	168	1
Emerging Curves		
Local Antiquities		
Sumerian Vistas		
Collapsed Structures		
The Deep End		
Saying Saying Away	168	133
The Clenched-Jaw School		

ARTICLES
A Note on Prosody	102	202
Comment		
[Josephine Miles]	151	204

REVIEWS
Three Poets	96	52
1450-1950, by Bob Brown		
Inscriptions: 1944-1956,		
by Charles Reznikoff		
Selected Poems,		
by Robert Duncan		
Reality Sandwiches, by Allen Ginsberg	104	186
Seven Books by Eight Poets	108	191
Lunes, by Robert Kelly, and Sightings		
by Jerome Rothenberg		
You, Mark Antony,		
Navigator upon the Nile,		
by Judson Crews		
The Dark Flags of Waking,		
by Robert Dana		
The Gathering, by David Bromige		
The Thing Said and Other Poems,		
by James L. Weil		
Peace Eye, by Ed Sanders		
Sleeping with One Eye Open,		
by Mark Strand		

BOOKS REVIEWED
Ommateum	89	45
Expressions of Sea Level	105	201
Tape for the Turn of the Year	107	330
Corsons Inlet		
Northfield Poems	111	43
Selected Poems	114	40
Briefings (Poems Small and Easy)	120	49
Collected Poems: 1951-1971	123	109
Sphere: The Form of a Motion	127	352

Diversifications	130	167
The Selected Poems 1951-1977	132	230
The Snow Poems		
Worldly Hopes	141	26
Lake Effect Country	143	295
The Selected Poems:		
Expanded Edition	151	360
Sumerian Vistas: Poems		
The Really Short Poems of...	159	101
Garbage	164	97

ARTICLES ABOUT
[Note]	166	177

ANAGNOSTAKIS, MANOLIS
ARTICLES ABOUT
Post-War Greek Poets,		
by Kimon Friar	139	99

ANANIA, JOSÉ
[See PORTOGALO, JOSÉ]

ANANIA, MICHAEL
POEMS
A Hanging Screen	126	125
Materials of June		
Afternoons		
Aesthetique du Râle	129	337

BOOKS REVIEWED
The Color of Dust	119	45
Riversongs	135	229

ANDELSON, PEARL
[See SHERRY, PEARL ANDELSON]

ANDERSON, DANIEL
POEMS
Executive Geochrone	167	130
Epilogue	170	157

ANDERSON, DOUGLAS MC CLURE
POEMS
Santa Fe Remembers	53	82

ANDERSON, ETHEL
BOOKS REVIEWED
Squatters Luck	62	352

ANDERSON, FORREST
BOOKS REVIEWED
Sea Pieces and Other Poems	48	49

ANDERSON, GERALD
POEMS
Consider This:	144	78

ANDERSON, JACK
POEMS
  A Poet's Guide to the Subway   120   78
  A Garden of Situations
  True Loves   124   63
  Ode to Pornography
  Young Man with Rifle
    Leaning from a Window   126   318
  The Gods   128   314

BOOKS REVIEWED
  The Invention of New Jersey   118   169

ANDERSON, JEAN
POEMS
  Forest Landscapes   51   23
    The Deer in the Glade
    In Molten Sunlight
    The Urns of Fruit
    The Pale Garden
    Bay Bridge

ANDERSON, JIM
POEMS
  Making the Strange Familiar   144   91
  Homework

ANDERSON, J(OHN) REDWOOD
BOOKS REVIEWED
  Transvaluations   42   228
  The Human Dawn   47   167
  Pillars to Remembrance   75   108

ANDERSON, JON
POEMS
  The Monument to Resignation   110   379
  Looking for Jonathan
  The Child Within Him   114   23
  Of Government   115   154
  The Next President
  The Mouths of the Poor
  The Robots, the City of Paradise
  Rowing at Dawn   116   141
  Creative Writing 307
  It's the Beginning; So Much for Sentiment
  Exile   117   372
  Level
  In Sepia
  The Inner Gate   122   91

BOOKS REVIEWED
  Looking for Jonathan   113   262
  In Sepia   126   103
  The Milky Way: Poems 1967-1982   143   295

ARTICLES ABOUT
  Rev. of The American Poetry Anthology
    (Ed. by Daniel Halpern)   128   106

ANDERSON, KATH M.
POEMS
  Coyote Gulch   166   210
  Tableau: 6:30 a.m.   170   135

ANDERSON, KATHERINE LUCAS
POEMS
  Annunciation   169   144

ANDERSON, LEE
POEMS
  Saturday as Usual   101   402

BOOKS REVIEWED
  The Floating World and Other Poems,
    in Poets of Today III   89   244
  Nags Head and Other Poems   99   178

ANDERSON, MARCIA LEE
POEMS
  Re Joyce   70   240

ANDERSON, MARGARET BARTLETT
BOOKS REVIEWED
  Robert Frost and John Bartlett:
    The Record of a Friendship   104   253

ANDERSON, MARGARET (C.)
BOOKS REVIEWED
  My Thirty Years' War   37   95
  The Little Review Anthology (Ed.)   83   290

ARTICLES ABOUT
  Our Contemporaries   5   299

ANDERSON, MARGARET STEELE
POEMS
  Purple   17   315

ANDERSON, MARK
POEMS
  Easter Eggs   156   35

ANDERSON, MARY LOUISA
BOOKS REVIEWED
  The Child and Other Verses   9   152

ANDERSON, MAXWELL
BOOKS REVIEWED
  You Who Have Dreams   27   337
  Winterset   48   221
  Eleven Verse Plays   57   258

ANDERSON, MELVILLE BEST
BOOKS REVIEWED
  The Divine Comedy of Dante Alighieri (Tr.)   20   165
  The Divine Comedy of Dante Alighieri (Tr.)   43   229

ANDERSON

POETRY

ANDERSON, PATRICK
POEMS
Hong Kong	61	643
Military Camp		
Poem ("A long time he dozed...")		
Wild Duck		
War Dead		
Drinker		
Shopping		
Dialectics		
Armaments Worker		
In the Hospital		
Mirrors		
The Airmen		
Hunter Returning	65	115
Landscape		
Bathroom		
Rink		
Night Rising		
The Map		
Mother's Boy		
Late Working		
Letter to a Girl on Holiday by a River	68	121
Camp		
Canoe		
Ars Poetica		
The Unfinished Hotel	71	301
Elevation		
The Length of the Legs		
For Dylan Thomas	73	323
Love Poem		
The Ball		
Sestina in Time of Winter	81	283
Soft Blizzard		
Parts of the Body		
Dear Son		
La Soirée Chez Nous		
A Seaside Fragment		

BOOKS REVIEWED
A Tent for April	67	224
The White Centre	69	284
The Colour as Naked	86	287

ANDERSON, SHERWOOD
POEMS
Mid-American Songs	10	281
Song of Stephen the Westerner		
American Spring Song		
A Visit		
Song of the Drunken Business Man		
Evening Song		
Song of Industrial America		

BOOKS REVIEWED
Mid-American Chants	12	155

ANDERSON, VIOLET
POEMS
Through the Barber Shop Window	73	77

ANDERSON, WENDELL B.
BOOKS REVIEWED
The Heart Must Be Half Eagle	77	114
Three on a Match (With Cerise Farallon and Judson Crews)	110	186

ANDERSON, W. L.
BOOKS REVIEWED
Poetry as Experience (With N. C. Stageberg)	84	43

ANDRADE, JORGE CARRERA
[See CARRERA ANDRADE, JORGE]

ANDRE, EUGENE ROBERT
POEMS
Cherry Market	49	306

ANDREEVA, TAMARA
POEMS
Night	40	262

ANDREWS, [LT.] C. E.
BOOKS REVIEWED
The Writing and Reading of Verse	16	113

ANDREWS, CLAUDIA EMERSON
POEMS
Wanda	156	76
The Way to Water	166	213
Flood		

ANDREWS, TOM
POEMS
Reading the Tao Te Ching in the Hospital	161	148
Praying with George Herbert in Late Winter		

ANGEL, RALPH
POEMS
The Loneliest Man in the World	149	195
And the Grass Did Grow		
Shadow Play		
In Every Direction	158	197

BOOKS REVIEWED
Anxious Latitudes	149	341

ANGELITA, [SISTER] MARY [B.V.M.]
BOOKS REVIEWED
Starshine and Candlelight	28	290

ANGELOU, MAYA
BOOKS REVIEWED
Oh Pray My Wings Are Gonna Fit Me Well	128	290

18

ANGERS, RICHARD
POEMS
   Three Portraits   41   310
    Spiritist
    Relic
    Ancien Régime

ANIBAL SANCHEZ, LUIS
POEMS
   Brother Dog
    (Tr. by Muna Lee)   26   130

ANONYMOUS
ARTICLES
   Correspondence: A Poet's Protest
    [Poem]   17   104

REVIEWS
   Poetical Works of Lionel Johnson
    [Two editions]   7   313

BOOKS REVIEWED
   Unconditioned Songs   4   166
   On the Four Quartets of T. S. Eliot   84   179

ARTICLES ABOUT
   Correspondence from Stanley Burnshaw   44   351

AN-SHIH, WANG
[See WANG AN-SHIH]

ANSON, JOHN S.
POEMS
   Tiresias   127   200
   To My Mother in the Mirror
   Trouble at School
   Spell   128   134
   The Gaze
   Clouds   131   145
   I Know the Star
   Early Frost
   Mothwings

TRANSLATIONS
   Poems by Conrad Ferdinand Meyer   131   322

ANT, HOWARD
POEMS
   Pavalatchie the Dwarf   100   290
   Too Much Judas

ANTHON, KATE SCOTT
ARTICLES ABOUT
   Rev. of *The Riddle of Emily Dickinson*,
    by Rebecca Patterson   80   242

ANTHONY, GEORGE
POEMS
   Post-Mortem   85   18

ANTIN, DAVID
POEMS
   The Marchers   109   18
   Allegory

BOOKS REVIEWED
   Definitions   112   56

ANTONINUS, [BROTHER]
[See also EVERSON, WILLIAM]
BOOKS REVIEWED
   The Crooked Lines of God   99   253
   The Hazards of Holiness   102   42

ANTONIO CUADRA, PABLO
BOOKS REVIEWED
   Songs of Cifar and the Sweet Sea:
    Selections from "Songs of Cifar, 1967-1977"
    (Tr. and ed. by Grace Schulman
    and Ann McCarthy de Zavala)   137   220

ANTONIO-MORA
[See PESSOA, FERNANDO]

ANTONIOU, DEMETRIOS
POEMS
   Poem ("To conquer this blank...")   78   167
   To the Cold Imagination
    (Tr. by Kimon Friar)

ANWAR, CHAIRIL
BOOKS REVIEWED
   Selected Poems
    (Tr. by Burton Raffel
    and Nurdin Salam)   104   115

ANZAI, FUYUE
POEMS
   Spain—III
    (Tr. by Satoru Satu
    and Constance Urdang)   88   97

AP GWILYM, DAFYDD
ARTICLES ABOUT
   Rev. of *The Rent That's Due to Love*
    (Tr. by Gwyn Williams)
    [Welsh poetry]   77   351
    [Note]   82   307

APOLLINAIRE, GUILLAUME
POEMS
   Poem for Lou
    (Tr. by Hubert Creekmore)   77   144
   Le Pont Mirabeau   77   265
   Zone
   The Pretty Redhead
   Toward the South
    (Tr. by Harry Duncan)

BOOKS REVIEWED
Selected Writings of...
    (Tr. by Roger Shattuck)   77   162
Alcools: Poems 1898-1913
    (Tr. by William Meredith)   105   136
Alcools
    (Tr. by Anne Hyde Greet)   111   124

ARTICLES ABOUT
The Disciples of Gertrude Stein,
  by Richard Aldington   17   35
Rev. of *Apollinaire: An Elegy*,
  by Walter Lowenfels   42   49
Surrealism in 1960:
  A Backward Glance,
  by Wallace Fowlie   95   365
Rev. of *Apollinaire:*
  Poet Among the Painters,
  by Francis Steegmuller   104   187
Rev. of *Apollinaire*,
  by Margaret Davies   107   267

APPLEBAUM, SYDNEY
POEMS
Winterpieces   49   310
Approach
Chorus

APPLEMAN, PHILIP
POEMS
State of Nature   132   68
Mr. Extinction, Meet Ms. Survival   133   151
Nostalgie de la Boue   134   330
The Voyage Home   137   342
Anniversary   142   261
The Trickle-Down Theory of Happiness
A Little Heart-to-Heart
  on Valentine's Day   145   270
"Are You Saved?"   146   288
Heading North   149   27
Gathering by the River   151   6
Heavenly Body   151   417

BOOKS REVIEWED
Open Doorways   130   293

APPLEWHITE, JAMES
POEMS
The Scorned   118   195
Highwater
Jogging on the New Construction   121   311
Poets, Now
The Man   123   85
Bordering Manuscript   125   249
Revisitings
The Sleeper   128   15
The Metals

To Earth   129   137
Atmosphere
Firewood
The Waters
Love Poem to a Bright Field
Science Fiction   138   156
A Catalogue of Trees   142   311
Barbecue Service
Marriage Portrait
Storm in the Briar Patch   158   272
Last Call   168   266

BOOKS REVIEWED
Foreseeing the Journey   144   40
River Writing, An Eno Journal   153   229

APULEIUS, LUCIUS
BOOKS REVIEWED
The Golden Ass
    (Tr. by Robert Graves)   93   395

AQUINAS, [SISTER] THOMAS [O.P.]
POEMS
Homing   42   75
Daily Augury   44   317

ARAGON, LOUIS
POEMS
Petite Suite Sans Fil
    (Tr. by Rolfe Humphries)   62   247
I Wait for Her Letter in the Twilight
    (Tr. by Rolfe Humphries)   63   306
Zone Libre   67   1
Elsa at the Mirror
    (Tr. by George Dillon)
Richard Coeur-de-Lion
    (Tr. by Sally Wood)   67   14
Elsa's Eyes   67   16
Night at Dunkirk
C
Night of Exile
Tears Are Alike
    (Tr. by William Jay Smith)

BOOKS REVIEWED
The Red Front
    (Tr. by E. E. Cummings)   42   281

ARTICLES ABOUT
On the Continent,
  by F. C. Weiskopf   56   332
The Conspiracy of the Poets,
  by Pierre Seghers
    (Tr. by William Jay Smith)   67   25
Rev. of *Aragon:*
  Poet of the French Resistance
  (Ed. by Hannah Josephson
  and Malcolm Cowley)   68   44

ARATUS
POEMS
From *The Phaenomena*
  (Tr. by John Hollander)   128   146

ARCHILOCHOS
POEMS
A Sheaf of Poems and Fragments
  (Tr. by Guy Davenport)   101   404

BOOKS REVIEWED
Carmina Archilochi:
The Fragments of Archilochos
  (Tr. by Guy Davenport)   105   329

ARENDT, HANNAH
ARTICLES ABOUT
After Reading Hannah Arendt,
  by Denis Donoghue   100   127

ARENS, EGMONT HEGEL
ARTICLES
Correspondence: To Carl Sandburg
  [Poem]   10   279

ARENSBERG, WALTER CONRAD
BOOKS REVIEWED
Idols   8   208

ARISTOPHANES
BOOKS REVIEWED
Lysistrata
  (Tr. by Dudley Fitts)   85   294
The Frogs
  (Tr. by Dudley Fitts)   88   337
Aristophanes: The Frogs
  (Tr. by Richmond Lattimore)   102   54
Aristophanes: The Clouds
  (Tr. by William Arrowsmith)
The Acharnians
  (Tr. by Douglass Parker)   102   56
The Birds
  (Tr. by William Arrowsmith)
The Birds
  (Tr. by Dudley Fitts)
The Frogs
  (Tr. by Dudley Fitts)
Ladies' Day
  [*Thesmophoriazusae*]
  (Tr. by Dudley Fitts)
Lysistrata
  (Tr. by Dudley Fitts)
The Congresswomen
  (Tr. by Douglass Parker)   113   188

ARISTOTLE
ARTICLES ABOUT
The Chicago Critics: Yes and Perhaps,
  by Martin J. Svaglic   82   157

ARKIN, DAVID
POEMS
Deus Ex Machina   26   188
New Love
Au Pis Aller

ARMANDA HUACUJA, E.
POEMS
Nostalgia   71   293

ARMENS, SVEN
POEMS
Love at Old Orchard Beach   83   199

ARMI, ANNA MARIA
BOOKS REVIEWED
Poems   59   340

ARMITAGE, BARRI
POEMS
Fall Ritual   148   336
Weights
Self-Portrait   149   264
Trading on Gravity
Double Helix   153   263

ARTICLES
Correspondence
  [Greg Kuzma, Martha Collins]   149   180

ARMS, GEORGE
BOOKS REVIEWED
Poetry Explication
  (Ed. with Joseph M. Kuntz)   77   289
The Fields Were Green:
A New View of Bryant,
Whittier, Holmes, Lowell,
and Longfellow, with a Selection
of Their Poems   84   98

ARMSTRONG, HAMILTON FISH
BOOKS REVIEWED
The Book of New York Verse (Ed.) 12   337

ARMSTRONG, M(ARTIN) D.
[MARTIN ARMSTRONG]
POEMS
The Procession   3   46
Man Seeks to Cage Delight   23   87

ARMSTRONG, VIRGINIA IRVING
POEMS
Tapestries   49   320
Sea-Gods
Interlude
The Duck Season

ARNETT, CARROLL
POEMS
Bushmill's   108   307
The Dare
Next
Song ("With you it is...")   112   103

BOOKS REVIEWED
Then   109   340
Not Only That   113   188

ARNHEIM, RUDOLF
BOOKS REVIEWED
Poets at Work: Essays
(With W. H. Auden, Karl Shapiro,
and Donald A. Stauffer)   72   311

ARNOLD, CRAIG
POEMS
Artichoke   169   256
Hot   170   152

ARNOLD, MARGUERITE
POEMS
Clinic   26   194
Residue
Divided
Joy

ARNOLD, MATTHEW
BOOKS REVIEWED
The Note-Books of...
(Ed. by Howard Foster Lowry,
Karl Young, and Waldo
Hilary Dunn)   81   196

ARTICLES ABOUT
Matthew Arnold's Centenary,
by Harriet Monroe   21   206
Rev. of *Emerson*
(Ed. by Alfred Kazin
and Daniel Aaron)   96   382

ARNSTEIN, FLORA J.
POEMS
Communication   38   306
Only the Dome
Plowing Song
Fishes
Gifts
Knowing No More
No Pledges   41   129
Bequest   41   317
No Winter   47   197

BOOKS REVIEWED
A Legacy of Hours   33   49

ARONSON, STEVEN M. L.
REVIEWS
Scattered Returns,
by L. E. Sissman   116   40

ARROWSMITH, WILLIAM
BOOKS REVIEWED
Cyclops and *Heracles* (Tr.),
in *Euripides II*   88   337
Hecuba and *Orestes* (Tr.),
in *The Complete Greek Tragedies:*
Euripides III, IV
(Ed. by David Grene
and Richmond Lattimore)   95   190
The Satyricon (Tr.)   96   247
Aristophanes: The Clouds (Tr.)   102   54
The Birds, by Aristophanes (Tr.)   102   56
The Satyricon of Petronius (Tr.)   107   264

ARTAUD, ANTONIN
ARTICLES ABOUT
Rev. of *The Sorrows of Priapus,*
by Edward Dahlberg   94   54

ARTHUR, CHARLOTTE
POEMS
Poems from Ireland   28   322
   Red Padraig
   Wind
   The Way of a Star
   Candle-Light and Dawn
For a Misty Day   32   19
In Ireland   34   320
   Connemara
   Black Ballad
Words Unspoken   46   147
   A Fantasy
   In the End
   For the Evening and the Morning

ARTICLES
Correspondence [AE]   47   174

ARVIN, NEWTON
BOOKS REVIEWED
Whitman   53   273

ASEKOFF, L. S.
POEMS
Day Lilies   155   266
The White Loft
Trace
Winter Roses
Kafka's Angels   157   135
In the House of the Deafman
Skywriters over Tokyo   157   216
Film Noir   157   280

On Certainty
Flowers by the Sea   161 325
Thule   163 139

ASH, JOHN
BOOKS REVIEWED
The Burnt Pages   161 339

ASHBERY, JOHN
[See also SYMINGTON,
JOEL MICHAEL, pseud.]
POEMS
And You Know   87 149
Grand Abacus
The Pied Piper
The Painter
Abstentions   89 341
To Redouté
Our Youth   91 163
The Idiot
A Blessing in Disguise   102 141
If the Birds Knew
Last Month
The Recent Past
Civilization and Its Discontents
Fragment   107 283
Sortes Vergilianae   114   1
For John Clare
It Was Raining in the Capital
An Outing
Scheherazade   123 104
As You Came from the Holy Land
A Man of Words
Grand Galop   124   1
Self-Portrait in a Convex Mirror 124 247
Syringa   130   4
Blue Sonata
The Ice-Cream Wars
Fantasia on "The Nut-Brown Maid" 130 260
Late Echo   134 187
Train Rising Out of the Sea
Not Only/But Also
Many Wagons Ago
The Sun
Five Pedantic Pieces
Flowering Death
Ostensibly   150 249
Adam Snow
Morning Jitters
Amid Mounting Evidence
Riddle Me
Unreleased Movie   151   7
Tahiti Trot   162 129
Leeward
Strange Things Happen at Night
A Poem of Unrest   166 187
Tower of Darkness
Theme
Sleepers Awake

TRANSLATIONS
Poems by Pierre Martory   162 132

ARTICLES
Comment
[David Morton,
Joel Michael Symington]   151 203

REVIEWS
Stanzas in Meditation,
by Gertrude Stein   90 250

BOOKS REVIEWED
Some Trees   89 307
The Tennis Court Oath   100 390
Rivers and Mountains   109 185
The Double Dream of Spring   117   50
A Nest of Ninnies
(With James Schuyler)   117   54
Three Poems   120 296
Self-Portrait in a Convex Mirror 127 349
As We Know   137   42
Houseboat Days
Shadow Train   140 236
A Wave   145 291
Selected Poems   148 228
April Galleons   152   98
Flow Chart   159 157
And the Stars Were Shining   165   31

ARTICLES ABOUT
Rev. of The Poets
of the New York School
(Ed. by John Bernard Myers)   119   39
Rev. by David Lehman   119 224
Rev. of John Ashbery:
An Introduction to the Poetry,
by David Shapiro   137   42
Rev. of Constant Defender,
by James Tate   145   99
Contemporary British Poetry:
A Romantic Persistence?
by John Bayley   146 227
Rev. of The Psycho-Political Muse:
American Poetry Since the Fifties,
by Paul Breslin   152 229
[Note]   160 240

ASHER, ELISE
POEMS
Moment in July   72 190
Ocean Resort
The Page   80 130
Sickbed   94 378

BOOKS REVIEWED
The Meandering Absolute   89   64

ASHLEY, RENÉE A.

POEMS

Missing You	159	253
Pressing the Body On	159	319
Sort of a Love Poem	163	283

BOOKS REVIEWED

Salt	161	99

ASHLEY, WINSTON

POEMS

A Sheaf of Flutes	48	142
When We Have Been and Have Returned		
Clark Street		
They that Saw You Told Me		
A Dance Last Night Next Door		
Separation		

ASHMAN, RICHARD

POEMS

The Crematory	89	26

ASHTON, E. B.

BOOKS REVIEWED

Primal Vision: Selected Writings		
of Gottfried Benn (Ed.)	97	387

ASKEW, WILSON

POEMS

Dream ("I rose and walked sunward...")	42	204
One Season to Another		

ASPEL, ALEXANDER

BOOKS REVIEWED

Contemporary French Poetry		
(Ed. with Donald Justice)	107	267

ASUNCION SILVA, JOSÉ

POEMS

Nocturne		
(Tr. by Muna Lee)	26	123

ATHERTON, HOPE

ARTICLES ABOUT

Rev. of Singularities,		
by Susan Howe	159	282

ATIK, ANNE

POEMS

Sonnets to Terry, Who Died Young	128	278

ATKINS, ELIZABETH

POEMS

High-School Portraits	38	260
Peter Pavlov		
Florence Dell		
August Manson		
"Broncho" Gallock		

Martha Harris		
Doloris Foster		
For a Freshman	41	252

REVIEWS

Topless Towers	57	270
The Arrow at the Heel,		
by Raymond Holden		
Poems and Portraits,		
by Christopher La Farge		
Love and Need,		
by Jean Starr Untermeyer	58	219
The Walls Do Not Fall, by H. D.	65	327

BOOKS REVIEWED

The Poet's Poet	22	168

ATKINS, KATHLEEN

POEMS

Loon Hunting	140	336
A Physics Problem		
You Conjure a Mother and Father	157	24

ATKINSON, CHARLES

POEMS

To Split a Round of Oak	144	215
The Patience of Dry Plants		
Plum		

ATKINSON, JENNIFER

POEMS

Hail on Stone Mountain	145	74
The Magic Words		
Fortune-Telling		
Philosophy Class	147	142
Choosing Happiness	148	125
The Dogwood Tree	150	328
Afterward		
Extradition	164	24
The Miraculous	165	311
Ancient of Days	170	324

BOOKS REVIEWED

The Dogwood Tree	159	32

ATLAS, JAMES

POEMS

From The Way of All Loss	113	317
The Celebration	115	26
The Death of Attila József	117	98
The Diary of Gustav Janouch	118	211
Isaac Rosenfeld Thinks About His Life		
Driving Through Small Towns in England	121	222

REVIEWS

A Chronicle of Younger Poets	113	428
The Blue Stairs,		
by Barbara Guest		

White Country,
  by Peter Schjeldahl
The Homer Mitchell Place,
  by John Engels
A Windmill Near Calvary,
  by Keith Waldrop
The Glass House:
  The Life of Theodore Roethke,
  by Allan Seager   114   327
His Toy, His Dream, His Rest,
  by John Berryman   115   43
Voyager: A Life of Hart Crane,
  by John Unterecker   116   256
What Is To Be Done?   119   45
  The Oblivion Ha-Ha,
  by James Tate
  The Color of Dust,
  by Michael Anania
  Letter to an Imaginary Friend,
  Parts I & II,
  by Thomas McGrath
  Highway to the Sky,
  by Michael Brownstein
  Meat Air: Poems 1957-1969,
  by Ron Loewinsohn
  The Boy Changed into a Stag,
  by Ferenc Juhász
  (Tr. by Kenneth McRobbie
  and Ilona Duczynska)
  The Twelve and Other Poems,
  by Alexander Blok
  (Tr. by Jon Stallworthy
  and Peter France)
  The Modern Poets:
  An American-British Anthology
  (Ed. by John Malcolm Brinnin
  and Bill Read)   119   169
Old Wines, New Bottles,
  Old Bottles, New Wines   121   229
  The Collected Poems and Epigrams,
  by J. V. Cunningham
  A Man Holding an Acoustic Panel,
  by David Shapiro
  Selected Poems,
  by Ford Madox Ford
  (Ed. by Basil Bunting)
  The Collected Poems
  of H. Phelps Putnam
  (Ed. by Charles R. Walker)
Preferences: 51 American Poets Choose from
  Their Own Work and from the Past
  (Ed. by Richard Howard)   125   52
Autobiography of the Present   125   295
  Selected Poems: In Five Sets,
  by Laura Riding
  Threats Instead of Trees,
  by Michael Ryan
  Return to a Place Lit by a Glass of Milk,
  by Charles Simic

Walking the Boundaries: Poems 1957-1974,
  by Peter Davison
Poems 4, by Alan Dugan
The Avenue Bearing the Initial of Christ
  into the New World: Poems 1946-1964,
  by Galway Kinnell
Thank You, Fog: Last Poems,
  by W. H. Auden   126   175

BOOKS REVIEWED
  Selected Poems and Texts,
  by Attila József
  (Tr. by John Batki)
  (Ed. with George Gömöri)   126   103

ATWOOD, MARGARET
POEMS
  For Archeologists   114   34
  Dream: Bluejay or Archeopteryx
  Three Desk Objects
  Carrying Food Home in Winter
  Projected Slide of an Unknown Soldier
  Hesitations Outside the Door   117   100
  ("You refuse to own")
  Songs of the Transformed   123   257
    Pig Song
    Bull Song
    Rat Song
    Crow Song
    Song of the Worms
    Owl Song
    Siren Song
    Fox/Fire Song
    Song of the Hen's Head
    Corpse Song

REVIEWS
  Four Poets from Canada   114   202
    Phrases from Orpheus, by D. G. Jones
    The Absolute Smile, by George Jonas
    An Idiot Joy, by Eli Mandel
    North of Summer, by Alfred Purdy
    Wild Grape Wine, by A. W. Purdy

BOOKS REVIEWED
  The Circle Game   112   201
  The Animals in That Country   115   430
  The Journals of Susannah Moodie   119   356
  Power Politics
  Power Politics   120   235
  You Are Happy   127   292
  Selected Poems   133   100
  Two-Headed Poems   140   102
  Murder in the Dark;
    Journal of Susannah Moodie; and
    New Oxford Book of Canadian
    Verse in English (Ed.)   144   297
  Morning in the Burned House   168   281

AUCLAIR, MARCELLE

ARTICLES ABOUT

Verse Drama on the Paris Stage,
by Ruby Haykin   82   294

AUDEN, W(YSTAN) H(UGH)

POEMS

Journey to Iceland   49   179
Poem ("O who can ever praise enough...")
Voltaire at Ferney   54   119
Poem ("He watched with all his...")   57   9
The Shield of Achilles   81   3
Doggerel by a Senior Citizen   115   185
Ode to the Medieval Poets   119   63
Poem ("O who can ever praise...")   121   1

TRANSLATIONS

Poems by Ondra Lysohorsky
(With Isobella Levatin)   116   273

REVIEWS

Visiting the Caves,
by William Plomer   49   223

BOOKS REVIEWED

Poems   38   35
Poems   38   101
The Orators: An English Study   42   110
Poems   47   43
The Poet's Tongue
(Ed. with John Garrett)   48   43
The Dog Beneath the Skin
(With Christopher Isherwood)   48   221
The Ascent of F6
(With Christopher Isherwood)   49   225
Look, Stranger!
Letters from Iceland
(With Louis MacNeice)   52   39
The Oxford Book of Light Verse (Ed.)   54   111
Another Time: Poems   56   40
The Double Man   58   148
For the Time Being   65   202
A Selection from the Poems
of Alfred, Lord Tennyson (Ed.)   65   335
The Collected Poetry of...   66   204
The Age of Anxiety   71   90
Slick But Not Streamlined,
by John Betjeman (Ed.)   71   162
Poets at Work: Essays
(With Karl Shapiro, Rudolf Arnheim,
and Donald A. Stauffer)   72   311
The Portable Greek Reader (Ed.)   73   284
The Portable Greek Reader (Ed.)   76   218
The Enchafed Flood, or The Romantic
Iconography of the Sea   76   291
Poets of the English Language
(Ed. with Norman Hall Pearson)   77   179

Nones   78   352
The Shield of Achilles   86   168
Mountains
The Magic Flute
(Tr. with Chester Kallman)   89   253
The Old Man's Road   90   47
The Criterion Book
of Modern American Verse (Ed.)   91   124
Homage to Clio   97   380
The Play of Daniel,
A Thirteenth-Century Musical Drama
(Ed. by Noah Greenberg)
[Narration]
Markings, by Dag Hammarskjöld
(Tr. with Leif Sjöberg)   106   356
The Dyer's Hand   107   118
About the House   108   119
Antiworlds, by Andrei Voznesensky
(Tr. with others)   110   40
Collected Shorter Poems 1927-1957   114   113
Collected Longer Poems   117   211
The Elder Edda, a Selection
(Tr. with Paul B. Taylor)   117   341
A Certain World: A Commonplace Book   118   349
City Without Walls & Other Poems   119   34
Slick But Not Streamlined,
by John Betjeman (Ed.)   121   48
Epistle to a Godson and Other Poems   122   344
Thank You, Fog: Last Poems   126   175
Collected Poems
(Ed. by Edward Mendelson)   131   159
Juvenilia: Poems, 1922-1928
(Ed. by Katherine Bucknell)   166   226

ARTICLES ABOUT

English Poetry Today, by Basil Bunting   39   264
Notes on English Poets,
by Michael Roberts   39   271
English Letter, by F. R. Leavis   43   215
Poetry of the Left, by Harriet Monroe   48   212
Poetry Politics in London,
by D. S. Savage   53   200
W. H. Auden:
The Search for a Public,
by David Daiches   54   148
The New Theatrum Poetarum,
by Alan S. Downer   60   206
Henry James and the Poets,
by Leon Edel   62   328
Rev. of New Poems: 1943
(Ed. by Oscar Williams)   64   86
The Poet's Perspectives,
by D. S. Savage   64   148
Correspondence
from Malcolm Cowley   65   345
Moods and Reactions,
by Stephen Spender   67   88

A New Engagement?
   by George Dillon   72   89
   [Note]   83   55
Conversation on Cornelia Street,
   by Howard Griffin   84   96
Rev. of *The Making of the Auden Canon*,
   by Joseph Warren Beach   92   116
Rev. of *Of the Festivity*,
   by William Dickey   95   248
   [Note]   98   65
Rev. of *The Poetry of W. H. Auden:*
   The Disenchanted Island,
   by Monroe K. Spears   104   264
Rev. of *A Reader's Guide to W. H. Auden*,
   by John Fuller   118   349
Rev. of *The Apple Barrel*,
   by Jon Stallworthy   127   98
Rev. of *Poems and Epistles*,
   by John Fuller   129   340
Rev. of *The New Oxford Book*
   of American Verse
   (Ed. by Richard Ellmann)   131   236
Rev. of *Early Auden*,
   by Edward Mendelson   139   292
Rev. of *The Penguin Book*
   of Homosexual Verse
   (Ed. by Stephen Coote)   144   166
Rev. of *Children in Exile*,
   by James Fenton   145   99
"Sacred Beings":
   Writers in Recorded Conversation,
   by Michael Milburn   146   101

AUSLANDER, JOSEPH
POEMS
I Have Waited for You Long   20   72
Little Lou
Enigma   23   299
To a Certain April Somewhere
Herodiade
Instead of Tears

BOOKS REVIEWED
Sunrise Trumpets   24   219
Cyclops' Eye   28   282
The Winged Horse:
   The Story of the Poets and Their Poetry
   (With Frank Ernest Hill)   31   349
Hell in Harness   35   346
Letters to Ladies
No Traveler Returns   46   291
More Than Bread   50   291
Riders at the Gate   55   162

AUSTER, PAUL
POEMS
Spokes   119   311

TRANSLATIONS
   Poem by Jacques Dupin   116   279

AUSTIN, JOHN
BOOKS REVIEWED
Poems for Men   18   223

AUSTIN, MARY
POEMS
Neither Spirit nor Bird   9   239
Prayer to the Mountain Spirit
High Places   15   181
   The Eagle's Song
   The Grass on the Mountain
   Black Prayers
   New-Mexican Love Song
   I Do Not Know
Whence?   17   192
Unworthy Love
Being Only a Dream   22   19
South-Western Poems   32   123
   Sounds
   Caller of Buffalo
   Rio Abajo
   Litany for New Mexico
The Dark Hours   37   86

ARTICLES
Sources of Poetic Influence
   in the Southwest   43   152

BOOKS REVIEWED
The Children Sing
   in the Far West   33   163

ARTICLES ABOUT
Obituary   45   59

AVISON, MARGARET
POEMS
Geometaphysics   70   318
The Iconoclasts
Perspective
Song but Oblique to '47
The Party
Hiatus   80   15
All Fools' Eve   91   173
Stray Dog, Near Ecully
Rich Boy's Birthday
   Through a Window
Prelude   93   366

ARTICLES
Poets in Canada
   [James Reaney, R. A. D. Ford,
   Goodridge MacDonald,
   R. G. Everson, Gordon LeClaire,
   Daryl Hine]   94   182

BOOKS REVIEWED
Winter Sun 98 118
The Dumbfounding 110 258
Poems 1940-1966 144 297

ARTICLES ABOUT
The Architecture of Vision,
    by Brewster Ghiselin 70 324

AXELROD, JOSEPH
ARTICLES
Cummings and Phonetics 65 88

AXINN, DONALD EVERETT
BOOKS REVIEWED
The Hawk's Dream and Other Poems 143 228

AYLING, ALAN
BOOKS REVIEWED
A Collection of Chinese Lyrics
    (With Duncan Mackintosh) 112 283

AYOUB, CHRISTIAN
POEMS
Pola Diva
    (Tr. by James Merrill) 114 71

AYRES, HARRY MORGAN
ARTICLES ABOUT
Poetry on Records, by Harry T. Moore 57 52

AYSCOUGH, FLORENCE
TRANSLATIONS
Poems by Li Hai-Ku, Wen Cheng-Ming,
    Ch'en Hung-Shou, Liang T'ung-Shu,
    T'ai Ta-Mien, Liu Shih-An, Lu Kun,
    T'ao Ch'ien, Wang Chang-Ling,
    and Wang Ching-Seng
    (Tr. with Amy Lowell) 13 233

ARTICLES
Written Pictures 13 268

BOOKS REVIEWED
*Tu Fu, The Autobiography
    of a Chinese Poet* (Tr.) 47 219
Travels of a Chinese Poet (Tr.)
Correspondence of a Friendship
    (With Amy Lowell)
    (Ed. by Harley Farnsworth MacNair) 69 54

ARTICLES ABOUT
Correspondence
    from Arthur Waley 14 55

B

BABCOCK, DONALD C.
BOOKS REVIEWED
New England Harvest   84   163

BACCHYLIDES
BOOKS REVIEWED
Complete Poems
(Tr. by Robert Fagles)   102   54

BACHELARD, GASTON
ARTICLES ABOUT
Paris Letter, by Wallace Fowlie   96   371

BACHMANN, INGEBORG
ARTICLES ABOUT
German Lyric Poetry Since 1945,
by Hans Egon Holthusen
(Tr. by Herman Salinger)   88   257

BACKHURST, PAUL
POEMS
Andy   131   197

BACON, FRANCIS
ARTICLES ABOUT
Rev. of The Complete Poems
of Marianne Moore   139   340

BACON, IRVING
POEMS
One Farmer   46   135

BACON, JOSEPHINE DASKAM
BOOKS REVIEWED
Truth o' Women:
Last Words from Ladies Long Vanished   24   341

BACON, LEONARD
BOOKS REVIEWED
The Song of Roland (Tr.)   9   156
Animula Vagula   29   170
Animula Vagula   32   282
Guinea-Fowl and Other Poultry
The Legend of Quincibald   33   343
Lost Buffalo and Other Poems   37   163
The Furioso   41   275

Dream and Action   45   223
The Goose on the Capitol   50   210
Rhyme and Punishment
Bullinger Bound and Other Poems   52   229
Day of Fire   64   39

BACON, MARTHA
BOOKS REVIEWED
Lament for the Chieftains   61   690
Things Visible and Invisible   72   281

BAER, WILLIAM
POEMS
Books   136   67
When She Is Silent

BAGG, ROBERT
POEMS
Sonnet by the Lakeside   89   98
'Laine   90   148
The Risen Eyelid   92   364
Confetti for a Red Haired Bride
Hallowe'en   95   229
Apollo and Daphne
Venus and Nausicaa
Poseidon and Demosthenes
Ronald Wyn
Epidaurus   120   40

BOOKS REVIEWED
Madonna of the Cello   98   245
The Scrawny Sonnets
and Other Narratives   125   166

ARTICLES ABOUT
Robert Bagg: A Postscript,
by James Merrill   98   250

BAGG, TERRY R.
POEMS
Sunburst, Icones Florarum Sanctorumque   114   234
Musical Offering
Perigee
Pavlov   117   231
Ballad for the Dead Narcissus   119   254

Reflections Approximately Divine
Small Homeric Overture
Recitatives (No Aria) for a Drowning   123   19
Three Puritans

BAGRITSKY, EDUARD
POEMS
  "My Honied Languor"
    (Tr. by Babette Deutsch)   70   248

BAILEY, DORIS ["D. E."]
POEMS
  Dante and Milton,
    Those Old and Bitter Men   61   652
  Is This Madness?
  Helpless and Fond,
    the Wolf and Lamb
  Killed in Action

BAIRD, MARTHA
BOOKS REVIEWED
  Nice Deity   89   64

BAIRD, TOM
ARTICLES ABOUT
  When Children Write Verse,
    by Maude Sumner Smith   56   154

BAKELESS, JOHN
POEMS
  Mountain Tops   13   253

BAKER, DAVID
POEMS
  Sunbathing   148   147
  Starlight   149   203
  The Supernatural: A Love Poem   154   278
  Red Shift
  Mercy
  Taxi After an Evening Shower   158   21
  Charming   159   323
  The Extinction of the Dinosaurs
  The Truth About Small Towns   161   329
  Holding Katherine
  Dust to Dust   163   205
  Abandoned Barn   164   4
  The Women

REVIEWS
  Culture, Inclusion, Craft   158   158
    Popular Culture,
      by Albert Goldbarth
    Let Evening Come,
      by Jane Kenyon
    The City in Which I Love You,
      by Li-Young Lee
    Ode to Anna Moffo,
      by Wayne Kostenbaum

Mystery Train,
  by David Wojahn
Powers of Congress,
  by Alice Fulton
Smarts   159   282
  Singularities, by Susan Howe
  [Hope Atherton]
  The Never-Ending,
    by Andrew Hudgins
  Bethlehem in Broad Daylight,
    by Mark Doty
  Star Ledger, by Lynda Hull
  Questions About Angels,
    by Billy Collins
Ecstasy and Irony   161   99
  Salt, by Renée Ashley
  Arreboles, by Boyer Rickel
  The Pilgrim Among Us,
    by Roberta Spear
  In the Year of the Comet,
    by Nicholas Christopher
  Looking for Luck,
    by Maxine Kumin
  Bread Without Sugar,
    by Gerald Stern
Plainness and Sufficiency   164   223
  Psalms, by April Bernard
  Incontinence, by Susan Hahn
  Devolution of the Nude,
    by Lynne McMahon
  Erasures, by Donald Revell
  Apocalyptic Narrative,
    by Rodney Jones
  [William Bradford]
On Restraint   168   33
  Weather Central, by Ted Kooser
  A Wedding in Hell,
    by Charles Simic
  Imperfect Thirst,
    by Galway Kinnell
  Song, by Brigit Pegeen Kelly
  Chickamauga,
    by Charles Wright
  [Walt Whitman,
    R. W. Emerson]
Romantic Melancholy,
  Romantic Excess   170   288
  The Woman Who Died in Her Sleep,
    by Linda Gregerson
  Loosestrife, by Stephen Dunn
  The Wellspring, by Sharon Olds
  The Marriage in the Trees,
    by Stanley Plumly
  Sun Under Wood,
    by Robert Hass

BOOKS REVIEWED
  Sweet Home, Saturday Night   160   219
  After the Reunion   167   223

BAKER, D(ONALD) W.
POEMS
Recital   91   370
Helen at Cocktails   97   293
The Room Within   104   26
The Mourner
Waiting   110   244
Seventeen
The Soldier

REVIEWS
Five Poets   109   401
    Sea Lion Caves, by Nelson Bentley
    An Eye for an I,
        by Harriet Zinnes
    27 Poems, by Roger Hecht
    Cipango's Hinder Door,
        by Edward Dahlberg
    The Stride of Time,
        by Richmond Lattimore
Five Poets   111   195
    Six Mile Corner, by Robert Dawson
    A Beginning, by William Burford
    Change of Address,
        by Kathleen Fraser
    Twenty Years of Hands,
        by Simon Perchik
    A Japanese Journal,
        by John Tagliabue
    Poems 1957-1967, by James Dickey   111   400

BAKER, HOWARD
POEMS
Carnival in New Orleans   57   227

BOOKS REVIEWED
    *A Letter from the Country
    and Other Poems*   58   266
    Ode to the Sea, and Other Poems   109   187

ARTICLES ABOUT
    Convention and Revolt,
        by Jessica Nelson North   34   212

BAKER, JAMES RUPERT
BOOKS REVIEWED
    Poems of Bishop Henry King (Ed.)   99   187

**BAKER, KARLE WILSON
    [CHARLOTTE WILSON]**
POEMS
Unser Gott   5   75
The Housemother   7   78
A Simple Song for America: 1917   10   296
To Get Wisdom   19   16
Meekness and Pride
Courage
Not in the Whirlwind

BOOKS REVIEWED
    Blue Smoke   15   164

ARTICLES ABOUT
    [Note on name]   5   97
    A Texas Prize Contest,
        by Harriet Monroe   21   91

BAKER, LEONE
POEMS
Spectre-Theme   17   198

BAKER, LOIS
POEMS
What Climbers Know   160   336
Tracers

BALABAN, JOHN
POEMS
Letters From Across the Sea   164   26

BOOKS REVIEWED
    After Our War   132   31

BALAKIAN, ANNA
ARTICLES
    Correspondence:
        Cryptology and Sublimity
        [Parker Tyler]   71   227

REVIEWS
    The Intimate Journals of Charles Baudelaire
        (Tr. by Christopher Isherwood)   72   228

BOOKS REVIEWED
    The Literary Origins of Surrealism   70   282

BALAKIAN, PETER
POEMS
A Country House   145   90
Wild Cherry
Fish Mouth
The Oriental Rug   147   78
Flat Sky of Summer   150   211
Father, 4-F, 1941
Domestic Lament   151   10
A Toast   154   256
The Color of Pomegranates

REVIEWS
    Collected Poems: 1948-1984,
        by Derek Walcott   148   169

BOOKS REVIEWED
    Sad Days of Light   144   107
    Reply from Wilderness Island   154   340

BALAKRISHNAN, T. K.
TRANSLATIONS
Poem by G. Sankara Kurup   93   259

BALANCHINE, GEORGE
ARTICLES ABOUT
Rev. of *Dancers, Buildings,*
and People in the Streets,
by Edwin Denby   111 268

BALCOM, NANITA MAC D.
POEMS
Secret Garden   34   137
Harvest

BALDWIN, CHARLES SEARS
BOOKS REVIEWED
Ancient Rhetoric and Poetic   27   283

BALDWIN, MERCY
POEMS
Gray Songs   27   190
Appreciation
Intangible Extremes

BOOKS REVIEWED
Gray Songs   30   232

ARTICLES ABOUT
[Note on name]   27   351

BALDWIN, TAMA
POEMS
Fatigue in California   142 338

BALL, ANGELA
POEMS
House   149 12
Tandem   153 197
Body
Possession   154 325

BALLOU, ROBERT O.
ARTICLES
Correspondence   28   176

BALMONT, KONSTANTIN
POEMS
With the Wind   12   258
On the Heights
(Tr. by Edith Chapman Tracy)

BALSEIRO, JOSÉ A.
BOOKS REVIEWED
Al Rumor de la Fuente   22   226

BANDEIRA, MANUEL
POEMS
Morning Star
(Tr. by H. R. Hays)   62   75

BANDYPADHYAY,
KARUNA NIDHAN
POEMS
Whispered
(Tr. by Lila Ray)   93   213

BANGS, JANET NORRIS
POEMS
The Sand Dunes   12   306
Care   21   21
April   24   12
Octaves   41   257
Peace
Time
Timepiece   54   317

BANGS, JOHN KENDRICK
BOOKS REVIEWED
The Foothills of Parnassus   4   166

BANNING, KENDALL
POEMS
Love Songs of the Open Road   1   110

BARAKA, IMAMU AMIRI
[See JONES, LE ROI]

BARBEAU, MARIUS
BOOKS REVIEWED
Folk Songs of French Canada
(Ed. with Edward Sapir)   28   348

ARTICLES ABOUT
Note on French-Canadian Folk-Songs,
by Edward Sapir   16   210

BARBER, DAVID
POEMS
The Favor   159 255
Little Overture   164 145
To the Trespasser

REVIEWS
Short Reviews   160 219
Green River: New and Selected Poems,
by Robert Morgan
Radio Sky, by Norman Dubie
Sweet Home, Saturday Night,
by David Baker
The Rain That Falls This Far,
by Dennis Hinrichsen
Covenant, by Alan Shapiro
Habits of Mind   162 224

Teodoro Luna's Two Kisses,
  by Alberto Ríos
Rapture, by Susan Mitchell
Two Trees, by Ellen Bryant Voigt
New and Selected Poems,
  by Mary Oliver
Collected Shorter Poems,
  by Hayden Carruth
Body and Soul   164   157
  About Love, by John Montague
  Constance, by Jane Kenyon
  The Devil's Tour, by Mary Karr
  No Nature, by Gary Snyder
Life Studies   166   38
  Entries, by Wendell Berry
  Each in a Place Apart,
    by James McMichael
  Stone Crop, by Jody Gladding
  Across the Layers:
    Poems Old and New,
    by Albert Goldbarth

BOOKS REVIEWED
  The Spirit Level   170   226

BARBER, JENNIFER
POEMS
  Summer As a Large, Reclining Nude   162   193

BARBER, MARY FINETTE
POEMS
  To a Man of Action   31   74
  Idle Acre   38   81
  Nantucket Sojourn   52   266
    Returning
    Survivals

BARBER, SOLON R.
POEMS
  Veracruz   37   18
  Sonora Desert   39   202
  Man of These Countries   47   306

BOOKS REVIEWED
  Cross-Country   42   52

BARBOUR, DOUGLAS
BOOKS REVIEWED
  Writing Right
    (Ed. with Marni L. Stanley)   144   297

BARBOUR, THOMAS
  [THOMAS BARBOUR II]
POEMS
  Having To Do with Poetry   72   240

BARCIA, JOSÉ RUBIA
  [See RUBIO BARCIA, JOSÉ]

BARCLAY, ROBERT EARL
BOOKS REVIEWED
  Etchings   13   167

BAREA, ARTURO
BOOKS REVIEWED
  Lorca, the Poet and His People
    (Tr. by Ilsa Barea)   76   46

BAREA, ILSA
BOOKS REVIEWED
  Lorca, the Poet and His People,
    by Arturo Barea (Tr.)   76   46

BARFIELD, OWEN
ARTICLES ABOUT
  The Aristocrats,
    by Morton Dauwen Zabel   34   37

BARKER, ERIC (WILSON)
POEMS
  Full Moon, West Coast   73   15

BOOKS REVIEWED
  A Ring of Willows   99   124

BARKER, GEORGE
POEMS
  Sequence   49   194
  Song for the Countess of Pemroke   57   15
  Anadyomene's Ballad   59   178
  My Dragonfly Roaring Your Engines
  Verses for an Anniversary
  O My Niobe Weeps
  Ode Against St. Cecilia's Day   74   133
  Elegy on the Death of Michael Roberts
  To My Son   78   316
  Prologue to The Degradations
    of Guatemozin   81   6
  Epithalamium   83   63
  Sonnets of the Triple-Headed Manichee
  Domestic Poem   86   8
  Cycle of Six Lyrics   88   287
    The Dove of the Seas
    The Rose and the Rod
    Heroes and Worms
    Swansong of the Hyena
    O Pearl and Breasted World
    Narcissus and the Star
  True Love True Love What Have I Done   98   273
  Memorial Stanzas for Louis MacNeice   104   1
  Formal Elegy on the Death
    of Oscar Williams   105   287
  Flight 462   110   38

ARTICLES
  The Face Behind the Poem
    [Alfred, Lord Tennyson,
    Gerard Manley Hopkins]   97   310

BOOKS REVIEWED
Selected Poems   59   159
Sacred and Secular Elegies   64   35
Love Poems   72   34
The True Confession of...   79   106
Collected Poems, 1930-1955   92   318
The True Confession of...   105   207
Collected Poems, 1930 to 1965   107   410

ARTICLES ABOUT
Aspects of English Poetry: 1932-1937,
   by Michael Roberts   49   210
London Letter, by D. S. Savage   51   277
Poetry on Records,
   by Harry Thornton Moore   58   345
Rev. of *New Poems: 1943*
   (Ed. by Oscar Williams)   64   86
The Lyricism of George Barker,
   by David Daiches   69   336

BARKER, MILDRED AMELIA
POEMS
Release   47   312
Not Again

BARKER, SHIRLEY
BOOKS REVIEWED
Dark Hills Under   43   290

BARKER, SUE TAMMINGA
POEMS
A Woman's Song   154   89
My Child

BARKER, WENDY
POEMS
Exorcism of a Nightmare   138   333
Black Sheep, Red Stars   146   11
Night Song
The Navy Blue Chair   148   23
Red Chair at the Piano Recital
Identifying Things   152   266
Giving Up the Dead   155   222
From the Attic at Thornfield   156   82
Reason of Lace   159   264
Taking a Language   162   257
Color Analysis

BOOKS REVIEWED
Winter Chickens and Other Poems   160   284
Let the Ice Speak

BARLOW, ROBERT
ARTICLES ABOUT
A Note on Robert Barlow,
   by Lawrence Hart   78   115

BARNARD, ELLSWORTH
BOOKS REVIEWED
Edwin Arlington Robinson: A Critical Study   81   187

BARNARD, MARY
POEMS
Shoreline   45   254
Spectral Tunes   46   25
   Faun in Exile
   Ondine
   Lai
Storm   52   256
Remarks on Poetry and the Physical World
The Tears of Princesses
Provincial II
Fable of the Ant and the Word   63   262
Height Is the Distance Down
Crossroads
On Arriving   151   12

BOOKS REVIEWED
Sappho (Tr.)   95   185
Time and the White Tigress   150   102

ARTICLES ABOUT
Poetry as a Jackdaw's Nest,
   by Sherman Conrad   58   90

BARNES, DICK
[See BARNES, R(ICHARD) G.]

BARNES, DJUNA
BOOKS REVIEWED
The Antiphon   93   47

BARNES, FLORENCE
POEMS
God's Man   25   308

BARNES, KAY
POEMS
Willow   168   85

BARNES, NELLIE
BOOKS REVIEWED
American Indian Love Lyrics (Ed.)   28   53

BARNES, R(ICHARD) G.
[DICK BARNES]
POEMS
Paradiso IX   165   280

TRANSLATIONS
Poems by Jorge Luis Borges
   (Tr. with Robert Mezey)   162   157

BARNES, RICHARD
POEMS
Every Failure Comes To Rest   142   65
The Salesman

Red Light
Concentrics   144   220
Watering the Lawn
To a Child Who Cut His Finger
    for the First Time   146   82
You
The Assassin   .

BARNES, WILLIAM
ARTICLES ABOUT
Hopkins' Ancestry: Part I,
    by Terence Heywood   54   209

BARNEY, DANFORD
BOOKS REVIEWED
Chords from Albireo   16   336
Chords from Albireo   16   340

BARNEY, WILLIAM D.
BOOKS REVIEWED
Permitted Proof   89   52

BARNFIELD, RICHARD
[RICHARD BARNEFIELD]
ARTICLES ABOUT
Rev. of The Penguin Book
    of Homosexual Verse
    (Ed. by Stephen Coote)   144   166

BARNSTONE, ALIKI
POEMS
Blue Is Greece   112   242

BARNSTONE, WILLIS
REVIEWS
Hispanic Chronicle   111   46
    Bestiary,
        by Pablo Neruda
        and Antonio Frasconi
        (Tr. by Elsa Neuberger)
    In the Middle of the Road,
        Selected Poems of Carlos
        Drummond de Andrade
        (Ed. and tr. by John Nist)
    Rafael Alberti, Selected Poems
        (Ed. and tr. by Ben Belitt)
    Jorge Guillén, Cántico:
        A Selection, Spanish Poems
        with English Translation
        (Ed. by Norman Thomas
        di Giovanni)
    [Federico García Lorca]

BOOKS REVIEWED
Eighty Poems of Antonio Machado (Tr.)   101   343
Greek Lyric Poetry (Tr.)   108   416
Sappho: Lyrics in the Original Greek
    with Translations

BARO, GENE
POEMS
Sonnet ("Poor dribbled death...")   76   76
Top-Ranking Funnymen   77   10
Buildings Where My Father Died
Exiles   85   153
Saints   92   355
The Secondary Players
Figures of Farewell
Mid-Winter   99   352
The Walk

REVIEWS
Phases of English Poetry,
    by Herbert Read   77   362
Key Poets   79   106
    Poor Men's Music,
        by Edith Sitwell
    The True Confession of George Barker
    The God in the Cave,
        by Randall Swingler
    Twinter's Wedding,
        by Jonathan Denwood
    The Common Festival,
        by Stanley Snaith
    Fugue for Our Time,
        by Dorian Cooke
    Three Letters to Nikolai Tikhonov,
        by Jack Lindsay
    Gentle Exercise,
        by Maurice Carpenter
    Aspects of Love, by Jack Beeching
    Forgive Me, Sire,
        by Norman Cameron
The Selected Poems of Horace Gregory   81   144
Under Milk Wood, by Dylan Thomas   87   119
Some British Poets   102   193
    The Flying Corset,
        by W. Price Turner
    A Smell of Burning,
        by Thomas Blackburn
    The Dark Window, by Robin Skelton
    Poems, Golders Green, by Dannie Abse
    Between Mars and Venus,
        by Robert Conquest
    The Blue-Fly in His Head,
        by John Heath-Stubbs
    Torse 3, by Christopher Middleton
    Weep Before God, by John Wain
    Poems from Limbo, by Rob Lyle
    Brief Candles, by Jack Bevan

BOOKS REVIEWED
Northwind and Other Poems,
    in Poets of Today VI
    (Ed. by John Hall Wheelock)   95   373
A View of Water   108   54
A View of Water   110   112

ARTICLES ABOUT
Review by Carolyn Kizer   102 393

BARON, MARY
BOOKS REVIEWED
Letters for the New England Dead   126 352

BARONTI, GERVE
BOOKS REVIEWED
In the Red Years   12 282

BAROT, RICK
POEMS
Occupations   168 202

BARR, TINA
POEMS
Circe   152 336

BARRACK, JACK
POEMS
Beached Whales   158 89
The Hiroshima Horse   164 194
Blackened Sunflowers, White Moths   168 229

BARRAULT, JEAN-LOUIS
ARTICLES ABOUT
Paris Letter, by Wallace Fowlie   96 371

BARRAX, GERALD WILLIAM
POEMS
Two Poems   110 164
Gunsmoke: 1957
Butterflies: 1965
From Five-Part Invention

REVIEWS
Four Poets   112 343
L'Autre, by Ron Loewinsohn
Characters in Certain Places,
by Theodore Enslin
The Mark, by Gail Dusenbery
Dusk Road Games,
by Robert Grenier

BARRES, MAURICE
ARTICLES ABOUT
As It Is in Paris,
by Jean Catel   25 268

BARRESI, DOROTHY
POEMS
Lifting   150 335
Late Summer News
Comeuppance
Chin Music   152 139
Nine of Clubs, Cleveland, Ohio   153 337

BARRET, ROBERT
POEMS
To God and Others   35 204
Strait Prayer
To One Woman
Lace Valentine
The Chase
Swinburne

BARRETT, KATHARINE ELLIS
POEMS
Poems of Patagonia   39 188
Westward
A Fact
Canaan
Ostrich
Lull

BARRETT, MARY LAWTHER
POEMS
Suddenly a Zebra   38 27

BARRETT, WILTON AGNEW
POEMS
Pictures   7 14
A New England Church
When I Heard You Were Dead   10 236
The Adventurer
An Awakening   15 140
Evangel   29 259

BOOKS REVIEWED
Songs from the Journey   20 160

BARRICELLI, JEAN-PIERRE
BOOKS REVIEWED
Giacomo Leopardi: Poems (Tr.)   107 333

BARRINGTON, PAULINE B.
POEMS
Sunrise at Santa Barbara   12 303
The Pomegranate Bush

BARROW, ELFRIDA DE RENNE
POEMS
Impressions   20 19
Recognition
Twilight
Death
I Wonder
Loose Leaves   22 67
Futility
Travelling
Habit and Custom and I
Concerning the World
Colors
The Wall Between
Presentiment
Insomnia

Hush
Underwings   27   250
  Interim
  Facing an Hour-Glass
  Twilight
  An Old Burying-Ground
  Silence Is a Stranger Here
  Penetralia
Autumnal   31   138
  Garden's End
  Earth Change
Ports   35   203
In the Calendar's Shadow   45   200
  New Year's Eve
  Lines of the Unknown

BARRY, FRANCIS
POEMS
  Less Feline   72   191

BARRY, IRIS
POEMS
  The Fledgling   8   187
  Impression ("The orchards...")
  Study
  Domestic
  Double
  Town-Mouse
  Enough Has Been Said of Sunset
  Impression ("At night...")
  Shadow Songs   20   312
    Lamentation
    Virgin Moon
    An Unposted Letter
    Nocturne

ARTICLES ABOUT
  Recent Magazines, by M. D. Zabel   39   166
  Letters to a Young Poet,
    by Ezra Pound   76   342

BARRY, PAUL
POEMS
  The House Below the Water   134   339
  Reconciliation
  September: The Literary Perspective
  Anatomical Illustration   145   271
  The Blind Girl Speaks
    of the Marvelous Things

BARTLETT, ALICE HUNT
BOOKS REVIEWED
  The Sea Anthology (Ed.)   27   343

BARTLETT, HELEN BIRCH
[HELEN LOUISE BIRCH]
POEMS
  Autumn Leaves   11   10
    Mid-October

Up in the Hills
Can This Be All?
Artist
Music
Forewarned
Prophets
  A Voice Breaks In Upon the Silence
Laughing in the Moonlight   13   78
Vertigo
And So the Days Go By
A Line-a-Day for Certain Lovers   15   248
  Remembrance
  Re-Encounter
  Undercurrents
  Premonitions
  The Bringers of Gifts
  Belshazzar
  Drift
  Epilogue ("Blue-purple...")
Lola in Silverpoint   21   248
  Lola Wears Lace
  The Moonlight Dance
  The Lake
October in Illinois   29   18
Sanctuary
Cat
Opiate

REVIEWS
  Minna and Myself,
    by Maxwell Bodenheim   13   342
  Kora in Hell: Improvisations,
    by William Carlos Williams   17   329

BOOKS REVIEWED
  Capricious Winds   31   94

BARTLETT, JOHN
ARTICLES ABOUT
  Rev. of *Robert Frost and John Bartlett:*
    The Record of a Friendship,
    by Margaret Bartlett Anderson   104   253

BARTLETT, LEE
POEMS
  Fishbones   138   100

BARTLETT, PHYLLIS
BOOKS REVIEWED
  Poems in Process   79   295

BARTON, MARY ELIZABETH
POEMS
  Perspective   43   78

BARTRA, AGUSTÍ
POEMS
  Refugee
    (Tr. by Rolfe Humphries)   59   77

Thou Art Not Cold
  (Tr. by Rolfe Humphries)   60   123
Far Off, They Are Lying
  (Tr. by Rolfe Humphries)   64   10

BARZUN, HENRI-MARTIN
ARTICLES ABOUT
  Paris, by Ezra Pound   3   26

BARZUN, JACQUES
BOOKS REVIEWED
  Selected Letters of Lord Byron (Ed.)   84   296
  Figaro's Marriage,
    by Beaumarchais (Tr.),
    in *Phaedra and Figaro*   100   41

BASHŌ, MATSUO [BASHŌ]
BOOKS REVIEWED
  The Narrow Road to the Deep North
    and Other Travel Sketches
    (Tr. by Nobuyuki Yuasa)   112   347

BASLER, ROY
POEMS
  Mr. Graves' White Goddess   96   220
  Old Photographs   106   345

BASS, CHARISSA TAYLOR
ARTICLES ABOUT
  Illumination, by Harriet Monroe   26   36

BASSAVANNA
POEMS
  Of Omens
    (Tr. by A. K. Ramanujan)   98   383

BASSETT, ANNA FLOURNOY
POEMS
  Farm Woman to the Earth   32   197

BATAILLE, NICOLAS
ARTICLES ABOUT
  Rimbaud in 1949, by Wallace Fowlie   75   166

BATE, WALTER JACKSON
BOOKS REVIEWED
  Coleridge   113   262

BATES, ARLO
ARTICLES ABOUT
  Notes Towards an Autobiography:
    The Childish Background (III),
    by William Carlos Williams   74   94

BATES, ESTHER WILLARD
BOOKS REVIEWED
  Edwin Arlington Robinson
    and His Manuscripts   65   209

BATES, KATHERINE LEE
ARTICLES
  Correspondence   8   157

BATES, MARGARET
ARTICLES ABOUT
  [Note]   84   119

BATKI, JOHN
TRANSLATIONS
  Poems by Attila József   116   281

BOOKS REVIEWED
  Selected Poems and Texts,
    by Attila József
    (Tr.) (Ed. by James Atlas
    and George Gömöri)   126   103

BAT-MIRIAM, YOHEVED
POEMS
  Like This Before You Just as I Am   92   228
  The Distance Spills Itself
    (Tr. by Ruth Finer Mintz)

BATTIN, WENDY
POEMS
  Practice at Dawn   163   274
  Seven   167   278
  Six of One,
  Frond   167   342

BAUDELAIRE, CHARLES
POEMS
  Spleen   98   343
  Autumn
  The Ruined Garden
  The Flawed Bell
  Meditation
  The Abyss
  The Injured Moon
    (Tr. by Robert Lowell)
  Châtiment de l'Orgueil   106   291
  Avec ses Vêtements Ondoyants...
    (Tr. by George Starbuck)

BOOKS REVIEWED
  Flowers of Evil
    (Tr. by George Dillon
    and Edna St. Vincent Millay)   48   158
  The Mirror of Baudelaire
    (Ed. by Charles Henri Ford)
    (Tr. by William Candlewood)   62   282
  Flowers of Evil
    (Tr. by Geoffrey Wagner)   72   105
  One Hundred Poems
    from Les Fleurs du Mal
    (Tr. by C. F. MacIntyre)
  Baudelaire, Rimbaud, Verlaine
    (Ed. by Joseph M. Bernstein)

The Intimate Journals of...
(Tr. by Christopher Isherwood) 72 228
Baudelaire on Poe: Critical Papers
(Tr. and ed. by Lois and
Francis E. Hyslop) 81 247
Poems of Baudelaire
(Tr. of *Les Fleurs du Mal*,
by Roy Campbell) 82 86
Pensées de Baudelaire
(Ed. by Henri Peyre)
Correspondance Générale
The Flowers of Evil
(Tr. by William Aggeler) 85 55
The Flowers of Evil
(Ed. by Marthiel
and Jackson Mathews) 103 316
Flowers of Evil
(Tr. by Florence Louie Friedman) 111 124

ARTICLES ABOUT
Correspondence from Theodore Stanton 11 168
Baudelaire,
by Morton Dauwen Zabel 43 38
Rev. of *Flowers of Evil*,
by Edwin Morgan 63 287
Rev. of *Baudelaire, a Criticism*,
by Joseph D. Bennett 66 48
Rev. of *Baudelaire*, by Jean-Paul Sartre 77 100
Rev. of *Connaissance de Baudelaire*,
by Henri Peyre 82 86
French Chronicle: Recent Publications,
by Wallace Fowlie 88 408
A Commemoration:
"Les Fleurs du Mal," 1857-1957,
by Wallace Fowlie 90 376
French Chronicle: Recent Publications,
by Wallace Fowlie 91 36
Recent French Publications,
by Wallace Fowlie 93 40
The Farmer and the Poet,
by Karl Shapiro 98 170
Rev. of *The Limits of Symbolism:
Studies of Five Modern French Poets*,
by Bernard Weinberg 112 41

BAUER, GRACE
POEMS
Frida Digresses on Red 156 9
Eve Recollecting the Garden
The Eye of the Beholder 158 334

BAUER, HAROLD
ARTICLES
Artist Versus Amateur 8 326

BAUGH, ALBERT C.
BOOKS REVIEWED
Literary History of England (Ed.) 113 262

BAUM, BERNARD
REVIEWS
Dylan Thomas: "Dog Among the Fairies,"
by Henry Treece 75 357

BAUM, PAULL FRANKLIN
BOOKS REVIEWED
The Principles of English Versification 22 218

BAUM, S. V.
BOOKS REVIEWED
E. E. Cummings and the Critics (Ed.) 102 341

BAUMEL, JUDITH
TRANSLATIONS
Poems by Patrizia Cavalli 155 135

BAWER, BRUCE
POEMS
Beach 148 225

REVIEWS
Short Reviews 144 345
Mirrors, by Robert Creeley
Axe Handles, by Gary Snyder
Afterlight, by Marc Hudson
Keeping Company,
by Gibbons Ruark
Riding to Greylock,
by Stephen Sandy
Tar, by C. K. Williams

BAX, CLIFFORD
BOOKS REVIEWED
Farewell My Muse 42 228

ARTICLES ABOUT
Rev. of *New Hyperion,
A Symposium of Poetry and Criticism*
(Ed. by Geoffrey Handley-Taylor) 78 45

BAXTER, CHARLES
POEMS
The Return of the Repressed 134 93
Two Theories of the Unconscious
Midwestern Poetics 148 26

BAXTER, JAMES K.
BOOKS REVIEWED
The Night Shift
(With Charles Doyle, Louis Johnson,
and Kendrick Smithyman) 94 44
The Rock Woman: Selected Poems 118 98
Runes 123 165

BAXTER, WARD
ARTICLES ABOUT
When Children Write Verse,
by Maude Sumner Smith 56 154

BAYES, RONALD (H.)
BOOKS REVIEWED
  Turtle Three   110   105
  X-ing Warm   114   251

BAYLEY, JOHN
ARTICLES
Contemporary British Poetry:
  A Romantic Persistence?
  [W. B. Yeats, Philip Larkin,
  Gavin Ewart, John Ashbery,
  A. Alvarez]   146   227

BAYLISS, JOHN
BOOKS REVIEWED
  New Road 1943
  (Ed. with Alex Comfort)   64   46

BAYNES, CARY F.
BOOKS REVIEWED
  The I Ching or Books of Changes (Tr.)   83   295

BAZIL, OSVALDO
POEMS
  Idyl (Tr. by Muna Lee)   26   147

BEACH, JOSEPH WARREN
POEMS
  Drypoints   6   53
    Rue Bonaparte
    The View at Gunderson's
    The Masseur
    The Point of View
    Jenny's Dancing
    Cave Talk
  On the Land   9   122
    The Black Land
    Succession
    The Red Land
  Dear Grace!   68   8
  Virtuoso   72   13
  Abstraction   81   108
  Horatian Ode   84   135
  Hard Timber
  Lares and Penates
  All My Knowing   87   288
  Early Morning   89   229

ARTICLES
  Rococo: The Poetry
  of Sacheverell Sitwell   74   217

REVIEWS
  The Theory of Poetry,
    by Lascelles Abercrombie   28   169
  The Theory of Poetry,
    by Lascelles Abercrombie   28   227
  Poetic Values, by John G. Neihardt   28   350
  Modern Poetry, by H. P. Collins   29   52

BOOKS REVIEWED
  The Making of the Auden Canon   92   116
  Obsessive Images, Symbolism in Poetry
  of the 1930's and 1940's
  (Ed. by William Van O'Connor)   98   332

ARTICLES ABOUT
  Joseph Warren Beach,
  by William Van O'Connor   91   192

BEALLE, ALFRED BATTLE
POEMS
  Peace   16   83
    Grasses and Sand
    The Adventurer

BEAMISH, RAE
BOOKS REVIEWED
  American Signatures (Ed.)   61   396

BEARDSLEY, DOUG
BOOKS REVIEWED
  Kissing the Body of My Lord   144   297

BEARDSLEY, GEORGIA
POEMS
  Night   38   245

BEASLEY, BRUCE
POEMS
  After an Adoration   157   127
  Consolation   161   251

BEATTY, JOHN (C.)
POEMS
  Sea Rain, and Sand   57   242
  The Suns Retire
  Poem ("The world is weighted...")
  Earl Baldwin of Bewdly   69   251

BEATY, JOHN O.
BOOKS REVIEWED
  An Introduction to Poetry
  (With Jay B. Hubbell)   22   168

BEAUMARCHAIS
BOOKS REVIEWED
  Figaro's Marriage
  (Tr. by Jacques Barzun),
  in Phaedra and Figaro   100   41

BEAUMONT, JEANNE (MARIE)
POEMS
  My Demure   157   263
  Pearl Hour   158   99
  Judging the Book by Its Cover   158   278
  Barometrics   160   269
  Two Bowls   163   27
  Placebo Effects   166   265

BEAUVAIS, PHYLLIS
POEMS
My Father Will Die   158   35

BECK, GARRARD
POEMS
Instruction   65   126
Autumn Negra

BECK, JOHN OSCAR
POEMS
A Plea to Indiana   25   231
On Parade   30   128
In the Laboratory
of the Great Chemist
The Cornfield

BOOKS REVIEWED
Windows in Dragon Town   26   109

BECK, RICHARD
BOOKS REVIEWED
Icelandic Poems and Stories (Ed.)   62   228

BECK, WARREN
REVIEWS
Ruins and Visions,
by Stephen Spender   61   386
The American Way of Poetry,
by Henry W. Wells   63   166
Lament for the Sleepwalker,
by Dunstan Thompson   70   217
Family Circle, by Eve Merriam   70   266
War as a Climate   74   48
Poems, by Rudolf Nassauer
Zero, by Pedro Salinas
(Tr. by Eleanor Turnbull)
Imagine the South,
by George Woodcock

BECKER, CHARLOTTE
POEMS
Echo   8   133

BECKER, LUCIEN
POEMS
Féerie Quotidienne
(Tr. by Wallace Fowlie)   80   344

BECKER, WILLIAM
REVIEWS
On the Margin of Yeats   81   331
The Interpretation of the Cuchulain
Legend in the Works
of W. B. Yeats,
by Birgit Bjersby
W. B. Yeats: The Tragic Phase,
by Vivienne Koch

BECKETT, SAMUEL
BOOKS REVIEWED
Thorns of Thunder, by Paul Eluard
(Ed. by George Reavey)
(Tr. with Denis Devlin,
David Gascoyne, Eugene Jolas,
Man Ray, George Reavey,
and Ruthven Todd)   48   347
An Anthology of Mexican Poetry
(Tr.) (Ed. by Octavio Paz)   95   379
Selected Poems, by Alain Bosquet
(Tr. with Charles Guenther,
Edouard Roditi, and Ruth Whitman)   104   115

BECKLEY, DARRELL J.
ARTICLES ABOUT
When Children Write Verse,
by Maude Sumner Smith   56   154

BECKWITH, RUSSELL
POEMS
Long Winter   42   87
Wing from the North
The Last Sunday
Landscapes
Rain Out of Season
White Drum Rolling
End and Beginning   51   182

BEDDOES, THOMAS LOVELL
ARTICLES ABOUT
Rev. of Thomas Lovell Beddoes, Eccentric
and Poet, by Royall H. Snow   34   111

BEDIENT, CALVIN
POEMS
White Snow Falling Without Wind   165   79

REVIEWS
Short Reviews   162   167
Magic City,
by Yusef Komunyakaa
American Gothic,
by Jonathan Holden
To Put the Mouth To,
by Judith Hall
After Estrangement,
by Molly Bendall
Short Reviews   163   336
My Tokyo, by Frederick Seidel
Debt, by Mark Levine
The Book of Light,
by Lucille Clifton
People Live, They Have Lives,
by Hugh Seidman
Short Reviews   165   31
First Language, by Ciaran Carson
The God of Indeterminacy,
by Sandra McPherson

The Great Fires: Poems 1982-1992,
  by Jack Gilbert
In a Time of Violence,
  by Eavan Boland
And the Stars Were Shining,
  by John Ashbery

BEECHING, JACK
POEMS
  Books Are So Much like Life   69   21

BOOKS REVIEWED
  Aspects of Love   79   106
  Penguin Modern Poets 16
    (With Harry Guest
    and Matthew Mead)   119   291

BEER, MORRIS ABEL
POEMS
  Moses   10   191
  Old China

BEER, PATRICIA
BOOKS REVIEWED
  The Loss of the Magyar   94   405
  Just Like the Resurrection   114   266

BEER, THOMAS
ARTICLES ABOUT
  Rev. of Stephen Crane,
    by John Berryman   78   298

BEHAN, BRENDAN
ARTICLES ABOUT
  Letter from Dublin,
    by John Montague   90   310

BEHN, ROBIN
POEMS
  Four Years After
    Your Deliberate Drowning   145   337
  Open Heart   152   88
  Angels

BOOKS REVIEWED
  Paper Bird   154   99

BEIER, ULLI
BOOKS REVIEWED
  African Poetry (Ed.)   111   266

BEINHACKER, ADA PERRY
ARTICLES
  Correspondence: Poetry on the Radio   36   227

BELEV, GEORGI
POEMS
  Train   159   20
  Tale
    (Tr. with Lisa Sapinkopf)

BELFORD, KEN
BOOKS REVIEWED
  Fireweed   115   353

BELIS, ANDREW
ARTICLES ABOUT
  A Letter from Ireland,
    by Joseph M. Hone   45   332

BELITT, BEN
POEMS
  Squill Song   36   17
  Blue and White Morning   38   17
  Wind Blows South   40   192
    Field Left Fallow
    The Deep Sleepers
    Contentious Heart
  This Fountainhead   42   260
    Tower of Grass
    Words for an Old Wound
  Goliath Stone   76   264
  Bullring: Plaza Mexico
  Smerdyakov with a Guitar   84   328
  Alyosha's Funeral Service
  Andaluz   89   74
  Country Songs   91   15
    Wasp and Windowscreen
    A Stand of Pine
  Battle-Piece   95   69
  Memorial Hospital   96   367
  Soldiers Asleep
  Life of Mrs. Cal   99   210
  The Hornet's House   101   5
  The Orphaning   103   219
  The Gorge
  Poem ("Salamander/that speaks...")
  Second Adam
  Dog in the Manger   110   71
  Flower Market: Cuernavaca
  The Termites: Taxco
  "Gayossa" Ambulance Service: Emergency
  Full Moon: The Gorge   125   269

TRANSLATIONS
  Poems by Pablo Neruda   79   204
  Poem by Federico García Lorca   85   187
  Poems by Pablo Neruda   98   359
  Poems by Antonio Machado   101   312
  Poem by Pablo Neruda   112   183

ARTICLES
  Pablo Neruda
    and the "Gigantesque"   80   116

REVIEWS
  The Collected Poems of Austin Clarke   49   288
  Trance and Monodrama   50   110

Landscape with Figures,
   by Lionel Wiggam
Stranger's Garment,
   by Gilbert Maxwell
Four Walls and The Emperor Heart,
   by Laurence Whistler   50   347
New Directions in Prose
   and Poetry (1936)
   (Ed. by James Laughlin IV)   51   45

BOOKS REVIEWED
The Five-Fold Mesh   53   214
Wilderness Stair   86   287
The Poet in New York,
   by Federico García Lorca (Tr.)   87   303
Selected Poems of Pablo Neruda
   (Tr. and ed.)   101   349
Juan de Mairena,
   by Antonio Machado
   (Ed. and tr.)   105   198
The Enemy Joy   105   324
Rafael Alberti, Selected Poems
   (Ed. and tr.)   111   46
The Double Witness   133   169

BELKNAP, JOHN
POEMS
Praefatio   36   74
Alibi
Bestiary
Candida
An Old Laugh of Li Po's

BELL, AUBREY F. G.
BOOKS REVIEWED
The Golden Treasury
   of Portuguese Verse (Ed.)   27   343

BELL, CHARLES G.
POEMS
Konigstein   82   264
Mississippi Return: Air-View   83   262
Sleepsong   84   203
Vineyard Idyl   85   10
From Delta Return   87   283
Litany of Women   114   298

ARTICLES
G. A. Borgese, Poet-Seer   82   40

BOOKS REVIEWED
Songs for a New America   84   163
Delta Return   89   110

ARTICLES ABOUT
Correspondence
   from Rolfe Humphries
   and James Dickey   89   391

BELL, JULIAN
ARTICLES ABOUT
Notes on English Poets,
   by Michael Roberts   39   271

BELL, MARVIN
POEMS
The Wisdom   103   166
The Admission
The Condition   105   169
What Songs the Soldiers Sang   105   381
The 3 Corners of Reality
The Coat of Arms
A Poor Jew
Things We Dreamt We Died For
Her Dream House
Walking Thoughts   108   101
The Bride in White
Time We Took To Travel
The Affair
A Picture of Soldiers   110   6
The War Piece
Memories of Bragg and Klein
Water, Winter, Fire
The Difference
Travel
On Returning to Teach
Give Back, Give Back
An Afterword to My Father   112   29
The Medicine
Wanting to Help
Verses Versus Verses
The Extermination of the Jews
Trial Novels
The Self-Made Man
The Ring   113   302
The Escape into You
The Drifting
More Going for Walks
On the Death of a Great Critic
Toward Certain Divorce
The Present
The Students
To the Sky   115   109
Put Back the Dark   115   415
In the Home
Lovesong
Service for Two
The Daily Grind
Homage to Alfred Stieglitz
The Music of the Spheres
Travels We Took in Our Time   117   304
Temper
Getting Lost in Nazi Germany
Constant Feelings
New Students   128   312
Landscape with Open Spaces   143   12
Draft Age

When I Run
The Moon Is Visible Tonight   151   13
How To Everything   155   391
The Book of the Dead Man (#27)   163   90
The Book of the Dead Man (#33)
The Book of the Dead Man (#44)   165   197
The Book of the Dead Man (#51)
The Book of the Dead Man (#54)
The Book of the Dead Man (#87)   170   313

ARTICLES
Correspondence: A Reply
    [John Gill]   112   210

REVIEWS
Four Young Poets   106   370
    Poems, by Bill Deemer
    Inventory, by Frank Lima
    The Sonnets,
        by Ted Berrigan
    The Man Who Bit the Sun,
        by Frederick Nicklaus
Two British Chronicles: II   107   410
    The Green Fig Tree,
        by Michael Parr
    In Flashlight,
        by Michael Hamburger
    Nature with Man, by Jon Silkin
    Collected Poems, 1930 to 1965,
        by George Barker
Four Anthologies   111   258
    A Controversy of Poets
        (Ed. by Paris Leary
        and Robert Kelly)
    Five Poets of the Pacific Northwest
        (Ed. by Robin Skelton)
    A Lermontov Reader
        (Ed. and tr. by Guy Daniels)
    The Modern Hebrew Poem Itself
        (Ed. by Stanley Burnshaw,
        T. Carmi, and Ezra Spicehandler)
Nine Canadian Poets   111   323
    Selected Poems, by F. R. Scott
    The Silver Wire and
        The Man in Yellow Boots,
        by George Bowering
    Home Free, by George Johnston
    The Glass Trumpet,
        by Miriam Waddington
    The Scarred Hull, by Frank Davey
    Ottawa Poems, by Wm. Hawkins
    During Rain, I Plant Chrysanthemums,
        by M. Lakshmi Gill
    The Windows, by Carlos Reyes
    *Sunday Afternoon
        at the Toronto Art Gallery*,
        by John Grube
Five Books   133   45

Collected Poems, 1953-1977,
    by Ernest Sandeen
Land Diving, by Robert Morgan
Night Talk and Other Poems,
    by Richard Pevear
Climb to the High Country,
    by Bill Hotchkiss
Cumberland Station, by Dave Smith
That We Keep Them Alive   136   164
    To a Blossoming Pear Tree,
        by James Wright
    Tread the Dark, by David Ignatow
    Rising and Falling,
        by William Matthews

BOOKS REVIEWED
    Poems for Nathan and Saul   111   189
    Things We Dreamt We Died For
    A Probable Volume of Dreams   118   98
    The Escape into You   120   296
    Residue of Song   126   346
    Stars Which See, Stars Which Do Not See 132   288
    *Drawn by Stones, by Earth,
        by Things That Have Been in the Fire* 145   348
    New and Selected Poems   152   35
    Iris of Creation   158   280
    The Book of the Dead Man   167   156

ARTICLES ABOUT
    Correspondence from John Gill   112   209
    Rev. of *The American Poetry Anthology*
        (Ed. by Daniel Halpern)   128   106

BELL, WILLIAM
POEMS
    The Popular Novelist Speaks   73   277

BELLAMANN, H(ENRY) (H.)
POEMS
    August Gardens   16   313
    Gargoyles of Notre Dame   19   85
    Edges
    Lullaby
    Peaks
    God
    The Artist
    High Trees   20   15
    The Gypsy   25   24
    Between Dimensions   36   16

ARTICLES
    Correspondence: Those Gardens
        [Amy Lowell]   21   342

BOOKS REVIEWED
    A Music-Teacher's Note-Book   18   223
    Cups of Illusion   23   108
    The Upward Pass   33   345

ARTICLES ABOUT
  What to Think? by Harriet Monroe
    [Mark Turbyfill]   28   215

BELLAMANN, KATHERINE
  BOOKS REVIEWED
    Two Sides of a Poem   88   329

BELLI, GIUSEPPI GIOACCHINO
  [GIUSEPPE GIOACHINO BELLI]
  POEMS
    Le Bbestie der Paradiso Terrestre   136   4
    The Beasts of the Earthly Paradise
    Cain
    Memory
    A Bad Moment
    The Resurrection of the Flesh
      (Tr. by Miller Williams)

  BOOKS REVIEWED
    The Roman Sonnets of...
      (Tr. by Harold Norse)   98   403

BELLINGER, ALFRED RAYMOND
  BOOKS REVIEWED
    Spires and Poplars   17   276

BELLM, DAN
  POEMS
    Silence   163   15
    Before Words   164   67
    Homage   170   262

BELLOC, HILAIRE
  BOOKS REVIEWED
    Verses   11   107

  ARTICLES ABOUT
    Hilaire Belloc (1870-1953)   83   119

BELLOW, BARBARA
  POEMS
    Evening Above East River   66   135
    For a Revolutionary in War Time   67   71

BELLOWS, HENRY ADAMS
  BOOKS REVIEWED
    The Poetic Edda (Tr.)   24   281

BELMONT, CYNTHIA
  POEMS
    Fields of Asphodel   167   211

BELOOF, ROBERT
  POEMS
    Interview with a Patron of the Pit   84   219
    An Easter Riddle Song   87   334

BELVIN, WILLIAM
  POEMS
    On a Recent Collegiate Basketball Scandal   79   278
    Men with Their Models   81   221
    This
    In Memory of Bryce Stavey
    To a Yellow Tea Rose   84   319
    A Blind Man's Bluff   85   265
    A Christening   89   218
    Satan on Economics

  REVIEWS
    Five Poets   90   114
      The Simon Passion,
        by Henry Birnbaum
      The Hidden Airdrome
        and Uncollected Poems,
        by Robert Price
      The Melting Clock,
        by Miriam Jans
      Spectre in the Fantastic Laboratory,
        by Jay Pell
      The Trespasser, by Lucien Stryk

  ARTICLES ABOUT
    Rev. of Poems from
      the Iowa Poetry Workshop
      (Ed. by Paul Engle)   79   284

BELY, ANDREY
  BOOKS REVIEWED
    The First Encounter
      (Tr. by Gerald Janecek)   136   40

BEMELMANS, LUDWIG
  BOOKS REVIEWED
    Madeline   55   221

BENARDETE, M. J.
  BOOKS REVIEWED
    And Spain Sings: Fifty Loyalist Ballads
      (Ed. with Rolfe Humphries)   52   43

BENAYA, MARGALIT
  TRANSLATIONS
    Poem by Yehuda Amichai   92   255

  ARTICLES ABOUT
    [Note]   93   56

BENBOW, MARGARET
  POEMS
    High Wind   136   98
    The Old Biograph Girl
    Bride and Bear
    The Queen of Everything   137   258
    Hard Freeze
    Cooking Lesson

Racine 1950
Laura's Visit to Aunt Lucrece   139   8
Crazy Arms: Earlene Remembers
Rose's Farm
Bogeyman: 1950   140   319
Out of Hand: Grant Park

BENDALL, MOLLY
POEMS
Conversations on the Plurality of Worlds   163   311
Fête on the Lake   164   264

BOOKS REVIEWED
After Estrangement   162   167

BENDER, VIOLET
POEMS
Wild Bird   45   7

BENDON, DOROTHE
POEMS
On Ararat   36   201

BOOKS REVIEWED
Mirror Images   40   291

BENDRE, D. R.
POEMS
The Secret
(Tr. by K. Raghavendra Rao)   93   265

BENEDICT, LIBBIAN
POEMS
I Am Afraid   28   311

BENEDIKT, MICHAEL
POEMS
Motions   102   96
The Country of the Hat   104   164
Tulips
Time
Pink Buds
Some Old Men   106   274
Landscape
An Enormous Dangling Sack-Like Net
The Eye
Events by Moonlight   108   388
Catching It All on the Way Back
The Villain
A Strained Credulity
Procession
Some Litanies   110   78
Fraudulent Days
From a Window
A Visual Face
Inside the Mystery   112   156
Before Going On
Thoughts

The Saint
The Wings of the Nose
The Debris of the Body
The Statue Speaks
Water   113   383
Money
The Sky
Four Psalms   115   97
On Earth   115   411
The Wonders of the Arm
The Tragic Landscape   117   363
Elegy for the Insects
Temporarily   128   313

REVIEWS
Choices and Risks   105   332
   Selected Poems,
     by Derek Walcott
   Selected Poems,
     by Kenneth Patchen
   The Quarry, by Richard Eberhart
   Collected Poems,
     by Theodore Roethke   109   262
   Poems: New and Selected,
     by Reed Whittemore   112   194
The Shapes of Nature   113   188
   Body Rags, by Galway Kinnell
   So Long at the Fair,
     by Miller Williams
   The Marches, by James Scully
   Covenants, by Robert Stock
   O'Ryan, by Charles Olson
   What the Grass Says,
     by Charles Simic
   The Binnacle, by Robert Peterson
   Waking Up Still Pickled,
     by Geof Hewitt
   Sled Hill Voices, by Aram Saroyan
   Not Only That, by Carroll Arnett
   Water I Slip Into at Night
     and 25 Stages of My Spine,
     by Margaret Randall
   Word Alchemy, by Lenore Kandel
   Baseball, by George Bowering
   The Buddha Uproar,
     by John Tagliabue
   Bean Spasms, by Ted Berrigan
     and Ron Padgett
   The Penguin Book
     of Modern Verse in Translation
     (Ed. by George Steiner)
   Poems from France
     (Ed. by William Jay Smith)
   Poems from the German
     (Ed. by Helen Plotz)
   Visions of Christ,
     by Rainer Maria Rilke
     (Ed. by Siegfried Mandel)
     (Tr. by Aaron Kramer)

Poems for People
  Who Don't Read Poems,
  by Hans Magnus Enzensberger
  (Tr. by Michael Hamburger,
  Jerome Rothenberg, and the author)
I Do Best Alone at Night,
  by Gunnar Ekelöf
  (Ed. and tr. by Robert Bly
  with Christina Paulson)
Poems after Martial
  (Tr. by Philip Murray)
Sixty Poems of Martial
  (Tr. by Dudley Fitts)
The Congresswomen of Aristophanes
  (Tr. by Douglass Parker)
The Experience of Literature
  (Ed. by Lionel Trilling)
Walking to Sleep, by Richard Wilbur   115   422
The Apotheosis of Darkness
  vs. Bardic Privilege   121   105
The Book of Nightmares,
  by Galway Kinnell
The Secret Meaning of Things,
  by Lawrence Ferlinghetti
The Common Shore,
  by Robert Kelly
Poems to Hear and See,
  by Ian Hamilton Finlay

BOOKS REVIEWED
  Changes   99   384
  Modern Spanish Theatre:
    An Anthology of Plays
    (Ed. with George Wellwarth)   113   338
  The Body   114   40
  Night Cries   130   285

BENÉT, LAURA
POEMS
  "Who Looks on Beauty"   30   11
  The Tree   37   317
  Lige Weedy's Fiddle   44   66
  Rulers   46   308

BOOKS REVIEWED
  Noah's Dove   35   49
  Basket for a Fair   45   103

BENET, MARIA M.
POEMS
  Recursion   168   334

BENÉT, STEPHEN VINCENT
BOOKS REVIEWED
  Young Adventure   16   53
  Heavens and Earth   19   340
  King David   24   341
  Tiger Joy   27   279

John Brown's Body   33   91
Burning City   48   276
Western Star   63   159
Stephen Vincent Benét and Edwin Muir
  [Recording]   101   275

ARTICLES ABOUT
  Obituary   62   56

BENÉT, WILLIAM ROSE
POEMS
  The Falconer of God   4   96
  On a Window Display in a Western City   6   234
  The Horse Thief   8   17
  Kites   10   232
  The Price   11   6
  Green and Gray   14   82
    Solid Earth
    Information
    Gray

ARTICLES
  A Point of Intention
    [John Gould Fletcher, Elinor Wylie]   59   350

BOOKS REVIEWED
  Merchants from Cathay   4   30
  The Falconer of God, and Other Poems   5   91
  The Great White Wall   9   322
  The Burglar of the Zodiac   15   48
  Poems for Youth:
    An American Anthology (Ed.)   28   114
  Man Possessed   32   159
  Twentieth-Century Poetry
    (Ed. with John Drinkwater
    and Henry Seidel Canby)   37   164
  Rip Tide: A Novel in Verse   44   108
  Starry Harness, New Poems
  Fifty Poets:
    An American Auto-Anthology (Ed.)
  Golden Fleece   47   223
  With Wings as Eagles   57   220
  The Dust Which Is God   59   213
  Contemporary Poets Series
    [Recording]   61   519
  Day of Deliverance:
    A Book of Poems in Wartime   65   101
  The Poetry of Freedom
    (Ed. with Norman Cousins)   67   46
  An Anthology of Famous English
    and American Poetry
    (Ed. with Conrad Aiken)   68   106

BENLOWES, EDWARD
ARTICLES ABOUT
  Hopkins' Ancestry: Part II,
    by Terence Heywood   54   271

BENN, GOTTFRIED
POEMS
   Psyche   80   266
   Alaska
   Cycle
   Icarus
   Opiate
   On the Edge of the Northern Seas
     (Tr. by Francis Golffing)

BOOKS REVIEWED
  Primal Vision:
    Selected Writings of Gottfried Benn
    (Ed. by E. B. Ashton)   97   387

ARTICLES ABOUT
  A Note on Gottfried Benn,
    by Francis Golffing   80   271
  German Lyric Poetry Since 1945,
    by Hans Egon Holthusen
    (Tr. by Herman Salinger)   88   257
  Rev. of *Contemporary German Poetry,*
    An Anthology (Tr. and ed.
    by Gertrude Clorius Schwebell)   111   336

BENNETT, ANNA ELIZABETH
POEMS
   Air Ways   40   252
   Wind
   Butterfly

BENNETT, BENJAMIN K.
POEMS
   For H K   113   41
   Alcaics
   Riverside Park   118   25
   Jardin du Luxembourg
   Ajax

BENNETT, BRUCE
POEMS
   Ready or Not   132   92
   Curious
   The Rendezvous

BENNETT, JOAN
BOOKS REVIEWED
  Five Metaphysical Poets
    [John Donne, George Herbert,
    Henry Vaughan, Richard Crashaw,
    Andrew Marvell]   108   65

BENNETT, JOSEPH (D.)
POEMS
   On Your Radio Tonight   63   145
   Isis and Osiris   81   9
   Earthly Love ("Cling together...")   85   5

   Earthly Love ("Abstaining from...") 90   73
   The Tomb at Rimini   109   167
   Marine
   The Death of Orpheus—A Journey 112   84
   Monsoon   117   357
   Return to Sea-Level

BOOKS REVIEWED
   Baudelaire, a Criticism   66   48
   Decembrist   80   294

BENNETT, MELBA BERRY
BOOKS REVIEWED
  The Stone Mason of Tor House:
    The Life and Times of Robinson Jeffers 111   333

BENSE, ROBERT
POEMS
   Contra August   158   276

BENSKO, JOHN
POEMS
   The Wild Horses of Asseateague Island 142   68
   Imagery Without Purpose   144   267
   Raising Cane
   My Wife's Desire
   The Implied Author   150   68

BENSON, A. C.
BOOKS REVIEWED
   Brontë Poems (Ed.)   9   259

BENSON, CORINNE
POEMS
   Proportion   71   300

BENSON, STELLA
POEMS
   If You Were Careless   16   309

BOOKS REVIEWED
   Twenty   14   225

BENTLEY, BETH (SINGER)
POEMS
   Aspects of Venus   94   27
   Country Lives   97   13
   Cowden's Farm   99   90
   Country Zoo
   Ondine   102   25
   In the Rain Forest
   A Sentimental Education   143   278

BENTLEY, BOOTH [Pseud.]
POEMS
   Formosa   21   247

BENTLEY, ERIC
REVIEWS
The Story of the Abbey Theatre,
by Peter Kavanagh   79 216

BOOKS REVIEWED
The Importance of Scrutiny.
Selections from Scrutiny:
A Quarterly Review, 1932-1948 (Ed.) 77 239
Manual of Piety (Die Hauspostille),
by Bertolt Brecht (Tr.) 111 336

BENTLEY, NELSON
POEMS
The Eye 86 328

BOOKS REVIEWED
Sea Lion Caves 109 401

BENTON, RITA
POEMS
Our Daily Bread 6 12

BENTON, WALTER [Pseud.]
POEMS
For Armistice 53 72
Dusk U. S. A.
Summary of the Distance
Between the Bomber and the Objective 59 72
With the Most Susceptible Element, the Mind,
Already Turned Under the Toxic Action—

BOOKS REVIEWED
This Is My Beloved 63 101
Never a Greater Need 74 50

BENVENUTA
[See also VON HATTINGBERG, MAGDA]
ARTICLES ABOUT
Rev. of Rilke and Benvenuta,
by Magda von Hattingberg
(Tr. by Cyrus Brooks) 76 92
Rilke Letters to Benvenuta
(Tr. by Heinz Norden) 77 276

BEOWULF
ARTICLES ABOUT
Rev. of Widsith, Beowulf,
Finnsburgh, Waldere, Deor
(Tr. by Charles Scott Moncrieff) 21 53
Rev. of Beowulf: A Verse Translation
into Modern English
(Tr. by Edwin Morgan) 83 44
Rev. of Beowulf
(Tr. by Kevin Crossley-Holland)
and The Beowulf Poet:
A Collection of Critical Essays
(Ed. by Donald K. Fry) 115 274

BERENBERG, D. P.
BOOKS REVIEWED
The Kid 44 55

BERG, STEPHEN
POEMS
The Room 91 309
Saint Ecuador 97 160
For a Friend on His Way Home 100 369
Wrists 104 160
And So On 106 394
Ollie, Answer Me 108 107
Going Upstairs to Bed
The Kiss 115 375
Unnamed Shapes
The Dead
Directions for Being Jesus
As the Days Pass and Darken
Nick's Photograph of Jeff, Me, and Arlene
The Soul
Heartache
Times 117 79
First Cold 121 81
In the Middle of Life
Don't Forget
From the Bridge 147 4
Nights After Reading

REVIEWS
Transparencies 116 260
Selected Poems by Eugene Guillevic
(Tr. by Denise Levertov)
Transparence of the World,
Poems by Jean Follain
(Tr. by W. S. Merwin)

BOOKS REVIEWED
Poems
(With Ronald Goodman
and Robert Mezey) 93 182
Bearing Weapons 104 47
Naked Poetry:
Recent American Poetry
in Open Forms
(Ed. with Robert Mezey) 116 35
The Queen's Triangle: A Romance 121 343
The Daughters 122 47
Grief: Poems and Versions of Poems 129 285
The New Naked Poetry:
Recent American Poetry
in Open Forms
(Ed. with Robert Mezey) 132 31

BERGÉ, CAROL
POEMS
Unfinished Poem 104 86
Winter Song 105 365

BOOKS REVIEWED
The Vulnerable Island   105   414
An American Romance   118   344

BERGENGRUEN, HANS
ARTICLES ABOUT
The Still Voice of German Poetry,
    by Edouard Roditi   68   208

BERGER, BRUCE
POEMS
Stout Brahms   142   269
Ambition
Transmigration   148   276
Family Reading   150   282
To Answer Your Question
The Wedding Gift
Facing the Music   153   10
These Arias
Impressionists
The Misconstrued   158   147
Science   160   148
Across, Down
Opus 28, The Preludes   162   11
Enigma Variations
Don't Ask

BERGER, CHARLES
REVIEWS
Laurels   140   35
    Hybrids of Plants and of Ghosts,
        by Jorie Graham
    Movable Islands, by Debora Greger
    Folly River, by Wendy Salinger
    Silks, by Roberta Spear
    Shooting Rats at the Bibb County Dump,
        by David Bottoms
    One Way to Reconstruct the Scene,
        by William Virgil Davis
    Natural Histories, by Leslie Ullman
    Walking Four Ways in the Wind,
        by John Allman
    Denizens, by Ronald Perry
    Quarterly Review of Literature Poetry Series
        (Ed. by T. and R. Weiss)
        [Ann Hébert]
    Wonders, by Karen Snow

BOOKS REVIEWED
James Merrill: Essays in Criticism
    (Ed. with David Lehman)   143   101

BERGER, MARGI
POEMS
Rumor   160   190
You'd Think You'd Hear the Sky
Skeleton   165   84

BERGGOLTS, OLGA
POEMS
My Insatiable Memory   124   192
To Boris Kornilov
Such a Dark Winter
The Return
My House
Infidelity
    (Tr. by Daniel Weissbort)

BERGHOLZ, HARRY
TRANSLATIONS
Poems by Josef Weinheber   85   35

ARTICLES
A Note on Josef Weinheber   85   42

BERGIN, THOMAS GODDARD
BOOKS REVIEWED
Anthology of the Provencal Troubadors
    (Ed. with Raymond Thompson Hill)   58   278

BERGMAN, ALEXANDER F.
POEMS
April 29th   56   305

BERGMAN, DAVID
POEMS
In the Waiting Room   149   136
Bonzai for Beginners

BOOKS REVIEWED
Cracking the Code   149   341

BERGSON, HENRI
ARTICLES ABOUT
Rev. of Imagism, a Chapter for the History
    of Modern Poetry,
    by Stanley K. Coffman, Jr.   78   294

BERGSTRAESSER, ARNOLD
BOOKS REVIEWED
Goethe's Image of Man and Society   75   232

BERKE, JUDITH
POEMS
The Retreat   153   203
Delmore
Custody   153   292
The Three Faces of Eve   156   7

BERKSON, BILL
POEMS
Trouble in Paradise   102   87
Moments
Clearing the Air   114   99
Shady Grove

REVIEWS
Fourteen Books   114 251
   Planet News, by Allen Ginsberg
   Salt & Core, by Rochelle Owens
   In. On. Or About the Premises,
     by Paul Blackburn
   Poems 1964-67,
     by Jerome Rothenberg
   The breath of once/Live Things/
    In the field with Poe,
     by Larry Eigner
   Rothschild's Lapwing,
     by John Temple
   X-ing Warm, by Ronald H. Bayes
   Blue House:
    Poems in the Chinese Manner,
     by Jim Chapson, James Liddy,
     and Thomas Hill
   So Many Rooms Has a House
    But One Roof,
     by Margaret Randall
   Urban Poetry, by Alfeo Marzi
   Surreal Songs, by John Judson
   Haiku,
     by John Esam, Tom Raworth,
     and Anselm Hollo
   The Man in the Treetop Hat,
     by Anselm Hollo
   Selected Poems,
     by Paavo Haavikko
     (Ed. and tr. by Anselm Hollo)

BOOKS REVIEWED
Saturday Night Poems   100 310

BERLIND, BRUCE
POEMS
  Dolly Pentreath   70 135
  The Incompatible   75 263
  Aetat 24   76 322
  Old Man in a Public Lavatory   96 213
  Borborygmus   101 256
  Metric
  Erotique
  Heidelberg 1963   105 240
  Sappho, Her Absences   160 73
  Meaning of Fragment:
   Fragment of Meaning   168 26

TRANSLATIONS
Poem by György Petri
  (Tr. with Mária Körösy)   164 85

REVIEWS
The Poems of Arthur Hugh Clough
  (Ed. by H. F. Lowry, A. L. P.
  Norrington, and F. L. Mulhauser)   82 27
A Poetry Chronicle   95 309

   Orpheus and Other Poems,
     by Robert Beum
   Poems and Translations,
     by Guy Daniels
   Two Laughters,
     by Joseph Joel Keith
   Men, Women, Vines,
     by Thomas Parkinson
   The Walks Near Athens,
     by Hollis Summers
   Several Houses, by Vi Gale

BOOKS REVIEWED
Bred in the Bone
  (Ed. with Henry Fischer)   68 106
Ways of Happening   96 375

BERNARD, APRIL
BOOKS REVIEWED
  Blackbird Bye Bye   155 283
  Psalms   164 223

BERNARD, OLIVER
POEMS
  Pavane   86 74
  For What Is Foreign
  At Hearne
  If the Bright Bird

BERNARDI, ADRIA
TRANSLATIONS
Poems by Gregorio Scalise   155 105

BERNHARD, SVEA
ARTICLES
Verner von Heidenstam   10 35

REVIEWS
Gustaf Froding—Selected Poems
  (Tr. by Charles Wharton Stork)   12 52

BERNHARDT, LYSIANE
POEMS
  La Neige à Poughkeepsie   13 136

BERNOS DE GASZTOLD, CARMEN
BOOKS REVIEWED
Prayers from the Ark
  (Tr. by Rumer Godden)   105 190

BERNSTEIN, CAROLE
POEMS
  Ricordo di Venezia   153 315
  Three-Toed Sloth   158 91
  Mah-Jongg, 1967   160 22
  Cure   161 77
  Familiar   165 312

BERNSTEIN, JOSEPH M.
BOOKS REVIEWED
Baudelaire, Rimbaud,
Verlaine (Ed.)   72   105

BERRIGAN, DANIEL
POEMS
More Like the Sea   92   301
Death   94   231
Saint John Baptist
Snowman
Elegy ("Permanent beauty...")
Parable
Great God Paused Among Men   97   363
Saint Matthew, Publican
Cry
Blind Man
A Statue of the Blessed Virgin,
Carved in Ivory
The Lens   100   283
Mortality
A Wonder of Origins;
Ironies
In Memoriam
Henry Moore in the Garden   104   12
We Are in Love,
the Celibates Gravely Say
A Dark Word
I Am Never Complete   111   31
The Unfinished Man
Of Fair Love the Mother
Somehow
This Crucifix
The Wedding

BOOKS REVIEWED
Time Without Number   92   178
Encounters   96   387
The World for Wedding Ring   102   250
No One Walks Waters   109   114
Night Flight to Hanoi:
War Diary with Eleven Poems   115   189
Selected and New Poems   125   .229

BERRIGAN, TED
POEMS
Words for Love   112   164

BOOKS REVIEWED
The Sonnets   106   370
Living with Chris   112   56
Bean Spasms
(With Ron Padgett)   113   188
In the Early Morning Rain   119   224

ARTICLES ABOUT
Review by Andrew Hoyem   113   426

BERRY, D C
POEMS
Geography   144   201
Pier, P. M.
Cow Bones
Davy Brokenleg
Daddy   146   79
Sir Walter Ralegh and the Milkweed
Dancer
Baby
Gulfport Lover's Confusion   160   192
Cigarette   163   261
Sailboat   168   150
Grandfather   170   285

BERRY, FRANCIS
BOOKS REVIEWED
Poetry and the Physical Voice   102   341

BERRY, JAMES
POEMS
What Is No Good?   146   224

BERRY, JOHN
POEMS
To the Widow's Castle   95   225
Winter Palace
The Hen Yard
Philosophical Congress
The Coming of Gods

BERRY, VIRGINIA
POEMS
Firelight Piece   67   302
This Virgin   79   23
The Garden Enclosed   86   230

BERRY, WENDELL
POEMS
Rain Crow   89   291
Elegy   91   357
Serenade in Black
Diagon   93   313
The River Voyagers   95   102
Nine Verses of the Same Song   96   133
The Country Town
in Early Summer Morning   100   351
Be Still in Haste
The Aristocracy
The Apple Tree
The Habit of Waking
From The Handing Down   106   1
Going   108   237
The Porch over the River
Marriage   110   148
Grace
The Burial of the Old

To Think of the Life of a Man
The Dead Calf
Do Not Be Ashamed
From *Window Poems*   112   1
September 2   116   77
Prayer After Eating   119   67
Anger Against Beasts
A Homecoming
To My Mother   151   14

REVIEWS
  Helmets,
    by James Dickey   105   130

BOOKS REVIEWED
  The Broken Ground   106   309
  Openings   113   421
  Findings   117   108
  Farming: A Hand Book   119   159
  The Country of Marriage   124   103
  The Wheel   143   39
  Collected Poems, 1957-1982   147   35
  Collected Poems, 1957-1982   152   35
  Sabbaths
  Entries   166   38

ARTICLES ABOUT
  [Note on misprint]   94   67
  Review by Paul Breslin   153   30

BERRYMAN, JOHN
POEMS
  The Dispossessed   72   1
  World's Fair
  Surviving Love
  The Traveler
  Fare Well
  The Cage   75   187
  Elegy, for Alun Lewis
  Innocent
  The Wholly Fail
  From *The Black Book*
    not him
    2 ("Luftmenschen...")
    the will
    waiting
  Scots Poem   79   25
  Sonnet 25   81   11
  Four Dream Songs   101   7
    ("The greens of the Ganges...")
    ("Henry's pelt was put on...")
    ("The high ones die, die...")
    ("Spellbound held subtle Henry...")
  Nine Dream Songs   103   1
    I ("In a motion of night...")
    II *Snow Line*
    III ("Henry Hankovitch, con guitar...")
    IV ("Some good people, daring ...")

  V ("Tell it to the forest fire...")
  VI [*To Mark Van Doren*] ("All virtues enter...")
  VII ("Hell is empty...")
  VIII ("He yelled at me in Greek...")
  IX ("He stared at ruin...")
  Fare Well   121   2
  From *Job*   136   35

REVIEWS
  The Long Way to MacDiarmid   88   52
    The Metal and the Flower,
      by P. K. Page
    Poets of Today: Poems and Translations,
      by Harry Duncan;
      Samurai and Serpent Poems,
      by Murray Noss;
      Another Animal: Poems,
      by May Swenson
    Bird in the Mulberry,
      by George Abbe
    A Character Invented,
      by LeRoy Smith
    Events and Signals, by F. R. Scott
    Leaves Without a Tree,
      by G. S. Fraser
    Selected Poems of Hugh MacDiarmid
      (Ed. by Oliver Brown)

BOOKS REVIEWED
  The Dispossessed   73   43
  Stephen Crane   78   298
  Homage to Mistress Bradstreet   90   244
  His Thought Made Pockets
    & the Plane Buckt   95   107
  77 Dream Songs   105   257
  Berryman's Sonnets   112   119
  His Toy, His Dream, His Rest   115   43
  Love & Fame   122   98
  Delusions, Etc.
  Collected Poems: 1937-1971
    (Ed. by Charles Thornbury)   156   158

ARTICLES ABOUT
  The New Intellectualism:
    The Dry Reaction,
    by W. T. Scott   58   86
  Rev. of *New Poems: 1943*
    (Ed. by Oscar Williams)   64   86
  The Things of the Eye,
    by Robert Fitzgerald   132   107
  Job, by John Berryman,
    by John Haffenden   136   39
  Rev. of *Selected Poems
    and Translations 1969-1991*,
    by William Matthews   161   286
  Finishes: Notes on Ambition
    and Survival,
    by Christian Wiman   169   217

BERTELE, RENÉ
BOOKS REVIEWED
Panorama de la Jeune
　Poésie Francaise (Ed.)　　　　　　　67　　42

BERTOCCI, ANGELO P.
POEMS
If the Diver　　　　　　　　　　　　58　　195

BOOKS REVIEWED
From Symbolism to Baudelaire　　　107　　267

BERTOLINO, JAMES
POEMS
Notes for an Elegy　　　　　　　　114　　383
A Seasonal Poem
Under Mayan Sun
From the New Window　　　　　　120　　148
Talisman　　　　　　　　　　　　123　　11

BOOKS REVIEWED
Drool, Poems　　　　　　　　　　116　　193
Maize, a Poem

BESWICK, KATHERINE
POEMS
Feminine Foot-Notes　　　　　　　36　　138
Marriage
To a Complacent Murderer
For Gareth

BETHELL, S. L.
ARTICLES ABOUT
Criticism and Orthodoxy,
　by D. S. Savage　　　　　　　　64　　279

BETJEMAN, JOHN
POEMS
Crematorium　　　　　　　　　　119　　98

BOOKS REVIEWED
Slick But Not Streamlined
　(Ed. by W. H. Auden)　　　　　71　　162
Collected Poems　　　　　　　　94　　124
Summoned by Bells　　　　　　　97　　390
Slick But Not Streamlined:
　Poems and Short Pieces
　(Ed. by W. H. Auden)　　　　121　　48
A Nip in the Air　　　　　　　　129　　226

BETSKY, SEYMOUR
REVIEWS
Palisades of Fear, by Ronald Bottrall　76　　109

BETTI, UGO
BOOKS REVIEWED
Three Plays
　(Tr. by Henry Reed)　　　　　　94　　350

BETTS, FRANK
BOOKS REVIEWED
The Iron Age　　　　　　　　　　10　　44

BETTS, THOMAS JEFFRIES
POEMS
Peking Camels　　　　　　　　　33　　307

BEUM, ROBERT (LAWRENCE)
POEMS
The Cholthoi Panel　　　　　　　90　　81
The Exhibition
Six A.M.
Chanty　　　　　　　　　　　　91　　298
Anniversary Birds
Sonnet XXI ("The widow's house...")　93　　310
11/20　　　　　　　　　　　　96　　92
A Dialogue with a Voice
Leaving Boston Harbor　　　　　97　　175
A Song ("Springing hard...")
A Definition
Good Night Song
On a Painting of Gethsemane　　120　　137

REVIEWS
William Carlos Williams,
　by Vivienne Koch　　　　　　80　　291
Epic and Lyric　　　　　　　　91　　266
　Hot Afternoons Have
　　Been in Montana:
　　Poems by Eli Siegel
　Some Time,
　　by Louis Zukofsky
Five Poets　　　　　　　　　　92　　384
　Hurrah for Anything,
　　by Kenneth Patchen
　Figures in the Shadows,
　　by Jess Cloud
　Eden Under Glass,
　　by Joanne de Longchamps
　If You, by Robert Creeley
　The Condition for All Poetry,
　　by William Packard

BOOKS REVIEWED
Abstract Spring　　　　　　　　77　　114
Twenty Poems　　　　　　　　　89　　52
Orpheus and Other Poems　　　　95　　309
Nine by Three
　(With Maxine Cassin
　and Felix Stefanile)　　　　　96　　375
Poems and Epigrams　　　　　　105　　270

BEVAN, JACK
BOOKS REVIEWED
Brief Candles　　　　　　　　　102　　193

BEVINGTON, HELEN
BOOKS REVIEWED
Dr. Johnson's Waterfall   69   234

BEWAS
POEMS
You-Me
(Tr. by Gobind L. Bhatia
and Tambimuttu)   93   254

BEWLEY, MARIUS
ARTICLES
The Cantabrigian Approach
[Cyril Connolly, Alan Pryce Jones,
F. R. Leavis]   75   282

REVIEWS
English Poetry and Its Contribution
to the Knowledge of a Creative Principle,
by Leone Vivante
[T. S. Eliot]   78   290

BEYE, HOLLY
BOOKS REVIEWED
XVI Poems: A Sampler   86   242

BEYER, WERNER W.
BOOKS REVIEWED
Keats and the Daemon King   70   168

BEYERS, MEREDITH
POEMS
Suggestions   20   141
Bit of Curls
Fat Man

BEZRUC, PETR
POEMS
Ostrava
(Tr. by David Daiches)   55   176

BHARTRIHARI
BOOKS REVIEWED
Bhartrihari: Poems
(Tr. by Barbara Stoler Miller)   112   347

BHATIA, GOBIND L.
TRANSLATIONS
Poem by Bewas
(Tr. with Tambimuttu)   93   254

BIALK, ELIZABETH
POEMS
Back o' the Yards   32   24
Across the Lake   36   314
City in Retrospect
Young Girl

BIANCHI, MARTHA DICKINSON
BOOKS REVIEWED
The Life and Letters of Emily Dickinson   26   97
Emily Dickinson Face to Face   42   345
Unpublished Poems,
by Emily Dickinson
(Ed. with Alfred Leete Hampson)   48   162

BICKERSTETH, G(EOFFREY) L.
BOOKS REVIEWED
Carducci: A Selection of His Poems,
with Verse Translations,
Notes and Three Introductory Essays
(Ed. and tr.)   4   198
The Paradise of Dante (Tr.)   43   229

BIDART, FRANK
BOOKS REVIEWED
Golden State   123   113
The Book of the Body   133   346
The Sacrifice   145   161
In the Western Night:
Collected Poems, 1965-90   157   96

BIENVENU, ROBERTA
POEMS
Divorce   140   325

BIERSTADT, EDWARD
BOOKS REVIEWED
Three Plays of the Argentine:
Juan Moreira, Santos Vega,
The Witches' Mountain (Ed.)
(Tr. by Jacob S. Fassett, Jr.)   17   52

BILAC, OLAVO
BOOKS REVIEWED
Diadems and Fagots
(With Pierre de Ronsard)
(Tr. by John Meem
and Yvor Winters)   23   113

BILGERE, GEORGE
POEMS
At the Vietnam Memorial   166   141
Buying a Touch Tone   168   267
Headstones   170   319

BILLER, MATTHEW
POEMS
Files Moving   49   262
Years
How Many?

BILLET, BONNIE
POEMS
Twelve Moons   138   271
The Vanishing Species

BINGHAM, MILLICENT TODD
BOOKS REVIEWED
Bolts of Melody,
New Poems of Emily Dickinson
(Ed. with Mabel Loomis Todd) 66 274
Ancestors' Brocades,
the Literary Debut of Emily Dickinson
Emily Dickinson: A Revelation 86 118

BINGHAM, ROBERT K.
POEMS
Jouissances 72 255

BINNEY, JAMES
POEMS
Song for Man and Coral 61 654

BINYON, LAURENCE
BOOKS REVIEWED
The Winnowing Fan:
Poems on the Great War 6 205
The Cause—Poems of the War 10 271
Selected Poems 21 337
The Golden Treasury
of Modern Lyrics (Ed.) 27 343
Dante's Inferno (Tr.) 43 229
The North Star and Other Poems 60 149

ARTICLES ABOUT
Correspondence
from Thomas W. Lamont 67 290

BIRCH, CYRIL
BOOKS REVIEWED
Anthology of Chinese Literature:
From Early Times to the
Fourteenth Century
(Ed. with Donald Keene) 109 272

BIRCH, HELEN LOUISE
[See BARTLETT, HELEN BIRCH]

BIRCH-BARTLETT, HELEN
[See BARTLETT, HELEN BIRCH]

BIRD, LAURA LEE
POEMS
Nuptial 40 248
Release 42 70
Sung at Dusk 42 253
Ascent
Bondage
After Dark
Evening
Waiting 44 194
The House
Surfeit
Perspective 46 205

Pursuit
Fulfilment
Twilight
Doom
Orphan 50 140
Plea
Auto-da-Fé

BIRNBAUM, HENRY
POEMS
A Family Group 87 8
A Sense of Hugging to Oneself 91 361
Orizons 94 156
The Great Heart of Lazar Shumsky 95 274
Parkside Public
A Place of Affection 99 164
The Apple
Abstract
The Tree
Living
Bedroom: Partially Descriptive

REVIEWS
The Poetry of Protest 94 408
American Voices,
by Walter Lowenfels
The Hotel Wentley Poems,
by John Wieners
The Diary of Alexander Patience;
The Papers of Professor Bold;
and *Something to Tell Mother,*
by Gil Orlovitz
A Poetry Chronicle 97 114
Anti-Poems,
by Nicamor Parra
(Tr. by J. Elliott)
Hymns to St. Geryon
and Other Poems,
by Michael McClure
Memoirs of an Interglacial Age,
by Philip Whalen
The Empire Finals at Verona,
by Jonathan Williams
The Orges Who Were His Henchmen,
by Judson Crews
No Other Time, by David Lyttle
Genius Is Desire,
by William Packard
O!, by Jess
The Happy Birthday of Death,
by Gregory Corso

BOOKS REVIEWED
The Simon Passion 90 114

BIRNEY, EARLE
BOOKS REVIEWED
David and Other Poems 63 172
Now Is Time 69 349

Twentieth Century Canadian Poetry,
  an Anthology (Ed.)   86   111
Ice Cod Bell or Stone   103   266
Memory No Servant   115   353

BISHOP, ELIZABETH

POEMS
Two Mornings and Two Evenings   50   181
  Paris, 7 A.M.
  A Miracle for Breakfast
  From the Country to the City
  Song ("Summer is over...")
The Mountain   81   12
A Miracle for Breakfast   121   3

TRANSLATIONS
Poems by Max Jacob   76   83
Play by João Cabral de Melo Neto   103   10
Poem by Carlos Drummond de Andrade   106   181

ARTICLES
Correspondence
  [Carlos Drummond de Andrade]   106   251

REVIEWS
Pantomime, a Journal of Rehearsals,
  by Wallace Fowlie   79   212
Come Hither (Ed. by Walter de la Mare)   93   50

BOOKS REVIEWED
North and South   69   228
Poems: North & South—A Cold Spring   87   179
The Diary of 'Helena Morley' (Tr. and ed.)   94   247
Questions of Travel   108   335
Geography III   133   346
The Complete Poems   142   231

ARTICLES ABOUT
[Note on misprint]   93   199
After Reading Hannah Arendt,
  by Denis Donoghue   100   127
Memorial Service for Elizabeth Bishop,
  by Penelope Laurans   135   227
Rev. of The Penguin Book
  of Homosexual Verse
  (Ed. by Stephen Coote)   144   166
Rev. of Becoming a Poet: Elizabeth Bishop
  with Marianne Moore and Robert Lowell,
  by David Kalstone
  (Ed. by Robert Hemenway)   157   159
Rev. of Elizabeth Bishop:
  The Biography of a Poetry,
  by Lorrie Goldensohn, and
  Elizabeth Bishop: Questions of Mastery,
  by Bonnie Costello   161   34
Four Letters to Stephen Yenser,
  by James Merrill   166   324

BISHOP, JOHN PEALE

POEMS
The Hunchback   18   131
Cravings   40   72
  Hunger and Thirst
  The Truth About the Dew
Forbears   42   190
  Beyond Connecticut Beyond the Sea
  My Grandfather Kept Peacocks
  The Ancestors
Homage to Audubon   49   239
  Conquest of the Wind
  Fourteen
  The Silence of the Sideboard
  Les Balcons Qui Revent
The Parallel   64   15
The Spare Quilt

ARTICLES
The Federal Poets' Number
  [Alfred Hayes, Raymond E. F. Larsson,
  Kenneth Fearing]   52   276

REVIEWS
The Assassins, by Frederick Prokosch   49   337
Reading the Spirit, by Richard Eberhart   50   164
Collected Poems, by Ford Madox Ford   50   336
Conversation at Midnight,
  by Edna St. Vincent Millay   51   99
Selected Poems, by John Masefield
  [Pablo Picasso]   53   144
The Collected Poems of A. E. Housman   56   144
Poetry and the Modern World,
  by David Daiches   58   210
3 Spanish American Poets
  [Carlos Pellicer, Pablo Neruda,
  Jorge Carrera Andrade]
  (Tr. by Lloyd Mallan, Mary and C. V.
  Wicker, and Joseph Leonard Grucci)   62   111

BOOKS REVIEWED
Green Fruit   12   165
Now with His Love   43   342
Selected Poems   58   96
John Peale Bishop and Maxwell Bodenheim
  [Recording]   101   275

ARTICLES ABOUT
Notebooks, 1924–1938,
  by Archibald MacLeish   73   88

BISHOP, MORRIS

POEMS
With the A. E. F.   13   308
  Ante Proelium
  Before My Fire in a French Village
  Le Père Segret
  The Piker
Ecclesiastes   19   314

A New Hampshire Boy
The Old Photograph 25 20
Dementia Praecox

ARTICLES
Correspondence: Serving in the A. E. F. 13 346
Correspondence: Disarmament
[Poem] 17 55

REVIEWS
Phaedra and Figaro: Phedre, by Racine
(Tr. by Robert Lowell),
and *Figaro's Marriage*, by Beaumarchais
(Tr. by Jacques Barzun) 100 41

BISHOP, ROBERT KNOX
BOOKS REVIEWED
Forty Poems 1935-43
(With John Claiborne Davis) 63 104

BISPHAM, G. TUCKER
POEMS
The Lacemaker of Ypres 7 236
Dread
Nocturne
Failure
Charm

BISSELL, TRIM
POEMS
Archaic Song 105 249

BISSETT, BILL
BOOKS REVIEWED
Lebanon Voices 115 353

BITTNER, NELSON DEL
POEMS
Night Thoughts Off Tarragonna 34 86
Phases
Whistles
Ships
Relinquishment 39 78
Saying Goodbye Under Lilacs in Rain
Plumes of the Great
Resurrected by a Bomb, By God 51 18
The Dolls 63 125
Blue Piano 70 140

REVIEWS
California Poets:
An Anthology of 244 Contemporaries
(Fwd. by Helen Hoyt) 42 233

BOOKS REVIEWED
Paper Faces 61 456

BJERSBY, BIRGIT
BOOKS REVIEWED
The Interpretation of the Cuchulain Legend
in the Works of W. B. Yeats 81 331

BLACK, JOHN
POEMS
A Poet's Epitaph 11 71

BLACK, MAC KNIGHT
POEMS
White Horizons 26 258
Sword Prayer
Structural Iron Workers
Street-Cleaner Stops for Lunch
Farm Wife
Bird of the Sun
Slag

BOOKS REVIEWED
Machinery 34 285
Thrust at the Sky and Other Poems 40 224

BLACK, SOPHIE CABOT
BOOKS REVIEWED
The Misunderstanding of Desire 165 219

BLACKBURN, PAUL
POEMS
Ritual IX 108 25
The Hour 109 153
Ritual VIII
The Evasion

BOOKS REVIEWED
The Dissolving Fabric 89 52
Sing-Song 112 56
The Cities 114 113
In. On. Or About the Premises 114 251

BLACKBURN, THOMAS
BOOKS REVIEWED
The Next Word 94 196
A Smell of Burning 102 193

BLACK MOUNTAIN REVIEW
BOOKS REVIEWED
The Black Mountain Review, 1-8 116 110

BLACKMUR, R. P.
POEMS
Alma Venus 29 11
Steriles Ritournelles 38 26
Funeral Business
Resurrection 40 261
A Labyrinth of Being 42 246
Lament of a Father-To-Be
Sonnet ("This marriage has...")
Sonnet ("Three silences made...")
Struggle-Bread
My Dog My Wife and Most Myself
An Elegy for Five 44 185
Of Lucifer 45 140

By Luckless Blood	47	15
Judas Priest	48	76
Scarabs for the Living	49	246
Nigger Jim	76	261
Mr. Virtue and the Three Bears	79	144

ARTICLES
Stickney's Poetry	42	158
A Note on Yvor Winters	57	144
An Adjunct to the Muses' Diadem:		
A Note on E. P.		
[Ezra Pound]	68	338

REVIEWS
Nobodaddy: A Play,		
by Archibald MacLeish	28	339
Doctor Donne and Gargantua,		
by Sacheverell Sitwell	38	162
Selected Poems,		
by William Vaughn Moody		
(Ed. by Robert Morss Lovett)	38	331
Eden Tree, by Witter Bynner	39	217
The Gates of the Compass,		
by Robert Hillyer	39	340
The Coming Forth by Day of Osiris Jones		
and *Preludes for Memnon,*		
by Conrad Aiken	40	39
Red Roses for Bronze, by H. D.	41	94
T. S. Eliot in Prose	42	44
The Poetry of T. S. Eliot,		
by Hugh Ross Williamson		
T. S. Eliot, by Thomas McGreevy		
Mr. Eliot Among the Nightingales,		
by Louis Grudin		
John Dryden and *Selected Essays,*		
by T. S. Eliot		
Ariadne, by F. L. Lucas	42	115
No Retreat, by Horace Gregory	42	217
Talifer, by Edwin Arlington Robinson	43	221
Icaro		
(Tr. by Ruth Draper)		
and *The Story of My Death,*		
by Lauro de Bosis	44	44
Rock and Shell,		
by John Wheelwright	44	282
Dream and Action,		
by Leonard Bacon	45	223
The Esthetic of Stéphane Mallarmé,		
by Hasye Cooperman	45	347
Horizons of Death,		
by Norman Macleod	46	108
A Tearless Glass, by Louis Grudin	47	162
XXIV Elegies,		
by John Gould Fletcher	47	344
Fire Testament, by Willard Maas	48	113
Poems 1919 to 1934,		
by Walter de la Mare	48	334

Collected Poems, 1909-1935, by T. S. Eliot	50	48
Shiloh. Fragments on a Famous Theme,		
by Edward Doro	50	166
Poetry and Sensibility:		
Some Rules of Thumb	71	271
Collected Poems, by Herbert Read		
Transport to Summer,		
by Wallace Stevens		

BOOKS REVIEWED
The Double Agent:		
Essays in Craft and Elucidation	49	52
The Expense of Greatness	57	335
The Second World	61	505
Language as Gesture	83	238
Four Poets on Poetry:		
Essays by R. P. Blackmur,		
Yvor Winters, Marianne Moore,		
and Mark Van Doren		
(Ed. by Don Cameron Allen)	96	382
R. P. Blackmur Reads His Works		
[Recording]	101	275
A Primer of Ignorance		
(Ed. by Joseph Frank)	112	356
Poems of…	133	290

ARTICLES ABOUT
Rev. of *Viva,* by E. E. Cummings	39	332
The Critical Method of R. P. Blackmur,		
by Delmore Schwartz	53	28
R. P. Blackmur and the Expense		
of Criticism,		
by Stanley Edgar Hyman	71	259
E. E. Cummings: The World of "Un,"		
by Carl Bode	86	358

BLACKPOOL, STANLEY
POEMS
Flashes over Basalt	44	72
The Woman in the Wheat		
Cold Rain		
The Stone Left Standing		
Flowering Night		

BLACKWELL, ALICE STONE
BOOKS REVIEWED
Armenian Poems (Tr.)	14	281
Some Spanish-American Poets (Tr.)	37	164

ARTICLES ABOUT
Rev. of *Studies in Spanish-American Literature,*		
by Isaac Goldberg	16	280

BLAIR, ARTHUR
POEMS
A Letter to the Moon	61	535
Boy Afraid		
The Saint: The Imagistic Self		

BLAIR, JOHN
POEMS
Cicada   153   211
Winter Storm, New Orleans

BLAIR, WALTER
BOOKS REVIEWED
Approaches to Poetry
(With W. K. Chandler)   84   43

BLAIR, WILFRID
BOOKS REVIEWED
The Life and Death of Mrs. Tidmuss,
an Epic of Insignificance   23   221

BLAKE, HOWARD (MILTON)
POEMS
Analyse des Amants   43   322
Rebellion
Argent Solipsism   47   19
Transcorporeal Wanted   56   11

REVIEWS
Daekargus, by William Fitzgerald   44   287
The Human Dawn,
by J. Redwood Anderson   47   167
Young Longfellow, by Lawrance Thompson   54   29
The Poetical Works of Edward Taylor
(Ed. by Thomas H. Johnson)   56   165
The Overturned Lake,
by Charles Henri Ford   60   48

BOOKS REVIEWED
Prolegomena to Any Future Poetry   51   221
The Island Self
(Ed. by Robert Kent)   125   352

BLAKE, PATRICIA
BOOKS REVIEWED
The Bedbug and Selected Poetry,
by Vladimir Mayakovsky (Ed.)   97   320
Antiworlds, by Andrei Voznesensky
(Ed. with Max Hayward)
(Tr. by W. H. Auden et al.)   110   40

BLAKE, WILLIAM
BOOKS REVIEWED
Selections from the Symbolical Poems of...
(Ed. by Fred E. Pierce)   9   315
The Land of Dreams   36   289
The Portable Blake
(Ed. by Alfred Kazin)   69   223
William Blake's Vala
(Ed. by H. M. Margoliouth)   90   321
The Poetry and Prose of...
(Ed. by David V. Erdman)   111   263
The Complete Writings of William Blake
with Variant Readings
(Ed. by Geoffrey Keynes)

ARTICLES ABOUT
Christmas and William Blake,
by Harriet Monroe   31   148
The Book of Hart Crane,
by M. D. Zabel   42   33
Rev. of William Blake:
The Politics of Vision,
by Mark Schorer   69   223
Rev. of Fearful Symmetry,
by Northrop Frye   71   101
Rev. of Blake: Prophet Against Empire,
by David V. Erdman   84   363
Rev. of The Letters of William Blake
(Ed. by Geoffrey Keynes);
William Blake's Vala
(Ed. by H. M. Margoliouth);
and William Blake:
The Finger on the Furnace,
by Laura DeWitt James   90   321
Rev. of William Blake:
A Reading of the Shorter Poems,
by Hazard Adams;
Blake's Apocalypse:
A Study in Poetic Argument,
by Harold Bloom;
A Study of the Illuminated
Books of William Blake,
by Geoffrey Keynes;
and William Blake,
by John Middleton Murry   107   65
Rev. of William Blake,
Poet and Painter,
by Jean H. Hagstrum   107   192
Rev. of Blake and Tradition,
by Kathleen Raine   117   43

BLAKESTON, OSWALD
BOOKS REVIEWED
Proems
(With Ruthven Todd, Patrick Evans,
Rayner Heppenstall, Edgar Foxall,
and Lawrence Durrell)   53   155

BLANCO, ANTONIO NICOLAS
[See NICOLAS BLANCO,
ANTONIO]

BLANCO FOMBONA, RUFINO
POEMS
Escape   26   153
By the Sea
(Tr. by Muna Lee)

BLAND, EDWARD
ARTICLES
Racial Bias and Negro Poetry
[Countee Cullen, Lewis Alexander,
Frank Horne, Claude McKay]   63   328

BLANDEN, CHARLES G.
BOOKS REVIEWED
The Chicago Anthology:
A Collection of Verse
from the Work of Chicago Poets
(Ed. with Minna Mathison)   12   337

**BLANDING,
HENRIETTE DE SAUSSURE**
POEMS
Nativity   37   130
Sung Before Death
Fisherman's Wife
White Leopard

BLANK, DOROTHY ANN
POEMS
Farmer's Wife   41   196

BLANSHARD, BRAND
ARTICLES ABOUT
Contemporary Poetry Criticism,
by J. V. Healy   61   672

BLANSHARD, RUFUS A.
BOOKS REVIEWED
A Reviewer's ABC:
Collected Criticism of Conrad Aiken
from 1916 to the Present (Ed.)   96   318

BLASER, ROBIN
BOOKS REVIEWED
The Moth Poem   107   121
Cups   116   193

BLASING, RANDY
POEMS
All Present   130   3
Over Drinks   142   267
Gilgamesh Visits Ephesus
Ramazan at New Phocaea
North End   145   206
Pirated Version   146   332
Kingdom Come
An Album Family   149   9
Richfield
Refuge   150   315
Golden Valley
Divining Rod
Calling   151   15
Within Limits   153   340
Triptych   154   77
White Bread
Burial Grounds   155   262
Permanent Ink   156   261
Lifelines
Mother Tongue   159   200
Chambers of the Heart   161   95
Man of Letters   162   333

Cardiogram
At Length   164   78
Rock Country   167   216
Wishful Thinking   168   311
BOOKS REVIEWED
To Continue   144   107
Graphic Scenes   166   166

BLAUNER, LAURIE
POEMS
The Art of Translation   155   213
Matisse in the Company of Strangers 161   324
Killing Time   165   146

**BLAUSTEIN, RACHEL
[See RACHEL]**

BLAYKER, MARY AVIS
POEMS
April Moods   28   19
Rain Girl
Guarded Truth

BLAZEK, DOUGLAS
POEMS
What We Once Knew   116   152
Usage of a Life
Fishing in a City
Bells & Bursting   119   315
A Personal Ecology
Nor Travels Nor Loves Anymore
There Is
Armchair Affidavit

REVIEWS
Falling into Triteness   124   167
Color Photos of the Atrocities,
by Kenneth Pitchford
Smudging, by Diane Wakoski
Dying to Survive,
by Carolyn Stoloff
Writings to an Unfinished Accompaniment,
by W. S. Merwin

BLISH, JAMES
POEMS
A Song for Music   78   14

BLISS, MARION LOUISE
POEMS
October   31   20
Dust Storm   46   88
Memorial   47   252
A Leaf Falls
Enduring Sojourn   50   258
The Earth Is Builded
Deeper than Drouth

BLISS, SYLVIA H.
BOOKS REVIEWED
   Quests   17   276

BLOCH, ARIEL
TRANSLATIONS
   From *Song of Songs: 5: 2-8, 2: 4-7*
     (With Chana Bloch)   163   83

BLOCH, CHANA
POEMS
   A Future   154   87
   The Family
   Rising To Meet It   156   16
   Afterlife
   White Petticoats
   Chez Pierre, 1961   156   213
   Signals
   Blue-Black   157   88
   The Captive   157   213
   The Secret Life   159   275
   The Ghost Worm Monster
   Inside
   Tuesday

TRANSLATIONS
   From *Song of Songs: 5: 2-8, 2: 4-7*
     (With Ariel Bloch)   163   83

BOOKS REVIEWED
   The Selected Poetry of Yehuda Amichai
     (Ed. and tr. with Stephen Mitchell)   150   286
   The Past Keeps Changing   160   284

BLOCH, JEAN-RICHARD
ARTICLES ABOUT
   Correspondence from George Dillon   67   49

BLOCK, ALLAN
POEMS
   The Meeting   65   186
   The Estate
   The Dog
   Three Songs for the Same Season   67   308
     ("Not at ship's wreck nor vessel's...")
     ("Across the neon cemeteries...")
     ("Will you love me with another...")
   Journey
   Diamond Boy

BLOCK, HASKELL M.
BOOKS REVIEWED
   Mallarmé and the Symbolist Drama   104   187

BLOCK, RALPH
POEMS
   After Rachmaninoff   15   302

BLODGETT, HAROLD W.
BOOKS REVIEWED
   Leaves of Grass,
     by Walt Whitman
     (Ed. with Sculley Bradley)   107   397

BLOK, ALEXANDER
BOOKS REVIEWED
   The Twelve and Other Poems
     (Tr. by John Stallworthy
     and Peter France)   119   45

ARTICLES ABOUT
   Alexander Blok,
     by Glenway Wescott   19   149
   New Trends in Soviet Russian Poetry,
     by Vera Sandomirsky   58   324
   Rev. of *The Poets of Russia 1890-1930,*
     by Renato Poggioli   97   320

BLOOM, HAROLD
BOOKS REVIEWED
   The Wind and the Rain: An Anthology
     of Poems for Young People
     (Ed. with John Hollander)   101   208
   Blake's Apocalypse:
     A Study in Poetic Argument   107   65
   Yeats   117   43
   The Anxiety of Influence:
     A Theory of Poetry   122   298
   A Map of Misreading   127   222
   Wallace Stevens:
     The Poems of Our Climate   131   165

ARTICLES ABOUT
   Rev. of *Somewhere Is Such a Kingdom,*
     by Geoffrey Hill   128   232

BLOOM, LLOYD
POEMS
   Hothouse Flowers   126   130
   Fenced Acres
   The Wreck
   After Her
   At the Window

BLOOM, ROBERT
POEMS
   Vintage Country   87   215

BLOOMFIELD, MAUREEN
POEMS
   Morning   129   257
   Ghosts
   Near the End of June
   The Long Ton
   Isuprel

BLOSSOM, LAUREL

POEMS

Doomed	132	327
Leaving		
Skate		
Next Time		
Trap	140	146
Under the Covers		
Normal	142	18
Back from the Dead		

BLOY, LEON

ARTICLES ABOUT

French Poetry and the Revival of Mysticism, by Eugene Jolas	56	264

BLUESTONE, STEPHEN

POEMS

The Unveiling	157	140

BLUM, ETTA

POEMS

In Corona	43	250
It Was Almost		
For Blake's Angels	94	22
From Theme: Variations	96	288
The Blackbird and the Gingko Tree	101	249
Fog at Brighton	103	162
Words for Eli	106	194
Passing the Rose Garden Touched What I Could	108	305
The Fountain, the Fire		
Three Poems	109	374
("Whatever it is I do...")		
("I am waiting...")		
("God is good...")		
Beit Guvrin	118	209
Only Because		

TRANSLATIONS

Poems by B. Alquit-Blum	104	88

REVIEWS

Five Poets	109	340
Then, by Carroll Arnett		
Men—In Good Measure, by Sam Bradley		
Go Read the River, by Dave Etter		
An Almanac for Twilight, by Jack Matthews		
Living in America, by Anne Stevenson		

BOOKS REVIEWED

Poems	51	219
The Space My Body Fills	128	290

BLUM, MORGAN

POEMS

Old Man at Window	61	360

REVIEWS

Riders at the Gate, by Joseph Auslander	55	162
The Connecticut River and Other Poems, by Reuel Denney	55	274
New Directions, 1940 (Ed. by James Laughlin)	58	164
The Mayfield Deer, by Mark Van Doren	60	43
The Diver, by E. L. Mayo	71	331
The Poetic Image and Poetry for You, by C. Day Lewis	72	322
Stephen Crane, by John Berryman [Thomas Beer]	78	298

BLUM, W. C.
[Pseud. of WATSON, J(AMES) SIBLEY]

REVIEWS

Book of Moments: Poems 1915-1954, by Kenneth Burke	87	362

BLUMENTHAL, MICHAEL (C.)

POEMS

The Flirtation	136	74
Life Goes On		
Days We Would Rather Know	138	203
Cheers	142	149
What a Time!	144	22
The Disappointments of Childhood		
Back from the Word Processing Course, I Say to My Old Typewriter		
Advice to My Students: How To Write a Poem	145	274
First Snow: Cambridge, Mass.	151	16
The Pleasures of Old Age	151	413
And the Wages of Goodness Are Not Assured	159	95
Ordinary Heartbreaks		
The Forces	164	150
Never To Have Loved a Child		
The Accountant		

TRANSLATIONS

Poem by Péter Kántor	170	129

BOOKS REVIEWED

Days We Would Rather Know	146	167
Laps		
Against Romance	152	161
The Wages of Goodness	162	96

BLUNDEN, EDMUND

BOOKS REVIEWED

The Waggoner	18	343
The Shepherd	21	104

Retreat   34   54
Near and Far   38   113
Halfway House   43   287
Poems 1930-1940   58   100
Shells by a Stream   67   225
Wayside Poems of the Seventeenth Century
    (Ed. with Bernard Mellor)   104   120

ARTICLES ABOUT
The Winter's Publishing in England,
    by R. Hughes   18   172
London Note,
    by Benjamin Gilbert Brooks   35   214
Poetry in the First World War,
    by David Daiches   56   323

BLUNT, WILFRID SCAWEN
  BOOKS REVIEWED
  Poems   22   337

  ARTICLES ABOUT
  Homage to Wilfrid Blunt,
      by Ezra Pound   3   220

BLY, ROBERT
  POEMS
  The Possibility of New Poetry   96   31
  This World Is a Confusion
      of Three Worlds
  Driving Through Ohio
  Clear Air of October   99   40
  Poem ("There is dust that is near us...")
  Images Suggested by Medieval Music
  The Confusion of America
  Awakening
  Fall Rain
  "Taking the Hands"   100   278
  Boards on the Ground
  Hunting Pheasants in a Cornfield
  Snowfall in the November Afternoon
  Watering the Horse
  A Late Spring Day in My Life
  After Working
  Late at Night During a Visit of Friends
  "Come with Me"   104   365
  Unanswered Letters
  The Beauty of Women
  Fall
  Driving North from San Francisco
  On a Cliff
  The Testament
  Poem in Praise of Solitude
  An American Dream   108   382
  Written near Rome
  The Life of Weeds
  Full Moon,
      Thinking of High School Girls
  A Journey with Women

March in Washington
    Against the Vietnam War
When the Dumb Speak   110   180
Hurrying Away from the Earth
Suddenly Turning Away
Looking at Some Flowers
The Hermit
Riderless Horses
A Dream on the Night of First Snow   118   33
After Long Busyness
A Caterpillar on the Desk
A Ramage for Awakening Sorrow   138   283
A Ramage for the Star Man, Mourning
The Moose
Herons
Prayer for My Father   151   17
Waking on the Farm   167   154
The Bear and the Man   170   9
A Boy on the Farm
He Wanted To Live His Life Over

TRANSLATIONS
Poem by César Vallejo   98   353

BOOKS REVIEWED
Twenty Poems of Georg Trakl
    (Tr. with James Wright)   100   319
Silence in the Snowy Fields   102   182
Twenty Poems of César Vallejo
    (Tr. with John Knoepfle
    and James Wright)   105   196
A Poetry Reading
    Against the Vietnam War
    (Ed. with David Ray)   109   345
The Light Around the Body   112   418
I Do Best Alone at Night,
    by Gunnar Ekelöf
    (Tr. and ed. with Christina Paulson)   113   188
Twenty Poems,
    by Pablo Neruda
    (Tr. with James Wright)   113   338
Neruda and Vallejo: Selected Poems (Ed.)
    (Tr. with John Knoepfle
    and James Wright)   120   304
The Sea and the Honeycomb:
    A Book of Tiny Poems (Ed.)   123   34
Twenty Poems of Tomas Transt-römer (Tr.)
David Ignatow: Selected Poems (Ed.)   128   37
Meditations on the Insatiable Soul   167   343

BOAS, GEORGE
  BOOKS REVIEWED
  The Hieroglyphics of Horapollo   77   168

BOAS, HARRIET BETTY
  BOOKS REVIEWED
  Madonna Dianora, a Play in Verse,
      by Hugo von Hofmannsthal (Tr.)   9   159

BOBROWSKI, JOHANNES
POEMS
East
  (Tr. by Michael Hamburger)   128   130

BOOKS REVIEWED
Shadow Land
  (Tr. by Ruth and Matthew Mead)   110   52

BOCK, FREDERICK
POEMS
The Force of Cassowaries   77   206
In Memory of PFC R.N.   86   234
The Heart on the Sand   88   219
Winter: The Statue of Pomona
The Vision of Dorinda
Rainfall on "The Puritans"
For the Queen of Franklin High   93   31
The Moonlight
Aubade: The Desert
The Picnic of Othello
"No Storms Trouble This Part of the Key"
The Sun of Poetry   98   71
Hymn to Reductive Thought
Ruin
The Cows   101   10
A Banner Day   102   217
For Richie
Vegetation
October Silence
Man Parked on Roadside   103   284
Summer Despite
Lost Image
The Recovery
Far   105   295
Catch a Man Forty
That Strait-Jacket Case
Crowd and Performer
Shadow of the Damson   112   384
Moving Day
Phenomenon
Tomato Juice   115   106
Snow and Ice
Mistaken Cats   116   22
Grasshoppers   132   97
Champs   133   331
Stock   138   19

REVIEWS
Poems 1947-1954, by Weldon Kees   88   191
The Invisible and the Manifest   89   64
  Nice Deity, by Martha Baird
  The Meandering Absolute,
    by Elise Asher
  The Hangman Ties the Holly,
    by Anne Wilkinson
  Family in the Forest,
    by Harold Witt

The Rudiment of an Eye,
  by W. Price Turner
Country Without Maps,
  by Jean Garrigue   106   229

BOOKS REVIEWED
The Fountains of Regardlessness   99   379

ARTICLES ABOUT
A Further Note, by Henry Rago
  [Poets of India]   93   272
Obituary   138   53

BODE, CARL
POEMS
Song ("Sit in the sun...")   76   328
Eastertide
And the Virgin   91   300

ARTICLES
E. E. Cummings: The World of "Un"
  [R. P. Blackmur]   86   358

REVIEWS
Contemporary Poetry, Vol. Ten
  (Ed. by Mary Owings Miller)   79   116

BOOKS REVIEWED
The Sacred Seasons   84   232

BODENHEIM, MAXWELL
POEMS
Sketches   4   187
  The Interne
  The Old Jew
  The Miner
  To an Enemy
  To a Discarded Steel Rail
The Camp Follower   5   65
Charcoals   7   73
  A Man to a Dead Woman
  The Crucifixion
  Thoughts While Walking
  Streets
  The Steam-Shovel
Sketches in Color   8   73
  Columns of Evening
  Happiness
  Suffering
  A Man to a Dead Woman
  The Window-Washers
  The Department Store
Songs to a Woman   14   76
The Cloud Descends   14   295
Sappho Answers Aristotle   18   61
  Impulsive Dialogue
  Emotional Monologue
  Feminine Talk

Philosophical Dialogue		
Concerning Roses	22	311
Sunlight on the Avenue	25	22
Old Theme		
The King of Spain	27	304
Emotion Speaks	33	138
One Generation	53	229
Margaret Calhoun		
Friendly Message to Certain Intellectuals		
To John Gould Fletcher	54	249
Sonnet ("His first time on...")	55	245
Advice to a Man	57	190
To Gertrude Stein		

ARTICLES
Correspondence:
A Reply to A. C. H.
[Lola Ridge]   14   170
Correspondence:
Words from a Departing Poet   16   227
Correspondence:
In Defense of Rodker
[John Rodker, Richard Aldington] 17   170
Correspondence:
Mr. Bodenheim is Dissatisfied
[Helen Hoyt]   26   48

BOOKS REVIEWED
Minna and Myself   13   342
Advice   18   39
Introducing Irony: A Book
of Poetic Short Stories and Poems 21 100
The Sardonic Arm   23   279
Returning to Emotion   30   104
The King of Spain   32   221
Lights in the Valley   60   219
Seven Poets in Search of an Answer
(With Joy Davidman, Langston Hughes,
Aaron Kramer, Alfred Kreymborg,
Martha Millet, and Norman Rosten)
(Ed. by Thomas Yoseloff)   64   289
John Peale Bishop and Maxwell Bodenheim
[Recording]   101   275

ARTICLES ABOUT
The Jew as Jewish Artist,
by Florence Kiper Frank   22   209
Maxwell Bodenheim,
by Harriet Monroe   25   320
[Note]   84   123

BODET, JAIME TORRES
[See TORRES BODET, JAIME]

BOE, DEBORAH
POEMS
Still-Life   147   316
Factory Work

Breaking Down		
And Yahweh Closed the Door		
Behind Noah	150	193
Mary of Bethany		
About Lazarus		

BOER, CHARLES
BOOKS REVIEWED
The Odes   116   51

BOGAN, LOUISE
POEMS
Beginning and End   20   248
Elders
Resolve
Knowledge
Leave-Taking
To a Dead Lover
Didactic Piece   31   314
Hypocrite Swift   39   12
The Sleeping Fury   49   119
M., Singing
Putting to Sea
Song for a Lyre   49   245
Untitled ("Tender and insolent...") 51   3
After the Persian   81   14
Night   101   12
Morning

TRANSLATIONS
Poems by Paul Valéry
(With May Sarton)   94   I

ARTICLES
Rilke in His Age   50   34
Correspondence   86   310
Correspondence to William Kolodny
(With Stanley Kunitz
and Robert Lowell)   100   412

REVIEWS
Collected Poems and
The Glory of the Nightingales,
by Edwin Arlington Robinson   37   216
The Frozen Ocean, by Viola Meynell 40 226
A Tale of Troy,
by John Masefield   41   332
Texts and Pretexts,
by Aldous Huxley   42   170
Blossoming Antlers,
by Winifred Welles   44   159
Wine from These Grapes,
by Edna St. Vincent Millay   45   277
Wheels and Butterflies,
William Butler Yeats   46   100
The Poet's Tongue
(Ed. by W. H. Auden
and John Garrett)   48   43

Unpublished Poems,
  by Emily Dickinson
  (Ed. by Martha Dickinson Bianchi
  and Alfred Leete Hampson)   48   162
The Old House in the Country,
  by Lizette Woodworth Reese   49   97
A Trophy of Arms. Poems: 1926-1935,
  by Ruth Pitter   51   43

BOOKS REVIEWED
Body of This Death   23   335
Dark Summer   35   158
The Sleeping Fury   50   158
Poems and New Poems   60   40
Collected Poems; 1923-53   85   165
Selected Criticism   87   370
The Golden Journey:
  Poems for Young People
  (Ed. with William Jay Smith)   108   343
The Blue Estuaries:
  Poems 1923-1968   114   330

ARTICLES ABOUT
A Few Women Poets,
  by Harriet Monroe   26   326
Contemporary Poetry Criticism,
  by J. V. Healy   61   672
Allen Tate: A Poet
  on Poetry, 1924-1944,
  by Ashley Brown   135   103
Rev. of *Summers of Vietnam*
  and Other Poems,
  by Mary Kinzie   158   41

BOGARDUS, EDGAR
POEMS
Le Puritain et la Putain   91   160

BOOKS REVIEWED
Various Jangling Keys   84   173

BOGEN, DON
POEMS
The Pageant   147   324
Romanesque
The Pond
Tableau   155   382
A Luddite Lullaby
La Clairière   162   83
Musée

BOGGS, TOM
POEMS
Valley   52   62
Prairie
For a New Boy
Rogue's Gallery   53   22
From Unfulfilled Delight

Bells   55   135
Poem ("Imagine the dread...")   57   19
Grackles   74   213

REVIEWS
Five Anthologies   57   221
  Eternal Passion in English Poetry
  (Ed. by Edith Wharton
  and Robert Norton)
  Immortal Lyrics
  (Ed. by Hudson Strode)
  An Anthology for
  the Enjoyment of Poetry
  (Ed. by Max Eastman)
  Behold, This Dreamer!
  (Ed. by Walter de la Mare)
  The Pocket Book of Verse
  (Ed. by M. E. Speare)

BOOKS REVIEWED
Lyrics in Brief (Ed.)   56   222
Arenas   63   99
American Decade (Ed.)   63   223
The Constant Mistress   67   270
Of Love   83   343

BOGIN, NINA
POEMS
Lappland: Ammarnäs   162   93
Two Poems
  ("A rock cleaved open...")
  ("Where did the words go?...")
Going Up the Hudson After Twenty Years   164   316

BOHM, ELIZABETH
POEMS
Quiet Morning   52   318
Stone Walls
The Unknown
Waste
The Milkweed Pod
September Water
Sea Death   57   302
Winter Afternoon
Victorian Parlor
Gossip
The Circle   63   137
Beast   68   83

BOISSARD, MAURICE
ARTICLES ABOUT
Our Contemporaries: Bond or Free?
  [Article excerpt]   18   53

BOISSEAU, MICHELLE
POEMS
Mental Hospital Graveyard   145   324
Votary

Sisters		
Counting	147	31
Arbor Day		
We Return to a Plain Sense of Things	150	280
Partial Eclipse		

BOOKS REVIEWED
No Private Life	159	32

BOLAND, EAVAN
POEMS
In Which the Ancient History		
I Learn Is Not My Own	161	218
Mother Ireland	167	93

BOOKS REVIEWED
Selected Poems	156	236
In a Time of Violence	165	31

ARTICLES ABOUT
A Map of Contemporary Irish Poetry,		
by Dennis O'Driscoll	167	94

BOLD, ALAN
BOOKS REVIEWED
To Find the New	114	266
A Perpetual Motion Machine	117	331
Penguin Modern Poets 15		
(With Edward Brathwaite		
and Edwin Morgan)	118	102
The State of the Nation	119	291

BOLT, THOMAS
BOOKS REVIEWED
Out of the Woods	155	283

BOLTON, CHARLES E.
POEMS
Fat	124	334

BOLTON, JOE
POEMS
Elegy for Roland Barthes	154	63

BOLTON, SARAH
ARTICLES ABOUT
Notes on Mid-Western Oblivion,		
by Pat Morrissette	34	346

BOMBERGER, CARL
POEMS
Inbred	52	323

BOND, BRUCE
POEMS
Planetarium	156	152
On Certainty	158	268
Taps	161	337
Host	168	273

BOND, DONALD F.
REVIEWS
New Poets from Old,		
by Henry W. Wells	59	102

BOND, GEORGE D.
ARTICLES ABOUT
A Texas Prize Contest,		
by Harriet Monroe	21	91

BOND, JUDITH S.
REVIEWS
Observing and Describing	58	275
The Black Butterfly, by Carl Grabo		
Renewal, by Pearl Hogrefe		
Here Only a Dove, by Sr. Maris Stella		
No Thunder on the Left or Anywhere	65	278
In This Our Day,		
by Edith Lovejoy Pierce		
The Middle Kingdom,		
by Christopher Morley		
Eighteen Poems, by James Boyd		

BOND, JULIANA ALLISON
POEMS
In the Morning	12	205

BOND, PEARL
POEMS
Sunday Afternoon	83	5

BONER, H.
POEMS
For a Monstrous Clever Fellow	29	319
Memoranda of Various Phenomena	34	1
Unfathomed Apparition		
Descent to the Sea		
Front-Page Stuff		
Portrait, etc.		
After Eight Years		
Nuevo Mexico		
Taos—Autumn		
Galveston		
Song Before Sleep		
Reflection		
Enchanted Mesa—New Mexico		
The Giant Cactus	38	321

BONHOMME, CLOVIS
ARTICLES ABOUT
Letter From Haiti,		
by Wallace Fowlie	94	398

BONN, JOHN LOUIS
POEMS
Epistles	45	205
To Gerard Manley Hopkins		
On Posthumous Fame		
On Philistines		

BONNEFOY, YVES
POEMS
  Cinq Poèmes   80   365
    ("Mais que se taise...")
    ("Visage séparé de ses branches...")
    ("Sur un fangeux hiver...")
    ("Le peu d'espace...")
    ("L'oiseau se portera...")
      (Tr. by Wallace Fowlie)
  Douve Parle   100   211
    ("Quelle parole a surgi...")
    Une Voix
    Une Autre Voix
    ("Si cette nuit est autre...")
  Douve Parle
    ("Quelquefois, disais-tu...")
    ("O fatale saison...")
    ("Que le verbe s'eteigne...")
    ("Demande au maître de la nuit...")
  Voix Basses et Phenix
  ("Mais que se taise celle qui veille...")
  ("Tais-toi puisqu'aussi bien nous...")
  L'Orangerie
    ("Ainsi marcherons-nous...")
  La Salamandre
    ("Et maintenant tu es Douve...")
    ("Toute une nuit...")
    ("Regarde-moi, regarde-moi...")
    ("Ainsi restions-nous éveillés...")
  ("Quand reparut la salamandre...")
  ("Cassandre, dira-t-il...")
  Justice
  ("Je prendrai dans mes mains...")
  ("L'orangerie sera ta residence...")
  Vérité
  ("Tu as pris une lampe...")
  Vrai Lieu
    ("Qu'une place soit faite a celui...")
    Lieu du Combat
    Lieu de la Salamandre
    Vrai Lieu du Cerf
    ("Le jour franchit le soir...")
      (Tr. by Galway Kinnell)
  From *Menaces du Témoin*   100   248
    A San Francisco, le Soir
  Le Visage Mortel
    ("Le jour se penche...")
    ("Il y a que la lampe brûlait...")
    Le Pont de Fer
  A Une Terre d'Aube
    Ici, Toujours Ici
      (Tr. by Jackson Mathews)

BOOKS REVIEWED
  On the Motion and
    Immobility of Douve
    (Tr. by Galway Kinnell)   113   262
  Dans le leurre du seuil   128   163

ARTICLES ABOUT
  Letters from the Midi,
    by Wallace Fowlie   100   258

BONNER, AMY
POEMS
  Pageantry   18   82
  Revelations
  Poise
  Words   30   27
  March   43   312
  Prelude to Sleep   55   186
  Man Subdues the Elements
  In Hollows of Sleep   61   606
  Freedom
  House Long Known   64   134
  Veiled Landscape
  Island Refuge   72   245
  Curve of Quiet

ARTICLES
  The Poetry Market:
    A Survey of American Periodicals   54   167
  Verse Drama and the Radio
    [L. H. Titterton, Davidson Taylor,
    Max Wylie, Norman Corwin,
    Robert Simon]   58   280

REVIEWS
  Three Lyric Poets   59   288
    Let Each Man Remember,
      by Josephine Jacobsen
    The Moving Tide,
      by Jessie B. Rittenhouse
    An American in Augustland,
      by Elliott Coleman

BONTEMPS, ARNA
BOOKS REVIEWED
  American Negro Poetry (Ed.)   103   394

BOOGHER, SUSAN M.
POEMS
  Alchemy   11   304
  The Harlot's Child
  War
  Fugitive   17   79

BOORUM, TED
POEMS
  Finnegans Wake   62   250
  Un-Natural Selection

BOOTH, EDWARD TOWNSEND
POEMS
  To a New England Girl   18   26
  To an Authentic Priest

BOOTH, EDWIN
ARTICLES ABOUT
   The Utterance of Poetry,
     by Harriet Monroe   19   266

BOOTH, LUELLA
BOOKS REVIEWED
   For the Record   109   53

BOOTH, PHILIP
POEMS
   Tenement Roof   82   258
   North   84   75
   Great Farm   85   340
   Adam
   Letter from a Distant Land   87   19
   Green Song   88   238
   Chart 1203
   Shag
   The Seiners
   Convoy   92   83
   These Men   94   92
   The Tower   96   7
   Spit   99   32
   August 1942   101   338
   The Heavy Poet   104   235
   Seeing Auden Off
   The Dancer
   Rain
   Refusing the Sea   107   310
   The Misery of Mechanics   111   19
   Crows   113   242
   Bolt
   Chekhov
   A Number of Ways of Looking At It   121   193
   Moment   127   267
   Creatures   144   264
   Saying It   147   13
   Presence   151   18
   Rule One   153   220
   Glove   154   13
   Times
   Heading Out
   March Again   161   313
   Outlook
   November Sun   163   72
   Ages   167   152
   Coming To   168   12

ARTICLES
   Comment   151   207

REVIEWS
   The Year One,
     by Kathleen Raine   83   106
   The Middle Passage,
     by Louis Coxe   97   46

BOOKS REVIEWED
   Letter From a Distant Land   94   333
   The Islanders   100   395
   Weathers and Edges   109   400
   Available Light   130   102
   Before Sleep   140   102
   Relations: Selected Poems, 1950-1985   149   94
   Selves   156   345
   Pairs: New Poems   166   289

BOOTHE, JAMES
POEMS
   Having Talked with Men   52   254
   Within the Houses, Love

BORAN, PAT
POEMS
   [The dead man's clothes]   167   74

BORDEN, ELLEN
[See STEVENSON, ELLEN]

BORDRY, PAUL
ARTICLES
   "Existentialisme, Drôle de Mot"
     [Jean-Paul Sartre]   69   152

BORDWELL, CONSTANCE
POEMS
   Paul Bunyan Speaks to the Boy   41   303

BORGES, JORGE LUIS
POEMS
   Adam Cast Forth   116   299
   One Morning in 1649
   A Rose and Milton
     (Tr. by Richard Eberhart)
   A Wolf   161   9
   May 20, 1928
   In Praise of Darkness
     (Tr. by Robert Mezey)
   Limits   162   157
   A Compass
   Sleep
   Written in a Copy of the
     Geste of Beowulf
     (Tr. by R. G. Barnes
     and Robert Mezey)
   On His Blindness   164   71
   From Fragments of an
     Apocryphal Evangelist
     (Tr. by Robert Mezey)

BORGESE, G(IUSEPPE) A(NTONIO)
ARTICLES
   Outline of a Poetics, I
     (Tr. by Frances Keene
     and Lucille Bunzl)   55   140

Outline of a Poetics, II
   (Tr. by Frances Keene
   and Lucille Bunzl)   55   204
Outline of a Poetics, III
   (Tr. by Frances Keene
   and Lucille Bunzl)   55   267

ARTICLES ABOUT
   G. A. Borgese, Poet-Seer,
   by Charles G. Bell   82   40

BORGES-ROSEN, CAROLE
POEMS
   Dreamseeker's Journey   165   338

BORJA, FRANCISCO
POEMS
   The Dead Man
   (Tr. by Lloyd Mallan)   62   70

BORRAZZO, BENEDICT
POEMS
   The Subway   73   83
   Directive
   Challenge from the Slums

BORROFF, MARIE
POEMS
   The Seeking   63   27
   Hospital   65   83
   Medicinae Doctor
   Death: Body and Mind
   Patient in Waiting
   Exhortation
   Reflections in Transit   66   308
   The Donors
   The Actor
   Understanding Poetry   148   194

BORUCH, MARIANNE
POEMS
   Rare Old Violins   156   276
   Driving After Supper   158   128
   Ash Wednesday   161   254

BOSANQUET, THEODORA
ARTICLES ABOUT
   Paul Valéry, by M. D. Zabel   45   90

BOSE, BUDDHADEVA
POEMS
   To an Unknown Dead   75   273
   The Crow
   Man   82   249
   Some Word To Say   84   8
   Versatility   93   209
   Holderlin   102   380
   For My Forty-Eighth Winter   116   285
   Two Birds

BOSQUET, ALAIN
POEMS
   Douce Terreur [3, 4, 5, 8]
   (Tr. by Wallace Fowlie)   80   355
   An Old Gentleman   166   159
   Another Era
   Everything Is Ready
   The Chain
   (Tr. by William Jay Smith)

BOOKS REVIEWED
   Anthologie de la Poésie
   Américaine (Ed.)   89   257
   Selected Poems
   (Tr. by Samuel Beckett,
   Charles Guenther, Edouard
   Roditi, and Ruth Whitman)   104   115
   Certaines Choses Naturelles,
   by James Laughlin (Tr.)   105   125

ARTICLES ABOUT
   Paris Letter,
   by Wallace Fowlie   96   371

BOSTELMANN, CARL JOHN
POEMS
   Skyscraper Builders   37   140
   Song at the Rise of the Full Moon
   The Deserts of Sleep
   With the South Wind   38   16
   Rediscovery
   Dawn Vigil   42   261
   Closed Season   45   322
       The Winter Hill
       Premonitory April

BOSTWICK, LAWRENCE
POEMS
   East Wind, West Wind   48   207
       Revery over Painted Porcelain
       Memorandum
       Portrait of a Poseur
       For a Friend
       Old Story

BOTKIN, BENJAMIN ALBERT
POEMS
   Meteor   37   85

BOTKIN, NANCY
POEMS
   Grief   170   89

BOTTOMLEY, GORDON
POEMS
   The Ploughman   9   181

BOOKS REVIEWED
   Scenes and Plays   36   112
   Collected Poems, by Isaac Rosenberg
      (Ed. with Denys Harding)   80   101
   Poems and Plays
      (Ed. by Claude Colleer Abbott)   86   363

ARTICLES ABOUT
   Rev. of *Georgian Poetry: 1913-1915*   8   255
   Rev. of *An Annual of New Poetry, 1917*   11   333

BOTTOMS, DAVID
POEMS
   Crawling Out at Parties   132   81
   The Catfish   133   85
   Watching Gators at Ray Boone's
      Reptile Farm
   Calling Across Water
      at Lion Country Safari
   In a U-Haul North of Damascus   137   251
   Rest at the Mercy House
   Hurricane
   A Home Buyer Watches the Moon
   In the Wilderness Motel   138   263
   In the Black Camaro   140   125
   Rendezvous: Belle Glade
   Wakulla: Chasing the Gator's Eye
   The Drowned
   The Boy Shepherds' Simile   141   169
   A Tent Beside a River   145   19
   The Desk
   Naval Photograph: 25 October 1942:
      What the Hand May Be Saying
   The Anniversary
   Ice   145   132
   Appearances   146   91
   Homage to Lester Flatt
   The Guitar   148   131
   On the Willow Branch
   The Resurrection
   In Heritage Farms, Settled   150   135
   Rats at Allatoona
   Armored Hearts   151   19
   A Night, Near Berkeley Springs   151   271
   In the Kitchen, Late   152   150
   Barriers
   Chinese Dragons   156   134
   Cemetery Wings   156   208
   Steve Belew Plays the National Steel   160   134
   In the Massachusetts Wilderness   161   138
   A Daughter's Fever   163   22
   Home Maintenance   165   68
   Homebuyer
   Warbler at Howell's Drive-In
   Horseshoes   167   277
   The Widower   168   270
   Their Father's Tattoo   170   265
   Bronchitis

BOOKS REVIEWED
   Shooting Rats at the Bibb County Dump   140   35
   In a U-Haul North of Damascus   143   295
   Under the Vulture-Tree   152   98
   Armored Hearts: Selected & New Poems   169   286

BOTTRALL, RONALD
POEMS
   Lost Heaven   49   186
   Mating Answer
   Exhortation to the Cloistered   53   78
   Darkened Windows
   Cassandra   72   136
   Cubes
   Wants   79   78
   Renewable Sacrament
   In Philistia
   Aspects of Darkness   135   29

BOOKS REVIEWED
   Festivals of Fire   46   285
   The Turning Path   55   101
   Farewell and Welcome   70   338
   Palisades of Fear   76   109
   Collected Poems   100   104

ARTICLES ABOUT
   English Letter, by F. R. Leavis   43   215

BOULTENHOUSE, CHARLES
POEMS
   Elegy ("In the white room...")   91   241

BOULTON, INEZ
[See also STARK, INEZ
CUNNINGHAM]
POEMS
   Waken Slowly!   70   196
   To Mr. Muscles

REVIEWS
   Take Them Stranger,
      by Babette Deutsch   65   268
   Correspondence of a Friendship,
      by Florence Ayscough and Amy Lowell
      (Ed. by Harley Farnsworth MacNair)   69   54
   Lough Derg, by Denis Devlin   69   169
   Declensions of the Air,
      by Louis Kent   79   119

BOURGEOIS, MAURICE
BOOKS REVIEWED
   John Millington Synge
      and the Irish Theatre   4   239

BOURJAILY, VANCE
POEMS
   News Item: Three Versions   69   256

BOURKE, SHARON
POEMS
  Two Nocturnes   96   365
  Café   101   245
  A Household Poem

BOURNE, RANDOLPH
ARTICLES
  Correspondence:
    The Retort Courteous
    (With Van Wyck Brooks)   12   341

ARTICLES ABOUT
  Mr. Bourne on Traps,
    by Harriet Monroe   12   90
  Correspondence
    from Alice Corbin Henderson   12   228
  "Aesthetic and Social Criticism,"
    by Harriet Monroe   13   37

BOURNURE, GABRIEL
ARTICLES ABOUT
  Rev. of Le Cahiers de la Pléiade
    (Ed. by Jean Paulhan)
    [St.-John Perse]   79   43

BOUTELLE, GRACE HODSDON
POEMS
  It Vanished   18   245

BOWE, AUGUSTINE
POEMS
  The Queen   57   250
  Dies Irae
  Conquest of the Mind
  Change   59   126
  Comet near Vega
  Great Armies
  It Minds Not
  The Frailty of Virtue
  The Felon
  The Strife
  There Is No Explaining
  It Took So Long
  The Crucifix
  Between
  What Distance
  The Weight of All this Air
  There Must Be Honesty in Kindness
  Rousseau in the Custom House   60   75
  Summer   63   28
  The Fanciful Engravure of the Sky
  The Reef
  The Worm Has Hope
  The Judge
  Doubt
  Numbers
  The Modern Saint   66   22

  So Fast, So Fast
  Country Burial
  I Thought of These Things
  Rilke
  Flux and Flow
  My Mother

REVIEWS
  Perennial,
    by Oliver St. John Gogarty   65   276

BOWE, JULIA (LE COUR)
TRANSLATIONS
  Article by Jacques Allamand   71   141
  Article by Juan Ramón Jiménez 82   216

ARTICLES
  Review of the Reviews
    [Spanish-American literary reviews] 62   116

REVIEWS
  12 Spanish American Poets
    (Ed. by H. R. Hays)   63   230
  Poèmes d'ici et de là-bas,
    by André Spire   65   342

ARTICLES ABOUT
  Obituary   149   242

BOWEN, DONNA
POEMS
  Return of the Lover   88   23

BOWERING, GEORGE
POEMS
  The White Station Wagon Strophes 110   88
  On Quadra Island   114   78
  Passport Doves

BOOKS REVIEWED
  Points on the Grid   105   270
  The Silver Wire   111   323
  The Man in Yellow Boots
  Baseball   113   188
  Rocky Mountain Foot   115   426
  The Contemporary Canadian
    Poem Anthology (Ed.)   144   297

BOWERING, MARILYN
BOOKS REVIEWED
  Giving Back Diamonds   144   297

BOWERS, CATHY SMITH
POEMS
  A Southern Rhetoric   160   80

BOWERS, EDGAR

POEMS

The Astronomers of Mont Blanc	99	151
An Afternoon at the Beach		
The Dream		
From *Autumn Shade*	105	290
The Field Marshal		
John	161	205

REVIEWS

From the Seventeenth Century	104	120
The Meditative Poem		
(Ed. by Louis L. Martz)		
The Songs and Sonets of John Donne		
(Ed. by Theodore Redpath)		
Wayside Poems of the Seventeenth Century		
(Ed. by Edmund Blunden		
and Bernard Mellor)		

BOOKS REVIEWED

The Form of Loss	89	244
The Astronomers	107	326
Living Together	125	229
For Louis Pasteur	158	214

BOWERS, FREDSON

BOOKS REVIEWED

Whitman's Manuscripts:		
Leaves of Grass, 1860 (Ed.)	87	183

BOWERS, KELLEY

POEMS

Television Poem	168	203

BOWERS, MILDRED

POEMS

Idyl	30	76
Strange		
Maybe		
Answer		
Two Men	33	257
James Marsh		
Sam Littleton		

BOWERS, NEAL

POEMS

Losses	147	7
Terminal	147	100
Living the Parable		
The Dance	148	68
For the Heart		
Bring Pies		
Night Builder	150	223
Apple Mechanics	150	270
Aliens		
Stump Speech	152	219
Extremities	154	208
Pockets		
The Rescue		

Apology for Solitude		
Thaw	156	6
RSVP	156	336
Tenth-Year Elegy		
Laws of Nature	157	78
Hymns	158	10
Dead Man Interview		
Art Thief	159	221
The Half Life	159	262
Repairs		
Communications	160	81
Forced Flowers	160	195
Family Matters		
Divining Love		
Divestments	162	76
Last		
The Center	162	338
Special Effects		
Applied Science		
Seized by the Days	165	149
The Music Never Gets Any Older		
Party Postmortem		
Making It Up		
Here	166	34
For the Ego		
Privileges		
Say It With Flowers	167	212
Results of the Questionnaire	167	311
Currency		
Harvest	168	227
Elegy for Two Voices	169	284
The Pose	169	323

BOOKS REVIEWED

Night Vision	163	97

BOWLES, PAUL FREDERIC

POEMS

Extract	39	131

BOWMAN, ARCHIBALD ALLEN

BOOKS REVIEWED

Sonnets from a Prison Camp	18	44

BOWMAN, LOUISE MOREY

POEMS

And Forbid Them Not	13	306
Cold Tragedy	24	308
Florence		
Venice		
Rome		
Waxworks	30	267
John Knox and Mary Queen		
John Milton and Cromwell		
Asides	39	310
The Asylum Farm		
Life History		
Study in Fragility	58	22
Hour		

Books Reviewed
  Moonlight and Common Day   21   43
  Dream Tapestries   27   99

BOWMAN, P. C.
Poems
  A Mobile by Alexander Rutsch   132   17
  Syntheses of Love

BOWRA, C. M.
Books Reviewed
  The Creative Experiment   75   217
  Selected Writings,
    by Boris Pasternak
    (Tr. with Babette Deutsch,
    Beatrice Scott, and Robert Payne)   76   238
  The Creative Experiment   93   117

BOYARS, ARTHUR
Books Reviewed
  The Face Behind the Face,
    by Yevgeny Yevtushenko
    (Tr. with Simon Franklin)   136   40

BOYD, JAMES
Books Reviewed
  Eighteen Poems   65   278

BOYD, MARION
Books Reviewed
  Silver Wands   24   280

BOYDEN, POLLY
[See CHASE, POLLY]

BOYE, KARIN
Articles About
  Rev. of *Half Sun Half Sleep,*
    by May Swenson   111   184

BOYLE, KAY
Poems
  Monody to the Sound of Zithers   21   125
  Harbor Song   25   252
  Depart   29   250
  To a Seaman Dead on Land
  Portrait
  A Poem of Gratitude   93   376
  Two Twilights
    for William Carlos Williams   95   356
  A Dialogue of Birds for Howard Nemerov
  Two Poems for a Poet   97   300
  Seascape for an Engraver   99   214
  Rendezvous

Articles
  Correspondence:
    Reactionary Composers   19   104

Books Reviewed
  A Statement   43   225
  A Glad Day   54   347
  American Citizen   65   333
  Collected Poems   102   250
  Testament for My Students   119   99

BOYLE, PETER
Poems
  The Colours of Ageing   169   7
  In a Provincial Capital
  Madrid, 1980

BOYNTON, LUELLA
Poems
  Sonnet ("Always with laughter...")   38   73
  Portrait   46   83

BRADBURY, JOHN
Reviews
  Reshuffling the Classics   72   336
    Readings in English Literature
      (Ed. by Gerald Bullett)
    The Shorter Poems
      of Walter Savage Landor
      (Ed. by J. B. Sidgwick)
    A Little Treasury of Great Poetry
      (Ed. by Oscar Williams)

BRADFORD, DOROTHY
Articles About
  Rev. of *The Misunderstanding of Desire,*
    by Sophie Cabot Black   165   219

BRADFORD, GAMALIEL
Articles
  Correspondence:
    A Word for Mr. Guest   20   114

BRADFORD, WILLIAM
Articles About
  Rev. by David Baker   164   223

BRADLEY, A. C.
Articles About
  Rev. of *The Verbal Icon,*
    by W. K. Wimsatt, Jr.   87   312

BRADLEY, ARDYTH
Poems
  Key   156   196

BRADLEY, F. H.
Articles About
  Rev. of *Knowledge and Experience*
    in the Philosophy of F. H. Bradley,
    by T. S. Eliot   106   239

BRADLEY, GEORGE
POEMS
An Arrangement of Sunlight
    at Hagia Sophia   134   86
Escape
Committed to Memory
Blue That Believes in Nothing   164   92

BOOKS REVIEWED
Terms To Be Met   149   31
The Fire Fetched Down   170   101

BRADLEY, KATHERINE
[See FIELD, MICHAEL,
pseud. with COOPER, EDITH]

BRADLEY, SAM
POEMS
African in This Different Land   105   247
An Impossible Situation
The Serpent Mound   115   14
Uncle Satyr
Be As Dear to Me As I Am to Myself   120   146
Cain on the Eve
An Elementary Keeping in Touch   125   132

BOOKS REVIEWED
Men—In Good Measure   109   340

BRADLEY, SCULLY
BOOKS REVIEWED
Leaves of Grass,
    by Walt Whitman
    (Ed. with Harold W. Blodgett)   107   397

BRADLEY, WILLIAM ASPENWALL
BOOKS REVIEWED
Old Christmas and Other Kentucky
    Tales in Verse   12   46

BRADSTREET, ANNE
BOOKS REVIEWED
The Works of...
    (Ed. by Jeannine Hensley)   112   127

ARTICLES ABOUT
Rev. of Homage to Mistress Bradstreet,
    by John Berryman   90   244

BRADY, MATHEW
ARTICLES ABOUT
[Note]   107   136

BRAGIN, MOE
POEMS
From an Eastern Farm   37   200
Night
The Farmer's Daughter

BRAINARD, JOE
BOOKS REVIEWED
I Remember   129   164

**BRAITHWAITE,
W(ILLIAM) S(TANLEY)**
BOOKS REVIEWED
Anthology of Magazine Verse for 1915 (Ed.)   7   318
Anthology of Magazine Verse (Ed.)   14   281
Anthology of Magazine Verse [Series] (Ed.)   27   343

ARTICLES ABOUT
Our Contemporaries,
    by Alice Corbin Henderson   3   187
Our Contemporaries,
    by Alice Corbin Henderson   5   193
Our Contemporaries   7   156
Our Contemporaries, by Harriet Monroe   8   211
Sir Oracle, by Harriet Monroe   9   211
Correspondence from Willard Wattles   10   52

BRAND, MILLEN
POEMS
Appeal in Grey   42   20
A Challenge
To Emily Dickinson
To One Newborn   43   193
Trapeze in Heaven
On the Roof
Grass
Rain in January
Children in San Diego   56   308
Morning   59   140
Joe Heimbucher   The Start   70   136
Dinner

BOOKS REVIEWED
Dry Summer in Provence   110   258

ARTICLES ABOUT
Correspondence from Edward Field
    [Richard Tillinghast]   110   433

BRAND-CAMMAERTS, TITA
BOOKS REVIEWED
Chants Patriotiques et Autres Poèmes
    and Les Trois Rois et Autres Poèmes,
    by Emile Cammaerts (Tr.)   10   331
Messines and Other Poems,
    by Emile Cammaerts (Tr.)   17   48

BRASH, EDWARD
POEMS
Airmail   114   11
Les Demoiselles of Piney Woods   134   285
The China Closet Neuron Loss   137   199
Some Feast
Forgotten Men 1   141   150

Forgotten Men 2
Forgotten Men 3: Geoffrey Graysbook
Kate Brash as Divorced Midget
The Argument
More Argument
Depression
Father of Twins
Vive E. E.
Wallace Stevens in Hartford
Rachel at Kitty Hawk

BRASSERT, JANET
TRANSLATIONS
Poem by Leopoldo Lugones   62   84

BRATHWAITE, EDWARD
BOOKS REVIEWED
Masks   114   56
Islands   118   102
Penguin Modern Poets 15
   (With Alan Bold and Edwin Morgan)
Other Exiles   130   230

BRAUN, HENRY
POEMS
The Shed   115   31
Scholars on Vacation   118   23
Old Groups
On Reading Late

BOOKS REVIEWED
The Virgil Woods   113   338

BRAUN, RICHARD EMIL
POEMS
Arrius the Affected   85   144

BOOKS REVIEWED
Companions to Your Doom   99   384
Children Passing   102   42

BRAUTIGAN, RICHARD
POEMS
Wood   115   30

BOOKS REVIEWED
The Galilee Hitch-Hiker   112   56
All Watched Over
   by Machines of Loving Grace   112   274
The Pill Versus
   the Springfield Mine Disaster   115   440
In Watermelon Sugar

BRAYMER, NAN
BOOKS REVIEWED
Modern Poetry from Spain
   and Latin America
   (Tr. with Lillian Lowenfels)   107   338

Where Is Vietnam?
   American Poets Respond
   (Ed. with Walter Lowenfels)   111   410

BREARLEY, HILDA
POEMS
Supper Party   39   24
Adagio

BREAZEALE, DANIEL
POEMS
The Radar Watcher   139   278

BRECHT, BERTOLT
POEMS
All of Us or None   67   140
Song of the Storm Trooper
The Burning of the Books
   (Tr. by H. R. Hays)
The Swamp
   (Tr. by Naomi Replansky)   71   128

BOOKS REVIEWED
Selected Poems
   (Tr. by H. R. Hays)   97   51
Manual of Piety (Die Hauspostille)
   (Tr. by Eric Bentley)   111   336
Poems 1913-56
   (Ed. by John Willett
   and Ralph L. Manheim)   137   220

ARTICLES ABOUT
The Poetry of Bertolt Brecht,
   by H. R. Hays   67   148
Rev. by David Lehman   123   173

BRÉE, GERMAINE
REVIEWS
Including the French   73   364
   Sonnets by Louise Labé
      (Tr. by Frederick Prokosch)
   Poems by Tristan Corbière
      (Tr. by Walter McElroy)

BREEN, ROBERT
ARTICLES ABOUT
Poetry Over WFMT   83   112
Poetry Over WFMT   85   118

BREGY, KATHERINE
POEMS
A Rouge Box   48   256

BREHM, JOHN
POEMS
Supplication at the River   142   70
Calling My Grandmother from New York
Insomnia: For My Grandfather   145   31

Autumn
Passage   162   347
Postcard from the Heartbreak Hotel   167   284
When My Car Broke Down   170   260
Incommunicado

BREIT, HARVEY
POEMS
The Hungered Circle   57   22

REVIEWS
Return Again, Traveler,
  by Norman Rosten   58   156
Poems on Several Occasions,
  by Josephine Miles   59   49
Selected Poems, by George Barker   59   159
The Dark Kingdom,
  by Kenneth Patchen   60   160
Paradox: The Ordinary Poet   60   341
  If There Is Time,
    by Hildegarde Flanner
  The Black Bull,
    by C. F. MacIntyre
  Have Come, Am Here,
    by José García Villa   61   632
  Notes Toward a Supreme Fiction,
    by Wallace Stevens   62   48
A Contrast   70   49
  The Quiet Center, by Edith Henrich
  The Long Reprieve,
    by Hubert Creekmore
  Figures for an Apocalypse,
    by Thomas Merton   73   46

BRERETON, GEOFFREY
ARTICLES ABOUT
French Chronicle: Recent Publications,
  by Wallace Fowlie   91   36

BRESLIN, PAUL
POEMS
Meditations on the Field Museum   134   63
Orpheus   143   285
Résumé   146   253
You Are Here   166   130
The Return   169   210

ARTICLES
Waking Up Over the Aeneid
  [Robert Fitzgerald, Dante,
  Hermann Broch, Wilfred Owen,
  Michael Casey, Christopher Lasch,
  Sigmund Freud, Robert Lowell, Virgil]   143   347

REVIEWS
Some Early Returns   134   107
  The Sun Fetcher,
    by Michael Dennis Browne

Queen of Darkness,
  by Celia Gilbert
Images of Kin: New and Selected Poems,
  by Michael S. Harper
Village Journal, by Greg Kuzma
The Difference Between Day and Night,
  by Bin Ramke
Black Mountain:
  A Critique of the Curriculum   136   219
  A Guide to the Maximus Poems
    of Charles Olson,
    by George F. Butterick
  Charles Olson: Call Him Ishmael,
    by Paul Christensen
  Selected Poems, by Edward Dorn
  Robert Creeley's Poetry:
    A Critical Introduction,
    by Cynthia Dubin Edelberg
  Olson's Push: Origin, Black Mountain
    and Recent American Poetry,
    by Sherman Paul
  Muthologos: The Collected Lectures
    & Interviews, Vol. I,
    by Charles Olson
    (Ed. by George F. Butterick)
  Life in the Forest,
    by Denise Levertov
  Charles Olson: The Scholar's Art,
    Robert von Hallberg
Warpless and Woofless Subtleties   137   42
  As We Know and Houseboat Days,
    by John Ashbery
  John Ashbery:
    An Introduction to the Poetry,
    by David Shapiro
Short Reviews   145   161
  The Sacrifice, by Frank Bidart
  The Best Hour of the Night,
    by Louis Simpson
  Characters from Proust,
    by Wallace Fowlie
  Continuing Conclusions:
    New Poems and Translations,
    by Richmond Lattimore
  Poems from Oby,
    by George MacBeth
  One-Legged on Ice,
    by Dannie Abse
  Opening the Hand,
    by W. S. Merwin
  The Water Inside the Water,
    by Susan Mitchell
  Summer Celestial,
    by Stanley Plumly
  Powers of Thirteen,
    by John Hollander
  Midsummer,
    by Derek Walcott
Four Poets: Collected and Selected   150   286

Collected Poems,
  by Geoffrey Hill
Collected Poems,
  by Charles Tomlinson
The Collected Poems of William Carlos
  Williams: Volume I, 1909-1939
  (Ed. by A. Walton Litz
  and Christopher MacGowan)
  [Donald Davie]
The Selected Poetry of Yehuda Amichai
  (Ed. and tr. by Chana Bloch
  and Stephen Mitchell)
The Simple, Separate Person and
  the Word En-Masse   153   30
Curriculum Vitae,
  by Lawrence Joseph
The Veil, by Denis Johnson
Dangerous Amusement, by Jon Davis
Objects of Affection, by Sharon Bryan
After the Lost War: A Narrative,
  by Andrew Hudgins
The Muse of Distance,
  by Alan Williamson
  [Wendell Berry, Walt Whitman,
  Sidney Lanier]
Poetry, Criticism, and the World   156   297
White Paper: On Contemporary
  American Poetry,
  by J. D. McClatchy
Poetry and the World,
  by Robert Pinsky
  [Robert Lowell, Amy Clampitt,
  Anthony Hecht, Jean Toomer,
  Philip Freneau, William Carlos
  Williams]
American Poetry:
  The Nineteenth Century
  (Ed. by John Hollander)
  [Walt Whitman, Emily
  Dickinson, Philip Freneau,
  Joseph Rodman Drake]   165   340
Heaney's Redress   168   337
The Spirit Level;
  The Redress of Poetry; and
  Crediting Poetry: The Nobel Lecture,
  by Seamus Heaney
  [Hugh MacDiarmid]
Four and a Half Books   170   226
Walking the Black Cat: Poems,
  by Charles Simic
Intensive Care:
  Selected and New Poems,
  by Miroslav Holub
Otherwise: New and Selected Poems,
  by Jane Kenyon
The Spirit Level, by David Barber
The Figured Wheel:
  New and Collected Poems 1966-1996,
  by Robert Pinsky

BOOKS REVIEWED
The Psycho-Political Muse:
  American Poetry Since the Fifties
  [Allen Ginsberg, Robert Lowell,
  Sylvia Plath, John Ashbery]   152   229

BRETON, ANDRÉ
BOOKS REVIEWED
Young Cherry Trees Secured Against Hares
  (Tr. by Edouard Roditi)   117   261

ARTICLES ABOUT
Rimbaud in 1949, by Wallace Fowlie   75   166
Letter From Haiti, by Wallace Fowlie   94   398
Surrealism in 1960: A Backward Glance,
  by Wallace Fowlie   95   365

BREWSTER, ELIZABETH
POEMS
In the Library   70   130
Fool's Song   71   250

BOOKS REVIEWED
The Way Home   144   297
Digging In

BREWTON, CATHERINE
POEMS
A Game of Relativity   153   22

BRIDGE, URSULA
BOOKS REVIEWED
W. B. Yeats and T. Sturge Moore,
  Their Correspondence (Ed.)   83   357

BRIDGES, LAWRENCE
POEMS
When the Wary Traveler Realized that Fate
  Was Part of Love's Journey   126   213
No Wonder

BRIDGES, ROBERT
BOOKS REVIEWED
October and Other Poems   17   344
Poems of Gerard Manley Hopkins (Ed.)   18   330
The Testament of Beauty   36   96
The Shorter Poems of...   39   280

ARTICLES ABOUT
The New Laureate, by Harriet Monroe   2   213
Robert Bridges' New Book,
  by Ezra Pound   7   40
Bridges as a Lyrist, by Harriet Monroe   36   146
Obituary   36   170
Hopkins in His Letters, by M. D. Zabel   46   210
Rev. of *Robert Bridges and Gerard Hopkins,*
  1863-1889: A Literary Friendship,
  by Jean-Georges Ritz   100   50

BRIDGWATER, PATRICK
BOOKS REVIEWED
    Twentieth-Century German Verse (Ed.)   104 245

BRIDSON, D. G.
POEMS
    Winter Purpose   45 195
    Winter Doubt
    Locomotive
    The Street Piano

REVIEWS
    One-Way Song, by Wyndham Lewis   45 165
    Variations on a Time Theme,
        by Edwin Muir   45 337
    Two Poets in Search of a Form   46 285
        Stony Limits and Other Poems
           and *At the Sign of the Thistle:*
           A Collection of Essays,
           by Hugh MacDiarmid
        Festivals of Fire,
           by Ronald Bottrall
        A Mad Lady's Garland,
           by Ruth Pitter   47 103
        The Noise of History,
           by John Lehmann   47 231

BRIDSON, G. D.
ARTICLES
    Broadcast Poetry in Britain   79 301

BRIERRE, JEAN
ARTICLES ABOUT
    Letter From Haiti
        by Wallace Fowlie   94 398

BRIGHAM, BESMILR
BOOKS REVIEWED
    Heaved from the Earth   120 235

BRIGHAM, JAMES
BOOKS REVIEWED
    Collected Poems 1931-1974,
        by Lawrence Durrell (Ed.)   140 170

BRIGHT, VERNE
POEMS
    Pioneer   34 23
    Death's Hour
    April Moments
    Elemental   37 322
    Honeycomb
    Gray Stone
    Good Soil   47 187
    Drought   49 72
        Goose-Grass Harvest
        Futile Furrow

BRILLIANT, ALAN
POEMS
    Searching for Signs   114 362

REVIEWS
    Five Pamphlets   116 125
        The Dream Telephone,
           by Dick Lourie
        Nothing You've Done,
           by Kirk Ruggles
        On Pain of Discovery,
           by Ottone M. Riccio
        The Webbing,
           by Drummond Hadley
        Promises, by Richard Flantz

BRINGHURST, ROBERT
POEMS
    Hachadura   126 311

BOOKS REVIEWED
    Selected Poems 1972-1982,
        The Beauty of the Weapons   144 297

BRINK, CAROL RYRIE
POEMS
    The Fairy Wife   28 312

BRINK, ROSCOE W.
POEMS
    Helen Is Ill   1 117

BOOKS REVIEWED
    Down the River   23 221

BRINKLEY, MAXINE
POEMS
    Signature   53 307
    Take Us the Foxes   62 138
    To My Ancestors

BRINNIN, JOHN MALCOLM
POEMS
    Prague   54 302
    Cadillac Square
    Address to the Refugees   56 293
    From *The Lincoln Lyrics*   57 309
    At the Band Concert   59 64
    Winter Term   60 65
    Spring Ritual   62 1
        Mardi Gras
        Letter to Statues
        The Fair of Summer
        Easter in the Field
        A Devotion for John Milton
        For My Pupils in the War Years
        Charades of Love

The Cafe Underground
Second Sight   64   59
The Blue Iris, the Backward Pupil
The Fortunate Isles
The Sorrows of Cold Stone   67   233
The Wind Is Ill
Faces, Faces
Fetes, Fates   69   25
Around the Egg
Angel Eye of Memory
The Worm in the Whirling Cross   71   61
Speech of the Wedding Guest   75   275
From *The Sorrows of Cold Stone*
In the Word Was the Beginning
A Love Song for Ash Wednesday
Flight 539   101   14

ARTICLES
  Muriel Rukeyser:
    The Social Poet and the
    Problem of Communication   61   554

REVIEWS
  America Was Promises,
    by Archibald MacLeish   56   43
  Song and Idea, by Richard Eberhart   61   508
  News of the Phoenix,
    by A. J. M. Smith   65   157

BOOKS REVIEWED
  The Lincoln Lyrics   61   622
  The Garden Is Political
  No Arch, No Triumph   66   32
  Modern Poetry: American and British
    (Ed. with Kimon Friar)   79   289
  The Sorrows of Cold Stone.
    Poems 1940-1950   80   159
  The Third Rose:
    Gertrude Stein and Her World   98   59
  The Selected Poems of...   103   387
  The Modern Poets:
    An American-British Anthology
    (Ed. with Bill Read)   104   245
  The Modern Poets:
    An American-British Anthology
    (Ed. with Bill Read)   119   169
  Skin Diving in the Virgins
    and Other Poems   119   342

ARTICLES ABOUT
  Rev. of *New Poems: 1943*
    (Ed. by Oscar Williams)   64   86
  The World in a Cross Word,
    by John Theobald   71   82

BRITTAIN, ROBERT
POEMS
  Epitaph ("Weep no penitential...")   44   199

TRANSLATIONS
  Poems by Nicolas Guillén   73   11

BRITTEN, ROLLO
POEMS
  Bird of Passion   2   98

BROADUS, EDMUND KEMPER
POEMS
  The Oracle   1   179
  A Gargoyle on Notre Dame
  An Aeroplane at Stonehenge   3   15

BOOKS REVIEWED
  The Laureateship: A Study
    of the Office of Poet Laureate
    in England, with Some Account
    of the Poets   21   164

BROADUS, KEMPER HAMMOND
POEMS
  Rough Ways   20   78
  Burnt Out
  Blizzard
  Philosophers   29   28

BROCH, HERMANN
ARTICLES ABOUT
  Waking Up Over the *Aeneid*,
    by Paul Breslin   143   347

BROCK, EDWIN
POEMS
  Nothing Is Too Much Trouble   122   265
  To His Love in Middle-Age   133   280
  Holy Cow

BOOKS REVIEWED
  The Portraits & the Poses   125   229
  The Blocked Heart   131   292

BRODERSON, LUCILLE
POEMS
  At Eighty-Five   157   11
  September Sunday   159   142
  This Is Your Old Age, Lucy
  Requiem

BRODEY, JIM
BOOKS REVIEWED
  Identikit   112   56

BRODSKY, GEORGE
POEMS
  Worship at Dawn   40   134
  Gauguin's Tahitian Olympia

BRODSKY, JOSEPH
POEMS
Part of Speech
   (Tr. by Daniel Weissbort)   131   311

BOOKS REVIEWED
Selected Poems
   (Tr. by George L. Kline)   127   42
To Urania
   (Tr. by Joseph Brodsky et al.)   153   106
So Forth   170   162

BRODY, ALTER
POEMS
Grandmother   21   134

ARTICLES
Correspondence:
   The Cowboy Theatre League   11   55

BOOKS REVIEWED
A Family Album   14   277

BROMIGE, DAVID
POEMS
Weight Less than the Shadow   110   30
Dictation   111   377
The New Age
We're All Young Once
Just Think
Hopeful

BOOKS REVIEWED
The Gathering   100   191
The Ends of the Earth   117   392
Tight Corners & What's Around Them   129   102

BROMLEY, PRISCILLA
POEMS
The Town   53   190
Burial

BROMWICH, DAVID
POEMS
Wandsworth Common   123   94
An Old People's Home in Southern California   125   204
Lines for Bill Evans
Conduct of Life   127   187
Separate Dwelling
From the Righteous Man
   Even the Wild Beasts Run Away   128   95
The Time and the Place   129   156
Mad Song   131   216
Oedipus, Pentheus   136   202

REVIEWS
Rules and Recipes   125   229
   Living Together, by Edgar Bowers

Town & Country Matters,
   by John Hollander
Notes from the Land of the Dead
   and Other Poems,
   by Thomas Kinsella
Selected and New Poems,
   by Daniel Berrigan
To Be of Use, by Marge Piercy
Flying Inland,
   by Kathleen Spivack
The Portraits & the Poses,
   by Edwin Brock
The Island Self, by Howard Blake
   (Ed. by Robert Kent)   125   352
Engulfing Darkness, Penetrating Light   127   234
   The Shires, by Donald Davie
Hazard, the Painter,
   by William Meredith
The Well-Wishers,
   by Edward Lucie-Smith
The Median Flow,
   by Theodore Enslin
The Woman Poems,
   by Joel Oppenheimer
Welcoming Disaster,
   by Jay Macpherson
Waving and Drowning   129   170
   45 Mercy Street, by Anne Sexton
   (Ed. by Linda Gray Sexton)
   Absence of Unicorns, Presence of Lions,
   by Michael Mott
Olson's Penny Arcade,
   by Elder Olson
Collected Poems, by Stevie Smith
Souvenirs and Prophecies:
   The Young Wallace Stevens,
   by Holly Stevens   132   166
I Showed Her My Darkness,
   She Gave Me a Stone   133   169
   China Trace, by Charles Wright
The Double Witness, by Ben Belitt
The Year of Our Birth,
   by Sandra McPherson
Eye Level, by Jane Shore
[Hart Crane]
Marianne Moore's Poems   139   340
   Marianne Moore: The Poet's Advance,
   by Laurence Stapleton
The Complete Poems of Marianne Moore
[Francis Bacon, T. S. Eliot]

BRONK, WILLIAM
POEMS
Midsummer   86   85

BOOKS REVIEWED
Light and Dark   90   386
The World, the Worldless   106   306
Life Supports: New and Collected Poems   141   105

BRONOWSKI, J(ACOB)
BOOKS REVIEWED
The Poet's Defense   55   340

BRONTË, ANNE
BOOKS REVIEWED
Brontë Poems
(Ed. by A. C. Benson)   9   259

BRONTË, BRANWELL
BOOKS REVIEWED
Brontë Poems
(Ed. by A. C. Benson)   9   259

BRONTË, CHARLOTTE
BOOKS REVIEWED
Brontë Poems
(Ed. by A. C. Benson)   9   259

BRONTË, EMILY
BOOKS REVIEWED
Brontë Poems
(Ed. by A. C. Benson)   9   259
The Complete Works of... Vol. I, Poetry
(Ed. by W. Robertson Nicoll
and Clement Shorter)

ARTICLES ABOUT
Edna St. Vincent Millay,
by Harriet Monroe   24   260
Rev. of *Gaudete; Cave Birds;*
and *Moortown*,
by Ted Hughes   138 297

BROOK, REEVES
POEMS
Shrouds   14   188

BROOKE, LOUISA
POEMS
Brick-Dust   15   255

BROOKE, RUPERT
POEMS
Retrospect   5   27
Nineteen-Fourteen   6   18
Peace
The Dead
The Soldier

BOOKS REVIEWED
The Collected Poems of...   7   262

ARTICLES ABOUT
The Death of Rupert Brooke,
by Harriet Monroe   6   136
The Brooke Letters,
by Henry B. Fuller   8   155

What Will He Do with It?   8   328
The Purposes of Stephen Spender,
by M. D. Zabel   45   208
Rev. of *Rupert Brooke,*
by Christopher Hassall   107 192

BROOKE, TUCKER
BOOKS REVIEWED
The Shakespeare Songs (Ed.)   35   337

BROOKE-ROSE, CHRISTINE
BOOKS REVIEWED
Gold   86   242

BROOKHOUSE, CHRISTOPHER
BOOKS REVIEWED
Scattered Light   118   290

BROOKS, BENJAMIN GILBERT
POEMS
Matinée Musicale at the Lune Rousse   29   200
The Vacuum
Mother Eugene   37   142
Morning Bathing Party

ARTICLES
A Word from London
[Edith Sitwell, T. S. Eliot,
Robert Graves, Sacheverell Sitwell]   28   40
London Note
[Edith Sitwell, Edmund Blunden,
Edgell Rickword]   35   214

BROOKS, CLEANTH
REVIEWS
The Destructive Element
and *Forward from Liberalism*,
by Stephen Spender   50   280
The Winter Sea, by Allen Tate   66   324
The Oxford Book of American Verse
(Ed. by F. O. Matthiessen)   79   36

BOOKS REVIEWED
Modern Poetry and the Tradition   55   154
The Well Wrought Urn   71   318
Understanding Poetry
(With Robert Penn Warren)   84   43
Literary Criticism: A Short History
(Ed. with William K. Wimsatt, Jr.)   91   320

ARTICLES ABOUT
A Glossary of the New Criticism,
by William Elton   73   153
A Glossary of the New Criticism,
by William Elton   73   232
A Glossary of the New Criticism,
by William Elton   73   296

Rev. of *Donne's Poetry*
  and Modern Criticism,
  by Leonard Unger   77   175
Rev. of *Critics and Criticism,*
  Ancient and Modern
  (Ed. by R. S. Crane)   82   98

BROOKS, CYRUS
BOOKS REVIEWED
  Rilke and Benvenuta,
    by Magda von Hattingberg (Tr.)   76   92

BROOKS, GWENDOLYN
POEMS
  Gay Chaps at the Bar   65   76
  "Still Do I Keep My Look, My Identity..."
  The Children of the Poor   73   318
  A Light and Diplomatic Bird
  The Bean Eaters   94   373
    Old Mary
    We Real Cool
    Strong Men, Riding Horses
    The Bean Eaters
  Henry Rago   115   95
  Winnie   151   20

ARTICLES
  Comment   151   202

BOOKS REVIEWED
  A Street in Bronzeville   67   164
  Annie Allen   76   52
  The Bean Eaters   99   247
  Selected Poems   103   387
  In the Mecca   113   421

BROOKS, PHYLLIS
POEMS
  Men like Bulls   108   313
  From Bulfinch
  To Relinquish   110   242

BROOKS, VAN WYCK
ARTICLES
  Correspondence:
    The Retort Courteous
    (With Randolph Bourne)   12   341

ARTICLES ABOUT
  "Aesthetic and Social Criticism,"
    by Harriet Monroe   13   37

BROOMELL, MYRON H.
POEMS
  Summary   37   24
  For a Septennial Anniversary   58   189
  Corpus Luminosum
  An Antinomy

Milestone
The Temporalities   60   257
Of Providence   61   659
Sonnet ("Still hold me close...")
Soliloquy, with Audience
The Eye
On My Shoulders
News Photo, 1906   64   314
The Waitress with the Big Pair of Eyes
The Time by Dialing
Marriage, or the Gist of Swedenborg
Lines for Ponce de Leon   67   244
The Material Accountant   68   17
From *The City Built on Sand*   70   16
Of Novel Disseizin   74   322
The Secretary   79   132

BOOKS REVIEWED
  The Time by Dialing   74   46
  The Outdoor Labyrinth   99   384

BROTHERSON, ROBERT
POEMS
  A Footnote on Saintliness   93   69

BROTHERTON, J. L.
POEMS
  Simulacra   66   314

BROUGHAM, ELEANOR M.
BOOKS REVIEWED
  Corn from Olde Fieldes—An Anthology
    of English Poems from the
    XIVth to the XVIIth Century (Ed.)   14   98

BROUGHTON, JAMES
POEMS
  Mama Is Gone   73   326
  The Gravity of Spilt Milk   92   10
  Beyond Her Depth
  Birthday Card
  The Birds of America   104   154
  The Gift of the Stag   106   192
  In the Wind's Eye

BOOKS REVIEWED
  The Ballad of Mad Jenny   77   114
  Musical Chairs   77   359
  An Almanac for Amorists   87   299
  True & False Unicorn   91   328
  Tidings   111   189

BROUGHTON, T. ALAN
POEMS
  Grace   133   27
  Inhibition
  Happiness
  Loneliness

Fear
Landscape with Vanishing Point   138   334
Hazards
Heroics   149   282
Aeneas Through the Looking Glass
Message from Herculaneum   154   21
Don Giovanni's Dream
An Old Riddle   156   19
Toward Light
Lyric ("First flakes...")   159   24
A Compliment   167   270

BOOKS REVIEWED
Far from Home   139   35
Dreams Before Sleep   143   163

BROWER, REUBEN A.
REVIEWS
Homer: The Odyssey
   (Tr. by Robert Fitzgerald)   98   397

BOOKS REVIEWED
The Poetry of Robert Frost:
   Constellations of Intention   104   253

BROWER, ROBERT H.
BOOKS REVIEWED
Superior Poems of Our Time,
   by Fujiwara Teika
   (Tr. with Earl Miner)   114   196

BROWN, ALICE
POEMS
Vision   3   81

BOOKS REVIEWED
Ellen Pryor   27   168

BROWN, ASHLEY
ARTICLES
Allen Tate: A Poet
   on Poetry, 1924-1944
   [Ezra Pound, Phelps Putnam,
   Léonie Adams, Louise Bogan,
   Yvor Winters, Wallace Stevens,
   Karl Shapiro, Robert Lowell]   135   103

BOOKS REVIEWED
The Achievement of Wallace Stevens
   (Ed. with Robert Haller)   102   269

ARTICLES ABOUT
[Note]   84   119

BROWN, AUDREY ALEXANDRA
BOOKS REVIEWED
A Dryad of Nanaimo   41   165

BROWN, BOB
BOOKS REVIEWED
1450-1950   96   52

BROWN, CLARENCE
BOOKS REVIEWED
Mandelstam   124   232
Osip Mandelstam: Selected Poems
   (Tr. with W. S. Merwin)

BROWN, CLARENCE ARTHUR
BOOKS REVIEWED
The Achievement
   of American Criticism (Ed.)   84   363

BROWN, E. K.
ARTICLES
The Development of Poetry
   in Canada, 1880-1940
   [Charles G. D. Roberts, Bliss Carman,
   Archibald Lampman, Duncan
   Campbell Scott, Marjorie Pickthall,
   Tom MacInnes, E. J. Pratt,
   Abraham Klein, Frank Scott,
   A. J. M. Smith, Robert Finch,
   Dorothy Livesay]   58   34

REVIEWS
The Hitleriad, by A. M. Klein   65   54
Three Russian Poets,
   Selections from Pushkin,
   Lermontov, and Tyutchev
   (Tr. by Vladimir Nabokov)   66   289
The Burning Glass,
   by Walter de la Mare   68   90
A Book of New Zealand Verse 1923-45
   (Ed. by Allen Curnow)   68   231
Recent Poetry from Canada   69   349
   Now Is Time, by Earle Birney
   The Blossoming Thorn,
      by John Coulter
   East of the City, by Louis Dudek
   When We Are Young,
      by Raymond Souster

BOOKS REVIEWED
On Canadian Poetry   63   281

BROWN, GLEN
POEMS
Maybe   161   98

BROWN, HARRY
POEMS
The Last of Mr. Gigginis   46   297
Plan for a Field
Epigrams for a Failing Voice
Return on a Shield   48   181

Hephaestus in Autumn
Patriarch
Silence Around an Old House
Prospective Conversation
The Madman Reincarnate
The Map of the Age   53   192
Fourth Elegy: The Poet Compared
  to an Unsuccessful General   71   173
The Wheel of Love, Like All Wheels,
  Comes Full Circle   90   137
Two Unrelated Facts
The Drowned
Ode 3 ("Her birth was one day...")   93   165
A Dialogue on a Sunny Morning...   113   7
Four Exercises
This Labyrinthine Garden   114   322
Caveat Everywhere
The Flesh Is Allowed Its Disasters

BOOKS REVIEWED
The End of a Decade   58   340
The Poem of Bunker Hill   59   283
The Violent   64   35
The Beast in His Hunger   75   366

ARTICLES ABOUT
The Poet with Wounds,
  by Hayden Carruth   71   217

BROWN, JIM
BOOKS REVIEWED
If There Are Any Noahs   115   353

BROWN, JOHN L.
REVIEWS
Panorama de la Jeune Poésie Francaise
  (Ed. by René Bertelé)   67   42

BROWN, KENNETH HUNTER
POEMS
A Vision   81   169

BROWN, MARION FRANCIS
POEMS
On a Hill   31   259

BROWN, MARY CHADBOURNE
POEMS
Requiem   33   21

BROWN, OLIVER
BOOKS REVIEWED
Selected Poems of Hugh MacDiarmid (Ed.)   88   52

BROWN, ROBERT
BOOKS REVIEWED
The Twittering Self   62   285

BROWN, ROLLO WALTER
BOOKS REVIEWED
Next Door to a Poet
  [E. A. Robinson]   50   150

BROWN, ROSELLEN
POEMS
Sestina for Three Voices   95   216

BOOKS REVIEWED
Some Deaths in the Delta   119   342

BROWN, S. G.
[See BROWN, STUART GERRY]

BROWN, SARAH-MARGARET
POEMS
From a Chicago "L"   19   251
Tryst   22   259

BROWN, SPENCER
REVIEWS
A Reader's Guide to T. S. Eliot,
  by George Williamson   82   287

BOOKS REVIEWED
My Father's Business and Other Poems,
  in *Poets of Today, III*   89   244

BROWN, STERLING (A.)
POEMS
The Young Ones   52   189

BOOKS REVIEWED
Southern Road   44   115

BROWN, STUART GERRY
[S. G. BROWN]
BOOKS REVIEWED
Reading Poems:
  An Introduction to Critical Study
  (Ed. with Wright Thomas)   59   346
Reading Poems
  (With Wright Thomas)   84   43

BROWNE, ANITA
ARTICLES ABOUT
Cattle in the Garden,
  by M. D. Zabel   38   268

BROWNE, EDWARD GRANVILLE
BOOKS REVIEWED
A Persian Anthology (Ed.)   32   96

BROWNE, MAURICE
POEMS
Nightfall   6   78
Silence of the Night   11   240

To My Heart   15   18
To Her Who Passes
Love Is More Cruel than Death

ARTICLES ABOUT
Various Views, by Harriet Monroe   8   140
Little Theatres and Poetic Plays,
    by Harriet Monroe   11   201

BROWNE, MICHAEL DENNIS
BOOKS REVIEWED
The Wife of Winter   119   234
The Sun Fetcher   134   107

BROWNE, WALDO R.
ARTICLES
Correspondence:
A Word from The Dial   6   51

BROWNELL, BAKER
POEMS
In Barracks   11   312
    Departure
    The Number
    Reveille
    On the Road
    Southward
    Major Fitzpatrick
    Freebourne's Rifle
    Private Rausch
    The Hurricane
    Taps
En Masse   13   255
Stones for Russia   15   12
Poems in Cadence   22   59
    Soil
    Words
    School-Teacher
    Work-Horse
Preludes to 1833   41   295
    Father Marquette
    Jean Baptiste Point de Sable
    Black Hawk

ARTICLES
Must Art Be Interesting?
    [Ford Madox Hueffer]   19   206
Correspondence:
    The Code of Minority
    [Yvor Winters]   19   347
Kinaesthetic Verse
    [Carl Sandburg]   22   36
Down South, by Harriet Monroe   44   92

REVIEWS
Aurelia and Other Poems,
    by Robert Nichols   19   162

BROWNELL, FLORENCE KERR
POEMS
Soft Rain   63   195
Torn Sky   64   201
Duality   70   195

BROWNING, ELIZABETH BARRETT
BOOKS REVIEWED
New Poems
    (With Robert Browning)
    (Ed. by Frederick G. Kenyon)   6   45

BROWNING, ROBERT
BOOKS REVIEWED
New Poems
    (With Elizabeth Barrett Browning)
    (Ed. by Frederick G. Kenyon)   6   45

BROWNJOHN, ALAN
BOOKS REVIEWED
Sandgrains on a Tray   117   108

BROWNJOHN, ALLEN
BOOKS REVIEWED
Travellers Alone   89   45
The Railings   102   393

BROWNRIGG, SHIRLEY
POEMS
The Dark Song   33   190

BROWNSTEIN, MICHAEL
POEMS
The Trumpets Are Coming   116   149
Strolling with the Adults

BOOKS REVIEWED
Highway to the Sky   119   45
Strange Days Ahead   132   31

BRUCE, CHARLES
POEMS
Note for a Textbook   70   71

BOOKS REVIEWED
Tomorrow's Tide   44   115

BRUCE, DEBRA
POEMS
An Argument About a Tree   152   138
Follow-Up Exam   164   213

BRUCE, GEORGE
BOOKS REVIEWED
Scottish Poetry, Number Two
    (Ed. with Maurice Lindsay
    and Edwin Morgan)   113   35

BRUCE, LENNART
BOOKS REVIEWED
Instructions for Undressing the Human Race,
  by Fernando Alegria
  (Tr. with Matthew Zion)   115   440

BRUNCKEN, HERBERT GERHARD
POEMS
Lazarus Silverloom   33   261

BOOKS REVIEWED
Last Parade   55   103

BRUNO, GIORDANO
POEMS
Sonnet ("Amor who makes me view...")
  (Tr. by Francis Golffing)   128   137

BRUSH, ALBERT
BOOKS REVIEWED
The Dark Tower   27   226

BRUSH, THOMAS
POEMS
Small Town   158   210
Lines on a Postcard of Lombard Street,
  San Francisco
Stars   159   145
In the Waiting Room   161   81
A Gift   162   325

BRUSOV, VALERY
[See BRYUSOV, VALERY]

DRUSSEL, CLARA
POEMS
The Book of Adelaide   59   142
Father Damien   62   16
Dream Taking Place in
  a Cathedral—Meeting with Angels
Unicorn Tapestry
Welfare Island
Serf Watching a Hunt   67   77
Fireworks Music   70   74
Tolstoy
Two German Women Sell a Guitar

BRYAN, SHARON
BOOKS REVIEWED
Salt Air   144   40
Objects of Affection   153   30

BRYANT, HELEN
POEMS
Bitterness   38   194
Busses in Oxford Street
Only the Blind
Asking No Benefit   39   135

BRYANT, LOUISE
ARTICLES ABOUT
Obituary   47   290

BRYANT, WILLIAM CULLEN
ARTICLES ABOUT
Aere Perennius,
  by Harriet Monroe   6   197
Rev. of The Fields Were Green,
  by George Arms   84   98

BRYHER, (A.) W(INIFRED)
[ANNIE WINIFRED ELLERMAN]
POEMS
Hellenics   17   136
  Blue Sleep
  Eos
  Wild Rose
Out of Boyhood   25   78
Gulls
Thessalian
Wish   45   146

REVIEWS
Hymen, by H. D.   19   333
Portrait of a Generation,
  by Robert McAlmon   28   280

BOOKS REVIEWED
Amy Lowell—A Critical Appreciation   13   97
Arrow Music   21   221
Gate to the Sea   93   320

ARTICLES ABOUT
[Notes from article]   13   105
A Symposium on Marianne Moore,
  by Harriet Monroe   19   208
The Forging of H. D.,
  by Gloria G. Fromm   153   160

BRYNES, OSCAR
POEMS
Autumnal   41   69
Temperate Zone   41   304
  Robin's-Egg Blue
  Matriculation
  Slow Evenings
  On the Road to the Holy Land
  Credo
  Finis
Two Sides of a Coin   44   145
  The Lemmings
  Everglades
Ephemera   46   246
  The Character of Stephen
  All in One Afternoon
  Heavy with Seeming

BOOKS REVIEWED
   The Day's Work   52   230

BRYSON, LYMAN
POEMS
   To a Certain Fair Lady   8   185

BOOKS REVIEWED
   Smoky Roses   9   324

**BRYUSOV, VALERY (IAKOVLEVICH)
[VALERY BRUSOV]**
POEMS
   Saint Sebastian
     (Tr. by Abraham Yarmolinsky)   14   79

BUBER, MARTIN
ARTICLES ABOUT
   Rev. of *The Way and Its Power*,
     by Arthur Waley   93   408

BUCHAN, JOHN
BOOKS REVIEWED
   The Northern Muse:
     An Anthology of Scots
     Vernacular Poetry (Ed.)   27   343

BUCHANAN, ALISON [Pseud.]
POEMS
   The Unloved   19   313

BUCK, HOWARD
POEMS
   Their Strange Eyes Hold No Vision   13   12
   Plush   24   231

BOOKS REVIEWED
   The Tempering   16   336

BUCKLEY, CHRISTOPHER
POEMS
   Flowers   134 210
   The Letters of Summer
   Walking Out the Appian Way
     Past the Circus of Maxentius   148 135
   Evening in Santorini
   Clouds in Summer   150 125
   On the Eiffel Tower
   Blue Autumn   150 311
   The Inverse Square Law
     of the Propagation of Light   151 22
   Last Night at Akrotiri   151 351
   Dark Time   153 255
   The Past
   Apologues of Winter Light   155 227
   Midlife   157 91
   Perseid Meteor Shower   158 133
   Reincarnation   159 83

   Isotropic
   Sycamore Canyon Nocturne   160 343
   Eschatology
   Equinox   164 332

BOOKS REVIEWED
   Other Lives   147 291
   Dust Light, Leaves   150 226
   Blossoms and Bones:
     On the Life and Work
     of Georgia O'Keeffe   154 283
   Blue Autumn   159 101

BUCKNELL, KATHERINE
BOOKS REVIEWED
   Juvenilia: Poems, 1922-1928,
     by W. H. Auden (Ed.)   166 226

BUDY, ANDREA HOLLANDER
POEMS
   Firmly Married   156 132
   History   165 93
   Ellis Island, September 1907
   Reading Aloud to My Mother   167 197
   Goodness   169 266

BUECHNER, FREDERICK
POEMS
   The Fat Man's Prescriptions   69   85

BUELL, FREDERICK
POEMS
   Replenishment   122 131
   Eros   141 325

BOOKS REVIEWED
   Theseus and Other Poems   121 348

BUFFINGTON, ROBERT
BOOKS REVIEWED
   The Equilibrist:
     A Study of John Crowe
     Ransom's Poems, 1916-1963   113 338

BUGEJA, MICHAEL J.
POEMS
   Trinity   163 316

BUKOWSKI, CHARLES
POEMS
   fingernails; nostrils; shoelaces   162 341
   a not so good night in the San Pedro
     of the world
   cold summer   164 214

BOOKS REVIEWED
   Run with the Hunted   102 42
   It Catches My Heart in Its Hands   104 258

BULKLEY, MARY E.
POEMS
Soliloquy by a Parachute Jumper   60   137

BOOKS REVIEWED
Speaking at Seventy   41   104

BULL, ARTHUR J.
POEMS
In Egypt's Land   70   317

BULL, KATHERINE
BOOKS REVIEWED
White Silences   16   222

BULLETT, GERALD
BOOKS REVIEWED
Winter Solstice   64   171
Readings in English Literature (Ed.)   72   336

BULLIS, JERALD
POEMS
Trumansburg Creek   139   328
Approaching Dinner
Raleigh and Marlowe Were Right
Carpe Diem
Pure Poetry   141   196
Barren Ground
Call To Worship
Of Ellipses and Deviations

BULLOCK, MICHAEL
BOOKS REVIEWED
Sunday Is a Day of Incest   100   191

BULOSAN, CARL
[CARLOS BULOSAN]
POEMS
The Unknown Quantity   47   263
Without Ceremony
Letter from America
In Time of Drought
Secret
No Story
Monuments
The Young Man Lost   50   326
Biography
Night Piece
Needing No Time
The Phoenix
These Are Also Living   52   259
Letter in Exile   60   12
Sunset and Evening Star
American History

ARTICLES
[Autobiographical sketch]   47   292

BOOKS REVIEWED
Letter from America   61   516

BUNKER, JOHN
BOOKS REVIEWED
Shining Fields and Dark Towers   17   276

BUNTING, BASIL
POEMS
Villon   37   27
The Word   37   260
Fearful Symmetry   39   251
Chomei at Toyama   42   301
Fishermen   45   13
To Violet   58   304
The Spoils   79   84
Briggflatts
[With notes]   107   213

ARTICLES
English Poetry Today
[Roy Campbell, T. S. Eliot,
J. J. Adams, J. G. Macleod,
Edgell Rickword, W. H. Auden]   39   264
[Commentary on Chomei at Toyama]   42   356
Correspondence   120   362

REVIEWS
Gemini, by John Collier   40   293

BOOKS REVIEWED
Redimiculum Matellarum   38   160
Poems: 1950   78   301
Loquitur   109   110
The Spoils   110   195
Selected Poems,
by Ford Madox Ford (Ed.)   121   229

ARTICLES ABOUT
Bunting: Formal Aspects,
by Thomas Cole   78   366

BUNZL, LUCILLE
TRANSLATIONS
Outline of a Poetics I,
by G. A. Borgese
(Tr. with Frances Keene)   55   140
Outline of a Poetics II,
by G. A. Borgese
(Tr. with Frances Keene)   55   204
Outline of a Poetics III,
by G. A. Borgese
(Tr. with Frances Keene)   55   267

BURCH, CLAIRE
POEMS
War's End   67   312
Chemistry Anonymous   68   184

The Brewers	71	238
Some People		
"Poem by Emily Dickinson"	74	205

BURDEN, JEAN
[JEAN PRUSSING]
POEMS

The Atomic Age—Pasadena, California	70	191
...But the Child Was Born Dead		
In Sorrow		
The Narrow Room	82	260
For a Sleeping Man	96	90
Premonition in the Midst of Plenty	132	259
On Coming Upon an Old Snapshot		
of Peter De Vries	133	149

REVIEWS

More Clinical Sonnets,		
by Merrill Moore		
[E. A. Robinson]	84	32
Sleep Without Armor,		
by Frances Minturn Howard	84	234

BOOKS REVIEWED

Naked as the Glass	103	316

BURFORD, WILLIAM
POEMS

O! To Be a Monarch	74	70
Fruit of the Mind		
A Scent of the Religious		
End of Season		
Discoveries	75	7
A History	75	326
Four Changes of World		
Celebrations	76	198
The Death of a Sensualist	77	137
In the Lovers' Room	80	209
The Sparrows		
On the Apparition of Oneself		
The Solitary Man	81	234
Let There Be Light	83	75
L'Education Feroce	84	125
El Dorado	88	304
Sea and Sky		
The Days of Love	90	164
Face of the Earth	92	172
The Sea Lavender	95	77
Clay God		
The Ambassadors		
South Harpswell		
The Poet's Brain		
Law of Motion		
The Swimmers	101	198
The Mouth		
The Land of Learning		

Barcelona	106	338
Space		
The Future? It Was the Beginning		
Lines	108	322
Cypris, Athene		

TRANSLATIONS

Poem by Max Jacob	76	86

ARTICLES

Correspondence		
[Louis Coxe, Ezra Pound]	92	195

REVIEWS

Hart Crane: The Life		
of an American Poet,		
by Philip Horton		
[Arthur Rimbaud]	91	117

BOOKS REVIEWED

Man Now	86	116
A World	103	192
A Beginning	111	195

BURGESS, R(OBERT) L(OUIS)
POEMS

Melissa	23	8
Tin Pan Elegy	28	244
San Franciscans	29	188
Junipero Serra		
Terry		
William Ralston		
Sutro		
Joaquin Miller		

REVIEWS

Continent's End, An Anthology		
of Contemporary California Poets		
(Ed. by George Sterling,		
Genevieve Taggard,		
and James Rorty)	27	217
The Physical Basis of Rime,		
by Henry Lanz	38	346

ARTICLES ABOUT

A Travel Tale,		
by Harriet Monroe	28	150

BURGH, MILTON
POEMS

Around the Mines	36	191
Copper Dust		
Mine Skyline		
Cabin		
Season's Flux		
The Blizzard		
December Thaw		

BURKARD, MICHAEL

POEMS

From *Elkin Poems*	118	156
From *Roots*		
Three Lost Poems	119	144
The Rafts	121	263
Some Time in the Winter	123	268
Gaslight		
L'Aveu		
Crescent	127	145
The Victim		
Wren: Three Mirrors		
Persona		

BURKE, KENNETH

POEMS

A Letter from the Center	93	14
To the Memory of E. E. Cummings	102	31
Here and Now	105	188
An Assertion to End On		
And Here I Am, Fighting Dandelions	107	363
Heavy, Heavy—What Hangs Over?		
A Count-In	113	29
A Juxtaposition		

ARTICLES

On Musicality in Verse		
[S. T. Coleridge]	57	31
Kinds of Criticism	68	272
"The Principle of Composition"		
[Edgar Allan Poe]	99	46

REVIEWS

Wine and Physic: A Poem and Six Essays		
on the Fate of Our Language,		
by Alexander Laing	45	294
Chorus for Survival,		
by Horace Gregory	46	227
On Imagination: Coleridge's Critical Theory,		
by I. A. Richards	47	52
One Season Shattered, by James Daly	48	282
The Double Agent:		
Essays in Craft and Elucidation,		
by R. P. Blackmur	49	52
Some Versions of Pastoral,		
by William Empson	49	347
The Mediterranean, and Other Poems and		
Reactionary Essays on Poetry and Ideas,		
by Allen Tate	50	96
New Poems,		
by Frederick Mortimer Clapp	50	226
Wordsworth and Milton, Poets and Prophets,		
by Herbert J. C. Grierson	51	37
The World's Body,		
by John Crowe Ransom	55	51
The Rime of the Ancient Mariner,		
by Samuel Taylor Coleridge		
[Robert Penn Warren]	70	42

Predilections,		
by Marianne Moore	87	239
The Encyclopaedic, Two Kinds Of	91	320
Literary Criticism: A Short History,		
by William K. Wimsatt, Jr.		
and Cleanth Brooks		
Anatomy of Criticism: Four Essays,		
by Northrop Frye		

BOOKS REVIEWED

Permanence and Change	47	347
The Philosophy of Literary Form	60	86
A Grammar of Motives	67	338
A Rhetoric of Motives	77	295
Leaves of Grass		
One Hundred Years After		
[Contrib.] (Ed. by Milton Hindus)	87	183
Book of Moments: Poems 1915–1954	87	362
Perspectives by Incongruity		
and *Terms for Order*		
(Ed. by Stanley Edgar Hyman)	106	366
Language as Symbolic Action:		
Essays in Life, Literature,		
and Method	111	416
Collected Poems, 1915–1967	113	338

ARTICLES ABOUT

The Arraignment,		
by J. Donald Adams	68	262
Speaking of Bookishness,		
by Herbert J. Muller	68	283
A Glossary of the New Criticism,		
by William Elton	73	232
A Glossary of the New Criticism,		
by William Elton	73	296
The Defense of Poetry,		
by Richard Eberhart	77	89

BURKE, ROYDON

BOOKS REVIEWED

Fantasy and Other Poems	27	169

BURKLUND, C(ARL) E(DWIN)

POEMS

Love Song for Mona	38	193
Song for a Night	52	252

BOOKS REVIEWED

New Michigan Verse (Ed.)	58	344

BURLESON, DERICK

POEMS

After This	158	66
Skipping School		
Democracy	164	197
In This Country		
Howdy	170	335
The Thief		

BURLIN, HELEN
TRANSLATIONS
    Poems by Edgar Degas   76   323

BURNE-JONES, EDWARD
ARTICLES ABOUT
    Rev. of *Visionary and Dreamer,*
      by David Cecil   118   343

BURNET, DANA
POEMS
    Antagonist   30   18

BURNETT, VIRGIL
POEMS
    The Mummy   118   342

REVIEWS
    Three Poetic Painters   118   343
      Rossetti and the Fair Lady,
        by David Sonstroem
      Visionary and Dreamer,
        by David Cecil

BURNHAM, DEBORAH
POEMS
    When the Unimaginable
      Becomes Easy   161   192
    Forgetting

BURNHAM, PHILIP
POEMS
    Nine Photographs of Descartes   135   137

BURNS, JERRY
BOOKS REVIEWED
    Acetylene Flowers   117   261

BURNS, JOHN
POEMS
    Ahab on His Wedding Night   85   342

BURNS, MICHAEL
POEMS
    The Widow on Route Three   153   69
    Trying To Know
    I Said It Could Have Been   158   13
    Cooking Breakfast After Reading
      Robert Penn Warren   160   281

BURNS, RALPH
POEMS
    Yes No Days   141   208
    Rid of Hogs
    Debris   147   261
    The Comfort of a Woman
    Lullaby   153   105

BOOKS REVIEWED
    Any Given Day   148   99

BURNS, ROBERT
BOOKS REVIEWED
    The Poems and Songs of...
      (Ed. by James Kinsley)   114   191

ARTICLES ABOUT
    Hugh MacDiarmid and Scottish Poetry,
      by David Daiches   72   202
    Rev. of *Selected Letters of Robert Burns*
      (Ed. by DeLancey Ferguson)   84   41
    Rev. of *The Russet Coat,*
      by Christina Keith   89   382

BURNS, ROBERT GRANT
POEMS
    Nutria   114   165
    Storm Warning
    Field Problem, and Midnight Convoy
    The Saviors   119   151

BURNS, VINCENT GODFREY
BOOKS REVIEWED
    The Red Harvest: A Cry for Peace (Ed.)   37   164

BURNSHAW, STANLEY
POEMS
    Eartha   37   297
      To the Earth
      Instead of Swords
      Restful Ground
      Forevermore
      Her Crown
      Blood of Earth
    Sun Voyage   99   96
    Seedling Air

TRANSLATIONS
    Poems by Anna Akhmatova   98   376

ARTICLES
    Vers-Libre in Full Bloom I
      [André Spire]   32   277
    Vers-Libre in Full Bloom II
      [André Spire]   32   334
    Correspondence
      [Walter Leuba]   33   52
    Correspondence
      [Objectivists, Louis Zukofsky]   38   51
    Correspondence:
      Stanley Burnshaw Protests   44   351

REVIEWS
    The Orphic Voice,
      by Elizabeth Sewell   99   387

BOOKS REVIEWED
  André Spire and His Poetry   44 347
  The Bridge   67 101
  The Poem Itself
    (Ed. with Dudley Fitts, Henri Peyre,
    and John Frederick Nims)   98 56
  Caged in an Animal's Mind   103 382
  The Modern Hebrew Poem Itself
    (Ed. with T. Carmi
    and Ezra Spicehandler)   111 258
  In the Terrified Radiance   122 344

ARTICLES ABOUT
  Correspondence from Walter Leuba   33 50
  Correspondence from Louis Zukofsky   38 51
  Art and Propaganda,
    by Harriet Monroe   44 210
  Poetry of the Left,
    by Harriet Monroe   48 212

BURNSIDE, JOHN
POEMS
  Hypothesis   166 198

BURR, AMELIA JOSEPHINE
BOOKS REVIEWED
  The Roadside Fire   2 26
  Selected Lyrics   32 114

BURR, DAVID STANFORD
POEMS
  An Abidance   157 147
  Dowsing for the Mole at Age Eight

BURR, GRAY
POEMS
  Cripple   69 24
  A Glance at the Album   86 277
  Lunar Tune
  Meadow Remembered
  Sunday at the Beach   132 144
  Mr. Thoben
  A Ramble

BOOKS REVIEWED
  A Choice of Attitudes   116 51

BURR, JANE
BOOKS REVIEWED
  City Dust   11 109

BURRIS, SIDNEY
POEMS
  On Living with a Fat Woman
    in Heaven   139 208
  Very True Confessions   149 330
  A Realm of Probability   162 142

BURROUGHS, JOHN
ARTICLES
  Correspondence
    [John Russell McCarthy,
    Emanuel Carnevali]   16 114

BURROWS, E(DWIN) G(RANT)
POEMS
  Murder for Tea   57 305
  Emigree   87 158
  The Sound of Love   89 169
  Uncles
  Landfall   91 297
  Landscape with Bo Tree   93 87
  From Music to Mire
  Nineteen Seventeen
  A Change in the Weather
  Nicias to the Athenians   96 104
  Camel Song
  The Day Grandmother Died   104 217
  Saratoga
  Limits   157 260
  The Statue

REVIEWS
  Three from Overseas   105 207
    Grooves in the Wind,
      by C. A. Trypanis
    Flight to Africa,
      by Austin Clarke
    The True Confession of George Barker

BOOKS REVIEWED
  Flower in My Ear
    Arts and Ethos of Ifaluk Atoll   104 245

BURSCH, JAMES F.
BOOKS REVIEWED
  My Worshipping Soul   77 215

**BURSK, CHRISTOPHER
[CHRIS BURSK]**
POEMS
  Jerusalem Road   137 138
  Plywood
  "The Only Thing Worse
    than the Terror Itself Would Be
    the Silence Afterward."
  Late Afternoon Shadows   143 31
  After Being by Myself All Day
  Sisters   148 90
  The Trees Keeping Their Place,
    Saying Nothing
  Rowing Cutthroat Creek
  The Museum of Fine Arts   151 23
  Don't Worry   165 7
  Does Poetry Matter?   166 279

BOOKS REVIEWED
Standing Watch   136   170

BURT, (MAXWELL) STRUTHERS
POEMS
Crepuscule   12   189

BOOKS REVIEWED
War Songs   63   172

BURT, NATHANIEL
BOOKS REVIEWED
Question on a Kite   78   45

BURT, STRUTHERS
    [See BURT, (MAXWELL)
    STRUTHERS]

BURTON, RICHARD
POEMS
An Impression   2   131
Song of Earth's Meaning

BUSCH, TRENT
POEMS
Aletha   144   94
Woman in a Swing
Staying
As Literature Comes of Age   146   271
Gay   168   77

BUSH, DOUGLAS
BOOKS REVIEWED
Science and English Poetry:
    A Historical Sketch, 1590-1950   76   352

ARTICLES ABOUT
Poetry and Advertising,
    by S. I. Hayakawa   67   204
Rev. of *Wordsworth:*
    Centenary Studies Presented at Cornell
    and Princeton Universities
    (Ed. by Gilbert T. Dunklin)   80   233

BUSHBY, D. MAITLAND
BOOKS REVIEWED
Golden Stallion (Ed.)   37   164

BUSS, KATE (NELDRAM)
POEMS
The Dead Pecos Town   11   81
Gargoyle   19   77

ARTICLES
Correspondence
    [Paul Claudel]   7   323
Armenian Poetry   9   41

BUTCHER, GRACE
POEMS
Getting What We Want   154   25
Reading the X-Ray:
    A Modern Mythology   158   31
Learning from Trees

BUTLER, CHARLES E.
POEMS
Hyde Park: The Serpentine   64   304
The Gift

BOOKS REVIEWED
Cut Is the Branch   66   280

BUTLER, DIANA
POEMS
Pregnant Woman   94   176

BUTLER, E. M.
BOOKS REVIEWED
Rainer Maria Rilke   61   441

BUTLER, GUY
ARTICLES ABOUT
Rev. of *Poets in South Africa*
    (Ed. by Roy Macnab)   95   244

BUTLER, JACK
POEMS
Timber Rattler   137   17
The Mantis
One Reason for Stars   142   263
The Lord Is Down
    in the Greek Theatre Again   151   468
The Key to Nothing   152   66
Practice

BUTLER, JESSIE STORRS
POEMS
Garçonne   32   259

BUTSCHER, EDWARD
REVIEWS
Fathers and Sons   130   167
    No Time for Good Reasons,
        by Brendan Galvin
    Why I Live in the Forest,
        by James Nolan
    Passage, by W. R. Moses
    Collected Poems,
        by James K. Feibleman
    The Kindness of Strangers:
        Poems 1969-1974,
        by Philip Whalen
    Diversifications,
        by A. R. Ammons

BUTTER, P. H.
BOOKS REVIEWED
   Edwin Muir: Man and Poet   112   206

BUTTERICK, GEORGE F.
BOOKS REVIEWED
   A Guide to the Maximus Poems
    of Charles Olson   136   219
   Muthologos:
    The Collected Lectures & Interviews,
    by Charles Olson (Ed.)

BUTTS, DOROTHY
POEMS
   The Passers-By   19   80
    The Parade
    To the Hills Around Northampton
    A Vanity
    Audience
    Listening
    May Basket
    The Transient
    Difference
    Please

BUXTON, JOHN
POEMS
   For D. L., Killed in the Last War   59   176
   Sonnet ("I saw men's homes burst...")
   To Edmund Blunden   61   361

BUZZELL, FRANCIS
POEMS
   Dancing to a Chewink's Song   2   209
   The Fisher Lad   3   214

BYER, KATHRYN STRIPLING
POEMS
   Old Orchard Road Again   141   71
   Like a Mother Who Never Sleeps, Rain
   Wide Open, These Gates

BYLANSEN, STEPHEN
POEMS
   To D. H. Lawrence   64   190
   Epithalaminuet

BYNNER, WITTER
[See also MORGAN,
EMANUEL, pseud.]
POEMS
   Apollo Troubadour   1   150
   One of the Crowd
   Neighbors
   The Hills of San José
   Grieve Not for Beauty
   The Mystic
   Passing Near
   To Celia   4   22

   Consummation
   During a Chorale by Cesar Frank
   Songs Ascending
   Passages from a Poem: The New World   6   1
   Presences   8   300
    A Thrush in the Moonlight
    A Mocking-Bird
    The Dead Loon
    To No One in Particular
    At the Touch of You
    The Earth-Clasp
    He Brought Us Clover-Leaves
    Wisdom
    Ecce Homo
   This Man   14   80
   Sea-Edge Songs   15   304
    The Enchanted Toad
    The Sand-Piper
    Grass-Tops
   The Fruits of the Earth   22   238
   A Young Girl   25   192
   The Singing Huntsman
   The Long Way
   There Are Too Many Dead
   To One in China
   Epithalamium and Elegy   27   16
   Chapala Poems   30   205
    Twilight
    The Storm Dragon
    A Zarape
    Asleep
    Along the Mountain-Margin of Mescala
    Montesuma
    La Francesa
    To My Mother
      Concerning a Chapala Sunset
    A Moth
    Calendar
   Color of Dreams   34   252
    Endion
    Undressing You
    This Happiness
   To a Careless Young Dog   38   132
   Winter Sonnets   39   186
   If Words Are Wise   41   11
   Face Alive   51   301
   Venus
   Change   53   129
   Sweet Chariot   53   289
   To Impossible Death
   Being of Sound and Disposing Mind
   One's Own Requiem
   Confessional   61   425
   Joe and Jack and Jennie
   Snow
   The Heart
   The Titanic   73   265
   Inscriptions on Chinese Paintings   89   240

Five Poems   100   35
  ("Again with spring...")
  ("Elegant are these ways...")
  ("The future ended...")
  ("From the jowl of a porpoise...")
  ("In the end...")
Four Poems   106   212
  ("I had an appointment with myself...")
  ("The blue heron all by himself...")
  ("He will walk here always...")
  ("Life and death might be the stakes...")

TRANSLATIONS
Poem by Charles Vildrac   13   243
Poems by Wang Wêi
  (Tr. with Kiang Kang-hu)   19   235

ARTICLES
Correspondence: Lines to W. B.   2   113
Correspondence: A Spectral Ghost   12   286
Translating Wang Wêi   19   272
Correspondence:
  From the President of the P.S.A.
  [Dorothy Dudley, Amy Lowell]   20   111
Ave Atque Vale
  [Arthur Davison Ficke]   68   56
Correspondence:
  Emanuel Morgan Demurs
  [Harvey Curtis Webster]   72   344

REVIEWS
New China in Verse,
  by Cheng Chi-Yu   65   222
Poems by Wang Wêi
  (Tr. by Chang Yin-Nan
  and Lewis C. Walmsley)
  [Kiang Kang-Hu, Amy Lowell]   96   309
The Summer Anniversaries,
  by Donald Justice   97   50

BOOKS REVIEWED
Tiger   3   184
The Little King   6   93
The New World   7   147
Grenstone Poems—A Sequence   12   227
The Beloved Stranger   15   281
A Book of Plays   22   158
A Book of Love,
  by Charles Vildrac (Tr.)   24   223
Young Harvard   27   170
Caravan   27   331

The Jade Mountain:
  A Chinese Anthology,
  by Kiang Kang-Hu (Tr.)   35   289
Indian Earth   36   276
Eden Tree   39   217
Guest Book   47   101
Against the Cold   57   217
The Way of Life, According to Laotzu.
  An American Version   66   40
Take Away the Darkness   72   44
Book of Lyrics   88   334
Iphigenia in Tauris (Tr.),
  in Euripides (Vol. II)   88   337
New Poems 1960   98   319

ARTICLES ABOUT
Various Views,
  by Harriet Monroe   8   140
Baiting the Public,
  by Alice Corbin Henderson   12   169
Correspondence: A Spectral Ghost,
  by Emanuel Morgan   12   286
Rev. of The Spectra Hoax,
  by William Jay Smith
  [Arthur Davison Ficke]   99   390

BYRNE, ALEXA
POEMS
On the Range   30   253
Wrangling
The Sheepherder

BYRNE, ELENA KARINA
POEMS
In Particular   158   30

BYRON, [LORD] [GEORGE GORDON]
BOOKS REVIEWED
Selected Poetry
  (Ed. by Leslie A. Marchand)   84   363

ARTICLES ABOUT
Byron, by Harriet Monroe   24   32
Rev. of Selected Letters of Lord Byron
  (Ed. by Jacques Barzun)   84   296
Rev. of His Very Self and Voice
  (Ed. by Ernest J. Lovell, Jr.)   87   372

BYRON, MAY
BOOKS REVIEWED
The Wind on the Heath,
  Ballads and Lyrics   2   107

C

"C. H."
[See HEAD, CLOYD]

"C. S."
ARTICLES
Correspondence: Imports from Africa   20   56

CABELL, JAMES BRANCH
POEMS
Post Annos   6   221

BOOKS REVIEWED
From the Hidden Way   9   324

CABOT, ELISE PUMPELLY
BOOKS REVIEWED
Arizona and Other Poems   17   276

CADDY, CAROLINE
POEMS
Editing the Moon   169   11
The Wind
Commonplace
Earthquake
Inoculation

ARTICLES ABOUT
Towards a Contemporary
Australian Poetics,
by John Kinsella   169   94

CADER, TERESA
POEMS
Empress Shōtoku Invents Printing in 770   166   80

CADES, HAZEL RAWSON
POEMS
Feel of Brambles   17   184

CADILLA, ALICIA
POEMS
The Boy Who Sells Sweet Oranges
(Tr. by H. R. Hays)   62   65

CAEIRO, ALBERTO
[See PESSOA, FERNANDO]

CAFAGNA, MARCUS
POEMS
Dybbuks   160   26

CAFFREY, JOHN
REVIEWS
English Institute Essays, 1949
(Ed. by Alan S. Downer)
[Arthur Mizener, Moody E. Prior,
Francis Fergusson, William Charvat]   77   48
The Rent that's Due to Love
(Tr. by Gwyn Williams)
[Welsh Poems]   77   351

CAGE, JOHN
ARTICLES ABOUT
Rev. of The Tradition of the New,
by Harold Rosenberg   102   341

CAHOON, HERBERT
BOOKS REVIEWED
Thanatopsis   76   229

CAIE, HARRIET
POEMS
"Who Wears Grief Long"   30   309

CAILLOIS, ROGER
ARTICLES ABOUT
Rev. of Le Cahiers de la Pléiade
(Ed. by Jean Paulhan)
[St.-John Perse]   79   43

CAIRNS, DOLORES
POEMS
Dust   42   264

CAIRNS, HUNTINGTON
REVIEWS
The Note-Books of Matthew Arnold
(Ed. by Howard Foster Lowry,
Karl Young, and Waldo Hilary Dunn)   81   196

BOOKS REVIEWED
The Limits of Art, an Anthology (Ed.)   74   353

CALDWELL, DORIS (PACKARD)
[See also SAGE, JOAN, pseud.]
POEMS
California Hills — 50 — 74
California Coast — 50 — 146

CALL, (FRANK) OLIVER
POEMS
In French Canada — 23 — 250
La Terre
The Sugar-Maker
The Raconteur

BOOKS REVIEWED
Blue Homespun — 24 — 283

CALLAGHAN, BARRY
BOOKS REVIEWED
As Close As We Came — 144 — 297

CALLAN, NORMAN
BOOKS REVIEWED
The Collected Poems of
Christopher Smart (Ed.) — 76 — 218

CALLAWAY, KATHY
BOOKS REVIEWED
Heart of the Garfish — 143 — 228

CAMBON, GLAUCO
REVIEWS
An Italian Chronicle — 94 — 350
The Penguin Book of Italian Verse
(Ed. by George Kay)
The Promised Land, and Other Poems
(Ed. by Sergio Pacifici)
Three Plays by Ugo Betti
(Tr. by Henry Reed)
Mandragola, by Niccolo Machiavelli
(Tr. by Anne and Henry Paolucci)
Petrarch at Vaucluse:
Letters in Verse and Prose
(Tr. by Ernest Hatch Wilkins)
Immediacies and Distances — 95 — 379
An Anthology of Mexican Poetry
(Ed. by Octavio Paz)
(Tr. by Samuel Beckett)
The Poems of St. John of the Cross
(Tr. by John Frederick Nims)
The Interior Distance,
by Georges Poulet
(Tr. by Elliott Coleman)
Recent Anthologies — 96 — 122
Modern Verse in English, 1900-1950
(Ed. by Lord David Cecil
and Allen Tate)
How Does a Poem Mean?,
by John Ciardi
The Poem—A Critical Anthology
(Ed. by Josephine Miles)

The "Usable" Dante — 96 — 323
Further Papers on Dante,
by Dorothy Sayers
De Sanctis on Dante,
by Francesco de Sanctis
(Ed. and tr. by Joseph Rossi
and Alfred Galpin)
Dante's Other World,
The "Purgatorio" as Guide
to The Divine Comedy,
by Bernard Stambler
Revolution and Tradition — 100 — 50
Reflections on a Literary Revolution,
by Graham Hough
A Primer of Ezra Pound,
by M. L. Rosenthal
Vision and Rhetoric:
Studies in Modern Poetry,
by G. S. Fraser
Robert Frost, the Trial by Existence,
by Elizabeth Shepley Sergeant
Robert Bridges and Gerard Hopkins,
1863-1889: A Literary Friendship,
by Jean-Georges Ritz
D. H. Lawrence,
The Failure and Triumph of Art,
by Eliseo Vivas
Between Aristotle and Plato — 102 — 198
A History of Literary Criticism
in the Italian Renaissance,
by Bernard Weinberg
The Age of Criticism:
The Late Renaissance in Italy,
by Baxter Hathaway
Tragedy and the Theory of Drama,
by Elder Olson
Metaphor and Reality,
by Philip Wheelwright
The New Romantics:
A Reappraisal of the New Criticism,
by Richard Foster
The Moment of Poetry
(Ed. by Don Cameron Allen)
Two Poets of New York — 102 — 266
By the Waters of Manhattan:
Selected Verse,
by Charles Reznikoff
The Materials, by George Oppen

CAMERON, J(AMES) M(UNRO)
POEMS
Only the Name Is Common to Horses — 98 — 203
The Night the Boy Sang
Inferences
South-West Passage
A Christmas Garland
for C. L. D. 1832-1898 — 141 — 129
Let Us Now Praise Famous Men
The Wizards

ARTICLES ABOUT
[Note]   98   269

CAMERON, MICHAEL
POEMS
"February"   133   258

CAMERON, NORMAN
BOOKS REVIEWED
Selected Verse Poems of Arthur Rimbaud (Tr.)   63   96
Ode to Bombed London,
    by Phillippe Soupault (Tr.)   68   54
Forgive Me, Sire   79   106
The Collected Poems of...   92   318

CAMMAERTS, ÉMILE
BOOKS REVIEWED
Chants Patriotiques et Autres Poèmes
    and Les Trois Rois et Autres Poèmes
    (Tr. by Tita Brand-Cammaerts)   10   331
Messines et Autres Poèmes   14   342
Messines and Other Poems
    (Tr. by Tita Brand-Cammaerts)   17   48

CAMO, PIERRE
ARTICLES ABOUT
Paris Letter, by Jean Catel   18   168

CAMPANA, DINO
ARTICLES ABOUT
Contemporary Italian Poetry,
    by Edward Williamson   79   159

CAMPBELL, ALICE ORMOND
POEMS
Modern Music   5   171

CAMPBELL, ALISTAIR
BOOKS REVIEWED
Mine Eyes Dazzle   81   335

CAMPBELL, CORY WADE
POEMS
Transformations   125   146

CAMPBELL, DORIS
POEMS
Anguish   21   131

CAMPBELL, FLOY
POEMS
The Dunes   24   254

CAMPBELL, GLADYS
POEMS
Inquiries   29   203
    Without Gift
    All That Is Beautiful
    For One Defenceless

Remembered Landing
A Prairie River
Never Silence
Alone in Fire   33   27
Not with Our Hearts
At Length
After Prayer
Inviolable
Old Enough
Memorial
Winter Songs   37   188
    After Summer
    Like Leaves
    Snow Will Come
    Drift of Days
Motion and Change   42   208
    Dreamer Who Runs
    Question
    No Escape
    Corante
    The Mover
Voyage   56   16

ARTICLES
Some Recollections of the Poetry Club
    at the University of Chicago
    [Harriet Moody, Harriet Monroe,
    Glenway Wescott, Elizabeth Madox
    Roberts, Robert Herrick]   107   110

REVIEWS
Flying Fish, by Grace Hazard Conkling   29   281
Verses New and Old, by John Galsworthy   30   168
A Stranger and Afraid, by Ted Olson   34   167
Slow Wall, by Leonora Speyer   56   217
Steeple Bush, by Robert Frost   71   145
Pleasure Dome: On Reading Modern Poetry,
    by Lloyd Frankenberg   76   294

CAMPBELL, ISABEL (JONES)
POEMS
("My love tonight is quiet...")   30   78
("My days, like swift wild birds...")
Women   48   206

CAMPBELL, JOHN R.
POEMS
Pastoral   161   278
Pornography

CAMPBELL, JOSEPH
POEMS
The Piper   1   33
The Irish Fairies   3   49
The Puca
Whence Comes the Stranger   5   67
On Waking   7   288
At Harvest

ARTICLES
Correspondence: The Dead Irish Poets
[Padraic Pearse]   8   272

BOOKS REVIEWED
Earth of Cualann   12   107

CAMPBELL, KATHLEEN (FOSTER)
POEMS
Not Fragments   55   246
Wake
Old Letters   74   22

REVIEWS
Two Islands   57   330
New Zealand Poems,
by Eileen Duggan
The Gap of Brightness,
by F. R. Higgins
Time and Low Tide   59   167
Angle of Earth and Sky,
by David Morton
Androscoggin, by Marsden Hartley

CAMPBELL, NANCY
POEMS
The Apple-Tree   6   223
The Monkey
The Magi   7   124
The Mother   15   307
Innocent Sleep   18   247

CAMPBELL, ROBERT BHAIN
BOOKS REVIEWED
The Task   67   282

CAMPBELL, ROY
ARTICLES
Memories of Dylan Thomas
at the B.B.C.   87   111

BOOKS REVIEWED
The Flaming Terrapin   25   217
Adamastor: Poems   38   98
Flowering Reeds   42   166
The Poems of St. John of the Cross (Tr.)   80   153
Poems of Baudelaire
(Tr. of Les Fleurs du Mal)   82   86
Light on a Dark Horse   82   169
Selected Poetry
(Ed. by Joseph M. Lalley)   113   262

ARTICLES ABOUT
English Poetry Today,
by Basil Bunting   39   264
Roy Campbell, by Edith Sitwell   92   42
Rev. of Poets in South Africa
(Ed. by Roy Macnab)   95   244

CAMPBELL, WALTER STANLEY
[See VESTAL, STANLEY, pseud.]

CAMPERT, REMCO
ARTICLES ABOUT
Down There on a Visit: Poetry
in the Netherlands,
by Turner Cassity   102   38

CAMPION, DAN
POEMS
Admonitions   167   143

CAMPION, THOMAS
POEMS
From Epigrammatum Liber Primus   130   90
From Epigrammatum Liber Secundus
(Tr. by Stephen Ratcliffe)

ARTICLES ABOUT
Campion's "Observations,"
by Richard Aldington   15   267
The 16th Century Lyric
in England: Part III,
by Yvor Winters   54   35
Rev. of England's Musical Poet,
Thomas Campion,
by Miles Merwin Kastendieck   56   51

CANBY, HENRY SEIDEL
BOOKS REVIEWED
Twentieth-Century Poetry
(Ed. with John Drinkwater
and William Rose Benét)   37   164

CANBY, MARION
POEMS
Ageless Narrative   36   245

BOOKS REVIEWED
High Mowing   44   55

CANDLEWOOD, WILLIAM
BOOKS REVIEWED
The Mirror of Baudelaire (Tr.)
(Ed. by Charles Henri Ford)   62   282

CANE, MELVILLE
BOOKS REVIEWED
January Garden   28   290
Behind Dark Spaces   38   345
A Wider Arc   70   278

CANFIELD, MARY CASS
POEMS
Tomb Epitaph   23   252
Rose
The Poet Outside

CANNÉLL, SKIPWITH
POEMS
Poems in Prose and Verse: A Sequence   2   171
  Invocation
  The Eagle
  Prelude
  Enigma
  The Mountains
  Nocturne in Pastels
  Nocturne Triste
  Nocturnes
Ikons   4   50
  The Blind Man
  The Dwarf Speaks
  Epilogue to the Crows
Monoliths   4   207
  The Prayer
  The Red Bridge
  The King
Songs of Hunger   6   127
  The Crown, the Plate and the Bowl
  The Temple of Hunger
  A Riddle
  The Lean Gray Rats

ARTICLES ABOUT
They Come and Go,
  by Harriet Monroe   36   326

CANNON, MOYA
POEMS
Viol   167   26
Viola d'Amore
Song in Windsor   170   12
Attention

CANTOR, ELI
POEMS
Song for the Times   49   24

CAPASSO, ALDO
ARTICLES ABOUT
Contemporary Italian Poetry,
  by Edward Williamson   79   233

CAPETANAKIS, DEMETRIOS
BOOKS REVIEWED
The Shores of Darkness   75   180

CAPLAN, RALPH
POEMS
Nowhere Lovelier than in Bars   77   263
And the Native Girls,
  What Were They Like, Really?

CAPON, R. F.
POEMS
Prothalamium   74   82

CAPRONI, GIORGIO
POEMS
The Elevator   155   30
I coltelli / The Knives
Delizia (e Saggezza) del bevitore /
  Drinker's Delight (and Wisdom)
Le parole / The Words
  (Tr. by Michael Palma)

ARTICLES ABOUT
Some Notes on Post-War Italian Poetry,
  by Paolo Cherchi and Joseph Parisi   155   161

CARBÓ, NICK
POEMS
Carta de Umm Al-Hákam
  Para Ben Quzman   168   200
Carta de Ben Quzman
  Para Umm Al-Hákam
Respuesta de Umm Al-Hákam

CARDEN, GUY
POEMS
Apprehension   44   69
Modern Interior
A Dancer   45   74
Weather   46   70
The Necessity   46   263

CARDONA-HINE, ALVARO
BOOKS REVIEWED
The Gathering Wave   99   313

CARDOZO, NANCY
POEMS
Primroses and Prayers   47   136
  Primrose Day
  Song ("Proud of your arrow...")
  The Giver
  Red-Haired Mask
  Unicorns and Candles
  The Prodigal

BOOKS REVIEWED
Helmet of the Wind   126   172

CARDUCCI, (GIOSUE)
BOOKS REVIEWED
Carducci: A Selection
  of His Poems, with Verse Translations,
  Notes and Three Introductory Essays,
  by G. L. Bickersteth   4   198

CARDWELL, GUY A.
POEMS
On Reaching Seventy-Three
Near Scott's Bluff on the Oregon Trail   95   208

CAREY, STEVE
BOOKS REVIEWED
 Smith Going Backward   117 261

CARGILL, OSCAR
REVIEWS
 Hart Crane's Sanskrit Charge:
 A Study of The Bridge,
 by L. S. Dembo [T. S. Eliot] 98 190

ARTICLES ABOUT
 Correspondence from Brom Weber
 [Hart Crane]   92 332

CARLIE, JULIA
POEMS
 Twilight Color   34 263

CARLILE, HENRY
POEMS
 The Job   115 167
 Endurances
 Dodo   126 87
 In Oceans, In Rivers 148 96
 Camouflage
 Hugo   151 24
 The Poet's Neighbor Talks Back 153 294
 Ugly Money   162 219
 Nature   170 8

BOOKS REVIEWED
 The Rough-Hewn Table 121 292

CARLIN, FRANCIS
BOOKS REVIEWED
 My Ireland—Songs and Simple Rhymes 13 165

CARLIN, KIM
POEMS
 Country Song   169 257

CARLIN, VUYELWA
POEMS
 Crazy Girl Candy   160 21

CARLOS, ALBERTO J.
BOOKS REVIEWED
 The Gaucho Martín Fierro,
 by José Hernández
 (Tr. by C. E. Ward)
 (Ed. with Frank G. Carrino) 113 338

CARLSEN, IOANNA
POEMS
 Fat   157 319
 Two Songs from a Car 159 135
  Hawk
  Love in Winter
 Love's Interest   160 200
 A Week Before Christmas 163 144

CARLSON, MARCIA
POEMS
 A Masque for Icarus   83 6

CARLSON, NANCY NAOMI
POEMS
 Subtitles   169 331

CARLTON, MARY
POEMS
 Of Tutankhamen's Tomb 98 207

CARLYLE, THOMAS
ARTICLES ABOUT
 The Hungry Generations,
 by Jessica Nelson North 34 90

CARMAN, BLISS
POEMS
 The Rainbird   4 49
 Lord of Morning   6 117
 Noon

BOOKS REVIEWED
 Earth Deities and Other
  Rhythmic Masques
  (With Mary Perry King) 6 205
 Later Poems   20 282
 The Oxford Book
  of American Verse (Ed.) 32 96
 Canadian Poetry in English
  (Ed. with Lorne Pierce
  and V. B. Rhodenhizer) 86 111

ARTICLES ABOUT
 The Development of Poetry
 in Canada, 1880-1940,
 by E. K. Brown   58 34

CARMER, CARL LAMSON
POEMS
 One Night in Calera   29 186
 Industrials   32 246
  Riding the Carriage
  Making the Mold
  Song for Orleans County, New York
  What the Black Driver Said
  Afric
  The Last White Man

BOOKS REVIEWED
 Deep South   36 284
 Taps Is Not Enough   67 101

CARMI, T.
POEMS
 She Is Asleep
  (Tr. by Ruth Finer Mintz) 92 258

BOOKS REVIEWED
The Modern Hebrew Poem Itself
  (Ed. with Stanley Burnshaw
  and Ezra Spicehandler)   III   258

**CARMICHAEL, WAVERLEY
  TURNER**
BOOKS REVIEWED
From the Heart of a Folk   16   287

CARNE-ROSS, D. S.
REVIEWS
Contemporary Greek   101   283
  Six Poets of Modern Greece
    (Tr. by Edmund Keeley
    and Philip Sherrard)
  The Complete Poems of Cavafy
    (Tr. by Rae Dalven)
  George Seferis: Poems
    (Tr. by Rex Warner)

CARNEVALI, EMANUEL ["E. C."]
POEMS
The Splendid Commonplace   11   298
  In This Hotel
  His Majesty the Letter-Carrier
  Drôlatique-Sérieux
  When It Has Passed
  To the Poets
  Sentimental Dirge
Walt Whitman   14   60
The Day of Summer   14   314
Neuriade   19   139
  Lake
  Sleep
  Aubade
  Encounter
  Sermon
  Hope
  Insomnia
  Smoke
  Funeral March
  Italian Song
  Old Accustomed Impudent Ghost
  Invocation to Death
The Return   24   85
Visiting Winds   32   179
  Furnished Room Rhapsody
  Sketch of Self
  Night
Observations   35   254
  Menta the Drunkard
  Some Things
  Shorties
Castles on the Ground   38   237
  The Mountains
  Cypresses
  Fireflies
  Chat While It Rains

Dead Books and Their Authors
Certain Families
Shorties

TRANSLATIONS
Poems by Arthur Rimbaud   37   262

ARTICLES
Correspondence:
  As He Sees It [Poem]   12   113
Correspondence:
  The Day of Victory   13   171
Five Years of Italian Poetry (1910-1915)
  [Corrado Govoni, Salvatore di Giacomo,
  Piero Jahier, Aldo Palazzeschi, Umberto
  Saba, Scipio Slataper, Giovanni Papini] 13   209
The Sandberg-Sarett Recital   15   271
Continental Magazines   16   54
Dante—and Today   18   323

REVIEWS
A Cabinet of Jade, by David O'Neil   12   225
A Few First Books   15   169
  Petals Blown Adrift,
    by Rose Florence Freeman
  Dreams and Gibes, by Edward Sapir
  The Omega and Other Poems,
    by Edward Shillito
  Out of Doors and *Gods and Devils*,
    by John Russell McCarthy
Pavannes and Divisions, by Ezra Pound 15   211
Scepticisms, by Conrad Aiken   15   283
McAroni Ballads, by T. A. Daly   16   278
Three Poets of Three Nations   17   48
  Messines and Other Poems,
    by Emile Cammaerts
    (Tr. by Tita Brand-Cammaerts)
  Life Immovable, by Kostes Palamas
    (Tr. by A. E. Phoutrides)
  The Soothsayer,
    by Verner von Heidenstam
  Tête d'Or, The Hostage;
    and *Three Poems of the War*,
    by Paul Claudel   17   222
Smoke and Steel, by Carl Sandburg   17   266
Sun-Up, by Lola Ridge   17   332
Collected Poems, by Walter de la Mare 18   36
Two Books of Refuge   18   46
  Black Marigolds
    (Tr. by E. Powys Mathers)
  The Dark Mother, by Waldo Frank
Explorations, by Robert McAlmon   20   155
Asia   20   346
  Early Persian Poetry,
    by A. J. Williams Jackson
  Selections from the Rubiyat of Hafiz
  Chips of Jade and Betel Nuts
    (Tr. by Arthur Guiterman)

The Garden of Bright Waters
    and *Colored Stars,*
    by E. Powys Mathers

BOOKS REVIEWED
    A Hurried Man   27   211

ARTICLES ABOUT
    The Glittering Metropolis,
        by Harriet Monroe   14   30
    Correspondence
    from John Burroughs
        [John Russell McCarthy]   16   114

CARNEY, JAMES
    BOOKS REVIEWED
        Mediaeval Irish Lyrics (Ed. and tr.)   113   35

CARPATHIOS, NEIL
    POEMS
        Same Sun, Same Moon, Same River   168   231

CARPENTER, ANNE NICODEMUS
    POEMS
        Depreciation   140   94
        Motel
        Ars Poetica

CARPENTER, BOGDANA
    TRANSLATIONS
        Poems by Zbigniew Herbert
            (Tr. with John R. Carpenter)   128   141

CARPENTER, EDMUND
    BOOKS REVIEWED
        Anerca: Eskimo Poems
            and Drawings (Ed.)   97   192

CARPENTER, EDWARD
    BOOKS REVIEWED
        Towards Democracy   21   331

CARPENTER, JOHN R.
    POEMS
        The Meeting   120   25
        The Sand Forest
        The Trolleycar
        The Face   123   203
        Satellite Factory
        Pomegranate
        Wild Plums
        Mistakes
        House of Water   126   135

    TRANSLATIONS
        Poems by Zbigniew Herbert
            (Tr. with Bogdana Carpenter)   128   141

REVIEWS
    Revalues   120   164
        The Blood of the Air,
            by Philip Lamantia
        The Wounded Mattress,
            by Sotère Torregian
        The Magellanic Clouds,
            by Diane Wakoski
        Poems for the Game of Silence 1960-1970,
            by Jerome Rothenberg
        The Stone Harp, by John Haines
        Regarding Wave, by Gary Snyder
    The Big Machine   125   166
        The History of the Growth of Heaven,
            by Andrei Codrescu
        Cochise, by Peter Wild
        The Buddhist Car and Other Characters,
            by James Schevill
        The Scrawny Sonnets and Other Narratives,
            by Robert Bagg
        Good News, by Greg Kuzma
        The Osprey Suicides,
            by Laurence Lieberman
        Hard Freight, by Charles Wright
        The Anonymous Lover, by John Logan

CARPENTER, MARGARET HALEY
    BOOKS REVIEWED
        Sara Teasdale: A Biography   97   392

CARPENTER, MAURICE
    BOOKS REVIEWED
        Gentle Exercise   79   106

CARPENTER, RHYS
    BOOKS REVIEWED
        The Tragedy of Etarre   1   131

CARPENTER, WILLIAM
    POEMS
        Night Fishing   138   259
        The Ice House   139   261

    BOOKS REVIEWED
        Rain   148   99

CARPER, THOMAS
    POEMS
        A Picture of the Reverend's Family
            with the Child of One   142   72
        A Conversation
        Daedalus Invents God
        Hercules' Descent into the Underworld
        The Monster in the Park   144   342
        Catching Fireflies   146   165
        Laundry at Night
        Creation
        The Beauty of Poetry   148   249

Oh Keep the Poet Hence
What People Make
Heavenly Park
The Abductors 150   137
The Attraction
Play on a French Beach
Burning Her Past
Nobody at Treblinka 151   493
At the Sistine Chapel:
    A View from the Floor 152   3
Fugue
The Resident Poet
On Sitting Down To Read
    the Dust Jacket Once Again
The Tranquil Life 154   277
Her Diamond Ring 156   133
A Guardian Tanya 156   192
Like the Spaniards 157   137
Even the Weariest River 158   14
Kollam 160   282
The Salvation of Faust 163   267
Sisyphus's Pet Rock

CARRALL, GODWIN TREZEVANT
POEMS
Your Voice 15   79

CARRERA ANDRADE, JORGE
POEMS
Ballot for Green 59   256
Movements of Nature
Clock
    (Tr. by Muna Lee)

ARTICLES
The New American and
    His Point of View Toward Poetry
    (Tr. by H. R. Hays)
    [Rubén Darío, Pablo Neruda] 62   88

BOOKS REVIEWED
Registro del Mundo 59   278
3 Spanish American Poets
    (With Carlos Pellicer
    and Pablo Neruda)
    (Tr. by Lloyd Mallan) 62   111
Secret Country
    (Tr. by Muna Lee) 70   159

CARRIER, CONSTANCE
POEMS
Theater 71   20
Death in the Afternoon 71   189
A Picnic in the Grove 73   327

BOOKS REVIEWED
The Middle Voice 86   295

CARRIER, WARREN
POEMS
Exile 83   189
Green I Walk 93   375

REVIEWS
Some Versions of Lorca 87   303
    The Gypsy Ballads of García Lorca
        (Tr. by Rolfe Humphries)
    The Selected Poems of...
        (Ed. by Francisco García Lorca
        and Donald M. Allen)
    The Poet in New York
        (Tr. by Ben Belitt)
    Ten Centuries of Spanish Poetry
        (Ed. by Eleanor Turnbull)
        [Angel del Río]
An "Agonist of the Intuition" 101   349
    Selected Poems of Pablo Neruda
        (Tr. and ed. by Ben Belitt)
    The Elementary Odes
        of Pablo Neruda
        (Tr. by Carlos Lozano)

BOOKS REVIEWED
Toward Montebello 109   118

CARRIGHAR, SALLY
ARTICLES
Correspondence: San Francisco's
    "Festival of Modern Poetry" 70   344

CARRINGTON, FITZ-ROY
BOOKS REVIEWED
The Quiet Hour (Ed.)   7   318

CARRINO, FRANK G.
BOOKS REVIEWED
The Gaucho Martín Fierro,
    by José Hernández
    (Tr. by C. E. Ward)
    (Ed. with Alberto J. Carlos) 113   338

CARRIÓN, ALEJANDRO
BOOKS REVIEWED
Five Young American Poets:
    Third Series, 1944
    (With Eve Merriam,
    John Frederick Nims, Jean Garrigue,
    and Tennessee Williams) 66   95

CARROLL, JAMES
BOOKS REVIEWED
Forbidden Disappointments 128   37

CARROLL, JIM
POEMS
The Distances 114   31

BOOKS REVIEWED
    Living at the Movies   125   162

CARROLL, PAUL
POEMS
    Un Voyage à Cythère   85   319
    Quomodo Sola Sedet Civitas   88   230
    Still Life: Tankard, Sun, and Avocado Plant   92   81
    The Cigar Store Indian's Gift to the Puritans   94   93

REVIEWS
    The Loyalties of Robinson Jeffers,
      by Radcliffe Squires   90   254
    The Looking Glass, by Isabella Gardner   101   215
    On Bear's Head, by Philip Whalen   117   338
    The Pleasures of Peace, by Kenneth Koch   119   104

BOOKS REVIEWED
    The Young American Poets (Ed.)   117   277
    Odes   118   169

CARRUTH, HAYDEN ["H. C."]
POEMS
    The University of Chicago   70   184
    Three Sonnets on the Necessity
      of Narrowly Escaping Death   71   244
    The Wreck of the Circus Train
    Men Leaning Forward
    Epithalamion
    Phylogenetic Meditation   73   208
    Renunciation   81   16
    Ends   82   11
    Directive
    Loss   85   1
    Inheritance
    Reflexive
    Under the Long Wind   85   311
    The Fat Lady   87   355
    I Also Love Thee Proserpine   89   362
    A Canon for Two Voices
    The Asylum   91   219
    Bedrock   93   357
    The Birth of Venus
    Depression
    The Street
    The Saving Way   96   335
    The Cheat
    Midsummer Letter   98   290
    Stanzas from the Reading Hour   101   17
    Spring Notes from Robin Hill   103   19
    The Smallish Son
    Contra Mortem   106   10
    Coming Down to the Desert
      at Lordsburg, N. M.   112   227
    The Cows at Night
    Dirge for Homecoming
    Sonnet ("Cry, crow...")

Fragments
    The Bearer   151   25
    Endnote   163   89
    The Heron   169   311
What Goes
    The Hyacinth Garden in Brooklyn   170   2
Nana
April Clean-Up
Stabat Mater

ARTICLES
    The Poet with Wounds [Harry Brown]   71   217
    Mr. Graham and the Dead Cigar
      [W. S. Graham, Randall Jarrell]   72   307
    Out of the Woods
      [New Criticism, William Elton]   73   151
    The Bollingen Award: What Is It?
      [Ezra Pound]   74   154
    The Anti-Poet All Told
      [Ezra Pound, Robert Hillyer]   74   274
    Malediction Against Radio Announcers   74   331
    Poet, Publisher, and the Tribal Chant   75   22
    The Editor [Response to symposium]   75   56
    The University and the Poet
      [Yvor Winters]   75   89
    Edwin Muir's Autobiography   87   50
    "To Fashion the Transitory"
      [Edwin Muir]   88   389
    Correspondence
      [Richard Murphy, Patrick Kavanagh]   102   62
    On a Picture of Ezra Pound   110   103
    "Islands Waited, Wait Still..."
      [Henry Rago]   115   130

REVIEWS
    Revaluation: Tradition and Development
      in English Poetry,
      by F. R. Leavis   72   41
    Three Academic Pieces, by Wallace Stevens   72   270
    Rage for Order, by Austin Warren   72   318
    Actfive and Other Poems,
      by Archibald MacLeish   73   287
    On the Limits of Poetry, by Allen Tate   74   54
    Yeats: The Man and the Masks,
      by Richard Ellmann   74   244
    Poets and Story-Tellers, by David Cecil   74   365
    Collected Poems, by Yvor Winters   82   151
    Dictionary of World Literature
      (Ed. by Joseph T. Shipley)   83   35
    The Collected Poems of Wallace Stevens   85   288
    Seven Books in Search of a Customer   86   168
      The Shield of Achilles and *Mountains,*
        by W. H. Auden
      Selected Poems, by Randall Jarrell
      The Center Is Everywhere,
        by E. L. Mayo
      The Salt Garden, by Howard Nemerov

The Scarecrow Christ and Other Poems,
  by Elder Olson
A Mantelpiece of Shells,
  by Ruthven Todd
An Autobiography, by Edwin Muir   87   50
The Persimmon Tree, by Peter Viereck   89 316
Great Praises, by Richard Eberhart   91   53
2,000 Poems, Mostly Good   91 124
  The Criterion Book
    of Modern American Verse
    (Ed. by W. H. Auden)
  The Mentor Book of Religious Verse
    (Ed. by Horace Gregory
    and Marya Zaturenska)
  The Silver Treasury of Light Verse
    (Ed. by Oscar Williams)
  Invitation to Poetry
    (Ed. by Lloyd Frankenberg)
  Fifteen Modern American Poets
    (Ed. by George P. Elliott)
  Poetry Now (Ed. by G. S. Fraser)
  New Lines (Ed. by Robert Conquest)
  Mavericks
    (Ed. by Howard Sergeant
    and Dannie Abse)
Four New Books   93 107
  A Crackling of Thorns,
    by John Hollander
  Overland to the Islands,
    by Denise Levertov
  In the Midnight Wood,
    by Cecil Hemley
  A Coney Island of the Mind,
    by Lawrence Ferlinghetti
Justine, by Lawrence Durrell   93 323
Three Poets   95 116
  Coming of Age: New and Selected Poems,
    by Babette Deutsch
  Heart's Needle, by W. D. Snodgrass
  A Bed of Strawberries, by Mary Phelps
A Reviewer's ABC: Collected Criticism
  of Conrad Aiken from 1916 to the Present
  (Ed. by Rufus A. Blanshard)   96 318
Collected Essays, by Allen Tate   99 123
Selected Poems, by Conrad Aiken   99 309
Imitations, by Robert Lowell   100   43
Further Unanswered Questions
  about Translating   100 198
  In the Stoneworks, by John Ciardi
  Dante's Purgatorio
    (Tr. by John Ciardi)
Problems of Maturity   101 205
  Come Dance with Kitty
    Stobling and Other Poems,
    by Patrick Kavanagh
  Selected Poems, by Francis Golffing
  Garland for the Winter Solstice,
    by Ruthven Todd

Waterlily Fire, by Muriel Rukeyser   101 358
Uses of Typology   101 424
  Selected Poems, by Anne Ridler
  Solstices, by Louis MacNeice
The Next Room of the Dream,
  by Howard Nemerov   102 389
Selected Poems, by Denis Devlin
  (Ed. by Allen Tate
  and Robert Penn Warren)   103 191
The Lordly Hudson, by Paul Goodman 104   44
A Peopled Landscape,
  by Charles Tomlinson   104 243
Poetic Mythology   104 369
  Shelburne Essays on American Literature,
    by Paul Elmer More
    (Ed. by Daniel Aaron)
  The Widening Gyre, by Joseph Frank
  Fables of Identity:
    Studies in Poetic Mythology,
    by Northrop Frye
  To the Palace of Wisdom:
    Studies in Order and Energy
    from Dryden to Blake,
    by Martin Price
  The Artistic Transaction and Essays
    on Theory of Literature,
    by Eliseo Vivas
  What Is Poetry?
    by John Hall Wheelock
The Bat-Poet, by Randall Jarrell   105 194
O Taste and See, by Denise Levertov 105 259
Upon Which To Rejoice   106 239
  Collected Poems 1909-1962 and
    Knowledge and Experience
    in the Philosophy of F. H. Bradley,
    by T. S. Eliot
  Notes on Some Figures
    Behind T. S. Eliot,
    by Herbert Howarth
  [Mrs. Trollope]
Three Poets   106 309
  Change of Weather,
    by Winfield Townley Scott
  The Broken Ground,
    by Wendell Berry
  Simeon, by Donald Finkel
For the Union Dead, by Robert Lowell 106 358
On Yeats and Others   107 192
  Swan and Shadow:
    Yeats's Dialogue with History,
    by Thomas R. Whitaker
  Selected Letters of Robert Frost
    (Ed. by Lawrance Thompson)
  Rupert Brooke, by Christopher Hassall
  William Blake, Poet and Painter,
    by Jean H. Hagstrum
  Testimony: The United States (1885-1890),
    by Charles Reznikoff   107 396

About the House, by W. H. Auden   108   119
Necessities of Life, by Adrienne Rich   109   267
Opposite Methods   109   400
  Weathers and Edges, by Philip Booth
  Staying Alive, by David Wagoner
Birds, by St.-John Perse
  (Tr. by Robert Fitzgerald)   110   184
All, The Collected Short Poems, 1956-1964,
  by Louis Zukofsky   110   420
Four Poets   111   43
  Nikal Seyn and Decoration Day,
    by Louis Coxe
    [John Nicholson]
  Planets, by Frederic Will
  An Upland Pasture,
    by Theodore Holmes
  Northfield Poems, by A. R. Ammons
Berryman's Sonnets, by John Berryman   112   119
Critic of the Month: I   112   418
  *O the Chimneys: Selected Poems,
  Including the Verse Play "Eli"*,
    by Nelly Sachs
  Poems and Antipoems, by Nicanor Parra
  Gallows Songs,
    by Christian Morgenstern
    (Tr. by W. D. Snodgrass
    and Lore Segal)
  The Lice, by W. S. Merwin
  Wodwo, by Ted Hughes
  The Light Around the Body,
    by Robert Bly
  The Blue Swallows,
    by Howard Nemerov
  The Hard Hours, by Anthony Hecht
  100 Poems, by Mark Van Doren
  New and Selected Poems,
    by Winfield Townley Scott
    (Ed. by George P. Elliott)
  Selected Poems: Summer Knowledge,
    by Delmore Schwartz
  Poems Written in Early Youth,
    by T. S. Eliot
  The Poems and Songs of Robert Burns
    (Ed. by James Kinsley)   114   191
  The Blue Estuaries: Poems 1923-1968,
    by Louise Bogan   114   330

BOOKS REVIEWED
  The Crow and the Heart   97   185
  Journey to a Known Place   101   209
  The Norfolk Poems of…   102   323
  A New Directions Reader
    (Ed. with J. Laughlin)   106   429
  Nothing for Tigers: Poems 1959-1964   107   253
  From Snow and Rock, from Chaos   124   103
  The Bloomingdale Papers   128   226
  The Selected Poetry of…
    (Ed. by Galway Kinnell)   149   94

*Tell Me Again How the White Heron Rises
  and Flies Across the Nacreous River
    at Twilight Toward the Distant Islands* 156 345
Collected Shorter Poems   162   224
Collected Longer Poems   167   343
*Scrambled Eggs & Whiskey:
  Poems 1991-1995*   170   162

ARTICLES ABOUT
  A Change of Editorship,
    by George Dillon   74   90
  The Poet and the University: A Reply,
    by Yvor Winters   75   170
  Correspondence from Richard Murphy
    [Patrick Kavanagh]   102   61
  Rev. of *Able Was I Ere I Saw Elba*,
    by Daniel Hoffman   132   170
  [Note]   156   242

CARRUTH, JOE-ANNE
[See MC LAUGHLIN, JOE-ANNE]

CARRY, MABEL D.
POEMS
  A Spring Song   6   74

CARSON, ANNE
BOOKS REVIEWED
  Plainwater: Essays and Poetry   168   281
  Glass, Irony and God

CARSON, ARTHUR
POEMS
  Bullfighter Story   86   92

CARSON, CIARÁN
POEMS
  Eesti   167   18
  Jacta Est Alea
  Vox et Praeterea Nihil

TRANSLATIONS
  Poem by Liam Ó Muirthile   167   69

BOOKS REVIEWED
  Belfast Confetti   160   34
  First Language   165   31

CARTER, DAVID
POEMS
  Seaward   38   22
  Downtown—New York

CARTER, JARED
POEMS
  Shaking the Peonies   137   272
  Ginseng
  Galleynipper   150   347

Improvisation	151	26
Soul Sleeping	153	157
Triage	154	140
For an Old Flame	156	69
Linen	165	155
Hawkmoth	166	85

BOOKS REVIEWED
Work, for the Night Is Coming	140	102

CARTER, LOUISE ADELE
POEMS
One Listens	6	237

CARTER, ROBERT A.
POEMS
The Minstrel in Search of a Legend	86	87

CARTER, THOMAS H.
BOOKS REVIEWED
Essays and Reviews	115	346

CARUS, HELENA
POEMS
Days After	25	304
Hymn of Primitive Women	37	133
Buddha, 480 B. C.	61	424
Norway	65	24

CARUS, PAUL
BOOKS REVIEWED
K'ung Fu Tze, a Dramatic Poem	6	205

CARVER, RAYMOND
POEMS
Happiness	145	251
For Tess		
Money		
My Crow		
Grief		
Shiftless	146	344
The Sensitive Girl		
Balsa Wood		
The Rest		
Mother	147	127
Mesopotamia		
Stupid		
The River	148	127
A Tall Order		
The Toes	151	27
The Net		
Margo	151	416
Wake Up	154	1
Another Mystery		
No Need		
Hummingbird		

ARTICLES
Comment [Ezra Pound]	151	204

BOOKS REVIEWED
Where Water Comes Together		
with Other Water	147	35
Ultramarine	150	226

CARY, LUCIAN
ARTICLES
Correspondence:
Mr. Cary Protests	6	104

REVIEWS
John M. Synge,		
by John Masefield	7	96

CASE, CHARLES ALBERT
ARTICLES
Correspondence:
The Allied Arts Again	19	169

ARTICLES ABOUT
Poetry and the Allied Arts,		
by Harriet Monroe	19	31

CASEMENT, ROGER
ARTICLES ABOUT
Correspondence
from Padraic Colum	8	268

CASEY, KATE
POEMS
Ode ("The quanta killed...")	95	22
In *Poems*		

CASEY, MICHAEL
ARTICLES ABOUT
Waking Up Over the *Aeneid,*		
by Paul Breslin	143	347

CASPER, LEONARD
ARTICLES
Apprenticed in Provence		
[Arnaut Daniel, Ezra Pound,		
Bertrans de Born]	81	203

REVIEWS
The City of Discontent,		
by Mark Harris		
[Vachel Lindsay]	82	355

BOOKS REVIEWED
Robert Penn Warren:		
The Dark and Bloody Ground	99	56

CASSIDY, INA SIZER
TRANSLATIONS
Translations from the Navajo	43	119
The Maid Who Became a Bear		
Reared Within the Mountains		

Song of the Mountain Sheep
Song of the Sun
Farewell of the Prophet
   (With Henry Tracy)
In the Valley of Nar-Sus-Sa

CASSIN, MAXINE
BOOKS REVIEWED
Nine by Three
   (With Robert Beum
   and Felix Stefanile)   96   375
A Touch of Recognition   102   49

CASSITY, TURNER
POEMS
Chronology   86   275
Earrings for the Virgin
The Quarter   89   361
Lotteria, Lotteria   91   306
Out of the Pit
The Mounted Bell
Astrology   94   34
Haitian Endymion
The Coast at Grand Isle
The Lumber Baron
The Flying Dutchman   96   28
Congo Colloquy
Woman
Johannesburg Requiem   97   290
Calvin in the Casino   99   281
Technique on the Firing Line
Marchen
A Clock with a Mirror Face,
   Presented to a Lady
Aubade
Catechism for Cape Malays   102   74
A Message from Mother Goddam
Meditation Under a Pith Helmet
The Shropshire Lad in Limehouse
Junker-Lied
In the Western Province
A Serenade for the Vicereine   104   346
Hotel des Indes
East Side, West Side
Any Year at Bad Irgendwo
Leda of the Grosse Freiheit
The Gardens of Proserpine
Period Piece   106   213
Love in Cincinnati
Pastoral with Ski-Lift
The Complaint of the Café Musicians
Nocturne   107   238
Grace at the Atlanta Fox
A Song in Subtitles
Epigoni Go French Line
By the Waters of Lexington Avenue   111   237
Cartography Is an Inexact Science

What the Sirens Sang   112   248
De Lesseps Go Home
A Ballade for Mr. Rhodes
Eva Beatified   114   183
The Condemned of Belgrano
Mascots
Pacelli and the Ethiop
Plot for a Guianese Operetta
The Airship Boys in Africa   116   211
Scenes from Alexander Raymond, or,
   The Return of Ming the Merciless   118   276
City of the Angels   120   282
The Love Life of Captain Hook   123   344
Postcard from a Cruise
Phantoms
A Dialogue with the Bride of Godzilla
Friendship of Fools
Plaza with a Cathedral
Cendrillon   126   74
Mélisande des Cheveux en Brosse
In the Kingdom of Jerusalem   127   342
Our Lady's Juggler
Favors
I the Swineherd
Morning on the Dodecanese Boulevard
Off Duty
A Walk with a Zombie
The Strange Case
   of Dr. Jekyll and Dr. Jekyll   131   136
Two Are Four
The Space Between the Andirons
Ghosts   138   197
Why Fortune Is the Empress
   of the World   146   161
Imputations
The Aswan Rowing Club
The Autoscopic Experience   148   205
Inducted
Prometheus in Polynesia   151   29
The Last Tauber-Lied   152   18
Persistence of Memory
Other-Directed
Monumental Is More Than
   a Question of Scale   159   209
At the Palace of Fine Arts
Meaner Than a Junkyard Dog;
   or, Turner's Evil Twin
Red Rust in the Sunset   162   265
Horizons and Myopia
A Word from Isobel   165   281
Christ of the Andes   166   79
Ex Machina   170   286

ARTICLES
Report from Goli
   [N. P. Van Wyk Louw,
   Elisabeth Eybers]   95   242

Down There on a Visit:
  Poetry in the Netherlands
  [Remco Campert, Gerrit Kouwenaar,
  Hugo Claus, Simon Vestdijk] 102 38
Correspondence 120 361
Comment 151 219

REVIEWS
Five Poets 103 192
  Quantities, by Richard Howard
  Views of Jeopardy, by Jack Gilbert
  A World, by William Burford
  Sonnet Variations,
    by Peyton Houston
  Arrivals and Departures,
    by Charles Gullans
  The Collected Poems of James Agee
  (Ed. by Robert Fitzgerald) 114 409

BOOKS REVIEWED
  Watchboy, What of the Night? 109 395
  Steeplejacks in Babel 125 44
  Hurricane Lamp 149 168
  Between the Chains 160 94

CASTAN, FRAN
POEMS
  First Month's Blessing 168 222

CASTLEMAN, MARIAN
ARTICLES
  Correspondence
  [Thomas Hornsby Ferril,
  John Ciardi] 65 108

REVIEWS
  The Poetry of Dorothy Wordsworth
  (Ed. by Hyman Eigerman) 57 280
  The New Zealand Group 59 343
    Recent Poems, by Allen Curnow,
    A. R. D. Fairburn, Denis Glover,
    and R. A. K. Mason
    Island and Time, by Allen Curnow
    Cold Tongue, by Denis Glover
  Civilian Singers 60 344
    Another England,
      by Dilys Bennett Laing
    Beyond This Wall,
      by John Robert Quinn
    Boy at Dusk and Other Poems,
      by Ralph Friedrich
    The Savage Century,
      by Charles Norman
    Time and Love, by Dorothy Dow
  Satires and Lyrics 61 456
    Paper Faces, by Nelson Del Bittner
    Open Letter, by Katherine M. Forkin
  Tenor of a Decade 63 223

American Decade
  (Ed. by Tom Boggs)
American Writing 1942
  (Ed. by Alan Swallow)
Supper Music 64 231
  Morning in Iowa, by Robert Nathan
  Trial by Time,
    by Thomas Hornsby Ferril
  Delay Is the Song,
    by Rosamond Haas
  Poems, by Dunstan Thompson 65 47

ARTICLES ABOUT
  Correspondence from John Ciardi 64 349
  Correspondence
    from Thomas Hornsby Ferril 64 351

CASWELL, DONALD
POEMS
  How It Works 167 332

CATEL, JEAN
POEMS
  Images Vaines 15 306

ARTICLES
  Correspondence: A Paris Letter
  [Guy Lavaud, Paul Moraud,
  Vincent Muselli] 16 343
  Correspondence: A Letter from Paris
  [Pierre Camo, Paul Valéry,
  George Duhamel, Stéphane Mallarmé,
  Jean Cocteau] 18 168
  Correspondence:
    Professor Phelps and Rostand 18 232
  Correspondence: A Letter from Paris
  [Jean Cocteau, Paul Valéry,
  Charles Vildrac] 19 229
  Correspondence: Paris Notes
  [Jean Cocteau, Paul Valéry] 20 287
  Literature of Repose
  [Paul Valéry] 23 96
  As It Is in Paris
  [Paul Valéry, Maurice Barrès,
  Jean Cocteau] 25 268
  The Poets Paris Is Reading
  [Max Jacob, Patrice de la Tour du Pin,
  Paul Eluard, Pierre Emmanuel] 67 39

ARTICLES ABOUT
  The American Image,
    by Henry B. Fuller 15 327
  Discovered in Paris,
    by Harriet Monroe 16 148

CATHER, WILLA
BOOKS REVIEWED
  April Twilights and Other Poems 22 221

CATHERON, LORRAINE
POEMS
Portrait—James Joyce   61   599
Bearings

CATTAFI, BARTOLO
POEMS
Mio amore non credere/
    My Love, Don't Believe   155   52
Questi piccoli uccelli/These Little Birds
Nella macchia mediterranea/
    In the Mediterranean Stain
    (Tr. by Dana Gioia)

CATULLUS, GAIUS VALERIUS
POEMS
Three from Gaius Valerius Catullus   94   148
    ("Whom do I give my...")
    ("Sparrow, my girl's pleasure...")
    ("Lament, o graces of Venus...")
        (Tr. by Celia and Louis Zukofsky)
Versions of Catullus
    (Tr. by Celia and Louis Zukofsky)   105   155
Peliaco Quondam
    (Tr. by Celia and Louis Zukofsky)   114   219
Ten Poems   128   125
    ("Greetings, girl!...")
    ("Lesbia, in the good old days...")
    ("Through many races...")
    ("Serving-boy, bring me...")
    ("You ask me, Lesbia...")
    ("To me he's on a level...")
    ("Catullus, you wretch...")
    ("O Sirmio, almost-island...")
    ("Fabullus, you'll have...")
    ("Flavius, you'd tell Catullus...")
        (Tr. by Martha Hollander)

BOOKS REVIEWED
The Poems of Catullus
    (Tr. by Horace Gregory)   39   93
Gaius Valerius Catullus,
    The Complete Poetry
    (Tr. by Frank O. Copley)   94   62
Poems
    (Tr. by Frederic Raphael
    and Kenneth McLeish)   136   40

ARTICLES ABOUT
Rev. of Collected Poems
    and The Man in the Wall,
    by James Laughlin   165   289

CAUDWELL, CHRISTOPHER
BOOKS REVIEWED
Illusion and Reality:
    A Study of the Sources of Poetry   53   40

CAUGHEY, M. L.
POEMS
Men Praise Mountains   35   127

CAUKIN, HELEN FERGUSON
BOOKS REVIEWED
American Writing: 1944
    (Ed. with Alan Swallow)   68   106

CAUSLEY, CHARLES
BOOKS REVIEWED
Survivor's Leave   83   343
Union Street   95   248
Collected Poems 1951-1975   129   233
Secret Destinations: Selected Poems 1977-1988 158   280

CAVAFIS, C. P.
[See C. P. CAVAFY]

CAVAFY, C(ONSTANTINE) P.
[C. P. CAVAFIS]
POEMS
Footfalls
    (Tr. by Andre Michalopoulos)   70   132
[Supplication]   98   30
[Anna Dalassené]
One of Their Gods
Dionysus and His Crew
Tomb of Iases
In the Month of Athyr
In a Famous Greek Colony, 200 B.C.
Perilous Things
Myres: Alexandria, A.D. 340
Aemilianus Monae Alexandrian,
    A.D. 628-655
    (Tr. by Rae Dalven)
The Pawn   120   257
The Mimiambi of Herodas
The Enemies
    (Tr. by Rae Dalven)
The Footsteps   120   266
The Ides of March
Theodotos
    (Tr. by Edmund Keeley
    and Philip Sherrard)

BOOKS REVIEWED
The Poems of...
    (Tr. by John Mavrogordato)   81   383
The Complete Poems of...
    (Tr. by Rae Dalven)   101   283

ARTICLES ABOUT
Cavafis and the Permanence
    of Greek History,
    by Edouard Roditi   81   389
Letter from Athens,
    by Vassilis Vassilikos   105   60

Rev. of *Modern Greek Poetry*
(Tr. and ed. by Rae Dalven)   123   34
Memorial Tribute,
by Rachel Hadas
[James Merrill]   166   334

CAVALCANTI, GUIDO
BOOKS REVIEWED
Guido Cavalcanti: Rime
(Ed. by Ezra Pound)   41   336

CAVALIERO, GLEN
BOOKS REVIEWED
The Ancient People   126   103

CAVALLI, PATRIZIA
POEMS
[*Qualcuno mi ha detto*]/
[*Someone told me*]   155   134
[*All'ombra di una metafora*]/
[*In the shadow of a metaphor*]
[*Eternità e morte insieme mi minacciano*]/
[*Together eternity and death threaten me*]
[*To simulate the burning of the heart*]
[*This time I won't permit the blue*]
[*Now that time seems all mine*]
(Tr. by Judith Baumel)

CAVIN, MIRIAM
POEMS
Wondering   30   260
Dirge

CAWEIN, MADISON
POEMS
Waste Land   1   104
My Lady of the Beeches
The Old Home   3   17
The Troubadour   5   149
The Wood Brook   8   134
The Dead Child

TRANSLATIONS
Poem by Konrad Ferdinand Meyer   8   135

BOOKS REVIEWED
Minions of the Moon   3   146
The Republic

ARTICLES ABOUT
The Death of Madison Cawein   5   195
[Note on *The Dead Child*]   8   329

CAYROL, JEAN
ARTICLES ABOUT
Marseille Letter,
by Jean Rivier   60   269

CECIL, [LORD] DAVID
BOOKS REVIEWED
Poets and Story-Tellers   74   365
Modern Verse in English, 1900-1950
(Ed. with Allen Tate)   96   122
Visionary and Dreamer
[Samuel Palmer,
Edward Burne-Jones]   118   343

CECIL, RICHARD
POEMS
The Architect of Glass Houses   124   74
True Sailing   127   73
Classical German Education
Elegy in a Pet Cemetery   144   343
Ballad of Dead Actresses   149   24
The Siren

CECIL, ROBERT
POEMS
Two Poems of Parting   69   68
("When the city changes...")
("When the train draws from...")

BOOKS REVIEWED
Time and Other Poems   89   45

CELA, CAMILO JOSÉ
[See JOSÉ CELA, CAMILO]

CELAC, SERGIU
TRANSLATIONS
Poems by Daniela Crăsnaru
(Tr. with Adam J. Sorkin)   159   18

CELAKOVSKY,
FRANTISEK LADISLAV
ARTICLES ABOUT
The Spirit of Czech Poetry,
by F. C. Weiskopf   55   200

CELAN, PAUL
POEMS
Homecoming   119   134
Below
Flower
Language Mesh
Night
All Souls
Draft of a Landscape
An Eye, Open
Radix, Matrix
Leap-Centuries
Think of It
(Tr. by Michael Hamburger)

ARTICLES ABOUT
    German Lyric Poetry Since 1945,
       by Hans Egon Holthusen
       (Tr. by Herman Salinger)   88   257

CENDRARS, BLAISE
  BOOKS REVIEWED
    Panama, or the Adventures
       of My Seven Uncles
       (Tr. by John Dos Passos)   39   224
    Selected Writings
       (Ed. by Walter Albert)   111   124

  ARTICLES ABOUT
    The Disciples of Gertrude Stein,
       by Richard Aldington   17   35

CENT, SION
  ARTICLES ABOUT
    Rev. of The Rent That's Due to Love
       (Tr. by Gwyn Williams)
       [Welsh poetry]   77   351

CERAVOLO, JOSEPH
  BOOKS REVIEWED
    Fits of Dawn   110   105
    Spring in This World of Poor Mutts   115   189

CERELLI, CARMEN
  ARTICLES ABOUT
    Correspondence from Carl Sandburg   9   218

CERVO, NATHAN
  POEMS
    The Caravan   114   371

CÉSAIRE, AIMÉ
  BOOKS REVIEWED
    State of the Union
       (Tr. by Clayton Eshleman
       and Denis Kelly)   112   56

CEYLON, S. R.
  BOOKS REVIEWED
    The Dusk Bazaar   46   53

CÉZANNE, PAUL
  ARTICLES ABOUT
    Rev. of Dans le leurre du seuil,
       by Yves Bonnefoy   128   163

CHADWICK, J. C.
  POEMS
    November Sun   7   80

CHAFFEY, HAROLD LELAND
  BOOKS REVIEWED
    Dust and Spray   30   233

CHAGALL, MARC
  ARTICLES ABOUT
    The Poetry of Robert Marteau,
       by Anne Winters   134   46

CHAIGNE, LOUIS
  ARTICLES ABOUT
    French Poetry and the Revival
       of Mysticism, by Eugene Jolas   56   264

CHAKRAVARTY, AMIYA
  POEMS
    The Traveler   93   221

  ARTICLES ABOUT
    [Note]   84   119

CHAMBERLAIN, BRENDA
  POEMS
    For Alun Lewis   66   303
    Midnight Mass   67   137

CHAMBERS, HENRY T.
  BOOKS REVIEWED
    Young Man's Country   46   53

CHAMBERS, R. W.
  BOOKS REVIEWED
    Form and Style in Poetry,
       by W. P. Ker (Ed.)   34   161

CHAMBERS, WHITTAKER
  POEMS
    October 21st, 1926   37   258

CHAMPION, MARTHA
  POEMS
    Poem ("There are places...")   37   265

  BOOKS REVIEWED
    Hellenic   43   225

CHANDLER, TOM
  POEMS
    Average Masterpiece   166   257
    Selling Door to Door

CHANDLER, W. K.
  BOOKS REVIEWED
    Approaches to Poetry (With Walter Blair) 84   43

CHANDRA, G. S. SHARAT
  POEMS
    I Feel Let Down   113   399
    Second Journey   119   65
    Of My 33rd Birthday
    The Woman in the Revolving Door   121   208
    Peasants Waiting for Rain   154   264

CHANG, DIANA
POEMS
Mood   69   74
At the Window
Knowing What Desires
  We Have Had

REVIEWS
Pakeha Poetry   81   335
  Mine Eyes Dazzle,
    by Alistair Campbell
  The Falcon Mask,
    by Hubert Witheford
  Roughshod Among the Lilies,
    by Louis Johnson
  The Bright Sea,
    by Pat Wilson

CHANG CHI
POEMS
Night Near the Maple Bridge
  (Tr. by Helen Burwell Chapin)   46   12

CHANG PENG CHUN
ARTICLES ABOUT
Correspondence
  from Dorothy Dudley   20   53

CHANG YIN-NAN
BOOKS REVIEWED
Poems by Wang Wêi
  (Tr. with Lewis C. Walmsley)   96   309

CHANNING, ANNE
[(MRS.) FAIRFIELD PORTER]
POEMS
Five Songs of Growth   45   16
  The Mother
  Wife of Time
  Early Respite
  Conspiracy
  Evening Song
In a Distant Suburb   51   256
That Is She

REVIEWS
Winter-Burning,
  by Lindley Williams Hubbell   52   354

CHAO TZE-CHIANG
TRANSLATIONS
Poems by Tu Fu   90   28

CHAPIN, HELEN BURWELL
POEMS
Two Sketches of Today   46   20
  T'ien-Lung Shan in May
  The Forbidden City

TRANSLATIONS
Poems by Ssu Wen-Ming, Lu Lun,
  Chang Chi, and Yu Wu-Ling   46   11
Poem by Fan Yun   46   310

BOOKS REVIEWED
Echoes   56   282

CHAPIN, HENRY
BOOKS REVIEWED
Leifsaga: A Narrative Poem
  of the Norse Discoveries of America   47   287
To the End of West   120   235

CHAPIN, KATHERINE GARRISON
[KATHERINE BIDDLE]
POEMS
Maya Sculpture   41   139
At Stonehenge   44   13
Assurances   47   318
  Sixth Sense
  Moon Shadow
  At Gettysburg
  Monument
Interval of Peace   59   204
Holiday 1941
Pastorale
Evening
This Lonely Light
Butterflies   92   77
Late Song

TRANSLATIONS
Poem by Gabriela Mistral   59   123

ARTICLES
The Quality of Poetry   59   90
T. S. Eliot at the National Gallery   70   328

REVIEWS
The Substance That Is Poetry,
  by Robert P. Tristram Coffin   61   636
Le Cahiers de la Pléiade
  (Ed. by Jean Paulhan)
  [St.-John Perse, Paul Claudel, Allen
  Tate, Valery Larbaud, Denis Devlin,
  Gabriel Bournure, Roger Caillois]   79   43
Anthologie de la Poésie Américaine
  (Ed. by Alain Bosquet)   89   257

BOOKS REVIEWED
Outside of the World   40   168
Time Has No Shadow   50   231
Plain-Chant for America   60   105
The Other Journey   97   185

ARTICLES ABOUT
[Note on Lament for the Stolen,
  by Genevieve Taggard]   53   286

CHAPLIN, RALPH
BOOKS REVIEWED
  Bars and Shadows — The Prison Poems   20   276

CHAPMAN, ARTHUR
BOOKS REVIEWED
  Out Where the West Begins   12   158

CHAPMAN, GEORGE
BOOKS REVIEWED
  Chapman's Homer:
    The Iliad (I) and The Odyssey (II)
    (Ed. by Allardyce Nicoll)   91   60

CHAPMAN, RAYNOR D.
POEMS
  Sonnet in a Cemetery   64   20
  City Spring
  Moon Deluge
  Familiarity

CHAPMAN, ROBIN S.
POEMS
  Catching Rabbits   154   275

CHAPPELL, FRED
POEMS
  Narcissus and Echo   142   320
  Message

CHAPSON, JIM
BOOKS REVIEWED
  Blue House:
    Poems in the Chinese Manner
    (With James Liddy and Thomas Hill)   114   251

CHAR, RENÉ
POEMS
  Les Transparents
    (Tr. by Richard Wilbur)   87   316
  The Inventors   89   333
  The Windowpane
  Put on Guard
  Anoukis and Later Jeanne
  The Slapped Adolescent
  Coral (Tr. by Charles Guenther)
  Companions in the Garden
    (Tr. by Charles Guenther)   94   37
  Chanson des Etages   104   278
  Post-Scriptum à "Lettera Amorosa"
  Sept Parcelles de Luberon
  Les Parages d'Alsace
    (Tr. by Wallace Fowlie)

ARTICLES ABOUT
  A Note on René Char,
    by Wallace Fowlie   83   49
  French Chronicle: Recent Publications,
    by Wallace Fowlie   88   408

  French Chronicle: Recent Publications,
    by Wallace Fowlie   91   36
  Letters from the Midi,
    by Wallace Fowlie   100   258

CHARLES, MARY [Pseud.]
POEMS
  A Prayer for Respite   51   132
  A Wish in a Museum
  What the Gipsies Left   51   313

CHARQUES, R. D.
BOOKS REVIEWED
  Contemporary Literature
    and Social Revolution   44   231

CHARTERS, ANN
BOOKS REVIEWED
  Olson/Melville:
    A Study in Affinity   116   110

CHARTERS, SAMUEL
BOOKS REVIEWED
  Days, or Days as Thoughts
    in a Season's Uncertainties   112   274
  Selected Poems, by Larry Eigner
    (Ed. with Andrea Wyatt)   126   172

CHARVAT, WILLIAM
ARTICLES ABOUT
  Rev. of English Institute Essays, 1949
    (Ed. by Alan S. Downer)   77   48

CHASE, M. M.
POEMS
  The Spiral Stair   47   310
  Who Has Not Dreamed?
  White
  Not Alone

**CHASE, POLLY
[POLLY BOYDEN]**
POEMS
  Firelight   25   17
  Bliss
  Little Things
  Stillborn
  Hands on a Card-Table
  Poems from a Suburb   28   14
    Suburban Idyl
    Broadway at Night
    Autumn Walk
    Palliative
    Married
    Discovery
    Encounter
  Contacts   30   183
    Form
    In a Museum

Dirge
Impact
Finalities
Remedy for Hurt
Fall of Leaves
Fall of Snow
Sunlit Labyrinth   35   138
First Snowfall
Respite
Narcissus Importuned
Branch of Willow
Inertia
Death Sentence
Sunday Afternoon: The Bronx   60   142
Gulls' Eggs in Eelgrass

BOOKS REVIEWED
Toward Equilibrium   36   223

CHASE, RICHARD
BOOKS REVIEWED
Leaves of Grass
   One Hundred Years After [Contrib.]
   (Ed. by Milton Hindus)   87   183

CHASE, RICHARD HARTLEY
BOOKS REVIEWED
A Canzonière   99   313

CHASIN, HELEN (S.)
POEMS
The Witch House at Salem: Winter   108   316
Leaving, or Being Left
An Empty Bed at the Asylum
Andalusia   113   387
The Poetess Ko Ogimi   116   78
June   120   133
Perspective
Poem Incorporating a Phrase from a Poem
   by Tom Lux Beginning with
   a Random Phrase from Coleridge   132   90
Changes   133   77
Before the Power Failure
   New York, July 1977

BOOKS REVIEWED
Coming Close and Other Poems   113   262

CHATAIN, ROBERT
POEMS
From *Years*   113   151
Curare   118   91
Map   118   313
The Crawl
Sane
Age of Reptiles   121   271
The Jewels
Nobody

Retraction   123   149
Connemara Wind Ode
World of Darkness
Curragh   134   131
Evasions of the Animal Hospital
Connemara Earth Ode

CHATARD, JEAN
POEMS
La Houle à Bout-Portant   116   374
Briser le Silence
Elans du Jour
Chaque Trace d'Envol
Oublier Tout
   (Tr. by Derk Wynand)

CHATTOPADHYAYA, H.
POEMS
Forgiveness   38   87

CHAUCER, GEOFFREY
ARTICLES ABOUT
Chaucer and Langland,
   by Harriet Monroe   6   297
Rev. of *The Living Chaucer*,
   by Percy V. D. Shelly   59   226

CHAVEZ, [FRAY] ANGELICO
BOOKS REVIEWED
Clothed with the Sun   55   338

CHEAVASA, MOIREEN FOX A
[See A CHEAVASA,
MOIREEN FOX]

CHEKHOV, ANTON
ARTICLES ABOUT
Rev. of *Grief*, by Stephen Berg   129   285

CHEN, KWEI
[See KWEI CHEN]

CHENEY, ANNE CLEVELAND
BOOKS REVIEWED
The Nameless One   8   264

CHENG CHI-YU
BOOKS REVIEWED
New China in Verse   65   222

CHENG HAO
POEMS
The Sudden Coming of Spring
   (Tr. by Louise S. Hammond)   20   253

CH'ENG HSI
BOOKS REVIEWED
An Anthology of Chinese Verse: Han, Wei,
   Chin, and the Northern Southern Dynasties
   (Tr. with J. D. Frodsham)   112   347

CHENG YU SUN
TRANSLATIONS
  Poems by Li Po   28   256

CH'EN HUNG-SHOU
POEMS
  On Seeing the Portrait
    of a Beautiful Concubine
    (Tr. by Amy Lowell
    and Florence Ayscough)   13   234

CH'EN TZU-ANG
POEMS
  In a Jade Cup
    (Tr. by Arthur Waley)   11   199

CHERCHI, PAOLO
ARTICLES
  Some Notes on Post-War Italian Poetry
    (With Joseph Parisi)
    [Sandro Penna, Vittorio Sereni,
    Mario Luzi, Giorgio Caproni,
    Edoardo Sanguineti, Andrea Zanzotto]   155   161

CHERRY, NATALIE
ARTICLES ABOUT
  Poetry Magazine on the Air   87   377

CHESS, RICHARD
POEMS
  At the Rabbi's Study Group   160   24
  Growing Up in a Jewish Neighborhood

CHESTERTON, G. K.
BOOKS REVIEWED
  Poems   7   267

CHEW, SAMUEL C.
BOOKS REVIEWED
  Swinburne   34   294

CHEYNE, ELIZABETH GIBSON
POEMS
  Partings   2   128
  A Poet to His Poems   6   284

CHEYNEY, RALPH
BOOKS REVIEWED
  Touch and Go   30   228
  How to Profit from That Impulse
    (Ed. with Lucia Trent
    and Benjamin Musser)   34   56

CH'I, KAO
[See KAO CH'I]

CHI, LU
[See LU CHI]

CHIARI, JOSEPH
BOOKS REVIEWED
  The Poetic Drama
    of Paul Claudel   86   108

CHILDE, W(ILFRED) R(OWLAND)
BOOKS REVIEWED
  The Escaped Princess   10   44
  The Gothic Rose   25   340
  Ivory Palaces   33   168

CHILDRESS, WILLIAM
POEMS
  From The Soldiers: The Mission   100   363
  Shellshock
  The Addict   106   207
  For Weldon Kees   108   100

CHILTON, ELEANOR CARROLL
BOOKS REVIEWED
  The Garment of Praise:
    The Necessity for Poetry
    (With Herbert Agar)   34   161

CHINOL, ELIO
BOOKS REVIEWED
  Il Dramma Divino e il Dramma
    Umano nel Paradiso Perduto   93   404

CHISHOLM, HUGH
POEMS
  Dirge for the Day   69   318

BOOKS REVIEWED
  The Prodigal Never Returns   71   327
  Winds, by St.-John Perse (Tr.)   82   345

CHITWOOD, M. LOUISA
ARTICLES ABOUT
  Notes on Mid-Western Oblivion,
    by Pat Morrissette   34   346

CHITWOOD, MICHAEL
POEMS
  Basement Barber   162   32
  Who Knows?   163   260
  Church Piano   164   76
  What Day Is This?
  After the Missionaries   166   78
  Chalk   169   334

CHOCANO, JOSÉ SANTOS
[See SANTOS CHOCANO, JOSÉ]

CHONG, LYNN
POEMS
  Sestina for Two Images (Bombay)   125   144

CHOULIARAS, YIORGOS
POEMS
   The Signals   162   136
   Demetrius Phalereus
   Occupied City
     (Tr. with David Mason)

CHOWN, HAROLD MEREDITH
POEMS
   To the Great Wind   50   264
   Winter
   The Eyot
   Indian Summer
   War
   The Bay   68   308
   To My Daughter

CHOYCE, A. NEWBERRY
BOOKS REVIEWED
   Songs While Wandering   18   39

CHRASTA, V. JAMES
POEMS
   This Hill of Stones   50   318

CHRISTENSEN, PAUL
BOOKS REVIEWED
   Charles Olson: Call Him Ishmael   136   219

CHRISTIANSEN, MARY
POEMS
   Songs   75   333
     ("The orchard...")
     ("Socrates...")
     ("The figtree swells...")
     ("Mass on a disk...")
   Songs   81   170
     ("Behind the field...")
     ("As the wind climbs...")

CHRISTOPH, CHARLES DE GUIRE
POEMS
   Reflections   17   199
   Neighbor Moon
   Profile
   Old Places
   Thought of Women
   Herons
   Improvisation

CHRISTOPHER, NICHOLAS
POEMS
   After a Long Illness   163   222
   The Fire at the Foundling Hospital   164   331

BOOKS REVIEWED
   On Tour with Rita   143   163
   A Short History of the Island of Butterflies   149   168

   Desperate Characters   154   283
   In the Year of the Comet   161   99
   5° and Other Poems   167   156

CHRISTOPHERSEN, BILL
REVIEWS
   Short Reviews   170   347
     Colander, by Michael McFee
     Common Carnage, by Stephen Dobyns
     Birds of the Night Sky/Stars of the Field,
       by Pamela Gross
     Fate's Kite: Poems, 1991-1995,
       by Dave Smith
     Heavy Grace, by Robert Cording
     Resurrection, by Nicole Cooley

CHRISTOPHERSON, MERRILL
POEMS
   Three Waves   55   191

CHUBB, ELMER
ARTICLES
   Correspondence   32   173

CHUBB, THOMAS CALDECOT
POEMS
   Hills Ruddy with Sumach   39   20
   Turkey Gobbler Land   44   260
   Dark Wings in the Night   58   250

REVIEWS
   Dante in English Verse   43   229
     The Divine Comedy of Dante Alighieri
      (Tr. by Jefferson Butler Fletcher)
     The Divine Comedy of Dante Alighieri
      (Tr. by Melville Best Anderson)
     Dante's Inferno
      (Tr. by Laurence Binyon)
     The Paradise of Dante
      (Tr. by Geoffrey L. Bickersteth)

BOOKS REVIEWED
   Ships and Lovers   42   292
   A Time to Speak   63   226

CHUN, CHANG PENG
[See CHANG PENG CHUN]

CHURCH, PEGGY POND
POEMS
   Song for Hanging Out Clothes   29   254
   Escape
   Drought   35   297
   Under Green and Brown Hills   43   131
     For an Afternoon Before Easter
     Burros
     Winter Sketch
   The Unceasing Fountain   48   6
     Again the Flowering

After the Rain
The Humming-Birds Coming
A Prayer for Rain
Of Fragments that Remained

BOOKS REVIEWED
    Foretaste   44   340

CHURCH, RICHARD
POEMS
    Waiting   25   135
    The Inept   49   201

CHURCHILL, CHARLES
ARTICLES ABOUT
    The Poetry of Charles Churchill: Part I,
        by Yvor Winters   98   44
    The Poetry of Charles Churchill: Part II,
        by Yvor Winters   98   104

CIARDI, JOHN
POEMS
    Letter for Those Who Grew Up Together   55   69
    On a Photograph of a German Soldier
        Dead in Poland   56   182
    Hometown   59   20
    Massachusetts Bay
    Aubade   61   372
    Poem from a Hired Room
    Love Makes No Music
    Ballad of How Adam Saw It   62   26
    Night Mail
    Record Crowds at Beaches
    Poem for a Soldier's Girl
    Girls Going to Church
    Night Piece for My Twenty-Seventh Birthday   63   59
    Mission
    Night Celestial
    Reveille for My Twenty-Eighth Birthday   64   179
    Reflections While Oiling a Machine Gun
    Mission
    Vagary of the Simple Heart
    Monday Morning Reveille
    First Snow on an Airfield
    Summer Evening
    Reverie During Briefing   66   85
    Elegy for a Seaman
    Goodmorning with Light
    P-51
    Journal
    Poem for My Twenty-Ninth Birthday   67   192
    Hometown After a War   69   1
    Balancing Act
    Ode for the Burial of a Citizen
    Serenade in a Drugstore
    Poem for My Thirtieth Birthday
    Letter to Virginia Johnson   70   117
    To Judith   71   240

Three Eggs Up   74   16
Metropolitan Ice Co.
To Judith Asleep
Flowering Quince   81   18
Measurements   82   12
Elegy for Jog
Domesticity
Temptation   82   145
Elegy for Sandro   84   1
Sunday Morning
Thoughts on Looking into a Thicket   86   63
On Looking East to the Sea
    with a Sunset Behind Me
Elegy ("My father was born...")
Some Figures for Who I Am   89   171
S.P.Q.R. — A Letter from Rome   91   287
To Lucasta, About That War
Love Poem   97   232
Everywhere That Universe
The Bird in Whatever Name
Divorced, Husband Demolishes House
Dragons
Launcelot in Hell
Death's the Classic Look   101   18
Credibility
Fast as You Can Count to Ten
Censorship   132   101
The Lungfish   132   269
For Instance
Machine
No White Bird Sings   133   340
Apprehendee Then Exited Vee-Hicle
On the Patio
A Crate of Sterling Silver Loving Cups
Thursday Also Happens   137   71
Ward Three: Faith
Mutterings   141   5
Obsolescence   141   63
The Project
Habitat
Friends   143   130
Quirks
True or False
Fortieth Anniversary Poem
A Trenta-Sei of the Pleasure We Take
    in the Early Death of Keats   148   281
Elegy for a Cave Full of Bones   151   471

TRANSLATIONS
    Paradiso: Canto Five
        [With notes]   107   75

ARTICLES
    Correspondence
        [Marian Castleman,
        Thomas Hornsby Ferril]   64   349
    Correspondence
        [Robert Lowell]   72   261

Correspondence: Letter from Harvard
  [Kenneth Rexroth, Marianne Moore,
  Winfield Townley Scott]   74   112

REVIEWS
  Crusade, by Captain John Waller   68   349

BOOKS REVIEWED
  Homeward to America   56   337
  Other Skies   72   99
  Live Another Day   75   361
  Dante's Inferno (Tr.)   85   225
  As If: Poems New and Selected   88   267
  I Marry You   93   46
  How Does a Poem Mean?   96   122
  39 Poems   96   230
  In the Stoneworks   100   198
  Dante's Purgatorio (Tr.)
  The Man Who Sang the Sillies   101   208
  John Ciardi and W. D. Snodgrass
    [Recording]   101   275
  In Fact   102   250
  Person to Person   106   231
  This Strangest Everything   111   184
  The Little That Is All   126   219
  For Instance   140   102
  Selected Poems   146   167

ARTICLES ABOUT
  Correspondence
    from Marian Castleman   65   108
  Humanism as the Father Face,
    by Harvey Curtis Webster   70   146
  John Ciardi: The Many Lives of Poetry,
    by John Frederick Nims   148   283

CIMA, ANNALISA
POEMS
  Da Ipotesi d'amore/
    From Hypotheses on Love   155   108
    ("Maybe natural analogies...")
    ("Beloved lover...")
    ("After the last flowers...")
    ("It began as a game...")
    ("And when you...")
    ("Tell me do you too...")
    ("You too will age...")
      (Tr. by Jonathan Galassi)

CIOLKOWSKA, MURIEL
POEMS
  Tonight   18   80
  Snow
  Presence

ARTICLES
  Correspondence:
    Machinery in Art   16   347

CIORAN, E. M.
ARTICLES ABOUT
  Rev. of No Traveller,
    by Richard Howard   155   283

CITINO, DAVID
POEMS
  Charcoal Sketch of Aged Couple
    in Peasant Dress, Circa 1880   152   95
  In the Kitchen, He Recalls a Passage
    from Suetonius
  Salt   157   320
  Winter   159   125
  My Father Shaves
    with Occam's Razor   162   261
  Smelling the Snow   165   128

CITKOWITZ, ISRAEL
POEMS
  Notes on Seasons   44   312
    Autumn
    The Prodigals of Summer

CLAIBORNE, CORNELIA PHELPS
POEMS
  Departure, 1939   67   72

CLAIRMONT, ROBERT
BOOKS REVIEWED
  Quintillions   34   56

CLAMPITT, AMY
POEMS
  Balms   137   82
  The Hickory Grove   139   142
  Gooseberry Fool
  Thermopylae   143   331
  Homer, A. D. 1982
  Dodona: Asked of the Oracle
  Leaving Yánnina
  Medusa   145   331
  Perseus
  Athene
  Westward   151   30

BOOKS REVIEWED
  The Kingfisher   143   163
  What the Light Was Like   147   156
  Archaic Figure   150   162
  Westward   157   33
  A Silence Opens   165   158

ARTICLES ABOUT
  Rev. of White Paper:
    On Contemporary American Poetry,
    by J. D. McClatchy   156   297

CLANCY, JOSEPH P.
BOOKS REVIEWED
   Medieval Welsh Lyrics (Tr.)   108   343

CLAPP, FREDERICK MORTIMER
POEMS
   Meditations   28   262
     Cuneiform
     Domus Domini
     Harvesting Ice
     Awake Too Soon
   Misguided   52   265

BOOKS REVIEWED
   On the Overland and Other Poems   9   324
   Joshua Trees   24   336
   New Poems   50   226
   Said Before Sunset   52   297
   Against a Background
     on Fire 1938-1943   64   343
   The Seeming Real   73   360

CLARK, ALAN J.
BOOKS REVIEWED
   First Awakenings:
     The Early Poems of Laura Riding
     (Ed. with Elizabeth Friedmann
     and Robert Nye)   164   39

CLARK, AXTON
POEMS
   Plateau Poems   43   125
     Rain on the Mesa
     New Mexico Processional
   The Meadowed Year   47   16
     Autumn Sonnets
       ("We stand, the harvesters...")
       ("Festivity in the equinox...")
     Desert Song for Sleep
     Deep Sea
   Tahoe Remembrance   50   306

BOOKS REVIEWED
   The Single Glow   43   165

CLARK, BADGER
[See CLARK,
CHARLES BADGER]

CLARK, BENNETT CHAMP
ARTICLES ABOUT
   Poets and Politicians,
     by Coleman Rosenberger
     [Archibald MacLeish]   65   322

CLARK, (CHARLES) BADGER
POEMS
   High Chin Bob   10   225

ARTICLES
   Correspondence: Coals of Fire
     from the Cowboy Poet   11   109

BOOKS REVIEWED
   Sun and Saddle Leather   12   158
   Grass-Grown Trails

ARTICLES ABOUT
   Our Cowboy Poet,
     by Alice Corbin Henderson   10   319
   Correspondence
     from William H. Skaling   11   56

CLARK, DAVID RIDGLEY
POEMS
   Old Chapel:
     A Poem in Favor of the World   88   144
   Pinnacle   92   154

CLARK, EUNICE
POEMS
   None Following   46   144
     Ariadne
     The Gone

CLARK, JOHN PEPPER
BOOKS REVIEWED
   Song of a Goat   103   394

CLARK, JOHN W.
POEMS
   The Tower   99   296
   The Tiger

BOOKS REVIEWED
   All the Time in the Dark   102   49

CLARK, LEADIE M.
BOOKS REVIEWED
   Walt Whitman's Concept
     of the American Common Man   87   183

CLARK, LEONARD
BOOKS REVIEWED
   Poems   58   159

CLARK, LUELLA
ARTICLES ABOUT
   Notes on Mid-Western Oblivion,
     by Pat Morrissette   34   346

CLARK, PATRICIA
POEMS
   Betrayal   160   153

CLARK, SAVILLE

POEMS

At Memphis   40   85
City
The Son of Senisub

CLARK, STEPHEN [Pseud.]

POEMS

Summer Visitors   136   84

CLARK, TOM [THOMAS CLARK]

POEMS

Birthday   105   102
A Winter Day
Pass by Blue Stone
The Trouble
A Look   107   353
Flora
Poem for Tom Pickard
A Red Wild Flower in North Africa
A Lamp
To J
Poem ("To simply talk...")
A Book of Magic
Purgatory   109   363
Inferno
Poem ("Like musical instruments...")
Fig. 1   111   143
The Song
Sonnet ("Five a.m. on East Fourteenth...")
Death in the Family
The City
The Lake: Coda
January Second   113   86
Now She Dwells Here
The Greeks   114   319
The Power of the Watchman
     Continually Increases Tenfold
Crows

REVIEWS

All: The Collected Short Poems, 1923-1958,
    by Louis Zukofsky   107   55
The Gestures of Deliberation   107   121
    The Place Where I Am Standing,
       by Theodore Enslin
    Black and White,
       by Gilbert Sorrentino
    The Moth Poem,
       by Robin Blaser
    A Line of Poetry, a Row of Trees,
       by Ronald Johnson
    Hands Up! by Edward Dorn
Seven Poets   108   408
    The Black President and Other Plays,
       by James Schevill
    Thousand-Year-Old Fiancée
       and Other Poems,
       by Robert Sward

The Disappearance of Mountains,
    by Max Finstein
The Recluse and Other Poems,
    by Allen Grossman
Angels Fall They Are Towers,
    by Judson Crews
Movements/Sequences,
    by Kenneth Irby
Lectiones, by Robert Kelly
Loquitur, by Basil Bunting   109   110
A Poetry Chronicle   110   105
    Touch of the Marvelous,
       by Philip Lamantia
    & It Is a Song; Faces and Forms;
       and The Going-On Poem,
       by Anselm Hollo
    Turtle Three, by Ronald Bayes
    Bertha and Other Plays,
       by Kenneth Koch
    Provisional Measures, by Charles Stein
    Fits of Dawn, by Joseph Ceravolo
    Dancers, Buildings, and People in the Streets,
       by Edwin Denby
    [Stéphane Mallarmé,
       George Balanchine]   111   268

BOOKS REVIEWED

Stones   115   440
Air   119   224

CLARK, WALTER VAN TILBURG

POEMS

Kindred   43   70
    Strength of Autumn End
    Of the Broken Brotherhood
Love as of Hawks   44   311

CLARKE, AUSTIN

POEMS

Flight to Africa   100   83
Old-Fashioned Pilgrimage   109   101

REVIEWS

An Irish Chronicle   103   185
    The Irish Comic Tradition,
       by Vivien Mercier
    William Butler Yeats:
       The Poet as a Mythmaker,
       by Morton Irving Seiden
    Yeats's Vision and the Later Plays,
       by Helen Hennessy Vendler

BOOKS REVIEWED

Pilgrimage and Other Poems   36   226
The Collected Poems of...   49   288
Too Great a Vine   94   264
Late Poems   100   104
Later Poems   102   330

Flight to Africa   105   207
The Son of Learning:
   A Comedy in Three Acts   105   404
Old-Fashioned Pilgrimage
   and Other Poems   112   131
Collected Poems   128   46

ARTICLES ABOUT
  Letter from Dublin,
    by John Montague   90   310
  A Map of Contemporary Irish Poetry,
    by Dennis O'Driscoll   167   94

CLARKE, GEORGE HERBERT
BOOKS REVIEWED
  At the Shrine   6   98
  A Treasury of War Poetry (Ed.)   12   284
  A Treasury of War Poetry (Ed.)   18   106
  The New Treasury of War Poetry,
    1939 to 1943 (Ed.)   63   346

CLARKE, HARLOW
POEMS
  An Old Woman   19   247
  I Complain in Passing

CLAUDEL, PAUL
POEMS
  The Blessed Lady Who Listens   56   240
  Souvenir
    (Tr. by Eugene Jolas)
  Dialogue from *La Ville*   87   130
  Heat of the Sun
  From the *Art Poétique*
  From the *Magnificat*
  The Infant Jesus of Prague
  The Virgin at Noon
  Saint Joseph
  Parable of Animus and Anima
  December 25, 1886
    (Tr. by Wallace Fowlie)

BOOKS REVIEWED
  The Tidings Brought to Mary
    (Tr. by Louise Morgan Sill)   9   321
  Tête d'Or   17   222
  The Hostage
  Three Poems of the War
  A Poet Before the Cross
    (Tr. by Wallace Fowlie)   95   50

ARTICLES ABOUT
  Paul Claudel, by F. S. Flint   6   200
  Correspondence
    from Kate Neldram Buss   7   323
  French Poetry and
    the Revival of Mysticism,
    by Eugene Jolas   56   264

Rev. of *Exile and Other Poems,*
  by St.-John Perse
  (Tr. by Denis Devlin)   74   343
Rev. of *Le Cahiers de la Pléiade*
  (Ed. by Jean Paulhan)
  [St.-John Perse]   79   43
Paul Claudel 1868-1955   86   58
Rev. of *The Poetic Drama of Paul Claudel,*
  by Joseph Chiari   86   108
Claudel: The Tidings that Are the Poem,
  by Wallace Fowlie   87   169
Paris Letter, by Wallace Fowlie   96   371

CLAUS, HUGO
ARTICLES ABOUT
  Down There on a Visit:
    Poetry in the Netherlands,
    by Turner Cassity   102   38

CLAUSEN, CHRISTOPHER
BOOKS REVIEWED
  The Place of Poetry:
    Two Centuries of an Art in Crisis   141   237

CLAWSON, H. PHELPS
BOOKS REVIEWED
  Questings   30   293

CLAY, DAVID M.
POEMS
  Motion   61   374

CLAY, WILLY
POEMS
  In Our Museum   163   251
  On Me, the Imported Skies   165   95

CLEARY, SUZANNE
POEMS
  Listening to the Poem   153   343
  Girl in Mourning
  Stock Footage

CLEGHORN, SARAH N.
POEMS
  The Socialist's Marriage   17   256

CLEMENS, SAMUEL LANGHORNE
[See TWAIN, MARK]

CLEMENTS, ALBERT (EDWARD)
POEMS
  Stark Yield   43   24
    The Stately Mind So Armed
  Sky Amazement
  Unoccupied Room   48   312
  Hung Out by My Feet
    on the Sunday Clothes Line   71   74

CLEWELL, DAVID
POEMS
    Two Alley Songs
       for the Vegetable Man: St. Louis   145   224
    New Year's Eve Letter to Friends
    Back to Life   147   272
    From the Other Side,
       Houdini Tries To Come
       Through for Bess   153   278
    I Can't Believe the Face on Mars   160   272
    America's Bed-and-Breakfasts
    Enough   168   72

CLIFTON, HARRY
POEMS
    A Spider Dance on the Bahnhofstrasse   167   35
    MacNeice's London

CLIFTON, LUCILLE
BOOKS REVIEWED
    Good News About the Earth   122   105
    The Book of Light   163   336

CLINE, LEONARD
BOOKS REVIEWED
    After-Walker and Other Poems   37   161

CLOETE, STUART
BOOKS REVIEWED
    The Young Men and the Old   59   51

CLOSE, UPTON [Pseud.]
[See HALL, JOSEF
WASHINGTON]

CLOSS, AUGUST
BOOKS REVIEWED
    Medusa's Mirror:
       Studies in German Literature   91   403

CLOUD, JESS
BOOKS REVIEWED
    Figures in the Shadows   92   384

CLOUGH, ARTHUR HUGH
BOOKS REVIEWED
    The Poems of...
       (Ed. by H. F. Lowry,
       A. L. P. Norrington,
       and F. L. Mulhauser)   82   27

CLOUGH, WILSON
BOOKS REVIEWED
    Brief Oasis   86   295

CLOVER, SAMUEL TRAVERS
ARTICLES
    Comments about Eunice Tietjens   6   266

CLOWER, JEAN
POEMS
    The Woman   89   163
    Corpus Mundi   93   5
    Night Sounds
    Principles of Flight
    Beauty and the Beast
    Stance
    The Birth of Athena

REVIEWS
    Four Poets   97   185
       In an Iridescent Time,
         by Ruth Stone
       Out in the Open,
         by Katherine Hoskins
       The Other Journey,
         by Katherine Garrison Chapin
       The Crow and the Heart,
         by Hayden Carruth

COADY, MICHAEL
POEMS
    The Public Record   167   80
    Watching "The Dead"
       in the Living Room
    Sister Imelda Rising on the Last Day

COAN, CATHERINE
POEMS
    Hunger   168   21

COATES, ARCHIE AUSTIN
POEMS
    Lavender   11   73

BOOKS REVIEWED
    City Tides   14   277

COATES, C(ARROL) T(URNER)
POEMS
    Morning of the Storm   69   144
    The Gull   70   65

REVIEWS
    The Shores of Darkness,
       by Demetrios Capetanakis   75   180

COATES, FLORENCE EARLE
BOOKS REVIEWED
    The Unconquered Air and Other Poems   1   131

COATES, GRACE STONE
POEMS
    The Intruder   18   27
    The Old Freighter Comes Back in a Ford   28   319
    Berries Sweet and Bitter   35   198
    Child Thoughts

    Aurora Argent
    Promise
    Mutterkorn

BOOKS REVIEWED
    Mead and Mangel-Wurzel   41   102

COATSWORTH, ELIZABETH (J.)
POEMS
    Vermilion Seals   15   130
      Light of Love
      Belated
      Spring in China
      The Ghouls
      The Curse
      Love Tower
      The Gate
    Cockle Shells   20   128
      The Ship
      The Cows
      Stream
      Broadway
      At Versailles
    The Coming   23   258
    Demeter
    All Goats
    Charms   24   250
    As Ghosts   28   254
    The Engineers
    Under the Sangre di Cristo   30   12
      Easter Rains at Taos
      The Carter
      No Snake in Springtime
    Aux Tuilleries—1790   33   76
    The Empresses
    So Far Away
    Morning and Evening
      Were the First Day   43   28

BOOKS REVIEWED
    Fox Footprints   22   163
    Atlas and Beyond   25   224
    Compass Rose   35   52

COBB, ANN
BOOKS REVIEWED
    Kinfolks   22   160

COBLENTZ, CATHERINE CATE
POEMS
    Doubters   42   15
    Triumph   48   257

COBLENTZ, STANTON A.
BOOKS REVIEWED
    The Lone Adventurer   31   96
    The Music Makers (Ed.)   68   106

COBURN, KATHLEEN
BOOKS REVIEWED
    The Notebooks of Samuel Taylor Coleridge
      Vol. I (Ed.)   91   385
    The Notebooks of Samuel Taylor Coleridge
      Vol. II (Ed.)   102   128

COCCIMIGLIO, VIC
POEMS
    Night Prayer   163   335

COCHRAN, DOROTHY C.
POEMS
    Strength   21   309

COCHRAN, LEONARD
POEMS
    On the Continuity of Deer, Falcons,
      and Other Things   115   110

COCTEAU, JEAN
POEMS
    From The Crucifixion
      (Tr. by Wallace Fowlie)   84   80

BOOKS REVIEWED
    Poésies—1917-1920   20   103
    Carte Blanche

ARTICLES ABOUT
    The Disciples of Gertrude Stein,
      by Richard Aldington   17   35
    Paris Letter, by Jean Catel   18   168
    Paris Letter, by Jean Catel   19   229
    Paris Notes, by Jean Catel   20   287
    As It Is in Paris, by Jean Catel   25   268
    A Note on Jean Cocteau,
      by Wallace Fowlie   84   85
    French Chronicle: Recent Publications,
      by Wallace Fowlie   88   408
    French Chronicle: Recent Publications,
      by Wallace Fowlie   91   36
    Paris Letter, by Wallace Fowlie   96   371

CODE, GRANT H.
POEMS
    Sea Quatrains   19   23
    Expecting Violets   33   188
    The Two Commandments
    Poet   38   140
    Nocturne
    Brief Sequence   43   313

REVIEWS
    Studies in Spanish-
      American Literature,
      by Isaac Goldberg   16   280

BOOKS REVIEWED
    Poems, by Joan Murray (Ed.)   70 335

CODRESCU, ANDREI
POEMS
    The Best Side of Me   119 74
    An Accident
    Truth & Ruffles
    Thieves, Seasons

BOOKS REVIEWED
    The History of the Growth of Heaven   125 166

COESTER, ALFRED
BOOKS REVIEWED
    Anthology of the Modernista Movement
      in Spanish America (Ed.)   26 169

COFFEY, DAIRINE
BOOKS REVIEWED
    The Dark Tower: Nineteenth Century
      Narrative Poems (Ed.)   111 410

COFFIN, ROBERT P. TRISTRAM
POEMS
    Dark to Dark   37 190
      Dead of Night
      Day's Diamond
      The Hill Place
      The End of Light
    Ancient Patterns   39 196
      When Man Swung a Scythe
      Towers of Silence
    Messages   44 261

BOOKS REVIEWED
    Golden Falcon   34 356
    Ballads of Square-Toed Americans   44 334
    The Yoke of Thunder
    Strange Holiness   47 229
    Saltwater Farm   51 267
    Maine Ballads   53 92
    There Will Be Bread and Love   60 155
    The Substance That Is Poetry   61 636

ARTICLES ABOUT
    Poetry on Records, by Harry T. Moore   57 52
    Poetry on Records,
      by Harry Thornton Moore   58 345

COFFMAN, STANLEY K., JR.
BOOKS REVIEWED
    Imagism, a Chapter
      for the History of Modern Poetry   78 294

COGSWELL, FRED
BOOKS REVIEWED
    Immortal Plowman   119 356

COHEN, DAVID
BOOKS REVIEWED
    Breakfast Rum   103 324

COHEN, HELEN LOUISE
BOOKS REVIEWED
    Lyric Forms from France   22 107

COHEN, J. M.
BOOKS REVIEWED
    The Penguin Book
      of Spanish Verse (Ed.)   93 188

COHEN, LEONARD
BOOKS REVIEWED
    The Energy of Slaves   123 173

COHEN, PHILIP
POEMS
    The Miracle of Transubstantiation   162 140

COHEN, ROBERT
POEMS
    Law   114 179

REVIEWS
    Five Books   115 189
      Spring in This World
        of Poor Mutts,
        by Joseph Ceravolo
      Little Johnny's Confession,
        by Brian Patten
      Poems Read in the Spirit
        of Peace & Gladness
        (Ed. by Doug Palmer)
      The Residual Years: Poems 1934-1948,
        by William Everson/
        Brother Antoninus
      Night Flight to Hanoi:
        War Diary with Eleven Poems,
        by Daniel Berrigan

COHEN, ROBERT DAVID
POEMS
    With a Missing Text   108 311
    Untitled Poem ("The lion faced...")
    September   111 288

COHEN, YAKOV
POEMS
    Tirzah
      (Tr. by Ruth Finer Mintz)   92 203

COLAHAN, ELLWOOD
POEMS
    The Waterfall   6 225
    Hand on a Harp   16 20
    Pilgrimage

COLANDER, VALERIE NIEMAN
POEMS
   Persephone in Suburbia   156   332

COLBY, JOAN
POEMS
   1943   143   317
   Geography   146   31
   Kay
   Blue Moon of Ixtab
   Target Fixation   148   82
   The Art of Dying   152   259

COLCORD, LINCOLN
BOOKS REVIEWED
   Vision of War   7   209

COLE, HENRI
POEMS
   Father's Jewelry Box   146   327
   Cape Cod Elegy   149   133
   A Half-Life   152   255

REVIEWS
   Short Reviews   156   36
     Unfinished Painting,
      by Mary Jo Salter
     Take Heart, by Molly Peacock
     God Hunger,
      by Michael Ryan
     The Little Voices of the Pears,
      by Herbert Morris
     Falling Deeply into America,
      by Gregory Djanikian
     Nurture, by Maxine Kumin
   Brief Reviews   158   41
     Boy on the Step, by Stanley Plumly
     Io at Night, by Laurie Sheck
     Summers of Vietnam and Other Poems,
      by Mary Kinzie
      [Theodore Roethke, Louise Bogan]
     Old and New Poems,
      by Donald Hall
     The Continuous Life, by Mark Strand

BOOKS REVIEWED
   The Look of Things   168   107

COLE, JAMES
POEMS
   Piano Lesson   114   376
   Faculty Offices, Circa 1985   148   195

COLE, KEVIN
POEMS
   Return   146   28
   Autistic Boy   148   221
   Indoor Pool

COLE, PETER
TRANSLATIONS
   Poems by Shmuel HaNagid   167   194

COLE, RICHARD
POEMS
   My Wife Believes in Reincarnation   155   331

COLE, THOMAS
POEMS
   The Violent Weaklings   71   17
   La Grande Jatte: Sunday Afternoon   76   335
   Spider   122   70

ARTICLES
   Bunting: Formal Aspects   78   366
   Correspondence
     [Galway Kinnell, Audrey McGaffin]   93   120

REVIEWS
   In Unison, by H. G. Livezey   81   252
   Ceremony and Other Poems,
     by Richard Wilbur   82   37

BOOKS REVIEWED
   A World of Saints   89   244

COLE, WILLIAM
BOOKS REVIEWED
   D. H. Lawrence,
     Poems Selected for Young People (Ed.)   112   127

COLEMAN, ELLIOTT
POEMS
   Winter Starret   51   180
   Baltimore Sonnets   72   252
   Sonnets on the Agnus Dei   80   16
   Sonnets on the Roman Light   85   138
   Joyce's Grave   92   291
   The Garden of Delights   94   178
   Mockingbirds at Fort McHenry   102   243
   Solo   106   278
   From *Rose Demonics*   109   237
   From *Agony on the Chenango River*   113   18

REVIEWS
   Man Now, by William Burford   86   116
   New England Saints and *Richard Crashaw,*
     A Study in Baroque Sensibility,
     by Austin Warren   91   273
   The Atlantic Book of British
     and American Poetry
     (Ed. by Dame Edith Sitwell)   95   182
   Three Plays of Racine:
     Phaedra, Britannicus, Andromache
     (Tr. by George Dillon)   100   47
   Eugenio Montale: Selected Poems   109   268
   Selected Poems, New and Old, 1923-1966,
     by Robert Penn Warren   110   416

BOOKS REVIEWED

An American in Augustland   59   288
27 Night Sonnets   75   298
A Glass Darkly   84   173
33 Night Sonnets   86   295
The Interior Distance,
  by Georges Poulet (Tr.)   95   379
Mockingbirds at Fort McHenry   104   47
The Metamorphoses of the Circle,
  by Georges Poulet
  (Tr. with Carley Dawson)   112   41
Rose Demonics   114   40

COLERIDGE, SAMUEL TAYLOR
BOOKS REVIEWED
Biographia Literaria
  (With Wordsworth's Preface
  and Essays on Poetry)
  (Ed. by George Sampson)   18   167
The Rime of the Ancient Mariner   70   42
The Notebooks of... Vol. I
  (Ed. by Kathleen Coburn)   91   385
The Notebooks of... Vol. II
  (Ed. by Kathleen Coburn)   102   128

ARTICLES ABOUT
Rev. of *The Road to Xanadu,*
  by John Livingston Lowes   30   283
Rev. of *On Imagination:*
  Coleridge's Critical Theory,
  by I. A. Richards   47   52
On Musicality in Verse,
  by Kenneth Burke   57   31
Rev. of *Critics and Criticism,*
  Ancient and Modern
  (Ed. by R. S. Crane)   82   98
Rev. of *Coleridge, Opium, and Kubla Khan,*
  by Elisabeth Schneider   84   179
Rev. of *Coleridge,*
  by Walter Jackson Bate   113   262
Rev. of *Somewhere Is Such a Kingdom,*
  by Geoffrey Hill   128   232

COLES, DON
POEMS
Recluse   134   89

COLES, KATHARINE
POEMS
Elegy for a Dog Larger Than Life   163   141
The Moth   169   260

COLES, ROBERT
ARTICLES
Bringing Poems to Medical School
  Teaching: A Memoir
  [L. E. Sissman]   152   294

COLLIER, JOHN
BOOKS REVIEWED
Gemini   40   293

COLLIER, MICHAEL
POEMS
Italian Genesis   127   270
Flyer   145   8
Consider the Garden
Tonight   146   273
Boats Near Luxor
The Diver   149   212
A Private Place
Breughel   161   92

BOOKS REVIEWED
The Clasp and Other Poems   150   162
The Folded Heart   156   158
The Neighbor   168   160

COLLIN, W. E.
REVIEWS
The Wind Our Enemy,
  by Anne Marriott   58   53

COLLINS, BILLY
POEMS
Winter Syntax   152   21
Books
A History of Weather
Student of Clouds   153   24
First Reader   153   327
American Sonnet
The Death of Allegory   155   276
Forgetfulness
The Afterlife   156   267
Mappamundi
Consolation   158   189
The Art of Drowning   159   19
Fiftieth Birthday Eve   159   137
Dancing Toward Bethlehem
Paperwork   159   189
Tuesday, June 4th, 1991   160   215
Thesaurus   161   195
The End of the World   161   315
Pin-Up
Cheers
Osso Buco   162   272
While Eating a Pear
Medium   163   217
Dear Reader
Romanticism   163   252
Days   164   348
Deathbeds   165   29
Influence   165   215
The Best Cigarette
The Biography of a Cloud

Forsythia	166	5
In the Room of a Thousand Miles	166	249
What I Learned Today		
Marginalia	167	249
The Listener		
Splitting Wood		
The Birds of America	168	129
Morning		
Lines Lost Among Trees		
Driving Through the Light	168	329
The First Line of a Poem	169	313
My Life		
Lines Composed Three Thousand Miles		
Away From Tintern Abbey		
Serpentine	170	217

BOOKS REVIEWED

The Apple That Astonished Paris	153	229
Questions About Angels	159	282

COLLINS, H. P.
BOOKS REVIEWED

Modern Poetry	29	52

COLLINS, LOYD, JR.
POEMS

He Goes Running	43	316

COLLINS, MARTHA
POEMS

Several Things	137	135
The Story We Know		

BOOKS REVIEWED

The Catastrophe of Rainbows	148	342

ARTICLES ABOUT

Correspondence from Barri Armitage,		
Sharon Dunn, Celia Gilbert,		
Mark Jarman, and Lloyd Schwartz		
[Greg Kuzma]	149	180

COLLINS, MICHAEL
ARTICLES ABOUT

[Note]	108	118

COLLINSWORTH,
MATT DOUGLAS
POEMS

Buffalo	168	80
My Father's Son		
A Vision Down on Red River		
Amid the Steady Green		

COLMAN, MARY ELIZABETH
POEMS

Answer	58	21

COLOMBO, JOHN ROBERT
BOOKS REVIEWED

Poetry 64 — Poésie 64		
(Ed. with Jacques Godbout)	104	385
Neo Poems	119	356

COLONNA, FRANCESCO
ARTICLES ABOUT

Rev. of *The Dream of Poliphilo,*		
by Linda Fierz-David		
[*Hypnerotomachia*]	77	168

COLSON, ETHEL M.
BOOKS REVIEWED

How to Read Poetry	15	224

COLUM, MARY M.
ARTICLES

The Later Yeats	7	258

BOOKS REVIEWED

From These Roots: The Ideas		
That Have Made Modern Literature	52	86

COLUM, PADRAIC ["P. C."]
POEMS

Three Irish Spinning Songs	3	208
("The Lannan Shee...")		
("One came before her and said...")		
("There was an oul' trooper...")		
The Sea Bird to the Wave		
The Wayfarer	6	22
Polonius and the Ballad Singers	6	161
To Any Poet	14	186
The Bison		
The Vultures		
The Wanderers		
Swift's Pastoral	17	175
The Poplar	41	22
The Story of Lowry Maen	47	1
After Speaking of One Who Died		
a Long Time Ago	94	179
Raftery		
Commemorating Michael Collins	108	116
The Poet Captain:		
Thomas MacDonagh	110	251

ARTICLES

Correspondence:		
The Dead Irish Poets		
[Joseph Mary Plunkett,		
Thomas MacDonagh]	8	268
Poetry and Oratory		
[John Philpot Curran]	9	200
Notes on *The Story of Lowry Maen*	47	55
Note on Michael Collins	108	118
[Note]	108	144

REVIEWS

Chap Books and Broadsheets   6   252

   The Old Ships,
      by James Elroy Flecker
   Spring Morning,
      by Frances Cornford
   The Contemplative Quarry,
      by Anna Wickham
   Songs, by Edward Shanks
   A Broadside, by Jack B. Yeats

Collected Poems, by AE   7   154

Reveries over Childhood and Youth,
   by William Butler Yeats   11   51

Poems, by Rainer Maria Rilke
   (Tr. by Jessie Lemont)   14   168

BOOKS REVIEWED

   Wild Earth and Other Poems   10   105
   The Children's Homer   15   345
   The Boy Apprenticed to an Enchanter   18   49
   Anthology of Irish Verse (Ed.)   21   51
   Dramatic Legends and Other Poems   22   215
   Creatures   32   53
   Old Pastures   38   224
   Poems   40   283
   The Story of Lowry Maen   51   213
   Collected Poems   83   357
   The Vegetable Kingdom   86   172
   Collected Poems
   Ten Poems   94   264
   Roofs of Gold (Ed.)   106   429

ARTICLES ABOUT

   Status Rerum, by Ezra Pound   1   123
   Praise from Mr. Colum,
      by Harriet Monroe   6   91
   Correspondence from
      John Gould Fletcher   7   213

COMBS, HOMER C.
POEMS
   Song ("I would so sing to you...")   54   259

COMBS, TRAM
BOOKS REVIEWED
   Ceremonies in Mind   96   238

COMER, JOHN
POEMS
   Three Prison Poems   120   76
      ("Often I remember to look out...")
      ("The last man's blood seeps...")
      ("I am concerned to judge myself...")

COMFORT, ALEX
POEMS
   The Lovers   60   133
   Image of Venus   62   135

BOOKS REVIEWED
   New Road 1943
      (Ed. with John Bayliss)   64   46
   The Song of Lazarus   68   116

COMPANIOTTE, JOHN
POEMS
   Words I've Lost Forever   161   201
   Burial at Sea

COMPTON, JENNIFER
POEMS
   Amulet   169   17
   The Pursuit of Poetry

COMSTOCK, MARY EDGAR
POEMS
   The Dancer   26   257

CONANT, (ISABEL) FISKE
[ISABEL HOWE FISKE]
POEMS
   Somewhere in France   13   74
   The Unknown Soldier   23   313
   Eleanora Duse   24   253
   Little History   25   69
      Old Aunt
      Lonely Farm
      Frail Flame
      Mary of the City
      Consequence

BOOKS REVIEWED
   Gabriel, a Pageant   1   131
   Songs Before Birth   2   107
   Many Wings   25   340
   Puritan   28   174

CONFUCIUS
BOOKS REVIEWED
   Great Digest & Unwobbling Pivot
      (Tr. by Ezra Pound)   81   127
   The Classic Anthology Defined by...
      (Tr. by Ezra Pound)   85   159

CONKLIN, GROFF
POEMS
   The Immense Power of Death   36   198
   Infinitude
   The Mortal Sound
   The Bud   42   314
   Thunder-Cloud
   Soul for Tears   48   148

CONKLING, ELSA
POEMS
   Summertime   8   193
      ("Babies are running all around...")

("Rosebushes on a happy day...")
("Oh, the apple-blossoms...")
("Gay as the flowers...")
("Clover tops are coming...")
("The violin makes brown music...")
("The daisies are shining...")
("O cherry tree...")
("I saw the clovers flow...")
("I think of you, Mr. Mapletree...")

CONKLING, GRACE HAZARD
POEMS
Symphony of a Mexican Garden   1   11
To the Mexican Nightingale   4   98
Ave Venezia
"I Will Not Give Thee All My Heart"
The Little Town
Refugees   7   70
"The Little Rose Is Dust, My Dear"
Out of Mexico   10   18
  Velardena Sunset
  Santa Maria del Rio
  The Museum
  Gulf View
  Spring Day
  Patio Scene
Songs for Places (Old Mexico)   11   129
  Guadalupe
  Popocatapetl
  Huasteca
  Tampico
  Cuernavaca
  Durango
  Orizaba
  Amecameca
  Vera Cruz
  San Luis Potosi
Diary Written on Peony Petals   16   304
Primaveral   18   144
From a Ship's Log   24   299
  Squalls of Rain
  Rough Sea
  Occasional Mist
  Strong Breeze
Guadeloupe   28   127
The Return   74   148

ARTICLES
Correspondence:
  Concerning Hilda Conkling   14   344

BOOKS REVIEWED
Afternoons in April   7   152
Variations on a Theme   22   93
Ship's Log   27   52
Flying Fish: A Book of Songs and Sonnets   29   281
Witch and Other Poems   36   47

CONKLING, HILDA
POEMS
("Rosy plum-tree...")   8   191
("There's dozens full of dandelions...")
("Oh wrinkling star...")
("The red moon comes...")
("Sparkle up, little tired flower...")
("Blossoms in the growing tree...")
("The garden is full of flowers...")
("I will sing you a song...")
A Little Girl's Songs   10   197
  Spring Song
  By Lake Champlain
  To a Mouse
  Water
  Sunset
Fairy Footsteps   12   202
  Autumn Song
  The Dream
  Butterfly ("Butterfly,/I like...")
  Evening
  Thunder Shower
  Red Cross Song
  Rose-Moss
  The Champlain Sandman
A Little Girl's Songs   14   204
  For You, Mother
  Morning
  Rose-Petal
  The Dew-Light
  Poplars
  Narcissus
  Yellow Summer-Throat
  Night Goes Rushing By
  Seagarde
  Easter
  Snow-Flake Song
  Poems
  Thoughts
  Snow-Storm
  Butterfly ("As I walked through...")
  Geography
Poems by a Child   16   200
  Moon in October
  Wishes
  My Mind and I
  Lilacs
  Orchid Lady
  To a Black Pansy
  Bare Butter-Nut Tree
  Leaves
  River
  The Cellar
  Japanese Picture
  To a Mother
Song Nets   20   261
  Snow Morning
  What I Said

Little Green Bermuda Poem
When Moonlight Falls
Elsa
Cloudy-Pansy
Field-Mouse
"I Wondered and Wondered"
Flowers Faded and Gone   22   251

BOOKS REVIEWED
Poems by a Little Girl   16   222
Shoes of the Wind   22   97

ARTICLES ABOUT
Correspondence
   from Edward Sapir, Grace Hazard
   Conkling, and Louise Driscoll   14   344

CONLEY, JOHN
REVIEWS
Hopkins Enshrined   74   292
   Poems of Gerard Manley Hopkins
      (Ed. by W. H. Gardner)
   Gerard Manley Hopkins,
      by W. H. Gardner
   Gerard Manley Hopkins,
      by K. R. Srinivasa Iyengar
   Gerard Manley Hopkins,
      by W. A. M. Peters
   Immortal Diamond
      (Ed. by Norman Weyand)

CONN, STEWART
POEMS
Marriage a Mountain Ridge   118   198

CONNOLLY, CYRIL
ARTICLES ABOUT
The Cantabrigian Approach,
   by Marius Bewley   75   282

CONNOLLY, GERALDINE
POEMS
Lydia   152   131
The Entropy of Pleasure   155   330
Face Lift   158   333
The New World   163   189

CONNOR, TONY
POEMS
Bringing In the House-Plants   137   84
Emptying the Fishtank
Reminiscences Remembered   138   198

BOOKS REVIEWED
With Love Somehow   102   330
Lodgers   107   406
Kon in Springtime   113   262
In the Happy Valley   120   107
New and Selected Poems   143   228

CONOLEY, GILLIAN
POEMS
*The Farmer's Daughter
   and the Travelling Salesman*   156   74

BOOKS REVIEWED
Tall Stranger   160   284

CONQUEST, ROBERT
REVIEWS
Eugene Onegin: A Novel in Verse,
   by Aleksandr Pushkin
   (Tr. by Vladimir Nabokov)   106   236

BOOKS REVIEWED
Poems   88   267
New Lines (Ed.)   91   124
Back to Life (Ed.)   97   192
Between Mars and Venus   102   193
*Arias from a Love Opera
   and Other Poems*   118   102

ARTICLES ABOUT
Rev. of *Poets of the 1950's:
   An Anthology of New English Verse*
   (Ed. by D. J. Enright)   89   260

CONRAD, PHILIP
ARTICLES
Correspondence: Visual Poetry
   [Jessica Nelson North]   32   112

BOOKS REVIEWED
Action, Didn't It   59   224

CONRAD, SHERMAN
POEMS
Of This Kind   45   15
Epistemology   50   19
Sonnet ("Hands, the brothers...")   60   312
The Room
Song ("My head held up...")
Song ("In dreams and morning...")   61   547
The Meal   104   36
Nights of Passage
Like Lazarus
Mother of God: Montserrat
One Hand Clapping

ARTICLES
Poetry as a Jackdaw's Nest
   [W. R. Moses, Mary Barnard,
   Randall Jarrell]   58   90

REVIEWS
Encounter in April, by May Sarton   50   229
Hounds on the Mountain,
   by James Still   51   347

Sophocles' Electra
   (Tr. by Francis Fergusson)   53   96
The War Poems of Alan Swallow   74   175

CONSTABLE, M. H.
POEMS
   Have Them Come In by Night   66   76

CONSTANTINE, DAVID
POEMS
   Sunken Cities   146   200

CONSTANTINOFF, R. P.
POEMS
   Marine   85   30

CONTE, GIUSEPPE
POEMS
   Da *Lei me diceva proprio così/*
   From *This Is Exactly*
   What She Told Me   155   126
   "Dopo Marx, Aprile"/
   "After Marx, April"
   "Trans-Europe-Express"
   (Tr. by Lawrence Venuti)

CONTOSKI, VICTOR
REVIEWS
   Eastern European Poetry   110   52
   Introduction to Modern Polish Literature
     (Ed. by Adam Gillon
     and Ludwik Krzyzanowski)
   Postwar Polish Poetry
     (Tr. and ed. by Czeslaw Milosz)
   Polish and Hungarian Poetry, 1945-1956,
     by George Gömöri
   Shadow Land: Johannes Bobrowski
     (Tr. by Ruth and Matthew Mead)

COOK, ALBERT
POEMS
   War in the Winter Kingdom   71   294
   Between Us   110   14
   Recessive

BOOKS REVIEWED
   The Charges   122   293

COOK, BRADFORD
ARTICLES ABOUT
   French Chronicle:
     Recent Publications,
     by Wallace Fowlie   88   408

COOK, FRANCIS C.
POEMS
   The Dead Hand   70   189

COOK, H. CALDWELL
ARTICLES ABOUT
   The Younger Bards,
     by Edward J. O'Brien   6   188

COOK, HAROLD (LEWIS)
POEMS
   ("Your hands—")   17   191
   ("All day her hair lay spread...")
   Standards   21   132
   Never Did I Dream
   A Sequence and Others   32   144
     Spell Against Death
     The Island
     Coward
     Fugue
     I Am a Slow Thing
   Space of Breath   34   301
     The Ghost
     Rejected Lover
     Warning
     Statement
   Things Descried   38   295
     Ode ("What is it that man knows...")
     Starlight
     To a Dead Lady
     Parable
     History
   Wintry Words   47   177
     From the Prologue to *All Hallows*
     Dies Irae
     Record for Another Age
     The Professor Meditates

BOOKS REVIEWED
   Spell Against Death   42   285

COOK, HOWARD WILLARD
BOOKS REVIEWED
   Our Poets of Today   14   159

COOK, NILLA CRAM
BOOKS REVIEWED
   The Way of the Swan:
     Poems of Kashmir (Ed.)   95   314

COOK, WILLARD
BOOKS REVIEWED
   Our Poets of Today   22   229

COOKE, DORIAN
POEMS
   Meditations   58   81

BOOKS REVIEWED
   Fugue for Our Time   79   106

COOKE, EDMUND VANCE
POEMS
Extenuations   27   18
Belshazzar
Seven Devils

BOOKS REVIEWED
From the Book of Extenuations   30   173

COOKE, LE BARON
POEMS
Autumnal Music   29   309
New England Spring   32   21
Provocative   32   321
Notes   36   313
Moonrise   39   21

COOKSLEY, (S.) BERT
POEMS
David   27   259
Side-Lights   30   307
From Forty to Eight
Fear
For Elaine
Late Visitor
Leaves from a Small Tree   33   293
Go Now and Speak Gently
Holiday
Brief Query
Portrait of Grief
A Lady Dies
The Ancient Miracle
Gray Lady
Love Flies
Moment of Silence

ARTICLES ABOUT
Give Him a Nobel Prize,
by Harriet Monroe   39   90

COOLBRITH, INA
BOOKS REVIEWED
Poems of Charles Warren Stoddard (Ed.) 12   279

ARTICLES ABOUT
California's Laureate, by Harriet Monroe 15   158

COOLEY, JULIA
[JULIA COOLEY ALTROCCHI]
POEMS
Spring Sorrow   7   280
In a Corridor of Statues
The Dreamers of Death   17   74

BOOKS REVIEWED
The Dance of Youth   11   48

COOLEY, NICOLE
POEMS
Undine   163   87

BOOKS REVIEWED
Resurrection   170   347

COOLEY, PETER
POEMS
The Way Back   126   338
Observances   128   195
From the Gulf
An Exorcism
Conclusion of a Letter to the Angel
Fathers and Sons   150   205
Seascape with Attendant Premonitions
The Boy Child
Holy Family: Audubon Zoo, New Orleans 153   91
The Soul
Psalm Before Sleep   162   35
Messengers   163   146
Poem on the First Day of School   164   347
Transcendentals   166   77
Poem on the First Day of Spring   168   13
Vespers
Sestina   169   213

ARTICLES ABOUT
Rev. of The American Poetry Anthology
(Ed. by Daniel Halpern)   128   106

COOLIDGE, CLARK
BOOKS REVIEWED
Flag Flutter & U.S. Electric   109   407
Space   119   224

COOMARASWAMY, ANANDA K.
BOOKS REVIEWED
Art and Swadeshi   2   226

COOMBS, PATRICIA
POEMS
Perhaps   79   262
The Critique   82   148
Parsifal
Uncle

COOPER, CHARLES W.
BOOKS REVIEWED
Preface to Poetry
(With John Holmes)   84   43

COOPER, DORIS
POEMS
Brevities   27   195
Ghosts
Autumn

COOPER, DOROTHY
POEMS
Like Divers   43   262
The Night-Hawk

Compensation
The Bridge 50 261

COOPER, EDITH
[See FIELD, MICHAEL, pseud.
with BRADLEY, KATHERINE]

COOPER, JANE
POEMS
The Builder of Houses 93 19

BOOKS REVIEWED
The Weather of Six Mornings 115 430
Green Notebook, Winter Road 166 104

COOPERMAN, HASYE
BOOKS REVIEWED
The Esthetic of Stéphane Mallarmé 45 347

COOPERMAN, STANLEY
BOOKS REVIEWED
The Owl Behind the Door 116 193

COOPER-STONE, ROBIN
POEMS
*To My Lover, Upon Seeing
a More Attractive Woman* 168 199

COOTE, STEPHEN
BOOKS REVIEWED
*The Penguin Book
of Homosexual Verse* (Ed.) 144 166

COPE, WENDY
ARTICLES ABOUT
A Letter from Britain [II],
by William Logan 157 290

COPLEY, FRANK O.
REVIEWS
From the Latin 96 247
The Satyricon, by Petronius
(Tr. by William Arrowsmith)
The Satires of Juvenal
(Tr. by Rolfe Humphries)
Ovid: The Metamorphoses
(Tr. by Horace Gregory)

BOOKS REVIEWED
*Gaius Valerius Catullus,
The Complete Poetry* (Tr.) 94 62

COPPARD, A. E.
BOOKS REVIEWED
Collected Poems 34 48

CORBETT, CHARLOTTE
POEMS
Jewish Shopkeeper 40 189

CORBIÈRE, TRISTAN
POEMS
The Contrary Poet
(Tr. by Randall Jarrell) 76 249

BOOKS REVIEWED
Poems by...
(Tr. by Walter McElroy) 73 364
Selections from Les Amours Jaunes
(Tr. by C. F. MacIntyre) 84 351

CORBIN, ALICE
[See HENDERSON,
ALICE CORBIN]

CORDAN, WOLFGANG
POEMS
Cain
(Tr. by Herman Salinger) 88 254

CORDING, ROBERT
POEMS
*A Boy Adds Black Vultures
to His Life-List* 144 97
A Cottage in the Country 149 143
*Elegy for John,
My Student Dead of AIDS*
Rock of Ages
The Gravity of Anonymity 151 464
Feeding the Birds 152 325
Ruffed Grouse
September 3 154 332
Thoor Ballylee
Going to Sea in a Sieve
Goat 157 153
The Cup 162 326
Unfinished Sampler 163 278
Astapovo 164 82
Self-Portrait 169 155
Narcissus 170 210

BOOKS REVIEWED
Heavy Grace 170 347

COREY, STEPHEN
POEMS
The Uselessness of American Counties 141 264
Freshman Lit & Comp 144 319
Animation
Preparing to Live Among the Old
The Blooming of Sentimentality 147 251
Ars Poetica 151 35
Complicated Shadows 151 391
*Editing Poems During
a Hospital Deathwatch* 163 224

BOOKS REVIEWED
All These Lands You Call One Country 162 37

CORKERY, CHRISTOPHER JANE

POEMS

Spoken Spanish	139	265
February 14		
Some Things a Prisoner Knew	141	339

BOOKS REVIEWED

Blessing	148	99

CORMAN, CID

POEMS

The Cockatoo	76	333
The Bearer	81	111
The Marriage of Bacchus and Ariadne	81	227
Invocation		
Backtalk from the Minotaur	83	138
The Groves of Colonos	85	73
After Reading Keats' Letters	88	152
The Desk	98	14
The Ways		
The Conversation		
The Infant	101	195
The Reason		
The Research		
The Day		
Memento	104	167
At Santo Spirito		
The Demonstration		
From Cahoots	141	259

TRANSLATIONS

Poems by Philippe Jaccottet	116	287

ARTICLES

Poetry for Radio	81	212

REVIEWS

The Kind of Act of, by Robert Creeley	83	340

BOOKS REVIEWED

The Precisions	87	53
The Descent from Daimonji	96	238
Livingdying	118	344

CORMIER, LOUIS

BOOKS REVIEWED

The Silent Cowboys of the East	119	356

CORN, ALFRED

POEMS

Chinese Porcelains at the Metropolitan	123	208
Dreambooks		
An Oregon Journal	124	264
Infinity Effect at the Hôtel Soubise	126	149
Parable at a Roman Fountain	127	134
Deception		
Darkening Hotel Room		
January	129	187
Nine to Five		
Spring and Summer Impression		
Some New Ruins		
Fire: The People	130	187
Sunday Mornings in Harlem		
Summer Vertigo		
Orlando Furioso: Sicilian Puppet Theater		
Fifty-Seventh Street and Fifth		
Photographs of Old New York		
Afternoon		
Short Story: A Covenant		
Audience	131	267
Prime Minister in Retirement		
Repertory		
Alcaics: Remembering Mykinai		
Tanagra		
Cornwall	135	145
Notes from a Child of Paradise	140	311
From Notes from a Child of Paradise	143	251
The Chi-Rho Page from the Book of Kells	151	35
An Xmas Murder	151	276
Infernal Regions and the Invisible Girl	156	287

ARTICLES

Comment	151	222

REVIEWS

Asylum	128	355
The Carpenter at the Asylum, by Paul Monette		
Climbing into the Roots, by Reg Saner		
Hindsight, Insight, Foresight	153	229
River Writing, An Eno Journal, by James Applewhite		
The Apple That Astonished Paris, by Billy Collins		
To the Place of Trumpets, by Brigit Pegeen Kelly		
The Wonder of Seeing Double, by Robert B. Shaw		
The Rain in the Trees, by W. S. Merwin		
The Calm at the Center of the Storm	155	283
Blackbird Bye Bye, by April Bernard		
Out of the Woods, by Thomas Bolt		
What Light There Is & Other Poems, by Eamon Grennan		
Between Angels, by Stephen Dunn		
No Traveller, by Richard Howard		
[E. M. Cioran, Wallace Stevens, Vera Lachmann]		
How To Enjoy Reading Poetry Again	157	33
The Transparent Man, by Anthony Hecht		
Grace Notes, by Rita Dove		

The Want Bone, by Robert Pinsky
Westward, by Amy Clampitt
Hermit with Landscape, by Daniel Hall
Near Changes, by Mona Van Duyn
Short Reviews   159   157
  Living in Time, by Rachel Hadas
  Lenten Anniversaries, Poems 1982-1989,
    by Ben Howard
  Even a Fist Was Once
    an Open Palm with Fingers,
    by Yehuda Amichai
    (Tr. by Barbara
    and Benjamin Harshav)
  Collected Poems, by Edwin Morgan
  Flow Chart, by John Ashbery
Looking Toward the Fin de Siècle   161   286
  Selected Poems
    and Translations 1969-1991,
    by William Matthews
    [John Berryman]
  The Man with Night Sweats,
    by Thom Gunn
  The Love Poems of May Swenson

BOOKS REVIEWED
  All Roads at Once   129   226
  A Call in the Midst of the Crowd   133   100
  The West Door   152   98
  Autobiographies   163   97

CORNEILLE, (PIERRE)
ARTICLES ABOUT
  Rev. of *Corneille*, by P. J. Yarrow   104   187

CORNELIUS, HELEN
POEMS
  The Wisdom of the Hand   38   77
  Day Hath Its Seasons   42   196
  Lunar Legend
  Pendulum

BOOKS REVIEWED
  In Tract of Time   49   99

CORNFORD, FRANCES
BOOKS REVIEWED
  Spring Morning   6   252
  Autumn Midnight   23   283
  Mountains and Molehills   47   225

CORNING, HOWARD MC KINLEY
POEMS
  Flame and Water   29   20
  Mountain Men
  Shadows in Marble   31   307
    Chant for the Brethren of Dust
    Snow Race
    Seeing How Surely Death

Windy Places   36   80
  Northwest Passage
  Green Councillors
  A Proud Man Walks in the Desert
  Song to Say a Farewell
Fruits of Rain   39   82
  Men Walk in Rain
  I Seek the Orchid
  The Meadow Brook Runs Over
Only the Windless Meadow   44   126

BOOKS REVIEWED
  These People   30   227
  The Mountain in the Sky   39   338

CORRINGTON, JOHN WILLIAM
BOOKS REVIEWED
  The Anatomy of Love and Other Poems   105   270
  Lines to the South and Other Poems   108   57

CORSO, GREGORY
BOOKS REVIEWED
  The Vestal Lady on Brattle   89   45
  Gasoline   93   182
  The Happy Birthday of Death   97   114

CORTES, MARGARET
POEMS
  Variations on Poems by Ezra Pound   131   63

CORWIN, NORMAN
ARTICLES ABOUT
  Verse Drama and the Radio,
    by Amy Bonner   50   200
  Rev. of *The War Poets, an Anthology*
    of the War Poetry of the 20th Century
    (Ed. by Oscar Williams)   67   344

CORY, DANIEL MAC GHIE
POEMS
  Only in Words   30   69

COSBUC, GEORGE
POEMS
  We Want Land
    (Tr. by Maurice Aisen)   4   146

COSTEA, LUCIANA
TRANSLATIONS
  Poems by Marin Sorescu
    (Tr. with W. D. Snodgrass
    and Dona Rosu)   159   191

COSTELLO, BONNIE
REVIEWS
  Orders of Magnitude   142   106
    Of the Great House,
    by Allen Grossman

One for the Rose, by Philip Levine
Flood, by William Matthews
Lord Dragonfly, by William Heyen
The Complete Poems,
   by Elizabeth Bishop   142   231

BOOKS REVIEWED
Elizabeth Bishop: Questions of Mastery   161   34

COTTER, JOSEPH S., JR.
BOOKS REVIEWED
The Band of Gideon   16   287

COTTON, JOHN
POEMS
Fragments   121   317
  (1. "As the plane rises...")
  (2. "Sundays are quiet...")
  (3. "Some windows already boarded...")
  (4. "The canal; a pub...")
  (5. "A day's drive...")
  (6. "From London fires spread...")
  (7. "Besieged by snow...")
  (8. "In the bay...")
  (9. "The end of a holiday...")
Fragments   127   266
  (I. "Did the grey climacteric...")
  (II. "Yet they say the horn...")
Fragments   134   156
  (15. "Remembered summers...")
  (16. "Now old friends...")
  (17. "These are it then...")

BOOKS REVIEWED
Old Movies and Other Poems   122   105
Kilroy Was Here   129   340

COULETTE, HENRI
POEMS
Brrr   117   366
Today I Begin My First Novel
The Prince of Frogs
Situation Comedy
At the Hotel des Saints Pères
Correspondence   156   136

BOOKS REVIEWED
The War of the Secret Agents
  and Other Poems   109   118
The Family Goldschmitt   121   348
The Collected Poems
  (Ed. by Donald Justice
  and Robert Mezey)   158   214

ARTICLES ABOUT
Rev. of *A Donald Justice Reader:*
  Selected Poetry and Prose   162   160

COULTER, JOHN
BOOKS REVIEWED
The Blossoming Thorn   69   349

COURNOS, JOHN
POEMS
The Rose
  [After K. Tetmaier]   3   132
Among the Rodins   10   299

ARTICLES
Pushkin: 1837-1937   49   328

REVIEWS
Eugene Onegin,
  by Alexander Pushkin
  (Tr. by Dorothea Prall Radin
  and George Z. Patrick)   50   294

BOOKS REVIEWED
Imagist Anthology 1930
  (With Richard Aldington,
  H. D., John Gould Fletcher,
  F. S. Flint, Ford Madox Ford,
  James Joyce, D. H. Lawrence,
  and William Carlos Williams)   36   213

COUROUCLI, JENNIFER
BOOKS REVIEWED
On This Athenian Hill   117   331

COURT, ARTELIA BOWNE
POEMS
Four Poems   92   92
  ("I am sitting dreamy...")
  ("when soldiers...")
  ("lying in a hammock...")
  ("please, please...")

COUSINS, NORMAN
BOOKS REVIEWED
The Poetry of Freedom
  (Ed. with William Rose Benét)   67   46

COVELL, ARTHUR
POEMS
Crusade   79   273

COVINO, MICHAEL
POEMS
Autumn Leaves   140   202
Prescribed Form

COWAN, CRAIG
POEMS
The Edge of Wilderness   125   272

COWELL, HARRY
POEMS
My Heart Is Full of You   27   239
Mountain Speech
Dan Adair

COWLEY, MALCOLM
POEMS
Three Portraits   15   76
Moonrise
Barn Dance
Danny
Here and There   21   233
Poem for Two Voices
Nocturnal Landscape
Interment
Sudden Encounter
Prophetic
Three Hills
Blue Juniata   29   61
Bones of a House
Chestnut Ridge
Laurel Mountain
Empty Barn, Dead Farm
Bill George
The Urn
The Streets of Air
The Dry Season   53   24
The Mother
The Firstborn
The Long Voyage
Roxane   59   115
Restaurateur with Music
The Eater of Darkness
The Lost People
Seven
The Source   72   18
Passport Blues   76   18
A Countryside, 1918-1968   112   149

ARTICLES
[Tribute to Harriet Monroe]   49   158
Poetry Project   52   224
Correspondence:
Auden's Versification   65   345

REVIEWS
Person, Place and Thing,
by Karl Jay Shapiro   61   620
For the Time Being,
by W. H. Auden   65   202

BOOKS REVIEWED
Blue Juniata   35   45
Aragon: Poet of the French Resistance
(Ed. with Hannah Josephson)   68   44
Blue Juniata: Collected Poems   114   335
Blue Juniata: A Life   149   94

ARTICLES ABOUT
Renewal of Youth,
by Harriet Monroe   19   146

COWPER, WILLIAM
BOOKS REVIEWED
Selected Letters of...
(Ed. by Mark Van Doren)   80   297
Selected Letters of...
(Ed. by Mark Van Doren)   84   296

COX, ELEANOR ROGERS
POEMS
To a Portrait of Whistler
in the Brooklyn Art Museum   11   24
Whistler's White Girl

BOOKS REVIEWED
Singing Fires of Erin   9   209

COX, JOHN HARRINGTON
BOOKS REVIEWED
Folk-Songs of the South (Ed.)   28   348

COX, MARK
POEMS
Things My Grandfather Must Have Said   149   209
I Want To Know What Love Is
Lemon Icing
Simile at the Side of the Road   152   79
Sonata   164   70

COX, NAOMI
POEMS
On Receiving the News   119   325

COX, WAYNE
TRANSLATIONS
Poems by Miquel Martí i Pol
(Tr. with Lourdes Manyé i Martí)   155   399

COXE, LOUIS O.
POEMS
Red Right Returning   65   131
Christmas Poem
Liberty Party
Dead Marine   66   312
For M.E.S. Before D-Day
V-J Day   69   18
Magnetic Pole, True Pole,
Axis of Torque, Axis of Spin   79   146
Death of Don Juan
Magna Mater
Ex Machina
Haying   80   208
Beowulf   83   260
Elegy: For a Child   84   264
Prodigal Son   86   155

Elegy ("Beyond the river...")   88   300
The Mythmakers
End of the Road
Fall of Leaf   90   227
The Hostage
After the Burst   91   225
The Waking
The Bush
The Last Hero   95   139
Swift's Tomb in Saint Patrick's   99   12
Sicilian Journey
Breaking the Barrier   101   20
The Falls   104   28
Crash Program
Friday, November 22, 1963
Suite for the Equinox   108   9
Two Poems   112   169
    I. Choosing a Career
    II. Stuck with It

REVIEWS
Edward Arlington Robinson,
    A Critical Study,
    by Ellsworth Barnard   81   187
Tilbury Town: Selected Poems
    of Edwin Arlington Robinson
    (Ed. by Lawrance Thompson)   84   108
Three Translations from the Classics   86   303
    The Poems of Sappho
        (Tr. by P. Maurice Hill)
    Euripides: Alcestis
        (Tr. by Richmond Lattimore),
        The Medea (Tr. by Rex Warner),
        The Heracleidae
        (Tr. by Ralph Gladstone),
        Hippolytus (Tr. by David Grene)
    The Metamorphoses of Ovid
        (Tr. by Rolfe Humphries)
Selected Criticism, by Louise Bogan   87   370
Selected Poems, by Ezra Pound
    [Hugh Kenner]   91   389
Two Views of Kazantzakis
    The Odyssey: A Modern Sequel,
    by Nikos Kazantzakis
        (Tr. by Kimon Friar)   95   179
    [Andonis Decavalles]

BOOKS REVIEWED
The Seafaring   73   355
The Second Man and Other Poems   88   267
The Wilderness and Other Poems   95   107
The Middle Passage   97   46
The Last Hero   107   258
Nikal Seyn and Decoration Day   111   43

ARTICLES ABOUT
Correspondence from William Burford
    and Robert Duncan [Ezra Pound]   92   195

COZZENS, EVANGELINE C.
POEMS
    Earth in Spring   40   11
    Pioneer   46   139

CRABTREE, R. A.
POEMS
    Interview Assignment   74   28

CRAFT, KEVIN
POEMS
    Incense   170   79

CRAIG, ALEXANDER
REVIEWS
    From Australia and New Zealand   94   44
        The Penguin Book of Australian Verse
            (Ed. by John Thompson,
            Kenneth Slessor, and R. G. Howarth)
        Poems 1949-57, by Allen Curnow
        Since Then, by Denis Glover
        The Night Shift, by James K. Baxter,
            Charles Doyle, Louis Johnson,
            and Kendrick Smithyman
        [R. A. Simpson, Evan Jones,
            Bertram Higgins]

CRAIG, GORDON
ARTICLES ABOUT
    Should He Be Educated?
        by Harriet Monroe   37   90

CRAMER, STEVEN
POEMS
    Pentimento   131   327
    The Hospitals   152   261
    The Battle of the Bands   154   317
    For the Bullies of West Morris High
    The Game   159   22
    The Work   164   96

REVIEWS
    Facts and Figures   156   100
        Night Landings,
            by Walter McDonald
        Dien Cai Dau,
            by Yusef Komunyakaa
        The Night Parade,
            by Edward Hirsch
        Black Wings, by Len Roberts
        The Burden Lifters,
            by Michael Waters
        Once Out of Nature,
            by Jim Simmerman
    Four True Voices of Feeling   157   96
        In the Western Night:
            Collected Poems, 1965-90,
            by Frank Bidart

Ararat, by Louise Glück
In the Room We Share,
  by Louis Simpson
Leaving Another Kingdom: Selected Poems,
  by Gerald Stern
Paying Attention   159   101
The Really Short Poems
  of A. R. Ammons
Blue Autumn,
  by Christopher Buckley
[William Wordsworth]
Fate, by Ai
Landscape at the End of the Century,
  by Stephen Dunn
Goddesses, Gods, and Devils   159   223
The Sacraments of Desire,
  by Linda Gregg
Selected Poems 1963-1983 and
  The Book of Gods and Devils,
  by Charles Simic
Self-Defense   161   159
The River at Wolf,
  by Jean Valentine
Meetings with Time,
  by Carl Dennis
Apocrypha, by Eric Pankey
What My Father Believed,
  by Robert Wrigley
Eva-Mary, by Linda McCarriston
[Daniel C. Dennett]

BOOKS REVIEWED
The World Book   163   39

CRANE, GEORGE
POEMS
The Effete   67   136

CRANE, HART
POEMS
At Melville's Tomb   29   25
Cutty Sark   31   27
O Carib Isle!
Eldorado   36   13
The Urn   41   177
  Reliquary
  Purgatorio
  The Circumstance
  Imperator Victus
  Havana Rose
  The Sad Indian
  The Visible The Untrue
  Reply
  By Nilus Once
  Phantom Bark
  A Postscript
  Enrich My Resignation
At Melville's Tomb   121   5

ARTICLES
Correspondence
  [*At Melville's Tomb*]   29   35

REVIEWS
Green River: A Poem for Rafinesque,
  by James Whaler   40   44

BOOKS REVIEWED
White Buildings   30   47
The Bridge   36   153
The Letters of Hart Crane, 1916-1932
  (Ed. by Brom Weber)   83   353

ARTICLES ABOUT
A Discussion with Hart Crane,
  by Harriet Monroe   29   34
Hart Crane and the American Mind,
  by Allen Tate   40   210
Rev. of *The Five Seasons*,
  by Phelps Putnam   40   335
The Book of Hart Crane,
  by Morton Dauwen Zabel   42   33
Poets as Leaders, by Harriet Monroe   48   330
Rev. of *Hart Crane*:
  The Life of an American Poet,
  by Philip Horton   50   219
[Note]   55   284
Disorder as Myth:
  Hart Crane's *The Bridge*,
  by Howard Moss   62   32
From the Introduction to
  The Oxford Book of American Verse,
  by F. O. Matthiessen   77   31
Falling Asleep over Grillparzer:
  An Interview with Robert Lowell,
  by John McCormick   81   269
Correspondence from Brom Weber
  [Babette Deutsch, Carl Schmitt]   84   245
Rev. of *Hart Crane*:
  The Life of an American Poet,
  by Philip Horton   91   117
Correspondence from Brom Weber
  [Oscar Cargill, Allen Tate,
  Yvor Winters]   92   332
Rev. of *Hart Crane's Sanskrit Charge*:
  A Study of The Bridge,
  by L. S. Dembo   98   190
Rev. of *The Poetry of...: A Critical Study*,
  by R. W. B. Lewis   114   113
Rev. of *Hart Crane*:
  An Introduction to the Poetry,
  by Herbert Leibowitz   115   346
Rev. of *Voyager: A Life of Hart Crane*,
  by John Unterecker   116   256
Rev. of *Fellow Feelings*,
  by Richard Howard   130   36

Rev. of *The New Oxford Book
  of American Verse*
  (Ed. by Richard Ellmann)   131   236
Rev. of *The Double Witness*,
  by Ben Belitt   133   169
Rev. of *The Penguin Book
  of Homosexual Verse*
  (Ed. by Stephen Coote)   144   166

CRANE, R(ONALD) S.
BOOKS REVIEWED
*Critics and Criticism,
  Ancient and Modern* (Ed.)   82   98

ARTICLES ABOUT
The Chicago Critics:
  Yes and Perhaps,
  by Martin J. Svaglic   82   157

CRANE, STEPHEN
BOOKS REVIEWED
The Poems of...: A Critical Edition
  (Ed. by Joseph Katz)   112   127

ARTICLES ABOUT
Stephen Crane, by Harriet Monroe   14   148
Rev. of *Stephen Crane*, by John Berryman   78   298
Rev. of *The Poetry of Stephen Crane*,
  by Daniel G. Hoffman   92   116

CRANMER-BYNG, L.
BOOKS REVIEWED
The Lute of Jade (Tr.)   14   281

CRAPSEY, ADELAIDE
BOOKS REVIEWED
Verse   21   333

ARTICLES ABOUT
The Great Adventure,
  by Alice Corbin Henderson   10   316

CRASE, DOUGLAS
POEMS
From *Six Places in New York State* 124   143
  Pultneyville
  The Pinnacle Range
  Genesee Falls
  Chimney Bluffs
Chelsea Square   127   1
Locale
In the Fall When It's Time To Leave
The Winter House
The Revisionist   128   87
The Lake Effect   129   202
Experience and What To Make of It
The Day Line   131   279
Gunpowder Morning in a Gray Room
The House at Sagg

REVIEWS
Collected Poems, by James Schuyler
  [Fairfield Porter, Anne Porter]   163   225

CRASHAW, RICHARD
ARTICLES ABOUT
Rev. of *Richard Crashaw,
  A Study in Baroque Sensibility*,
  by Austin Warren   57   160
Rev. of *Richard Crashaw,
  A Study in Baroque Sensibility*,
  by Austin Warren   91   273
Rev. of *Six Metaphysical Poets:
  A Reader's Guide*,
  by George Williamson   112   356

CRĂSNARU, DANIELA
POEMS
Lethal Dose   159   18
Breath
  (Tr. by Adam J. Sorkin
  and Sergiu Celac)

CRAWFORD, FRANCES
POEMS
Who Sees the Panic   74   76

CRAWFORD, JACK, JR.
POEMS
Sleepwalkers   91   180
The Wound of Innocence   94   100
Empty House
Goddess of the Doorbell
A Breast Humming
The Ship   105   304
Camels Pass in Smoke
Behind the Brow
Bright Flesh
I Stand as on a Battleground
The Surf Rider   111   157

REVIEWS
Suddenly Falling Earth   105   410
  Song of the Archer,
    by Mary Shumway
  The Sky of Orange Whispers,
    by Howard Hart
  A Change of View, by Philip Legler
  In My Father's House,
    by William Goodreau

CRAWFORD, JOHN (W.)
POEMS
Night   18   308
  Nadir
  Sumach
  Brackish Well
  Endymion

Portraits   22   24
   Dirge for Griselda
   Ishmael
   The Young Bacchus
   Pilgrim
   Fox-Fire
   Purr   24   133

ARTICLES
Correspondence:
   A Word of Protest   17   287

CRAWFORD, NELSON ANTRIM
["N. A. C."]
POEMS
   The Carrying of the Ghost   15   188
   Fragilities   19   24
    Song ("These are the words...")
    Lake
    Companionship
    Impotence
    Branches
   Cats and Zinnias   34   315

ARTICLES
Correspondence:
   A Kansas Prize   17   171

REVIEWS
   New War Poets   16   336
    The Tempering, by Howard Buck
    Chords from Albireo,
     by Danford Barney
    There and Here, by Allen Tucker
    Poems, by Cecil Roberts
    The Poets in Picardy, by E. deStein
    Poems in Captivity, by John Still
   Broken Lights, by Glenn Hughes   17   98
   Jehovah, by Clement Wood   17   167
   Europe: A Book for America,
    by Samuel Roth   17   341
   Teacher-Poets   18   44
    The Roamer and Other Poems,
     by George Edward Woodberry
    Sonnets from a Prison Camp,
     by Archibald Allen Bowman
   The Little School, by T. Sturge Moore   18   50
   Fairies and Fusiliers
    and Country Sentiment,
    by Robert Graves   18   105
   Before Dawn,
    by Irene Rutherford McLeod   18   166
   New Poems, by D. H. Lawrence   18   336
   As the Wind Blows, by Eden Philpotts   19   53
   The Professor as Critic   19   54
    The Function of the Poet
     and Other Essays,
     by James Russell Lowell

   The Kinds of Poetry and Other Essays,
    by John Erskine
   Poems, by Iris Tree   19   165
   On English Poetry, by Robert Graves   20   344
   Translating Old English   21   53
    Old English Poetry: Translations
     into Alliterative Verse,
     by J. D. Spaeth
    Widsith, Beowulf,
     Finnsburgh, Waldere, Deor
     (Tr. by Charles Scott Moncrieff)
   The Laureateship: A Study of the Office
    of Poet Laureate in England,
    by Edmund Kemper Broadus   21   164
   Arrow Music, by Bryher   21   221
   Poems, by Margaretta Schuyler   21   222
   Folk Songs—Warranted Not to Shock   22   105
    American Ballads and Songs
     (Ed. by Louise Pound)
    Songs of the Cowboys
     (Ed. by N. Howard Thorp)
   Less Lonely, by Alfred Kreymborg   24   269
   The Poetic Edda
    (Tr. by Henry Adams Bellows)   24   281
   From Whitman to Sandburg
    in American Poetry,
    by Bruce Weirick   25   167
   Poetry Yesterday and Today   27   283
    Ancient Rhetoric and Poetic,
     by Charles Sears Baldwin
    The Background of Gray's Elegy,
     by Amy Louise Reed
    An Anatomy of Poetry,
     by A. Williams-Ellis
   Paintrock Road, by Edwin Ford Piper   31   91
   Branches of Adam,
    by John Gould Fletcher   31   216
   The House of Silk,
    by Audrey Wurdemann   31   226
   God's Drum, by Hartley Alexander   31   286
   The Classical Tradition in Poetry,
    by Gilbert Murray   32   289
   Our Singing Strength,
    by Alfred Kreymborg   36   110

BOOKS REVIEWED
   The Carrying of the Ghost   25   45

CRAWFORD, TERRY
BOOKS REVIEWED
   Lost Neighbourhood   119   356

CREAGH, JOHN
POEMS
   Leaves in a Dark Wind   43   20
    The Old House
    The Rounding of the Wave
    Against Gods

Lamentation
After Parting

CREEKMORE, HUBERT
POEMS

Sonnets in Slanting Rhymes   42   200
   Coincidence of Birds
   Before a Leyden Jar
It's Me, Oh Lord, Standing with a Gun...   65   310
An Old Story of How...   73   131
Agony Column
Mallarmé in His Study   84   74

TRANSLATIONS
Poem by Guillaume Apollinaire   77   144
Poems by Stéphane Mallarmé   80   28

REVIEWS
Poems 1943-1949, by Francis Golffing   76   57
A Treasury of Russian Verse
   (Ed. by Avrahm Yarmolinsky)   80   95

BOOKS REVIEWED
Personal Sun   56   340
The Stone Ants   64   48
The Long Reprieve   70   49
A Little Treasury of World Poetry (Ed.)   82   281
Lyrics of the Middle Ages (Ed.)   97   195

CREELEY, ROBERT
POEMS

Sing Song   90   293
The Hill   94   11
The Herd
The Door (I)
A Gift of Great Value
My Love
The Names
Going to Bed
The Door (II)
The Rose   96   71
The First Time
The Woman
Jack's Blues
Air: "The Love of a Woman"
Out of Sight
The Cracks
For Fear
The Gesture
Song ("What I took in my hand...")
The Rescue   98   76
For Love
The Rhythm   99   373
The Invitation   101   23
The Woman   104   133
The Pattern
The Mechanic
Walls

"I Keep to Myself Such Measures..."
The Dream
Hello
Quick-Step
Variations
The Chance
The Window
Walking
The Language
The Answer   106   26
Dimensions
A Night Sky
The World
The Shame   107   318
A Reason
The Window
To Bobbie
The Statue
A Prayer
The Flower
The Circle
Song ("I wouldn't/embarrass you...")
Enough   109   287
The Eye
Water
Here
Of Years
Intervals
Song ("How simply/for another...")
Chicago   112   331
The Friends
Place
The Puritan Ethos
America
I'll Be Here
Mr. Warner
The Province
Names
So Big   115   113

REVIEWS
"To Build Castles in Spain"   93   188
   Ten Centuries of Spanish Verse
     (Ed. by Eleanor L. Turnbull)
   The Penguin Book of Spanish Verse
     (Ed. by J. M. Cohen)
"Her Service is Perfect Freedom"   93   395
   The White Goddess, Five Pens in Hand,
     and *The Poems of...*,
     by Robert Graves
   The Golden Ass,
     by Lucius Apuleis
     (Tr. by Robert Graves)
   The Twelve Caesars,
     by Gaius Suetonius Tranquillus
     (Tr. by Robert Graves)
Letters, by Robert Duncan   96   55
Ways of Looking   98   192
   Parvenus & Ancestors, by Barriss Mills

Experiment Theatre Anthology #1
  (Ed. by Carol Ely Harper)
Ko, or A Season on Earth,
  by Kenneth Koch
Mexico City Blues, by Jack Kerouac
A Red Carpet for the Sun,
  by Irving Layton
The Heart in Naked Hunger
  and *The Feel of Sun & Air*
  Upon Her Body,
  by Judson Crews
The Fascinating Bore   100   324
Swinburne: Poems
  (Ed. by Bonamy Dobrée)
Swinburne: A Selection
  (Ed. by Edith Sitwell)
"Think What's Got Away..."   102   42
The Hazards of Holiness,
  by Brother Antoninus
Traveling Through the Dark,
  by William Stafford
Imperatives, by Anthony Ostroff
Uncle Dog, by Robert Sward
Children Passing,
  by Richard Emil Braun
A Wedge of Words, by Frederic Will
A Local Pride, by Raymond Souster
Run with the Hunted,
  by Charles Bukowski
Letter to an Imaginary Friend,
  by Thomas McGrath
My Friend Tree,
  by Lorine Niedecker
All: The Collected Short Poems,
  1923-1958, by Louis Zukofsky
[William Carlos Williams]   107   52
Human Universe and Other Essays,
  Proprioception, and *A Bibliography*
  on America for Ed Dorn,
  by Charles Olson   109   40

BOOKS REVIEWED
The Kind of Act of   83   340
All That Is Lovely in Men   89   52
The Whip   92   110
If You   92   384
For Love: Poems 1950-1960   101   421
The Island   104   45
The Gold Diggers and Other Stories   108   341
Words   111   256
Selected Writings by Charles Olson (Ed.)   111   413
Numbers (With Robert Indiana)   116   110
Pieces   117   195
A Quick Graph:
  Collected Notes and Essays
  (Ed. by Donald Allen)   119   99
Mirrors   144   345
Selected Poems   160   157

ARTICLES ABOUT
[Note]   82   367
Rev. of *The New American Poetry:*
  1945-1960 (Ed. by Donald M. Allen)   98   242
Rev. of *Robert Creeley's Poetry:*
  A Critical Introduction,
  by Cynthia Dubin Edelberg   136   219

CRENNER, JAMES (T.)
POEMS
Song to a Crippled Child   98   208
Notes for a Wedding Anniversary   109   83
Reading Habits
Museums   150   161

CRESSON, ABIGAIL (W.)
POEMS
Challenge   23   139
A Child   28   255
Ridicule   30   323

CREW, HELEN COALE
POEMS
Irish Song   19   192

CREWS, JUDSON [J. C. CREWS]
POEMS
A Kingdom's Utter Rail   75   145
Concerning Less of the Sea
Cattle the Meadows Spread
The Poise of Restless Wonder
Sallow Sallow the Sign Yet Wreathed   76   132
The Concession Pilate Never Made
Kine Level the Mane Desire
What Babylon Was Built About   83   258
The Lovers   85   337
Matadora
The Artist   88   17
Sole the Fabled Dim Recess
The River   91   239
Excelsior
Winter Edge   93   157
Aftermath of War   95   292
The Ruin in Our Flesh
The Poet Facing Up to Life   105   308
Perfection

BOOKS REVIEWED
A Poet's Breath   77   114
The Anatomy of Proserpine   86   242
The Wrath Wrenched Splendor of Love   90   386
To Wed Beneath the Sun
The Orges Who Were His Henchmen   97   114
The Heart in Naked Hunger   98   192
The Feel of Sun & Air upon Her Body
Hermes Past the Hour   104   258
You, Mark Antony,
  Navigator upon the Nile   108   191

Angels Fall They Are Towers 108 408
The Stones of Konarak 110 186
Three on a Match
  (With Wendell B. Anderson
  and Cerise Farallon)

CRILL, HILDRED
POEMS
Elsewhere Condition 160 1

CRISICK, MAUREEN MICUS
POEMS
Suppose 164 191

CRISWELL, CLOYD MANN
BOOKS REVIEWED
Asiatic Station 70 108

CROFT-COOKE, RUPERT
POEMS
Downstairs 32 194
That Pueblo
Three Miles from Tilbury

CROFTS, FREEMAN WILLS
ARTICLES ABOUT
Dagger of the Mind,
  by James Sandoe 68 146

CROMWELL, GLADYS
POEMS
The Fugitive 10 21
The Crowning Gift
Songs of the Dust 11 306
  Folded Power
  The Mould
  Autumn Communion
  Star Song

BOOKS REVIEWED
Poems 16 105

ARTICLES ABOUT
A Gold Star for Gladys Cromwell,
  by Harriet Monroe 13 326
The P.S.A. Prizes and Ours,
  by Harriet Monroe 17 88
A Few Women Poets,
  by Harriet Monroe 26 326

CRONIN, EDWARD J.
REVIEWS
The Good and the Bad 61 516
Mill Talk and Other Poems,
  by Leslie Nelson Jennings
The Nameless, by Lew Williams
Letter from America,
  by Carlos Bulosan

CRONYN, GEORGE W.
BOOKS REVIEWED
*The Path on the Rainbow—An Anthology
of Songs and Chants from the Indians
of North America* (Ed.) 14 41

CROOK, EDWARD L.
[See CROOK, KILE]

CROOK, KILE
[EDWARD L. CROOK]
POEMS
Memorial to Larry 33 59
The Safe Spartans 48 251

CROSBY, CARESSE
BOOKS REVIEWED
Painted Shores 33 47
The Stranger
Impossible Melodies

CROSBY, HARRY
POEMS
Fragment 34 78

BOOKS REVIEWED
Sonnets for Caresse 32 111
Red Skeletons

ARTICLES ABOUT
Obituary 35 293

CROSS, LESLIE
POEMS
Bleak and Pink Airs 48 323
Plague
Merry-Go-Round
Aprille's Crazy Day
The Crossroads

CROSS, WILBUR L.
ARTICLES ABOUT
The Pulitzer Award System,
  by Harriet Monroe 30 210

CROSSLEY-HOLLAND, KEVIN
BOOKS REVIEWED
Beowulf (Tr.) 115 274

CROTHERS, SAMUEL MC CHORD
ARTICLES ABOUT
Our Contemporaries 9 160

CROW, FLORENCE (MONROE)
POEMS
Let Me Remember 46 312
Country Afternoon
Thrown-Out Field

CROW, MARTHA FOOTE
POEMS
   Religion   9   133
   Ghosts of Past Time

BOOKS REVIEWED
   Christ in the Poetry of Today:
     An Anthology (Ed.)   12   340

CROWDER, RICHARD
ARTICLES
   Mr. MacNeice and Miss Sitwell   63   218

REVIEWS
   Three Poets   66   53
     The Gates of Silence,
      by Wrey Gardiner
     The Wounds of the Apostles,
      by Fred Marnau
     Three Poems,
      by Fred Marnau, Wrey Gardiner,
      and Nicholas Moore
   The Sun Never Sets   66   170
     100 Poems,
      by Edward Thompson
     As Iron Hills,
      by Flexmore Hudson

CROWELL, F. H.
BOOKS REVIEWED
   Cape Cod in Poetry
     (Ed. with J. F. Crowell)   27   343

CROWELL, J. F.
BOOKS REVIEWED
   Cape Cod in Poetry
     (Ed. with F. H. Crowell)   27   343

CROWLEY, J. V.
POEMS
   Donne's Brook...   96   293
   Siloam

CROWN, RACHEL
POEMS
   Where Are No Trees   87   148
   Boy with Snake   90   159

CROZIER, ANDREW
BOOKS REVIEWED
   Train Rides   117   261

CRUICKSHANK, HELEN
ARTICLES ABOUT
   Some Poets of the
     Scottish Renaissance,
     by Tom Scott   88   43

CRUIKSHANK, DOROTHY
[DOROTHY CRUIKSHANK
COCHRAN]
POEMS
   The Puritan   28   253

CRUZ, VICTOR HERNANDEZ
[See HERNANDEZ CRUZ,
VICTOR]

CUADRA, PABLO ANTONIO
[See ANTONIO CUADRA, PABLO]

CUCCHI, MAURIZIO
POEMS
   [Il mio risveglio è stato nel tuo nome]/
     [I am awakened]   155   124
   Sorrow
     (Tr. by Michael Palma)

CULL, DAVID
BOOKS REVIEWED
   Cancer Rising   119   356

CULLEN, COUNTEE (P.)
POEMS
   Shadowed   24   76
     Simon the Cyrenian Speaks
     Three Epitaphs
   Threnody for a Brown Girl   26   78
   Epitaphs   26   204
   For Amy Lowell   27   189
   Then   29   75
     Two Thoughts of Death
     The Wind Bloweth Where It Listeth

BOOKS REVIEWED
   Color   28   50
   Copper Sun   31   284
   Caroling Dusk (Ed.)   32   96
   The Black Christ and Other Poems   35   286
   On These I Stand   70   222

ARTICLES ABOUT
   Racial Bias and Negro Poetry,
     by Edward Bland   63   328

CULLEN, WINIFRED
POEMS
   Movie   66   194
   New England
   Defend Her in Time of Trouble

CULLUM, J. W.
POEMS
   Roses, Revisited, in a Paradoxical Autumn   136   93
   The Eucharist of the Holy Ghost
     at Key West   141   225

CULTER, RICHARD
BOOKS REVIEWED
Odd Pieces   96   179

CUMBERLEGE, MARCUS
BOOKS REVIEWED
Oases   116   120

CUMMINGS, E(DWARD) E(STLIN)
POEMS
("mortals)...")   53   169
("these children singing in stone a...")
("nouns to nouns...")
("when what hugs stopping earth...")
("up into the silence the green...")
("six...")
("love is more thicker than forget...")
("anyone lived in a pretty how town...")   56   233
("you which could grin three smiles...")
("a pretty a day...")
("i say no world...")
("If you can't eat you got to...")
("one's not half two...")   62   179
("what if a much of a which...")
("rain or hail...")
("might these be thrushes climbing...")
("if everything happens that can't...")
("this(let's remember)day...")   70   293
("neither awake...")
("infinite jukethrob smoke...")
("jake hates...")
("whose are these(wraith...")
("this is a rubbish...")
("if(touched by love's own secret)...")
("if a cheerfulest Elephantangel-child..")   74   187
("a thrown a...")
("open his head,baby...")
("possibly thrice we glimpsed—")
("(im)c-a-t(mo)...")
("in/Spring comes(no-...")
("now all the fingers of this tree...")
("dim/i/nu/tiv...")   76   187
("spirit colossal...")
("jack's white horse(up...")
("!/o(rounD)moon,how...")
("if the Lovestar grows most big...")
("crazy jay blue)...")
("if up's the word...")
("dive for dreams...")   80   125
("all nearness pauses, while a star...")
("unlove's the heavenless hell...")
("i carry your heart with me...")
("spring!may—")
("rosetree,rosetree...")   81   20
("how many moments
    must(amazing each...")   97   273
("'though your sorrows not...")
("why / don't / be...")
("2 little whos...")

("your homecoming will be my...")
("timeless...")   99   71
("if seventy were young...")
("for any ruffian of the sky...")
("pity his how illimitable plight...")
("without the mercy of...")
("annie died the other day...")
("O the sun comes up-up-up...")
("now that, more nearest...")   101   25
Seven Poems, I ("mortals...")   121   6

ARTICLES
Eleven Quotations
    [*Letters to a Young Poet*,
    by Rainer Maria Rilke]   74   91
Correspondence   85   248

BOOKS REVIEWED
Tulips and Chimneys   23   211
XLI Poems   29   164
is 5
Him   31   345
Viva   39   332
Eimi   42   277
The Red Front, by Louis Aragon (Tr.)   42   281
Tom   48   221
Collected Poems   52   284
50 Poems   59   162
Contemporary Poets Series
    [Recording]   61   519
One Times One   64   158
Anthropos: The Future of Art   70   211
i: six nonlectures   86   353
Poems 1923-1954
Adventures in Value
    (With Marion Morehouse)   102   341
Selected Letters of...
    (Ed. by F. W. Dupee
    and George Stade)   115   277

ARTICLES ABOUT
Visual Poetry,
    by Jessica Nelson North   31   334
Cummings and Phonetics,
    by Joseph Axelrod   65   88
Notebooks, 1924-1938,
    by Archibald MacLeish   73   88
Prosody as the Meaning,
    by Karl Shapiro   73   336
Poetry on Records,
    by Harry T. Moore   79   353
E. E. Cummings:
    The World of "Un,"
    by Carl Bode   86   358
Rev. of *E. E. Cummings and the Critics*
    (Ed. by S. V. Baum)   102   341
Poets Aloud, by Donald Hall   139   297

CUNARD, NANCY
BOOKS REVIEWED
Wheels, An Anthology of Verse (Ed.) 10 41

CUNLIFFE, J. W.
BOOKS REVIEWED
Poems of the Great War (Ed.) 12 284

CUNNINGHAM, C. [Pseud.]
POEMS
The Alien 13 253

CUNNINGHAM, HOUSE
POEMS
With the Feet on the Ground 76 145
The Draft of a Finale
Foundation

CUNNINGHAM, J. S.
BOOKS REVIEWED
The Powers That Be 118 102

CUNNINGHAM, J. V. ["J. V. C."]
POEMS
Sonnet on a Still Night 40 21
Horoscope 81 23
Epigram 81 175
Love Letter 101 26
Two Love Poems 103 26
 Miramar Beach
 Perfect Imperfection
From *To What Strangers?*
 What Welcome? 103 281

ARTICLES
The Ancient Quarrel
 Between History and Poetry 74 336
The Poetry of Wallace Stevens 75 149

REVIEWS
The Journey and Other Poems,
 by Yvor Winters 40 163

BOOKS REVIEWED
The Helmsman 60 279
The Judge Is Fury 71 50
Doctor Drink 77 114
The Exclusions of a Rhyme 97 181
Tradition and Poetic Structure 98 332
The Journal of John Cardan,
 Together with the Quest of the Opal
 and the Problem of Form 105 262
To What Strangers, What Welcome
The Collected Poems and Epigrams 121 229

ARTICLES ABOUT
Rev. of *Forms of Discovery,*
 by Yvor Winters 114 113

CUNNINGHAM, NORA B.
POEMS
Giving 21 133
February 23 257

CURNOW, ALLEN
POEMS
Discovery 59 324
Rite of Spring
In Summer Sheeted Under...
"Sailing or Drowning..." 60 203
Attitudes for a New Zealand Poet 63 74
When the Hulk of the World 76 78
To Forget Self and All 86 342
He Cracked a Word

ARTICLES
Correspondence:
 The Pacific Is Narrower 59 349

BOOKS REVIEWED
Recent Poems
 (With A. R. D. Fairburn,
 Denis Glover, and R. A. K. Mason) 59 343
Island and Time
Sailing or Drowning 65 51
A Book of New Zealand
 Verse 1923-45 (Ed.) 68 231
Poems 1949-57 94 44

CURRAN, EDWIN
POEMS
The March Thaw 11 310
The Lions 19 59

BOOKS REVIEWED
First Poems 15 53
Second Poems

CURRAN, G. E.
BOOKS REVIEWED
The Last Judgment 28 104

CURRAN, JOHN PHILPOT
ARTICLES ABOUT
Poetry and Oratory,
 by Padraic Colum 9 200

CURREY, R. N.
POEMS
Now that the War Is Here 56 306
Among Strangers 58 252
Spring Offensive
This Other Planet:
 Three Poems on Exile 63 128
South India 64 197
 Men and Gods
 Hindu Temple

Siva		
Ganesh		
Hindu Women		
Cattle		
Hill Station		
Elephants, Rajputana	69	197

CURRY, HELEN
POEMS
| *American Story* | 71 | 254 |

CURRY, MARY C.
BOOKS REVIEWED
| *The Poems of…* | 77 | 215 |

CURRY, OTWAY
ARTICLES ABOUT
| Notes on Mid-Western Oblivion, | | |
| by Pat Morrissette | 34 | 346 |

CURRY, WALTER CLYDE
BOOKS REVIEWED
| *Milton's Ontology,* | | |
| *Cosmogony, and Physics* | 93 | 404 |

CURTIS, CHRISTINE TURNER
POEMS
| *Quenched* | 25 | 140 |

CURTIS, NATALIE
ARTICLES
| Again the Negro | | |
| [Vachel Lindsay] | 11 | 147 |

ARTICLES ABOUT
[Note]	10	110
On the Need of Scholarships		
for the Study of Indian Culture,		
by Alice Corbin Henderson	22	325

CURTISS, MINA
BOOKS REVIEWED
| *Olive, Cypress, and Palm* (Ed.) | 37 | 164 |

CURTIUS, ERNST ROBERT
BOOKS REVIEWED
European Literature		
and the Latin Middle Ages		
(Tr. by Willard R. Trask)	84	158

CURZON, DAVID
POEMS
| *A Day in 1609* | 169 | 19 |

CUSCADEN, R. R.
BOOKS REVIEWED
| *Ups & Downs of a Third Baseman* | 103 | 324 |

CUSHING, EDWARD
POEMS
| *The Old Man* | 23 | 255 |

CUSHING, FRANK HAMILTON
ARTICLES ABOUT
| Aboriginal Poetry I, | | |
| by Harriet Monroe | 9 | 251 |

CUTHBERT, CLIFTON
POEMS
| *Decline* | 43 | 23 |

CUTLER, BRUCE
POEMS
From *A West Wind Rises: The Massacre*	100	381
Sun City	104	363
Waking	108	303
Prognosis	153	156

REVIEWS
The Facts of Human Defeat	93	404
Il Dramma Divino		
e il Dramma Umano		
nel Paradiso Perduto,		
by Elio Chinol		
Milton's Ontology,		
Cosmogony, and Physics,		
by Walter Clyde Curry		
Milton, by Rose Macaulay		
Heroic Knowledge, by Arnold Stein		
Like Prelates of the Grove	99	187
Image and Meaning: Metaphoric		
Traditions in Renaissance Poetry,		
by Don Cameron Allen		
Poems of Bishop Henry King		
(Ed. by James Rupert Baker)		
The Poems of Lord Vaux		
(Ed. by Larry P. Vonalt)		
A Long Reach, Strong Speech	103	387
The Selected Poems		
of John Malcolm Brinnin		
Selected Poems,		
by Gwendolyn Brooks		
Poems 2, by Alan Dugan		
The City of Satisfactions,		
by Daniel Hoffman		
The Wheel of Summer,		
by Joseph Langland		
The Complete Poems		
of Frederick Goddard Tuckerman		
(Ed. by N. Scott Momaday)		
[Yvor Winters]	107	401
What We Are, and Are Not	108	269
Knock upon Silence,		
by Carolyn Kizer		
Selected Poems, by Louis Simpson		

"D. D."
[See DUDLEY, DOROTHY]

"D. E."
[See BAILEY, DORIS]

"D. H."
[See HINE, DARYL]

DACEY, PHILIP
POEMS
The Rowboat   124   71
From the Clearing   129   252
Hopkins Under Ether   132   73
Praiseful Mouths   135   153
Upon Sending His Child Support Check
    to L. L. Bean and His Check
    for the Sleeping Bags to His Ex-Wife   148   328

DAGERMAN, STIG
POEMS
From "Birgitta Suite"
    (Tr. by Thomas and Vera Vance)   103   231

ARTICLES ABOUT
A Note on Stig Dagerman,
    by Thomas Vance   103   255

D'AGUIAR, FRED
ARTICLES ABOUT
A Letter from Britain,
    by William Logan   157   222

DAHLBERG, EDWARD
POEMS
A Classical Regularity   37   203
Kansas City West Bottoms
For Louis Zukofsky   78   278
Trust Is a Fool   81   97
Two Poems   83   193
    ("Ocean begat ground...")
    ("The spirit is a vast marsh...")
Five Poems   95   144
    ("He who has never tasted...")
    ("The world is a wound...")
    ("Do I not know that the Mother...")

    ("No one knows himself...")
    ("Much flesh walks upon the earth...")

ARTICLES
How Do You Spell Fool?
    [Edouard Roditi]   78   54

REVIEWS
Ushant, an Autobiographical Narrative,
    by Conrad Aiken   81   313
Studies in Classic American Literature,
    by D. H. Lawrence   83   347

BOOKS REVIEWED
The Flea of Sodom   77   236
The Sorrows of Priapus   94   54
Because I Was Flesh   105   397
Cipango's Hinder Door   109   401

ARTICLES ABOUT
Correspondence from Elizabeth Pollet
    [Conrad Aiken]   82   176
Does Poetry Have a "Policy"?
    by Karl Shapiro   82   178
    [Note on misquotations]   82   183

DAICHES, DAVID
POEMS
Cosmogony   53   70
Spring in November
Scotland from America, 1938   57   237
Ulysses' Library
Remembering a Farm
    in East Lothian, Scotland   59   328
Six War Poems   60   235
    Manifesto
    ("If the wind blows...")
    ("This is a strange thing...")
    ("When I was one and twenty...")
    From Chicago
    ("Fall from the slow-drawn days...")
War Poem for Britain   63   71
1947   71   121
Paradise Mislaid   98   79
Notes for a History of Poetry

TRANSLATIONS
  Poems by Petr Bezruc,
    Jiri Wolker, and Laco Novomesk   55   176

ARTICLES
  W. H. Auden: The Search for a Public   54   148
  Poetry in the First World War
    [Wilfrid Wilson Gibson,
    Siegfried Sassoon, Edmund Blunden,
    Wilfrid Owen]   56   323
  Poetry and the Post-Medieval Mind
    [Henry Rago, Dante]   57   374
  Poets and the War   59   208
  Contemporary Poetry in Britain
    [M. J. Tambimuttu, Dylan Thomas,
    Henry Treece, G. S. Fraser,
    J. F. Hendry, Nicholas Moore,
    Tom Scott, D. S. Savage,
    Francis Scarfe]   62   150
  Correspondence:
    Reply to Mr. O'Connor   62   292
  The Poetry of Karl Shapiro   66   266
  The Lyricism of George Barker   69   336
  Hugh MacDiarmid and Scottish Poetry   72   202

REVIEWS
  Orion Marches, by Michael Roberts   55   335
  Another Time: Poems, by W. H. Auden   56   40
  The Last Ditch, by Louis MacNeice   57   152
  Awake! and Other Wartime Poems,
    by W. R. Rodgers   60   94
  The Craftsman and the Poet   64   35
    The Violent, by Harry Brown
    Sacred and Secular Elegies,
      by George Barker
  The Shield of Achilles, by Horace Gregory 64   334
  Poems, New and Selected,
    by Richard Eberhart   66   92
  Questions and Answers   71   45
    Collected Poems, by Sidney Keyes
    Fossils of a Future Time?
      by W. J. Turner

BOOKS REVIEWED
  Poetry and the Modern World   58   210
  Leaves of Grass One Hundred Years After
    [Contributor]
    (Ed. by Milton Hindus)   87   183

ARTICLES ABOUT
  Correspondence from Henry Rago   58   108
  Correspondence
    from William Carlos Williams   58   112
  Correspondence
    from William Van O'Connor   62   291
  Correspondence
    from William Van O'Connor   63   55
  [Note]   84   58

DAIKIN, LESLIE H.
  BOOKS REVIEWED
    Good-Bye Twilight (Ed.)   55   279

DAILY, ELWOOD
  POEMS
    Medieval Exhibit   69   198
    Highway Bridge

DALE, PETER
  BOOKS REVIEWED
    The Storms   114   266
    Mortal Fire   131   292

DALL, IAN
  POEMS
    Island Droves   33   22

DALTON, A. C.
  BOOKS REVIEWED
    Flame and Adventure   24   341

DALTON, HENRY
  POEMS
    Opera Matinée   61   608
    Threat of Blindness
    Short Story

DALTON, POWER
  POEMS
    Impulse   23   71
    Gulls
    Flail

  BOOKS REVIEWED
    Star Pollen   22   223
    Turning Earth   25   337

DALVEN, RAE
  TRANSLATIONS
    Poems by C. P. Cavafy   98   31
    Poems by Yannis Ritsos   103   306
    Poems by Yannis Ritsos   116   292
    Poems by C. P. Cavafy,
      Yannis Ritsos, Angelos Sikelianus,
      and Kostes Palamas   120   257
    Poem by Alexandra Placotari   145   335

  ARTICLES
    A Note on Yannis Ritsos   103   334

  REVIEWS
    Theatre and Lyric   102   54
      Aristophanes: The Frogs
        (Tr. by Richmond Lattimore)
      Aristophanes: The Clouds
        (Tr. by William Arrowsmith)
      Bacchylides: Complete Poems
        (Tr. by Robert Fagles)

BOOKS REVIEWED
    The Complete Poems of Cavafy (Tr.)   101   283
    Modern Greek Poetry (Tr. and ed.)   123   34

DALY, DANIEL
POEMS
    Milk Cartons   154   91

DALY, JAMES
POEMS
    Finalities   25   250
      Words of the Weaver of Nets
      Sculpture
      Excursion
      Crest of Slow Fire
    Interludes   28   27
      The Eagle
      Fodder
      Faith
      Another Phoenix
      For the Praiser of Perilous Lips
      Flight
    Filaments of Fable   33   312
      Lament
      A Very Old Woman
      In the Mind
      Diomedes' Horses
    Death from Natural Causes   51   307
    Epithalamion: A Fragment
    Wary Travelers Suspect
    For a Talkative Woman
    Stone-Steep the Pier
    City   52   178
    Lutany at Brink of Armageddon   55   20
    The Dreamed Flight
    A Nausicaa Remembers
    Stokowski in the Park
    A.D. 1940: An Epigraph   56   138
    Franchester Farm
    Chaplin on Fifth Avenue   60   186
    Moment of Summer
    The Asker
    Diamond Point
    Still-Life: Corner
      in a Montclair Sun-Room   62   193

REVIEWS
    Tamar and Other Poems,
      by Robinson Jeffers   26   278
    Dionysus in Doubt,
      by Edwin Arlington Robinson   27   40
    This Was a Poet: A Critical
      Biography of Emily Dickinson,
      by George Frisbie Whicher   53   312
    Mortal Sequence,
      by Charlotte Wilder   55   217
    Walt Whitman: Poet of Democracy,
      by Hugh l'Anson Fausset   61   687

BOOKS REVIEWED
    The Guilty Sun   29   346
    One Season Shattered   48   282
    Poems 1923-1943   64   223

ARTICLES ABOUT
    Obituary   65   114

DALY, T. A.
BOOKS REVIEWED
    McAroni Ballads   16   278

DALY, TOM
ARTICLES ABOUT
    Our Contemporaries:
    Bound or Free?
    [Free verse]   18   53

DALZIEL, KATHLEEN
POEMS
    The Lakes of Connewarre   41   130
    Hill Water   46   146

DAMAS, LEON
BOOKS REVIEWED
    African Songs of Love,
      War, Grief, & Abuse   103   394

DAME, HAZEL STEVENS
BOOKS REVIEWED
    This Too-Brief Moment   77   215

DAMON, S. FOSTER
POEMS
    Bound Wings   24   7
      In the Third Person
      Burning Bush
    Three Lyrics from an Unfinished
      Revolutionary Poem   43   324
      Dawn Song to His First-Born
      Sung at a Private Dinner
      Another Dinner Song
    From *The Moulton Tragedy*   60   115
      The New Cellar Hole
      Abigail at the Window
      Old Lydia Blaisdell,
        the Cross-Roads Witch

ARTICLES
    Francis Daniel Pastorius   44   37

BOOKS REVIEWED
    Eight More Harvard Poets
      (Ed. with Robert Hillyer)   24   162
    Astrolabe   31   167
    Tilted Moons   35   340
    Amy Lowell: A Chronicle
      with Extracts from Her Correspondence   47   212

DANA, ROBERT (PATRICK)
POEMS
My Glass Brother   85   196
For Sister Mary Apolline   91   17
Some Versions of Silence   108   111
At the Vietnam War Memorial   146   285
Rat   158   87
Anniversary   162   260

REVIEWS
Five Anthologies   110   47
  Poetry in Australia
    (Ed. by T. Inglis Moore
    and Douglas Stewart)
  The Golden Treasury
    (Ed. by Francis Turner Palgrave
    and John Press)
  The Mentor Book of Irish Poetry
    (Ed. by Devin A. Garrity)
  The Fugitive Poets
    (Ed. by William Pratt)
  Poems on Poetry
    (Ed. by Robert Wallace
    and James G. Taaffe)
  [John Press, Laura Riding]

BOOKS REVIEWED
The Dark Flags of Waking   108   191
Some Versions of Silence   111   329

DANIEL, ARNAUT
POEMS
A Strict Lady Strictly Guarded
  (Tr by Richmond Lattimore)   101   63

ARTICLES ABOUT
Apprenticed in Provence,
  by Leonard Casper   81   203

DANIEL, JOHN
POEMS
The Meal   153   94
To the Scrub Jay on My Office Mate's Desk
For Our Fifth Anniversary, Seven Days Late 156 129
The Rising Wind
In Sky Lakes Wilderness   157   82
The Echoing Lake
Dependence Day
To My Mother   162   318

DANIELL, ROSEMARY
BOOKS REVIEWED
A Sexual Tour of the Deep South   128   290

DANIELS, EARL
POEMS
Birth   24   77
Death
Weather Moods   42   252

DANIELS, GUY
BOOKS REVIEWED
Poems and Translations   95   309
A Lermontov Reader (Ed. and tr.)   111   258
The Complete Plays
  of Vladimir Mayakovsky (Tr.)   114   40

DANNER, MARGARET
POEMS
Far from Africa   81   176
  Garnishing the Aviary
  Dance of the Abakweta
  The Visit of the Professor of Aesthetics
Etta Moten's Attic   84   320
Best Loved of Africa   89   23
The Painted Lady

D'ANNUNZIO, (GABRIELE)
ARTICLES ABOUT
Rev. of The Furioso,
  by Leonard Bacon   41   275

DANTE (ALIGHIERI)
POEMS
Paradiso: Canto Five
  (Tr. by John Ciardi)   107   75
From Dante's Inferno   162   143
  Canto XVI
  Canto XVII
  (Tr. by Robert Pinsky)
From Dante's Purgatorio (Canto V)
  (Tr. by W. S. Merwin)   162   152

BOOKS REVIEWED
The Divine Comedy
  (Tr. by Henry Johnson)   9   104
The Divine Comedy...
  (Tr. by Melville Best Anderson)   20   165
The Divine Comedy...
  (Tr. by Jefferson Butler Fletcher)   43   229
The Divine Comedy...
  (Tr. by Melville Best Anderson)
Dante's Inferno
  (Tr. by Laurence Binyon)
The Paradise of...
  (Tr. by Geoffrey L. Bickersteth)
Inferno (Tr. by John Ciardi)   85   225
Dante's Purgatorio
  (Tr. by John Ciardi)   100   198

ARTICLES ABOUT
Dante—and Today,
  by Emanuel Carnevali   18   323
Dante and Contemporaneousness,
  by Harriet Monroe
  [John Erskine]   23   264
The Medievalism of T. S. Eliot,
  by Leo Shapiro   56   202

Poetry and the Post-Medieval Mind,
  by David Daiches   57   374
Rev. of *The Idea of a Theatre*,
  by Francis Fergusson   77   227
Conversation on Cornelia Street:
  A Dialogue with W. H. Auden,
  by Howard Griffin   83   96
Rev. of *Dante's Drama of the Mind*,
  by Francis Fergusson   86   108
Rev. of *Further Papers on Dante*,
  by Dorothy Sayers;
  De Sanctis on Dante,
  by Francesco De Sanctis;
  Dante's Other World, the "Purgatorio"
  as Guide to The Divine Comedy,
  by Bernard Stambler   96   323
Rev. of *The Sweetness and Greatness*
  of Dante's Divine Comedy,
  by Robert Duncan   111   402
Waking Up Over the *Aeneid*,
  by Paul Breslin   143   347

DAO, GIA [See GIA DAO]

DARGAN, E. PRESTON
POEMS
  Heartily Know   6   14
  Erect
  For a Map of Mars

DARGAN, OLIVE TILFORD
BOOKS REVIEWED
  Lute and Furrow   23   285

DARÍO, RUBÉN
POEMS
  Litany for Our Lord Don Quixote
  (Tr. by Muna Lee)   26   135

BOOKS REVIEWED
  Prosas Profanas
  (Tr. by Charles B. McMichael)   22   165

ARTICLES ABOUT
  Rubén Darío,
  by Salomon de la Selva   8   200
José Santos Chocano,
  by John Pierrepont Rice   11   260
New Tendencies,
  by Ernesto Montenegro   26   161
The New American and His
  Point of View Toward Poetry,
  by Jorge Carrera Andrade
  (Tr. by H. R. Hays)   62   88

DARR, ANN
BOOKS REVIEWED
  The Myth of a Woman's Fist   127   164

D'ARRIGO, STEFANO
POEMS
  Tu che nel mondo hai parola ancora/
  You Who Still Possess Speech   155   42
  Avevi alito, un corpo/
  You Had Breath, a Body
  (Tr. by Stephen Sartarelli)

DARYUSH, ELIZABETH
POEMS
  The Look   73   16
  Loved Faces

BOOKS REVIEWED
  Selected Poems   74   304
  Selected Poems   124   45

DAS, JIBANANANDA
POEMS
  Twenty Years After   93   216

DA SAN GEMIGNANO, FOLGORE
BOOKS REVIEWED
  A Wreath for San Gemignano
  (Ed. and tr. by Richard Aldington)   68   293

DATTA, SUDHINDRANATH
POEMS
  Camel-Bird   93   218

DAUER, LESLEY
POEMS
  Falling   162   69

DAUER, ROSAMOND
POEMS
  Burial Places   124   262
  Seasonal Adjustment

DAVENPORT, GUY
POEMS
  The Resurrection
  in Cookham Churchyard   110   321

TRANSLATIONS
  Poems and fragments
  by Archilochus   101   404

REVIEWS
  Four Modes of Translation   107   264
    The Revelation of John
      (Tr. by Richmond Lattimore)
    Poems from the Greek Anthology
      (Tr. by Kenneth Rexroth)
    The Comedies of Terence
      (Tr. by Laurence Echard)
      (Ed. by Robert Graves)
    The Satyricon of Petronius
      (Tr. by William Arrowsmith)

From the Greek   108   416
  Greek Lyric Poetry
    (Tr. by Willis Barnstone)
  Sappho: Lyrics in the Original Greek
    with Translations,
    by Willis Barnstone
  Patrocleia of Homer: A New Version,
    by Christopher Logue

BOOKS REVIEWED
  Carmina Archilochi:
    The Fragments of Archilochos (Tr.)   105   329

ARTICLES ABOUT
  Rev. of Valley of
    the Many-Colored Grasses,
    by Ronald Johnson   115   47

DAVENPORT, RUSSELL (W.)
POEMS
  Songs from the Dusk   28   136
  Movement for an Imaginary Violin
  Song from Memory
  Song to the New Moon

BOOKS REVIEWED
  My Country   66   106

DAVEY, FRANK
BOOKS REVIEWED
  City of the Gulls and Sea   108   45
  Bridge Force   109   123
  The Scarred Hull   111   323

DAVIDMAN, JOY
POEMS
  Stark Lines   47   193
  Resurrection
  Amulet
  Doubts and Certainties   49   323
  Variations on a Theme
  The Half-Hearted
  Shadow Dance
  Odi et Amo

BOOKS REVIEWED
  Letter to a Comrade   54   33
  War Poems of the United Nations (Ed.)   63   346
  Seven Poets in Search of an Answer
    (With Maxwell Bodenheim,
    Langston Hughes, Aaron Kramer,
    Alfred Kreymborg,
    and Norman Rosten)
    (Ed. by Thomas Yoseloff)   64   289

DAVIDSON, DONALD
POEMS
  Aunt Maria and the Gourds   40   76

ARTICLES
  The Southern Poet and His Tradition   40   94
  In Memory of John Gould Fletcher
    [Amy Lowell]   77   154

BOOKS REVIEWED
  An Outland Piper   24   341
  The Tall Men   31   222
  Fugitives: An Anthology of Verse   32   102
  Lee in the Mountains, and Other Poems   54   108
  The Long Street   100   395
  Poems, 1922-1961   109   189

ARTICLES ABOUT
  Correspondence from Allen Tate   25   169
  A Note on Three Southern Poets,
    by Robert Penn Warren   40   103
  Present-Day Tendencies,
    by Harriet Monroe   48   152

DAVIDSON, GUSTAV
POEMS
  Beauty   26   203
  Eaglet   35   84
  Tai
  Rock

ARTICLES
  Correspondence
    [Robert Graves]   103   200

BOOKS REVIEWED
  Twenty Sonnets   29   229
  Mortal Hunger   64   48
  Thirst of the Antelope   67   170

DAVIDSON, WILLIAM
POEMS
  One Savage Word   40   69
  The Loneliest Born   44   68

DAVIE, DONALD
POEMS
  In California   100   71
  Sculptures in Hungary
  New York in August
  Coastal Redwoods
  Agave in the West
  On Not Deserving
  Hyphens
  Autumn Imagined   102   312
  Hot Hands
  Where Depths Are Surfaces
  Vying
  The Red Mills
  July
  A Battlefield

ARTICLES
England as Poetic Subject   100 121

REVIEWS
Enigma   91   56
   Letters of James Joyce
    (Ed. by Stuart Gilbert)
   Collected Poems, by James Joyce
   [W. B. Yeats]

BOOKS REVIEWED
Articulate Energy   93   325
A Winter Talent   94   250
The Forests of Lithuania   97   260
A Sequence for Francis Parkman   100   104
  New and Selected Poems
Ezra Pound: Poet as Sculptor   106   361
Events and Wisdoms   108   399
Collected Poems 1950-1970   122   289
The Shires   127   234
In the Stopping Train   133   227

ARTICLES ABOUT
Rev. of Poets of the 1950's:
  An Anthology of New English Verse
  (Ed. by D. J. Enright)   89   260
Letter from Dublin,
  by John Montague   90   310
Rev. of The Collected Poems
  of William Carlos Williams: Volume I
  (Ed. by A. Walton Litz
  and Christopher MacGowan)   150   286

DAVIES, ADA
POEMS
Poem ("See in the screen of steel...")   78   80

DAVIES, ANEIRIN TALFAN
BOOKS REVIEWED
Dylan Thomas's Choice
  (Ed. with Ralph Maud)   106   429

DAVIES, MARGARET
BOOKS REVIEWED
Apollinaire   107   267

DAVIES, MARY CAROLYN
POEMS
Cloistered   7   130
The Death Watch
Intuition
A Day   10   244
  Sun Prayer
  Wind Prayer
  The Grapes
  Dusk
  A Girl's Songs
Wanderings   14   308

In the Middle West
Sea Gulls
The Apple Tree Said
I Pray You
Portrait of a House   20   131
The Last of the Cowboys
The Wise Lovers   22   133
Out of the West   24   134
  A Dedication
  The Hunting Season
  Pine-Woman
  Out of the Earth
  A Poet to a Lover
The Lighter of Flames   27   246
Complimentary Ticket   30   315

BOOKS REVIEWED
The Drums in Our Street   14   220
Marriage Songs   24   339
Penny Show   32   55

DAVIES, W(ILLIAM) H.
BOOKS REVIEWED
Collected Poems   11   99
Selected Poems   27   44
Secrets
The Poems of...   48   232
Love Poems
The Complete Poems of...   107   406

ARTICLES ABOUT
Rev. of The Listeners,
  by Walter de la Mare   8   312

DAVIS, ANDREW
POEMS
A Krater: Achilles and Ajax
  Playing Backgammon   168   18

DAVIS, BETTY MILLER
POEMS
To Phedre   77   78
Holy Thursday Communion   78   322
Only Beneath Whose Awful Hand

REVIEWS
Secular Lyrics of the XIVth
  and XVth Centuries
  (Ed. by Russell Hope Robbins)   81   258

DAVIS, BRAD
POEMS
Stepping Through Mercury   170   68

DAVIS, CATHERINE
POEMS
The Raven's Plight   75   207
Plato and the Serpent

   The Leaves
   Arachne: An Ode
   Cold Comfort   106   204

REVIEWS
   27 Night Sonnets,
      by Elliott Coleman   75   298
   Four Poets   88   273
      The Nets, by Brewster Ghiselin
      Upon This Rock, by James Kirkup
      The Book, by Harvey Shapiro
      The Traveler, by Don Stanford

DAVIS, DICK
  ARTICLES ABOUT
   A Letter from Britain [II],
      by William Logan   157   290

DAVIS, ETHEL M.
  POEMS
   Song ("Over what is lovely...")   42   19

DAVIS, FANNIE STEARNS
  POEMS
   Profits   1   182
   Two Songs of Conn the Fool
     Moon Folly
     Warning
   Storm Dance
   In an Old Lodging-House   5   269
   Tonight

  BOOKS REVIEWED
   Myself and I   2   223
   Crack o' Dawn   6   45

DAVIS, FRANK MARSHALL
  BOOKS REVIEWED
   Black Man's Verse   48   293

DAVIS, GLOVER
  POEMS
   Monuments   106   282
   The Giant   114   17
   Columns   120   345
   The Orphan   121   143
   Mouths
   Body Armor   123   12
   Telescope/Kaleidescope   132   11

  BOOKS REVIEWED
   Bandaging Bread and Other Poems   121   343

DAVIS, H. L.
  POEMS
   Primapara   14   1
   The Sweet-Tasting
   Running Vines in a Field

   A Field by the River
   In the Field
   The Gypsy Girl
   The Spirit
   My Step-Grandfather
   Oakland Pier: 1918
   The Old Are Sleepy
   Flags
   The Valley Harvest
   [Rpt. in The Prize Poems]   15   108
     Proud Riders
     In the Field
     My Step-Grandfather
     The Valley Harvest
   In This Wet Orchard   16   117
   Stalks of Wild Hay
   Baking Bread
   The Rain-Crow
   The Threshing-Floor
   From a Vineyard
   The Market-Gardens
   October: "The Old Eyes"
   To the River Beach
   Open Hands   21   18
   Dog-Fennel
   Far-Western Pastorals   25   289
     Binding Hands
     Mid-September
     The River People
     The Dead Bird
     Renewing Windbreak
     A Hill Come Out of the Sea
     The Deep Water
   White Petal Nanitch   29   177
   Pico y Pala   32   299
     Steel Gang
     Cloudy Day
     Rivers to Children
   In Argos   42   61
   New Birds

  ARTICLES
   Correspondence
     [Robinson Jeffers]   29   292
   [Note]   33   348

  REVIEWS
   The Township Line,
     by Albert Frederick Wilson   17   343
   October and Other Poems,
     by Robert Bridges   17   344
   Ballads of the Singing Bowl,
     by Marjorie Allen Seiffert   30   338
   The Women at Point Sur,
     by Robinson Jeffers   31   274

  ARTICLES ABOUT
   [Note]   46   354

DAVIS, JOHN CLAIBORNE
BOOKS REVIEWED
   Forty Poems 1935-43
     (With Robert Knox Bishop)   63   104

DAVIS, JON
POEMS
   White Body, Green Moss   146   88
   Essay on Joy Beginning with
     Mozart's Sinfonia Concertante
     in B-Flat Major   151   359
   Essay: The Yearbook   151   463

BOOKS REVIEWED
   Dangerous Amusements   153   30

DAVIS, KI
POEMS
   Two Lovers   141   327

DAVIS, LELAND
POEMS
   A Ghetto Catch   22   16
   The Peril of Happiness

DAVIS, MELODY
POEMS
   Pink   157   275
   Topos   158   131
   It Only Starts   170   287

DAVIS, ROBERT GORHAM
REVIEWS
   Selected Poems,
     by Vernon Watkins   73   170

DAVIS, WILLIAM VIRGIL
POEMS
   The Polar Bear   118   81
   The Pond
   After the Funeral   121   206
   In a Room   124   78
   The Science of Numbers:
     or Poetry as Pure Mathematics
   Windows   154   98
   For My Father   158   36
   The Orchard

BOOKS REVIEWED
   One Way to Reconstruct
     the Scene   140   35

DAVISON, EDWARD
POEMS
   The Owl   27   254
   Password
   Any Street

ARTICLES
   Correspondence: Mr. Davison Protests
     [Eunice Tietjens]   46   352

BOOKS REVIEWED
   Harvest of Youth   29   348
   The Ninth Witch   42   228
   Collected Poems: 1917-1939   62   338

ARTICLES ABOUT
   The Cuckoo School of Criticism,
     by Eunice Tietjens   46   96
   [Note]   46   353

DAVISON, PETER
POEMS
   Artemis   98   209
   Sacrificial Mask
   Under Protection   114   304
   The Public Garden
   The Grandmother
   The Visitant
   Walking the Boundaries:
     North by the Creek   124   9
   July Meeting   134   205
   Swimming 1935   140   269
   The Money Cry
   Not a Dilemma
   The Revenant   144   141
   Remembering Eurydice
   Moving into Memory
   Equinox 1980   151   37
   The War of the Pelicans   152   194
   Mother & Child #3   152   277
   What Ails You   170   142

BOOKS REVIEWED
   The Breaking of the Day   105   201
   The City and the Island   110   267
   Pretending To Be Asleep   118   228
   Walking the Boundaries:
     Poems 1957-1974   125   295
   Hello, Darkness: The Collected Poems
     of L. E. Sissman (Ed.)   133   100
   A Voice in the Mountain   133   227
   Barn Fever and Other Poems   140   293
   Praying Wrong: New and Selected Poems,
     1957-1984   147   227

DAVISON, SCOTT
TRANSLATIONS
   Poems by Cesare Pavese   161   13

DAVITT, MICHAEL
POEMS
   3AG   167   50

DAWKINS, JOHN
POEMS
Bare Poem   72   19

DAWSON, CARLEY
BOOKS REVIEWED
The Metamorphoses of the Circle,
by Georges Poulet
(Tr. with Elliott Coleman)   112   41

DAWSON, GRACE STRICKLER
POEMS
The Victor   26   193
Conversation   32   203
Sundown   40   206

DAWSON, MITCHELL
POEMS
New Days   23   191
Dry Ochre
Gulls' Eyes Are Cold
Any Night
No and Yes

REVIEWS
Birds, Beasts and Flowers,
by D. H. Lawrence   23   273
Three Victorians   24   160
Poems of Arthur O'Shaughnessy
(Ed. by William Alexander Percy)
A Selection from the Poems
of Michael Field
[Katherine Bradley, Edith Cooper]
The Flaming Terrapin,
by Roy Campbell   25   217

DAWSON, ROBERT
BOOKS REVIEWED
Six Mile Corner   111   195

DAWSON-SCOTT, C. A.
BOOKS REVIEWED
Bitter Herbs   23   54

DAY, DOUGLAS
BOOKS REVIEWED
Swifter than Reason: The Poetry
and Criticism of Robert Graves   104   264

DAY, SARAH
POEMS
Deep Sleep   169   20

ARTICLES ABOUT
Towards a Contemporary
Australian Poetics,
by John Kinsella   169   94

DAY-LEWIS, CECIL
[CECIL DAY LEWIS]
POEMS
Epitaph for an Enemy   39   249
Winter Night
From The Magnetic Mountain   41   244
Address to the Mother
Condemned
Elegy Before Death   81   24

REVIEWS
Paging Mankind   49   225
The Ascent of F 6,
by W. H. Auden and
Christopher Isherwood
Look, Stranger!,
by W. H. Auden

BOOKS REVIEWED
From Feathers to Iron   42   288
The Magnetic Mountain
Collected Poems 1929-1933   47   158
A Hope for Poetry
Short Is the Time   67   96
The Georgics of Virgil (Tr.)   71   337
The Poetic Image   72   322
Poetry for You
Poems 1943-1947   74   114
Christmas Eve   86   242
Pegasus and Other Poems   92   309
The Collected Poems
of Wilfred Owen (Ed.)   104   41
Requiem for the Living   104   375
The Lyric Impulse   108   65
Selected Poems   112   131
The Whispering Roots
and Other Poems   119   342

ARTICLES ABOUT
Notes on English Poets,
by Michael Roberts   39   271
English Letter, by F. R. Leavis   46   274
Poetry of the Left,
by Harriet Monroe   48   212
A Letter from England,
by Geoffrey Grigson   49   101
Rev. of New Poems: 1943
(Ed. by Oscar Williams)   64   86
Rev. of The Marine Cemetery,
by Paul Valéry
(Tr. by Sidney Alexander)   76   172

DAZIEL, BRADFORD DUDLEY
BOOKS REVIEWED
Sarton Selected:
An Anthology of the Journals,
Novels and Poems of May Sarton (Ed.)   160   284

DEACON, ANNE [Pseud.]
POEMS
   The Traveller   17   75

DE ACOSTA, MERCEDES
POEMS
   Through Windows   17 185
   Lumbermen
   Soiled Hands
   Unreality
   To Vouletti
   Spring Sounds   26   16
   Offering
   In New Mexico   38 143

BOOKS REVIEWED
   Moods   17 276
   Archways of Life   19 345
   Streets and Shadows   23 222

DEAN, ELMA
POEMS
   Sestina for a Certain Coast 66 184
   Female   72 247

DEAN, LEONARD F.
BOOKS REVIEWED
   Shakespeare: Modern Essays
      in Criticism (Ed.)   92 189

DE ANDRADE, CARLOS DRUMMOND
[See DRUMMOND DE ANDRADE,
CARLOS]

DEANE, JOHN F.
POEMS
   Father   167 89

DE ANGELIS, MILO
POEMS
   Year   155 151
   Chi ha osato/He Who Has Dared
   Ti benderai?/
      Will You Put on the Blindfold?
   Il narratore/The Narrator
   Annuario/Yearbook
      (Tr. by Lawrence Venuti)

DEBEE, RAJLUKSHMEE
POEMS
   The House   93 211

DE BORN, BERTRANS
ARTICLES ABOUT
   On Near Perigord,
      by Ezra Pound   7 143
   Apprenticed in Provence,
      by Leonard Casper   81 203

DE BORNELH, GIRAUT
POEMS
   Alba (Tr. by Stephen Orgel) 116 356

DE BOSIS, LAURO
BOOKS REVIEWED
   Icaro (Tr. by Ruth Draper) 44 44
   The Story of My Death

DE BOSSCHÈRE, JEAN
BOOKS REVIEWED
   The Closed Door
      (Tr. by F. S. Flint)   12 48

DE BRAGANCA, NADEJDA
POEMS
   A Million Miles Apart   33 26
   To a Thinker   36 79

DE BRIMONT, A.
BOOKS REVIEWED
   Tablettes de Cire   10 160

DE BULLET, GENE
POEMS
   Looking Through   40 79
   Question
   Invitation
   The Dreamers

DE CAMPOS, ALVARO
[See PESSOA, FERNANDO]

DE CASSERES, BENJAMIN
BOOKS REVIEWED
   The Shadow-Eater   22 284

DECAUNES, LUC
ARTICLES ABOUT
   Marseille Letter, by Jean Rivier 60 269

DECAVALLES, ANDONIS
[ANDONIS DECAVALLAS]
POEMS
   Letter from Ithaca
      (Tr. by Kimon Friar) 78 181
   A Greek Trireme   88 310
   Tragedia Minima
   The Well
   Time of Judgement
      (Tr. by Kimon Friar)
   Robert Traill Spence Lowell
      (Tr. by Kimon Friar) 139 79

REVIEWS
   Two Views of Kazantzakis
      The Odyssey: A Modern Sequel,
        by Nikos Kazantzakis
        (Tr. by Kimon Friar) 95 175

[Louis O. Coxe]
The Plant, The Well,
    The Angel: A Trilogy,
    by Vassilis Vassilikos
    (Tr. by Edmund and Mary Keeley)   105   65

ARTICLES ABOUT
    Contemporary Greek Poetry,
    by Kimon Friar   78   145
    Post-War Greek Poets,
    by Kimon Friar   139   99

DE CHAZAL, MALCOLM
    POEMS
        From Sens-Plastique
        (Tr. by Richard Howard)   116   327

DECKER, DOROTHY
    ARTICLES ABOUT
        Correspondence
        from Will Wharton
        [Decker Press, Ervin Tax]   77   58

DECKER, JAMES
    ARTICLES ABOUT
        Correspondence
        from Will Wharton
        [Decker Press, Ervin Tax]   77   58

DE CORTE, MARCEL
    ARTICLES ABOUT
        French Poetry and
        the Revival of Mysticism,
        by Eugene Jolas   56   264

DEEMER, BILL
    POEMS
        Diana   107   98
        Poem ("The room is damp...")
        Poem ("Asleep, electric heaters...")

    BOOKS REVIEWED
        Poems   106   370

DE FOE, MARK
    POEMS
        Dream Lover   150   323
        Heat

DE FORD, MIRIAM ALLEN
    [MIRIAM DE FORD COLLIER]
    POEMS
        The Musicmaker's Child   5   169
        Faun   14   78
        Wisdom Through Tears
        Under the Cliff   19   18
            Shadow Canyon
            Themes

Will It Be Like This?
Traveler's Ditty   22   136
Ronsard   24   309
Milka   26   27
Aspects of Life   29   135
    Remittance Man
    Heloise
    Words
One of Those Accidents   33   253
Prelude to an Execution
Tule Fog   39   134
Bright Horseman
Sonnets in Farewell   46   138
    ("When you go from me...")
    ("Now you are gone...")
Litany   52   203

REVIEWS
    A Legacy of Hours,
    by Flora J. Arnstein   33   49

ARTICLES ABOUT
    [Note on misprint]   5   248

DE FORD, SARA
    POEMS
        In the Cave of the Giant Despair   114   170
        The Sleeping Beauty

DE FREES, MADELINE
    POEMS
        The Dovecove: Its Head Keepers   143   22

    BOOKS REVIEWED
        When Sky Lets Go   133   346
        Magpie on the Gallows   143   39

DEGAS, EDGAR
    POEMS
        Six Sonnets   76   323
            Thoroughbred
            The Parrot
            Dancer
            (To Mademoiselle Sanlaville)
            (To Mme. Caron...)
            Young Dancer
            (Tr. by Helen Burlin)

DE GASZTOLD, CARMEN BERNOS
    [See BERNOS DE GASZTOLD,
    CARMEN]

DE GIOVANNI, NORMAN THOMAS
    BOOKS REVIEWED
        Jorge Guillén, Cántico:
        A Selection, Spanish Poems
        with English Translation (Ed.)   111   46

DE GONGORA Y ARGOTE, LUIS
ARTICLES ABOUT
  Correspondence
    from William Carlos Williams   78 107

DE GOURMONT, REMY
POEMS
  Epigrammes   5 164
    Je N'Aime Plus
    La Vasque

ARTICLES
  A French Poet on Tradition
    (Tr. by Richard Aldington)   4 154
  French Poets and the War
    (Tr. by Richard Aldington)   5 184

ARTICLES ABOUT
  Vers Libre and Metrical Prose,
    by Amy Lowell   3 213
  In Memoriam, by Harriet Monroe   7 98
  Remy de Gourmont, by Ezra Pound   7 197
  Rev. of Six French Poets,
    by Amy Lowell   7 202

DE IBARBOUROU, JUANA
POEMS
  Bond (Tr. by Muna Lee)   26 151

DE JONG, DAVID CORNEL
POEMS
  Soft Measures   38 12
    Slow Dance
    I Hope at Dawn
    Walking Fieldward
  Cool Weather   42 201
  Father at Evening   45 316
  Soliloquy During Sorrow
  Aubade
  Question   47 316
  Simple Legend   52 70
  Easter Hymn   54 10
  Historical Note
  Armistice Again   57 178
  Night of Cats and Fathers
  Such Sweet Sorrow
  For the Weather About Us   59 267
  In Due Season
  Pleasant Streets
  Suburban Life and Death   61 431
  Eve of the Innocents   62 145
  Oh! Evening Star
  Nocturne
  Parade in Berlin
  Domination of June
  Spring Song   64 192
  Far Distant Star
  Ditty

Days and Battles Go On
For Our Past Years
Spring, 1944
Love Story   66 138
Milestone   68 13
When It Is Done
Beach Scene
Soliloquy
Appointment with Mr. Baxter   71 295
In the Respectful Evening
Delights of Husbandry
The Fevers of Spring
The Importance of the Inner Life
Deciphering the Elephant   73 321
Thanksgiving to Wise and Solid Old Men   76 200
A Little Sleep at Night
The Return
Still Traveling on Sunday
Dutch Ditty   80 198
Fever of the Blood Comes in June   84 209
Thomasina Refuted
The Old Man Had Few Fancies
Master   86 23
Eglantine: A Souvenir
Adagio: On a Summer's Beach
Travel Log   89 298
The Youthful Expectations
Pavan on a Beach
The Janitor's Face   91 11
There Is a Railroad Track
Preparing for a Love Nest on the Plains
Old Men Observing Small Boy Crying   92 371
Do Re Mi of Young
  Watching and Waiting
Song of a Little Experience
I Never Lost Faith in Angels   94 384
Yellow Tom
The Smallness and Strangeness
Pensive and Sceptical   96 277
Adolescence
Flight Outward
Angel
Possibly an Alien Here   97 366
To Mary, with Love
Cup of Mercy
Man Who in Faith Is Rooted
Choir of Reality
Lent Within and Without   100 155
Demiurgic
And Out Comes Summer
Assailed from Without   104 9
Born in a County-Seat
Ritual   106 286
Survivor
Family Court Ltd.   109 7
North of Hackensack
Honeymoon
Erelong Remembered   111 21

    Direction North
    Every Saturday
    All American

REVIEWS
    New and Selected, and a First Volume   102   125
      Hold April, by Jesse Stuart
      Long Feud, by Louis Untermeyer
      Trio in a Mirror, by Dorothy Donnelly

BOOKS REVIEWED
    Across the Board   62   170
    Domination of June   66   45
    Outside the Four Walls of Everything   99   320
    Elks, Mooses, Lions and Other Escapes   104   115

DEKIN, TIMOTHY
POEMS
    For Edgar Bowers   128   328

DEKKER, GEORGE
BOOKS REVIEWED
    The Cantos of Ezra Pound:
      A Critical Study   106   361

**DE LACOSTE, HENRY
DE BOUILLANE**
ARTICLES ABOUT
    Rimbaud in 1949, by Wallace Fowlie   75   166

DE LA JARA, LUIS
BOOKS REVIEWED
    Espigas   22   226

DE LA MARE, WALTER
POEMS
    The Reawakening   10   12
    Two Epitaphs
      ("Ye say we sleep...")
      ("O passer-by, beware!")
    The Hostage   19   124
    Things   56   242
    Antiques
    Lethe
    Secret
    A Character   58   117
    The Secret
    Enough
    A Fiddler
    A Tailor
    Crops
    Immanent
    Poetry
    The Very Self
    The Jackdaws   60   185
    Harvest Home   62   140
    A Dull Boy
    Finished With   81   27

BOOKS REVIEWED
    The Listeners   8   312
    Songs of Childhood   11   106
    Motley and Other Poems   14   335
    Collected Poems   18   36
    The Veil and Other Poems   21   210
    Down-Adown Derry
    A Child's Day   24   341
    Stuff and Nonsense   31   53
    Selected Poems   32   108
    Poems 1919 to 1934   48   334
    Memory   54   288
    Behold, This Dreamer!   57   221
    Collected Poems   58   146
    The Burning Glass   68   90
    Winged Chariot and Other Poems   80   213
    The Winnowing Dream   86   242
    Come Hither (Ed.)   93   50
    Tom Tiddler's Ground (Ed.)   103   261

ARTICLES ABOUT
    Master of Silences:
      Walter de la Mare 1873-1956,
      by William Jay Smith   91   112
    [Note on misprint in review]   93   199

DE LAMARTINE, ALPHONSE
ARTICLES ABOUT
    Rev. of *The Life of Lamartine*,
      by H. Remsen Whitehouse   14   108

DE LA SELVA, SALOMON
POEMS
    My Nicaragua   11   77
    Two Spanish Folk-Songs
      The Tiny Maiden
      The Merchant

ARTICLES
    Rubén Darío   8   200

REVIEWS
    Strains of Yesterday   11   281
      Glad of Earth,
        by Clement Wood
      Main Street,
        by Joyce Kilmer

DE LA TOUR DU PIN, PATRICE
ARTICLES ABOUT
    French Poetry
      and the Revival of Mysticism,
      by Eugene Jolas   56   264
    Marseille Letter,
      by Jean Rivier   60   269
    The Poets Paris Is Reading,
      by Jean Catel   67   39

DE LAUGHTER, MARGARET
POEMS
In the Night Watches   18   252
Invocation
Pierrot and Columbine
Requiem
Toward Evening
A Pantoun   22   119
Knowledge

DE LAUTRÉAMONT, (COMTE)
[Pseud. of DUCASSE, ISIDORE]
BOOKS REVIEWED
Lautréamont par lui-même,
by Marcelin Pleynet   112   41

ARTICLES ABOUT
Surrealism in 1960:
A Backward Glance,
by Wallace Fowlie   95   365

DE LIBERO, LIBERO
ARTICLES ABOUT
Contemporary Italian Poetry,
by Edward Williamson   79   233

DELIUS, ANTHONY
ARTICLES ABOUT
Rev. of *Poets in South Africa*
(Ed. by Roy Macnab)   95   244

DELL, FLOYD
POEMS
Apologia   6   67
Song ("Blue eyes, brown eyes...") 15   22

ARTICLES
Correspondence:
A Winged Word   6   319

DE LONGCHAMPS, JOANNE
POEMS
Idyll   85   203
Delivered From a Heaviness of Love 89   156
Between the City Gates and the Sea 90   284
Blind, I Speak to the Cigarette
The Hungry Lions   96   26

BOOKS REVIEWED
Eden Under Glass   92   384
The Hungry Lions   103   324
The Wishing Animal   119   107

ARTICLES ABOUT
Correspondence
from Kenneth Lillquist   120   59

DE LOS SANTOS, MARISA
POEMS
Because I Love You,   167   267

DEL RIO, ANGEL
ARTICLES ABOUT
Rev. of *The Poet in New York,*
by Federico García Lorca
(Tr. by Ben Belitt)   87   303

DE LUCCHI, LORNA
BOOKS REVIEWED
An Anthology of Italian Poems,
13th-19th Century (Ed. and tr.) 24   52

DEL VALLE, ROSAMEL
POEMS
Shadow of the Fish
(Tr. by Lloyd Mallan)   62   76

DEL VASTO, LANZA
ARTICLES ABOUT
Marseille Letter,
by Jean Rivier   60   269

DE MADARIAGA, SALVADOR
BOOKS REVIEWED
Spanish Folk Songs (Ed. and tr.) 22   101

DE MAIRENA, JUAN
[Pseud. of MACHADO, ANTONIO]
ARTICLES ABOUT
Rev. of *Juan de Mairena:*
Epigrams, Maxims, Memoranda,
and Memoirs of an Apocryphal Professor,
with an Appendix of Poems
from The Apocryphal Songbooks,
by Antonio Machado
(Ed. and tr. by Ben Belitt) 105   198

DEMBO, L. S.
BOOKS REVIEWED
Hart Crane's Sanskrit Charge:
A Study of The Bridge   98   190
The Confucian Odes of Ezra Pound:
A Critical Appraisal   106   361
Conceptions of Reality
in Modern American Poetry 111   203

DE MELO NETO, JOÃO CABRAL
POEMS
From "The Death and Life
of a Severino"
(Tr. by Elizabeth Bishop)   103   10

ARTICLES ABOUT
Rev. of *Modern Brazilian Poetry*
(Ed. by John Nist)   103   261

DE MENEZES, EMILIO
ARTICLES ABOUT
Emilio de Menezes,
by Evelyn Scott   16   40

DEMETILLO, RICAREDO
POEMS
The God My Father Chiseled
with His Tongue   79   271

DEMETZ, PETER
BOOKS REVIEWED
Marx, Engels, and the Poets:
Origins of Marxist Literary Criticism
(Tr. by Jeffrey L. Sammons)   112   206

**DE MONTALK, [COUNT]
GEOFFREY POTOCKI**
POEMS
Old Green Wines   37   67
Clare
To the Countess Zinka Chrapowicka
From Battersea Bridge at Midnight
My First London Fog

BOOKS REVIEWED
Surprising Songs   39   288

DE NAIR, ALICE
POEMS
Light as Air   34   324
Enter Fool
Day

ARTICLES ABOUT
[Note]   35   57

DEN BOER, JAMES
BOOKS REVIEWED
Learning the Way   113   262
Trying To Come Apart   119   296

DENBY, EDWIN
POEMS
Wind Song   28   142
During Music
Winter

BOOKS REVIEWED
Mediterranean Cities   89   307
Dancers, Buildings,
and People in the Streets
[Stéphane Mallarmé,
George Balanchine]   111   268
Collected Poems   129   164
The Complete Poems
(Ed. by Ron Padgett)   150   36

DENMAN, PETER
TRANSLATIONS
Poem by Biddy Jenkinson   167   23

DENNETT, DANIEL C.
ARTICLES ABOUT
Review by Steven Cramer   161   159

DENNEY, REUEL
POEMS
Three Declarations   39   200
The Hunters
A Defeat
Morning Song
Invocation   45   78
The Laboratory Midnight   51   117
The Game
The Dance
The Sleeping Woman
The Iroquois
The Old Northwest
McSorley's Bar
The Knowers   57   4
Days of Dictation
The Rememberer   74   8
The Drunk Oil Rigger   76   337
Noah
A Nisei Who Died of Relocation
An Evangeline Postcard, from Louisiana
Thisbe
The Ceremony   81   29
A Lakeshore Promenade   82   66
The City Park
A Weatherman's Delight   83   249
Summer Round
In Praise of Adam
Fixer of Midnight, and Other Portraits   86   254

REVIEWS
The Modern Mind,
by Michael Roberts   52   106
Natural History,
by Raymond Holden   52   156
Proems, by Ruthven Todd,
Patrick Evans, Rayner Heppenstall,
Edgar Foxall, Lawrence Durrell,
and Oswald Blakeston   53   155
A Glad Day, by Kay Boyle   54   347
Weep and Prepare,
by Raymond E. F. Larsson   57   394
Selected Poems and Undercliff,
Poems 1946-1953,
by Richard Eberhart   85   102
Invitations to the Listener: Nine
Young Poets and Their Audiences   89   45
Time and Other Poems,
by Robert Cecil

The Vestal Lady on Brattle,
  by Gregory Corso
Ommateum,
  by A. R. Ammons
Pictures of the Gone World,
  by Lawrence Ferlinghetti
Black Rain,
  by Katue Kitasono
In the Midst of My Fever,
  by Irving Layton
All Devils Fading,
  by Martin Seymour-Smith
Travellers Alone,
  by Allen Brownjohn
Time of Hawks,
  by Joseph L. Grucci

BOOKS REVIEWED
The Connecticut River
  and Other Poems   55   274
In Praise of Adam   101   203

ARTICLES ABOUT
Correspondence
  from August Derleth
  [Raymond E. F. Larsson]   58   170

DENNIS, CARL
POEMS
Clara Hopes for a Lie   137   265
The Sweetness of the Law
News from Cleveland
Steamboat Days   141   266
The Connoisseur
What Happened Then
On the Way to School   143   197
Fear of the Dark
The Dream of Fair Women
Little League   146   158
The Greenhouse Effect   146   266
Winter Light   147   145
Heinrich Schliemann
The Task   149   21
Fairy Tales
Last Words   150   267
The Deacon's Complaint
Horace and I   151   38
No Shame   154   27
Waking on Sunday   154   65
Soon
If I Need To See You
The Window   157   79
Defining Time
Spring Letter   158   63
Help from the Audience   160   264
Holy Brethren
Bimini Queen

To Reason   163   258
Loss   164   86
Still Life
As If   164   341
Orpheus   166   72
Old Woman
Book Fair
Rescue   167   329
Two Gods   169   140
Eternal Poetry   169   318
Habit   170   76
Cut Flowers

BOOKS REVIEWED
Climbing Down   130   342
Signs and Wonders   137   102
The Near World   147   291
Meetings with Time   161   159

DENSMORE, FRANCES
ARTICLES ABOUT
Aboriginal Poetry II,
  by Carl Sandburg   9   254

DENWOOD, JONATHAN
BOOKS REVIEWED
Twinter's Wedding   79   106

DE OTERO, BLAS
BOOKS REVIEWED
Twenty Poems of...
  (Tr. by Hardie St. Martin)   107   338

DE PALCHI, ALFREDO
TRANSLATIONS
Poems by Lucio Piccolo
  (With Sonia Raiziss)   98   387
Article by Eugenio Montale
  [Lucio Piccolo]   98   392

DE PLEDGE, ORIAN C.
POEMS
Autumn   57   183

DEPPE, THEODORE
POEMS
Red Pigeons   168   92

DE QUENTAL, ANTHERO
BOOKS REVIEWED
Sonnets and Poems
  (Tr. by S. Griswold Morley)   23   225

DE RACHEWILTZ, MARY
ARTICLES ABOUT
Rev. of *"Ezra Pound Speaking"*
  (Ed. by Leonard W. Doob)   134   292

DE RÉGNIER, HENRI
ARTICLES ABOUT
Vers Libre and Metrical Prose,
by Amy Lowell   3   213
Rev. of *Six French Poets*,
by Amy Lowell   7   202

DE RENEVILLE, ROLLAND
BOOKS REVIEWED
L'Expérience Poétique   53   218

ARTICLES ABOUT
French Poetry and
the Revival of Mysticism,
by Eugene Jolas   56   264

DERLETH, AUGUST W.
POEMS
Calliope Music   48   141
Poems for Someone Loved   64   74
Humbly in the Dark: A Prayer
The Hawk as Time
The Solitary

ARTICLES
Correspondence
[Reuel Denney,
Raymond E. F. Larsson]   58   170

BOOKS REVIEWED
Rind of Earth   62   50
And You, Thoreau!   65   338
Selected Poems   66   223
The Edge of Night   67   168

DE RONSARD, PIERRE
POEMS
Comme On Voit sur la Branche   85   200
Estre Indigent
Je Faisois ces Sonnets
(Tr. by George Dillon)

BOOKS REVIEWED
Diadems and Fagots
(With Olavo Bilac)
(Tr. by John Meem
and Yvor Winters)   23   113
Poems (Tr. and ed. by Nicholas Kilmer)   136 40

DERRY, ALICE
POEMS
Every Day of Her Girlhood in Montana   142 76
The House   144 68

DERRY, SELMA
POEMS
From a Crown of Snow   25   310
Out of the Singing Throat

The Virgin's Complaint
Medallion
Desolate

DERWOOD, GENE
POEMS
Camel   85   269
Shelter
Third Madrigal

BOOKS REVIEWED
The Poems of...   89   43

DE SANCTIS, FRANCESCO
BOOKS REVIEWED
De Sanctis on Dante
(Ed. and tr. by Joseph Rossi
and Alfred Galpin)   96   323

DESCHERE, CAROL
POEMS
Chance   36   251

DESHE, MICHAEL
ARTICLES ABOUT
Postscript: The Younger Poets,
by Simon Halkin   92   259

DE STEIN, E(DWARD)
BOOKS REVIEWED
The Poets in Picardy   16   336

DE TABLEY, LORD
BOOKS REVIEWED
Poems (Ed. by John Drinkwater)   27   164

DE TOLEDANO, RALPH
POEMS
Devotional   50   324

DE UNAMUNO, MIGUEL
POEMS
Cloud-Music   101 319
Bull
(Tr. by Anthony Kerrigan)

DEUTSCH, BABETTE
POEMS
Sea-Music   11   191
Semper Eadem   18   190
Fourth Dimension
Overtones
Reflections
Knowledge
Tak for Sidst   19   259
The Young Man Remembers   23   243
Forbidden
Forgotten

By Way of Contrast   34   256
    Moment at Croton Dam
    Soirée
After Music   49   130
Midsummer Night   52   250
Truro Hour
At the Cape
The Remnant   53   115
Escape Denied   55   13
To Napoleon, in an Evil Time   56   70
Memory   57   297
The Day's Lesson   60   183
Recovery
Le Temps Retrouvé   63   138
The Faraway Island   64   262
    On the Beach
    The Two Voices
    Sankaty at Sunset
    On the Cliff
The Net   66   70
Bull
The Lotus   67   314
Visit to the Zoo   75   75
The Poem ("The painter of Dante's...")   76   136
Paradigm   81   163
July Day   86   231
Barges on the Hudson   87   147
Suspension   90   141
Unearthly Toy   92   71
Admonition   96   170
The Mother   97   348
Lizard at Pompeii   101   194

TRANSLATIONS
Poems by Wilhelm Klemm,
    Rainer Maria Rilke, Franz Werfel,
    Georg Heym, Albert Ehrenstein,
    Richard Schaukal, and Arno Holz
    (With Avrahm Yarmolinsky)   21   141
Poems by Eduard Bagritsky,
    Stepan Shschipachev, Yevgeny
    Dolmatovsky, Mikhail Matusovsky,
    E. Serebrovskaya, Anna Akhmatova,
    and Boris Pasternak   70   248

ARTICLES
A Note on Modern German Poetry
    [Arno Holz, Rainer Maria Rilke,
    Franz Werfel]   21   149
[Notes on Translations]   70   290
[Note on misprint]   86   123
Correspondence   120   361

REVIEWS
Picture-Show, by Siegfried Sassoon   16   159
Lancelot, by Edwin Arlington Robinson   16   217
The Collected Poems of Sara Teasdale   51   148

Land of the Free,
    by Archibald MacLeish   52   153
Selected Poems, by John Gould Fletcher   52   347
Wartime Letters
    of Rainer Maria Rilke, 1914-1921
    (Tr. by M. D. Herter-Norton)   56   271
The Expense of Greatness,
    by R. P. Blackmur   57   335
The Double Man, by W. H. Auden   58   148
The Listening Landscape,
    by Marya Zaturenska   58   337
Out of the Jewel, by Rolfe Humphries   61   393
Street Songs, by Edith Sitwell   61   684
Miracle and Mystery   66   274
    Bolts of Melody, New Poems
        of Emily Dickinson
        (Ed. by Mabel Loomis Todd
        and Millicent Todd Bingham)
    Ancestors' Brocades, The Literary
        Debut of Emily Dickinson,
        by Millicent Todd Bingham
The Bridge: Poems 1939-1944,
    by Ruth Pitter   68   103
Little Friend, Little Friend,
    by Randall Jarrell   69   98
J. B. Yeats: Letters to His Son,
    W. B. Yeats, and Others, 1869-1922
    (Ed. by Joseph Hone)   69   291
John Skelton, A Selection
    from His Poems
    (Ed. by Vivian De Sola Pinto)   82   95
English Folk Songs from
    the Southern Appalachians
    (Coll. by Cecil J. Sharp
    and ed. by Maud Karpeles)   83   37
Love's Argument, by Adele Greef   83   230
The Letters of Hart Crane, 1916-1932
    (Ed. by Brom Weber)   83   353
A Key to Modern British Poetry,
    by Lawrence Durrell   84   106
The Desert Music and Other Poems,
    by William Carlos Williams   85   351
[Addendum to Desert Music]   86   123
Poems Old and New,
    by John Hall Wheelock   89   319
The Notebooks
    of Samuel Taylor Coleridge Vol. I
    (Ed. by Kathleen Coburn)   91   385
The Notebooks
    of Samuel Taylor Coleridge Vol. II
    (Ed. by Kathleen Coburn)   102   128
Platform Verse   102   400
    Yevtushenko: Selected Poems
        (Tr. by Robin Milner-Gulland
        and Peter Levi)
    Red Cats
        (Tr. by Anselm Hollo)

BOOKS REVIEWED
Banners   15   164
Modern Russian Poetry
  (Ed. and tr. with Avrahm Yarmolinsky)   20   228
Contemporary German Poetry
  (Ed. and tr. with Avrahm Yarmolinsky)   24   52
Honey Out of the Rock   28   102
Epistle to Prometheus   38   166
Fire for the Night
Potable Gold
One Part Love   55   332
Poems from the Book of Hours,
  by Rainer Maria Rilke (Tr.)   61   441
Take Them Stranger   65   268
Selected Writings,
  by Boris Pasternak
  (Tr. with C. M. Bowra,
  Beatrice Scott, and Robert Payne)   76   238
A Treasury of Russian Verse
  (Ed. by Avrahm Yarmolinsky) (Tr.)   80   95
Poetry in Our Time   82   282
Animal, Vegetable, Mineral   86   48
Poetry Handbook—A Dictionary of Terms   92   116
Coming of Age: New and Selected Poems   95   116
Collected Poems: 1919-1962   103   382
Two Centuries of Russian Verse
  (Ed. with Avrahm Yarmolinsky)   114   113
The Collected Poems of...   115   277

ARTICLES ABOUT
Correspondence from Brom Weber
  [Hart Crane]   84   245

DE VIGNY, (ALFRED VICTOR)
POEMS
  To the Deaf-Mutes
    (Tr. by George Dillon)   70   68

DEVLIN, CHRISTOPHER
BOOKS REVIEWED
  Poor Kit Smart   99   375

DEVLIN, COLLEEN
POEMS
  The Toast   143   213

DEVLIN, DENIS
POEMS
  Farewell and Good   57   300

BOOKS REVIEWED
  Thorns of Thunder,
    by Paul Eluard
    (Ed. by George Reavey)
    (Tr. with Samuel Beckett,
    David Gascoyne, Eugene Jolas,
    Man Ray, George Reavey,
    and Ruthven Todd)   48   347

Lough Derg   69   169
Exile and Other Poems,
  by St.-John Perse (Tr.)   74   343
Selected Poems
  (Ed. by Allen Tate and
  Robert Penn Warren)   103   191

ARTICLES ABOUT
Rev. of *Le Cahiers de la Pléiade*
  (Ed. by Jean Paulhan)
  [St.-John Perse]   79   43
A Map of Contemporary Irish Poetry,
  by Dennis O'Driscoll   167   94

DE VRIES, PETER ["P. D."]
POEMS
  Late Song   51   196
  Love Song   53   308
  Song for a Son
  Mirror
  Conscript   58   184
  My Heart Is A   62   142

ARTICLES
  On Being Thirty   61   380
  Voice in Babel [Charles Péguy]   62   208
  A Note on This Issue   62   272
  James Thurber: The Comic Prufrock   63   150

REVIEWS
  Fusion and Confusion   52   236
    *The Garden of Disorder
    and Other Poems*,
      by Charles Henri Ford
    *Christopher Columbus
    and Other Poems*,
      by Sydney Salt
  Basic Verities, by Charles Péguy
    (Tr. by Ann and Julian Green)   62   208
  One Times One, by E. E. Cummings   64   158

ARTICLES ABOUT
  [Note]   61   699
  For the Record,
    by George Dillon   73   28

DEY, RICHARD MORRIS
POEMS
  Landfall: Grenada   128   25
  Afterward
  From *Wind Against the Tide*   133   205

DE ZAVALA, ANN MC CARTHY
BOOKS REVIEWED
  *Songs of Cifar and the Sweet Sea: Selections
  from "Songs of Cifar, 1967-1977,"*
    by Pablo Antonio Cuadra
    (Tr. and ed. with Grace Schulman)   137   220

DHIKTEOS, ARIS
POEMS
St. Mark
(Tr. by Kimon Friar)   139   77

ARTICLES ABOUT
Post-War Greek Poets,
by Kimon Friar   139   99

DHIMOULAS, ATHOS
POEMS
Sic Transit
(Tr. by Kimon Friar)   139   82

ARTICLES ABOUT
Post-War Greek Poets,
by Kimon Friar   139   99

DHOUKARIS, DHIMITRIS
POEMS
The Grammar of the Body
(Tr. by Kimon Friar)   139   94

ARTICLES ABOUT
Post-War Greek Poets,
by Kimon Friar   139   99

DIAZ MIRON, SALVADOR
POEMS
The Dead Man
(Tr. by Muna Lee)   26   133

DI BIASIO, RODOLFO
POEMS
*Poemetto dell'alba e della notte/
Poem of the Dawn and the Night*
(Tr. by Stephen Sartarelli)   155   94

DICKEY, JAMES (L.)
POEMS
Of Holy War   79   24
The Child in Armor   82   137
The Anniversary
The Angel of the Maze   86   147
The Father's Body   89   145
The First Morning of Cancer   90   97
Dover: Believing in Kings   92   283
The Game   94   211
The Landfall
The Signs
The Enclosure
The Performance
The String
Below the Lighthouse
Into the Stone
Antipolis   97   153
A View of Fujiyama after the War
Inside the River

The Hospital Window   99   236
A Dog Sleeping on My Feet
After the Night Hunt
The Gamecocks
Below Ellijay   101   27
The Being   102   281
Why in London the Blind Are Saviors
A Folk-Singer of the Thirties
The Firebombing   104   63
Blood   114   149
Diabetes
    Sugar
    Under Buzzards
Venom
The Cancer Match
Pine: Taste, Touch and Sight
Of Holy War   121   7
Five Poems from Puella   137   313
The Little More   150   208
Gila Bend   151   40
The Six

ARTICLES
Correspondence:
An Exchange on *Delta Return*
[Charles Bell, Rolfe Humphries]   89   391
Comment   151   202

REVIEWS
Five Poets   89   110
The Scattered Causes,
by Samuel French Morse
Antennas of Silence,
by Ernest Sandeen
Friday's Child,
by Wilfred Watson
Delta Return, by Charles Bell
An American Takes a Walk,
by Reed Whittemore
Sheepfold Hill, by Conrad Aiken   94   41
Five Poets   94   117
The Sum, by Alan Stephens
A Local Habitation,
by Ellen Kay
A Book of Kinds,
by Margaret Tongue
Passage After Midnight,
by William Pillin
The Death of Venus,
by Harold Witt
Five First Books   97   316
Myths and Texts, by Gary Snyder
The Year of the Green Wave,
by Bruce Cutler
Bone Thoughts,
by George Starbuck
To Bedlam and Part Way Back,
by Anne Sexton

What a Kingdom It Was,
  by Galway Kinnell
[Ezra Pound]
The Morning Song of Lord Zero,
  by Conrad Aiken   103   187
First and Last Things   103   316
  The Hawk and the Lizard,
    by Gene Frumkin
  The Imaged Word,
    by Rolf Fjelde
  Blind Man's Holiday,
    by R. G. Everson
  Final Solutions,
    by Frederick Seidel
  Naked as the Glass,
    by Jean Burden
  New Poems, by Robert Graves
  Affinities, by Vernon Watkins
  The Beginning and the End,
    by Robinson Jeffers
  Collected Poems,
    by Ralph Hodgson
  The Collected Later Poems,
    by William Carlos Williams
  Charles Baudelaire:
    The Flowers of Evil
    (Ed. by Marthiel
    and Jackson Mathews)
  Sequence, Sometimes Metaphysical,
    by Theodore Roethke   105   119

BOOKS REVIEWED
  Into the Stone and Other Poems,
    in *Poets of Today, VII*   99   178
  Drowning with Others   101   412
  Helmets   105   130
  Two Poems of the Air   105   131
  The Suspect in Poetry   107   332
  Buckdancer's Choice   109   44
  Poems 1957-1967   111   400
  Babel to Byzantium:
    Poets and Poetry Now   115   346
  The Eye-Beaters, Blood, Victory,
    Madness, Buckhead and Mercy   118   228
  Drowning with Others   121   54
  The Zodiac   137   349
  The Strength of Fields

ARTICLES ABOUT
  Correspondence from Conrad Aiken   103   402
  Rev. of *Selected Poems*
    of Edwin Arlington Robinson
    (Ed. by Morton Dauwen Zabel)   108   187

DICKEY, R. P.
BOOKS REVIEWED
  Running Lucky   118   234
  Acting Immortal   122   47

DICKEY, WILLIAM H.
POEMS
  Quae Lucis Miseris
    Tam Dira Cupido? Dicam.   85   333
  For Easter Island or Another Island
  Oxford. 16 October 1555
  A Vision, Caged   90   291
  Of the Festivity   92   296
  Teaching Swift to Young Ladies   94   165
  Exemplum   99   1
  In the Appropriate Moment
  Autumnal
  Father Unknown
  After the Romantics
  Droll Story
  Parallels in Darkness
  Continued in Our Next
  Three Speeches After the Event   100   177
  Islands   102   368
  Rehabilitation   105   166
  Sonnet: The Platonic Form   115   11
  Parliamentary Procedure   117   296
  At the Middle of It
  The Bullhorn
  The Poet's Farewell to His Teeth   120   220
  Here's Mars
  Alone I Care for Myself
  The Death of Mr. Thrale
  Aubrey's Brief Lives   134   344
  Gloryosky, Zero!   140   164
  Seizure
  Those Destroyed by Success
  Rather than Musick   143   282
  Novgorod
  Semi-Private   166   145
  Hat   166   271
  Coming of Television News
    and the National Guard
  The Arrival of the Titanic   167   140
  The Death of John Berryman   167   218
  Coming Back by Night   170   311

REVIEWS
  Revelations and Homilies   99   124
    Adam Before His Mirror,
      by Ned O'Gorman
    Halfway, by Maxine W. Kumin
    Abraham's Knife and Other Poems,
      by George Garrett
    The Ungrateful Garden,
      by Carolyn Kizer
    A Ring of Willows, by Eric Barker
    For Love: Poems 1950-1960,
      by Robert Creeley   101   421
  In the Convention   104   375
    Weather and Season,
      by Michael Hamburger

Requiem for the Living,
    by C. Day Lewis
The Burning Perch,
    by Louis MacNeice
The Owl in the Tree,
    by Anthony Thwaite

BOOKS REVIEWED
Of the Festivity   95   248
Interpreter's House   104   104
More Under Saturn   122   47
The Rainbow Grocery   141   170
The Sacrifice Consenting
The Education of Desire   170   162

DICKINSON, EMILY
BOOKS REVIEWED
The Single Hound   5   134
The Complete Poems of...   26   97
Further Poems of...   35   164
Letters of...
    (Ed. by Mabel Loomis Todd)   41   219
Unpublished Poems
    (Ed. by Martha Dickinson Bianchi
    and Alfred Leete Hampson)   48   162
Bolts of Melody, New Poems of...
    (Ed. by Mabel Loomis Todd
    and Millicent Todd Bingham)   66   274

ARTICLES ABOUT
Rev. of *The Life and Letters*
    of Emily Dickinson,
    by Martha Dickinson Bianchi   26   97
Christina Rossetti
    and Emily Dickinson,
    by M. D. Zabel   37   213
Emily Dickinson Face to Face,
    by Martha Dickinson Bianchi   42   345
Rev. of *This Was a Poet,*
    by George Frisbie Whicher   53   312
Rev. of *Ancestors' Brocades,*
    The Literary Debut of Emily Dickinson,
    by Millicent Todd Bingham   66   274
Rev. of *The Riddle of Emily Dickinson,*
    by Rebecca Patterson   80   242
Rev. of *Emily Dickinson: A Revelation,*
    by Millicent Todd Bingham   86   118
Rev. of *The Poetry of Emily Dickinson,*
    by Ruth Miller   115   346
Review by Sandra M. Gilbert   160   284
Rev. of *American Poetry:*
    The Nineteenth Century
    (Ed. by John Hollander)   165   340

DICKINSON, PATRIC
BOOKS REVIEWED
Selected Poems   114   397

DICKSON, JOHN
POEMS
Feeding the Neighbor's Cat   139   12
The Runaway
A Tale of Two Cities   141   145
Cinderella
Rosehill   142   143
Quiet Zone
Damocles   143   344
Fugue
Fossil Fuel   147   8
Suicide Pact   149   266
Little Brother
Delayed Decision
Preservation of the Species   153   285
Good Old Boy   154   143
Looking Ahead   156   263
Filling in the Past   158   65
Second Chance   160   10
Fast Food Restaurant
As It Was in the Beginning   162   214
Echoes of a Native Land   164   137
After The Rubaiyat   167   281

BOOKS REVIEWED
Waving at Trains   150   162

DI GIACOMO, SALVATORE
ARTICLES ABOUT
Five Years of Italian
    Poetry (1910-1915),
    by Emanuel Carnevali   13   209

DI GIOVANNI, NORMAN THOMAS
BOOKS REVIEWED
Jorge Guillén, Cántico:
    A Selection, Spanish Poems
    with English Translation (Ed.)   111   46

DI LASSO, ORLANDO
POEMS
Matona, Mia Cara
    (Tr. by W. D. Snodgrass)   157   270

DILLARD, ANNIE
POEMS
The Heart   125   260
A Natural History
    of Getting Through the Year
Quatrain of the Body's Sleep

DILLER, MARY BLACK
POEMS
Yuletide Notes   35   136
    The Song of the Lowly
    Lord of the Waters

DILLON, GEORGE (H.)
["G. D.", "G. H. D."]
POEMS
Preludes   26   235
    The World Goes Turning
    Compliment to Mariners
    Elemental
    Toe Ballet
    No Question
    Song on Death
Sequence   28   237
    Serenader
    As Dancers
    Love Like Fear
    En Route
    Fairy Tale
    The Hard Lovers
    To Losers
    Again
    Fall of Stars
Snow   29   247
The Hours of the Day   34   241
The Cure
Four Sonnets
    ("Your life, so rarefied...")
    ("I think you are closer to me...")
    ("Yours is the Attic and ambiguous...")
    ("Suddenly on a winter's day...")
The Loiterer
Beauty Intolerable
A Dreamer of Leaves
Spring Remembered
In Passing
Marching Song
Salutation at Dawn
After Image
Malediction Against Wars   35   70
Address to the Doomed   37   4
What Artifice   38   119
Fabric of Light
The Dead Elm on the Hilltop
This Dream Is Strange
The Constant One
The Summery Night Before the Frost
The Traveler   49   145
Sonnet ("I am saved by love...")   113   412

TRANSLATIONS
Poems by Jean Rivier   59   29
Poems by Louis Aragon   67   1
Poems by Paul Eluard   67   5
Poems by Henri Michaux   67   10
To the Deaf-Mutes (After Vigny)   70   68
Poems by Pierre de Ronsard   85   200

ARTICLES
Poetry in the Colleges   29   151
Spring Cleaning   30   36

[Note: Resignation]   31   230
[Tribute to Harriet Monroe]   49   145
Another Year   57   30
Correspondence   61   639
Correspondence
    [Henri Michaux, T. S. Eliot,
    Paul Valéry, Jean-Richard Bloch]   67   49
A Note on the Obvious
    [Ezra Pound]   68   322
The "Little Magazine" Gimmick   71   41
A New Engagement?
    [John Gould Fletcher,
    Stephen Spender, W. H. Auden]   72   89
For the Record
    [Margedant Peters, Katinka Loeser,
    Peter DeVries, J. F. Nims, Tom Lea]   73   28
A Change of Editorship   74   90

REVIEWS
Once in a Blue Moon,
    by Marion Strobel   26   346
Selected Poems and Secrets,
    by W. H. Davies   27   44
Nor Youth Nor Age, by Harold Vinal   27   48
Dream Tapestries,
    by Louise Morey Bowman   27   99
The Northeast Corner,
    by Frederick R. McCreary   27   167
Blue Norther, by Therese Lindsey   27   169
Selected Poems of Charles Hanson Towne   27   170
The Sea-Wall, by Lyon Sharman   27   282
Poems, by Mabel Simpson   27   334
Color, by Countee Cullen   28   50
The Last Judgment, by G. E. Curran   28   104
Cyclops' Eye, by Joseph Auslander   28   282
Episodes and Epistles, by "W. L."
    [Walter Lowenfels]   28   342
New Poems and Old, by Muriel Stuart   29   45
Brief Notices   29   56
    Poems, by Irwin Edman
    Concerto in A Minor,
        by Charles Whitby
Coach into Pumpkin,
    by Dorothy E. Reid   29   101
Children of the Sun, by James Rorty   29   343
Returning to Emotion,
    by Maxwell Bodenheim   30   104
A Jeweled Screen, by Ann Hamilton   30   112
The White Rooster and Other Poems,
    by George O'Neil   30   159
Kensington Gardens and Lampoons,
    by Humbert Wolfe   30   222
Angels and Earthly Creatures,
    by Elinor Wylie   34   230
Time's Profile, by Hildegarde Flanner   35   162
The Shakespeare Songs
    (Ed. by Tucker Brooke)   35   337

Selected Poems, by Conrad Aiken	37	221
Chosen Poems, by Harriet Monroe	46	336
Esthétique du Mal, by Wallace Stevens	68	97
War and the Poet		
(Ed. by Richard Eberhart		
and Selden Rodman)	69	46
Style and the Many-Headed Beast	86	287
Collected Poems, by James Stephens		
Collected Poems,		
by Oliver St. John Gogarty		
Selected Poems, by Mark Van Doren		
Wilderness Stair, by Ben Belitt		
Kingdom of Diagonals,		
by Kenneth Slade Alling		
The Colour as Naked,		
by Patrick Anderson		
A Spring Journey and Other Poems		
of 1952-1953, by James Kirkup		
The Diary of Dr. Eric Zeno,		
by Gil Orlovitz		
Eden Two-Way, by Chad Walsh		
Sara Teasdale: A Biography,		
by Margaret Haley Carpenter		
[Vachel Lindsay]	97	392
Alcools: Poems 1898-1913,		
by Guillaume Apollinaire		
(Tr. by William Meredith)	105	136
BOOKS REVIEWED		
Boy in the Wind	31	343
The Flowering Stone	39	328
Flowers of Evil,		
by Charles Baudelaire		
(Tr. with Edna St. Vincent Millay)	48	158
Three Plays of Racine:		
Phaedra, Britannicus, Andromache (Tr.)	100	47
ARTICLES ABOUT		
An Announcement	60	348
[Note]	61	463
[Note on erroneous attribution]	114	138

DILLON, JOHN
POEMS

A Face at Fate	58	78

DIMOCK, EDWARD C., JR.
TRANSLATIONS

Vaishnava Lyrics		
(Tr. with Denise Levertov)	107	176

ARTICLES

A Note on the Vaishnava Lyrics	107	182

BOOKS REVIEWED

In Praise of Krishna:		
Songs from the Bengali		
(Ed. and tr. with Denise Levertov)	111	407

DINE, REITZA
[See **WIRTSHAFTER,
REITZA DINE**]

DINGS, FRED
POEMS

Words for a Perfect Evening	166	99
The Fire		
Revelations		
Migratory Flight		
The Past		
The Man and the Cemetery Effigy	167	217
Chains of Change	167	333
Letter to Genetically		
Engineered Super Humans		

DIONISOTTI, C.
BOOKS REVIEWED

The Oxford Book		
of Italian Verse, 2nd ed.		
(Ed. by St. John Lucas)	82	277

DI PALMA, RAYMOND
BOOKS REVIEWED

The Gallery Goers	120	115

DI PIERO, W. S.
POEMS

On a Picture by Cézanne	159	218

TRANSLATIONS

Poems by Franco Fortini	155	36

BOOKS REVIEWED

The Restorers	161	339

DI PRIMA, DIANE
BOOKS REVIEWED

The New Handbook of Heaven	104	258

DIRCKS, HELEN
BOOKS REVIEWED

Passenger	17	276

DISCH, TOM
[**THOMAS M. DISCH**]
POEMS

A Turkish Holiday	117	154
In a Time of Plague		
Phaedra	118	216
A Questionnaire		
D. W. Richmond Gives Directions		
to the Architect of His Tomb		
The Clouds	119	272
The Vowels of Another Language		
The Vegetables		
Apollo 14		
The Prisoners of War	120	332

Ode on the Source of the Clitumnus   121   187
Tearing It Apart
May
The Fourth Law
Eternity   123   87
Homage to the Carracci   124   336
The Poltergeist
The Color Blue   129   31
Descriptions of the Wilderness   129   249
High Purpose in Poetry: A Primer   132   84
To Our Christmas Tree   133   139
Abecedary
Poems
Luxe, Calme, et Désespoir
Entropic Villanelle   144   205
Working on a Tan
The Return to Nature   146   125
The Dot on the i   148   198
The Viewers and the Viewed:
    Eurailpass Verses, 1985
To the Young Mercenaries
In Defense of Forest Lawn   148   253
The Argument Resumed;
    Or, Up Through Tribeca
Medusa at Her Vanity   151   42
Why This Tie, Why That   152   15
A Stroll Through Moscow
Three People and Their Feelings   159   195
Red Tulips in 1947
Remarks Concerning
    the Fitness of All Things
Villanelle for Charles Olson
The Garage Sale
    as a Spiritual Exercise   163   147
Christmas Guilt
Signs of Spring
    in a Depressed Economy   164   8
In Praise of History   165   187
Capital Punishment
The Lipstick on the Mirror
A Sestina for Susan Sontag   167   324
The Shelf   168   152
What Else Is There   169   141
Hooray for Hollywood   170   199

ARTICLES
Christopher Fry: An Appreciation
    [Thomas Hardy]   166   280

REVIEWS
The Occasion of the Poem   160   94
    Heaven and Earth: A Cosmology,
        by Albert Goldbarth
    What Work Is
        and New Selected Poems,
        by Philip Levine
    Between the Chains,
        by Turner Cassity

Someone Going Home Late,
    by Daryl Jones
Madoc: A Mystery,
    by Paul Muldoon
Having an Oeuvre   163   285
    Selected Poetry and
        Tesserae and Other Poems,
        by John Hollander
    Collected Poems: 1953-1993,
        by John Updike
    What We Don't Know
        About Each Other,
        by Lawrence Raab
    Sweet Ruin, by Tony Hoagland
    The Palms, by Charlie Smith

BOOKS REVIEWED
    Dark Verses & Light   162   96

DISMORR, BLANCHE
POEMS
    Charlotte Bronte   18   83

DITTA, JOSEPH M.
POEMS
    Winter Poem   130   88
    In Another City

DIVINE, CHARLES
BOOKS REVIEWED
    The Road to Town   27   348

DIVOIRE, FERNAND
ARTICLES ABOUT
    Orchestral Poetry,
        by Charles K. Meschter   24   327

DIXEY, H. G.
BOOKS REVIEWED
    Darien   23   286

DIXON, ALAN
POEMS
    What Dignity Is Not   138   336
    Taking Leave
    Eastbourne and Charleston   166   253
    Les Maîtres

DIXON, DEAKIN
[See also DIXON, JEANNIE BEGG]
POEMS
    Hints of Beauty   48   307
    The Valley
    Vestige
    New Wine
    Wonder

ARTICLES ABOUT
    [Note on names]   48   357

DIXON, JEANNIE BEGG
  [See also DIXON, DEAKIN]
  POEMS
    Tied Sheaves   41   85

  ARTICLES ABOUT
    [Note on names]   48   357

DIXON, RICHARD WATSON
  ARTICLES ABOUT
    Hopkins in His Letters, by M. D. Zabel   46   210

DJANIKIAN, GREGORY
  POEMS
    The Journey   140   322
    Literally Speaking
    The Theft   145   216
    These Are the Gifts
    Clouds   148   164
    Grandmother's Rugs
    In the Elementary School Choir   149   221
    How I Learned English
    When I First Saw Snow
    Alexandria, 1953   151   43
    The Boy Who Had Eleven Toes   152   70
    Late at Night in Bed
    Mrs. Caldera's House of Things   154   92
    The Visit   158   25
    In Alexandria   158   140
    Absences   164   311
    The Physics of Traveling Away   167   263

  ARTICLES
    Comment   151   224

  BOOKS REVIEWED
    Falling Deeply into America   156   36
    About Distance   170   37

DJI-NAN, SENG
  [See SENG DJI-NAN]

DOBRÉE, BONAMY
  BOOKS REVIEWED
    Swinburne: Poems (Ed.)   100   324

DOBSON, AUSTIN
  BOOKS REVIEWED
    The Poetical Works of...   27   164

  ARTICLES ABOUT
    From Queen Anne to George the Fifth,
      by Harriet Monroe   19   90

DOBYNS, STEPHEN
  POEMS
    Name-Burning   113   253
    Waking, the Cheering Begins

    Finding the Direction   115   319
    The Ways of Keys
    Passing the Word
    Counterparts
    Contingencies   117   385
    When You're Dancing,
      Make the Whole World Dance with You
    Taking a Crack at It
    Clouds   119   337
    The Survival Variation   121   336
    Six Poems on Not Moving
    Six Poems on Moving
    Play in Four Acts   124   316
    A Separate Time   132   215
    Morning Song
    Song for Making the Birds Come
    Song for Putting Aside Anger
    How Sweet and Proper It Is   135   210
    Oatmeal Deluxe
    A Place in Maine
    Arrested Saturday Night
    It's Like This
    Six Poems After Balthus   138   187
      The Greedy Child
      The Guitar Lesson
      The Street
      Patience
      The Cherry Tree
      The Room
    Six Poems After Balthus   139   1
      Girl in White
      Landscape at Champrovent
      The Mountain
      The Golden Days
      The Triangular Field
      Katia Reading
    General Matthei Drives Home
      Through Santiago   142   249
    Between Hamburg and Buenos Aires
    The Invitation   147   278
    Cemetery Nights V
    Theseus Within the Labyrinth
    Querencia
    Long Story   151   44
    Thoughts at Thirty-Thousand Feet   152   92
    Freight Cars
    Brink
    Adam   154   125
    Rootless
    Utopian Melodies   154   316

  REVIEWS
    Five Poets   117   392
      The Ends of the Earth,
        by David Bromige
      Sitting Around,
        by Greg Kuzma
      Hard Loving, by Marge Piercy

The Torches,
  by James Tate
New and Selected Poems,
  by David Wagoner

BOOKS REVIEWED
Concurring Beasts   122   105
Griffon   132   31
Heat Death   138   231
The Balthus Poems   143   39
Black Dog, Red Dog   146   293
Cemetery Nights   150   226
Body Traffic   158   342
Velocities   164   285
Common Carnage   170   347

DODD, BILL
POEMS
The Piper   113   314
Apartment
Getting Up and Going to Work

BOOKS REVIEWED
Aloud   112   56

DODD, LEE WILSON
POEMS
The Temple   5   172
Only Not To Be Too Early Old
The Comrade
Mirella Dances   7   18
Age and Youth   18   22
Riddle
Vacuum   23   144
Sic Transit Gloria   38   146

ARTICLES
Correspondence:
  The Parting [Poem]   8   215

BOOKS REVIEWED
The Middle Miles and Other Poems   8   264
The Great Enlightenment,
  A Satire in Verse with
  Other Selected Verses   35   167

ARTICLES ABOUT
Obituary   42   298

DODGE, ANNE ATWOOD
POEMS
Ephemeral   26   200
  Earth Speaks
  Vision
  Incredible
In an Orchard   29   313
Pilgrimage

DODGE, HENRY NEHEMIAH
BOOKS REVIEWED
Christus Victor   30   353

DODSON, M. F.
POEMS
Do Not Frighten Me with Size   81   168

DODSON, OWEN
REVIEWS
Fields of Wonder,
  by Langston Hughes   71   279

BOOKS REVIEWED
Powerful Long Ladder   69   175

DOLE, NATHAN HASKELL
POEMS
The Summer Sea   6   225

ARTICLES ABOUT
Farewell to Two Poets,
  by Harriet Monroe   46   219

DOLIN, SHARON
POEMS
If My Mother   162   315
The Visit

DOLMATOVSKY, YEVGENY
POEMS
Frost (Tr. by Babette Deutsch)   70   250

DOLSON, EUGENE C.
POEMS
John Reed   30   265

DOMINO, RUTH
POEMS
The Word
  (Tr. by Daniel Hoffman
  and Jerre Mangione)   104   85

DONAGHY, MICHAEL
POEMS
Machines   152   341
Shibboleth
Cage,   156   126
Liverpool   157   277
Erratum
A Reprieve   160   133
Lives of the Artists   161   189
The Heirloom
Reliquary   165   323

DONAHOE, WADE
POEMS
If Not Love Then Nothing   76   72
A Consequence of the Storm

DONALDSON, ROBERT A.
BOOKS REVIEWED
En Repos and Elsewhere Over There
(With Lansing Warren)   14   220

DONNE, J. B.
TRANSLATIONS
Poems by Pablo Neruda   74   315

DONNE, JOHN
BOOKS REVIEWED
The Songs and Sonets of...
(Ed. by Theodore Redpath)   104   120

ARTICLES ABOUT
The Mechanism of Sensibility,
by Morton Dauwen Zabel   34   150
The 16th Century Lyric
in England: Part III,
by Yvor Winters   54   35
Hopkins' Ancestry: Part II,
by Terence Heywood   54   271
Poetry and Nature, by D. S. Savage   61   496
Rev. of *Donne's Poetry
and Modern Criticism,*
by Leonard Unger   77   175
Rev. of *The School of Donne,*
by A. Alvarez   99   261
Rev. of *Five Metaphysical Poets,*
by Joan Bennett   108   65
Rev. of *Six Metaphysical Poets:
A Reader's Guide,*
by George Williamson   112   356

DONNELLY, DOROTHY
POEMS
Three-Toed Sloth   85   31
Les Fleurs d'Amour
Alexandrina   86   249
Perennial Landscape
Greek Coins
Charm   88   298
*For Peter Who Cried Because
He Could Not Catch the Moth*
People   90   270
Trio in a Mirror   94   362
Two Figures in a Golden Light   97   178
Origin of Species   101   392
To Three Old Ladies
Faces   141   7

REVIEWS
Through the Chinese Eye   96   57
Ch'u Tz'u, The Songs of the South
(Tr. by David Hawkes)
*Why I Live on the Mountain,
30 Chinese Poems*
(Tr. by C. H. Kwôck
and Vincent McHugh)

Chinese Love Poems
(Ed. by D. J. Klemer)
Five Poets   100   395
Selected Poems, by Charles Norman
Poems, by Francis Fergusson
Book Like a Bow Curved,
by Raymond E. F. Larsson
The Long Street,
by Donald Davidson
The Islanders, by Philip Booth

BOOKS REVIEWED
Trio in a Mirror   102   125

DONOGHUE, DENIS
ARTICLES
After Reading Hannah Arendt
[Elizabeth Bishop]   100   127

REVIEWS
For Civility   96   382
Emerson: A Modern Anthology
(Ed. by Alfred Kazin
and Daniel Aaron)
*Four Poets on Poetry:
Essays by R. P. Blackmur, Yvor Winters,
Marianne Moore, and Mark Van Doren*
(Ed. by Don Cameron Allen)
James Joyce, by Richard Ellmann
Bird in the Bush: Obvious Essays,
by Kenneth Rexroth
[Matthew Arnold, Edwin Muir,
Edith Sitwell, Thomas Hardy]

ARTICLES ABOUT
Rev. of *Poems of R. P. Blackmur*   133   290

DONOSO, ARMANDO
BOOKS REVIEWED
*Nuestros Poetas:
Antología Chilena Moderna* (Ed.)   26   170

DONOVAN, VIRGINIA LODGE
POEMS
Pyriphlegethon   53   245

DONZELLA, D. W.
POEMS
Stonehenge   119   333

DOOB, LEONARD W.
BOOKS REVIEWED
*"Ezra Pound Speaking":
Radio Speeches of World War II* (Ed.) 134   292

DOOLITTLE, HILDA ["H. D."]
POEMS
*Verses, Translations,
and Reflections from "The Anthology"* 1   118

Hermes of the Ways
Priapus
Epigram
Hermonax   3   164
Acon
The Wind Sleepers   5   265
Storm
The Pool
The Garden
Moonrise
Hymen   15   117
Hesperides   19   26
    Fragment XXXVI ("I know not what...")
    Song ("You are as gold...")
    At Baia
Thetis   22   143
All Mountains   27   83
Leucadian Artemis
Halcyon   30   119
Birds in Snow   33   142
Triplex
Apollo at Delphi   41   320
    His Song
    His Presence
    His Ecstasy
Elegy and Choros, from Electra-Orestes   45   135
Sigel XV   52   139
From Episode I
Last Winter   77   125
In Time of Gold   91   149
Nails for Petals
Sometimes and After
Regents of the Night   94   71
Delphi   139   223

BOOKS REVIEWED
Some Imagist Poets—An Anthology   6   150
Some Imagist Poets: 1916   8   255
The Poets' Translation Series I-VI   9   101
Sea-Garden   9   266
Some Imagist Poets, 1917   11   339
Some Imagist Poets   14   281
Poets' Translation Series, Second Set
    [Choruses from Iphigenia in Aulis
    and Hippolytus, by Euripides] (Tr.)   18   284
Hymen   19   333
Heliodora and Other Poems   25   160
Imagist Anthology 1930
    (With Richard Aldington,
    John Cournos, John Gould Fletcher,
    F. S. Flint, Ford Madox Ford,
    James Joyce, D. H. Lawrence,
    and William Carlos Williams)   36   213
Red Roses for Bronze   41   94
Ion of Euripides (Tr.)   51   160
The Walls Do Not Fall   65   327
Tribute to the Angels   67   341

The Flowering of the Rod   70   36
By Avon River   75   223
Tribute to Freud   89   326
Selected Poems   91   256
Selected Poems   91   260
Bid Me to Live   99   54
Helen in Egypt   100   186
Hermetic Definition   124   162
Trilogy: The Walls Do Not Fall;
    Tribute to the Angels;
    The Flowering of the Rod

ARTICLES ABOUT
Sara Teasdale's Prize,
    by Harriet Monroe   12   264
H. D., by Harriet Monroe   26   268
H. D.: An Appreciation,
    by Denise Levertov   100   182
Review by Andrew Hoyem   113   426
The Forging of H. D.,
    by Gloria G. Fromm   153   160
Review by Sandra M. Gilbert   160   284

DOPLICHER, FABIO
POEMS
    A Diderot/To Diderot
      (Tr. by Stephen Sartarelli)   155   98

DORGAN, THEO
POEMS
    Seven Versions of Loss Eternal   167   70

D'ORGE, JEANNE
POEMS
    The Beggar   10   242
    The Statue
    Matins

BOOKS REVIEWED
    Voice in the Circle   88   334

DORN, EDWARD
POEMS
    This March Afternoon   103   304
    Daffodil Song
    Dark Ceiling
    The Sundering U.P. Tracks   109   359
    The First Note

REVIEWS
    The Moving Target,
      by W. S. Merwin   104   184

BOOKS REVIEWED
    The Newly Fallen   99   313
    Hands Up!   107   121
    The North Atlantic Turbine   113   426
    Gunslinger: Book I

The Collected Poems: 1956-1974   130   285
Selected Poems   136   219

DORO, EDWARD
  BOOKS REVIEWED
    The Boar and Shibboleth   44   111
    Shiloh. Fragments
      on a Famous Theme   50   166
    Mr. Zenith and Other Poems   62   285

DORSET, EDMUND
  POEMS
    Steel-Gray Lines   24   196
      To a Lady
      To Another
      In the Village
      A Comforter
      On Failure

DORSETT, ROBERT
  POEMS
    The Death of Boethius   137   95

DOS PASSOS, JOHN
  POEMS
    Crimson Tent   28   188

  BOOKS REVIEWED
    Panama, or the Adventures
      of My Seven Uncles,
      by Blaise Cendrars (Tr.)   39   224

DOTY, MARK
  POEMS
    Shaker Orchard   147   33
    Ararat   152   24
    The Death of Antinoüs   156   98
    Demolition   158   208
    To Bessie Drennan   159   155

  BOOKS REVIEWED
    Bethlehem in Broad Daylight   159   282

DOUGHTY, CHARLES
  ARTICLES ABOUT
    Hopkins' Ancestry: Part I,
      by Terence Heywood   54   209

DOUGHTY, ISABEL PERRY
  POEMS
    In Search   44   84
      Patterns Are Made to Break
      There Is a Wild Weed
      What Wordless Way?

DOUGHTY, LE GARDE S.
  POEMS
    Grub!   53   246
    Blind Boy with Accordion

Sabbatical Return, Without Music
Pastoral, Nineteen Forty-One   58   196
I Lie, Thou Liest
Nocturne on Gunny   60   316
World at Night   63   134
The Land, the Labor
Old Men at Air Base   63   320
Epilogue to History   66   10
War, Deep South
Humanist   74   263

  REVIEWS
    Effects and Sound Effects   60   163
      Galanty Show,
        by Josiah Titzell
      A Day in Manhattan,
        by A. M. Sullivan

DOUGHTY, LEONARD
  POEMS
    Master Francois Villon
      Greets Death   32   86

DOUGLAS, GAVIN
  ARTICLES ABOUT
    Rev. of *Late Mediaeval*
      Scots Poetry
      (Ed. by Tom Scott)   113   35

DOUGLAS, KEITH
  BOOKS REVIEWED
    The Collected Poems of...
      (Ed. by John Waller
      and G. S. Fraser)   79   356

DOUGLAS, MONA
  POEMS
    Seaward   34   136

DOVE, RITA
  POEMS
    November for Beginners   139   63
    Agosta the Winged Man
      and Rasha the Black Dove
    Dusting
    Flirtation   141   10
    Pomade   144   324
    The Wake
    Old Folk's Home, Jerusalem   147   12
    Ars Poetica   151   45
    The Breathing, the Endless News   153   196
    Demeter's Prayer to Hades   161   23
    Sonnet ("Nothing can console me...")
    Protection
    The Venus of Willendorf
    Her Island   166   63

BOOKS REVIEWED
The Yellow House on the Corner   145   36
Museum
Grace Notes   157   33
Mother Love   167   343
The Darker Face of the Earth

DOW, DOROTHY
POEMS
Handful of Ashes   19   130
  The Captive
  Waiting
  Futility
  Bound
Covenant   22   123
Spring Picture   24   69
Two at Tea
Cabaret
Heimweh
Today Will Never Come Back   36   128
Phantom
Rivals
Even Though   38   314
  Portrait
  Plea
What I Have Felt   54   319
O Loveliest Voice   57   304

BOOKS REVIEWED
Will-o'-the-Wisp   27   281
Time and Love   60   344

DOWD, F. HARRISON
POEMS
His Acre   44   259

DOWDEN, GEORGE
BOOKS REVIEWED
Flight from America   109   123
Because I Am Tired of the Night

DOWLING, ALLAN
BOOKS REVIEWED
A Poet's Youth   66   284

DOWNER, ALAN S.
ARTICLES
The New Theatrum Poetarum
  [T. S. Eliot, W. H. Auden,
  Christopher Isherwood,
  Louis MacNeice, Stephen Spender,
  Delmore Schwartz]   60   206

REVIEWS
Climates of Tragedy,
  by William Van O'Connor   62   344
Morality Plays   67   101

Taps Is Not Enough, by Carl Carmer
The Bridge, by Stanley Burnshaw

BOOKS REVIEWED
English Institute Essays, 1949 (Ed.)
  [Arthur Mizener, Moody E. Prior,
  Francis Fergusson, William Charvat]   77   48

DOWNEY, HARRIS
POEMS
Revisit   50   194
At the Clavier

DOWNING, BEN
POEMS
Pieces of Pangaea   162   268
Ranakpur
Saudades
Onomathesia   163   130
Naming the Ford   165   73

REVIEWS
Brief Reviews
  After the Reunion, by David Baker   167   223
  The Post Office Murals Restored,
    by Robert B. Shaw
  The Parts of Light, by Vicki Hearne
  The Only World, by Lynda Hull

DOWSON, ERNEST
ARTICLES ABOUT
Rev. of Ernest Dowson,
  by Victor Plarr   6   43

DOYLE, ARTHUR
POEMS
In the Ward   25   248
Voices
The Moon
Death Lies In

DOYLE, CAMILLA
POEMS
In Pockthorpe   26   308
House in the Chilterns

BOOKS REVIEWED
Poems   24   341

DOYLE, CHARLES
BOOKS REVIEWED
The Night Shift
  (With James K. Baxter, Louis Johnson,
  and Kendrick Smithyman)   94   44

DOYLE, JAMES
POEMS
The Village   156   200

DOYLE, MARION
POEMS
Brevities   42   202
  Mountain Woman
  Birthday
  Exile
  Seventy's Dinner
Earth-Run   48   200
  Autumn Orchard
  First Furrow

DOYLE, MIKE
REVIEWS
Made in Canada?   119   356
  Made in Canada:
    New Poems of the Seventies
    (Ed. by Douglas Lochhead
    and Raymond Souster)
  The Cosmic Chef:
    An Evening of Concrete
    (Ed. by b p nichol)
  So Far, So Good, by Raymond Souster
  The Great Bear Lake Meditations,
    by J. Michael Yates
  Contemporary Poetry of British Columbia
    (Ed. by J. Michael Yates)
  Neo Poems,
    by John Robert Colombo
  The Man with Seven Toes,
    by Michael Ondaatje
  Cancer Rising, by David Cull
  By the Light of the Silvery McLune:
    Media Parables, Poems, Signs, Gestures,
    and Other Assaults on the Interface,
    by Lionel Kearns
  The Happy Hungry Man,
    by George Jonas
  Year of the Quiet Sun,
    by Ian Young
  Body, by Robert Flanagan
  The Journals of Susannah Moodie
    and *Power Politics*,
    by Margaret Atwood
  Plainsongs, by Dorothy Livesay
  Gnu Soup, by Heinz Fischer
  Immortal Plowman,
    by Fred Cogswell
  Inside Me, by Kathleen Forsythe
  The Hitch Hiker, by Frank Gillis
  Lost Neighbourhood,
    by Terry Crawford
  Catching the Sun's Fire,
    by Brenda Fleet
  The Silent Cowboys of the East,
    by Louis Cormier
  Cables to Rage, by Audre Lorde
  An Irish Album, by Robin Skelton
  Playing the Jesus Game,
    by Alden Nowlan

BOOKS REVIEWED
  Earth Meditations: One to Five   120   107
  Stonedancer   131   225
  A Steady Hand   144   297

DRACHLER, JACOB
BOOKS REVIEWED
  African Heritage (Ed.)   103   394

DRAKE, CAROL CHRISTOPHER
POEMS
  Immigrant   89   99

DRAKE, JOSEPH RODMAN
ARTICLES ABOUT
  Rev. of *American Poetry:*
    The Nineteenth Century
    (Ed. by John Hollander)   165   340

DRAKE, LEAH BODINE
POEMS
  Vestal   62   188
  Luna   64   305
  Leonardo Before His Canvas   74   208
  Legendary Tapestries: Semele   83   202

DRAKE, NICK
POEMS
  Static   167   257

DRANSFIELD, JANE
POEMS
  The Loons   38   76

DRANSFIELD, MICHAEL
ARTICLES ABOUT
  Towards a Contemporary
    Australian Poetics,
    by John Kinsella   169   94

DRAPER, RUTH
BOOKS REVIEWED
  Icaro, by Lauro de Bosis (Tr.)   44   44

DRAVO, MARGARET DUNCAN
POEMS
  Revelation   27   81

DRAYTON, MICHAEL
ARTICLES ABOUT
  The 16th Century Lyric
    in England: Part II,
    by Yvor Winters   53   320

DREISER, THEODORE
ARTICLES ABOUT
  Rev. of *Caius Gracchus*,
    by Odin Gregory   17   337

Dorothy Dudley's Frontiers,
   by Harriet Monroe   43   208

DRESBACH, D. P.
POEMS
   Photosynthesis   161   327

DRESBACH, GLENN WARD
POEMS
   Songs for a Violin   7   68
   One Face in the Crowd   10   130
   ("When my dream-robe is tattered...")
   ("When I am dead, oh, speak to me...")
   The Dreamers   10   297
   Nocturne
   In New Mexico   14   192
   ("I saw a grown girl coming down...")   16   136
   ("You saw me staring at the girl...")
   ("A gypsy passed me with a song...")
   ("I would build myself a house...")
   To One Beloved   17   19
   Songs of the Plains   19   187
   In Western Mountains   20   76
   The Syrian Peddler   23   314
   Desert Rain
   ("Dip your hand in the...")   26   74
   ("I found in the arms of a valley...")
   ("O thrush, in what deep glades...")
   After the Rain   29   193
   Birds in the Wind   31   186
   Snowbird
   Mountain Water
   The Gnawing Mouse
   Song ("These I asked not, but...")
   Autumnal   33   11
      The Cavern
      Woodland Incident
      Song ("Remembering how mint...")
      The Little Spring Flows Clear Again
      A Toast in Autumn
      Autumn Crickets
      Cider
      Discards
      Flesh
   Songs Out-of-Doors   36   239
      Early Morning in a Glade
      The Desert
      Wings into Sunset
      Mission Bell
   Century of Progress Hymn   42   138
   The Field   55   310
   Slow Defeat
   No Fire Left
   The Last Corn Shock   59   198
   Stone Wall

BOOKS REVIEWED
   The Road to Everywhere   9   324
   Morning, Noon and Night   18   281

   In Colors of the West   22   344
   The Enchanted Mesa
      and Other Poems   25   47
   Cliff Dwellings and Other Poems   30   349
   The Wind in the Cedars   36   43
   Star-Dust and Stone
   Selected Poems   40   346

DREW, ELIZABETH
BOOKS REVIEWED
   Discovering Poetry   44   231
   T. S. Eliot:
      The Design of His Poetry   75   112

DREWRY, CARLETON
POEMS
   Castle of the Child   55   180
   Fields of Fear
   Time in the Trees   65   194
   Pause
   This Tree   66   307

BOOKS REVIEWED
   Proud Horns   42   339

DREYSPRING, MARY
POEMS
   July in Michigan   34   202

DRINKWATER, JOHN
POEMS
   Sunrise on Rydal Water   7   122
   Invocation   8   297
   Reciprocity   11   68
   Union   17   134

BOOKS REVIEWED
   Abraham Lincoln, a Play   15   159
   Pawns   19   94
   Mary Stuart
   Poems
   New Poems   27   158
   Poems by Lord de Tabley (Ed.)   27   164
   Twentieth-Century Poetry
      (Ed. with Henry Seidel Canby
      and William Rose Benét)   37   164

ARTICLES ABOUT
   Rev. of *An Annual*
      of New Poetry, 1917   11   333
   Visitors from the Other Side,
      by Harriet Monroe   15   93
   Mr. Yeats and the Poetic Drama,
      by Harriet Monroe   16   32
   Drinkwater on Abercrombie,
      by Harriet Monroe   18   30
   Poetry on Records,
      by Harry T. Moore   57   52

DRISCOLL, JACK
POEMS
Spying   149   325
Houdini
Elegy: Charles Atlas (1893-1972)

DRISCOLL, LOUISE
POEMS
"Passe Rosa"   3   51
The Metal Checks [Drama]   5   49
The Lilacs   6   75
A Village Church
Old Roofs   11   237
Harbury
The Garden of the West   13   138
Treasure   15   82
Premonition   15   311
Keep My Hand   19   17
The Owl   22   141
Bargain   24   194
Mountain Stream
Verities   26   199
Whispers   28   198
    Charm
    Portrait
Patronage   32   200
Here Lie
Madman   33   189

ARTICLES
Correspondence:
    Concerning Hilda Conkling   14   344

BOOKS REVIEWED
The Garden of the West   21   217
Garden Grace   24   283

DRIVER, TOM F.
BOOKS REVIEWED
Poems of Doubt and Belief
    (Ed. with Robert Pack)   106   429

DRUMMOND, DONALD (F.)
POEMS
Five Times Zero   69   204
Intuitive Essential   74   259
The Blood of the Lamb
Anthropomorphism
Aftermath of Ahab   75   268
Jet Plane
Orestes to His Mother
Valediction to Culprit and Judge
The Middle-Age of Reason   79   196
Leda
Of a Dead Woman

REVIEWS
The Waldport Poems, by William Everson   65   281

BOOKS REVIEWED
No Moat No Castle   76   302
The Battlement   89   244
The Drawbridge   102   118
The Grey Tower   110   258

DRUMMOND, JOHN
ARTICLES ABOUT
[Note: Ezra Pound]   52   302

**DRUMMOND DE ANDRADE,
    CARLOS**
POEMS
Travelling in the Family
    (Tr. by Elizabeth Bishop)   106   181

BOOKS REVIEWED
In the Middle of the Road, Selected Poems
    (Ed. and tr. by John Nist)   111   46

ARTICLES ABOUT
Excerpt of letter from Elizabeth Bishop   106   251

DRURY, FINVOLA
POEMS
Those Garages   78   272
House with Tulips   80   138

DRURY, JOHN
BOOKS REVIEWED
Arclight Dusks   28   290

DRURY, JOHN
POEMS
Decoys   134   218
Side Panels: Adam and Eve   136   274
    1. After Cranach
    2. After Dürer

DRYDEN, BRIDGET
POEMS
A la Recherche d'un Dieu Perdu   33   72

DRYDEN, JOHN
BOOKS REVIEWED
Selected Works of John Dryden
    (Ed. by William Frost)   86   118

ARTICLES ABOUT
The Poetics of Translation,
    by Edouard Roditi   60   32
The Poetry of Charles Churchill: Part I,
    by Yvor Winters   98   44
Rev. of Dryden's Poetry, by Earl Miner   112   356
Rev. of Contexts of Dryden's Thought,
    by Philip Harth   115   196
Rev. of The Anxiety of Influence,
    by Harold Bloom   122   298

DUBERMAN, MARTIN
BOOKS REVIEWED
   James Russell Lowell   111   333

DUBIE, NORMAN
POEMS
   Ibis   127   63
   The Negress: Her Monologue of Dark Crêpe
      with Edges of Light   128   285
   The Ambassador Diaries
      of Jean de Bosschère and Edgar Poe   129   324
   The World Isn't a Wedding
      of the Artists of Yesterday: 132   66
   The Scrivener's Roses   133   93
   Pictures at an Exhibition   136   203
   Revelations   142   218

BOOKS REVIEWED
   In the Dead of the Night   128   290
   The Illustrations   132   288
   The Everlastings   137   169
   Selected and New Poems   145   99
   Radio Sky   160   219

DUBLE URRUTIA, DIEGO
POEMS
   From The Mines
      (Tr. by Muna Lee)   26   121

DU BOIS, MELANIE
POEMS
   Rug on the Floor of My Mind   165   156

DU BOUCHET, ANDRÉ
ARTICLES ABOUT
   Letters from the Midi,
      by Wallace Fowlie   100   258

DUCASSE, ISIDORE
[See DE LAUTREAMONT,
(COMTE)]

DUCKER, BRUCE
POEMS
   The Cricket in the City   158   86
   Picnic   160   255

DUCZYNSKA, ILONA
BOOKS REVIEWED
   The Boy Changed into a Stag,
      by Ferenc Juhász
      (Tr. with Kenneth McRobbie) 119   45

DUDEK, LOUIS
BOOKS REVIEWED
   Unit of Five
      (With Ronald Hambleton,
      P. K. Page, Raymond Souster
      and James Wreford)   66   334

   East of the City   69   349
   Europe   88   329

DUDIS, ELLEN KIRVIN
POEMS
   Lily Morning   119   314

DUDLEY, CAROLINE
POEMS
   Concerning a Nobleman   7   283
   Chaotic Peace

DUDLEY, DOROTHY ["D. D."]
POEMS
   La Rue de la Montagne Sainte-Geneviève 6   119
   November in the Park   7   67
   Paderewski   10   189
   The Moon
   Pine River Bay   11   124
   Fandangle   22   80
   Interlude
   Branch
   Under-Current

ARTICLES
   Correspondence:
      Notes from the P.S.A. Annual Dinner
      [Chang Peng Chun, Amy Lowell,
      Carl Sandburg]   20   53

REVIEWS
   In the Town and *On the Road,*
      by Douglas Goldring   8   262
   Goblins and Pagodas
      by John Gould Fletcher 9   43
   Celtic Songs   9   209
      Singing Fires of Erin,
         by Eleanor Rogers Cox
      Songs of the Fields,
         by Francis Ledwidge
   Women's Eyes
      (Tr. by Arthur William Ryder) 9   274
   Roads and *What Is Your Legion?*
      by Grace Fallow Norton 11   164
   Al Que Quiere!
      by William Carlos Williams 12   38
   Toward the Gulf,
      by Edgar Lee Masters 12   150
   The Mystic Warrior,
      by James Oppenheim 19   216
   Legends, by Amy Lowell 19   330
   New Hampshire, by Robert Frost 23   328
   Roman Bartholow,
      by Edwin Arlington Robinson 24   96

ARTICLES ABOUT
   Correspondence
      from Witter Bynner   20   111

Dorothy Dudley's Frontiers,
  by Harriet Monroe
  [Theodore Dreiser]   43   208

DUDLEY, HELEN
POEMS
  To One Unknown   1   10
  Song ("A few more windy days...")   4   186
  Reed-Song   11   128
  Dirge
  Against the Sun   16   80
  Cootham Lane

DUER, DAVID
POEMS
  Of Two Minds   154   187

DUERDEN, RICHARD
POEMS
  Bee: Flowers   105   89
  Circle, Death, Magic
  Well Well
  Today the Sun's Up
  The Medium or Web   107   245
  The Host, March 1965
  Song Coyote Stole from the Navajo   110   231
  Gregorian Chant 2

REVIEWS
  Eyes and "I"   108   125
    Routines, by Lawrence Ferlinghetti
    King Lord/Queen Freak, by Ed Sanders
    Two Hands, by James Koller

BOOKS REVIEWED
  The Fork   108   198

DUERR, EDWIN
POEMS
  Interval for a Song   36   84

DUFAULT, PETER KANE
POEMS
  The Jay's Cry   76   140
  Drowning of a Fly
  Hill Walk, November, 1948

BOOKS REVIEWED
  For Some Stringed Instrument   91   268

DUFF, E. L.
BOOKS REVIEWED
  Bohemian Glass   10   44

DUFF, JAMES L.
POEMS
  After Calvary   38   10
  Pilate

  Caiaphas
  Iscariot
  John
  The Major   38   315

DUFF, NAOMI
POEMS
  Before Her Statue   37   134
  Old Song
  The Theft

DUFFEY, BERNARD
REVIEWS
  Leaves of Grass,
    by Walt Whitman
    (Ed. by Harold W. Blodgett
    and Sculley Bradley)   107   397

DUFFY, CAROL ANN
ARTICLES ABOUT
  A Letter from Britain,
    by William Logan   157   222

DUFFY, WILLIAM
POEMS
  An Old Man's Walk   98   211
  Bachelor Place

DUGAN, ALAN
POEMS
  Aubade: Chant of the Innocents   65   196
  Aside
  Young Girl   68   196
  Soldier
  The Christian Scientist I Love
  Family Scene: Young Vet and Relatives
  The Martyr   70   9
  Poem ("At twelve noon...")
  The Explorer
  Niagara Falls
  Tuesday
  April
  Song for a Deformed Prince   82   311
  Prison Song
  Oasis
  To Sleep
  Natural Enemies of the Conch
  Imperial Song for Warmth   84   214
  The Branches of Water or Desire   88   7
  Portrait
  Landfall
  Notes Toward a Spring Offensive   95   269
  How We Heard the Name
  On an East Wind from the Wars
  Actual Vision of Morning's Extrusion
  Philodendron
  Free Variation on a Translation from Greek 100   1
  Three as a Magic Number

To a Red-Headed Do-Good Waitress
851
Dedication for a Building
From Heraclitus   101   29
What the Hell, Rage,
    Give in to Natural Graces
Fabrication of Ancestors
Admonitor: A Pearl for Arrogance   102   8
On Trees
Variation on a Theme by Stevens
Accommodation to Detroit
Winter's Onset from
    an Alienated Point of View
Flower Grower in Aquarius   109   217
Conspiracy of Two Against the World
The Working World's Bloody Flux
His Hands Have Five Knives Each
On Being Out-Classed by Class
Barefoot for a Scorpion
Poem ("Oh that was not a scrap...")
Poem ("Flowering balls!...")
Variation of Themes by Roethke & Eliot
On Rape Unattempted
On Zero
Stentor and Mourning   120   355
Aside   121   8

REVIEWS
    Three Books, a Pamphlet,
        and a Broadside   100   310
    Saturday Night Poems,
        by Bill Berkson
    Works and Days, by Irving Feldman
    Starting from San Francisco and *Berlin,*
        by Lawrence Ferlinghetti
    The Dancing Beasts, by Harold Norse

BOOKS REVIEWED
    Poems   98   245
    Poems 2   103   387
    Poems 3   112   270
    Collected Poems   119   301
    Poems 4   125   295
    New and Collected Poems 1961-1983   145   291

DUGGAN, EILEEN
BOOKS REVIEWED
    New Zealand Poems   57   330

DUHAMEL, GEORGES
ARTICLES ABOUT
    Georges Duhamel Returns   14   227
    Paris Letter, by Jean Catel   18   168

DUJARDIN, EDOUARD
BOOKS REVIEWED
    De Stéphane Mallarmé au prophète Ezéchiel,
        et essai d'une théorie de réalisme symbolique   16   164

DUKES, THOMAS
POEMS
    Snow in Ohio   161   143
    Minerva, Ohio   162   345

DULL, HAROLD
POEMS
    The Night of the Perseids   108   90

DUMONT, HENRY
POEMS
    Sestina ("To thee, O fairest...")   21   126

DUMONT, JULIA L.
ARTICLES ABOUT
    Notes on Mid-western Oblivion,
        by Pat Morrissette   34   346

DUNBAR, OLIVIA HOWARD
BOOKS REVIEWED
    A House in Chicago
        [Harriet Moody]   71   277

DUNBAR, VIRGINIA ESTERLY
POEMS
    The Equator   78   202
    The Titan

DUNBAR, WILLIAM
ARTICLES ABOUT
    Rev. of *Late Mediaeval Scots Poetry*
        (Ed. by Tom Scott)   113   35

DUNCAN, HARRY
POEMS
    January Thaw   81   31
    A Bugler, Dying   81   356

TRANSLATIONS
    Poems by Guillaume Apollinaire   77   265

REVIEWS
    Collected Poems of Herman Melville
        (Ed. by Howard P. Vincent)   72   167
    The Undersea Mountain, by Harold Norse   83   335

BOOKS REVIEWED
    Poems and Translations   88   52

DUNCAN, ISADORA
ARTICLES ABOUT
    Golden Moments,
        by Harriet Monroe   31   206

DUNCAN, ROBERT
POEMS
    A Spring Memorandum   60   76
    A Pair of Uranian Garters for Aurora Bligh

A Morning Letter   90   350
The Temple of the Animals
There's Too Much Sea on the Big Sur
Poem ("When the immortal blond...")
A Ride to the Sea
Brought to Love   91   377
To Vow
Metamorphosis
Re-
Words Open Out upon Grief
August Sun
A Storm of White,   93   369
Food for Fire, Food for Thought,   95   29
Under Ground
Bone Dance
Returning to Roots of First Feeling
The Law   99   168
Two Dicta of William Blake / Variations
After a Passage in Baudelaire   101   32
Risk   101   383
The Continent   103   28
The Fire   106   32
In the Place of a Passage 22   108   1
Benefice: Passages 23
Orders: Passages 24
Passages 28: The Light   110   141
Eye of God: Passages 29
Passages 31: The Concert   113   179
Passages 32

ARTICLES
Correspondence
    [Louis Coxe, Ezra Pound]   92   196

REVIEWS
Selected Poems, by H.D.   91   256
True & False Unicorn,
    by James Broughton   91   328
The Sorrows of Priapus,
    by Edward Dahlberg
    [D. H. Lawrence, Antonin Artaud]   94   54
Two Poems of the Air,
    by James Dickey   105   131

BOOKS REVIEWED
Heavenly City, Earthly City   72   48
Medieval Scenes   77   114
Caesar's Gate   89   52
Selected Poems   96   52
Letters   96   55
Roots and Branches   106   427
As Testimony: The Poem and the Scene
The Years as Catches   111   402
The Sweetness and Greatness
    of Dante's Divine Comedy
Of the War: Passages 22-27
Medea at Kolchis, the Maiden Head

Bending the Bow   114   40
The First Decade:
    Selected Poems, 1940-1950   116   110
Derivations: Selected Poems, 1950-1956
Roots and Branches
Tribunals: Passages 31-35   121   343

ARTICLES ABOUT
Rev. of The New American Poetry: 1945-1960
    (Ed. by Donald M. Allen)   98   242
Rev. of Poemas Humanos,
    by César Vallejo
    (Tr. by Clayton Eshleman)   114   193
Rev. of The New Oxford Book
    of American Verse
    (Ed. by Richard Ellmann)   131   236

DUNCAN, THOMAS W.
POEMS
Chromosomes   34   20
1960: The Last War   39   79
One Who Came in Night   49   73
The Strolling Girls   52   73
Six O'Clock in February   65   250
Aries

BOOKS REVIEWED
Elephants at War   50   57

DUNETZ, LORA
REVIEWS
First Poems,
    by Marvin Solomon   83   227

DUNHAM, VERA
BOOKS REVIEWED
Nostalgia for the Present,
    by Andrei Voznesensky
    (Ed. with Max Hayward)   136   40

DUNKLIN, GILBERT T.
BOOKS REVIEWED
Wordsworth: Centenary Studies Presented
    at Cornell and Princeton Universities (Ed.)   80   233

DUNN, DOUGLAS
BOOKS REVIEWED
Terry Street   126   219
The Happier Life

ARTICLES ABOUT
A Letter from Britain,
    by William Logan   157   222

DUNN, SHARON
ARTICLES
Correspondence
    [Greg Kuzma, Martha Collins]   149   180

DUNN, STEPHEN
POEMS
Men in Winter   119   220
From *The Monastery of Work and Love*   133   153
  Welcome
  Work
  The Photograph in the Hallway
  Movie Night
Fairy Tale   138   35
Workers
Elementary Poem
In the Blowdown Zone   139   161
The Snow Leopard
The End of the World
Corners   140   330
Eggs
Rubbing
Elegy ("Those men going home...")   142   141
Ignorance   146   259
Saints
Portrait
All that We Have   147   253
Sleeping with Ghosts
Aerial in the Pines
Hawk   149   291
On the Way to Work
Poetry
Sweetness   150   149
Tenderness
Cleanliness
Loveliness
Emptiness
Why I Think I'm a Writer   151   46
Naturally   153   150
Letting the Puma Go
Happiness
Kindness
Landscape at the End of the Century   155   335
Little Essay on Communication
Beautiful Women
Loves
Stations   157   268
The Snowmass Cycle   160   327
Language   162   311
Bank Street   164   136
Fallacies   166   28
Loosestrife   167   187
After Making Love   167   254
Meaninglessness   167   335
Nocturne
Homage   168   8

BOOKS REVIEWED
Looking for Holes in the Ceiling   127   352
Work and Love   141   170
Local Time   149   168
Between Angels   155   283

Landscape at the End of the Century   159   101
New and Selected Poems: 1974-1994   165   219
Loosestrife   170   288

DUNN, WALDO HILARY
BOOKS REVIEWED
The Note-Books of Matthew Arnold
  (Ed. with Howard Foster Lowry
  and Karl Young)   81   196

DUNNE, SEÁN
POEMS
One Sunday in the Gearagh   167   31
Russians in Paris

DUNNING, RALPH CHEEVER
POEMS
The Home-Coming   7   179
Falling Leaves   24   183
  Sentimental
  Dead Youth
  On a Passing Funeral
  April
The Four Winds   26   1
  My Garden
  That Mythical Entity
  Stonehenge
  Driftwood
  A Passing Woman
  Laws
  Concerning a Secret
  Bitter Sweet
  The Return
  Trumpets
  In the Snow
  Shadows
Education of Barbara   33   140

BOOKS REVIEWED
The Four Winds   26   339
Rococo   30   108
Windfalls   34   292

**DUNSANY, [LORD]
[EDWARD PLUNKETT]**
ARTICLES ABOUT
Visitors from the Other Side,
  by Harriet Monroe   15   93

DUPEE, F. W.
BOOKS REVIEWED
Selected Letters of E. E. Cummings
  (Ed. with George Stade)   115   277

DUPIN, JACQUES
POEMS
The Frugal Path
  (Tr. by Paul Auster)   116   279

DURAND, LIONEL
ARTICLES ABOUT
  The Forging of H. D.,
    by Gloria G. Fromm   153 160

DURCAN, PAUL
ARTICLES ABOUT
  A Map of Contemporary Irish Poetry,
    by Dennis O'Driscoll   167 94

**DURHAM, ELIZABETH
  MALCOLM**
POEMS
  Divagations   27 188

DURLING, DWIGHT
POEMS
  Time Casts Shadows   43 242
    Mind's Winter
    In Ceaseless Changes
    Scope in Earth and Air
    Poverty Parish

DURRELL, LAWRENCE
BOOKS REVIEWED
  Proems
    (With Ruthven Todd, Patrick Evans,
    Rayner Heppenstall, Edgar Foxall,
    and Oswald Blakeston)   53 155
  A Key to Modern British Poetry   84 106
  Selected Poems   91 396
  Justine   93 323
  Collected Poems   98 53
  Collected Poems 1931-1974
    (Ed. by James Brigham)   140 170

DURST, DORIS
POEMS
  From China and Hawaii   44 76
    An Urn of Tears
    Now They Can Be Gay
    Can It Be?

DUSENBERY, GAIL
POEMS
  I Carried with Me Poems   108 171
  Two Poems
    ("Your citadel/is secure...")
    ("I recline on a cloud couch...")

BOOKS REVIEWED
  The Mark   112 343

DUTRAIT, JEAN
ARTICLES ABOUT
  Marseille Letter,
    by Jean Rivier   60 269

DUTTON, GEOFFREY
BOOKS REVIEWED
  Bratsk Station
    and Other New Poems,
    by Yevgeny Yevtushenko
    (Tr. with Tina Tupinika-Glaessner)   111 121

DUTTON, MARGAN
POEMS
  Winter Poem   49 319
  The Mountains   51 310
  The Instinct   57 365
  Press No Petal   61 538
  To Be Poor
  The Starlings and the Serpent

DU VON, JAY
POEMS
  November   41 79
  ("Here by the unremembering...")   42 256
  ("As for myself...")
  ("Together there is strength...")
  Communications   48 127
    Flight from the Sun
    For Patrouska at Fifteen
    Monody
    Plaint of a Friend

DWYER, MARY H.
POEMS
  Return   35 315

DWYER, SUSAN
POEMS
  Sestina for the 26-Letter Athlete   126 91
  The Lies of Sleeping Dogs:
    A Fable
  Little Song for Pythagoras'
    Rubber Band

DYBEK, STUART
POEMS
  Kiddie Corner   135 18
  Angelus   149 158
  Tomorrow
  Night Walk
  Autobiography
  Island   151 48
  Today, Tonight   163 328
  Overhead Fan   169 278

BOOKS REVIEWED
  Brass Knuckles   139 35

DYCK, E. F.
BOOKS REVIEWED
  The Mossback Canon   144 297

POEMS
Aurelius Augustinus   53   249

DYKSTRA, LESLIE
POEMS
Poor Butterfly   26   19
Bitter Days   37   198
Tornado
Famine

DYMENT, CLIFFORD
POEMS
Secret Idiom   46   251
Final Decision
Sanctuary
The Flower
Straight or Curly?   49   202

BOOKS REVIEWED
Straight or Curly?   50   233

"E. C."
[See CARNEVALI, EMANUEL]

"E. H. L."
ARTICLES
Correspondence: To Miss Monroe
in the Carolinas
[Poem]   10   166

"E. L. M."
[See MASTERS, EDGAR LEE]

"E. M."
[See MARSH, EDWARD]

"E. P." [See POUND, EZRA]

"E. R." [See ROSS, W. W. E.]

"E. T."
[See TIETJENS, EUNICE]

"E. W." [See WYATT, EDITH]

EARLEY, TOM
BOOKS REVIEWED
The Sad Mountain   119   159

EARNSHAW, RUTH
POEMS
In the General Motors Building   42   325
For a Day in May   46   81

EARP, T. W.
BOOKS REVIEWED
Contacts   10   44

EASON, T. W.
POEMS
Childhood   49   189

EASTAWAY, EDWARD
[Pseud. of THOMAS, EDWARD]
POEMS
Old Man   9   247
The Word
The Unknown

ARTICLES ABOUT
Rev. of An Annual of New Poetry, 1917   11   333
[Note about name]   12   102

EASTMAN, MAX
BOOKS REVIEWED
Child of the Amazons   3   31
Colors of Life   13   322
Kinds of Love   39   51
An Anthology
for the Enjoyment of Poetry (Ed.)   57   221

ARTICLES ABOUT
Poetry a Zest for Life, by Harriet Monroe 2   140
Lazy Criticism,
by Alice Corbin Henderson   9   144
A Radical-Conservative,
by Harriet Monroe   13   322

EATON, CHARLES EDWARD
POEMS
The Bright Plain   58   201
Tropical Burial   66   128
Evening Ritual
A Dry Hot Night   68   188
The Garden Party   75   271
Flamboyante   77   260
The Marriage of Martyrs
The Heart Tattoo   81   113
The Bride Is a Motive of Memory   89   343
Such Force as Blinds the Giant   92   153

BOOKS REVIEWED
The Bright Plain   63   101
The Greenhouse in the Garden   89   373
Countermoves   102   402

EATON, W. D.
BOOKS REVIEWED
The War in Verse and Prose (Ed.)   14   281

EBERHART, NELLE RICHMOND
BOOKS REVIEWED
From the Land of the Sky-Blue Water
and Other Songs for Music   30   353

EBERHART, RICHARD

POEMS

Things Known	31	80
Under the Hill		
Looking Down		
The Village Daily		
Schopenhauer		
Windy		
Twenty-Two		
Search		
Song ("Cover me over, clover...")		
The Slope Sun—1927	35	122
Wentworth Place		
L'Apres-Midi d'un Faune		
The Kiss of Stillness		
Night Watch on the Pacific		
Sumatra Shore Leave		
"To Come Closer unto Thee"	51	190
Anglo-Saxon Song		
Poem ("If I could only live...")		
Song for the Death of My Uncle in Illinois		
From Poem in Construction	56	140
To H. E. B.	60	1
New Hampshire, February		
Of Truth: The Protagonist Speaking		
Dublin Afternoon		
To Evade the Whirlwind		
The Dream		
The Blindness of Poets		
From The Kite	68	202
The Wind as an Abstract God		
Aerialism		
Meditation by an Old Barn		
in the Heat of Summertime		
From Letter I	72	14
Indian Summer	76	10
Politics		
Talk at Dawn		
Order and Disorder		
Forms of the Human		
The Forum		
The Apparition	77	311
The Skier and the Mountain	81	33
Easter Absolutes	81	357
Blessed Are the Angels in Heaven		
Grape Vine Shoots		
The Voyage		
Order Again		
The Lost Poem		
On the Fragility of Mind	82	261
Jealousy		
Seeing Is Deceiving		
The Giantess	85	94
World's Havoc		
The Project		
Sunday in October	85	273
A Young Greek, Killed in the Wars		
Attitudes	88	318

Only in the Dream		
Thrush Song at Dawn		
Light From Above	95	1
The Blue Grains		
The Spider		
A Testament		
Late Summer		
Riches		
The Struggle	101	34
Dream Journey of the Head and Heart		
Hark Back		
Winter Kill		
Mexico Phantasmagoria	110	400
United 555	117	39
Time Passes		
Vermont Idyll	121	79
Plain Song Talk		
Offering to the Body	134	342
Speculative Nature Note		
Singular, Desolate, Out of It	151	49
Speech of Acceptance		

TRANSLATIONS

Poems by Jorge Luis Borges	116	299

ARTICLES

[Note on Dublin Afternoon]	60	112
Correspondence	61	698
The Defense of Poetry		
[Harvard Poetry Conference]		
[John Crowe Ransom,		
Stephen Spender, Peter Viereck,		
Marianne Moore, Randall Jarrell,		
Pierre Emmanuel, Kenneth Burke]	77	89

REVIEWS

M: 1000 Autobiographical Sonnets,		
by Merrill Moore	54	160
The Turning Path,		
by Ronald Bottrall	55	101
A Mixed Bag	56	274
Poems, by Glyn Jones		
Poems, by Roy Fuller		
38 Poems, by Henry Treece		
Planets and Angels,		
by Eugene Jolas	57	276
Collected Poems,		
by Walter de la Mare	58	146
New Directions 1941		
(Ed. by James Laughlin)	60	165
Gerard Manley Hopkins,		
Priest and Poet,		
by John Pick	62	347
Selected Poems,		
by John Crowe Ransom	67	212
The Dispossessed, by John Berryman	73	43
The Green Wave, by Muriel Rukeyser	73	173

The Labyrinth, by Edwin Muir   75   239
The Dream of Alcestis,
  by Theodore Morrison   78   49
Poetry in Our Time, by Babette Deutsch   82   282
The Collected Poems of Edith Sitwell   87   48
Hölderlin, Leopardi, and H.D.   91   260
  Selected Poems of Hölderlin
    (Tr. and ed. by J. B. Leishman)
  Poems from Giacomo Leopardi
    (Tr. by John Heath-Stubbs)
  Selected Poems, by H.D.
  A Dirty Hand: The Literary Notebooks
    of Winfield Townley Scott   115   345

BOOKS REVIEWED
  A Bravery of Earth   36   343
  Reading the Spirit   50   164
  Song and Idea   61   508
  Poems, New and Selected   66   92
  War and the Poet
    (Ed. with Selden Rodman)   69   46
  Burr Oaks   73   226
  The Brotherhood of Men   74   172
  An Herb Basket   77   114
  Selected Poems   85   102
  Undercliff, Poems 1946-1953
  Undercliff, Poems 1946-1953   85   106
  Great Praises   91   53
  Collected Verse Plays   102   115
  The Quarry   105   332
  Selected Poems 1930-1965   109   44
  Shifts of Being   113   262

ARTICLES ABOUT
  Rev. of *New Directions 1942*
    (Ed. by James Laughlin)   61   693

EBERSTEIN, MYRTLE
POEMS
  Woman-Songs of the Herero   16   71
    Song of Mocking for an Old Woman
    Song for Shredding Bark
    Song of a Woman with Twins

EBERTS, MAX
POEMS
  Program for the Class of '87   168   159

EBRIGHT, FREDERICK
POEMS
  Obituary for the Unknown   66   17

ECHARD, LAURENCE
BOOKS REVIEWED
  The Comedies of Terence
    (Ed. by Robert Graves)   107   264

ECKMAN, FREDERICK
POEMS
  The Starlings   86   262
  The Sign   90   158
  Old Man, Phantom Dog   93   162
  After Work
  Love Lies A-Bleeding   96   222
  Penelope
  Three Huntresses
  Vocations   102   161
  A Retrospect

REVIEWS
  Six Poets, Young or Unknown   89   52
    Permitted Proof,
      by William D. Barney
    Twenty Poems, by Robert Beum
    Pictures of the Gone World,
      by Lawrence Ferlinghetti
    The Dissolving Fabric,
      by Paul Blackburn
    All That Is Lovely in Men,
      by Robert Creeley
    Caesar's Gate, by Robert Duncan
  Neither Tame nor Fleecy   90   386
    The Maximus Poems/11-22,
      by Charles Olson
    The Improved Binoculars,
      by Irving Layton
    Howl and Other Poems,
      by Allen Ginsberg
    The Wrath Wrenched Splendor of Love
      and *To Wed Beneath the Sun,*
      by Judson Crews
    Superman Unbound,
      by Harold Witt
    River Full of Craft,
      by Felix Stefanile
    Light and Dark,
      by William Bronk
    Adam's Footprint,
      by Vassar Miller
    Selected Poems, When We Were Here
      Together, and *Poemscapes,*
      by Kenneth Patchen   92   389

BOOKS REVIEWED
  Cobras and Cockle Shells   95   122
  The Epistemology of Loss   104   47

ECKRICH, CATHERINE
POEMS
  Ipso Jure   140   27

ECKSTROM, FANNIE HARDY
BOOKS REVIEWED
  Minstrelsy of Maine
    (Ed. with Mary Winslow Smyth)   32   96

EDDY, LUCY
POEMS
Valley and Mesa   11   248
Iris
The Flowering Acacia
Ophelia Roses
Red Eucalyptus Blossoms
The Jacaranda
The Olive Tree
Bougainvillea
Sea-Gardens—Avalon
New-Born
Lullabies
The Singing Sands
Rider of Sun Fire   16   253

EDE, H. S.
ARTICLES ABOUT
Rev. of The Sleeping Lord
and Other Fragments,
by David Jones   125   233

EDEL, LEON
ARTICLES
Henry James and the Poets   62   328

REVIEWS
Hath Not a Jew... by A. M. Klein   58   51
New Poems: 1940
(Ed. by Oscar Williams)   58   215
A Treasury of Great Poems
(Ed. by Louis Untermeyer)   62   45

EDELBERG, CYNTHIA DUBIN
BOOKS REVIEWED
Robert Creeley's Poetry:
A Critical Introduction   136   219

EDEN, HELEN PARRY
BOOKS REVIEWED
Bread and Circuses   6   45

EDGAR, PELHAM
REVIEWS
Brébeuf and His Brethren, by E. J. Pratt   58   48

EDGE, MARY ALLEN
POEMS
Beginnings   22   135

EDGERTON, GLADYS
POEMS
Love's Passing   18   254
My Sepulchre

EDMAN, IRWIN
BOOKS REVIEWED
Poems   29   56

ARTICLES ABOUT
Fifteen Years,
by Harriet Monroe   31   32

EDMUNDS, ABE CRADDOCK
BOOKS REVIEWED
Mass and Other Poems   30   114
Geese Are Swan   41   105

EDSALL, FLORENCE S.
[FLORENCE S. SMALL]
POEMS
Stolen Moments   30   22
City in Mist
Sky in Early March
April Snow
Magnolia Blossoms
Fantasy
Closed Eyelids
Play of Light   36   69
The Magic Sieve
Roman Candles
Tricked   37   129
Miracle   57   236

EDSON, RUSSELL
BOOKS REVIEWED
The Very Thing that Happens   105   414
The Clam Theater   124   292

EDWARDS, JOHN
REVIEWS
The Translations of Ezra Pound   83   233

BOOKS REVIEWED
A Preliminary Checklist
of the Writings of Ezra Pound (Ed.)   83   29

EDWARDS, OSMAN
BOOKS REVIEWED
The Cloister, a Play in Four Acts,
by Emile Verhaeren (Tr.)   8   96

EFIRD, SUSAN
POEMS
The Fruit and Vegetable Stand   128   340
Rain
Nebuchadnezzar's Robes   130   94

EGAN, MOIRA
POEMS
Notes on a Potion   170   80
The Perverse Whelk

EGUREN, JOSÉ M.
POEMS
Ballad   62   86
The Dead
(Tr. by H. R. Hays)

EHRENSTEIN, ALBERT
POEMS
Homer
  (Tr. by Babette Deutsch
  and Avrahm Yarmolinsky)   21   144

EICH, GUNTER
POEMS
Changed Landscape   116   362
Clearings in the Woods
  (Tr. by Teo Savory)

ARTICLES ABOUT
German Lyric Poetry Since 1945,
  by Hans Egon Holthusen
  (Tr. by Herman Salinger)   88   257

EICHHORN, DOUGLAS
BOOKS REVIEWED
Rituals, a Book of Poems   116   193

EIGERMAN, HYMAN
BOOKS REVIEWED
*The Poetry of
  Dorothy Wordsworth* (Ed.)   57   280

EIGNER, LARRY
POEMS
Six Poems   100   359
  ("Piercing the wall the window...")
  ("They would not rent or sell...")
  ("The surgical waters...")
  ("Ply with chocolates...")
  ("the knowledge of death...")
  ("Walls or clear fields...")
Six Poems   103   227
  ("much space along the/wall...")
  ("stand on one foot...")
  ("The clock/breaks...")
  ("Where is an attic...")
  ("50 cars/don't matter...")
File
Five Poems   105   313
  ("the baby cries he...")
  ("to make myself a world...")
  ("the water dripping...")
  ("the green garage door...")
  ("empty the apartment...")
Seven Poems   108   39
  ("the earth you may as well...")
  ("newspaper circling...")
  ("blackbird/blue sky...")
  ("a penny/in the road...")
  ("The dark bird white bird...")
  ("the distances are shortened...")
  ("sliding down the/bannister...")
Three Poems   110   18
  ("the pipes how many...")

  ("the feet of Icarus...")
  ("the birds/risen to a tree...")
Eight Poems   111   383
  ("summer and winter...")
  ("The wind-bell...")
  ("shadows, birds...")
  ("varieties of quiet...")
  ("among various hills...")
  ("how/are things...")
  ("down there in the street...")
  ("the tree/roots water...")
Three Poems   113   256
  ("the strength of a wing...")
  ("dangerous/diving...")
  ("the air/stirs...")
#292 ("in the air")   115   105

BOOKS REVIEWED
On My Eyes   100   400
Another Time in Fragments   113   426
*The breath of once/Live Things/
  In the field with Poe*   114   251
Selected Poems
  (Ed. by Samuel Charters
  and Andrea Wyatt)   126   172

EISELEY, LOREN (C.)
POEMS
The Deserted Homestead   35   142
Tasting the Mountain Spring   54   316
The Spider
Safe in the Toy Box   128   345
Knossus
Two Hours from Now   130   33

BOOKS REVIEWED
The Innocent Assassins   126   44

EKELÖF, GUNNAR
POEMS
Four Poems   131   338
  Oecus
  ("Heard in a dream...")
  Ghazal
  The Hypnogogue
  (Tr. by Rika Lesser)

BOOKS REVIEWED
I Do Best Alone at Night
  (Ed. and tr. by Robert Bly
  with Christina Paulson)   113   188

ELDRIDGE, PAUL
POEMS
My Years   15   254
*To a Courtesan
  a Thousand Years Dead*   26   317

BOOKS REVIEWED
Vanitas   17   276

ELIOT, T(HOMAS) S(TEARNS)
POEMS
The Love Song of J. Alfred Prufrock   6   130
The Boston Evening Transcript   7   21
Aunt Helen
Cousin Nancy
Observations   8   292
    Conversation Galante
    La Figlia che Piange
    Mr. Apollinax
    Morning at the Window

ARTICLES
[Note]   53   342
Ezra Pound   68   326
A Letter   76   88

REVIEWS
The Poets' Translation Series, I-VI   9   101

BOOKS REVIEWED
Prufrock and Other Observations   10   264
Poems   16   157
The Sacred Wood   17   345
The Waste Land   21   325
Ash Wednesday   36   330
Journey of the Magi
A Song for Simeon
Animula
Dante
Marina   30   337
Triumphal March   41   152
Difficulties of a Statesman
John Dryden   42   44
Selected Essays
Sweeney Agonistes   42   106
The Rock: A Pageant Play   45   161
After Strange Gods
Murder in the Cathedral   47   279
Murder in the Cathedral   48   221
Collected Poems, 1909-1935   50   48
Essays Ancient and Modern   50   51
Anabasis,
    by St.-John Perse (Tr.)   50   90
The Family Reunion   54   264
Old Possum's Book of Practical Cats   55   221
The Dry Salvages   59   338
Four Quartets   63   44
The Cocktail Party   85   47
The Confidential Clerk
Murder in the Cathedral
    [Old Vic Company Recording]   85   113
The Cultivation of Christmas Trees   86   41
On Poetry and Poets   92   121

The Elder Statesman   95   36
Collected Poems 1909-1962   106   239
Knowledge and Experience
    in the Philosophy of F. H. Bradley
To Criticize the Critic:
    Eight Essays on Literature and Education   108   265
Poems Written in Early Youth   112   418
The Waste Land: A Facsimile
    and Transcript of the Original Drafts
    Including the Annotations of Ezra Pound
    (Ed. by Valerie Eliot)   121   156

ARTICLES ABOUT
A Note on T. S. Eliot's Book,
    by Max Michelson   12   36
Mr. Jepson's Slam,
    by Harriet Monroe   12   208
A Word from London,
    by Benjamin Gilbert Brooks   28   40
Rev. of Fugitives:
    An Anthology of Verse   32   102
The Mechanism of Sensibility,
    by Morton Dauwen Zabel   34   150
English Poetry Today,
    by Basil Bunting   39   264
Notes on English Poets,
    by Michael Roberts   39   271
Rev. of The Poetry of T. S. Eliot,
    by Hugh Ross Williamson;
    T. S. Eliot by Thomas McGreevy;
    and Mr. Eliot Among the Nightingales,
    by Louis Grudin   42   44
The Use of the Poet, by M. D. Zabel   44   32
English Letter, by F. R. Leavis   44   98
Poetry for the Theatre,
    by M. D. Zabel   45   152
A Letter from England,
    by Geoffrey Grigson   49   101
Rev. of The Achievement of T. S. Eliot,
    by F. O. Matthiessen   50   54
The Medievalism of T. S. Eliot,
    by Leo Shapiro   56   202
Poetry on Records,
    by Harry T. Moore   57   52
Religion and Sensibility,
    by Henry Rago   57   314
The New Theatrum Poetarum,
    by Alan S. Downer   60   206
Contemporary Poetry Criticism,
    by J. V. Healy   61   672
Little Gidding: Introductory to a Reading,
    by James Johnson Sweeney   62   214
James Thurber: The Comic Prufrock,
    by Peter DeVries   63   150
Correspondence from George Dillon   67   49
Moods and Reactions,
    by Stephen Spender   67   88

Rev. of *A History*
of American Poetry, 1900-1940,
by Horace Gregory
and Marya Zaturenska   69   210

T. S. Eliot at the National Gallery,
by Katherine Garrison Chapin   70   328

A Note on Seriousness in Poetry,
by Stephen Spender   72   92

To Write Poetry Nowadays You Have
to Have One Foot in the Grave,
by Gilbert Neiman   74   30

Poetry on Records,
by Harry T. Moore   74   367

Rev. of *T. S. Eliot:*
The Design of His Poetry,
by Elizabeth Drew   75   112

Rev. of *Collected Poems,*
by William Empson   75   150

Rev. of *The Creative Experiment,*
by C. M. Bowra   75   217

From the Introduction to
The Oxford Book of American Verse,
by F. O. Matthiessen   77   31

Rev. of *The Art of T. S. Eliot,*
by Helen Gardner   77   41

Rev. by Parker Tyler   77   168

Rev. of *The Idea of a Theatre,*
by Francis Fergusson   77   227

The Vocation of the Poet
in the Modern World,
by Delmore Schwartz   78   223

Rev. of *English Poetry and Its Contribution*
to the Knowledge of a Creative Principle,
by Leone Vivante   78   290

Rev. of *The Autobiography*
of William Carlos Williams   80   89

Rev. of *A Reader's Guide to T. S. Eliot,*
by George Williamson   82   287

Verse Drama on the Paris Stage,
by Ruby Haykin   82   294

Rev. of *On the* Four Quartets
of T. S. Eliot, by Anonymous   84   179

T. S. Eliot's Voice and His Voices,
by Delmore Schwartz   85   170

T. S. Eliot's Voice and His Voices,
by Delmore Schwartz   85   232

Jorge Guillén, Marianne Moore,
and T. S. Eliot: Some Recollections,
by Wallace Fowlie   90   103

[Note]   95   382

Rev. of *Hart Crane's Sanskrit Charge,*
by L. S. Dembo   98   190

Letter to a Foreign Friend,
by George Seferis
(Tr. by Nanos Valaorites)   105   50

T. S. Eliot: A Memoir and a Tribute,
by Henry Rago   105   392

Rev. of *Notes on Some Figures*
Behind T. S. Eliot,
by Herbert Howarth   106   239

Rev. of *Poets of Reality:*
Six Twentieth-Century Writers,
by J. Hillis Miller   110   254

The Vocation of Poetry,
by Henry Rago   110   328

Rev. of *T. S. Eliot:*
The Dialectical Structure
of His Theory of Poetry,
by Fei-Pai Lu   111   203

Rev. of *T. S. Eliot: Moments and Patterns,*
by Leonard Unger   112   52

Poets Aloud, by Donald Hall   139   297

Rev. of *The Complete Poems*
of Marianne Moore   139   340

Comment by Wallace Fowlie   151   208

Rev. of *A History of Modern Poetry,*
Volume II: Modernism and After,
by David Perkins   151   296

Rev. of *Tell Me Again*
How the White Heron...
by Hayden Carruth   156   345

ELIOT, VALERIE
BOOKS REVIEWED
The Waste Land: A Facsimile
and Transcript of the Original Drafts
Including the Annotations of Ezra Pound,
by T. S. Eliot (Ed.)   121   156

ELLEDGE, JIM
REVIEWS
Familiar and New Voices   144   107
People Live Here:
Selected Poems, 1949-1983,
by Louis Simpson
Proud and On My Feet,
by J. W. Rivers
Shouting at No One,
by Lawrence Joseph
To Continue,
by Randy Blasing
Sad Days of Light,
by Peter Balakian
Triumphs   146   293
To Hold in My Hand:
Selected Poems, 1955-1983,
by Hilda Morley
Leaving the Door Open,
by David Ignatow
Black Dog, Red Dog,
by Stephen Dobyns
Willingly, by Tess Gallagher
Rejoicings: Poems 1966-1972
and *Paradise Poems,*
by Gerald Stern

ELLENBOGEN, GEORGE
BOOKS REVIEWED
  Winds of Unreason   94   186

ELLIDGE, GEORGE
BOOKS REVIEWED
  Three Prayers for Pilots,
    by Jules Roy (Tr.)   68   54

ELLIOTT, G. R.
BOOKS REVIEWED
  English Poetry of the Nineteenth Century
    (Ed. with Norman Foerster)   27   164

ELLIOTT, GEORGE P.
POEMS
  Pastorale   63   136
  The Cyclone
  Madonna and Child   65   181
  To a Bird Outside the Window
  Insurance Salesman   85   25
  Crematorium

BOOKS REVIEWED
  Fifteen Modern American Poets (Ed.)   91   124
  Fever & Chills   100   390
  New and Selected Poems,
    by Winfield Townley Scott (Ed.)   112   418
  From the Berkeley Hills   118   351

ELLIOTT, J.
BOOKS REVIEWED
  Anti-Poems,
    by Nicamor Parra (Tr.)   97   114

ELLIS, AMANDA M.
BOOKS REVIEWED
  Rebels and Conservatives: Dorothy and
    William Wordsworth and Their Circle   113   262

ELLIS, MARTHA
POEMS
  Watching in a Sickroom   59   327

ELLIS, VIVIAN LOCKE
BOOKS REVIEWED
  Collected Lyrical Poems   73   177

ELLMANN, RICHARD
TRANSLATIONS
  Poem by Henri Michaux   73   258

REVIEWS
  Atonic and Archaic Verse from England   74   304
    Selected Poems,
      by Sacheverell Sitwell
    Selected Poems,
      by Elizabeth Daryush

BOOKS REVIEWED
  Yeats: The Man and the Masks   74   244
  James Joyce   96   382
  The New Oxford Book
    of American Verse (Ed.)   131   236

ELLYSON, JOHN REGNAULT
POEMS
  A Colloquy in Sleep   8   186

ELMENDORF, MARY J.
POEMS
  Three Stories   32   88
    Jasper
    Beauty's the Thing
    White Rose
  Tales of Women   38   250
    Two Wives
    Blind
  October   41   81

ELMSLIE, KENWARD
POEMS
  Alabama   96   97
  Adele the Vaudeville Martinet
  Fringe People
  Communique for Orpheus

ELON, FLORENCE
POEMS
  Room 9639   142   22
  Hothouse Art
  Bequest

ELOVIC, BARBARA
POEMS
  Afterwards   140   162
  Schooling   144   30
  Intentions
  Light Years   146   338
  3/4 Time

ELSON, REBECCA A. W.
POEMS
  The Last Animists   161   131
  These Two Candles, Saint Pantelehm   164   322

ELTON, WILLIAM
ARTICLES
  A Note on Robert Lowell   71   138
  A Glossary of the New Criticism
    [William Empson, Cleanth Brooks,
    Robert Penn Warren, I. A. Richards,
    John Crowe Ransom]   73   153
  A Glossary of the New Criticism
    [Kenneth Burke, Allen Tate,
    I. A. Richards, Yvor Winters,
    Cleanth Brooks, Robert Penn Warren,
    John Crowe Ransom]   73   232

A Glossary of the New Criticism
[Cleanth Brooks, John Crowe Ransom,
Yvor Winters, I. A. Richards,
Kenneth Burke, Allen Tate,
Robert Penn Warren]   73   296

REVIEWS
The Age of Anxiety, by W. H. Auden   71   90
A Map of Verona and Other Poems,
by Henry Reed   72   165

ARTICLES ABOUT
Out of the Woods,
by Hayden Carruth   73   151
Correspondence
from Reed Whittemore   73   370

ELUARD, PAUL
POEMS
Liberty   67   5
Understand Who Will
(Tr. by George Dillon)

BOOKS REVIEWED
Thorns of Thunder
(Ed. by George Reavey)
(Tr. by Samuel Beckett, Denis Devlin,
David Gascoyne, Eugene Jolas,
Man Ray, George Reavey,
and Ruthven Todd)   48   347

ARTICLES ABOUT
The Poets Paris Is Reading,
by Jean Catel   67   39
To Write Poetry Nowadays You
Have to Have One Foot in the Grave,
by Gilbert Neiman   74   30

ELY, GLADYS
POEMS
The Lane   92   367
Eximious Old Friendships Are
Moral Spontaneity: A Love Poem
Woodchuck Rampant

ELYTIS, ODYSSEUS (ALEPOUDELIS)
POEMS
Poem ("I know the night no longer...") 78   174
Aegean Melancholy
The Shape of Boeotia
(Tr. by Kimon Friar)
The Genesis (From Axion Esti)
(Tr. by Edmund Keeley
and George Savidis)   105   1
This Then Is I (From Axion Esti)   105   21
The Sleep of the Brave
(From Six and One Regrets for the Sky)
(Tr. by Ruth Whitman)

ARTICLES ABOUT
Contemporary Greek Poetry,
by Kimon Friar   78   145
The Genesis: A Commentary,
by Edmund Keeley   105   16
Letter from Athens,
by Vassilis Vassilikos   105   60

EMANUEL, LYNN
POEMS
Frying Trout While Drunk   142   78
The Photograph of Ramona Posing
While Father Sketches Her in Charcoal
When Father Decided
He Did Not Love Her Anymore

BOOKS REVIEWED
Hotel Fiesta   147   102

EMBERIKOS, ANDREAS
POEMS
Spring as Always   78   166
Moment of Porphery
(Tr. by Kimon Friar)

ARTICLES ABOUT
Contemporary Greek Poetry,
by Kimon Friar   78   145

EMERSON, DOROTHY
POEMS
Sparks   32   257
The Stir
Note
Roadside   43   73
The Wall   45   70
Come Soon   132   77
Space Divides   133   216
Imagined Girl

EMERSON, NATHANIEL B.
ARTICLES ABOUT
Nature Themes
in Ancient Hawaiian Poetry,
by Vaughan MacCaughey   10   205

EMERSON, RALPH WALDO
BOOKS REVIEWED
Emerson: A Modern Anthology
(Ed. by Alfred Kazin
and Daniel Aaron)   96   382

ARTICLES ABOUT
Emerson in a Loggia,
by Harriet Monroe   10   311
Correspondence
from Ernest Nelson   11   166

Rev. of *American Renaissance:*
Art and Expression in the Age of
Emerson and Whitman,
by F. O. Matthiessen   60   334
Review by David Baker   168   33

EMERSON, RICHARD WIRTZ
ARTICLES
Poet, Publisher,
and the Tribal Chant   75   34

BOOKS REVIEWED
Symbol and Reality   77   114

EMERY, CLARK
ARTICLES ABOUT
[Note]   84   119

EMERY, JANE
POEMS
In a Cafe   36   310
Hora

EMMANUEL, PIERRE
ARTICLES ABOUT
Marseille Letter, by Jean Rivier   60   269
The Conspiracy of the Poets,
by Pierre Seghers
(Tr. by William Jay Smith)   67   25
The Poets Paris Is Reading,
by Jean Catel   67   39
The Defense of Poetry,
by Richard Eberhart   77   89
Recent French Publications,
by Wallace Fowlie   93   40

EMORY, WILLIAM CLOSSON
POEMS
Solids   32   254
Thesis
Winter Song
On One November Morning   33   66
Moments   36   87
That Night
Suicide
Swift Moment
On Hearing a Symphony of Sibelius
Evening on the Lake
Poem for a Dark Girl   38   141
Painted Beak in My Heart   40   16

BOOKS REVIEWED
Be Still   35   229

EMPSON, WILLIAM
POEMS
Reflection from Rochester   49   68
Bacchus IV   49   188

Bacchus III   56   18
Bacchus IV   59   266

ARTICLES
A London Letter   49   218
Correspondence
[Geoffrey Grigson]   49   237
Correspondence
[Geoffrey Grigson]   50   116

REVIEWS
More Poems, by A. E. Housman   49   228
Modern Poetry and the Tradition,
by Cleanth Brooks   55   154

BOOKS REVIEWED
Seven Types of Ambiguity   43   98
Some Versions of Pastoral   49   347
Collected Poems of...   74   234
Collected Poems   76   150

ARTICLES ABOUT
Notes on English Poets,
by Michael Roberts   39   271
English Letter, by F. R. Leavis   46   274
Correspondence
from Geoffrey Grigson   50   115
A Glossary of the New Criticism,
by William Elton   73   153
Rev. of *Critics and Criticism,*
Ancient and Modern
(Ed. by R. S. Crane)   82   98

ENDICOFF, MAX
POEMS
The City   6   233

ENGELS, FRIEDRICH
ARTICLES ABOUT
Rev. of *Marx, Engels, and the Poets:*
Origins of Marxist Literary Criticism,
by Peter Demetz
(Tr. by Jeffrey L. Sammons)   112   206

ENGELS, JOHN
POEMS
The Old Duke   95   165
Gothic Pieta   97   372
The Fire
De Pere: Feeding a Child, 5:30 A.M. 101   399
Poem on the Death of the Gardener's Wife

REVIEWS
Two Religious Poets   99   253
The Crooked Lines of God,
by Brother Antoninus
The Gravel Ponds,
by Peter Levi, S.J.

Five Poets   102   402
    Light in the West,
        by Judson Jerome
    The Sketches of Lewis Turco
    Guarded by Women,
        by Robert Pack
    Countermoves,
        by Charles Edward Eaton
    Voyages from Troy,
        by Ronald Perry

BOOKS REVIEWED
    The Homer Mitchell Place   113   428
    Signals from the Safety Coffin   129   102
    Vivaldi in Early Fall   140   346

ENGLE, PAUL
POEMS
    Girl of Wind   37   78
    Turret Lathe
    Elegy ("It was as though...")   39   13
    Lost Things   41   314
    America Remembers   42   121
    New Times on the Plains   44   86
        The Last Cup
        Letter to Sam
        Burning My Boyhood's Poems
        Earth in Our Blood
    Extreme   55   115
    Weather
    Divination
    Moving In
    Bird
    Fern
    Our Human Strength
    America 1941   58   293
    On the Birth of My Child
    Elements
    Henry David Thoreau
    Emily Dickinson
    Contrary
    Letter After Drouth
    American Child III   66   1
    Night Scene   77   63
    Fossil
    Beasts
    USA   81   35
    Amagansett Beach   86   273
    Sick
    Colette   88   321
    A Dedication   95   27
    The Sound of Red
    Hercules   101   38
    Etruscan Vase in Form of a Clock
    Venus and the Lute Player
    In a Bar near Shibuya Station, Tokyo   105   185
    Taichung, Taiwan, Republic of China
    Dancer: Four Poems   133   339

    Images of China   138   291
    Drop of Water   151   50
    Door   156   194

ARTICLES
    Poet and Professor Overture   79   267
    Comment
        [Harriet Monroe]   151   201

REVIEWS
    Western Star,
        by Stephen Vincent Benét   63   159

BOOKS REVIEWED
    Worn Earth   42   220
    American Song   45   285
    Break the Heart's Anger   48   228
    Corn   54   342
    West of Midnight   60   102
    American Child   67   215
    The Word of Love   79   111
    Poems from the
        Iowa Poetry Workshop (Ed.)   79   284
    American Child   89   122
    Poems in Praise   96   230
    Poet's Choice
        (Ed. with Joseph Langland)   103   261
    A Woman Unashamed
        and Other Poems   107   326

ARTICLES ABOUT
    Poetry of the Left,
        by Harriet Monroe   48   212

ENGLISH, MAURICE
POEMS
    Lines   59   81
    Reasons for Love   99   17
    The Chorus
    "Quand C'est Minuit dans le Siècle"
    Copernicus, Darwin, Freud   136   264

REVIEWS
    The First Morning,
        by Peter Viereck   84   89

ENGONOPOULOS, NIKOS
POEMS
    The Hydra of Birds   78   172
    The Apprentice of Sorrow
    Poetry 1948
        (Tr. by Kimon Friar)

ARTICLES ABOUT
    Contemporary Greek Poetry,
        by Kimon Friar   78   145
    Letter from Athens,
        by Vassilis Vassilikos   105   60

ENNIS, JOHN
POEMS
Hydroturbines   167   27

ENRICO, H(AROLD)
POEMS
Isolde   79   260

ENRIGHT, D. J.
BOOKS REVIEWED
Commentary on Goethe's Faust   75   232
Poets of the 1950's: An Anthology
  of New English Verse (Ed.)   89   260
The Typewriter Revolution & Other Poems   122   47
The Terrible Shears   127   292

ENSLIN, THEODORE
POEMS
Times of Day   108   248
Degrees   110   397
A Photograph of Wives
This Is a Catbird Watching a King

REVIEWS
This in Which,
  by George Oppen   108   339
American Scenes,
  by Charles Tomlinson   109   112

BOOKS REVIEWED
The Place Where I Am Standing   107   121
This Do (& The Talents)   109   195
Characters in Certain Places   112   343
The Median Flow   127   234

ENSLOW, CONSTANCE
POEMS
Improvisations   22   14
Purple
Profile
Lavender

ENZENSBERGER, HANS MAGNUS
POEMS
Cultivate Your Garden
  (Tr. by Edouard Roditi)   88   250
die hebammen
  (Tr. by Michael Hamburger)   98   378

BOOKS REVIEWED
Poems for People Who Don't Read Poems
  (Tr. with Michael Hamburger
  and Jerome Rothenberg)   113   188

EPSTEIN, DANIEL MARK
BOOKS REVIEWED
No Vacancies in Hell   125   44

ERBA, LUCIANO
POEMS
Lo Svagato   94   308
Terra e Mare
  (Tr. by Robert Fitzgerald)
La Grande Jeanne   155   62
Vanitas Varietatum
The Forties
  (Tr. by Charles Wright)

ERDMAN, DAVID V.
BOOKS REVIEWED
Blake: Prophet Against Empire   84   363
The Poetry and Prose
  of William Blake (Ed.)   111   263

ERDRICH, LOUISE
POEMS
Fooling God   154   223

BOOKS REVIEWED
Jacklight   146   38

ERSKINE, ALBERT
ARTICLES
Poet, Publisher,
  and the Tribal Chant   75   30

ERSKINE, JOHN
BOOKS REVIEWED
The Kinds of Poetry
  and Other Essays   19   54

ARTICLES ABOUT
Dante and Contemporaneousness,
  by Harriet Monroe   23   264
The Pulitzer Award System,
  by Harriet Monroe   30   210

ERSKINE, MALCOLM EDWARD
POEMS
In the Garden   10   198

ERULKAR, MARY
POEMS
Street Song   93   244
The Third Continent

REVIEWS
The World in India   95   314
  Modern Indian Poetry: An Anthology
    (Ed. by A. V. Rajeswara Rau)
  Green and Gold:
    Stories and Poems from Bengal
    (Ed. by Humayun Kabir)
  The Way of the Swan:
    Poems of Kashmir
    (Ed. by Nilla Cram Cook)

ERWIN, MARGARET
POEMS
Twisted Skeins   28   20
  Lachesis the Tangler
  Premonition
  Remembering

BOOKS REVIEWED
Canyon Garden   24   278

ERWIN, SÉAN
POEMS
Recovery   164   216

ESAM, JOHN
BOOKS REVIEWED
Haiku
  (With Tom Raworth
  and Anselm Hollo)   114   251

**ESCUDERO MOSCOSO,
  GONZALO**
POEMS
Overtones
  (Tr. by Muna Lee)   26   131

ESHLEMAN, CLAYTON
POEMS
Seppuku   103   359
  "The Koreans"
  The Second
  February 25
  The Ascent
The Book of Yorunomado   106   257
Poem to Accompany Mary   109   75
Nonomiya   111   76
  Sensing Duncan
  To Crane
  Little Moon Worm
Poem ("A woman whose open / eyes...")
The Book of Barbara   112   109

BOOKS REVIEWED
Mexico & North   103   256
Lachrymae Mateo   112   56
State of the Union,
  by Aimé Cesaire
  (Tr. with Denis Kelly)
Poemas Humanos,
  by César Vallejo (Tr.)   114   193
Indiana   118   174
César Vallejo:
  The Complete Posthumous Poetry
  (Tr. with José Rubia Barcia)   137   220

ESLER, RICHARD
POEMS
Seasonal   40   10

At the Grave of Hart Crane   41   68
Remembrance of Waters   43   258
Year's End   47   135

ESPAILLAT, RHINA P.
POEMS
Changeling   158   255
Cutting Bait
Gardening   164   141
Last Day   167   155

**ESSENIN, SERGEI
[SERGEY YESENIN]**
POEMS
From Transfiguration
  (Tr. by Alexander Kaun
  and Roberta Holloway)   27   76

ARTICLES ABOUT
New Trends in Soviet Russian Poetry,
  by Vera Sandomirsky   58   324

ESSINGER, CATHRYN
POEMS
Growing Accustomed to Green   160   262
You Are Right
The Philosophy Professor Discusses
  the Nature of the Self-Conscious Mind   168   320
Not To Reply
For Six Friends   170   316

ESTANG, LUC
POEMS
Le Monde Eclate   80   335
L'Arbre
Enterrement
  (Tr. by Wallace Fowlie)

ESTAVAN, LAWRENCE
POEMS
It Is My Fault   52   183

ETTER, DAVE
POEMS
Jane's Blue Jeans   134   98
Living in the Middle
When Sister Pearl Does Her Homework   139   206
Body
Librarian   141   222
Moonlight Yodel
Gone with the Grain   143   88
Black Sunflowers
The Railroad Wave

BOOKS REVIEWED
Go Read the River   109   340
Last Train to Prophetstown   117   322
Alliance, Illinois   144   231

209

EURIPIDES

BOOKS REVIEWED

Poet's Translation Series, Second Set
[Choruses from *Iphigenia in Aulis*
and *Hippolytus* (Tr. by H. D.)]   18   284
The Alcestis
(Tr. by Dudley Fitts
and Robert Fitzgerald)   50   108
Ion (Tr. by H. D.)   51   160
Euripides: Alcestis
(Tr. by Richmond Lattimore);
The Medea (Tr. by Rex Warner);
The Heracleidae
(Tr. by Ralph Gladstone);
Hippolytus (Tr. by David Grene)   86   303
Euripides (Vol. II): Cyclops and *Heracles*
(Tr. by William Arrowsmith);
Iphigenia in Tauris
(Tr. by Witter Bynner);
Helen (Tr. by Richmond Lattimore)   88   337
Euripides III: Hecuba
(Tr. by William Arrowsmith);
Andromache
(Tr. by John Frederick Nims);
The Trojan Women
(Tr. by Richmond Lattimore);
Ion (Tr. by Ronald Frederick Willetts);
in *The Complete Greek Tragedies*
(Ed. by David Grene
and Richmond Lattimore)   95   190
Euripides IV: Rhesus
(Tr. by Richmond Lattimore);
The Suppliant Women
(Tr. by Frank Jones);
Orestes (Tr. by William Arrowsmith);
Iphigenia in Aulis
(Tr. by Charles R. Walker);
in *The Complete Greek Tragedies*
(Ed. by David Grene
and Richmond Lattimore)

ARTICLES ABOUT

Rev. of *The Idea of a Theatre*,
by Francis Fergusson   77   227
Rev. of *The Dream of Alcestis*,
by Theodore Morrison   78   49
Rev. of *Herakles*,
by Archibald MacLeish   112   199

EVANS, ABBIE HUSTON

POEMS

Breton Song   22   138
Outdoor Rhymes   23   76
    First Concerns
    Mid-May
    The Bird-Tree
    Love's Fool
The Woman   29   253
The Poet   34   323

The Well
On This Hill   36   295
    The Mineral Collection
    Moonrise
    What Once I Was
    Jones's Pasture
    Wing-Spread
    In Conclusion
Country Miracle   52   307
Slow Gain
First Night of Fall
Time's Citizen
To a Forgotten Dutch Painter

REVIEWS

The Name of a Rose,
    by Helen Hoyt   39   158

BOOKS REVIEWED

Outcrop   32   341
The Bright North   53   339
Fact of Crystal   99   320

EVANS, DONALD

BOOKS REVIEWED

Sonnets from the Patagonian   5   38
Ironica   14   276

EVANS, FLORENCE WILKINSON

BOOKS REVIEWED

The Ride Home   4   201

EVANS, GEORGE

POEMS

Isaac   149   336
Study of My Father
Northern Island   150   131
The Dowser
Pachinko King   157   276

EVANS, OLIVER

POEMS

Banks, Etc.   67   313
Of Atom Age   68   200
For All You People   69   84
The Art of Mr. Pavel Tchelitchew   70   302
Elegy for Miss Curtis   72   70
Old Men Watching Baseball

BOOKS REVIEWED

Young Man with a Screwdriver   77   215

EVANS, PATRICK

POEMS

Christmas, Great Britain   61   482
Memories of Boyhood
*Poem from the Autobiography of
    an Old Landowner, Who Died Recently* 62   260

ARTICLES
    Correspondence   61   579
    Correspondence   62   57

BOOKS REVIEWED
    Proems
        (With Ruthven Todd,
        Rayner Heppenstall, Edgar Foxall,
        Lawrence Durrell,
        and Oswald Blakeston)   53   155

EVERSON, LANDIS
POEMS
    These Friends of Yours   85   331
    Famine   88   370
    The Last Marriage

EVERSON, R. G.
POEMS
    Incident at Montreal   96   352
    Whistling Swans
    Outgoing Tide
    Digging Potato Hills
    One Dark Night
    All Fools' Day

BOOKS REVIEWED
    A Lattice for Momos   94   186
    Blind Man's Holiday   103   316
    Wrestle with an Angel   109   53
    Selected Poems: 1920/1970   120   107

ARTICLES ABOUT
    Poets in Canada,
        by Margaret Avison   94   182

EVERSON, RONALD
POEMS
    Leerie   36   140
    Over Antin

**EVERSON, WILLIAM
    [(BROTHER) ANTONINUS]
    [See also HERBER,
    WILLIAM, pseud.]**
POEMS
    The Watchers   50   130

    We in the Fields
    Dust and the Glory

ARTICLES
    Correspondence
        [William Herber, pseud.]   56   108

BOOKS REVIEWED
    San Joaquin   56   220
    The Masculine Dead   63   52
    Ten War Elegies
    The Waldport Poems   65   281
    War Elegies   66   284
    Poems: mcmxlii   68   227
    Single Source   110   258
    *The Residual Years:
        Poems 1934-1948*   115   189
    Man-Fate   127   98

EVERWINE, PETER
POEMS
    Designs on a Point of View   91   23

BOOKS REVIEWED
    The Broken Frieze   93   182

EWART, GAVIN
BOOKS REVIEWED
    Poems and Songs   54   284

ARTICLES ABOUT
    London Letter,
        by D. S. Savage   51   277
    Contemporary British Poetry:
        A Romantic Persistence?
        by John Bayley   146   227

EWING, RICARDO
POEMS
    The Fine Duel   40   138

EYBERS, ELISABETH
ARTICLES ABOUT
    Report from Goli,
        by Turner Cassity   95   242

"F. D. W."
BOOKS REVIEWED
Little Verse for a Little Clan   4   163

"F. P."
ARTICLES
A New Poetry Society   19   351

"F. P. A."
[See ADAMS, FRANKLIN P.]

"F. S."
REVIEWS
Carducci: A Selection of His Poems
  (Ed. and tr. by G. L. Bickersteth)   4   198

FABER, GEOFFREY
BOOKS REVIEWED
The Buried Stream,
  Collected Poems 1908-1940   60   225

FABILLI, MARY
BOOKS REVIEWED
Aurora Bligh and Early Poems   118   98

FACOS, JAMES
POEMS
Shivaree   72   188
The Captive   78   258

FAGAN, KATHY
POEMS
Daughter   135   329

FAGIN, LARRY
BOOKS REVIEWED
The Parade of the Caterpillars   117   261

FAGLES, ROBERT
BOOKS REVIEWED
Bacchylides: Complete Poems (Tr.)   102   54

FAHEY, DIANE
POEMS
Macaws   169   22
Snow
Teiresias

FAINLIGHT, RUTH
POEMS
The Wild Hunt   121   280
Fire-Queen
At Home at Last   125   294
Passions   141   318
Grandmas
The Prism

BOOKS REVIEWED
Cages   114   266
To See the Matter Clearly   118   102
Another Full Moon   131   292

FAIRBURN, A. R. D.
POEMS
From a Younger Country   34   131
After-Times
The Runner
New Zealand
Twilight
Byways of Love   39   22

BOOKS REVIEWED
Recent Poems
  (With Allen Curnow,
  Denis Glover, and R. A. K. Mason)   59   343

FAIRCHILD, B. H.
POEMS
Flight   145   29
Old Men Playing Basketball   162   223

FAIRCHILD, DONALD
POEMS
Man with Blue Eyes   70   14
Confusion

FAIRCHILD, HOXIE N(EALE)
BOOKS REVIEWED
Religious Trends
  in English Poetry: VI (1920-1965)   115   196

FAIRCLOUGH, GEORGE T.
POEMS
Furious as a Lute   75   8

FALCK, COLIN
BOOKS REVIEWED
  Backwards into the Smoke   126   103

FALCONER, NORTH [Pseud.]
POEMS
  Gold of Evening   48   264

FALLON, PETER
POEMS
  Easter   167   84
  Again

BOOKS REVIEWED
  Selected and New Poems,
    by Michael Hartnett (Ed.)   168   107

FANDEL, JOHN
POEMS
  Cavalero   80   12
  Hearse   81   181
  Chant at Aquidneck: Pars Verna   92   359
  Driving Home Through Night Fog   136   141
  75 Mirrors   141   271

REVIEWS
  Decembrist,
    by Joseph Bennett   80   294

FANG, ACHILLES
REVIEWS
  Out of China   107   196
    The Art of Chinese Poetry,
      by James J. Y. Liu
    The Poet Kao Ch'i: 1336-1374,
      by F. W. Mote
    Twentieth Century Chinese Poetry:
      An Anthology
      (Ed. and tr. by Kai-Yu Hsu)
    Cold Mountain:
      100 Poems by Han-Shan
      (Ed. and tr. by Burton Watson)

ARTICLES ABOUT
  Rev. of *The Classic Anthology*
  Defined by Confucius
  (Tr. by Ezra Pound)   85   159

FAN YUN
POEMS
  A Song of Separation
    (Tr. by Helen Burwell Chapin)   46   310

FARALLON, CERISE
BOOKS REVIEWED
  Three on a Match
    (With Wendell B. Anderson
    and Judson Crews)   110   186

FARBER, NORMA
POEMS
  Inform Yourself Completely   75   212
  This Dew, These Eyes   79   324
  Make Me No Lazy Love   91   245

BOOKS REVIEWED
  Poets of Today II
    (With Robert Pack
    and Louis Simpson)   88   329

FARGAS, LAURA
POEMS
  To the Person Who Stole My Camera   156   131
  Erg   157   70
  Grass the Fine Body Hairs of Earth   162   194
  "Actively Speciating Even Now"

FARGNOLI, PATRICIA
POEMS
  Still Water   170   34

FARJEON, ELEANOR
BOOKS REVIEWED
  Singing Games for Children   15   345
  Edward Thomas:
    The Last Four Years   95   52
  First and Second Love   95   248

FARLEY, JEAN
POEMS
  A Better Mousetrap   76   144
  Like Pinocchio   77   332

REVIEWS
  The Poet Laureate and Others   78   45
    On the Hill and
      My Favourite English Poems,
      by John Masefield
    New Hyperion, a Symposium
      of Poetry and Criticism
      (Ed. by Geoffrey Handley-Taylor)
    Recollections of the Gala,
      by Nicholas Moore
    Arma Virumque Cano,
      by John Walker
    Question on a Kite,
      by Nathaniel Burt
    The Simple Songs
      of Khatchik Minasian

BOOKS REVIEWED
  Figure and Field   119   107

FARLEY, PARKE [Pseud.]
POEMS
  If War Is Right   5   56

FARMILOE, DOROTHY
BOOKS REVIEWED
  21 x 3
    (With Len Gasparini
    and Eugene McNamara)   115 353

FARNSWORTH, ROBERT
POEMS
  Music for Piano and Electrical Storm 139 135
  Sampler

FARRAN, DON
ARTICLES ABOUT
  [Note]   32 296

FARRELL, KATE
POEMS
  Last Spring   125 290

FASSETT, JACOB S., JR.
BOOKS REVIEWED
  Three Plays of the Argentine:
  Juan Moreira, Santos Vega,
  The Witches' Mountain (Tr.)
  (Ed. by Edward Bierstadt)   17 52

FAULKNER, WILLIAM
BOOKS REVIEWED
  A Green Bough   43 48

FAUSSET, HUGH L'ANSON
BOOKS REVIEWED
  Walt Whitman: Poet of Democracy 61 687
  Poets and Pundits: A Collection of Essays 72 329

FAUST, FREDERICK
BOOKS REVIEWED
  Dionysus in Hades   41 165

FAWCETT, BRIAN
BOOKS REVIEWED
  Aggressive Transport   144 297

FAWCETT, SUSAN
POEMS
  Black Water Diving   160 257

FAY, JULIE
POEMS
  Provencal Laundry   144 72

FEARING, KENNETH
POEMS
  The City Takes a Woman 30 190
  Caricature of Felice Ricarro
  Rain
  Old Men
  Longshot Blues   48 68

  Hold the Wire   52 173
  A Dollar's Worth of Blood, Please
  American Rhapsody   53 12
  To a Daffodil, or Perhaps a Little Gossip
    About Flaubert
  SOS
  Discussion After the Fifth or Sixth 56 82
  Pay-Off
  5 A.M.
  King Juke   61 663
  Confession Overheard in a Subway
  4 A.M.   64 188
  The Face in the Bar Room Mirror 71 24
  The Juke-Box Spoke and the Juke-Box Said:
  Newspaperman

ARTICLES
  Poetry at the Writers' Congress 54 228
  U. S. Writers in War   56 318

REVIEWS
  The Spider and the Clock,
    by S. Funaroff   53 50

BOOKS REVIEWED
  Poems   49 282
  Dead Reckoning   54 26
  Collected Poems of...   57 264
  Afternoon of a Pawnbroker 63 163
  Stranger at Coney Island 74 118
  New and Selected Poems 90 325

ARTICLES ABOUT
  The Federal Poets' Number,
    by John Peale Bishop 52 276
  The Meaning of Kenneth
    Fearing's Poetry,
    by Macha Rosenthal 64 208

FECHHEIMER, LEE S.
POEMS
  America to Her Flag   10 201

FEDERMAN, DAVID
ARTICLES
  Correspondence:
    More on Louis Zukofsky 107 271

FEENEY, MARY
BOOKS REVIEWED
  A World Rich in Anniversaries,
    by Jean Follain
    (Tr. with William Matthews) 137 220

FEIBLEMAN, JAMES K.
BOOKS REVIEWED
  Journey to the Coastal Marsh 70 108
  Collected Poems   130 167

FEINBERG, CHARLES E.
BOOKS REVIEWED
  Walt Whitman,
    A Selection of the Manuscripts,
    Books and Association Items (Ed.)   87   183

FEINBLATT, EBRIA
ARTICLES
  Correspondence
    [Stephen Spender]   72   342

FEINMAN, ALVIN
BOOKS REVIEWED
  Preambles and Other Poems   107   183

FEINSTEIN, ELAINE
BOOKS REVIEWED
  Marina Tsvetayeva:
    Selected Poems (Tr.)   124   232

FEINSTEIN, ROBERT N.
POEMS
  Heaven Can't Wait   148   259

FEI-PAI LU
BOOKS REVIEWED
  T. S. Eliot: The Dialectical Structure
    of His Theory of Poetry   111   203

FELD, ROSS
POEMS
  A Set of Poems for Jack Spicer   112   11
  A Plum for Edward Dahlberg   115   16
  Hindenburg

FELDMAN, IRVING
POEMS
  Song ("I'm in love...")   74   81
  When We Go Walking
  Loss   87   287
  Artist and Model   102   155
  Elegy for a Suicide   109   4
  Father and Son   126   150
  The Bathers   137   1
  Progress
  Social Constructions of Reality
    at Coney Island   138   227
  Just Another Smack   139   198
  You Know What I'm Saying?   168   333
  Episode   169   253
  Bad Brunch
  For J. M., His Poems   169   322
  Fifteen Minutes

BOOKS REVIEWED
  Works and Days   100   310
  The Pripet Marshes   107   258
  Magic Papers   119   159

  Lost Originals   122   351
  Leaping Clear   130   41
  New & Selected Poems   136   295
  All of Us Here   149   168
  The Life and Letters   169   286

FELDMAN, RUTH
TRANSLATIONS
  Poem by Cesare Pavese
    (Tr. with Brian Swann)   116   302
  Poem by Lucio Piccolo
    (Tr. with Brian Swann)   116   303

FELSHIN, SIMON
BOOKS REVIEWED
  Poems for the New Age   27   348

FENDELL, SOLOMON J. D.
POEMS
  Love Lasts Like a Lily   12   77

FENG YIEN CHI
POEMS
  Three Desires
    (Tr. by Elizabeth Y. Gilbert
    and Su Kai Ming)   50   137

FENOLLOSA, ERNEST
TRANSLATIONS
  Play by Motokiyo   4   35

ARTICLES ABOUT
  Notebooks 1924-1938,
    by Archibald MacLeish   73   33

FENTON, CARROLL LANE
POEMS
  "E Be Than"   18   24

FENTON, EDWARD
POEMS
  Parley in Algiers   63   191
  Twilight Song for a Bombed City   65   25
  Aubade
  Whom?
  You
  A Dove, a Dog, a Dancing Mouse   66   257
  The Orchard's Floor

BOOKS REVIEWED
  Soldiers and Strangers   67   162

FENTON, JAMES
BOOKS REVIEWED
  Children in Exile: Poems 1968-1984   145   99

ARTICLES ABOUT
  A Letter from Britain, by William Logan   157   222

A Letter from Britain [II],
  by William Logan   157   290

FENWORTH, REBEKAH
POEMS
  Rain   40   139

FERGUSON, DE LANCEY
BOOKS REVIEWED
*Selected Letters
  of Robert Burns* (Ed.)   84   41

FERGUSON, VIRGINIA MARIAN
POEMS
  Moth Wings   40   196
  A Girl Among the Seasons
  Eucalyptus
  Peacock Prefix
  Games
  The Deer

FERGUSSON, FRANCIS
POEMS
  The Westerner   42   252
  Mr. Lyle Hereford
  The Big Branch: A Memorandum   98   297

REVIEWS
The Psychology of Art,
  by André Malraux
  [Joseph Frank]   76   288

BOOKS REVIEWED
Sophocles' Electra (Tr.)   53   96
The Idea of a Theatre   77   227
Dante's Drama of the Mind   86   108
Poems   100   395

ARTICLES ABOUT
Rev. of *English Institute Essays, 1949*
  (Ed. by Alan S. Downer)   77   48

FERLINGHETTI, LAWRENCE
BOOKS REVIEWED
Pictures of the Gone World   89   45
Pictures of the Gone World   89   52
A Coney Island of the Mind   93   107
*One Thousand Fearful Words
  for Fidel Castro*   99   313
Starting from San Francisco   100   310
Berlin
*Unfair Arguments with Existence:
  Seven Plays for a New Theater*   104   258
Routines   108   125
The Secret Meaning of Things   121   105

ARTICLES ABOUT
Correspondence from Henry Rago   90   260

FERRELL, KATE
POEMS
  Last Spring   125   290

FERRIL, THOMAS HORNSBY
POEMS
  One Mountain Hour   24   127
  Words for Leadville   49   1
  Grandmother's Old Dear Friend   75   258
  *The Children Are Coming
    Slowly Up the Stairs*   97   230

ARTICLES
Correspondence
  [Objectivists]   38   291
Correspondence
  [Marian Castleman]   64   351

BOOKS REVIEWED
High Passage   30   165
Westering   48   169
Trial by Time   64   231
New and Selected Poems   83   282
New and Selected Poems   89   373

ARTICLES ABOUT
[Note]   31   113
Correspondence
  from John Ciardi   64   349
Correspondence
  from Marian Castleman   65   108

FERRINI, VINCENT
BOOKS REVIEWED
Injunction   63   104
Blood of the Tenement   66   284
In the Arriving   98   319
Mirandum   104   258

FERRY, DAVID
POEMS
  Cythera   118   31
  A Night-Time River Road
  To Sally
  Photographs from a Book   131   204

BOOKS REVIEWED
On the Way to the Island   99   178

FEYERABEND, BARBARA
POEMS
  Femina Aegyptiaca   121   326
  Anza
  The Painter of Animals   128   86

FIACC, PADRAIC
POEMS
  Initial Deception   167   72

FIALLO, FABIO
POEMS
Full Moon
   (Tr. by Muna Lee)   26   148

FIAMENGO, MARYA
BOOKS REVIEWED
The Quality of Halves   94   186

FICHMAN, YAKOV
POEMS
Midnight
   (Tr. by Ruth Finer Mintz)   92   205

FICKE, ARTHUR DAVISON
["A. D. F."]
[See also KNISH, ANNE, pseud.]
POEMS
Poetry   I   I
Swinburne, an Elegy   I   137
To a Child—Twenty Years Hence
Portrait of an Old Woman
The Three Sisters
Among Shadows
A Watteau Melody
I Am Weary of Being Bitter   5   275
The Birdcage
Don Giovanni
Like Him Whose Spirit
Snowtime
Meeting
To Rupert Brooke   6   113
Four Japanese Paintings   9   77
   The Pine Branch
   Pines on a Mountain
   The Wave Symphony
   Buddha Appearing
     from Behind Mountains
Perspective of Co-Ordination 18   28
World Beyond World
Leaf-Movement
Old Wives' Tale   18   72
Holy Writ
The Book of Lu T'ang Chu
Buddha at Nadika   22   243
Epitaph for a Certain Sculptor 22   309
"In That Dim Monument
   Where Tybalt Lies"
Memorial for Dead Friends   39   73
O Beauty Infinite   41   8
On Dying
America Is Happy Tonight   53   176
Portrait ("Oh burning eyes...")
Portrait ("You, silver-throat...")

ARTICLES
From a Note Book   10   145

REVIEWS
Madonna Dianora,
  by Hugo von Hofmannsthal
   (Tr. by Harriet Betty Boas)   9   159
The Way of Life, According to Laotzu.
  An American Version,
  by Witter Bynner   66   40

BOOKS REVIEWED
Mr. Faust   3   184
Twelve Japanese Painters   4   29
Sonnets of a Portrait Painter 6   36
The Man on the Hill-Top   6   247
An April Elegy   10   323
Out of Silence and Other Poems 24   154
The Selected Poems of...   29   275
The Secret, and Other Poems 49   286
Tumultuous Shore   60   155

ARTICLES ABOUT
Poetry's Banquet
  [Poem for W. B. Yeats]   4   25
Various Views,
  by Harriet Monroe   8   140
Baiting the Public,
  by Alice Corbin Henderson 12   169
Ave Atque Vale, by Witter Bynner 68   56
Rev. of *The Spectra Hoax,*
  by William Jay Smith
  [Witter Bynner]   99   390

THE FIDDLEHEAD
BOOKS REVIEWED
Five New Brunswick Poets 103   266

FIEDLER, LESLIE (A.)
POEMS
"Thou Shalt Surely Die..." 69   194
  O All!
  No Ghost Is True
A Jahrzeit for Papa Jay   75   17
A Lament for Little Farfel: 75   264
To the Unbeautiful in Spring
On Leaving Cambridge   76   125
A Pair of Posies for John Skelton
Memories of Winter
Poem for St. Valentine's Day 77   69
Child's Play
A Boy by the Sea
Children at the Show
A Bloody Husband
Your Green Stone Hair   78   208
To Margaret: Against Waking
The Sea   83   10
The Quarry
Extra Ecclesiam...
The Lion   85   197

Three Train Poems   90   294
A Prayer Before Departure   137   78

REVIEWS
Bad Poetry and the Tradition   77   215
  Blossom Time, by Zula Hall
  The Poems of Mary C. Curry
  This Too-Brief Moment,
    by Hazel Stevens Dame
  Incident in Silver, by A. M. Sullivan
  Trajectory,
    by Granville Paul Smith
  My Worshipping Soul,
    by James F. Bursch
  Lodestone, by Sjanna Solum
  Another Challenge,
    by Irwin Burbank Abrams
  The Green Leaf,
    by Robert Nathan
  A Star by Day,
    by David McCord
  Barnyard Year, by Fred Lape
  This Time This Tide,
    by Rosamond Haas
  Young Man with a Screwdriver,
    by Oliver Evans
  Tightrope in the Dark,
    by Sidney Alexander
  Second Poems,
    by Meade Harwell
    [Albert Ralph Korn]
Tribute to Freud, by Hilda Doolittle   89   326
Poems of a Jew, by Karl Shapiro
    [Delmore Schwartz]   96   171

BOOKS REVIEWED
  Leaves of Grass
    One Hundred Years After
    [Contributor]
    (Ed. by Milton Hindus)   87   183

FIELD, EDWARD
POEMS
  The Telephone   98   213
  Goats
  Who Is Sylvia
  The Book of Sorrow   124   327
  Open Sesame
  Ant
  The Farewell

ARTICLES
  Correspondence
    [Millen Brand,
    Richard Tillinghast]   110   433

BOOKS REVIEWED
  Variety Photoplays   112   276
  A Full Heart   134   226

FIELD, EUGENE
ARTICLES
  An Unpublished Letter
    from Eugene Field,
    by Harriet Monroe   28   268

FIELD, MICHAEL
  **[Pseud. of BRADLEY, KATHERINE,
  and COOPER, EDITH]**
  BOOKS REVIEWED
    A Selection from the Poems of...   24   160

FIELD, SARA BARD
POEMS
  My City   25   190
  Wind and Water
  *Could You Not Watch with Me
    One Little Hour*
  Into the Shadow
  People   28   314
    Lovers
    Spinster
    Poet's Child
    To Kay
    Wild Flowers
  Wings   49   20
  Dark Song
  Unweighted Dead

REVIEWS
  *A Tree in Bloom
    and Other Verses*,
    by Hildegarde Flanner   26   112
  Words for the Chisel,
    by Genevieve Taggard   28   221

BOOKS REVIEWED
  The Pale Woman   32   50
  Barabbas   41   226

FIELDS, ANN
POEMS
  Pueblo Sketches   99   158

FIELDS, KENNETH
POEMS
  Lemons   126   96
  They Say Wyoming
  Keening
  Hummingbird

BOOKS REVIEWED
  Sunbelly   126   352

FIERZ-DAVID, LINDA
BOOKS REVIEWED
  The Dream of Poliphilo   77   168

FIGGIS, DARRELL
ARTICLES ABOUT
  Correspondence
    from Padraic Colum   8   268

FIGMAN, ELLIOT
POEMS
  This Morning   146   324
  The Tunnel
  The Silence
  Station Music   150   11
  Night and Day   159   273

FIGUEIRA, GASTON
POEMS
  Little Ballad of a Sailor
    (Tr. by Lloyd Mallan)   62   83

FILLER, LOUIS
BOOKS REVIEWED
  The Unknown
    Edwin Markham   111   333

FINCH, ROBERT
POEMS
  Scroll-Section   58   18
  Words
  Being Remembered
  The Formula

BOOKS REVIEWED
  Poems   74   44

ARTICLES ABOUT
  The Development of Poetry
    in Canada, 1880–1940,
    by E. K. Brown   58   34

FINCKE, GARY
POEMS
  The Girl Who Breathes
    Through a Hole in Her Neck   136   92
  The Local Cemetery   146   68
  A Murder of Crows
  Bourbon, Red Meat, Salt, Grease   149   219
  Enlisting
  Walking   154   266
  The Double Negatives of the Living   156   143
  The REM Sleep of Birds
  The Hunza Dream   158   27
  Reaching the Deaf   158   263
  The Conversation of Elephants
  The Stuttering Cures
  The Elephant Paintings   159   219

BOOKS REVIEWED
  The Double Negatives of the Living   162   37
  Inventing Angels   166   166

FINERTY, JOHN F.
POEMS
  May-Day at Sea   24   84
  Love

FINK, ELOISE BRADLEY
POEMS
  That Other Fellow— From
    the River Front   142   81

FINK, ROBERT A.
POEMS
  Consider   148   84
  Mother's Day
  The Need for Order
  Mesquite   150   33
  In the Hospital Waiting Room   154   199

FINK, ROBERT O.
POEMS
  Preferences   32   26

FINKEL, DONALD
POEMS
  Of All the Ways to Die   83   316
  Two Steps of a Lame Man   89   360
  The Day of the Dead   91   236
  The Imbecile
  Loss of Hearing   93   311
  The Great Wave: Hokusai
  Negative   101   387
  Sonic Boom
  The Father
  The Husband
  The Bachelor
  For Noah, My Son, Sleeping
  Bones
  Planh   105   358
  Metaphysic of Snow
  Vogelfanger
  The Phrygian Version   151   51
  In Dickens' House   152   343

REVIEWS
  Selected Poems of Octavio Paz
    and Sun Stone
    by Octavio Paz
    (Tr. by Muriel Rukeyser)   104   382

BOOKS REVIEWED
  The Clothing's New Emperor
    and Other Poems, in Poets of Today VI
    (Ed. by John Hall Wheelock)   95   373
  Simeon   106   309
  A Joyful Noise   109   114
  Answer Back   113   338
  The Garbage Wars   119   99
  Adequate Earth   122   351

A Mote in Heaven's Eye   127   292
What Manner of Beast   141   170
Selected Shorter Poems   152   35

FINKELSTEIN, CAROLINE
POEMS
Seeing the Light   138   89
Stories of Houses
The Soul in the Bowl   156   150
Not Responsible   157   139
For That Husband   158   321
With Fox Eyes
Vacation   164   252
Brief
An Opinion
Garden in the Field   166   94
Brief   167   255
My Testimony   168   136

BOOKS REVIEWED
Windows Facing East   150   102

FINLAY, IAN HAMILTON
BOOKS REVIEWED
Ocean Stripe Series 4   112   125
6 Small Songs in 3's
4 Sails
Glasgow Beasts,
    an a Burd Haw, an, aw, a Fush
6 Small Pears for Eugen Gomringer
Autumn Poem
Poems to Hear and See   121   105

FINNE, DIDERIK
POEMS
Hydroponically Speaking   128   272

FINNEGAN, ALICE W(INIFRED)
[See also JEREMY, (SISTER)
MARY]
POEMS
Song for Viaticum   34   319
November   43   77

FINNIGAN, JOAN
BOOKS REVIEWED
A Dream of Lilies   108   45

FINSTEIN, MAX
BOOKS REVIEWED
The Disappearance of Mountains   108   408
There's Always a Moon in America   113   426

FISCHER, AARON
POEMS
Lockjaw   134   95
Three Versions

FISCHER, ALLEN C.
POEMS
An Idea Without Wings   153   6
Rare Earths
Ménage à Trois
Highnotes

FISCHER, HEINZ
BOOKS REVIEWED
Gnu Soup   119   356

FISCHER, HENRY
BOOKS REVIEWED
Bred in the Bone
    (Ed. with Bruce Berlind)   68   106

FISCHER, RAYMOND (P.)
POEMS
A Year   20   84
A Woman Complains of Rain at Dawn   25   72
November   35   82
Time   144   39
An Aged Man Remembers April

ARTICLES
Correspondence:
    Our Motto [Poem]   14   347

FISH, KAREN
POEMS
Flames Behind Your Head   170   32
The Cistern
Driving in Spring   170   63

FISH, WILLISTON
POEMS
Swan Creek   2   206

FISHER, ALFRED YOUNG
BOOKS REVIEWED
The Ghost in the Underblows   57   391

FISHER, HENRY G.
POEMS
The Closet-Drinker   73   137

FISHER, ROY
BOOKS REVIEWED
Collected Poems 1968   116   51

FISHER, VARDIS
BOOKS REVIEWED
Sonnets to an Imaginary Madonna   30   353

FISHER, VIRGINIA
POEMS
Spirit Sons, Spirit Lovers   88   234

FISKE, ISABEL HOWE
    [ISABELLE HOWE FISKE]
    [See CONANT, FISKE]

FITCH, ANITA
  POEMS

The Wayfarers	1	108
Les Cruels Amoureux		
The Faeries' Fool	8	236

FITTS, DUDLEY
  POEMS

Southwest Passage	36	126
Chaconne for Quietus	39	29
O'Byrne Redvx	97	288
Palamedes: A Mystical Colloquy	98	296
On a Phrase from John XIX:22		

  TRANSLATIONS

Poem by Silvino Ocampo	68	245
Poem by Pablo Neruda	70	124
Poems by Martial	91	157
Poems by Martial	98	381

  REVIEWS

The Winter Alone, by Evelyn Scott	36	338
Driven, by Leroy MacLeod	38	48
The Serpent in the Cloud,		
by Theodore Morrison	38	342
Surprising Songs,		
by Count Geoffrey		
Potocki de Montalk	39	288
Flower of Evil, by Edwin Morgan	63	287
Prose Poems from "The Illuminations,"		
by Arthur Rimbaud		
(Tr. by Helen Rootham)	64	44
Selected Poems, by Robert Penn Warren	65	94
Essay on Rime, by Karl Shapiro	68	39
A Wreath for San Gemignano		
(Ed. and tr. by Richard Aldington)	68	293
Residence on Earth, by Pablo Neruda		
(Tr. by Angel Flores)	70	150
The Iron Pastoral,		
by John Frederick Nims	71	149
Ships and Other Figures,		
by William Meredith	73	111
The Travelers, by Henry Rago	75	229
O Dulce Convivium!	79	150
An Examination of Ezra Pound		
(Ed. by Peter Russell)		
The Letters of Ezra Pound, 1907-1941		
(Ed. by D. D. Paige)		
An Introduction to the Economic		
Nature of the United States;		
What Is Money For?		
and Social Credit: An Impact,		
by Ezra Pound		

Five Young Poets	94	333
Letter from a Distant Land,		
by Philip Booth		
The Green Wall, by James Wright		
True Minds, by Marie Ponsot		
The Opulent Citizen,		
by LeRoy Smith, Jr.		
The Deserted Altar,		
by David L. Posner		
Medusa in Gramercy Park,		
by Horace Gregory	100	387

  BOOKS REVIEWED

Two Poems	43	225
Ten Introductions:		
A Collection of Modern Verse		
(Ed. with Genevieve Taggard)	46	112
The Alcestis of Euripides		
(Tr. with Robert Fitzgerald)	50	108
Poems 1929-1936	51	107
An Anthology of Contemporary		
Latin American Poetry (Ed.)	62	231
Oedipus Rex		
(Tr. with Robert Fitzgerald)	76	299
Aristophanes: Lysistrata (Tr.)	85	294
Aristophanes: The Frogs (Tr.)	88	337
The Poem Itself		
(Ed. with Stanley Burnshaw, Henri		
Peyre, and John Frederick Nims)	98	56
The Birds (Tr.)	102	56
The Frogs (Tr.)		
Ladies' Day (Thesmophoriazusae) (Tr.)		
Lysistrata (Tr.)		
Sixty Poems of Martial (Tr.)	113	188

  ARTICLES ABOUT
  Rev. of Sappho

(Tr. by Mary Barnard)	95	185

FITZELL, LINCOLN
  POEMS

Grass of Ruins	41	70
A Desert Paradox		
The Road to San Joaquin		
Through a Gate		
Ancestors' House		
Hymn to Labor	43	14
Snow Burial		
Romance		
A Weathered Grove	44	202
Knoll Oak		
Entity		
Indian		
Museum Piece		
Rough Ground	48	194
Country Air		
Contemporary		
Fragment		

Echoes from a Precipice   52   128
Church Picnic

BOOKS REVIEWED
Selected Poems   87   53

ARTICLES ABOUT
The New Intellectualism:
   The Dry Reaction,
   by W. T. Scott   58   86

FITZGERALD, EDWARD
ARTICLES ABOUT
Rev. of *The Original Rubaiyyat*
   of Omar Khayyam
   (Tr. by Robert Graves
   and Omar Ali-Shah)   113   262

FITZGERALD, EDWARD J.
POEMS
Renewals   49   22
Saddle the Horses
Abandoned Hill
Colonial House

FITZGERALD, ELLEN
ARTICLES
A Modern Epic of War
   [Thomas Hardy]   5   288

REVIEWS
John Millington Synge
   and the Irish Theatre,
   by Maurice Bourgeois   4   239
Poems of Heinrich Heine
   (Ed. and tr. by Louis Untermeyer)   11   279

FITZGERALD, GERALD
POEMS
Death and the Maiden   88   25
Three Orpheus Songs   89   152
   ("Fear, Orpheus, if it ever...")
   ("See the little Circus boy...")
   ("Suddenly, noon among us...")

FITZGERALD, MICHAEL
POEMS
The Landscape
   That Is Not There   170   25

FITZGERALD, ROBERT
POEMS
Mutations   38   264
Midsummer
Charles River Nocturne
Winter Night
Night Prayer
The Memory of Flowers

Himeros   43   185
Metaphysician
For the Others
Metaphysical   89   271
Figlio Maggiore   99   79
Φύσις   101   40

TRANSLATIONS
Poems by Luciano Erba   94   309
Poems by Alfredo Rizzardi   94   319
Poem by Virgil   136   1

ARTICLES
A Letter from Sestri Levante   89   176
The Things of the Eye
   [Robert Lowell, Randall Jarrell,
   John Berryman, George Santayana]   132   107
A Springfield Memoir
   [Vachel Lindsay, Elisabeth Lindsay,
   Harriet Monroe]   141   33

REVIEWS
These Our Matins, by Michael Roberts   38   229
Ten Poems,
   by Kathleen Tankersley Young   38   339
The Uncelestial City,
   by Humbert Wolfe   39   54
New Bearings in English Poetry,
   by F. R. Leavis   41   112
New Signatures and *New Country*
   (Ed. by Michael Roberts)   44   46
Footnotes to These Days   48   340
   Thanksgiving Before November,
      by Norman Macleod
   Before the Brave,
      by Kenneth Patchen
Adam & Eve & the City,
   by William Carlos Williams   49   94
The Deer Come Down,
   by Edward Weismiller   50   45
Primitivism and Decadence,
   by Yvor Winters   50   173
The Man with the Blue Guitar
   and Other Poems,
   by Wallace Stevens   51   153
Poems, by Etta Blum   51   219
Homer: The Odyssey
   (Tr. by E. V. Rieu)
   [T. E. Lawrence]   72   28

BOOKS REVIEWED
Poems   48   166
The Alcestis of Euripides
   (Tr. with Dudley Fitts)   50   108
A Wreath for the Sea   64   111
Oedipus Rex
   (Tr. with Dudley Fitts)   76   299

Oedipus at Colonus (Tr.)   85   225
In the Rose of Time: Poems 1931-1956   90   110
Paul Valéry, Plays (Tr. with David Paul)   97   121
Homer: The Odyssey (Tr.)   98   397
Chronique, by St.-John Perse (Tr.)   99   194
Birds, by St.-John Perse (Tr.)   110   184
The Collected Poems of James Agee (Ed.)   114   409
The Collected Short Prose
    of James Agee (Ed.)   114   411
Spring Shade: Poems 1931-1970   119   296

ARTICLES ABOUT
Waking Up Over the Aeneid,
    by Paul Breslin   143   347

FITZGERALD, WILLIAM
POEMS
The Harridan at Heart   48   255
Death of Leah   51   248

REVIEWS
Prolegomena to Any Future Poetry,
    by Howard Blake   51   221
New Directions, 1938
    (Ed. by James Laughlin IV)   53   209
In What Hour,
    by Kenneth Rexroth   57   158

BOOKS REVIEWED
Daekargus   44   287

FJELDE, ROLF
POEMS
Cold Comfort
    from an Old Air   85   12

REVIEWS
Promises, Poems 1954-1956,
    by Robert Penn Warren   92   49

BOOKS REVIEWED
Washington, a Poem in Six Parts   86   242
The Imaged Word   103   316

FLACCUS, KIMBALL
POEMS
Look to the North Star   43   202

ARTICLES
Correspondence:
    Selden Rodman's Anthology
    [T. C. Wilson]   53   162

BOOKS REVIEWED
In Praise of Mara   43   225
Avalanche of April   45   342
The White Stranger   56   101

FLAGG, SUE SKIPWITH
POEMS
Sung Upward   42   205

FLANAGAN, ROBERT
BOOKS REVIEWED
Body   119   356

FLANDERS, JANE
POEMS
Wild Asters   134   259
Late Report from Miss Harriet Robinson's
    Third Grade   140   137
Cloud Painter   144   249
Homage to Leonardo   150   158
The Hard Way   161   90

BOOKS REVIEWED
The Students of Snow   143   228
Timepiece   154   99

FLANNER, HILDEGARDE
POEMS
Communion   17   245
Notes of Song   23   306
    To a Tree in Bloom
    Singing
    Moment
    Trees
    To a Dear Friend
Written in the West   30   299
    A Bird Sings at Night
    Storm
    The Rain
    Burial of the Mocking Bird
    To My Books Who Perished by Fire
    God Pity Them
    A Wreath for Ashes
Green Galleries   34   134
    Superior People
    Ascent
    Pacific Winter
Prayer for This Day   43   177
Ascent
Orpha's Song
Driving-Clock
Towers Like These
The Ballad of Santa Monica
Native Hours   46   61
    This Land Is America
    Myth and Actual
    Entreaty on a Hill
    Hope for This
    A Way to Know
Women of My Day   48   78
Traffic   50   310
    Noon on Alameda Street
    He May Come Late
    Moon and Motor

REVIEWS
The Trumpeting Crane,
    by Helene Magaret   45   291
The Collected Poems of John Galsworthy   46   168
Poems, Et Cetera,
    by David Greenhood   46   289
Dance of Fire, by Lola Ridge   47   40
Mountains and Molehills,
    by Frances Cornford   47   225
A Spectacle for Scholars,
    by Winifred Welles   48   285
In Tract of Time, by Helen Cornelius   49   99
Selected Poems,
    by Marsden Hartley
    (Ed. by Henry W. Wells)   68   220

BOOKS REVIEWED
Young Girl and Other Poems   18   223
A Tree in Bloom and Other Verses   26   112
Time's Profile   35   162
If There Is Time   60   341

FLANTZ, RICHARD
BOOKS REVIEWED
Promises   116   125

FLECKER, JAMES ELROY
BOOKS REVIEWED
The Old Ships   6   252
The Collected Poems of...   20   282

FLEET, BRENDA
BOOKS REVIEWED
Catching the Sun's Fire   119   356

FLEMING, ARCHIBALD
BOOKS REVIEWED
The Island Called Pharos   48   111

FLEMING, HAROLD (LEE)
POEMS
Sure of What the Birds Know   89   24
The Lens Grinder
Elocution at Thirty   92   293
The Hour Before the Coming of the Night
The Farm   95   159
An Atmosphere
Rainbow, Rainbow...
In This Fleshmill   98   88
Now It Is Morning   140   151

BOOKS REVIEWED
Elizabeth Newt   112   353

FLEMING, RAY
POEMS
One on One in Basketball   117   233
In the Boboli Gardens

FLEMING, RUDD
ARTICLES ABOUT
[Note]   84   119

FLETCHER, FRANCES
BOOKS REVIEWED
The Banquet and Other Poems   27   226

FLETCHER, JEFFERSON BUTLER
BOOKS REVIEWED
The Divine Comedy
    of Dante Alighieri (Tr.)   43   229

FLETCHER, JOHN GOULD
POEMS
Irradiations   3   85
The Blue Symphony   4   211
The Old South   6   181
New York
Arizona Poems   7   271
    The Well in the Desert
    Mexican Quarter
    Cliff Dwelling
    Rain in the Desert
Modern Lamentations   9   137
    Give and Take
    The Everlasting Contradiction
    Blind People
    Why the War?
Chicago Notes   11   139
    Lake Front at Night
    The Monadnock
    La Salle Street—Evening
    War Angles
Russia   12   22
At the Turn of the Year   15   142
Rain
Down the Mississippi   17   1
    Embarkation
    Heat
    Full Moon
    The Moon's Orchestra
    The Stevedores
    Night Landing
    The Silence
Prayers   22   6
To the Unknown God   29   119
At the Dream's-Edge Shore   40   64
The Blue Elegy
Big River   42   149
Elegy as Epithalamium   43   59
Children of the Sun
By the Rio Grande   45   23
    Desert
    The Dancers in the Plaza
    Nomad's Song
    Sonnets of Life
Requiem for H. M.   49   165

Ascent of Monadnock   51   14
The Ozarks   55   248
Memorial for 1940   58   65
Los Angeles Smog   76   194
Along the Highway, Rogers to Fayetteville
Charles Baudelaire   84   279
William Blake
Sonnets at Sunset
    ("Except when unexpected...")
    ("Strange that this inner fire...")
    ("This is the shape...")
Evening of Life

ARTICLES
Miss Lowell's Discovery:
    Polyphonic Prose   6   32
A Poet's Declaration of Rights   7   88
Correspondence [Padraic Colum]   7   213
Living History [Amy Lowell]   10   149
Correspondence: "Hard" and "Soft"
    [Ezra Pound]   12   111
The Land of Enchantment   43   150
Correspondence [J. V. Healy]   44   355
Correspondence [W. T. Scott]   58   230
Correspondence: History, Criticism,
    and the Audience
    [Karl Shapiro]   72   110

REVIEWS
Images Old and New,
    by Richard Aldington   8   49
Sea-Garden, by H. D.   9   266
Selections from the Symbolical Poems
    of William Blake
    (Ed. by Fred E. Pierce)   9   315
Moments of Vision,
    by Thomas Hardy   12   96
Look! We Have Come Through!
    by D. H. Lawrence   12   269
Georgian Poetry, 1916-1917   12   332
Chinese Poems
    (Tr. by Arthur Waley)   13   273
Last Poems, by Edward Thomas   14   103
Collected Poems, by Thomas Hardy   16   43
Real Property, by Harold Monro   21   38
The Orators, by W. H. Auden   42   110
Last Poems, by D. H. Lawrence
    (Ed. by Richard Aldington
    and Giuseppe Orioli)   42   163
Poems, by Stephen Spender   42   225
The Single Glow, by Axton Clark   43   165
Give Your Heart to the Hawks,
    by Robinson Jeffers   43   338
Discovering Poetry
    or Discovering Revolution   44   231
    Discovering Poetry,
    by Elizabeth Drew

Contemporary Literature
    and Social Revolution,
    by R. D. Charques
The Sun Turns West,
    by Alice Corbin   44   279
Man with a Bull-Tongue Plow,
    by Jesse Stuart   45   217
American Song, by Paul Engle   45   285
Poems of People,
    by Edgar Lee Masters   49   343
Edgar Allan Poe, by Edward Shanks   50   353
Illusion and Reality,
    by Christopher Caudwell   53   40
Whitman—Without and Within   53   273
    Whitman, by Newton Arvin
    Walt Whitman
    and the Springs of Courage,
    by Haniel Long
Two Plainsmen   54   342
    Corn, by Paul Engle
    The High Plains,
    by Kenneth Porter
Clothed with the Sun,
    by Fray Angelico Chavez   55   338
Lorca in English   56   343
    Poems of F. García Lorca
    (Tr. by Stephen Spender
    and J. L. Gili)
    The Poet in New York
    and Other Poems,
    by Federico García Lorca
    (Tr. by Rolfe Humphries)
    Blood Wedding,
    by Federico García Lorca
    (Tr. by Gilbert Neiman)
The Dust Which Is God,
    by William Rose Benét   59   213
Stars, Fixed and Variable   60   149
    And In the Human Heart,
    by Conrad Aiken
    The North Star and Other Poems,
    by Laurence Binyon
Four Quartets, by T. S. Eliot   63   44
The Triumph of Life
    (Ed. by Horace Gregory)   64   107
Poems 1923-1943, by James Daly   64   223
The Selected Poems
    1912-1944 of Alfred Kreymborg   66   215
Poet to Poet
    (Ed. by Houston Peterson
    and William S. Lynch)   66   345
The War Poets, An Anthology
    (Ed. by Oscar Williams)   67   344
One-Dimensional America   69   171
    Brady's Bend and Other Ballads,
    by Martha Keller
    No Rain from These Clouds,
    by Kenneth Porter

BOOKS REVIEWED
  Fire and Wine   3   111
  The Dominant City
  Some Imagist Poets—An Anthology   6   150
  Irradiations: Sand and Spray   7   44
  Some Imagist Poets: 1916   8   255
  Goblins and Pagodas   9   43
  Some Imagist Poets, 1917   11   339
  Japanese Prints   13   340
  The Tree of Life
  Some Imagist Poets   14   281
  Breakers and Granite   19   155
  Preludes and Symphonies   21   270
  Branches of Adam   31   216
  The Black Rock   33   222
  Imagist Anthology 1930
    (With Richard Aldington,
    John Cournos, H. D., F. S. Flint,
    Ford Madox Ford, James Joyce,
    D. H. Lawrence, and William
    Carlos Williams)   36   213
  XXIV Elegies   47   344
  Selected Poems   52   347
  South Star   58   334
  The Burning Mountain   69   353

ARTICLES ABOUT
  John Gould Fletcher, by Harriet Monroe   27   206
  A Note on Three Southern Poets,
    by Robert Penn Warren   40   103
  Correspondence
    from John A. Holmes   42   355
  Correspondence from Ezra Pound   43   292
  Correspondence from J. V. Healy   44   354
  On the Great River,
    by Harriet Monroe   46   268
  Poetry on Records,
    by Harry Thornton Moore   58   345
  Correspondence
    from William Rose Benét
    [Elinor Wylie]   59   350
  Correspondence from Edouard Roditi   67   173
  Correspondence
    from Margaretta W. Wright   70   54
  A New Engagement?
    by George Dillon   72   89
  In Memory of John Gould Fletcher,
    by Donald Davidson   77   154
  Rev. of *Johnswood*,
    by Charlie May Simon   84   284

FLEXNER, HORTENSE
POEMS
  Voyage   12   79
  Decoration for Valor   13   316
  Holiday Crowd   19   317
  Winged Victory

  Adopted Son   30   70
  Contemporary
  The Word   33   137
  Threat   34   254
  The Scientist Dies
  Lost Tenants   65   13
  Interval
  Storm Warning   72   186

ARTICLES
  Correspondence: To a Minor Poet
    [Poem]   16   348

BOOKS REVIEWED
  Clouds and Cobblestones   17   276
  Clouds and Cobblestones   20   102
  This Stubborn Root   38   109
  North Window   62   277

FLINT, F(RANK) S(TEWART)
POEMS
  Four Poems in Unrhymed Cadence   2   136
    ("London, my beautiful...")
    ("Dear one!")
    ("Under the lily shadow...")
    In the Garden
  In London   7   227
    Cones
    Gloom
    Terror
    Evil
    War-Time
  Children   11   192
  In the Cathedral

ARTICLES
  Imagisme   1   198
  Paul Claudel   6   200

BOOKS REVIEWED
  Some Imagist Poets—An Anthology   6   150
  Cadences   8   260
  Some Imagist Poets, 1917   11   339
  The Closed Door,
    by Jean de Bosschère (Tr.)   12   48
  Some Imagist Poets   14   281
  Otherworld   17   44
  Imagist Anthology 1930
    (With Richard Aldington,
    John Cournos, H. D., John
    Gould Fletcher, Ford Madox Ford,
    James Joyce, D. H. Lawrence,
    and William Carlos Williams)   36   213

FLINT, MICAH
ARTICLES ABOUT
  Notes on Mid-Western Oblivion,
    by Pat Morrissette   34   346

FLINT, R(OBERT) W.
REVIEWS
The Art of T. S. Eliot,
    by Helen Gardner   77   41
Beyond the Mountains,
    by Kenneth Rexroth   78   356
*Wordsworth: Centenary Studies Presented
    at Cornell and Princeton Universities*
    (Ed. by Gilbert T. Dunklin)
    [Douglas Bush, Lionel Trilling] 80   233

FLOCK, MIRIAM
POEMS
*If Ontogeny Does Not Recapitulate
    Phylogeny, Then What Is Metaphor?* 161   203

FLOOK, MARIA
POEMS
Strangers: Many Perfect Examples   138   96
The Late-Shift Comptroller
Against Spring   142   325
Discreet
Affidavit   144   32
The Improper Persons   145   259
The Sapling   148   21
Child Burial   148   341

ARTICLES
Comment
    [Henry Rago]   151   217

BOOKS REVIEWED
Reckless Wedding   143   163
Sea Room   150   37

FLORES, ANGEL
TRANSLATIONS
Poem by Pablo Neruda   69   13

BOOKS REVIEWED
Selected Poems by Pablo Neruda (Tr.) 65   225
Residence on Earth,
    by Pable Neruda (Tr.)   70   150
*Anthology of French Poetry
    from Nerval to Valéry
    in English Translation* (Ed.)   93   40
*An Anthology of German Poetry
    from Hölderlin to Rilke* (Ed.)   97   387

FLORY, SHELDON
POEMS
The Kindred of the Wild   114   10
Portents

FLOWERS, NANCY
POEMS
Little Things   40   199
The Truth I Seek

FLUCHÈRE, HENRI
ARTICLES ABOUT
Verse Drama on the Paris Stage,
    by Ruby Haykin   82   294

FLYNN, JAN
POEMS
The Dreamer   26   196
A Silver Night

FOERSTER, NORMAN
BOOKS REVIEWED
*English Poetry
    of the Nineteenth Century*
    (Ed. with G. R. Elliott)   27   164

FOERSTER, RICHARD
POEMS
Sleep   144   79
EEG   146   163
Transfigured Nights
Mozart's Death   151   295
Playland   151   400
Strategy   154   274
Love Affair   156   285
Disposing of His Ashes   158   319
The Hours   159   313
Atmospherics   161   32
Life Drawing   162   192
The Clearing   164   324
The Failure of Similes
Holyrood Abbey
Valentines   165   249
Icebound   167   139
In the Moment   168   192
Constable's Cloud Studies
The Book Cover   168   314
Geological Survey   169   264
Fiddleheads   170   151

BOOKS REVIEWED
Sudden Harbor   163   39
Patterns of Descent   165   97

FOGEL, EPHIM G.
POEMS
Landscape with Bayonets   66   196

FOLLAIN, JEAN
BOOKS REVIEWED
Transparence of the World, Poems by...
    (Tr. by W. S. Merwin)   116   260
A World Rich in Anniversaries
    (Tr. by Mary Feeney
    and William Matthews)   137   220

FOLSOM, FRANKLIN
POEMS
These Days   44   8
   Exploration
   An Unemployed Man's Holiday
   Our New Regimens
   Dilettante
   My Hand
   Complete Sight
A Room in a House   50   134
   After Moving to a Quiet Room
   Students to Workers
   The Intellectual in 1937

FOMBEURE, MAURICE
POEMS
Cris de la Rue   80   325
Métempsychose
   (Tr. by Wallace Fowlie)

ARTICLES ABOUT
Recent French Publications,
   by Wallace Fowlie   93   40

FOMBONA, RUFINO BLANCO
[See BLANCO FOMBONA,
RUFINO]

FOOTE, ALVIN
BOOKS REVIEWED
Poems   56   106

FOOTE, ELLIS
BOOKS REVIEWED
Layman's Fall:
   A Fantasy in the Joyous Mode   73   294

FOOTE, ELVIRA
BOOKS REVIEWED
Aspen Leaves   36   52

FORBES, CALVIN
POEMS
Poem on My Birthday   115   42
The Chocolate Soldiers   116   157
Good Morning Blues
Gabriel's Blues

BOOKS REVIEWED
Blue Monday   126   219

FORBES, JOHN
ARTICLES ABOUT
Towards a Contemporary
   Australian Poetics,
   by John Kinsella   169   94

FORD, BORIS
BOOKS REVIEWED
The Pelican Guide to English Literature (Ed.)   92   393

FORD, CHARLES HENRI
POEMS
Choice   37   25
This Is the Rock
Left Instantly Designs   37   286
Pension Ballad   54   192
Platitude
The Bad Habit
The Overturned Lake   56   19
Dismemberment   79   325

ARTICLES
Note on Hymn and
   Left Instantly Designs
   (With Parker Tyler)   37   287

BOOKS REVIEWED
The Garden of Disorder and Other Poems   52   236
ABC's   56   340
The Overturned Lake   60   48
The Mirror of Baudelaire
   (Tr. by William Candlewood) (Ed.)   62   282
Poems for Painters   66   340
Sleep in a Nest of Flames   76   234

ARTICLES ABOUT
Surrealist Influence
   in Contemporary English
   and American Poetry,
   by H. R. Hays   54   202

FORD, FORD MADOX
["F. M. F.", FORD MADOX
HUEFFER]
POEMS
On Heaven   4   75
What the Orderly Dog Saw   9   293
The Silver Music   12   19
The Sanctuary
A House   17   291
Seven Shepherds   22   122
Buckshee I-V   39   233
Buckshee VI-VIII   39   317

ARTICLES
Impressionism—Some Speculations [I]   2   177
Impressionism—Some Speculations II   2   215
Poeta Nascitur... [Ezra Pound]   29   326
Poeta Nascitur [Ezra Pound]   121   41

REVIEWS
The Sleeping Fury,
   by Louise Bogan   50   158

BOOKS REVIEWED
Collected Poems   4   111
Antwerp   6   153

On Heaven and Poems
   Written on Active Service   13   219
Imagist Anthology 1930
   (With Richard Aldington, John Cournos,
   H. D., John Gould Fletcher, F. S. Flint,
   James Joyce, D. H. Lawrence,
   and William Carlos Williams)   36   213
Collected Poems   50   336
Buckshee   111   184
Selected Poems
   (Ed. by Basil Bunting)   121   229

ARTICLES ABOUT
Status Rerum, by Ezra Pound   1   123
Their Wide Range,
   by Harriet Monroe   17   322
Must Art Be Interesting?
   by Baker Brownell   19   206
The Editor in France,
   by Harriet Monroe   23   90
[Quote from speech]   50   236
Obituary   54   290

FORD, GENA
POEMS
In the Eye   108   29
Another Day, Another Alba
The Nude on the Bathroom Wall
Today, the World
Lines for a Hard Time   110   96

BOOKS REVIEWED
Tall Tales from Far Corners   102   335
A Planting of Chives   107   258

FORD, JULIA ELLSWORTH
BOOKS REVIEWED
Snickerty Nick   15   345
Imagina   36   289

FORD, R. A. D.
ARTICLES ABOUT
Poets in Canada,
   by Margaret Avison   94   182

FORD, WEBSTER
[Pseud. of MASTERS, EDGAR LEE]
ARTICLES ABOUT
Our Contemporaries [Poems]   5   42
[Note on pseudonym]   5   247

FORD, WILLIAM
POEMS
On Putting the Grandchild to Bed   143   319
The Eskimo Ivory Exhibition   145   208
Crossing Indian Land
At Mt. Rushmore   151   459
The Summer of Twelve

Doctor Doctorum   154   327
Audition   158   332
Love in Middle Age   164   256

FORGOTSON, E. S.
POEMS
Elderly Nobody Erases Self
   in Central Park   96   94

REVIEWS
Poets of the New Decade   58   159
   Poems, by Leonard Clark
   The Secret Field,
      by Christopher Lee
   The White Island,
      by George Woodcock
   Letter in Wartime,
      by H. B. Mallalieu
   Inscapes, by Francis Scarfe
Selected Poems, by John Wheelwright   59   45
Lights in the Valley,
   by Maxwell Bodenheim   60   219
Montparnasse and the Cosmos   61   396
   American Signatures
      (Ed. by Rae Beamish)
   Vertical: A Yearbook
      for Romantic-Mystic Ascensions
      (Ed. by Eugene Jolas)
   Cloth of the Tempest,
      by Kenneth Patchen   63   278
   Seven Poets in Search of an Answer
      (Ed. by Thomas Yoseloff)
      [Maxwell Bodenheim, Joy Davidman,
      Langston Hughes, Aaron Kramer,
      Alfred Kreymborg, Martha Millet,
      Norman Rosten]   64   289
Social Poetry: Four Recent Specimens 66   106
   My Country,
      by Russell W. Davenport
   Smile, Ichabod,
      by Hugo Manning
   Exile from a Future Time,
      Posthumous Poems,
      by Sol Funaroff
   Preface to Maturity,
      by Selwyn S. Schwartz
   A Masque of Reason,
      by Robert Frost   66   156
   The Granite Butterfly,
      by Parker Tyler   69   231

ARTICLES ABOUT
Correspondence
   from Waldemar Hansen   70   113

FORKIN, KATHERINE M.
BOOKS REVIEWED
Open Letter   61   456

FORSTER, LOUIS, JR.
REVIEWS
Against the Cold,
   by Witter Bynner   57   217
Open House,
   by Theodore Roethke   58   222

FORSYTH, JAMES LAW
POEMS
Poem ("If I should never see...")   58   200

FORSYTHE, KATHLEEN
BOOKS REVIEWED
Inside Me   119   356

FORT, PAUL
POEMS
Louis Eleventh, Curious Man   18   293
The Miraculous Catch
The Lament of the Soldiers
The Return
The Little Silent Street
Eternity
   (Tr. by John Strong Newberry)

BOOKS REVIEWED
Les Enchanteurs   15   42
Barbe Bleue, Jeanne d'Arc et Mes Amours
Chansons à la Gauloise
Selected Poems and Ballads of...
   (Tr. by John Strong Newberry)   21   161

ARTICLES ABOUT
Vers Libre and Metrical Prose,
   by Amy Lowell   3   213
Rev. of *Six French Poets,*
   by Amy Lowell   7   202

FORTINI, FRANCO
POEMS
Dalla Cina/Out of China   155   36
1944-1947
The Trees
One September Night
You Look Out and See
   (Tr. by W. S. Di Piero)

FOSSO, D. R.
POEMS
Opposing   130   21
Salute
Volume

FOSTER, JOHN L.
POEMS
The Narrow Road
   Through the Deep West   120   277

TRANSLATIONS
Two "Songs of Heart's Ease":
   Translated from the Ancient Egyptian   114   176
   From *Papyrus Harris 500*   116   304

FOSTER, KATHLEEN
POEMS
The Lonely One   30   313

FOSTER, RICHARD
BOOKS REVIEWED
The New Romantics,
   a Reappraisal of the New Criticism   102   198

FOULKE, MILDRED PLUMA
POEMS
The Creation to the Creator   24   22

FOULKE, WILLIAM DUDLEY
BOOKS REVIEWED
Some Love Songs of Petrarch (Tr.)   7   207

FOWLIE, WALLACE
TRANSLATIONS
Poem by St.-John Perse   79   12
Poems by Francis Ponge,
   Pierre Seghers, Maurice Fombeure,
   André Frenaud, Luc Estang,
   Lucien Becker, Jean Rousselot,
   Alain Bosquet, Georges Guy,
   and Yves Bonnefoy   80   316
Poem by Jean Cocteau   84   80
Letter from St.-John Perse   86   179
Poem by St.-John Perse   86   189
Poems by Paul Claudel   87   130
Poems by Pierre Jean Jouve,
   René Char, Jean Grosjean,
   and Jean-Claude Renard   104   275

ARTICLES
Rimbaud in 1949
   [Akakia Viala, Nicolas Bataille,
   André Breton, Henry de Bouillane
   de Lacoste]   75   166
Homage to Max Jacob
   [Pablo Picasso]   75   352
Paul Valéry [Stéphane Mallarmé]   76   279
Jules Laforgue   78   216
St.-John Perse   79   31
Mallarmé [Paul Verlaine]   80   37
Foreword
   [French Poets, Francis Ponge]   80   311
Henri Michaux   81   265
A Note on René Char   83   49
A Note on Jean Cocteau   84   85
Claudel: The Tidings that
   Are the Poem   87   169

French Chronicle: Recent Publications
[Valery Larbaud, William Jay Smith,
Jean Cocteau, Charles Baudelaire,
René Char, Jackson and Marthiel
Mathews, Georges Poulet, Henry
Miller, Arthur Rimbaud, Daisy Aldan,
Stéphane Mallarmé, Bradford Cook]   88   408

Jorge Guillén, Marianne Moore,
T. S. Eliot: Some Recollections
[Christopher Morley]   90   103

A Commemoration:
"Les Fleurs du Mal," 1857-1957
[A. E. Housman, André Gide,
Paul Valéry]   90   376

French Chronicle: Recent Publications
[Geoffrey Brereton, Jules Laforgue,
Paul Valéry, Wallace Stevens,
Charles Baudelaire, Jean Cocteau,
Charles Péguy, René Char]   91   36

Recent French Publications
[Dorothy Sayers, C. F. MacIntyre,
Stéphane Mallarmé, Jules Laforgue,
Patricia Terry, Paul Verlaine, Brian
Hill, Angel Flores, Charles Baudelaire,
Enid Starkie, Maurice Fombeure,
Pierre Emmanuel, Claude Vigée]   93   40

Letter From Haiti
[Emile Roumer, Félix
Morrisseau-Leroy, Jean Brierre,
Clément Magloire-Saint-Aude,
Clovis Bonhomme, Arthur Rimbaud,
André Breton]   94   398

Surrealism in 1960: A Backward Glance
[Guillaume Apollinaire,
André Breton, Lautréamont]   95   365

Paris Letter
[Jean-Louis Barrault, Paul Claudel,
Alain Bosquet, St.-John Perse,
Gaston Bachelard, Jean Cocteau]   96   371

In Tribute to St.-John Perse   97   255

Jorge Guillén   99   243

Letters from the Midi: I
[Yves Bonnefoy, St.-John Perse,
René Char, André du Bouchet,
Gaetan Picon]   100   258

Letters from the Midi: II
[Henri Mondor, Stéphane Mallarmé]   100   261

French Poetry Today   104   322

Comment
[Karl Shapiro, Isabella Gardner,
Henry Rago, T. S. Eliot, M. D. Zabel] 151   208

REVIEWS
Across the Board,
by David Cornel DeJong   62   170

Men and Saints,
by Charles Péguy
(Tr. by Ann and Julian Green)   66   42

Exile and Other Poems,
by St.-John Perse
(Tr. by Denis Devlin)   74   343

Selected Writings of Guillaume Apollinaire
(Tr. by Roger Shattuck)   77   162

Baudelaire Today   82   86
Poems of Baudelaire
(Tr. of Les Fleurs du Mal,
by Roy Campbell)
Pensées du Baudelaire (Ed.) and
Connaissance du Baudelaire,
by Henri Peyre
Correspondance Générale,
by Charles Baudelaire

Winds, by St.-John Perse
(Tr. by Hugh Chisholm)   82   345

Tristan Corbière.
Selections from Les Amours Jaunes
(Tr. by C. F. MacIntyre)   84   351

Paul Valéry and the Civilized Mind,
by Norman Suckling   85   300

Poetry and Prophecy   86   108
Modern Poetry
and the Christian Tradition,
by Amos N. Wilder
The Poetic Drama of Paul Claudel,
by Joseph Chiari
Dante's Drama of the Mind,
by Francis Fergusson

One Hundred Poems
from the Japanese,
by Kenneth Rexroth   88   116

Paul Valéry, Plays
(Tr. by David Paul
and Robert Fitzgerald)   97   121

Chronique, by St.-John Perse
(Tr. by Robert Fitzgerald)
[Dag Hammarskjöld]   99   194

The Poet and the Machine,
by Paul Ginestier
(Tr. by Martin B. Friedman)   101   292

Sainte-Beuve: Selected Essays
(Tr. by Francis Steegmuller
and Norbert Guterman)   103   183

Four Poets and Two Dramatists   104   187
The Poetry of Villon,
by John Fox
Apollinaire: Poet Among the Painters,
by Francis Steegmuller
Mallarmé and the Symbolist Drama,
by Haskell M. Block
The Design of Rimbaud's Poetry,
by John Porter Houston
Corneille, by P. J. Yarrow
The Art of Jean Racine,
by Bernard Weinberg

The Enemy Joy, by Ben Belitt   105   324

A French Chronicle   107   267

Contemporary French Poetry
  (Ed. by Alexander Aspel
  and Donald Justice)
From Symbolism to Baudelaire,
  by Angelo Bertocci
Idée Fixe, by Paul Valéry
  (Tr. by David Paul)
Apollinaire, by Margaret Davies
Selected Works of Alfred Jarry
  (Ed. by Roger Shattuck
  and Simon Watson Taylor)
Three Critical Approaches to Poetry   112   41
Lautréamont par lui-même,
  by Marcelin Pleynet
The Limits of Symbolism:
  Studies of Five Modern French Poets,
  by Bernard Weinberg
The Metamorphoses of the Circle,
  by Georges Poulet
  (Tr. by Carley Dawson
  and Elliott Coleman)
Selected Essays,
  by William Troy
  (Ed. by Stanley Edgar Hyman)   112   116

BOOKS REVIEWED
Rimbaud   70   102
Pantomime, A Journal of Rehearsals   79   212
Mallarmé   83   278
Seamarks,
  by St.-John Perse (Tr.)   93   332
A Poet Before the Cross,
  by Paul Claudel (Tr.)   95   50
Characters from Proust   145   161

ARTICLES ABOUT
[Note]   75   184

FOX, JOHN
BOOKS REVIEWED
The Poetry of Villon   104   187

FOX, JOSEF W.
REVIEWS
Glory for Me,
  by MacKinlay Kantor   68   51

FOX, MOIREEN
  [See A CHEAVASA,
  MOIREEN FOX]

FOX, SUSAN
POEMS
Penelope Gardening   150   35

FOXALL, EDGAR
POEMS
Slow Rhythms   43   72
  Evening in Sight of Liverpool

The Winter Woods
On Reading Milton at Midnight

BOOKS REVIEWED
Proems
  (With Ruthven Todd, Patrick Evans,
  Rayner Heppenstall, Lawrence Durrell,
  and Oswald Blakeston)   53   155

FOY, JOHN
POEMS
From *Rue des Martyrs*   165   147
  3 ("In that cold...")
  15 ("In holey socks...")
  21 ("Sick of decision...")
From *Rue des Martyrs*   166   142
  12 ("The question isn't...")

FRANCE, PETER
BOOKS REVIEWED
The Twelve and Other Poems,
  by Alexander Blok
  (Tr. with Jon Stallworthy)   119   45

FRANCIS, HELEN M.
POEMS
Delilah   27   191

FRANCIS, ROBERT
POEMS
Evening Ride   56   253
Statement   60   64
Encounter   66   126
Part for the Whole
Two Words   68   246
His Wealth
Fortune
The Oxen
The Hawk
The Big Tent   73   84
Portrait
Cold   84   271
Sailboat, Your Secret   86   233

BOOKS REVIEWED
Stand with Me Here   49   340
The Sound I Listened For   63   226
The Orb Weaver   97   109
Come Out into the Sun:
  Poems New and Selected   108   272
The Trouble with Francis
  (An Autobiography)   121   102
Collected Poems, 1936-1976   131   106
Late Fire, Late Snow:
  New and Uncollected Poems   163   39

FRANDEGARIS, C. [Pseud.]
POEMS
Scarf-Dancer   26   311

FRANGOPOULOS, T. D.
POEMS
Death of the Solitary Man
(Tr. by Kimon Friar)   139   90

ARTICLES ABOUT
Post-War Greek Poets,
by Kimon Friar   139   99

FRANK, FLORENCE KIPER
POEMS
To J. L.   5   23
A Girl Strike-Leader
City of Huge Buildings
The Jewish Conscript   5   66
New Life   11   136
  With Child
  Attack
  The Moment
  Afterwards
  Within My Arms
For Barbara   17   70
  Sleep the Mother
  Elf-Child
  ("Some certainty? Some light...")
  ("Suppose you have just a person...")
  ("Woman and freedom!")
Women   21   83
  Dialogue
  Married
  Interior
  Baby
December   27   183
Prairie Night   30   140
Abnegation
February Rain   39   308
The Cord
Note for Tourists   54   9

ARTICLES
The Jew as Jewish Artist
[Maxwell Bodenheim]   22   209
New York Plays
[Eugene O'Neill]   25   327
New York Plays
[Henrik Ibsen, Franz Werfel,
Eugene O'Neill]   28   95
[Note]   29   231

BOOKS REVIEWED
*The Jew to Jesus
and Other Poems*   8   264

FRANK, JOHN FREDERICK
POEMS
Dead Man   59   201
Coffee Hour   71   133

FRANK, JOSEPH
BOOKS REVIEWED
The Widening Gyre   104   369
A Primer of Ignorance,
by R. P. Blackmur (Ed.)   112   356

ARTICLES ABOUT
Rev. of *The Psychology of Art*,
by André Malraux   76   288

FRANK, RACHEL
TRANSLATIONS
Poems by Juan Ramón Jiménez   82   209

ARTICLES
Juan Ramón Jiménez:
The Landscape of the Soul
[J. B. Trend, Emmy Neddermann]   82   224

FRANK, WALDO
BOOKS REVIEWED
The Dark Mother   18   46

FRANKAU, GILBERT
BOOKS REVIEWED
A Song of the Guns   10   271

FRANKENBERG, LLOYD
POEMS
Gone to Summer   52   134
The Years of Enormous Addresses   68   257
Jerusalem   75   197
The Harbor
Scarecrow Suite   76   266

REVIEWS
One Irish   59   51
  Veterans and Other Poems,
  by Donagh McDonagh
  The Young Men and the Old,
  by Stuart Cloete
Poems in War   59   98
  Poems, by Terence Tiller
  A Dream Observed and Other Poems,
  by Anne Ridler
  A Book for Priscilla: Poems,
  by Nicholas Moore
Plain-Chant for America,
  by Katherine Garrison Chapin   60   105
The Short and the Long of It   63   228
  XI Poems, by Alan Swallow
  The Virginia Poems,
  by Francis Coleman Rosenberger
  The Proud People,
  by Joseph Joel Keith
Letter Home, by George Abbe   65   154
Selected Poems,
  by August Derleth   66   223

To Marry Strangers,
  by Winfield Townley Scott   67   157

BOOKS REVIEWED
  The Red Kite   56   46
  Pleasure Dome:
    On Reading Modern Poetry   76   294
  Invitation to Poetry (Ed.)   91   124
  A James Stephens Reader (Ed.)   102   324

FRANKLIN, SIMON
  BOOKS REVIEWED
    The Face Behind the Face,
      by Yevgeny Yevtushenko
      (Tr. with Arthur Boyars)   136   40

FRANKS, DAVID
  BOOKS REVIEWED
    Touch   110   186

FRANTZ, LAURENT B.
  POEMS
    Freight Car   41   199

FRASCONI, ANTONIO
  BOOKS REVIEWED
    Bestiary (With Pablo Neruda)   111   46

FRASER, G. S.
  POEMS
    Speech of a Sufferer   97   353
    Catullus: XXII
    Ovid: Amores, I, 5
    Penelope to Ulysses

  REVIEWS
    Technology and Insight   106   366
      Perspectives by Incongruity and *Terms*
      for Order, by Kenneth Burke
      (Ed. by Stanley Edgar Hyman)
      Aesthetics, by Paul Valéry
      (Tr. by Ralph Manheim)

  BOOKS REVIEWED
    The Collected Poems of Keith Douglas
      (Ed. with John Waller)   79   356
    Leaves Without a Tree   88   52
    Poetry Now (Ed.)   91   124
    Vision and Rhetoric:
      Studies in Modern Poetry   100   50

  ARTICLES ABOUT
    Contemporary Poetry in Britain,
      by David Daiches   62   150

FRASER, KATHLEEN
  POEMS
    A Child Drowns in the Sea
      of Its Own Imagining   101   178

  Giants with Capes of Gold   106   205
  The Baker's Daughter   108   318
  Grass
  Poem Wondering if I'm Pregnant

  BOOKS REVIEWED
    Change of Address   111   195

FRASER, MARGARET
  POEMS
    Though Color Should Fail   35   86
    To the Poet in Autumn   43   25
    Lost Icicle   46   145
    Delicate Destruction   47   18

FRASER, MARJORIE FROST
  POEMS
    America   46   320
    No Common Hand
    Grief

FRAZIER, T(OM)
  POEMS
    From My Tenth Year   79   266

FREDE, RICHARD
  POEMS
    At the Auto Sales & Service   165   76
    Vitae

FREDERICK, JOHN T(OWNER)
  POEMS
    The Orchard   15   17
    Notes on Natural History   111   169

FREDERICKS, CLAUDE
  ARTICLES
    Poet, Publisher, and the Tribal Chant
      (With Milton Saul)   75   24

FREDERICKS, T. PAGET
  BOOKS REVIEWED
    Green Pipes: Poems and Pictures 36   289

FREEDMAN, B. M.
  POEMS
    Malay Boy   30   79

FREEDMAN, MICHELE
  REVIEWS
    Collected Poems,
      by Louise Townsend Nicholl   84   175

FREEMAN, ARTHUR
  POEMS
    Beauty, Sleeping   100   293
    Troilus and Cressida
    The Occupation   106   413

REVIEWS
Five Poets   109   189
    Poems, 1922-1961,
        by Donald Davidson
    The Wrong Angel,
        by Stanley Moss
    A Private Mythology,
        by May Sarton
    White Blossoms,
        by Robert Mezey
    The Horse Opera and Other Poems,
        by Mac Hammond

BOOKS REVIEWED
    Apollonian Poems   100   191
    Estrangements   110   258
    Assays of Bias   119   342

FREEMAN, JOSEPH
POEMS
    Bitter Wine   21   308
    Renunciation
    Be Still Today

FREEMAN, MASON A., JR.
POEMS
    The Triple Shroud   18   256
    The Way
    Once More
    Epigrams
    From the Vedic

FREEMAN, ROSE FLORENCE
BOOKS REVIEWED
    Petals Blown Adrift   15   169

FREEMAN, TOM
POEMS
    Cruel Fellowship   31   254

FREER, AGNES LEE
[See LEE, AGNES]

FREIS, RICHARD
POEMS
    Life Story   130   256
    The Beach Motel

FRENAUD, ANDRÉ
POEMS
    Veille
        (Tr. by Wallace Fowlie)   80   329

FRENEAU, PHILIP
ARTICLES ABOUT
    Rev. of Poetry and the World,
        by Robert Pinsky   156   297

Rev. of American Poetry:
    The Nineteenth Century
    (Ed. by John Hollander)   165   340

FRENCH, BRYANT MOREY
POEMS
    ("See the sculptured head...")   51   140
    ("Slow though we are in ideas...")

FRENCH, JOSEPH LEWIS
BOOKS REVIEWED
    Lotus and Chrysanthemum (Ed.)   32   96

FRERE, HOOKHAM
ARTICLES ABOUT
    Rev. of Aristophanes: Lysistrata
    (Tr. by Dudley Fitts)   85   294

FREUD, SIGMUND
ARTICLES ABOUT
    Rev. of Tribute to Freud, by H. D.   89   326
    Waking Up Over the Aeneid,
        by Paul Breslin   143   347
    The Forging of H. D.,
        by Gloria G. Fromm   153   160

FREYRE, RICARDO JAIMES
[See JAIMES FREYRE, RICARDO]

FREZZA, LUCIANA
POEMS
    Le Due Cugine   94   324
    Paesaggio
        (Tr. by Barbara Arnett Melchiori)

FRIAR, KIMON
POEMS
    In Childhood's Chair   90   217

TRANSLATIONS
    Poems by Anghelos Sikelianos,
        George Seferis, Nikos Kazantsakis,
        Takis Papatzonis, Andreas Emberikos,
        Demetrios Antoniou, Nikiforos
        Vrettakos, Alexander Matsas,
        Nikos Engonopoulos, Odysseus Elytis,
        Nikos Gatsos, Miltos Sahtouris, Andonis
        Decavalles, and Nanos Valaoritis   78   154
    Poems by Andonis Decavalles   88   310
    Poems by Takis Varvitsiotis, Aris
        Dhikteos, Andonis Decavalles,
        Eleni Vakalo, Athos Dhimoulas,
        P. D. Papadhitsas, Aristotle Nikolaidis,
        Aris Alexandhrou, T. D. Frangopoulos,
        Tasos Livadhitis, Dhimitris Dhoukaris,
        Nikos Karouzos, and Yannis
        Papadhopoulos   139   76
    Poem by Yannis Kondos   151   52

ARTICLES
Medusa-Mask   55   322
Contemporary Greek Poetry
   [Anghelos Sikelianos, Nikos
   Kazantzakis, George Seferis,
   Takis Papatzonis, Alexander Matsas,
   Nikiforos Vrettakos, Andreas Emberikos,
   Nikos Engonopoulos, Miltos Sahtouris,
   Odysseus Elytis, Nikos Gatsos,
   Andonis Decavallas, Nanos Valaoritis]   78   145
A Note on the Prosody   78   152
On the Road to Knossos   89   190
Post-War Greek Poets
   [Manolis Anagnostakis, Takis
   Sinopoulos, Miltos Sahtouris,
   Aris Alexandhrou, Tasos Livadhitis,
   Dhimitris Dhoukaris, Aristotle
   Nikolaidis, T. D. Frangopoulos,
   Andonis Decavalles, Takis Varvitsiotis,
   Aris Dhikteos, Nikos Karouzos,
   Yannis Papadhopoulos, D. P.
   Papadhitsas, Eleni Vakalo,
   Athos Dhimoulas]   139   99

REVIEWS
Collected Poems: 1917-1939,
   by Edward Davison   62   338
New Poems: 1943
   (Ed. by Oscar Williams)   64   86
Europa and the Bull, by W. R. Rodgers   82   358
Collected Poems, 1921-1951,
   by Edwin Muir   84   27

BOOKS REVIEWED
Modern Poetry: American and British
   (Ed. with John Malcolm Brinnin)   79   289
The Odyssey: A Modern Sequel,
   by Nikos Kazantzakis (Tr.)   95   175
The Odyssey: A Modern Sequel,
   by Nikos Kazantzakis (Tr.)   95   179

ARTICLES ABOUT
Correspondence
   from Norman Rosten   65   346

FRIEDLAENDER, V. H.
POEMS
Bus-Ride in a Fog   21   74
New Year   25   197

FRIEDMAN, FLORENCE LOUIE
BOOKS REVIEWED
Flowers of Evil,
   by Charles Baudelaire (Tr.)   111   124

FRIEDMAN, JEFF
POEMS
The Record-Breaking Heat Wave   136   335
The Mannikin

FRIEDMAN, MARTIN B.
BOOKS REVIEWED
The Poet and the Machine,
   by Paul Ginestier (Tr.)   101   292

FRIEDMAN, SUSAN STANFORD
ARTICLES ABOUT
The Forging of H. D.,
   by Gloria G. Fromm   153   160

FRIEDMANN, ELIZABETH
BOOKS REVIEWED
First Awakenings:
   The Early Poems of Laura Riding
   (Ed. with Alan J. Clark
   and Robert Nye)   164   39

FRIEDRICH, RALPH
POEMS
Under the Stars   49   11
Forethought
A Spell Is Broken
Ruined City

BOOKS REVIEWED
Boy at Dusk and Other Poems   60   344

FRIEND, ROBERT
POEMS
City Nightfall   50   191
Home
The Wish
Bridges
History
The Journey   51   22
The Impossible Sea   55   136
Exile
The Myth
The Somnambulist
The Underworld of Love   67   255
Spring Suicides
The Irrational Source   72   196

TRANSLATIONS
Poems by Nathan Alterman   92   236
Poem by Yehuda Amihai   92   254
Poems by Leah Goldberg   124   324

BOOKS REVIEWED
Shadow on the Sun   58   340

ARTICLES ABOUT
[Note on translation]   93   56

FRIESEKE, FRANCES
POEMS
Dew Shining   48   204
Prisoner
Realization

FRIMAN, ALICE
POEMS
  Angel Jewell   153   200
  Stars   155   203
  Birthday in Autumn   157   26
  Invitation to a Minor Poet   159   31

FRISARDI, ANDREW
REVIEWS
  Short Reviews   170   101
    Elephant Rocks, by Kay Ryan
    The Fire Fetched Down,
      by George Bradley
    The Chain, by Tom Sleigh
    Cities of Memory, by Ellen Hinsey
    Strange Relation, by Daniel Hall

FRITZ, MARTHA
POEMS
  January Thaw   119   189
  Between You and Sleep
  The Visitor

FRODING, GUSTAF
BOOKS REVIEWED
  Selected Poems
    (Tr. by Charles Wharton Stork)   12   52

FRODSHAM, J. D.
BOOKS REVIEWED
  An Anthology of Chinese Verse:
    Han, Wei, Chin, and the Northern
    Southern Dynasties
    (Tr. with Ch'eng Hsi)   112   247
  The Murmuring Stream:
    The Life and Works of Hsieh Ling-Yun 114 196

FROMM, GLORIA G.
ARTICLES
  The Forging of H. D.
    [Norman Holmes Pearson,
    Susan Stanford Friedman, Barbara Guest,
    D. H. Lawrence, Janice Robinson,
    Bryher, Albert Gelpi, Sigmund Freud,
    Lionel Durand]   153   160

FROMM, HAROLD
REVIEWS
  A History of Modern Poetry, Volume II:
    Modernism and After,
    by David Perkins
    [James Tuttleton, Charles Olson,
    W. B. Yeats, William Wordsworth,
    T. S. Eliot]   151   296
  The Psycho-Political Muse:
    American Poetry Since the Fifties,
    by Paul Breslin
    [Allen Ginsberg, Robert Lowell,
    Sylvia Plath, John Ashbery]   152   229

FROST, ELISABETH
POEMS
  3 Grace Court West   168   262

FROST, ELIZABETH HOLLISTER
POEMS
  The Moor   34   259
  The House
  Saturday   54   138
  Old Age of Youth
  Ultimate Snow

BOOKS REVIEWED
  The Lost Lyrist   34   110
  Hovering Shadow   36   112

FROST, EVELYN GRAHAM
POEMS
  Memory   40   190

FROST, FRANCES (M.)
POEMS
  Unbound   31   195
  Disappearances   36   250
    Confession To Be Read After Death
    Earthward
  Fusion   42   249
  Last Generation   44   74
  Pursuit   48   249
  Legend of Sail Rock
  Great Chebeague
  Sunday Afternoon   74   209

BOOKS REVIEWED
  Blue Harvest   39   161
  These Acres   41   163
  Woman of This Earth   45   50
  Road to America   51   223
  Mid-Century   70   98

FROST, RICHARD
POEMS
  Villanelle of the Circus Villains   98   216
  Hunting in Deep Creek
  Marriage   140   139
  The Standing Broad Jump

FROST, ROBERT
POEMS
  The Code—Heroics   3   167
  Snow   9   57
  The Witch of Coös   19   175
  The Flower-Boat   22   242
  At Woodward's Gardens   48   1
  Ten Mills
    Precaution
    The Span of Life
  Pertinax

Assertive
Tendencies Cancel
Untried
Money
Ring Around
Not All There
In Dives' Dive
The Prophets Really Prophesy as Mystics/
  The Commentators Merely by Statistics   101   41

ARTICLES
Correspondence   92   398
Remarks on the Occasion
  of the Tagore Centenary
  [Mrs. William Vaughn Moody]   99   106

BOOKS REVIEWED
A Boy's Will   2   72
North of Boston   5   127
Mountain Interval   9   202
New Hampshire   23   328
West-Running Brook   33   333
Selected Poems
A Further Range   49   45
Collected Poems of...: 1939   54   218
A Witness Tree   60   146
A Masque of Reason   66   156
Steeple Bush   71   145
A Masque of Mercy   72   38
In the Clearing   101   200
The Letters of Robert Frost
  to Louis Untermeyer
  (Ed. by Louis Untermeyer)   104   253
Selected Letters of...
  (Ed. by Lawrance Thompson)   107   192
Collected Poems, Prose & Plays
  (Ed. by Richard Poirier
  and Mark Richardson)   168   232

ARTICLES ABOUT
Our Contemporaries,
  by Alice Corbin Henderson   6   99
Robert Frost's Quality,
  by Alice Corbin Henderson   8   327
Rev. of *An Annual of New Poetry, 1917*   11   333
Discovered in Paris,
  by Harriet Monroe   16   148
Robert Frost, by Harriet Monroe   25   146
Rev. of *Robert Frost*,
  by Gorham B. Munson   31   292
Rev. of *Robert Frost* [Recording]   58   105
Rev. of *New Poems: 1943*
  (Ed. by Oscar Williams)   64   86
Rev. of *A History of American Poetry,*
  1900-1940,
  by Horace Gregory
  and Marya Zaturenska   69   210

From the Introduction to
  The Oxford Book of American Verse,
  by F. O. Matthiessen   77   31
Why We're Still Here, by Henry Rago   87   360
[Note]   90   398
[Note]   97   327
[Note]   98   127
Rev. of *Robert Frost, the Trial by Existence*,
  by Elizabeth Shepley Sergeant   100   50
[Note on misprint]   101   227
Rev. of *Robert Frost and John Bartlett:*
  The Record of a Friendship,
  by Margaret Bartlett Anderson;
  Robert Frost: Farm-Poultryman
  (Ed. by Edward Connery Lathem
  and Lawrance Thompson);
  The Poetry of Robert Frost:
  Constellations of Intention,
  by Reuben A. Brower;
  The Major Themes of Robert Frost,
  by Radcliffe Squires   104   253
Rev. of *Robert Frost: The Early Years*,
  by Lawrance Thompson   110   425
Rev. of *New and Collected Poems*,
  by Archibald MacLeish,
  and *Available Light*, by Philip Booth   130   102
Rev. of *Collected Poems, 1936-1976*,
  by Robert Francis   131   106
Rev. of *Robert Frost*,
  by Richard Poirier   132   226
Review by Samuel Hynes   135   342
Review by William H. Pritchard   136   295
MacLeish Revisited,
  by William Pritchard   141   291
Rev. of *The Selected Poetry*
  of Hayden Carruth
  (Ed. by Galway Kinnell)   149   94

FROST, WILLIAM
BOOKS REVIEWED
Selected Works
  of John Dryden (Ed.)   86   118

FRUMKIN, GENE
POEMS
Lament for an Old Pressman   95   164
This Great Burden of Loving   96   283
The Dragon
We Come Into the Gospel Country
The Builder of Clouds   99   358
A Man Preserved in Stone   104   18
King of Daydreams
Winter Passage   111   306
Placitas Night

BOOKS REVIEWED
The Hawk and the Lizard   103   316
The Rainbow-Walker   117   261

FRY, CHRISTOPHER
ARTICLES ABOUT
  Christopher Fry
    and the Redemption of Joy,
    by Monroe K. Spears   78   28
  London Letter: The Publishing Season,
    by John McCormick   85   176
  Christopher Fry: An Appreciation,
    by Thomas M. Disch   166 280

FRY, DONALD K.
BOOKS REVIEWED
  The Beowulf Poet:
    A Collection of Critical Essays (Ed.)   115 274

FRY, ROGER
BOOKS REVIEWED
  Poems,
    by Stéphane Mallarmé (Tr.)
    (With commentaries
    by Charles Mauron)   49 350

FRYE, NORTHROP
REVIEWS
  Blake on Trial Again   69 223
    William Blake:
      The Politics of Vision,
      by Mark Schorer
    The Portable Blake
      (Ed. by Alfred Kazin)
    Slick But Not Streamlined,
      by John Betjeman
      (Ed. by W. H. Auden)   71 162
    The Georgics of Virgil
      (Tr. by Cecil Day Lewis)   71 337
    La Wallonie, 1886-1892:
      The Symbolist Movement in Belgium,
      by Andrew Jackson Mathews 72 231
    Slick But Not Streamlined,
      by John Betjeman
      (Ed. by W. H. Auden)   121   48

BOOKS REVIEWED
  Fearful Symmetry:
    A Study of William Blake   71 101
  Anatomy of Criticism: Four Essays 91 320
  Fables of Identity:
    Studies in Poetic Mythology   104 369

ARTICLES ABOUT
  Review by James Reaney   94 186
  Rev. of *The Collected Poems*
    of E. J. Pratt   95 248

FRYER, CECILY
POEMS
  In a Gale   12   75
  Conscience

FUCHS, RUDOLPH
BOOKS REVIEWED
  Gedichte aus Reigate   58 272

FUESS, CLAUDE M.
BOOKS REVIEWED
  The Little Book of Society Verse
    (Ed. with Harold C. Stearns) 22 168

FUJITA, JUN
POEMS
  Tanka   15   68
    ("A frail hepatica...")
    ("The air is still...")
    ("The storm has passed...")
    ("A sloping sand plain...")
    ("The brook has gone...")
    ("On a country road...")
    ("Across the frozen marsh...")
    ("Graves are frozen...")
  Tanka   18 128
    To Elizabeth
    Spring
    May Moon
    Storm
    November
    A Leaf
    December Moon
    Echo
  Japanese Brush-Strokes   22 126
    Two Leaves
    Oblivion
    Mist
  Projections   31 101
    Morning Woods
    Storm
    Dried Whispers
    Snow

REVIEWS
  Waley on the "Uta"   16 283
    Japanese Poetry: The "Uta,"
      by Arthur Waley
    Moons of Nippon,
      by Edna Worthley Underwood
    Seen and Unseen and *Selected Poems,*
      by Yone Noguchi   20 162

BOOKS REVIEWED
  Tanka: Poems in Exile   26   44

ARTICLES ABOUT
  Correspondence
    from Arthur Waley   17 103

FULLER, ETHEL ROMIG
POEMS
  Dust of Silver   31 310
    Knitting Factory

Dust Motes
Poverty Buys
Labyrinth
Winter Orchard
Of a Cross
Miracles Old and New   33   132
Madonna Mary
Trilliums
The Airmail Arrives
Doing Dishes
Thrushes in the Dawn
Sea   34   255
Winter Rhymes   35   128
Hills to Christmas
On Frosty Nights
First Snow
Winter Sunset
Remembering Rocks   43   69

BOOKS REVIEWED
White Peaks and Green   37   55

FULLER, HENRY B. ["H. B. F."]
POEMS
Postponement   7   240
Toward Childhood   9   189

ARTICLES
The Brooke Letters   8   155
The American Image
   [Jean Catel]   15   327

REVIEWS
Some Love Songs of Petrarch
   (Tr. by William Dudley Foulke)   7   207
—And Other Poets,
   by Louis Untermeyer   8   321
The Divine Comedy, by Dante
   (Tr. by Henry Johnson)   9   104
Special Editions and Translations   9   156
   The Sonnets of Shakespeare,
      Variorum Edition
      (Ed. by Raymond M. Alden)
   The Song of Roland
      (Tr. by Leonard Bacon)
Two Essayists   16   288
   A New Study of English Poetry,
      by Henry Newbolt
   Formative Types in English Poetry,
      by George Herbert Palmer
Coleridge's Biographia Literaria
   (With Wordsworth's Preface
   and Essays on Poetry)
   (Ed. by George Sampson)   18   167
The Divine Comedy of Dante Alighieri
   (Tr. by Melville Best Anderson)   20   165
The Road to Xanadu,
   by John Livingston Lowes   30   283
Swinburne, by Samuel C. Chew   34   294

BOOKS REVIEWED
   Lines Long and Short   10   155

ARTICLES ABOUT
Henry B. Fuller,
   by Harriet Monroe   35   34

FULLER, JOHN
POEMS
Witch   93   16
Sleeping
In a Railway Compartment
Jealous
White Queen
Peasant Woman: Rhodes   99   153
Shy
The Self-Conscious Lover
The Curable Romantic   146   187
Aubade ("Woken by the pale...")
Bud

BOOKS REVIEWED
Fairground Music   102   393
The Tree that Walked   113   262
A Reader's Guide to W. H. Auden   118   349
Poems and Epistles   129   340

ARTICLES ABOUT
A Letter from Britain [II],
   by William Logan   157   290

FULLER, R. B.
POEMS
Poem ("To disregard the pimple...")   54   82

FULLER, REX GEORGE
POEMS
Portrait of an Old Lady   24   131

FULLER, ROY
POEMS
Sonnet ("The crumbled rock...")   55   73
Soliloquy in an Air-Raid   57   352
The Growth of Crime   59   59
The Bay   59   317
The Festival   60   204
The Wood   61   479
Spring 1943   62   266
In Hospital   63   259
On Seeing the Leni Riefenstahl Film
   of the 1936 Olympic Games   71   239
The Middle Years   85   16

BOOKS REVIEWED
Poems   56   274
The Middle of a War   63   50
A Lost Season   67   218
Brutus's Orchard   92   378

Collected Poems   102   330
Buff   108   399
New Poems   114   397

ARTICLES ABOUT
A Letter from Britain [II],
   by William Logan   157   290

FULTON, ALICE
POEMS
What I Like   141   224
Doing the Evolution Shuffle   142   192
Plumbline
My Second Marriage
   to My First Husband   143   205
Babies
Aviation
Traveling Light
Fierce Girl Playing Hopscotch   145   340
Nugget and Dust
The Body Opulent   147   319
Another Troy
Trouble in Mind   151   53
Self-Storage   153   79
A Union House

REVIEWS
The State of the Art   150   162
   Archaic Figure,
      by Amy Clampitt
   The Clasp and Other Poems,
      by Michael Collier
   Chinese Architecture,
      by Aleda Shirley
   Forms of Conversion,
      by Allison Funk
   The Enchanted Room,
      by Maurya Simon
   Waving at Trains,
      by John Dickson
Main Things   151   360
   The Selected Poems:
      Expanded Edition and Sumerian Vistas,
      by A. R. Ammons
   The Tattooed Lady in the Garden,
      by Pattiann Rogers
   The Beautiful Noon
      of No Shadow,
      by Susan Ludvigson
   Second Language,
      by Lisel Mueller
   At the Edge of the Orchard Country,
      by Robert Morgan
   Mermaids in the Basement:
      Poems for Women and
      The Nearness of You,
      by Carolyn Kizer
   [Fanny Osbourne Stevenson]

On the Plains of Fancy   159   32
   The Dogwood Tree,
      by Jennifer Atkinson
   No Private Life, by Michelle Boisseau
   Bright Moves, by J. Allyn Rosser
   Sea Room, by Maria Flook
   The Six-Cornered Snowflake
      and Other Poems;
         The Six-Cornered Snowflake;
      and Zany in Denim,
         by John Frederick Nims
   [René Girard]

BOOKS REVIEWED
Dance Script with Electric Ballerina   145   99
Palladium   149   31
Powers of Congress   158   158
Sensual Math   168   281

FULTON, ROBIN
POEMS
Frontiers   126   319
The Waiting-Room

FUNAROFF, S(OL)
POEMS
Factory Night   51   145
I Dreamed I Was Master   51   302
Strange World   52   138
To Federico García Lorca   52   185

REVIEWS
The Day's Work,
   by Oscar Brynes   52   230

BOOKS REVIEWED
We Gather Strength
   (With Herman Spector, Joseph Kalar,
   and Edwin Rolfe)   44   50
The Spider and the Clock   53   50
Exile from a Future Time,
   Posthumous Poems   66   106

FUNK, ALLISON
POEMS
The Ghost of Elinor Wylie   147   263
Forms of Conversion
Elegy ("To endure this place...")
This Scar   152   134
Turning Forty   161   33
After Dark   162   195
Faultline
Blondin
Sea Change   166   215

BOOKS REVIEWED
Forms of Conversion   150   162

FUNKHOUSER, ERICA
POEMS
    Earth Day in Provincetown   139   200
    Cryogenics   145   139
    Apple Tree   154   69
    Tae Kwon Do
    Grief
    Identification   155   403
    Valentine   157   251

BOOKS REVIEWED
    Natural Affinities   145   36

FUREY, BILL
BOOKS REVIEWED
    Night Letters   144   297

FURLONG, WALTRINA
POEMS
    The Sling of Vision   93   76

FUSSELL, EDWIN
POEMS
    Black Cross   86   91

BOOKS REVIEWED
    Edwin Arlington Robinson   92   121
    Your Name Is You   130   102

FUSSELL, PAUL, JR.
BOOKS REVIEWED
    Theory of Prosody
      in Eighteenth-Century England   84   363
    Poetic Meter and Poetic Form   110   119

G

"G. D." or "G. H. D."
[See DILLON, GEORGE]

"G. M."
[See MARGULIES, GEORGE]

GABIS, RITA
POEMS
Antique Doll   170   134

GAILLARD, ANDRÉ
ARTICLES ABOUT
Marseille Letter, by Jean Rivier   60   269

GAINES, RUTH
POEMS
I Heard a Flute   2   166
Paris, 1917   13   11

GALAHAD, JOSEPH ANDREW
POEMS
Sic Passim   19   20
Recalled
A Mood   20   123

GALASSI, JONATHAN
POEMS
Change of Weather   118   13
King Caesar's Windows   118   260
Names   129   154

TRANSLATIONS
Poems by Eugenio Montale   155   1
Poems by Annalisa Cima   155   109
Poems by Valerio Magrelli   155   159

REVIEWS
Scattered Craft   118   290
  Scattered Light,
    by Christopher Brookhouse
  From Under the Hill of Night: Poems,
    by Paul Petrie
  Elegies for the Hot Season,
    by Sandra McPherson
  The Zigzag Walk: Poems, 1963-1968,
    by John Logan

An Open Idiom   121   343
  The Queen's Triangle: A Romance,
    by Stephen Berg
  Bandaging Bread and Other Poems,
    by Glover Davis
  Digging for Indians,
    by Gary Gildner
  The Inhabitant: Poems,
    by Lewis Turco
  Terms and Renewals,
    by Peter Wild
  Tribunals: Passages 31-35,
    by Robert Duncan
Dealing with Tradition   123   113
  Preaching to the Converted,
    by Peter Porter
  A Postcard from Don Giovanni,
    by Grey Gowrie
  Lives, by Derek Mahon
  Written on Water,
    by Charles Tomlinson
  Desert of the Lions,
    by Michael Schmidt
  Poems 1970-1972,
    by Robert Graves
  Wintering Out,
    by Seamus Heaney
  Happy Enough: Poems 1935-1972,
    by George Johnston
  Golden State,
    by Frank Bidart
Determined Forms   129   164
  The Western Approaches:
    Poems 1973-75,
    by Howard Nemerov
  Collected Poems,
    by Edwin Denby
  Collected Poems,
    by George Oppen
  I Remember,
    by Joe Brainard

GALE, VI
POEMS
The Spit   87   213
The Old Fishstation

BOOKS REVIEWED
   Several Houses   95   309
   Love Always   109   118

GALL, SALLY M.
BOOKS REVIEWED
   Maximum Security Ward and Other Poems,
      by Ramon Guthrie (Ed.)   145   348

GALLAGHER, KATHERINE
POEMS
   The Ash Tree   169   25

ARTICLES ABOUT
   Towards a Contemporary
     Australian Poetics,
     by John Kinsella   169   94

GALLAGHER, TESS
POEMS
   Rijl   150   343
   Dim House, Bright Face
   Small Garden Near a Field
   If Poetry Were Not a Morality   151   54
   Redwing

BOOKS REVIEWED
   Under Stars   136   170
   Willingly   146   293
   Amplitude:
     New and Selected Poems   155   229

GALLAGHER, WILLIAM D.
ARTICLES ABOUT
   Notes on Mid-Western Oblivion,
     by Pat Morrissette   34   346

GALLATIN, DAVID
BOOKS REVIEWED
   Machines & Illusions   96   179

GALLER, DAVID
POEMS
   Outdoors One Makes
     Most Strange, My Lady   87   199
   The Great Vox: A Dumb Show
   The Graces of Autumn
   Snow Scene   90   85
   For Robert Graves
   The Beetle   92   34
   The Carousel
   Whistle Stop
   Ascendance
   Joseph
   Jericho
   Fields of Flowers   94   23
   In the Maze
   The Witness   96   14

A Trial of Masters
   from the Travelling Fair
To My Father
The Heap of Craft
The Dybbuk
A Chronicle of the Flyer's Death   98   96
The Glacier   101   180
Emblem: The Spring at Rest
Nocturne: A City Park
The Badlands
The Hand   103   236
The Root
Self-Hatred
The Bow
Trust   105   361
The Habit
The Hall
The Partridge   108   162
The Hundred Years
To My Lust
Orpheus   113   247
Marsyas   116   92
Alba: The Furies   118   311
Questions   120   271
For Eurydice: A Song of Ascent   123   326
Narcissus: To Himself
Doing   127   265
To A. J., On the Death of Her Bird   128   277
To My Wife   140   144

ARTICLES
   Edwin Muir   94   330

REVIEWS
   Three Poets   96   185
     Saint Judas, by James Wright
     Colonel Johnson's Ride and Other Poems,
       by Robert Huff
     Apples from Shinar,
       by Hyam Plutzik
   Seven Poets   99   379
     Initial A,
       by David Schubert
       (Ed. by Theodore Weiss
       and Judith E. Kranes)
     Skeleton of Light,
       by Thomas Vance
     The Fountains of Regardlessness,
       by Frederick Bock
     Poets of Today VIII: The Mother
       of the Amazons and Other Poems,
       by Albert Herzing;
       Fires of Home: Poems,
       by John M. Ridland;
       Suits for the Dead: Poems,
       by David R. Slavitt
     The Royal Tiger's Face,
       by Marvin Solomon

Versions from Fyodor Tyutchev: 1803-1873
  (Tr. by Charles Tomlinson)   101 418
The Use of Anthologies   103 261
  Tom Tiddler's Ground
    (Ed. by Walter de la Mare)
  The Crystal Cabinet
    (Ed. by Horace Gregory
    and Marya Zaturenska)
  Poet's Choice
    (Ed. by Paul Engle
    and Joseph Langland)
  Modern American Poetry
    and *Modern British Poetry*
    (Ed. by Louis Untermeyer)
  The Mentor Book
    of Major American Poets
    (Ed. by Oscar Williams
    and Edwin Honig)
  Modern German Poetry: 1910-1960
    (Ed. by Michael Hamburger
    and Christopher Middleton)
  Modern Brazilian Poetry
    (Ed. by John Nist)
    [João Cabral de Melo Neto]
  Dear Men and Women: New Poems,
    by John Hall Wheelock   110 123
Three Recent Volumes   110 267
  Rhymes and More Rhymes of a PFC,
    by Lincoln Kirstein
  Selected Poems, by Robert Hayden
  The City and the Island,
    by Peter Davison

BOOKS REVIEWED
  Walls and Distances   98 118
  Leopards in the Temple, Poems   113 35

GALLUP, DICK
POEMS
  The Door to the Future   111 316
  After Alcman
  Where I Hang My Hat
  Death and the Maiden

BOOKS REVIEWED
  Where I Hang My Hat   119 224

GALLUP, DONALD
BOOKS REVIEWED
  A Bibliography of Ezra Pound   106 361

GALLUP, GEORGE H.
BOOKS REVIEWED
  *Best Creative Work in American
  High Schools 1928-9* (Ed.)   38 282

GALPIN, ALFRED
BOOKS REVIEWED
  De Sanctis on Dante
    (Tr. and ed. with Joseph Rossi)   96 323

GALSWORTHY, JOHN
BOOKS REVIEWED
  Verses New and Old   30 168
  The Collected Poems of...   46 168

GALT, JOHN
BOOKS REVIEWED
  The Common Ground   106 369

GALVIN, BRENDAN
POEMS
  Tautog   133 41
  Stethoscope
  Black Bear in October   143 35
  Workout
  Whirl Is King
  Fall Squashes   145 65
  Fog Township   148 63
  Pole Beans
  Mayflies
  Kale Soup   153 84
  War in the Garden
  My Grandmother Steals Her Last Trout   154 85
  Carrowkeel   154 329
  Hearing Irish Spoken
  Backtalk
  For a Daughter Gone Away   156 329

BOOKS REVIEWED
  No Time for Good Reasons   130 167
  Wampanoag Traveler   156 345
  Saints in Their Ox-Hide Boat   161 223

GALVIN, MARTIN
POEMS
  Universal Donor   164 219
  Introductions   168 98

GALVIN, PATRICK
BOOKS REVIEWED
  Heart of Grace   92 309

GAMBLE, ISABEL
REVIEWS
  The Permanence of Yeats
    (Ed. by James Hall
    and Martin Steinmann)   76 227
  New Chapbooks   77 114
    The Heart Must Be Half Eagle,
      by Wendell B. Anderson
    Abstract Spring,
      by Robert Lawrence Beum
    The Ballad of Mad Jenny,
      by James Broughton
    A Poet's Breath, by Judson Crews
    Doctor Drink, by J. V. Cunningham
    Medieval Scenes, by Robert Duncan
    An Herb Basket, by Richard Eberhart

Symbol and Reality,
  by Richard Wirtz Emerson
Five Poets, 1949
  (Golden Goose Chap Book 5)
  [Harold G. Miller]
Mr. P. Squiggle's Reward,
  by Dennis McCalib
Industrial Sonnets,
  by Clarence Alva Powell
Two Conceits,
  by Allen Tate
My Country Dreams,
  by Wightman Williams
Three Poems,
  by Yvor Winters

GAMES, JULIA GARCIA
  [See GARCIA GAMES, JULIA]

GAMMANS, HAROLD W.
  BOOKS REVIEWED
  Common Men and Women   12   282

GANTZ, JEFFREY
  POEMS
  Monochrome   129   157
  De Val Der Opstandige Engelen
  The Dark Wood
  Our Incorruptible Snow

GARCIA GAMES, JULIA
  POEMS
  Ode to England
    (Tr. by Lloyd Mallan)   62   73

GARCÍA LORCA, FEDERICO
  POEMS
  Rider's Song   50   8
  Little Ballad of Three Rivers
    (Tr. by Rolfe Humphries)
  Ode to Walt Whitman
    (Tr. by Ben Belitt)   85   187
  Gacela of the Remembrance of Love
    (Tr. by James Wright)   96   151
  Somnambulist Ballad
    (Tr. by W. D. Snodgrass)   157   271

  BOOKS REVIEWED
  *Lament for the Death
  of a Bullfighter and Other Poems*
    (Tr. by A. L. Lloyd)   51   167
  Poems of...
    (Tr. by Stephen Spender
    and J. L. Gili)   56   343
  *The Poet in New York
  and Other Poems*
    (Tr. by Rolfe Humphries)
  Blood Wedding (Bodas de Sangre)
    (Tr. by Gilbert Neiman)

Selected Poems of...
  (Tr. by Stephen Spender
  and J. L. Gili)   63   96
Three Tragedies
  (Tr. by Richard O'Connell
  and James Graham-Luján)   75   114
The Gypsy Ballads of García Lorca
  (Tr. by Rolfe Humphries)   87   303
The Selected Poems of...
  (Ed. by Francisco García Lorca
  and Donald M. Allen)
The Poet in New York
  (Tr. by Ben Belitt)

ARTICLES ABOUT
Dimensions of Imagery and Action
  in the Work of García Lorca,
  by Edwin Honig   63   32
Rev. of *García Lorca*, by Edwin Honig   64   225
Rev. of *New Directions 1944*
  (Ed. by James Laughlin)   66   161
Rev. of *Contemporary Spanish Poetry*
  by Eleanor L. Turnbull.
  (With Pedro Salinas)   67   265
Rev. of *The Creative Experiment,*
  by C. M. Bowra   75   217
Rev. of *Lorca, the Poet and His People,*
  by Arturo Barea
  (Tr. by Ilsa Barea)   76   46
Verse Drama on the Paris Stage,
  by Ruby Haykin   82   294
Rev. of *After Lorca*, by Jack Spicer   93   182
Rev. of *Rafael Alberti, Selected Poems*
  (Ed. and tr. by Ben Belitt)   111   46

GARCÍA LORCA, FRANCISCO
  BOOKS REVIEWED
  The Selected Poems of García Lorca
    (Ed. with Donald M. Allen)   87   303

GARCIA VILLA, JOSÉ
  POEMS
  Quiet Songs   40   136
    Communion
    Songs to be Whispered
    Invisible
  Parliament of Giraffes   58   136
  ("her day-rose is much sweet...")
  ("I can no more hear Love's...")
  ("Bring the pigeons watermelons...")   60   308
  ("In Picasso you see Blue...")
  ("Because thy smile is primavera...")
  Theseus   81   82

  BOOKS REVIEWED
  Have Come, Am Here   61   632
  Volume Two   75   290
  Selected Poems and New   93   329

GARDELS, SUSAN
POEMS
Warblers at Eve   140   199
Plains Song

GARDINER, WREY
BOOKS REVIEWED
The Gates of Silence   66   53
Three Poems
(With Fred Marnau
and Nicholas Moore)

GARDNER, HELEN
BOOKS REVIEWED
The Art of T. S. Eliot   77   41

GARDNER, ISABELLA
POEMS
The Panic Vine   79   70
Cadenza
The Last Trump
Cowardice
The Milkman   80   7
This Neighborhood
Fall in Massachusetts
Three Rings or Five Rings
The Grocery Bouquet
It Rained Last Night   81   37
Southwest of True North   84   257
The Widow's Yard   90   368
"...And Thou No Breath at All?"   99   100
A Word from the Piazza del Limbo   105   225
The Accomplices   109   100
The Telephone   130   208

REVIEWS
Reservations, by Valentin Iremonger   82   291

BOOKS REVIEWED
The Looking Glass   101   209
The Looking Glass   101   215
West of Childhood: Poems 1950-1965   109   44

ARTICLES ABOUT
Comment by Wallace Fowlie   151   208

GARDNER, W. H.
BOOKS REVIEWED
Poems of Gerard Manley Hopkins (Ed.)   74   292
Gerard Manley Hopkins

GARIOCH, ROBERT
ARTICLES ABOUT
London Letter:
The Publishing Season,
by John McCormick   85   176
Some Poets of the Scottish Renaissance,
by Tom Scott   88   43

GARLAND, HAMLIN
POEMS
Magic   3   37
A Gray Sunset
To a Captive Crane
The Mountains Are a Lonely Folk

GARLAND, MARIE TUDOR
POEMS
The Desert   25   14

GARLAND, MAX
POEMS
Cappuccino at the Marconi Hotel in Venice 156 210
The Postal Confessions
Fedoras
Revisiting the Sistine Chapel   159   92
County Night   163   21
Mirror   163   199

GARNETT, DAVID
BOOKS REVIEWED
The Golden Echo   86   118

GARNETT, EDWARD
ARTICLES ABOUT
American Verse and English Critics,
by Alice Corbin Henderson   11   207

GARNETT, LOUISE AYRES
POEMS
The Return   6   175
Flowers of War   13   14
The Lilies of France
Know Thyself
Comrades
Arbor-Vitae   14   192
Songs of Silence   15   137
Little Chief
Song ("Do you never tire...")
Hound at Night
Reflections
Outcast
The Prodigal
Armenian Fields   15   288
Resurgam   19   117
Birth
Life
Death
Re-Birth
Open Casements   21   254
Soul at Play
The Teacup
Young Loveliness
The Bargain
Immortal Death
The Rover   24   130
Ballad of the Door-Stone   27   311

Design	39	307
They Who Listen	41	73
Candles Burning	47	128
The Feast of Light		
Christmas Night		
Exhalation		

ARTICLES
Correspondence:
For Armenian Orphans [Poem]	15	288

Correspondence:
Poet and Composer as Allies		
[Henry Hadley]	19	102

BOOKS REVIEWED
Eve Walks in Her Garden	30	110

GARNIER, CHARLES-MARIE
ARTICLES ABOUT
[Note]	53	164

GARREN, CHRISTINE
BOOKS REVIEWED
Afterworld	167	156

GARRETT, CHARLOTTE
POEMS
Drawn to That Time	101	253

GARRETT, GEORGE
BOOKS REVIEWED
Abraham's Knife and Other Poems	99	124
For a Bitter Season	112	337

GARRETT, JOHN
BOOKS REVIEWED
The Poet's Tongue		
(Ed. with W. H. Auden)	48	43

GARRIGUE, JEAN
POEMS
Movie	66	242
The Maimed Grasshopper Speaks Up	80	249
Gravepiece		
The Pony		
Poem ("Fate, heat...")		
Cantabile for Single Voice	81	117
A Figure for J. V. Meer	86	282
Declamation After the Three Bears		
Soliloquy in the Cemetery of Père Lachaise	88	243
Incantatory Poem	90	335
The Chess Dance		
This Swallow's Empire	93	133
One Third of a Dream		
Another Third		
Notation		
Dialog in the Dark Tower		
Her Spring Song	97	32

Song II ("And now my spring...")		
Three Poems	103	33
Of Provence and the River Var		
How I Loved		
On the Legend of a Dancer		
The Adam Tree	104	335
"When Shall We Set Sail for Happiness"		
— Baudelaire		
French Country Circus		
The Flux of Autumn	110	359
Consecration Piece		
Little Ballad		
Why the Heart Has Dreams		
Is Why the Mind Goes Mad	119	284
Lead in the Water	120	341

REVIEWS
In the American Grain,		
by William Carlos Williams	90	315
The Collected Poems of Dylan Thomas	94	111

BOOKS REVIEWED
Five Young American Poets:		
Third Series, 1944		
(With Eve Merriam, John Frederick		
Nims, Tennessee Williams,		
and Alejandro Carrión)	66	95
The Ego and the Centaur	73	118
The Monument Rose	83	176
A Water Walk by Villa D'Este	96	118
Country Without Maps	106	229
Antiworlds, by Andrei Voznesensky		
(Tr. with others)	110	40
New and Selected Poems	112	121
Studies for an Actress and Other Poems	127	44

GARRISON, THEODOSIA
POEMS
The Windows	12	253

BOOKS REVIEWED
The Dreamers and Other Poems	12	165

GARRISON, TROY
POEMS
"Remembrance of Things Past"	54	188
Girl on a Bicycle		
When I Was Very Old	56	244
Sunlight and Its Shadow		
Christmas		
Early Night		
Birth of My Anger		
Filipino Rain	66	26

REVIEWS
Pilgrims in Four Spheres	58	226
Proud Universe, by Sydney King Russell		
Core of Fire, by Kenneth Slade Alling		

Five Times the World,
  by John Russell McCarthy
New Journey, by Sydney Salt

GARRITY, DEVIN A.
BOOKS REVIEWED
  The Mentor Book of Irish Poetry (Ed.)   110   47

GARTH, CECIL
BOOKS REVIEWED
  The Song of the Five   6   257

GARVIN, KATHARINE
POEMS
  New York   50   22

GARVIN, MARGARET ROOT
BOOKS REVIEWED
  A Walled Garden and Other Poems   2   107

GARVIN, VIOLA GERARD
BOOKS REVIEWED
  Dedication   34   106

GASCOIGNE, GEORGE
ARTICLES ABOUT
  The 16th Century Lyric
  in England: Part I,
  by Yvor Winters   53   258

GASCOYNE, DAVID
BOOKS REVIEWED
  Thorns of Thunder, by Paul Eluard
  (Ed. by George Reavey)
  (Tr. with Samuel Beckett,
  Denis Devlin, Eugene Jolas,
  Man Ray, George Reavey,
  and Ruthven Todd)   48   347
  Night Thoughts   92   309
  Collected Poems   108   399

ARTICLES ABOUT
  London Letter, by D. S. Savage   51   277
  Surrealist Influence in Contemporary
  English and American Poetry,
  by H. R. Hays   54   202
  Rev. of *Defending Ancient Springs,*
  by Kathleen Raine   114   113

GASKELL, RONALD
POEMS
  Caesar   143   334

GASPARINI, LEN
BOOKS REVIEWED
  21 x 3
  (With Dorothy Farmiloe
  and Eugene McNamara)   115   353

GASTIGER, JOSEPH
POEMS
  Why I Need Glasses   146   156

GATSOS, NIKOS
POEMS
  Part II from *Amorgos*   78   177
  Death and the Knight (1513)
  (Tr. by Kimon Friar)
  Part I from *Amorgos*
  (Tr. by Edmund Keeley)   105   24

ARTICLES ABOUT
  Contemporary Greek Poetry,
  by Kimon Friar   78   145
  Letter from Athens,
  by Vassilis Vassilikos   105   60

GAUER, JIM
POEMS
  What the Fire Conceals from Itself   136   152
  The Visit
  Measuring the Distance   138   13
  This Feeds on the Light

GAUTIER, THÉOPHILE
POEMS
  Art (Tr. by James Michie)   142   153

ARTICLES ABOUT
  The Hard and the Soft in French Poetry,
  by Ezra Pound   11   264

GAVIN, JOHN H.
POEMS
  Creeds   20   80
  Immortality

GAVIN, MARY
POEMS
  The Curtains
  (With Cloyd Head)   16   1

ARTICLES
  Note on *The Curtains*
  (With Cloyd Head)   16   39

GEDDES, GARY
BOOKS REVIEWED
  The Inner Ear (Ed.)   144   297

GEDDES, VIRGIL
POEMS
  Implications   21   314
  Prelude for Darkness
  Excruciation
  Denouement
  Summons at Night   52   194

REVIEWS
Poems 1918-21, by Ezra Pound 21   95
Selected Poems and Ballads of Paul Fort
    (Tr. by John Strong Newberry) 21   161
The Pier-Glass, by Robert Graves 21   215
Selected Poems, by Laurence Binyon ... 21   337
Modern American Poets
    (Ed. by Conrad Aiken) 22   53
The Sardonic Arm,
    by Maxwell Bodenheim 23   279

BOOKS REVIEWED
Forty Poems 29   172

GEE, KENNETH
POEMS
("And there were other ways to live...") 56   194
South
A Child Could See 62   136
Yesterday 65   318
Apples in Orchards
Winter
Sonnet ("I live the summer...")
Homecoming 69   14
Say It Was Autumn
The Drowned 72   78

GEIGER, DON
POEMS
Speed of Sound 83   317
Aunt Mabel 88   24
Hart Crane II 96   87

REVIEWS
Passages from Finnegans Wake.
    A Free Adaptation for the Theatre,
    by Mary Manning 91   335
The Voice, the Poet, and the Poem ... 101   275
    R. P. Blackmur Reads His Works
    John Hollander Reads His Works
    Vernon Watkins Reads His Works
    Stephen Vincent Benét and Edwin Muir
    [Recording]
    John Peale Bishop
    and Maxwell Bodenheim
    [Recording]
    Robert Hillyer and John Hall Wheelock
    [Recording]
    I. A. Richards and Oscar Williams
    [Recording]
    John Ciardi and W. D. Snodgrass
    [Recording]

BOOKS REVIEWED
Unexpected Truce 89   373

GEIGER, TIMOTHY
POEMS
That Past 157   94

GELPI, ALBERT
ARTICLES ABOUT
The Forging of H. D.,
    by Gloria G. Fromm 153   160

GEMMELL, JEAN
POEMS
Three Dimensions 48   316
Love's Labor
City Late 86   80

GENEGA, PAUL
POEMS
Neighbors 158   22

GENSLER, KINERETH
POEMS
December 143   139
Birds
Writing Poetry 160   72

GEORGE, ANITA
POEMS
From Sappho 164   140
    Fragment 105(a)
    Fragment 105(c)

GEORGE, DIANA HUME
BOOKS REVIEWED
Selected Poems of Anne Sexton
    (Ed. with Diane Wood
    Middlebrook) 154   151

GEORGE, EMERY
POEMS
Moiré 127   259
Sunray
Solstice 130   249

GEORGE, FAYE
POEMS
Kore 157   212
Like Anne Shirley's House 160   213
No One Plays the Piano
Daphne 163   88
Only the Words 166   163
What She Looked Out Upon 168   268
The Sudden Tug of the Familiar 169   148
Plum 170   35
Night Piece
My Father's People 170   271

GEORGE, LEGARE
POEMS
("There is a flame, there is a bird...") 30   316
("Could she emerge in blood and bone...")
("My love came to me when...")
("A truth I touched but could not...")

GEORGE, STEFAN
BOOKS REVIEWED
Poems
    (Tr. by Carol North Valhope
    and Ernst Horwitz)   62   334

ARTICLES ABOUT
Stefan George 1868-1933,
    by Morton Dauwen Zabel   43   333

GEORGIA, POETRY SOCIETY OF
[See POETRY SOCIETY
OF GEORGIA]

GEPHART, PATTERSON
POEMS
Night Scoop   74   214

GERBER, DAN
POEMS
In the Still Night   170   208
Tarawa

GERLACH, L(EE) F.
POEMS
For Peter   102   305

REVIEWS
Pillars to Remembrance,
    by John Redwood Anderson   75   108

GEROULD, GORDON HALL
BOOKS REVIEWED
Poems of James Thomson, "B.V." (Ed.)   32   229

GERRY, W. H.
POEMS
Observations   49   304
    Dear Friends
    Le Coq d'Or
    On Listening to a Clavichord
    Apologia
    Cemetery   52   79

GERSTENBERG, ALICE
ARTICLES ABOUT
"Grotesques" and "Overtones,"
    by Harriet Monroe   7   193

GESSLER, CLIFFORD (FRANKLIN)
POEMS
The Villager   18   132
    Your Horses
    Nevertheless
    Concentric Circles
    Prayer
In Hawaii   24   10
    Petals of Darkness
    Slants

    Star-Dancers
Two Hawaiian Poems   25   12
    Beorhtgar to the Dusk-Woman
        of the Sea-Caves
    Dark Bamboos
Go Then   29   13
Stars Behind the Sky   31   15
Patterns in Shadow   35   186
    From Old Hawaii
    Steel Smile
    Of Sorrows
Island Love Song   46   197
The Voyage   47   246
    Haunted Island
    Lagoon Evening
    Three Things
Tehuantepec Journey   58   316
Mexico   60   258

BOOKS REVIEWED
Slants   26   106
Kanaka Moon   33   46
Tropic Earth   65   218

GETTY, NORRIS
POEMS
Details   61   488
Winter
Nina
Review

ARTICLES
Correspondence   61   698

GHALIB
POEMS
From The Ghazals
    (Tr. by Aijaz Ahmad
    and W. S. Merwin)   116   335

GHISELIN, BREWSTER
POEMS
Lost Life   37   308
Land Birds by the Sea   50   251
Day in the Fields   54   72
Rattlesnake
Headland
Bath of Aphrodite   57   10
Needle To Be Threaded   64   73
Venice at Noonday   65   245
Gull in the Great Basin Desert   66   9
Ego   77   9
Red   77   254
The Food of Birds
Formation of the Soul   80   135
End of Childhood
The Field
Of Freedom   81   38

A Calm   81   349
The Nets   84   346
In Search of Man   90   156
Ascent   101   193
This Is Vietnam   120   320
Dolphins   121   312
Credo
April-June, 1970
Let There Be Light   122   130
On the Cutting Block   124   153
Palimpsest of Air, Earth, Water, Fire
Bittern   132   249
Of Shapes and Shadows
A View of Little Scope
Explication of Evening
For the Eighth Decade
On the Loom of Light
Rose of the Winds:
    A Wreath for Allen   135   88
Poetry
Equinox   135   325
Apocalypse
Semblance on Semblance   137   284
Theft
Flame   141   321
The Well-Beloved
Green Wave of Cuyutlan
Honor and Honors   152   5

ARTICLES
    The Birth of a Poem
        [Bath of Aphrodite]   69   30
    Reading Sprung Rhythms
        [G. M. Hopkins, Harold Whitehall] 70   86
    The Architecture of Vision
        [Margaret Avison]   70   324

REVIEWS
    English Prosody and Modern Poetry,
        by Karl Shapiro
        [Gerard Manley Hopkins]   72   332
    Poems from the Iowa Poetry Workshop
        (Ed. by Paul Engle)
        [William Belvin, James B. Hall] 79   284
    The Poetry of Dylan Thomas,
        by Elder Olson   87   118

BOOKS REVIEWED
    Against the Circle   69   162
    The Creative Process (Ed.)   81   133
    The Nets   88   273
    Country of the Minotaur   119   342

GHISELIN, OLIVE
POEMS
    Mazatlan Jungle   140   12
    Sarcophagi

GHOSE, MANMOHAN
BOOKS REVIEWED
    Songs of Love and Death   29   49

GHOSE, ZULFIKAR
POEMS
    View from the Observatory   118   86

GIA DAO
POEMS
    Seeking the Hermit in Vain
        (Tr. by Louise S. Hammond)   20   252

GIBB, ROBERT
POEMS
    Blues for December 21st   145   127
    Coming into the Body
    Lines in a Slow Thaw
    The Race   156   339
    Saying Farewell to the Displays
        in the Carnegie Museum   164   317
    Wood Frog   168   256

GIBBON, MONK
BOOKS REVIEWED
    The Masterpiece and the Man:
        Yeats as I Knew Him   98   59

GIBBONS, REGINALD
BOOKS REVIEWED
    The Ruined Motel   141   170

GIBBS, BARBARA
POEMS
    In a Garden   73   211
    The Garden: Duration
    Dry Canyon, September
    Petition to This Room,
        To Allow Me To Work   90   142
    California, An Ode   91   152
    The Fountain   93   363
    The Meeting-Place of the Colors
    Lion
    Distance   109   158
    Sand-Pit

ARTICLES
Preview
    [Henry Rago]   71   341

REVIEWS
    Local Measures, by Josephine Miles   69   49
    North and South,
        by Elizabeth Bishop   69   228
    Presentations of Baudelaire   72   105
        Flowers of Evil,
            by Charles Baudelaire
            (Tr. by Geoffrey Wagner)

One Hundred Poems
    from Les Fleurs du Mal
    (Tr. by C. F. MacIntyre)
Baudelaire, Rimbaud, Verlaine
    (Ed. by Joseph M. Bernstein)
The Wound and the Weather,
    by Howard Moss   72   276
The Ego and the Centaur,
    by Jean Garrigue   73   118
Collected Poems, by Stephen Spender   86   237
Opus Posthumous—Poems, Plays, Prose,
    by Wallace Stevens
    (Ed. by Samuel French Morse)   92   52
Five Recent Volumes   94   189
    The Dark Houses, by Donald Hall
    One Squeaking Straw,
        by Richard Lyons
    The Two Freedoms, by Jon Silkin
    The Triumph of the Muse,
        by John Heath-Stubbs
    A Cage of Spines,
        by May Swenson
Merwin as Translator   101   353
    Poema del Cid,
        by Ramón Menendez Pidal
        (Tr. by W. S. Merwin)
    The Satires of Persius
        (Tr. by W. S. Merwin)
    Spanish Ballads
        (Tr. by W. S. Merwin)

BOOKS REVIEWED
    The Green Chapel   94   339
    Poems Written in Berlin   95   107

GIBBS, JOSIAH WILLARD
ARTICLES ABOUT
    Review by Linda Gregerson   167   287

GIBRAN, KAHLIL
BOOKS REVIEWED
    The Madman   14   277
    The Forerunner:
        His Parables and Poems   18   39
    The Prophet   23   216

GIBSON, MARGARET
POEMS
    The Inheritance   137   9

BOOKS REVIEWED
    Long Walks in the Afternoon   143   295
    The Vigil: A Poem in Four Voices   167   287

GIBSON, STEPHEN (M.)
POEMS
    The Peat-Cutters   132   326
    Woman with Chrysanthemums   159   217

GIBSON, W. W.
POEMS
    Play   63   147

GIBSON, WALKER
REVIEWS
    Summoned by Bells,
        by John Betjeman   97   390

GIBSON, WILFRID (WILSON)
POEMS
    The Tram   4   102
    On Hampstead Heath
    A Catch for Singing
    In the Orchestra   6   24
    Battle   6   239
        The Going
        The Joke
        Nightmare
        In the Ambulance
        Hit
        The Housewife
        Hill-Born
        The Fear
        Back
    Color   7   277
    Oblivion
    Tenants
    Gold
    The News   9   165

BOOKS REVIEWED
    Borderlands and Thoroughfares   5   134
    Battle and Other Poems   9   90
    Livelihood   10   108
    Neighbors   18   39
    The Golden Room, and Other Poems   34   297
    Islands   42   228
    The Alert   60   109

ARTICLES ABOUT
    Rev. of An Annual of New Poetry, 1917   11   333
    Poetry in the First World War,
        by David Daiches   56   323

GIBSON, WILL
POEMS
    Homecoming Piece   64   18
    Kaw River: Heron
    Colorado Poems   65   171
        Little Elegy
        A Letter from Colorado
        Gopher Skull
        Hymn on Thatchtop
        Mountain Song
        A Little Bestiary
        "Rock Said, Old Giants"
        Timberline

Three Tunes on a Ground Bass, and Coda   66   320
  A Street Song
  Bondsman
  Balaam
  Night Shift

GIBSON, WILLIAM
POEMS
  Moses Rock   70   300
  Pod   74   311
  Circe
  The Sorrow Bush
  Orchard   80   132
  Jack Sprat

BOOKS REVIEWED
  Winter Crook   72   278

GIDE, ANDRÉ
ARTICLES ABOUT
  Rev. of André Gide,
    by Klaus Mann   63   276
  A Commemoration:
    "Les Fleurs du Mal" 1857- 1957,
    by Wallace Fowlie   90   376
  Rev. of Duino Elegies,
    by Rainer Maria Rilke
    (Tr. by A. Poulin, Jr.)   131   345

GIDLEY, MICK
POEMS
  From Passion-Love:
    A Cycle of Poems   109   161

GIDLOW, ELSA
  [ELSIE A. GIDLOW]
POEMS
  At the Top of the World   15   24
  Never Any Fear
  Litany of Unrest   31   262
  Twentieth-Century Songs   35   316
    New York: Dance at Full Moon
    No Peace
    The Skyscraper
  In the Unknown Streets   42   80
  From a California Valley   46   192

ARTICLES
  Correspondence:
    Science and the Poets   42   236
  The Western Writers' Congress   49   293

REVIEWS
  This Is Our Own,
    by Marie de L. Welch   56   104

BOOKS REVIEWED
  On a Grey Thread   24   109

GIDLOW, ELSIE A.
  [See GIDLOW, ELSA]

GIFFORD, FANNIE STEARNS
POEMS
  Death in the Sun   17   312
  Apology

GIFFORD, HENRY
TRANSLATIONS
  Versions of César Vallejo
    (With Charles Tomlinson)   109   229

REVIEWS
  Poets of Russia   97   320
    The Poets of Russia 1890-1930,
      by Renato Poggioli
    The Bedbug and Selected Poetry,
      by Vladimir Mayakovsky
      (Ed. by Patricia Blake)
    [Alexander Blok, Boris Pasternak]
    The Penguin Book of Russian Verse
      (Ed. by Dimitri Obolensky)   100   124
    The Master of Pain   105   196
      Vallejo, by Xavier Abril
      Twenty Poems of César Vallejo
        (Tr. by John Knoepfle, James Wright,
        and Robert Bly)

BOOKS REVIEWED
  Versions from Fyodor Tyutchev
    (Tr. with Charles Tomlinson)   100   104
  Castilian Ilexes:
    Versions from Antonio Machado
    (Tr. with Charles Tomlinson)   105   198

GILBERT, ANNE KELLEDY
POEMS
  Snow   39   307

GILBERT, BERNARD
ARTICLES ABOUT
  Bernard Gilbert,
    by John Rodker   30   274

GILBERT, CELIA
POEMS
  Journey   136   73
  Persephone Ascending   147   150
  Crossing
  She's Painted a Blue Fish, a Red Apple   151   57
  Requiem   152   282
  The Death of St. Francis
  After-Image
  The Sabbath   153   63
  Primapara   156   14
  An Evening Meal   158   127
  Absence   160   193

ARTICLES
Correspondence
[Greg Kuzma, Martha Collins]   149   180

BOOKS REVIEWED
Queen of Darkness   134   107
Bonfire   145   36

GILBERT, ELIZABETH Y(OLANDE)
TRANSLATIONS
Poems by Ou Yang Hsiu
and Feng Yien Chi
(Tr. with Su Kai Ming)   50   136

GILBERT, GERRY
BOOKS REVIEWED
White Lunch   108   45

GILBERT, HELEN
POEMS
Sunday in November   27   82

GILBERT, JACK
POEMS
It Is Difficult To Speak of the Night   105   252
Bartleby at the Wall
What Is There To Say
Fidelity
The Sirens Again

BOOKS REVIEWED
Views of Jeopardy   103   192
The Great Fires: Poems 1982-1992   165   31

GILBERT, MORRIS
POEMS
Prussians Don't Believe in Dreams   10   14
To a French Aviator Fallen in Battle
Episodes   14   22
The Thing
Epitaph on a Madman's Grave
Why He Cornered the Market
Disillusion
From the Near East   18   140
Cape Helles
The Boulghar Dagh
Prediction   20   200

BOOKS REVIEWED
A Book of Verse   12   165

GILBERT, RUDOLPH
POEMS
The Christ Spirit   25   141
Russia

GILBERT, SANDRA M.
POEMS
The Suits   119   271

The Fog Dream   122   321
The Dream of Shooting Stars
Indiana: The Invitation   127   18
The Dream of the Intruder
For the Muses   128   288
Sculpture: Naiad/Fountain   131   67
Elegy ("The pages of history open...")
My Grandmother in Paris   135   204
Rissem   136   191
Thinking About an Old Friend
To a Man Who Advises Maturity
The Mothers at Seventy
Sitting   139   336
Eating Your Words
Blood Pressure
Simplicity   142   211
In the Forest of Symbols
History
In the Golden Sala   147   132
For Miss Lewis and Miss Newton
After Thanksgiving   149   204
Gold Tooth
Against Poetry   151   59
Seizure   152   285
Memory Fails
Rain/Insomnia/North Coast
About the Beginning   158   154
The Magi in Florida   159   97
In the Garage of the Retirement Complex
Indoor Camellia
Water Music   164   29
The Mountains   167   275
Autumn/Como/Essay   168   324

REVIEWS
Out of the Women's Museum   127   44
Studies for an Actress and Other Poems,
by Jean Garrigue
Ordinary Things,
by Jean Valentine
Futures, by Sandra Hochman
An Attic of Ideals, by Karen Swenson
The Jane Poems, by Kathleen Spivack
Armed Love, by Eleanor Lerman
[Huub Oosterhuis, Judith Herzberg]
A Platoon of Poets   128   290
A Sexual Tour of the Deep South,
by Rosemary Daniell
The Art of Love, by Kenneth Koch
Dancing on the Grave of a Son of a Bitch,
by Diane Wakoski
Oh Pray My Wings
Are Gonna Fit Me Well,
by Maya Angelou
In the Dead of the Night,
by Norman Dubie
The Space My Body Fills,
by Etta Blum

On the Edge of the Estate   129   296
  The New York Head Shop
    and Museum,
    by Audre Lorde
  Cheap, by Ruth Stone
On Burning Ground?   139   35
  Far from Home,
    by T. Alan Broughton
  The Loneliness Factor, by Carol Oles
  The Public Hug, by Robert Hershon
  Nervous Horses, by Vicki Hearne
  Giselle Considers Her Future,
    by Evan Zimroth
  Trader, by Robert Mazzocco
  Brass Knuckles, by Stuart Dybek
  Killing Floor, by Ai
  Coming to Terms,
    by Josephine Miles
  The Names of a Hare in English,
    by David Young
Six Reviews   147   156
  What the Light Was Like,
    by Amy Clampitt
  My Mother's Body, by Marge Piercy
  Hemispheres,
    by Grace Schulman
  Wyndmere, by Carol Muske
  The Lamplit Answer,
    by Gjertrud Schnackenberg
  Assumptions, by Marilyn Hacker
Six Poets in Search of a History   150   102
  Windows Facing East,
    by Caroline Finkelstein
  Ghost Money, by Lynda Hull
  Collected Poems,
    by Elizabeth Jennings
  Time and the White Tigress,
    by Mary Barnard
  The Pose of Happiness,
    by Gail Mazur
  Dream Work, by Mary Oliver
  [Robert Lowell, D. H. Lawrence]
How These New Homegirls Sing   160   284
  Sarton Selected
    (Ed. by Bradford Dudley Daziel)
    [May Sarton]
  Heroes in Disguise, by Linda Pastan
  The Cult of the Right Hand,
    by Elaine Terranova
  Bears Dancing in the Northern Air,
    by Christiane Jacox Kyle
  Winter Chickens and Other Poems
    and Let the Ice Speak,
    by Wendy Barker
  The Past Keeps Changing,
    by Chana Bloch
  Tall Stranger, by Gillian Conoley
  Out of Canaan,
    by Mary Stewart Hammond

String Light, by C. D. Wright
An Atlas of the Difficult World:
    Poems 1988-1991, by Adrienne Rich
  [Hilda Doolittle, Marianne Moore,
    Emily Dickinson, Walt Whitman]
Family Values   164   39
  First Awakenings:
    The Early Poems of Laura Riding
    (Ed. by Elizabeth Friedmann,
    Alan J. Clark, and Robert Nye)
  New and Collected Poems,
    by Grace Paley
  Mars and Her Children, by Marge Piercy
  Red Trousseau, by Carol Muske
  The Father, by Sharon Olds
Looks of Memory and Desire   168   281
  The Dear Past
    and Other Poems 1919-1994,
    by Janet Lewis
  An Early Afterlife, by Linda Pastan
  The Other Side/El Otro Lado,
    by Julia Alvarez
  The Woman Who Fell From the Sky,
    by Joy Harjo
  Morning in the Burned House,
    by Margaret Atwood
  Red Suitcase, by Naomi Shihab Nye
  Sensual Math, by Alice Fulton
  Plainwater: Essays and Poetry,
    by Anne Carson
  Glass, Irony and God, by Anne Carson

BOOKS REVIEWED
  In the Fourth World   138   170
  Emily's Bread   146   38
  Blood Pressure   154   151
  The Ghost Volcano   169   156

GILBERT, STUART
  BOOKS REVIEWED
    Letters of James Joyce (Ed.)   91   56

GILBERT, WARREN
  BOOKS REVIEWED
    The Joy Ride and Other Poems   32   345

GILBOA, AMIR
  POEMS
    Against the Wind   92   248
    Birth
    Isaac
    Moses
    On a Recollected Road
    Evening of Whirlwind
    The Lock of Weeping
    If They Show Me a Stone and I Say Stone
    Their Past Laughter Will Strike Them
    Song Yet Song
      (Tr. by Ruth Finer Mintz)

GILCHRIST, ANNE
BOOKS REVIEWED
  The Letters of Anne Gilchrist
  and Walt Whitman
    (Ed. by Thomas B. Harned)   14   106

GILCHRIST, MARIE (EMILIE)
POEMS
  Stones in the Road   26   318
  The Diviner
  Beyond
  Judgment
  An Unofficial Epitaph
  Reason Speaks
  Re-Agent   43   197
  November Letter   65   65

BOOKS REVIEWED
  Wide Pastures   31   228

GILDART, ROBERT
POEMS
  Syllables of Silence   46   89
  Portraits of the Living
  Sonnet ("These dreams of you...")

GILDNER, GARY
POEMS
  Jabón   137   146
  String   153   127
  Cabbage in Polish

BOOKS REVIEWED
  Digging for Indians   121   343
  Nails   127   292

GILES, BRIAN
BOOKS REVIEWED
  A Dead Sparrow   92   309

GILES, HERBERT A.
ARTICLES ABOUT
  On Translating Chinese Poetry II,
    by Eunice Tietjens   20   328

GILI, J. L.
BOOKS REVIEWED
  Poems of F. García Lorca
    (Tr. with Stephen Spender)   56   343
  Selected Poems of Federico García Lorca
    (Tr. with Stephen Spender)   63   96

GILL, ERIC
ARTICLES ABOUT
  Eric Gill, by Morton D. Zabel   37   41

GILL, FRANCES
POEMS
  Outside   35   308

GILL, JOHN
POEMS
  Rending the Veil   44   15

ARTICLES
  Correspondence:
    A Strong Word for Canada
    [Marvin Bell]   112   209

BOOKS REVIEWED
  Young Man's Letter   112   276

ARTICLES ABOUT
  Correspondence
    from Marvin Bell   112   210

GILL, JOHN J.
POEMS
  Traffic   83   140
  Lover's Choice   85   91
  Comparison of Flowers   86   157

GILL, M. LAKSHMI
BOOKS REVIEWED
  During Rain,
  I Plant Chrysanthemums   111   323

GILLESPIE, JOHN
POEMS
  Le Siffleur du Bois   28   138
  Poignards
  Song ("I loved a long time...")   32   20
  Requiem ("Because my love was left...")

GILLESPIE, JONATHAN
POEMS
  Survivor   130   80

GILLESPIE, RICHARD CHARLES
POEMS
  To One Who Sings of Water   28   194

GILLETTE, CHARLES
POEMS
  Quarter to Eight   29   190

GILLILAND,
WINONA MONTGOMERY
POEMS
  Images from Hangchow   46   22
    Pavilion of the Peaceful Lake
    Three Pools and the Printed Moons
    The Lagoon of Fish and Flowers
    Evening Illumination of Thunder Peak
    Willow Bay
    The Winding Hall of Fragrant Breezes
  The Faithful Shadow   49   260
    Moon Magic
    Nostalgia

Gray Pigeons
In August 50 262

GILLIS, FRANK
BOOKS REVIEWED
The Hitch Hiker 119 356

GILLIS, PETER C.
POEMS
Kneeling 114 372

GILLMAN, RICHARD
POEMS
Girl Bathers and the Gulls 71 21
College Girls 72 135

GILLON, ADAM
BOOKS REVIEWED
Introduction to Modern Polish Literature
  (Ed. with Ludwik Krzyzanowski) 110 52

GILMAN, DUGAN
POEMS
After Eating Salt Fish 115 391

BOOKS REVIEWED
Upstate 120 235

GILMORE, LOUIS
POEMS
Inventions 12 132
  Deity
  Earth
  Pause
Toward Parnassus 119 263
Toward Utopia
Toward Zion
Toward Tahiti
Toward the North Pole
Toward Nirvana

ARTICLES
Correspondence:
  Unbound [Poem] 10 278

GILMORE, WILLIAM
REVIEWS
The Last Look and Other Poems,
  by Mark Van Doren 51 164
Sebastian, by Rayner Heppenstall 52 104

GILPIN, LAURA
POEMS
The Bath 144 71

GIMÉNEZ-ROSELLÓ, CARMEN
POEMS
Tree, Tree, Tree 170 207

GINESTIER, PAUL
BOOKS REVIEWED
The Poet and the Machine
  (Tr. by Martin B. Friedman) 101 292

GINS, MADELINE
BOOKS REVIEWED
Word Rain 118 35

GINSBERG, ALLEN
POEMS
Written in My Dream
  by W. C. Williams 148 256

ARTICLES
Correspondence:
  Lamantia as Forerunner 103 271

BOOKS REVIEWED
Howl and Other Poems 90 386
Kaddish and Other Poems, 1958-1960 100 329
Reality Sandwiches 104 186
Planet News 114 251
Ankor Wat 114 401
The Fall of America:
  Poems of these States 1965-71 124 292

ARTICLES ABOUT
Creative Glut, by Karl Shapiro 135 36
Rev. of *The Psycho-Political Muse:*
  American Poetry Since the Fifties,
  by Paul Breslin 152 229

GINSBERG, LOUIS
POEMS
Hymn to Evil 30 200
Soon at Last 31 249
The Everlasting Minute 37 313
Beyond Our Sight
Eighteen 62 13
Bridal Party 70 70

GIOIA, DANA
POEMS
My Secret Life 139 203
The Journey, the Arrival, and the Dream 141 142
Thanks for Remembering Us 143 7
Cuckoos
The Country Wife
The Sunday News
My Confessional Sestina
The Next Poem 146 262
Cruising with the Beachboys
The End
Night Watch 151 60
The Gods of Winter 151 285
Speaking of Love

TRANSLATIONS
  Poems by Mario Luzi   155   25
  Poems by Bartolo Cattafi   155   53
  Poems by Valerio Magrelli   155   157

ARTICLES
  Comment   151   225

REVIEWS
  Eight Poets   140   102
    Work, for the Night Is Coming,
      by Jared Carter
    A World of Difference,
      by Heather McHugh
    Views and Spectacles:
      New and Selected Shorter Poems,
      by Theodore Weiss
    Waking to My Name:
      New and Selected Poems,
      by Robert Pack
    Before Sleep, by Philip Booth
    Two-Headed Poems,
      by Margaret Atwood
    In a Pig's Eye, by Robert Siegel
    For Instance, by John Ciardi

  BOOKS REVIEWED
    Daily Horoscope   149   31

GIORNO, JOHN
  BOOKS REVIEWED
    Balling Buddha   119   224

GIOVANNITTI, ARTURO
  BOOKS REVIEWED
    Arrows in the Gale   6   36

GIRARD, RENÉ
  ARTICLES ABOUT
    Review by Alice Fulton   159   32

GITLIN, TODD
  BOOKS REVIEWED
    Campfires of the Resistance:
      Poetry from the Movement (Ed.)   123   34

GIUDICI, GIOVANNI
  POEMS
    Da *La Bovary c'est moi/*
      From *Madame Bovary C'est Moi*   155   70
    Poesie per una voce/Poem for One Voice
    An Evening Like So Many Others
      (Tr. by Charles Wright)

GIULIANI, ALFREDO
  POEMS
    Brucio e l'Imminenza l'Ombra
      Che Sale Riconosco   94   312
    Il Cuore Zoppo
      (Tr. by Ben Johnson)

GLADDING, JODY
  BOOKS REVIEWED
    Stone Crop   166   38

GLADSTONE, RALPH
  BOOKS REVIEWED
    The Heracleidae (Tr.)   86   303

GLAENTZER, HELEN
  POEMS
    The Coming   32   265

GLAENZER, RICHARD BUTLER
  POEMS
    From a Club Window   4   141
    Rodin
    Star-Magic
    The Tapestry   7   126
    The Chasm
    Pomegranate
    Bermuda   10   122
    Quandary
    The Passage
    Crayons of Dominica   13   250
      Under the Saman
      The Little Donkey
      First Growth
      Caribbean Nights
    Between the Brackets   24   20

  BOOKS REVIEWED
    Beggar and King   12   279

GLASCOCK, K(ATHERYN) IRENE
[IRENE GLASSCOCK]
  POEMS
    Daylight   22   83

  ARTICLES ABOUT
    A Texas Prize Contest,
      by Harriet Monroe   21   91

GLASER, ELTON
  POEMS
    Dancing Lessons   149   259
    Winter Inset
    Confluences at San Francisco   153   131
    In Another Life   166   29
    Midnight at the Club Imaginaire   170   193

GLASS, MALCOLM
  POEMS
    Superstitions   150   90
    Living on Light   152   187
    Legerdemain
    Soaring: Goal and Return
    The Truth About Polar Bears   153   228
    Disguised   157   89

GLASSCO, JOHN
POEMS
 For Cora Lightbody, R. N.   118 165

BOOKS REVIEWED
 A Point of Sky   108 45
 Selected Poems   126 50
 Montreal

GLASSCOCK, IRENE
[See GLASCOCK, K. IRENE]

GLATSTEIN, JACOB
POEMS
 Small Door of a Dream
  (Tr. by Doris Vidaver) 146 256

GLAZE, ANDREW
POEMS
 Marine Biology   76 63
 Three Songs About One Thing
 Antigua
 The Big Eye   78 260
 Henry Buck
 Ludwig Rellstab's Visit to Beethoven 83 197
 A Cut of Copernicus   87 281

BOOKS REVIEWED
 The Trash Dragon of Shensi 133 227
 I Am the Jefferson County Courthouse 140 346

GLAZNER, GREG
POEMS
 New Stars   144 63
 The Valley
 Red Tide, a Beach of Salvage 150 143

GLEASON, GEORGE SCOTT
POEMS
 Song of the Saw   37 318

GLEASON, HAROLD WILLARD
POEMS
 Domestication   38 25

GLEASON, MADELINE
POEMS
 For All Living   48 190
  These Are Her Wonders
  Alone My Thoughts
  We Are Like These
  Show Me the Resurrection
 The Surviving Mirror   57 138
 Complaint
 Land's End   61 668
  Extremes Must Meet
  There Is a Season
  Yet All Remains the Same
  The Franciscan Fathers in California

BOOKS REVIEWED
 Poems   66 102

GLENN, LAURA
POEMS
 Precarious   142 82

GLINES, ELLEN
POEMS
 The Caribbean   24 18
 Borinquen
 Today
 R.I.P. Amor
 Pegasus   27 136
 La Jazmincita
 Grapes   30 28
 Challenge
 Vampire
 On the Road to Skull Hill 31 129
 Equations   32 204
  Fourth Floor Back
  Little Elegy
  Armistice
  Conqueror
 The Victory of Samothrace Speaks
  to the Mutilated of a Great War 33 70
 Hyena   34 24
 Porto Rico Beaches   35 189
  Weather
  Causeway
  November Afternoon
  Level Sun
  Rose-Gold

GLOVER, DENIS
BOOKS REVIEWED
 Recent Poems
  (With Allen Curnow, A. R. D.
  Fairburn, and R. A. K. Mason) 59 343
 Cold Tongue
 Since Then   94 44

GLOVER, GUY
POEMS
 In Act Is Fact   59 251

GLÜCK, LOUISE
POEMS
 Monologue at Nine A.M. 108 33
 Dead End
 Anniversary
 Grandmother in the Garden 109 382
 The Egg
 The Undertaking   118 63
 The Fortress
 Land's End
 The Magi
 Archipelago
 The Shad-Blow Tree

BOOKS REVIEWED
Firstborn — 117 322
The House on Marshland — 127 292
Descending Figure — 138 231
The Triumph of Achilles — 148 36
Ararat — 157 96
The Wild Iris — 162 96
Meadowlands — 169 339

GLYNN, JOHN FRANCIS
BOOKS REVIEWED
Songs from the Silence — 27 170

GODBOUT, JACQUES
BOOKS REVIEWED
Poetry 64 — Poésie 64
(Ed. with John Robert Colombo) — 104 385

GODDEN, RUMER
BOOKS REVIEWED
Prayers from the Ark,
by Carmen Bernos de Gasztold (Tr.) — 105 190

GODOLPHIN, FRANCIS R. B.
BOOKS REVIEWED
The Latin Poets (Ed.) — 76 218

GODOY Y ALCAYAGA, LUCILA
[See MISTRAL, GABRIELA, pseud.]

GOEDICKE, PATRICIA
POEMS
Looking Through the Window at the Future — 118 143
Spitfire
Love Song: For the Four Corners
The Core — 122 198

GOETHE, JOHANN WOLFGANG VON
POEMS
Song of the Traveller at Evening — 116 345
Mignon
Death of a Fly
To Charlotte Von Stein
Anacreon's Grave
Permanence in Change
(Tr. by John Frederick Nims)

BOOKS REVIEWED
Goethe's Faust.
A New American Translation,
by C. F. MacIntyre — 61 406
Faust: Parts One and Two
(Tr. and ed. by George Madison Priest)
The Sorrows of Young Werther,
The New Melusina, Novelle
(Tr. by Victor Lange) — 75 232
Faust, Part One
(Tr. by Philip Wayne)

Goethe's Faust, Parts I and II
(Tr. by Louis MacNeice) — 81 393
Goethe's Faust [Pt. I; sections of pt. II]
(Tr. and ed. by Walter Kaufmann) — 101 287

ARTICLES ABOUT
Rev. of *Commentary on Goethe's* Faust,
by D. J. Enright; *Goethe the Poet,*
by Karl Vietor (Tr. by Moses Hadas);
and *Goethe's Image of Man and Society,*
by Arnold Bergstraesser — 75 232
Notes on Language and
Its Deconstruction,
by Erich Heller — 145 229

GOETZ, PHILIP BECKER
POEMS
Charwomen — 5 112

BOOKS REVIEWED
Lyrics and Meditations — 28 290

GOGARTY, OLIVER ST. JOHN
POEMS
Ode ("Empyrean is the source...") — 58 233
Croker of Ballinagarde — 61 430
To an Old Tenor — 63 12
High Tide at Malahide — 64 79
Between Brielle and Manasquan
Farrell O'Reilly — 68 70
The Three — 69 10
Faith
Hope
Charity
The Supreme Crown — 85 267

BOOKS REVIEWED
Wild Apples — 37 349
An Offering of Swans
Selected Poems — 45 55
Perennial — 65 276
Collected Poems — 86 287

ARTICLES ABOUT
Poetry on Records,
by Harry Thornton Moore — 58 345
Oliver St. John Gogarty,
by Vivian Mercier — 93 35

GOKAK, V. K.
POEMS
On Womanhood — 93 262

GOLDBARTH, ALBERT
POEMS
Survival — 117 365
The Bittersweet Comfort of Motley Detail — 122 325
Goat / Cat / Dog — 136 127

Closer
Thoreau/Who Directed Le Boucher/ & Pope
Weave   137   280
Hey Sweetie
Sympathetic Magic
Blue Flowers   138   338
Pleasures
Before
Worlds   140   1
Sitting in the Margin
Reel Estate
Edgewater Hospital
"[The Importance of Artists' Biographies]   141   91
A Film
A Theory of Wind
The Well
From The Agnostic's Holy Sonnets   142   225
Diagrams
These Likenesses
That Gap
"The Numbering at Bethlehem"   143   141
Vestigial   144   293
Scar/Beer/Glasses
"We're Just About To Observe
    the Edge of the Universe"   145   210
Problem Solving
You Hum
Steerage   146   74
Poem Whose Last Sentence Is 17 Syllables
    After a Suggestion
Brotherly
A Monument   148   260
Seeing
The More Modest the Definition of Heaven,
    the Oftener We're There
Again   149   13
At the Heart   149   257
Parnassus
Assembly
A Hum
The Way the Novel Functions   151   62
The Multiverse   151   329
The Quest for the Source of the Nile
In the Midst of Intrusive Richness   153   316
A Letter
After Seeing the Impressionist Group Exhibit
    in Kansas City, We Drive Back
    Through Flatness to Wichita   155   214
The Talk Show
Vigil
Sentimental   156   190
The Title for a Collection of Poems
    Appears from Out of Nowhere   157   335
Finely Written Labels
Alveoli   161   63
"When Wild Beasts Charge,
The Amounts
The Bonds   162   71

Effect Over Distance
Arguing Bartusiak   163   131
Spaces
The Yoking of the Two Modes
Away   164   343
"Y'Call Someplace Paradise,
    Kiss It Goodbye"
Thread Through History   166   90
"A Wooden Eye. An 1884 Silver Dollar.
    A Homemade Explosive.
    A Set of False Teeth.
    And a 14-Karat Gold Ashtray."
Prepositions   167   198
Circa 1861
Because It Happened
Trails of Fire and Spirits   168   90
Various Ulia   168   274
Poem Beginning with a Quote
    from Keith Laumer's Galactic Odyssey
    and Ending with a Quote
    from Mika Waltari's The Egyptian   169   133
Ancestored-Back Is the Overpresiding
    Spirit of This Poem
Past Presidents of the Counters Club   170   281

BOOKS REVIEWED
Jan. 31   127   352
Comings Back   132   31
Original Light:
    New and Selected Poems 1973-1983   145   99
Arts & Sciences   150   36
Popular Culture   158   158
Heaven and Earth: A Cosmology   160   94
Across the Layers: Poems Old and New   166   38

GOLDBAUM, HELEN
POEMS
    The Tree   54   311
    In the Shadow of Great Times
    The Human Touch   58   255
    Fellow Stockholders:
    A New Year   61   548
    Reflections on War as Art

GOLDBERG, BARBARA
POEMS
    Cautionary Tales   142   83
    Teeth
    Night Watch   153   272
    What Is Served

GOLDBERG, ISAAC
BOOKS REVIEWED
    Studies in Spanish-American Literature   16   280

GOLDBERG, LEAH
POEMS
    Dialogue   92   238

Remembrance of Beginnings of Things
On This Day
Will Truly Yet Come...
   (Tr. by Ruth Finer Mintz)
From *On the Flowering*
   (Tr. by Sholom J. Kahn)
White Poplar Leaves   124   324
From *Love Songs from an Ancient Book*
   (1. "I have not seen you...")
   (5. "We did not know how...")
     (Tr. by Robert Friend)

ARTICLES ABOUT
[Note on Translations]   93   56

GOLDEN GOOSE CHAP BOOKS
BOOKS REVIEWED
Five Poets: 1949
[Chap Book 5]   77   114

GOLDENSOHN, BARRY
POEMS
Sybyl the Psychoanalysand
   in the Subways   115   263
Aerial Photo
New Center of Gravity
Noli Me Tangere
Worn Bearing Cross
Flaubert and Emma Bovary
The Returned Utopians   117   166
The Alert Scribe
13th Anniversary
Visual Contact
The Letter Killeth, the Letter Giveth Life
Light
The Morning of Execution   118   323
The Man of Words Encounters the Circle of
   Infinite Radius Whose Center Is Everywhere
   and Whose Circumference Is Nowhere
Time and the String
   Quartet Domesticate Eros
The Art of the Angler   124   12
A Landscape with Ornamental Morals   124   321
War and Peace   143   313
Home   144   258
The Drawing of Thomas Wyatt by Holbein
The Toy   147   289
Witness   150   198
Her Husband Speaks After Her Death
Before Beethoven's Creation of Music
   as Personal Expression   165   25
Law and Sensibility   165   91
Arch of Titus
Point Lobos   168   206
Aphrodites

BOOKS REVIEWED
The Marrano   154   340

GOLDENSOHN, LORRIE
POEMS
Gemini   135   199
Farm Woman
My Mother's Safety
Promises   152   289
Anesthesia
The World as Conscious Will
Timor Mortis   167   141

REVIEWS
Flights Home   144   40
   Foreseeing the Journey,
     by James Applewhite
   Only the World, by Constance Urdang
   Picture Bride, by Cathy Song
   Jurgis Petraskas,
     by Anthony Petrosky
   Salt Air, by Sharon Bryan
   Quarry, by Carol Oles
   Translations of the Gospel
     Back into Tongues,
     by C D Wright
   Poems 1960-1967,
     by Denise Levertov

BOOKS REVIEWED
Elizabeth Bishop:
   The Biography of a Poetry   161   34

GOLDFARB, SIDNEY
BOOKS REVIEWED
Speech, for Instance   115   281
Messages   120   235

GOLDING, ARTHUR
ARTICLES ABOUT
Rev. of *Ovid: The Metamorphoses*
   (Tr. by Horace Gregory)   95   185

GOLDING, LOUIS
POEMS
Numbers   18   198
Full of Laughter   20   196
Beauty a Ghost   24   192
The Passer-By
The Midnight Singer   26   312
Older Heliopolis
From the Mediterranean   29   132
   Sicily and England
   Greece Remembered
   Beauty's Wars
A Springtime Lost   33   300
The Jolly God
Calm Lady

BOOKS REVIEWED
Prophet and Fool   24   333

GOLDMAN, MICHAEL
POEMS
The Change   99   365
Nothing
The Rothko Paintings
Lyric (II)
For an Older Poet
Resistance to Music   103   251
The Skill
Caverned from the Storm
Natural Selection   121   255
Prayer: For Our Eyes
Together
Verdict
Minimal
Abuse
What the Night Says   141   342
Dinner Is Served
Recovery

BOOKS REVIEWED
First Poems   108   130

GOLDMARK, PAULINE
BOOKS REVIEWED
The Gypsy Trail,
    an Anthology for Campers
    (Ed. with Mary Hopkins)   6   98

GOLDRING, DOUGLAS
POEMS
Calle Memo o Loredan   4   217
Hill House
Voyages   6   79

BOOKS REVIEWED
Streets   3   146
A Country Boy
In the Town   8   262
On the Road

ARTICLES ABOUT
Rev. of Catholic Anthology—1914-1915   8   94

GOLDSMITH, BEATRICE
POEMS
Weeds in Rain   42   328
    Melancholia
    Rain
    Eternity
    Wraith
Lullaby for a Failure   44   313
The Immutable Transit   49   266
    Phase
    Transit
    Escape
    Finis
Nocturne   54   122

GOLDSMITH, OLIVER
ARTICLES ABOUT
Rev. of The Oxford Book of Irish Verse
    (Ed. by Donagh MacDonagh
    and Lennox Robinson)   94   260

GOLDSTEIN, LAURENCE
POEMS
Homesick in Los Angeles   146   73
Posies   153   329
Elderly Surfer   154   270

GOLDSWORTHY, PETER
POEMS
Descartes at Bell's Beach   169   26
Lullaby
Eye of the Needle

GOLEMBIEWSKI, ALISON
POEMS
The Gold Pistol   138   317

GOLFFING, FRANCIS (C.)
POEMS
A Ballade of Reckoning   66   246
Dialogue at Midnight
A Friend's Retort
The Higher Empiricism
Cradle Song for a Young Sailor
The Manikin   69   16
Nightfall
After the Slaying
September Sonnet   70   312
Variations on a Theme
Lines to a Man Whose
    Marriage Went Suddenly to Pieces
Song ("Sailors contend with sails...")
An Exhortation
Artemis
Four Epigrams   77   256
Drinking at Dusk   87   33
Dry Gold
The Cross   88   158
On Prescience
To a Recent Believer
The Arizona Desert, Filmed   91   232
The Sibyl   93   85
The Tomb of Stéphane Mallarmé
A Monologue   118   340
Couplets and Quatrains   121   209
Survival Training
A German Lady   128   264
To a Hammer

TRANSLATIONS
Poems by Gottfried Benn   80   266
Poems by Giordano Bruno,
    Vincenzo Monti, Alessandro Tassoni,
    and Metastasio   128   137

ARTICLES

The Hazards of Criticism
   [J. Donald Adams]   68   265
A Note on Gottfried Benn   80   271

REVIEWS

The Phoenix and the Tortoise,
   by Kenneth Rexroth   65   260
*A Selection from the Poems
   of Alfred, Lord Tennyson*
   (Ed. by W. H. Auden)   65   335
Germany—A Winter's Tale,
   by Heinrich Heine
   (Tr. by Herman Salinger)   66   56
The Soldier, by Conrad Aiken   66   159
The Plain and the Stratosphere   66   340
   Generation of Journey,
      by Jacob Sloan
   Poems for Painters,
      by Charles Henri Ford
The Edge of Night, by August Derleth   67   168
Facets of Convention   67   225
   Shells by a Stream,
      by Edmund Blunden
   Silent Fame, by Loyd Haberly
   Far from the Land,
      by James Monahan
   No Mortal Blow,
      by Charles Glenn Wallis   67   288
A Grammar of Motives,
   by Kenneth Burke   67   338
Sonnets to Orpheus, Duino Elegies,
   by Rainer Maria Rilke
   (Tr. by Jessie Lemont)   68   100
A Blear Ball, by Wightman Williams   68   166
A Little Treasury of Modern Poetry
   (Ed. by Oscar Williams)   69   109
Transfigured Night, by Byron Vazakas
   [William Carlos Williams]   69   158
Prose Poems from the Illuminations,
   by Arthur Rimbaud
   (Tr. by Louise Varese)   69   286
James Hurnard, a Victorian Character
   (Ed. by G. R. Hamilton)   70   106
Farewell and Welcome,
   by Ronald Bottrall   70   338
The Image and the Law,
   by Howard Nemerov   71   94
The Beautiful Changes,
   by Richard Wilbur   71   221
Love Poems, by George Barker   72   34
Two Longer Poems   73   294
   Layman's Fall, by Ellis Foote
   The Ninth Continent,
      by Lindley Williams Hubbell
The Signature of All Things,
   by Kenneth Rexroth   76   159
Quandary and Statement   77   359

   Musical Chairs,
      by James Broughton
   Paris Poems, by Harry Roskolenko
Recent German Criticism: A Chronicle   91   403
   Medusa's Mirror, by August Closs
   Reason and Energy,
      by Michael Hamburger
   The Disinherited Mind,
      by Erich Heller

BOOKS REVIEWED
   Poems 1943-1949   76   57
   Selected Poems   101   205
   Collected Poems   140   170

ARTICLES ABOUT
   Correspondence from Jessie Lemont
   [Rainer Maria Rilke]   69   57

GOLL, CLAIRE
   BOOKS REVIEWED
   *Die Neue Welt: Eine Anthologie
      Jungster Amerikanischer Lyrik* (Tr.)   22   168

GOLL, IVAN [YVAN GOLL]
   POEMS
   John Landless Is Landsick
      (Tr. by Clark Mills)   57   252

   BOOKS REVIEWED
   *Le Cinq Continents: Anthologie
      Mondiale de Poésie Contemporaine*   24   52
   Selected Poems
      (Ed. by Paul Zweig)   114   40
   Lackawanna Elegy
      (Tr. by Galway Kinnell)   122   105

   ARTICLES ABOUT
   [Note]   85   244

GOMEZ JAIME, ALFREDO
   POEMS
   Problem (Tr. by Muna Lee)   26   127

GÖMÖRI, GEORGE
   BOOKS REVIEWED
   Polish and Hungarian Poetry, 1945-1956 110   52
   Selected Poems and Texts,
      by Attila József
      (Tr. by John Batki)
      (Ed. with James Atlas)   126   103

GONET, JILL
   POEMS
   Daughters and Sons   168   318
   Existential Good Humor

GONGORA
**[See DE GONGORA Y ARGOTE,
LUIS]**

GONNE, MAUD
ARTICLES ABOUT
Rev. of *The Senate Speeches of W. B. Yeats*
(Ed. by Donald R. Pearce)   98   253

GONZALES, LAURENCE
POEMS
Forgery   117   34

GONZALES, N. V. M.
POEMS
Notations   43   198
Circus Song
At Puerto
Virginia
The Lady on the Operating-Table

GONZALES MARTINEZ, ENRIQUE
POEMS
Wring the Neck of the Swan
(Tr. by Muna Lee)   26   134

GONZALES ROJO, ENRIQUE
BOOKS REVIEWED
Elegías Romanas y Otros Poemas   61   680

GONZALEZ, A. R.
[Pseud. of HIPP, DOROTHY]
TRANSLATIONS
Poem by Carlos R. Mondaca   38   309

ARTICLES
Some Chilean Poets
[Carlos Mondaca, Manuel Magallanes
Moure, Gabriela Mistral]   38   329

GOODELL, ELBRA DICKINSON
POEMS
Gift Perennial   35   141

GOODENOUGH, J. B.
POEMS
Gathering Constellations   157   76
Nightmare

GOODMAN, ALICE
POEMS
The Chemical Blonde   139   251

GOODMAN, BRENT
POEMS
The Brother Swimming
Beneath Me   168   96

GOODMAN, MIRIAM
POEMS
Father's Mirror   154   150
Losing the Words   160   71
Widowed,   162   270

Anxiety of Ten O'Clock
Hungry

GOODMAN, MITCHELL
POEMS
Waiting   113   248

GOODMAN, PAUL
POEMS
"To Undo the Work of the Creation—" 56   184
Electra
"Dreams Are the Royal Road
to the Unconscious"   70   139
For Janet Fairbanks   71   127
Introduction and Ballade   73   311
Candelabra of Jacques Lipchitz
Stanzas
My Friend Below
In Lydia
"Gemelle Castor et Gamelle Castoris" 75   77
Couplets
Proposal for a Shrine of Dionysus
at Patchogue, Long Island
Classical Quatrain
Attributed to Linus
Little Ode   76   262
The Parallax   77   204
Anacreontic
Evening (After Rameau and Cézanne) 78   20
Birthday   78   275
A Meal
Quaker Hill
Sentences of Nietzsche   80   131
On My Fortieth Birthday   81   113
A Walk (For Noel)   82   259
Poem ("Fever is beautiful...")   83   264
March 1954   85   29
Wellfleet Harbor   86   339
The Car Barn Under Coogan's Bluff 88   306
Long Lines   90   210
Song ("When the couple passed me...")
My Daughter Very Ill
Two Poems of the Way
We Have a Verb "Stood Up"   92   374
"No"
The Past
A Rough Wall
The Great Black Hound Upstairs—
Lavender   94   290
On the Lake
Lines in Spite
Our Yellow Kite   96   344
The Cape Cod Canal
Motorcycle Song
Haiku ("Sleep is honey, but...")
The "Weepers Tower" in Amsterdam   97   359
Haiku ("Sowing, ignorant...")   102   304
A Firefly

ARTICLES
The Chance for Popular Culture   74   157

REVIEWS
Song in the Meadow,
  by Elizabeth Madox Roberts   57   43
Prison Within Prison:
  Three Elegies on Hebrew Themes,
  by Edouard Roditi   60   282
A Beginning, by Robert Horan   73   166
Terror and Decorum, by Peter Viereck   73   289
The Song of the Cold, by Edith Sitwell   74   239
New British Poets
  (Ed. by Kenneth Rexroth)   75   237
Strike Through the Mask!
  by Peter Viereck   76   99
Orpheus, by Muriel Rukeyser   77   234
The Cliff's Edge, by Eithne Tabor   78   243
Journey to Love,
  by William Carlos Williams   87   366
Poems 1906-26,
  by Rainer Maria Rilke
  (Tr. by J. B. Leishman)
  and Gedichte 1906 bis 1926
  (Ed. by Ernst Zinn)   93   192

BOOKS REVIEWED
Five Young American Poets,
  Second Series 1941
  (With Jeanne McGahey, Clark Mills,
  David Schubert, and Karl Shapiro)   60   215
The Structure of Literature   84   363
Red Jacket   89   118
The Copernican Revolution   89   120
Day
The Lordly Hudson   104   44
Hawkweed   112   337
North Percy   114   401
Tragedy & Comedy: Four Cubist Plays   119   99
Homespun of Oatmeal Gray   120   235
Collected Poems
  (Ed. by Taylor Stoehr)   128   100

ARTICLES ABOUT
Correspondence
  from John Hall Wheelock   76   306

GOODMAN, RONALD
BOOKS REVIEWED
Poems
  (With Stephen Berg
  and Robert Mezey)   93   182

GOODREAU, WILLIAM
BOOKS REVIEWED
The Many Islands   100   191
In My Father's House   105   410

GOOGE, BARNABE
ARTICLES ABOUT
The 16th Century Lyric
  in England: Part I, by Yvor Winters   53   258

GORBANEVSKAYA, NATALYA
POEMS
Aphrodite   124   209
Memory of Pyarvalka
My Dear, Dear One
Hold Out a Handful of Snow
And Tomorrow You'll Not
  Find Even a Trace
But What Is There on This Dark Floor
Whose Dreams Die Out
  (Tr. by Daniel Weissbort)

GORBOVSKY, GLEB
POEMS
From Yakut Five-Liners
  (Tr. by Daniel Weissbort)   124   213

GORDON, DON
POEMS
Atomic Theory   37   309
Hospital Room   63   258
The Beachhead   64   252
The General   82   252
The Neurotics   84   337
The Middle Passage   86   322

BOOKS REVIEWED
Statement   64   171

GORDON, FRANK S.
POEMS
Along the South Star Trail   9   221
  The Tom-Tom
  Sa-A Narai
  On the War-Path
  Night
Gold in the Desert   12   140
  Morning Hymn
  The Smoke Prayer
  I Have But One Love
  Startled Waters
  Dirge for One Dying
  By Genesseret

ARTICLES
Correspondence:
  A Word from Dr. Gordon   9   329

ARTICLES ABOUT
[Note]   10   110

GORDON, GEORGE
[See BYRON, (LORD)]

GORDON, IAN A.
POEMS
  For Us No More
    in Epic Encounter   63   264

GORE-BOOTH, CONSTANCE
[See MARKIEVICZ, (COUNTESS)]

GORE-BOOTH, EVA
BOOKS REVIEWED
  Selected Poems   45   214
  Prison Letters of Countess Markievicz
    (With Poems by Eva Gore-Booth)

GORHAM, SARAH
POEMS
  Hymn to the Intellect   158   261

GORLIN, DEBRA
POEMS
  In Bold Relief   138   77
  Parents

GORMAN, HERBERT (S.)
POEMS
  Tea Hour   23   24
  For This My Body   24   245
  Desultory Epistles   28   119
    Mine Adversary
    Colloquy in Brass
    The Birds
    The Fountain
    Inquisition in Mist
    Viaticum
  Worldlings   31   1
    Proem
    Chanson de Chateaulaire
    Madame de Vaudraucourt
      and White Simone Stroll in the Park

REVIEWS
  The Hundred and One Harlequins,
    by Sacheverell Sitwell   24   331
  The Poems of Seumas O'Sullivan   25   52
  The Sea, by James Oppenheim   25   333
  The Temptation of Anthony,
    by Isidor Schneider   33   276
  Spring Plowing, by Charles Malam   33   287

BOOKS REVIEWED
  The Barcarole of James Smith
    and Other Poems   21   213
  A Victorian American [Longfellow]   29   266

GORMAN, WILLIAM
REVIEWS
  The Boar and Shibboleth,
    by Edward Doro   44   111

GORMLEY, GREGG J.
POEMS
  Farming with Boustrophedon   139   276

GOSSE, EDMUND
BOOKS REVIEWED
  The Life of Algernon Charles Swinburne   11   322

GOTLIEB, PHYLLIS
BOOKS REVIEWED
  Ordinary, Moving   118   35

GOTTLIEB, ELAINE (S.)
REVIEWS
  Australian Romantics   62   352
    Squatters Luck,
      by Ethel Anderson
    Dramas from the Sky
      and The Gift of Blood,
      by Max Harris

BOOKS REVIEWED
  Dimensions of Midnight,
    by Cecil Hemley (Ed.)   110   427

GOTTLIEB, SAUL
POEMS
  Standards   63   245

ARTICLES
  Correspondence   62   58

GOTTSCHALK, LAURA RIDING
[See RIDING, LAURA]

GOULD, EDWARD R.
POEMS
  Letitia Passes   39   26

GOULD, GERALD
BOOKS REVIEWED
  My Lady's Book   5   192

GOULD, WALLACE
POEMS
  In Maine   17   82
    The Pilgrimage
    The Last Tableau
    Diversion
    Postlude

BOOKS REVIEWED
  Children of the Sun—Rhapsodies
    and Poems   13   44

GOVE, PHILIP B.
BOOKS REVIEWED
  Webster's Third
    New International Dictionary (Ed.)   100   190

GOVONI, CORRADO
ARTICLES ABOUT
Five Years of Italian Poetry (1910-1915),
    by Emanuel Carnevali   13   209
Contemporary Italian Poetry,
    by Edward Williamson   79   159

GOW, A. S. F.
BOOKS REVIEWED
   A. E. Housman, A Sketch   52   94
   The Greek Bucolic Poets (Tr.)   84   112

GOWER, M. G. [Pseud.]
POEMS
   Poet and Peasant   39   252
   The Statue and the Lord
   The Return of the Argo
   Cassation   41   312

GOWRIE, GREY
[LORD GOWRIE,
GREY RUTHVEN]
POEMS
   A Postcard from Don Giovanni 117   190

BOOKS REVIEWED
   A Postcard from Don Giovanni 123   113

GOYEN, WILLIAM
POEMS
   Three Artifices   74   84

GOZZANO, GUIDO
POEMS
   Invernale   136   10
   A Wintry Scene
   Totò Merúmeni
   Ketty
     (Tr. by Michael Palma)

ARTICLES ABOUT
Contemporary Italian Poetry,
    by Edward Williamson   79   159

GRABO, CARL H.
POEMS
   Sonnet ("In crumbling texture...") 56   254
   Mountain Shower
   Spain
   Folk Rhyme
   Religieuse   59   19

BOOKS REVIEWED
   The Black Butterfly   58   275

GRAHAM, DAVID (M.)
POEMS
   Dusk   136   89

   The Outskirts of Everything 146   22
   A Lot of Boys Bar
   American Gothic
   Self-Portrait with Nostalgia 147   203
   Self-Portrait with Self-Doubt
   The Editorial We
   The Day I Cannot Stop Crying 148   269
   Self-Portrait with Stage Fright
   Comfortable Smoke   150   318
   The Mind's Eye
   Kinds of Jazz
   Bad Dogs   156   193

GRAHAM, JORIE
POEMS
   Mirror Prayer   143   93
   Expecting

BOOKS REVIEWED
   Hybrids of Plants and of Ghosts 140   35

GRAHAM, LORENZ
BOOKS REVIEWED
   How God Fix Jonah   70   165

GRAHAM, MARCUS
[ROBERT PARSONS]
BOOKS REVIEWED
   An Anthology
    of Revolutionary Poetry (Ed.) 37   164

GRAHAM, STEPHEN
ARTICLES ABOUT
Two Trampers—and a Poem,
    by Maurice Lesemann   22   212

GRAHAM, VICKI
POEMS
   Positions   160   313
   Cape Blanco

GRAHAM, W. S.
POEMS
   Other Guilts as Far   69   315
   At Whose Sheltering Shall the Day Sea 71   308
   The Constructed Space   93   30
   Malcolm Mooney's Land 108   393
   The Beast in the Space   110   1
   Clusters Traveling Out   112   178

REVIEWS
   Losses,
    by Randall Jarrell   72   302

BOOKS REVIEWED
   The White Threshold   82   272
   The Nightfishing   86   295
   Malcolm Mooney's Land 118   228

ARTICLES ABOUT
Mr. Graham and the Dead Cigar,
  by Hayden Carruth   72   307

GRAHAME, ROBERTA M.
POEMS
  Watch Night   55   189

GRAHAM-LUJÁN, JAMES
BOOKS REVIEWED
  Three Tragedies,
    by Federico García Lorca
    (Tr. with Richard O'Connell)   75   114

GRANDBOIS, ALAIN
BOOKS REVIEWED
  Selected Poems   108   45

GRANICH, IRWIN
POEMS
  Surrender   16   134

GRANNIS, ANITA
POEMS
  A Fillet of Thorn   19   75

GRANSDEN, K. W.
BOOKS REVIEWED
  Any Day   100   191

GRANT, STEPHEN
POEMS
  Second Marriage   115   232

GRANVILLE, CHARLES
POEMS
  Poems of the Hour   11   187
  For Parents of the Slain
  The Question
  The Mourner
  The Bayonet Charge
  Under Orders

GRASS, GÜNTER
POEMS
  Open Wardrobe
    (Tr. by Michael Hamburger)   98   154

BOOKS REVIEWED
  Selected Poems
    (Tr. by Michael Hamburger
    and Christopher Middleton)   111   336

GRAVES, ALFRED PERCEVAL
POEMS
  O Drimin Dhu Deelish   2   161
  The Sea Singer
  Lough Leane   30   82

GRAVES, HARLEY
[Pseud. of WILKINSON,
MARGUERITE]
POEMS
  Songs from the Woods   10   292
  White Magic
  A Thought When Noon Is Hot
  Before Dawn in Camp
  I Came To Be Alone

ARTICLES ABOUT
  Correspondence: A Confession,
    by Marguerite Wilkinson   12   56

GRAVES, ROBERT
POEMS
  Songs and Catches   14   252
  Dicky
  Hawk and Buckle
  The Cupboard
  The Lord-Chamberlain Tells
    of a Famous Meeting   21   257
  In the Beginning Was a Word   30   16
  The Cool Web
  The Bait
  Return of the Goddess Artemis   71   22
  Intercession in Late October
  The Jackals' Address to Iris   75   257
  With the Gift of a Ring   79   125
  Cry Faugh!
  The Foreboding
  The Straw
  Hercules at Nemea
  The Sacred Mission   81   39
  From the Embassy   82   14
  Ouzo Unclouded   101   43
  Myrrhina   103   182
  The Cupboard   121   9

ARTICLES
  [Note]   59   170
  Correspondence   86   186
  Correspondence:
    Gold, in Medals and in Poems   104   53

BOOKS REVIEWED
  Fairies and Fusiliers   18   105
  Country Sentiment
  On English Poetry   20   344
  The Pier-Glass   21   215
  Oxford Poetry, 1921
    (Ed. with Alan Porter
    and Richard Hughes)   24   162
  Collected Poems   55   157
  Poems 1938-1945   70   98
  The White Goddess   73   362
  Collected Poems 1955   87   175

The White Goddess	93	395
Five Pens in Hand		
The Poems of...		
The Golden Ass,		
by Lucius Apuleius (Tr.)		
The Twelve Caesars,		
by Gaius Suetonius Tranquillus (Tr.)		
More Poems	100	104
Collected Poems	100	305
The Penny Fiddle: Poems for Children	101	208
Oxford Addresses on Poetry	102	341
New Poems	103	316
Man Does, Woman Is	106	294
The Comedies of Terence (Ed.)		
(Tr. by Laurence Echard)	107	264
Collected Poems 1966	110	409
The Original Rubaiyyat of Omar Khayaam,		
A New Translation		
with Critical Commentaries		
(Tr. with Omar Ali-Shah)	113	262
On Poetry: Collected Talks & Essays	116	107
Poems: 1970-1972	123	113

ARTICLES ABOUT

A Word from London,		
by Benjamin Gilbert Brooks	28	40
Poets and Mushrooms,		
by Charles Tomlinson	100	104
Correspondence		
from Gustav Davidson	103	200
Rev. of *Swifter than Reason:*		
The Poetry and Criticism of Robert Graves,		
by Douglas Day	104	264
Rev. of *A Bibliography*		
of the Works of Robert Graves,		
by Fred H. Higginson	110	409
Rev. of *Barbarous Knowledge:*		
Myth in the Poetry of Yeats,		
Graves, and Muir,		
by Daniel Hoffman	112	52

GRAVES, STEVEN
POEMS

Ivory Spheres in a Chinese Carving	129	161
Small Anthem	131	19
The Cancellation		

GRAY, ALICE WIRTH
POEMS

A Present for Poor Monsieur Proust	136	82
Zoo Prepares to Adopt Metric System		

GRAY, ALLAN
POEMS

Aubade ("The curtains fill...")	129	335
A Family Argument		
Two Theories for the Muses' Mother	130	140

GRAY, DARRELL
POEMS

Elephants	115	401
Poem ("The lightning arranges us...")		
Today Is Water		
For the Future Occupants		
The Thought		
Planets		

BOOKS REVIEWED

Scattered Brains	128	37

GRAY, DON
BOOKS REVIEWED

The Silence Outside Things	116	193

GRAY, MARY
POEMS

Belleau Hill	14	193

GRAY, ROBERT
ARTICLES ABOUT

Towards a Contemporary		
Australian Poetics,		
by John Kinsella	169	94

GRAY, ROLAND PALMER
BOOKS REVIEWED

Songs and Ballads of Maine Lumberjacks		
with Other Songs from Maine (Ed.)	27	343

GRAY, THOMAS
ARTICLES ABOUT

Rev. of *The Background of Gray's Elegy,*		
by Amy Louise Reed	27	283
Rev. of *Selected Letters of Thomas Gray*		
(Ed. by Joseph Wood Krutch)	84	296

GRAYBEAL, MARIE (A.)
POEMS

Swimmer	78	82
Gloom for Gloaming		
Poem ("The enraged swimmer...")	93	74
Poem ("He dreams death...")		

REVIEWS

Poems 1906-26 and		
Gedichte 1906 bis 1926,		
by Rainer Maria Rilke	93	192

GRAZIANO, FRANK
BOOKS REVIEWED

James Wright: The Heart of the Light		
(Ed. with Peter Stitt)	157	343

GREEF, ADELE
BOOKS REVIEWED

Love's Argument	83	230

GREEN, ANN
BOOKS REVIEWED
Basic Verities, by Charles Péguy
  (Tr. with Julian Green)   62   208
Men and Saints, by Charles Péguy
  (Tr. with Julian Green)   66   42

GREEN, HATTIE CORA
ARTICLES
Magazines of Poetry
  in the Class Room   22   273

GREEN, JANE BANNARD
BOOKS REVIEWED
Letters of Rainer Maria Rilke, 1892-1910
  (Tr. with M. D. Herter Norton)   67   221

GREEN, JIM
BOOKS REVIEWED
Beyond Here   144   297

GREEN, JULIAN
BOOKS REVIEWED
Basic Verities, by Charles Péguy
  (Tr. with Ann Green)   62   208
Men and Saints, by Charles Péguy
  (Tr. with Ann Green)   66   42

GREEN, SAMUEL
POEMS
At the Pond's Edge   164   257

GREEN, T. H.
ARTICLES ABOUT
Rev. of *Somewhere
Is Such a Kingdom*,
  by Geoffrey Hill   128   232

GREENBERG, ALVIN
BOOKS REVIEWED
The Metaphysical Giraffe   115   47

GREENBERG, BARBARA L.
POEMS
Rondeau of the Wide Awake   127   68

GREENBERG, BATYAH
TRANSLATIONS
Poem by Anda Pinkerfeld-'Amir   92   232

GREENBERG, ELIEZER
BOOKS REVIEWED
A Treasury of Yiddish Poetry
  (Ed. with Irving Howe)   118   354

GREENBERG, NOAH
BOOKS REVIEWED
The Play of Daniel (Ed.)   97   380

GREENBERG, SAMUEL
BOOKS REVIEWED
Poems by...
  (Ed. by Harold Holden
  and Jack McManis)   71   158

GREENBERG, URI ZVI
POEMS
We Were Not Likened to Dogs
  (Tr. by Ruth Finer Mintz)   92   215

GREENE, GRAHAM
BOOKS REVIEWED
Babbling April   28   112

ARTICLES ABOUT
Dagger of the Mind,
  by James Sandoe   68   146

GREENE, JEFFREY
POEMS
Arolla   160   335

GREENE, JONATHAN
POEMS
Where the Blinding Sun   114   388
Horror Rations: A Meditation
Where the Comfort

GREENE, RALPH E.
POEMS
The Comedian Retires   25   197

GREENHOOD, DAVID
POEMS
The Worker   17   138
Thanks for a Season
A Psalm for Cathleen Ni Hoolihan   20   74
Liberty
Today   23   84
Impeachment
The Hungry
Elvira   41   204
Five O'Clock Near Lamy   42   148
Summer Accident   50   263

REVIEWS
Joshua Trees,
  by Frederick Mortimer Clapp   24   336

BOOKS REVIEWED
Poems, Et Cetera   46   289

ARTICLES ABOUT
Free Verse Again,
  by Margery Swett
  [Mansfield]   25   153

GREENLEE, JOHN (MC KINLEY)
POEMS
  Straight Talk   41   80
    Journeyman
    The People Are At Peace
  Protests   43   200
    Through with Troubled Waters
    When Neap Tides Leave the Piers
  Dipping Upward   46   78
    Ohio Lanes and Wells
    Cold Ambition

GREENSLET, FERRIS
ARTICLES
  Correspondence:
    About a Poet's Contract   41   167

ARTICLES ABOUT
  Our Contemporaries
    [Amy Lowell]   5   299
  The Pulitzer Award System,
    by Harriet Monroe   30   210

GREENWALD, MARTHA
POEMS
  The Story of the Day   163   29
  Sunday Afternoon Palindrome
    1813   166   19
  Edward Hopper Watching
    The Petrified Forest, 1936   170   197

GREENWAY, WILLIAM
POEMS
  Heart   142   85
  The Weaning
  Our Father Who Art on Third   148   272
  The Best Days of Your Life
  Entrance   152   129
  Small Road to Nowhere
  Boomers
  Intensive Care   155   220
  Hypochondria   159   14
  Anniversary   161   257
  Seventh Heaven   163   155
  For My Friends, Who Complain
    That I Never Write Anything Happy
    Them   163   202
  Progress
  Beneath the Plaza of Illustrious Hombres   164   337
  Dreams of the Blind Girl
  Toothache   165   13
  One Owner   165   71
  Yearn   166   164

GREENWOOD, JULIA WICKHAM
POEMS
  The Kind Heart   13   17

GREER, HILTON ROSS
BOOKS REVIEWED
  Voices of the Southwest,
    A Book of Texan Verse (Ed.)   22   344

GREER, LAURIE
POEMS
  Almanack: 21 July   166   225
  Dark Matters   167   132
  Blessing of the Hands   167   208
  Snowdrops / Candlemas Bells

GREER, SCOTT
POEMS
  The Return of Aegean Apollo   68   249
  From Los Pesares   76   330
  Nightshades   85   20
  Parties
  The Beaches of Summer
  Human Interest Story   85   256
  Danse Macabre
  Noon Fire   92   360
  Patterns of Conquest   101   247

BOOKS REVIEWED
  The Landscape Has Voices   70   108

GREET, ANNE HYDE
BOOKS REVIEWED
  Alcools, by Guillaume Apollinaire (Tr.)   111   124

GREGER, DEBORA
POEMS
  Dream Lecture, June   144   251
  Passage Overland
  Two Rodin Torsos
  The Rome of Keats   145   28
  The 1,002nd Night   150   140
  Narcissus
  The Snow Woman   153   138
  Sleeping Beauty
  The Boy Juliet   156   84
  Cleopatra in the Afterworld
  Blue Mirrors   157   329
  The Widower, His Weeds   158   207
  Easter 1991   162   16
  In the Museum of the Eighteenth Century
  Eve at the Paradise
  Les Très Riches Heures de Paris   163   125
  The Mosaic of Creation
  Psyche and Eros in Florida   163   262
  The Twilight of England   164   200
  Sacre Conversazioni   165   138
  Lives of the North American Martyrs
  The Cloud of Unknowing
  The British Museum   166   21
  The Blessing of the Throats

BOOKS REVIEWED
  Movable Islands   140   35
  And   149   31
  The 1002nd Night   158   280
  Off-Season at the Edge of the World   166   289

GREGERSON, LINDA
POEMS
  The Three-Legged Dog
    at the Heart of Our Home   136   76
  Wife
  Frame
  An Arbor   157   129
  Good News
  The Resurrection of the Body   162   14
  Bleedthrough   168   218

REVIEWS
  Short Reviews   145   36
    The Dead and the Living,
      by Sharon Olds
    American Primitive,
      by Mary Oliver
    Bonfire, by Celia Gilbert
    Portraits and Elegies,
      by Gjertrud Schnackenberg
    The Hands in Exile,
      by Susan Tichy
    Natural Affinities,
      by Erica Funkhouser
    The Going Under of the Evening Land,
      by Mekeel McBride
    The Yellow House on the Corner
      and *Museum,*
      by Rita Dove
  Short Reviews   151   419
    The Minute Hand, by Jane Shore
    The Boat of Quiet Hours,
      by Jane Kenyon
    Partial Account: New and Selected Poems,
      by William Meredith
    War Stories: Poems
      About the Long Ago and Now,
      by Howard Nemerov
    Above the Land, by Julie Agoos
    Flesh and Blood,
      by C. K. Williams
    In Time & Place,
      by John Hollander
    [John Milton]
    In Other Words, by May Swenson   154   233
  Short Reviews   155   229
    Zone Journals, by Charles Wright
    Amplitude: New and Selected Poems,
      by Tess Gallagher
    Lovesick, by Gerald Stern
    A Walk with Tom Jefferson,
      by Philip Levine
    Selected Poems, by James Schuyler   155   351

Short Reviews   167   287
  Like Most Revelations,
    by Richard Howard
  The Vigil: A Poem in Four Voices,
    by Margaret Gibson
  A Muriel Rukeyser Reader.
    (Ed. by Jan Heller Levi)
  The Knot, by Alice Jones
  [Mark Strand, Josiah Willard Gibbs]

BOOKS REVIEWED
  The Woman Who Died in Her Sleep   170   288

GREGG, FRANCES
POEMS
  Pageant   5   165
  To H. D.

GREGG, LINDA
BOOKS REVIEWED
  The Sacraments of Desire   159   223

GREGH, FERNAND
ARTICLES ABOUT
  As It Is in Paris,
    by Harriet Monroe   27   266

GREGOR, ARTHUR
POEMS
  Ritual   71   78
  Blackout
  The Mind Placed in a Room   73   330
  Voyage   75   83
  Red Boots, a Balalaika
  Octavian Shooting Targets   78   268
  Kenya Drums   84   66
  A Mode of Hangings   89   29
  Song Without Words   92   79
  Hand, Hand   96   167
  Twenty or So
  Lack of Stand
  Basic Movements   105   379
  Short Poem   108   225
  Enchanted Flowers
  The Unworldliness that He Creates   111   175
  The Statue   115   18
  Gift of the Firebird   118   145
  Addressed to the Firebird
  Ruined Tracks   120   338

REVIEWS
  Terraces of Light,
    by Marya Zaturenska   98   186

BOOKS REVIEWED
  Basic Movements   112   44
  Figure in the Door   113   35
  A Bed by the Sea   117   108

Selected Poems	121	234
The Past Now	130	41

GREGORY, ALLENE

POEMS

Litany	13	13

GREGORY, [LADY] AUGUSTA

BOOKS REVIEWED

Visions and Beliefs in the West of Ireland (Ed.; notes by W. B. Yeats)	18	49

GREGORY, HORACE

POEMS

The Sailor	26	197
The Boy of Twenty		
Prisoner's Song	31	10
Flora		
Where Caesar Fell		
Into Earth		
Interior: The Suburbs	35	237
Columbo Dominico		
O Mors Aeterna		
O Metaphysical Head		
A Tombstone with Cherubim	37	306
Valediction to My Contemporaries	41	237
A Wreath for Margery		
Men of Three Ages	44	239
Reunion at Washington Square		
River Marquette:		
Winter and Spring, 1675		
My Portrait, My Signature		
Fortune for Mirabel	51	8
Pandarus, the Wheel, and Mirabell	64	297
Landscape from a Window:		
Hudson River School		
The Last of Mirabel	67	119
The Material Witness Escapes		
from the "Coq d'Or":		
An Incident with a Moral		
Rabinowitz, the Piano-Tuner, Speaks		
The Rehearsal	78	137
The Aquatic Gardens: Washington, D. C.		
The Cage of Voices		
Haunted Odysseus: The Last Testament		
On a Celtic Mask by Henry Moore	97	335
Three Allegories of Bellini		
After Ovid: The Burning of the Locks	99	306
Peace in Our Time	122	63
Death & Empedocles 444 B.C.		
The Glass Box: A Domestic Fable 1972		
Plessis-du-Parc-Lès-Tours 1483		
Balquhidder at Morning	134	134
Nature & the Architect	139	133

ARTICLES

Correspondence:		
The February Number	38	51

Prologue as Epilogue	48	92
[Tribute to Harriet Monroe] (With Marya Zaturenska)	49	157
The "Vita Nuova" of Baroque Art in the Recent Poetry of Edith Sitwell	66	148
The Isolation of Isaac Rosenberg [D. H. Lawrence, Wilfred Owen]	68	30
The "Romantic" Heritage in the Writings of Dylan Thomas	69	326

REVIEWS

The Seventh Hill, by Robert Hillyer	32	165
The King of Spain, by Maxwell Bodenheim	32	221
The Tower, by W. B. Yeats	33	41
Good Morning America, by Carl Sandburg	33	214
The Long Leash, by Jessica Nelson North	33	340
The Red Front, by Louis Aragon (Tr. by E. E. Cummings)	42	281
From Feathers to Iron and The Magnetic Mountain, by C. Day Lewis	42	288
Recent Poetry 1923-1933 (Ed. by Alida Monro)	44	113
This Side of Poetry	44	291
Sense and Poetry, by John Sparrow		
Criticism and Poetry, by F. L. Lucas		
Selected Poems, by Oliver St. John Gogarty	45	55
Amaranth, by Edwin Arlington Robinson	45	158
Permit Me Voyage, by James Agee	46	48
How to Read; The ABC of Reading; Make It New; The ABC of Economics; Social Credit: An Impact; and Eleven New Cantos (XXXI to XLI), by Ezra Pound	46	279
An Anthology of Light Verse (Ed. by Louis Kronenberger)	48	47
Poets in the Theatre	48	221
Winterset, by Maxwell Anderson		
Panic, by Archibald MacLeish		
Murder in the Cathedral, by T. S. Eliot		
Tom, by E. E. Cummings		
The Dog Beneath the Skin, by W. H. Auden and Christopher Isherwood		
Collected Plays, by W. B. Yeats		
A Contrast in Satires	49	282
Poems, by Kenneth Fearing		
Second Hymn to Lenin, by Hugh MacDiarmid		
The Vigil of Venus (Tr. by Allen Tate)	64	30
A Soul for Sale, by Patrick Kavanagh	71	324
Holes in the Sky, by Louis MacNeice	74	301

By Avon River, by H. D.   75   223
The Metamorphosis
    of the Classical Heritage   76   218
    The Portable Greek Reader
        (Ed. by W. H. Auden)
    The Latin Poets
        (Ed. by Francis R. B. Godolphin)
    The Classical Tradition,
        by Gilbert Highet
    The Collected Poems of Christopher Smart
        (Ed. by Norman Callan)
    The Pleasures of Pope
        (Ed. by Peter Quennell)   77   340
Winged Chariot and Other Poems,
    by Walter de la Mare
    [Robert Louis Stevenson]   80   213
The Poems of C. P. Cafavy
    (Tr. by John Mavrogordato)   81   383
The Autobiography of William Butler Yeats   84   153

BOOKS REVIEWED
    Chelsea Rooming House   38   41
    The Poems of Catullus (Tr.)   39   93
    No Retreat   42   217
    Chorus for Survival   46   227
    New Letters in America (Ed.)   51   206
    Poems 1930-1940   58   152
    The Triumph of Life:
        Poems of Consolation for
        the English-speaking World (Ed.)   64   107
    The Shield of Achilles,
        Essays on Beliefs in Poetry   64   334
    A History of American Poetry, 1900-1940
        (With Marya Zaturenska)   69   218
    The Selected Poems of…   81   144
    The Mentor Book of Religious Verse
        (Ed. with Marya Zaturenska)   91   124
    Ovid: The Metamorphoses (Tr.)   95   185
    Ovid: The Metamorphoses (Tr.)   96   247
    Medusa in Gramercy Park   100   387
    The Crystal Cabinet
        (Ed. with Marya Zaturenska)   103   261
    Collected Poems   105   134
    Another Look   128   300

ARTICLES ABOUT
    Correspondence from Ezra Pound   47   55

GREGORY, MARY
TRANSLATIONS
    Poem by Kostes Palamas   130   211

GREGORY, MARYA ZATURENSKA
[See ZATURENSKA, MARYA]

GREGORY, ODIN
BOOKS REVIEWED
    Caius Gracchus   17   337

GREGSON, JAMES R.
ARTICLES ABOUT
    The Editor in England,
        by Harriet Monroe   23   32

GRENE, DAVID
REVIEWS
    The Odes of Pindar
        (Tr. by Richmond Lattimore)   70   340
    Oedipus Rex
        (Tr. by Dudley Fitts
        and Robert Fitzgerald)   76   299

BOOKS REVIEWED
    Oedipus the King (Tr.)   85   225
    Hippolytus (Tr.)   86   303
    The Complete Greek Tragedies:
        Euripides III, IV
        (Ed. with Richmond Lattimore)   95   190

GRENFELL, JULIAN
ARTICLES ABOUT
    Rev. of *Soldier Poets*   10   271

GRENIER, ROBERT
POEMS
    St. Emily of the Body   112   96
    Bird Song
    Warm

BOOKS REVIEWED
    Dusk Road Games   112   343

GRENNAN, EAMON
POEMS
    The Coming Day   149   65
    At Home in Winter
    Houseplants in Winter
    The Cave Painters   157   324
    Sitting in a Field on a Windy Day
    A Few Last Lines of Laundry
    Dog   163   75
    Leaving the Garden   167   6
    Alli Dying
    Streak of Light
    Night by the Harbor   170   82

BOOKS REVIEWED
    What Light There Is & Other Poems   155   283
    As If It Matters   161   223

GREVILLE, FULKE
[(LORD) BROOKE]
ARTICLES ABOUT
    The 16th Century Lyric
        in England: Part II,
        by Yvor Winters   53   320

GREY, JEANNETTE
POEMS
   Soft Airs   40   256
      She Wakes the Lilies
      Antithesis
      Far Land

GRIEG, MICHAEL
BOOKS REVIEWED
   Guide to the City   96   238

GRIER, ELDON
BOOKS REVIEWED
   A Friction of Lights   104   385

GRIER, MARY
POEMS
   Winter's End   39   302
      Spring Day in March
      Snow in the Loop

GRIERSON, FRANCIS
ARTICLES
   Stéphane Mallarmé   2   104

GRIERSON, HERBERT J. C.
BOOKS REVIEWED
   Wordsworth and Milton,
      Poets and Prophets. A Study
      of Their Reactions to Political Events   51   37
   Criticism and Creation   78   285

GRIEVE, CHRISTOPHER MURRAY
  [See MAC DIARMID, HUGH, pseud.]

GRIFFIN, ELIZABETH F.
POEMS
   In Flood   52   23

GRIFFIN, HOWARD
POEMS
   Washington House   69   11
      The Detective Story
   The Party   73   25
   The Gladiatore Farnese   95   202
      The Analyst

ARTICLES
   Conversation on Cornelia Street:
      A Dialogue with W. H. Auden
      [William Shakespeare, Dante]   83   96

BOOKS REVIEWED
   Cry Cadence   71   327

GRIFFIN, WALTER
POEMS
   Corvus   153   98

      Stanley Smith Is Dead
   Mother's Day   154   97
   Outlaws   158   19
      Other Cities
   At the All Night Cafeteria   166   196

GRIFFITH, D. W.
ARTICLES ABOUT
   The New Era,
      by Harriet Monroe   9   195

GRIFFITH, E. V.
BOOKS REVIEWED
   Answers   96   179

GRIFFITH, LL. WYN
POEMS
   Valediction   49   203

GRIFFITH, WILLIAM
POEMS
   Woodwinds   6   123
      Hadleyburg
      Little Songs of the Forest
   He Forgets Yvonne   8   298
      Pierrette Goes

BOOKS REVIEWED
   Loves and Losses of Pierrot   12   165
      City Pastorals and Other Poems
   Loves and Lasses of Pierrot   27   162

GRIGSON, GEOFFREY
POEMS
   The Professionals   59   26
      No Get-Away
      June
   Scent of Women   117   174
      Incident of Wolves and Water
      Poor Tom, Poor Scullion
      Short History of Old Art
   The Oculi   119   28
      The Chapel
      No Sprinkling of Bright Weeds
      Pawlonia
      Aprés la Chasse
      A Myth Enacted
      Hill of the Bees
      Return to Florence
   After All, White Doves   120   337
   The Gods and the Colonels 121   126
      Spleen Again of the Night: Picnic
      The Cyprian's Spring
      The Cold Spring
      Desultory Summer Poem
      As Dufy Paints
      To Dijon, Under Snow
      Water Voice of a Dove

Through Butterflies
A Dozen Facts of London
Burial
Television To-Night   125   32
Two A.M. in the Archipelago
Angles and Circles
His Swans   128   65
The Corner
To Hermes
Bright Piece out of a Dead Sea
Death for the Undying   131   147
Joan of Arc's Stone, Le Crotoy   132   254
Annotation
Fearing Invasion

ARTICLES
A Letter from England
  [Cecil Day Lewis, T. S. Eliot]   49   101
Correspondence
  [William Empson]   50   115
Correspondence:
  Poetry Politics in London Continued
  [D. S. Savage]   54   52

REVIEWS
Poetry by the Manufacturing Chemist   80   159
  The Sorrows of Cold Stone,
    by John Malcolm Brinnin
  American Sampler.
    A Selection of New Poetry
    (Ed. by Francis Coleman Rosenberger)

BOOKS REVIEWED
  A Skull in Salop and Other Poems   116   46
  Poems & Poets

ARTICLES ABOUT
  Correspondence from William Empson   49   237
  Correspondence from William Empson   50   116
  Poetry Politics in London,
    by D. S. Savage   53   200

GROBMANN, EDITH
POEMS
  Eurydice   66   16
  Syndrome   69   260

GROFF, ALICE
ARTICLES
  Correspondence
    [Alice Corbin Henderson]   8   158

GROFF, DAVID
POEMS
  The Sense of Well-Being   154   232

GROS, LEON-GABRIEL
ARTICLES ABOUT
  Marseille Letter, by Jean Rivier   60   269

GROSHOLZ, EMILY
POEMS
  The River-Painter   128   17
  Gathering of Friends,
    After the Fall of the Sung Dynasty
  The Old Fisherman   144   195
  Siesta
  Thirty-Six Weeks   158   156
  The Great Blizzard   165   133

BOOKS REVIEWED
  Shores and Headlands   154   283

GROSJEAN, JEAN
POEMS
  Graduel   104   296
  Hiver
    (Tr. by Wallace Fowlie)

GROSS, HARVEY
POEMS
  The Tapestry   83   18
  Plans for an Orderly Apocalypse
  Seven Views of the City

BOOKS REVIEWED
  Sound and Form in Modern Poetry:
    A Study of Prosody from Thomas Hardy
    to Robert Lowell   107   332
  Plans for an Orderly Apocalypse   113   262

GROSS, PAMELA
POEMS
  Losing the Eight Colors   157   327
  The Hive   160   261
  Some Notes in the Margin   163   28
  Matthew Paris Maps the Move of the Hive   165   206

BOOKS REVIEWED
  Birds of the Night Sky/Stars of the Field 170   347

GROSS, SUZANNE
BOOKS REVIEWED
  Sand Verbena   104   108

GROSSBARDT, ANDREW
POEMS
  The Mummies of Guanajuato   132   338
  Photo from Costa Rica

GROSSMAN, ALLEN
POEMS
  Trucks   89   168
  The Secret Religionist   90   144
  Norma
  I Am in Babylon Dying
  Pain
  Pompeii   94   239

The Jealousy of the Hawk   99   285
The Middleman
O Great O North Cloud   129   321
The Runner
Nightmare
The Holdout   134   157
An Inventory of Destructions   140   14

BOOKS REVIEWED
The Recluse and Other Poems   108   408
And the Dew Lay All Night upon My Branch 130   41
The Woman on the Bridge
    over the Chicago River   137   169
Of the Great House   142   106
The Bright Nails Scattered
    on the Ground: Love Poems   149   31

GROSSMAN, FLORENCE
POEMS
Sewing Box   136   86
Tree
Still Life   142   17
Cobwebs   158   93

GROSZMANN, LORE
TRANSLATIONS
Poems by Christian Morgenstern
    (With W. D. Snodgrass)   98   365

GROUITCH, [MADAME] SLAVKO
ARTICLES ABOUT
The Servian Epic, by Harriet Monroe   1   195

GROVER, EDWIN OSGOOD
BOOKS REVIEWED
Dartmouth Lyrics, by Richard Hovey (Ed.)   27   164

GRUBE, JOHN
BOOKS REVIEWED
Sunday Afternoon at the Toronto Art Gallery 111   323

GRUBER, RUTH
POEMS
Leaves Burning in the Autumn   47   24

GRUCCI, JOSEPH L(EONARD)
BOOKS REVIEWED
3 Spanish American Poets (Tr.)
    [Pablo Neruda]   62   111
Time of Hawks   89   45

GRUDIN, LOUIS
POEMS
Miniatures   11   126
"All Roads Lead to Rome"   20   306
Jest

REVIEWS
Introducing Irony;
    A Book of Poetic Short Stories and Poems,
    by Maxwell Bodenheim   21   100

Preludes and Symphonies,
    by John Gould Fletcher   21   270
Towards Democracy,
    by Edward Carpenter   21   331

BOOKS REVIEWED
Charlatan   24   103
Mr. Eliot Among the Nightingales   42   44
A Tearless Glass   47   162

GRUDSKY, LEO
POEMS
Family Portrait   17   80
Melodrama
In the Mirror

GRUMBINE, HARVEY C.
BOOKS REVIEWED
Humanity or Hate: Which? (Ed.)   14   281

GUENTHER, CHARLES
TRANSLATIONS
Poems by René Char   89   333
Poem by René Char   94   37
Poems by Leopold Sedar Senghor   103   179

ARTICLES
A Note on Leopold Sedar Senghor   103   199

REVIEWS
Seamarks, by St.-John Perse
    (Tr. by Wallace Fowlie)   93   332

BOOKS REVIEWED
Selected Poems,
    by Alain Bosquet
    (Tr. with Samuel Beckett,
    Edouard Roditi, and Ruth Whitman) 104   115

GUERNSEY, BRUCE
POEMS
Back Road   135   209
The Owl   141   137
The Seeing-Eye Dog
The Photographer of Funerals
The Search   154   129

GUEST, BARBARA
POEMS
Dido to Aeneas   98   218
Green Awnings
The Return of the Muses   105   174
Fan Poems

BOOKS REVIEWED
Poems: The Locations of Things,
    Archaics, The Open Skies   103   256
The Blue Stairs   113   428
Moscow Mansions   124   45

ARTICLES ABOUT
The Forging of H. D.,
  by Gloria G. Fromm 153   160

GUEST, EDGAR (A.)
ARTICLES ABOUT
Newspaper Verse,
  by Harriet Monroe 19   324
Correspondence
  from Gamaliel Bradford 20   114
The Laureate They Deserve?
  by Margery Swett (Mansfield) 25   38

GUEST, HARRY
BOOKS REVIEWED
Penguin Modern Poets 16
  (With Jack Beeching
  and Matthew Mead) 119   291

GUEVARA, MAURICE KILWEIN
POEMS
Tombstones 161   263
Cofradía

GUHA, NARESH
POEMS
Supernatural
  (Tr. by Lila Ray) 93   214

GUILFORD, CHUCK
POEMS
Below the Dam 128   338
Song ("Everything's falling...")

GUILLÉN, JORGE
BOOKS REVIEWED
Cántico: A Selection,
  Spanish Poems with English Translation
  (Ed. by Norman Thomas di Giovanni) 111   46
Affirmation: A Bilingual
  Anthology, 1919-1966
  (Tr. by Julian Palley) 113   338

ARTICLES ABOUT
Jorge Guillén, Marianne Moore,
  T. S. Eliot: Some Recollections,
  by Wallace Fowlie 90   103
Jorge Guillén,
  by Wallace Fowlie 99   243

GUILLÉN, NICOLAS
POEMS
Federico (Tr. by Lloyd Mallan) 62   66
Sabas (Tr. by L. C. Kaplan) 62   69
Madrigals 73   11
Words in the Tropics
Guadalupe, W. I.
  (Tr. by Robert Brittain)

GUILLERMO, GELACIO
POEMS
Pan de Sal 118   208

GUILLEVIC, EUGÈNE
POEMS
Parallels 116   358
Right Angle
Acute Angle
Rectangle
  (Tr. by Teo Savory)

BOOKS REVIEWED
Selected Poems
  (Tr. by Denise Levertov) 116   260

GUINEY, LOUISE IMOGEN
ARTICLES ABOUT
Two Poets Have Died,
  by Harriet Monroe 17   208

GUITERMAN, ARTHUR
BOOKS REVIEWED
Chips of Jade and Betel Nuts (Tr.) 20   346
I Sing the Pioneer 30   293
Death and General Putnam,
  and 101 Other Poems 50   210
Gaily the Troubador

GULICK, ALIDA CAREY
POEMS
Dusk at Noon 77   330
Ein' Feste Burg

GULLANS, CHARLES
POEMS
Satyr 125   131
"Philosopher Standing,
  Holding a Book" 132   158
The Source 140   283

BOOKS REVIEWED
Arrivals and Departures 103   192

GULLBERG, HJALMAR
POEMS
Stellaria 126   13
For the Demigods
  (Tr. by Judith Moffett)
There Is a Lake
  and Nothing Ever More 128   152
Delos, an Ode to the Young
  (Tr. by Judith Moffett)

GUMILYOV, NIKOLAI
ARTICLES ABOUT
Rev. of Three Poets of Modern Russia,
  by Leonid I. Strakhovsky 76   112

GUND, HERMAN
POEMS
   The Lake Poems   49   128
   Carnival   52   322
   Queens

GUNN, ANDER
BOOKS REVIEWED
   Positives (With Thom Gunn)   111   405

GUNN, THOM
POEMS
   During an Absence   86   125
   Human Condition
   A Plan of Self Subjection
   Lines for a Book
   Merlin in the Cave:
      He Speculates Without a Book
   Legal Reform
   Autumn Chapter in a Novel
   The Corridor
   High Fidelity
   The Unsettled Motorcyclist's Vision
      of His Death   90   32
   Waking in a Newly-Built House, Oakland
   In Santa Maria del Popolo   93   1
   Black Jackets
   The Annihilation of Nothing
   In the Tank   101   44
   Taylor Street   109   69
   The Old Man in the Britannia
   No Speech from the Scaffold
   Snowfall
   The Produce District
   The Messenger   116   1
   Being Born
   The Discovery of the Pacific
   Patch Work   151   63

ARTICLES
   Comment   151   214

REVIEWS
   Eight Poets   89   244
      The Form of Loss,
        by Edgar Bowers
      The Battlement,
        by Donald F. Drummond
      A World of Saints,
        by Thomas Cole
      Three Priests in April,
        by Stephen Stepanchev
      Poets of Today, III:
        The Floating World and Other Poems,
        by Lee Anderson;
        My Father's Business and Other Poems,
        by Spencer Brown;
        The Green Town,
        by Joseph Langland

   Villa Narcisse, by Katherine Hoskins
   The Calm Style   92   378
      Brutus's Orchard, by Roy Fuller
      The Open Sea and Other Poems,
        by William Meredith
      Home Truths,
        by Anthony Thwaite
      The Forever Young and Other Poems,
        by Pauline Hanson
   Certain Traditions   97   260
      Collected Poems,
        by J. C. Squire
      The Prodigal Son,
        by James Kirkup
      Collected Poems,
        by William Plomer
      Ballad of the Mari Lwyd
        and *Cypress and Acacia,*
        by Vernon Watkins
      The Forests of Lithuania,
        by Donald Davie
      Lupercal, by Ted Hughes
      Florida East Coast Champion,
        by Rod Taylor   121   239

BOOKS REVIEWED
   The Sense of Movement   92   318
   The Sense of Movement   95   107
   My Sad Captains   100   104
   A Geography   111   189
   Positives (With Ander Gunn)   111   405
   Touch   113   35
   Moly   124   103
   My Sad Captains
   To the Air   126   352
   Selected Poems 1950-1975   138   107
   The Man with Night Sweats   161   286
   Collected Poems   165   289

GURGANUS, ALLAN
ARTICLES
   An Introduction
      [James Merrill]   166   350

GURI, HAYIM
POEMS
   The Spring   92   246
   Song and Me
      (Tr. by Ruth Finer Mintz)

ARTICLES ABOUT
   Postscript: The Younger Poets,
      by Simon Halkin   92   259

GURLEY, GEORGE H., JR.
POEMS
   Bird Songs   144   20
   Burning of the Books

GURLEY, JAMES
POEMS
Biosophy,
an Optimist's Manifesto   169   131

GURNEY, IVOR
ARTICLES ABOUT
Finishes: Notes
on Ambition and Survival,
by Christian Wiman   169   217

GUSTAFSON, INGEMAR
ARTICLES ABOUT
Rev. of *Half Sun Half Sleep,*
by May Swenson   111   184

GUSTAFSON, RALPH
POEMS
From Sweden   51   144
Seascape   52   313
Begin Living O How   55   130
We Shall Know Hurt
Atlantic Crossing   57   23
Excelling the Starry Splendor of This Night   61   427

BOOKS REVIEWED
A Little Anthology
of Canadian Poets (Ed.)   63   281
Flight into Darkness   66   100
The Penguin Book
of Canadian Verse (Ed.)   94   186
Rocky Mountain Poems   98   319
Rivers Among Rocks

GUSTAVSON, JEFFREY
POEMS
Is Light   163   94

GUTERMAN, NORBERT
BOOKS REVIEWED
Sainte-Beuve: Selected Essays
(Tr. with Francis Steegmuller)   103   183

GUTHRIE, RAMON
POEMS
L'Enfance de la Sirene   100   365
Anatomy of the Week   117   84
The Poster by the Mailbox   120   333

BOOKS REVIEWED
Maximum Security Ward   119   159
Maximum Security Ward
and Other Poems
(Ed. by Sally M. Gall)   145   348

GUTMANN, ASSIA
BOOKS REVIEWED
Poems, by Yehuda Amichai (Tr.)   116   120

GUY, GEORGES
POEMS
From *Lettre à Theo Léger*
(Tr. by Wallace Fowlie)   80   361

GWILLIM, JOY
POEMS
I Wept When Horses Bit Me   134   90
It Covers Me
The Ritual

GWILYM, DAFYDD AP
[See AP GWILYM, DAFYDD]

GWYNN, R. S.
POEMS
Among Philistines   141   340

"H. A."
[See ALLEN, HERVEY]

"H. B. F."
[See FULLER, HENRY B.]

"H. C."
[See CARRUTH, HAYDEN]

"H. D."
[See DOOLITTLE, HILDA]

"H. H."
[See HOYT, HELEN]

"H. M."
[See MONROE, HARRIET]

"H. S. M."
REVIEWS
War Poetry Again   12   285
    A Book of Verse on the Great War
      (Ed. by W. R. Wheeler)
    The Muse in Arms
      (Ed. by E. B. Osborn)
    Fifes and Drums

HAAG, JOHN
POEMS
Footnotes from
    the Book of Nature   170   224

HAAS, ROSAMOND
BOOKS REVIEWED
Delay Is the Song   64   231
This Time This Tide   77   215

HAAVIKKO, PAAVO
BOOKS REVIEWED
Selected Poems
    (Ed. and tr. by Anselm Hollo)   114   251

HABER, TOM BURNS
ARTICLES
Correspondence: The Housman Text
    [Laurence Housman, Donald Justice]   96   392

BOOKS REVIEWED
Complete Poems,
    by A. E. Housman (Ed.)   96   44

HABERLY, LOYD
BOOKS REVIEWED
Poems   41   165
Silent Fame   67   225

HACKER, MARILYN
POEMS
Chanson de l'Enfant Prodigue   120   276
An Alexandrite Pendant for My Mother   122   202
Under the Arc de Triomphe: October 17   123   10
Lines Declining a Transatlantic
    Dinner Invitation   132   82
Third Snowfall   133   134
The Hang-Glider's Daughter   135   133
Burnham Beeches   136   134
A Man with Sons
Gerda in the Eyrie   138   204
A Chaplet for Judith Landry   141   261
April Interval I   144   1
April Interval III
April Interval IV

BOOKS REVIEWED
Presentation Piece   126   44
Separations   129   285
Taking Notice   138   231
Assumptions   147   156
Going Back to the River   158   214

HADAS, MOSES
BOOKS REVIEWED
Goethe the Poet,
    by Karl Vietor (Tr.)   75   232
The Greek Poets (Ed.)   84   112

HADAS, PAMELA (WHITE)
POEMS
From Building Waking   127   214
Plain Lisa   133   222
From The Bandit Queen's Abandonment:
    Belle Starr Remembering   137   217

To Make a Dragon Move:
   From the Diary of an Anorexic   140   261
Ringling Bros. Present:
   The Lucky Lucie Lamort

BOOKS REVIEWED
   Designing Women   135   229

HADAS, RACHEL
POEMS
   Waiting   128   7
   Twelfth Birthday   169   268
   Committee Meeting   170   141

ARTICLES
   Memorial Tribute
   [James Merrill,
   C. P. Cavafy]   166   334

BOOKS REVIEWED
   Slow Transparency   145   99
   Pass It On   156   158
   Living in Time   159   157
   Mirrors of Astonishment   164   97
   The Empty Bed   169   286

HADLEY, DRUMMOND
BOOKS REVIEWED
   The Webbing   116   125

HADLEY, HENRY
ARTICLES ABOUT
   Correspondence
   from Louise Ayres Garnett   19   102

HAFFENDEN, JOHN
ARTICLES
   Job, by John Berryman   136   39

HAFIZ
BOOKS REVIEWED
   Selections from the Rubaiyat of...   20   346

HAGEDORN, HERMANN
POEMS
   Early Morning at Bargis   6   180
   Fatherland   6   280
   The Cabaret Dancer   7   125

ARTICLES
   As to Preaching   2   142

BOOKS REVIEWED
   Poems and Ballads   1   131
   The Great Maze and the
      Heart of Youth—A Poem and a Play   9   90
   Edwin Arlington Robinson   54   92

HAGELSTANGE, RUDOLF
POEMS
   All Is Dust
      (Tr. by Herman Salinger)   88   255

HAGIWARA, KYOJIRO
POEMS
   The Family   88   87
   I Will Suffer From What
      My Father Suffered From
      (Tr. by Satoru Satu
      and Constance Urdang)

HAGIWARA, SAKUTARO
POEMS
   Tortoise   88   102
   Song Without a Name
   Littoral Zone
   Death of a Frog
   The White Moon
   A Dish of Skylarks

HAGSTRUM, JEAN H.
BOOKS REVIEWED
   William Blake, Poet and Painter:
      An Introduction to the Illuminated Verse   107   192

HAGUE, RICHARD
POEMS
   Time-Lapse Photography:
      A Mouse Corpse Devoured by Maggots   163   331
   The Poem Starts To Start Over   169   330
   Pitch Pine   170   278

HAHN, SUSAN
POEMS
   Melancholia   141   218
   Looking Out on Africa
   Agoraphobia   144   136
   Waiting at the Gate
   Small Green   150   76
   Oral Interpretation
   Flowers   153   296
   Between Rosh Hashanah and Yom Kippur   158   327
   Calendar   159   206
   The Hemlock Society   160   85
   Insomnia   162   329
   Incontinence
   Pneumonia   165   267
   Disorderly Conduct
   Poison
   The Lovers
   February Day   167   269

BOOKS REVIEWED
   Incontinence   164   223

HAI-KU, LI
   [See LI HAI-KU]

HAINES, JOHN
POEMS
   This Dark Water   103   242

BOOKS REVIEWED
   Winter News   109   118
   Twenty Poems   120   107
   The Stone Harp   120   164

HAISLIP, JOHN
BOOKS REVIEWED
   Not Every Year   123   34

HA JIN
POEMS
   Ways of Talking   164   196

HALD, PETER
POEMS
   Narcissus in New York   79   275

HALE, NANCY
ARTICLES
   The Other Side of the Cove   98   313

HALE, OLIVER
POEMS
   The Loss   66   182
   Portraits
   The History   71   305
   The Brittle Glass
   Vantage Point: Subway   76   272
   Where Towers Form

HALE, SWINBURNE
BOOKS REVIEWED
   The Demon's Notebook   22   344

HALE, WILLIAM GARDNER
ARTICLES
   Correspondence: Pegasus Impounded
      [Ezra Pound]   14   52

HALEY, LAURA MARGARET
POEMS
   Whispers   36   24
   The Ghost
   Night Song

HALEY, VANESSA
POEMS
   Dead Horses   136   70
   At the Smithsonian
   The Housesitter   142   220
   Home

HALGREN, PAULETTE
POEMS
   Summer at Home   79   265

HALKIN, SIMON
ARTICLES
   Postscript: The Younger Poets
      [Hayim Guri, Michael Deshe,
      Yitzhak Shalev]   92   259

HALL, AMANDA (BENJAMIN)
POEMS
   The Dish-Washer   15   310
   O Singer! O Dancer!
   The Haunted Well   22   18
   The Ballad of the Three Sons   24   289
   The Sale   29   314
   Now Must the Huntsman   51   138
   New England Sabbath   56   197

BOOKS REVIEWED
   The Dancer in the Shrine
      and Other Poems   28   345

HALL, CAROL
POEMS
   An Old Woman's Words
      to Her Young Cat   90   356
   To a Woman Seen Eating
      the Evening Paper

HALL, DANIEL
POEMS
   Winged Torso of Eros   158   194
   A Fifties 4th

BOOKS REVIEWED
   Hermit with Landscape   157   33
   Strange Relation   170   101

HALL, DONALD
POEMS
   A Second Stanza for Dr. Johnson   84   201
   The Lone Ranger
   Syllables of a Small Fig-Tree
   Matter of Fact   86   263
   Lycanthropy Revisited
   Jamaica
   Bamboo
   Some Americans in Paris   88   225
   The Morning Porches
   Amos
   T. R.   92   169
   Caribbean
   The Kiss   93   29
   The Days   100   31
   The Beau of the Dead
   The Footsteps
   The Sun
   The Stump   104   93
   Wells
   Assassin

"Internal and External Forms"
The Grave, the Mine
Apples   113   88
Swan
The Table
The Blue Wing
This Room
Poem Beginning with
    a Line of Wittgenstein   133   279
For an Early Retirement
Apology for Old Clothes
Adultery at Forty
At Eagle Pond   143   25
Sums   148   93
A Beard for a Blue Pantry   165   283
Goggles and Helmet
Extended Care
The Words
Without   167   144
Midwinter Letter   170   17

ARTICLES
    Poets Aloud
        [Ted Hughes, Robert Lowell,
        Sylvia Plath, T. S. Eliot,
        Ezra Pound, William Carlos Williams,
        Robert Penn Warren, E. E. Cummings,
        Philip Levine]   139   297

REVIEWS
    A Diet of Dissatisfaction   87   299
        An Almanac for Amorists,
            by James Broughton
        Rainbow at Midnight,
            by Lawrence Lipton
        The Colours of Memory,
            by George Reavey
        The Diamond Cutters,
            by Adrienne Cecile Rich
    Claims on the Poet   88   398
        Things of This World,
            by Richard Wilbur
        The Misanthrope, by Molière
            (Tr. by Richard Wilbur)
        Tenebrae, and
        The Poetry and Voice of Geoffrey Hill
        [Recording]   136   102

BOOKS REVIEWED
    The Harvard Advocate (Ed.)   78   241
    To the Loud Wind and Other Poems   87   53
    Exiles and Marriages   88   183
    The Dark Houses   94   189
    A Poetry Sampler (Ed.)   104   245
    Contemporary American Poetry (Ed.)
    A Roof of Tiger Lilies   107   125
    The Alligator Bride:
        Poems New and Selected   118   98

The Yellow Room   119   234
Kicking the Leaves   134   226
The Happy Man   150   36
Old and New Poems   158   41
The Museum of Clear Ideas   163   158

ARTICLES ABOUT
    [Note]   159   51
    [Note]   164   245

HALL, EILEEN
    BOOKS REVIEWED
        The Fountain and the Bough   53   223

HALL, HAZEL
    POEMS
        To a Phrase   12   194
        Needlework   16   18
        Repetitions   18   86
            Two Sewing
            Instruction
            Three Songs for Sewing
            Cowardice
            Flash
        Walkers   21   185
            Hunger
            Shawled
            The Hurrier
            A Whistler in the Night
            They Who Walk in Moonlight
            Pedestrian
            Footfalls
        Songs of Farewell   24   173
            Before Quiet
            Song To Be Known Before Death
            Pleasantry
            The Relinquisher
            Submergence
            Protest
            A Woman Ponders
            Experienced Griever
            Hearsay
            Sleep Charm
            Death Defied

    BOOKS REVIEWED
        Curtains   19   100
        Walkers   22   276
        Cry of Time   33   272

    ARTICLES ABOUT
        Hazel Hall, by Harriet Monroe   24   210
        A Few Women Poets,
            by Harriet Monroe   26   326

HALL, HERBERT J.
    POEMS
        Sea and Land   3   14

HALL, J. C.
   BOOKS REVIEWED
      The Summer Dance   81   254

HALL, JAMES
   ARTICLES ABOUT
      Notes on Mid-western Oblivion,
         by Pat Morrissette   34   346

HALL, JAMES
   REVIEWS
      Winter Crook, by William Gibson   72   278
      Red Wine and Yellow Hair,
         by Kenneth Patchen   75   115
      Fingerboard, by Marshall Schacht   76   361

   BOOKS REVIEWED
      The Permanence of Yeats
         (Ed. with Martin Steinmann)   76   227

HALL, JAMES B.
   POEMS
      Gaspar's Ferry: End of Ohio Roads   76   138
      Pastoral   79   77
      Seasonal   79   280
      In Bailey Woods   80   254
      The Hunt Within   82   15
      Grandmother   88   160
      Pilgrims: Uncle Sid   97   15

   ARTICLES ABOUT
      Rev. of *Poems from the
         Iowa Poetry Workshop*
         (Ed. by Paul Engle)   79   284

HALL, JAMES BAKER
   POEMS
      *four year old brown & grey
         Ford family car, dirty*   132   98
      Whenever He Leaves   134   200
      Her Hand
      *A Thin Strip of Bright Light Falls
      Sitting Between Two Mirrors*   140   133
      I Move
      Adam's Love Song   143   135
      Fresh Snow at Dusk
      The Child
      Establishing Longitude   146   35
      *Organdy Curtain, Window,
         South Bank of the Ohio*
      Welcoming the Season's First Insects
      On the Day of Balanchine's Death   146   98
      Identifying the Body
      Final

   REVIEWS
      A Poetry Chronicle   104   47
         Mockingbirds at Fort McHenry,
            by Elliott Coleman

      The Heron,
         by Constance Hunting
      To Peel an Apple,
         by William Packard
      The Epistemology of Loss,
         by Frederick Eckman
      A Sigh Is the Sword,
         by Herman Salinger
      A View from Africa,
         by Marvin Solomon
      Bearing Weapons,
         by Stephen Berg

HALL, JAMES NORMAN
   BOOKS REVIEWED
      The Friends   55   103

HALL, JIM
   POEMS
      Sorting the Photos   135   281
      False Statements   140   205
      The First One
      Woolgathering   142   319
      One-Liners   148   74
      Working to the Top
      Ourselves
      Tennis Elbow

HALL, JOHN
   POEMS
      Candlemas   63   198
      Earthbound

**HALL, JOSEF WASHINGTON
   [UPTON CLOSE, pseud.]**
   TRANSLATIONS
      Poem from Chinese   26   319

HALL, JUDITH
   BOOKS REVIEWED
      To Put the Mouth To   162   167

HALL, KAY DE BARD
   POEMS
      Heat Wave   66   310

HALL, RUTH
   POEMS
      The Wolf at the Door   8   233
      The Anniversary

HALL, ZULA
   BOOKS REVIEWED
      Blossom Time   77   215

HALLER, ROBERT
   BOOKS REVIEWED
      The Achievement of Wallace Stevens
         (Ed. with Ashley Brown)   102   269

HALLERMAN, VICTORIA
POEMS
   We Grew Up Playing Bomb Shelter   144 89
   Seeing, Being Seen
   A Sculpture by George Segal   148 87
   The Road Home
   Slippage: A Writing-Room Idyll
   Beneath the Interstate   152 77
   Egret   165 130

HALLEY, ANNE
POEMS
   News from Another Province   141 80
   Oh a Quick Man

HALLIDAY, DAVID
BOOKS REVIEWED
   The Black Bird   144 297

HALLIDAY, MARK
POEMS
   A Kind of Reply   154 314
   Location   158 187
   Ketchup and Heaven   160 32
   There
   The White Helmet   162 337
   1946   163 255

HALLIWELL, J. O.
ARTICLES ABOUT
   Rev. of The Oxford Dictionary
     of Nursery Rhymes
     (Ed. by Iona and Peter Opie)   84 167

HALPER, ALBERT
BOOKS REVIEWED
   Chicago Side-Show   43 225

HALPERIN, MARK
POEMS
   April 1945   134 5
   A Servant
   On the Steps of Temple Shalom   156 23

HALPERN, DANIEL
POEMS
   Return   135 333
   Late
   The Storm   136 267
   Summer Constellations
   The End of Vigil
   Summer Storm   143 146
   The Afternoon: Mid-December

BOOKS REVIEWED
   Traveling on Credit   125 162
   The American Poetry Anthology (Ed.)   128 106

HALPERN, MARTIN
BOOKS REVIEWED
   Two Sides of an Island   103 324

HAMBLETON, RONALD
BOOKS REVIEWED
   Unit of Five
    (With Louis Dudek, P. K. Page,
    Raymond Souster,
    and James Wreford)   66 334

HAMBURGER, MICHAEL
POEMS
   The Body   99 29
   Old Woman
   Arctic Explorer
   Travelling IV   119 94
    (1. "In winter light...")
    (2. "Earth. That must be...")
    (3. "Where am I? Bare trees...")
    (4. "And you? How near...")
    (5. "Too late I take back...")
    (6. "Last of my needs...")
   Travelling V   119 287
    (1. "Now or before...")
    (2. "I move on...")
    (3. "As do his, who forsook...")
    (4. "Slowly, detained by love...")
    (5. "Gone. Lost. Half-forgotten...")
   Travelling VI   124 68
    (1. "Autumn again...")
    (2. "There will be a second...")
    (3. "Hardly one name...")
    (4. "And at last it comes...")
   Grape and Nut Letter   128 280
   Travelling VII
    (1. "So much forgotten. Care...")
    (2. "So much forgotten. As leaves...")
    (3. "Somewhere she walks...")
    (4. "No season now...")
    (5. "I move on, I stop...")
    (6. "Where am I? Here and there...")
   Variations: In Suffolk   133 283

TRANSLATIONS
   Poem by Georg Trakl   98 151
   Poem by Günter Grass   98 154
   Poem by Hans Magnus Enzensberger   98 379
   Poems by Paul Celan   119 134
   Poems by Phillippe Jaccottet   122 147
   Poems by Peter Huchel, Johannes
    Bobrowski, and Ernst Meister   128 130
   Poems by Marin Sorescu   136 25

ARTICLES
   Correspondence   120 363

REVIEWS
   A Book of Modern German
     Lyric Verse 1890-1955
     (Ed. by Willam Rose)   97   393
   Duino Elegies, by Rainer Maria Rilke
     (Tr. by David Young)
     [William Carlos Williams]   134   234

BOOKS REVIEWED
   Reason and Energy:
     Studies in German Literature   91   403
   Hölderlin (Tr. and ed.)   101   287
   Hugo von Hofmannsthal:
     Poems and Verse Plays (Ed.)
   Modern German Poetry: 1910-1960
     (Ed. with Christopher Middleton)   103   261
   Weather and Season   104   375
   In Flashlight   107   410
   In Flashlight   110   112
   Selected Poems, by Günter Grass
     (Tr. with Christopher Middleton)   111   336
   Poems for People Who Don't Read Poems,
     by Hans Magnus Enzensberger
     (Tr. with Jerome Rothenberg
     and the author)   113   188
   Travelling   118   102
   The Truth of Poetry:
     Tensions in Modern Poetry
     from Baudelaire to the Nineteen-Sixties   119   99
   Ownerless Earth: New & Selected Poems   124   45

HAMEIRI, AVIGDOR
POEMS
   Passover in Jerusalem
     (Tr. by Ruth Finer Mintz)   92   213

HAMILL, CHARLES H.
ARTICLES
   [Tribute to Harriet Monroe]   49   159

HAMILL, PAUL
POEMS
   Specifically Themselves   139   281

HAMILTON, ALEXANDER
ARTICLES ABOUT
   Rev. of *Hamilton,*
     by Chard Powers Smith   37   53

HAMILTON, ANNE
BOOKS REVIEWED
   A Jeweled Screen   30   112
   Broken Crescendo   56   220

HAMILTON, DAVID O(SBORNE)
POEMS
   Hoofs and Haloes   18   239
   Te Deum

   The Idiot
   Beauty in Fourth Street
   Our Time
   Once More the Moon   22   13
   Creation
   The North Wind   31   315
   Epitaph ("I was the master of this...")
   Even Then   36   83
   Words   57   135
   Whoever

BOOKS REVIEWED
   Four Gardens   17   276

HAMILTON, FLORA BRENT
POEMS
   Silhouette   33   259

HAMILTON, G(EORGE) R(OSTREVOR)
BOOKS REVIEWED
   A Soul of Wit,
     A Choice of English Verse Epigrams (Ed.)   27   343
   James Hurnard, a Victorian Character (Ed.)
     [Passages from *The Setting Sun*]   70   106

HAMILTON, GORDON
POEMS
   In the Red Cross   14   199

HAMILTON, HORACE
POEMS
   Ivy Colleague   99   302
   Town on the Equator   125   151

HAMILTON, IAN
BOOKS REVIEWED
   Pretending Not To Sleep   110   195

HAMILTON, JULIAN H.
POEMS
   Elvira   73   215

HAMILTON, MARION ETHEL
POEMS
   Pink Blossoms   13   311
   Hallowe'en   27   26
   In Stillness   36   20
     California Afternoon
     Shadow
   Moor Winds   38   254
     Dream
     Windy Night
     High Tide
   Circles   41   132
   Moment   44   195
   Children on a Hill   49   129

BOOKS REVIEWED
   The Ultimate Lover and Other Poems   33   168

HAMILTON, PATRICK
ARTICLES ABOUT
  Dagger of the Mind,
    by James Sandoe   68   146

HAMILTON, ROBIN
POEMS
  Nightpiece: London, 1888   142   322
  Learning the Code,
    Coding the Life

HAMILTON, STEVE
POEMS
  Hommage to Tristan   132   20

HAMILTON, VIRGINIA
POEMS
  Poems at Dusk   46   318
  Three in Firelight
  No Thunder
  The Possessed   60   190

HAMMARSKJÖLD, DAG
BOOKS REVIEWED
  Markings
    (Tr. by Leif Sjöberg
    and W. H. Auden)   106   356

ARTICLES ABOUT
  Rev. of Chronique,
    by St.-John Perse
    (Tr. by Robert Fitzgerald)   99   194

HAMMER, LOUIS
BOOKS REVIEWED
  Bone Planet   117   322

HAMMOND, ELEANOR
POEMS
  Transition   16   133
  Words Unuttered   23   312
  Loneliness
  You Said

HAMMOND, LOUISE STRONG
TRANSLATIONS
  Poems by Seng Dji-Nan,
    Gia Dao, Yeh Shih, Cheng Hao,
    and Wang An-Shih   20   252

REVIEWS
  The Works of Li Po
    (Tr. by Shigeyoshi Obata)   22   334

ARTICLES ABOUT
  On Translating Chinese Poetry,
    by Eunice Tietjens   20   268

HAMMOND, MAC
[MC MULLEN HAMMOND]
POEMS
  Snapshot   76   135
  In Memory of V. R. Lang   104   221
  An Indian Miniature   133   322
  High Fidelity   142   31
  The Final Note

REVIEWS
  The Collected Poems of Keith Douglas
    (Ed. by John Waller and G. S. Fraser) 79   356

BOOKS REVIEWED
  The Horse Opera and Other Poems   109   189
  Cold Turkey   118   35

HAMMOND, MARY STEWART
BOOKS REVIEWED
  Out of Canaan   160   284

HAMMOND, MC MULLEN
[See HAMMOND, MAC]

HAMMOND, PERCY
ARTICLES ABOUT
  Correspondence
    from Carl Sandburg   9   218

HAMPSON, ALFRED LEETE
BOOKS REVIEWED
  Unpublished Poems,
    by Emily Dickinson
    (Ed. with Martha Dickinson Bianchi)   48   161

HA NAGID, SHMUEL
POEMS
  I Quartered the Troops for the Night   167   194
  The Critique
  The Heart Holds Hidden Knowledge
    (Tr. by Peter Cole)

HANDLEY-TAYLOR, GEOFFREY
BOOKS REVIEWED
  New Hyperion, a Symposium
    of Poetry and Criticism (Ed.)   78   45

HANDLIN, JIM
POEMS
  Akbar's Algebra   138   75
  Remnants

HANES, LEIGH (BUCKNER)
POEMS
  Song of the New Hercules   33   117
  Seasonals   36   70
  Spring Rhapsody
  Trees in a Winter Storm

Elegiac   42   76
  Harvested
  Whisper

BOOKS REVIEWED
  Song of the New Hercules   37   345

HANFORD, JAMES HOLLY
BOOKS REVIEWED
  A Restoration Reader (Ed.)   86   118

HANNIGAN, PAUL
BOOKS REVIEWED
  Laughing   120   49

HANSEN, WALDEMAR
POEMS
  Poem ("If love is true...")   69   254
  Avez-Vous Quelque Chose à Declarer?   72   84

ARTICLES
  Correspondence:
    The Butterfly as a Strategy
    [Parker Tyler, E. S. Forgotson]   70   113
    London Letter [Edith Sitwell]   73   280

HAN-SHAN
BOOKS REVIEWED
  Cold Mountain:
    100 Poems by Han-Shan
    (Ed. and tr. by Burton Watson)   107   196

HANSON, ISABEL
POEMS
  Creation   47   133

HANSON, K(ENNETH) O.
POEMS
  Copalis Beach   73   18

BOOKS REVIEWED
  The Distance Anywhere   112   276
  The Uncorrected World   124   343

HANSON, PAULINE
POEMS
  The Return   75   82
  The Ways   78   256
  So Beautiful Is the Tree of Night   90   225
  From as Far as Once
  And Everywhere Ghost   93   22
  Stars   97   210
  In Oracles of Listening   101   333
  We Meet   106   388

BOOKS REVIEWED
  The Forever Young   74   357
  The Forever Young and Other Poems   92   378

HANZLICEK, C. G.
POEMS
  Heart   153   18
  Adrenalin
  Imagination

HAO, CHENG
[See CHENG HAO]

HAPGOOD, ISABEL F.
BOOKS REVIEWED
  The Epic Songs of Russia (Tr.)   9   271

HARD, WALTER
BOOKS REVIEWED
  A Mountain Township   45   57

HARDEKOPF, FERDINAND
ARTICLES ABOUT
  Modern German Poetry: I,
    by Reginald H. Wilenski   5   178

HARDIN, CHARLOTTE
BOOKS REVIEWED
  Dream Fugue   28   56

HARDING, DENYS
BOOKS REVIEWED
  Collected Poems,
    by Isaac Rosenberg
    (Ed. with Gordon Bottomley)   80   101

HARDING, PHILIP M.
POEMS
  Bridal Tower   34   258
  "A Richer Dust"   39   74
  "Wunder Um Verdun"
  American Cemetery
  Second Childhood   41   201
  Sonnet for a Smile at Dusk
  Naked Interval
  Dirge for Golden Strings
  Post-Jazz
  1929   43   251

HARDY, EVELYN
BOOKS REVIEWED
  Thomas Hardy: A Critical Biography   85   356

HARDY, JOHN EDWARD
POEMS
  Louisiana Foxhunt   93   24
  Bavarian Prospect, 1960   99   93

REVIEWS
  Donne's Poetry and Modern Criticism,
    by Leonard Unger
    [John Crowe Ransom,
    Allen Tate, Cleanth Brooks]   77   175

Celebration at Dark,
   by William Jay Smith   78 237
Imagism, a Chapter for the History
  of Modern Poetry,
   by Stanley K. Coffman, Jr.   78 294
Stephen Crane, Whitman, Auden,
  and a Poetry Handbook   92 116
  Poetry Handbook, by Babette Deutsch
  The Poetry of Stephen Crane,
   by Daniel G. Hoffman
  A Critical Guide to Leaves of Grass,
   by James E. Miller, Jr.
  The Making of the Auden Canon,
   by Joseph Warren Beach
You, Robert Penn Warren   99 56
  Robert Penn Warren:
   The Dark and Bloody Ground,
   by Leonard Casper
  You, Emperors, and Others:
   Poems 1957-60,
   by Robert Penn Warren

BOOKS REVIEWED
  Certain Poems   95 304
  The Curious Frame:
   Seven Poems in Text and Context 102 269

HARDY, THOMAS
BOOKS REVIEWED
  Satires of Circumstance, Lyrics and Reveries,
   with Miscellaneous Pieces 5 240
  The Dynasts 5 288
  Moments of Vision 12 96
  Collected Poems 16 43

ARTICLES ABOUT
  A Modern Epic of War,
   by Ellen FitzGerald 5 288
  Thomas Hardy, by Harriet Monroe 31 326
  Form in Modern Poetry,
   by D. S. Savage 65 30
  Rev. of *Thomas Hardy:*
   A Critical Biography,
   by Evelyn Hardy 85 356
  Rev. of *Four Poets on Poetry:*
   Essays by R. P. Blackmur, Yvor Winters,
   Marianne Moore, and Mark Van Doren
   (Ed. by Don Cameron Allen) 96 382
  Review by Samuel Hynes 135 342
  Rev. of *Juvenilia: Poems, 1922-1928,*
   by W. H. Auden
   (Ed. by Katherine Bucknell) 166 226
  Christopher Fry: An Appreciation,
   by Thomas M. Disch 166 280

HARE, AMORY
BOOKS REVIEWED
  Sonnets 30 353

HARING, PHYLLIS
POEMS
  The Tunnel 67 144
  Holiday for Strings 68 73
  Overture to Strangers 71 123
  Jungle
  Non-European Hospital
  Poker-Face
  Here Comes a Candle to Light Me to Bed 73 133
  The Alchemist 76 327
  Oman the Diver 86 341

HARJO, JOY
BOOKS REVIEWED
  The Woman
   Who Fell From the Sky 168 281

HARMON, WILLIAM
POEMS
  A Lament in Four Fragments 141 313
  Five Poems 144 26
   1 ("Ask me no questions...")
   2 ("O. Wow. O...")
   3 ("Crepuscular autumnal moribund...")
   4 ("O how I O endlessly think...")
   5 ("Way back in my hand-wrestling...")

REVIEWS
  The Place of Poetry:
   Two Centuries of an Art in Crisis,
   by Christopher Clausen 141 237
  Kumin and Kinnell (and Kilmer) 142 50
   Our Ground Time Here Will Be Brief:
   New and Selected Poems,
   by Maxine Kumin
   Selected Poems,
   by Galway Kinnell
  The Argot Merchant Disaster:
   Poems New and Selected,
   by George Starbuck 142 350

BOOKS REVIEWED
  Treasury Holiday 119 342
  Legion: Civic Choruses 123 165
  One Long Poem 143 228

HARMS, JAMES
POEMS
  Mexican Christmas 149 156
  Penance 152 146
  Mrs. Worthington 164 23
  From Ocean Park to Healdsburg 164 93

HARNED, THOMAS B.
BOOKS REVIEWED
  The Letters of Anne Gilchrist
   and Walt Whitman (Ed.) 14 106

HARNEY, JOHN PAUL
POEMS
   Alternatives for My Son   95   285

HARPER, CAROL ELY
BOOKS REVIEWED
   Experiment Theatre Anthology #1 (Ed.)   98   192

HARPER, MICHAEL S.
POEMS
   New Season   111   311
   Village Blues
   For Bud
   Savage
   The Black Angel
   Blues Alabama

BOOKS REVIEWED
   History Is Your Own Heartbeat   122   293
   Debridement   123   173
   Song: I Want a Witness   126   172
   Images of Kin: New and Selected Poems   134   107

HARPER, R(OBERT) D.
REVIEWS
   The Still Centre, by Stephen Spender   57   46
   Shelley, by Newman Ivey White   57   386
   Poetic Drama:
      An Anthology of Plays in Verse
      (Ed. by Alfred Kreymborg)   60   276
   Three Poets and the War   63   172
      War Songs, by Struthers Burt
      David and Other Poems, by Earle Birney
      Prose Chants and Proems,
        by Ross Nichols

HARRIES, LYNDON
BOOKS REVIEWED
   Swahili Poetry   103   394

HARRIGAN, ANTHONY
REVIEWS
   First Poems, by James Merrill   78   233

BOOKS REVIEWED
   Ten Poets Anthology   74   55

HARRINGTON, KATHERINE S.
POEMS
   Whispering Grass   29   87

HARRINGTON, MICHAEL
POEMS
   ("If possibility...")   80   256
   ("A prayer must...")
   James Joyce
   ("The street lights...")
   Young Girls: First Communion

HARRIS, MARK
BOOKS REVIEWED
   The City of Discontent
      [Vachel Lindsay]   82   355

HARRIS, MAX
BOOKS REVIEWED
   Dramas from the Sky   62   352
   The Gift of Blood

HARRIS, PHYLLIS
POEMS
   Phonograph   109   165
   Bolinas   112   397

HARRIS, SYDNEY J(USTIN)
POEMS
   I Come to Bury Caesar   47   147

HARRISON, AUSTIN
ARTICLES ABOUT
   An International Episode,
      by Harriet Monroe   13   94

HARRISON, JAMES
BOOKS REVIEWED
   Flying Dutchman   144   297

HARRISON, JEFFREY
POEMS
   The Hummingbird Feeder   144   336
   Bathtubs, Three Varieties   152   86
   The One That Got Away
   Mycology   159   12
   Adirondack Moosehead   160   347
   Swifts at Evening
   Political Poem   161   216
   Entry in a Baby Book: Two Weeks   161   331
   Shaker Chair
   Convenience Store   166   156

BOOKS REVIEWED
   The Singing Underneath   154   99

HARRISON, JIM
POEMS
   Dead Doe   106   328
   Complaint
   Return
   Poem ("Form is the woods...")
   David
   Suite to Fathers   109   321

REVIEWS
   Tape for the Turn of the Year
      and *Corsons Inlet*, by A. R. Ammons   107   330
   California Hybrid   108   198
      The Fork, by Richard Duerden

Against the Silences To Come,
  by Ron Loewinsohn
The Process,
  by David Meltzer
On Out and *Hermit Poems,*
  by Lew Welch

BOOKS REVIEWED
Plain Song   108   272
Locations   117   322

HARRISON, KEITH
  BOOKS REVIEWED
  Points in a Journey   114   266

HARRISON, MARTIN
  POEMS
  Saintliness   169   29

HARRISON, PAMELA
  POEMS
  So, Caravaggio   157   322
  Field in Snow   161   140

HARRISON, T. W.
  BOOKS REVIEWED
  Earthworks   110   112

HARRISON, TONY
  BOOKS REVIEWED
  Newcastle Is Peru   117   331
  The Loiners   119   159

  ARTICLES ABOUT
  A Letter from Britain,
    by William Logan   157   222

HARS, THEODORE
  POEMS
  Tocqueville's America   125   333

HARSENT, DAVID
  BOOKS REVIEWED
  A Violent Country   118   102

HARSHAV, BARBARA
  BOOKS REVIEWED
  *Even a Fist Was Once
    an Open Palm with Fingers,*
    by Yehuda Amichai
    (Tr. with Benjamin Harshav)   159   157

HARSHAV, BENJAMIN
  BOOKS REVIEWED
  *Even a Fist Was Once
    an Open Palm with Fingers,*
    by Yehuda Amichai
    (Tr. with Barbara Harshav)   159   157

HART, HENRY (H.)
  POEMS
  The Spring Competitions   146   283
  Mystery Play   151   292
  Icarus on Stone Mountain   158   135

  TRANSLATIONS
  Poem by Wang Wêi   35   259

  BOOKS REVIEWED
  Poems of the Hundred Names   85   225

HART, HOWARD
  BOOKS REVIEWED
  The Sky of Orange Whispers   105   410

HART, JOHN BARKLEY
  POEMS
  Squatters   81   363
  *The Wife of the Superintendent
    of the Granaries*   86   270

  BOOKS REVIEWED
  The Flight of Mr. Sun   96   238

HART, JOSEPH KINMONT
  BOOKS REVIEWED
  Prophet of a Nameless God   32   114

HART, LAWRENCE
  ARTICLES
  About the Activist Poets
    [Rosalie Moore, Jeanne McGahey,
    Robert Horan, Amelia MacIntyre]   78   99
  A Note on Robert Barlow   78   115
  A Note on the Activists   93   102

  ARTICLES ABOUT
  Correspondence
    from William Carlos Williams
    [Luis de Gongora y Argote]   78   107

HART, LOUISE
  POEMS
  Song-Drops   10   200
  Winter
  The Spider's Web
  Inscription on a Sun-Dial

HART, MARJORIE COMSTOCK
  POEMS
  Winter Farm   27   258
  Love

HART, RICHARD (L.)
  POEMS
  These Are Cats   38   196
  An Inhibited Persian

The Grand Eunuch
   A Mother with Young Kittens
Letter from Madrid   71   179
Dream   78   85
The Returner   87   332

BOOKS REVIEWED
  A Winter's Journey   66   343

HARTH, PHILLIP
  BOOKS REVIEWED
   Contexts of Dryden's Thought   115   196

HARTLEY, MARSDEN
  POEMS
   Kaleidoscope   12   195
    In the Frail Wood
    Spinsters
    Her Daughter
    After Battle
   Sunlight Persuasions   16   59
    The Festival of the Corn
    Español
    Girl with the Camelia Smile
    The Topaz of the Sixties
    The Asses' Out-House
    To C—
    Saturday
   Scenes   40   22
    Brautigam
    Window-Washer—Avenue C

  ARTICLES
   Tribute to Joyce Kilmer   13   149
   The Business of Poetry   15   152

  BOOKS REVIEWED
   Twenty-Five Poems   23   105
   Androscoggin   59   167
   Selected Poems
    (Ed. by Henry W. Wells)   68   220

HARTMAN, CHARLES O.
  POEMS
   To Shadow   123   212
   Lying Awake 8/24/72
   A Little Song
   Before My Father Before Me   125   263
   To A and B,
    My Friends Who Are Not in Books
   3:00
   Milkweed
   Inflation
   The Stone Lions   128   251
   Fire in the Library
   The Essayist   131   99
   Stars: Flat, Blue, Large Stars. Nothing.
   Double Mock Sonnet   132   159

Daddy Long-Legs
Over a Cup of Tea   135   135
Two Poems About Grass
Not Oscar Wilde in Duluth   138   265
Terzanelle
Pal Is a Romany World   142   38
Digging In
New Hampshire

HARTMAN, GEOFFREY (H.)
  POEMS
   Spring Offensive   120   330
   Sicilian Sketches   121   251
   A Winter Afternoon in New Haven
   The Garden   127   33
   Genius Loci   131   138

  REVIEWS
   Methods and the Man   98   332
    In Pursuit of Poetry,
     by Robert Hillyer
    Obsessive Images, Symbolism in Poetry
     of the 1930's and 1940's,
     by Joseph Warren Beach
     (Ed. by William Van O'Connor)
    Tradition and Poetic Structure,
     by J. V. Cunningham

HARTMUS, LAURENCE
  POEMS
   Shards   28   23
   Iron
   City

HARTNETT, MICHAEL
  POEMS
   IX [Do Neasa]   167   60
   XVIII [In Memoriam Sheila Hackett]
   XXVI ("Across the road...")
   Parables for Clane

  BOOKS REVIEWED
   Selected and New Poems
    (Ed. by Peter Fallon)   168   107

  ARTICLES ABOUT
   A Map of Contemporary Irish Poetry,
    by Dennis O'Driscoll   167   94

HARTOG, DIANA
  BOOKS REVIEWED
   Matinee Light   144   297

HARTSOCK, ERNEST
  POEMS
   April Mile   34   21
   Strange Splendor   35   192
   Gist of Glory

BOOKS REVIEWED
Strange Splendor   38   45

HARVEY, ANDREW
BOOKS REVIEWED
No Diamonds, No Hat, No Honey   147   227

HARVEY, FRANCIS
POEMS
The Wheelwright and the Boy   167   12
Fishermen
The Space Between
Love Letters
Sheepmen

HARVEY, SAVILA
POEMS
For My Thirtieth Birthday   51   70
Summer at the Beach   66   140

HARVEY, SHIRLEY
POEMS
Rainy Days   13   75

BOOKS REVIEWED
The Christmas Trail and Other Poems   9   155

HARWELL, MEADE
BOOKS REVIEWED
Second Poems   77   215

HARWOOD, LEE
BOOKS REVIEWED
The White Room   118   102
Landscapes

HARWOOD, RUTH
POEMS
Working-Hour Songs   19   310
The Shoe Factory
Making Little Clothes
Always and Always
Dolorous   28   258

HASENCLEVER, WALTER
ARTICLES ABOUT
On the Continent,
   by F. C. Weiskopf   56   332

HASHIMOTO, SHARON
POEMS
The Mirror of Matsuyama   157   13
Dandelion

HASKELL, DENNIS
POEMS
Evening Flight   169   31
Natural Piety

The Recognition
The Unsuccessful Interview

ARTICLES ABOUT
Towards a Contemporary
   Australian Poetics,
   by John Kinsella   169   94

HASLEY, LOUIS
ARTICLES
Correspondence   72   343

HASS, ROBERT
POEMS
San Pedro Road   114   12
Lines on Last Spring
The Failure of Buffalo To Levitate

BOOKS REVIEWED
Praise   135   229
Twentieth Century Pleasures   145   345
Unattainable Earth, by Czeslaw Milosz
   (Tr. with the author)   149   168
Provinces, by Czeslaw Milosz
   (Tr. with the author)   161   223
Facing the River, by Czeslaw Milosz
   (Tr. with the author)   169   286
Sun Under Wood   170   288

HASS, ROBERT B.
POEMS
Humpback   163   333
Lullaby for the Mathematician

HASSALL, CHRISTOPHER
BOOKS REVIEWED
Rupert Brooke   107   192

HASSMER, WARREN
POEMS
Cloud of an Ancient Rage   90   27
A Darkening Threshold   93   151
Quiet Bird in the Big Night   97   24

HASTE, GWENDOLEN
POEMS
In the Office   19   260
The Guardians
Aileen
In Montana   23   194
Exotic
The Wind
Colter's Hell   29   192
The Horseman   36   132

REVIEWS
Songs of the Coast Dwellers,
   by Constance Lindsay Skinner   36   278

BOOKS REVIEWED
  Young Land   38   111

HASTINGS, ELIZABETH [Pseud.]
  POEMS
  Summer Forgets   46   202
    In Every Field and Meadow
    Something Remembered
    The Curse
    In All the Sun-Pooled Spaces

HASTINGS, NANCY PETERS
  POEMS
  Left   157   68

HATFIELD, LEE
  BOOKS REVIEWED
  Breakfast in Mycenae   102   49

HATHAWAY, BAXTER
  BOOKS REVIEWED
  *The Age of Criticism,
    the Late Renaissance in Italy*   102   198

HATHAWAY, WILLIAM
  POEMS
  Still Life   144   218
  In Each Day   148   203

  BOOKS REVIEWED
  The Gymnast of Inertia   144   231
  Fish, Flesh, & Fowl   147   227

HATTERSLEY, MICHAEL E.
  POEMS
  Body Knowledge   163   37
  Taking the Century by the Throat   163   200

HAUGEN, EINAR
  REVIEWS
  Anthology of Norwegian Lyrics
    (Ed. by Charles Wharton Stork)   62   54

  ARTICLES ABOUT
  [Note on misprint]   62   175

HAUGH, IRENE
  POEMS
  Evening on Road, Dun Laoghaire   40   194

HAUGHAWOUT, MARGARET E.
  BOOKS REVIEWED
  Pittsburg College Verse 1924-30 (Ed.)   38   282

HAUPTMANN, GERHART
  ARTICLES ABOUT
  Honors and Prizes,
    by Harriet Monroe   29   92

HAUSER, JACOB
  POEMS
  Miracle   36   303
  Weather Notes   46   257
    Siesta at Zenith
    Lilac Evening Sand
    Weather Chronicles

HAUSMAN, GERALD
  BOOKS REVIEWED
  Circle Meadow   123   236

HAVIRD, DAVID
  POEMS
  Midnight Oil   129   75
  Outside De Bruhl's Cafe
  A Sentimental Journey

HAWKES, DAVID
  BOOKS REVIEWED
  Ch'u Tz'u, The Songs of the South (Tr.)   96   57
  A Little Primer of Tu Fu   112   283

HAWKINS, DOROTHY
  POEMS
  Epigram   28   135

HAWKINS, HUNT
  POEMS
  My Cat Jack   133   158

HAWKINS, WILLIAM
  BOOKS REVIEWED
  Louis Riel (In *Two Longer Poems*,
    with *The Seasons of Miss Nicky*,
    by Harry Howith)   108   45
  Ottawa Poems   111   323

HAWKRIDGE, EMMA
  POEMS
  The Painted Desert   15   194
  Hopi Sun-Christening
  I Hope   37   316
  Siva

HAXTON, BROOKS
  POEMS
  Breakfast Ex Animo   140   63
  Bones   143   291
  Tongue
  Hand and Foot   147   92
  My Friends   150   16
  Northbound

HAY, ELIJAH
  [Pseud. of SEIFFERT,
  MARJORIE ALLEN]
  ARTICLES ABOUT
  Baiting the Public,
    by Alice Corbin Henderson   12   169

Rev. of *The Spectra Hoax*,
  by William Jay Smith   99   390

HAY, GEORGE CAMPBELL
ARTICLES ABOUT
  Some Poets of
    the Scottish Renaissance,
    by Tom Scott   88   43

HAY, JOHN
POEMS
  Post Mortems   58   134
  Lebensraum ("The golden maps...")
  Wake Island   60   9
  Dispute for Death   61   545
  Lebensraum ("The golden maps...")   62   267
  City Ball Game   64   136
  New Continents   67   196
    Twilight Travelers
    Poem ("All colors, derelicts...")
    Concert in Panama City
  Politics   84   322
  The Living Air
  The Power of Speech
  Running Eternally
  An American Summer   86   21
  Order
  Digging a Neighbor's Grave

REVIEWS
  The Ghost in the Underblows,
    by Alfred Young Fisher   57   391

BOOKS REVIEWED
  A Private History   71   334

HAY, SARA HENDERSON
BOOKS REVIEWED
  This, My Letter   56   220
  The Stone and the Shell   95   248

HAYAKAWA, S. I(CHIYE)
POEMS
  To One Elect   44   319

ARTICLES
  Poetry and Advertising
    [Robert Hillyer, Douglas Bush,
    Archibald MacLeish]   67   204

REVIEWS
  Tu Fu, The Autobiography of a Chinese Poet
    and Travels of a Chinese Poet
    (Tr. by Florence Ayscough)   47   219
  Leifsaga: A Narrative Poem
    of the Norse Discoveries of America,
    by Henry Chapin   47   287
  Selected Poems, by AE   48   290

Collected Poems,
  by E. E. Cummings   52   284
Collected Poems, 1922-1938,
  by Mark Van Doren   54   157
Cafés and Cathedrals,
  by C. F. MacIntyre   56   161
The Linguistic Approach to Poetry 60   86
  The Nature of Literature,
    by Thomas Clark Pollock
  The Philosophy of Literary Form,
    by Kenneth Burke
  Reason in Madness,
    by Allen Tate
Nevertheless,
  by Marianne Moore   65   262

ARTICLES ABOUT
[Note]   65   228

HAYDEN, ROBERT (E.)
POEMS
  O Daedalus, Fly Away Home 62   192

BOOKS REVIEWED
  Selected Poems   110   267
  Angle of Ascent   130   221

HAYES, ALFRED
POEMS
  Singleman   48   64
  A Little Nightmusic   52   177
  The Imitation of Faust   56   198
  Nebuchadnezzar   59   121
  A Ride on the Carousel   62   318
  The Chapel
  The Slaughter-House
  The Child in the Dark   65   313
  The Loggia   67   59
  The Englishman in the Piazza di Spagna 68   128
  From The Fall of Rome   69   179
  The Shrunken Head   73   68
  An Epistle to the Gentiles

BOOKS REVIEWED
  The Big Time   64   292

ARTICLES ABOUT
  The Federal Poets' Number,
    by John Peale Bishop   52   276

HAYES, RAPHAEL
POEMS
  St. Anthony in the Desert   57   364

HAYKIN, RUBY
POEMS
  Zigzagging in Paris   77   324

ARTICLES

Verse Drama on the Paris Stage
[T. S. Eliot, Henri Fluchère,
Robinson Jeffers, Julien Philbert,
Federico García Lorca, Marcelle
Auclair, Henri Pichette, Jean Vilar,
Jules Supervielle]   82   294

HAYS, H. R.
POEMS

Villon   29   191
Voyage into Myth   43   259
Portrait of the Artist as a Tree   45   14
For Minor Beauty   46   243
Backward Child
Melody of Rocking-Chairs
Defenseless Spring   52   208
Mystery   60   130
Desert Spectacle
Lullaby
The Liberators   61   421
To an American Flyer

TRANSLATIONS

Poem by Ramón López Velarde   57   16
Poem by Pablo Neruda   62   62
Poem by Alicia Cadilla   62   65
Poems by Ramón López Velarde   62   71
Poem by Manuel Bandeira   62   75
Poem by Luis Palés Matos   62   79
Poems by Gabriela Mistral   62   80
Poems by José M. Eguren   62   86
Article by Jorge Carrera Andrade   62   88
Poems by Bertolt Brecht   67   140

ARTICLES

Surrealist Influence in Contemporary
English and American Poetry
[Dylan Thomas, Harold Rosenberg,
Charles Henri Ford, George
Gascoigne (sic. David Gascoyne)]   54   202
A Mexican Symbolist
[Ramón López Velarde]   57   40
Correspondence
[John Theobald, Herbert Read]   67   115
The Poetry of Bertolt Brecht   67   148

REVIEWS

In Memoriam, 1933,
by Charles Reznikoff   46   230
Collected Poems of Laura Riding   54   101
Narration with a Red Piano,
by J. Calder Joseph   58   273
Shakespeare in Harlem,
by Langston Hughes   60   223
The Epic of Latin American Literature,
by Arturo Torres Rioseco   62   105

Trance Above the Streets,
by Harold Rosenberg   62   342
García Lorca, by Edwin Honig   64   225
A World Within a War,
by Herbert Read   66   220
A Penetential Primer,
by Katherine Hoskins   67   228
The Collected Poems of Henry Treece   69   346
The Fall of the Magicians,
by Weldon Kees   70   330

BOOKS REVIEWED

12 Spanish American Poets (Ed.)   63   230
The Selected Writings
of Juan Ramón Jiménez (Tr.)   92   184
Selected Poems of Bertolt Brecht (Tr.)   97   51
Selected Poems 1933-67   113   262

ARTICLES ABOUT

[Note on misprint]   60   233
Correspondence from John Theobald
[Herbert Read]   67   114

HAYS, LEE
POEMS

Deadbuggy   57   134

HAYWARD, MAX
TRANSLATIONS

Poems by Anna Akhmatova
(Tr. with Stanley Kunitz)   122   96

BOOKS REVIEWED

Antiworlds, by Andrei Voznesensky
(Ed. with Patricia Blake)
(Tr. with others)   110   40
Hope Against Hope
and Hope Abandoned,
by Nadezhda Mandelstam (Tr.)   124   232
Poems of Akhmatova,
by Anna Akhmatova
(Tr. with Stanley Kunitz)
Nostalgia for the Present,
by Andrei Voznesensky
(Ed. with Vera Dunham)   136   40

HAZEL, ROBERT
POEMS

Little Horn   77   257
Dynamo
Washington, 1958   92   271
The Red and the Black   96   225

REVIEWS

Three New Volumes   94   339
The Green Chapel, by Barbara Gibbs
In Time Like Air, by May Sarton
Plays and Poems, by Elder Olson

BOOKS REVIEWED
Poems 1951-1961   101   279

HAZO, SAMUEL
BOOKS REVIEWED
Once for the Last Bandit   122   168
Quartered   126   219
Inscripts   129   285

HEAD, CLOYD
POEMS
Grotesques   9   1
War Sequence   13   6
   Prelude
   The Marne
   They March Through the Streets of Paris
   The German Empire — Bismarck,
      Von Moltke
   Epilogue ("When all is done....")
The Curtains
   (With Mary Gavin)   16   1

ARTICLES
Note on *Grotesques*
   (With Harriet Monroe)   9   31
Note on *The Curtains*
   (With Mary Gavin)   16   39
Influence of the Art-Theatre
   on Poetic Drama   19   37

REVIEWS
Four Plays for Dancers,
   by William Butler Yeats   19   288
A Book of Plays,
   by Witter Bynner   22   158

ARTICLES ABOUT
"Grotesques" and "Overtones,"
   by Harriet Monroe   7   193
Little Theatres and Poetic Plays,
   by Harriet Monroe   11   201

HEAD, GWEN
POEMS
Not Sleeping   129   263

HEAGY, H. LEE
POEMS
Magnets of Fire   114   238

HEAL, EDITH
ARTICLES ABOUT
Rev. of *I Wanted to Write a Poem*,
   by William Carlos Williams   94   127

HEALY, ALEXIS
POEMS
Necropsy   73   8

HEALY, J(OHN) V(INCENT)
POEMS
Disturbers   39   312
The Thief
On Shore
Fall Wind
Against the Wall I-III   42   82
Visit to Erebus   43   306
Portrait of a Governor   53   295
Straits of Belle Isle
Palm Springs
Murray Bay   55   236
Faces Seen in Dreams
The Thirtieth Year of My Age   60   306
Substance of Shadow   64   128

ARTICLES
Correspondence
   [John Gould Fletcher]   44   354
Contemporary Poetry Criticism
   [Louise Bogan, Ezra Pound,
   Brand Blanshard, T. S. Eliot]   61   672
Addendum [Ezra Pound]   68   347

REVIEWS
Flowering Reeds, by Roy Campbell   42   166
The Metaphysical Poets,
   by J. B. Leishman   47   169
Cantos LII-LXXI; Ezra Pound's
   ABC of Economics; Polite Essays;
   and *Culture*, by Ezra Pound   57   200
Shores of Darkness,
   by Edward B. Hungerford   61   403
The New Criticism,
   by John Crowe Ransom   61   575
The Life of W. B. Yeats,
   by Joseph M. Hone   62   223
An Act of Life, by Theodore Spencer   64   229
Selected Poems of Herman Melville
   (Ed. by F. O. Matthiessen)   66   47
Letters of Rainer Maria Rilke, 1892-1910
   (Tr. by Jane Bannard Green
   and M. D. Herter Norton)   67   221

ARTICLES ABOUT
Correspondence
   from John Gould Fletcher   44   355
Correspondence from Gorham Munson
   [Ezra Pound]   57   399

HEANEY, SEAMUS
POEMS
Gifts of Rain   119   280
May
A Dog Was Crying
   To-Night in Wicklow Also   167   1
Remembered Columns
Mycenae Nightwatch

BOOKS REVIEWED
   Door into the Dark   117   108
   Wintering Out   123   113
   North   129   233
   Station Island   147   35
   The Haw Lantern   154   340
   Seeing Things   160   157
   The Spirit Level   168   337
   The Redress of Poetry
   Crediting Poetry: The Nobel Lecture

ARTICLES ABOUT
   "Sacred Beings":
     Writers in Recorded Conversation,
     by Michael Milburn   146   101
   A Letter from Britain,
     by William Logan   157   222
   A Map of Contemporary Irish Poetry,
     by Dennis O'Driscoll   167   94
   Finishes: Notes
     on Ambition and Survival,
     by Christian Wiman   169   217

HEAP, JANE
POEMS
   Notes   10   132

HEARN, LAFCADIO
BOOKS REVIEWED
   Japanese Lyrics (Tr.)   7   89

HEARNE, VICKI
POEMS
   On R. L. S. and Happiness   138   255
   The Claim of Speech

BOOKS REVIEWED
   Nervous Horses   139   35
   The Parts of Light   167   223

HEARST, JAMES
POEMS
   Frost   36   320
   Clover Swaths   40   249
   Fall Ploughing   43   189
   Even Though Snow   47   66
     Barns in November
     Inquiry
     The Grail
   Speaking of Iowa   56   260
     Morning Song
     The Sun at Noon
     False Warning
     After the Son Died
     The Same in This as Other Lands
   The Fence Row   60   201
   Burn the Cocoons   64   78
   The Oracle   78   274

   Success   92   299
   Landmark   100   367
   Limited View
   Hen Pheasant   106   405
   Forsythia
   Behind the Stove
   Hard Way To Learn   134   17
   No Nightingales, No Nymphs

BOOKS REVIEWED
   Country Men   50   344
   The Sun at Noon   63   99

HEATH-STUBBS, JOHN
BOOKS REVIEWED
   The Charity of the Stars   74   169
   Poems from Giacomo Leopardi (Tr.)   91   260
   The Triumph of the Muse   94   189
   Helen in Egypt, and Other Plays   95   304
   The Blue-Fly in His Head   102   193
   Selected Poems   109   126

ARTICLES ABOUT
   A Letter from Britain [II],
     by William Logan   157   290

HÉBERT, ANNE
BOOKS REVIEWED
   The Tomb of the Kings
     (Tr. by Peter Miller)   112   201

ARTICLES ABOUT
   Rev. of *Quarterly Review*
     of Literature Poetry Series
     (Ed. by T. and R. Weiss)   140   35

HECHT, ANTHONY
POEMS
   To Phyllis   76   319
   Alceste in the Wilderness
   La Condition Botanique   79   73
   Double Sonnet   81   40
   Spring for Thomas Hardy   82   17
   Tarantula, or The Dance of Death   101   45
   Alceste in the Wilderness   121   10
   The Venetian Vespers   133   1
   A Love for Four Voices: Homage
     to Franz Joseph Haydn   138   1
   On Translation   141   11
   Anthem
   Horatian Virtue
   For James Merrill: An Adieu   166   316
   Death Sauntering About   168   249
   Death the Mexican Revolutionary
   Death the Archbishop
   Death the Painter
   Death the Copperplate Printer
   Death the Punchinello

ARTICLES
[Merrill Memorial Tribute]   166   339

BOOKS REVIEWED
The Hard Hours   112   418
Millions of Strange Shadows   131   103
The Venetian Vespers   137   297
The Transparent Man   157   33
Flight Among the Tombs   170   162

ARTICLES ABOUT
[Note]   152   242
Rev. of White Paper:
    On Contemporary American Poetry,
    by J. D. McClatchy   156   297

HECHT, BEN
POEMS
Snow Monotones   11   246

HECHT, ROGER
POEMS
Summer's End   86   332
Man at a Window   92   160

REVIEWS
Collected Poems, by Elder Olson   104   181
Poetry in Pamphlets   110   112
    Preghiere, by Geoffrey Hill
    Those Other Growths,
      by Ted Walker
    Earthworks,
      by T. W. Harrison
    Flower Poems, by Jon Silkin
    Eleven Poems, by Ken Smith
    In Flashlight,
      by Michael Hamburger
    A View of Water, by Gene Baro
    Fables from Life,
      by W. Price Turner

BOOKS REVIEWED
27 Poems   109   401

HECHT, S. THEODORE
POEMS
Table for Christmas   37   255

HEDGES, ADA HASTINGS
POEMS
Now   31   79
Release

HEDIN, ROBERT
POEMS
Tornado   140   28
On Tuesdays They Open
    the Local Pool to the Stroke-Victims

HEDLEY, LESLIE WOOLF
BOOKS REVIEWED
Abraxes & Other Poems   99   247

HEFFERNAN, MICHAEL
POEMS
The Table   114   386
Rage Seated
A Figure of Plain Force   119   322
The Apparition
How the Archangel Answered   121   220
February 1st   132   103
Ten Past Eleven   137   271

REVIEWS
Place for Love   136   170
    Rites of Strangers, by Phyllis Janowitz
    Standing Watch, by Christopher Bursk
    Adirondacks, by Greg Kuzma
    Under Stars, by Tess Gallagher
    Listeners at the Breathing Place,
      by Gary Miranda

HEIFETZ, HAROLD
POEMS
Ritual for the Night   66   252

HEINE, HEINRICH
POEMS
The Phoenix   74   257
Leaning Against the Mast
    (Tr. by Vernon Watkins)

BOOKS REVIEWED
Poems of...
    (Ed. and tr. by Louis Untermeyer)   11   279
Germany—A Winter's Tale
    (Tr. by Herman Salinger)   66   56
The North Sea
    (Tr. by Vernon Watkins)   81   149

ARTICLES ABOUT
Correspondence
    from Louis Untermeyer   7   212
Rev. of Heinrich Heine:
    Paradox and Poet
    (The Life and The Poems),
    by Louis Untermeyer   52   46

HEINEMANN,
    KATHERINE ARNSTEIN
BOOKS REVIEWED
Brandings   116   193

HEINESEN, WILLIAM
POEMS
Rain in Leningrad
    (Tr. by George Johnston)   128   151

HEINZELMAN, KURT
POEMS
  Fear a Joke Inside   128   63
  Proteus's Children   131   223

REVIEWS
  Five Poets of the Commonwealth   131   225
    Rites of Passage: Selected Translations,
      by Edwin Morgan
    Stonedancer, by Mike Doyle
    Turns, by Richard Outram
    Will's Dream, by Philip Roberts
    Shabbytown Calendar,
      by Thomas W. Shapcott

HELD, DENNIS
POEMS
  Reuben, Sunday Morning, 1967   161   144
  Night Cats at the Grain Elevator   168   260

HELLAAKOSKI, AARO
POEMS
  Hauen Laulu (Tr. by Meri Lehtinen)   98   348

HELLER, ERICH
ARTICLES
  Notes on Language and Its Deconstruction:
    On Translating and Stephen
    Mitchell's Translation of Rilke
    [Socrates, J. W. von Goethe]   145   229

REVIEWS
  The Selected Poetry of Rainer Maria Rilke
    (Ed. and tr. by Stephen Mitchell)   145   229

BOOKS REVIEWED
  The Disinherited Mind   91   403
  *The Artist's Journey into the Interior
    and Other Essays*   110   254

HELLER, SAMUEL
POEMS
  Meditation   24   182

HELLERSTEIN, KATHRYN
POEMS
  Illusion-Making Craft   129   11

HELSTON, JOHN
BOOKS REVIEWED
  Aphrodite and Other Poems   4   69

HELTON, ROY
BOOKS REVIEWED
  Outcasts in Beulah Land   14   277
  Lonesome Water   39   221
  Come Back to Earth   68   163

HELWIG, DAVID
BOOKS REVIEWED
  The Rain Falls Like Rain   144   297

HEMENWAY, ISABEL (WOLFE)
POEMS
  Youth   36   25

HEMENWAY, ROBERT
BOOKS REVIEWED
  *Becoming a Poet: Elizabeth Bishop
    with Marianne Moore and Robert Lowell,*
    by David Kalstone (Ed.)   157   159

HEMINGWAY, ERNEST (M.)
POEMS
  Wanderings   21   193
    Mitrailliatrice
    Oily Weather
    Roosevelt
    Riparto d'Assalto
    Champs d'Honneur
    Chapter Heading

ARTICLES ABOUT
  Program: "Objectivists" 1931,
    by Louis Zukofsky   37   268
  Program: "Objectivists" 1931,
    by Louis Zukofsky   121   45
  MacLeish Revisited,
    by William Pritchard   141   291

HEMLEY, CECIL
POEMS
  The Gentle Women   65   184
  Empress of Oceans
  Observing Birds   66   136
  A Visitor at Breakfast
  The Sea Is Acquisitive   67   186
  The Continents Have Been Discovered
  A Nocturne
  At Shale Springs
  The Mirrors
  Homecoming
  The Chamber of the Dead   73   271

BOOKS REVIEWED
  Twenty Poems   89   373
  In the Midnight Wood   93   107
  Dimensions of Midnight: Poetry and Prose
    (Ed. by Elaine Gottlieb)   110   427

**HENDERSON, ALICE CORBIN
[ALICE CORBIN, "A. C. H."]**
POEMS
  America   1   81
  Symbols
  The Star
  Nodes
  Fallen   5   72
  Old Songs for New   5   99
    O World
    Humoresque

Two Voices
Love Me at Last
One City Only   7   163
Music
The Pool
Apparitions
Color Note
Song ("A king's but a puppet...")
In the Desert   9   232
Indian Songs
    Listening
    Buffalo Dance
    Where the Fight Was
    The Wind
    Courtship
    Fear
    Parting
The Great Air Birds Go Swiftly By   10 176
New Mexico Songs   11 82
    Los Conquistadores
    Three Men Entered the Desert Alone
    Old Timer
    Pedro Montoya of Arroyo Hondo
    In the Sierras
    A Song from Old Spain
Red Earth   13 194
    Muy Vieja Mexicana
    On the Acequia Madre
    El Rito de Santa Fe
Candle-Light and Sun
    Candle-Light
    The Mask
    Rain-Prayer
    Fame
    Song of Sunlight
"Songs from a Book of Airs"   16 28
    Go Touch the Silent Strings
    The Storm Bird
    Song ("I know you beautiful...")
    I Saw the World Go By
    Summons
    Epitaph ("Earth, draw thy...")
New Mexico Folk-Songs   16 254
    The Ballad of Macario Romero
    Madre Maria
    Manzanita
    Chula La Manaña
    El Coyotito
    Christ Is Born in Bethlehem
    Coplas
    Cundiyo
    Petrolino's Complaint
Horoscope   24 302
Another Spring
The Wood
Flame
Loss
Song ("Take the moment...")
New Mexico Sky   43 128

La Carreta del Muerto
Tomorrow's Sun
Rivers
This Soil

ARTICLES
    A Perfect Return
        [Walt Whitman, Paul Scott Mowrer]   1   87
    Poetic Prose and Vers Libre
        [Yone Noguchi]   2   70
    Our Contemporaries
        [William Stanley Braithwaite,
        Herman Scheffauer]   3   187
    "Too Far from Paris"
        [Nicholas Vachel Lindsay,
        W. B. Yeats]   4   105
    Poetry and War   5   82
    Contemporary Poetry
        and the Universities   5   176
    Our Contemporaries
        [William Stanley Braithwaite]   5   193
    Art and Photography
        [Amy Lowell, Robert Frost]   6   99
    Our Friend the Enemy
        [Raymond F. Alden,
        Edgar Lee Masters]   6   259
    Poetic Drama   7   31
    What Would Walt Think?
        [John L. Hervey]   7   48
    A Partisan Verdict
        [Joyce Kilmer, Rabindranath Tagore] 7   50
    Mr. Masefield's Lecture   7   301
    A New School of Poetry   8   103
    The Rejection Slip   8   197
    Correspondences   8   254
    Of Editors and Poets   8   308
    A New Quarterly
        [Form, Austin O. Spare,
        Francis Marsden]   8   323
    Robert Frost's Quality   8   327
    A Jitney-Bus Among Masterpieces   9   39
    Lazy Criticism [Max Eastman]   9   144
    The Seven Arts
        [James Oppenheim]   9   214
    Aboriginal Poetry III   9   256
    Home Rule [Vachel Lindsay]   9   328
    The Hawk's Well [W. B. Yeats]   10 163
    Wanted: A Song for America   10 165
    The Vigilantes   10 218
    Cowboy Songs and Ballads
        [John A. Lomax, H. H. Knibbs]   10 255
    The Great Adventure
        [Adelaide Crapsey]   10 316
    Our Cowboy Poet
        [Charles Badger Clark]   10 319
    American Verse and English Critics
        [Edward Garnett]   11 207

Send American Poets   12   37
"Our Contributors"   12   94
Baiting the Public
   [Witter Bynner, Arthur Davison
   Ficke, Ann Knish, Emanuel Morgan,
   Elijah Hay]   12   169
Correspondence: Of Puritans,
   Philistines and Pessimists
   [Randolph Bourne, Amy Lowell]   12   228
Mannerisms of Free Verse   14   95
A Note on Primitive Poetry   14   330
Science and Art Again I
   [Charles Steinmetz]   15   204
The Folk Poetry of These States   16   264
   [Notes on *New Mexico Folk-Songs*]   16   291
Correspondence [Resignation]   21   55
On the Need of Scholarships
   for the Study of Indian Culture
   [Natalie Curtis]   22   325

REVIEWS

Interpretations, by Zoë Akins   1   97
Lyrical Poems, by Lucy Lyttelton
The Daffodil Fields, by John Masefield   2   76
Child of the Amazons, by Max Eastman   3   31
The Kingdom of All-Souls,
   and Two Other Poems,
   by George Edward Woodberry   3   69
Minions of the Moon and *The Republic*,
   by Madison Cawein   3   146
Streets and *A Country Boy*,
   by Douglas Goldring
The Poems of Paul Mariett
Some Letters of William Vaughn Moody
   (Ed. by Daniel Gregory Mason)
Poetic Dramas   3   184
   The Americans,
      by Edwin Davies Schoonmaker
   Mr. Faust,
      by Arthur Davison Ficke
   The Wolf of Gubbio,
      by Josephine Preston Peabody
   Tiger, by Witter Bynner
Des Imagistes: An Anthology   5   38
Sonnets from the Patagonian,
   by Donald Evans   5   41
Saloon Sonnets with Sunday Flutings,
   by Allen Norton   5   41
The Shadow of Aetna,
   by Louis V. Ledoux   5   92
Two Kings   5   131
   Philip the King and Other Poems,
      by John Masefield
   The King of the Dark Chamber,
      by Rabindranath Tagore
The Sharing, by Agnes Lee   5   294
The Congo and Other Poems,
   by Vachel Lindsay   5   294

Spoon River Anthology,
   by Edgar Lee Masters   6   145
Antwerp, by Ford Madox Hueffer   6   153
Poems, by John Rodker
Sing-Songs of the War,
   by Maurice Hewlett
Irradiations: Sand and Spray,
   by John Gould Fletcher   7   44
Japanese Poetry   7   89
   The Spirit of Japanese Poetry,
      by Yone Noguchi
   Japanese Lyrics
      (Tr. by Lafcadio Hearn)
      [Ernest Fenollosa]
The Collected Poems of Rupert Brooke   7   262
New Anthologies   7   318
   The Quiet Hour
      (Ed. by Fitz-Roy Carrington)
   The Little Book of American Poets
      (Ed. by Jessie B. Rittenhouse)
   Anthology of Magazine Verse for 1915
      (Ed. by William Stanley Braithwaite)
Wild Earth and Other Poems,
   by Padraic Colum   10   105
Songs of the Soil, by Fenton Johnson   10   158
Poems, by Ralph Hodgson   11   41
Streets and Faces, by Scudder Middleton   11   47
An Annual of New Poetry, 1917
   [Gordon Bottomley, John Drinkwater,
   Edward Eastaway, Robert Frost,
   W. W. Gibson, T. Sturge Moore,
   R. C. Trevelyan]   11   333
Some Imagist Poets, 1917
   [Richard Aldington, H. D.,
   John Gould Fletcher, F. S. Flint,
   D. H. Lawrence, Amy Lowell]   11   339
Poems, by Edward Thomas   12   102
The Last Blackbird,
   by Ralph Hodgson   12   105
Earth of Cualann, by Joseph Campbell   12   107
Mid-American Chants,
   by Sherwood Anderson   12   155
Far-Western Verse   12   158
   Out Where the West Begins,
      by Arthur Chapman
   Riders of the Stars
      and *Songs of the Outlands*,
      by Henry Herbert Knibbs
   Sun and Saddle-Leather
      and *Grass-Grown Trails*,
      by Badger Clark
Art Versus Formulae   12   279
   Poems of Charles Warren Stoddard
      (Ed. by Ina Coolbrith)
   First Offerings: Sonnets and Lyrics,
      by Samuel Roth
   Gardens Overseas,
      by Thomas Walsh

Beggar and King,
  by Richard Butler Glaenzer
Ships in Port,
  by Lewis Worthington Smith
War Poetry Again   12   284
  A Treasury of War Poetry
    (Ed. by George Herbert Clarke)
  Poems of the Great War
    (Ed. by J. W. Cunliffe)
More Anthologies,
  Chiefly Topographical   12   337
  The Chicago Anthology
    (Ed. by Charles G. Blanden
    and Minna Mathison)
  Sunflowers: A Book of Kansas Poems
    (Ed. by Willard Wattles)
  Christ in the Poetry of Today
    (Ed. by Martha Foote Crow)
Green Branches and *Reincarnations*,
  by James Stephens   13   161
My Ireland—Songs and Simple Rhymes,
  by Francis Carlin   13   165
The Old Huntsman,
  by Siegfried Sassoon   13   283
Japanese Prints and *The Tree of Life*,
  by John Gould Fletcher   13   340
*The Path on the Rainbow—An Anthology
  of Songs and Chants from the
  Indians of North America*
    (Ed. by George W. Cronyn)   14   41
Chamber Music—Old and New   14   98
  Chamber Music, by James Joyce
  Corn from Olde Fieldes
    (Ed. by Eleanor M. Brougham)
On "The Movement"   14   159
  The New Era in American Poetry,
    by Louis Untermeyer
  *The Advance of English Poetry
    in the Twentieth Century*,
    by William Lyon Phelps
  Our Poets of Today,
    by Howard Willard Cook
The Sad Years, by Dora Sigerson   14   219
Twenty, by Stella Benson   14   225
Convention and Revolt in Poetry,
  by John Livingston Lowes   14   269
Songs of the Celtic Past,
  by Norreys Jephson O'Conor   14   341
Poems About God,
  by John Crowe Ransom   16   51
Songs of the Cattle Trail and Cow Camp,
  by John A. Lomax   16   273
Two English Poets   16   331
  Poems: First Series,
    by J. C. Squires
  The Queen of China and Other Poems,
    by Edward Shanks
Many Many Moons, by Lew Sarett   17   158

The New Adam, by Louis Untermeyer   17   212
Rhymes of a Homesteader,
  by Elliott C. Lincoln   18   51
Poetic Origins and the Ballad,
  by Louise Pound   18   227
Poems, by Wilfred Owen   18   276

BOOKS REVIEWED
  The New Poetry
    (Ed. with Harriet Monroe)   12   214
  The New Poetry
    (Ed. with Harriet Monroe)   14   281
  Red Earth: Poems of New Mexico   18   157
  The New Poetry
    (Ed. with Harriet Monroe)   27   343
  The Turquoise Trail (Ed.)   37   164
  The Sun Turns West   44   279

ARTICLES ABOUT
  Correspondence from Alice Groff   8   158
  Correspondence
    from Edgar Lee Masters   12   345
  Correspondence from Minna Mathison   13   172
  [Note on *Song of Sunlight*]   13   287
  Correspondence
    from Maxwell Bodenheim   14   170
  A Few Women Poets,
    by Harriet Monroe   26   326
  Obituary   74   370
  Rev. of *Harriet Monroe
    and the Poetry Renaissance*,
    by Ellen Williams   131   39

HENDERSON, ALICE OLIVER
  POEMS
    Ribbons in the Sun   6   195

HENDERSON, DANIEL
  POEMS
    Friendship   20   127
    The Mormon Trail   27   319
    An East-Side Funeral   29   317
    Enemies   33   78
    The Return
    Coin Watcher: Hudson Tubes

  BOOKS REVIEWED
    Life's Minstrel   17   276
    Harp in the Winds   27   162

HENDERSON, HELENA
  POEMS
    Arrest   76   71

HENDERSON, ROSE
  POEMS
    Spring—New Mexico   12   15

HENDERSON, RUTH EVELYN
POEMS
   Festivities   31   245
     The Party
     Crossing the Range
     Interim
     Half-Heard
   First Crossing   54   130
   Postcard from Geneva

HENDRICKS, BRENT
POEMS
   In His Sleep, My Father Inspects
     the Work of the Army Corps
     of Engineers   154   147

HENDRICKS, FLORA
POEMS
   Death That Need Not Have Been   53   244

HENDRICKS, WALTER
POEMS
   Limitation   52   130
   Spider Against Fly
   Bird in My Room
   Dead Tree   66   183

BOOKS REVIEWED
   Flames and Fireflies   29   350

HENDRICKSON, JOHN R.
ARTICLES
   Correspondence:
     An Exchange on Ezra Pound   91   209

HENDRY, DIANA
POEMS
   Trespassing   134   76
   Bank Holiday Sunday on the Canal

HENDRY, J. F.
POEMS
   Midnight Air Raid   57   184
   A Trojan Chorus   69   321
   She or Ariel
   Consummatum Est
   Hymen
   A Theme for Flutes
   Rescue-Party
   Eros and Agape   100   297

ARTICLES ABOUT
   Contemporary Poetry in Britain,
     by David Daiches   62   150

HENKE, MARK
POEMS
   Campania   157   285

HENLEY, ELIZABETH
POEMS
   The Mythologic Prize Pony   85   134
   The Puritan Conflict   86   162
   The Rose-Cut   95   351

ARTICLES ABOUT
   [Note on Zinaida Lazda]   93   413

HENNING, MARLYS
POEMS
   Tardigrade   41   84

HENRI, ADRIAN
BOOKS REVIEWED
   Tonight at Noon   115   61

HENRICH, EDITH
[EDITH KLEM]
POEMS
   Premises   47   74
   Hostility
   The Death of a Nun
   Love Song in April
   Evening
   Morning   58   256
   A Day on Gospel Hill   68   18
   American Town   69   202
   The Quiet Center

BOOKS REVIEWED
   The Quiet Center   70   49
   Person in the World   87   53

ARTICLES ABOUT
   [Note on name]   58   291

HENRICI, ANTHONY
POEMS
   Toward Winter   45   68
   A Trip Through the Mountains
   Our Winter Comrade

HENRIE, CAROL
POEMS
   Limits   140   77
   Crows on the Road in Rain

HENRY, GERRIT
POEMS
   Night and Day   119   335
   The Lecturer's Aria   123   162

REVIEWS
   Starting from Scratch   124   292
     The Fall of America:
       Poems of these States 1965-71,
       by Allen Ginsberg

Two Citizens, by James Wright
The Clam Theater, by Russell Edson
(Asian Figures), by W. S. Merwin
Fever Coast, by Carter Ratcliff

HENRY, LAURIE
POEMS
  Restoring the Chateau
    of the Marquis de Sade   142   88

HENRY, LEIGH
ARTICLES ABOUT
  New International Magazines   19   224

HENRY, S. W.
POEMS
  Black Satin   27   243

HENSEL, GLADYS
POEMS
  The Shepherd Hymn   16   139

HENSLEY, JEANNINE
BOOKS REVIEWED
  The Works of Anne Bradstreet (Ed.)   112   127

HENSON, RICHARD
POEMS
  Invocation   41   251
  If You Are Lost   43   315

HEPPENSTALL, RAYNER
POEMS
  Shadow Shapes   43   308
    Theme Nocturne
    A Thought of Your Unfaith
    For Safety of Her Image
  Humility   46   132
  Perfection

REVIEWS
  Open the Sky, by John Pudney   46   51

BOOKS REVIEWED
  Sebastian   52   104
  Proems
    (With Ruthven Todd, Patrick Evans,
    Edgar Foxall, Lawrence Durrell,
    and Oswald Blakeston)   53   155

HERALD, LEON (SERABIAN)
[LEON SRABIAN HERALD]
POEMS
  A Trifoliate   20   314
    Beauty
    My Wedding
    In Your Eyes
  Memories from My Village   24   246
  Tornado   26   320

Two Canticles   32   198
  A Wary Woman
  So to Me
Personals   38   82
  Scene from Hamlet
  To M. M.
  Lesson to the Sun

BOOKS REVIEWED
  This Waking Hour   28   167

HERBER, WILLIAM
[Pseud. of EVERSON, WILLIAM]
POEMS
  The Sign   55   243

ARTICLES ABOUT
  [Note on name]   56   108

HERBERT, GEORGE
ARTICLES ABOUT
  Hopkins' Ancestry: Part II,
    by Terence Heywood   54   271
  Rev. of Six Metaphysical Poets:
    A Reader's Guide,
    by George Williamson   112   356
  Rev. of George Herbert's Lyrics,
    by Arnold Stein   115   196

HERBERT, ZBIGNIEW
POEMS
  Mother   128   141
  Remembering My Father
    (Tr. by John R. Carpenter
    and Bogdana Carpenter)

BOOKS REVIEWED
  Selected Poems
    (Tr. by Czeslaw Milosz
    and Peter Dale Scott)   114   40
  Mr. Cogito   164   285

HERFORD, OLIVER
BOOKS REVIEWED
  Poems from Life (Ed.)   23   57

HERNÁNDEZ, JOSÉ
BOOKS REVIEWED
  The Gaucho Martín Fierro
    (Tr. by C. E. Ward)
    (Ed. by Frank G. Carrino
    and Alberto J. Carlos)   113   338

HERNÁNDEZ, MIGUEL
POEMS
  Elegy for Ramón Sijé   101   325
  From The Unending Lightning
    (Tr. by Edwin Honig)

HERNANDEZ CRUZ, VICTOR
BOOKS REVIEWED
Snaps   116   120

HERNANDEZ MIYARES, ENRIQUE
POEMS
The Most Fair
(Tr. by Muna Lee)   26   128

HERRERA, FLAVIO
POEMS
Hai Kais
(Tr. by Nora B. Thompson)   74   194

HERRERA REISSIG, JULIO
POEMS
Night   26   149
Interment
The Quarrel
Heraldic Decoration
(Tr. by Muna Lee)

HERRICK, ROBERT
ARTICLES ABOUT
Some Recollections of the Poetry Club
at the University of Chicago,
by Gladys Campbell   107   110

HERRIDGE, ROBERT
POEMS
Vision with Commentary   54   84

HERSCHBERGER, RUTH
POEMS
Our Absence Was Designed   78   22
Summer Mansion
Displays of Skill
The Kiss   81   41
The Huron   83   23
The Song Sparrow Chided
Hunt
Sweet Beast, Dear Cobra
The Robin
The Mouse
Mulberry Street
Thou Shalt Have Trouble Trying Me   86   140
The Big Buck and the Little Buck
The Hiding Virtues
Now Ride Us in a Boat,
Any Round-Bottomed
No, No, I Cannot Tell It
Boating at Yaddo
A Conceit   98   143
Grouse in a Writers' Colony
So If You Love Me

TRANSLATIONS
Poem by Vladimir Mayakovsky
(Tr. with Marina Prychodko)   102   100

BOOKS REVIEWED
A Way of Happening   73   357
Nature & Love Poems   118   41

HERSHON, ROBERT
BOOKS REVIEWED
The Public Hug   139   35

HERSKOVITS, FRANCES
TRANSLATIONS
Dahomean Songs   45   75
To the Envious
To the Sun God
For the Earth God
Song for the Dead

ARTICLES ABOUT
[Note on translations]   45   119

HERTER, SUZETTE
POEMS
To a Flower   8   77

HERTER NORTON, M. D.
[M. D. HERTER-NORTON]
BOOKS REVIEWED
Translations from the Poetry
of Rainer Maria Rilke   55   96
Wartime Letters
of Rainer Maria Rilke, 1914-1921 (Tr.)   56   271
Sonnets to Orpheus,
by Rainer Maria Rilke (Tr.)   61   441
Letters of Rainer Maria Rilke, 1892-1910
(Tr. with Jane Bannard Green)   67   221
The Notebooks of Malte Laurids Brigge,
by Rainer Maria Rilke (Tr.)   76   92
The Lay of the Love and Death
of Cornet Christopher Rilke,
by Rainer Maria Rilke (Tr.)   95   373

ARTICLES ABOUT
Rev. of Thirty-One Poems,
by Rainer Maria Rilke
(Tr. by Ludwig Lewisohn)   69   103

HERVEY, JOHN L.
ARTICLES ABOUT
Our Contemporaries,
by Alice Corbin Henderson   7   48

HERZ, NAT
ARTICLES
Correspondence [Eli Siegel]   80   303

HERZBERG, JUDITH
ARTICLES ABOUT
Rev. of Ordinary Things,
by Jean Valentine
[Huub Oosterhuis]   127   44

HERZING, ALBERT
POEMS
   Canticle I   79   272

BOOKS REVIEWED
   The Mother of the Amazons
     and Other Poems, in Poets of Today VIII   99   379

HESELTINE, NIGEL
POEMS
   Death and the Maiden   56   248

HESS, HARRY WARREN
Poems
   Three Women   33   24
   Forced Flower
   Names
   Proselyte Unmade

HESSE, EVA
BOOKS REVIEWED
   Dichtung und Prosa,
     by Ezra Pound (Tr.)   83   357

HESSE, HERMANN
ARTICLES
   "Bad" Poetry
     (Tr. by Roy Temple House)   70   202

BOOKS REVIEWED
   Hours in the Garden and Other Poems
     (Tr. by Rika Lesser)   136   40

ARTICLES ABOUT
   A Note on Hermann Hesse's Verse,
     by Clyde W. Park   70   206

HESTER, MICHELE
POEMS
   Bees at Termes   156   209

HESTER, WILLIAM
POEMS
   Didactos   61   478

HEWETT, DOROTHY
POEMS
   Goodbye Forever   169   37
   Her Ghost
   His Ghost

ARTICLES ABOUT
   Towards a Contemporary
     Australian Poetics,
     by John Kinsella   169   94

HEWITT, GEOF
BOOKS REVIEWED
   Waking Up Still Pickled   113   188

   Quickly Aging Here:
     Some Poets of the 1970's (Ed.)   118   46

HEWLETT, DOROTHY
BOOKS REVIEWED
   Adonais: A Life of John Keats   53   159

HEWLETT, MAURICE
BOOKS REVIEWED
   Helen Redeemed and Other Poems   2   72
   Sing-Songs of the War   6   153
   The Song of the Plow   9   324

HEYEN, WILLIAM
POEMS
   Kamikaze   110   27
   Depth of Field   114   15
   The King's Men
   The Return   118   27
   The Snapper
   The Swan   119   150
   The Trail Beside the River Platte   123   16
   Papyrus   126   334
   Mustard
   Watermelon
   Anise
   Fires   128   267
   The Singer   132   95
   Lord Dragonfly   132   187
   To a Warplane
   Anthem
   The Field   133   127
   The Crow
   A Story from Chekhov   135   120
   Mantle
   The Buffalo
   Redwings
   Ram Time   138   22
   Arrows
   Catbird
   Post Mortem: Literary Criticism
   The Oregon Coast at Seal Rock:
     Thinking of Wallace Stevens at Seventy   139   158
   The Berries
   Mother and Son   142   209
   Between Flights

REVIEWS
   Responsibilities: Four Poets   111   329
     The Course, by Robert Huff
     The Book of the Green Man,
      by Ronald Johnson
     Some Versions of Silence,
      by Robert Dana
     The Lost Pilot, by James Tate
   Sensibilities   115   426
     Beyond Power,
      by M. L. Rosenthal

Fidelities, by Vernon Watkins
Midpoint, by John Updike
Rocky Mountain Foot,
    by George Bowering
Four Realities   122   237
Poems from Three Decades,
    by Richmond Lattimore
A Book of Change,
    by Frederick Morgan
Conjure: Selected Poems, 1963-1970,
    by Ishmael Reed
Of All the Dirty Words,
    by Richard Shelton

BOOKS REVIEWED
Depth of Field   118   351
Noise in the Trees: Poems and a Memoir   126   219
Lord Dragonfly   142   106

HEYM, GEORG
POEMS
Evening
    (Tr. by Babette Deutsch
    and Avrahm Yarmolinsky)   21   144

HEYWARD, DU BOSE
POEMS
The Mountain Woman   16   191
The Mountain Graveyard   18   246
Charleston Poems   20   1
    Dusk
    Edgar Allan Poe
    Matins
Milestones   23   130
New England Landscape
The Equinox
Pirate Legend   23   308

ARTICLES
Poetry South
    (With Hervey Allen)
    [Edgar Allan Poe, Sidney Lanier]   20   35

BOOKS REVIEWED
Carolina Chansons:
    Legends of the Low Country
    (With Hervey Allen)   22   89
Sky-Lines and Horizons   25   164

ARTICLES ABOUT
Poets as Prosers,
    by Harriet Monroe   28   328

HEYWOOD, JASPER
ARTICLES ABOUT
The 16th Century Lyric
    in England: Part II,
    by Yvor Winters   53   320

HEYWOOD, TERENCE
POEMS
A Flamingo's Egg   52   22
Rags of Time
The Whale   52   253
Notes for a Bestiary   55   250
Not Without Hazard
Linguistic
Grisaille
Holy Living and Wholly Dying

ARTICLES
Hopkins' Ancestry: Part I
    [Walt Whitman, Charles Doughty,
    William Barnes]   54   209
Hopkins' Ancestry: Part II
    [John Donne, George Herbert,
    Edward Benlowes]   54   271

BOOKS REVIEWED
Facing North
    (With Edward Lowbury)   97   192

HIBBARD, ADDISON
BOOKS REVIEWED
The Lyric South (Ed.)   37   164

HICKEY, FLORENCE MAYNE
POEMS
Shadowed Scarlet   26   190
They Told Me
Out of Character
Ending

HICKLER, ROSALIE (DUNLAP)
POEMS
Spring Music   36   21
Autumnal   36   301
September
January Thaw
Night on a Mountain
Sacraments
On This Still Air   49   13

BOOKS REVIEWED
Lower than the Angels   46   232

HICKS, JOHN V.
POEMS
O But What Sun   98   220
I Know You and I Am Troubled   99   362
The Hungerers

HICKY, DANIEL WHITEHEAD
POEMS
Snowstorm   35   323

HICOK, BOB
POEMS
   Rothko's Last Meditation   166   37
   Ha'ish hu ha'ish   170   345

BOOKS REVIEWED
   The Legend of Light   169   339

HIERONYMUS, R. E.
POEMS
   To a Steam Turbine-Generator   30   20
   "Interconnection"   33   304

HIGGINS, BERTRAM
POEMS
   The Confrontation   42   269

ARTICLES ABOUT
   Rev. of *The Penguin Book*
     of Australian Verse
     (Ed. by John Thompson,
     Kenneth Slessor, and R. G. Howarth)   94   44

HIGGINS, BRIAN
BOOKS REVIEWED
   The Only Need   100   191

HIGGINS, F. R.
BOOKS REVIEWED
   The Gap of Brightness   57   330

ARTICLES ABOUT
   A Letter from Ireland,
     by Joseph M. Hone   44   213

HIGGINSON, FRED H.
BOOKS REVIEWED
   A Bibliography of the
     Works of Robert Graves   110   409

HIGHAM, CHARLES
BOOKS REVIEWED
   Spring and Death   83   343

HIGHET, GILBERT
BOOKS REVIEWED
   The Classical Tradition   76   218

HILBERRY, CONRAD
POEMS
   The Sea   132   335
   A Christmas Poem   133   125
   The Moon Seen as a Slice of Pineapple   136   325
   The Expatriate
   Nuestra Señora de la Salud
   Christmas, Mexico   137   148
   A Procession of Ants, Chanting   140   277
   The Frog   141   284

HILDEBIDLE, JOHN
POEMS
   For Nicholas, at Two   145   264
   Leah's Morning Song

HILDEBRAND, TIM
POEMS
   The Silver   115   386
   Her Back
   Once in the Water

HILL, BRIAN
ARTICLES ABOUT
   Recent French Publications,
     by Wallace Fowlie   93   40

HILL, CREIGHTON
[HUGH CREIGHTON HILL]
POEMS
   Chrysalides   43   16
   Triangle in a Quandary   95   281

HILL, DANA
POEMS
   The Fools   24   306
   She Is Like
   Temptation

HILL, FRANK ERNEST
BOOKS REVIEWED
   The Winged Horse: The Story
     of the Poets and Their Poetry
     (With Joseph Auslander)   31   349
   Stone Dust   33   131

HILL, GEOFFREY
POEMS
   Wreaths   90   80

BOOKS REVIEWED
   For the Unfallen   102   393
   Preghiere   110   112
   King Log   114   397
   Mercian Hymns   120   170
   Somewhere Is Such a Kingdom:
     Poems 1952-1971   128   232
   Tenebrae   136   102
   The Poetry and Voice of...
     [Recording]
   Collected Poems   150   286
   New and Collected Poems, 1952-1992   165   158

ARTICLES ABOUT
   A Letter from Britain,
     by William Logan   157   222

HILL, HUGH CREIGHTON
[See HILL, CREIGHTON]

HILL, LEWIS
POEMS
   For the Complaint of Love   82   136

HILL, MARVIN LUTER
POEMS
   Doris   34   25

HILL, P. MAURICE
BOOKS REVIEWED
   The Poems of Sappho (Tr.)   86   303

HILL, RAYMOND THOMPSON
BOOKS REVIEWED
   Anthology of the Provençal Troubadors
     (Ed. with Thomas Goddard Bergin)   58   278

HILL, THOMAS
BOOKS REVIEWED
   Blue House: Poems in the Chinese Manner
     (With Jim Chapson and James Liddy)   114   251

HILL-LEVITT, LESLIE
POEMS
   Afternoon: Manhattan   66   133
   Island Song

HILLMAN, BRENDA
POEMS
   Walking the Dunes   130   83
   On the Pier
   An Effort To Enter into Morning

HILLMAN, CAROLYN
POEMS
   Two Christmas Poems   15   134
     Sugar Mice
     Wreaths
   A Portrait   23   17

HILLYER, ROBERT (SILLIMAN)
POEMS
   Arabesque   24   241
   Autumn   27   69
   A Miscellany   29   82
     XXth Century
     Watching
     Portrait
     Pastoral
   Pastorals   32   310
   A Voice in the Night   71   23

BOOKS REVIEWED
   Eight More Harvard Poets
     (Ed. with S. Foster Damon)   24   162
   The Hills Give Promise, and Carmus:
     A Symphonic Poem   25   281
   The Halt in the Garden   29   284

   The Seventh Hill   32   165
   The Gates of the Compass   39   340
   Collected Poems   45   99
   A Letter to Robert Frost   51   267
   Pattern of a Day   58   103
   Poems for Music, 1917-1947   73   177
   The Suburb by the Sea   82   34
   In Pursuit of Poetry   98   332
   Robert Hillyer and John Hall Wheelock
     [Recording]   101   275

ARTICLES ABOUT
   Poetry on Records,
     by Harry Thornton Moore   58   345
   Poetry and Advertising,
     by S. I. Hayakawa   67   204
   The Anti-Poet All Told,
     by Hayden Carruth
     [Ezra Pound]   74   274

HILTON, DAVID
POEMS
   Salty Dog Asleep   116   13
   Above Passion
   The Furnished Cottage
   The Excursionists
   Making Love

BOOKS REVIEWED
   The Shot Goes In   118   98

HIND, C. LEWIS
BOOKS REVIEWED
   200 Best and Second Best Poems (Ed.)   32   96

HINDUS, MILTON
POEMS
   Self Wears Vanity
     To Make Itself Invisible   51   193

REVIEWS
   The Migrants and *A Suite for France*,
     by Clark Mills   59   285
   Modern Poetry and Antique Diction   60   285
     This Last Devotion,
       by Hugh Western
     Bathsheba,
       by Virginia Horton Rogers
   Pure and Otherwise   61   629
     Three Lyric Poets
       (Ed. by Alan Swallow)
       [Byron Herbert Reece,
       Alice Moser, Tom H. McNeal]
     Motley's the Only Wear,
       by Tom H. McNeal
     The Jervis Bay and Other Poems,
       by Michael Thwaites
   The Necessity of Vision   61   696

Rock and Cumulus,
    by Richard Leon Spain
Steep Acres, by Daniel Smythe
Modernity and Convention   62   285
    Songs for America,
        by Sydney King Russell
    Mr. Zenith and Other Poems,
        by Edward Doro
    The Twittering Self,
        by Robert Brown
Soft and Loud   63   226
    No Boundary,
        by Lenore G. Marshall
    The Sound I Listened For,
        by Robert Francis
    A Time to Speak,
        by Thomas Caldecot Chubb
The Equation of Sensibility
    with Expression   64   39
    Day of Fire, by Leonard Bacon
    Enrico Considers,
        by John Russell McCarthy
Time of Year, by Samuel French Morse   64   337
Workshop (Ed. by Oscar Williams)   65   283
Ha! Ha! Among the Trumpets,
    by Alun Lewis   67   286

BOOKS REVIEWED
    Leaves of Grass
        One Hundred Years After (Ed.)
        [William Carlos Williams,
        Richard Chase, Leslie A. Fiedler,
        Kenneth Burke, David Daiches,
        J. Middleton Murry]   87   183

HINE, DARYL ["D. H."]
    POEMS
        Where Your Heart Is
            There Your Treasure Is Also   91   367
        Elegiacs   115   83
        Linear A   120   287
        Vowel Movements   123   299
        Daylight Saving: A January Journal   131   187
        Codex
        Doctor Faustus' Welcome Home
        Copied in Camoes
        Coma Berenices
        After the Solstice
        Vivid Season of Decay   138   315
        Sapphics   141   14
        Window or Wall

    TRANSLATIONS
        Homeric Hymn to Aphrodite   116   313
        Poem by Theocritus   128   155

    ARTICLES
        Correspondence   120   361

REVIEWS
    Several Makers: Poets and Translators   113   35
        Mediaeval Irish Lyrics
            (Ed. and tr. by James Carney)
        Late Mediaeval Scots Poetry
            (Ed. by Tom Scott)
        Scottish Poetry, Number Two
            (Ed. by George Bruce, Maurice
            Lindsay, and Edwin Morgan)
        Contemporary Portuguese Poetry
            (Ed. and tr. by Jean R. Langland)
        An Anthology of Modern Yiddish Poetry
            (Ed. and tr. by Ruth Whitman)
        Polish Writing Today
            (Ed. by Celina Weniewska)
        Collected Poems, 1930-1965,
            by A. D. Hope
        After Experience, Poems,
            by W. D. Snodgrass
        The Damages, Poems,
            by Richard Howard
        Touch, by Thom Gunn
        Figure in the Door, by Arthur Gregor
        The Light Under Islands, Poems,
            by Radcliffe Squires
        Lanced in Light, Poems,
            by Larry Rubin
        Leopards in the Temple, Poems,
            by David Galler
        Cry Ararat!, Poems New and Selected,
            by P. K. Page
        [Sedulius Scotus, Gavin Douglas,
            William Dunbar]
    Collected Longer Poems, by W. H. Auden   117   211
    The Palm at the End of the Mind:
        Selected Poems and a Play
        by Wallace Stevens
        (Ed. by Holly Stevens)   119   171

    BOOKS REVIEWED
        The Devil's Picture Book   100   191
        The Wooden Horse   109   53
        Daylight Saving   134   167

    ARTICLES ABOUT
        Poets in Canada,
            by Margaret Avison   94   182
        Announcement,
            by Henry Rago   113   60

HINMAN, BERTHA
    POEMS
        Primitive   96   102
        Beside These Sheltered Waters

HINRICHSEN, DENNIS
    POEMS
        Testament   156   63
        Poem of Mercy

BOOKS REVIEWED
The Attraction of Heavenly Bodies   143   295
The Rain That Falls This Far   160   219

HINSEY, ELLEN
BOOKS REVIEWED
Cities of Memory   170   101

HINTON, LEONARD
POEMS
Three Moods in Love   32   314
Modern Marriage
Tribute
A Man to His World

HIPP, DOROTHY
[See GONZALEZ, A. R.]

HIRSCH, EDWARD
POEMS
How To Get Back to Chester   133   37
For the Sleepwalkers   137   151
Edward Hopper and the House
   by the Railroad (1925)   140   219
Moving Toward a Blue Unicorn
Fever   143   271
Poor Angels
The Renunciation of Poetry   163   31

REVIEWS
Twentieth Century Pleasures,
   by Robert Hass   145   345

BOOKS REVIEWED
For the Sleepwalkers   140   346
Wild Gratitude   148   99
The Night Parade   156   100
Earthly Measures   165   158

HIRSCHMAN, JACK
POEMS
From One Finger from the Seasons   102   97
The Baseball Poem   106   398

TRANSLATIONS
Poems by Malka Haifetz Tussman   102   381

ARTICLES
A Note on Malka Tussman   102   406

REVIEWS
Five Poets   112   274
All Watched Over
   by the Machines of Loving Grace,
   by Richard Brautigan
Days, or Days as Thoughts
   in a Season's Uncertainties,
   by Samuel Charters

The Difference Between,
   by Christine LaBelle
Apocalypse Rose,
   by Charles Plymell
Burning Snake,
   by Charles Potts

BOOKS REVIEWED
Interchange   105   414

HIRSH, EDWARD L.
POEMS
Memorial Day   70   309

HIRSHFIELD, JANE
POEMS
A Sweetening
All Around Me As It Falls   160   254

HITCH, ALFRED
POEMS
Wander Song   3   20
Alone
Quatrains
The Desert
Beauty   10   241

BOOKS REVIEWED
Poems and Essays   18   223

HITCHCOCK, ANNE
POEMS
The Women   88   143
Chinese Poetry   92   358

HITCHCOCK, GEORGE
BOOKS REVIEWED
Tactics of Survival   105   414

HITCHCOCK, LILA
POEMS
Burns's Stanza   70   133
Artist Dormant
The Glance

HIVNOR, ROBERT
BOOKS REVIEWED
Playbook: Five Plays for a New Theater
   (With Lionel Abel, Junjo Kinoshita,
   James Merrill, and I. A. Richards) 89   253

HIX, H. L.
POEMS
Villanelle After Wittgenstein   158   314

HOAGLAND, KATHLEEN
BOOKS REVIEWED
1000 Years of Irish Poetry (Ed.)   73   53

HOAGLAND, TONY
POEMS
   Volunteer   153   146
   The Miracle
   Safeway   158   15
   Emigration

BOOKS REVIEWED
   Sweet Ruin   163   285

HOBSBAUM, PHILIP
BOOKS REVIEWED
   In Retreat and Other Poems   114   266
   Coming Out Fighting   118   98

HOBSON, ALFRED JOHN
BOOKS REVIEWED
   A Song of David   43   290

HO CHI-FANG
POEMS
   A Night Scene
     (Tr. by Harold Acton)   46   16

HOCHMAN, SANDRA
POEMS
   Not Having a Child   104   230
   The Spy   110   157
   Living Without Treasures

BOOKS REVIEWED
   Manhattan Pastures   104   108
   Love Letters from Asia   113   262
   Earthworks   120   49
   Futures   127   44

ARTICLES ABOUT
   Rev. of *Buckdancer's Choice*,
    by James Dickey   108   44

HOCKENHULL, DONALD
POEMS
   Arriving Manchester   67   243
   Some Fields Remain   69   70
    Europe, 1946
    Flight
    With Sausages
    Culture, 1946
    "Da gwyddwn ban oeddwn iau
     Ba dir yn y byd oreu"
    Winter, 1946

HODGE, RUPERT
POEMS
   Pedant   51   19
   Discovery   51   76
   And Times There Are   53   306
   Blind

HODGSON, RALPH
BOOKS REVIEWED
   Poems   11   41
   The Last Blackbird   12   105
   The Skylark and Other Poems   94   124
   Collected Poems   103   316

ARTICLES ABOUT
   Rev. of *Georgian Poetry: 1913-1915*   8   255
   Rev. of *The Listeners*,
    by Walter de la Mare   8   312
   [Note]   99   135

HOEY, ALLEN
POEMS
   Dividing the Firmament
    Hourly in Rome   154   258

HOFFENSTEIN, SAMUEL
POEMS
   Cloud   34   76
   Hill

HOFFMAN, DANIEL (G.)
POEMS
   In the Beginning   89   221
   Cowhead   96   21
   A Legacy   99   292
   A Letter to Wilbur Frohock
   Gestures
   A Deliverance   102   310
   Entering Doorways   106   209
   In the Republic of the Troll King
   This Day   109   89
   Testament
   Other Poems
   When My Wiser Brother
   A Historian   115   101
   A Special Train
   Aphrodite
   An Old Photo in an Old Life   117   80
   Comanches   119   17
   Stone
   Blood
   The Poem ("Arriving at last...")
   Window   120   198
   Door
   Path
   Shell
   Burning Bush   121   321
   At the Roman Wall, 1956   131   328
   Haunted Houses
   Fables   151   64

TRANSLATIONS
   Poem by Ruth Domino
    (Tr. with Jerre Mangione)   104   85

REVIEWS
   Graves—A Ghost and a Skeleton Key   110   409
      Collected Poems 1966,
         by Robert Graves
      A Bibliography of the
         Works of Robert Graves,
         by Fred H. Higginson
   Constraints and Self-Determinations   114   335
      Blue Juniata: Collected Poems,
         by Malcolm Cowley
      White-Haired Lover, by Karl Shapiro
      The Last Day and the First,
         by Theodore Weiss
      Selected Poems, by Robin Skelton
      The Collected Poems
         of Anne Wilkinson and a Prose Memoir
         (Ed. by A. J. M. Smith)
      The Battle of Aughrim,
         by Richard Murphy

BOOKS REVIEWED
   The Poetry of Stephen Crane   92   116
   A Little Geste, and Other Poems   100   404
   The City of Satisfactions   103   387
   Barbarous Knowledge:
      Myth in the Poetry of Yeats,
      Graves, and Muir   112   52
   Striking the Stones   113   338
   Broken Laws   118   228
   The Center of Attention   125   354
   Able Was I Ere I Saw Elba:
      Selected Poems   132   170
   Brotherly Love   140   346
   Hang-Gliding from Helicon:
      New and Selected Poems 1948-1988   154   99

HOFFMAN, FREDERICK J.
   ARTICLES
      Marianne Moore:
         Imaginary Gardens and Real Toads   83   152
      Williams and His Muse   84   23

   REVIEWS
      The Shaping Spirit:
         A Study of Wallace Stevens,
         by William Van O'Connor   76   355
      The Uses of Literature   111   203
         Conceptions of Reality
            in Modern American Poetry,
            by L. S. Dembo
         Literature Inside Out:
            Ten Speculative Essays,
            by Frederic Will
         T. S. Eliot: The Dialectical Structure
            of His Theory of Poetry,
            by Fei-Pai Lu
         The New England Conscience,
            by Austin Warren

   Language as Symbolic Action:
      Essays on Life, Literature, and Method,
      by Kenneth Burke   111   416

BOOKS REVIEWED
   The Little Magazine:
      A History and a Bibliography
      (Ed. with Charles Allen
      and Carolyn F. Ulrich)   70   274

HOFFMAN, GEORGE EDWARD
   POEMS
      Sandpipers   44   200

HOFFMAN, HAROLD
   POEMS
      Killdeer   23   196
      Belated

HOFMANN, MICHAEL
   POEMS
      White Noise   140   91
      Author, Author   142   194
      Not Talking   146   221

   BOOKS REVIEWED
      Nights in the Iron Hotel   145   99

   ARTICLES ABOUT
      A Letter from Britain, by William Logan   157   222

HOGAN, CHARLES BEECHER
   BOOKS REVIEWED
      A Bibliography of
         Edwin Arlington Robinson   50   150

HOGARTH, WILLIAM
   ARTICLES ABOUT
      The Poetry of Charles Churchill: Part I,
         by Yvor Winters   98   44

HOGBEN, CAROL
   POEMS
      ("Far cry below my flying children...")   75   86
      ("Your slim self, sharpened white...")
      Flower Clock Almanack   78   15
      The Bare Peak
      For Harold & Elisabeth
      Theagony

HOGG, ROBERT
   BOOKS REVIEWED
      The Connexions   109   123

HOGREFE, PEARL
   POEMS
      In the Open   44   134
         Poplar in Storm
         Renewal

BOOKS REVIEWED
Renewal   58   275

HOKE, TRAVIS
POEMS
Supreme Laughter   9   180
The Ultimate

HOLBERG, RUTH LANGLAND
POEMS
Rockport Water-Colors   35   195
    Still Water
    Tide-Fear
    Ebbing
    End
Song for the Beloved   39   138
Strange Fruit
Ice Tree

HOLBROOK, DAVID
BOOKS REVIEWED
Dylan Thomas and Poetic Dissociation   108   65

HOLDEN, HAROLD
BOOKS REVIEWED
Poems by Samuel Greenberg
    (Ed. with Jack McManis)   71   158

HOLDEN, JONATHAN
POEMS
Salvation   125   283
Fire
How To Throw Apples
Night Game
Sandia Mountain
One-Ring Circus   136   197
Losers   140   210
The Third Party
Full Moon, Rising   143   27
Scraping the House
Shoptalk   146   144
Rereading Old Love Letters
Sex Without Love
Wading
Against Paradise   149   321
Home
Some Basic Aesthetics   151   65
After Closing Luigi Cremona's
    Projective Geometry   151   353
The Colors of Passion   156   197
Combine

BOOKS REVIEWED
Against Paradise   158   342
American Gothic   162   167

HOLDEN, MOLLY
BOOKS REVIEWED
To Make Me Grieve   115   61

HOLDEN, RAYMOND (PECKHAM)
POEMS
Passers-By   12   134
Sugaring   16   198
Night Above the Tree Line   20   124
Sonnets to Speak a Name   29   78
The Systems and Fellowmen   30   320
Whom Wisdom Bewitched
To Quiet the Bitter Heart
Quarrel   40   203
Cold Clouds   43   66
    Storm over Rockefeller Center
    To the Sun
Outcry   45   147
    You Must Not Listen
    O Wind of Music
    Song in Danger
    We, Who from Breath...
Matter in Agony   48   21
Rockefeller Plaza Night
"But When I Became a Man..."   50   325
The Mind Has Studied Flight   51   254
Variations on a Theme by Circumstance   54   320

REVIEWS
Spell Against Death,
    by Harold Lewis Cook   42   285
Collected Poems, by Robert Hillyer   45   99
Ten Introductions:
    A Collection of Modern Verse
    (Ed. by Genevieve Taggard
    and Dudley Fitts)   46   112
No Traveler Returns,
    by Joseph Auslander   46   291
Six Sides to a Man, by Merrill Moore   47   49
Strange Holiness,
    by Robert P. Tristram Coffin   47   229
First Symphony,
    by Harold Trowbridge Pulsifer   47   283
Address to the Living, by John Holmes   50   170

BOOKS REVIEWED
Granite and Alabaster   24   222
Natural History   52   156
The Arrow at the Heel   57   270

HÖLDERLIN, FRIEDRICH
BOOKS REVIEWED
Some Poems of...
    (Tr. by Frederic Prokosch)   63   169
Selected Poems of...
    (Tr. and ed. by J. B. Leishman)   91   260
Hölderlin
    (Tr. and ed. by Michael Hamburger)   101   287

HOLLAND, JON BEN
POEMS
Carnival   33   260

HOLLAND, ROBERT

REVIEWS

Six or Seven Fools   129   285
  Grief: Poems and Versions of Poems,
    by Stephen Berg
  Riding the Earthboy 40,
    by James Welch
  Transplants,
    by Cynthia Macdonald
  Inscripts, by Samuel Hazo
  Separations, by Marilyn Hacker
  Vital Signs: New and Selected Poems,
    by David Slavitt
  [Anton Chekhov]
Lost and Found   133   346
  100 Chameleons, by Dennis Saleh
  Half-Tones, by Pamela Stewart
  When Sky Lets Go,
    by Madeline DeFrees
  The Book of the Body,
    by Frank Bidart
  31 Letters and 13 Dreams,
    by Richard Hugo
  Geography III,
    by Elizabeth Bishop

HOLLANDER, JOHN

POEMS

The Jewels and the Gracchi   87   217
The Observatory   90   221
Aristotle to Phyllis   94   19
The Whole Story   97   75
The Altarpiece Finished   98   17
Riddle/Answer
For the Passing of Groucho's Pursuer
The Find
Sent with a Bottle of
  Burgundy for a Birthday   100   13
The Right Wave   102   371
Five Shaped Poems   109   175
  Normal Bell-Curve
  Swan and Shadow
  Crise de Coeur
  Graven Image
  Broken Column
From Sonnets to Roseblush   115   1
The Curse   117   41
String Player in the Shack   118   264
The Long and the Short of It
Two Slices of Sequoia
Hall of Ocean Life
Sunday A. M. Not in Manhattan
As the Sparks Fly Upward
Another Firefly
Kinds of Kindling
Glimpses of the Birds   122   36
Breadth. Circle. Desert.
  Monarch. Month. Wisdom.

Remembering the Fountain   123   63
After Callimachus
The Hidden Ones
Leaving Delos
A Description of the Celebrated Statue
  of the Storyteller at Ioannapolis
Mount Blank   124   128
The Pictures
A Cup of Tremblings
The Same Question
Reflections on Espionage   125   63
From Spectral Emanations   129   214
  Orange
  Commentary on Orange
  Yellow
  Commentary on Yellow
  In Place of Indigo,
    Who Fled Our Spectrum
  Violet
  After Violet
Thirteens   138   125
Looking East in Winter   145   95
Vintage Absence
The Court of Love: Special Sessions
O I [Cat poem]
Coordinating Conjunction   151   66
For a Tall Headstone   152   8
About the Canzone   153   347
Garden Sundial   157   315
Stable Ego
A Watched Pot
Lazy Susan
Forget How To Remember
  How To Forget   165   153
Arachne   166   87
Two Predators   167   322

TRANSLATIONS

Poem by Aratus   128   146

ARTICLES

Notes [Reflections on Espionage]   125   115
[Merrill Memorial Tribute]   166   341

REVIEWS

Goodbye Earth and Other Poems,
  by I. A. Richards   93   392
Life Studies,
  by Robert Lowell   95   41
Yeats,
  by Harold Bloom   117   43
The Anxiety of Influence:
  A Theory of Poetry,
  by Harold Bloom   122   298
A Map of Misreading,
  by Harold Bloom
  [John Milton, Edmund Spenser,
  Gershom Scholem]   127   222

BOOKS REVIEWED
A Crackling of Thorns   93   107
The Wind and the Rain:
  An Anthology of Poems for Young People
  (Ed. with Harold Bloom)   101   208
John Hollander Reads His Works
  [Recording]   101   275
Movie-Going   102   118
Visions from the Ramble   107   326
Poems of Our Moment (Ed.)   113   262
The Night Mirror   120   296
Town & Country Matters   125   229
The Head of the Bed   126   352
Reflections on Espionage   130   41
Blue Wine and Other Poems   136   295
Powers of Thirteen   145   161
In Time & Place   151   419
Selected Poetry   163   285
Tesserae and Other Poems
American Poetry:
  The Nineteenth Century (Ed.)   165   340

HOLLANDER, MARTHA
POEMS
Gray Elegy   123   6
In the Museum   155   281
Giorgione's Tempest: *Another Story*   159   272
The Web   160   341

TRANSLATIONS
Poems by Catullus   128   125

HOLLERER, WALTER
ARTICLES ABOUT
German Lyric Poetry Since 1945,
  by Hans Egon Holthusen
  (Tr. by Herman Salinger)   88   257

HOLLEY, HORACE
POEMS
Creative   6   73
Twilight at Versailles
Lovers
Cross Patch   8   23
The Fool   17   247

BOOKS REVIEWED
Divinations and Creation   11   222

HOLLEY, MARGARET
POEMS
A Critique of Pure Reason   157   339
Eastering
The Tree of Life
Koan
Galileo in the Snow   161   207
The Gallery of Owls

HOLLINGSHEAD, ROSEMARY
BOOKS REVIEWED
Feet in the Earth   144   297

HOLLINGSWORTH, ROBERT CLARK
POEMS
A Man of the Road   55   242

HOLLO, ANSELM
POEMS
The Days: Air   110   24
Journey
Any News from Alpha Centauri   113   259
Poem ("a painting with no...")
The Lights Going On in the Rooms
  Strung Out Back Through the Years

TRANSLATIONS
Poem by Tomaz Salamun
  (Tr. with Tomaz Salamun)   122   197

BOOKS REVIEWED
Red Cats (Tr.)   102   400
& It Is a Song   110   105
Faces and Forms
The Going-On Poem
Here We Go   110   195
Selected Poems
  of Andrei Voznesensky (Tr.)   111   121
The Man in the Treetop Hat   114   251
Haiku
  (With John Esam
  and Tom Raworth)
Selected Poems,
  by Paavo Haavikko (Ed. and tr.)
The Coherences   117   261

HOLLOWAY, JOHN
BOOKS REVIEWED
The Minute and Longer Poems   91   45
New Poems   118   351

HOLLOWAY, ROBERTA
POEMS
Sorrow   23   318
At Night   41   248
  Maze at Midnight
  Wake for Another Day
Remembering Atlas   50   207
The Wide Day
The Lovely Children
Invitation to Many Voices

TRANSLATIONS
Poem by Sergey Yesenin
  (With Alexander Kaun)   27   76

HOLLOWELL, GRACE BAER
POEMS
  Lines from Dust   32   325
    Summer Idyl
    Song of the Yellow-Green Willow
    How Praise Her
    Perhaps
    City Dwelling
    To My Stepson
  Sketches in Color   38   28
    Josephine Sciba
    Of Her Enemy
    Cash-Girl
    Wisdom
  In the Pearl   47   308
    In Place of Snow
    Dear Mexico
  Exemption   57   239
  Creed
  Das Rhinegold
  Angels   60   19
  On the Road to Reality   75   206
  When the Light Is in the Pearl 77   26

HOLME, JAMIE SEXTON
POEMS
  Dissolution   34   82
    The Flesh
    The Spirit
    The Builder

HOLMES, CALVIN RUSSELL
POEMS
  Madonna   22   253

HOLMES, CLELLON
POEMS
  Fear in the Afternoon   72   181
  Doctor Trustus: Man of Good Will 73   203
  "Les Italiennes"
  "The Palpable Elysium"   76   139

ARTICLES
  A Concerned Neutrality   74   46

REVIEWS
  A Second Book of Danish Verse
    (Ed. by Charles Wharton Stork) 71   339
  The Time by Dialing,
    by Myron Broomell   74   46

HOLMES, ELIZABETH
POEMS
  Things Past   155   404
  Taking a History   165   329
  Belly
  Doorstep

HOLMES, JANET
POEMS
  The Erotics of Detail   165   263

HOLMES, JOHN (A.)
POEMS
  Peter at His Mirror   30   264
  Remembering You, Long After
  A Prologue for Poems   34   199
  In a College Coffee-House
  Noon Waking
  To Music First
  Incredible Greeting   40   314
  The Mask the Living Wear   43   245
  Unlikely Tale   47   79
  To Keep and Not To Keep   58   246
  The Praise of Poetry
  Election   68   260
  Silence
  Cow Be Killed   84   262
  The Laws   95   279
  Hearing Margaret, Aged Four
  Between Thousand and Thousands 101   265

ARTICLES
  Correspondence:
    A Dissenting Opinion
    [John Gould Fletcher,
    Stephen Spender]   42   355

REVIEWS
  The Sword on the Table,
    by Winfield Townley Scott   61   454
  Natalie Maisie and Pavilastukay,
    by John Masefield   61   514
  Autolycus in Limbo,
    by Vincent Starrett   62   350
  The Ear and the Mind   64   343
    Against a Background on Fire 1938-1943,
      by Frederick Mortimer Clapp
    The Seven Sleepers,
      by Mark Van Doren
  Album of Destiny, by Jesse Stuart 66   168
  Cut Is the Branch,
    by Charles E. Butler   66   280
  The Remembered Land,
    by Alan Swallow   69   52
  Poems 1928-1948, by Edouard Roditi 75   243
  Mortal Summer,
    by Mark Van Doren   85   362
  Collected Poems, by Charlotte Mew
    [Alida Monro]   86   240

BOOKS REVIEWED
  Address to the Living   50   170
  The Poet's Work   56   222
  Map of My Country   63   289

A Little Treasury of Love Poems (Ed.)   77   179
Preface to Poetry
    (With Charles W. Cooper)   84   43
The Fortune Teller   100   404

ARTICLES ABOUT
Poetry on Records,
    by Harry Thornton Moore   58   345

HOLMES, OLIVER WENDELL
ARTICLES ABOUT
Rev. of The Fields Were Green,
    by George Arms   84   98

HOLMES, THEODORE
POEMS
The Dressing of a Young Girl   90   214
A Single Man at the Fire
On Becoming of Age   92   31
When the Child
    Would Accommodate the Adult Again
J.   94   174
The Abandoned   95   328
The Doll
A Trilogy of Three Women
Portrait of a Woman   101   238
The Sea
In the Deep Woods
Winter Park with Beeches   106   283
Woman and Horse
Her Body   112   166
Experience
Storm Day   116   89
The Apple Tree

REVIEWS
The Letters of Rainer Maria Rilke
    and Princess Marie von Thurn und Taxis
    (Tr. by Nora Wydenbruck)   94   59
A Water Walk by Villa D'Este,
    by Jean Garrigue   96   118
Bertolt Brecht and Others   97   51
    Selected Poems of Bertolt Brecht
        (Tr. by H. R. Hays)
    New Young German Poets
        (Tr. by Jerome Rothenberg)
Advice to a Prophet and Other Poems,
    by Richard Wilbur   100   37
Wit, Nature, and the Human Concern   100   319
    Nude Descending a Staircase,
        by X. J. Kennedy
    Twenty Poems of Georg Trakl
        (Tr. by James Wright and Robert Bly)

BOOKS REVIEWED
Ship on the Beach   107   183
An Upland Pasture   111   43
Poems from Donegal   129   102

HOLOUBEK, MARY BARBARA
POEMS
Epitaph ("She stood in silence...")   42   207
Fickle

HOLSTEIN, LUDWIG
POEMS
Father, Where Do the Wild Swans Go?
    (Tr. by Charles Wharton Stork)   21   73

HOLTHUSEN, HANS EGON
POEMS
Man of Action   82   330
My Life, My Death
With Roses in Raron

ARTICLES
German Lyric Poetry Since 1945
    (Tr. by Herman Salinger)
    [Oskar Loerke, Wilhelm Lehmann,
    Elizabeth Langgasser, Gunter Eich,
    Karl Krolow, Heinz Piontek,
    Walter Hollerer, Gottfried Benn,
    Ingeborg Bachmann, Paul Celan]   88   257

BOOKS REVIEWED
Rainer Maria Rilke:
    A Study of His Later Poetry
    (Tr. by J. P. Stern)   82   342

ARTICLES ABOUT
Hans Egon Holthusen:
    The Panther and the Prophet,
    by Herman Salinger   82   333

HOLUB, MIROSLAV
BOOKS REVIEWED
Intensive Care:
    Selected and New Poems   170   226

HOLZ, ARNO
POEMS
From Phantasus
    (Tr. by Babette Deutsch
    and Avrahm Yarmolinsky)   21   147

ARTICLES ABOUT
A Note on Modern German Poetry,
    by Babette Deutsch   21   149

HOMER
POEMS
Hymn to Aphrodite
    (Tr. by Daryl Hine)   116   313

BOOKS REVIEWED
The Children's Homer,
    by Padraic Colum   15   345
Homer: The Odyssey: A New Translation
    (Tr. by E. V. Rieu)   72   28

Chapman's Homer: The Iliad (I)
  and *The Odyssey (II)*
   (Ed. by Allardyce Nicoll)   91   60
Homer: The Odyssey
  (Tr. by Robert Fitzgerald)   98 397
Patrocleia: A New Version,
  by Christopher Logue   108 416
The Odyssey
  (Tr. by Richmond Lattimore) 114 113
Rev. of *Kings: An Account of*
  Books 1 and 2 of Homer's Iliad,
  by Christopher Logue   160 157

ARTICLES ABOUT
  Rev. of *The Odyssey:*
   A Modern Sequel,
   by Nikos Kazantzakis
   (Tr. by Kimon Friar)   95 175

HOMER, ART
POEMS
  Commuter's Log   150   10
  Nocturne Moderne   154 262
  Cottonwood Blue

HONDA, H. H.
BOOKS REVIEWED
  The Manyoshu:
   A New and Complete Translation (Tr.) 112 347

HONE, JOSEPH M.
ARTICLES
  Letter from Ireland
   [M. M. Rossi]   43 274
  A Letter from Ireland
   [Alida Monro, Frank O'Connor,
   F. R. Higgins]   44 215
  A Letter from Ireland
   [Andrew Belis, AE]   45 332
  A Letter from Ireland
   [W. B. Yeats]   49 332

REVIEWS
  Good-Bye Twilight
   (Ed. by Leslie H. Daikin)   55 279

BOOKS REVIEWED
  Life of George Moore   49 355
  The Life of W. B. Yeats   62 223
  J. B. Yeats: Letters to His Son, W. B. Yeats,
   and Others, 1869-1922 (Ed.)   69 291

HONG TCHE-KONG
POEMS
  ("Autumn has come. All is empty...")
   (Tr. by George Margulies
   and Willard R. Trask)   46   7

HONIG, EDWIN
POEMS
  Odyssey   58   80
  Summer: University Town   62 196
  Rustler   72 180
  As a Great Prince
  A Graver Story   74 197
  Pray Eros   81 297
  Island Storm   82 254
  Poetry and Pedantry   90 160
  The White Explorers
  Young December in Old Pollentia   96   23

TRANSLATIONS
  Poems by Miguel Hernández   101 325

ARTICLES
  Dimensions of Imagery and
   Action in the Work of García Lorca   63   32
  Correspondence
   [William Justema]   65 165
  The Paterson Impasse   74   37

REVIEWS
  Three Mythmakers   62 282
   Some Odes of Pindar
    (Tr. by Richmond Lattimore)
   The Mirror of Baudelaire
    (Tr. by William Candlewood)
    (Ed. by Charles Henri Ford)
   The Teeth of the Lion,
    by Kenneth Patchen
  Rilke and Hölderlin   63 169
   Poems, by Rainer Maria Rilke
    (Tr. by Jessie Lemont)
   Some Poems of Friedrich Hölderlin
    (Tr. by Frederic Prokosch)
  Private Papers, by William Justema   64 347
  The Giant Weapon, by Yvor Winters   65   43
  Paterson (Book I),
   by William Carlos Williams   69 277
  Paterson (Book II) and *The Clouds,*
   Aigeltinger, Russia, etc.,
   by William Carlos Williams   74   37
  Three Tragedies,
   by Federico García Lorca
   (Tr. by Richard O'Connell
   and James Graham-Luján)   75 114
  Illegitimate Sonnets, by Merrill Moore   80   58
  The Poems of Gene Derwood   89   43

BOOKS REVIEWED
  García Lorca   64 225
  The Moral Circus   87   53
  The Gazabos: 41 Poems   97 109
  The Mentor Book of Major American Poets
   (Ed. with Oscar Williams)   103 261

Survivals   108   57
Spring Journal: Poems   114   40

ARTICLES ABOUT
Correspondence from William Justema   65   164

HOOD, MARY WINIFRED
POEMS
His Vision of the Angel of Death   165   135
St. Caspar del Bufalo
St. Catherine dei Ricci

HOOGESTRAAT, JANE
POEMS
Background Music   163   80

HOOPER, PATRICIA
POEMS
The Stone Boy   99   33
Desert   119   25
Annunciations   161   320
Maples   168   223
Perennials

HOPE, A. D.
POEMS
The School of Night   114   172
The Apotelesm of W. B. Yeats
Parabola   120   280

ARTICLES
Correspondence   120   363

BOOKS REVIEWED
Poems   100   104
Collected Poems, 1930-1965   113   35
New Poems: 1965-1969   118   223
The Cave and the Spring: Essays on Poetry

ARTICLES ABOUT
Towards a Contemporary
Australian Poetics,
by John Kinsella   169   94

HOPE, WELBORN
POEMS
In Indian Territory   39   193
The Squatter   42   206
Oklahoma Poems   44   256
Southwestern Tornado
A Squatter's Wife
The Vanished River
In Early Spring   46   87
Moonrise After Midnight   46   316

HOPKINS, GERARD MANLEY
BOOKS REVIEWED
Poems of... (Ed. by Robert Bridges)   18   330

The Note-Books and Papers of...
(Ed. by Humphry House)   50   274
Further Letters of...
(Ed. by Claude Colleer Abbott)   53   150
Poems of... (Ed. by W. H. Gardner)   74   292
*Further Letters of
Gerard Manley Hopkins*, 2d ed.
(Ed. by Claude Colleer Abbott)   92   113

ARTICLES ABOUT
The Poetry of Gerard Hopkins,
by Joyce Kilmer   4   241
Quality in Madness,
by Jessica Nelson North   34   270
Gerard Manley Hopkins, by M. D. Zabel   37   152
Notes on English Poets,
by Michael Roberts   39   271
Hopkins in His Letters, by M. D. Zabel   46   210
Hopkins' Ancestry: Part I,
by Terence Heywood   54   209
Hopkins' Ancestry: Part II,
by Terence Heywood   54   271
The Rebellious Will of
Gerard Manley Hopkins,
by Frajam Taylor   59   270
Rev. of *Gerard Manley Hopkins,
Priest and Poet*, by John Pick   62   347
Rev. of *Gerard Manley Hopkins,*
by Eleanor Ruggles   65   142
Reading Sprung Rhythms,
by Brewster Ghiselin   70   86
Rev. of *English Prosody and Modern Poetry,*
by Karl Shapiro   72   332
Rev. of *Gerard Manley Hopkins,*
by W. H. Gardner;
Gerard Manley Hopkins
by K. R. Srinivasa Iyengar;
Gerard Manley Hopkins,
by W. A. M. Peters;
and *Immortal Diamond*
(Ed. by Norman Weyand)   74   292
The Face Behind the Poem,
by George Barker   97   310
Rev. of *Robert Bridges and Gerard Hopkins,
1863-1889: A Literary Friendship,*
by Jean-Georges Ritz   100   50
Rev. of *Worldly Hopes,*
by A. R. Ammons   141   26

HOPKINS, JOYCE
POEMS
University: Old Time   37   251

HOPKINS, MARY
BOOKS REVIEWED
*The Gypsy Trail,
an Anthology for Campers*
(Ed. with Pauline Goldmark)   6   98

HOPKINS, RUTH E.
POEMS
Morning   32   196

HORACE
ARTICLES ABOUT
Oliver St. John Gogarty,
    by Vivian Mercier   93   35

HORACIO, GERMAN
BOOKS REVIEWED
A Cry in the Dark
    (With Humberto Rivas)   66   350

HORAN, ROBERT
POEMS
Triumph of Icarus   83   147

BOOKS REVIEWED
A Beginning   73   166

ARTICLES ABOUT
About the Activist Poets,
    by Lawrence Hart   78   99

HORDER, JOHN
BOOKS REVIEWED
A Sense of Being   115   61

HORGAN, PAUL
POEMS
Exotics   24   138
The Temples and the Gongs
Litany
Winter Night
The Mask   26   205
Her Frown
Her Empty Eyes
Her Hidden Smile
Westward   43   144
The Prairie Sleepers
The Branding
Threads of Sky
Last Indian Sign

HORIGUCHI, DAIGAKU
POEMS
A Seascape
    (Tr. by Hisakazu Kaneko)   101   174

HORN, EDWARD
POEMS
Poems for Small Apartments   56   193
The Brilliant
Recall

HORNE, FRANK
ARTICLES ABOUT
Racial Bias and Negro Poetry,
    by Edward Bland   63   328

HORNE, LEWIS
POEMS
Conundrums of Color   146   93
Silent Things
Homage to G. G.

HORNIK, JESSICA
POEMS
Native   170   65

HORRELL, JOE
POEMS
For the Romanticists   53   136
North Carolina Idyl   54   247

ARTICLES ABOUT
The Poet and Pedant Symposium,
    by Margedant Peters   57   194

HORTON, PHILIP
REVIEWS
Twelve Poets of the Pacific
    (Ed. by Yvor Winters)   51   48

BOOKS REVIEWED
Hart Crane:
    The Life of an American Poet   50   219
Hart Crane:
    The Life of an American Poet   91   117

HORVATH, BROOKE
POEMS
Accademia: Florence   153   313
My Girl   156   154
Winding My Watch   169   262

HOSAIN, SHAHID
BOOKS REVIEWED
First Voices: Six Poets from Pakistan (Ed.)   109   272

HOSKEN, RAYMOND
POEMS
The Secret Lake   45   71
Wanderings   47   301
The Span in the Rain
Locusts
Gulls in Snow

HOSKINS, KATHERINE
POEMS
To Apollo Musagetes   91   107
When the Snow Falls
Where Is It That We Go?
Three for Friendship   97   7
Out of Environment   103   289
Explication de Texte
Now Plus Then
December   108   11

Da Ming
Baucis and Philemon   118   92
Poem ("I think I must be dying...")

REVIEWS
The Modern Poets:
    A Critical Introduction,
    by M. L. Rosenthal   99   259
On the Poet and His Craft:
    Selected Prose of Theodore Roethke
    (Ed. by Ralph J. Mills, Jr.)   107   400
Randall Jarrell 1914-1965
    (Ed. by Robert Lowell, Peter Taylor,
    and Robert Penn Warren)   112   118

BOOKS REVIEWED
A Penetential Primer   67   228
Villa Narcisse   89   244
Out in the Open   97   185
Excursions:
    New and Selected Poems   111   184

HOSPERS, JOHN
BOOKS REVIEWED
Meaning and Truth in the Arts   72   326

HOTCHKISS, BILL
POEMS
White World   137   189

BOOKS REVIEWED
Climb to the High Country   133   45

HOUGH, GRAHAM
POEMS
Heliograph   49   185

BOOKS REVIEWED
Reflections on a Literary Revolution   100   50
Legends and Pastorals   100   104

HOURMOUSIADES, KRITON
TRANSLATIONS
Letter from Vassilis Vassilikos   105   60

HOUSE, HUMPHRY
BOOKS REVIEWED
The Note-Books and Papers
    of Gerard Manley Hopkins (Ed.)   50   274

HOUSE, ROY TEMPLE
POEMS
To a Dead Mouse in a Trap   14   17
Dialogue   65   309

TRANSLATIONS
Article by Hermann Hesse   70   202

HOUSMAN, A(LFRED) E(DWARD)
BOOKS REVIEWED
A Shropshire Lad   20   282
Last Poems   22   41
The Name and Nature of Poetry   43   52
More Poems   49   228
The Collected Poems of...   56   144
Complete Poems
    (Ed. by Tom Burns Haber)   96   44

ARTICLES ABOUT
Rev. of A. E. Housman, a Sketch,
    by A. S. F. Gow   52   94
Dr. Johnson and A Shropshire Lad,
    by Charles Norman   60   264
A Commemoration:
    "Les Fleurs du Mal" 1857-1957,
    by Wallace Fowlie   90   376
Correspondence: The Housman Text
    [Tom Burns Haber, Donald Justice]   96   392

HOUSMAN, LAURENCE
ARTICLES ABOUT
Rev. of Complete Poems of A. E. Housman
    (Ed. by Tom Burns Haber)   96   44
Correspondence:
    The Housman Text: An Exchange
    [Tom Burns Haber, Donald Justice]   96   392

HOUSTON, G. CRAIG
BOOKS REVIEWED
Selected Works of
    Rainer Maria Rilke, vol. I, Prose (Tr.)   97   323

HOUSTON, JOHN PORTER
BOOKS REVIEWED
The Design of Rimbaud's Poetry   104   187

HOUSTON, MARGARET BELLE
POEMS
Memory   18   241

HOUSTON, PEYTON
POEMS
The Speaking Wind   49   124
Dancer Over America
In Winter
Seeing a Carved Roman Gem:
    First Century
Thoughts on Good and Evil: 1936

BOOKS REVIEWED
Sonnet Variations   103   192

HOVEY, RICHARD
BOOKS REVIEWED
Dartmouth Lyrics
    (Ed. by Edwin Osgood Grover)   27   164

HOW, LOUIS
BOOKS REVIEWED
  The Youth Replies and Other Verses   2   107
  A Hidden Well: Lyrics and Sonnets   9   324

HOWARD, BEN
POEMS
  The Granite   121   333
  Break
  Redwood
  Wild Turkey in the Rain   122   204
  Seclusion
  Ice Leaf   123   72
  Incision   124   75
  Gourd   125   258
  Winter Report   127   7
  Noon
  Orion's Crossing
  The Diver
  Evidence of Movement   129   131
  Refuge
  Two Deer   130   258
  Sluice   131   291
  Cartographies   144   212
  Fado
  Views   146   257
  Fair Exchange
  Because You Asked for a Bedtime Story   148   265
  1985
  In the Regions of Belief   153   332
  Lute Music
  Sabula   154   214
  For the Calvinists
  The Minor Poets: An Afterlife   155   280
  November   157   74
  Lament for the Holy Places
  Westward   163   220

REVIEWS
  Naturalist, Feminist, Professor   126   44
    The Innocent Assassins,
      by Loren Eiseley
    Presentation Piece,
      by Marilyn Hacker
    The End of Nature,
      by Chad Walsh
    The Book of Folly; The Death Notebooks;
      and *The Awful Rowing Toward God*,
      by Anne Sexton   127   286
  Four Voices   130   285
    The Collected Poems of Weldon Kees
      (Ed. by Donald Justice)
    The Collected Poems: 1956-1974,
      by Edward Dorn
    Night Cries,
      by Michael Benedikt
    "A" 22 & 23, by Louis Zukofsky

British Wells   131   292
    Letters to Vernon Watkins,
      by David Jones
    I That Was Born in Wales,
      by Vernon Watkins
      (Ed. by Gwen Watkins
      and Ruth Pryor)
    Feng, by John Wain
    Collected Poems: 1941-1975,
      by Sidney Goodsir Smith
    The Little Time-Keeper,
      by Jon Silkin
    Mortal Fire, by Peter Dale
    The Blocked Heart,
      by Edwin Brock
    Another Full Moon,
      by Ruth Fainlight
    Sons of My Skin:
      Selected Poems 1954-1974,
      by Peter Redgrove
      (Ed. by Marie Peel)
Chords and Keys   137   105
    Collected Poems, by F. T. Prince
    A Familiar Tree,
      by Jon Stallworthy
    Selected Poems: 1951-1974
      and *The Shaft*,
      by Charles Tomlinson
Five Latitudes   153   106
    To Urania, by Joseph Brodsky
      (Tr. by Joseph Brodsky et al.)
    Selected Poems: 1938-1988,
      by Thomas McGrath
    Flight and Pursuit, by Dick Allen
    Dreams by No One's Daughter,
      by Leslie Ullman
    Selected Poems,
      by Jayanta Mahapatra
Incarnate Lights   154   99
    New and Collected Poems,
      by Richard Wilbur
    Hang-Gliding from Helicon:
      New and Selected Poems 1948-1988,
      by Daniel Hoffman
    Tales of the Supernatural,
      by Maura Stanton
    Timepiece, by Jane Flanders
    The Singing Underneath,
      by Jeffrey Harrison
    The Gaza of Winter,
      by Donald Revell
    Paper Bird, by Robin Behn
Places and Losses   154   340
    The Haw Lantern,
      by Seamus Heaney
    The Sunset Maker,
      by Donald Justice
    The Imperfect Paradise,
      by Linda Pastan

The Marrano, by Barry Goldensohn
Reply from Wilderness Island,
  by Peter Balakian
New Englanders   156   345
  Tell Me Again
    How the White Heron Rises...,
    by Hayden Carruth
  Selves, by Philip Booth
  The Town of No,
    by Wesley McNair
  Wampanoag Traveler,
    by Brendan Galvin
  [Louis MacNeice, T. S. Eliot]
Another Shore   157   343
  Above the River: The Complete Poems,
    by James Wright
  James Wright: The Heart of the Light
    (Ed. by Peter Stitt
    and Frank Graziano)
World and Spirit, Body and Soul   158   342
  House of Light,
    by Mary Oliver
  Sigodlin, by Robert Morgan
  Body Traffic, by Stephen Dobyns
  Against Paradise,
    by Jonathan Holden
Together and Apart   160   34
  The Collected Poems,
    by John Logan
    (Ed. by A. Poulin, Jr.,
    and Jerome Mazzaro)
  Passwords, by William Stafford
  Home Course in Religion,
    by Gary Soto
  Belfast Confetti, by Ciarán Carson
Secular Believers   161   223
  Provinces, by Czeslaw Milosz
    (Tr. by Czeslaw Milosz
    and Robert Hass)
  Selected Poems, by Derek Mahon
  Saints in Their Ox-Hide Boat,
    by Brendan Galvin
  As If, by James Richardson
  As If It Matters,
    by Eamon Grennan
Masters of Transience   163   158
  Firefall, by Mona Van Duyn
  The Museum of Clear Ideas,
    by Donald Hall
  A Dream of Mind,
    by C. K. Williams
  Travels, by W. S. Merwin
Histories and Selves   165   97
  Each in His Season,
    by W. D. Snodgrass
  Selected Poems: 1968-1987,
    by Paul Muldoon
  The City of Women,
    by Sherod Santos

  Patterns of Descent,
    by Richard Foerster
Forms and Discoveries   167   343
  Collected Longer Poems,
    by Hayden Carruth
  Meditations on the Insatiable Soul,
    by Robert Bly
  Mother Love and *The Darker*
    Face of the Earth,
    by Rita Dove
Forms and Discoveries   168   107
  The Look of Things, by Henri Cole
  Selected and New Poems,
    by Michael Hartnett
    (Ed. by Peter Fallon)
  Samhain, by Robin Skelton

BOOKS REVIEWED
  Lenten Anniversaries,
    Poems 1982-1989   159   157

HOWARD, FRANCES MINTURN
POEMS
  Owl in Science Museum   118   321
  Signals
  Antelope — Royal Gardens, Athens

BOOKS REVIEWED
  Sleep Without Armor   84   234

HOWARD, JOHN R.
BOOKS REVIEWED
  Poems of Heroism
    in American Life (Ed.)   21   276

HOWARD, JOHN WESTON
POEMS
  Simple Song   72   133

HOWARD, JOHN ZOLLIE
POEMS
  Warning   28   139

HOWARD, KATHARINE
POEMS
  Belgium   7   133
  The Host of Dreams   10   190
  Beauty Possessed Me   29   80

BOOKS REVIEWED
  The Little God   10   217

HOWARD, RICHARD
POEMS
  Landed: A Valentine   87   220
  Agreement with Sir Charles Sedley
  209 Canal   103   351
  The Difference

Crepuscular   109   245
Secular Games
The Demolition   114   289
Aubade: Donna Anna to Juan, Still Asleep
Freshwater: An Idyll
May 26 1969: The Grievance   115   111
Giovanni da Fiesole On the Sublime,
    or Fra Angelico's Last Judgment   117   1
Compulsive Qualifications   122   154
A Phenomenon of Nature   123   286
"Richard, What's That Noise?"   127   256
Charles Garnier   131   101
Famed Dancer Dies of Phosphorus Poisoning   151   68
Triangulations   151   402
To a Librettist at Liberty   159   201
A Lost Art   161   280

TRANSLATIONS
Poem by Malcolm de Chazal   116   327

REVIEWS
Five Poets   101   412
    The Colossus and Other Poems,
        by Sylvia Plath
    All My Pretty Ones,
        by Anne Sexton
    The Jacob's Ladder,
        by Denise Levertov
    Drowning with Others,
        by James Dickey
    Thank You and Other Poems,
        by Kenneth Koch
Poetry Chronicle   102   182
    A West Wind Rises,
        by Bruce Cutler
    In England's Green &,
        by Jonathan Williams
    Silence in the Snowy Fields,
        by Robert Bly
    The Heads of the Town
        Up to the Aether,
        by Jack Spicer
    Private Dooms & Public Destinations,
        by James Schevill
    Destroyed Works,
        by Philip Lamantia
    The Center of the Circle,
        by Bink Noll
    The Pitch: Poems and Plays,
        by V. R. Lang
Poetry Chronicle   102   250
    Gunsight, by Theodore Weiss
    In Fact, by John Ciardi
    Collected Poems, by Kay Boyle
    The World for Wedding Ring,
        by Daniel Berrigan
    Sestina for a Far-Off Summer,
        by Richmond Lattimore

Snapshots of a Daughter-in-Law,
    by Adrienne Rich
Innocence by Association   104   245
    A Western Sampler
        (Ed. by editors of Talisman)
    A Poetry Sampler and
        Contemporary American Poetry
        (Ed. by Donald Hall)
    Twentieth-Century German Verse
        (Ed. by Patrick Bridgwater)
    The Penguin Book of Religious Verse
        (Ed. by R. S. Thomas)
    The Mentor Book of Major British Poets
        from William Blake to Dylan Thomas
        (Ed. by Oscar Williams)
    The Modern Poets:
        An American-British Anthology
        (Ed. by John Malcolm Brinnin
        and Bill Read)
    Flower in My Ear:
        Arts and Ethos of Ifaluk Atoll,
        by Edwin Grant Burrows
Some Poets in Their Prose   105   397
    The Letters of Wyndham Lewis
        (Ed. by W. K. Rose)
    Because I Was Flesh,
        by Edward Dahlberg
    Poetry and Fiction,
        by Howard Nemerov
    Blues People:
        Negro Music in White America,
        by LeRoi Jones
The Bourgeois Poet, by Karl Shapiro   106   225
Poetry Chronicle   106   296
    Rhymes of a PFC,
        by Lincoln Kirstein
    Figures of the Human,
        by David Ignatow
    Sun City, by Bruce Cutler
    A Time of Bees,
        by Mona Van Duyn
    New & Selected Poems,
        by Thomas McGrath
Nothing for Tigers: Poems 1959-1964,
    by Hayden Carruth   107   253
Hispanic Chronicle   107   338
    Selected Poems of Jaime Torres Bodet
        (Tr. by Sonja Karsen)
    Twenty Poems of Blas de Otero
        (Tr. by Hardie St. Martin)
    Modern Poetry from Spain
        and Latin America
        (Tr. by Nan Braymer
        and Lillian Lowenfels)
A Canadian Chronicle   108   45
    A Dream of Lilies,
        by Joan Finnigan
    City of the Gulls and Sea,
        by Frank Davey

Kyoto Airs, by Roy Kiyooka
Elephants, Mothers & Others,
   by John Newlove
White Lunch, by Gerry Gilbert
Two Longer Poems:
   The Seasons of Miss Nicky,
     by Harry Howith,
     and *Louis Riel*, by William Hawkins
Moving in Alone, by John Newlove
Selected Poems, by Alain Grandbois
The Colour of the Times,
   by Raymond Souster
A Point of Sky,
   by John Glassco
Birth of a Shark,
   by David Wevill
Nights and Days, by James Merrill   108   329
British Chronicle   108   399
   Collected Poems and
     Essays on Literature and Society,
     by Edwin Muir
   Buff, by Roy Fuller
   Pompeian Dog,
     by C. A. Trypanis
   Collected Poems,
     by David Gascoyne
   Events and Wisdoms,
     by Donald Davie
British Chronicle   110   195
   The Spoils, by Basil Bunting
   Here We Go, by Anselm Hollo
   Prince of the Plague Country,
     by Richard Packer
   In a Blue Smoke,
     by James Liddy
   Bricks, by R. J. Wathen
   Pretending Not To Sleep,
     by Ian Hamilton
   Adam at Evening,
     by David Wright
   Collected Poems,
     by Bernard Spencer
   [Ezra Pound]
Near the Ocean, by Robert Lowell   110   413
Letters of Wallace Stevens
   (Ed. by Holly Stevens)   111   39
Masters and Friends   113   338
   Collected Poems, by Dilys Laing
   Collected Poems 1915-1967,
     by Kenneth Burke
   Selected Poems,
     by Vernon Watkins
   Striking the Stones,
     by Daniel Hoffman
   Answer Back, by Donald Finkel
   The Perfect Fiction,
     by Gilbert Sorrentino
   The Virgil Woods,
     by Henry Braun

Twenty Poems,
   by Pablo Neruda
   (Tr. by Robert Bly
   and James Wright)
Affirmation:
   A Bilingual Anthology, 1919-1966,
   by Jorge Guillén
   (Tr. by Julian Palley)
The Gaucho Martín Fierro,
   by José Hernández
   (Tr. by C. E. Ward)
   (Ed. by Frank G. Carrino
   and Alberto J. Carlos)
Modern Spanish Theatre:
   An Anthology of Plays
   (Ed. by Michael Benedikt
   and George Wellwarth)
   [Valle-Inclán]
Masters & Friends, by Paul Valéry
   (Tr. by Martin Turnell)
   (Ed. by Jackson Matthews)
Selected Writings,
   by Jules Supervielle
Yeats' Autobiography,
   by Joseph Ronsley
The Equilibrist: A Study
   of John Crowe Ransom's
   Poems, 1916-1963,
   by Robert Buffington
Selected Letters of Theodore Roethke
   (Ed. by Ralph J. Mills, Jr.)
Second Nature, by Howard Moss   114   331
Essays of Four Decades,
   by Allen Tate   116   43
On Poetry: Collected Talks and Essays,
   by Robert Graves   116   107
The Double Dream of Spring,
   by John Ashbery   117   50
A Beginning, a Middle,
   and an Ode to Terminus   119   34
   Green Business,
     by John N. Morris
   Good Luck in Cracked Italian,
     by Richard Hugo
   City Without Walls & Other Poems,
     by W. H. Auden
Pursuits and Followings   120   296
   Three Poems, by John Ashbery
   The Escape into You,
     by Marvin Bell
   The Night Mirror,
     by John Hollander
   Midnight Was My Cry,
     by Carolyn Kizer
Five Poets   121   54
   The Colossus and Other Poems,
     by Sylvia Plath
   All My Pretty Ones,
     by Anne Sexton

The Jacob's Ladder,
  by Denise Levertov
Drowning with Others,
  by James Dickey
Thank You and Other Poems,
  by Kenneth Koch
Four Originals   122   351
  Collected Poems
    of John Wheelwright
  Lost Originals,
    by Irving Feldman
  Adequate Earth,
    by Donald Finkel
  Native Grass,
    by Paul Smyth
Centers of Attention   125   354
  1933, by Philip Levine
  The Center of Attention,
    by Daniel Hoffman
Three Found Poets   126   346
  Residue of Song,
    by Marvin Bell
  Sleeping in the Woods,
    by David Wagoner
  Turtle Island, by Gary Snyder
Self-Portrait in a Convex Mirror,
  by John Ashbery   127   349
Art or Knack?   129   226
  All Roads at Once,
    by Alfred Corn
  Sadness and Happiness,
    by Robert Pinsky
  Boning the Dreamer,
    by Terry Stokes
  A Nip in the Air,
    by John Betjeman
  Millions of Strange Shadows,
    by Anthony Hecht   131   103
Report from the Academy   132   226
  Five Temperaments,
    by David Kalstone
  Robert Frost,
    by Richard Poirier

BOOKS REVIEWED
Quantities   103   192
The Damages, Poems   113   35
Alone with America:
  Essays on the Art of Poetry
  in the United States Since 1950   117   258
Findings   119   342
Preferences: 51 American Poets
  Choose from Their Own Work
  and from the Past (Ed.)   125   52
Fellow Feelings   130   36
Lining Up   145   291
No Traveller   155   283
Like Most Revelations   167   287

HOWARTH, HERBERT
  BOOKS REVIEWED
  Notes on Some Figures
    Behind T. S. Eliot   106   239

HOWARTH, R. G.
  BOOKS REVIEWED
  The Penguin Book of Australian Verse
    (Ed. with John Thompson
    and Kenneth Slessor)   94   44

HOWE, FANNY
  POEMS
  Remember   122   23
  Slide
  The Angels
  Not as Much
  By Halves
  The Law
  Ice

  BOOKS REVIEWED
  Eggs   118   295

HOWE, IRVING
  BOOKS REVIEWED
  A Treasury of Yiddish Poetry
    (Ed. with Eliezer Greenberg)   118   354

HOWE, M. A. DE WOLFE
  BOOKS REVIEWED
  Songs of September   46   53

HOWE, MARIE
  POEMS
  What the Angels Left   143   79
  What Belongs to Us
  The Fourth Visit
  Lullaby   147   287
  Apology

HOWE, SUSAN
  BOOKS REVIEWED
  Singularities   159   282

HOWELL, ELIZABETH
  POEMS
  Smoke at Night   34   85
  Buffoon   42   81

HOWELLS, THOMAS
  POEMS
  Status   54   244
  The Equal Passion
  Vigil
  Plan   55   312

  ARTICLES
  Correspondence: Reply to Mr. Winters   63   293

REVIEWS
  Poetry and Crisis,
    by Martin Turnell   55   86
  England's Musical Poet,
    Thomas Campion,
    by Miles Merwin Kastendieck   56   51
  "Where To, Where Now?"   56   340
    First Manifesto,
      by Thomas McGrath
    Personal Sun,
      by Hubert Creekmore
    ABC's, by Charles Henri Ford
  Selected Poems, by John Peale Bishop   58   96
  Public Speaking and Private Glimpses   62   277
    The World in Your Hand,
      by Theodore Spencer
    North Window,
      by Hortense Flexner
    The Anatomy of Nonsense,
      by Yvor Winters   63   86
  At the Gates, by Boris Todrin   65   160

ARTICLES ABOUT
  Correspondence
    from Yvor Winters   63   291

HOWES, BARBARA
POEMS
  In the Cold Country   73   249
  Relatives
  North Oxford
  The Nuns Assist at Childbirth
  The Heart of Europe
  Portrait of an Artist
  Lament   76   262
  Tramontana   89   136
  A Lullaby
  The Triumph of Time
  Delivery Room
  To W. H. Auden on His Fiftieth Birthday   90   129
  Lignum Vitae
  Death of a Vermont Farm Woman   94   359
  On Falling Asleep in a Mountain Cabin
  The Triumph of Pride
  The Triumph of Truth
  A Conversation   101   47
  Dream of a Good Day
  At the Blue Mill Tavern
  Headlong   102   71
  Thinking of K.H.S.
  A Stand of Birches
  The Dressmaker's Dummy as Scarecrow   103   343
  Town Meeting Tuesday
  What Bird
  Troy Weight Taken
  The Governess's Tale
  A Round
  Footnote

For J. S.   107   170
Quilt of a Formal Pattern
The Crane Chub—Barbados
The Cicisbeae
The Lonely Box
Radar and Unmarked Cars
Ouroborus   113   78
A Drachma for Myself
Barn-Razing in Pownal   135   34
A Thanksgiving Guernsey

REVIEWS
  Poems: A Selection,
    by Léonie Adams   87   45
  Robert Frost: The Early Years,
    by Lawrance Thompson   110   425

BOOKS REVIEWED
  The Undersea Farmer   74   166
  In the Cold Country   86   295
  Light and Dark   96   114
  Looking Up at Leaves   109   270
  The Blue Garden   122   344

HOWITH, HARRY
BOOKS REVIEWED
  The Seasons of Miss Nicky
    (In *Two Longer Poems* with *Louis Riel,*
    by William Hawkins)   108   45
  Total War   115   353

HOWRY, ERLE
POEMS
  Time   40   81

HOYDAL, KARSTEN
POEMS
  White Night   116   333
  Stones
    (Tr. by George Johnston)

HOYEM, ANDREW
POEMS
  Diana   109   86
  "When We Meet I Will Wear a Rose"
  Love Seat
  Zeal
  Other People, Other Places   113   389
  Chateau
  Circumambulation of Mt. Tamalpais   117   289
  Of a Ruined Roman Sculpture
  While in Waiting
  Up in the Air
  Filtres
  512 Cubic Furlongs
  Financial Statement   122   326
  Rhetorical Questions
  Morning Glory

Alimentary   131   282
Eating the Afterbirth

REVIEWS
I Like to (B)eat People Up   113   426
  The North Atlantic Turbine
    and *Gunslinger: Book I,*
    by Edward Dorn
  There's Always a Moon in America,
    by Max Finstein
  Another Time in Fragments,
    by Larry Eigner
  [Hilda Doolittle, Ted Berrigan]

BOOKS REVIEWED
  Articles   119   342

HOYT, HELEN ["H. H."]
POEMS
Ellis Park   2   159
The Bubbling Fountain   4   180
Poems of Life and Death   6   227
  Annunciation
  The New-Born
  Rain at Night
  Since I Have Felt the Sense of Death
  Action Poem
Desertion   6   267
City Pastorals   9   277
  Poem To Be Danced
  Under the Tree
  The Dancer
  To a Vine the Workmen Cut Down
  Arches
  Continuance
  Sky-Humor
  The Letter
  Kin
  Hey Nonino
  Men-Folks
The Harp   13   118
  I Have Found My Beloved
  Stature
  Name
  Difference
  Unity
  Happiness Betrays Me
  Triumph
  Interlude
  At the Museum
  Memory
  Oh We Shall Meet
  Ascension
  The Root
In a Certain City   15   291
  Chicago
  Encounter
  Automobiles on Sunday
  By the Lake

Night
The Stone-Age Sea
When We Are Asleep
Creator
Headstone
There Was a Time
October Letter   23   1
Your Words
Chant of Rejoicing
Day's End
The Stone
The Bride and the Matron
Flower and Flame
Gravid
Recompense
Poems for Amis   32   239
  Crescent Moon
  A Woman and Mountains
  At Daybreak
  Are You a Freesia?
  Game
  In the White Crib
  First Walking
  Portrait at Five
  Dahlias
The Dream   34   307
Like Something of Earth
The Elf
The Fern
The Picture
For One Who Died in Spring   37   310
  Orchard Branches
  The Clock
  The Locks of Hair
Vaunting of Fire   44   16
Estuaries of Fire
Reflections on Lot's Wife   46   189
  Obediences of Women
  Women and Janus

ARTICLES
  Correspondence: Desertion [Poem]   6   267
  Correspondence: A Declaration [Poem]   9   330
  Our Contemporaries: *Others* Redivivus   10   109
  [Tribute to Harriet Monroe]   49   140

REVIEWS
  Livelihood, by Wilfrid Wilson Gibson   10   108
  The Jig of Forslin, by Conrad Aiken   10   162
  Pilgrimage, by Eric Shepherd   11   108
  City Dust, by Jane Burr   11   109
  The Book of Self,
    by James Oppenheim   11   219
  Others, An Anthology of the New Verse
    (Ed. by Alfred Kreymborg)   11   274
  The Answering Voice — One Hundred
    Love Lyrics by Women
    (Ed. by Sara Teasdale)   11   278

Grenstone Poems—A Sequence,
  by Witter Bynner   12   227
Three Whitman Books   14   106
  Visits to Walt Whitman in 1890-1891,
    by J. Johnston and J. W. Wallace
  The Letters of Anne Gilchrist
  and Walt Whitman
    (Ed. by Thomas B. Harned)
  Patriotic Poems of Walt Whitman
Negro Poets   16   287
  Fifty Years and Other Poems,
    by James Weldon Johnson
  Songs of My People,
    by Charles Bertram Johnson
  From the Heart of a Folk,
    by Waverley Turner Carmichael
  The Band of Gideon,
    by Joseph S. Cotter, Jr.

BOOKS REVIEWED
  Apples Here in My Basket   24   214
  Leaves of Wild Grape   36   346
  The Name of a Rose   39   158
  California Poets:
    An Anthology of 244
    Contemporaries (Fwd.)   42   233

ARTICLES ABOUT
  [Note on joining staff]   13   288
  Correspondence
    from Maxwell Bodenheim   26   48
  A Few Women Poets,
    by Harriet Monroe   26   326

HSI, CH'ENG
[See CH'ENG HSI]

HSIEH LING-YUN
ARTICLES ABOUT
  Rev. of *The Murmuring Stream:*
  The Life and Works of…,
    by J. D. Frodsham   114   196

HSU, KAI-YU
[See KAI-YU HSU]

HSIU, OU YANG
[See OU YANG HSIU]

HSU-LING
POEMS
  Fighting at Lung-Tou
    (Tr. by Arthur Waley)   11   254

HSU TSE-MO
POEMS
  The Five Old Men Peaks
    (Tr. by Harold Acton)   46   14

ARTICLES ABOUT
  Contemporary Chinese Poetry,
    by Harold Acton   46   39

HUACUJA, E. ARMANDA
[See ARMANDA HUACUJA, E.]

HUBBELL, JAY B.
BOOKS REVIEWED
  An Introduction to Poetry
    (With John O. Beaty)   22   168

HUBBELL, LINDLEY WILLIAMS
POEMS
  Sinner   30   138
  Where Music Is
  Song ("If love should bring…")
  Tower   51   253
  Old Books
  Something the Matter   75   204
  ("When storms rage on…")   80   202
  ("Why, when the rat ambled…")
  ("Being born under the difficult sign…")

BOOKS REVIEWED
  The Tracing of a Portal   38   344
  Winter-Burning   52   354
  The Ninth Continent   73   294
  Long Island Triptych and Other Poems   74   44

HUCHEL, PETER
POEMS
  View from the Winter Window
    (Tr. by Michael Hamburger)   128   130

HUCKFIELD, LEYLAND
POEMS
  Haunted Reaping   6   172
  The Muse in Church

HUDDLE, DAVID
POEMS
  Asylum   156   77

HUDDLESTON, MABEL BARKER
POEMS
  The Roof-Garden   16   81

HUDEBURG, CHARLES
POEMS
  Last Year's Flowers Photographed   52   192
  A Song ("Lovely, the weight…")

HUDGINS, ANDREW
POEMS
  Audubon Examines a Bittern   140   84
  Air View of an Industrial Scene   141   216
  Julia Tutwiler State Prison for Women

Madonna of the Pomegranate	144	271
My Mother's Hands		
November Garden: An Elegy	145	63
Sentimental Dangers	147	1
Compost: An Ode		
All of Us Beneath Red Cowboy Hats	147	194
The Green Christ		
Burial Insurance	161	261
Tools: An Ode	164	155
Song of the Drunkards Whose Throats		
Will Be Cut in a Moment	170	201
Airport Boulevard		
Stump		
In Alesia	170	325

BOOKS REVIEWED

Saints & Strangers	148	36
After the Lost War: A Narrative	153	30
The Never-Ending	159	282
The Glass Hammer: A Southern Childhood	165	219

HUDGINS, L. E.
[ELIZABETH HUDGINS]
POEMS

At the News-Stands	79	256
When Hock-Cart Rolls		
How Haunting Are the Shafts		

HUDIBURG, EDWARD
POEMS

Adventures of the Damned and Blessed	70	18

HUDSON, ETHEL DE KOVEN
POEMS

Thief's Funeral	41	319

HUDSON, FLEXMORE
BOOKS REVIEWED

As Iron Hills	66	170

HUDSON, HOYT (H.)
POEMS

Pastor Almost Sees God	64	22
Gastropod at Prayer		

ARTICLES
Robinson and Praed
[E. A. Robinson,

Winthrop Mackworth Praed]	61	612

HUDSON, MARC
POEMS

Winter, Aeneas Valley	131	208
Home		
Elegy for Martin Heidegger		

BOOKS REVIEWED

Afterlight	144	345

HUDSON, THOMAS DAVID
POEMS

The Inheritors	54	85

HUDZIK, ROBERT
POEMS

The Luck of Creatures	158	90

HUEFFER, FORD MADOX
[See FORD, FORD MADOX]

HUEFFER, VIOLET HUNT
[See HUNT, VIOLET]

HUELIN, E. SCOTTON
BOOKS REVIEWED

Poems	6	257

HUFF, ROBERT
POEMS

Falcon	77	24
The Snows		
Burning		
The Course	99	26
Getting Drunk with Daughter		
On the Death		
of Theodore Roethke	107	360
To Francey		
For Philip Booth		
While the Now Generation		
Basks in Its Brand New Milky Way	132	201
Lines for William Golding		
Auld Lang Syne	147	140

REVIEWS
The Lamb, the Clocks,

the Blue Light	109	44
Richard Eberhart:		
Selected Poems 1930-1965		
West of Childhood:		
Poems 1950-1965,		
by Isabella Gardner		
Buckdancer's Choice,		
by James Dickey		
[Sandra Hochman]		

BOOKS REVIEWED
Colonel Johnson's Ride

and Other Poems	96	185
The Course	111	329

HUGHES, D. J.
POEMS

Kokoro	94	379

HUGHES, DOROTHY BERRY
POEMS

The Hand	65	133

HUGHES, GLENN
BOOKS REVIEWED
  Broken Lights   17   98
  Imagism and the Imagists   38   169

HUGHES, GLYN
BOOKS REVIEWED
  Neighbours   118   344

HUGHES, LANGSTON
POEMS
  Blues   29   88
    Hard Luck
    Po' Boy Blues
    Red Roses
    Suicide
  The Quick and the Dead   39   16
    Lover's Return
    Sylvester's Dying Bed
    Sailor
    Dying Beast
    God
  Out of Work   56   20
  Love Again Blues
  Dust Bowl   58   72
  Southern Mammy Sings
  Crossing Jordan
  Black Maria
  Folks Who Knock at Madam's Door   62   310
    Madam's Calling Cards
    Madam and the Charity Child
    Madam and the Rent Man
  Crowing Hen Blues
  Seashore Through Dark Glasses   69   248
  Blues on a Box
  Who But the Lord?
  Yesterday and Today
  Blues in Stereo   98   288

REVIEWS
  Ziba, by James Pipes   64   41

BOOKS REVIEWED
  Fine Clothes for the Jew   31   44
  Shakespeare in Harlem   60   223
  Seven Poets in Search of an Answer
    (With Maxwell Bodenheim,
    Joy Davidman, Aaron Kramer,
    Alfred Kreymborg, Martha Millet,
    and Norman Rosten)
    (Ed. by Thomas Yoseloff)   64   289
  Fields of Wonder   71   279
  One-Way Ticket   75   300
  Selected Poems of Gabriela Mistral (Tr.) 92 106
  Poems from Black Africa (Ed.)   103   394
  New Negro Poets: U. S. A. (Ed.)   106   429
  The Panther and the Lash   112   337

HUGHES, MARY GRAY
POEMS
  Query   167   220

HUGHES, R(ICHARD)
POEMS
  Dirge   18   248

ARTICLES
  Correspondence:
    The Winter's Publishing in England
    [Edmund Blunden, Wilfred Owen]   18   172

BOOKS REVIEWED
  Oxford Poetry, 1921
    (Ed. with Alan Porter
    and Robert Graves)   24   162

HUGHES, TED
POEMS
  Bawdry Embraced   88   295
  The Drowned Woman   89   296
  The Casualty   90   279
  The Ancient Heroes and the Pilot
  The Jaguar
  The Martyrdom of Bishop Ferrar
  A Woman Unconscious   94   296
  Cat and Mouse
  To Paint a Water-Lily
  Lupercalia
  Dully Gumption's Addendum   100   92
  Poem to Robert Graves Perhaps   103   152
  On Westminster Bridge
  After Lorca
  Heatwave
  Era of Giant Lizards
  Small Hours
  Bawdry Embraced   121   12

BOOKS REVIEWED
  The Hawk in the Rain   92   178
  Lupercal   97   260
  Wodwo   112   418
  Crow   119   291
  Moon-Whales   132   31
  Gaudete   138   297
  Cave Birds: An Alchemical Cave Drama
  Moortown
  The Collected Poems,
    by Sylvia Plath (Ed.)   142   170

ARTICLES ABOUT
  Poets and Mushrooms,
    by Charles Tomlinson   100   104
  Poets Aloud, by Donald Hall   139   297
  A Letter from Britain,
    by William Logan   157   222

HUGO, RICHARD (F.)
POEMS
    Skykomish River Running   93   308
    Back of Gino's Place   96   208
    Kapowsin
    Argo
    In Stafford Country   102   23
    Tahola
    Point No Point   108   236
    South Italy, Remote and Stone   112   19
    On Hearing a New Escalation   120   319
    Approaching the Castle   122   125
    Old Scene
    In Your Blue Dream
    Indian Girl
    Last Days
    Beaverbank   127   23
    Birthday
    Graves
    The Small Oil Left
      in the House We Rented in Boulder
    Belt
    Mill at Romesdal   134   19
    Ferniehirst Castle
    Mecox Bay

BOOKS REVIEWED
    A Run of Jacks   101   279
    Death of the Kapowsin Tavern   107   125
    Good Luck in Cracked Italian   119   34
    The Lady in Kicking Horse Reservoir   124   103
    What Thou Lovest Well,
      Remains American   127   292
    31 Letters and 13 Dreams   133   346
    The Triggering Town   138   46
    Selected Poems
    Making Certain It Goes On:
      The Collected Poems of...   145   291

HULL, LYNDA
POEMS
    Insect Life of Florida   148   148
    Chinese New Year
    Shore Leave   153   75
    Slick Packages
    Utopia Parkway   157   207

BOOKS REVIEWED
    Ghost Money   150   102
    Star Ledger   159   282
    The Only World   167   223

HULL, ORA MAY
POEMS
    Anger of the Bull   88   357
    The Great Lakes
    Edith Cavell

    I Believe in Your Country   92   352
    A Seated Figure
    By Marriage I Make Evil

HULLIHAN, ROBERT
POEMS
    Returning Late to Camp   73   78
    Summer 1944
    Semester of Night

HULME, T. E.
ARTICLES ABOUT
    Rev. of *Imagism, a Chapter*
      for the History of Modern Poetry,
      by Stanley K. Coffman, Jr.   78   294

HUMES, HARRY
POEMS
    My Father Planted Tomatoes in Coal Ash   154   133

HUMPHREY, JAMES
BOOKS REVIEWED
    Argument for Love   120   115

HUMPHREY, ROBERT
POEMS
    Metamorphosis   72   61

HUMPHRIES, ROLFE
POEMS
    On an Official Occasion   51   59
    Song for Later Summer
    "—Not Love, but Ardor"
    Green Mountain Scene
    Song, Diminishing   51   318
    Song Heard in a New House
    Draft Ode for a Phi Beta Kappa Occasion   54   136
    Et Nos Mutamur   57   351
    The Five Dreams   58   302
    The Statue
    Coming Home   64   254
    Night Game   65   18
    A Landscape, and a Lady
    Caveamus   66   81
    Second Spell   68   127
    Song from the Gaelic, Maybe
      ("The fond summer numbers...")   81   112
    Song from the Gaelic, Maybe
      ("The fond summer numbers...")   81   304
    Wmffre the Sweep   86   144
    For a Wordfarer
    The Lament of Llywarch Hen   87   263
    Oak
    Rain in Jackson Heights   90   370
    Among the Paeligni
    With Garb of Proof   113   407
    A Song for Mortimer

TRANSLATIONS
  Poems by Federico García Lorca   50   8
  Poem by Agustí Bartra   59   77
  Poem by Agustí Bartra   60   123
  Poem by Louis Aragon   62   247
  Poem by Louis Aragon   63   306
  Poem by Agustí Bartra   64   10

ARTICLES
  [Note]   53   55
  Correspondence:
    An Exchange on *Delta Return*
    [Charles Bell]   89   391

REVIEWS
  The Poems of Catullus
    (Tr. by Horace Gregory)   39   93
  The Signature of Pain, by Alan Porter   39   342
  Thurso's Landing and Other Poems
    and *Descent to the Dead*,
    by Robinson Jeffers   40   154
  The Name and Nature of Poetry,
    by A. E. Housman   43   52
  Journeyman of Letters   44   108
    Rip Tide and *A Starry Harness*,
      by William Rose Benét
    Fifty Poets: An American Auto-Anthology
      (Ed. by William Rose Benét)
  Poems, by Marie de L. Welch   44   228
  Two Pastoralists   45   50
    Woman of This Earth,
      by Frances Frost
    The Crows, by David McCord
  Before Disaster, by Yvor Winters   45   288
  New Writing V
    (Ed. by John Lehmann)   52   351
  Dawn Is Forever, by E. Merrill Root   54   225
  The Dry Salvages, by T. S. Eliot   59   338
  From the Greek   88   337
    Greek Lyrics
      (Tr. by Richmond Lattimore)
    Euripides (Vol. II): Cyclops and *Herakles*
      (Tr. by William Arrowsmith);
    Iphigenia in Tauris
      (Tr. by Witter Bynner);
    Helen (Tr. by Richmond Lattimore)
    Aristophanes: The Frogs
      (Tr. by Dudley Fitts)

BOOKS REVIEWED
  Europa and Other Poems and Sonnets   36   286
  And Spain Sings: Fifty Loyalist Ballads
    (Ed. with M. J. Benardete)   52   43
  The Poet in New York and Other Poems,
    by Federico García Lorca (Tr.)   56   343
  Out of the Jewel   61   393
  The Summer Landscape   65   330

  Forbid Thy Ravens   72   219
  The Wind of Time   75   364
  The Metamorphoses of Ovid (Tr.)   86   303
  The Gypsy Ballads of García Lorca (Tr.)   87   303
  Poems Collected and New   88   404
  Green Armor on Green Ground
  The Satires of Juvenal (Tr.)   96   247
  Collected Poems of...   108   337
  Coat on a Stick   118   351

ARTICLES ABOUT
  [Note on title:
    Lament of Llywarch Hen]   87   380

HUNG, WILLIAM
  BOOKS REVIEWED
    Tu Fu, China's Greatest Poet   83   295

HUNGERFORD, EDWARD B.
  BOOKS REVIEWED
    Shores of Darkness   61   403

HUNGERFORD, NED
  BOOKS REVIEWED
    Hidden Path   19   167

HUNG-SHOU, CH'EN
[See CH'EN HUNG-SHOU]

HUNT, MARJORIE
  POEMS
    Gathering of the Distance   111   239
    Two Woods, Two Weathers
    Going to Bed in the Sea

HUNT, RICHARD
  POEMS
    To a Golden-Crowned Thrush   8   68
    The Scarlet Tanager   10   295
    Gas-Lamp Ghost   12   11
    Song in Early April

HUNT, ROBERT
  POEMS
    Cross-Roads Merchant   37   320
    Legend for a Sundial
    Period Piece   63   14

  BOOKS REVIEWED
    The Early World   51   226

HUNT, VIOLET
[VIOLET HUNT HUEFFER]
  POEMS
    A Call in Hell   5   219
    What the Civilian Saw   9   295
    Is It Worth While   12   21

HUNT, WILLIAM
POEMS
An Exclusion of the Stars   110   95
Of the Map that Changes   112   25
Through the Trees
Winter Indoors
The Ladder You Offer   115   311
After a Fine Day We Found This
This Is a Way
Two Days
How We Resemble Curtains   124   13
At Times We Wake
From the Beginning
Close by the Prisoner of Death
The Pleasures of Magicians
The Magic Sleep
   and the Memory of Waking   128   254
Events Disappear
The Spirits of Clairvoyance
For What Took Place
The Night's Distance
We Are Friends
There Are Bodies

REVIEWS
Poetry Without Letters   111   266
   The Unwritten Song, Vol. I
      (Ed. by Willard R. Trask)
   African Poetry
      (Ed. by Ulli Beier)
Positives,
   by Thom Gunn and Ander Gunn   111   405
Night Light, by Donald Justice   112   272
Voices, by Antonio Porchia
   (Tr. by W. S. Merwin)   120   113
Auto-Necrophilia, by Bill Knott   122   103

BOOKS REVIEWED
Of the Map that Changes   127   98

HUNTER, PAUL
POEMS
Moonrise   114   364
Back Side Front Side   121   214

HUNTING, CONSTANCE
POEMS
After the Stravinsky Concert   96   359
A Dream of Heavenly Love
   and Redemption in the Wood
Afternoon of a Contemporary Poet

BOOKS REVIEWED
The Heron   104   47

HUNTINGTON, JULIA WELD
POEMS
Off the Highway   18   81

HURD, HARRY ELMORE
BOOKS REVIEWED
Christ in the Breadlines:
   A Book of Poems for Christmas and Lent
   (With Kenneth L. Porter
   and Seymour Gordon Link)   42   168

HURKEY, ROOAN
BOOKS REVIEWED
Romances   99   313

HURLOW, MARCIA L.
POEMS
The Sisterhood   153   299
For the Linguist Doing Field Work   155   212
The Pantheist Who Loved His Wife   156   8
Praying for Father   156   338
Nuclear Romance   159   274
Other Evidence   165   85
Milin An Elorn

HURNARD, JAMES
BOOKS REVIEWED
James Hurnard, a Victorian Character
   [From The Setting Sun]
   (Ed. by G. R. Hamilton)   70   106

HUSBAND, JOHN DILLON
POEMS
Toward Another Spring   63   318
At Last Be Still

HU SHIH
ARTICLES ABOUT
Contemporary Chinese Poetry,
   by Harold Acton   46   39

HUSS, AVRAHAM
POEMS
The Green Refrain
   (Tr. by Ruth Finer Mintz)   92   257

HUTCHINGS, PAT
POEMS
Winter Keeps Us Close   141   67

HUTCHINS, MAUDE PHELPS
POEMS
Lately I Walk Lightly   57   356
She Waited and Waited
There Is Something Appealing
Gothic Lover
I Asked Her   60   301
Absent-Minded Poet in Washington
Suitor
Gold
Club Sorrow   72   9
Preoccupied Poet

Epigram
Letter to a Lady on the Nightmare Side

HUTCHINSON, PEARSE
POEMS
  Tomar   80   207

HUTCHINSON, ROBERT
POEMS
  Lives of the Ancient Poets   105   377
  Margaret
  The Battle in Amherst: E. D.

BOOKS REVIEWED
  The Kitchen Dance   88   183

HUTCHINSON, VELMA BYERS
POEMS
  Widowed   30   85

HUTCHINSON, VERONICA S.
BOOKS REVIEWED
  Chimney-Corner Poems (Ed.)   36   289

HUTCHISON, COLLISTER
[See HUTCHISON, HAZEL
C(OLLISTER)]

HUTCHISON, HAZEL C(OLLISTER)
[COLLISTER HUTCHISON]
POEMS
  Adoration   17   15
  In France   23   80
    Reims
    Paris Impression
    Inheritance
  Landscape Poems   25   188
  Croquis   30   74
  From Fire in a Field   33   145
  Anyway   59   177

HUTCHISON, JOSEPH
POEMS
  Shadowy Trees   157   288
  The Wound
  What I Know   161   256
  Black River   162   348

BOOKS REVIEWED
  House of Mirrors   162   37

HUTCHISON, PERCY
ARTICLES ABOUT
  Recent Magazines, by M. D. Zabel   39   166

HUTTON, MARY
POEMS
  Four   76   143

Five
The Sleeping Beauty   78   84

HUXLEY, ALDOUS
BOOKS REVIEWED
  The Burning Wheel   10   44
  Leda   17   217
  The Cicadas and Other Poems   39   285
  Texts and Pretexts:
    An Anthology with Commentaries   42   170
  The Collected Poetry of…
    (Ed. by Donald Watt)   120   230

HUXLEY, JULIAN
POEMS
  Spitsbergen Summer   39   248

BOOKS REVIEWED
  The Captive Shrew   42   228

HUYLER, FRANK
POEMS
  In Vitro   160   7

HYDE, LEWIS
BOOKS REVIEWED
  A Longing for the Light: Selected Poems
    of Vicente Aleixandre (Tr.)   136   40

HYMAN, STANLEY EDGAR
ARTICLES
  Correspondence: More Relegating
    [John Masefield, John M. Schealer]   71   117
  R. P. Blackmur and the Expense
    of Criticism   71   259

REVIEWS
  Thanks Before Going, by John Masefield
    [D. G. Rossetti]   70   333
  Forces in Modern British Literature 1885-1946,
    by William York Tindall   71   165
  The White Goddess, by Robert Graves   73   362

BOOKS REVIEWED
  The Armed Vision   73   228
  Perspectives by Incongruity
    and *Terms for Order,*
    by Kenneth Burke (Ed.)   106   366
  Selected Essays, by William Troy (Ed.)   112   116

HYNES, SAMUEL
REVIEWS
  The Odds on Edward Thomas   135   342
    Collected Poems of Edward Thomas
    (Ed. by R. George Thomas)
    Edward Thomas: A Poet for His Country,
    by Jan Marsh
    [Thomas Hardy, Robert Frost]

HYSLOP, FRANCIS E., JR.
BOOKS REVIEWED
Baudelaire on Poe: Critical Papers
(Tr. and ed. with Lois Hyslop)   81   247

HYSLOP, LOIS
BOOKS REVIEWED
Baudelaire on Poe: Critical Papers
(Tr. and ed. with Francis E. Hyslop, Jr.)   81   247

I

IBSEN, HENRIK
ARTICLES ABOUT
New York Plays,
    by Florence Kiper Frank   28   95

IDEMA, JAMES M.
POEMS
The So and So Memorial Library   70   22
To Pearson   70   242

IDLE, E. DOREEN
POEMS
Holiday   56   131

IGLEHART, EMILY POWERS
POEMS
Colored Shadows   34   143
    Silence
    Man
    The Moon by Day
    Fulfilment

IGNATOW, DAVID
POEMS
The Mountain Is Stripped   93   82
And Step
A Semblance
I Felt
Job's Anger
To Nowhere   103   353
If My Hand
As I Stumble
Beautiful and Kind
On the Death of Winston Churchill   108   16
All Quiet
Rescue the Dead   109   156
The Hope
For Nobody Else   110   178
Like Smoke   112   104
Here I Am   120   321
In a Dream   122   76
The Building   134   269
I Love To Fly
Live It Through
A Cloud Creates   137   277
Listening   149   255

The Self
Witness   151   70
From *Six Love Poems*   151   398
    ("We are seated...")
    ("What would life be...?")
    ("Let's see how natural...")
If
Between Us   156   135
We   165   282
For Rose   168   276
For Jane Kenyon

ARTICLES
Comment   151   219

REVIEWS
Engagements   99   247
    Selected Poems,
        by Gil Orlovitz
    Abraxes & Other Poems,
        by Leslie Woolf Hedley
    Selected Poems: 1945-49,
        by James Schevill
    The Bean Eaters,
        by Gwendolyn Brooks

BOOKS REVIEWED
Poems   74   118
The Gentle Weight Lifter   87   53
Say Pardon   98   245
Figures of the Human   106   296
Rescue the Dead   113   262
Poems 1934-1969   118   228
Selected Poems
    (Ed. by Robert Bly)   128   37
Tread the Dark   136   164
Leaving the Door Open   146   293
New and Collected Poems: 1970-1985   149   94
Against the Evidence:
    Selected Poems 1934-1994   165   219

ARTICLES ABOUT
"Sacred Beings":
    Writers in Recorded Conversation,
    by Michael Milburn   146   101

IKEMOTO, TAKASHI
TRANSLATIONS
Poems by Shinkichi Takahashi
(Tr. with Lucien Stryk)   116   364

ILIO, DOMINADOR I.
POEMS
Diplomat Listening to Speech
of Another Diplomat   79   276

IMBS, BRAVIG
POEMS
Four Poems for Valeska   34   266
("Pines on this plain...")
("Near this slow river slept...")
("Wheeling aloft and chanting...")
("The stars float high...")

INDIANA, ROBERT
BOOKS REVIEWED
Numbers
(With Robert Creeley)   116   110

INEZ, COLETTE
POEMS
Empty Parenthesis   126   22
Service for Two,
I Shall Dine with Myself
Blind Mouths
Far in the Blindness of Time   127   268
November Lord
Meeting in Germany   132   136

INGALLS, DANIEL H. H.
BOOKS REVIEWED
Sanskrit Poetry from
Vidyakara's "Treasury" (Tr.)   114   196

INGALLS, JEREMY
POEMS
The Error of the Tyrant   58   306
In Time of Civil Wars
If None Will Listen
Apotheosis of Four Poets   61   366
Time and Eternity   63   24
Questions Concerning Madness
Fright

REVIEWS
The Revolutionists,
by Selden Rodman   61   511
Map of My Country,
by John Holmes   63   289
Moderate Fable,
by Marguerite Young   65   215
American Citizen, by Kay Boyle   65   333
No Arch, No Triumph,
by John Malcolm Brinnin   66   32

BOOKS REVIEWED
The Metaphysical Sword   59   218
Tahl   67   106
These Islands Also   96   314

INGPEN, ROGER
BOOKS REVIEWED
The Letters of
Percy Bysshe Shelley (Ed.)   8   204

INGWERSEN, JOHN
POEMS
Poem ("To the north...")   109   378

**IOWA FEDERATION
OF WOMEN'S CLUBS**
BOOKS REVIEWED
Silk of the Corn   41   284

IPUCHE, PEDRO LEANDRO
[See LEANDRO IPUCHE, PEDRO]

IQBAL, MOHAMMED
POEMS
Sicily (Tr. by Saadath Ali Kahn)   93   233

IRBY, KENNETH
POEMS
For Gordon Clark   105   94
"Only Love Is Holy and Love's Ecstasy"
"The Faults Along Which the
Tremor Runs" — Robert Duncan   107   365
Fragments for Bill Dodd

REVIEWS
"The World Dances Between Our Eyes"   105   414
The Unknowing Dance,
by Chad Walsh
Tactics of Survival,
by George Hitchcock
The Vulnerable Island,
by Carol Bergé
The Very Thing that Happens,
by Russell Edson
Interchange,
by Jack Hirschman
Round Dances,
by Robert Kelly

BOOKS REVIEWED
Movements/Sequences   108   408

IREMONGER, VALENTIN
BOOKS REVIEWED
Reservations   82   291

IRION, MARY JEAN
POEMS
The Green Gatherers at Sounion   157   155

IRIS, SCHARMEL
POEMS
  After the Martyrdom   5   115
  Lament
  The Mad Woman
  Early Nightfall
  Lake Michigan at Night   10   300
  Your Neighbor and Mine
  The Old Man
  War-Time Cradle Song
  Before the Cathedral   91   101
  Vincent
  How Shall I Sing Again

BOOKS REVIEWED
  Lyrics of a Lad   6   93

IRVING, HENRY
ARTICLES ABOUT
  The Utterance of Poetry,
    by Harriet Monroe   19   266

IRWIN, JOHN T.
REVIEWS
  Four Practitioners   118   351
    Coat on a Stick, by Rolfe Humphries
    From the Berkeley Hills,
      by George P. Elliott
    New Poems, by John Holloway
    Depth of Field, by William Heyen

ISAACS, WILBUR
POEMS
  Boy in Virginia   66   249

ISHERWOOD, CHRISTOPHER
BOOKS REVIEWED
  The Dog Beneath the Skin
    (With W. H. Auden)   48   221

  The Ascent of F 6
    (With W. H. Auden)   49   225
  The Intimate Journals
    of Charles Baudelaire (Tr.) 72   228

ARTICLES ABOUT
  The New Theatrum Poetarum,
    by Alan S. Downer   60   206

ISLAS, ARTURO
POEMS
  Hostility   131   199
  Motherfucker or The Exile
  Drunk

IUPPA, M. J.
POEMS
  Chrysalis   162   36

IVES, MABEL LORENZ
BOOKS REVIEWED
  Chinese Love Songs   76   357

IVIE, KELLY
POEMS
  Gull Lake Reunion   136   88

IWAI, SANNOSUKE
POEMS
  Fruit
    (Tr. by Satoru Satu
    and Constance Urdang)   88   71

IYENGAR, K. R. SRINIVASA
BOOKS REVIEWED
  Gerard Manley Hopkins   74   292

J

"J. N."
  [See NORTH, JESSICA NELSON]

"J. N. N."
  [See NORTH, JESSICA NELSON]

JACCOTTET, PHILLIPPE
  POEMS
  Five Poems   116   287
    ("Grapes and figs...")
    ("I would like only to remove...")
    ("'Who will help me?'...")
    ("I lifted up my eyes...")
    ("And I now utterly...")
      (Tr. by Cid Corman)
  Notebook Poems from *La Semaison*
      (Tr. by Michael Hamburger)   122   147

JACKSON, A. J. WILLIAMS
  BOOKS REVIEWED
  Early Persian Poetry   20   346

JACKSON, ALAN
  BOOKS REVIEWED
  The Grim Wayfarer   118   102

JACKSON, DAVID
  REVIEWS
  The Collected Short Prose of James Agee
      (Ed. by Robert Fitzgerald)   114   411

  ARTICLES ABOUT
  Rev. of *Mirabell: Books of Number*,
      by James Merrill   135   161

JACKSON, FLEDA BROWN
  POEMS
  The Pupil   168   87
  Monarchs   168   144
  Wild Raspberries

JACKSON, JESSICA
  POEMS
  Song ("As I lie sick abed...")   22   261
  The Grunchin' Witch   24   255

JACKSON, JOHN
  POEMS
  Lambing, Upstate New York   162   1
  The Dead Orchard   163   13
  Cardinals
  Quartet   168   126

JACKSON, LAURA RIDING
  [See RIDING, LAURA]

JACKSON, PHYLLIS
  POEMS
  Prairie Mother   24   191

JACKSON, RICHARD
  POEMS
  Some Haphazard Notes
    After an Evening Storm   120   36
  The Room
  Prologue of a Man Going Blind
  Poem with Variable Refrain
  A Hand in the Tree   151   484
  Eight Ball

JACOB, HEINRICH EDUARD
  ARTICLES ABOUT
  The New Poets of Germany,
      by Morton Dauwen Zabel   34   94

JACOB, JOHN
  POEMS
  Kingsrider   130   85
  Area

JACOB, MAX
  POEMS
  Rainbow   76   83
  Patience of an Angel
  Banks
  Hell Is Graduated
      (Tr. by Elizabeth Bishop)
  Ballad of the Country Exile
      (Tr. by Harvey Shapiro)   76   85
  Love of the Neighbor
      (Tr. by William Burford)   76   86

ARTICLES ABOUT
The Poets Paris Is Reading, by Jean Catel   67   39
Homage to Max Jacob,
  by Wallace Fowlie   75   352

JACOBS, PAUL DU BOIS
POEMS
A Blue Ridge Elegy   168   272
Wintering at the End of the Mississippi   169   142

JACOBSEN, JOSEPHINE
POEMS
This Is the Hour   48   326
  Winter Castle
  The Passionate Place
  Non Sum Dignus
The Secret Flame   50   201
  Who Shall Escape the Lord?
  Love Song
  The Faithful
  Caprice
Virgin in Glass   51   142
Poet, When You Rhyme
Immortal Element   54   195
Holiday
The Bathers   56   24
Artist's Sustenance
For Wilfred Owen   56   315
Midnight Eden   59   265
Respite—1942
Weather Report from the State Asylum   78   267
Time Exposure   82   144
Florida Friday   83   80
Mr. Tuninpp's Day   86   14
The Animal Inside the Animal   91   229
Poems for My Cousin   94   82
The Revolutionary   98   287
Reindeer and Engine   103   374
The Three Children
Homage to Henri Christophe
Return from Delphi   108   301
In the Crevice of Time   113   166
Arrival   117   20
Destinations
The Planet
Ghosts at Khe Son   120   348
Ascetic's Soliloquy   123   342
Winter Forecast
Border   135   196
A Motel in Troy, N. Y.   137   66
The Nightwatchman
The Monosyllable   139   16
A Dream of Games   145   82
The Presences   148   161
Swimmer's Tide   151   208
Poetry Review   160   79
The Ugly Old Lady   164   139

REVIEWS
For Both Letter and Spirit   89   378
  Children of the Ladybug,
    by Robert Thom
  The Trial of Thomas Cranmer,
    by Anne Ridler
Whittemore, Engle, Scott, Ciardi   96   230
  The Self-Made Man,
    by Reed Whittemore
  Poems in Praise,
    by Paul Engle
  Scrimshaw,
    by Winfield Townley Scott
  39 Poems, by John Ciardi
Helen in Egypt, by H. D.   100   186
Five Poets   105   201
  The Buzzard and the Peacock,
    by Ned O'Gorman
  Wedding Night of a Nun,
    by Lynne Lawner
  The Breaking of the Day,
    by Peter Davison
  Birds, by Judith Wright
  Expressions of Sea Level,
    by A. R. Ammons
Three Poets   118   166
  Violence and Glory,
    Poems: 1962-1968,
    by James Schevill
  Let Not Your Hart,
    by James Seay
  To See, To Take,
    by Mona Van Duyn

BOOKS REVIEWED
Let Each Man Remember   59   288
The Human Climate   84   173
The Animal Inside   109   395
The Shade-Seller   126   103
The Chinese Insomniacs   141   349
The Sisters: New and Selected Poems   152   35
In the Crevice of Time   170   37

ARTICLES ABOUT
[Note on misprint]   96   327

JAEGER, LOWELL
POEMS
How He Cut Himself Shaving   162   262

JAHIER, PIERO
ARTICLES ABOUT
Five Years of Italian Poetry (1910-1915),
  by Emanuel Carnevali   13   209

JAIME, ALFREDO GOMEZ
  [See GOMEZ JAIME, ALFREDO]

JAIMES FREYRE, RICARDO
POEMS
Aeternum Vale
  (Tr. by Muna Lee)   26   119

JAKOB, MAX
REVIEWS
Die Hellen Naechte, by Hans Sahl   60   228
Poems, by Stefan George
  (Tr. by Carol North Valhope
  and Ernst Morwitz)   62   334

JAMES, BERTHA TEN EYCK
POEMS
L'ung-Chien Kun
  [The Dragon of the Universe]   22   254
Eve and Adam   29   194
A Wind Goes
Miracle   36   248
Lost Youth
At Verdun   37   70
Bereft   39   298
In Childhood
Breathless Love
Harvest Deferred
A Painted Scroll of Summer
What Use
To a Dead Child   41   128
For My Father   43   318
In Taos   47   20
On a Thread   49   74
  The Observer
  Madonna Enthroned
  Dutch Garden
  La Muta
Southern Journey   54   14
On Being Ten Years Married
Down Such a Street

REVIEWS
Compass Rose,
  by Elizabeth Coatsworth   35   52
The Black Christ and Other Poems,
  by Countée Cullen   35   286
Lost Buffalo and Other Poems,
  by Leonard Bacon   37   163
The Secret Bird,
  by Jessie B. Rittenhouse   38   112
Student Verse   38   282
  Dartmouth Verse
  The Rollins Book of Verse 1929
    (Ed. by Jessie B. Rittenhouse)
  University of Southern
    California Poems, 1930
  Illini Poetry 1924-9
    (Ed. by Prof. Paul Landis)
  Pittsburg College Verse 1924-30
    (Ed. by Margaret E. Haughawout)

First the Blade: California Intercollegiate
  Anthology of Verse II-III (1929-30)
Selected Poems by Students
  in Hamline University
Miscellany, 1930 [Univ. of Tulsa]
A Year Book of Stanford Writing
The Echo: A Magazine of Verse,
  Autumn 1930 [College Poetry Guild]
Hunter College Echo: A Quarterly
Troubador, Univ. of Oregon Issue
Marshall Script. Spring 1930
The Dial (Poetry Number, Spring 1930)
  [St. Mary's College]
Saplings: A Literary Yearbook
  of the American High School
Chrysalid, A Selection
  of Student Writing, 1929-30
Best Creative Work
  in American High Schools 1928-9
  (Ed. by George H. Gallup)
Ink Spots [Garden City, L.I.]
The Beacon [Glencoe, Ill.]

BOOKS REVIEWED
Nine Dragons   33   160

JAMES, CHARLES BREGA
POEMS
("My love is like a bird with...")   27   194
("O silver-throated fawn...")

JAMES, HENRY
ARTICLES ABOUT
The Poetics of Henry James,
  by M. D. Zabel   45   270
Henry James and the Poets,
  by Leon Edel
  [W. H. Auden, Weldon Kees,
  William Abrahams]   62   328
Rev. of Ushant,
  an Autobiographical Narrative,
  by Conrad Aiken   81   313
Ghosts and Benedictions,
  by Hugh Kenner   113   109

JAMES, LAURA DE WITT
BOOKS REVIEWED
William Blake:
  The Finger on the Furnace   90   321

JAMES, SETH
POEMS
Strong Roots   38   246
The Thug
Murderer
The Blind
One Room Apartment
A Young Girl
The Steel Hand

JAMES, THOMAS (b. 1946)
POEMS
   Waking Up   115   248
   Reasons   117   308

JAMES, THOMAS (b. 1948)
POEMS
   This Green Earth   132   336

JAMESON, R. D.
BOOKS REVIEWED
   The Concert and Other Studies   17   276

JAMMES, FRANCIS
POEMS
   Il Va Neiger...   89   157
   Quand Verrai-Je les Iles...
   L'Ane Savant
      (Tr. by L. L. Lee)

BOOKS REVIEWED
   La Vierge et les Sonnets   15   42
   Le Poète et l'Inspiration   21   47

ARTICLES ABOUT
   Rev. of Six French Poets, by Amy Lowell   7   202
   French Poetry and the
      Revival of Mysticism,
      by Eugene Jolas   56   264

JANECEK, GERALD
BOOKS REVIEWED
   The First Encounter,
      by Andrey Bely (Tr.)   136   40

JANOWITZ, PHYLLIS
BOOKS REVIEWED
   Rites of Strangers   136   170

JANS, MIRIAM
BOOKS REVIEWED
   The Melting Clock   90   114

JANSON, ELLEN (MARGARET)
POEMS
   Tableaux   19   196
     Scherzo
     Tryst
     Incense Smoke
     Night in the City
     The Unknown
   Think of Me as a Passer-By   22   127
   Rhador
   We Shall Be Buried Far Apart

JANZEN, JEAN
POEMS
   Identifying the Fire   158   274
   St. Basil's Cathedral   159   148

   The Gardens of the Body   162   9
   Toward the End of the Century
   Magnolia   166   200
   Claiming the Dust

JARMAN, MARK
POEMS
   The Desire of Water   121   323
   This Way   122   83
   From Another Planet   124   76
   Though We No Longer Possess It
   The Same Clay   127   80
   To the Point
   Goodbye to a Poltergeist   130   146
   Days of '74   151   392
   Shyness of the Muse
     in an Almond Orchard   152   220

ARTICLES
Correspondence
   [Greg Kuzma, Martha Collins]   149   181

JARMAN, WRENNE
BOOKS REVIEWED
   Nymph in Thy Orisons   99   313

JARRELL, RANDALL
POEMS
   The Ways and the Peoples   54   187
   Aesthetic Theories: Art as Expression   60   72
   Time and the Thing-in-Itself in a Textbook
    Man
   Absent with Official Leave   62   262
   Port of Embarkation
   Come to the Stone...
   The Emancipators
   A Lullaby   64   265
   A Front
   Losses
   The Angels at Hamburg
   The Sick Nought
   A Pilot from the Carrier   66   117
   The Dream of Waking
   Mail Call
   Gunner
   Leave
   Protocols
   The Learners
   Terms   72   291
   The Sleeping Beauty:
     Variation of the Prince
   The King's Hunt
   Afterwards
   Hohensalzburg   74   1
   Goodbye, Wendover;
     Goodbye, Mountain Home   74   137
   An English Garden in Austria
     (Seen After Der Rosenkavalier)   75   311

Seele im Raum
The Traveller   77   146
The Face
The Princess Wakes in the Wood
Charles Dodgson's Song
Deutsch Durch Freud
A Conversation with the Devil   78   1
A Girl in a Library
The Survivor Among Graves   81   42
The Lonely Man   84   311
The Meteorite
Windows
Aging
The One Who Was Different   101   50
The Blind Man's Song
Field and Forest
The Lost World   103   37
Thinking of the Lost World   103   149
The Ways and the Peoples   121   15

TRANSLATIONS
  Poem by Tristan Corbière   76   249

BOOKS REVIEWED
  Blood for a Stranger   61   626
  Little Friend, Little Friend   69   98
  Losses   72   302
  The Seven-League Crutches   79   335
  Pictures from an Institution   86   46
  Selected Poems   86   168
  A Sad Heart at the Supermarket   102   269
  The Bat-Poet   105   194
  The Lost World   106   425
  Selected Poems
    (Ed. by William H. Pritchard)   158   100

ARTICLES ABOUT
  The New Intellectualism:
    The Dry Reaction,
    by W. T. Scott   58   86
  Poetry as a Jackdaw's Nest,
    by Sherman Conrad   58   90
  Mr. Graham and the Dead Cigar,
    by Hayden Carruth   72   307
  The Defense of Poetry,
    by Richard Eberhart   77   89
  [Note on misprint]   78   246
  Rev. of *Randall Jarrell 1914–1965*
    (Ed. by Robert Lowell, Peter Taylor,
    and Robert Penn Warren)   112   118
  The Things of the Eye,
    by Robert Fitzgerald   132   107
  Rev. of *Randall Jarrell:*
    A Literary Life,
    by William H. Pritchard   158   100

JARRY, ALFRED
  BOOKS REVIEWED
    Selected Works
      (Ed. by Roger Shattuck
      and Simon Watson Taylor)   107   267
    Selected Works
      (Ed. and tr. by Roger Shattuck
      and Simon Watson Taylor)   111   124

JARVIS, KATHLEEN
  BOOKS REVIEWED
    Poems of Christina Rossetti (Ed.)   89   385

JAUSS, DAVID
  POEMS
    Quotations for a Winter Evening   157   158
    Smile   157   334
    Never   160   256
    Homage to John Cage   165   16

JAY, MAURICE
  POEMS
    Slabs   115   33

JEFFARES, (A.) NORMAN
  REVIEWS
    The Senate Speeches of W. B. Yeats
      (Ed. by Donald R. Pearce)
      [Maud Gonne]   98   253

  BOOKS REVIEWED
    W. B. Yeats: Man and Poet   112   52

  ARTICLES ABOUT
    Letter from Ireland,
      by Patrick Kavanagh   74   286

JEFFERS, ROBINSON
  POEMS
    The Women on Cythaeron   31   175
    The Trumpet
    Birth-Dues
    Come, Little Birds   55   1
    9, 19, 1939   57   171
    Finland Is Down
    Great Men
    The Stars Go Over the Lonely Ocean
    The Bloody Sire
    Greater Grandeur   71   5
    Real and Half Real
    Their Beauty Has More Meaning
    Orca
    Fire   77   187
    The Beauty of Things
    Animals
    The World's Wonders
    Time of Disturbance

The Old Stone-Mason		
To Death		
Hungerfield	80	63

BOOKS REVIEWED
Tamar and Other Poems	26	278
Roan Stallion, Tamar and Other Poems	28	160
The Women at Point Sur	31	274
Cawdor and Other Poems	33	336
Dear Judas	35	279
Thurso's Landing and Other Poems	40	154
Descent to the Dead: Poems Written in Ireland and Great Britain		
Give Your Heart to the Hawks	43	338
Solstice and Other Poems	49	279
Such Counsels You Gave to Me, and Other Poems	51	209
The Selected Poetry of...	55	30
Be Angry at the Sun	59	148
The Double Axe	73	351
Hungerfield and Other Poems	84	226
The Beginning and the End	103	316

ARTICLES ABOUT
A Travel Tale, by Harriet Monroe	28	150
Correspondence from H. L. Davis	29	292
The Hawk and the Stone, by Frajam Taylor	55	39
Poetry on Records, by Harry Thornton Moore	58	345
Poetry on Records, by Harry T. Moore	79	353
Verse Drama on the Paris Stage, by Ruby Haykin	82	294
Rev. of *The Loyalties of Robinson Jeffers*, by Radcliffe Squires	90	254
Rev. of *The Loyalties of Robinson Jeffers*, by Radcliffe Squires	104	264
Rev. of *The Stone Mason of Tor House: The Life and Times of Robinson Jeffers*, by Melba Berry Bennett	111	333

JEFFERSON, THOMAS
ARTICLES ABOUT
Rev. of *Brother to Dragons*, by Robert Penn Warren	83	167

JEFFRESS, DEAN (P.)
POEMS
Thomas Mann	58	135
March	63	310
Some Winter Touch Has Rimed the Sun		
Having Exchanged These Views		
Week-End Party		
Asylum	64	309
Hope Was Abandoned		
Noon Leaves No Shadows		

He Made His Terror		
Transaction in a Restaurant		
Furnished Room		
Destroyer Graveyard		
Fog on the Town		

JEFFREY, WILLIAM
ARTICLES ABOUT
Some Poets of the Scottish Renaissance, by Tom Scott	88	43

JENKINS, DAVID CLAY
POEMS
Quentin Compson	79	277

JENKINS, DONALD
POEMS
Night at the Ocean: A Walk	86	76
The Nameless Ocean		

JENKINS, OLIVER
POEMS
Pinpoint Exhibit	31	190
Faithful		
Prodigy		
Cigarette		

BOOKS REVIEWED
Heavenly Bodies	32	288

JENKINS, WENDY
POEMS
On Reading	169	40
Caddy in Amantla		

JENKINSON, BIDDY [Pseud.]
POEMS
Cumann na bPíobairí/At the Pipers' Club (Tr. by Peter Denman)	167	22

ARTICLES ABOUT
A Map of Contemporary Irish Poetry, by Dennis O'Driscoll	167	94

JENKS, TUDOR
POEMS
The Idol	2	200

JENNETT, SÉAN
BOOKS REVIEWED
The Cloth of Flesh	67	274

JENNINGS, ELIZABETH
POEMS
The Painter	90	151
Sister of Charity		
Port Meadow, Oxford	114	102
On Writing an Autobiography		
A Game of Tennis		

The Workers
A Summing-Up
From Homer   121   258
Penelope
Need
Decision
Rhodes   130   87

BOOKS REVIEWED
A Way of Looking   89   193
A Sense of the World   95   107
Poetry Today (Ed.)   100   104
An Anthology
    of Modern Verse 1940-60 (Ed.)
Song for a Birth or a Death   102   330
Collected Poems 1967   114   266
The Animals' Arrival   118   102
Growing-Points   129   340
Collected Poems   150   102

ARTICLES ABOUT
London Letter: Some New Figures,
    by John McCormick   83   269
A Letter from Britain, by William Logan   157   222

JENNINGS, FRANCES
POEMS
Thunderstorm at the Zoo   37   185
Last Double
Husk
The Cabin   39   314
Set for Macbeth

JENNINGS, KATE
BOOKS REVIEWED
Fish Store   126   208
The Man in the Moon   127   72
Harvest Moon   129   1

JENNINGS, LESLIE NELSON
POEMS
Gardens There Were   12   254
God's House
Eidolon   17   311
Girders   32   250

ARTICLES
Correspondence:
    When Spoon River Came
    [Poem]   10   220

BOOKS REVIEWED
Mill Talk and Other Poems   61   516

JENSEN, LAURA
BOOKS REVIEWED
Bad Boats   134   226
Memory   143   163

JEPSON, EDGAR
ARTICLES
Words and the Poet   10   97

ARTICLES ABOUT
Mr. Jepson's Slam,
    by Harriet Monroe   12   208
An International Episode,
    by Harriet Monroe   13   94

JEREMY, [SISTER] MARY, O.P.
[See also FINNEGAN, ALICE]
POEMS
As If a Star   47   250
    The Departure
    Untimed
Night-Piece   55   307
Gerard Manley Hopkins: 1844-1944   64   11
Ever to Scourges   89   81

JEROME, JUDSON
POEMS
Deer Hunt   86   84
The Violence   88   236
Instructions for Acting   96   356
On Mountain Fork   113   85

BOOKS REVIEWED
Light in the West   102   402

JESS
BOOKS REVIEWED
O!   97   114

JESSON, FREDERICK SHEA
POEMS
Worship   16   312
    Earth-Song
    A Certain Girl
    The Archer
North Ohio Village   21   77

JHAVERI, MANSUKKLAL
POEMS
To My Child   93   232

JIMÉNEZ, JUAN RAMON
[See RAMON JIMÉNEZ, JUAN]

JIN, HA [See HA JIN]

JOHN, CECIL [Pseud.]
POEMS
On the Edge   21   24
    Gone Under
    The White Father
    The Toss
In Africa   24   26

The First-Born
The Old-Timer
The Exile
Disillusion
Unforgotten
Ha!
To Africa
Tanganyika
The Last Wilderness   28   180
Sic Transit
The Semliki
The Grave at Kibati
Two Soldiers
The Doctor
The Poacher
Moonlight
Answered
Irrevocable
Finis
Knowledge
Exit
Jungle Exile   39   293
Resurgence
The Love Cure
Contrast
Debt of Honor
Salvage
On Receiving a Letter
A Testament

ARTICLES ABOUT
They Come and Go,
by Harriet Monroe   36   326

JOHN, GEORGE (W.)
POEMS
("Aunt Ida...")   70   303
("Where shall we begin...")
("It is a long time...")
("Which has it?")

BOOKS REVIEWED
A Garland About Me   81   243

ARTICLES ABOUT
Gertrude Stein,
by Henry Rago   69   93

JOHNS HOPKINS UNIVERSITY
BOOKS REVIEWED
Lectures in Criticism   74   353

JOHNS, ORRICK
POEMS
Songs of Deliverance   3   172
The Song of Youth
Virgins
No Prey Am I

Sister of the Rose   5   223
The Rain
The Battle of Men and God
The Haunt
Country Rhymes   9   285
Old Youth
The Door
The Tree Toad
The Horns of Peace
Dilemma
Bess   12   80
Revisit at Forty   37   177
The Land
Winter Voices
Old Man
The Cardinal Bird
Snow
Joseph   39   122
Sun Image
The Quiet I
Here and There   41   16
Fall Equinox
To the Body
Critic

ARTICLES
Correspondence:
Mr. Johns Rises to Protest   16   230

BOOKS REVIEWED
Asphalt   11   44
Black Branches   16   162
Wild Plum: Lyrics   29   221

JOHNS, RICHARD
POEMS
The Sphinx   37   264

JOHNSON, A(LBERT) E.
POEMS
Birth of the Heart   36   317
Memorandum for Midnight   45   324

JOHNSON, ARTHUR
POEMS
Lyra Vernalis   4   15

JOHNSON, BEN
TRANSLATIONS
Poems by Alfredo Giuliani   94   313

JOHNSON, CAROL
POEMS
Elegy ("Brow and mouth to quiet...")   95   210
The Loser   97   86
Natural History
A Journey Through Spain   101   252

ARTICLES
The Poet as Liturgist 97 179

REVIEWS
The Vision and the Poem 96 387
Selected Poems,
by Thomas Merton
Encounters,
by Daniel Berrigan

BOOKS REVIEWED
Figure for Scamander and Others 107 183
Reason's Double Agents 110 254

JOHNSON, CHARLES BERTRAM
BOOKS REVIEWED
Songs of My People 16 287

JOHNSON, COURTNEY
POEMS
The Man from Nothing 79 282

JOHNSON, DENIS
POEMS
The Story 134 101
The Boarding
Surreptitious Kissing
Nude

BOOKS REVIEWED
The Incognito Lounge 143 163
The Veil 153 30
The Throne of the Third Heaven
of the Nations Millennium
General Assembly 170 90

JOHNSON, DON
POEMS
The Children's Hour 136 94
The Sergeant 137 210

JOHNSON, EDWARD
POEMS
Boy at the Piano 37 26

JOHNSON, FENTON
POEMS
Three Negro Spirituals 12 136
The Lost Love
How Long, O Lord!
Who Is That A-Walking
in the Corn?
Two Negro Spirituals 19 128
A Dream
The Wonderful Morning

BOOKS REVIEWED
Songs of the Soil 10 158

JOHNSON, GEOFFREY
POEMS
As of Yesterday 35 76
The Blackberry-Picker
Notre Dame, Bruges
John the Scrivener
The Outcast 38 318
Partition 60 318
Marginal
Mistress Fell 64 66

BOOKS REVIEWED
Changing Horizons 42 228

JOHNSON, GREG
POEMS
Visiting the Sick 152 257
The Foreign Element
Aid and Comfort 156 72
Sexual Outlaw
Spinster 157 15
Withholding the Last Word 158 253
Insomnia
Lines on Turning Forty 161 255

JOHNSON, HENRY
BOOKS REVIEWED
The Divine Comedy,
by Dante (Tr.) 9 104

JOHNSON, IDA JUDITH
POEMS
The Minstrel 12 70
Flood

JOHNSON, JAMES WELDON
BOOKS REVIEWED
Fifty Years and Other Poems 16 287
The Book of American
Negro Spirituals (Ed.) 27 221
God's Trombones:
Seven Negro Sermons in Verse 30 291
Saint Peter Relates an Incident,
Selected Poems 49 49

JOHNSON, JOSEPHINE
POEMS
November Wind 33 71
Bankrupt 37 135
Tight-Rope 41 256
The Mortal Companion 42 250
Autumn Song
Interval 44 144
Year's End 45 198
Summary in August 48 267
Lost Shepherd
The Poet to His Friend

Solstice
Prelude to Winter
On a Cartoon by Blake   54   7
A Polar Word   58   318
In the Park

BOOKS REVIEWED
Year's End   52   233

JOHNSON, JOSEPHINE W.
POEMS
Persons Seen   40   82
  Changeling
  But for Ourselves
  Love

JOHNSON, KATE KNAPP
POEMS
For Now   140   274
Anniversary

JOHNSON, LIONEL
BOOKS REVIEWED
Poetical Works of...
  [Two editions]   7   313

JOHNSON, LOUIS
POEMS
A Love Poem   73   332
The Sandwich Man   83   82
Age of Discovery   87   271
The Quick and the Dead
Nimrod   89   228

BOOKS REVIEWED
Roughshod Among the Lilies   81   335
New Zealand Poetry Yearbook (1953) (Ed.) 86 111
The Night Shift
  (With James K. Baxter, Charles Doyle,
  and Kendrick Smithyman)   94   44

JOHNSON, LUCY BLACK
POEMS
Economic Theory   74   198

JOHNSON, MAURICE
POEMS
The Beach Before Midnight   70   197

JOHNSON, MERYL
POEMS
Lucille in the Garden   81   352

JOHNSON, ROBERT UNDERWOOD
ARTICLES ABOUT
The Critic's Sense of Humor   8   106

JOHNSON, RONALD
POEMS
Sweet Orange, Sour,
  Osage & Mock-Orange   103   48
Four Orphic Poems   104   210
From The Book of the Green Man 106   37
Letters to Walt Whitman   108   152
The Unfoldings   113   96
Poem ("Out from this floor...") 120   144
The Core

BOOKS REVIEWED
A Line of Poetry, a Row of Trees 107   121
The Book of the Green Man   111   329
Valley of the Many-Colored Grasses
  [Guy Davenport]   115   47

JOHNSON, ROY IVAN
POEMS
Moon Song   22   137

JOHNSON, SAM F.
POEMS
Boat Ride on Lake Shabomeka   126   215
Feet
Hand
Eye Rising   159   205

JOHNSON, SAMUEL
ARTICLES ABOUT
Dr. Johnson and A Shropshire Lad,
  by Charles Norman   60   264

JOHNSON, SIDDIE JOE
POEMS
Beside the Lake   34   138
  Shore Road
  Heron Flight
Cruel Beauty   38   185

JOHNSON, THOMAS
POEMS
A Grammarian Takes the Morning Air 120 135
Rightly, It Would Be Morning
The Physics of Autobiography 126   63

JOHNSON, THOMAS H.
BOOKS REVIEWED
The Poetical Works
  of Edward Taylor (Ed.)   56   165

JOHNSON, TOM
POEMS
Wallace Stevens   132   152
How Plato Was Right
The Fear of Oversleeping   133   138
Vermeer   135   265

The Chinese Wall   145   16
Mystery Story   154   202

JOHNSON, W. R.
  POEMS
    Signs for Travelers   86   329
    Hunting Tale
    The Cabin Builders

JOHNSON, WILLARD
  POEMS
    Interior   27   198

JOHNSON, WILLIAM
  ARTICLES ABOUT
    Rev. of An Apology
      for Loving the Old Hymns,
      by Jordan Smith   143   163

JOHNSTON, ANDREW
  POEMS
    In White   169   261

JOHNSTON, GEORGE
  POEMS
    October   117   3
    Shadowy
    Ongoing
    The Day that Would Never Come
    Wild Apples   118   139
    Indoors
    Self-Portrait
    Pride of Ownership
    Who Bomb?   120   326
    Sue Power and I See Cathleen Off 124   151
    Fuel

  TRANSLATIONS
    Poems by Christian Matras
      and Karsten Hoydal   116   330
    Poems by Olafur Johann Sigurdsson
      and William Heinesen   128   148

  REVIEWS
    Our Germanic Epic   115   274
    Beowulf
      (Tr. by Kevin Crossley-Holland)
    The Beowulf Poet:
      A Collection of Critical Essays
      (Ed. by Donald K. Fry)
    The Elder Edda, a Selection
      (Tr. by Paul B. Taylor
      and W. H. Auden)   117   341

  BOOKS REVIEWED
    The Cruising Auk   96   47
    Home Free   111   323
    Happy Enough: Poems 1935-1972   123   113

JOHNSTON, J.
  BOOKS REVIEWED
    Visits to Walt Whitman in 1890-1891
      (With J. W. Wallace)   14   106

JOHNSTON, ROBERT A.
  POEMS
    Stop And   64   260

JOHNSTONE, J. K.
  BOOKS REVIEWED
    The Bloomsbury Group   92   121

JOLAS, EUGENE
  POEMS
    Return to a Frontier   54   184
    Lumor   56   22
    Lorraine Childhood   60   250

  TRANSLATIONS
    Poems by Paul Claudel   56   240

  ARTICLES
    French Poetry and the Revival of Mysticism
      [Charles Péguy, Léon Bloy,
      Paul Claudel, Francis Jammes,
      Louis Chaigne, Patrice de la Tour du Pin,
      O. V. de L. Milosz, Pierre-Jean Jouve,
      Jacques Maritain, Raissa Maritain,
      Rolland de Renéville, Marcel de Corte] 56   264

  REVIEWS
    The Spiritual Aspects of the New Poetry,
      by Amos N. Wilder   57   49

  BOOKS REVIEWED
    Anthologie de la Nouvelle
      Poésie Américaine (Ed.)   33   165
    Thorns of Thunder, by Paul Eluard
      (Ed. by George Reavey)
      (Tr. with Samuel Beckett,
      Denis Devlin, David Gascoyne,
      Man Ray, George Reavey,
      and Ruthven Todd)   48   347
    Planets and Angels   57   276
    Vertical: A Yearbook
      for Romantic-Mystic Ascensions (Ed.) 61   396
    Wanderpoem, or Angelic Mythamorphosis
      of the City of London   69   103

  ARTICLES ABOUT
    Recent Magazines, by M. D. Zabel 38   348
    Recent Magazines, by M. D. Zabel 48   351

JONAS, GEORGE
  BOOKS REVIEWED
    The Absolute Smile   114   202
    The Happy Hungry Man   119   356

JONAS, GERALD
POEMS
   Hieroglyphs   168   277
   Cartography   169   251

JONAS, ROSALIE
POEMS
   The Foundling Hospital   3   91

JONAS, STEPHEN
BOOKS REVIEWED
   Transmutations   110   186
   Exercises for Ear   115   47

JONES, ALAN PRYCE
ARTICLES ABOUT
   The Cantabrigian Approach,
      by Marius Bewley   75   282

JONES, ALICE
POEMS
   Persephone   156   334
   Prayer   158   78
   Brother and Sister   159   279
   Thirteen   163   271
   Thirst
   The Dream
   Solo   167   204
   Light
   Birds   168   106
   Coast   170   69
   Reach

BOOKS REVIEWED
   The Knot   167   287

JONES, ALICE LOUISE
POEMS
   The Pelican   17   21

JONES, D. G.
BOOKS REVIEWED
   Phrases from Orpheus   114   202

JONES, DARYL
BOOKS REVIEWED
   Someone Going Home Late   160   94

JONES, DAVID
POEMS
   The Wall   87   68
   The Tutelar of the Place   97   203

BOOKS REVIEWED
   The Anathemata   83   295
   In Parenthesis   101   426
   The Tribune's Visitation   118   102
   The Sleeping Lord and Other Fragments   125   233
   Letters to Vernon Watkins   131   292

ARTICLES ABOUT
   [Note on misprint]   87   380
   [Note]   97   271

JONES, EVAN
ARTICLES ABOUT
   Rev. of *The Penguin Book of Australian Verse*
      (Ed. by John Thompson,
      Kenneth Slessor, and R. G. Howarth)   94   44

JONES, FRANK
REVIEWS
   The Armed Vision,
      by Stanley Edgar Hyman   73   228
   The Portable Greek Reader
      (Ed. by W. H. Auden)   73   284
   The Undersea Farmer,
      by Barbara Howes   74   166
   The Edge of Being,
      by Stephen Spender   74   348
   Goethe: Tombstones and Milestones   75   232
      The Sorrows of Young Werther,
         The New Melusina, Novelle,
         by J. W. von Goethe
         (Tr. by Victor Lange)
      Faust, Part One,
         by J. W. von Goethe
         (Tr. by Philip Wayne)
      Commentary on Goethe's Faust,
         by D. J. Enright
      Goethe the Poet,
         by Karl Vietor
         (Tr. by Moses Hadas)
      Goethe's Image of Man and Society,
         by Arnold Bergstraesser
      Criticism and Creation,
         by Herbert J. C. Grierson   78   285

BOOKS REVIEWED
   The Suppliant Women (Tr.),
      in *The Complete Greek Tragedies:*
      Euripides IV
      (Ed. by David Grene
      and Richmond Lattimore)   95   190

JONES, GLYN
BOOKS REVIEWED
   Poems   56   274

JONES, HERBERT
BOOKS REVIEWED
   The Well of Being   18   162
   The Blue Ship   20   280
   Finlay   24   340

JONES, HOWARD MUMFORD
POEMS
   University Sketches   8   7

The Professor Muses
Aphrodite
November on the Lake Michigan Dunes   9   125

BOOKS REVIEWED
A Little Book of Local Verse   7   209
Gargoyles   15   164
The Romanesque Lyric,
  by Philip Schuyler Allen
  [Translations]   33   227
The Theory of American Literature   110   119

ARTICLES ABOUT
Rev. of Personae,
  by Ezra Pound   30   216

JONES, JILL
POEMS
Interspersed   169   44
Disrepair

ARTICLES ABOUT
Towards a Contemporary
Australian Poetics,
  by John Kinsella   169   94

JONES, LEILA
POEMS
Alembic   50   20
The Shadow
Lost Swan   54   243

JONES, LE ROI
[IMAMU AMIRI BARAKA]
POEMS
Balboa, the Entertainer   100   14
As a Possible Lover
Valery as Dictator   103   157
The Liar
Snake Eyes
Like Rousseau   105   161
History as Process

REVIEWS
A Dark Bag   103   394
American Negro Poetry
  (Ed. by Arna Bontemps)
Poems from Black Africa
  (Ed. by Langston Hughes)
Song of a Goat,
  by John Pepper Clark
Heavensgate,
  by Christopher Okigbo
African Songs of Love,
  War, Grief, & Abuse,
  by Leon Damas
24 Poems,
  by Jean-Joseph Rabearivelo

African Heritage
  (Ed. by Jacob Drachler)
Swahili Poetry, by Lyndon Harries

BOOKS REVIEWED
Blues People:
  Negro Music in White America   105   397
The System of Dante's Hell   109   332

JONES, LLEWELLYN
ARTICLES
Correspondence:
Naming Verse Patterns
  [Amy Lowell]   21   281

REVIEWS
Poetry Under the Scalpel   34   161
The Criticism of Literature,
  by Elizabeth Nitchie
The Craft of Poetry,
  by Clement Wood
Form and Style in Poetry,
  by W. P. Ker
  (Ed. by R. W. Chambers)
The Garment of Praise,
  by Eleanor Carroll Chilton
  and Herbert Agar

BOOKS REVIEWED
First Impressions   28   285

JONES, LOUISE
POEMS
When Love Is Gone   20   18

JONES, MARY HOXIE
POEMS
Admonition   43   256
On Second Thought
Let Him Who Is Without Sin
The Offering

JONES, PAUL
POEMS
Better Tomorrow   162   127

JONES, PAUL FORTIER
ARTICLES
Correspondence:
About Mr. Underwood's Prize   13   228

JONES, RICHARD
POEMS
Things   153   132
My Painting
Song of the Old Man   156   139
Certain People
Scars   161   28
Lanterns

BOOKS REVIEWED
    At Last We Enter Paradise   161 339

JONES, RODNEY
POEMS
    After Storms   143 326
    For Those Who Miss
      the Important Parts
    Meditation on Birney Mountain
    Life on Sundays   151 71
    An Explanation of the Exhibit   153 214
    Carpe Diem
    Mortal Sorrows   166 125
    An Errand for My Grandmother
    The First Space-Travelers

BOOKS REVIEWED
    Apocalyptic Narrative   164 223

JONES, RUTH LAMBERT
POEMS
    I Would Entreat You   25 76
    Alarum   29 255

JONES, T. H.
POEMS
    The Pride of the Morning   85 264

JONG, ERICA
POEMS
    Where It Begins   117 309
    Narcissus, Photographer
    Touch
    Books
    Climbing You   118 201
    The Universal Explicator
    The Wives of Mafiosi
    The Man Who Can Only Paint Death
    Seminar
    Middle Aged Lovers I   151 72

BOOKS REVIEWED
    Fruits & Vegetables   119 296
    Half-Lives   123 353

JONSON, BEN
ARTICLES ABOUT
    The 16th Century
      Lyric in England: Part III,
      by Yvor Winters   54 35
    Rev. of Revaluation: Tradition
      and Development in English Poetry,
      by F. R. Leavis   72 41

JOOST, NICHOLAS
REVIEWS
    The Riddle of Emily Dickinson,
      by Rebecca Patterson   80 242

Baudelaire on Poe: Critical Papers
    (Tr. and ed. by Lois
    and Frances E. Hyslop, Jr.)   81 247
Poetics, Reprints, Poetry Texts   84 363
    The Achievement of American Criticism
      (Ed. by Clarence Arthur Brown)
    The Selected Poetry of Lord Byron
      (Ed. by Leslie A. Marchand)
    Blake: Prophet Against Empire,
      by David V. Erdman
    The Structure of Literature,
      by Paul Goodman
    Theory of Prosody
      in Eighteenth-Century England,
      by Paul Fussell, Jr.
Briefer Notices   85 55
    More Modern American Poets,
      by James G. Southworth
    Medieval People, by Eileen Power
    The Flowers of Evil,
      by Charles Baudelaire
      (Tr. by William Aggeler)
    Leopardi: A Study in Solitude,
      by Iris Origo
    Lira Española:
      Representative Spanish Lyric Poets
      (15th-20th Centuries)
      (Ed. by Diego Marin)
    Portraits of Keats, by Donald Parson
    La Fontaine: The Man and His Work,
      by Monica Sutherland
Brief Notices   86 118
    A Restoration Reader
      (Ed. by James Holly Hanford)
    The Haunted Man:
      A Portrait of Edgar Allan Poe,
      by Philip Lindsay
    The English Epic and Its Background,
      by E. M. W. Tillyard
    Emily Dickinson: A Revelation,
      by Millicent Todd Bingham
    Selected Works of John Dryden
      (Ed. by William Frost)
    Greek Tragedy: A Literary Study,
      by H. D. F. Kitto
    The Golden Echo,
      by David Garnett
    Leaves of Grass, by Walt Whitman
    Verse and Worse, A Private Collection
      (Ed. by Arnold Silcock)

JORDAN, JUDY
POEMS
    In the 25th Year
      of My Mother's Death   168 271

JORDAN, JUNE
BOOKS REVIEWED
    Some Changes   121 292

JOSÉ CELA, CAMILO
POEMS
Inventory of the Dark
    (Tr. by Anthony Kerrigan)   101   322

ARTICLES ABOUT
The Color of Seed,
    by Anthony Kerrigan   101   345

JOSEPH, [CHIEF]
ARTICLES ABOUT
Chief Joseph on War
    [Poem]   5   92

JOSEPH, J. CALDER
POEMS
Subject Matter   55   192
A Path Alone
Rhapsody in D Sharp   57   254
Hospital

BOOKS REVIEWED
Narration with a Red Piano   58   273

JOSEPH, LAWRENCE
POEMS
Curriculum Vitae   147   85
Any and All
I Pay the Price
On Nature   151   74
An Awful Lot Was Happening   152   68

BOOKS REVIEWED
Shouting at No One   144   107
Curriculum Vitae   153   30

JOSEPHS, LAURENCE
POEMS
A Letter   74   267
The Paper Chase, 1880
Rimbaud in Abyssinia
For the Afflicted, Vision Turns to Stone
"There Is No Lack of Hell
    in that Mad Nest"   77   259
Poem for a World Traveler   78   264
Trompe L'Oeil
The Garden   95   90
A Mirror, a Window, a Pool

REVIEWS
The New Barbarian,
    by Winthrop Palmer   79   347

JOSEPHSON, HANNAH
BOOKS REVIEWED
Aragon: Poet of the French Resistance
    (Ed. with Malcolm Cowley)   68   44

JOSEPHSON, MATTHEW
POEMS
The Last Lady   17   20

JOSHI, UMASHANKAR
POEMS
The Death of a Poet   93   230

JOUVE, PIERRE JEAN
POEMS
Ténèbre   104   273
A la Beauté
    (Tr. by Wallace Fowlie)

BOOKS REVIEWED
Présences   1   165

ARTICLES ABOUT
French Poetry and the
    Revival of Mysticism,
    by Eugene Jolas   56   264

JOYCE, JAMES
POEMS
Simples   10   72
Tutto è Sciolto
Flood
A Flower Given to My Daughter
Night Piece
On the Beach at Fontana   11   70
Alone
She Weeps over Rahoon
Night Piece   121   16

BOOKS REVIEWED
Chamber Music   14   98
Imagist Anthology 1930
    (With Richard Aldington,
    John Cournos, H. D.,
    John Gould Fletcher, F. S. Flint,
    Ford Madox Ford, D. H. Lawrence,
    and William Carlos Williams)   36   213
Chamber Music
    (Ed. by William York Tindall)   85   109
Collected Poems   91   56

ARTICLES ABOUT
Poets as Prosers, by Harriet Monroe   28   328
Why Not Laugh? by Harriet Monroe   33   206
Poems and Pictures,
    by Morton Dauwen Zabel   34   217
The Lyrics of James Joyce,
    by M. D. Zabel   36   206
James Joyce (1882-1941),
    by Thornton Wilder   57   370
The Vocation of the Poet
    in the Modern World,
    by Delmore Schwartz   78   223

Joyce's Chambermade Music,
   by W. Y. Tindall   80   105
Rev. of *In Memoriam James Joyce.*
   A Vision of World Language,
   by Hugh MacDiarmid   88   48
Rev. of *Letters of James Joyce*
   (Ed. by Stuart Gilbert)   91   56
Rev. of *Passages from Finnegans Wake.*
   A Free Adaptation for the Theatre,
   by Mary Manning   91   335
Rev. of *James Joyce,* by Richard Ellmann   96   382

JÓZSEF, ATTILA
POEMS
   Glasses   116   281
   O Europe
   On Evening Clouds
   A Fine Summer Evening
   (Tr. by John Batki)

BOOKS REVIEWED
   Selected Poems and Texts
   (Tr. by John Batki)
   (Ed. by James Atlas
   and George Gömöri)   126   103

JUDSON, ALICE CLAY
POEMS
   Mist Reflections   58   75
   Beyond the Candle   61   550
   Birth Is a Gift
   Three Seasons of Growth   72   17

JUDSON, JOHN
POEMS
   Psalm Above Santa Fe   151   347

BOOKS REVIEWED
   Surreal Songs   114   251

JUDSON, MARGARET
POEMS
   In the Night   13   254

JUHÁSZ, FERENC
BOOKS REVIEWED
   The Boy Changed into a Stag
   (Tr. by Kenneth McRobbie
   and Ilona Duczynska)   119   45
   Selected Poems (With Sandor Weöres)   119   342

JULLICH, GEOFFREY
POEMS
   Eight Line Stanzas   127   208

JUNG, C(ARL) G.
BOOKS REVIEWED
   Essays on a Science of Mythology
   (With C. Kerényi)   77   168

JUNKINS, DONALD
POEMS
   Processions   102   92

BOOKS REVIEWED
   The Sunfish and the Partridge   108   121

JURGELIONIS, KLEOFAS
TRANSLATIONS
   Lament   8   138

JUSTEMA, WILLIAM
POEMS
   To Last Violets   56   14
   I Have a Friend
   Private Papers   62   14
     Without Keys
     One Last Look
     I Try My New Toys
   The Snake House, Bronx Zoo   65   66
   New York
   Of Innocence   69   257
   A Dream

ARTICLES
   Correspondence
   [Edwin Honig]   65   164

BOOKS REVIEWED
   Private Papers   64   347

ARTICLES ABOUT
   Correspondence from Edwin Honig   65   105

JUSTICE, DONALD
[DON JUSTICE]
POEMS
   "Here Lies Love"   73   87
   Aboard! Aboard!   81   354
   Landscape
   On a Painting by Patient B
     of the Independence State Hospital
     for the Insane   85   90
   Variations on a Neo-Classic Theme   88   365
   Here in Katmandu
   Southern Gothic   92   292
   From *Bad Dreams*   95   149
   Love's Map
   After a Line by John Peale Bishop   98   286
   Poem ("Time and the weather...")
   For the Suicides of Two Years Ago   105   349
   The Evening of the Mind
   About My Poems
   At a Rehearsal of "Uncle Vanya"
   Memory of a Porch
   To the Hawks   108   79
   Men at Forty
   The Man Closing Up

Lethargy	113	329
Portrait with Brown Hair		
The Assassination		
A Letter	119	326
White Notes		

ARTICLES
  Correspondence:
    The Housman Text
    [Laurence Housman,
    Tom Burns Haber]   96   392

REVIEWS
  The Copernican Revolution and *Day*,
    by Paul Goodman   89   120
  Sacred and Secular   91   41
    The Strange Islands,
      by Thomas Merton
    Collected Poems,
      by Kathleen Raine
    A Swimmer in the Air,
      by Howard Moss
  Orpheus Descending, with Battle of Angels
    and *Suddenly Last Summer*,
    by Tennessee Williams   93   402
  Complete Poems,
    by A. E. Housman
    (Ed. by Tom Burns Haber)   96   44
  The Exclusions of a Rhyme,
    by J. V. Cunningham
    [Yvor Winters]   97   181

BOOKS REVIEWED
  The Summer Anniversaries   97   50
  *The Collected Poems
    of Weldon Kees* (Ed.)   98   319
  A Local Storm   105   264
  Contemporary French Poetry
    (Ed. with Alexander Aspel)   107   267
  Night Light   112   272
  Departures   125   44
  *The Collected Poems
    of Weldon Kees* (Ed.)   130   285
  The Sunset Maker   154   340
  The Collected Poems of Henri Coulette
    (Ed. with Robert Mezey)   158   214
  *A Donald Justice Reader:
    Selected Poetry and Prose*   162   160
  New and Selected Poems   168   160

ARTICLES ABOUT
  [Note]   159   51

JUVENAL
BOOKS REVIEWED
  The Satires of...
    (Tr. by Rolfe Humphries)   96   247

JUVONEN, HELVI
POEMS
  The Chantarelle
    (Tr. by Meri Lehtinen)   98   351

"K. L."
[See LOESER, KATINKA]

"K. M. B."
REVIEWS
Les Poètes de la Guerre   7   320

KABIR, HUMAYUN
[HUMAYAN KABIR]
POEMS
Prisoners   93   220

TRANSLATIONS
Poem by Rabindranath Tagore   93   203

BOOKS REVIEWED
Green and Gold:
   Stories and Poems from Bengal (Ed.)   95   314
One Hundred and One:
   Poems by Rabindranath Tagore (Ed.)   111   407

KADOW, AUGUST
POEMS
The Migrant Birds   77   331
White   79   195
Royal Poinciana   82   70
The Diving Bell
"Why Should I Not
   Love Childhood Still?"   84   70
Key West   89   225

KAFKA, FRANZ
ARTICLES ABOUT
Rev. of Rage for Order,
   by Austin Warren   72   318
Rev. of You Can't Have Everything,
   by Richard Shelton   132   31

KAGAWA, BUNICHI
POEMS
Under the Skyscrapers   36   246
   Hunger
   July
   Soaring Hour
News   43   196
   The Village Spring

The Rumor
Silent Intimacy   47   192

KAHN, GUSTAVE
ARTICLES ABOUT
As It Is in Paris,
   by Harriet Monroe   27   266

KAHN, HANNAH
POEMS
Notation in Time   116   20
Without Compass

KAHN, MARCELLA
POEMS
Sidelong Glances   43   254
   He Does Not Read
   She Asks Forgiveness
   At Sunset

KAHN, SAADATH ALI
TRANSLATIONS
Poem by Mohammed Iqbal   93   233

KAHN, SHOLOM J.
TRANSLATIONS
Poem by Rachel   92   214
Poem by Leah Goldberg   92   242

KAI-YU HSU
BOOKS REVIEWED
Twentieth Century Chinese Poetry:
   An Anthology (Ed. and tr.)   107   196

KALAR, JOSEPH
BOOKS REVIEWED
We Gather Strength
   (With Herman Spector,
   Edwin Rolfe, and S. Funaroff)   44   50

KALLMAN, CHESTER
POEMS
Song ("I tip-toed naked...")   84   12
A Romance
The Souvenir
Night Music

Storm at Castelfranco
The Capital of Away   115   178
Dead Center
The Matrix
Salome Dance
Like as Not

ARTICLES
Correspondence   120   363

BOOKS REVIEWED
The Magic Flute
     (Tr. with W. H. Auden)   89   253
Storm at Castelfranco   89   307
Absent and Present   104   108
The Sense of Occasion   120   47

KALSTONE, DAVID
BOOKS REVIEWED
Five Temperaments   132   226
Becoming a Poet: Elizabeth Bishop
     with Marianne Moore and Robert Lowell
     (Ed. by Robert Hemenway)   157   159

KANDEL, LENORE
BOOKS REVIEWED
Word Alchemy   113   188

KANEKO, HISAKAZU
TRANSLATIONS
Poems by Fuyuji Tanaka,
     Taro Yamamoto, Jukichi Yagi,
     Shinkichi Takahashi,
     and Daigaku Horiguchi   101   169

KANEKO, MITSUHARU
POEMS
Demons and a Poet
     (Tr. by Satoru Satu
     and Constance Urdang)   88   72

KANELOS, PETER
POEMS
In the Cave of Skulls   164   320

KANFER, ALLEN
POEMS
Moses   83   136
Jacob   85   205
Like Two Old Theologians   88   232
Never Counsel a Lovely Lady
The Lonely Fugitive   91   294
The Giraffe
A Mountain Standing Strong
Moses
We Wander in Each Other's Woods   94   30
Fear Is a Formal Matter
Teaching a Child To Read   97   26

Past Anger
Tomorrow's Weather   99   290
The Frostbitten Mourner and Beethoven 101   242
The Portrait   103   249
Love and Snow
Sermon
Separation
Seven Wonders of the World   115   12

KANG-HU, KIANG
[See KIANG KANG-HU]

KANTOR, MAC KINLAY
BOOKS REVIEWED
Turkey in the Straw, a Book
     of American Ballads and Primitive Verse   48   169
Glory for Me   68   51

KÁNTOR, PÉTER
POEMS
Moonlight Monlogue for the New Kitten
     (Tr. by Michael Blumenthal)   170   129

KAO CH'I
POEMS
Buffalo Herder's Song
     (Tr. by George Margulies
     and Willard R. Trask)   46   6

ARTICLES ABOUT
Three Chinese Poets of Long Ago,
     by George Margulies
     and Willard R. Trask   46   46
Rev. of The Poet Kao Ch'i: 1336-1374,
     by F. W. Mote   104   264
Rev. of The Poet Kao Ch'i: 1336-1374,
     by F. W. Mote   107   196

KAPLAN, ALLAN
POEMS
Poem ("I don't know whether...")   115   227

KAPLAN, HAROLD
POEMS
The Dying Acrobat   73   199

KAPLAN, L. C.
TRANSLATIONS
Poem by Jacques Roumain   62   61
Poem by Nicolas Guillén   62   69

KAPLAN, MILTON (A.)
POEMS
The Top Spins   59   63

ARTICLES
Radio and Poetry
     [Archibald MacLeish]   64   270

REVIEWS
   Mass Chants and Other Poems,
     by Alan Baer Rothenberg   66   348

KAPLAN, MIRIAM
  POEMS
   City Scenes   41   258
     Servants
     Ghetto Sabbath Night
     The Head Waitress
     In Madison Square
     Judas
   Snares   48   196
     Nirvana
     The Roomers
     The Puppet

KAPLAN, SUSAN
  POEMS
   The Servant's Choice   148   274

KAPP, DAVID
  POEMS
   Judgment Day   70   79
   One Small Voice

KAPPEL, ANDREW J.
  POEMS
   One Kiss, Five Pups, and No Conclusion   145   285

KAPSTEIN, ISRAEL JAMES
  POEMS
   New York Skyline   32   130
   New York   35   322

KARADJICH, VUK STEFANOVICH
  ARTICLES ABOUT
   Serbian Poetry, by F. C. Weiskopf   61   438

KARANDIKAR, VINDA
  POEMS
   Early Morning
     (Tr. by P. Machwe)   93   239

KARLFELDT, ERIK AXEL
  POEMS
   The Wooden Castle
     (Tr. by Charles Wharton Stork)   40   145
   Easter Week
     (Tr. by Charles Wharton Stork)   42   14

  BOOKS REVIEWED
   Arcadia Borealis: Selected Poems of...
     (Tr. by Charles Wharton Stork)   56   284

  ARTICLES ABOUT
   Erik Axel Karlfeldt, Swedish Poet,
     by Charles Wharton Stork   40   152

KARNI, YEHUDA
  POEMS
   A Woman's Prayer   92   209
   Put Me into the Breach
     (Tr. by Ruth Finer Mintz)

KAROUZOS, NIKOS
  POEMS
   Misery in the Chest
     (Tr. by Kimon Friar)   139   95

  ARTICLES ABOUT
   Post-War Greek Poets,
     by Kimon Friar   139   99

KARPELES, MAUD
  BOOKS REVIEWED
   English Folk Songs
     from the Southern Appalachians (Ed.)
     (Coll. by Cecil J. Sharp)   83   37

KARR, MARY
  POEMS
   The Last Paris Poem   138   132
   Diogenes Tries To Forget
   The New Year
   My New Diet
   Lipstick
   The Distance   140   230
   Predictions
   The Magnifying Mirror
   Witnessing My Father's Will
   Report
   Hard Knocks   142   155
   Vigil
   Diogenes Passes the Time
   Diogenes the Bartender Closes Up
   For My Children
   Diogenes Invents a Game   145   86
   Soft Mask   148   330
   Etching of the Plague Years   156   70
   Final Position   157   16
   Don Giovanni's Confessor   159   258

  REVIEWS
   Stealing the Language: The Emergence
     of Women's Poetry in America,
     by Alicia Suskin Ostriker   149   294

  BOOKS REVIEWED
   The Devil's Tour   164   157

KARSEN, SONJA
  BOOKS REVIEWED
   Selected Poems
     of Jaime Torres Bodet (Tr.)   107   338

KASCHNITZ, MARIE LUISE
POEMS
  Hiroshima   136   342
  A Map of Sicily
  Toward Evening
  Can't Forget
  My Curiosity
    (Tr. by Lisel Mueller)

KASDORF, JULIA
POEMS
  First Gestures   165   261

KASISCHKE, LAURA
POEMS
  Palm   157   262
  The Driver's Lullaby   158   129
  Happy Birthday   162   88

KASTENDIECK, MILES MERWIN
BOOKS REVIEWED
  England's Musical Poet,
    Thomas Campion   56   51

KATZ, JOSEPH
BOOKS REVIEWED
  The Poems of Stephen Crane:
    A Critical Edition (Ed.)   112   127

KATZ, NAOMI
POEMS
  Poems After the Fact   48   16
    Orphans of a Dream
    Perfection
    Atelier
    Penelope in Wood
    Apostate

KATZIN, OLGA
BOOKS REVIEWED
  Peeps at Parnassus   34   175

KAUFMAN, HERBERT
BOOKS REVIEWED
  Poems   2   107

KAUFMAN, KENNETH C.
POEMS
  Big Lige   43   141

BOOKS REVIEWED
  Level Land   47   281

KAUFMAN, SHIRLEY
POEMS
  For a Cold Night   108   378
  Getting There   117   28
  Apples

In Touch
  The Dream   121   322
  Annunciation   140   208

BOOKS REVIEWED
  Gold Country   125   44

KAUFMANN, WALTER
BOOKS REVIEWED
  Goethe's Faust
    [Part I; Sections from Part II]
    (Tr. and ed.)   101   287

KAUN, ALEXANDER (S.)
TRANSLATIONS
  Poem by Sergey Yesenin
    (With Roberta Holloway)   27   76

REVIEWS
  The Epic Songs of Russia
    (Tr. by Isabel F. Hapgood)   9   271

BOOKS REVIEWED
  Soviet Poets and Poetry   63   343

KAVANAGH, PATRICK
ARTICLES
  Letter from Ireland
    [Lord Longford,
    Norman Jeffares]   74   286

BOOKS REVIEWED
  A Soul for Sale   71   324
  Recent Poems   94   264
  Come Dance with Kitty Stobling
    and Other Poems   101   205
  Self Portrait   106   234
  Come Dance with Kitty Stobling,
    and Other Poems
  Collected Poems

ARTICLES ABOUT
  Letter from Dublin,
    by John Montague   90   310
  Correspondence
    from Richard Murphy
    [Hayden Carruth]   102   61
  A Map of Contemporary Irish Poetry,
    by Dennis O'Driscoll   167   94

KAVANAGH, PETER
BOOKS REVIEWED
  The Story of the Abbey Theatre   79   216

KAVANAUGH, JAMES
BOOKS REVIEWED
  There Are Men Too Gentle
    to Live Among Wolves   119   342

KAY, ELLEN
BOOKS REVIEWED
    A Local Habitation   94   117

KAY, GEORGE
BOOKS REVIEWED
    The Penguin Book
    of Italian Verse (Ed.)   94   350

KAYDEN, EUGENE M.
BOOKS REVIEWED
    Poems by Boris Pasternak (Tr.)   96   108

KAYE-SMITH, SHEILA
BOOKS REVIEWED
    Saints in Sussex:
    Poems and Plays   30   293

KAZANTZAKIS, NIKOS
[NIKOS KAZANTSAKIS]
POEMS
    Voyage with Charon
    (Tr. by Kimon Friar)   78   162

BOOKS REVIEWED
    The Odyssey: A Modern Sequel
    (Tr. by Kimon Friar)   95   175
    The Odyssey: A Modern Sequel
    (Tr. by Kimon Friar)   95   179

ARTICLES ABOUT
    Contemporary Greek Poetry,
    by Kimon Friar   78   145

KAZIN, ALFRED
BOOKS REVIEWED
    The Portable Blake (Ed.)   69   223
    Emerson: A Modern Anthology
    (Ed. with Daniel Aaron)   96   382

KEARNEY, LAWRENCE
POEMS
    K-Mart   132   198
    Delight
    Portrait of the Artist as a Nice Guy   137   328
    Elegy ("At the door of your room...")

BOOKS REVIEWED
    Kingdom Come   138   231

KEARNS, LIONEL
BOOKS REVIEWED
    Pointing   115   353
    By the Light of the Silvery McLune:
    Media Parables, Poems, Signs, Gestures,
    and Other Assaults on the Interface   119   356

KEAST, W. R.
ARTICLES ABOUT
    Rev. of *Critics and Criticism,*
    Ancient and Modern
    (Ed. by R. S. Crane)   82   98

KEATING, DIANE
BOOKS REVIEWED
    No Birds or Flowers   144   297

KEATS, JOHN
ARTICLES ABOUT
    A Keats Memorial
    [Amy Lowell]   16   231
    A Word About Keats,
    by Harriet Monroe   18   150
    Rev. of *John Keats,*
    by Amy Lowell   26   220
    Correspondence
    from Edgar Lee Masters   26   349
    Rev. of *Adonais: A Life of John Keats,*
    by Dorothy Hewlett   53   159
    Rev. of *Keats and the Daemon King,*
    by Werner W. Beyer   70   168
    Rev. of *The Finer Tone:*
    Keats' Major Poems,
    by Earl Wasserman   84   37
    Rev. of *Selected Letters of...*
    (Ed. by Lionel Trilling)   84   296
    Correspondence
    from William Van O'Connor:
    Keats-Shelley Memorials   84   366
    Rev. of *Portraits of Keats,*
    by Donald Parson   85   55
    Rev. of *Keats,*
    by John Middleton Murray   92   121
    Rev. of *John Keats,*
    by Robin Mayhead   113   262
    Finishes: Notes
    on Ambition and Survival,
    by Christian Wiman   169   217

KEELEY, DOROTHY
[See ALDIS, DOROTHY KEELEY]

KEELEY, EDMUND
TRANSLATIONS
    Poem by Odysseus Elytis
    (With George Savidis)   105   1
    Poem by Nikos Gatsos   105   24
    Poems by Takis Sinopoulos
    (With George Savidis)   105   36
    Poems by George Seferis
    (With Philip Sherrard)   105   44
    Poems by C. P. Cavafy
    (With Philip Sherrard)   120   266

ARTICLES
The Genesis: A Commentary   105   16
Amorgós: A Commentary   105   33

BOOKS REVIEWED
Six Poets of Modern Greece
    (Tr. with Philip Sherrard)   101   283
The Plant, the Well, the Angel: A Trilogy,
    by Vassilis Vassilikos
    (Tr. with Mary Keeley)   105   65
Collected Poems 1924-1955,
    by George Seferis
    (Tr. with Philip Sherrard)   114   113
Angelos Sikelianos: Selected Poems
    (Tr. with Philip Sherrard)   137   220
Ritsos in Parentheses (Tr.)

KEELEY, MARY
    BOOKS REVIEWED
    The Plant, the Well, the Angel: A Trilogy,
        by Vassilis Vassilikos
        (Tr. with Edmund Keeley)   105   65

KEENE, DONALD
    BOOKS REVIEWED
    Japanese Literature:
        An Introduction for Western Readers   88   109
    An Anthology of Japanese Literature
        from the Earliest Era
        to the Mid-Nineteenth Century (Ed.)
    The Japanese Discovery of Europe:
        Honda Toshiaki and Other
        Discoverers 1720-1798
    Anthology of Chinese Literature:
        From Early Times to the
        Fourteenth Century
        (Ed. with Cyril Birch)   109   272

KEENE, FRANCES
    TRANSLATIONS
    Outline of a Poetics I,
        by G. A. Borgese
        (Tr. with Lucille Bunzl)   55   140
    Outline of a Poetics II,
        by G. A. Borgese
        (Tr. with Lucille Bunzl)   55   204
    Outline of a Poetics III,
        by G. A. Borgese
        (Tr. with Lucille Bunzl)   55   267

KEENER, LUANN
    POEMS
    Vultures   168   259

KEENS, WILLIAM
    POEMS
    Skull House, Heart Flower   129   276
    How It Feels To Walk on the Moon

KEES, WELDON
    POEMS
    The Inquiry   52   196
    Poem
        ("Mind's residue is vein-violet...")
    The Speakers   54   70
    Statement with Rhymes
    White Collar Ballad   56   72
    Poem ("Memories rich as Proust's...")
    Praise to the Mind
    On a Painting by Rousseau   58   127
    Henry James at Newport   59   16
    For H. V. (1901-1927)
    After the Trial
        ("Prurient tapirs gamboled...")   61   493
    Note to be Left on the Table
        ("The eye no longer single...")
        ("And when your beauty...")
    Crime Club   62   322
    Report of the Meeting
    Sestina: Travel Notes
    Xantha Street
    That Winter
    The Locusts, the Plaza, the Room   71   14
    Problems of a Journalist
    Dog
    Small Prayer
    Equinox   72   233
    Interregnum
    The Upstairs Room
    Return of the Ghost
    Turtle   77   18
    The Coming of the Plague
    Covering Two Years
    The Umbrella   77   326
    January

    REVIEWS
    Collected Poems of Kenneth Fearing   57   264
    50 Poems,
        by E. E. Cummings   59   162
    Sixteen Hundred Poems   59   346
        The Viking Book of Poetry
        of the English-Speaking World
        (Ed. by Richard Aldington)
        Reading Poems
        (Ed. by Wright Thomas
        and Stuart Gerry Brown)

    BOOKS REVIEWED
    The Last Man   63   349
    The Fall of the Magicians   70   330
    Poems 1947-1954   88   191
    The Collected Poems of...
        (Ed. by Donald Justice)   98   319
    The Collected Poems of...
        (Ed. by Donald Justice)   130   285

ARTICLES ABOUT
Henry James and the Poets,
by Leon Edel — 62 328
[Note on disappearance] — 88 199

KEGG, MARTIN MATTHEW
POEMS
Pow-Wow Shots — 139 221

KEISCH, HEINRICH
ARTICLES ABOUT
On the Continent,
by F. C. Weiskopf — 56 332

KEITH, CHRISTINA
BOOKS REVIEWED
The Russet Coat
[Robert Burns] — 89 382

KEITH, JOSEPH JOEL
POEMS
To Rise — 52 260
Of One Unwed
The Sister of Witches
The Farmer

BOOKS REVIEWED
The Proud People — 63 228
The Long Nights — 64 339
Two Laughters — 95 309

KEITHLEY, GEORGE
BOOKS REVIEWED
The Donner Party — 122 173

KELLER, DAVID
POEMS
Longing — 144 84
The Doorstop in the Shape
of a Calico Cat
The Applicants
for the Correspondence Course — 148 196

KELLER, MARTHA E.
POEMS
Flinders — 25 74
Mazed
A Song for Caesar
Arachne
The Lovers
Sheep
Herbs and Simples — 64 68
Seizure
Mrs. McGraw
Small Choice
Lost Hollow
Headstone

BOOKS REVIEWED
Mirror to Mortality — 51 223
Brady's Bend and Other Ballads — 69 171
Brady's Bend and Other Ballads — 70 226

ARTICLES ABOUT
Correspondence
from Margaretta W. Wright — 70 54

KELLEY, EDITH SUMMERS
POEMS
A Wish — 37 72
A Rich Woman

KELLEY, LEONE
POEMS
Snow — 15 180

KELLEY, REEVE SPENCER
POEMS
Winesburg and Willoughby — 103 241

KELLOGG, CHARLOTTE
POEMS
Closer than Wind — 48 202
Walking Alone
Return to the Desert

KELLOGG, HANSON
POEMS
Four Disinterested Prayers — 75 205

KELLY, BRIGIT PEGEEN
POEMS
The Convent Park Beneath My Window
at the Hotel Charles — 141 205
Mount Angel
The Valiant — 144 335
Napa Valley — 146 9
Doing Laundry on Sunday — 146 159

BOOKS REVIEWED
To the Place of Trumpets — 153 229
Song — 168 33

KELLY, DAVE
BOOKS REVIEWED
Instructions for Viewing a Solar Eclipse — 122 168

KELLY, DENIS
BOOKS REVIEWED
State of the Union,
by Aimé Césaire
(Tr. with Clayton Eshleman) — 112 56

KELLY, GRACE VERONICA
POEMS
"Katey Rhue" — 30 83

KELLY, RICHARD
POEMS
   First Night   104   233

KELLY, ROBERT
BOOKS REVIEWED
   Round Dances   105   414
   Lunes
     (With *Sightings*,
       by Jerome Rothenberg)   108   191
   Lectiones   108   408
   A Controversy of Poets
     (Ed. with Paris Leary)   111   258
   Finding the Measure   114   40
   Songs   118   355
   The Common Shore   121   105
   Kali Yuga   122   293
   Flesh:Dream:Book

KELLY-DE WITT, SUSAN
POEMS
   Francis in Ecstasy   159   91
   Odalisque   164   88

KEMMERER, JOHN
BOOKS REVIEWED
   Two Stories   43   225

KEMP, HARRY
BOOKS REVIEWED
   The Cry of Youth   5   192

KEMP, LYSANDER
POEMS
   Reveille Here and Now   66   250
   On a Wall in Puerto Rico
   Landscape, Puerto Rico   68   24
   The Faulty Hag
   Tumbando Cana   71   28
   Invitation to the Dance
   The Vacation   89   230

BOOKS REVIEWED
   The Northern Stranger   70   159

KENNEDY, CELIA MARY
POEMS
   The Lie   24   251

KENNEDY, GERTA
POEMS
   Tracks   72   243

KENNEDY, KATHARINE
  [See also RUSS, PENELOPE, pseud.]
POEMS
   Luminous Body   63   78
   Image in the Waters

TRANSLATIONS
   Poems from the Zuni   50   254

KENNEDY, LEO
POEMS
   Of One Dead   35   258
   Time that Wears Granite Thin   58   14
   Three Sonnets in Sequence
     Fall Horoscope
     Afternoon of the Damned
     Winter Solstice
   End of Epos

REVIEWS
   An American Generation   63   104
     Forty Poems 1935-43,
       by Robert Knox Bishop
       and John Claiborne Davis
     Injunction, by Vincent Ferrini

BOOKS REVIEWED
   The Shrouding   44   345

KENNEDY, X. J.
POEMS
   Nude Descending a Staircase   95   224
   B Negative   97   278
   Narcissus Suitor
   At Colonus
   One A. M. with Voices   98   305
   Barking Dog Blues
   The Man in the Manmade Moon
   Ant Trap   113   325
   National Shrine
   Peace and Plenty
   On a Well-Dressed Man Much Married   132   157
   Jack and Jill
   A Word from Hart Crane's Ghost
   On Being Accused of Wit   151   75
   City Churchyard   152   6

ARTICLES
  Comment
   [Henry Rago]   151   215

REVIEWS
   Five Poets in Search of Six Lines   98   118
     Winter Sun, by Margaret Avison
     Wilderness of Ladies,
       by Eleanor Ross Taylor
     Walls and Distances,
       by David Galler
     Outlanders, by Theodore Weiss
     The Drunk in the Furnace,
       by W. S. Merwin
     The New American Poetry: 1945-1960
       (Ed. by Donald M. Allen)
       [Robert Creeley, Denise Levertov,
       Robert Duncan, Charles Olson]   98   242

Twelve from Small Presses   99   313
    The Gathering Wave,
        by Alvaro Cardona-Hine
    Early Rain, by Bert Meyers
    Wild Lace, by Natalie S. Robins
    Mountain, Fire, Thornbush,
        by Harvey Shapiro
    A Canzoniere,
        by Richard Hartley Chase
    The Newly Fallen,
        by Edward Dorn
    *One Thousand Fearful Words
        for Fidel Castro*,
        by Lawrence Ferlinghetti
    Romances, by Rooan Hurkey
    Nymph in Thy Orisons,
        by Wrenne Jarman
    Populations of the Heart,
        by Walter H. Kerr
    Stills & Movies,
        by Ralph Pomeroy
    The Penalty of Adam,
        by Frederick Staver
The Boy from Iowa,
    by Reed Whittemore   101   356
Aristophanes in American   102   56
    The Acharnians
        (Tr. by Douglass Parker)
    The Birds
        (Tr. by William Arrowsmith)
    *The Birds; The Frogs; Ladies' Day
        [Thesmophoriazusae]; and Lysistrata*
        (Tr. by Dudley Fitts)
Underestimations   103   330
    *To Mix with Time:
        New and Selected Poems*,
        by May Swenson
    On the Edge, by Philip Levine
    The Nesting Ground,
        by David Wagoner
    Collected Poems: 1925-1948,
        by Louis MacNeice
    Emblems of a Season of Fury,
        by Thomas Merton   104   378
The Poet in the Playpen   105   190
    *Puss in Boots, The Sleeping Beauty,
        & Cinderella: A Retelling
        of Three Classic Fairy Tales
        Based on the French of Charles Perrault*,
        by Marianne Moore
    Prayers from the Ark,
        by Carmen Bernos de Gasztold
        (Tr. by Rumer Godden)
    The Adventures of Tom Bombadil,
        by J. R. R. Tolkien
The Tin Can,
    by William Jay Smith   109   184
The Devalued Estate   114   266
    The Storms, by Peter Dale

Collected Poems 1967,
    by Elizabeth Jennings
Points in a Journey,
    by Keith Harrison
In Retreat and Other Poems,
    by Philip Hobsbaum
The Second Life: Selected Poems,
    by Edwin Morgan
Cages, by Ruth Fainlight
To Find the New, by Alan Bold
*A Look Round the Estate:
    Poems 1957-1967*,
    by Kingsley Amis
Just Like the Resurrection,
    by Patricia Beer
A Tenth and Four Fifths   141   349
    The Chinese Insomniacs,
        by Josephine Jacobsen
    *A Woman Under the Surface:
        Poems and Prose Poems*,
        by Alicia Ostriker
    The Fortunate Traveller,
        by Derek Walcott
    Recoveries: A Poem,
        by Theodore Weiss
    The Southern Cross,
        by Charles Wright

BOOKS REVIEWED
    Nude Descending a Staircase   100   319
    Growing into Love   117   195
    Emily Dickinson in Southern California 124 343
    *Celebrations After the Death
        of John Brennan*   128   226
    Cross Ties: Selected Poems   147   227
    Dark Horses   163   39

KENNER, HUGH
    ARTICLES
    Stele for Hephaestus
        [Wyndham Lewis]   90   306
    Correspondence:
        An Exchange on Ezra Pound   91   210
    Ghosts and Benedictions
        [Henry James, Ezra Pound,
        Eli Siegel, William Carlos Williams] 113 109
    Correspondence: Pound's Text   113   285
    Stele for Hephaestus
        [Wyndham Lewis]   121   50

    REVIEWS
    The Charity of the Stars,
        by John Heath-Stubbs   74   169
    Poets of the Pacific, Second Series
        (Ed. by Yvor Winters)   76   104
    Collected Poems,
        by William Empson
        [T. S. Eliot]   76   150

Poems: 1950, by Basil Bunting   78   361

Vaudeville for a Princess,
    by Delmore Schwartz   79   50

Paterson, Parts I-IV,
    by William Carlos Williams   80   276

Gold in the Gloom   81   127
    Confucius: Great Digest
        and Unwobbling Pivot
        (Tr. by Ezra Pound)
    Ezra Pound and the Cantos,
        by Harold H. Watts

Light on a Dark Horse, by Roy Campbell   82   169

Ezra Pound and Provision of Measures   83   29
    A Preliminary Checklist
        of the Writings of Ezra Pound
        (Ed. by John Edwards)
    The Spirit of Romance
        and Guide to Kulchur,
        by Ezra Pound

Language as Gesture,
    by R. P. Blackmur   83   238

Seedless Fruit   83   295
    The Anathemata, by David Jones
    The I Ching or Book of Changes
        (Tr. by Cary F. Baynes)
    Tu Fu, China's Greatest Poet,
        by William Hung

Some Elders   83   357
    Collected Poems,
        by Padraic Colum
    W. B. Yeats and T. Sturge Moore,
        Their Correspondence
        (Ed. by Ursula Bridge)
    Dichtung und Prosa,
        by Ezra Pound
        (Tr. by Eva Hesse)
    Women of Trachis,
        by Sophocles
        (Tr. by Ezra Pound)

Subways to Parnassus   84   43
    Approaches to Poetry,
        by Walter Blair
        and W. K. Chandler
    Understanding Poetry,
        by Cleanth Brooks
        and Robert Penn Warren
    Reading Poems,
        by Wright Thomas
        and S. G. Brown
    Preface to Poetry,
        by Charles W. Cooper
        and John Holmes
    Reading Poetry,
        by Fred Millett
    Introduction to Poetry,
        by Mark Van Doren
    Poetry as Experience,
        by N.C. Stageberg
        and W. L. Anderson

Poems for Study,
    by Leonard Unger
    and William Van O'Connor

Poetry and Life,
    by Clyde S. Kilby

Hellas Without Helicon   84   112
    Aeschylus' Oresteia
        (Tr. by Richmond Lattimore)
    The Greek Poets
        (Ed. by Moses Hadas)
    The Greek Bucolic Poets
        (Tr. by A. S. F. Gow)

Two Critics   84   179
    Coleridge, Opium, and Kubla Khan,
        by Elisabeth Schneider
    On the Four Quartets of T. S. Eliot,
        by Anonymous

Four Outsiders   84   296
    Selected Letters of Thomas Gray
        (Ed. by Joseph Wood Krutch)
    Selected Letters of William Cowper
        (Ed. by Mark Van Doren)
    Selected Letters of John Keats
        (Ed. by Lionel Trilling)
    Selected Letters of Lord Byron
        (Ed. by Jacques Barzun)

The Fables of La Fontaine
    (Tr. by Marianne Moore)   84   356

The Cocktail Party
    and The Confidential Clerk,
    by T. S. Eliot   85   47

The Classic Anthology
    Defined by Confucius
    (Tr. by Ezra Pound)   85   159

Problems in Faithfulness and Fashion   85   225
    Sophocles: Three Tragedies:
        Oedipus the King
        (Tr. by David Grene),
        Oedipus at Colonus
        (Tr. by Robert Fitzgerald),
        Antigone (Tr. by Elizabeth Wyckoff)
    Poems of the Hundred Names,
        by Henry H. Hart
    Dante's Inferno
        (Tr. by John Ciardi)
    The Metamorphoses of Ovid
        (Tr. by A. E. Watts)
    Aristophanes: Lysistrata
        (Tr. by Dudley Fitts)
        [Hookham Frere]   85   294

Plea for Metrics   86   41
    Canto 85, by Ezra Pound
    The Cultivation of Christmas Trees,
        by T. S. Eliot
    Three Elegies of Quintilius,
        by Peter Russell

Regional Muses   86   111
    New Zealand Poetry Yearbook (1953)
        (Ed. by Louis Johnson)

Twentieth Century Canadian Poetry,
   An Anthology   .
   (Ed. by Earle Birney)
Canadian Poetry in English
   (Ed. by Bliss Carman, Lorne
   Pierce, and V. B. Rhodenhizer)
Any Number Can Play   86   242
   Washington, A Poem in Six Parts,
      by Rolf Fjelde
   Short Stories, by James Merrill
   XVI Poems: A Sampler,
      by Holly Beye
   The Anatomy of Proserpine,
      by Judson Crews
   An Oxford Odyssey,
      by John Theobald
   Gold, by Christine Brooke-Rose
   The White Kid,
      by George Moor
   The Winnowing Dream,
      by Walter de la Mare
   Christmas Eve,
      by C. Day Lewis
Whitman's Multitudes   87   183
   Leaves of Grass
      One Hundred Years After
      (Ed. by Milton Hindus)
   The Solitary Singer,
      by Gay Wilson Allen
   Walt Whitman Abroad
      (Ed. by Gay Wilson Allen)
   Whitman's Manuscripts:
      Leaves of Grass, 1860
      (Ed. by Fredson Bowers)
   Walt Whitman's Concept
      of the American Common Man,
      by Leadie M. Clark
   Walt Whitman:
      A Selection of the Manuscripts,
      Books and Association Items
      (Ed. by Charles E. Feinberg)
   One-Way Song;
      The Demon of Progress in the Arts;
      and *The Human Age,* Vol. II,
      by Wyndham Lewis   87   247
   Pope's Dunciad,
      A Study of Its Meaning,
      by Aubrey Williams   88   277
   The Necklace,
      by Charles Tomlinson   88   324
   Section: Rock Drill;
      85-95 de los Cantares
      and *Sophokles' Women of Trachis,*
      by Ezra Pound   90   237
   Glow-Worms and Antimacassars   92   121
      On Poetry and Poets,
         by T. S. Eliot
      Keats,
         by John Middleton Murry

   Edwin Arlington Robinson,
      by Edwin S. Fussell
   Middleton's Tragedies,
      by Samuel Schoenbaum
   The Bloomsbury Group,
      by J. K. Johnstone
   Eras & Modes in English Poetry,
      by Josephine Miles
   Precious Rubbish,
      by Theodore L. Shaw
   The Selected Letters
      of William Carlos Williams
      (Ed. by John C. Thirlwall)   92   174
   The Pelican Guide to English Literature
      (Ed. by Boris Ford)   92   393
   Seeing is Believing,
      by Charles Tomlinson   93   335
   Gaius Valerius Catullus,
      The Complete Poetry
      (Tr. by Frank O. Copley)   94   62
   Paterson, Book Five and
      I Wanted To Write a Poem,
      by William Carlos Williams
      [Edith Heal]   94   127
   A Laughter in the Mind,
      by Irving Layton   94   413
   The Elder Statesman, by T. S. Eliot
      [Alison Leggat]   95   36
   A Marianne Moore Reader   102   109
   "A" 1-12, by Louis Zukofsky
      [Ezra Pound]   111   112
   The Earliest English Poems
      (Tr. by Michael Alexander)
      [Ezra Pound]   111   395
   James and the Children,
      by Eli Siegel   113   109

BOOKS REVIEWED
   The Translations
      of Ezra Pound (Intro.)   83   233

ARTICLES ABOUT
   [Note]   84   119
   Correspondence
      from John R. Hendrickson   91   209
   Rev. of *Selected Poems,* by Ezra Pound   91   389

KENNERLEY, MITCHELL
BOOKS REVIEWED
   The Lyric Year (Ed.)   1   128

KENNEY, JAMES C.
POEMS
   Invasion   65   9

KENNEY, RICHARD
POEMS
   The Hours of the Day   128   214

Notes from Greece   131   249
From *The Encantadas*   142   1
Ocelots, Etc.   151   76
Lucifer   159   63

ARTICLES
Comment   151   221

BOOKS REVIEWED
The Evolution of the Flightless Bird   145   291
Orrery   148   36

KENSETH, ARNOLD
POEMS
Footnote for John Smith   59   86

KENT, ARTHUR V.
POEMS
The Wild Honey of Wisdom   8   13
The Leader

KENT, H. R.
POEMS
The Spider Who Lives by Thinking   120   153
April at the Ruins   126   1

KENT, JEAN
POEMS
The Baby Magpie's Catwalk   169   46

KENT, LOUIS
POEMS
The Stair   71   69
The Clerk's Good Night   74   323
Midsummer
Leviathan North and South   76   205
Winter in Glass
American Death   78   19

BOOKS REVIEWED
Declensions of the Air   79   119

KENT, MARGARET
POEMS
The Stammerers   134   71
The Uneasy
Limits
Last Signals   137   23
Watching the Island

KENT, ROBERT
BOOKS REVIEWED
The Island Self, by Howard Blake (Ed.)   125   352

KENYON, BERNICE (LESBIA)
BOOKS REVIEWED
Songs of Unrest   25   49
Meridian: Poems 1923-1932   44   42

KENYON, FREDERICK G.
BOOKS REVIEWED
New Poems,
   by Robert Browning
   and Elizabeth Barrett Browning (Ed.)   6   45

KENYON, JANE
POEMS
Teacher   141   278
Evening Sun
Coming Home at Twilight
   in Late Summer
Inpatient   144   34
Whirligigs
Inertia   146   133
Trouble with Math
   in a One-Room Country School
On the Aisle   150   147
The Blue Bowl
After an Illness, Walking the Dog   151   78
Three Songs at the End of Summer   152   311
Having It Out with Melancholy   161   86
Reading Aloud to My Father   165   287
Happiness
Man Sleeping   167   146
The Call
Afternoon at MacDowell
Dutch Interiors
Mosaic of the Nativity: Serbia, Winter, 1993

BOOKS REVIEWED
The Boat of Quiet Hours   151   419
Let Evening Come   158   158
Constance   164   157
Otherwise: New & Selected Poems   170   226

KENYON, THEDA
BOOKS REVIEWED
Scarlet Anne   56   48

KER, W. P.
BOOKS REVIEWED
Form and Style in Poetry:
   Lectures and Notes
   (Ed. by R. W. Chambers)   34   161

KERÉNYI, C.
BOOKS REVIEWED
Essays on a Science of Mythology
   (With C. G. Jung)   77   168

KERMODE, FRANK
BOOKS REVIEWED
The Living Milton (Ed.)   115   196

KEROUAC, JACK
BOOKS REVIEWED
Mexico City Blues   98   192

KERR, HAROLD
POEMS
From the Interrogations   46   130
    Adamant Tree
    Coward
    Voice from the Womb

KERR, WALTER H.
POEMS
In Dream   119   155
The Esrever Boys on Safari
Consorting with Silences
The View from Khufu's Tongue
Xmass

BOOKS REVIEWED
Populations of the Heart   99   313

KERRIGAN, ANTHONY
POEMS
Haitian Themes   70   138
Druidical   84   78
Wildness Bred into a Plant
Childhood Vision of Virtu   96   148
Canicular Acrostic
For Two Ladies Ascending a Bus   105   167
The Zion of Echoing Sound

TRANSLATIONS
Poems by Miguel de Unamuno   101   319
Poem by Camilo José Cela   101   322

ARTICLES
The Color of Seed
    [Camilo José Cela]   101   345

REVIEWS
James Joyce, Chamber Music
    (Ed. by William York Tindall)   85   109
The Vegetable Kingdom
    and *Collected Poems,*
    by Padraic Colum   86   172

KERSHNER, BRANDON
POEMS
Dredging   138   326

KESSLER, EDWARD
POEMS
Grey Squirrel   98   141
Pain   165   327

KESSLER, JASCHA
POEMS
Requiem for an Abstract Artist   89   293
Routine Assignment   91   364
Reading   121   290

REVIEWS
Trial and Error   121   292
    Directionscore:
       Selected and New Poems,
       by Don L. Lee
    Something Human,
       by Barry Spacks
    No Jerusalem But This,
       by Samuel Menashe
    Time's Web, by Ruth Moore
    Wrecking Crew, by Larry Levis
    The Rough-Hewn Table,
       by Henry Carlile
    I Am the Bitter Name,
       by C. K. Williams
    Some Changes,
       by June Jordan

BOOKS REVIEWED
American Poems (Ed.)   106   429

KEYES, SIDNEY
BOOKS REVIEWED
Collected Poems   71   45

KEYNES, GEOFFREY
BOOKS REVIEWED
The Letters of William Blake (Ed.)   90   321
A Study of the Illuminated
    Books of William Blake:
    Poet, Printer, Prophet   107   65
The Complete Writings of William Blake
    with Variant Readings (Ed.)   111   263

KEYSNER, BLANCHE WHITING
POEMS
Frosty Morning   35   137

KHAYAAM, OMAR
BOOKS REVIEWED
The Original Rubaiyyat of Omar Khayaam,
    A New Translation with
    Critical Commentaries,
    by Robert Graves and Omar Ali-Shah   113   262

KIANG KANG-HU
TRANSLATIONS
Poems by Wang Wêi
    (Tr. with Witter Bynner)   19   235

BOOKS REVIEWED
The Jade Mountain:
    A Chinese Anthology
    (Tr. by Witter Bynner)   35   289

ARTICLES ABOUT
Rev. of *Poems by Wang Wêi*
    (Tr. by Chang Yin-nan
    and Lewis C. Walmsley)   96   309

KIDD, WALTER (EVANS)
[See also PENDLETON,
CONRAD, pseud.]
POEMS
  Words in the Wind   31   322
    Black Orchards
    Sea-Petals
    Cattle Shading In
    The Old Ranch Widow
    New England Bachelor
    Her Marble Sleep
  Cold Harvest   34   203
    The Woman at the Edge of Town
    Black Frost with Wind
    After the Freeze
    A Snowy Orchard
    Black-Raspberry Patch
  A Measure of Earth   50   144
    Praise for Stars
    Frigid Interval
    Soil Mate

REVIEWS
  Cry of Time,
    by Hazel Hall   33   272

KIKUCHI, CARL
POEMS
  Watercolor   157   333

KILBY, CLYDE S.
BOOKS REVIEWED
  Poetry and Life   84   43

KILLIGREW, ANNE
ARTICLES ABOUT
  Correspondence
    from Edouard Roditi   67   173

KILMER, ALINE
POEMS
  Charmian's Song   18   74
  For All Ladies of Shalott
  The Heart Knoweth
    Its Own Bitterness
  Novelette   21   15
    Diagonals
    Ignis Fatuus
    Week-End
    Release
    Escape
  Against the Wall   25   10
    Complaint
    Falcon

BOOKS REVIEWED
  Candles That Burn   17   276
  The Poor King's Daughter 28   48
  Selected Poems   36   102

ARTICLES ABOUT
  A Few Women Poets,
    by Harriet Monroe   26   326

KILMER, JOYCE
POEMS
  Trees   2   160
  Easter   4   14
  A Blue Valentine   9   289
  The Thorn

ARTICLES
  The Poetry
    of Gerard Hopkins   4   241

BOOKS REVIEWED
  Trees and Other Poems   5   140
  Main Street and Other Poems 11   281

ARTICLES ABOUT
  A Partisan Verdict,
    by Alice Corbin Henderson
    [Rabindranath Tagore]   7   50
  Joyce Kilmer, by Harriet Monroe 13   31
  Tribute to Joyce Kilmer,
    by Marsden Hartley   13   149
  The "Great Poem,"
    by Harriet Monroe   41   90
  Review by William Harmon 142   50

KILMER, NICHOLAS
BOOKS REVIEWED
  Poems of Pierre de Ronsard
    (Tr. and ed.)   136   40

KIM, SUE KWOCK
POEMS
  Occupation   164   193
  On Pike Street   165   274

KIMBALL, ALICE MARY
BOOKS REVIEWED
  The Devil Is a Woman   34   100

KIMBRELL, JAMES
POEMS
  Empty House   165   209
  True Descenders   165   278
  A Greeting   168   23
  Memory
  The Gatehouse Heaven 170   249

KIMMEL, STANLEY
POEMS
  Sketches from Underground 24   316
    The Secret Spring
    Joe
    In the Wheat-Field

Rust
Strike
Autumn Wind
Sketches of My People   36   186
  Dagos
  Niggers
  Little Egypt
  Going to Work at Daybreak
  Prairie
  Toil
  Illinois Central
  John Beem

BOOKS REVIEWED
  The Kingdom of Smoke:
    Sketches of My People   43   47

KIMPEL, BEN
  REVIEWS
    Beowulf: A Verse Translation
      into Modern English,
      by Edwin Morgan   83   44
    European Literature
      and the Latin Middle Ages,
      by Ernst Robert Curtius
      (Tr. by Willard R. Trask)   84   158
    Johnswood, by Charlie May Simon
      [John Gould Fletcher]   84   284

KING, FRANCIS
  POEMS
    Germinal   63   308
    Oxford   65   300
    Seance
    Villa Serbelloni   130   251
    Down by the Lake, Up at the Villa
    Intruders
    Lago di Como
    Dawn

KING, [BISHOP] HENRY
  BOOKS REVIEWED
    Poems of...
      (Ed. by James Rupert Baker)   99   187

KING, MARY PERRY
  BOOKS REVIEWED
    Earth Deities and Other Rhythmic Masques
      (With Bliss Carman)   6   205

KIN-LAU, WAN
  [See WAN KIN-LAU]

KINNELL, GALWAY
  POEMS
    The Wolves   83   145
    The Feast   84   71
    Across the Brown River   85   210

Lilacs
Alewives Pool
Canada Warbler   87   349
Ah Moon
Peer Gynt
Yesterday from My Fever
Braemar
Seven Streams of Nevis   90   346
The Descent   92   85
Where the Track Vanishes   94   170
For Ruth   95   352
The Supper After the Last
The Homecoming of Emma Lazarus   98   85
Ruins Under the Stars   103   348
The Mystic River   106   53
The Poem   108   217
The Correspondence-School Instructor
  Says Goodbye to His Poetry Students
The Poetry Shelf
In the Anse Galet Valley   110   406
In the Farmhouse
How Many Nights
The Shoes   115   114
Memories of My Father   156   341
Neverland   165   26

TRANSLATIONS
  Poems by Yves Bonnefoy   100   213

REVIEWS
  Out of America   84   163
    New England Harvest,
      by Donald C. Babcock
    Songs for a New America,
      by Charles G. Bell
  Four First Volumes   92   178
    Meditations in an Emergency,
      by Frank O'Hara
    The Hawk in the Rain,
      by Ted Hughes
    The Imagined Country,
      by Audrey McGaffin
    Time Without Number,
      by Daniel Berrigan
  On My Eyes, by Larry Eigner   100   400

BOOKS REVIEWED
  What a Kingdom It Was   97   316
  Flower Herding on Mount Monadnock   105   264
  Black Light   109   332
  The Poems of Francois Villon (Tr.)   111   124
  Body Rags   113   188
  On the Motion
    and Immobility of Douve,
    by Yves Bonnefoy (Tr.)   113   262
  The Book of Nightmares   121   105
  Lackawanna Elegy, by Yvan Goll (Tr.)   122   105

The Avenue Bearing the Initial of Christ
   into the New World: Poems 1946-1964   125   295
Mortal Acts, Mortal Words   137   297
Selected Poems   142   50
The Selected Poetry
   of Hayden Carruth (Ed.)   149   94
When One Has Lived a Long Time Alone   158   214
Imperfect Thirst   168   33

ARTICLES ABOUT
[Note]   83   305
Correspondence from Thomas Cole
   [Audrey McGaffin]   93   120

KINOSHITA, JUNJO
BOOKS REVIEWED
Playbook: Five Plays for a New Theater
   (With Lionel Abel, Robert Hivnor,
   James Merrill, and I. A. Richards)   89   253

KINSELLA, JOHN
POEMS
The Hunt   169   48
Death of a Roo Dog
Dam & Globe of Death
Drowning in Wheat
The Disappearing   170   74

ARTICLES
Towards a Contemporary
   Australian Poetics
   [Judith Wright, Michael Dransfield,
   John Tranter, Les Murray, Anthony
   Lawrence, Robert Adamson,
   John Forbes, Robert Gray, Tracy Ryan,
   Sarah Day, Jill Jones, Caroline Caddy,
   Katherine Gallagher, Dorothy Hewett,
   Peter Rose, Geoff Page, Dennis Haskell,
   A. D. Hope]   169   94

KINSELLA, THOMAS
POEMS
Mirror in February   100   102
The Force of Eloquence
Ritual of Departure   110   98
At the Ocean's Edge   151   79
[I put my hand in my bosom]   167   90
Dream
Natural Life

REVIEWS
Some Irish Poets   102   324
   A Garland for the Green,
      by Ewart Milne
   Poisoned Lands,
      by John Montague
   A James Stephens Reader
      (Ed. by Lloyd Frankenberg)

BOOKS REVIEWED
Another September   94   264
Poems and Translations   100   104
Poems and Translations   100   191
Nightwalker and Other Poems   113   262
Notes from the Land of the Dead
   and Other Poems   125   229

ARTICLES ABOUT
A Letter from Britain [II],
   by William Logan   157   290
A Map of Contemporary Irish Poetry,
   by Dennis O'Driscoll   167   94

KINSLEY, JAMES
BOOKS REVIEWED
The Poems and Songs
   of Robert Burns (Ed.)   114   191

KINSOLVING, SALLY BRUCE
POEMS
Anguish   20   307
Surprise   30   81
Tranquil   36   131

KINZIE, MARY
POEMS
Monologue Before an Innocent Being
   Prisoned in a Tree   128   317
The Advance of Summer
The Human Face   129   331
The Bamberger Reiter
Olympiad   131   93
Accidie
Chagall in His Sickness
Nature Morte
Nereid's Song   132   25
The Childhood of Homer
The Muse of Satire
Superbia: A Triumph with No Train
Their Story   136   283
Novum Organum
Old Postcard   145   257
Half Rations   154   219

REVIEWS
How Could Fools Get Tired!   132   31
   Strange Days Ahead,
      by Michael Brownstein
   Comings Back, by Albert Goldbarth
   Moon-Whales, by Ted Hughes
   The New Naked Poetry:
      Recent American Poetry in Open Forms
      (Ed. by Stephen Berg
      and Robert Mezey)
   After Our War, by John Balaban
   Goodwill, Inc., by Dennis Schmitz
   Griffon, by Stephen Dobyns

You Can't Have Everything,
  by Richard Shelton
Selected Poems, by Lucien Stryk
[Franz Kafka]
Sentences, by Howard Nemerov   138   344
Applied Poetry   154   151
  Selected Poems of Anne Sexton
    (Ed. by Diane Wood Middlebrook
    and Diana Hume George)
  I'm Deadly Serious,
    by Chris Wallace-Crabbe
  Home Free, by Diana O'Hehir
  Blood Pressure, by Sandra M. Gilbert
  It Was Fever That Made the World,
    by Jim Powell
  A Schedule of Benefits,
    by John N. Morris
  [C. S. Lewis]

BOOKS REVIEWED
  Summers of Vietnam and Other Poems   158   41

KIPLING, RUDYARD
  BOOKS REVIEWED
    The Years Between   15   277

  ARTICLES ABOUT
    "The Greatest Living Poet,"
      by Harriet Monroe   21   322
    Kipling as a Poet,
      by Harriet Monroe   48   32

KIRBY, SHEELAH
  BOOKS REVIEWED
    The Yeats Country   102   341

KIRBY-SMITH, H. T.
  POEMS
    Eric on the Drums   132   132
    The Commercial Traveler
    Remembers Lost Love

KIRCHWEY, KARL
  POEMS
    Barium   167   205

KIRK, R. R.
  ARTICLES ABOUT
    Rev. of Yanks—A Book
      of A. E. F. Verse   13   329

KIRKPATRICK, DORIS
  POEMS
    Release   38   191

KIRKUP, JAMES
  BOOKS REVIEWED
    A Spring Journey
      and Other Poems of 1952-1953   86   287

Upon This Rock   88   273
The Prodigal Son   97   260

KIRN, WALTER
  POEMS
    Small Farmer   150   272
    No Surmise
    The Detective Agency

KIRSANOV, SEMJEN
  ARTICLES ABOUT
    New Trends in Soviet Russian Poetry,
      by Vera Sandomirsky   58   324

KIRSTEIN, LINCOLN
  BOOKS REVIEWED
    Rhymes of a PFC   106   296
    Rhymes and More Rhymes of a PFC   110   267

KITAGAWA, FUYUHIKO
  POEMS
    Festival   88   85
    A Horse and the Landscape
      (Tr. by Satoru Satu
      and Constance Urdang)

KITAHARA, HAKUSHU
  POEMS
    The Water Surface   88   99
    Okaru and Kampei
      (Tr. by Satoru Satu
      and Constance Urdang)

KITASONO, KATUE
  BOOKS REVIEWED
    Black Rain   89   45

KITTO, H. D. F.
  BOOKS REVIEWED
    Greek Tragedy: A Literary Study   86   118

KIYOOKA, ROY
  BOOKS REVIEWED
    Kyoto Airs   108   45

KIZER, ASHLEY
  [MABEL ASHLEY KIZER]
  POEMS
    Lost Quarry   35   303

KIZER, CAROLYN
  POEMS
    Complex Autumnal   87   208
    The Ungrateful Garden   89   160
    The Intruder
    The Great Blue Heron   92   28
    A Widow in Wintertime
    A Muse of Water   93   380
    Love Song

Plaint of the Poet in an Ignorant Age
Two Poets by the Lake   97   224
Not Writing Poems About Children
To a Visiting Poet in a College Dormitory
After Tu Fu   103   63
Thwarted   105   163
Food of Love   118   71
Heart's Limbo
Children   134   23
Afternoon Happiness   143   156
Thrall
Bitch
A Child's Guide to Central Ohio
The Valley of the Fallen   147   63
Ingathering
Pearl   148   318
Medicine   166   144
Arthur's Party   166   256
Poem for Your Birthday   167   326

TRANSLATIONS
Poem by Edouard J. Maunick
  (Tr. with Edouard J. Maunick)   112   257
Poems by Shu Ting
  (Tr. with Y. H. Zhao)   149   253

REVIEWS
Poems Collected and New and
  Green Armor on Green Ground,
  by Rolfe Humphries   88   404
Four English Poets   91   45
  The Minute and Longer Poems,
    by John Holloway
  Devil, Maggot and Son,
    by Christopher Logue
  A Case of Samples,
    by Kingsley Amis
  Still and All, by Burns Singer
Mirrors and Windows: Poems,
  by Howard Nemerov   93   178
The Uses of Intelligence   94   250
  Poems, by Richmond Lattimore
  Poems 1947-1957,
    by William Jay Smith
  A Winter Talent, by Donald Davie
Collected Poems,
  by Hugh MacDiarmid   102   177
Poets Old and Young   102   393
  The Bluebells and Other Verse,
    by John Masefield
  A Tropical Childhood,
    by Edward Lucie-Smith
  Fairground Music, by John Fuller
  The Railings, by Alan Brownjohn
  For the Unfallen, by Geoffrey Hill
  Pantaloon, by Philip Toynbee
  The Wallace, by Sidney Goodsir Smith
  [Gene Baro]

The Feast of Domitian   119   291
  Crow, by Ted Hughes
  A Man in My Position,
    by Norman MacCaig
  The State of the Nation,
    by Alan Bold
  Memoirs in Oxford,
    by F. T. Prince
  The Last of England,
    by Peter Porter
  Penguin Modern Poets 16:
    Jack Beeching, Harry Guest,
    Matthew Mead

BOOKS REVIEWED
  The Ungrateful Garden   99   124
  Knock Upon Silence   108   269
  Midnight Was My Cry   120   296
  Yin   145   348
  YIN: New Poems   147   102
  Mermaids in the Basement:
    Poems for Women   151   360
  The Nearness of You

ARTICLES ABOUT
  [Note]   147   51

KLAPPERT, PETER
POEMS
  From The Idiot Princess
    of the Last Dynasty   133   311
    Pontius O'Connor
    Doctor O'Connor and the Laughter of War
    Saint Matthew the Paranoiac

BOOKS REVIEWED
  Lugging Vegetables to Nantucket   122   344
  The Idiot Princess of the Last Dynasty   146   38

KLAVAN, ANDREW
POEMS
  This Morning   156   125

KLEIN, A(BRAHAM) M.
POEMS
  A Sequence of Songs   35   22
    Exultation
    Exit
    Love Call
    Tremblement du Coeur
    First Sight
    Song of Love
    Quarrel
    New Version
    Doubt
    Home
    Finale
  The Psalter of A. M. Klein   58   6
    Psalm 151

Psalm 154
Psalm 155
Upon the Heavenly Scarp   59   315
Sennet from Gheel
Come Two, Like Shadows   61   595
Indian Reservation: Caughnawaga   66   318
Grain Elevator   70   175
The Cripples
For the Sisters of the Hotel Dieu
Air-Map
The Breakup
M. Bertrand
Frigidaire

ARTICLES
Correspondence   66   229

BOOKS REVIEWED
Hath Not a Jew   58   51
The Hitleriad   65   54
Poems   66   104
The Rocking Chair,
and Other Poems   75   105

ARTICLES ABOUT
The Development of Poetry
in Canada, 1880-1940,
by E. K. Brown   58   34
Rev. of New Directions 1944
(Ed. by James Laughlin)   66   161

KLEINMAN, H. H.
BOOKS REVIEWED
The Religious Sonnets
of Dylan Thomas: A Study
in Imagery and Meaning   104   264

KLEINPOPPEN, PAUL
POEMS
Anniversary   130   147
Domination of Yellow

KLEINSCHMIDT, EDWARD
POEMS
Random Panic in the U. S. A.   144   101
Tonight Insomnia   145   194
Antagonisms   146   341
The World Without
Winter Fathers, 1963   147   331
Without Thinking
University of Iowa Hospital, 1976
Departure Tax   149   206
Consider/Desire
The Prime Mover   150   133
"Nothing Is But What Is Not"   153   5
The Death of Literature   158   273
The World   162   312

KLEINZAHLER, AUGUST
POEMS
Watching Dogwood Blossoms Fall
in a Parking Lot off Route 46   164   262
The Damselfly

BOOKS REVIEWED
Red Sauce, Whiskey and Snow   168   160

KLEM, EDITH
[See HENRICH, EDITH]

KLEMER, D. J.
BOOKS REVIEWED
Chinese Love Poems (Ed.)   96   57

KLEMM, WILHELM
POEMS
Night
(Tr. by Babette Deutsch
and Avrahm Yarmolinsky)   21   141

KLIMKOWSKY, BRIAN
POEMS
El Caracol   129   136

KLINE, GEORGE L.
BOOKS REVIEWED
Selected Poems, by Joseph Brodsky (Tr.)   127   42

KLOSS, PHILLIPS
BOOKS REVIEWED
Arid   44   115

KNAPP, MARJORIE
POEMS
Tenth Birthday   44   12
Steeds   50   205

KNAUBER, CHARLES FRANCIS
POEMS
Spring Song   74   77
The Public Bird Is Not Always a Dove
The Thing X
But When in Time   75   15
Vigil   77   143

KNEVELS, MARY EASTWOOD
POEMS
Stone Walls   2   130
Rocks
Wood Paths by the Sea   10   70
The Hills

KNIBBS, H(ENRY) H(ERBERT)
BOOKS REVIEWED
Songs of the Outlands, Ballads
of the Hoboes, and Other Verse   6   45

Riders of the Stars   12   158
Songs of the Outlands
Saddle Songs   23   57

ARTICLES ABOUT
Cowboy Songs and Ballads,
    by Alice Corbin Henderson   10   255

KNIGHT, LULU W(EEKS)
POEMS
The Wind in the Trees   8   184

KNIGHT, LYNNE
POEMS
Her Story   163   263
Not Even They Could Stop It,
    and They Were Myth   165   251
O, Penelope!   167   271
Now There Were More of Them

KNISH, ANNE
[Pseud. of FICKE,
ARTHUR DAVISON]
ARTICLES ABOUT
Baiting the Public,
    by Alice Corbin Henderson   12   169
Rev. of The Spectra Hoax,
    by William Jay Smith   99   390

KNISTER, RAYMOND
POEMS
The Hawk   24   25

REVIEWS
Songs of Unrest,
    by Bernice Lesbia Kenyon   25   49
The Hills Give Promise, and Carmus:
    A Symphonic Poem,
    by Robert Silliman Hillyer   25   281
Even Excellence   25   340
    Many Wings,
        by Isabel Fiske Conant
    The Gothic Rose,
        by Wilfred Rowland Childe
    Hawaiian Hilltop,
        by Genevieve Taggard   26   108

KNODEL, ARTHUR
BOOKS REVIEWED
Saint-John Perse:
    A Study of His Poetry   110   254

KNOEPFLE, JOHN
POEMS
On the Passing of a Sternwheel Tow   93   147
Keelboatman's Horn
Little Harpe's Head
Time's Out

Children in the Leaves   99   303
The Washer of Bodies

BOOKS REVIEWED
Twenty Poems of César Vallejo
    (Tr. with James Wright
    and Robert Bly)   105   196
Rivers into Islands   108   130
The Intricate Land   120   115
Neruda and Vallejo: Selected Poems
    (Tr. with Robert Bly
    and James Wright)
    (Ed. by Robert Bly)   120   304

KNOTT, BILL
[See also SAINT GERAUD, pseud.]
BOOKS REVIEWED
Nights of Naomi (Plus 2 Songs)   120   107
Auto-Necrophilia   122   103

ARTICLES ABOUT
Review by Ralph Mills, Jr.   113   282

KNOX, ANN B.
POEMS
The Boy Brings His Blind
    Grandmother a Stone Bird   157   30
Circles   159   254
Bereave: 165   18

KNOX, CAROLINE
POEMS
I Have Met Freddy   132   105
Herbert Smith   132   283
The Fat Baby
Walden Remaindered
The Foamy-Necked Floater
Hittites
The Crybaby at the Library   133   333
Green Animals
The Phoenix
Sports
The Cavendish Club   137   152
Nancy Drew
Sol Invictus

KOBYLARZ, PHILIP
POEMS
A Bill, Posted   168   100

KOCH, KENNETH
POEMS
Poem for My Twentieth Birthday   67   80
Ladies for Dinner, Saipan
The Trip from California
Schoolyard in April   70   17
You Know All This   72   244
In Love with You   86   18

Pregnancy	87	259
The Horse	89	87
Permanently		
Meeting You at the Piers		
Gigue		
Locks	90	199
Down at the Docks		
Thanksgiving		
Thank You	94	74
You Were Wearing		
Taking a Walk with You	96	39
From "Angelica,"		
an Opera [Act II]	101	56
From Seine	106	70
Sleeping with Women	113	225
Poem for My Twentieth Birthday	121	17
From The Art of Love	121	63
The Art of Poetry	125	187
On Beauty	126	28
From The Duplications	127	311
What People Say About Paris	151	80
Talking to Patrizia	160	204
Vous Êtes Plus Beaux		
que Vous ne Pensiez	168	209

REVIEWS

New Books by Marianne Moore		
and W. H. Auden	90	47
Like a Bulwark,		
by Marianne Moore		
The Old Man's Road,		
by W. H. Auden		
Alfred and Guinevere,		
by James Schuyler	93	321

BOOKS REVIEWED

Poems	84	232
Kô, or A Season on Earth	98	192
Thank You and Other Poems	101	412
Bertha and Other Plays	110	105
When the Sun Tries To Go On	114	401
The Pleasures of Peace	119	104
Thank You and Other Poems	121	54
The Art of Love	128	290
The Duplications	132	288
On the Great Atlantic Rainway,		
Selected Poems 1950-1988	170	90

ARTICLES ABOUT

Another Word on Kenneth Koch,		
by Frank O'Hara	85	349
On Kenneth Koch Again: A Rebuttal,		
by Harry Roskolenko	86	177
Rev. of The Poets		
of the New York School		
(Ed. by John Bernard Myers)	119	39
Rev. by David Lehman	119	224

KOCH, VIVIENNE
REVIEWS

The Continuity of Poetic Language,		
by Josephine Miles	79	360
The Autobiography		
of William Carlos Williams	80	89
The Metaphysical Passion,		
by Sonia Raiziss	81	328
A Coat of Many Colors and		
Moon's Farm and Other Poems,		
by Herbert Read	89	322
Three Lives	98	59
The West-Going Heart:		
A Life of Vachel Lindsay,		
by Eleanor Ruggles		
The Third Rose:		
Gertrude Stein and Her World,		
by John Malcolm Brinnin		
The Masterpiece and the Man:		
Yeats as I Knew Him,		
by Monk Gibbon		

BOOKS REVIEWED

William Carlos Williams	76	177
William Carlos Williams	80	291
W. B. Yeats: The Tragic Phase	81	331

KOEHLER, G. STANLEY
POEMS

New Construction	90	23
Peace and the Pacific		
A Blue Day	95	156
Man Overboard		
Encounter at Salerno		

KOENIG, ELEANOR
[C. O'ROURKE]
POEMS

The Grave Woman	32	206
Two Dialogues	35	87
The Shade		
Two on an Old Pathway		
Autumn Pigeons	39	137

BOOKS REVIEWED

Herb Woman and Other Poems	30	114
Two on an Old Pathway	36	280

KOESTENBAUM, WAYNE
BOOKS REVIEWED

Ode to Anna Moffo	158	158
Rhapsodies of a Repeat Offender	165	219

KOETHE, JOHN
POEMS

Process	110	28
Your Day		
Personal Life	115	19

Satie's Suits
Summer
Mission Bay
Domes   117   89
Tiny Figures in Snow   119   187
Kinderszenen   128   22
Partial Clearance

REVIEWS
Freely Espoused   117   54
    Freely Espousing, by James Schuyler
    Poems from Deal, by David Shapiro
    The Pit and Other Poems,
        by Lucien Stryk
    A Nest of Ninnies,
        by John Ashbery
        and James Schuyler
The Poetry Room   120   49
    The World Before Us,
        by Theodore Weiss
    Briefings (Poems Small and Easy),
        by A. R. Ammons
    Earthworks, by Sandra Hochman
    The Poetry Room,
        by Lewis MacAdams, Jr.
    Laughing, by Paul Hannigan
    No Place for Hiding,
        by John L'Heureux

KOGURE, KATSUHIKO
POEMS
    The Face
        (Tr. by Satoru Satu
        and Constance Urdang)   88   69

KOHN, WALTER F.
POEMS
    The Poet Sings   27   130

KOLLER, JAMES
BOOKS REVIEWED
    Two Hands   108   125

KOLLWITZ, KÄTHE
ARTICLES ABOUT
    [Note]   143   240

KOLMAR, RICHARD
BOOKS REVIEWED
    Games   109   407

KOLODINSKY, ALISON
POEMS
    Adoption   160   151

KOLODNEY, WILLIAM
ARTICLES ABOUT
    Correspondence from Louise Bogan,
        Stanley Kunitz, and Robert Lowell 100   412

KOMUNYAKAA, YUSEF
POEMS
    Blessing the Animals   170   220
    Quatrains for Ishi   170   330

BOOKS REVIEWED
    Dien Cai Dau   156   100
    Magic City   162   167

KONDO, AZUMA
POEMS
    Poem ("In the mirror the reverse...") 88   82
    The Country
    Afternoon
        (Tr. by Satoru Satu
        and Constance Urdang)

K'ONG CHAO-NGAN
POEMS
    ("Early autumn startles the leaves...")
        (Tr. by George Margulies
        and Willard R. Trask)   46   7

KONDOS, YANNIS
POEMS
    Old Stories
        (Tr. by Kimon Friar)   151   52

KOOSER, TED
POEMS
    The Witness   143   69
    A Birthday Card
    The Sigh
    The Mouse
    The Urine Specimen
    Lobocraspis Griseifusa   166   86
    New Moon   166   217

BOOKS REVIEWED
    Weather Central   168   33

KORIYAMA, NAOSHI
TRANSLATIONS
    Poems by Sachiko Yoshihara
        and Kio Kuroda
        (Tr. with Edward Lueders)   143   320

KORN, ALBERT RALPH
ARTICLES ABOUT
    Rev. by Leslie Fiedler   77   215

KORNMANN, RUDOLPH EDWARD
POEMS
    Slow Rhythms   36   306
        Chant Before Thought
        Mother
        Whirl of Dust

KÖRÖSY, MÁRIA
TRANSLATIONS
Poem by György Petri
(Tr. with Bruce Berlind)   164   85

KORSON, GEORGE
BOOKS REVIEWED
Coal Dust on the Fiddle   63   106

KOUWENAAR, GERRIT
ARTICLES ABOUT
Down There on a Visit:
Poetry in the Netherlands,
by Turner Cassity   102   38

KOVAL, ALEXANDER
POEMS
The Elect and the Damned
(Tr. by Edouard Roditi)   88   252

KRAMER, AARON
BOOKS REVIEWED
Seven Poets in Search of an Answer
(With Maxwell Bodenheim,
Joy Davidman, Langston Hughes,
Alfred Kreymborg, Martha Millet,
and Norman Rosten)
(Ed. by Thomas Yoseloff)   64   289
Visions of Christ,
by Rainer Maria Rilke (Tr.)
(Ed. by Siegfried Mandel)   113   188

KRAMER, ARTHUR (J.)
POEMS
Moment   22   304
Shadows
The Old Age of Eve   31   143
Victory   56   124
Vampire

REVIEWS
Along the Wind,
by Chard Powers Smith   29   289
Harvest of Youth,
by Edward Davison   29   348

KRAMER, LARRY
POEMS
Wild Onions   159   149
The Public Monuments   159   207
For a Poet
of the Previous Generation   169   321

KRANES, JUDITH E.
BOOKS REVIEWED
Initial A,
by David Schubert
(Ed. with Theodore Weiss)   99   379

KRAPF, NORBERT
POEMS
Rural Lines after Brueghel   124   338

KRAUSS, RUTH
BOOKS REVIEWED
There's a Little Ambiguity
Over There Among the Bluebells   117   261

KREHBIEL, EVANS
POEMS
Ripples   12   206
That Little Girl Next Door
Logic
Travels
Trees

KRESENSKY, RAYMOND
POEMS
Pioneer Poems   35   145
Men Are Oxen
The Lean Gods
Purple Pool
Maple Blood   39   185

BOOKS REVIEWED
Emmaus   41   105

KRESH, DAVID
POEMS
The   138   92
"St. Jude Pray for Us...
Almost Without Hope"   143   18
To Rio

KREYMBORG, ALFRED ["A. K."]
POEMS
Old Manuscript   7   239
Toadstools   10   27
Love Was Dead All Day
Lanes
Again
Courtship
Sir Hobbledehoy
1914
Dirge
When the Willow Nods   11   287
Indian Sky   15   196
Cradle   15   260
To W. C. W. M. D.
Spirit
Pianissimo   20   175
Italian Stream   22   130
Madonna di Campagna   22   313
When They Require Gardens
...And White the White Invokes
Another Grieving Forest
...The Kingdom of the Air

A Ribbon Two Yards Wide
The Likeness of His Yesterdays
The Huddled Ones Behold
A Drop of Any Sea
Learning   25   73
Tobacco Smoke   27   260
Manhattan Epitaphs   30   246
    Fame
    Oblivion
    Wind and Wind
    Two Weeks
    Hobo
    Contemporary
    This Grave
    Thieves
    Poet
    Humanity
Cape Cod   32   192
    The Lost Sail
    The Hand of Understanding
Miss O'Connor at Yaddo   38   144
One Face   51   243
Slow Blue   54   197
Spring and Winter   73   76
December Tenth   87   156
Warm Sun   93   145

ARTICLES
    Correspondence [Poem]   8   158
    On Being Reviewed   11   212
    The Sixteenth to the Twentieth
        [Philip Sidney]   12   330
    Touring America on Pegasus   16   90
    Dread and Poetry   5a   aa9
    [Note on Book: Seventeen and One]   62   234

REVIEWS
    The New Poetry
        (Ed. by Harriet Monroe
        and Alice Corbin Henderson)   12   214
    Cornhuskers, by Carl Sandburg   13   155
    The Ghetto and Other Poems,
        by Lola Ridge   13   335
    A Woman of Thirty,
        by Marjorie Allen Seiffert   16   219
    Collected Poems, 1918-1938,
        by Genevieve Taggard   54   280
    From Another World:
        The Autobiography of Louis Untermeyer 55 281
    The White Stranger,
        by Kimball Flaccus   56   101
    Wheel of Paper,
        by Mary Owings Miller   75   295

BOOKS REVIEWED
    Others: An Anthology
        of the New Verse (Ed.)   8   151

Mushrooms: A Book of Free Forms   9   51
Others: An Anthology of the New Verse (Ed.) 11   274
Others   14   281
Others for 1919—An Anthology
    of New Verse (Ed.)   17   150
Plays for Merry Andrews   18   218
Less Lonely   24   269
Scarlet and Mellow   29   226
Funnybone Alley   33   164
Manhattan Men   35   168
Our Singing Strength   36   110
The American Caravan
    (Ed. with Lewis Mumford
    and Paul Rosenfeld)   38   156
The Planets: A Modern Allegory   54   164
Poetic Drama: An Anthology
    of Plays in Verse (Ed.)   60   276
Seven Poets in Search of an Answer
    (With Maxwell Bodenheim,
    Joy Davidman, Langston Hughes,
    Aaron Kramer, Martha Millet,
    and Norman Rosten)
    (Ed. by Thomas Yoseloff)   64   289
The Selected Poems 1912-1944 of...   66   215

ARTICLES ABOUT
    Rev. of Catholic Anthology—1914-1915   8   94
    Little Theatres and Poetic Plays,
        by Harriet Monroe   11   201
    Kreymborg's Plays for Poem-Mimes,
        by Marjorie Allen Seiffert   13   224
    Correspondence
        from John W. Crawford   17   287
    Kreymborg's Millions   18   174
    New International Magazines   19   224
    Poets as Prosers, by Harriet Monroe   28   328

KRIEGER, MURRAY
    BOOKS REVIEWED
        The Play and Place of Criticism   112   356
        The Play and Place of Criticism   114   113

KRIEGER, NORTON
    POEMS
        Common Threat   52   184

KRIEGER, ROBERT
    POEMS
        The Elk   85   145
        Night at the Fish Traps
        The Delay   89   103
        A Now Famous Escape
        Flowering Antler   93   153
        6 A. M.   104   161
        Some Quarrels Do Not Stop
            in Reno, Nevada
        Island Storm

KRINKIN, A(LEXANDRA) V.
REVIEWS
Selected Writings,
  by Boris Pasternak
  (Tr. by C. M. Bowra,
  Babette Deutsch, Beatrice Scott,
  and Robert Payne)   76   238
The Solstice Tree,
  by Julia Randall
  (Ed. by Mary Owings Miller)   85   366

KROGFUS, MILES
POEMS
Sun Photographs   136   90

KROLL, ERNEST
POEMS
Washington, D. C.   71   182
Miners   73   80
Homer with a Camera   83   17
April 20, 1953
Marin No More in Maine   85   131
Passing East of Hartford   90   22

BOOKS REVIEWED
The Pauses of the Eye   88   267

KROLL, JUDITH
POEMS
Akbar's Tomb   122   87
A Walk in India
Hotel Metropole   134   274
Report to the Dead
Climacteric   137   204
Thinking About History   142   146
Freedom

BOOKS REVIEWED
In the Temperate Zone   126   219

KROLOW, KARL
POEMS
Oranges Three, Lemons Two
  (Tr. by Herman Salinger)   88   253

ARTICLES ABOUT
German Lyric Poetry Since 1945,
  by Hans Egon Holthusen
  (Tr. by Herman Salinger)   88   257

KRONEN, STEVE
POEMS
London, 1943   161   153
The World's Deserts

KRONENBERGER, LOUIS
BOOKS REVIEWED
An Anthology of Light Verse (Ed.)   48   47

KRUTCH, JOSEPH WOOD
BOOKS REVIEWED
Selected Letters of Thomas Gray (Ed.)   84   296

KRZYZANOWSKI, LUDWIK
BOOKS REVIEWED
Introduction to Modern Polish Literature
  (Ed. with Adam Gillon)   110   52

**KUEFFNER, LOUISE
(MALLINCKRODT)**
POEMS
The Crag   6   226

ARTICLES
Correspondence:
  Notes on German Poetry   6   211

BOOKS REVIEWED
Moods of Manhattan   18   223

KUEPPER, PHILIP
POEMS
A Coloring Fire   125   327

KUGEL, JAMES
POEMS
A Defender of the City   115   170
From The Assemblyman   125   224
  ("A heart-beat strung...")
From The Assemblyman   126   201
  ("PSALM: Like agéd Europeans...")
Ah Gunslinger! Weary of Time

KUHLKE, R. H.
POEMS
Fall Pause   57   130
Nocturne

KUMIN, MAXINE (W.)
POEMS
One Dead Friend   96   33
My Quotable Friend
Song ("Everything imitates...")   100   26
The Spell
The Masochist   114   77
Song for Seven Parts of the Body   119   12
The Eternal Lover
Heaven as Anus   120   340
The Knot   122   333
The Selling of the Slaves
The Excrement Poem   128   250
In April, in Princeton   132   1
The Archaeology of a Marriage
Grandchild   141   148
Sundays in March   145   342
On Reading an Old Baedeker
  in Schloss Leopoldskron   148   187

The Festung, Salzburg
Night Launch
"Primitivism" Exhibit
A Calling
Marianne, My Mother, and Me   150   63
Nurture   151   83
With the Caribou
Finding the One Brief Note   157   69
The Poets' Garden   157   201
The Geographic Center
Progress
In a Different Country   164   249
Youth Orchestra, with Dogs
Cross-Country Skiing   165   131
Almost Spring, Driving Home,
    Reciting Hopkins   166   7
Chores   168   151

BOOKS REVIEWED
Halfway   99   124
The Privilege   108   121
The Retrieval System   133   227
Our Ground Time Here Will Be Brief:
    New and Selected Poems   142   50
The Long Approach   148   36
Nurture   156   36
Looking for Luck   161   99

ARTICLES ABOUT
Rev. of The Complete Poems,
    by Anne Sexton   142   170
Rev. of Sarah's Choice,
    by Eleanor Wilner   156   224

KUN, LU [See LU KUN]

KUNISCH, HERMANN
ARTICLES ABOUT
The Still Voice of German Poetry,
    by Edouard Roditi   68   208

KUNITZ, STANLEY [J.]
POEMS
The Moon at the Door   34   181
    Vita Nuova
    Prophecy on Lethe
    Poem ("O heart: this is a dream...")
    Twilight
    First Love
    Postscript
    A Daughter of the Sun Is She
    Last Words
Nameless Men   44   299
    The Guilty Man
    The Old Clothes Man
    The Man in the Park
The Harsh Judgment   58   59
My Surgeons

The Last Question
The Tutored Child
The Illusionist
The Supper Before Last
Reflection by a Mailbox   62   268
The Daughters of the Horseleech
This Day This World
Between the Acts
"What Have You Done?"
The Thief   87   254
Goose Pond
Off Point Lotus
The Dark and the Fair   90   1
A Spark of Laurel
The Approach to Thebes
Three Floors   101   61
After the Last Dynasty
Robin Redbreast   115   92
The Game
The Mulch

TRANSLATIONS
Poems by Anna Akhmatova
    (Tr. with Max Hayward)   122   96

ARTICLES
A Lesson from Rilke   45   328
Correspondence
    to William Kolodney
    (With Louise Bogan
    and Robert Lowell)   100   412

REVIEWS
The Collected Poems of Edith Sitwell   37   339
Chelsea Rooming House,
    by Horace Gregory   38   41
Vale and Other Poems, by AE
    [George William Russell]   38   276
The Poems of Wilfred Owen   40   159
Naked Heel, by Leonora Speyer   41   100
Six English Poets   42   228
    Farewell My Muse, by Clifford Bax
    Islands, by Wilfrid Gibson
    Changing Horizons,
        by Geoffrey Johnson
    The Ninth Witch,
        by Edward Davison
    Transvaluations,
        by J. Redwood Anderson
    The Captive Shrew,
        by Julian Huxley
Proud Horns, by Carleton Drewry   42   339
Collected Poems of Harold Monro
    (Ed. by Alida Monro)   44   162
A Mountain Township, by Walter Hard   45   57
Thing of Sorrow, by Elder Olson   45   279
A Winter Diary and Other Poems,
    by Mark Van Doren   47   46

Collected Poems 1929-1933
  and *A Hope for Poetry*,
  by C. Day Lewis   47   158
The Poems of... and *Love Poems*,
  by W. H. Davies   48   232
Vigils, by Siegfried Sassoon   48   292
In Sight of Mountains,
  by C. A. Millspaugh   50   43
Time in the Rock, by Conrad Aiken   50   103
The Ten Principal Upanishads
  (Tr. by Shree Purohit Swami
  and W. B. Yeats)   51   216
From These Roots: The Ideas
  That Have Made Modern Literature,
  by Mary M. Colum   52   86
Poems 1930-1940,
  by Horace Gregory   58   152
What Are Years,
  by Marianne Moore   59   96
Be Angry at the Sun,
  by Robinson Jeffers   59   148
Poems and New Poems,
  by Louise Bogan   60   40
Five Young American Poets,
  Second Series 1941
  [Paul Goodman, Jeanne McGahey,
  Clark Mills, David Schubert,
  Karl Shapiro]   60   215
The Flowering of the Rod, by H. D.   70   36
The Lost Son and Other Poems,
  by Theodore Roethke   73   222
Annie Allen, by Gwendolyn Brooks   76   52
Thanatopsis, by Herbert Cahoon   76   229
Viaticum, by Robert Thom
Five Points of the Compass   88   183
  Cycle for Mother Cabrini,
    by John Logan
  Exiles and Marriages, by Donald Hall
  The Kitchen Dance,
    by Robert Hutchinson
  The Deaths at Paragon, Indiana,
    by John Woods
  Prefabrications, by Josephine Miles
  Homage to Mistress Bradstreet,
    by John Berryman   90   244

BOOKS REVIEWED
  Intellectual Things   36   218
  Passport to the War   64   165
  Selected Poems 1928-1958   93   174
  Antiworlds, by Andrei Voznesensky
    (Tr. with others)   110   40
  Poems of Akhmatova,
    by Anna Akhmatova
    (Tr. with Max Hayward)   124   232
  The Poems of Stanley Kunitz 1928-1978   136   347
  Passing Through: The Later Poems
    New and Selected   169   286

ARTICLES ABOUT
  "Sacred Beings":
    Writers in Recorded Conversation,
    by Michael Milburn   146   101

KUNTZ, JOSEPH M.
  BOOKS REVIEWED
    Poetry Explication
      (Ed. with George Arms)   77   289

KUO MO-JO
  ARTICLES ABOUT
    Contemporary Chinese Poetry,
    by Harold Acton   46   39

KUPPNER, FRANK
  ARTICLES ABOUT
    A Letter from Britain [II],
    by William Logan   157   290

KURODA, KIO
  POEMS
    A Guerrilla's Fantasy
      (Tr. by Naoshi Koriyama
      and Edward Lueders)   143   321

KURUP, G. SANKARA
  POEMS
    The Moment
      (Tr. by T. K. Balakrishnan)   93   259

KUSHNER, ALEKSANDR
  POEMS
    I Sat on the Edge of My Seat   124   218
    In the Hotel
    Compared with the Signs of Winter
    Long Does the Prose-Writer Write
    Flora
    On a Dark-Blue December Morning
    We're Not Entertained by the News
    I See the Twelfth Century Distinctly
      (Tr. by Daniel Weissbort)

KUSHNER, DALE
  POEMS
    Ravaged Sarajevo   164   192

KUTCHINS, LAURIE
  POEMS
    Summerless   168   228

KUUSISTO, STEPHEN
  POEMS
    Summer at North Farm   154   273

KUZMA, GREG
  POEMS
    My Father and I Steal
      an Engine from a Sawmill   114   368

In the Morning   116   160
Hose and Iron
The Pelican   118   151
The Map
Nightfall
Midnight
After Midnight in a Small Town
Poetry   119   125
Turning Off the TV
The Process   120   86
House
The Age of Carpets
The Face
Peace, So That   120   329
The New House   122   134
The Abandoned Farm   123   215
Asparagus Beside the Road
The Coming of Night   124   79
Summer
The Weak
Melons
The Brook   125   336
Another Day
August   128   97
The Dump
From Translations from the English   148   277
A Day in Late November   151   85
Hearing Sirens   156   149

REVIEWS
The Catastrophe of Rainbows,
    by Martha Collins   148   342

BOOKS REVIEWED
Sitting Around   117   392
Good News   125   166
The Buffalo Shoot   128   226
Village Journal   134   107
Adirondacks   136   170

ARTICLES ABOUT
Correspondence
    from Barri Armitage, Sharon Dunn,
    Celia Gilbert, Mark Jarman,
    and Lloyd Schwartz
    [Martha Collins]   149   180

KWAN, MOON
    [See MOON KWAN]

KWEI CHEN
POEMS
Whiffs   33   139
    On Reading Romeo and Juliet
    Fragrance
    Solitude

KWÔCK, C. H.
BOOKS REVIEWED
Why I Live on the Mountain,
    30 Chinese Poems
    (Tr. with Vincent McHugh)   96   57

KYGER, JOANNE
POEMS
The Pigs for Circe in May   108   175

KYLE, CHRISTIANE JACOX
POEMS
A Late Epithalamion   164   135

BOOKS REVIEWED
Bears Dancing
    in the Northern Air   160   284

KYNETT, BARBARA
POEMS
The Roads Taken   141   328

L

"L. H. B."
BOOKS REVIEWED
Joyful Sorrow (Ed.) 18 106

"L. U."
[See UNTERMEYER, LOUIS]

LABE, LOUISE
BOOKS REVIEWED
Sonnets
(Tr. by Frederic Prokosch) 73 364

LA BELLE, CHRISTINE
BOOKS REVIEWED
The Difference Between 112 274

LA BOMBARD, JOAN
POEMS
The Sibyl 92 89
If We Were Water-Voice

LACHMANN, VERA
ARTICLES ABOUT
Rev. of *No Traveller*,
by Richard Howard 155 283

LACOSTE, HENRY DE BOUILLANE DE
[See DE LACOSTE,
HENRY DE BOUILLANE]

LADD, GABRIELLE
POEMS
The College Greenhouse: March 97 347

LADD, MIKE
POEMS
From *Shadow Stories* 169 53
Angela
Plato's Cave

LADER, BRUCE
POEMS
Wait Till You're Twenty-One 164 153

LAEDLEIN, LAURA LANDIS
POEMS
Time 23 133

LA FARGE, CHRISTOPHER
POEMS
Portraits 56 250

BOOKS REVIEWED
Hoxsie Sells His Acres 45 228
Each to the Other: A Novel in Verse 56 281
Poems and Portraits 57 270

LAFFITTE, SOPHIE
TRANSLATIONS
Poem by Anna Akhmatova
[In French] 98 376

LA FOLLETTE, MELVIN WALKER
POEMS
Didactic Sonnet 84 198
Shark Eggs
Dear Ronn,
Portage 88 26
Lake Beaver
Elegy ("Your ace of hearts...") 99 25

BOOKS REVIEWED
The Clever Body 96 375

LA FONTAINE
[JEAN DE LA FONTAINE]
BOOKS REVIEWED
The Fables of...
(Tr. by Marianne Moore) 84 356

ARTICLES ABOUT
Rev. of *La Fontaine:
The Man and His Work*,
by Monica Sutherland 85 55

LAFORGUE, JULES
POEMS
The Clowns
(Tr. by William Jay Smith) 78 210

ARTICLES ABOUT
Irony, Laforgue,
and Some Satire,
by Ezra Pound 11 93

Notes on the Metaphysics
of Jules Laforgue,
by Edwin Morgan   69   266
Jules Laforgue,
by Wallace Fowlie   78   216
Rev. of *Jules Laforgue
and the Ironic Inheritance*,
by Warren Ramsey   83   331
French Chronicle:
Recent Publications,
by Wallace Fowlie   91   36
Recent French Publications,
by Wallace Fowlie   93   40

LAGDEN, MERVYN
POEMS
Sea-Church   79   332
The Roman Villa

LAING, A. K.
POEMS
Thoughts Locking Antlers   28   131
Mountain Moment

LAING, ALEXANDER
REVIEWS
Fandango, by Stanley Vestal   33   158
The Legend of Quincibald,
by Leonard Bacon   33   343
Sweet Water and Bitter,
by Virginia Moore   34   53
Peeps at Parnassus,
by Olga Katzin   34   175
Machinery, by MacKnight Black   34   183
O City Cities,
by R. Ellsworth Larsson   35   230
New Legends, by Hervey Allen   35   342
Buck Fever,
by Henry Morton Robinson   36   107

BOOKS REVIEWED
Fool's Errand   35   54
Wine and Physic:
A Poem and Six Essays
on the Fate of Our Language   45   294

LAING, DILYS (BENNETT)
POEMS
Nautilus   60   23
Eros Out of the Sea   64   137
Occult Adventure   65   191
Genesis and Exodus   68   11
Root and Branch
The Bell
Rescue   72   74
The Uncreation
Welcome Song
Harsh Return   75   332

Time Is All a Year   79   321
The Proud
To Dolores Preserved
Dance of Burros   81   174
Afternoon of a Forethinker   82   72
Capsule Dragon   82   255
Saint Giotto of Assisi   83   256
I Shall Know
The Catch   85   13
Picasso's Candlefire   97   362
The Swift Ships
Flowers out of Rock   104   14

BOOKS REVIEWED
Another England   60   344
Birth Is Farewell   66   51
Walk Through Two Landscapes   76   231
Poems from a Cage   101   209
Collected Poems   113   338

LAIRD, WILLIAM [Pseud.]
POEMS
A Very Old Song   2   129
Traumerei at Ostendorff's   4   219
Ascription
Buds   7   233

LAKE, LAURA
POEMS
Petition   81   355

LAKE, PAUL
POEMS
Narcissus Reflets   163   163

LAL, P.
POEMS
The Chinese Doll   93   247

BOOKS REVIEWED
The Dhammapada (Tr.)   112   347

LALLEY, JOSEPH M.
BOOKS REVIEWED
Selected Poetry,
by Roy Campbell (Ed.)   113   262

LAMANTIA, PHILIP
BOOKS REVIEWED
Erotic Poems   70   47
Ekstasis   96   238
Destroyed Works   102   182
Touch of the Marvelous   110   105
The Blood of the Air   120   164

ARTICLES ABOUT
Correspondence
from Allen Ginsberg   103   271

LAMAR, FRANCES KITCHELL
POEMS
  Earth Dominant   46   237
    Outworn Tune
    Betrayal
    Solet
    Child
    Tomb's Changeling
    Bones of the Year
    Double
    Darkness-Hearted
    Death in Black Rain
    Mad Song
  New Folklore   49   307
    Sceptic
    Progress
    To a Child, Wishing
    Old Man

LAMARTINE
[See DE LAMARTINE, ALPHONSE]

LAMB, JESSICA
POEMS
  The Opening Question   158   277

LAMDAN, YITZHAK
POEMS
  In the Hot Wind   92   217
  Israel
    (Tr. by Ruth Finer Mintz)

LAMONT, JESSIE
[See LEMONT, JESSIE]

LAMONT, [MRS.] THOMAS W.
ARTICLES
  Correspondence
    [Laurence Binyon]   67   290

LAMPMAN, ARCHIBALD
BOOKS REVIEWED
  At the Long Sault   64   171

ARTICLES ABOUT
  The Development of Poetry
    in Canada, 1880-1940,
    by E. K. Brown   58   34

LAMPMAN, REX H.
ARTICLES
  Correspondence:
    With the Army of Occupation
    [Poem]   14   113

LANDIS, PAUL
BOOKS REVIEWED
  Illini Poetry 1924-9 (Ed.)   38   282

LANDOR, WALTER SAVAGE
BOOKS REVIEWED
  The Shorter Poems of...
    (Ed. by J. B. Sidgwick)   72   336

LANE, MERVIN
POEMS
  Pushing Upward   125   280
  The Receptive

LANE, RED
BOOKS REVIEWED
  Collected Poems   115   353

LANG, JON
POEMS
  Winter Night   130   23
  Winter Tree
  Winter Music
  Winter Landscape

LANG, V. R.
POEMS
  The Suicide   74   69
  Philosopher-King
  At the Meeting of Two Families   75   81
  The Pitch   75   266
  The Elizabethans and Illusion   76   130
  Incantation to an Age of Stone
  25 Years   81   116
  Already Ripening Barberries Are Red   83   131
  Waiting and Peeking   84   77
  I Too Have Lived in Arcadia   86   27
  Poem ("Lately by language...")   89   367
  Pique-Dame
  Death of Another Swan—Miami
  From Poems to Preserve the Years at Home
  Poem ("Then all the listening...")

BOOKS REVIEWED
  The Pitch: Poems and Plays   102   182

LANGBRIDGE, ROSAMOND
POEMS
  The White Moth   20   194
  The Gentle Housewife

LANGE, VICTOR
BOOKS REVIEWED
  The Sorrows of Young Werther;
    The New Melusina; Novelle,
    by J. W. von Goethe (Tr.)   75   232

LANGGASSER, ELIZABETH
ARTICLES ABOUT
  German Lyric Poetry Since 1945,
    by Hans Egon Holthusen
    (Tr. by Herman Salinger)   88   257

LANGLAND, JEAN R.
BOOKS REVIEWED
Contemporary Portuguese Poetry
(Ed. and tr.)   113   35

LANGLAND, JOSEPH
POEMS
The Moving Hand   57   355
Dry Grass   64   140
Light in Autumn   81   295
A Little Homily for the
Holy Seasons of the Spirit   84   141
Any Hot Springs: A Bellhop's Portrait   84   332
Willows
Odour of Cut Flowers   85   148
In the Park
Choice   89   358
Myself in You   96   88
Ballad of Poor Will   98   277
The Wheel of Summer   101   259
Singing in Late Summer   105   237
From Conversations in Half-Song   111   363
At the American Well
A Luncheon Date
From Conversations from Childhood
The Victrola

REVIEWS
Poems, Books of Poems,
and Character   103   256
Mexico & North,
by Clayton Eshleman
Poems: The Locations of Things,
Archaics, The Open Skies,
by Barbara Guest
Three Ages of Lake Light,
by David Ross

BOOKS REVIEWED
The Green Town,
in Poets of Today, III   89   244
Poet's Choice
(Ed. with Paul Engle)   103   261
The Wheel of Summer   103   387

LANGLAND, WILLIAM
ARTICLES ABOUT
Chaucer and Langland,
by Harriet Monroe   6   297

LANGLAS, JAMES
POEMS
Waiting To Adopt a Child   156   21
A Loss of Memory   160   3
Sickness
Connections   160   150
Crossing   164   148
Another Birthday

LANGTON, DANIEL J.
POEMS
A Day Dream   98   142
First Things   133   32
Again
Everything Is Clear Except Events   159   30

LANIER, DAVID
POEMS
This Far, in Snow   167   134

LANIER, LARRY
POEMS
The Deathing   126   81
Field Guide
Summer Night
The Fish   129   89
The Pen King
Household

LANIER, SIDNEY
ARTICLES ABOUT
Poetry South,
by Hervey Allen
and DuBose Heyward   20   35
Rev. of After the Lost War: A Narrative,
by Andrew Hudgins   153   30

LANYON, CARLA LANYON
POEMS
The Dancer   47   249

BOOKS REVIEWED
The Crag   48   49

LANZ, HENRY
BOOKS REVIEWED
The Physical Basis of Rime   38   346

LAO TZU
BOOKS REVIEWED
The Way of Life
(Tr. by Witter Bynner)   66   40
The Way and Its Power,
a Study of the Tao Te Ching
and Its Place in Chinese Thought,
by Arthur Waley   93   408

LAPE, FRED
BOOKS REVIEWED
Barnyard Year   77   215

LAPIN, ADAM
POEMS
Only His Breath   40   20

LARBAUD, VALERY
POEMS
Four Poems of a Multimillionaire   85   249
My Muse

The Gift of Oneself
The Death of Atahuallpa
Poet's Wish
   (Tr. by William Jay Smith)

ARTICLES ABOUT
  Rev. of *Le Cahiers de la Pléiade*
   (Ed. by Jean Paulhan)
   [St.-John Perse]   79   43
  French Chronicle: Recent Publications,
   by Wallace Fowlie   88   408

LARDAS, KONSTANTINOS
  BOOKS REVIEWED
  And In Him, Too; In Us   107   183

LARKIN, MARGARET
  POEMS
  Nikral ("These are the charming...")   24   132
  A Snake Poem
  If Only   28   200
  For One Too Faithful
  Nikral ("Nikral in her narrow bed...")

LARKIN, PHILIP
  BOOKS REVIEWED
  The Less Deceived   89   193
  The Whitsun Weddings   106   294
  Collected Poems
   (Ed. by Anthony Thwaite)   155   408

  ARTICLES ABOUT
  Rev. of *Poets of the 1950's:*
   An Anthology of New English Verse
   (Ed. by D. J. Enright)   89   260
  Contemporary British Poetry:
   A Romantic Persistence?
   by John Bayley   146   227

LAROCCHI, MARICA
  POEMS
  Da *In questa forma/*
   From *In This Way*   155   114
  Don't Jump Out of Your Skin
  Sailing to Aphinar
   (Tr. by Beverly Allen)

LARSON, ANN
  POEMS
  Prologue   78   91

**LARSSON, RAYMOND
E(LLSWORTH) F.**
  POEMS
  Leda   30   67
  From *The Various Tree*   43   203
  Tufts of Sunlight   46   248
  Compline of the Men of Peace   52   179

BOOKS REVIEWED
  O City Cities   35   230
  Wherefore: Peace   43   225
  Weep and Prepare   57   394
  Book Like a Bow Curved   100   395

ARTICLES ABOUT
  The Federal Poets' Number,
   by John Peale Bishop   52   276
  Correspondence from August Derleth
   [Reuel Denney]   58   170

LASCH, CHRISTOPHER
  ARTICLES ABOUT
  Waking Up Over the *Aeneid*,
   by Paul Breslin   143   347

LASDUN, JAMES
  ARTICLES ABOUT
  A Letter from Britain [II],
   by William Logan   157   290

LASSON, ROBERT
  POEMS
  Italian Child's Ditty   72   129
  God Shed His Grace on Me

LATHAM, AGNES M. C.
  ARTICLES ABOUT
  Toward Posthumous Fame,
   by Jessica Nelson North
   [Walter Ralegh]   34   335

LATHEM, EDWARD CONNERY
  BOOKS REVIEWED
  Robert Frost: Farm-Poultryman
   (Ed. with Lawrance Thompson)   104   253

  ARTICLES ABOUT
  Rev. of *Collected Poems, Prose, & Plays,*
   by Robert Frost
   (Ed. by Richard Poirier
   and Mark Richardson)   168   232

LATTIMORE, RICHMOND
  POEMS
  Symbols   45   72
   The Eidolon Again
   Dyad
  Past and Present   49   254
   Prelude for a History
   Two Octobers
  The Brink   77   76
  The Pearl
  Sea Changes   88   13
  Marginals
  Leilah
  Landscape with Story

Note on the L and N
Three Greek Virgins   92   149
Green and White   95   75
The Pillow and the Book
Easter   98   7
Remorse
Failure
The First Seven Years
Wild Mourning Doves
The Painter's Eye
Wabash Blues   102   369
Of Seven Sins   106   185
The Sticks
Coastal Stuff   134   256
Sliding Scales
Western Ways
Flesh Tones   138   149
Bone Structure

TRANSLATIONS
Poem from The Iliad, Book 22   79   63
Poem by Arnaut Daniel   101   63

REVIEWS
The Alcestis of Euripides
   (Tr. by Dudley Fitts
   and Robert Fitzgerald)   50   108
Ion of Euripides (Tr. by H. D.)   51   160

BOOKS REVIEWED
Some Odes of Pindar (Tr.)   62   282
The Odes of Pindar (Tr.)   70   340
Aeschylus' Oresteia (Tr.)   84   112
Alcestis (Tr.)   86   303
Greek Lyrics (Tr.), and Helen (Tr.),
   in Euripides (Vol. II)   88   337
Poems   94   250
The Poetry of Greek Tragedy   95   190
The Trojan Women (Tr.),
   in The Complete Greek Tragedies:
   Euripides III
   (Ed. with David Grene)
Rhesus (Tr.),
   in The Complete Greek Tragedies
   (Ed. with David Grene)
Aristophanes: The Frogs (Tr.)   102   54
Sestina for a Far-Off Summer   102   250
The Revelation of John (Tr.)   107   264
The Stride of Time   109   401
The Odyssey of Homer (Tr.)   114   113
Poems from Three Decades   122   237
Continuing Conclusions:
   New Poems and Translations   145   161

LAUGHLIN, J(AMES)
[JAMES LAUGHLIN IV]
POEMS

Easter in Pittsburgh   55   314

The Avalanche   66   72
The Shape of Love
The Prisoner   77   325
How Fortunate   89   150
A Long Night of Dreaming   132   5
The Person   136   157
The Child   139   222
No My Dear   142   166
You Came as a Thought   144   133
Absolute Love   149   251
Request for Confirmation
My Ambition   151   87
Then and Now   153   325
The Sacks   156   145
Ave Atque Vale
Layers   157   342
Little Bits of Paper   160   74
The Shameful Profession
The Lost Song   163   82
Anima Mea   165   210
The Calendar of Fame
Those To Come   168   25

ARTICLES
Gists and Piths:
   From the Letters
   of Pound and Williams   139   229

BOOKS REVIEWED
New Directions
   in Prose and Poetry (1936) (Ed.)   51   45
New Directions
   in Prose and Poetry, 1937 (Ed.)   51   311
New Directions, 1938 (Ed.)   53   209
New Directions, 1940 (Ed.)   58   164
New Directions 1941 (Ed.)   60   165
New Directions, 1942 (Ed.)   61   693
New Directions 1944 (Ed.)   66   161
New Directions 9 (Ed.)   68   352
Certaines Choses Naturelles
   (Tr. by Alain Bosquet)   105   125
A New Directions Reader
   (Ed. with Hayden Carruth)   106   429
Selected Poems   135   297
Selected Poems: 1935-1985   149   94
The Owl of Minerva   152   98
Collected Poems   165   289
The Man in the Wall
The Country Road   170   37

ARTICLES ABOUT
[Note]   55   223
[Note on misprint]   66   174

LAUGHLIN, LEILA
REVIEWS

From the Bengali   111   407

One Hundred and One:
  Poems by Rabindranath Tagore
  (Ed. by Humayun Kabir)
In Praise of Krishna:
  Songs from the Bengali
  (Ed. and tr. by Edward C. Dimock
  and Denise Levertov)
Moon, For What Do You Wait?:
  Poems by Tagore
  (Ed. by Richard Lewis)
  [W. B. Yeats, Ezra Pound]

LAURANS, PENELOPE
ARTICLES
  Memorial Service
    for Elizabeth Bishop
    [Robert Lowell]   135   227

REVIEWS
  Selected Poems,
    by James Laughlin   135   297

LAURIE, PETER
POEMS
  Noel   133   160
  Pomona
  Exile
  On the Death of the Poet   134   213

LAUTRÉAMONT, (COMTE) DE
[See DE LAUTRÉAMONT,
(COMTE)]

LAVAUD, GUY
ARTICLES ABOUT
  Correspondence from Jean Catel   16   343

LAWDER, DOUGLAS
POEMS
  Trying To Write Again   113   22
  Traveling Without Lights

LAWNER, LYNNE
POEMS
  From *Cracked Obelisk at Aswan*   134   249
  Sorceress   137   269

BOOKS REVIEWED
  Wedding Night of a Nun   105   201

LAWRENCE, ANTHONY
POEMS
  Baiting Bush Rats   169   56
  The Sapphic Stanza
  Insects
  Signatures

ARTICLES ABOUT
  Towards a Contemporary
    Australian Poetics,
    by John Kinsella   169   94

LAWRENCE, D(AVID) H(ERBERT)
POEMS
  Green   3   115
  All of Roses
  Fireflies in the Corn
  A Woman and Her Dead Husband
  The Wind, the Rascal
  The Mother of Sons
  Illicit
  Birthday
  Grief   5   102
  Memories
  Weariness
  Service of All the Dead
  Don Juan
  Song ("Love has crept...")
  Resurrection   10   139
  Moonrise   12   186
  People
  Tommies in the Train   13   258
  War Baby
  Obsequial Chant
  Bread Upon the Waters
  Pentecostal
  Nostalgia
  War Films   14   178
    Mother's Son in Salonika
    Casualty
    Message to a Perfidious Soldier
    The Jewess and the V. C.
    Sighs
    The Child and the Soldier
    Zeppelin Nights
    Daughter of the Great Man
    Prisoner at Work in a Turkish Garden
    Mourning
    The Grey Nurse
    Neither Moth nor Rust
  The Evening Land   21   59
  Turkey-Cock
  Saint Matthew   22   27
  Birthday   121   18

BOOKS REVIEWED
  Love Poems and Others   2   149
  Some Imagist Poets—An Anthology 6   150
  Some Imagist Poets: 1916   8   255
  Amores   9   264
  Some Imagist Poets, 1917   11   339
  Look! We Have Come Through!   12   269
  Some Imagist Poets   14   281
  New Poems   18   336
  Birds, Beasts and Flowers   23   273
  Collected Poems   35   273
  Pansies
  Imagist Anthology 1930
    (With Richard Aldington, John Cournos,
    H. D., John Gould Fletcher, F. S. Flint,
    Ford Madox Ford, James Joyce,
    and William Carlos Williams)   36   213

Last Poems
  (Ed. by Richard Aldington
  and Giuseppe Orioli)   42   163
Studies in Classic American Literature   83   347
The Complete Poems of...
  (Ed. by Vivian De Sola Pinto
  and F. Warren Roberts)   106   218
Poems Selected for Young People
  (Ed. by William Cole)   112   127

ARTICLES ABOUT
  Our Contemporaries:
    Autumn Leaves from England   7   99
  Visitors from the Other Side,
    by Harriet Monroe   15   93
  D. H. Lawrence, by Harriet Monroe   36   90
  An Elegy for D. H. Lawrence,
    by William Carlos Williams   45   311
  Moods and Reactions,
    by Stephen Spender   67   88
  The Isolation of Isaac Rosenberg,
    by Horace Gregory   68   30
  Poetry on Records,
    by Harry T. Moore   79   353
  The Poetry of Kenneth Rexroth,
    by Lawrence Lipton   90   168
  The Unemployed Magician,
    by Karl Shapiro   91   194
  Rev. of The Sorrows of Priapus,
    by Edward Dahlberg   94   54
  Rev. of D. H. Lawrence,
    the Failure and Triumph of Art,
    by Eliseo Vivas   100   50
  Rev. of Dream Work, by Mary Oliver   150   182
  The Forging of H. D.,
    by Gloria G. Fromm   153   160

LAWRENCE, FRIEDA
ARTICLES ABOUT
  Poetry on Records, by Harry T. Moore   79   353

LAWRENCE, GORDON
POEMS
  Ginkgo   37   202

LAWRENCE, HARRIET PAINE
POEMS
  Stars in the Sea   23   83

LAWRENCE, REBECCA PARK
POEMS
  Ecce Mysterium   6   176

LAWRENCE, T. E.
ARTICLES ABOUT
  Rev. of Lawrence, the Last Crusade,
    by Selden Rodman, and Ornament
    of Honor, by E. H. R. Altounyan   50   285

Rev. of Homer: The Odyssey:
  A New Translation
  (Tr. by E. V. Rieu)   72   28

LAWSON, PAUL
POEMS
  The Cloud   113   396
  Survey

LAYTON, IRVING
POEMS
  Drill Shed   63   256
  Newsboy
  The Swimmer   66   123

BOOKS REVIEWED
  Here and Now   67   282
  In the Midst of My Fever   89   45
  The Improved Binoculars   90   386
  A Laughter in the Mind   94   186
  A Laughter in the Mind   94   413
  A Red Carpet for the Sun   98   192
  The Shattered Plinths   115   353
  A Wild Peculiar Joy   144   297

LAZDA, ZINAIDA
ARTICLES ABOUT
  [Note]   93   413

LEA, SYDNEY
POEMS
  Over Brogno   150   93

LEA, THOMAS C.
["T. C. L."]
REVIEWS
  1000 Years of Irish Poetry
    (Ed. by Kathleen Hoagland)   73   53

ARTICLES ABOUT
  For the Record,
    by George Dillon   73   28

LEACOCK, STEPHEN
BOOKS REVIEWED
  Hellements of Hickonomics:
    In Hiccoughs of Verse Done in
    Our Social Planning Mill   50   210

LEADER, PAULINE
POEMS
  The Rejected Lover: A Block of Images   31   256
  The Delusion
  Poem to Emily Dickinson   36   85

LEANDRO IPUCHE, PEDRO
BOOKS REVIEWED
  Alas Nuevas   22   226

LEAR, DAVID
POEMS
Casual Seed   46   76
Laocoon
Venus Pandemos

LEARY, PARIS
POEMS
Aunt Honey Van Lear   100   288
Oxford Commination   135   283
Gaudeamus Igitur

BOOKS REVIEWED
Views of the Oxford Colleges
    and Other Poems,
    in Poets of Today VII   99   178
A Controversy of Poets
    (Ed. with Robert Kelly)   111   258
The Snake at Saffron Walden   127   98

LEAVENWORTH, COMAN
POEMS
Admonition   61   485
The Repeating Heart   68   192
In the Garden   71   188

LEAVIS, F. R.
ARTICLES
English Letter
    [W. H. Auden, Ronald Bottrall]   43   215
English Letter
    [T. S. Eliot]   44   98
English Letter
    [Cecil Day Lewis, Stephen Spender,
    Naomi Mitchison, William Empson,
    Isaac Rosenberg]   46   274

BOOKS REVIEWED
New Bearings in English Poetry:
    A Study of the Contemporary Situation   41   112
How To Teach Reading:
    A Primer for Ezra Pound   44   53
Revaluation: Tradition
    and Development in English Poetry   72   41

ARTICLES ABOUT
Correspondence
    from William Carlos Williams   44   174
Toward Standards of Criticism,
    by M. D. Zabel   45   40
The Little Magazine
    as a Cultural Journal,
    by William Van O'Connor   72   339
The Cantabrigian Approach,
    by Marius Bewley   75   282
Rev. of The Importance of Scrutiny
    (Ed. by Eric Bentley)   77   239
[Note]   84   58

LEAVIS, Q(UEENIE) D.
ARTICLES ABOUT
Titans, Tea-Hounds,
    Rasslers, and Reviewers,
    by M. D. Zabel   41   326

LEBRUN, RICO
ARTICLES ABOUT
A Note on the Lebrun Drawings   107   109

LECHLITNER, RUTH
POEMS
Afterward   26   24
Summer Evening
October Afternoon   35   27
Kansas Boy   39   84
How Many Summers   40   313
Change Must Be Served   51   295
Ordeal by Tension
Connecticut Countryside
A Winter's Tale   56   298
Only the Years   58   131
Quiz Program
At the Road's Turn   59   322
Elegy   63   194
Night in August   68   258
Lines for the Year's End   73   72

REVIEWS
Robin Landing, by Stanley Young   52   164
Said Before Sunset,
    by Frederick Mortimer Clapp   52   297
The Fountain and the Bough,
    by Eileen Hall   53   223
The Complete Collected Poems (1906-1938)
    of William Carlos Williams   54   326
Death at Sea, by Frederic Prokosch   57   327
Last Poems of Elinor Wylie   62   164
Love Letter from an Impossible Land,
    by William Meredith   64   227
The Circus, by Clark Mills   65   152
The Collected Poetry of W. H. Auden   66   204
New Directions 9
    (Ed. by James Laughlin)   68   352

BOOKS REVIEWED
Tomorrow's Phoenix   51   157
Only the Years   68   224
The Shadow on the Hour   90   325

LE CLAIRE, GORDON
ARTICLES ABOUT
Poets in Canada, by Margaret Avison   94   182

LE CRON, HELEN COWLES
POEMS
The Wife   2   97

LEDBETTER, J. T.
  POEMS
    My Father's Voice   169   151

LEDOUX, LOUIS V.
  BOOKS REVIEWED
    The Shadow of Aetna   5   92
    George Edward Woodberry—A Study
      of His Poetry   11   103
    The Story of Eleusis—A Lyrical Drama   11   105
    Yzdra, a Tragedy

LEDWIDGE, FRANCIS
  BOOKS REVIEWED
    Songs of the Fields   9   209

LEE, AGNES
  [AGNES LEE FREER, "A. F.",
  "A. L. F."; see also "A. L."]
  POEMS
    The Silent House [Drama]   1   173
    The Sharing [Drama]   3   95
    On the Jail Steps   5   25
    A Statue in a Garden
    Three Guests   6   285
    At Dawn
    Long Distance Line
    Eastland Waters   7   234
    Shakespeare   8   16
    The Answer   10   61
    Evening
    The Doll
    Claude Debussy   12   74
    Peace   13   117
    Pictures of Women   13   200
      An Old Woman with Flowers
      The Slacker
      The Broken Tie
      Bark-Bound
      In the Morgue
      The Sweeper
    Sleep Poems   16   128
      Old Lizette on Sleep
      The Ancient Singer
      Mrs. Malooly
      The Ilex Tree
    The Jilt   19   69
    The Blunted Age
    Lyrics of the Shadows   24   257
      Brief Return
      The Lack
      The Ghost's Ethic
      Fickle Ivy
      Hospital Doors
    The Tower   27   138
    A Lonely Man
    The Years
    In a Bed by the Sea

    A Meditation
    Howard Shaw, Architect   28   179
    The Glove-Worker   29   130
    A Man Walks Home   31   16
    In an Old Homestead
    Having Read Lenotre
    Rheumatic   34   322
    They Pass   36   183
      Voices on the Drive
      Music
      At a Symphony Concert
      Enemies
      Black Flowers and White
    Aeneas Sleeps   37   80
    Edison   39   128
    A Half-Memory   41   12
    After the Terror
    Slumber Lyrics   42   322
      He Dreamed
      The Radio
      Only This
      Italian Planes at Rest
        on Lake Michigan
    The Drought   44   191
    Love Letters of a Surgeon   44   264
    Vi et Armis   50   200
    Boast of Heredity   53   130
    Saint Anne's Lullaby
    To an Early Friend

  ARTICLES
    [Tribute to Harriet Monroe]   49   156

  REVIEWS
    Two Belgian Poets   8   96
      Maurice Maeterlinck, a Critical Study,
        by Una Taylor
      Poems by Maurice Maeterlinck
        (Tr. by Bernard Miall)
      Poems of Emile Verhaeren
        (Tr. by Alma Strettel)
      The Cloister, a Play in Four Acts,
        by Emile Verhaeren
        (Tr. by Osman Edwards)
    Le Prisonnier des Mondes,
      by Jean Le Roy   9   48
    London, One November,
      by Helen Mackay   9   152
    Collected Poems,
      by Condé Benoist Pallen
    The Child and Other Verses,
      by Mary Louisa Anderson
    Madonna Dianora,
      by Hugo von Hofmannsthal
      (Tr. by Harriet Betty Boas)   9   159
    Harvest Moon,
      by Josephine Preston Peabody   9   269
    Poems, by Alan Seeger   10   38

A Flock from Oxford   10   44
    The Escaped Princess,
      by W. R. Childe
    Thursday's Child, by E. Rendall
    Bohemian Glass, by E. L. Duff
    Contacts, by T. W. Earp
    The Iron Age, by Frank Betts
    The Two Worlds, by Sherard Vines
    The Burning Wheel,
      by Aldous Huxley
    Op. I, by Dorothy Sayres
    A Vagabond's Wallet,
      by S. Reid-Heyman
   Songs of a Baby's Day, by Frances Shaw   10   216
   Chants Patriotiques et Autres Poèmes
    and *Les Trois Rois et Autres Poèmes,*
    by Emile Cammaerts
    (Tr. by Tita Brand-Cammaerts)   10   331
   Ardors and Endurances,
    by Robert Nichols   12   274
   Barbed Wire and Other Poems,
    by Edwin Ford Piper   12   276
   The Poets of Modern France,
    by Ludwig Lewisohn   13   52
   The Life of Lamartine,
    by H. Remsen Whitehouse   14   108
   The Jargon of Master Francois Villon,
    by Jordan Herbert Stabler   14   287
   Messines et Autres Poèmes,
    by Emile Cammaerts   14   342
   Fleurs de Lys
    (Tr. and ed. by Wilfred Thorley)   18   111
   La Mêlée Symboliste, by Ernest Raynaud   18   113
   Paul Verlaine, by Harold Nicolson   20   223
   The Open Sea, by Edgar Lee Masters   21   154
   The Bare Hills, by Yvor Winters   32   41
   Flowers of Evil, by Charles Baudelaire
    (Tr. by George Dillon and
    Edna St. Vincent Millay)   48   158

   BOOKS REVIEWED
   The Sharing   5   294
   Faces and Open Doors   21   267
   New Lyrics and a Few Old Ones   38   221
   Under One Roof   58   269

   ARTICLES ABOUT
   A Few Women Poets,
    by Harriet Monroe   26   326
   Agnes Lee, by Harriet Monroe   39   324
   Agnes Lee, by Yvor Winters   54   335

LEE, AL
  POEMS
   The Magical Mystery Submarine   113   391
   Sturm und Drang Confessed in Tranquility
   Going Whoring   117   248
   The Federal Reserve Bank of New York

LEE, ALFRED M.
  POEMS
   The Swarming of the Fish   95   283
   The Diamond Ladies

LEE, BORGHILD
  POEMS
   Norse-Immigrant Ballads   31   250
    My Mother's Mother Speaks
    Newcomer Ragna
   Saint Per   33   126
   Irony   34   322

LEE, CHARLES
  BOOKS REVIEWED
   The Stuffed Owl
    (Ed. with D. B. Wyndham Lewis)   37   164

LEE, CHRISTOPHER
  BOOKS REVIEWED
   The Secret Field   58   159

LEE, DENNIS
  BOOKS REVIEWED
   Kingdom of Absence   115   353
   Civil Elegies

LEE, DON L.
  [See MADHUBUTI, HAKI R.]

LEE, HARRY
  BOOKS REVIEWED
   High Company   18   223

LEE, JOHN B.
  BOOKS REVIEWED
   To Kill a White Dog   144   297

LEE, L. L.
  TRANSLATIONS
   Poems by Francis Jammes   89   157

LEE, LAURIE
  BOOKS REVIEWED
   My Many-Coated Man   89   193
   The Edge of Day, a Boyhood
    in the West of England   99   54
   The Sun My Monument   100   104

LEE, LAWRENCE
  POEMS
   In Time of War   56   312
   While We Are Safe
   The Syllable Will Be Heard

  BOOKS REVIEWED
   The Tomb of Thomas Jefferson   58   103

LEE, LI-YOUNG
BOOKS REVIEWED
   The City in Which I Love You   158   158

LEE, MUNA
POEMS
   Footnotes   7   175
   Songs of Many Moods   10   228
      A Song of Happiness
      Mahhavis
      Shadows
      Wind-Blown
      Compensation
   These Are But Words   20   235
      The Sonnet ("What other form...")
      ("I have been happy...")
      ("I have a thousand pictures...")
      ("Life of itself will be cruel...")
      ("There have been many Junes...")
      ("You have not known...")
      ("It would be easy to say...")
      ("I make no question...")
      ("No love can quite forego...")
      ("It will be easy to love you...")
      ("Of you, the beloved...")   22   124
      ("Running water...")
   So Many Ways
   Tropic Dawn   35   321
   Carib Summer   41   19
      Garden Episode
      Song Before Outcry
      Protest Against Security
      Epithalamium
      Ballad ("She wandered singing ")
   Sentence   45   80
   Alcatraz

TRANSLATIONS
   Poems by Alfonsina Storni, Leopoldo
     Lugones, Fernandez Moreno,
     Ricardo Jaimes Freyre, Gabriela Mistral,
     Diego Duble Urrutia, Manuel
     Magellanes Moure, José Asunción Silva,
     Guillermo Valencia, Luis C. López,
     Alfredo Gómez Jaime, Enrique
     Hernández Miyares, José Manuel Poveda,
     Diwaldo Salom, Luis Anibal Sánchez,
     Gonzálo Escudero Moscoso, Luis G.
     Urbina, Luis Rosado Vega, Salvador
     Díaz Mirón, Enrique Gonzáles Martinez,
     Rubén Darío, José Santos Chocano,
     Antonio Nicolas Blanco, Luis Palés Matos,
     Luis Llorens Torres, Osvaldo Bazil,
     Fabio Fiallo, Julio Herrera Reissig,
     Juana de Ibarbourou, Rufino Blanco
     Fombona, and Andrés Mata   26   117
   Folk-Songs of the Pampas   26   138
   Poems by Jorge Carrera Andrade   59   256

ARTICLES
   A Word from the Translator   26   168
REVIEWS
   Clouds and Cobblestones,
     by Hortense Flexner   20   102
   Songs from the Journey,
     by Wilton Agnew Barrett   20   160
   The Garden of the West,
     by Louise Driscoll   21   217
   Spanish Folk Songs
     (Ed. and tr. by Salvador de Madariaga)   22   101
   Prosas Profanas, by Rubén Darío
     (Tr. by Charles B. McMichael)   22   165
   Poetry Under Three Flags   22   226
     Espigas, by Luis de la Jara
     Al Rumor de la Fuente,
       by José A. Balseiro
     Alas Nuevas, by Pedro Leandro Ipuche
   Diadems and Fagots,
     by Olavo Bilac and Pierre de Ronsard
     (Tr. by John Meem and Yvor Winters)   23   113
   Sonnets and Poems,
     by Anthero de Quental
     (Tr. by S. Griswold Morley)   23   225
   Poems, by George Santayana   23   338
   Anthology of the Modernista Movement
     in Spanish America
     (Ed. by Alfred Coester)   26   169
   Poemas, by Jaime Torres Bodet   26   172
   Level Land, by Kenneth C. Kaufman   47   281
   Registro del Mundo,
     by Jorge Carrera Andrade   59   278
   Selected Poems by Pablo Neruda
     (Tr. by Angel Flores)   65   225

BOOKS REVIEWED
   Sea-Change   23   51
   Secret Country,
     by Jorge Carrera Andrade (Tr.)   70   159

ARTICLES ABOUT
   A Few Women Poets,
     by Harriet Monroe   26   326
   [Note on misprint]   62   354

LEE, PETER H.
TRANSLATIONS
   Two Medieval Korean Poems   98   357

BOOKS REVIEWED
   Anthology of Korean Poetry:
     From the Earliest Era to the Present (Tr.)   109   272

LEE, ROBERT E.
ARTICLES ABOUT
   Rev. of *Lee: A Dramatic Poem*,
     by Edgar Lee Masters   29   336

LEED, JACOB

POEMS

Two Poems   108   309
    ("this morning/three times...")
    ("often I've/thought who...")
Four Poems   111   290
    ("A shower, but there's more rain...")
    In Small Town Ohio
    ("No lines do right...")
    ("out there/a soggy bird...")

LEEKLEY, RICHARD

POEMS

Testimony After Jeremiah   44   262
This Native Place
Ode After Donne's Sermons   47   204
Near the Palmolive Building
Prelude to My Son
Remembrance of Karl Lockner   53   235
Sun-Up   57   362

LEET, JUDITH

POEMS

Distraught, Alarmed, Uncomforted   132   213
Sum   137   162
On Participating in Four Forms
    of Planetary Motion
The Play of the Mind
Returning Lewis to His Freedom
Early Friday Evening Observations   139   17
A Revisionist's Mozart   142   131
Returning Alive from Diverse Routes
    and Far Travels

LE FANU, SHERIDAN

ARTICLES ABOUT

Dagger of the Mind,
    by James Sandoe   68   146

LE GALLIENNE, RICHARD

BOOKS REVIEWED

The Lonely Dancer,
    and Other Poems   4   30

**LÉGER, ALEXIS ST. LÉGER
[See PERSE, ST.-JOHN]**

LEGGAT, ALISON

ARTICLES ABOUT

Rev. of The Elder Statesman,
    by T. S. Eliot   95   36

LEGGE, JAMES

ARTICLES ABOUT

On Translating Chinese Poetry, II,
    by Eunice Tietjens   20   328
Correspondence
    from Amy Lowell   21   167

LEGLER, PHILIP (FERGUSON)

POEMS

On the Death of a Test Pilot: A Footnote   88   381
Landscape for a Wife   93   289
Week End Visit   97   162
Bedstraw   110   390

REVIEWS

Collected Poems, by Marianne Moore   83   158
Four First Volumes   99   184
    The Wandering Jew,
      by Robert Mezey
    Forms of Exile, by John Montague
    Eyes Without a Face,
      by Kenneth McRobbie
    First Poems, by Lewis Turco
Three Poets   109   411
    Fox on a Barn Door,
      by Ted Walker
    The Striders,
      by A. K. Ramanujan
    Poems 1955-1965,
      by Dom Moraes
Live or Die, by Anne Sexton   110   125

BOOKS REVIEWED

A Change of View   105   410

LE GUIN, URSULA K.

BOOKS REVIEWED

Hard Words   140   346

LEHMAN, DAVID

POEMS

Poem ("As the day cuts off...")   114   247
The Anatomy of Your Body
Excursion
Two Sonnets   117   26
    ("It's hardly there, and then...")
    ("Listen! The garbage pouring...")
This Unmentionable Feeling   118   88
From Goodbye Instructions
    ("They're real.—Those angels...")
    ("A dream in which I fell...")
Goodnight Poem
New Year's Day   119   195
Four Poems from Good-Bye Instructions
    ("We are waiting—all of us...")
    ("A statue may be rising...")
    ("And somewhere along the line...")
    ("These ladders never go anywhere...")
Edvard Munch   123   142
How To Think   125   271
And About Time   126   209
Two Sonnets, in 1972
    February
    May
October Classic

Journey into the Eye   128   36
The Heroic Couple   130   209
In Praise of Robert Penn Warren   135   85
Ode ("People in the middle ages...")
In Praise of A. R. Ammons   136   148
Amnesia   144   203

REVIEWS
When the Sun Tries To Go On   114   401
    When the Sun Tries To Go On,
        by Kenneth Koch
    Ankor Wat, by Allen Ginsberg
    Notes of Woe, by James Tate
    Short History of the Fur Trade,
        by Adrien Stoutenburg
    North Percy, by Paul Goodman
The Whole School   119   224
    Great Balls of Fire, by Ron Padgett
    North, by Tony Towle
    Where I Hang My Hat,
        by Dick Gallup
    Chic Death/Poems,
        by Gerard Malanga
    Air, by Tom Clark
    In the Early Morning Rain,
        by Ted Berrigan
    Balling Buddha, by John Giorno
    Space, by Clark Coolidge
    Giant Night, by Anne Waldman
    [John Ashbery, Kenneth Koch,
        Frank O'Hara]
Politics   123   173
    Monster, by Robin Morgan
    Debridement, by Michael S. Harper
    The Energy of Slaves,
        by Leonard Cohen
    Burning the Empty Nests,
        by Gregory Orr
Holocaust   128   37
    Holocaust, by Charles Reznikoff
    Settling Down, by Ira Sadoff
    David Ignatow: Selected Poems
        (Ed. by Robert Bly)
    Forbidden Disappointments,
        by James Carroll
    Scattered Brains, by Darrell Gray
    Collected Poems,
        by W. H. Auden
        (Ed. by Edward Mendelson)   131   159

BOOKS REVIEWED
James Merrill: Essays in Criticism
    (Ed. with Charles Berger)   143   101

LEHMANN, JOHN
POEMS
    In Two Cities   46   322
        His Hands
        So Many Voices

BOOKS REVIEWED
    The Noise of History   47   231
    New Writing (Ed.)   51   206
    New Writing V (Ed.)   52   351
    Forty Poems   63   50

ARTICLES ABOUT
    London Letter: Some New Figures,
        by John McCormick   83   269

LEHMANN, WILHELM
ARTICLES ABOUT
    German Lyric Poetry Since 1945,
        by Hans Egon Holthusen
        (Tr. by Herman Salinger)   88   257

LEHMER, DERRICK N(ORMAN)
POEMS
    The Ballad of Fightery Dick   36   1
    The Feud   38   88
    Eviction
    Xanadu   42   131
        The Giant
        The Spirit
        The High Priest
        The Adversary
        The Poet

ARTICLES
    Correspondence:
        Mr. Rorty's Indians   39   165

BOOKS REVIEWED
    Fightery Dick and Other Poems:
        A Book of Free Ballads   48   169

ARTICLES ABOUT
    Correspondence
        from James Rorty   39   228

LEHTINEN, MERI
TRANSLATIONS
    Poems by Aaro Helaakoski,
        Eeva-Liisa Manner, Lauri Viita,
        Aila Meriluoto, and Helvi Juvonen   98   348

LEIBOWITZ, HERBERT
BOOKS REVIEWED
    Hart Crane: An Introduction to the Poetry 115   346

LEIGHTON, LAWRENCE
REVIEWS
    A. E. Housman, a Sketch,
        by A. S. F. Gow   52   94

LEISHMAN, J. B.
BOOKS REVIEWED
    Rainer Maria Rilke: Poems (Tr.)   45   344
    The Metaphysical Poets   47   169

Requiem and Other Poems,
   by Rainer Maria Rilke (Tr.)   50   34
Sonnets to Orpheus,
   by Rainer Maria Rilke (Tr.)
Duino Elegies, by Rainer Maria Rilke
   (Tr. with Stephen Spender)   55   96
Selected Poems of Hölderlin
   (Tr. and ed.)   91   260
Poems 1906-26, by Rainer Maria Rilke (Tr.)   93   192
Selected Works of Rainer Maria Rilke,
   Vol. II, Poetry (Tr.)   97   323

LEITCH, MARY SINTON
  BOOKS REVIEWED
   The Waggon and the Star   22   168

LEITHAUSER, BRAD
  POEMS
   Canoeing at Night   123   217
   Alternate Landscape   129   96
   Along Lake Michigan
   Dead Elms by a River
   Anonymous' Lament   151   88
   Parallel Lifelines
   First Birthday   156   153

  ARTICLES
   Comment   151   221

  BOOKS REVIEWED
   Hundreds of Fireflies   141   170
   The Mail from Anywhere   158   280

  ARTICLES ABOUT
   Review by William H. Pritchard   143   228

LEMONT, JESSIE
  [JESSIE LEMONT TRANSIL,
  JESSIE LAMONT]
  TRANSLATIONS
   Poem by Rainer Maria Rilke   18   319
   Poem by Rainer Maria Rilke   66   84
   Poem by Rainer Maria Rilke   68   195

  ARTICLES
   Correspondence
   [Francis Golffing, Rainer Maria Rilke]   69   57

  BOOKS REVIEWED
   Poems of Rainer Maria Rilke (Tr.)   14   168
   Poems, by Rainer Maria Rilke (Tr.)   63   169
   Sonnets to Orpheus, Duino Elegies,
    by Rainer Maria Rilke (Tr.)   68   100

LE NOIR, PHIL
  POEMS
   Western Poems   16   248
   Down on the Ol' Bar-G

   Ol' Dynamite
   The Puncher Poet

LENTRICCHIA, FRANK, JR.
  REVIEWS
   Some Coordinates of Modern Literature   108   65
    Five Metaphysical Poets,
     by Joan Bennett
    The Lyric Impulse,
     by C. Day Lewis
    Tree and Leaf, by J. R. R. Tolkien
    Dylan Thomas and Poetic Dissociation,
     by David Holbrook
   Wallace Stevens: Emergence of the Poet   109   201
    Wallace Stevens:
     An Anatomy of Figuration,
     by Eugene Nassar
    The Clairvoyant Eye:
     The Poetry and Poetics
     of Wallace Stevens,
     by Joseph N. Riddel
    Introduction to Wallace Stevens,
     by Henry W. Wells
   Attitudes Toward Literature   110   119
    The Poem of the Mind:
     Essays on Poetry, English and American,
     by Louis Martz
    The Theory of American Literature,
     by Howard Mumford Jones
    Poetic Meter and Poetic Form,
     by Paul Fussell, Jr.
    Poets on Poetry
     (Ed. by Howard Nemerov)

  BOOKS REVIEWED
   The Gaiety of Language:
    An Essay on the Radical Poetics
    of W. B. Yeats and Wallace Stevens   115   346

LEO, JOHN ROBERT
  REVIEWS
   Finding the Imagination   129   102
    Tyorkin & The Stovemakers:
     Poetry and Prose
     by Alexander Tvardovsky
     (Ed. and tr. by Anthony Rudolf)
    Poems from Donegal,
     by Theodore Holmes
    Gathering the Bones Together,
     by Gregory Orr
    Mining the Darkness,
     by Stephen Stepanchev
    Signals from the Safety Coffin,
     by John Engels
    Tight Corners & What's Around Them,
     by David Bromige

LEON, ABELARDO SANCHEZ
  [See SANCHEZ LEON, ABELARDO]

LEONARD, DOROTHY
POEMS
   Silent   35   28
   Away
   The Fighters   37   77
   Logic   39   195

LEONARD, WILLIAM ELLERY
POEMS
   Indian Summer   3   11
   Afterthought   23   186
     I Never Knew
     The Visitor
     Because I've Learned

BOOKS REVIEWED
   The Vaunt of Man and Other Poems   2   26
   Two Lives   27   272
   Tutankhamen and After
   Gilgamesh: Epic of Old Babylonia (Tr.)   44   289
   A Man Against Time   67   260

ARTICLES ABOUT
   Obituary   64   176

LEONHARD, RUDOLPH
POEMS
   Die Letzten Tage   57   185

LEOPARDI, GIACOMO
BOOKS REVIEWED
   Poems from...
     (Tr. by John Heath-Stubbs)   91   260
   Giacomo Leopardi. Poems
     (Tr. by Jean-Pierre Barricelli)   107   333

ARTICLES ABOUT
   The Century of Leopardi,
     by Morton Dauwen Zabel   50   270
   Rev. of Leopardi: A Study in Solitude,
     by Iris Origo   85   55
   Rev. of Leopardi
     and the Theory of Poetry,
     by G. Singh   107   333

LEOPOLD, NIKIA
POEMS
   Snow into Evening   165   129

LE PAN, DOUGLAS
POEMS
   Stragglers   119   1
   Song in October
   The Double
   Hysterica Passio

BOOKS REVIEWED
   Something Still Hard to Find   144   297

LERMAN, ELEANOR
BOOKS REVIEWED
   Armed Love   127   44
   Come the Sweet By and By   130   342

LERMONTOV, MIKHAIL
BOOKS REVIEWED
   Three Russian Poets
     (With Alexander Pushkin
     and Fyodor Tyutchev)
     (Tr. by Vladimir Nabokov)   66   289
   A Lermontov Reader
     (Ed. and tr. by Guy Daniels)   111   258

LERNER, LAURENCE
BOOKS REVIEWED
   Domestic Interior   94   405

LE ROY, JEAN
BOOKS REVIEWED
   Le Prisonnier des Mondes   9   48

LESEMANN, MAURICE
POEMS
   A Man Walks in the Wind   16   12
   Brushwood
     To Himself in Autumn
     The Crying Cranes
     Tramps
     Appointment
     No Poem
   Dark Rain: New Mexico   22   257
   Storm-Gathering
   Sheep Herders   29   1
   Ranchers
   The Death of a Hill Girl
   Lost   34   121
   On a Fly-Leaf
   Earth Never Knows
   Prometheus
   Burglars
   City Asleep
   Night Pieces   40   1
     Noctiflora
     Transport
     Round Trip
     New Year's Eve
   Mountain Quail   55   7
   The Dam   68   1
   Enemy
   On an Evening of Bright Meteors
   The Leave-Taking
   The Train

ARTICLES
   Two Trampers—And a Poem
     [Vachel Lindsay,
     Stephen Graham]   22   212

REVIEWS
Poems, by Wilfrid Scawen Blunt   22   337
XLI Poems and is 5,
    by E. E. Cummings   29   164
Personae: The Collected Poems
    of Ezra Pound   30   216

ARTICLES ABOUT
[Note on misprint]   40   116

LESLIE, SHANE
BOOKS REVIEWED
Verses in Peace and War   12   165

LESLIE, SHAW
BOOKS REVIEWED
An Anthology of Catholic Poets (Ed.)   30   114

LESSER, RIKA
POEMS
Translation   129   39
Losses   131   342
About Her   170   273

TRANSLATIONS
Poems by Gunnar Ekelöf   131   338

REVIEWS
Duino Elegies and The Sonnets to Orpheus,
    by Rainer Maria Rilke
    (Tr. by A. Poulin, Jr.)
    [André Gide]   131   345

BOOKS REVIEWED
Hours in the Garden and Other Poems,
    by Hermann Hesse (Tr.)   136   40
Etruscan Things   143   295

LE SUEUR, MERIDEL
POEMS
Nests   24   80

LEUBA, WALTER
ARTICLES
Correspondence:
    Mr. Leuba Wants To Know
    [Stanley Burnshaw]   33   50

BOOKS REVIEWED
Poems Out of a Hat   74   50

ARTICLES ABOUT
Correspondence from Stanley Burnshaw   33   52

LEVANT, HOWARD
POEMS
The Pious Squire Regrets
    His Year's Sins of Lust   89   166

Pleasures of the Imagination
Connection in October
An Old Traveler   96   350
Pathetic Fallacy
Later

LEVATIN, ISOBELLA
TRANSLATIONS
Poems by Ondra Lysohorsky
    (With W. H. Auden)   116   273

LEVCHEV, VLADIMIR
POEMS
The Refugee
    (Tr. with Henry Taylor)   168   32

LEVENDOSKY, CHARLES
BOOKS REVIEWED
Perimeters   118   295

LEVERTOV, DENISE
POEMS
To the Snake   93   10
A Happening
The Departure
Seems Like We Must Be Somewhere Else
The Room
A Ring of Changes   94   240
The Communion
A Straw Swan Under the Christmas Tree
Come into Animal Presence   96   1
Six Variations
A Map of the Western Part
    of the County of Essex in England
The Well   97   282
The Illustration—A Footnote
Matins   99   21
Summer 1961   100   175
Living with a Painting   101   65
Another Spring
Claritas   102   211
Leaving Forever
In Abeyance
The Crack
Eros at Temple Stream
A Cure of Souls
The Resolve
Eight Poems   103   66
    The Prayer
    Losing Track
    In Mind
    About Marriage
    Melody Grundy
    Looking-Glass
    Our Bodies
    The Runes
Olga Poems   106   81
Life at War   108   149

A Vision   109   357
An Interim   113   69
Invocation   115   90
Wings of a God
The Distance   120   346

TRANSLATIONS
Vaishnava Lyrics
  (Tr. with Edward C. Dimock, Jr.)   107   176

ARTICLES
H. D.: An Appreciation   100   182
Some Notes on Organic Form   106   420

REVIEWS
"A" 1-12, by Louis Zukofsky
  [William Carlos Williams]   97   102
Ace of Pentacles, by John Wieners   105   326

BOOKS REVIEWED
Here and Now   91   120
Overland to the Islands   93   107
With Eyes at the Back of Our Heads   96   314
The Jacob's Ladder   101   412
O Taste and See   105   259
In Praise of Krishna:
  Songs from the Bengali
  (Ed. and tr. with Edward C. Dimock) 111   407
The Sorrow Dance   112   123
Selected Poems by Eugene Guillevic (Tr.) 116 260
Relearning the Alphabet   118   97
The Jacob's Ladder   121   54
Life in the Forest   136   219
Candles in Babylon   143   39
Poems 1960-1967   144   40

ARTICLES ABOUT
Rev. of The New American Poetry: 1945-1960
  (Ed. by Donald M. Allen)   98   242

LEVI, ADELE
POEMS
Summer News   78   75

LEVI, JAN HELLER
BOOKS REVIEWED
A Muriel Rukeyser Reader (Ed.)   167   287

LEVI, PETER [S. J.]
BOOKS REVIEWED
The Gravel Ponds   99   253
Water, Rock and Sand   102   330
Yevtushenko: Selected Poems
  (Tr. with Robin Milner-Gulland)   102   400
Poems, by Richard Selig (Ed.)   105   336
Pancakes for the Queen of Babylon:
  Ten Poems for Nikos Gatsos   116   193

LEVIN, MARSHALL N.
ARTICLES
Correspondence: Points at Issue
  [Stephen Spender]   72   343

LEVIN, PHILLIS
POEMS
On Marble   150   3
Machines
Grace

LEVINE, MARK
BOOKS REVIEWED
Debt   163   336

LEVINE, PHILIP
POEMS
The Toys   86   78
Summer   90   30
Night Thoughts Over a Sick Child   93   95
Gangrene   96   214
Hunted
For Fran   97   214
Sierra Kid
In a Vacant House   100   19
The Reply
My Poets   102   163
The Horse
It's Mother   104   355
The Book   106   400
Common Entrances
They Got Our Leader   109   94
Looking for Levine
Spanish Lesson   111   167
What We Did to What We Were   114   88
Noon
Alone   118   136
The Way Down
Here
Letters for the Dead   119   79
This War   120   324
Death Bearing   121   84
I've Been Asleep
Losing You
One by One   122   254
Bad Penny
I Am Always
The Falling Sky   128   74
A Woman Waking
Saturdays in Heaven
Bloodstone
Here and Now   130   319
My Name   134   311
The First Truth
Salt
That Day
To Cipriano, in the Wind
Buying Earth

Keep Talking	136	311
Having Been Asked		
"What Is a Man?" I Answer		
The Radio		
One		
The Myth		
For the Country	143	63
Sweet Will	145	313
Look		
The Present		
Jewish Graveyards, Italy		
Winter Words	149	127
The Whole Soul		
Long Gone March	149	313
Keats in California	151	88
The Right Cross	152	125
Burned	156	311
Photography	164	15
One Day		
Tristan		

REVIEWS

Three Poets	93	399
Woman in Apartment,		
by Cynthia Pickard		
Magellan, by Ann Stanford		
Western Reaches, by Leonard Nathan		
W. S. Merwin:		
Selected Translations 1948-1968	115	187

BOOKS REVIEWED

On the Edge	103	330
Not This Pig	113	262
Pili's Wall	120	235
1933	125	354
The Names of the Lost	130	293
Ashes: Poems New and Old	137	169
Seven Years from Somewhere		
One for the Rose	142	106
Selected Poems	147	35
Sweet Will		
A Walk with Tom Jefferson	155	229
What Work Is	160	94
New Selected Poems		
The Simple Truth	167	156

ARTICLES ABOUT

Poets Aloud, by Donald Hall	139	297
[Note]	150	244

LEVINE, ROSALIND
POEMS

And Solomon Sang in Arden	80	206
The Shadow Bird	81	173
Butterflies	83	9
A Permissive Climate	85	86
Enchanted Blueprint		

Three Songs at Midsummer	86	160
Sparrow over the Snow		
Only the Juke-Box		
Washing Blueberries		
From The Pomegranate	87	354
Space Design	91	303
Poems of Commitment	96	347

REVIEWS

New and Selected Poems,		
by Thomas Hornsby Ferril	83	282
Six Young Poets	93	182
After Lorca, by Jack Spicer		
Gasoline, by Gregory Corso		
The Broken Frieze,		
by Peter Everwine		
Poems, by Stephen Berg,		
Ronald Goodman,		
and Robert Mezey		

LEVINSON, S(ALMON) O.
ARTICLES

[Tribute to Harriet Monroe]	49	159

LEVIS, LARRY
POEMS

To a Wall of Flame in a Steel Mill,		
Syracuse, New York, 1969	136	137
To a Woman Glancing Up from the River		
Elegy With a Chimneysweep		
Falling Inside It	170	22

BOOKS REVIEWED

Wrecking Crew	121	292
The Dollmaker's Ghost	140	293
Winter Stars	148	99

LEVITT, LESLIE HILL
[See HILL-LEVITT, LESLIE]

LEVY, HOWARD
POEMS

Mozart	161	285

LEVY, JERRE
ARTICLES ABOUT

The Neural Lyre: Poetic Meter,		
the Brain, and Time,		
by Frederick Turner		
and Ernst Pöppel	142	277

LEVY, LEO B.
POEMS

After Love	57	11

LEVY, NEWMAN
ARTICLES ABOUT

Poetry on Records, by Harry T. Moore	57	338

LEVY, ROBERT J.
POEMS
On Making Love
After Having Made Love 155 328
Meditation on Virginia Woolf's
Final Diary Entry, Written
Three Weeks Before Her Suicide ... 156 92
On Looking at a Photo of Myself,
Age 10, After a Tonsillectomy ... 159 15
The Parents 159 127
Beyond Recipes

LEWIS, ALUN
BOOKS REVIEWED
Ha! Ha! Among the Trumpets ... 67 286

LEWIS, C(ECIL) DAY
[See DAY-LEWIS, CECIL]

LEWIS, C(LIVE) S(TAPLES)
ARTICLES ABOUT
Review by Mary Kinzie 154 151

LEWIS, D. B. WYNDHAM
BOOKS REVIEWED
The Stuffed Owl
(Ed. with Charles Lee) 37 164

LEWIS, EDWIN H.
ARTICLES ABOUT
Poetic Parallels,
by Harriet Monroe 35 328

LEWIS, EMILY W(ESTWOOD)
POEMS
The Learned Princess 36 249

LEWIS, H. H.
POEMS
Farmhands' Refrain 52 115
Lest Sympathy Function
Oink
Freedom, Inc.
Don't Judge Him Too Harshly
Insult for Insult 60 256

BOOKS REVIEWED
Red Renaissance 47 227
Thinking of Russia
Salvation
Road to Utterly

LEWIS, JANET (LOXLEY)
POEMS
Cold Hills 16 140
Austerity
The End of the Age
Geology

Fossil
The Indians in the Woods 21 190
In the Woods
A Song for the Wife of Manibozho
A Gull-Following Song
A Song for the Grandmother
Manibush and the Grandmother
Time and Treasure 40 245
Child in a Garden
The Clock
The Hangar 51 184
On an Old Woman Dying
At Carmel Highlands
A Lullaby 53 123
Old Love 65 198
A Farewell
The April Hill
Lines with a Gift of Herbs
For Louise 126 218
Sunday Morning at the Artists' House ... 151 90

ARTICLES
Comment [Harriet Monroe] 151 199

REVIEWS
Sign of Capricornus, by Kathryn Worth ... 51 270
Fifty-One Poems, by Mary Webb ... 73 49

BOOKS REVIEWED
The Indians in the Woods 21 335
The Wheel in Midsummer 32 222
The Earth-Bound 69 220
Poems Old and New 1918-1978 .... 140 346
The Dear Past and Other Poems 1919-1994 ... 168 281

ARTICLES ABOUT
Convention and Revolt,
by Jessica Nelson North 34 212

LEWIS, KENNETH
POEMS
Incompleteness 48 314
Permanence
Heritage
City Easter

LEWIS, LISA
POEMS
Silence 141 335
The Consequences of Minutes

LEWIS, MAY
POEMS
Sad Songs 30 136
The Grapes Are Sour
Music
Charity
Here at High Morning 35 21

Not Simple Daisy	41	316
As They Seem	47	70
False Friend		
White Field of Stone		
The Buried Heart		
How Otherwise	49	70
Equilibrium		
Spell		
And Piranesi Admired Dungeons		
Circular Pattern	52	324
Progress		
Strikers		

BOOKS REVIEWED
| Red Drumming in the Sun | 41 | 230 |

LEWIS, NORMAN
POEMS
| Ugly Hour | 60 | 191 |
| So Many Men | 61 | 486 |

LEWIS, R. W. B.
BOOKS REVIEWED
| The Poetry of Hart Crane: A Critical Study | 114 | 113 |

LEWIS, RICHARD
BOOKS REVIEWED
| Moon, For What Do You Wait?: Poems by Tagore (Ed.) | 111 | 407 |
| Out of the Earth I Sing (Ed.) | 113 | 262 |

LEWIS, SINCLAIR
ARTICLES ABOUT
| Honors and Prizes, by Harriet Monroe | 29 | 92 |

LEWIS, WYNDHAM
BOOKS REVIEWED
One-Way Song	45	165
One-Way Song	87	247
The Demon of Progress in the Arts		
The Human Age, Vol. II		
The Letters of... (Ed. by W. K. Rose)	105	397

ARTICLES ABOUT
Our Contemporaries [Blast]	5	42
Stele for Hephaestus, by Hugh Kenner	90	306
Stele for Hephaestus, by Hugh Kenner	121	50

LEWISOHN, LUDWIG
BOOKS REVIEWED
| The Poets of Modern France | 13 | 52 |
| Thirty-One Poems, by Rainer Maria Rilke (Tr.) | 69 | 103 |

LEX, BARBARA
ARTICLES ABOUT
| The Neural Lyre: Poetic Meter, the Brain, and Time, by Frederick Turner and Ernst Pöppel | 142 | 277 |

L'HEUREUX, JOHN
BOOKS REVIEWED
| No Place for Hiding | 120 | 49 |

LIANG T'UNG-SHU
POEMS
| Calligraphy (Tr. by Amy Lowell and Florence Ayscough) | 13 | 235 |

LIBBEY, ELIZABETH
POEMS
The Gesture	132	311
Love Poem		
Déjà Vu		
Girl Sitting Alone in Her Room		
Putting Things By		
Late One Night	137	192
Themselves		
Apparent Horizon		
The Kiss	142	43
The Act of Letting Go		
Eavesdropper Out Walking		
Afterword		

BOOKS REVIEWED
| Songs of a Returning Soul | 143 | 163 |

LIBEN, MEYER
POEMS
These Unalterable Configurations	59	244
That Single Glance, That Nervous Scowl		
Waiting for Each Other To Die		
Of the Ceaseless Coming and Going		
Still the Stupefaction	65	317

LIBERA, SHARON
POEMS
| Second Child | 153 | 193 |

LIBERO, LIBERO DE
[See DE LIBERO, LIBERO]

LIDDY, JAMES
BOOKS REVIEWED
In a Blue Smoke	105	404
In a Blue Smoke	110	195
Blue House: Poems in the Chinese Manner (With Jim Chapson and Thomas Hill)	114	251
Blue Mountain	119	159

LIEBENTHAL, JEAN
POEMS
   Explorer   166   143
   Unknown Woman in
      My Grandmother's Photograph   170   131
   Map
   Rehearsal

LIEBERMAN, ELIAS
POEMS
   The Professor Sneezes   53   252

BOOKS REVIEWED
   Man in the Shadows   56   220

LIEBERMAN, LAURENCE
POEMS
   The Mountain Hoax   103   244
   Skin Song   110   236
   The House Skin
   Lobsters in the Brain Coral   117   81
   Daibutsu   124   277

REVIEWS
   Art in Transition   109   395
      Advantages of Dark,
         by Robert Watson
      Watchboy, What of the Night?
         by Turner Cassity
      The Cutting Edge,
         by John Woods
      The Animal Inside,
         by Josephine Jacobsen
      Battle Report,
         by Harvey Shapiro
      New and Selected Poems,
         by Jean Garrigue   112   121
   Poetry Chronicle   112   337
      Of Flesh and Bone,
         by John Frederick Nims
      Hawkweed, by Paul Goodman
      The Panther and the Lash,
         by Langston Hughes
      For a Bitter Season,
         by George Garrett
      Amulet, by Carl Rakoski
      New and Selected Poems,
         by Peter Viereck
   A Confluence of Poets   114   40
      Shall We Gather at the River,
         by James Wright
      The Heart's Garden The Garden's Heart,
         by Kenneth Rexroth
      The Speed of Darkness,
         by Muriel Rukeyser
      Bending the Bow,
         by Robert Duncan
      The Collected Poems,
         by Kenneth Patchen

      Selected Poems, by Karl Shapiro
      Rose Demonics,
         by Elliott Coleman
      Of Being Numerous,
         by George Oppen
      Cables to the Ace,
         by Thomas Merton
      Onions and Roses, by Vassar Miller
      Spring Journal: Poems,
         by Edwin Honig
      The Body, by Michael Benedikt
      Finding the Measure,
         by Robert Kelly
      Zbigniew Herbert: Selected Poems
         (Tr. by Czeslaw Milosz
         and Peter Dale Scott)
      Yvan Goll: Selected Poems
         (Ed. by Paul Zweig)
      The Complete Plays
        of Vladimir Mayakovsky
         (Tr. by Guy Daniels)
      The Unwritten Song (Volume II)
         (Ed. and tr. by Willard R. Trask)
      Masks, by Edward Brathwaite
      Selected Poems,
         by A. R. Ammons
   Poet-Critics and Scholar-Critics   115   346
      Babel to Byzantium:
        Poets and Poetry Now,
         by James Dickey
      To Abolish Children
        and Other Essays,
         by Karl Shapiro
      Introduction to Poetry:
        Commentaries on Thirty Poems,
         by Mark Van Doren
      Essays and Reviews,
         by Thomas H. Carter
      Poetic Closure:
        A Study of How Poems End,
         by Barbara Herrnstein Smith
      The Gaiety of Language:
        An Essay on the Radical Poetics
        of W. B. Yeats and Wallace Stevens,
         by Frank Lentricchia
      The Poetry of Emily Dickinson,
         by Ruth Miller
      Hart Crane:
        An Introduction to the Poetry,
         by Herbert Leibowitz
   The Book of Mourning   124   280
      The Story of Our Lives,
         by Mark Strand
      The Owl's Insomnia,
         by Rafael Alberti
         (Ed. and tr. by Mark Strand)

BOOKS REVIEWED
   The Unblinding   113   421
   The Osprey Suicides   125   166

God's Measurements   140   293
The Mural of Wakeful Sleep   147   35

LIETZ, ROBERT
POEMS
Three Airmen Regroup at Casey's Topless   146   251

LI HAI-KU
POEMS
An Evening Meeting
  (Tr. by Amy Lowell
  and Florence Ayscough)   13   233
After How Many Years
  (Tr. by Amy Lowell
  and Florence Ayscough)   13   239

LII TYNG KWEI
[LII TYNGKWEI]
POEMS
Fugitive Journey   56   12
While I Study Abroad   73   74

LILLIE, MARIA ELMENDORF
POEMS
The Recluse   7   284

LILLQUIST, KENNETH
POEMS
Rosemount   115   228
The Realization
Outside Mattoon
Macoupin County

ARTICLES
Correspondence
  [Nancy Sullivan,
  Joanne de Longchamps]   120   59

LIMA, FRANK
BOOKS REVIEWED
Inventory   106   370

LIM-WILSON, FATIMA
POEMS
Raising the Dead   164   327
Prima Gravida   165   314
Upon Overhearing Tagalog   167   330
Teaching My Son His Abakadas   168   88
Casting Call   170   200

LINCOLN, ABRAHAM
ARTICLES ABOUT
The "Great Poem," by Harriet Monroe   41   90

LINCOLN, ELLIOTT C.
BOOKS REVIEWED
Rhymes of a Homesteader   18   51

LIND, L(EVI) ROBERT
[L. R. LIND]
POEMS
At Key West   46   321
Poem After War   47   321
To an Aging Tennis Player   51   66
Twelve Gauge Sonnet

ARTICLES ABOUT
[Note]   84   119

LINDEMAN, JACK
POEMS
August 1   91   242
August 2
August 5
Letter Man   95   88
Wartime   97   166
Obituary
New Arrival   102   19
Surgery, Please   114   163

REVIEWS
Three Poets   97   109
  The Orb Weaver, by Robert Francis
  Morning Worship,
    by Mark Van Doren
  The Gazabos: 41 Poems,
    by Edwin Honig

LINDER, CARL
POEMS
Flowing Backwards   105   99
The Younger Man
The Accident
Glass

LINDH, STEWART
POEMS
The Clasp   122   199
Settler
The Tongue His Touch

LINDNER, CARL
POEMS
The Door   160   2
Outside Activities   163   214

LINDSAY, ELISABETH
ARTICLES ABOUT
A Springfield Memoir,
  by Robert Fitzgerald
  [Vachel Lindsay]   141   33

LINDSAY, ELIZABETH CONNER
REVIEWS
Echoes,
  by Helen Burwell Chapin   56   282

LINDSAY, JACK
BOOKS REVIEWED
   Three Letters to Nikolai Tikhonov   79   106

LINDSAY, MAURICE
BOOKS REVIEWED
   Scottish Poetry, Number Two
   (Ed. with George Bruce
   and Edwin Morgan)   113   35

LINDSAY, NICHOLAS VACHEL
[See LINDSAY, VACHEL]

LINDSAY, PHILIP
BOOKS REVIEWED
   The Haunted Man:
   A Portrait of Edgar Allan Poe   86   118

LINDSAY, VACHEL
[NICHOLAS VACHEL LINDSAY]
POEMS
   General William Booth
    Enters Into Heaven   1   101
   The Moon Is a Mirror   2   119
    A Sense of Humor
    The Soul of the Gambler
    What the Miner in the Desert Said
    What the Moon Saw
    The Moon Is Compared to a City
    The Moon Is a Knight in Armor
    Euclid
    Drying Their Wings
    Yet Gentle Will the Griffin Be
    What the Rattlesnake Said
    The Recreant Queens
    The Scissors-Grinder
    What the Young Rhymer Said
   Aladdin and the Jinn   4   12
   Poems To Be Chanted   4   123
    The Firemen's Ball
    The Santa Fé Trail—A Humoresque
    The Black Hawk War of the Artists
   The Chinese Nightingale   5   199
   Booker Washington Trilogy   8   109
    A Negro Sermon: Simon Legree
    John Brown
    King Solomon and the Queen of Sheba
   For America at War   10   169
    Our Mother Pocahontas
    Niagara
    Mark Twain and Joan of Arc
   The Soap-Box   11   14
   How Samson Bore Away
    the Gates of Gaza
   The Empire of China
    Is Crumbling Down   12   291
   Whimseys   14   256
    Kalamazoo

    The Modest Jazz-Bird
    Davy Jones' Door-Bell
    The Conscientious Deacon
    The Horrid Voice of Science
    My Lady Is Compared to a Young Tree
   How a Little Girl Sang   22   237
   The Forest Ranger's Honeymoon   28   1
    The Writhing Imperfect Earth
    Begging Pardon
    The Old Mail Coach to Belton
    The Dragon-Fly Guide
    To the Tallest Aspen
    The Deer of Quartz Lake
    The Fawns and the Stranger
    The City of Glass
    The Golden Orchids
    A Great Shadowy Day
    The Rat-Souled Foe the City Fears
    One More Song
   Every Soul Is a Circus   33   1
    My Brothers of the Poet Trade
    A Million Singing Circuses
    The Long Street Lifts
    The Pontoon Bridge Miracle
    Beside Her Carriage
   Poems He Left Us   40   179
    Is Wisdom Such a Thing?
    To a Girl in a Sun Suit
    When I Gave My Lady
    a Double Rosebud
    The Poet in the Orchard of Art
    In Memory
    Epitaph for Jeb Stuart

ARTICLES
   Mr. Lindsay on "Primitive Singing"   4   161
   Correspondence:
    A Plea to the Colleges   7   160
   Notes on the
    Booker Washington Trilogy   8   146
   Correspondence   11   54
   Correspondence:
    Mr. Lindsay Protests Against Jazz   21   285

REVIEWS
   Twelve Japanese Painters,
    by Arthur Davison Ficke   4   29
   Yanks—A Book of A. E. F. Verse
    [R. R. Kirk, Russell Lord]   13   329

BOOKS REVIEWED
   General William Booth Enters into Heaven,
    and Other Poems   3   179
   The Congo and Other Poems   5   294
   The Chinese Nightingale and Other Poems   11   214
   The Golden Whales of California and
    Other Rhymes in the American Language   16   101
   Collected Poems   22   330

Going to the Stars   29   217
The Candle in the Cabin—A Weaving
    Together of Script and Singing
Collected Poems
Every Soul Is a Circus   36   46

ARTICLES ABOUT
Incarnations, by Harriet Monroe   2   101
"Too Far from Paris,"
    by Alice Corbin Henderson   4   105
Poem-Games, by Harriet Monroe   9   88
Home Rule, by Alice Corbin Henderson   9   328
Again the Negro, by Natalie Curtis   11   147
Notes and Queries from Mr. Lindsay,
    by Harriet Monroe   17   262
Two Trampers—and a Poem,
    by Maurice Lesemann   22   212
Vachel Lindsay, by Harriet Monroe   24   90
[Note]   33   54
Lindsay, by Harriet Monroe   39   206
Poetry's Old Letters,
    by Harriet Monroe   47   30
Rev. of Vachel Lindsay:
    A Poet in America,
    by Edgar Lee Masters   47   337
Poetry on Records,
    by Harry T. Moore   57   338
From the Introduction to
    The Oxford Book of American Verse,
    by F. O. Matthiessen   77   31
Rev. of The City of Discontent,
    by Mark Harris   82   355
Rev. of Sara Teasdale: A Biography,
    by Margaret Haley Carpenter   97   392
Rev. of The West-Going Heart:
    A Life of Vachel Lindsay,
    by Eleanor Ruggles   98   59
A Springfield Memoir,
    by Robert Fitzgerald   141   33

LINDSEY, THERESE
BOOKS REVIEWED
Blue Norther   27   169

LINEAWEAVER, MARIAN
POEMS
Child Afraid   65   125

LINEHAN, MOIRA
POEMS
Vow of Stability   165   326

LING-YUN, HSIEH
[See HSIEH LING-YUN]

LINK, GORDDEN
POEMS
The Deaf   60   248

LINK, SEYMOUR GORDON
POEMS
The Mulatto   35   26
Things Against the Sky
The Sculptor Year   52   195

BOOKS REVIEWED
Christ in the Breadlines: A Book
    of Poems for Christmas and Lent
    (With Kenneth W. Porter
    and Harry Elmore Hurd)   42   168

LIN KENG
POEMS
A Group of Nature Poems   46   17
    The Country in Spring
    Rainy Windy Evening
    Red Sun
    Forget
    Daybreak
        (Tr. by Harold Acton)

LINN, MABEL
POEMS
Spring   10   82
Madrigal

LIOTTA, P. H.
POEMS
The Story I Can't Tell   151   473
Epithalamion   156   127

BOOKS REVIEWED
Rules of Engagement: Poems 1974-1991   162   37

LI PO [RIHAKU]
POEMS
Exile's Letter
    (Tr. by Ezra Pound)   5   258
Goodfellowship
    (Tr. by Moon Kwan)   18   130
The Long War   28   256
Sorrow Untold
The Green Water
    (Tr. by Cheng Yu Sun)

BOOKS REVIEWED
The Works of...
    (Tr. by Shigeyoshi Obata)   22   334

LIPPMANN, ALICE D.
POEMS
Fifth Avenue Sky-Scrapers   14   19
Vagabonds
Which?   42   79

LIPSITZ, LOU
BOOKS REVIEWED
Cold Water   112   48

LIPTON, LAWRENCE
ARTICLES
The Poetry of Ewart Milne   86   366
The Poetry of Kenneth Rexroth
   [D. H. Lawrence]   90   168

BOOKS REVIEWED
Rainbow at Midnight   87   299

LISTER, QUEENE B.
POEMS
I Never Knowed   30   197
"Why Is Night?"   36   197

LITSEY, EDWIN CARLILE
POEMS
Plowman   35   83

LITSEY, SARAH
POEMS
Arc de Triomphe   33   64
For Elinor Wylie   33   303
Attic Dialogue   37   194
Dan Tabour

LITTLE, RICHARD HENRY
BOOKS REVIEWED
Line Book   27   343

LITTLEDALE, MARY
POEMS
Winter Wood   49   257

LITZ, A. WALTON
BOOKS REVIEWED
The Collected Poems
   of William Carlos Williams:
   Volume I, 1909-1939
   (Ed. with Christopher MacGowan)   150   286

LIU, JAMES J. Y.
BOOKS REVIEWED
The Art of Chinese Poetry   107   196
The Chinese Knight-Errant   112   283

LIU SHIH-AN
POEMS
One Goes a Journey
   (Tr. by Amy Lowell
   and Florence Ayscough)   13   236

LIU, SHIH SHUN
[See SHIH SHUN LIU]

LIU, TIMOTHY
POEMS
A Boston Fourth   168   230
Ode to Bunker Hill

LIVADHITIS, TASOS
POEMS
Craft   139   92
The Juggler with the Oranges
It Has Been Written...
   (Tr. by Kimon Friar)

ARTICLES ABOUT
Post-War Greek Poets, by Kimon Friar   139   99

LIVESAY, DOROTHY
POEMS
Lorca   58   30
Nocturne

BOOKS REVIEWED
Day and Night   65   220
Plainsongs   119   356

ARTICLES ABOUT
The Development of Poetry
   in Canada, 1880-1940,
   by E. K. Brown   58   34

LIVESAY, FLORENCE RANDAL
TRANSLATIONS
Slavic Songs   7   25
   Old Ruthenian Folk-Song
   Song of the Cossack
   Where Luck Lies
   The Lover—In Strawberry Time
   The Day Before the Wedding
Old Folk-Songs of Ukraina   9   74
   The Kalina
   Song of Departure
   Ruthenian Lovers
   My Field, My Field
Old Folk Songs of Ukraina   14   24
   The Return of Drebenucha
   Song of the Drowning Cossack
   Marusenka's Wedding
   Parting
   The Battlefield
Two Ukrainian Folk Songs   23   16
   Song for the Lady Dmitrova
   Kolada or Christmas Song

ARTICLES
The Ukraine and Its Song   14   36
Canadian Poetry Today
   [Duncan Campbell Scott]   27   36

BOOKS REVIEWED
Songs of Ukraina, with Ruthenian Poems (Tr.)   9   273
Songs of Ukraina (Tr.)   14   281

LIVEZEY, H. G.
BOOKS REVIEWED
In Unison   81   252

LIVINGSTONE, TRISTRAM [Pseud.]
POEMS
   Dream   51   311

LI-YOUNG LEE
  [See LEE, LI-YOUNG]

LLORENS TORRES, LUIS
POEMS
   Bolivar (Tr. by Muna Lee)   26   146

LLOYD, A. L.
BOOKS REVIEWED
   *Lament for the Death
   of a Bullfighter and Other Poems,*
     by Federico García Lorca (Tr.)   51   167

LOCHHEAD, DOUGLAS
BOOKS REVIEWED
   Made in Canada: New Poems of the Seventies
    (Ed. with Raymond Souster)   119   356

LOCKE, EDWARD
POEMS
   Crossing the Heights   170   338

LOCKETT, ROWENA
POEMS
   Nursemaid on the Sand   41   124
   Enlightened
   Above the Sea

LOCOCK, C. D.
BOOKS REVIEWED
   A Selection from Modern Swedish Poetry (Tr.)   37   164

LOERKE, OSKAR
ARTICLES ABOUT
   German Lyric Poetry Since 1945,
    by Hans Egon Holthusen
    (Tr. by Herman Salinger)   88   257

LOESER, KATINKA ["K. L."]
POEMS
   Cafe: Retrospect   57   244
   The Defender
   Alerte
   To Eight
   In This Time
   In Season   60   27
   Straight and Level Flying
   Spring Is the Time for Flowers
   Alien
   The Landing   64   24
   Three Songs for a Woman
   To Remember

REVIEWS
   Action, Didn't It, by Philip Conrad   59   224
   The Last Man, by Weldon Kees   63   349

ARTICLES ABOUT
   For the Record,
    by George Dillon   73   28

LOEWENTHAL, JESSE
POEMS
   Match   37   261

LOEWINSOHN, RON
POEMS
   Flowers, Because They've Come To Be   108   178
   From *The Step*
   From *Waiting for Spring*   112   105

REVIEWS
   Some Uses of Landscape   109   123
    Flight from America and
     Because I Am Tired of the Night,
     by George Dowden
    Bridge Force, by Frank Davey
    The Connexions, by Robert Hogg

BOOKS REVIEWED
   Watermelons   96   179
   The World of the Lie   104   258
   Against the Silences To Come   108   198
   L'Autre   112   343
   Meat Air: Poems 1957-1969   119   45
   The Step   122   293

LOGAN, JOHN
POEMS
   A Chance Visit to Mother Cabrini's Bones   81   350
   Spring Chill
   Mother Cabrini Crosses the Andes   83   67
   The Death of Southwell   85   278
   *Reflection on the Date
    of a Book: October 26*   88   368
   Lines for a Young Wanderer in Mexico   94   164
   On the Death of Keats   109   1
   Carmel: Point Lobos   109   388
   Big Sur: Partington Cove
   The Library   134   144

REVIEWS
   i: six nonlectures
    and *Poems 1923-1954,*
    by E. E. Cummings   86   353

BOOKS REVIEWED
   Cycle for Mother Cabrini   88   183
   The Zigzag Walk: Poems: 1963-1968   118   290
   The Anonymous Lover   125   166
   The Bridge of Change   140   293
   The Collected Poems
    (Ed. by A. Poulin, Jr.,
    and Jerome Mazzaro)   160   34

LOGAN, WILLIAM
POEMS
  Medusae   127   203
  Mise en Scène
  Totenlieder   130   201
  The Object
  Three Lives
    Joseph Conrad
    Camilla, Daughter of Metalous
    A Valentine for Matthew Arnold
  The Moth Disturbs the Night
  In December, Thirty-One Moons   131   125
  The Desert of Reminiscence
  Anamnesis
  Monocular
  Animal Actors on
    the English Stage After 1642   151   91
  The Age of Ballroom Dining   151   483
  Larkin   166   151
  Flamingoes   170   215
  Achilles
  For the Hostages   170   340

ARTICLES
  A Letter from Britain
    [Seamus Heaney, Geoffrey Hill,
    Ted Hughes, James Fenton,
    Tony Harrison, Michael Hofmann,
    Derek Mahon, Michael Longley,
    Paul Muldoon, Tom Paulin,
    Sorley Maclean, Douglas Dunn,
    Fred D'Aguiar, Elizabeth Jennings,
    Carol Ann Duffy, Medbh McGuckian,
    Andrew Motion, Blake Morrison]   157   222
  A Letter from Britain [II]
    [Jeffrey Wainwright, Dick Davis,
    Clive Wilmer, John Fuller, James
    Fenton, Craig Raine, Wendy Cope,
    Fiona Pitt-Kethley, John Whitworth,
    Frank Kuppner, Peter Reading,
    James Lasdun, Thomas Kinsella,
    Roy Fuller, John Heath-Stubbs,
    E. J. Scovell]   157   290

REVIEWS
  Language Against Fear   130   221
    Viper Jazz, by James Tate
    The Picnic in the Cemetery,
      by Constance Urdang
    Returning Your Call,
      by Leonard Nathan
    Angle of Ascent,
      by Robert Hayden
    Sea Grapes, by Derek Walcott
  Short Reviews   145   99
    Constant Defender, by James Tate
    [John Ashbery]
    Nights in the Iron Hotel,
      by Michael Hofmann

  Dance Script with Electric Ballerina,
    by Alice Fulton
  Original Light:
    New and Selected Poems 1973-1983,
    by Albert Goldbarth
  Selected and New Poems,
    by Norman Dubie
  Slow Transparency,
    by Rachel Hadas
  Great Tranquillity:
    Questions and Answers,
    by Yehuda Amichai
    (Tr. by Glenda Abramson
    and Tudor Parfitt)
  Children in Exile: Poems 1968-1984,
    by James Fenton
    [W. H. Auden]
  Inner Translations   160   157
  Selected Poems,
    by Robert Creeley
  The Rest of the Way,
    by J. D. McClatchy
  The Rabbiter's Bounty:
    Collected Poems and The Boys
    Who Stole the Funeral:
    A Novel Sequence,
    by Les Murray
  Kings: An Account of Books 1 and 2
    of Homer's Iliad,
    by Christopher Logue
  Seeing Things,
    by Seamus Heaney

LOGUE, CHRISTOPHER
BOOKS REVIEWED
  Devil, Maggot and Son   91   45
  Songs   94   405
  Patrocleia of Homer: A New Version   108   416
  Kings: An Account of Books 1 and 2
    of Homer's Iliad   160   157

LOHF, KENNETH A.
POEMS
  Picasso at Vallauris   94   26
  Les Saltimbanques   95   294

LOMAX, JOHN A.
BOOKS REVIEWED
  Songs of the Cattle Trail
    and Cow Camp   16   273

ARTICLES ABOUT
  Cowboy Songs and Ballads,
    by Alice Corbin Henderson   10   255

LOMBARDI, VINCENT
ARTICLES ABOUT
  Rev. of The Strength of Fields,
    by James Dickey   137   349

LONG, H. C.
POEMS
Through the Window Near His Bed   7   132
The Ides of March

LONG, HANIEL
POEMS
On the Road   12   83
  Song of Young Burbage
  The Herd Boy
  Shoes
  The Cuban in the States
  Madness
  Dead Men Tell No Tales
  A Book on Economics
  The Cause of This I Know Not
  Song ("Poppies paramour...")
  Star-Dust
  The Terror
  Seeger
Girl-Athletes   23   12
Easter 1933   43   138
The Women of My Blood   57   18
To a Friend Who Won Out

REVIEWS
The Beloved Stranger,
  by Witter Bynner   15   281
The Poetic Mind, by F. C. Prescott   22   342

BOOKS REVIEWED
Poems   18   101
Atlantides   45   226
Walt Whitman and
  the Springs of Courage   53   273

LONG, LILY A.
POEMS
The Singing Place   1   47
Immured
He Buildeth His House   8   183
The Poet's Part

LONG, ROBERT
POEMS
What It Is   136   286
Thruway
Poem ("Someone you loved is dead...")
Saying One Thing
Old Story   138   194
Strange Insects
In the Red
Interior Decoration   143   15
In the Unfinished House
Goodbye
Dreaming   144   209
Hot Air
Perfect Sunset

Return to Nowheresville   159   320
Tie City

LONG, ROBERT HILL
POEMS
Hatteras   150   17
Fin de Siècle
The Third River   154   144
The Mouse   156   79
The Conspiracy   163   195
Closing My Eyes in Heaven   168   187

**LONGFELLOW,
HENRY WADSWORTH**
ARTICLES ABOUT
Rev. of A Victorian American,
  by Herbert S. Gorman   29   266
Rev. of Young Longfellow,
  by Lawrance Thompson   54   29
Rev. of Early American Poets
  (Ed. by Louis Untermeyer)   81   261
Rev. of The Fields Were Green,
  by George Arms   84   98

LONGFORD, [LORD]
ARTICLES ABOUT
Letter from Ireland,
  by Patrick Kavanagh   74   286

LONGLEY, JUDY
POEMS
Gauguin and Bonnard   156   205
Delta Journal
Flores, Flores por los Muertos   162   29
Garden Wedding   162   199
Hunting Lodge,
  Wakullah Springs, Florida
Doppelgänger   167   219
June Again   170   127

LONGLEY, MICHAEL
POEMS
The Quilt   167   64
The Design

BOOKS REVIEWED
No Continuing City   118   288

ARTICLES ABOUT
A Letter from Britain,
  by William Logan   157   222
A Map of Contemporary Irish Poetry,
  by Dennis O'Driscoll   167   94

LOOMIS, JON
POEMS
Common Prayer   162   327
Insomnia

LOPEZ, LUIS C.
POEMS
Village Night
   (Tr. by Muna Lee)   26   126

LÓPEZ VELARDE, RAMÓN
POEMS
The Anchor
   (Tr. by H. R. Hays)   57   16
What Delightful Madness   62   71
If You Die Unwed
   (Tr. by H. R. Hays)

ARTICLES ABOUT
A Mexican Symbolist,
   by H. R. Hays   57   40

LORCA, FEDERICO GARCÍA
[See GARCÍA LORCA, FEDERICO]

LORCA, FRANCISCO GARCÍA
[See GARCÍA LORCA, FRANCISCO]

LORD, RUSSELL
BOOKS REVIEWED
Voices from the Fields:
   A Book of Country Songs
   by Farming People (Ed.)   52   299

ARTICLES ABOUT
Rev. of Yanks—A Book
   of A. E. F. Verse   13   329

LORDE, AUDRE
BOOKS REVIEWED
Cables to Rage   119   356
The New York Head Shop
   and Museum   129   296

LORIMER, EMILIA STUART
POEMS
Fish of the Flood   1   9

LOTHIAN, ALEXANDER
BOOKS REVIEWED
The Golden Treasury
   of the Greeks (Tr.)   18   284

LOTT, RICK
POEMS
Nocturne for Autumn   149   7
Exile   158   85

LOUGEE, DAVID
POEMS
If the Seas Unmask   77   16
My Love's Mad Music
Lament   79   81

Charade   86   235
Mountain View   95   163
On Behalf of the Ivory Tower   100   29
The Moment
Lines from the End of a Play   102   239
Old Man in a Wheelchair
Childhood

REVIEWS
A Little Treasury of British Poetry
   (Ed. by Oscar Williams)   81   191
Quite Early One Morning and
   Adventures in the Skin Trade,
   by Dylan Thomas   87   114
Dylan Thomas: Letters
   to Vernon Watkins
   (Ed. by Vernon Watkins)   94   114

LOUNBERG, KATHERINE
POEMS
Lonely Places   36   263
   This Forgotten Pasture
   The Walk in the Swamp
   Sybil
   The Valley Widow

LOURIE, DICK
BOOKS REVIEWED
The Dream Telephone   116   125

LOURIE, IVEN
POEMS
Sea Fever   111   310
Comprehension

LOUW, N. P. VAN WYK
ARTICLES ABOUT
Report from Goli,
   by Turner Cassity   95   242

LOVELACE, SKYLER
POEMS
Rock, Scissors, Paper   158   84
Gyroscope   158   132

LOVELL, ERNEST J., JR.
BOOKS REVIEWED
His Very Self and Voice (Ed.)
   [Lord Byron]   87   372

LOVELL, JAMES
POEMS
A Letter Out of Silence   40   258
A Legacy

LOVETT, ROBERT MORSS
ARTICLES
[Tribute to Harriet Monroe]   49   160

REVIEWS
  The Flowering Stone,
    by George Dillon   39   328
  A Poet's Life: Seventy Years
    in a Changing World,
    by Harriet Monroe   52   30
  The Poetry of Freedom
    (Ed. by William Rose Benét
    and Norman Cousins)   67   46

BOOKS REVIEWED
  Selected Poems
    of William Vaughn Moody (Ed.)   38   331

LOWBURY, EDWARD
  BOOKS REVIEWED
  Facing North
    (With Terence Heywood)   97   192

LOWE, ROBERT LIDDELL
  POEMS
    "Never Again"   35   314
    God's Hands
    This Glittering Grief   39   14
    Acre of Song
    Beauty and Sorrow
    Sir Isaac Newton   56   136
    An Old Man Talking in His Sleep
    The Liable Tree

  ARTICLES
    Correspondence   61   698

  REVIEWS
    The Iron Dish, by Lynn Riggs   37   347
    Wait for These Things,
      by George Abbe   57   332
    Tropic Earth, by Clifford Gessler   65   218
    Partial Success   65   338
      The Devious Way,
        by Theodore Morrison
      And You, Thoreau!,
        by August Derleth
      Soldiers and Strangers,
        by Edward Fenton   67   162
    Three at Mid-Century   70   98
      Mid-Century, by Frances Frost
      Poems 1938-1945, by Robert Graves
      Dublin Poems, by Seumas O'Sullivan
      Heroes and Heroines,
        by Reed Whittemore   71   97
    Poems, by William Jay Smith   73   116

LOWELL, AMY
  [See also "A. L."]
  POEMS
    Apology   2   134
    A Blockhead

  The Cyclists   4   1
  The Foreigner
  A Lady
  Music
  The Bungler
  Anticipation
  A Gift
  The Forsaken
  The Coal Picker   4   178
  The Bombardment   5   60
  Venus Transiens   6   9
  Solitaire
  Red Slippers
  Chalks: Black, Red, White   6   269
    Lead Soldiers
    Vernal Equinox
    Fenway Park
    May Evening in Central Park
    Aliens
    Strain
    The Painter on Silk
  Pyrotechnics   8   76
  1777   8   219
    The Trumpet-Vine Arbor
    The City of Falling Leaves
  Lacquer Prints   9   302
    Streets
    Desolation
    Sunshine
    Illusion
    A Year Passes
    A Lover
    To a Husband
    From China
    Autumn
    Ephemera
    Document
    The Emperor's Garden
    One of the "Hundred Views of Fuji,"
      by Hokusai
    Disillusion
    Paper Fishes
    Meditation
    The Camellia Tree of Matsue
  The Landlady of the Whinton Inn
    Tells a Story   11   171
  Appuldurcombe Park   12   260
  The Bookshop   14   310
  Peach-Color to a Soap-Bubble
  The Artist
  Autumn
  Balls
  Good Gracious!
  The Day That Was That Day!   17   59
  Twenty-Four Hokku on a Modern Theme   18   124
  Southern April   21   117
    Charleston, South Carolina
    The Middleton Place

Magnolia Gardens
A South Carolina Forest
The Vow
Eleanora Duse   22   234
Evelyn Ray   23   117
The Green Parrakeet
The Madonna of Carthagena   27   117

TRANSLATIONS
Poems by Li Hai-Ku, Wen Cheng-Ming,
Ch'en Hung-Shou, Liang T'ung-Shu,
T'ai Ta-Mien, Liu Shih-An, Lu Kun,
T'ao Ch'ien, Wang Chang-Ling,
and Wang Ching-Seng
(Tr. with Florence Ayscough)   13   233

ARTICLES
Vers Libre and Metrical Prose
[Henri de Régnier, Fiona Macleod,
Paul Fort, Remy de Gourmont]   3   213
Nationalism in Art   5   33
Correspondence:
Miss Lowell Not the Editor
[Some Imagist Poets]   6   52
Correspondence:
Miss Lowell on Translating Chinese
[Helen Waddell, James Legge,
Eunice Tietjens]   21   167

REVIEWS
Myself and I, by Fannie Stearns Davis   2   225
Flashlights, by Mary Aldis   8   318
Profiles from China, by Eunice Tietjens   10   326
These Times, by Louis Untermeyer   11   157
Growing Pains, by Jean Starr Untermeyer 14   47

BOOKS REVIEWED
A Dome of Many Colored Glass   2   107
Sword Blades and Poppy Seed   5   134
Some Imagist Poets—An Anthology   6   150
Six French Poets:
Studies in Contemporary Literature
[Émile Verhaeren, Albert Samain,
Remy de Gourmont, Henri de Régnier,
Francis Jammes, Paul Fort]   7   202
Some Imagist Poets: 1916   8   255
Men, Women and Ghosts   9   207
Tendencies in Modern American Poetry   11   151
Some Imagist Poets, 1917   11   339
Can Grande's Castle   13   97
Some Imagist Poets   14   281
Pictures of the Floating World   15   332
Legends   19   330
John Keats   26   220
What's O'Clock   27   154
East Wind   29   160
Ballads for Sale   31   338

Correspondence of a Friendship
(With Florence Ayscough)
(Ed. by Harley Farnsworth MacNair)   69   54

ARTICLES ABOUT
[Note on misprint]   4   72
Our Contemporaries
[Ferris Greenslet]   5   299
Miss Lowell's Discovery: Polyphonic Prose,
by John Gould Fletcher   6   32
Our Contemporaries,
by Alice Corbin Henderson   6   99
Various Views, by Harriet Monroe   8   140
[Note on Lacquer Prints]   9   331
Living History, by John Gould Fletcher   10   149
Correspondence
from Alice Corbin Henderson   12   228
Rev. of Amy Lowell, by W. Bryher   13   97
That Bookshelf, by Harriet Monroe   15   39
A Keats Memorial   16   231
Correspondence from Dorothy Dudley   20   53
Correspondence from Witter Bynner   20   111
On Translating Chinese Poetry II,
by Eunice Tietjens   20   328
[Note from Eunice Tietjens]   21   172
Correspondence from Llewellyn Jones   21   281
Correspondence from Roberts Walker   21   284
Correspondence from Henry Bellamann   21   342
Apologia, by Eunice Tietjens   22   267
Amy Lowell, by Harriet Monroe   25   32
Memories of Amy Lowell,
by Harriet Monroe   26   100
The Amy Lowell Scholarships,
by Harriet Monroe   26   276
Rev. of Amy Lowell: A Chronicle
with Extracts from Her Correspondence,
by S. Foster Damon   47   212
Rev. of A History
of American Poetry, 1900-1940,
by Horace Gregory
and Marya Zaturenska   69   210
In Memory of John Gould Fletcher,
by Donald Davidson   77   154
Rev. of Poems by Wang Wêi
(Tr. by Chang Yin-nan
and Lewis C. Walmsley)   96   309
Rev. of Harriet Monroe and
the Poetry Renaissance,
by Ellen Williams   131   39

LOWELL, JAMES RUSSELL
BOOKS REVIEWED
The Function of the Poet and Other Essays 19   54

ARTICLES ABOUT
The Glittering Metropolis,
by Harriet Monroe   14   30

Rev. of *The Fields Were Green*,
  by George Arms   84   98
Rev. of *James Russell Lowell*,
  by Martin Duberman   111   333

LOWELL, ROBERT
POEMS
  The Ghost (After Sextus Propertius)   68   297
  The Fat Man in the Mirror   70   238
  Child's Song   101   67
  Jonathan Edwards
    in Western Massachusetts
  Four Spanish Sonnets   103   74
    ("I saw the musty shingles...")
    ("You search in Rome for Rome?...")
    ("This structure you admire...")
    ("The whistling arrow flies...")

TRANSLATIONS
  Poems by Charles Baudelaire   98   343

ARTICLES
  Correspondence to William Kolodney
    (With Louise Bogan
    and Stanley Kunitz)   100   412

REVIEWS
  Collected Poems,
    by Yvor Winters   98   40

BOOKS REVIEWED
  Land of Unlikeness   65   264
  Lord Weary's Castle   70   262
  Life Studies   95   41
  Phedre, by Racine (Tr.),
    in *Phaedra and Figaro*   100   41
  Imitations   100   43
  For the Union Dead   106   358
  The Old Glory   108   189
  Near the Ocean   110   413
  Randall Jarrell 1914-1965
    (Ed. with Peter Taylor
    and Robert Penn Warren)   112   118
  Prometheus Bound   115   281
  Notebook 1967-68   116   191
  Notebook   119   159
  History   123   304
  The Dolphin
  For Lizzie and Harriet
  The Oresteia of Aeschylus (Tr.)   137   220

ARTICLES ABOUT
  A Note on Robert Lowell,
    by William Elton   71   138
  Correspondence from John Ciardi   72   261
  Falling Asleep over Grillparzer:
    An Interview with Robert Lowell,
    by John McCormick   81   269

Rev. of *Robert Lowell:*
  The First Twenty Years,
    by Hugh B. Staples   102   269
  [Note]   103   139
Rev. of *The Poetic Themes of...*
  by Jerome Mazzaro   109   198
Rev. of *Herakles*,
  by Archibald MacLeish   112   199
Rev. of *Somewhere Is Such a Kingdom*,
  by Geoffrey Hill   128   232
The Things of the Eye,
  by Robert Fitzgerald   132   107
Allen Tate:
  A Poet on Poetry, 1924-1944,
    by Ashley Brown   135   103
Memorial Service for Elizabeth Bishop,
  by Penelope Laurans   135   227
Poets Aloud, by Donald Hall   139   297
Rev. of *Presence*, by Alan Williamson   143   163
Waking Up Over the *Aeneid*,
  by Paul Breslin   143   347
"Sacred Beings":
  Writers in Recorded Conversation,
    by Michael Milburn   146   101
Rev. of *The Pose of Happiness*,
  by Gail Mazur   150   102
Rev. of *The Psycho-Political Muse:*
  American Poetry Since the Fifties,
    by Paul Breslin   152   229
Rev. of *White Paper:*
  On Contemporary American Poetry,
    by J. D. McClatchy   156   297
Rev. of *Becoming a Poet: Elizabeth Bishop*
  with Marianne Moore and Robert Lowell,
  by David Kalstone
  (Ed. by Robert Hemenway)   157   159
Rev. of *Randall Jarrell: A Literary Life*,
  by William H. Pritchard   158   100
Rev. of *Elizabeth Bishop:*
  The Biography of a Poetry,
    by Lorrie Goldensohn   161   34
Finishes: Notes on Ambition and Survival,
  by Christian Wiman   169   217

LOWENFELS, LILLIAN
BOOKS REVIEWED
  Modern Poetry from Spain
  and Latin America
  (Tr. with Nan Braymer)   107   338

LOWENFELS, WALTER
POEMS
  4 to the Rain   29   306
  Cloudburst
  Rain in the Desert
  It Rains All Night
  Farmland
  Homer   52   255

ARTICLES
  Correspondence
    [Objectivists]   38   289

BOOKS REVIEWED
  Episodes and Epistles   28   342
  Finale of Seem: A Lyrical Narrative   42   49
  Apollinaire: An Elegy
  Sonnets of Love and Liberty   88   329
  American Voices   94   408
  Some Deaths   106   306
  Poets of Today (Ed.)   106   429
  Where Is Vietnam? American Poets Respond
    (Ed. with Nan Braymer)   III   410

LOWENSTEIN, TOM
POEMS
  The Death of Dido   131   218

LOWES, JOHN LIVINGSTON
BOOKS REVIEWED
  Convention and Revolt in Poetry   14   269
  The Road to Xanadu
    [S. T. Coleridge]   30   283

LOWRY, H(OWARD) F(OSTER)
BOOKS REVIEWED
  The Note-Books of Matthew Arnold
    (Ed. with Karl Young
    and Waldo Hilary Dunn)   81   196
  The Poems of Arthur Hugh Clough
    (Ed. with A. L. P. Norrington
    and F. L. Mulhauser)   82   27

LOWY, SIMON
POEMS
  The Classic Pose   127   75

LOY, MINA
BOOKS REVIEWED
  Lunar Baedecker   23   100

ARTICLES ABOUT
  The Editor in France, by Harriet Monroe   23   90

LOZANO, CARLOS
BOOKS REVIEWED
  The Elementary Odes of Pablo Neruda (Tr.)   101   349

LUCAS, E. V.
BOOKS REVIEWED
  Remember Louvain, A Little Book
    of Liberty and War (Ed.)   6   98

LUCAS, F. L.
BOOKS REVIEWED
  Ariadne   42   115
  Criticism and Poetry   44   291

LUCAS, ST. JOHN
BOOKS REVIEWED
  The Oxford Book
  of Italian Verse (Ed.)
    (2nd ed. by C. Dionisotti)   82   277

LU CHI
ARTICLES ABOUT
  Rev. of *Poetry and Experience*,
    by Archibald MacLeish   99   191

LUCIA, JOSEPH P.
POEMS
  Move Toward Me   158   146

LUCIE-SMITH, EDWARD
BOOKS REVIEWED
  A Tropical Childhood   102   393
  Towards Silence   115   61
  Holding Your Eight Hands: An Anthology
    of Science Fiction Verse (Ed.)   117   115
  The Well-Wishers   127   234

LUCINA, MARY
POEMS
  Footprints   164   272

LUCKHARDT, HERTHA D.
POEMS
  Brevities   47   248
  Soirée
  Storm
  The Passing

LUDVIGSON, SUSAN
POEMS
  The Widow   136   142
  Some Notes on Courage   139   210
  After He Called Her a Witch   141   79
  When Love Becomes   145   269
  Happiness: The Forbidden Subject   157   209
  New Orleans Feather Sculptor
    Dies of Knife Wounds
  Listening   164   220
  This Move into the Abstract
  Gratitude
  A Day Like Any Other   166   11

BOOKS REVIEWED
  The Swimmer   146   38
  The Beautiful Noon
    of No Shadow   151   360

LUEDERS, EDWARD
TRANSLATIONS
  Poems by Sachiko Yoshihara
    and Kio Kuroda
    (Tr. with Naoshi Koriyama)   143   320

LU FU LI
POEMS
Quatrain ("Here where ten thousand..")
   (Tr. by George Margulies
   and Willard R. Trask)   46   6

LUGONES, LEOPOLDO
POEMS
Journey
   (Tr. by Muna Lee)   26   118
Death of the Moon
   (Tr. by Janet Brassert)   62   84

LUHAN, MABEL DODGE
POEMS
False Start   28   133

LUHRS, MARIE
POEMS
Lights in a Pool   23   316
   Flash
   Fugitive
   Rainy Night
   Murderous Weapons
Patterns for Weavers   27   77
   Pursuit of Beauty
   The Tapestry
   This World of Spring
   Cry
   Said the Devil
   Premonition
Leaves from Five Trees   31   68
   Cylix: Bacchante
   Ennui of an Empress
   A Death
   The Grassy Bank
   Child-Sight
Notes in Passing   36   242
   Celebration
   On Horseback
   Women Dream
   Death Before Death
Ascent   41   140
Seasons   44   205
   Sorrow in Summer
   Autumnal
New Grief   48   248
For the Glory of Italy   51   179

REVIEWS
First Poems, by Edwin Muir   27   50
Ship's Log,
   by Grace Hazard Conkling   27   52
Will-o'-the-Wisp, by Dorothy Dow   27   281
Kam and Pages from the
   History of Zachy Trenoy,
   by Ruth Manning-Sanders   27   339
The Brothers Sitwell   28   274

The Thirteenth Caesar,
   by Sacheverell Sitwell
Out of the Flame,
   by Osbert Sitwell
Animula Vagula, by Leonard Bacon   29   170
Citadels, by Marguerite Wilkinson   29   223
The Halt in the Garden,
   by Robert Hillyer   29   284
Enough Rope, by Dorothy Parker   30   52
Rococo, by Ralph Cheever Dunning   30   108
Two Gentlemen in Bonds,
   by John Crowe Ransom   30   162
These People,
   by Howard McKinley Corning   30   227
Lost Eden, by E. Merrill Root   30   229
Autobiographies: Reveries over Childhood
   and Youth and The Trembling of the Veil,
   by W. B. Yeats   30   279
Poetical Works of William Butler Yeats,
   Vol. I, Lyrical Poems;
   Vol. II, Dramatic Poems   30   346
Capricious Winds,
   by Helen Birch Bartlett   31   94
The Lone Adventurer,
   by Stanton A. Coblentz   31   96
Rustic Elegies, by Edith Sitwell   31   224
Little Henrietta,
   by Lizette Woodworth Reese   31   283
Boy in the Wind, by George Dillon   31   343
Selected Poems, by Walter de la Mare   32   108
Lost Address, by Chard Powers Smith   33   44
Nursery Rhymes for Children of Darkness,
   by Gladys Oaks   33   225
The Upward Pass,
   by Henry Bellamann   33   345
This Stubborn Root,
   by Hortense Flexner   38   109

LUJAN, JAMES GRAHAM
TRANSLATIONS
Poem by Gabriela Mistral
   (Tr. with Richard O'Connell)   63   204

LU KUN
POEMS
From the Straw Hut
   Among the Seven Peaks
   (Tr. by Amy Lowell
   and Florence Ayscough)   13   237

LULL, RODERICK ALLYN
POEMS
In the Prison   29   22
   Church
   Condemned
   The Yard
   At the Death Hour
   Freedom

LU LUN
POEMS
   Spring Longings at Ch'ang-An   46   11
   Among the Hills
     (Tr. by Helen Burwell Chapin)

LUNDAHL, GENE
POEMS
   A Father to His Young Son   98   221

LURIE, ALISON
POEMS
   The Archer with His Arrow   70   126
   In a Good Year
   Trees, Being Neighbors

LUX, THOMAS
POEMS
   Poem Beginning with
     a Random Phrase from Coleridge   132   89
   The Night So Bright a Squirrel Reads   137   158
   After a Few Whiffs
     of Another World
   It's the Little Towns I Like
   His Spine Curved Just Enough
   Backyard Swing Set   153   210

LU, FEI-PAI
[See FEI-PAI LU]

LU YU
POEMS
   The Pedlar of Spells
     (Tr. by Arthur Waley)   11   200

LUZI, MARIO
POEMS
   Nell'imminenza dei quarant'anni/
     On Approaching Forty   155   24
   Hunt
     (Tr. by Dana Gioia)
   From *Tutto perso, tutto parificato?/*
     (All Lost, All Made Equal?)   155   27
     [*Stolen? that is exactly how*]
     [*They speculate on a fall*]
     [*Can they?*]
     [*"Hurry and become the past..."*]
     (Tr. by Stephen Sartarelli)

ARTICLES ABOUT
   Some Notes on
     Post-War Italian Poetry,
     by Paolo Cherchi
     and Joseph Parisi   155   161

LYLE, ROB
BOOKS REVIEWED
   Poems from Limbo   102   193

LYMAN, DEAN B., JR.
POEMS
   Pomegranates   12   76

BOOKS REVIEWED
   Last Lutanist   24   280

LYMAN, HENRY
TRANSLATIONS
   Poem by Aleksis Rannit   131   321

LYMAN, JACK
REVIEWS
   Irish Anthologies   21   51
     Anthology of Irish Verse
     (Ed. by Padraic Colum)
     Irish Poets of Today
     (Ed. by L. D'O. Walters)

LYMAN, W. W.
BOOKS REVIEWED
   Figs from California (Ed.)   21   276
   Figs from California (Ed.)   24   162

LYNCH, GENEVIEVE LOUISE
POEMS
   Nostalgia   24   78
   Immigrants
   Alcestis

LYNCH, THOMAS (P.)
POEMS
   A Death   138   327
   The Old Dilemma
   The Grandmothers   139   324
   The Widow
   A Dog with Character

BOOKS REVIEWED
   Skating with Heather Grace   152   98

LYNCH, WILLIAM S.
BOOKS REVIEWED
   Poet to Poet, A Treasury of Golden Criticism
     (Ed. with Houston Peterson)   66   345

LYON, LILIAN BOWES
POEMS
   The Glittering North   49   198

LYONS, NATHAN
BOOKS REVIEWED
   Jones Very: Selected Poems (Ed.)   111   333

LYONS, RICHARD
POEMS
   Constellation   147   219

Books Reviewed
   One Squeaking Straw   94   189

LYSOHORSKY, ONDRA
Poems
   Poet   116   273
   Room for All
   At the Circus
   Trees in Courtyards
     (Tr. by Isobella Levatin
     and W. H. Auden)

LYSTER, M. [Pseud.]
Poems
   The Painted Saint in the Wood   15   23
   Dawn

LYTTELTON, LUCY
Books Reviewed
   Lyrical Poems   1   97

LYTTLE, DAVID
Books Reviewed
   No Other Time   97   114

M

"M. A. S."
[See SEIFFERT,
MARJORIE ALLEN]

"M. D. Z."
[See ZABEL,
MORTON DAUWEN]

"M. G."
[See GAVIN, MARY]

"M. M."
[See MICHELSON, MAX]

"M. S."
[See STROBEL, MARION]

MAAS, WILLARD
POEMS
  Studies in Hyperbole   38   186
    Ten O'Clock Promenade
    Challenge Out of the Heart
  Strong Men Love a Building   42   84
  Esoterics of the Fox
  Melody for a Swan Song
  Memory of Winds   43   320
    Address to the Heart at the Lake's Edge
    A Wind Stirring
    Winter Atavism
  Contemporary Legend   51   235
  Transcontinental
  No Word for the Young
  Darkness Coming
  Song ("What will the evening tell...")
  Journey and Return   52   209
  The Secret on the Urn   56   8
  Tableau at Cocktail Hour
  Morning, Memorial, Monolith   74   13

ARTICLES
  A Brief Statement   52   227

REVIEWS
  We Gather Strength,
    by Herman Spector, Joseph Kalar,
    Edwin Rolfe, and S. Funaroff   44   50

  U. S. 1, by Muriel Rukeyser   52   101
  Special Laughter, by Howard Nutt   58   162

BOOKS REVIEWED
  Fire Testament   48   113
  Concerning the Young   53   336

MAC ADAMS, LEWIS, JR.
BOOKS REVIEWED
  The Poetry Room   120   49

MACARTNEY, FREDERICK T.
BOOKS REVIEWED
  Poems   17   276

MACAULAY, ROSE
BOOKS REVIEWED
  Milton   93   404

ARTICLES ABOUT
  A London Letter,
    by Richard Aldington   15   227

MACAULAY, THOMAS BABINGTON
ARTICLES ABOUT
  Oliver St. John Gogarty,
    by Vivian Mercier   93   35

MAC BETH, GEORGE
BOOKS REVIEWED
  The Night of Stones   117   108
  Collected Poems 1958-1970   120   170
  Shrapnel   127   159
  A Poet's Year
  Poems from Oby   145   161

MAC CAIG, NORMAN
POEMS
  Beach Talk   86   81
  A Good Day   100   87
  Walking in a Rain Storm
  Upper Circle
  Things in Each Other
  Drinking Fountain
  Brackloch

REVIEWS
  Figs and Thistles,
    by Sydney Goodsir Smith   96 320

BOOKS REVIEWED
  Riding Lights   87 53
  The Sinai Sort   91 268
  A Common Grace   102 330
  A Man in My Position   119 291

ARTICLES ABOUT
  Poets and Mushrooms,
    by Charles Tomlinson   100 104

MAC CAUGHEY, VAUGHAN
ARTICLES
  Nature Themes
    in Ancient Hawaiian Poetry
    [Nathaniel B. Emerson]   10 205

MAC DIARMID, HUGH
[Pseud. of GRIEVE,
CHRISTOPHER MURRAY]
POEMS
  Of Life and Death   55 128
  My Heart Always Goes
    Back to the North   72 175
  Speech, My Beloved   101 72

BOOKS REVIEWED
  Stony Limits and Other Poems 46 285
  At the Sign of the Thistle:
    A Collection of Essays
  Second Hymn to Lenin   49 282
  In Memoriam James Joyce.
    A Vision of World Language 88 48
  Selected Poems of...
    (Ed. by Oliver Brown)   88 52
  Collected Poems   102 177
  Collected Poems of...
    (Ed. by John C. Weston) 112 131

ARTICLES ABOUT
  Hugh MacDiarmid and Scottish Poetry,
    by David Daiches   72 202
  Some Poets of
    the Scottish Renaissance,
    by Tom Scott   88 43
  Review by Paul Breslin   168 337

MAC DONAGH, DONAGH
POEMS
  Six Men and Their Dog   50 14
  Water and Time Divide
    the World Too Much   56 81

BOOKS REVIEWED
  Veterans and Other Poems   59 51

  The Oxford Book of Irish Verse:
    XVII Century-XX Century
    (Ed. with Lennox Robinson) 94 260

MAC DONAGH, THOMAS
BOOKS REVIEWED
  Literature in Ireland:
    Studies Irish and Anglo-Irish 8 309

ARTICLES ABOUT
  Correspondence
    from Padraic Colum   8 268

MACDONALD, CYNTHIA
BOOKS REVIEWED
  Amputations   123 241
  Transplants   129 285
  Alternate Means of Transport 148 36

MAC DONALD, GOODRIDGE
ARTICLES ABOUT
  Poets in Canada,
    by Margaret Avison   94 182

MAC DONALD, JESSIE
POEMS
  The Debt   17 316
  A Prayer

MAC DONALD, WILSON
BOOKS REVIEWED
  Out of the Wilderness   30 353

MAC EWEN, GWENDOLYN
BOOKS REVIEWED
  The Rising Fire   104 385
  A Breakfast for Barbarians 109 53

MAC FADYEN, JANET
POEMS
  Hymn   166 82

MAC GILLIVRAY, ARTHUR [S.J.]
ARTICLES
  Correspondence
    [Edna St. Vincent Millay]   90 259

MAC GOWAN, CHRISTOPHER
BOOKS REVIEWED
  The Collected Poems
    of William Carlos Williams:
    Volume I, 1909-1939
    (Ed. with A. Walton Litz) 150 286

MAC GREEVY, THOMAS
POEMS
  Moments Musicaux   99 85
  Breton Oracles

MACHADO, ANTONIO
[ANTONIO MACHADO Y ALVAREZ]
[See also DE MAIRENA, JUAN, Pseud.]
POEMS
Portrait   98   384
Poem CXXXVI (xxi and xv)
    (Tr. by John Frederick Nims)
To José María Palacio   101   303
The Draw-Wheel
The Ephemeral Past
O Luminous Late Day!
Grey Olives
Proverbs and Canticles
Winter Sun
    (Tr. by Charles Tomlinson)
From The Apocryphal Songbook:
    Abel Martín
    (Tr. by Ben Belitt)   101   312

BOOKS REVIEWED
Eighty Poems of...
    (Tr. by Willis Barnstone)   101   343
Juan de Mairena: Epigrams, Maxims,
    Memoranda, and Memoirs
    of an Apocryphal Professor,
    with an Appendix of Poems
    from "The Apocryphal Songbooks"
    (Ed. and tr. by Ben Belitt)   105   198
Castilian Ilexes: Versions from...
    (Tr. by Charles Tomlinson
    and Henry Gifford)

MACHIAVELLI, NICCOLÒ
BOOKS REVIEWED
Mandragola
    (Tr. by Anne and Henry Paolucci)   94   350

MACHWE, P.
TRANSLATIONS
Poem by Devendra Satyarthi   93   228
Poem by Rajendra Shah   93   231
Poems by Mangesh Padgaonkar
    and Vinda Karandikar   93   238

MAC INNES, MAIRI
BOOKS REVIEWED
Splinters   83   172

MAC INNES, TOM
ARTICLES ABOUT
The Development of Poetry
    in Canada, 1880-1940,
    by E. K. Brown   58   34

MAC INTYRE, AMELIA
ARTICLES ABOUT
About the Activist Poets,
    by Lawrence Hart   78   99

MAC INTYRE, C(ARLYLE) F.
[CARLYLE MC INTYRE]
POEMS
Rodomontades   16   76
    The Brimming Cup
    Compensations
    The Untamed
    The Green Door
    The Mourners
    Lady of Autumn
    The House of Laurels
On the Road   20   70
    Promenading
    The Scissor-Grinder
    The Visit
Home Brew   37   74
    Interim
    In the "Golden Lark"
    Three Topers in a Shanty
Sonata in Hollywood   46   119
    The Sycamore
    Consolation
    In the Fog
    One Knocking at a Door
    Hawk
    Snake
    April Skies
    White
    The Full Cup
    Toward You
    These Still Acres
    House
Night Letter to a Man Lost
    in Mid-Ocean   51   250
By a Patriot's Grave
Sincerely Not Artesian
"Revenge Is Not a Food To Be Eaten Hot"
The Old Woman Waits for Spring   53   300
The Ex-Senator
Aqueduct of Claudius   55   8
Autumn in Arles
Idyl Beside the Lower Tiber
Retired Actress
Spring Dance of the Bedouins
Chrysanthemums
From Electra Hid an Axe   56   257
Mariposa Lilies   59   82
Black Wind
Green Sloughage
Skyscraper
The Begetting of John Doe Jr.
Vista in a Garden

BOOKS REVIEWED
The Brimming Cup   43   225
Poems   50   289
Cafés and Cathedrals   56   161
The Black Bull   60   341

Goethe's Faust,
   a New American Translation   61   406
Rainer Maria Rilke:
   Fifty Selected Poems (Tr.)   61   441
One Hundred Poems
   from Les Fleurs du Mal (Tr.)   72   105
Tristan Corbière: Selections
   from Les Amours Jaunes (Tr.)   84   351

ARTICLES ABOUT
   Recent French Publications,
      by Wallace Fowlie   93   40

MACKAY, HELEN
   BOOKS REVIEWED
      London, One November   9   152

MAC KAY, L. A.
   POEMS
      Polyphemus Madden'd   58   25
      Aubade

MACKAY, MARGARET MACKPRANG
   POEMS
      Under a Peking Peach-Tree   46   21

MACKAYE, ARVIA
   POEMS
      The Purple Gray   8   191

MACKAYE, CHRISTY
   BOOKS REVIEWED
      Wind in the Grass   41   105

MACKAYE, PERCY
   BOOKS REVIEWED
      Uriel and Other Poems   1   131
      Rip Van Winkle   19   51
      The Skippers of Nancy Gloucester   24   283
      The Gobbler of God   32   352

MACKENZIE, JEAN KENYON
   BOOKS REVIEWED
      The Venture   28   56

MACKENZIE, W. ROY
   BOOKS REVIEWED
      Ballads and Sea Songs
      from Nova Scotia (Ed.)   33   166

MACKERETH, JAMES A.
   POEMS
      Espied   25   66

MACKESY, MARJORIE
   [MARJORIE MACKERY]
   POEMS
      The Children's Room   39   23

ARTICLES ABOUT
   [Note on name]   39   114

MACKIE, ALBERT D.
   ARTICLES ABOUT
      Some Poets of the
         Scottish Renaissance,
         by Tom Scott   88   43

MACKINTOSH, DUNCAN
   BOOKS REVIEWED
      A Collection of Chinese Lyrics,
         by Alan Ayling (Tr.)   112   283

MACKINTOSH, E. A.
   BOOKS REVIEWED
      A Highland Regiment and Other Poems 14   220
      War the Liberator and Other Pieces

MACKLIN, ELIZABETH
   POEMS
      Leaving One of the State Parks
         After a Family Outing   135   207

MACLAINE, CHRISTOPHER
   ARTICLES
      We and They: The Artist in California 72   256

MAC LANE, MARY
   ARTICLES ABOUT
      Fire of Youth,
         by Harriet Monroe   10   154

MAC LEAN, KATHARINE ALLISON
   POEMS
      Artemidora Buried in Egypt   30   319

MACLEAN, SORLEY
   ARTICLES ABOUT
      A Letter from Britain,
         by William Logan   157   222

MAC LEISH, ARCHIBALD
   POEMS
      Ars Poetica   28   126
      Published Correspondence   33   184
         Epistle to the Rapalloan
         Unanswered Letter to a Lady Novelist
         Communication to Leon-Paul Fargue
      Discovery of This Time   57   1
      Hypocrite Auteur   81   45
      Five Poems from the 1920s   137   63
         Vernissage
         Birth of Eventually Venus
         Poem ("Who of us all...")
         Project for an Aesthetic
         Poem Dedicated to the Advancement
            of Aviation

ARTICLES
Nevertheless One Debt   38   208
In Challenge Not Defense   52   212
Correspondence
    [Harold Rosenberg]   52   342
A Note on Alexis Saint Léger Léger   59   330
Notebooks, 1924-1938
    [Ernest Fenollosa]   73   33
Notebooks, 1924-1938
    [E. E. Cummings,
    John Peale Bishop]   73   88
Correspondence   85   124

BOOKS REVIEWED
The Happy Marriage and Other Poems   28   44
The Pot of Earth
Nobodaddy: A Play   28   339
Streets in the Moon   29   278
The Hamlet of A. MacLeish   33   219
New Found Land   36   270
Conquistador   40   216
Before March   43   225
Frescoes for Mr. Rockefeller's City
Panic   48   221
Land of the Free   52   153
Air Raid: A Verse Play for Radio   54   164
America Was Promises   56   43
Contemporary Poets Series
    [Recording]   61   519
Actfive and Other Poems   73   287
Poetry and Experience   99   191
Herakles: A Play in Verse   112   199
New and Collected Poems, 1917-1976   130   102
Collected Poems: 1917-1982   149   94

ARTICLES ABOUT
Archibald MacLeish,
    by Harriet Monroe   38   150
The Age of Power,
    by Harriet Monroe   41   268
Cinema of Hamlet,
    by M. D. Zabel   44   150
Poetry of the Left,
    by Harriet Monroe   48   212
The God in the Car,
    by Harold Rosenberg   52   334
Poetry on Records,
    by Harry T. Moore   57   338
Radio and Poetry,
    by Milton A. Kaplan   64   270
Poets and Politicians,
    by Coleman Rosenberger   65   322
Poetry and Advertising,
    by S. I. Hayakawa   67   204
[Note]   83   116
MacLeish Revisited,
    by William H. Pritchard   141   291

MAC LENNAN, TOBY
BOOKS REVIEWED
    Singing the Stars   144   297

MACLEOD, CATHERINE STUART
POEMS
    That Which Means Spring   41   253

MACLEOD, FIONA
ARTICLES ABOUT
    Vers Libre and Metrical Prose,
        by Amy Lowell   3   213

MACLEOD, JOSEPH GORDON
POEMS
    Foray of Centaurs   39   259
        The Great West Road
        Piccadilly Circus
    The Slug   43   260

BOOKS REVIEWED
    The Ecliptic   38   35
    The Ecliptic   38   101

ARTICLES ABOUT
    English Poetry Today,
        by Basil Bunting   39   264

MAC LEOD, LEROY
BOOKS REVIEWED
    Driven   38   48

MACLEOD, NORMAN
POEMS
    Song for the Turquoise People   37   253
    Time of the Year   38   203
        The Lyrical Absolutes
        Cloud Symbols
        City of Flowers
        Autumn in New Mexico
        Song Before Winter
        Fragrance of Life
        Cosmic Moment
    Biography in Blues   41   144
        Before We Were Lost in the Mountains
        Song on a Dark Night
        Bivisional Horizon
        Pilgrimage
        Out of Esthetic Air
        Fort Bridger: Wyoming
        Late with Fear
    Reflections   42   241
        Television of Darkness
        Penultimate Tower
        Journey Imagined
        Squaw to the Rock
        Uptown
        Groves of Defeat
        Exile Without Return

In Winter   47   202
   Boys in the North Country
   Banners of Desperation
Fragments of Time   50   252
   Dieppe: Summer of 1932
   With All Due Reverence
   Autumn
   Drunkard Out of the Country
The Coffin of Print   54   255
After the Bombing of Barcelona
The Milkman
The Girls Are Dancing at Santo Domingo
Song when Returning from Cutting Wheat
Occasional Intelligence by Radar   91   168
Lament

BOOKS REVIEWED
   Horizons of Death   46   108
   Thanksgiving Before November   48   340
   We Thank You All the Time   59   220

ARTICLES ABOUT
   [Note]   55   111

MAC LOW, JACKSON
REVIEWS
   Collected Poems,
    by Isaac Rosenberg
    (Ed. by Gordon Bottomley
    and Denys Harding)   80   101
   So Late into the Night,
    Fifty Lyrics 1944-1948,
    by Sydney Goodsir Smith   86   52

MAC NAB, ROY
BOOKS REVIEWED
   Poets in South Africa: An Anthology (Ed.) 95   244

MAC NAIR, HARLEY FARNSWORTH
BOOKS REVIEWED
   Correspondence of a Friendship,
    by Florence Ayscough
    and Amy Lowell (Ed.)   69   54

MAC NEICE, LOUIS
POEMS
   Prognosis   56   59
   Obituary
   O'Connell Bridge
   Entirely
   Order to View
   I Am That I Am
   Three Thousand Miles
   The British Museum Reading Room
   Perdita
   Stylite
   The Springboard   61   375

BOOKS REVIEWED
   Poems   48   115
   Out of the Picture   51   104
   Poems   51   339
   Letters from Iceland
    (With W. H. Auden)   52   39
   The Earth Compels   53   280
   The Last Ditch   57   152
   Springboard: Poems, 1941-1944   68   44
   Holes in the Sky   74   301
   Goethe's Faust, Parts I and II (Tr.) 81 393
   Ten Burnt Offerings   84   101
   Visitations   92   318
   Solstices   101 424
   Collected Poems: 1925-1948   103 330
   The Burning Perch   104 375
   The Mad Islands and The Administrator:
    Two Radio Plays   105 404

ARTICLES ABOUT
   Louis MacNeice:
    The Artist as Everyman,
    by Julian Symons   56   86
   The New *Theatrum Poetarum,*
    by Alan S. Downer   60   206
   Mr. MacNeice and Miss Sitwell,
    by Richard Crowder   63   218
   Rev. of *New Poems: 1943*
    (Ed. by Oscar Williams)   64   86
   The Poet's Perspectives,
    by D. S. Savage   64   148
   Rev. of *Tell Me Again*
    How the White Heron...
    by Hayden Carruth   156 345
   A Map of Contemporary Irish Poetry,
    by Dennis O'Driscoll   167 94

MAC NEILL, EOIN
ARTICLES ABOUT
   Correspondence
    from Padraic Colum   8   268

MACPHERSON, JAY
POEMS
   The Ark   89   267
   A Garden Shut   90   341
   The Old Man
   A World of Words
   Like Adamant
   Inside the Angel
   The Beauty of Job's Daughters   93   146
   The Way Down   123 1
    Karloff Poem
    In That Cellar
    The Well
    Orion
    They Return
   To the Unknown God   128 69

BOOKS REVIEWED
The Boatman 91 268
Welcoming Disaster 127 234

MAC QUEEN, JOHN
BOOKS REVIEWED
The Oxford Book of Scottish Verse
    (Ed. with Tom Scott) 111 410

MAC SHANE, FRANK
REVIEWS
A Range of Six 118 295
    Eggs, by Fanny Howe
    Perimeters,
        by Charles Levendosky
    Swallow the Lake, by Clarence Major
    A Book of Dying and
        The Door Standing Open,
        by Robert Mezey
    Elegies and Odes, by William Moebius
    Collecting Evidence,
        by Hugh Seidman

MAC SHERRY, CHARLES
REVIEWS
The Island and the World 88 109
    Japanese Literature:
        An Introduction for Western Readers
        and *The Japanese Discovery of Europe,*
        by Donald Keene
    An Anthology of Japanese Literature
        from the Earliest Era to
        the Mid-Nineteenth Century
        (Ed. by Donald Keene)

MAC SWEENEY, BARRY
BOOKS REVIEWED
The Boy from the Green Cabaret
    Tells of His Mother 115 61

MACY, ETHEL WOODRUFF
POEMS
Brevities 30 144
    Inconstant
    Doric
Meditation 33 256
Futility

MADÁCH, IMRE
BOOKS REVIEWED
The Tragedy of Man
    (Tr. by Paul Vajda and
    Charles Henry Meltzer) 47 285

MADDOW, BEN
POEMS
Obsequy 38 79
Elegy upon a Certificate of Birth 85 194
Psalm of Twelve Fridays 105 355

MADDOX, MARJORIE
POEMS
Cartography 154 197
Chimera

MADELEVA, [SISTER] M.
BOOKS REVIEWED
Knights Errant and Other Poems 23 286

MADGE, CHARLES
POEMS
Delusions 49 207

BOOKS REVIEWED
The Disappearing Castle 50 342

MADHUBUTI, HAKI R.
[See LEE, DON L.]
BOOKS REVIEWED
Directionscore: Selected and New Poems 121 292

MADIGAN, MARK
POEMS
Letter to Monet 150 160

MADIGAN, RICK
POEMS
Sacraments 159 146

MADUEÑO, AMALIO
POEMS
Las Cruces 162 68

MAETERLINCK, MAURICE
BOOKS REVIEWED
Poems by...
    (Tr. by Bernard Miall) 8 96

ARTICLES ABOUT
Rev. of *Maurice Maeterlinck, a Critical Study,*
    by Una Taylor 8 96
Visitors from the Other Side,
    by Harriet Monroe 15 93

MAGALLANES MOURE, MANUEL
[MANUEL MAGELLANES
MOURE]
POEMS
Table Talk
    (Tr. by Muna Lee) 26 122

ARTICLES ABOUT
Some Chilean Poets, by A. R. Gonzalez 38 329

MAGARET, HELENE
POEMS
The Thoroughbred 36 134
To a Lover Who Bewildered Me
Decreed 39 192

An Hour
The Branch
The Hunters   40   309
An Incident   47   260

BOOKS REVIEWED
The Trumpeting Crane   45   291

MAGAVERN, SAM
POEMS
Master, Man, and Woman   164   84

MAGEE, MICHAEL
POEMS
The Hand   121   260
It Is the Stars that Govern Us
Nightwatch
Murder Weapon

MAGEE, WES
POEMS
On the Esplanade   133   33

MAGINNES, AL
POEMS
Earworm   158   267
Jobs   160   145
Harness   163   140

**MAGLOIRE-SAINT-AUDE,
CLEMENT**
ARTICLES ABOUT
Letter From Haiti, by Wallace Fowlie 94   398

MAGOWAN, ROBIN
POEMS
Secrecies   114   98
On This Day
Poem
Bear's Level Campground   121   283
The House of the Dawn   123   219
In Memory of Nancy Ling (Perry)   125   346

REVIEWS
Pancakes for You and Me   116   193
    The Owl Behind the Door,
        by Stanley Cooperman
    Drool, Poems and Maize, a Poem,
        by James Bertolino
    Cups, by Robin Blaser
    Brandings,
        by Katherine Arnstein Heinemann
    Mia Poems, by Burton Raffel
    The Correspondences: Poems 1965-1967,
        by James L. Weil
    Greyhound: A Poem Sequence,
        by Joseph Somoza
    The Silence Outside Things, by Don Gray

Rituals, a Book of Poems,
    by Douglas Eichhorn
Pancakes for the Queen of Babylon:
    Ten Poems for Nikos Gatsos,
    by Peter Levi, S.J.

BOOKS REVIEWED
Voyage Noir   103   324
Voyages   112   56

MAGRELLI, VALERIO
POEMS
[Ricevo da te questa tazza]/[This Red Cup] 155 156
[Each photographed face]
[I have often imagined that glances]
[This handwriting wears itself away]
    (Tr. by Dana Gioia)
[I love uncertain gestures]   155   159
[There's silence between one page and another]
    (Tr. by Jonathan Galassi)

MAGRITTE, RENÉ
ARTICLES ABOUT
Rev. of Mysteries of the Horizon,
    by Lawrence Raab   127   352

MAHAPATRA, JAYANTA
POEMS
Dawn   125   139
A Rain
A Rain of Rites
The Whorehouse in a Calcutta Street
Pain   126   339
Village
Desire
The Face
The Moon Moments
The Life
Now When We Think of Compromise
The House   128   187
A Wind of Judgment
The Retreat
Flight
A Sailboat of Occasions
Glass
The Day After My Friends
    Became Godly and Great
Shadows   130   18
Ash
Song of the Past   131   211
The Storm
The Wound
A Kind of Happiness
Of Independence Day   150   203
Doors   151   96
Another Hour's Bell   152   278
Farewell   159   17
Heroism   166   276

BOOKS REVIEWED
A Rain of Rites   130   342
A Father's House
Selected Poems   153   106

MAHON, DEREK
POEMS
Chinatown   167   10

BOOKS REVIEWED
Night-Crossing   114   397
Lives   123   113
Selected Poems   161   223

ARTICLES ABOUT
A Letter from Britain, by William Logan   157   222
A Map of Contemporary Irish Poetry,
   by Dennis O'Driscoll   167   94

MAHONY, CHRISTINA HUNT
ARTICLES
A Note on "The Watch-Fire,"
   by W. B. Yeats
   (With Edward O'Shea)   135   224

MAIAKOVSKY, VLADIMIR
[See MAYAKOVSKY, VLADIMIR]

MAIER, JENNIFER
POEMS
33   170   30

MAILER, NORMAN
BOOKS REVIEWED
Deaths for the Ladies   102   118

MAJOR, CLARENCE
BOOKS REVIEWED
Swallow the Lake   118   295

MAKUCK, PETER
POEMS
Feeders   149   29
Woodsmoke   165   5
Close   168   261

MALAM, CHARLES
POEMS
Closed Doors   33   128
Thirtieth Storey   35   252
Breaking Ground
Spring Grinding   52   78
Night on the Mountain
The Monument in the Square   53   74

BOOKS REVIEWED
Spring Plowing   33   287
Upper Pasture   36   169

MALANGA, GERARD
POEMS
Sonnet XLVI   105   108
Some Clouds
New Stars Develop in Orion   107   373
The Third Person
October in New York
Human Sunlight: A Sonnet   109   327
Nice Things
Coming Up for Air
Two Poems for Benedetta Barzini   112   23

REVIEWS
Bottom: On Shakespeare
   and *After I's,*
   by Louis Zukofsky   107   60
Three Firsts   108   130
   Rivers into Islands,
     by John Knoepfle
   First Poems,
     by Michael Goldman
   January,
     by David Shapiro
Lingua Franca et Jocundissima   123   236
   Life Notes,
     by Anne Waldman
   Personae Non Gratae,
     by Paul Mariah
   Circle Meadow,
     by Gerald Hausman
Traveling & Living   125   162
   Traveling on Credit,
     by Daniel Halpern
   Living at the Movies,
     by Jim Carroll

BOOKS REVIEWED
The Last Benedetta Poems   115   47
Chic Death/Poems   119   224

MALING, A(RTHUR) G(ORDON)
POEMS
Passé   68   199
The Cemeterian   69   201
Weapon   70   239

MALKOFF, KARL
REVIEWS
History, Biography, and Criticism   112   206
   Marx, Engels, and the Poets:
     Origins of Marxist Literary Criticism,
     by Peter Demetz
     (Tr. by Jeffrey L. Sammons)
   Edwin Muir: Man and Poet,
     by P. H. Butter
   Seven Modern American Poets:
     An Introduction
     (Ed. by Leonard Unger)

BOOKS REVIEWED
Theodore Roethke:
An Introduction to the Poetry   112   52

MALLALIEU, H. B.
POEMS
("In the grim valley the iron...")   52   81
("I will walk to your wish...")
("Everywhere in the past...")
Cul-de-Sac   54   260
Calenture
The Photograph
Epilogue
Poems in Time of War   56   27
Days of Waiting   61   353
Lines from Europe   70   23
Samothrace   116   76
Lines to an Ambassador   117   36
Confrontation with a Stork   117   381
A Berkshire Landscape
The Bow in the Attic
Lines to Roy Fuller
Variation on a Theme of Cavafy   120   272
Portrait
Future Shock
Empedocles on Etna   123   89
Conversation near Cadiz, 1493
The Last Week in the Working Life of an
    Executive on Reaching Retirement Age   125   213
Voyage to Naxos   130   321

ARTICLES
Correspondence: Malice Rebuked
[D. S. Savage]   54   55

BOOKS REVIEWED
Letter in Wartime   58   159

MALLAN, LLOYD
TRANSLATIONS
Poems by Nicolas Guillén   62   66
Poem by Francisco Borja   62   70
Poem by Julia García Games   62   73
Poem by Rosamel del Valle   62   76
Poem by José Portogalo   62   77
Poem by Gastón Figueira   62   83

REVIEWS
Five Mexican Poets   61   680
    Entre la Piedra y la Flor,
        by Octavio Paz
    Algunos Poemas, by Alfonso Reyes
    Exágonos, by Carlos Pellicer
    Decima Muerte,
        by Xavier Villaurrutia
    Elegías Romanas y Otros Poemas,
        by Enrique González Rojo
Towers of Rhetoric   66   350

A Cry in the Dark,
    by German Horacio
    and Humberto Rivas
The Towers of Manhattan,
    by A. Ortiz-Vargas

BOOKS REVIEWED
3 Spanish American Poets (Tr.)
    [Jorge Carrera Andrade]   62   111
Selected Poems, by Rafael Alberti (Tr.)   67   166

MALLARMÉ, STÉPHANE
POEMS
Homage to Richard Wagner   80   28
The Tomb of Edgar Poe
The Tomb of Charles Baudelaire
The Tomb of Paul Verlaine
    (Tr. by Hubert Creekmore)

BOOKS REVIEWED
Poems
    (Tr. by Roger Fry.
    With commentaries
    by Charles Mauron)   49   350

ARTICLES ABOUT
Stéphane Mallarmé,
    by Francis Grierson   2   104
Rev. of De Stéphane Mallarmé
    au prophète Ezéchiel,
    by Edouard Dujardin   16   164
Paris Letter, by Jean Catel   18   168
Rev. of The Esthetic
    of Stéphane Mallarmé,
    by Hasye Cooperman   45   347
Paul Valéry, by Wallace Fowlie   76   279
Mallarmé, by Wallace Fowlie   80   37
Rev. of Mallarmé,
    by Wallace Fowlie   83   278
French Chronicle:
    Recent Publications,
    by Wallace Fowlie   88   408
Recent French Publications,
    by Wallace Fowlie   93   40
Rev. of The Poetry
    of Boris Pasternak
    (Ed. and tr. by George Reavey)   96   108
Letters from the Midi: II,
    by Wallace Fowlie   100   261
Rev. of Mallarmé and
    the Symbolist Drama,
    by Haskell M. Block   104   187
Rev. of Dancers, Buildings,
    and People in the Streets,
    by Edwin Denby   111   268
Rev. of The Limits of Symbolism:
    Studies of Five Modern French Poets,
    by Bernard Weinberg   112   41

MALLEY, JEAN
POEMS
   The Quilt   115   337
   A Stale Piece
   Untitled ("Words do not grow...")
   The Past
   Strength
   Ghost

MALONEY, JOHN OWEN
POEMS
   Laura-by-the-Sea   137   28
   For William Carlos Williams
   Raining Towards Aries
   Water
   Loose Ladder

MALRAUX, ANDRÉ
BOOKS REVIEWED
   The Psychology of Art   76   288

MANDEL, ELI
BOOKS REVIEWED
   An Idiot Joy   114   202

MANDEL, SIEGFRIED
BOOKS REVIEWED
   Visions of Christ,
     by Rainer Maria Rilke (Ed.)
     (Tr. by Aaron Kramer)   113   188

MANDELBAUM, ALLEN
POEMS
   From *The Ardent Forest*   86   86
   From *Chelmaxioms*   125   351
     The Song of Offspring
TRANSLATIONS
   Poems by Salvatore Quasimodo   84   187
ARTICLES
   Ungaretti's *La Terra Promessa:*
     A Commentary and Some Examples   88   168
BOOKS REVIEWED
   Life of a Man, by Giuseppe Ungaretti (Ed.)   93   329
   The Selected Writings
     of Salvatore Quasimodo (Tr.)   98   403

MANDELSTAM, NADEZHDA
BOOKS REVIEWED
   Hope Against Hope
     (Tr. by Max Hayward)   124   232
   Hope Abandoned
     (Tr. by Max Hayward)

MANDELSTAM, OSIP
POEMS
   КАМЕНЬ /   136   21
   From *Stone*
   (Tr. by Robert Tracy)

BOOKS REVIEWED
   Selected Poems
     (Tr. by Clarence Brown
     and W. S. Merwin)   124   232

ARTICLES ABOUT
   Rev. of *Three Poets*
     of Modern Russia,
     by Leonid I. Strakhovsky   76   112
   Rev. of *Mandelstam,*
     by Clarence Brown   124   232

MANEY, JILL MARION
POEMS
   Lesson   154   338

MANGAN, SHERRY
POEMS
   Passage   38   200
   P. P. C.
   Revenant   41   190

REVIEWS
   Selected Poems,
     by Richard Rowley   38   231
   The Tracing of a Portal,
     by Lindley Williams Hubbell   38   344
   Kinds of Love,
     by Max Eastman   39   51
   Guido Cavalcanti: Rime
     (Ed. by Ezra Pound)   41   336
   Seven Types of Ambiguity,
     by William Empson   43   98

BOOKS REVIEWED
   No Apology for Poetrie,
     and Other Poems
     Written 1922-1931   45   339

MANGIONE, JERRE
TRANSLATIONS
   Poem by Ruth Domino
     (Tr. with Daniel Hoffman)   104   85

MANHEIM, RALPH
BOOKS REVIEWED
   Aesthetics,
     by Paul Valéry (Tr.)   106   366
   Bertolt Brecht: Poems 1913-56
     (Ed. with John Willett)   137   220

MANIFOLD, JOHN
POEMS
   Song ("My dark-headed Kathchen...")   67   145
   Quins
   "Ces Longues Nuicts d'Hyver"
   For the Mercenaries
   Schrammel-Musik   81   49

BOOKS REVIEWED
   Selected Poems   69   43

MANLEY, FRANK
POEMS
   Heliogabalus   129   81
   Erasmus in Love

MANLY, JOHN M.
REVIEWS
   Romance, Vision, and Satire,
      by Jessie L. Weston   2   145

MANN, KLAUS
BOOKS REVIEWED
   André Gide   63   276

MANNER, EEVA-LIISA
POEMS
   Moon Games
    (Tr. by Meri Lehtinen)   98   350

MANNERS, MARGARET
POEMS
   No Definition Rises from these Ashes   65   22
   Particular Speech

MANNHEIM, RALPH L.
   [See MANHEIM, RALPH]

MANNING, CLARENCE A.
BOOKS REVIEWED
   An Anthology
    of Czechoslovak Poetry (Ed.)   37   164

MANNING, ELIZABETH
BOOKS REVIEWED
   Willie Lamberton   33   229

MANNING, FREDERIC
POEMS
   Simaetha   2   99
   At Even
   From Demeter
   Sacrifice   8   181
   Anacreontic   9   186

BOOKS REVIEWED
   Eidola   13   281

ARTICLES ABOUT
   Farewell to Two Poets,
    by Harriet Monroe   46   219

MANNING, HUGO
BOOKS REVIEWED
   Smile, Ichabod   66   106
   Beyond the Terminus of Stars   74   362

MANNING, MARY
BOOKS REVIEWED
   Passages from Finnegans Wake.
    A Free Adaptation for the Theatre   91   335

MANNING-SANDERS, RUTH
POEMS
   Sea Stories   27   233
    Legend
    Martha Wish-You-Ill
    Hands
    Eleven Saved
    Solitary Places
   Monstrous Happenings   30   239
    "Darkness"
    One Two Three and Four
    Mr. Benny
    The Poultry Farm
    Away

BOOKS REVIEWED
   Karn   27   339
   Pages from the History of Zachy Trenoy
   The City   32   348

MANNON, STORM
POEMS
   Cueillez   72   79
   Deth Cam Drivynge

MANSFIELD, MARGERY (SWETT)
POEMS
   Winter Wife   15   247
   Song of an Impudent Day   21   310
   A Ballet
   Corpus Christi   25   117
   Fable of a Little Sister   28   324
   Warnings   30   132
    Little Fugue
    Poets... Not Only
   This Is New England   32   305
   Brothers of the Grass   36   321
    Ode on the Absence of Joy
    The Wind Is My Neighbor
    When No One Hears
   Song ("Tenaciously as sleep...")   38   189
   Hand   41   82
   Song for Music
   A Berkshire Settler   42   258
    Nostalgia
    Explanation
   The Snake   46   317
   Farewell to a Winged Horse   48   13
   It Stopped Ticking   52   270
   Blessing Mrs. Larkin   56   189

ARTICLES
   The Laureate They Deserve?
    [Edgar A. Guest, Ivan Swift]   25   38

Free Verse Again
  [David Greenhood, Ernest Walsh]   25   153
Poetry Recitals in New York   28   158
Yaddo   29   333
Wasting the Poets' Time   31   37
[Note]   33   349

REVIEWS
  Finders: More Poems in American,
    by John V. A. Weaver   22   48
  Shoes of the Wind,
    by Hilda Conkling   22   97
  Orioles and Blackbirds, by Hi Simons   22   156
  Star Pollen, by Power Dalton   22   223
  Walkers, by Hazel Hall   22   276
  Sea-Change, by Muna Lee   23   51
  Cups of Illusion,
    by Henry Bellamann   23   108
  College Poetry   24   162
    Eight More Harvard Poets
      (Ed. by S. Foster Damon
      and Robert Hillyer)
    Collected Verse,
      by the Poetry Club
      of the University of Chicago
    Illini Poetry, 1918-23
      (Ed. by Bruce Weirick)
    Figs from California
      (Ed. by W. W. Lyman)
    Verse, 1905-1923,
      by students of the
      University of Missouri
    Poems,
      by the Writers' Club
      of Michigan Agricultural College
    University Anthology
      (Ed. by Joseph Francis Paxton)
      [Univ. of Oklahoma]
    Oxford Poetry, 1921
      (Ed. by Alan Porter, Richard Hughes
      and Robert Graves)
    Oxford Poetry, 1922
  Hill Solitudes,
    by Benjamin Rosenbaum   24   275
  Prophet and Fool, by Louis Golding   24   333
  The Enchanted Mesa and Other Poems,
    by Glenn Ward Dresbach   25   47
  The Haunted House and Other Poems and
    The Three Sphinxes and Other Poems,
    by George Sylvester Viereck   25   221
  Turning Earth, by Power Dalton   25   337
  The Crimson Cloak,
    by Lois Seyster Montross   25   341
  Slants, by Clifford Gessler   26   106
  A Few Nineteenth-Century Voices   27   164
    Poems by Lord de Tabley
      (Ed. by John Drinkwater)
    The Poetical Works of Austin Dobson

  Dartmouth Lyrics,
    by Richard Hovey
    (Ed. by Edwin Osgood Grover)
  English Poetry of the Nineteenth Century
    (Ed. by G. R. Elliott
    and Norman Foerster)
  The Dancer in the Shrine,
    by Amanda Benjamin Hall   28   345
  Songs of Love and Death,
    by Manmohan Ghose   29   49
  Forty Poems, by Virgil Geddes   29   172
  Scarlet and Mellow,
    by Alfred Kreymborg   29   226
  Lilliput, by Roberta Teale Swartz   30   285
  Upper Night, by Scudder Middleton   31   50
  Robert Frost, by Gorham B. Munson   31   292
  A Stranger in Heaven, by Harold Vinal 32   225
  Heavenly Bodies, by Oliver Jenkins   32   288
  The Joy Ride and Other Poems,
    by Warren Gilbert   32   345
  Nine Dragons, by Bertha Ten Eyck James 33   160
  Collected Poems,
    by Margaret Widdemer   33   284
  Jealous of Dead Leaves,
    by Shaemas O'Sheel   34   51
  A Woman at Dusk and Other Poems,
    by Arthur Stringer   34   108
  Fool's Errand, by Alexander Laing   35   54
  The Great Enlightenment,
    by Lee Wilson Dodd   35   167
  Green Nakedness,
    by Benjamin Rosenbaum   36   51
  Selected Poems, by Aline Kilmer   36   102
  Leaves of Wild Grape, by Helen Hoyt   36   346

BOOKS REVIEWED
  Workers in Fire: A Book About Poetry 51   273

ARTICLES ABOUT
  Correspondence
    from George Sylvester Viereck   25   342
  [Note on name]   28   233

MANUEL, C. H.
POEMS
  A Litter of Honey   47   140
    Suspended Hour
    Senses
    Silver Bird
    Counsel
    Daphne
    Mirror
    Sweets and Bitter

MANUEL POVEDA, JOSÉ
POEMS
  Withdrawal
    (Tr. by Muna Lee)   26   128

MANWARING, [MISS]
ARTICLES ABOUT
Jorge Guillén, Marianne Moore,
T. S. Eliot: Some Recollections,
by Wallace Fowlie   90   103

MANYÉ I MARTÍ, LOURDES
TRANSLATIONS
Poems by Miquel Martí i Pol
(Tr. with Wayne Cox)   155   399

THE MANYOSHU
ARTICLES ABOUT
The Manyoshu: The Nippon
Gakujutsu Shinkokai Translation
of One Thousand Poems,
with the Texts in Romaji   107   404

MARCH, AUSIAS
POEMS
LXVIII
(Tr. by John Frederick Nims)   98   354

MARCH, J(OSEPH) M(ONCURE)
POEMS
Autumn Prophecy   16   311

BOOKS REVIEWED
The Set-Up   33   279

MARCHAND, LESLIE A.
BOOKS REVIEWED
The Selected Poetry
of Lord Byron (Ed.)   84   303

MARCO, ANGELA [Pseud.]
POEMS
Marble Yard   32   87

MARCUS, MORTON
POEMS
The Wolf Without His Teeth   141   285

BOOKS REVIEWED
Origins   115   47

MARCUS, PETER
POEMS
Statue of Eros Without Wings   160   208

MARFIELD, DWIGHT HUNTER
POEMS
A Love Song   30   142

MARGGRAFF, ROBERTA
POEMS
Vanishing   167   213

MARGOLIOUTH, H. M.
BOOKS REVIEWED
William Blake's Vala (Ed.)   90   321

MARGOLIS, GARY
POEMS
The Visit   134   78
Town Meeting   140   334
Away from Any Uniform   147   207
Having Watched "The Day After"
If You Asked
Did You Bring Me Anything?   151   97
The Groves of Argos   151   478
Some Nation Who's Been Slighted   153   71

MARGOLIS, WILLIAM J.
BOOKS REVIEWED
The Little Love of Our Yearning   102   335

MARGULIES, GEORGE ["G. M."]
TRANSLATIONS
Poems by Yuan Chieh,
the Emperor Yang, Lu Fu Li,
Kao Ch'i, Siue Tao-Heng,
Hong Tche-Kong,
and K'ong Chao-Ngan
(With Willard R. Trask)   46   3
Chinese Folk Songs   46   8
Songs of the Fourth Century A.D.
Songs of the Fifth Century A.D.
Song of the Sixth Century A.D.
(With Willard R. Trask)

ARTICLES
Three Chinese Poets of Long Ago
(With Willard R. Trask)
[Yuan Chieh, the Emperor Yang,
Kao Ch'i]   46   46

MARIAH, PAUL
POEMS
The Swimmer Who Never Swam   116   163
From Concordances with Dali   118   66
Old Age, Adolescence, Infancy 1940   123   220
The Disintegration
of the Persistence of Memory 1952-1954
Saint Surrounded by Three Pi-Mesons 1956

BOOKS REVIEWED
Personae Non Gratae   123   236

MARIAN, GEORGE
[Pseud. of UHLMAN, GEORGE]
POEMS
The Home-Coming   14   200

MARIANI, PAUL
POEMS
Then   167   151

MARIETT, PAUL
BOOKS REVIEWED
   The Poems of…   3   146

MARIN, DIEGO
BOOKS REVIEWED
   Lira Española:
   Representative Spanish Lyric Poets
   (15th-20th Centuries) (Ed.)   85   55

MARIN, LUIS MUNOZ
[See MUNOZ MARIN, LUIS]

MARING, HELEN
POEMS
   She Says   33   258
     Reversed
     Lean Wind
   Cherry-Bloom   40   7

MARINI, MYRA
POEMS
   Peace Be Unto Her   43   80
   Young Thinker

MARIS, [SISTER] STELLA
[See STELLA, (SISTER) MARIS]

MARITAIN, JACQUES
ARTICLES
   The Poetic Sense   81   369

BOOKS REVIEWED
   Situation de la Poésie
   (With Raissa Maritain)   53   218
   Creative Intuition in Art and Poetry 87   308
   The Situation of Poetry
   (With Raissa Maritain)

ARTICLES ABOUT
   French Poetry and the
   Revival of Mysticism,
   by Eugene Jolas   56   264

MARITAIN, RAISSA
BOOKS REVIEWED
   Situation de la Poésie
   (With Jacques Maritain)   53   218
   The Situation of Poetry
   (With Jacques Maritain)   87   308

ARTICLES ABOUT
   French Poetry and the
   Revival of Mysticism,
   by Eugene Jolas   56   264

MARKHAM, EDWIN
BOOKS REVIEWED
   The Shoes of Happiness and Other Poems 6   308
   The Book of Poetry (Ed.)   32   96

ARTICLES ABOUT
   Edwin Markham, 1852-1940,
   by Charles Hanson Towne   56   30
   Obituary   56   54
   Rev. of *The Unknown*
   Edwin Markham,
   by Louis Filler   111   333

MARKIEVICZ, [COUNTESS]
[CONSTANCE GORE-BOOTH]
BOOKS REVIEWED
   Prison Letters of…
   (With poems by Eva Gore-Booth) 45   214

MARKOV, VLADIMIR
BOOKS REVIEWED
   Modern Russian Poetry
   (Ed. with Merrill Sparks)   114   113

MARKS, GIGI
POEMS
   Instrument   170   14
   Breath
   Melting

MARKS, JEANNETTE
POEMS
   Sea-Gulls   15   308
   Rosy Miller
   Shadow Songs   17   314
     Rose Toada
     Ebony
     The Broken Door
   All Day   25   77
     Weariness
     Window-Bars

BOOKS REVIEWED
   Willow Pollen   20   99

MARKS, MARGARET (JULIA)
POEMS
   Behind the Shades   33   196
     To the Other Woman
     Last Night
     Young Widow
   Muffled   38   188
     Song Lost
     Why Will You Beckon

MARKUN, LEO
POEMS
   Two Realities   31   21
   My Song   35   29

MARKUS, YVONNE
POEMS
   Anabasis   56   135

MARLATT, EARL
POEMS
Love Untold — 11 134
People
Toward Silence — 30 7
Lent
Cloistered

MARLETTO, CHARLOTTE
BOOKS REVIEWED
Jewel of Our Longing — 74 236

MARLIS, STEFANIE
POEMS
Star Dust — 162 220
Saturn — 164 68

MARNAU, FRED
BOOKS REVIEWED
The Wounds of the Apostles — 66 53
Three Poems
(With Wrey Gardiner
and Nicholas Moore)
New Road:
Directions in European Art and Letters,
Number 4 (Ed.) — 72 222

MARRIOTT, ANNE
POEMS
Prairie Graveyard — 58 27
Traffic Light

BOOKS REVIEWED
The Wind Our Enemy — 58 53

MARSDEN, FRANCIS
ARTICLES ABOUT
A New Quarterly
[Form, Austin O. Spare] — 8 323

MARSH, EDWARD ["E. M."]
BOOKS REVIEWED
Georgian Poetry, 1918-1919 (Ed.) — 16 108

MARSH, HALLOCK
POEMS
Song of Ah Hing — 50 21

MARSH, JAN
BOOKS REVIEWED
Edward Thomas:
A Poet for His Country — 135 342

MARSHALL, HERBERT
BOOKS REVIEWED
Selected Poems,
by Andrei Voznesensky (Tr. and ed.) — 110 40
Yevtushenko Poems (Tr.) — 111 121

MARSHALL, JACK
POEMS
Convalescence in Tarrasa — 102 236
Bacon's Van Gogh — 106 208
The Feeding Machine — 114 94

BOOKS REVIEWED
The Darkest Continent — 112 48
Bearings — 124 45

MARSHALL, LENORE (G.)
POEMS
Against the Wind — 47 200
They Vie with Waves
After Illness
Argument on Immortality — 65 75

BOOKS REVIEWED
No Boundary — 63 226
Latest Will — 115 430

MARTEAU, ROBERT
POEMS
Royauté (Tr. by Anne Winters) — 134 34

BOOKS REVIEWED
Salamander: Selected Poems of...
(Tr. by Anne Winters) — 137 220

ARTICLES ABOUT
The Poetry of Robert Marteau,
by Anne Winters — 134 46

MARTIAL
[MARCUS VALERIUS MARTIALIS]
POEMS
In Labienvm — 91 157
Ad Maximvm
In Nestorem
Ad Caecilianvm
(Tr. by Dudley Fitts)
In Vacerram VIII:69 — 98 380
Ad Septicianvm XI:107
Ad Mamercvm II:88
De Gemello di Maronilla I:10
(Tr. by Dudley Fitts)
Three Translations from the Epigrams — 159 25
V:X
VII:XLVI
XII:XL
(Tr. by William Matthews)
From Martial's Epigrams (X:XLVII)
(Tr. by William Matthews) — 165 157

BOOKS REVIEWED
Poems after Martial
(Tr. by Philip Murray) — 113 188
Sixty Poems of... (Tr. by Dudley Fitts)

MARTÍ I POL, MIQUEL
POEMS
Rooms   155   399
After All
If I Talk About Death
   (Tr. by Wayne Cox and
   Lourdes Manyé i Martí)

MARTIN, CHARLES
POEMS
Four for Theodore Roethke   115   249
Remembering the Box
Heroic Attitudes
East Sixty-Fifth   118   162
Work in Progress
After
Sonnet ("My paradise, my urban...")
Scenes Drawn from Life
   in Buffalo, New York   121   137
Leaving Buffalo
Persistence of Ancestors
Orgy with Toads   123   156
Erogenous Zones
Sharks at the New York Aquarium   127   191
Love in the City of Light Bent Back
Proposal for a Monument of Pears
Calvus in Ruins   129   33
Dido and Aeneas   144   130
Lines Freely Taken from Callimachus

BOOKS REVIEWED
Room for Error   134   226

MARTIN, CHRISTOPHER
POEMS
Mock Interview   119   200
News from Guatemala
Yes or No
Girls that Swim
Curious Death
Georgian Green

MARTIN, DAVID
POEMS
The Cemetery   114   20
Intercourse

MARTIN, HERBERT WOODWARD
POEMS
From Final W.   155   402

MARTIN, JAMES
POEMS
Letter to Virginia Woolf   117   240
Leaving Arles   132   15

REVIEWS
Knife Sharpeners   118   344
   Neighbours, by Glyn Hughes

An American Romance,
   by Carol Bergé
Livingdying,
   by Cid Corman
Darker, by Mark Strand
Questions of Style   126   103
Giraffe, by Stanley Plumly
In Sepia,
   by Jon Anderson
The Ancient People,
   by Glen Cavaliero
Backwards into the Smoke,
   by Colin Falck
Selected Poems and Texts,
   by Attila József
   (Tr. by John Batki)
   (Ed. by James Atlas
   and George Gömöri)
Radiation,
   by Sandra McPherson
The Shade-Seller,
   by Josephine Jacobsen
Collected Poems: 1930-1973,
   by May Sarton
[Boris Pasternak]

MARTIN, JAMES BEVERLEY
POEMS
Songs for Judith   44   142
Messenger
The Soul Compared to a Mullet Seed   45   250
Sonnet ("I named You over...")
A Conceit on Her Sleeping Eyes
To William Blake

MARTIN, PATRICIA
POEMS
Would You Care to Leave a Message?   68   254
Sub Rosa
Of an Ivory Tower

MARTIN, PHILIP
POEMS
Christmas Ghosts   139   149

BOOKS REVIEWED
Voice Unaccompanied   121   348

MARTIN, PORTIA
POEMS
Isolate   26   22
Return

MARTIN, ROBERT K.
REVIEWS
Fellow Feelings,
   by Richard Howard
[Hart Crane]   130   36

The New Oxford Book of American Verse
  (Ed. by Richard Ellmann)
  [F. O. Matthiessen, Herman Melville,
  E. A. Robinson, George Santayana,
  Hart Crane, Wallace Stevens,
  Robert Duncan, W. H. Auden]   131   236
The Penguin Book of Homosexual Verse
  (Ed. by Stephen Coote)
  [Walt Whitman, Richard Barnfield,
  W. H. Auden, Hart Crane,
  Elizabeth Bishop, Theocritus]   144   166

MARTINEZ, ENRIQUE GONZALES
[See GONZALES MARTINEZ,
ENRIQUE]

MARTORY, PIERRE
  POEMS
  Passing the Frontier   162   132
  Coming and Going
  Wine
  Elegy ("Adieu near those fields...")
    (Tr. by John Ashbery)

MARTZ, LOUIS L.
  REVIEWS
  Varieties of Criticism   110   254
    The Artist's Journey into the Interior
    and Other Essays,
      by Erich Heller
    Saint-John Perse:
      A Study of His Poetry,
      by Arthur Knodel
    Reason's Double Agents,
      by Carol Johnson
    Poets of Reality:
      Six Twentieth-Century Writers,
      by J. Hillis Miller
    A Colder Fire:
      The Poetry of Robert Penn Warren,
      by Victor H. Strandberg
    [William Carlos Williams,
      Wallace Stevens, T. S. Eliot]

  BOOKS REVIEWED
  The Meditative Poem (Ed.)   104   120
  The Poem of the Mind:
    Essays on Poetry, English and American   110   119

MARUYAMA, KAORU
  POEMS
  A Distant View of the School   88   90
  A Rhinoceros and a Lion
    (Tr. by Satoru Satu
    and Constance Urdang)

MARVELL, ANDREW
  ARTICLES ABOUT
  Poetry and Nature, by D. S. Savage   61   496

Rev. of *Six Metaphysical Poets:*
  A Reader's Guide,
  by George Williamson   112   356

MARX, KARL
  ARTICLES ABOUT
  Rev. of *Marx, Engels, and the Poets:*
    Origins of Marxist Literary Criticism,
    by Peter Demetz
    (Tr. by Jeffrey L. Sammons)   112   206

MARZ, ROY
  POEMS
  Charlotte to Emily   75   260
  The Abstract Nude
  The Buzzard
  Night Walker
  Campagna Picnic   77   135
  Mrs. Simmons to Astolfo
  Pietà
  Vittoria Colonna   78   280
  Buonarotti to His Public and God
  Savonarola
  Housecleaning
  Black Is the Color   80   140
  The Probation
  Leonardo on the Annunciations
  The Sisters
  The Italian Lesson
  The Cat at the Last Supper   81   365
  The Disciple
  The Bird Is God
  Etruscan Burial
  The Fugitive   82   325
  The Elephant Graveyard
  Martyrs
  Leonardo on the Annunciations   84   149
  Annunciation of the Unknown Master:
    Galleria Accademia, Florence
  Virgin to Angel as Bird: Botticelli
  The Donatello Annunciation: Santa Croce
  Boy Buried on Sunday   86   280
  The Blind Man
  Life of the Virgin   88   131
  The Paulownia Tree   90   162
  The Poem's Words
  The Legacy
  The Children   95   8
  The Blue Tablecloth
  Targets
  The Count and the Rose   102   374
  Frameless

  ARTICLES ABOUT
  [Note on misprints]   95   259

MARZI, ALFEO
  BOOKS REVIEWED
  Urban Poetry   114   251

MASEFIELD, JOHN
BOOKS REVIEWED
  The Story of a Round House
    and Other Poems   1   160
  The Daffodil Fields   2   76
  Philip the King and Other Poems   5   131
  John M. Synge   7   96
  Good Friday and Other Poems   8   43
  Lollingdon Downs   10   320
  Reynard the Fox, or the Ghost Heath Run   17   40
  Enslaved
  Right Royal   18   279
  Selected Poems   22   330
  Tristan and Isolt   32   109
  Midsummer Night,
    and Other Tales in Verse   34   111
  Minnie Maylor's Story
    and Other Tales and Scenes   40   344
  A Tale of Troy   41   332
  End and Beginning: A Play   44   106
  A Letter from Pontus   48   338
  Selected Poems   53   144
  Gautama the Enlightened   60   109
  Natalie Maisie and Pavilastukay   61   514
  Wonderings   64   171
  Thanks Before Going
    [D. G. Rossetti]   70   333
  On the Hill   78   45
  My Favourite English Poems
  Poems: Complete Edition with Recent Poems   86   49
  The Bluebells and Other Verse   102   393

ARTICLES ABOUT
  In Danger, by Harriet Monroe   2   68
  Mr. Masefield's Lecture,
    by Alice Corbin Henderson   7   301
  Rev. of *Georgian Poetry: 1913-1915*   8   255
  A London Letter,
    by Richard Aldington   15   226
  Reading Aloud, by Harriet Monroe   31   271
  Correspondence
    from John M. Schealer
    and Stanley Edgar Hyman   71   112

MASON, DANIEL GREGORY
BOOKS REVIEWED
  Some Letters
    of William Vaughn Moody (Ed.)   3   146

MASON, DAVID
POEMS
  In the Islands   158   139
  Questions at Christmas   167   150

TRANSLATIONS
  Poems by Yiorgos Chouliaras
    (Tr. with the author)   162   136

MASON, F. W.
POEMS
  From South Africa   40   142
    Black Madonna
    The Stricken Tree
    The Captive Lion
    The Pioneer's Grave

MASON, FRANCIS CLAIBORNE
POEMS
  Land's End   38   136
  First Sight

BOOKS REVIEWED
  This Unchanging Mask   34   56

MASON, LAWRENCE
ARTICLES ABOUT
  The Utterance of Poetry,
    by Harriet Monroe   19   266

MASON, MASON JORDAN
BOOKS REVIEWED
  The Constipated Owl   96   179
  A Legionere
  The Twenty-Third of Love   104   258

MASON, R. A. K.
BOOKS REVIEWED
  Recent Poems
    (With Allen Curnow,
    A. R. D. Fairburn,
    and Denis Glover)   59   343

MASON, ROSALIND
POEMS
  Poems of Happiness   8   125
    Vision
    Fair Weather and I Happy
    Happiness
    A Child's Grace

MASON-MANHEIM, MADELINE
BOOKS REVIEWED
  Hill Fragments   27   226

MASSECK, CLINTON JOSEPH
POEMS
  At Thirty He Sings of a Day in Spring   8   230
  Down the Wind

MASSINGHAM, H. J.
BOOKS REVIEWED
  Poems About Birds (Ed.)   23   111

MASSON, LOYS
ARTICLES ABOUT
  Marseille Letter,
    by Jean Rivier   60   269

The Conspiracy of the Poets,
by Pierre Seghers
(Tr. by William Jay Smith)   67   25

MASTERMAN, J(OHN) C.
ARTICLES ABOUT
Rev. of *Reflections on Espionage*,
by John Hollander   130   41

MASTERS, CHARLIE (SCOTT)
POEMS
This Animal   63   11

MASTERS, DEXTER
POEMS
Before the Hourglass   37   139

MASTERS, EDGAR LEE
[See also FORD, WEBSTER, pseud.]
POEMS
Ollie M'Gee   5   42
Doc Hill
The Hill
Silence   5   209
The Conversation   7   55
Arabel
All Life in a Life   7   292
In Memory of Bryan Lathrop   8   180
Canticle of the Race   11   1
 Song of Men
 Song of Women
 Song of the Human Spirit
The World's Desire   14   14
From "Domesday Book"   14   117
 Henry Murray
 At Fairbanks
 George Joslin on "La Menken"
Keats to Fanny Brawne   17   181
Worlds   21   28
Ode to Autumn   22   249
The Return   22   291
Mind Flying Afar   23   242
Peterkin   32   119
I Will Stand Guard
Two Lychee Nuts   32   308
 Yee Lem of Keokuk
 Wah Tom and Black Mag
Harriet Monroe   49   153
Milwaukee Avenue   52   1
Jake Mann
Sunken Realms   52   272

ARTICLES
Correspondence:
 A "Spoon River" Boost   6   103
What Is Poetry?   6   306
Mars Has Descended   10   88

Correspondence: A Correction   12   345
The Artist Revolts   22   206
Correspondence:
 What Is Great Poetry?
 [John Keats]   26   349
Correspondence:
 Letter to Harriet Monroe
 [Poem]   48   175

REVIEWS
You and I, by Harriet Monroe   5   188
Faces and Open Doors, by Agnes Lee   21   267
The World at My Shoulder,
 by Eunice Tietjens   52   356

BOOKS REVIEWED
Spoon River Anthology   6   145
Songs and Satires   8   148
The Great Valley   9   202
Toward the Gulf   12   150
Starved Rock   16   151
Domesday Book   18   214
The Open Sea   21   154
The New Spoon River   25   273
Lee: A Dramatic Poem   29   336
Selected Poems
Jack Kelso: A Dramatic Poem   34   177
Lichee Nuts   38   104
Vachel Lindsay: A Poet in America   47   337
Invisible Landscapes   48   41
Poems of People   49   343
The Golden Fleece of California   50   215
Whitman   50   350
The New World   51   213
More People   55   211
Illinois Poems   59   164

ARTICLES ABOUT
Our Contemporaries,
 by Alice Corbin Henderson   6   259
Correspondence from Lee Wilson Dodd   8   215
The P. S. A. Prizes and Ours,
 by Harriet Monroe   17   88
Correspondence
 from Jessie B. Rittenhouse   17   227
Edgar Lee Masters,
 by Harriet Monroe   24   204
Poets as Prosers,
 by Harriet Monroe   28   328
Poetry's Old Letters,
 by Harriet Monroe   47   30

MASTERS, MARCIA (LEE)
POEMS
The True Gait   58   192
Tomorrow
The River

Sojourn in the Country
Late Summer
The Darkness   62   130
A Hand Is a World
Telephone
Thoughts After Parting
All Day
There Is a Country
Portrait for a Young Man
The Memory   86   321
The Graveyard at Genoa   88   223
Mansion at Sundown   90   365
Impressions of My Father   93   91
At My Mother's Bedside   96   24
Figure   102   377

BOOKS REVIEWED
Intent on Earth   109   48

MASTERSON, DAN
POEMS
The Outing   130   34
The Lawn
Safe Distance   137   207

MASTIN, FLORENCE RIPLEY
POEMS
School Room Sketches   11   195
  Americus
  Roderick
  Lucretia
  Isidor
  David
Your Hands   20   247
From the Telephone
Hearing the Frogs   32   85
Flying   40   130
After Morphia   42   315
Frost Flowers   43   317
A Moment   46   129
This Crystal Snow   47   21
Interior   50   24
Now I Have Died   57   299
Teacher on Strike   70   311

BOOKS REVIEWED
Green Leaves   13   167
Cobwebs of Cable   48   345

MATA, ANDRES
POEMS
Soul and Landscape
  (Tr. by Muna Lee)   26   154

MATANLE, STEPHEN
POEMS
Errand   159   213

MATHERS, E(DWARD) POWYS
BOOKS REVIEWED
Black Marigolds (Tr.)   18   46
The Garden of Bright Waters   20   346
Colored Stars

MATHESON, MARY M.
POEMS
Shifting Winds   22   23

MATHEWS, A. J.
[See MATHEWS, JACKSON]

MATHEWS, AIDAN CARL
POEMS
Way Out   167   52
When
Handicap

MATHEWS, ESTHER
POEMS
Song ("I can't be talkin'...")   53   76
The Pharisees

MATHEWS, JACKSON
[A. J. MATHEWS,
ANDREW JACKSON MATHEWS]
TRANSLATIONS
Poems by Yves Bonnefoy   100   249

REVIEWS
A Barbarian in Asia,
  by Henri Michaux   75   100
The Marine Cemetery,
  by Paul Valéry
  (Tr. by Sidney Alexander)
  [Cecil Day-Lewis]   76   172

BOOKS REVIEWED
La Wallonie, 1886-1892:
  The Symbolist Movement in Belgium   72   231
Charles Baudelaire: The Flowers of Evil
  (Ed. with Marthiel Mathews)   103   316

ARTICLES ABOUT
French Chronicle:
  Recent Publications,
  by Wallace Fowlie   88   408

MATHEWS, MARTHIEL
BOOKS REVIEWED
Charles Baudelaire: The Flowers of Evil
  (Ed. with Jackson Mathews)   103   316

ARTICLES ABOUT
French Chronicle:
  Recent Publications,
  by Wallace Fowlie   88   408

MATHIAS, ROLAND
POEMS
Freshwater West   75   I
Olchon
Pas Seul
Pas de Deux

MATHIEU, BERTRAND
TRANSLATIONS
Poems by Yannis Ritsos   125   I

MATHISON, MINNA
ARTICLES
Correspondence: A Word of Protest
[Alice Corbin Henderson]   13   172

BOOKS REVIEWED
The Chicago Anthology: A Collection
of Verse from the Works of Chicago Poets
(Ed. with Charles G. Blanden)   12   337

MATOS, LUIS PALES
[See PALES MATOS, LUIS]

MATOS, PABLO
REVIEWS
Nuestros Poetas:
Antología Chilena Moderna
(Ed. by Armando Donoso)   26   170

MATRAS, CHRISTIAN
POEMS
The Company of the Blind   116   330
So Deep, So Deep
(Tr. by George Johnston)

MATSAS, ALEXANDER
POEMS
Midday Contemplation at Delos   78   170
The Seduction
(Tr. by Kimon Friar)

ARTICLES ABOUT
Contemporary Greek Poetry,
by Kimon Friar   78   145

MATSON, MABEL CORNELIA
POEMS
What Grief?   16   85

MATSON, SUZANNE
POEMS
After "Charming"   142   90
The Sunday Drunk
The Sunbather

MATTAWA, KHALED
POEMS
For Al-Tayib Salih   158   142

MATTHEWS, JACK
POEMS
Montana Night at Twenty Below   96   161
Remembered
Things   137   68
It
The World's Oldest Authority on Keats
Woman Sitting   138   324
The Instant
On the Etiology of Ghosts
That Poems Should Be Printed
on Recyclable Paper Is Only Right
Inverse Proportions   141   201
Interview with the Poet's Mother
The Civil War Photograph

BOOKS REVIEWED
An Almanac for Twilight   109   340

MATTHEWS, JACKSON
BOOKS REVIEWED
Masters & Friends,
by Paul Valéry (Ed.)
(Tr. by Martin Turnell)   113   338

MATTHEWS, W. K.
BOOKS REVIEWED
Anthology of Modern Estonian Poetry
(Ed. and tr.)   84   236

MATTHEWS, WILLIAM
POEMS
The Explorer   117   160
Sandlot Basketball
Example
Apathy
The Visionary Picnic   119   278
Poems from Right   142   187
("Right as rain you are...")
("Gauche, sinister...")
("Four months of his life...")
("Too right, my son accuses me...")
("On the way to the rink...")
Poems from Wrong
("There's some wrong...")
("By itself...")
("It's too quiet...")
("Maybe what's wrong...")
("What's wrong is to live...")
School Days   151   98
What a Little Moonlight Can Do   154   249
Nabokov's Blues
Onions
The Scalpel
Short Farewells
Reticence   159   25
The Buddy Bolden Cylinder
Mingus at The Showplace

Three Translations
from Martial's *Epigrams*
Last Words   161   198
Visiting Hours
A Telegram from the Muse
The Time of Our Lives   162   125
Time
A Serene Heart at the Movies
Room Full of Used
Baby Furniture for Sale   165   332
Portrait of the Artist
as a Young Clarinettist
The Place on the Corner   170   195
The Tempo Room

TRANSLATIONS
Three Translations
from Martial's *Epigrams*   159   25
V:X
VII:XLVI
XII:XL
From Martial's *Epigrams (X:XLVII)*   165   157
From Horace's *Satires*   167   314
I, i
I, iii

BOOKS REVIEWED
Ruining the New Road   118   234
Sleek for the Long Flight   123   241
Rising and Falling   136   164
A World Rich in Anniversaries,
by Jean Follain
(Tr. with Mary Feeney)   137   220
Flood   142   106
A Happy Childhood   146   167
Foreseeable Futures   150   226
Blues If You Want   156   158
Selected Poems
and Translations 1969-1991   161   286
Time & Money   168   160

ARTICLES ABOUT
[Note]   170   181

MATTHIAS, JOHN
POEMS
Epilogue for Toby Barkan:
From a New Home   123   223
For John Garvick after His Visit:
Suffolk, Fall   124   18
Clarification for Robert Jacoby:
After Many Years   125   276

REVIEWS
Travellers   124   45
Ownerless Earth:
New & Selected Poems,
by Michael Hamburger

H'm, by R. S. Thomas
From Glasgow to Saturn,
by Edwin Morgan
Selected Poems,
by Elizabeth Daryush
Moscow Mansions,
by Barbara Guest
Bearings, by Jack Marshall
The Sleeping Lord and Other Fragments,
by David Jones
[H. S. Ede]   125   233
Songs and Conversations   127   98
The Apple Barrel and Hand in Hand,
by Jon Stallworthy
The Snake at Saffron Walden,
by Paris Leary
Correspondences, by Anne Stevenson
American Handbook,
by David Steingass
Of the Map that Changes,
by William Hunt
Man-Fate, by William Everson
[W. B. Yeats, W. H. Auden]
Somewhere Is Such a Kingdom:
Poems 1952-1971,
by Geoffrey Hill
[Harold Bloom, S. T. Coleridge,
Jon Silkin, T. H. Green,
Robert Lowell]   128   232
Pointless and Poignant   129   340
Poems and Epistles, by John Fuller
Growing-Points,
by Elizabeth Jennings
Living in a Calm Country,
by Peter Porter
Kilroy Was Here,
by John Cotton
Love and Other Deaths,
by D. M. Thomas
[W. H. Auden]

BOOKS REVIEWED
Bucyrus   122   47
Turns   129   233
Crossing   137   169

MATTHIESSEN, F. O.
ARTICLES
From the Introduction to
The Oxford Book of American Verse
[E. A. Robinson, Walt Whitman,
Hart Crane, Vachel Lindsay,
Robert Frost, T. S. Eliot]   77   31

BOOKS REVIEWED
The Achievement of T. S. Eliot   50   54
American Renaissance:
Art and Expression in the Age
of Emerson and Whitman   60   334

Selected Poems of Herman Melville (Ed.)   66   47
The Oxford Book of American Verse (Ed.)   79   36

ARTICLES ABOUT
Rev. of *Contemporary Poetry*, Volume Ten
  (Ed. by Mary Owings Miller)   79   116
Rev. of *The New Oxford Book*
  of American Verse
  (Ed. by Richard Ellmann)   131   236

MATUSOVSKY, MIKHAIL
POEMS
Long Roads
  (Tr. by Babette Deutsch)   70   251

MAUD, RALPH
BOOKS REVIEWED
Dylan Thomas's Choice
  (Ed. with Aneirin Talfan Davies)   106   429

MAUNICK, EDOUARD J.
POEMS
Sept Versants Sept Syllabes
  (Tr. with Carolyn Kizer)   112   256

MAURA, [SISTER] M.
POEMS
Professor of Medieval Balladry   69   78
Class in Surveying

MAURON, CHARLES
BOOKS REVIEWED
Poems, by Stéphane Mallarmé
  (Tr. by Roger Fry)
  [Commentaries]   49   350

MAVITY, NANCY BARR
BOOKS REVIEWED
A Dinner of Herbs   23   286

MAVROGORDATO, JOHN
POEMS
Entropy   49   14

BOOKS REVIEWED
Elegies and Songs   45   231
The Poems of C. P. Cavafy (Tr.)   81   383

MAXIS STELLA, (SISTER)
[See STELLA, (SISTER) MARIS]

MAXWELL, GILBERT
POEMS
Mortality   42   316
  Boy and Hawk
  Farewell
From a Piazza in the South   46   74
Symbol for Static Grief
Forfeits   50   206

BOOKS REVIEWED
Look to the Lightning   44   226
Stranger's Garment   50   110

MAY, HENRY F., JR.
POEMS
Curtains   48   318
After Reading a Carmel Poet

MAY, WONG
[See WONG MAY]

MAYAKOVSKY, VLADIMIR
POEMS
A Talk with a Tax Collector
  (Tr. by Ruth Herschberger
  and Marina Prychodko)   102   100

BOOKS REVIEWED
The Bedbug and Selected Poetry
  (Ed. by Patricia Blake)   97   320
The Complete Plays of...
  (Tr. by Guy Daniels)   114   40

ARTICLES ABOUT
New Trends in Soviet Russian Poetry,
  by Vera Sandomirsky   58   324

MAYERS, FLORENCE CASSEN
POEMS
Fishing Blues   162   277
Your Poem: Boat to Saltaire

MAYES, FRANCES
POEMS
The Untying of a Knot   153   290

MAYHALL, JANE
BOOKS REVIEWED
Givers & Takers   118   41

MAYHEAD, ROBIN
BOOKS REVIEWED
John Keats   113   262

MAYNARD, THEODORE
BOOKS REVIEWED
Our Best Poets   22   108
The Book of Modern Catholic Verse (Ed.)   30   114
Exile, and Other Poems   34   111

MAYO, E. L.
POEMS
Colloquy   52   123
Beyond the Iron Gate   54   17
The Phoenix and the Turtle
The Questioners   57   182
The Diver   59   22

Sonnet for Redheads
The Positivists
Sooth for the Chancellor
The Windless Oaks   60   295
1939
The Forgotten Soldier
In the Web
Prelude and Fugue
Elegy ("He will mount Jacob's ladder...")
The Uninfected   67   248
In the Time of the Great Wind
To Urizen
Pillar of Smoke   73   268
Variations on a Line
    from Shakespeare's Sixty-Fifth Sonnet
Fiscal Year: A Report
The Last   77   12
Spring Is Coming
Letter to My Grandfather's Picture
Homage to Vincent   80   260
The Word of Water   83   137
Twinkling   90   367
The Third Tower   92   166
Icarus
The Factory
What Shall I Say of You?   98   304
On Growing Invisible   111   28
Substance
At the Odds
The Sparrows

REVIEWS
The Angel of Our Thirst,
    by Herman Salinger   79   298
Two Twayne Poets   81   324
    The Catch, by T. Weiss
    Immediate Sun,
        by Rosemary Thomas
The Roads Taken   88   334
    Voice in the Circle, by Jeanne d'Orge
    Book of Lyrics, by Witter Bynner
Five Poets and the Public
    Speech Tradition   111   333
    Jones Very: Selected Poems
        (Ed. by Nathan Lyons)
    Whitman: Explorations in Form,
        by Howard J. Waskow
    James Russell Lowell,
        by Martin Duberman
    The Unknown Edwin Markham,
        by Louis Filler
    The Stone Mason of Tor House:
        The Life and Times of Robinson Jeffers,
        by Melba Berry Bennett

BOOKS REVIEWED
The Diver   71   331
The Center Is Everywhere   86   168
Summer Unbound   93   46

MAZUR, GAIL
POEMS
    Spring Planting   148   5
    Ware's Cove   150   215
    A Small Plane from Boston to Montpelier
    Ice   151   270
    Foliage   152   318
    Another Tree   158   33

REVIEWS
    Brief Reviews   156   224
        Sarah's Choice, by Eleanor Wilner
            [Maxine Kumin]
        Green Age, by Alicia Ostriker
        Days of Awe, by Maurya Simon
        The Book of Winter, by Sue Owen
        Splitting and Binding, by Pattiann Rogers

BOOKS REVIEWED
    The Pose of Happiness   150   102

MAZZARO, JEROME
POEMS
    Early Autumn   128   311
    The Lesson   131   69
    Autumn Landscape
    The Visit
    Quadrille

REVIEWS
    Selected Poems, Third Edition,
        by John Crowe Ransom   117   275

BOOKS REVIEWED
    The Poetic Themes of Robert Lowell   109   198
    The Collected Poems, by John Logan
        (Ed. with A. Poulin, Jr.)   160   34

MAZZOCCO, ROBERT
BOOKS REVIEWED
    Trader   139   35

MC ADAMS, JANET
POEMS
    Flood   154   265

MC ALEAVEY, DAVID
POEMS
    A Sheaf of Light   124   133
    Fire-Boned
    Driving; Driven   134   146
    Reading Mark Trail   138   160

MC ALLISTER, CLAIRE
POEMS
    Paradox   85   17
    Ovid's Mulberry   97   349
    The Body Is a Divining Rod
    Poem About My Father
    Memorial Place

BOOKS REVIEWED
Arms of Light   106   369

MC ALMON, ROBERT (M.)
POEMS
Flying   13   317
  Aero-Laughter
  Aero-Metre
  Consecration
  Consummation
  Volplanetor
  Perspicuity
The Via Dolorosa of Art   17   117
  White Males
  Today's Music
  Form Destructionist—Sculptor
Contributions   27   12
  Completion
  For Instance
  Query
Fortuno Carraccioli   37   247

ARTICLES
Correspondence:
  Concerning Kora in Hell   18   54

BOOKS REVIEWED
Explorations   20   155
Portrait of a Generation   28   280
North America,
  Continent of Conjecture   36   112

ARTICLES ABOUT
[Note]   37   110

MC AULEY, JAMES (J.)
POEMS
Winter Drive   120   334
Private Devotions   121   88
World on Sunday
In the Gardens
Trakl: Salzburg   123   69
Moulting Lagoon   128   249
Timepiece   133   36
The Boy Who Knew Nine Languages   141   140

ARTICLES
Correspondence   121   170

ARTICLES ABOUT
Australian Poetry 1940–1980:
  A Personal View,
  by John Tranter   169   86

MC AULIFFE, MARTIN L., JR.
POEMS
The Stone Frog   79   194
Bimini

MC BETH, VARLEY
POEMS
Sawyer   76   81

MC BLAIR, ROBERT
POEMS
Virginia Portraits   29   26
  Poet Laureate of Albemarle County
  Change
  Cavalier
  Ancestral Oil Portrait
Antelope with Cattle   38   125
  Cattle
  Half-Breed MacPherson
  Requiem

MC BRIDE, MEKEEL
POEMS
Reversals on a Day That Begins with Rain   137   338
Or Failing
Aubade
Castaway   144   197
My Story As Told By Someone Else   150   72
The Earliest Maps

BOOKS REVIEWED
The Going Under of the Evening Land   145   36

MC CABE, VICTORIA
POEMS
Outline for a Life of Balzac   159   331

MC CAFFREY, PHILLIP
POEMS
Gourds   145   64

MC CALIB, DENNIS
BOOKS REVIEWED
Mr. P. Squiggle's Reward   77   114

MC CALL, VIRGINIA ARMITAGE
POEMS
In Nineteen-Thirty-Four   47   82
  Ode to Books
  Lost
  Saint Swithen's

MC CANN, DAVID
POEMS
David   130   1
Morning Light

MC CARRISTON, LINDA
POEMS
Riding Out at Evening   140   153
Quincey's Harvest Moon
On Horseback
Bucked

Driveway
    Aubade: November   143   74
    Late Afternoon

BOOKS REVIEWED
    Talking Soft Dutch   146   38
    Eva-Mary   161   159

MC CARRON, HUGH
  BOOKS REVIEWED
    Realization: A Philosophy of Poetry   51   227

MC CARTHY, JOHN RUSSELL
  POEMS
    The Hero   5   57
    Adventuring   8   237
    Goldenrod
    Come Down, Walt!   14   59
    Wild Aster   15   141
    How Can I Go   35   81
    Ever Thus   41   254
      Walls
      Ingenious
      Happy Are We
    Savor of God   42   136
    Sequoian Notes   50   204
      Memories
      Laying On of Hands
    O Idiot Heart   52   268
    Have No Fear
    Friendship Broken
    Such a Morning   60   310
    Each to His Choice
    No Tower Needed

  BOOKS REVIEWED
    Out of Doors   15   169
    Gods and Devils
    For the Morning   27   226
    Five Times the World   58   226
    Enrico Considers   64   39

  ARTICLES ABOUT
    Correspondence from John Burroughs
      [Emanuel Carnevali]   16   114

MC CARTHY, MARY
  ARTICLES ABOUT
    Rev. of *Pictures from an Institution*,
      by Randall Jarrell   86   46

MC CARTHY, THOMAS
  POEMS
    The Garden of Sempervirons 167   5

MC CARTY, DIXIE
  POEMS
    The Infidel   29   131

MC CAUGHIE, DAVID L.
  POEMS
    In These Gardens   50   78
    Les Voyageurs
    Antitheme
    Dirge (Andante)
    L'Automne

MC CAULEY, SHANE
  POEMS
    Prelude   169   60
    Living
    Puppetmaker
    I

MC CLANAHAN, REBECCA
  POEMS
    Ex-Brother-in-Law   163   150
    Afterglow
    Sidekick
    Teaching a Nephew To Type 169   338

MC CLATCHY, J. D.
  POEMS
    The Pleasure of Ruins   125   19
    A Poem Is a Cafe
    Suffering the Cut   130   28
    Scenes from Another Life
    The Luna Moth   144   311
    Ovid's Farewell
    First Steps   146   311
    Achill Island   151   92
    Fog Tropes   152   249
    An Essay on Friendship 155   315
    Three Dreams About Elizabeth Bishop 158   249
    My Mammogram   164   210
    Dervish   166   314
    Flies   170   344

  TRANSLATIONS
    Poems by Pier Paolo Pasolini
      (Tr. with David Stivender) 155   47
    Poems by Giovanni Raboni
      (Tr. with David Stivender) 155   89

  ARTICLES
    Setting the Hard Tasks
      [Harriet Monroe, Ezra Pound] 141   39
    Comment   151   220

  REVIEWS
    Dialects of the Tribe   130   41
      Reflections on Espionage,
        by John Hollander
      The Mind-Reader, by Richard Wilbur
      Fireweeds, by Theodore Weiss
      The Past Now, by Arthur Gregor
      The Collector of Cold Weather,
        by Lawrence Raab

And the Dew Lay All Night
   Upon My Branch,
   by Allen Grossman
Leaping Clear, by Irving Feldman
[J. C. Masterman]
Selected Poems 1923-1975,
   by Robert Penn Warren   131   169
Grace and Rude Will   132   288
   The Compass Flower,
      by W. S. Merwin
   Stars Which See,
      Stars Which Do Not See,
      by Marvin Bell
   The Illustrations,
      by Norman Dubie
   Regions with No Proper Names,
      by Dick Allen
   Round and Round: A Triptych,
      by Dabney Stuart
   A Swim Off the Rocks,
      by Howard Moss
   The Duplications,
      by Kenneth Koch
Daylight Saving, by Daryl Hine   134   167
Figures in the Landscape   138   231
   Taking Notice,
      by Marilyn Hacker
   Descending Figure,
      by Louise Glück
   Classic Ballroom Dances,
      by Charles Simic
   Heat Death, by Stephen Dobyns
   What Moves Is Not the Wind,
      by James Nolan
   Kingdom Come,
      by Lawrence Kearney
   The Shore, by David St. John
   Summer Palaces,
      by Peter Scupham
All Told   140   170
   Collected Poems 1931-1974,
      by Lawrence Durrell
      (Ed. by James Brigham)
   The Collected Shorter Poems 1947-1977,
      by Robin Skelton
   Collected Poems,
      by Francis Golffing
Short Reviews   140   346
   Vivaldi in Early Fall, by John Engels
   I Am the Jefferson County Courthouse,
      by Andrew Glaze
   For the Sleepwalkers,
      by Edward Hirsch
   Brotherly Love,
      by Daniel Hoffman
   Hard Words,
      by Ursula K. LeGuin
   Poems Old and New 1918-1978,
      by Janet Lewis

Trying to Surprise God,
   by Peter Meinke
White Monkeys, by Bin Ramke
Northern Spy, by Chase Twichell
Swimmer in the Spreading Dawn,
   by Kathleen Spivack
So This Is the Map, by Reg Saner
Yellow Stars and Ice,
   by Susan Stewart
Waiting for My Life,
   by Linda Pastan
Enough Said: Poems 1974-1979,
   by Philip Whalen
Short Reviews   143   163
   Second Sight, by Jonathan Aaron
   Dreams Before Sleep,
      by T. Alan Broughton
   The Kingfisher, by Amy Clampitt
   On Tour with Rita,
      by Nicholas Christopher
   Reckless Wedding, by Maria Flook
   Memory, by Laura Jensen
   The Incognito Lounge,
      by Denis Johnson
   Songs of a Returning Soul,
      by Elizabeth Libbey
   The Vernacular Republic,
      by Les A. Murray
   The Expectations of Light,
      by Pattiann Rogers
   Accidental Weather, by Sherod Santos
   An Apology for Loving the Old Hymns,
      by Jordan Smith
   Presence, by Alan Williamson
   Icehouse Lights, by David Wojahn
   [William Johnson, Robert Lowell]
Weaving and Unweaving   145   291
   New and Collected Poems 1961-1983,
      by Alan Dugan
   Making Certain It Goes On:
      The Collected Poems of Richard Hugo
   Lining Up,
      by Richard Howard
   The Evolution of the Flightless Bird,
      by Richard Kenney
   A Wave, by John Ashbery
Mortal Listeners   149   31
   Collected Poems: 1928-1985,
      by Stephen Spender
   A Few Days, by James Schuyler
   The Unlovely Child,
      by Norman Williams
   Terms To Be Met,
      by George Bradley
   Daily Horoscope, by Dana Gioia
   The Key to the City,
      by Anne Winters
   And, by Debora Greger
   Palladium, by Alice Fulton

The Bright Nails Scattered
on the Ground: Love Poems,
by Allen Grossman
Masks and Passions   154   29
The Collected Poems
of Octavio Paz 1957-1987
(Ed. by Eliot Weinberger)
(Tr. by Eliot Weinberger et. al.)
[Gabriela Mistral]
Collected Poems,
by Charles Tomlinson
The Diversions of Purley,
by Peter Ackroyd
Poems 1963-1983, by C. K. Williams
Streamers, by Sandra McPherson
The Inner Room,
by James Merrill
Amid the Groves,
Under the Shadowy Hill,
the Generations Are Prepared   158   280
Secret Destinations:
Selected Poems 1977-1988,
by Charles Causley
The Use of Fire,
by Reynolds Price
Iris of Creation, by Marvin Bell
The World of the Ten Thousand Things:
Poems 1980-1990, by Charles Wright
The Mail from Anywhere,
by Brad Leithauser
The 1002nd Night, by Debora Greger
Promised Lands, by Peter Sacks

BOOKS REVIEWED
Scenes from Another Life   141   170
Stars Principal   149   168
White Paper:
On Contemporary American Poetry   156   297
The Rest of the Way   160   157

MC CLELLAN, EDWIN
REVIEWS
The Manyoshu: The Nippon
Gakujutsu Shinkokai Translation
of One Thousand Poems,
with the Texts in Romaji   107   404

MC CLELLAN, WALTER
POEMS
Tosti's Goodbye   17   14

MC CLOSKEY, MARK
POEMS
The Smell of the Woods   103   168
A Change for the Better   105   245
Out of Touch   108   235
The Insurance Agent   111   15
Our Kingdom

Meetings, Departures
Stars
The Wedding   113   168
New Country, Excessive Snow
Pig   116   94
Too Dark

REVIEWS
Seven Poets   105   270
Take With Me Now
That Enormous Step,
by Eric Pfeiffer
Picture-Poem Primer, by Paul Reps
A Very Particular Hill,
by Gael Turnbull
Points on the Grid,
by George Bowering
The Lightfall,
by Armand Schwerner
The Anatomy of Love
and Other Poems,
by John William Corrington
Poems and Epigrams,
by Robert Beum
Three Poets   107   125
A Roof of Tiger Lilies,
by Donald Hall
Death of the Kapowsin Tavern,
by Richard Hugo
The Changes,
by Samuel French Morse
Five Poets   108   272
Plain Song, by Jim Harrison
Love Makes the Air Light,
by Raymond Roseliep
The Puritan Carpenter,
by Julia Randall
Dependencies, by Lisel Mueller
Come Out into the Sun,
by Robert Francis
Three English Poets   109   126
Selected Poems,
by John Heath-Stubbs
Nonsequences: Self Poems,
by Christopher Middleton
Symptoms of Loss,
by Hugo Williams
Dimensions of Midnight:
Poetry and Prose,
by Cecil Hemley
(Ed. by Elaine Gottlieb)   110   427
The Moral Features of Seven Poets   118   98
Coming Out Fighting,
by Philip Hobsbaum
Greed, Parts 3 and 4,
by Diane Wakoski
A Probable Volume of Dreams,
by Marvin Bell
The Shot Goes In, by David Hilton

The Alligator Bride:
    Poems New and Selected,
    by Donald Hall
Aurora Bligh and Early Poems,
    by Mary Fabilli
The Rock Woman: Selected Poems,
    by James K. Baxter

BOOKS REVIEWED
    Goodbye, But Listen   113   262

MC CLURE, JOHN
POEMS
    To His Lady, Philosophy   7   286
    Owl-Blasted   20   135

BOOKS REVIEWED
    Airs and Ballads   12   165

MC CLURE, MICHAEL
POEMS
    2 for Theodore Roethke   87   218
    The Child   102   152
    Mad Sonnet ("When spirit has no edge...")
    Mad Sonnet ("We shall be free...")

BOOKS REVIEWED
    Hymns to St. Geryon and Other Poems   97   114
    Dark Brown   100   329
    The New Book/A Book of Torture   100   404
    The Blossom, or Billy the Kid   112   276
    The Beard
    Little Odes & The Raptors   115   47

MC CLUSKEY, KATHERINE WISNER
POEMS
    Envyings   16   194
    A Heat Wave
    Summer Phases   20   254
        The Spree
        Transit
        A Parable
        Wholly Happy
    In an Arizona Valley   24   248
        Dust-Storm
        Heat

MC COMBS, JUDITH
POEMS
    The Habit of Fire   127   205
    In Praise of the Natural Flowing
    Changeling Dream   146   340
    Burden   152   270

MC CORD, DAVID
POEMS
    Recession   34   314
    After Spring   40   132

    Afternoon of a Toad   134   281
    Early Warning
    One of Two, Three of Four, One of Eight
    Look Alive

BOOKS REVIEWED
    Floodgate   32   171
    The Crows   45   50
    What Cheer (Ed.)   68   106
    A Star by Day   77   215

MC CORMACK, T. M.
POEMS
    Love Poem   113   318

MC CORMACK, TOM
POEMS
    Crimes Committed on Winter   124   323

MC CORMICK, JOHN
ARTICLES
    Falling Asleep over Grillparzer:
        An Interview with Robert Lowell
        [John Crowe Ransom, Hart Crane]   81   269
    London Letter: Some New Figures
        [Elizabeth Jennings, Kathleen Raine,
        John Wain, Tom Scott, John Lehmann]   83   269
    London Letter: The Publishing Season
        [Robert Garioch, Vernon Watkins,
        Christopher Fry]   85   176

REVIEWS
    Goethe's Faust, Parts I and II
        (Tr. by Louis MacNeice)   81   393
    Splinters, by Mairi MacInnes   83   172

MC CORMICK, VIRGINIA
POEMS
    Dido   29   81

MC CORMMACH, CAROL
POEMS
    Gestures   121   328
    Triumph 650

MC COURT, EDNA WAHLERT
POEMS
    Voices   16   84
        You and I
        Query
        Strangers

MC COY, SAMUEL
POEMS
    Dirge for a Dead Admiral   1   187
    Spring-Song
    A Sweetheart: Thompson Street
    The Off-Shore Wind

BOOKS REVIEWED
  Merchants of the Morning   17   276

MC CRAE, JOHN
  BOOKS REVIEWED
    In Flanders Fields   14   220

MC CREARY, F(REDERICK) R.
  POEMS
    Hillside Poems   19   255
      Winter Rain
      A Naked Maple
      Noontime
      Judges
      Alone on the Hill
    May-Day   24   82
      Buttons
      Buds
      Sand-Memory

  BOOKS REVIEWED
    The Northeast Corner   27   167

MC CREARY, WILLIAM HAROLD
  POEMS
    Harvest   38   84
    Empty Room
    Renunciation

MC CULLAR, MARY RAY
  POEMS
    Offering   42   326
    Purple of Sleep   43   134
      Water and Stone
      Sotto Voce
    Under this Willow   46   142
    Vista   49   76
    Pace
    Swan
    Indian Summer
    The Light, the Bough

MC CULLOUGH, HELEN CRAIG
  BOOKS REVIEWED
    Tales of Ise: Lyrical Episodes
      from Tenth-Century Japan (Tr.)   114   196

MC DONALD, WALTER
  POEMS
    Catching the Light at Lake Raven   144   332
    Fathers and Sons
    For Dawes, on Takeoff
    Memento Mori
    Buzzing in a Biplane   146   275
    The Middle Years
    Whatever It Takes
    When Children Think
      You Can Do Anything   149   280

    Losing a Boat on the Brazos
    The Songs We Fought For   153   100
    Coming Home
    Father's Straight Razor   156   147
    Starting a Pasture   157   151
    Wishing for More than Thunder   160   187
    The Digs in Escondido Canyon

  BOOKS REVIEWED
    After the Noise of Saigon   152   161
    The Flying Dutchman
    Night Landings   156   100

MC DOWELL, ROBERT
  POEMS
    The Move   126   207
    Elegy in August   170   277

MC ELROY, WALTER
  POEMS
    The Undersea Casino   73   278

  BOOKS REVIEWED
    Poems by Tristan Corbière (Tr.)   73   364

MC FADDEN, ATHENA
  POEMS
    Your Words   20   134

MC FARLAND, ELIZABETH
  POEMS
    Exiles   70   137

MC FEE, MICHAEL
  POEMS
    Cold Quilt   149   28
    First Radio   149   329
    Shooting Baskets at Dusk   153   89
    Bach, Beethoven, Brahms, Mendelssohn,
      Mozart, Schubert, and Schumann
    Ever After   153   209
    Sad Girl Sitting on a Running Board   154   207
    Scanning the Poetry Shelves in Heaven   157   218
    Paper   158   328
    Multi-Purpose Protractor
    Answering Machine   161   258
    Grave Grass
    The All-Dog Siren Choir   162   252
    Pas de Deux
    Clotheslines
    The Bat   166   259
    Champagne
    Poem Typed on an Old Machine
      With a Bi-Chrome Ribbon   169   337

  BOOKS REVIEWED
    Colander   170   347

MC FEE, WILLIAM
ARTICLES ABOUT
   The Wrong-Headed Poets,
      by Jessica Nelson North   34   156

MC GAFFIN, AUDREY
BOOKS REVIEWED
   The Imagined Country   92   178

ARTICLES ABOUT
   Correspondence from Thomas Cole
      [Galway Kinnell]   93   120

MC GAHEY, JEANNE
POEMS
   Recurrent Dream   56   13
   Threat for Suburban   63   130
   Road to Chicago
   The Leaders   78   92
   Fantasy for Planet
   The Dolls
   Poem for January
   Ballad ("Of the flesh that lately...")   93   78
   Refusal for Heaven
   Family Circle   102   241

ARTICLES
   Rosie the Riveter
      [Rosalie Moore]   78   109

BOOKS REVIEWED
   Five Young American Poets,
      Second Series 1941
      (With Paul Goodman, Clark Mills,
      David Schubert, and Karl Shapiro)   60   215

ARTICLES ABOUT
   About the Activist Poets,
      by Lawrence Hart   78   99
   The Beat and the Unbeat,
      by Rosalie Moore   93   104

MC GANN, JEROME (J.)
POEMS
   Prescriptions   114   95

REVIEWS
   Religious Poetry   115   196
      The Christian Tradition
         in Modern British Verse Drama,
         by William V. Spanos
      Christopher Smart,
         Scholar of the University,
         by Arthur Sherbo
      Contexts of Dryden's Thought,
         by Phillip Harth
      George Herbert's Lyrics,
         by Arnold Stein

      Religious Trends in English Poetry:
         VI (1920-1965),
         by Hoxie N. Fairchild
      The Living Milton
         (Ed. by Frank Kermode)
      English Religious Lyric
         in the Middle Ages,
         by Rosemary Woolf
      Blake and Tradition,
         by Kathleen Raine   117   45
      Poetry and Truth   117   195
      The Best Beast,
         by Stevie Smith
      Growing into Love,
         by X. J. Kennedy
      Anonymous Sins and Other Poems,
         by Joyce Carol Oates
      Pieces, by Robert Creeley
      New Poems: 1965-1969
         and The Cave and the Spring:
         Essays on Poetry,
         by A. D. Hope   118   223
      The Importance of Being Ordinary   125   44
      Steeplejacks in Babel,
         by Turner Cassity
      Departures,
         by Donald Justice
      Gold Country,
         by Shirley Kaufman
      No Vacancies in Hell,
         by Daniel Mark Epstein
      Breaking Open,
         by Muriel Rukeyser
      The Page-Turner,
         by David Shapiro

MC GINLEY, PHYLLIS
BOOKS REVIEWED
   One More Manhattan   51   223

**MC GOVERN,
JANET B. MONTGOMERY**
BOOKS REVIEWED
   The Butterflies of Taiwan
      and Other Fantasies   32   55

MC GOVERN, MARGARET
BOOKS REVIEWED
   The Lost Year   36   169

MC GOVERN, MARTIN
POEMS
   Christmas, Colorado   145   143
   Toward an Epithalamion   147   15
   All Hallows Eve/Anniversary
   For Charles and Mary Lamb   149   86
   Processionalia   154   72
   Summer Indians   154   320

MC GRANE, JULIA (BLAUVELT)
POEMS
   Earth's Last Maturity   53   81
   Familiar Pattern   59   258
   Ideologies
   Transition Period
   Arch-Remedy
   For Undiminished Grief
   Heart Affords a Smile   61   604
   Yet Rest To Rise

MC GRATH, THOMAS
POEMS
   Sentiments for a Valediction   54   242
   Song ("Lovers in ladies' magazines..")   64   130
   A Letter for Marian
   Celebration for June 24
   Deep South   64   306
   University Days
   Crash Report   68   26
   Encounter
   Late Arrivals
   Homecoming
   Same Old Jazz   86   156
   The Buffalo Coat   104   361
   For Eugenia
   A Coal Fire in Winter
   All the Dead Soldiers   109   385
   The End of the Line
   The Restless Night

BOOKS REVIEWED
   First Manifesto   56   340
   To Walk a Crooked Mile   74   50
   Figures from a Double World   88   329
   Letter to an Imaginary Friend   102   42
   New & Selected Poems   106   296
   Letter to an Imaginary Friend, Parts I & II   119   45
   Selected Poems: 1938-1988   153   106

MC GREEVY, THOMAS
BOOKS REVIEWED
   T. S. Eliot   42   44

MC GUCKIAN, MEDBH
POEMS
   Ylang-Ylang   146   203

BOOKS REVIEWED
   On Ballycastle Beach   158   214

ARTICLES ABOUT
   A Letter from Britain, by William Logan   157   222
   A Map of Contemporary Irish Poetry,
      by Dennis O'Driscoll   167   94

MC GUIRE, HARRY
POEMS
   The Young Man   38   24

MC GURRIN, BUCKLEY
POEMS
   Ephemera   22   22
   Love on a Spring Night
   Sayonara

MC HUGH, HEATHER
POEMS
   Lines   137   286
   What the Old Women See
   Acts of God
   Remains To Be Seen
   Mind
   Elevated

BOOKS REVIEWED
   A World of Difference   140   102
   Hinge & Sign   166   166

MC HUGH, VINCENT
Books Received
   The Blue Hen's Chickens   70   278
   Why I Live on the Mountain,
      30 Chinese Poems
      (Tr. with C. H. Kwôck)   96   57

MC INTYRE, AMELIA SNYDER
POEMS
   "..The Flowers of Orcus Remember Thee"   59   139

MC INTYRE, CARLYLE (F.)
[See MAC INTYRE, CARLYLE]

MC KAIN, DAVID
POEMS
   A Neighbor   107   91
   Monologue

MC KAY, CLAUDE
BOOKS REVIEWED
   Selected Poems of...   83   287

ARTICLES ABOUT
   Racial Bias and Negro Poetry,
      by Edward Bland   63   328

MC KEAN, JAMES
POEMS
   Bus Ride, Pie de la Cuesta   138   91
   Lost in Amsterdam   145   261
   Headlong   148   27
   Stump Farm

MC KENNY, MARGARET
POEMS
   Sweetpeas   16   193

MC KENZIE, ALEX
POEMS
   Tracking   161   21

MC KENZIE, RODERICK
POEMS
   Harbor   46 73

MC KEON, RICHARD P.
ARTICLES ABOUT
   Rev. of *Critics and Criticism,*
     Ancient and Modern
     (Ed. by R. S. Crane)   82 98

MC KIM, E.
POEMS
   ("horses move across...")   117 38

MC KINNEY, IRENE
POEMS
   Visiting My Gravesite:
     Talbott Churchyard, West Virginia   143 288

MC KINNEY, ISABEL
POEMS
   When Singing April Came   12 13

MC KINSEY, MARTIN
TRANSLATIONS
   Poems by Yannis Ritsos   158 204

MC LANE, JAMES L., JR.
BOOKS REVIEWED
   Spindrift   17 276

MC LAREN, FLORIS CLARK
POEMS
   There Was a Bridge   30 17

MC LAUGHLIN, JOE-ANNE
[JOE-ANNE CARRUTH;
JOE-ANNE
MC LAUGHLIN-CARRUTH]
POEMS
   Half Note for Hayden   157 265
   Muse Tune
   To the Tune of Fats Waller's
     "Rockin' Chair"
   The Parents They Would Be   161 273
   Ode for Adam
   Coming Home from the Circus
   My Son Makes Me Promise
     Not To Say "Bear"
   A Brood of Critics; a Mischief of Poets   168 313
   Evening Star   169 152

MC LAUGHLIN-CARRUTH, JOE-ANNE
[See MC LAUGHLIN, JOE-ANNE]

MC LAUGHLIN, KATHY
POEMS
   Suicide Pond   79 261

MC LEAN, JIM
BOOKS REVIEWED
   The Secret Life of Railroaders   144 297

MC LEISH, KENNETH
BOOKS REVIEWED
   The Poems of Catullus
     (Tr. with Frederic Raphael)   136 40

MC LEMORE, DOROTHY JEAN
POEMS
   On Composing   47 80

MC LEOD, IRENE RUTHERFORD
BOOKS REVIEWED
   Swords for Life   11 48
   Before Dawn   18 166

MC LEOD, LE ROY
POEMS
   Adolescent   29 320
   A Boy Ploughing

MC LUHAN, H. M.
ARTICLES ABOUT
   [Note]   84 119

MC LUHAN, MARSHALL
REVIEWS
   Dream and Responsibility,
     by Peter Viereck   84 93

MC MAHAN, BRYAN MICHAEL
ARTICLES ABOUT
   [Note]   46 294

MC MAHON, LYNNE
POEMS
   All Lycra and Spandex   164 65
   Zachary at Three

BOOKS REVIEWED
   Devolution of the Nude   164 223

MC MANIS, JACK
BOOKS REVIEWED
   Poems by Samuel Greenberg
     (Ed. with Harold Holden)   71 158

MC MICHAEL, CHARLES B.
BOOKS REVIEWED
   Prosas Profanas,
     by Rubén Darío (Tr.)   22 165

MC MICHAEL, JAMES
POEMS
   The Vegetables   117 71
   The Admiral Benbow   120 141

Terce

The Inland Lighthouse

Sluice   122   84

Prime

The Great Garret, or 100 Wheels

The Very Rich Hours   122   209

Its Time   123   135

Clear Teeth

Lauds

Sext   125   11

Nones

Vespers

He Finds the Mansion

BOOKS REVIEWED

Against the Falling Evil   122   105

Each in a Place Apart   166   38

MC MURRAY, EARL

POEMS

Keeping Quiet   145   87

A Perfect Stranger

A Man in a House

MC NAIR, WESLEY

POEMS

The Bald Spot   136   292

The Poetic License

Hair on Television   138   157

The Fat Enter Heaven

Small Towns Are Passing   141   286

Mute   144   9

Big Cars

Remembering Aprons   144   156

The Faith Healer

The Portuguese Dictionary

The Man with the Radios   151   93

After My Stepfather's Death   152   148

The Revival   152   275

Trying To Find Her Teeth   157   19

ARTICLES

Comment

  [John Frederick Nims]   151   223

BOOKS REVIEWED

The Town of No   156   345

My Brother Running and Other Poems   165   219

MC NAMARA, EUGENE

BOOKS REVIEWED

21 x 3

  (With Dorothy Farmiloe

  and Len Gasparini)   115   353

MC NAUGHT, ELMOND FRANKLIN

POEMS

Green and Gray   10   201

Spring Morning

Gray Morning

Sparkles   12   205

MC NEAL, THOMAS H(ILL)

POEMS

Seven Songs of Earth   34   68

Portrait

Woman's Song

A Woman Looking into Her Glass

Her Child Was Dead

The Sign

At Parting

The Grief

Spring Song

BOOKS REVIEWED

Three Lyric Poets

  (With Alice Moser and

  Byron Herbert Reece)

  (Ed. by Alan Swallow)   61   629

Motley's the Only Wear

MC NEIL, C. R.

POEMS

Definition   79   329

Woolworth

MC NEIL, FLORENCE

BOOKS REVIEWED

The Overlanders   144   297

MC NEILL, LOUISE

POEMS

Nora Kane   53   183

Tillie Sage

BOOKS REVIEWED

Time Is Our House   61   690

MC NULTY, TED

POEMS

Antietam   158   320

MC PEEK, JAMES A. S.

POEMS

Ether Darkness   36   305

MC PHEE, ROSALIND

BOOKS REVIEWED

What Place Is This   144   297

MC PHERSON, JAMES L.

POEMS

To Carol   67   68

For Belgium

The Party Is Over   72   62

Walking at Night Two Years Later

Inventory

MC PHERSON, SANDRA

POEMS

Autumnal	114	374
His Body	116	31
Some Meanings of Silence		
Eschatology		
A Community	118	94
The War Surplus Store		
Triolets		
Holding Pattern	119	213
Seaweeds	121	94
Some Engravings of Pierré Joseph Redoute		
A Little Fire		
Siberia		
Page	122	187
The Empty House		
Poem ("The name of his boat...")		
Triolet		
Letter After the Poems of a Friend	124	139
Letter by Air		
Extract		
Fresh Flowers		
Poem Whose First Stanza Is		
Martin Heidegger on Georg Trakl	126	187
The Heredity of Systems		
Metaphors		
In a Garden		
Seeing Dr. H, Teacher of Villanelles,		
10 Years Later		
Sentience		
Studies in the Imaginary	128	323
For Neruda: Political Landscape	131	332
Smoking: Notes		
Salamanders		
Umbra		
The Clown	133	249
Veteran		
He, Like Everyone		
Writing to a Prisoner		
Corresponding		
The Jet Engine	135	249
Haze		
Lullaby		
Debut		
Black Soap		
Living Glass	138	163
Singing Teakettle		
Preparing the Will, Three Generations		
Diary—May 15, 1980—Twin Cities		
Urban Ode	140	187
Peter Is Here		
Only Once		
Wings and Seeds: For My Birth Mother		
Presbyterian, 1983	151	94
Postcard to the Musician	156	187
Lowell Fulson, Age 66, Eli's Mile High Club,		
Oakland, California		
Affirmation Against Critics	157	1

Mixing the Patches		
Genius of Fog at Ecola Creek Mouth	159	5
The Study of Genius	164	63
My Theory of Mockingbirds	165	212
Edge Effect	166	203
Research Trail, Cold Canyon, November		
Chalk-Circle Compass	169	332

BOOKS REVIEWED

Elegies for the Hot Season	118	290
Radiation	126	103
The Year of Our Birth	133	169
Patron Happiness	143	295
Streamers	154	29
The God of Indeterminacy	165	31
Edge Effect: Trails and Portrayals	169	339
The Spaces Between Birds:		
Mother/Daughter Poems 1967-1995		

MC QUILKIN, RENNIE

POEMS

Hands	138	86
The Other Woman		
Isobel at 87	139	219
Miss Caroline		
Rendezvous in a Country Churchyard	140	152
Peter Farr	141	276
Doing Time at Gilead Regional	144	16
Ladders to Glory, Woods Hole		
At the Bar		
Eviction	147	201
Visit	150	148
Going Under	160	147
The Tracking	161	141
Birthday at the Motor Vehicle Dept.	162	335

MC RAY, PAUL

POEMS

Mósa—Mohave	152	215

MC ROBBIE, KENNETH

POEMS

Nanook	96	155
Squirrels		
The Movement of the Worlds		
The Rite of Spring		

REVIEWS

Canadian Chronicle	103	266
The First Five Years:		
A Selection from		
The Tamarack Review		
(Ed. by Robert Weaver)		
Sun Stone, by Octavio Paz		
(Tr. by Peter Miller)		
A Shifting Pattern,		
by Peter Miller		

Ice Cod Bell or Stone,
   by Earle Birney
The Things Which Are,
   by Alden Nowlan
Five New Brunswick Poets
Twelve Letters to a Small Town,
   by James Reaney
The Sea Is Also a Garden,
   by Phyllis Webb
Collected Poems, by A. J. M. Smith

BOOKS REVIEWED
Jupiter C for the Missile Age, 4 Poems   94 186
Eyes Without a Face   99 184
The Boy Changed Into a Stag,
   by Ferenc Juhász
   (Tr. with Ilona Duczynska)   119 45

MC VICKAR, DOROTHY
POEMS
Long Days   18 84
Heaphy Herself
Eve and Mrs. Pengilly   30 263

MEAD, MARGARET
POEMS
Misericordia   35 253

MEAD, MATTHEW
BOOKS REVIEWED
Shadow Land: Johannes Bobrowski
   (Tr. with Ruth Mead)   110 52
Penguin Modern Poets 16
   (With Jack Beeching
   and Harry Guest)   119 291

MEAD, RUTH
BOOKS REVIEWED
Shadow Land: Johannes Bobrowski
   (Tr. with Matthew Mead)   110 52

MEADE, J. V.
POEMS
To a Woman Who Is Not All Myth   79 281
Winter's End   82 140

MEADOWCROFT, CLARA PLATT
BOOKS REVIEWED
A Wind Blowing Over   27 226

MEARNS, DAVID C.
ARTICLES
Correspondence
   [Karl Shapiro]   92 331

MEARS, ALICE MONKS
POEMS
Always the Timid   57 133
Prowhead   58 183

Nocturne for the Town   60 259
New Tale   61 658
Always the Hill Remembered   64 202
O Hollywood   74 21
Springshine   84 335

BOOKS REVIEWED
Brief Enterprise   68 227

MEDINA, PABLO
POEMS
The Ivory Tower   140 97
Return to Dunbarton Oaks

MEE, SUZI
POEMS
Sebastian   114 369
Brighton Beach Line   130 82

MEEK, JAY
POEMS
Voyager Music   147 154

MEEKER, ARTHUR, JR.
REVIEWS
Two Anthologies   52 299
   American Naval Songs and Ballads
     (Ed. by Robert W. Neeser)
   Voices from the Fields
     (Ed. by Russell Lord)
   The Oxford Book of Light Verse
     (Ed. by W. H. Auden)   54 111
Lyric and Narrative   56 48
   Strange Dimension,
     by Florence Dickinson Stearns
   Scarlet Anne, by Theda Kenyon

MEEKER, MARJORIE
POEMS
At Sea   14 70
Daisies
Songs of Night   19 182
   Ode to Myself Trying to Sleep
   In Darkness
   By a Window
   Song for a May Night
   Color of Water
   Lonely Sky and Sea
   Comrades
Wake-Song   22 118
Words Said in an Attic   23 233
Sonnets
   ("Now here is love...")
   ("With names and gifts...")
Airs for a Flute
Before You Came
Where My Step Falters
Memorial Sonnets   25 258

When I Am Old
Color of Water   31   59
  Beach Fire
  On the Beach
  Intercession
  The Hidden Scorn of the Heart
  Words Said for Farewell
  Certainly Oceans
  This Wary Winter
  Pear Orchard in Spring
  Before First Frost
  Winter Solstice
  For Rockwell Kent's Twilight of Man
The House on the Marshes   44   130
A Sign Awaited   50   72
  Wild Oranges
  Once I Called Time
  Bay of Dolphins
  The Day Before the Storm

BOOKS REVIEWED
  Color of Water   32   217

MEEM, JOHN
  BOOKS REVIEWED
  Diadems and Fagots,
    by Olavo Bilac and Pierre de Ronsard
    (Tr. with Yvor Winters)   23   113

MEHROTRA, ARVIND KRISHNA
  POEMS
  Engraving of a Bison on Stone   128   83

MEI, YUAN
  [See YUAN MEI]

MEINKE, PETER
  POEMS
  Azaleas   133   144
  The Artist
  Elephant Tusks
  Playing Badminton:
    Sunday Afternoon 1968
  The Gift of the Magi   141   127
  Atomic Pantoum   142   20
  Exodus with Children   152   136
  The Dead Tree
  Apples   165   275
  Mazzaroli's Cannon
  J   167   280

  BOOKS REVIEWED
  Trying to Surprise God   140   346
  Liquid Paper: New and Selected Poems   162   96

MEISSNER, BILL
  POEMS
  So Many Americans,
    Driving Late on Country Roads   148   267

MEISTER, ERNST
  POEMS
  Winterly
    (Tr. by Michael Hamburger)   128   132

MELARTIN, RIKKA
  POEMS
  Untitled   142   94
  Territories

MELCHIORI, BARBARA ARNETT
  TRANSLATIONS
  Poems by Luciana Frezza   94   325

MELENDEZ, ENGRACIA
  POEMS
  Agave Flowers   23   136
  In Berkeley
  Rubén Darío
  Mi Marido
  Defense
  Lontananza

MELLOR, BERNARD
  BOOKS REVIEWED
  Wayside Poems of the Seventeenth Century
    (Ed. with Edmund Blunden)   104   120

MELNYCZUK, ASKOLD
  POEMS
  The Way of the World   141   324
  The Sunday Before Easter   144   35
  Chorale: In April   146   29
  The Usual Immigrant Uncle Poem   153   130
  After a Snowfall on the Second Day
    of Spring in 1992   161   326

MELTZER, CHARLES HENRY
  BOOKS REVIEWED
  The Tragedy of Man,
    by Imre Madách
    (Tr. with Paul Vajda)   47   285

MELTZER, DAVID
  BOOKS REVIEWED
  Ragas   96   179
  The Process   108   198
  Luna   122   293

MELVILLE, HERMAN
  BOOKS REVIEWED
  Selected Poems of...
    (Ed. by F. O. Matthiessen)   66   47
  Collected Poems of...
    (Ed. by Howard P. Vincent)   72   167

  ARTICLES ABOUT
  Rev. of *Olson/Melville: A Study in Affinity,*
    by Ann Charters   116   110

Rev. of *The New Oxford Book
of American Verse*
(Ed. by Richard Ellmann)   131   236

MEMMER, PHILIP
POEMS
Letter to a Friend   163   256

MENASHE, SAMUEL
BOOKS REVIEWED
The Many Named Beloved   100   104
No Jerusalem But This   121   292

MENCKEN, H. L.
ARTICLES ABOUT
Mephistopheles and the Poet,
by Harriet Monroe   28   210
Recent Magazines,
by M. D. Zabel   39   166

MENDELSON, EDWARD
BOOKS REVIEWED
Collected Poems,
by W. H. Auden (Ed.)   131   159
Early Auden   139   292

MENENDEZ PIDAL, RAMON
BOOKS REVIEWED
Poema del Cid
(Tr. by W. S. Merwin)   101   353

MEOGO, PERO
POEMS
*Song of the Girl Who Tore
Her Dress at the Spring*
(Tr. by Yvor Winters)   29   302

MERCHANT, W. MOELWYN
POEMS
Breaking the Code   119   11

MERCIER, VIVIAN
ARTICLES
Oliver St. John Gogarty
[W. B. Yeats, Lord Macaulay,
Ezra Pound, Horace]   93   35

REVIEWS
Ovid and Sappho in Translation   95   185
Ovid: The Metamorphoses
(Tr. by Horace Gregory)
Sappho
(Tr. by Mary Barnard)
[A. E. Watts, Arthur Golding,
Dudley Fitts]

BOOKS REVIEWED
The Irish Comic Tradition   103   185

MEREDITH, GEORGE
ARTICLES ABOUT
Meredith as a Poet,
by Harriet Monroe   32   210
Rev. of *Shadow Train,*
by John Ashbery   140   236

MEREDITH, WILLIAM
POEMS
Words After Midnight, Forbidding Remorse   60   18
"When Do We Inherit Them..."
Love Letter from an Impossible Land   63   239
Quartet in F Major
Reductio Ad Absurdum Blues
In Strange Events
Ten-Day Leave
String Quartet   69   134
Against Excess of Sea or Sun or Reason
Battlewagon   70   66
A Figure from Politics
The Impressment
In a Copy of Yeats' Poems
An Account of a Visit to Hawaii   81   345
The Illiterate   82   270
A Wasteland Sonnet
The Deciduous Trees
The Fish-Vendor   87   13
Bachelor   88   165
Pastoral
A Botanical Trope
Roots   99   232
For His Father   101   74
Iambic Feet Considered as Honorable Scars
Sonnet   113   412
Reading My Poems from World War II   115   343
My Mother's Life   136   187
The Revenant
Stages
Grace   151   99

ARTICLES
Correspondence   120   363

REVIEWS
The Big Road, by Norman Rosten   69   101
As Ten As Twenty, by P. K. Page   70   208
Poems, by Joan Murray
(Ed. by Grant Code)   70   335
Other Skies, by John Ciardi   72   99
Ten Poets Anthology
(Ed. by Anthony Harrigan)   74   55
Volume Two, by José García Villa   75   290
A Gift to Both Languages   88   113
The Pillow-Book of Sei Shonagon
(Tr. by Arthur Waley)
The No Plays of Japan,
by Arthur Waley
[Lady Murasaki, Ezra Pound, Seami]

Poetry and the
   Counter-Broadway Theater   89   253
   Playbook: Five Plays for a New Theater,
      by Lionel Abel, Robert Hivnor,
      Junjo Kinoshita, James Merrill,
      and I. A. Richards
   The Magic Flute
      (Tr. by W. H. Auden
      and Chester Kallman)
Advice to a Prophet and Other Poems,
   by Richard Wilbur   100   40
In the Clearing, by Robert Frost   101   200
The Dyer's Hand,
   by W. H. Auden   107   118
Love & Fame and Delusions, Etc.,
   by John Berryman   122   98

BOOKS REVIEWED
   Love Letter from an Impossible Land   64   227
   Ships and Other Figures   73   111
   The Open Sea and Other Poems   92   378
   Alcools: Poems 1898-1913,
      by Guillaume Apollinaire (Tr.)   105 136
   The Wreck of the Thresher and Other Poems 107 326
   Earth Walk: New and Selected Poems   118 228
   Hazard, the Painter   127 234
   The Cheer   139 171
   Partial Accounts: New and Selected Poems 151 419

ARTICLES ABOUT
   [Note on erroneous attribution]   114 138

MERIDETH, ROBERT
   REVIEWS
   Collected Poems,
      by Paul Goodman
      (Ed. by Taylor Stoehr)   128 100

MERILUOTO, AILA
   POEMS
   Wading Girl
      (Tr. by Meri Lehtinen)   98   351

MERKER, KARL KIMBER
   POEMS
   Poem for Con   95   92

MERRIAM, EVE
   POEMS
   Ask Your Grocer Tomorrow
      for This Glamorous Product   57   6
   October-Midst
   The Escape
   The Circulation of Newspapers
      Rises Greatly in Time of War
   Poem for the Seventh Day
   Lullaby
   Jew   58   310

I Anonymous
Ditty for Departing Troops
The Democratic Dime
Funeral Service
Imagine Yourself
Furniture   60   200
How Do You Know?   61   467
Blackout
The Word
Above All Great and Public Grief
A. W. O. L.
Summer Heat
Library
"Morning or Midnight, the Same Hour"   63   140
Home Town
The Coward
Brother
For a Soldier's Birthday   64   246
The Dusty Young Men
South Pacific   65   303
Memo to Myself   69   259
Abstraction   74   24
Movie Star in the Projection Room

BOOKS REVIEWED
   Five Young American Poets:
      Third Series, 1944
      (With John Frederick Nims,
      Jean Garrigue, Tennessee Williams,
      and Alejandro Carrión)   66   95
   Family Circle   70   266

MERRILL, JAMES
   POEMS
   From Theory of Vision   67   293
      The Green Eye
      The Cosmological Eye
      Perspectives of the Lonesome Eye
   The Formal Lovers
   The Broken Bowl   69   246
   Accumulations of the Sea   70   1
   River Poem
   The Flint Eye
   Suspense of Love
   Variations: The Air Is Sweetest
      that a Thistle Guards   72   117
   Europa
   Kite Poem
   Figures in a Legendary Glade   74   125
   The Peacock
   Poem in Spring
   Conservatory
   Periwinkles
   The Octopus   78   324
   Fire Poem
   Hotel de L'Univers et Portugal
   Who Guessed Amiss the Riddle of the Sphinx
   The Lovers

The Greenhouse	81	50
Salomé	87	295
For a Second Marriage		
Mirror	91	281
A Valentine in Crayons		
At Mamallapuram		
Laboratory Poem		
Italian Lesson		
Walking All Night		
Scenes of Childhood	96	195
Lover by Full Moon		
The Power Station		
Angel		
Six Leaves from the Album		
in the Waiting-Room	98	159
A Tenancy		
The Mad Scene	101	75
From the Cupola	107	143
Matinees	114	71
Another April	118	1
Seaside Doorway, Summer Dawn		
Banks of a Stream Where Creatures Bathe		
The Black Mesa		
Komboloi		
Desert Motel with Frog Amulet		
Flèche d'Or		
From *Theory of Vision*	121	19
The Green Eye		
McKane's Falls	122	313
The Will	125	37
O	131	1
The Blue Grotto	141	16
After the Ball		
Alessio and the Zinnias	151	101
Nine Lives	156	249
Christmas Tree	166	313
The Charioteer of Delphi	166	337
Last Words		
The Victor Dog	166	340
Mirror	166	348

TRANSLATIONS
Poem by Christian Ayoub	114	71

ARTICLES
Robert Bagg: A Postscript	98	250
Comment	151	213
Four Letters to Stephen Yenser [Elizabeth Bishop]	166	324

BOOKS REVIEWED
First Poems	78	233
Short Stories	86	242
Playbook: Five Plays for a New Theater (With Lionel Abel, Robert Hivnor, Junjo Kinoshita, and I. A. Richards)	89	253
The Country of a Thousand Years of Peace and Other Poems	94	199

Water Street	102	260
Nights and Days	108	329
The (Diblos) Notebook	109	332
The Fire Screen	117	388
Braving the Elements	122	163
Divine Comedies	129	40
Mirabell: Books of Number	135	161
Scripts for the Pageant	137	297
From the First Nine: Poems 1946-1976	143	101
The Changing Light at Sandover		
Late Settings	147	291
The Inner Room	154	29
Selected Poems 1946-1985	162	282
The Changing Light at Sandover		
A Scattering of Salts	166	354

ARTICLES ABOUT
Rev. of *James Merrill: Essays in Criticism* (Ed. by David Lehman and Charles Berger)	143	101
Rev. of *The Arkansas Testament*, by Derek Walcott	152	98
In Memory of James Merrill, by Joseph Parisi	166	311
Metamorphoses, by Stephen Yenser	166	331
Memorial Tribute, by Rachel Hadas	166	334
Memorial Tribute, by Anthony Hecht	166	339
Memorial Tribute, by John Hollander	166	341
An Introduction, by Allan Gurganus	166	350

MERRILL, STUART
ARTICLES ABOUT
The Death of Stephen Phillips, by Harriet Monroe	7	260

MERRYMAN, MILDRED PLEW
POEMS
The Housewife	21	78
Old Folk		
Choctawhatchee Sonnets	25	244
By an Indian Grave		
Memory		
L'envoi		
Two Ladies	36	196
Epitaph for Tabitha		
Local Color		

MERTEN, JACK
POEMS
Children at Play	17	77

MERTON, THOMAS (JAMES)
POEMS
The Night Train	60	20
The Dark Morning		
Poem: 1941		

A Dirge		
St. Malachy	73	255
From the Legend of St. Clement		
Sincerity	89	140
Seneca	103	381
Notes for a New Liturgy	112	254

BOOKS REVIEWED

Thirty Poems	65	264
A Man in the Divided Sea	69	165
Figures for an Apocalypse	73	46
The Tears of the Blind Lions	76	224
The Strange Islands	91	41
Selected Poems	96	387
Original Child Bomb	102	118
Emblems of a Season of Fury	104	378
Cables to the Ace	114	40

MERWIN, W. S.

POEMS

Variations on the Gothic Spiral	71	304
Half Roundel	80	13
On the Subject of Poetry	80	264
Colloquy at Peniel	81	52
Toro	83	72
Spider	83	320
The Sapphire	84	255
Bear	85	214
Camel		
The Other Tree	86	228
The Master	87	323
Corps de Ballet		
Thorn Leaves in March		
The Shipwreck		
Small Woman on Swallow Street	89	345
Whaler		
Mercy		
The Highway		
Air	99	203
Lost Month		
Reunion		
Despair		
By Day and By Night		
In the Gorge		
Separation		
The Defeated		
Noah's Raven		
Witnesses		
Foreign Summer		
Bread and Butter	101	76
Before That		
The Students of Justice	102	384
For the Grave of Posterity		
Mountain Town		
An Island in the Harbor		
Spring		
The Last One	104	339

Pieces for Other Lives		
Bread at Midnight		
It Is March		
Among the Eyes		
Some Last Questions		
The Gods	107	299
Looking East at Night		
April		
Whenever I Go There		
How We Are Spared	109	235
The Dream Again		
Death of a Favorite Bird		
Provision		
The Dragonfly		
The Hydra	110	100
Is That What You Are		
An End in Spring		
Divinities		
Encounter	113	147
Do Not Die		
Not These Hills		
Esther		
Inscription Facing Western Sea	116	71
The Calling Under the Breath		
Sunset After Rain		
In the Time of the Blossoms		
The Sadness		
Looking Back	117	179
Something I've Not Done		
At the Same Time		
Tool		
Memory of the Loss of Wings		
Malayan Figures	118	16
Exercise	120	98
The Second Time		
Song of Man Chipping an Arrowhead		
The Day		
The Chase		
Animals from Mountains		
A Purgatory		
After the Alphabets	151	102
A Last Look		
The Overpass	152	78
Search Party	159	251
After the Spring	160	125
A Summer Night		
Mirage		
Panes		
The Stranger	161	1
The Hummingbird		
Fox Sleep		
Entry	163	10
Color Merchants		
Oak Time		
Traces	164	1
The Bird		
Returning Season		
The View	164	313

Passing
Untouched
Old Sound   165   334
The Shortest Night
Distant Morning
The Time Before
Before a Departure in Spring   166   12
Ceremony After an Amputation
A Night Fragrance
Lament for the Makers   166   317
Portrait   167   221
Completion
Sixth-Floor Walk-Up   169   125
Returns After Dark
Legend
Portovenere
The Old Year
Whoever You Are   170   28
The Causeway

TRANSLATIONS
Poems by Juan Ramón Jiménez   82   187
Poems by Ghalib
    (Tr. with Aijaz Ahmad)   116   335
From Dante's *Purgatorio* (Canto V)   162   152

ARTICLES
Correspondence   120   362

REVIEWS
Early American Poets
    (Ed. by Louis Untermeyer)   81   261
In Memoriam James Joyce.
    A Vision of World Language,
    by Hugh MacDiarmid   88   48

BOOKS REVIEWED
A Mask for Janus   82   34
The Drunk in the Furnace   98   118
Poema del Cid,
    by Ramón Menendez Pidal (Tr.)   101   353
The Satires of Persius (Tr.)
Spanish Ballads (Tr.)
The Moving Target   104   184
The Lice   112   418
W. S. Merwin:
    Selected Translations 1948-1968   115   187
Transparence of the World,
    Poems by Jean Follain (Tr.)   116   260
Voices, by Antonio Porchia (Tr.)   120   113
Twenty Love Poems
    and a Song of Despair,
    by Pablo Neruda (Tr.)   120   304
Writings to an Unfinished Accompaniment   124   167
Osip Mandelstam: Selected Poems
    (Tr. with Clarence Brown)   124   232
(Asian Figures)   124   292
The Compass Flower   132   288

Opening the Hand   145   161
The Rain in the Trees   153   229
Travels   163   158
The Vixen   170   37

ARTICLES ABOUT
"Sacred Beings":
    Writers in Recorded Conversation,
    by Michael Milburn   146   101
[Note]   158   354

MESA, LAUREN
POEMS
The Progress   144   255
Evening Walk
The Years We Will Know Them   151   343

MESCHTER, CHARLES K.
ARTICLES
Orchestral Poetry
    [Fernand Divoire]   24   327

MESIC, MICHAEL
POEMS
Three Stanzas   115   38
[Rev. of The Young American Poets]   117   277
Three Hymns to Hypnos   121   201
Gaudi   125   147
Night Letter
Swallows
Model Solar System

TRANSLATIONS
Poems by Pushkin and Mimnermus   116   343

REVIEWS
The Young American Poets
    (Ed. by Paul Carroll)   117   277
The Sense of Occasion,
    by Chester Kallman   120   47
Three of Them   124   232
    Hope Against Hope and Hope Abandoned,
        by Nadezhda Mandelstam
        (Tr. by Max Hayward)
    Mandelstam, by Clarence Brown
    Osip Mandelstam: Selected Poems
        (Tr. by Clarence Brown
        and W. S. Merwin)
    Poems of Akhmatova
        (Tr. by Stanley Kunitz
        with Max Hayward)
    Marina Tsvetayeva: Selected Poems
        (Tr. by Elaine Feinstein)

MESIC, PENELOPE
REVIEWS
Brief Reviews   143   295
    The Forces of Plenty,
        by Ellen Bryant Voigt

475

In a U-Haul North of Damascus,
    by David Bottoms
The Milky Way: Poems 1967-1982,
    by Jon Anderson
Patron Happiness,
    by Sandra McPherson
Stone, Paper, Knife,
    by Marge Piercy
Etruscan Things, by Rika Lesser
Long Walks in the Afternoon,
    by Margaret Gibson
The White Words,
    by Baron Wormser
Lake Effect Country,
    by A. R. Ammons
The Attraction of Heavenly Bodies,
    by Dennis Hinrichsen
In the House of the Judge,
    by Dave Smith

MESSBARGER, REBECCA
TRANSLATIONS
    Poem by Giampiero Neri   155   75
    Poems by Carlo Villa   155   81

METASTASIO, (PIETRO)
POEMS
    Sonnet ("Why, froward goddess...")
        (Tr. by Francis Golffing)   128   140

MEUTTMAN, MARGARET MOORE
POEMS
    Noel   27   135

MEW, CHARLOTTE
BOOKS REVIEWED
    Saturday Market   20   152
    Collected Poems   86   240

**MEYER, CONRAD FERDINAND
[KONRAD FERDINAND MEYER]**
POEMS
    The Dead Child
        (Tr. by Madison Cawein)   8   135
    Black-Shadow-Giving Chestnut   131   322
    Sheet Lightning
    Huss's Prison
        (Tr. by John S. Anson)

MEYER, EMMA VORIES
POEMS
    To a Tree   30   196

MEYER, JOHN H.
REVIEWS
    Mallarmé, by Wallace Fowlie   83   278
    Poems and Plays,
        by Gordon Bottomley
        (Ed. by Claude Colleer Abbott) 86   363

**MEYER, KONRAD FERDINAND
[See MEYER, CONRAD
FERDINAND]**

MEYERS, BERT
BOOKS REVIEWED
    Early Rain   99   313

MEYNELL, ALICE
POEMS
    Maternity   1   181

BOOKS REVIEWED
    Poems   4   69

ARTICLES ABOUT
    Of Two Poets, by Harriet Monroe   21   262
    Rev. of Alice Meynell: A Memoir,
        by Viola Meynell   35   349

MEYNELL, VIOLA
POEMS
    The Blind Man's Morning   47   126
    Late Tidings

BOOKS REVIEWED
    Alice Meynell: A Memoir   35   349
    The Frozen Ocean   40   226

MEZEY, ROBERT
POEMS
    It Is June, This Jesting Heat   99   83
    Dark Head   98   11
    To Philip Levine, on the Day of Atonement
    To the Goddess
    Vetus Flamma

TRANSLATIONS
    Poems by Jorge Luis Borges   161   9
    Poems by Jorge Luis Borges
        (Tr. with R. G. Barnes)   162   157
    Poems by Jorge Luis Borges   164   71

BOOKS REVIEWED
    Poems
        (With Stephen Berg
        and Ronald Goodman)   93   182
    The Wandering Jew   99   184
    The Lovemaker   100   404
    White Blossoms   109   189
    Naked Poetry:
        Recent American Poetry in Open Forms
        (Ed. with Stephen Berg)   116   35
    A Book of Dying   118   295
    The Door Standing Open
    The New Naked Poetry:
        Recent American Poetry in Open Forms
        (Ed. with Stephen Berg)   132   31

The Collected Poems of Henri Coulette
   (Ed. with Donald Justice)   158   214

MHAC AN TSAOI, MÁIRE
POEMS
   Shoa   167   38

MIALL, BERNARD
BOOKS REVIEWED
   Poems,
     by Maurice Maeterlinck (Tr.)   8   96

MICHALOPOULOS, ANDRE
TRANSLATIONS
   Poem by C. P. Cafavis   70   132

MICHAUX, HENRI
POEMS
   Response in Unhappiness   67   10
   A Girl of Budapest
   On the Road to Death
   But You, When Will You Come?
   Destiny
     (Tr. by George Dillon)
   The Jetty
     (Tr. by Richard Ellmann)   73   258

BOOKS REVIEWED
   A Barbarian in Asia   75   100

ARTICLES ABOUT
   Correspondence
     from George Dillon   67   49
   Henri Michaux,
     by Wallace Fowlie   81   265

MICHAUX, WILLIAM
POEMS
   Lucretius   63   253

MICHELANGELO (BUONARROTI)
BOOKS REVIEWED
   The Complete Poems of...
     (Tr. by Joseph Tusiani)   98   403

MICHELSON, MAX ["M. M."]
POEMS
   O Brother Tree   6   170
   The Bird
   May in the City   8   63
     The Newcomers
     Love-Lyric
     Midnight
     The Willow Tree
     Storm
     The Red Light
     In the Park
     A Hymn to Night

Winds of March   9   296
   "Newly Seeded"
   Night Moods
   On a Windy Afternoon
   Off
   Fire
   Knowledge
   The Adversary
   A Polish Girl
   Portrait
   Gone
   Playing Horse
   Traveler
The Tired Woman   11   255
Masks   13   83
   A Helen
   Girls
   Myrrh
   Pain
   A Lady Talking to a Poet
   The Golden Apple
   A Dilettante
   The Traitor
   A Rich Gentleman
   A Petit Bourgeois
   La Mort de Paul Verlaine
   Death
   To a Woman Asleep
     in a Street-Car
The Haunted Hat-Shop   17   233

ARTICLES
   A Note on T. S. Eliot's Book   12   36
   Poetry as an Art   12   325

REVIEWS
   Catholic Anthology—1914-1915
     [John Rodker, Carl Sandburg,
     Alfred Kreymborg, Douglas Goldring,
     Ezra Pound]   8   94
   Others: An Anthology of the New Verse
     (Ed. by Alfred Kreymborg)   8   151
   Idols, by Walter Conrad Arensberg   8   208
   Cadences, by F. S. Flint   8   260
   The Tidings Brought to Mary,
     by Paul Claudel
     (Tr. by Louise Morgan Sill)   9   321
   Lustra, by Ezra Pound   11   330
   The Closed Door,
     by Jean de Bosschère
     (Tr. by F. S. Flint)   12   48
   The Wild Swans at Coole,
     Other Verses and a Play in Verse,
     by William Butler Yeats   13   42

ARTICLES ABOUT
   Correspondence
     from Frances Shaw   13   107

MICHIE, JAMES
TRANSLATIONS
   Poem by Théophile Gautier   142   153

BOOKS REVIEWED
   Possible Laughter   94   405

MICUS, EDWARD
POEMS
   Crows   158   83

MIDDLEBROOK, DIANE WOOD
BOOKS REVIEWED
   Selected Poems
     of Anne Sexton
     (Ed. with Diana Hume George)   154   151

MIDDLETON, CHRISTOPHER
POEMS
   Aesthetics for Benetto Gulgo   87   232
   The Suspense
   After a Noise in the Street   139   74

BOOKS REVIEWED
   Torse 3   102   193
   Modern German Poetry: 1910-1960
     (Ed. with Michael Hamburger)   103   261
   Nonsequences: Self Poems   109   126
   Selected Poems,
     by Gunter Grass
     (Tr. with Michael Hamburger)   111   336

MIDDLETON, JESSE EDGAR
BOOKS REVIEWED
   Sea-Dogs and Men at Arms—a Canadian
     Book of Songs   14   220

MIDDLETON, LILLIAN
POEMS
   Ego   26   75

MIDDLETON, RICHARD
BOOKS REVIEWED
   Poems and Songs
     (Second Series)   3   33

MIDDLETON, SCUDDER
POEMS
   A Woman   10   24
   The Stranger
   To an Old Couple
   Answer   23   74
   The Beast

BOOKS REVIEWED
   Streets and Faces   11   47
   The New Day   15   164
   Upper Night   31   50

MIDDLETON, THOMAS
ARTICLES ABOUT
   Rev. of Middleton's Tragedies,
     by Samuel Schoenbaum   92   121

MIGEL, PARMENIA
POEMS
   Portrait   28   313

MILAM, MAY THOMAS
POEMS
   Open a Door   20   25
   Jenice

MILBURN, MICHAEL
POEMS
   The Initial-Tree   143   24

ARTICLES
   "Sacred Beings":
     Writers in Recorded Conversation
     [W. S. Merwin, Howard Nemerov,
     Stanley Kunitz, Robert Lowell,
     W. H. Auden, W. D. Snodgrass,
     Czeslaw Milosz, Adrienne Rich,
     James Wright, Seamus Heaney,
     Robert Penn Warren, Muriel Rukeyser,
     David Ignatow]   146   101

MILES, CHARLOTTE
POEMS
   The Hill of the Hawks   73   142

MILES, JOSEPHINE
POEMS
   Local Habitation   44   304
     On Inhabiting an Orange
     Desert
     To Town
     Land Grant
     Imperative
     Physiologus
   Driver Saying   48   79
   Sunday   48   320
   Custom of Exercise   53   236
     Seminar
     Smoker
     Scholarly Procedure
     Enlightenment
     Gardeners
   Residential Area   58   240
     Outside
     Childe
     Dewey and Dancer
     Midweek
     Ode ("Jake's store past...")
     What Followed
   Merchant Marine   63   76
   Highway

War Time
Ad
Despairer   65   252
Friend
Measurement
Redemption
Players
Merchants
Speaker
Three Poems for New York   77   322
  ("Into our brick acropolis...")
  ("Iron as wrought wrings...")
  ("At most times of the day...")
A Foreign Country   79   311
The Day the Winds   81   54
Winter   81   300
Evangel
If Conference Keeps You   84   276
Sale
Quartos
Heir
Yard   92   139
Three Stages
Increment
Conjure
Italian
View
To Time
Iowa and West   94   141
Dream
Dialogue
Berg
Location
Love at a Distance   100   302
Turn
Rehearsal
Power
King   108   324
Civilian
Edge
Freedoms
Sundays
Countryside
The Hampton Institute Album   110   365
The National Parks
Vigils   139   21
Balance
Faces
Sleep

Articles
  The Pathetic Fallacy
    and the Thing in Itself   63   210

Reviews
  The Nature of Poetry,
    by Donald A. Stauffer   68   290

Books Reviewed
  Lines at Intersection   55   277
  Poems on Several Occasions   59   49
  Local Measures   69   49
  *The Continuity of Poetic Language:
    Studies in English Poetry
    from the 1540s to the 1940s*   79   360
  Prefabrications   88   183
  Eras & Modes in English Poetry   92   121
  The Poem—A Critical Anthology (Ed.)   96   122
  Poems 1930-1960   102   260
  Civil Poems   111   189
  *To All Appearances:
    Poems New and Selected*   128   226
  Coming to Terms   139   35

Articles About
  Comment by A. R. Ammons   151   204

MILLAR, MARGARET
Articles About
  Dagger of the Mind, by James Sandoe   68   146

MILLAY, EDNA ST. VINCENT
Poems
  Kin to Sorrow   10   234
  The Little Tavern
  Afternoon on a Hill
  Figs from Thistles   12   130
    First Fig
    Second Fig
    The Unexplorer
    Thursday
    The Penitent
  She Is Overheard Singing   14   66
  Recuerdo
  The Bean-Stalk   16   74
  The Concert   22   72
  ("Women have loved before...")   37   1
  ("I know my mind and I have made...")
  ("Even in the moment of our...")
  Inert Perfection   53   1
  Song for Young Lovers in a City
  The Fitting
  What Savage Blossom
  Intention to Escape from Him
  The Road to the Past
  Sonnet in Tetrameter
  Truce for a Moment
  Sonnet ("My earnestness...")   54   61
  Rendezvous
  Modern Declaration
  The True Encounter
  The Plaid Dress
  This Dusky Faith
  The Snow Storm
  Two Voices

BOOKS REVIEWED

Renascence and Other Poems	13	167
Second April	19	151
The King's Henchman	30	42
Three Plays		
The Buck in the Snow	33	210
Fatal Interview	38	216
Wine from These Grapes	45	277
Flowers of Evil,		
by Charles Baudelaire		
(Tr. with George Dillon)	48	158
Conversation at Midnight	51	99
Huntsman, What Quarry?	55	47
Make Bright the Arrows	57	389
Collected Lyrics of...	63	334
Collected Poems of...		
(Ed. by Norma Millay)	90	52

ARTICLES ABOUT

Edna St. Vincent Millay,		
by Harriet Monroe	24	260
Correspondence		
from Arthur Mac Gillivray		
and Reed Whittemore	90	259

MILLAY, KATHLEEN
POEMS

Witch	33	252
Ignorance		

BOOKS REVIEWED

The Evergreen Tree	32	169
The Hermit Thrush	35	170
The Beggar at the Gate	41	105

MILLAY, NORMA
BOOKS REVIEWED

Collected Poems		
of Edna St. Vincent Millay (Ed.)	90	52

MILLER, BARBARA STOLER
BOOKS REVIEWED

Bhartrihari: Poems (Tr.)	112	347

MILLER, BOB
POEMS

Opaque Clouds	58	317

MILLER, CHARLES
POEMS

Epilogue for Pilate	58	124

MILLER, FRED R.
POEMS

She of the Walled Garden	45	262

MILLER, HAROLD G.
ARTICLES ABOUT

Rev. of *Five Poets: 1949*	77	114

MILLER, HENRY
BOOKS REVIEWED

Stand Still Like the Hummingbird	102	269

ARTICLES ABOUT

French Chronicle:		
Recent Publications,		
by Wallace Fowlie	88	408

MILLER, J. CORSON
POEMS

Departure	33	195

BOOKS REVIEWED

Cup of the Years	46	53

MILLER, J. HILLIS
BOOKS REVIEWED

Poets of Reality:		
Six Twentieth-Century Writers		
[Joseph Conrad, W. B. Yeats,		
T. S. Eliot, Dylan Thomas,		
Wallace Stevens,		
William Carlos Williams]	110	254

MILLER, JAMES E., JR.
BOOKS REVIEWED

A Critical Guide to Leaves of Grass	92	116

MILLER, JASON
POEMS

Veil	117	235
The Call		
Tenement Sky		
Web		
Gate		

MILLER, JOHN N.
POEMS

Night Game	114	378
Prince Charming		

MILLER, JOHN S., JR.
POEMS

Ravage	8	296

MILLER, MABEL
POEMS

I Too Have Wings	28	141

MILLER, MARY BRITTON
BOOKS REVIEWED

Songs of Infancy and Other Poems	32	350
Without Sanctuary	40	286
Intrepid Bird	47	99

MILLER, MARY OWINGS
POEMS

New View	62	134
Cobh	79	334

Woman and Sea Horse	87	279
Renewal	96	299

BOOKS REVIEWED

Wheel of Paper	75	295
Contemporary Poetry, Volume Ten (Ed.)	79	116
The Solstice Tree, by Julia Randall (Ed.)	85	366
High Sun over Yram	99	320

MILLER, MAY

POEMS

Measurement	73	138
Instant Before Sleep		
Brief Negro Sermon		

MILLER, PETER

POEMS

Notes from Uxmal	97	28

REVIEWS

The Oxford Book of Canadian Verse (Ed. by A. J. M. Smith)	99	324

BOOKS REVIEWED

Meditation at Noon	94	186
Sun Stone, by Octavio Paz (Tr.)	103	266
A Shifting Pattern		
The Tomb of the Kings, by Anne Hébert (Tr.)	112	201

MILLER, PHILIP

POEMS

God!	160	317
The Long and the Short of It		
Death Camp Documentary in Gray and White	162	141
Winning	162	319
Fathers		
What It Comes Down To		

MILLER, ROBERT

POEMS

The Bats Fly	44	190

MILLER, RUTH

BOOKS REVIEWED

Selected Poems	115	61
The Poetry of Emily Dickinson	115	346

MILLER, VASSAR

POEMS

On a Weekend in September	143	274

BOOKS REVIEWED

Adam's Footprint	90	386
Wage War on Silence	99	178
My Bones Being Wiser	104	104
Onions and Roses	114	40

MILLET, MARTHA

POEMS

Never Before	50	322
Grey Afternoon	53	298

BOOKS REVIEWED

Seven Poets in Search of an Answer (With Maxwell Bodenheim, Joy Davidman, Langston Hughes, Aaron Kramer, Alfred Kreymborg, and Norman Rosten) (Ed. by Thomas Yoseloff)	64	289

MILLETT, FRED

BOOKS REVIEWED

Reading Poetry: A Method of Analysis with Selections for Study	84	43

MILLIGAN, CLARENCE P.

POEMS

Idyl	34	257

MILLS, BARRISS

BOOKS REVIEWED

Parvenus & Ancestors	98	192

MILLS, CLARK

POEMS

Five for Jules Romains	49	299
Proem		
Portrait		
Fragment		
The Hounds in Autumn		
Crossing: Webster Groves		
Catalina	51	20
Catechism	57	345
Fable		
The Green Gown		
Port-Royal		
Sleeper		
Postscript		
A Few Faces from the Crowd	60	192

TRANSLATIONS

Poem by Ivan Goll	57	252
Poems by André Spire	59	192

BOOKS REVIEWED

The Migrants	59	285
A Suite for France		
Five Young American Poets, Second Series 1941 (With Paul Goodman, Jeanne McGahey, David Schubert, and Karl Shapiro)	60	215
The Circus	65	152

MILLS, RALPH J., JR.

ARTICLES

For the Word, For the Silence
  [Henry Rago]   115   127

REVIEWS

Lives of the Poets   98   245
  Poems, by Alan Dugan
  Say Pardon, by David Ignatow
  Madonna of the Cello,
    by Robert Bagg
  I Am! Says the Lamb,
    by Theodore Roethke   100   54
Recent Prose   102   269
  Riverside Drive, by Louis Simpson
  Stand Still like the Hummingbird,
    by Henry Miller
  Assays, by Kenneth Rexroth
  A Sad Heart at the Supermarket,
    by Randall Jarrell
  Robert Lowell: The First Twenty Years,
    by Hugh B. Staples
  The Achievement of Wallace Stevens
    (Ed. by Ashley Brown
    and Robert Haller)
  John Crowe Ransom,
    by John L. Stewart
  The Continuity of American Poetry,
    by Roy Harvey Pearce
  The Curious Frame:
    Seven Poems in Text and Context,
    by John Edward Hardy
The Far Field, by Theodore Roethke   105   122
Two British Chronicles: I   107   406
  The Complete Poems of W. H. Davies
  Lodgers, by Tony Connor
  The Snow Leopard, by Paul West
Three Younger Poets   109   114
  Poems Selected and New,
    by Jon Silkin
  No One Walks Waters,
    by Daniel Berrigan
  A Joyful Noise, by Donald Finkel
Five Anthologies   109   345
  From the Hungarian Revolution
    (Ed. by David Ray)
  A Poetry Reading
    Against the Vietnam War
    (Ed. by Robert Bly and David Ray)
  Metaphrasis: An Anthology
    from the University of Iowa
    Translation Workshop 1964-1965
    (Ed. by Frederic Will)
  Master Poems of the English Language
    (Ed. by Oscar Williams)
  American Poetry
    (Ed. by Gay Wilson Allen,
    Walter B. Rideout,
    and James K. Robinson)

Collected Poems, by Herbert Read   110   45
Three Poets in Fine Editions   112   127
  The Works of Anne Bradstreet
    (Ed. by Jeannine Hensley)
  The Poems of Stephen Crane:
    A Critical Edition
    (Ed. by Joseph Katz)
  D. H. Lawrence, Poems Selected
    for Young People
    (Ed. by William Cole)
Critic of the Month: V   113   262
  Literary History of England
    (Ed. by Albert C. Baugh)
  American Poets
    from the Puritans to the Present,
    by Hyatt Waggoner
  Colonial American Poetry
    (Ed. by Kenneth Silverman)
  The Edge of the Image,
    by A. Kingsley Weatherhead
  John Keats, by Robin Mayhead
  Coleridge, by Walter Jackson Bate
  Rebels and Conservatives:
    Dorothy and William Wordsworth
    and Their Circle,
    by Amanda M. Ellis
  100 Postwar Poems
    (Ed. by M. L. Rosenthal)
  Poems of Our Moment
    (Ed. by John Hollander)
  I Am the Darker Brother
    (Ed. by Arnold Adoff)
  Out of the Earth I Sing
    (Ed. by Richard Lewis)
  The Original Rubaiyyat of
    Omar Khayyam, A New Translation
    with Critical Commentaries,
    by Robert Graves
    and Omar Ali-Shah
    [Edward Fitzgerald]
  The Poems of St. John of the Cross
    (Tr. by John Frederick Nims)
  On the Motion and Immobility of Douve,
    by Yves Bonnefoy
    (Tr. by Galway Kinnell)
  Selected Poetry,
    by Roy Campbell
    (Ed. by Joseph M. Lalley)
  Kon in Springtime,
    by Tony Connor
  Signs and Cities,
    by Elizabeth Sewell
  The Tree That Walked,
    by John Fuller
  Nightwalker and Other Poems,
    by Thomas Kinsella
  Shifts of Being,
    by Richard Eberhart
  Selected Poems 1933-67, by H. R. Hays

Love Letters from Asia,
  by Sandra Hochman
The Harvesters' Vase,
  by Ned O'Gorman
A Voyage to America and Other Poems,
  by Bruce Cutler
Rescue the Dead,
  by David Ignatow
Not This Pig, by Philip Levine
Coming Close and Other Poems,
  by Helen Chasin
Goodbye, But Listen,
  by Mark McCloskey
Plans for an Orderly Apocalypse,
  by Harvey Gross
Learning the Way,
  by James Den Boer
Looking for Jonathan,
  by Jon Anderson
The Naomi Poems: Corpse and Beans,
  by Saint Geraud
A Pig, and Several Poets   117   331
  An Ear in Bartram's Tree:
    Selected Poems 1957-1967,
    by Jonathan Williams
  A Trampoline: Poems 1952-1964,
    by Gael Turnbull
  Reversals, by Anne Stevenson
  Newcastle Is Peru,
    by Tony Harrison
  North Bank Night,
    by Edward Storey
  On This Athenian Hill,
    by Jennifer Couroucli
  A Perpetual Motion Machine,
    by Alan Bold
  Pig, by Jeff Nuttall
Six Poets   122   105
  Concurring Beasts,
    by Stephen Dobyns
  Against the Falling Evil,
    by James McMichael
  Good News About the Earth,
    by Lucille Clifton
  Old Movies and Other Poems,
    by John Cotton
  Lackawanna Elegy,
    by Yvan Goll
    (Tr. by Galway Kinnell)

BOOKS REVIEWED
  On the Poet and His Craft:
    Selected Prose of Theodore Roethke (Ed.)   107   400
  Contemporary American Poetry   109   198
  Selected Letters of Theodore Roethke (Ed.)   113   338

MILLSPAUGH, C. A.
POEMS
  Past Pitch of Grief   41   74

The Porcelain Clay   42   25
  Narrative
  Words from This Land
  Elegy by the Water
  A Pattern for Night
  Processional
Out of a Soundless Land   45   1
  The Angels in the Mountains
  Song ("Silent, silent, still...")
  Who Flies from Frost
  Before Wisdom Comes
  I Thought of Shelley
  Sonnet ("I wait in the...")
  Prothalamion
  Assignation
Season Unknown   47   295
  For the Making of Worlds
  The Shadow
  My Father the Sun
  The Earthly Heaven
  Brutes Have Wings
  A Woman Praying for Her Son
  A Season There Is
Under Midnight over Indiana   48   310
Hierarchy   51   314
Orpheus Alone
The Ability to Translate
Herman Melville
The Tower of Desire   56   247

REVIEWS
  Poems, by Robert Fitzgerald   48   166
  Poems, by Michael Roberts   48   343
  The Secret, and Other Poems,
    by Arthur Davison Ficke   49   286
  Country Men, by James Hearst   50   344
  Harvard Has It   51   267
    A Letter to Robert Frost,
      by Robert Hillyer
    Saltwater Farm,
      by Robert P. Tristram Coffin
    Lee in the Mountains,
      and Other Poems,
      by Donald Davidson   54   108

BOOKS REVIEWED
  In Sight of Mountains   50   43

MILNE, A. A.
BOOKS REVIEWED
  When We Were Very Young   27   162

MILNE, EWART
POEMS
  Sierran Aftermath   57   308
  The Woman on the Rock   88   125
  Could I Believe
  The Gifts of the Oracle

BOOKS REVIEWED
  Life Arboreal   86 366
  Galion
  Diamond Cut Diamond
  Boding Day
  Jubilo
  Listen Mangan
  Letter from Ireland
  Forty North Fifty West
  A Garland for the Green   102 324

MILNER-GULLAND, ROBIN
BOOKS REVIEWED
  Yevtushenko: Selected Poems
    (Tr. with Peter Levi)   102 400

MILOSZ, CZESLAW
BOOKS REVIEWED
  Postwar Polish Poetry (Tr. and ed.) 110 52
  Zbigniew Herbert: Selected Poems
    (Tr. with Peter Dale Scott) 114 40
  Bells in Winter
    (Tr. by the author
    and Lillian Vallee)   136 40
  Unattainable Earth
    (Tr. by Robert Hass)   149 168
  Provinces
    (Tr. with Robert Hass) 161 223
  Facing the River
    (Tr. with Robert Hass) 169 286

ARTICLES ABOUT
  "Sacred Beings": Writers
    in Recorded Conversation,
    by Michael Milburn   146 101

MILOSZ, O. V. DE L.
ARTICLES ABOUT
  French Poetry and the
    Revival of Mysticism,
    by Eugene Jolas   56 264

MILTON, JOHN
ARTICLES ABOUT
  Rev. of *Wordsworth and Milton,*
    Poets and Prophets. A Study
    of Their Reactions to Political Events,
    by Herbert J. C. Grierson 51 37
  Rev. of *Il Dramma Divino e*
    il Dramma Umano nel Paradiso Perduto,
    by Elio Chinol;
    Milton's Ontology, Cosmogony,
    and Physics, by Walter Clyde Curry;
    Milton, by Rose Macaulay;
    Heroic Knowledge,
    by Arnold Stein   93 404
  The Poetry of Charles Churchill: Part I,
    by Yvor Winters   98 44

  Rev. of *The Living Milton*
    (Ed. by Frank Kermode) 115 196
  Rev. of *A Map of Misreading,*
    by Harold Bloom   127 222
  Rev. of *In Time & Place,*
    by John Hollander   151 419

MIMNERMUS
POEMS
  On Old Age
    (Tr. by Michael Mesic) 116 344

MINASIAN, KHATCHIK
BOOKS REVIEWED
  The Simple Songs of...   78 45

MINDLIN, MEIR
TRANSLATIONS
  Poem by Yehuda Amichai   92 256

ARTICLES ABOUT
  [Note on translations]   93 56

MINER, EARL
BOOKS REVIEWED
  Dryden's Poetry   112 356
  Superior Poems of Our Time,
    by Fujiwara Teika
    (Tr. with Robert H. Brower) 114 196

MING, SU KAI
[See SU KAI MING]

MINITER, EDITH
POEMS
  Confidences   23 21
  Bureau
  Huckleberries

MINOR, DRUMMOND
REVIEWS
  Tensions, by James Schevill 72 226

MINTON, HELENA
POEMS
  Artifacts   138 71
  Bread
  Letter from Shuyak Island, Alaska

MINTY, JUDITH
POEMS
  Palmistry for Blind Mariners 123 330
  Harbors
  Sailing by Stars
  Grand Valley
  Look to the Back of the Hand
  From *Yellow Dog Journal—Fall* 135 9
  The Gray Whale   146 3

MINTZ, RUTH FINER
TRANSLATIONS
Poems by Yakov Cohen, Yakov Fichman,
    David Shimoni, Yehuda Karni,
    Zalman Shneur, Avigdor Hamieri,
    Uri Zvi Greenberg, Yitzhak Lamdan,
    Avraham Shlonsky, Yoheved Bat-Miriam,
    Shin Shalom, Nathan Alterman,
    Leah Goldberg, David Rokeah,
    Hayim Guri, Amir Gilboa,
    Avaraham Huss, and T. Carmi   92   203

ARTICLES
Contributors   92   266

ARTICLES ABOUT
[Note on translations]   93   56

MIRANDA, GARY
POEMS
The Must-Be-Admired Things   130   14
Survivor
The Thickets of Sleep   131   133
Collision
Salmon Ladder
    at the Government Locks, Seattle   135   202
Still Lifes: Hoh Rain Forest

BOOKS REVIEWED
Listeners at the Breathing Place   136   170

MIRICK, EDITH
POEMS
Drought   43   74
Window of Night
("The casement, now drawn inward...")

MIROLLO, GABRIELLA
POEMS
The Poet at Two Rejects the Beach   164   270
Cellini's Saltcellar   165   250

MIRON, SALVADOR DIAZ
[See DIAZ MIRON, SALVADOR]

MISHKIN, JULIA
POEMS
This Country   136   149
Something Like Lust
9/21/78
On Reading Certain Novels
    of Henry James   139   258
Ice Water
The Bad Nostalgia   143   152

MISRA, MARENDRA
TRANSLATIONS
Poem by Kalandi Charan Panigrahi
    (Tr. with Lila Ray)   93   243

MISRA, VIDYA NIWAS
BOOKS REVIEWED
Modern Hindi Poetry:
    An Anthology (Ed.)   109   272

**MISTRAL, GABRIELA
[Pseud. of GODOY Y ALCAYAGA,
LUCILA]**
POEMS
Ecstasy
    (Tr. by Muna Lee)   26   120
God Wills It
    (Tr. by Katherine Garrison Chapin) 59   123
Drinking   62   80
Slow Rain
    (Tr. by H. R. Hays)
Woman: the Mad One
    (Tr. by Richard O'Connell
    and James Graham Lujan)   63   204

BOOKS REVIEWED
Selected Poems of...
    (Tr. by Langston Hughes)   92   106

ARTICLES ABOUT
Some Chilean Poets,
    by A. R. Gonzalez   38   329
Rev. of The Collected Poems
    of Octavio Paz 1957-1987
    (Ed. by Eliot Weinberger)   154   29

MITALSKY, FRANK
POEMS
Ladder Into the Clouds   26   242
    Sustenance
    Lightning
    Beauty
    The Poet
    Rabbit in the Moonlight
    Sleep
    Distance
Stolen Fire   30   134
    Angles
    Stallion
    Girl in Green
    Elegy to a Lover
    Walking at Night

MITCHAM, JUDSON
POEMS
The Foolishness of God
    Is Wiser than Men   164   73

MITCHELL, BURROUGHS
REVIEWS
Thirty Pieces,
    by Sydney Salt   46   166

MITCHELL, C. BRADFORD
POEMS
  Ghostly Consolation   51   68
  Of Wasted Time
  Solid Geometry

MITCHELL, JOAN
POEMS
  Autumn   47   129

MITCHELL, JULIAN
POEMS
  Lament for the Cowboy Life   98   222
  Epitaph for an Airman

MITCHELL, MARION STROBEL
[See STROBEL, MARION]

MITCHELL, ROGER
POEMS
  Cinderella   137   149
  Return to a Small Town   156   201

REVIEWS
  Nine Poets   147   227
    Praying Wrong:
      New and Selected Poems, 1957-1984,
      by Peter Davison
    No Diamonds, No Hat, No Honey,
      by Andrew Harvey
    Fish, Flesh, & Fowl,
      by William Hathaway
    Cross Ties: Selected Poems,
      by X. J. Kennedy
    The House, by Bink Noll
    History of My Heart,
      by Robert Pinsky
    Late Stars, by Jeffrey Skinner
    Anniversary of the Air,
      by Michael Waters
    Eternity's Woods,
      by Paul Zweig

MITCHELL, RUTH COMFORT
POEMS
  St. John of Nepomuc   7   183

MITCHELL, STEPHEN
BOOKS REVIEWED
  The Selected Poetry
    of Rainer Maria Rilke (Ed. and tr.)   145   229
  The Selected Poetry
    of Yehuda Amichai
    (Ed. and tr. with Chana Bloch)   150   286

MITCHELL, STEWART
BOOKS REVIEWED
  Poems   20   49

MITCHELL, SUSAN
BOOKS REVIEWED
  The Water Inside the Water   145   161
  Rapture   162   224

MITCHELL, SUSANNA VALENTINE
POEMS
  Ten Years   45   265

BOOKS REVIEWED
  Journey Taken by a Woman   47   164

MITCHISON, NAOMI
ARTICLES ABOUT
  English Letter,
    by F. R. Leavis   46   274

MITCHNER, STUART
POEMS
  Verisimilitude   163   215
  At Stephen Crane's Funeral
  Coleridge
  Louise Brooks As Lulu   166   274
  The Bijou Hotel

MIXTER, FLORENCE K(ILPATRICK)
POEMS
  To a Child   11   138
  Sanctuary   14   250
  Ritual
  The Death of an Artist
  All Souls' Eve   18   242
  Chinese Epitaph
  Alchemy
  Invocation
  Lullaby

BOOKS REVIEWED
  Out of Mist   19   222

MIYARES, ENRIQUE HERNANDEZ
[See HERNANDEZ MIYARES,
ENRIQUE]

MIYOSHI, TATSUJI
POEMS
  Nostalgia
    (Tr. by Satoru Satu
    and Constance Urdang)   88   79

MIZENER, ARTHUR
REVIEWS
  The Well Wrought Urn,
    by Cleanth Brooks   71   318
  Burr Oaks, by Richard Eberhart   73   226
  The Brotherhood of Men,
    by Richard Eberhart   74   172
  Live Another Day, by John Ciardi   75   361

The Tears of the Blind Lions,
  by Thomas Merton   76   224

ARTICLES ABOUT
  Rev. of *English Institute Essays, 1949*
    (Ed. by Alan S. Downer)   77   48

MOE, HENRY ALLEN
  ARTICLES
  Correspondence   26   232

MOEBIUS, WILLIAM
  BOOKS REVIEWED
  Elegies and Odes   118   295

MOFFETT, JUDITH
  POEMS
  Wash in Eight Colors   121   330
  Cows and Corn
  Glossolalia   123   17
  Indecent Exposure   126   6
  Comeuppance
  Cecropia Terzine
  Plaint of the Summer Vampires
  Diehard   127   125
  Signatories
  Bending the Twig
  Passage   131   29
  Moving Parts
  Relay
  Fadeout
  Twinings Orange Pekoe
  Going to Press   133   198
  From *Variations on a Theme*   136   273
    Leaf Lesson
  Sympathy Card, One Year Later   158   40

  TRANSLATIONS
  Poems by Hjalmar Gullberg   126   13
  Poems by Hjalmar Gullberg   128   152

  REVIEWS
  Life More and Less Abundantly   127   164
    101 Different Ways of Playing Solitaire
      and Other Poems,
      by Belle Randall
    The Scenic Route,
      by Fleur Adcock
    The Dark Side of the Earth,
      by Paul Zweig
    The Myth of a Woman's Fist,
      by Ann Darr
    Gathering Firewood:
      New Poems and Selected,
      by David Ray
    Boxcars, by David Young
    Divine Comedies,
      by James Merrill   129   40

Able Was I Ere I Saw Elba: Selected Poems,
  by Daniel Hoffman
  [Hayden Carruth, Yvor Winters]   132   170

MOFFITT, JOHN
  BOOKS REVIEWED
  The Living Seed   102   49

MOHANTY, G. P.
  POEMS
  The Doves of My Eyes
    (Tr. by J. M. Mohanty)   93   241

MOHANTY, J. M.
  TRANSLATIONS
  Poem by G. P. Mohanty   93   241

MOHN, EARL
  POEMS
  Three Poems for Mad Anne   62   252
    Scratchings
    Dirge and Recovery
    The Poet at Work

MO-JO, KUO
  [See KUO MO-JO]

MOLESWORTH, CHARLES
  POEMS
  The Name "Pacific Foam" Is Easy 115   238
    Series
  A Walk in the City   118   77
  Stanzas Occasioned by a View   120   71
  The Blue Heron   122   191
  Nightstorm   125   129
  Passages from an Early History of Love 128   84

  REVIEWS
  Some Locals   120   107
    Twenty Poems, by John Haines
    In the Happy Valley, by Tony Connor
    Earth Meditations: One to Five,
      by Mike Doyle
    Poems: 1962-69, by Jeff Nuttall
    Ransoms, by Leslie Norris
    Selected Poems: 1920/1970,
      by R. G. Everson
    Pop. By 1940: 40,000, by Harold Witt
    Nights of Naomi (Plus 2 Songs),
      by Bill Knott

MOLIÈRE
[JEAN-BAPTISTE POQUELIN]
  POEMS
  Tartuffe, I, ii-v
    (Tr. by Richard Wilbur)   98   369
  Tartuffe [From Act II]
    (Tr. by Richard Wilbur)   101   133

BOOKS REVIEWED
   The Misanthrope
     (Tr. by Richard Wilbur)   88   398
   The School for Wives
     (Tr. by Richard Wilbur)   120   230

MOMADAY, N. SCOTT
BOOKS REVIEWED
   The Complete Poems
     of Frederick Goddard Tuckerman (Ed.)   107   401
   Angle of Geese and Other Poems   126   352

MONAHAN, JAMES
BOOKS REVIEWED
   Far from the Land   67   225

MONCRIEFF, CHARLES SCOTT
BOOKS REVIEWED
   Widsith, Beowulf, Finnsburgh,
     Waldere, Deor (Tr.)   21   53

MONDACA, CARLOS R.
POEMS
   Amor
     (Tr. by A. R. Gonzalez)   38   309

ARTICLES ABOUT
   Some Chilean Poets,
     by A. R. Gonzalez   38   329

MONDOR, HENRI
ARTICLES ABOUT
   Letters from the Midi, II:
     On Henri Mondor,
     by Wallace Fowlie   100   261

MONETTE, PAUL
POEMS
   The Safety in Numbers   127   38
   The Wedding Letter   129   278

BOOKS REVIEWED
   The Carpenter at the Asylum   128   355

ARTICLES ABOUT
   Rev. of *The American Poetry Anthology*
     (Ed. by Daniel Halpern)   128   106

MONRO, ALIDA (KLEMANTASKI)
BOOKS REVIEWED
   Recent Poetry 1923-1933 (Ed.)   44   113
   Collected Poems
     of Harold Monro (Ed.)   44   162

ARTICLES ABOUT
   A Letter from Ireland,
     by Joseph M. Hone   44   215
   Rev. of *Collected Poems*,
     by Charlotte Mew   86   240

MONRO, HAROLD
POEMS
   Strange Meetings   8   286
   Introspection   15   298
   City Storm
   Officers' Mess (1916)   17   238
   Fate   19   252
   Pale Adventure   32   75
     Journey to Reclaim a Ghost
     Rumor

BOOKS REVIEWED
   Children of Love   6   36
   Trees   9   90
   Real Property   21   38
   The Earth for Sale   36   282
   Collected Poems of...
     (Ed. by Alida Monro)   44   162

ARTICLES ABOUT
   Our Contemporaries,
     by Harriet Monroe   5   246
   The Editor in England,
     by Harriet Monroe   23   32
   Poetry's Old Letters,
     by Harriet Monroe   47   30
   Harold Monro:
     A Study in Integration,
     by D. S. Savage   60   324

MONROE, HARRIET ["H. M."]
POEMS
   Nogi   1   50
   Mother Earth   2   13
   Our Canal   3   153
   Love Songs
   Lullaby
   The Inner Silence
   Now
   Poems of Travel   4   224
     The Ocean Liner
     A Garden in the Desert
     The Giant Cactus of Arizona
     In the Louvre
     The Tower
     The Childless Woman
     The Wonder of It
   Mountain Poems   6   215
     The Water Ouzel
     The Pine at Timber-Line
     A Lady of the Snows
     On the Porch
     Mountain Song
   To W. J. C.   9   73
   A Letter of Farewell   9   175
   Vernon Castle   11   311
   Carolina Wood-Cuts   12   1
     The Blue Ridge

White
The Oak
Azaleas
The Mocking-Bird
The Fringe-Bush
The Laurel
My Porch
The Mountaineer's Wife
The Rose-Bush
The Question
The Meeting
April—North Carolina
America   13   133
Supernal Dialogue   19   125
Notes of Travel   20   188
  On the Train
  At O'Neill's Point
  In the Yellowstone
  Utah
  In High Places
The Difference   21   175
  1823
  1923
A Song ("Who is it I love?")   22   132
Ten Years Old   23   199
At the Prado   23   291
  Their God
  Velasquez
  Titian on Charles V, Philip II,
    and the Empress Isobel
  El Greco
  Murillo
  Fra Angelico's Annunciation
  Rubens
  Goya
  Durer's Portrait of Himself
Poems by the Way   31   295
  The Quest
  In March
  For Helen
  The Death of the Khalifa
  To Lindbergh Flying
  Winds of Texas
  Galveston
  The Sacramento Valley
From Far Lands   35   I
  Back Home
  On the Ocean
  Egypt
  Her Majesty
  Sakkara
  A Golden Statuette in the Cairo Museum
  The Assouan Dam
  Jerusalem
  Constantinople
  Under the Moon
  The Theatre of Dionysus
  Delphi
  Apollo of Olympia

  Olympia
  Salamis
  Rome
  Botticelli
  Venice
  Dalmatia
  A Croatian Crucifix
  The Mestrovic Chapel at Cavtat
  The Memorial to American Doctors
    at Selce
Pavlova Dead   37   301
Winter Fruits   39   175
  At the Edge
  The Song ("The song I heard...")
  Heroes of Peace
  The Graf Zeppelin
  Radio
  The Man of Science Speaks
  A Dirge ("Put out the lights...")
  Grade Crossing
  O Little Earth
  Plaint
Eighty Degrees   41   77
Chicago 1933   42   147
Balbo's Air Armada   42   324
Every-Day Types   44   322
  The American
  The Hitch-Hiker
  Communist I
  Communist II
  Capitalist I
  Capitalist II
The Temple of Heaven   46   I
Jane Addams   46   187
At the Edge   49   131
  A Garden in the Desert
  High Places
  Olympia
  Plaint
  A Farewell
  Nogi   121   21

ARTICLES
  As It Was   I   19
  The Motive of the Magazine   I   26
  Moody's Poems   I   54
  The Open Door   I   62
  "That Mass of Dolts"
    [Ezra Pound]   I   168
  The Servian Epic
    [Mme. Slavko Grouitch]   I   195
  The New Beauty   2   22
  Tradition   2   67
  In Danger
    [John Masefield, Stephen Phillips]   2   68
  Incarnations
    [Nicholas Vachel Lindsay,
    Rabindranath Tagore]   2   101

Poetry a Zest for Life		
[Max Eastman]	2	140
The New Laureate		
[Robert Bridges]	2	213
Our Modern Epic		
[Panama Canal]	3	23
Rhythms of English Verse, I	3	61
Rhythms of English Verse, II	3	100
"Sobriety and Earnestness"	3	141
Poetry's Banquet		
[W. B. Yeats]	4	25
The Enemies We Have Made		
[The Dial]	4	61
"The Poet's Bread and Butter"		
[The Nation]	4	195
The Poetry of War		
[Carl Sandburg]	4	237
A Word to Our Readers	4	245
The Audience: II	5	31
Christmas, 1914	5	125
Our Contemporaries		
[Harold Monro]	5	246
The Fight for the Crowd	5	280
The Shakespearean Motive	6	29
Give Him Room	6	81
Praise from Mr. Colum	6	91
The Death of Rupert Brooke	6	136
Aere Perennius		
[William Cullen Bryant]	6	197
In Cathay	6	244
Chaucer and Langland	6	297
Its Inner Meaning		
[Conrad Aiken, Imagism]	6	307
Our Contemporaries		
[Poetry magazines]	6	315
Our Birthday	7	30
At the Fair	7	35
A Nation-Wide Art	7	84
In Memoriam		
[Remy de Gourmont, Alan Seeger]	7	98
Christmas and the Poets	7	140
"Grotesques" and "Overtones"		
[Cloyd Head, Alice Gerstenberg]	7	193
The Question of Prizes	7	246
The Death of Stephen Phillips	7	260
Shakespeare	8	32
Down East [Zoë Akins]	8	85
Various Views		
[Witter Bynner, Arthur Ficke,		
Amy Lowell, Maurice Browne]	8	140
How Not To Do It	8	195
Our Contemporaries		
[William Stanley Braithwaite]	8	211
New Banners	8	251
James Whitcomb Riley	8	305
Note on Grotesques		
(With Cloyd Head)	9	31
The Future of the Magazine	9	33
Truth and the Paradox	9	87
Poem-Games		
[Vachel Lindsay]	9	88
Then and Now	9	141
The New Era		
[D. W. Griffith]	9	195
Sir Oracle		
[William Stanley Braithwaite]	9	211
Aboriginal Poetry I		
[Frank Hamilton Cushing]	9	251
Hard Times Indeed		
[The Atlantic]	9	308
The City and the Tower	10	32
Colonialism Again	10	92
What May War Do		
[Carl Sandburg]	10	142
Fire of Youth		
[Mary MacLane]	10	154
[A Song for America]	10	165
Will Art Happen?	10	203
To the Wilderness	10	259
Emerson in a Loggia	10	311
These Five Years		
[Ezra Pound]	11	33
A Word to the Carping Critic		
[George Soule]	11	89
Christmas and War	11	144
Little Theatres and Poetic Plays		
[Alfred Kreymborg, Maurice Brown,		
Cloyd Head]	11	201
Back to China		
[Ezra Pound, Eunice Tietjens]	11	271
Academic Back-Water	11	283
The War and the Artist	11	320
Dr. Patterson on Rhythm	12	30
Mr. Bourne on Traps	12	90
The New Internationalism	12	146
Mr. Jepson's Slam		
[T. S. Eliot]	12	208
The New Postal Rate	12	212
Sara Teasdale's Prize		
[H. D., Ezra Pound]	12	264
[Note to Emanuel Morgan]	12	288
The Great Renewal	12	320
Joyce Kilmer	13	31
The Other Stars in the Poets' Flag	13	34
"Aesthetic and Social Criticism"		
[Randolph Bourne,		
Van Wyck Brooks]	13	37
A Century in Illinois	13	90
An International Episode		
[Edgar Jepson, Ezra Pound,		
Austin Harrison]	13	94
Poetry an Essential Industry		
[Conrad Aiken]	13	96
Christmas Indeed	13	146

[Note on John Curtis Underwood
and Paul Fortier Jones]   13   230
The Viereck Incident
[George Sylvester Viereck]   13   265
A Radical-Conservative
[Max Eastman]   13   322
A Gold Star for Gladys Cromwell   13   326
The Glittering Metropolis
[James Russell Lowell, William
Carlos Williams, Emanuel Carnevali]   14   30
Walt Whitman   14   89
Stephen Crane   14   148
A Year After   14   209
Editorial Amenities
[Joseph Pulitzer]   14   262
Back to Nature   14   328
What Next?   15   33
That Bookshelf
[Amy Lowell]   15   39
A Word to the Colossus   15   90
Visitors from the Other Side
[W. B. Yeats, Maurice Maeterlinck,
D. H. Lawrence, Lord Dunsany,
Siegfried Sassoon, John Drinkwater]   15   93
A Scientist's Challenge
[Charles P. Steinmetz]   15   149
California's Laureate
[Ina Coolbrith]   15   158
Science and Art Again II
[C. P. Steinmetz]   15   208
Mr. Robinson's Jubilee   15   265
Those We Refuse   15   321
Mr. Yeats and the Poetic Drama
[Wallace Stevens, John Drinkwater,
Zoë Akins]   16   32
Men or Women?   16   146
Discovered in Paris
[Jean Catel, Robert Frost,
Carl Sandburg]   16   148
New English Magazines   16   168
Dr. Chubb on the Platform
[Paul Shorey]   16   205
In Texas and New Mexico   16   324
The Death of Mr. Reedy   16   328
Frugality and Deprecation
[Herman George Scheffauer]   17   30
The P.S.A. Prizes and Ours
[Gladys Cromwell, John G. Neihardt,
Edgar Lee Masters]   17   88
The Christmas Clock   17   148
What Are They Doing?   17   204
Two Poets Have Died
[John Reed, Louise Imogen Guiney]   17   208
Notes and Queries from Mr. Lindsay   17   262
[Note on Others]   17   288
Their Wide Range
[Ford Madox Hueffer, Lew Sarett]   17   322

Drinkwater on Abercrombie   18   30
Southern Shrines   18   91
The Death of "B. L. T."
[Bert Leston Taylor]   18   97
Two New Magazines   18   115
A Word About Keats   18   150
Here in Cass Street   18   208
The Nebraska Laureate
[John G. Neihardt]   18   212
Midsummer Delite   18   264
John Adams' Prophecy   18   327
Poetry and the Allied Arts
[Charles Albert Case]   19   31
From Queen Anne to George the Fifth
[Austin Dobson]   19   90
Renewal of Youth
[Malcolm Cowley]   19   146
The Hope of Peace   19   204
A Symposium on Marianne Moore
[Rev. essay]   19   208
The Utterance of Poetry
[Lawrence Mason, Edwin Booth,
Henry Irving]   19   266
Newspaper Verse
[Edgar Guest]   19   324
This Southern Number   20   31
Moving   20   88
Prosody   20   148
Shelley   20   206
A New Pulitzer Prize
[Edwin Arlington Robinson]   20   215
Nature the Source   20   266
Mea Culpa   20   323
Ten Years Old
[Lew Sarett]   21   32
Flamboyance   21   89
A Texas Prize Contest
[George D. Bond, Irene Glasscock,
Karle Wilson Baker]   21   91
The Christmas Symbol   21   148
Matthew Arnold's Centenary   21   206
Of Two Poets
[Alice Meynell,
Josephine Preston Peabody]   21   262
"The Greatest Living Poet"
[Rudyard Kipling]   21   322
The King's Tomb   22   32
Au Revoir   22   88
The Editor in England
[Harold Monro, Edith Sitwell,
Richard Aldington, Muriel Stuart,
James R. Gregson]   23   32
The Editor in France
[Erik Satie, Ford Madox Ford,
Ezra Pound, Mina Loy]   23   90
The Nativity in Art   23   150
Poets the Self-Revealers   23   206

Dante and Contemporaneousness		
[John Erskine]	23	264
A Cavalier of Beauty		
[Wallace Stevens]	23	322
Byron	24	32
Vachel Lindsay	24	90
In New York	24	146
Edgar Lee Masters	24	204
Hazel Hall	24	210
Edna St. Vincent Millay		
[Emily Brontë]	24	260
Once More the Revolution		
[Robert L. Wolf]	24	266
Carl Sandburg	24	320
Amy Lowell	25	32
A Western Travel-Tale	25	90
Robert Frost	25	146
Edwin Arlington Robinson	25	206
Sara Teasdale	25	262
Maxwell Bodenheim	25	320
Marjorie Allen Seiffert	26	32
Illumination		
[Charissa Taylor Bass]	26	36
Ezra Pound	26	90
Pan-American Concord	26	155
Memories of Amy Lowell	26	208
In Texas and Oklahoma		
[Stanley Vestal]	26	214
H. D.	26	268
The Amy Lowell Scholarships	26	276
A Few Woman Poets		
[Helen Hoyt, Muna Lee,		
Aline Kilmer, Louise Bogan,		
Agnes Lee, Eunice Tietjens,		
Alice Corbin, Grace Fallow Norton,		
Lola Ridge, Marion Strobel,		
Elinor Wylie, Genevieve Taggard,		
Hazel Hall, Gladys Cromwell]	26	326
Another Birthday	27	32
Lew Sarett and		
Our Aboriginal Inheritance	27	88
This Christmas	27	148
A Word About Prosody	27	149
John Gould Fletcher	27	206
As It Is in Paris		
[Paul Valéry, Gustave Kahn,		
André Rivoire,		
Fernand Gregh]	27	266
The Impossible	27	324
Typographical Queries		
[Sara Teasdale]	28	32
Mr. Turbyfill's Poem	28	92
A Travel Tale		
[Robinson Jeffers,		
Robert Louis Burgess]	28	150
Mephistopheles and the Poet		
[H. L. Mencken]	28	210
What To Think?		
[Mark Turbyfill]	28	215
An Unpublished Letter		
from Eugene Field	28	268
Poets as Prosers		
[Carl Sandburg, Alfred Kreymborg,		
Edgar Lee Masters, DuBose Heyward,		
Julia Peterkin, Eunice Tietjens,		
Edith Wyatt, Elinor Wylie,		
James Joyce, Glenway Wescott]	28	328
Nomads	29	32
A Discussion with Hart Crane	29	34
Honors and Prizes		
[Sinclair Lewis, Gerhart Hauptmann,		
W. B. Yeats]	29	92
For Christmas	29	150
Two Poets Say Farewell		
[Allen Upward, George Sterling]	29	208
And Ernest Walsh	29	213
Observations in the Obvious	30	32
Going East		
[Lizette Woodworth Reese]	30	90
Why Not Poets?	30	150
The Pulitzer Award System		
[Leonora Speyer, Wilbur L. Cross,		
Ferris Greenslet, John Erskine]	30	210
The Procession Moves	30	270
"In Lighter Vein"		
[Keith Preston, Bert Leston Taylor]	30	330
Fifteen Years		
[Irwin Edman]	31	32
Wanted—A Theme	31	86
Christmas and William Blake	31	148
Golden Moments		
[Isadora Duncan]	31	206
Reading Aloud		
[John Masefield]	31	271
The Vinal Books	31	289
Thomas Hardy	31	326
Marguerite Wilkinson	31	332
Books and Tomorrow	32	32
In Florida	32	95
Again New York		
[Eugene O'Neill]	32	150
Meredith as a Poet	32	210
Rossetti		
[D. G. Rossetti]	32	270
The "Voice" and the "Singer"	32	330
Looking Backward		
[Francois Porché]	33	32
The Armistice	33	88
Christmas		
(With Jessica Nelson North)	33	148
Why Not Laugh?		
[Gertrude Stein, James Joyce]	33	206
Elinor Wylie	33	266
A Prize for Peace	33	324

A Travel Tale of Egypt	34	222
A Travel Tale of Greece	34	278
A Final Travel-Chapter	34	338
Henry B. Fuller	35	34
More About Greece	35	41
Subsidies and Prizes	35	92
The Incomparable Gift	35	150
Valéry's Epigrams	35	208
Poetic Parallels [Edwin H. Lewis, Percy Bysshe Shelley]	35	328
The Radio and the Poets	36	32
D. H. Lawrence	36	90
Bridges as a Lyrist	36	146
The Soaring Scientific Mind [Paul Valéry]	36	266
They Come and Go [Cecil John, Patrick Orr, Clara Shanafelt, Skipwith Cannéll]	36	326
Coming of Age	37	34
Should He Be Educated? [Gordon Craig, Ellen Terry]	37	90
Christmas Again	37	150
Sailing to Byzantium	37	208
The Arrogance of Youth [Louis Zukofsky]	37	328
"Greatest Women"	38	32
Leadership	38	92
Archibald MacLeish	38	150
A Midsummer Interlude	38	326
Birthday Reflections	39	32
Give Him a Nobel Prize [Bert Cooksley]	39	88
Christmas Again	39	146
Lindsay	39	206
Agnes Lee	39	324
Volume Forty	40	30
Advantages	40	150
Another Chance	40	270
A Poet's Contract	40	330
Twenty Years	41	30
The "Great Poem" [Abraham Lincoln, Joyce Kilmer]	41	90
Christmas 1932	41	150
Ernest Walsh	41	208
The Age of Power [Archibald MacLeish]	41	268
Sara Teasdale	42	30
Mexico [Diego Rivera]	42	92
"The Century of Progress" and Our Prize	42	152
A Bull in the China Shop [Martin Schutze]	42	212
Between the Lake and the River	42	272
In the Aboriginal Mode [Hartley Alexander]	42	332
Twenty-One	43	32
Nature's New Revelation	43	88
A Christmas Greeting	43	164
Stedman's Centenary	43	268
In These Days	43	328
Down South [Baker Brownell]	44	92
Art and Propaganda [Stanley Burnshaw]	44	210
This Changing World	44	330
Another Birthday	45	32
In Peking	46	30
A Department of Science Art and Literature?	46	92
Robinson as Man and Poet	46	150
Farewell to Two Poets [Frederic Manning, Nathan Haskell Dole]	46	219
On the Great River [Mark Twain, John Gould Fletcher]	46	268
Office Visitors	46	328
Poetry's Old Letters [Harold Monro, Edgar Lee Masters, Vachel Lindsay, Ezra Pound]	47	30
The Season of Gifts	47	150
Joy in Great Art [Rebecca West]	47	208
Honor to Lizette Reese	47	277
Kipling as a Poet	48	32
Present-Day Tendencies [John Crowe Ransom, Donald Davidson]	48	152
Poetry of the Left [W. H. Auden, Stephen Spender, Cecil Day-Lewis, Stanley Burnshaw, Archibald MacLeish, Edwin Rolfe, Paul Engle, Kenneth Patchen, Muriel Rukeyser]	48	212
Both Slave and Free	48	270
Poets as Leaders [Hart Crane]	48	330
Twenty-Four Years	49	30
[Her Last Letters]	49	166

REVIEWS

The Poems of Rosamund Marriott Watson	1	94
The Adventures of Young Maverick, by Hervey White		
The Iscariot, by Eden Philpotts		
The Lyric Year (Ed. by Mitchell Kennerly)	1	128
A Little Book of Modern Verse (Ed. by Jessie B. Rittenhouse)	3	144
The Works of Francis Thompson	3	179

General William Booth Enters
  into Heaven and Other Poems,
  by Nicholas Vachel Lindsay
Aphrodite and Other Poems,
  by John Helston   4   69
Poems, by Alice Meynell
Love and Liberation,
  by John Hall Wheelock   4   163
Little Verse for a Little Clan,
  by F. D. W.
The Ride Home,
  by Florence Wilkinson Evans   4   201
Challenge, by Louis Untermeyer
The Sea Is Kind,
  by T. Sturge Moore   5   84
Beyond the Stars and Other Poems,
  by Charles Hanson Towne   5   90
Borderlands and Thoroughfares,
  by Wilfrid Wilson Gibson   5   134
Sword Blades and Poppy Seed,
  by Amy Lowell
The Single Hound,
  by Emily Dickinson
The Cry of Youth, by Harry Kemp   5   192
My Lady's Book, by Gerald Gould
Satires of Circumstance,
  by Thomas Hardy   5   240
Open Water, by Arthur Stringer
Arrows in the Gale,
  by Arturo Giovannitti   6   36
Sonnets of a Portrait Painter,
  by Arthur Davison Ficke
Children of Love,
  by Harold Monro
Crack o' Dawn,
  by Fannie Stearns Davis   6   45
Songs of the Outlands,
  Ballads of the Hoboes,
  and Other Verse,
  by Henry Herbert Knibbs
Bread and Circuses,
  by Helen Parry Eden
New Poems,
  by Robert Browning and
  Elizabeth Barrett Browning
  (Ed. by Frederick G. Kenyon)
Songs from the Clay,
  by James Stephens   6   93
The Night Watchman and Other Poems,
  by Vance Thompson
The Little King, by Witter Bynner
Lyrics of a Lad, by Scharmel Iris
Some Imagist Poets—An Anthology
  [D. H. Lawrence, H. D., Richard
  Aldington, John Gould Fletcher,
  Amy Lowell, F. S. Flint]   6   150
Visions and Revisions,
  by John Cowper Powys   6   205

Earth Deities and
  Other Rhythmic Masques,
  by Bliss Carman and
  Mary Perry King
K'ung Fu Tze, a Dramatic Poem,
  by Paul Carus
The Winnowing Fan:
  Poems on the Great War,
  by Laurence Binyon
The Shoes of Happiness and Other Poems,
  by Edwin Markham   6   308
The Poet in the Desert,
  by Charles Erskine Scott Wood
The New World, by Witter Bynner   7   147
Rivers to the Sea, by Sara Teasdale
The Factories with Other Lyrics,
  by Margaret Widdemer
New Poets   7   209
  Vision of War,
    by Lincoln Colcord
  A Little Book of Local Verse,
    by Howard Mumford Jones
The Song of Hugh Glass,
  by John G. Neihardt   7   264
Beyond the Breakers and Other Poems,
  by George Sterling   7   307
Good Friday and Other Poems,
  by John Masefield   8   43
The Man Against the Sky,
  by Edwin Arlington Robinson
Chicago Poems, by Carl Sandburg   8   90
Songs and Satires,
  by Edgar Lee Masters   8   148
Two Anthologies   8   255
  Some Imagist Poets: 1916
  Georgian Poetry: 1913-1915
    [H. D., Gordon Bottomley,
    John Gould Fletcher, D. H. Lawrence,
    Amy Lowell, Richard Aldington,
    John Masefield, Ralph Hodgson]
The Middle Miles and Other Poems,
  by Lee Wilson Dodd   8   264
The Jew to Jesus and Other Poems,
  by Florence Kiper Frank
Today and Tomorrow,
  by Charles Hanson Towne
The Nameless One,
  by Anne Cleveland Cheney
Mushrooms: A Book of Free Forms,
  by Alfred Kreymborg   9   51
The Great Maze and the Heart of Youth,
  by Hermann Hagedorn   9   90
Battle and Other Poems,
  by Wilfrid Wilson Gibson
Trees, by Harold Monro
A Marriage Cycle,
  by Alice Freeman Palmer   9   151
Frost and Masters   9   202

Mountain Interval, by Robert Frost
The Great Valley,
   by Edgar Lee Masters
Men, Women and Ghosts,
   by Amy Lowell   9   207
Songs of Ukraina, with Ruthenian Poems
   (Tr. by Florence Randal Livesay)   9   273
Other Books of Verse   9   324
   The Quest, by John G. Neihardt
   The Song of the Plow,
     by Maurice Hewlett
   From the Hidden Way,
     by James Branch Cabell
   The Road to Everywhere,
     by Glenn Ward Dresbach
   Smoky Roses, by Lyman Bryson
   The Son of Merope and Other Poems,
     by Antoinette de Coursey Patterson
   Horizons, by Robert Alden Sanborn
   A Hidden Well, by Louis How
   On the Overland and Other Poems,
     by Frederick Mortimer Clapp
Lundy's Lane and Other Poems,
   by Duncan Campbell Scott   10   49
Lines Long and Short,
   by Henry B. Fuller   10   155
Merlin, by Edwin Arlington Robinson   10   211
Sappho in Levkas and Other Poems,
   by William Alexander Percy   10   213
The Flower from the Ashes
and *The White Messenger*,
   by Edith M. Thomas   10   215
The Little God, by Katharine Howard   10   217
War Poems   10   271
   Rhymes of a Red Cross Man,
     by Robert W. Service
   War Flames,
     by John Curtis Underwood
   A Song of the Guns,
     by Gilbert Frankau
   The Cause—Poems of the War,
     by Lawrence Binyon
   All's Well, by John Oxenham
   Soldier Poets:
     Songs of the Fighting Men
     [Julian Grenfell]
Lollingdon Downs,
   by John Masefield   10   320
Asphalt, by Orrick Johns   11   44
Swords for Life,
   by Irene Rutherford McLeod   11   48
The Dance of Youth, by Julia Cooley
A Modern Solitary   11   103
   Ideal Passion—Sonnets,
     by George Edward Woodberry
   *George Edward Woodberry—A Study
     of His Poetry*,
     by Louis V. Ledoux

The Story of Eleusis
and *Yzdra, A Tragedy*,
   by Louis V. Ledoux   11   105
Songs of Childhood,
   by Walter de la Mare   11   106
Verses, by Hilaire Belloc   11   107
Tendencies in Modern American Poetry,
   by Amy Lowell   11   151
The Chinese Nightingale,
   by Vachel Lindsay   11   214
The Wind in the Corn,
   by Edith Franklin Wyatt   11   218
Divinations and Creation,
   by Horace Holley   11   222
*Retrogression and
Other Poems* and *Pencraft*,
   by William Watson   11   225
Reverie: A Little Book of Poems for H.D.,
   by Richard Aldington   12   44
The Poems of Frank Dempster Sherman
   (Ed. by Clinton Scollard)   12   109
First Books and Others   12   165
   Airs and Ballads, by John McClure
   A Book of Verse, by Morris Gilbert
   Verses in Peace and War,
     by Shane Leslie
   Loves and Losses of Pierrot and
     City Pastorals and Other Poems,
     by William Griffith
   Green Fruit,
     by John Peale Bishop
   The Dreamers and Other Poems,
     by Theodosia Garrison
Verses—Bond and Free   12   282
   Elegy in Autumn, by Clinton Scollard
   Common Men and Women,
     by Harold W. Gammans
   In the Red Years, by Gervé Baronti
The Book of New York Verse
   (Ed. by Hamilton Fish Armstrong)   12   337
Children of the Sun,
   by Wallace Gould   13   44
Miss Lowell and Polyphonic Prose   13   97
   Can Grande's Castle,
     by Amy Lowell
   Amy Lowell, by W. Bryher
*Nocturne of Remembered Spring
and Other Poems*,
   by Conrad Aiken   13   102
First Books of Verse   13   167
   Renascence and Other Poems,
     by Edna St. Vincent Millay
   Green Leaves,
     by Florence Ripley Mastin
   Etchings, by Robert Earl Barclay
   *On Heaven and Poems
     Written on Active Service*,
     by Ford Madox Hueffer   13   219

Eidola, by Frederic Manning   13   281
Colors of Life, by Max Eastman   13   322
The Springtide of Life:
  Poems of Childhood,
  by Algernon Charles Swinburne   13   344
Other Poets of the War   14   220
  In Flanders Fields,
    by John McCrae
  A Highland Regiment and Other Poems
    and *War the Liberator and Other Pieces,*
    by E. A. Mackintosh
  Sea-Dogs and Men at Arms,
    by Jesse Edgar Middleton
  En Repos and Elsewhere Over There,
    by Lansing Warren and
    Robert A. Donaldson
  The Drums in Our Street,
    by Mary Carolyn Davies
  Forward March! by Angela Morgan
  The Chosen Nation,
    by Irwin St. John Tucker
  The Old Road to Paradise,
    by Margaret Widdemer   14   273
Ironica, by Donald Evans   14   276
Journeymen Poets   14   277
  The Madman, by Kahlil Gibran
  Lanterns in Gethsemane,
    by Willard Wattles
  A Family Album,
    by Alter Brody
  Outcasts in Beulah Land,
    by Roy Helton
  City Tides, by Archie Austin Coates
Anthologies   14   281
Motley and Other Poems,
  by Walter de la Mare   14   335
The Burglar of the Zodiac,
  by William Rose Benét   15   48
First Poems and Second Poems,
  by Edwin Curran   15   53
Abraham Lincoln, a Play,
  by John Drinkwater   15   159
On Their Way   15   164
  Gargoyles,
    by Howard Mumford Jones
  Banners,
    by Babette Deutsch
  The New Day,
    by Scudder Middleton
  Blue Smoke, by Karle Wilson Baker
For Beginners   15   224
  New Voices,
    by Marguerite Wilkinson
  How to Read Poetry,
    by Ethel M. Colson
A Hundred and Seventy Chinese Poems (Tr.)
  and *More Translations from the Chinese,*
  by Arthur Waley   15   337

Dust and Light, by John Hall Wheelock   15   343
Children's Books   15   345
  Snickerty Nick,
    by Julia Ellsworth Ford
  Singing Games for Children,
    by Eleanor Farjeon
  The Children's Homer,
    by Padraic Colum
  The Golden Whales of California,
    by Vachel Lindsay   16   101
Poems, by Gladys Cromwell   16   105
King George's Poets   16   108
  Georgian Poetry, 1918-1919
    (Ed. by Edward Marsh)
  A Miscellany of British Poetry (1919)
    (Ed. by W. Kean Seymour)
  Wheels, 1919
    (Ed. by Edith Sitwell)
Two Child Poets   16   222
  Poems by a Little Girl,
    by Hilda Conkling
  White Silences,
    by Katherine Bull
Reynard the Fox and *Enslaved,*
  by John Masefield   17   40
The Song of Three Friends,
  by John G. Neihardt   17   94
Others for 1919
  (Ed. by Alfred Kreymborg)
  [Wallace Stevens]   17   150
A Score of First Books   17   276
  Candles That Burn,
    by Aline Kilmer
  The Hesitant Heart,
    by Winifred Welles
  Arizona and Other Poems,
    by Elise Pumpelly Cabot
  The Cobbler in Willow Street
    and Other Poems,
    by George O'Neil
  The Dark Wind, by W. J. Turner
  Escape and Fantasy,
    by George Rostrevor
  Quests, by Sylvia H. Bliss
  Songs of the Dead,
    by Margaret Napier
  Poems, by Charles Reznikoff
  A Whisper of Fire,
    by Agnes Ryan
  Passenger, by Helen Dircks
  Moods, by Mercedes de Acosta
  Clouds and Cobblestones,
    by Hortense Flexner
  Merchants of the Morning,
    by Samuel McCoy
  Life's Minstrel,
    by Daniel Henderson
  Vanitas, by Paul Eldridge

Spindrift, by James L. McLane, Jr.

Shining Fields and Dark Towers,
    by John Bunker

Spires and Poplars,
    by Alfred Raymond Bellinger

Four Gardens,
    by David Osborne Hamilton

Poems, by Frederick T. Macartney

The Concert and Other Studies,
    by R. D. Jameson

Celtic Fairies   18   49

   Visions and Beliefs in the West of Ireland
    (Ed. by Lady Gregory,
    notes by W. B. Yeats)

   Irish Fairy Tales,
    by James Stephens

   The Boy Apprenticed to an Enchanter,
    by Padraic Colum

Pins for Wings,
  by Emanuel Morgan   18   52

Recent Anthologies   18 106

   *The Oxford and
    Cambridge Miscellany: June, 1920*

   A Queen's College Miscellany

   A Treasury of War Poetry
    (Ed. by George Herbert Clarke)

   Dreams and Voices
    (Ed. by Grace Hyde Trine)

   Joyful Sorrow (Ed. by L. H. B.)

   *Lillygay: An Anthology
    of Anonymous Poems*

   *American and British Verse
    from* The Yale Review

   Modern British Poetry
    (Ed. by Louis Untermeyer)

   Contemporary Verse Anthology
    (Ed. by Charles Wharton Stork)

A Contrast   18 162

   In American,
    by John V. A. Weaver

   The Well of Being,
    by Herbert Jones

Domesday Book, by Edgar Lee Masters 18 214

The Three Taverns and Avon's Harvest,
    by Edwin Arlington Robinson 18 273

Morning, Noon and Night,
    by Glenn Ward Dresbach 18 281

The Poet in the Desert and
   Maia—A Sonnet Sequence,
    by Charles Erskine Scott Wood 18 283

Youth and the Desert   18 339

   The Bitterns,
    by Glenway Wescott

   The Immobile Wind, by Yvor Winters

Poems, by Marianne Moore 19 208

Nets to Catch the Wind,
    by Elinor Wylie 19 220

Out of Mist,
    by Florence Kilpatrick Mixter 19 222

The Lifted Cup,
    by Jessie B. Rittenhouse 19 344

Archways of Life,
    by Mercedes de Acosta 19 345

Ireland Unfreed: Poems of 1921,
    by Sir William Watson 19 346

Plays of Edmond Rostand
   (Tr. by Henderson
   Daingerfield Norman) 20 51

*Bars and Shadows—the Prison Poems
   of Ralph Chaplin* 20 276

Slabs of the Sun-Burnt West,
    by Carl Sandburg 20 332

Moonlight and Common Day,
    by Louise Morey Bowman 21 43

Odes and Lyrics,
    by Hartley Burr Alexander 21 158

The Veil and Other Poems
   and *Down-Adown Derry*,
    by Walter de la Mare 21 210

The Master-Mistress,
    by Rose O'Neill 21 219

The Bride of Huitzil and
   Wampum and Old Gold,
    by Hervey Allen 21 226

A Contrast   21 325

   The Waste Land, by T. S. Eliot

   The Box of God, by Lew Sarett

Last Poems, by A. E. Housman 22 41

American Poetry, 1922—A Miscellany 22 50

Carolina Chansons,
   by DuBose Heyward
   and Hervey Allen 22 89

Our Best Poets,
    by Theodore Maynard 22 108

Dramatic Legends and Other Poems,
    by Padraic Colum 22 215

Maine Coast, by Wilbert Snow 23 45

Bitter Herbs, by C. A. Dawson-Scott 23 54

Lunar Baedecker, by Mina Loy 23 100

Twenty-Five Poems,
    by Marsden Hartley 23 105

Tulips and Chimneys,
    by E. E. Cummings 23 211

Two Novel-Poems   23 221

   Down the River,
    by Roscoe W. Brink

   The Life and Death of Mrs. Tidmuss,
    by Wilfrid Blair

A Gate of Cedar, by Katharine Morse 23 224

Autumn Midnight, by Frances Cornford 23 283

Lute and Furrow,
    by Olive Tilford Dargan 23 285

Wild Cherry,
    by Lizette Woodworth Reese 23 341

After Disillusion, by Robert L. Wolf 23 343

The Tide Comes In, by Clement Wood 24 51

Three Foreign Anthologies   24   52
  Les Cinq Continents,
    by Ivan Goll
  An Anthology of Italian Poems,
   13th-19th Century
    (Tr. by Lorna de Lucchi)
  Contemporary German Poetry
    (Ed. and tr. by Babette Deutsch
    and Avrahm Yarmolinsky)
Charlatan, by Louis Grudin   24   103
King of the Black Isles,
  by J. N. Nicolson   24   105
On a Gray Thread, by Elsa Gidlow   24   109
Out of Silence and Other Poems,
  by Arthur Davison Ficke   24   154
We Have Kept the Faith, by H. Stuart   24   158
Apples Here in My Basket,
  by Helen Hoyt   24   214
Voyage, by Harold Vinal   24   221
Granite and Alabaster,
  by Raymond Holden   24   222
Here You Have Me, by Robert Roe   24   276
Canyon Garden, by Margaret Erwin   24   278
The Elfin Pedlar and
  Tales Told by Pixy Pool,
  by Helen Douglas Adam   24   279
Finlay, by Herbert Jones   24   340
Barbed Wire and Wayfarers,
  by Edwin Ford Piper   25   42
The Carrying of the Ghost,
  by Nelson Antrim Crawford   25   45
The Dark Night, by May Sinclair   25   99
Sky-Lines and Horizons,
  by DuBose Heyward   25   164
The New Spoon River,
  by Edgar Lee Masters   25   273
Harvest, by David Morton   25   283
Ballad and Lyrical Poems,
  by John Shaw Neilson   25   284
Tanka: Poems in Exile,
  by Jun Fujita   26   44
Windows in Dragon Town,
  by John Oscar Beck   26   109
John Keats, by Amy Lowell   26   220
Profiles from Home,
  by Eunice Tietjens   26   227
Hesperides, by Ridgeley Torrence   26   286
Earth Moods and Other Poems,
  by Hervey Allen   27   96
What's O'Clock, by Amy Lowell   27   154
The Road to Welles-Perennes,
  by Daniel Sargent   27   160
Thistle-Down Verse   27   162
  Loves and Lasses of Pierrot,
    by William Griffith
  Harp in the Winds,
    by Daniel Henderson

When We Were Very Young,
  by A. A. Milne
Brief Notices   27   168
Ellen Pryor, by Alice Brown   27   168
Fantasy and Other Poems,
  by Roydon Burke   27   169
Young Harvard, by Witter Bynner   27   170
Songs from the Silence—A Book
  of Prison Verse,
  by John Francis Glynn   27   170
A Hurried Man,
  by Emanuel Carnevali   27   211
The Sainted Courtesan
  and *The Drums of Yle,*
  by J. N. Nicholson   27   216
Two Lives and *Tutankhamen and After,*
  by William Ellery Leonard   27   272
Poets of America,
  by Clement Wood   27   287
You Who Have Dreams,
  by Maxwell Anderson   27   337
Many Anthologies   27   343
  The New Poetry
    (Ed. by Harriet Monroe
    and Alice Corbin Henderson)
  Modern American Poetry
    and *Modern British Poetry*
    (Ed. by Louis Untermeyer)
  The Home Book of Modern Verse
    (Ed. by Burton E. Stevenson)
  The Golden Treasury of Modern Lyrics
    (Ed. by Lawrence Binyon)
  The Little Book of Modern British Verse
    (Ed. by Jessie B. Rittenhouse)
  By Haunted Stream
    (Ed. by L. A. G. Strong)
  Anthology of Magazine Verse [Series]
    (Ed. by W. S. Braithwaite)
  The Best Poems of 1924
    (Ed. by L. A. G. Strong)
  The Best Poems of 1924
    (Ed. by Thomas Moult)
  The Northern Muse:
   An Anthology of Scots Vernacular Poetry
    (Ed. by John Buchan)
  The Golden Treasury of Irish Verse
    (Ed. by Lennox Robinson)
  The Golden Treasury of Portuguese Verse
    (Ed. by Aubrey F. G. Bell)
  Cape Cod in Poetry
    (Ed. by J. F. and F. H. Crowell)
  Songs and Ballads of Maine Lumberjacks
   with Other Songs from Maine
    (Ed. by Roland Palmer Gray)
  The Sea Anthology
    (Ed. by Alice Hunt Bartlett)
  The Magic Carpet
    (Ed. by Mrs. Waldo Richards)

Love and Laughter
  (Ed. by Matthew Prothero)
The Soul of Wit,
  A Choice of English Verse Epigrams
  (Ed. by George Rostrevor Hamilton)
Carolyn Wells' Book
  of American Limericks
Column Poets
  (Ed. by Keith Preston)
Line Book,
  by Richard Henry Little
The Happy Marriage
  and *The Pot of Earth,*
  by Archibald MacLeish   28   44
The Poor King's Daughter,
  by Aline Kilmer   28   48
Honey Out of the Rock,
  by Babette Deutsch   28   102
Golden Pheasant,
  by Kathryn White Ryan   28   110
Anthologies for Children   28   114
  Silver Pennies:
    Modern Poems for Boys and Girls
    (Ed. by Blanche Thompson)
  Fifty New Poems for Children
  Poems for Youth:
    An American Anthology
    (Ed. by William Rose Benét)
  The Listening Child
    (Ed. by Lucy W. Thatcher)
  Nurse Lovechild's Legacy
Roan Stallion, Tamar and Other Poems,
  by Robinson Jeffers   28   160
Fiddler's Farewell,
  by Leonora Speyer   28   218
First Impressions, by Llewellyn Jones   28   285
Folk-Song Collections   28   348
  Folk-Songs of the South
    (Ed. by John Harrington Cox)
  Folk Songs of French Canada
    (Ed. by Marius Barbeau
    and Edward Sapir)
  Ballads and Songs of the Shanty Boy
    (Ed. by Franz Rickaby)
  Spanish Folk Songs of New Mexico
    (Ed. by Mary R. Van Stone)
The Sleeping Beauty; Troy Park;
  and *Poetry and Criticism,*
  by Edith Sitwell   29   41
Legend, by Paul Sandoz   29   56
Not Poppy, by Virginia Moore   29   97
Dark of the Moon, by Sara Teasdale   29   157
East Wind, by Amy Lowell   29   160
Going to the Stars; The Candle in the Cabin;
  and *Collected Poems,*
  by Vachel Lindsay   29   217
Poe and Longfellow   29   266
  Israfel, by Hervey Allen

A Victorian American,
  by Herbert S. Gorman
The Shoeing of Jerry-Go-Nimble and
  Other Dialect Poems and *Dale Lyrics,*
  by Dorothy Una Ratcliffe   29   286
Lee: A Dramatic Poem
  and *Selected Poems,*
  by Edgar Lee Masters   29   336
The King's Henchman
  and *Three Plays,*
  by Edna St. Vincent Millay   30   42
Collected Poems of John G. Neihardt   30   99
Eve Walks in Her Garden,
  by Louise Ayres Garnett   30   110
Red Flag, by Lola Ridge   30   154
The Inner Harbor, by Wilbert Snow   30   170
I Come Singing,
  by H. Thompson Rich   30   171
From the Book of Extenuations,
  by Edmund Vance Cook   30   173
Touch and Go, by Ralph Cheyney   30   228
You That Come After,
  by Mary Siegrist   30   230
The Arrow of Lightning,
  by Beatrice Ravenel   30   288
The Traveller and Other Poems,
  by Iris Tree   30   290
God's Trombones,
  by James Weldon Johnson   30   291
Cliff Dwellings,
  by Glenn Ward Dresbach   30   349
The Pack of Autolycus
  (Ed. by Hyder Edward Rollins)   30   352
7 P.M. and Other Poems,
  by Mark van Doren   31   47
Tristram, by Edwin Arlington Robinson   31   160
The Tall Men, by Donald Davidson   31   222
Ballads for Sale, by Amy Lowell   31   338
Hale's Pond, by James Whaler   32   47
The Pale Woman, by Sara Bard Field   32   50
Sonnets for Caresse and *Red Skeletons,*
  by Harry Crosby   32   111
Sea-Drinking Cities,
  by Josephine Pinckney   32   162
Color of Water, by Marjorie Meeker   32   217
Outcrop, by Abbie Huston Evans   32   341
Songs of Infancy and Other Poems,
  by Mary Britton Miller   32   350
Painted Shores; The Stranger;
  and *Impossible Melodies,*
  by Caresse Crosby   33   47
John Brown's Body,
  by Stephen Vincent Benét   33   91
Stone Dust, by Frank Ernest Hill   33   151
Here, There and Everywhere
  and *Everything and Anything,*
  by Dorothy Aldis   33   162

Songs of a Baby's Day,
    by Frances Shaw   33   164

The Buck in the Snow,
    by Edna St. Vincent Millay   33   210

West-Running Brook and *Selected Poems,*
    by Robert Frost   33   333

Collected Poems, by Richard Aldington   34   42

Poetry of the Orient
    (Ed. by Eunice Tietjens)   34   102

The Lost Lyrist,
    by Elizabeth Hollister Frost   34   110

Jack Kelso: A Dramatic Poem,
    by Edgar Lee Masters   34   177

Blue Juniata, by Malcolm Cowley   35   45

This Delicate Love,
    by Winifred Welles   35   217

Along Old Trails,
    by William Haskell Simpson   35   226

Collected Poems and *Pansies,*
    by D. H. Lawrence   35   273

Firehead, by Lola Ridge   36   36

The Wind in the Cedars
    and *Star-Dust and Stone,*
    by Glenn Ward Dresbach   36   43

Every Soul Is a Circus,
    by Vachel Lindsay   36   46

Gold Coast Customs and Other Poems,
    by Edith Sitwell   36   101

Seesaw, by May Williams Ward   36   106

Arrowheads, by Lilian White Spencer   36   109

Imagist Anthology 1930
    (Richard Aldington, John Cournos,
    H. D., John Gould Fletcher,
    F. S. Flint, Ford Madox Ford,
    James Joyce, D. H. Lawrence,
    and William Carlos Williams)   36   213

Toward Equilibrium,
    by Polly Chase Boyden   36   223

Pilgrimage and Other Poems,
    by Austin Clarke   36   226

Indian Earth, by Witter Bynner   36   276

Two on an Old Pathway,
    by Eleanor O'Rourke Koenig   36   280

The Earth for Sale, by Harold Monro   36   282

Deep South, by Carl Carmer   36   284

Balm in Gilead, by Helene Mullins   36   288

Books for Children   36   289
    Chimney-Corner Poems
        (Ed. by Veronica S. Hutchinson)
    The Land of Dreams,
        by William Blake
    Green Pipes,
        by T. Paget Fredericks
    Old Swedish Fairy Tales,
        by Anna Wahlenberg
        (Tr. by Antoinette
        de Coursey Patterson)

Imagina, by Julia Ellsworth Ford

Nightlights,
    by Dorothy Una Ratcliffe

A Bravery of Earth,
    by Richard Eberhart   36   343

L'Influence du Symbolisme Francais
    sur La Poésie Américaine (de 1910 à 1920),
    by René Taupin   37   44

Hamilton: A Poetic Drama in Three Acts,
    by Chard Powers Smith   37   53

White Peaks and Green,
    by Ethel Romig Fuller   37   55

My Thirty Years' War,
    by Margaret Anderson   37   95

After-Walker and Other Poems,
    by Leonard Cline   37   161

Turning Point, by John V. A. Weaver   37   230

Strange Splendor, by Ernest Hartsock   38   45

Adamastor: Poems, by Roy Campbell   38   98

Lichee Nuts, by Edgar Lee Masters   38   104

Young Land, by Gwendolen Haste   38   111

Fatal Interview,
    by Edna St. Vincent Millay   38   216

Wings Against the Moon, by Lew Sarett   39   155

Matthias at the Door,
    by Edwin Arlington Robinson   39   212

The Mountain in the Sky,
    by Howard McKinley Corning   39   338

Jane Matthew and Other Poems,
    by Eda Lou Walton   40   165

Outside of the World,
    by Katherine Garrison Chapin   40   168

Conquistador, by Archibald MacLeish   40   216

Thrust at the Sky and Other Poems,
    by MacKnight Black   40   224

Boy with a Silver Plow,
    by Dennis Murphy   40   232

Poems, by Padraic Colum   40   283

Without Sanctuary,
    by Mary Britton Miller   40   286

Mirror Images, by Dorothe Bendon   40   291

Minnie Maylor's Story
    and Other Tales and Scenes,
    by John Masefield   40   344

Selected Poems,
    by Glenn Ward Dresbach   40   346

Old Prairie du Chien, by Laura Sherry   40   348

Mead and Mangel-Wurzel,
    by Grace Stone Coates   41   102

Speaking at Seventy, by Mary E. Bulkley   41   104

Wind in the Grass, by Christy Mackaye   41   105

Mortal Triumph and Other Poems,
    by Selden Rodman   41   161

These Acres, by Frances Frost   41   163

Barabbas, by Sara Bard Field   41   226

Red Drumming in the Sun,
    by May Lewis   41   230

The Furioso, by Leonard Bacon   41   275
Lord Juggler and Other Poems,
    by Roberta Teale Swartz   41   279
Lost Warrior, by Sydney King Russell   41   281
Harvest of Time,
    by Harold Trowbridge Pulsifer   41   283
Worn Earth, by Paul Engle   42   220
The Kingdom of Smoke,
    by Stanley Kimmel   43   47
Strange Victory, by Sara Teasdale   43   96
Forgotten Frontiers,
    by Dorothy Dudley
    [Theodore Dreiser]   43   208
Any Spring, by Dorothy Aldis   43   346
Meridian: Poems 1923-1932,
    by Bernice Kenyon   44   42
Look to the Lightning,
    by Gilbert Maxwell   44   226
Ideas of Order, by Wallace Stevens   47   153
*Amy Lowell: A Chronicle with Extracts
    from Her Correspondence,*
    by S. Foster Damon   47   212
Vachel Lindsay: A Poet in America,
    by Edgar Lee Masters   47   337
Black Man's Verse,
    by Frank Marshall Davis   48   293

BOOKS REVIEWED
You and I   5   188
The New Poetry
    (Ed. with Alice Corbin Henderson)   12   214
The New Poetry
    (Ed. with Alice Corbin Henderson)   14   281
The New Poetry
    (Ed. with Alice Corbin Henderson)   27   343
*Chosen Poems:
    A Selection from My Books of Verse*   46   336
*A Poet's Life:
    Seventy Years in a Changing World*   52   30

ARTICLES ABOUT
Correspondence
    from John W. Crawford
    [*Others for 1919*]   17   287
Correspondence
    from Louis Untermeyer   22   109
Our Contemporaries   22   286
Correspondence from Robert O. Ballou
    [English typography]   28   176
[Note]   40   354
Microcosm, by Eunice Tietjens   41   43
The Romance of It, by Marion Strobel   41   47
An Adventure Story,
    by Jessica Nelson North   41   50
Harriet Monroe:
    December 23, 1860-September 26, 1936,
    by Morton Dauwen Zabel   49   85

[Note]   49   117
Tribute to Harriet Monroe
    [Ezra Pound, Eunice Tietjens,
    Helen Hoyt, Edith Franklin Wyatt,
    Marion Strobel, George Dillon,
    Jessica Nelson North, Lew Sarett,
    Geraldine Udell, Edgar Lee Masters,
    Carl Sandburg, Wallace Stevens,
    Marianne Moore, Agnes Lee,
    Horace Gregory, Marya Zaturenska,
    Malcolm Cowley, Charles H. Hamill,
    S. O. Levinson, Robert Morss Lovett,
    Morton Dauwen Zabel,
    John Gould Fletcher]   49   136
[Excerpts from clippings, correspondence
    from Mrs. Arthur Thompson
    about Harriet Monroe's death]   49   173
Poetry's Quarter-Century,
    by M. D. Zabel   51   28
[Note]   52   241
Rev. of *A History of American
    Poetry, 1900-1940,*
    by Horace Gregory
    and Marya Zaturenska   69   210
Harriet Monroe Memorial   83   245
H. M.: In Memory,
    by Morton Dauwen Zabel   97   241
Some Recollections of the Poetry Club
    at the University of Chicago,
    by Gladys Campbell   107   110
Rev. of *Harriet Monroe
    and the Poetry Renaissance:
    The First Ten Years
    of Poetry, 1912-22,*
    by Ellen Williams   131   39
A Springfield Memoir,
    by Robert Fitzgerald   141   33
Setting the Hard Tasks,
    by J. D. McClatchy   141   39
Comments by Janet Lewis,
    Elder Olson, and Paul Engle   151   199

MONTAGUE, JOHN
POEMS
Speech for an Ideal Irish Election   94   376
Murphy in Manchester   97   84
Old Mythologies
All Legendary Obstacles   106   408
Remission   167   56
Psychic Surgery
Lost Worlds
Between

ARTICLES
Return to Europe   89   180
Letter from Dublin
    [Patrick Kavanagh, Austin Clarke,
    Brendan Behan, Donald Davie]   90   310

REVIEWS
Isolation and Cunning:
Recent Irish Verse   94   264
Too Great a Vine,
by Austin Clarke
Recent Poems,
by Patrick Kavanagh
Ten Poems, by Padraic Colum
Another September,
by Thomas Kinsella

BOOKS REVIEWED
Forms of Exile   99   184
Poisoned Lands   102   324
About Love   164   157

ARTICLES ABOUT
A Map of Contemporary
Irish Poetry,
by Dennis O'Driscoll   167   94

MONTALE, EUGENIO
POEMS
Sul Muro Grafito   92   96
Barche Sulla Marna
Su Una Lettera Non Scritta
(Tr. by Sonia Raiziss)
Tre poesie inedite/
Three Unpublished Poems   155   I
É solo un vizio/
It's Only an Error
20 Gennaio o 30 anni/
January 20 or Age 30
Ex Abrupto
Cinque Poesie da La Bufera e Altro/
Five Poems from
The Storm and Other Things
L'Orto/The Orchard
Proda di Versilia/Coast of Versilia
The Hitler Spring
The Magnolia's Shadow
The Prisoner's Dream
(Tr. by Jonathan Galassi)

ARTICLES
Lucio Piccolo's *Canti Barocchi*
(Tr. by Sonia Raiziss
and Alfredo de Palchi)   98   392

BOOKS REVIEWED
Selected Poems   109   268
The Storm & Other Poems
(Tr. by Charles Wright)   136   40

ARTICLES ABOUT
Contemporary Italian Poetry,
by Edward Williamson   79   159

MONTENEGRO, ERNESTO
ARTICLES
New Tendencies
[Rubén Darío]   26   161

MONTGOMERY, LOIS
POEMS
The Gift   31   71

MONTGOMERY, MARION
BOOKS REVIEWED
Stones from the Rubble   109   48

MONTGOMERY,
ROSELLE MERCIER
BOOKS REVIEWED
Many Devices   34   III

MONTGOMERY, STUART
POEMS
Circe   110   304

MONTI, VINCENZO
POEMS
Sonnet ("A vulgar thought...")
(Tr. by Francis Golffing)   128   138

MONTROSS, LOIS SEYSTER
BOOKS REVIEWED
The Crimson Cloak   25   341

MONYPENNY, KATHLEEN
POEMS
Deep Sea Tides   45   204

MOODEY, J(OHN) S(OUTHWORTH)
POEMS
End of Fall   47   134
November
Dove Hunting
Green Key   57   124
Indian Blanket   58   191
Song ("Bright in the morning...")   69   23

MOODY, HARRIET
[(MRS.) WILLIAM VAUGHN
MOODY]
ARTICLES ABOUT
Rev. of *A House in Chicago*,
by Olivia Howard Dunbar   71   277
Remarks on the Occasion
of the Tagore Centenary,
by Robert Frost   99   106
Some Recollections
of the Poetry Club
at the University of Chicago,
by Gladys Campbell   107   110

MOODY, WILLIAM VAUGHN
POEMS
    I Am the Woman   I   3

BOOKS REVIEWED
    Some Letters of...
        (Ed. by Daniel Gregory Mason)   3   146
    Selected Poems of...
        (Ed. by Robert Morss Lovett)   38   331

ARTICLES ABOUT
    Moody's Poems,
        by Harriet Monroe   I   54

MOOLTEN, DAVID
POEMS
    Gypsy   163   193

MOON KWAN
TRANSLATIONS
    Poems by Li Po
        and Wang Wêi   18   130

MOON, SAMUEL
POEMS
    A Dialogue of Poets   105   366
    What Is Love?
    The Moment of Turning
    Composing an Eclogue
    The Shape of Space
    At the Divide   109   24
    This Twisting
    A Late Conversation
    My Wife, I Will Try
    The River   111   163
    The Plane
    Man in the Landscape
    Trying To Read   113   406

REVIEWS
    The Lost World, by Randall Jarrell   106   425
    The Old Glory, by Robert Lowell   108   189
    The Gold Diggers and Other Stories,
        by Robert Creeley   108   341
    Canadian Chronicle   112   201
        Extended, by Dorothy Roberts
        Exsultate, Jubilate,
            by Richard Outram
        The Tomb of the Kings,
            by Anne Hébert
            (Tr. by Peter Miller)
        The Circle Game,
            by Margaret Atwood

MOOR, GEORGE
POEMS
    On a Family Regathering
        Seen One Night Through a Window   68   179

Madame Rachel's Outburst
The Brontes
Saxophones and Insomnia
Day's End
Song of Death's Envoy to Violet   70   72
Death's Love Song
Old Man and Woman   71   76
Willows
Boy   73   198

BOOKS REVIEWED
    The White Kid   86   242

MOORE, AGNES D(ONGAN)
POEMS
    Globe Amaranth   47   262
    Downpour   48   317
    Take Care!   50   323

MOORE, BARBARA
POEMS
    Autumn   71   73
    To the Orphans   144   164
    Photograph Album

MOORE, CATHERINE
[CATHERINE MOORE PICARD]
POEMS
    The Burden   34   130
    Blizzard   47   188

MOORE, GEORGE B.
POEMS
    The Transformation of Nature   160   88

MOORE, HARRY T(HORNTON)
ARTICLES
    Poetry on Records
        [E. K. Rand, Harry Morgan Ayres,
        John Drinkwater, R. P. Tristram Coffin,
        T. S. Eliot]   57   52
    Poetry on Records
        [Ogden Nash, Newman Levy,
        Otis Skinner, Viola Allen,
        William Shakespeare, Vachel Lindsay,
        Archibald MacLeish]   57   338
    Poetry on Records   58   105
        Robert Frost
        Theodore Spencer
        Carl Sandburg's American Songbag
    Poetry on Records
        [Robinson Jeffers, Oliver St. John
        Gogarty, Robert Hillyer, George Barker,
        John Gould Fletcher, John Holmes,
        Robert P. Tristram Coffin]   58   345
    Correspondence   62   290
    Poetry on Records
        [T. S. Eliot]   74   367

Poetry on Records
  [Edith Sitwell, E. E. Cummings,
  Robert Penn Warren, William
  Carlos Williams, Robinson Jeffers,
  D. H. Lawrence, Frieda Lawrence]   79   353

BOOKS REVIEWED
  Selected Letters
    of Rainer Maria Rilke (Ed.)   101   287

MOORE, MARIANNE
POEMS
  Pouters and Fantails   6   70
    That Harp You Play So Well
    To an Intra-Mural Rat
    Counseil to a Bacheler
    Appellate Jurisdiction
    The Wizard in Words
  Part of a Novel, Part of a Poem,
    Part of a Play   40   119
    The Steeple-Jack
    The Student
    The Hero
  No Swan So Fine   41   7
  Imperious Ox, Imperial Dish   45   61
    The Buffalo
    Nine Nectarines and Other Porcelain
  Pigeons   47   61
  Walking-Sticks and Paperweights
    and Watermarks   49   59
  Then the Ermine: 81   55
  Three Fables of La Fontaine   83   1
    The Fox and the Goat
    The Fox and the Bust
    The Fox Shorn of His Tail
  More Fables from La Fontaine   83   311
    The Hen that Laid the Golden Eggs
    The Dog Who Dropped
      Substance for Shadow
    The Woods and the Woodman
  The Wizard in Words   121   22

ARTICLES
  [Tribute to Harriet Monroe]   49   155

REVIEWS
  Laconics, by W. W. E. Ross   38   280
  Marina, by T. S. Eliot   38   337
  A Draft of XXX Cantos,
    by Ezra Pound   39   37
  Jonathan Gentry,
    by Mark Van Doren   40   222
  Letters of Emily Dickinson
    (Ed. by Mabel Loomis Todd)   41   219
  The Winding Stair and
    Words for Music Perhaps
    and Other Poems,
    by W. B. Yeats   42   40

Sweeney Agonistes, by T. S. Eliot   42   106
Sonnets, by W. W. E. Ross (E.R.)   42   114
Eimi, by E. E. Cummings   42   277
The Ukiyoye Primitives,
  by Yone Noguchi   43   92
Collected Poems 1921-1931,
  by William Carlos Williams   44   103
Murder in the Cathedral,
  by T. S. Eliot   47   279
Owl's Clover and *Ideas of Order,*
  by Wallace Stevens   49   268
Gate to the Sea, by A. W. Bryher   93   320
The Diary of 'Helena Morley'
  (Tr. and ed. by Elizabeth Bishop)   94   247

BOOKS REVIEWED
  Poems   19   208
  Observations   26   39
  What Are Years   59   96
  Contemporary Poets Series
    [Recording]   61   519
  Nevertheless   65   262
  Collected Poems   83   158
  The Fables of La Fontaine (Tr.)   84   356
  Predilections   87   239
  Like a Bulwark   90   47
  O To Be a Dragon   96   112
  Four Poets on Poetry:
    Essays by R. P. Blackmur, Yvor Winters,
    Marianne Moore, and Mark Van Doren
    (Ed. by Don Cameron Allen)   96   382
  A Marianne Moore Reader   102   109
  Puss in Boots, The Sleeping Beauty,
    & Cinderella: A Retelling
    of Three Classic Fairy Tales
    Based on the French of Charles Perrault 105   190
  Tell Me, Tell Me   110   423
  The Complete Poems of...   114   113
  The Complete Poems of...   139   340

ARTICLES ABOUT
  A Symposium on Marianne Moore,
    by Harriet Monroe
    [Rev. essay]   19   208
  [Note on error]   39   114
  [Note on error]   42   179
  A Literalist of the Imagination,
    by M. D. Zabel   47   326
  Rev. of *New Poems: 1943*
    (Ed. by Oscar Williams)   64   86
  Form in Modern Poetry,
    by D. S. Savage   65   30
  The Direction of the Little Magazine,
    by William Van O'Connor   71   281
  Correspondence:
    Letter from Harvard,
    by John Ciardi   74   112

The Defense of Poetry,
  by Richard Eberhart   77   89
Marianne Moore:
  Imaginary Gardens
  and Real Toads,
  by Frederick J. Hoffman   83   152
Jorge Guillén, Marianne Moore,
  T. S. Eliot: Some Recollections,
  by Wallace Fowlie   90   103
The Vocation of Poetry,
  by Henry Rago   110   328
Rev. of *Marianne Moore:*
  The Poet's Advance,
  by Laurence Stapleton   139   340
[Note on symposium]   150   47
Rev. of *Becoming a Poet: Elizabeth Bishop*
  with Marianne Moore and Robert Lowell,
  by David Kalstone
  (Ed. by Robert Hemenway)   157   159
Review by Sandra M. Gilbert   160   284

MOORE, MARY
POEMS
  Cosmology of the Irish Mother   156   331
  Fontanel   163   136
  Doors   164   91

MOORE, MERRILL
POEMS
  Hospital Poems   34   61
    Armamentaria
    Transfusion
    Rana Americana
    Inanition
    Other Humors
    Grey Roofs
    Shock
    Anesthesia
    Hymn for Water
  Over This Ice Here These Winds Know   40   70
  The Winter's Grey Inn
  The Esthetic Problem Entire
  So Ordered   42   262
    Leave the Telling of Jokes
    Fidelitas
  Poetry Is Also Like Riding on a Train   83   8
  Fragrance: Peonies in 1937   85   92
  Deaconing Is an Honorable Persuasion   86   272

ARTICLES
  Correspondence   62   288

BOOKS REVIEWED
  The Noise that Time Makes   36   104
  Six Sides to a Man: New Sonnets   47   49
  M: 1000 Autobiographical Sonnets   54   160
  Illegitimate Sonnets   80   58
  More Clinical Sonnets   84   32

MOORE, NICHOLAS
POEMS
  Two Poems   56   130
    ("Fivesucked the feature...")
    ("The moment when we were alone...")
  On Christmas Eve   63   126
  Children Gathering Flowers
  Poetry as Clover
  Fire and Disease   64   302
  The Legend
  The Monument   65   193
  The Orange Bed   66   295
  Mr. Ullubux Umpires a Cricket Match
  The Portfolios of Doom
  Something Is Possible
  Song ("Since the struggle...")
  Stalks
  Girls and Birds   69   191
  Horace Hawspice at a Desk
    in Denmark Street   70   59
  The Adventures of Y
  The Common Weather
  The Phallic Symbol   71   183
  For J. J. J. Slipfeather
  In the Course of the Rider
  Happy Without Sex
  October in the University
  No, No, Go Not, Said Mr. Kyew   72   194
  The Maroon Suit   73   134
  When I First Held Your Naked Body
  The Truth About the Ogre
  The Dream of Ravens
  The Azure Tower   74   215
  Unity Quitbread at Eltham   75   135
  Alteration
  Coffee-Coloured Horses of the Moon   151   103

BOOKS REVIEWED
  A Book for Priscilla: Poems   59   98
  Three Poems
    (With Fred Marnau
    and Wrey Gardiner)   66   53
  Recollections of the Gala   78   45

ARTICLES ABOUT
  Contemporary Poetry in Britain,
    by David Daiches   62   150

MOORE, PRENTISS
POEMS
  From the Library of Alexandria   143   83
  Porfyry in Exile
  Wisdom of the Mediterranean
  The 101 Views of Fuji

MOORE, RICHARD
POEMS
  The Clowns   67   184

Seascape
The Fish   83   205
Marriage Blues   119   209
The Tennis Ball
Pond Thoughts
Sonnet ("She had no choice...")
Pyramids   122   259
Continuity
The Playground   138   16
Friends
On Coming to Nothing
Poets   139   211
For Gertrude   146   149
Signals

REVIEWS
    Two New Editions of Blake   111   263
        The Poetry and Prose of William Blake
            (Ed. by David V. Erdman)
        The Complete Writings
            of William Blake
            with Variant Readings
            (Ed. by Geoffrey Keynes)

MOORE, ROBERT THOMAS
    BOOKS REVIEWED
        Poetry Awards 1952 (Ed.)   82   363

MOORE, ROSALIE
    POEMS
        The Grasshopper's Man   74   63
        Stand Before Him as Would
        The Easter of the Mill   76   31
        Summer Camp: Wane   78   63
        The Enchantment
        Bird and Bell
        Sun at Veracruz
        Venice
        Poem ("The peerless vacancy...")
        Crusade of the Children   81   57
        Of Singles and Doubles   82   19
        View of Rome Circa 1200
        Joy and the Presence of Snakes   85   347
        Latin Lecturer   89   205
        The Manicure
        Life of a King
        Richard in England   93   63
        Poem for a Commencement
        The Party   99   149
        Poet as Bullfighter   101   79
        Death of the Story Teller   110   222
        Sea Look
        Love Poem
        What He Sees

    ARTICLES
        The Beat and the Unbeat
            [Jeanne McGahey]   93   104

REVIEWS
    Beyond the Terminus of Stars,
        by Hugo Manning   74   362
    Graphiti from Elsinore,
        by Will Wharton   76   170
    Further Letters of
        Gerard Manley Hopkins, 2nd ed.
        (Ed. by Claude Colleer Abbott)   92   113

BOOKS REVIEWED
    The Grasshopper's Man
        and Other Poems   75   98

ARTICLES ABOUT
    About the Activist Poets,
        by Lawrence Hart   78   99
    Rosie the Riveter,
        by Jeanne McGahey   78   109

MOORE, RUTH
    BOOKS REVIEWED
        Time's Web   121   292

MOORE, T. INGLIS
    BOOKS REVIEWED
        Poetry in Australia
            (Ed. with Douglas Stewart)   110   47

MOORE, T. STURGE
    [See STURGE MOORE, T.]

MOORE, VIRGINIA
    POEMS
        Wishes   27   257
        Grief
        Wind Want
        Smells   31   199
        Old Age   32   322
        Justified Bird
        Angels...   55   127
        Dark the Approach   57   354
        The Ashless Fire
        The Banshee   59   247

    REVIEWS
        The Living Chaucer,
            by Percy V. D. Shelly   59   226

    BOOKS REVIEWED
        Not Poppy   29   97
        Sweet Water and Bitter   34   53

MORABADI, JIGAR
    POEMS
        Ghazal
            (Tr. by Rahm Ali Alhashmi
            and Tambimuttu)   93   235

MORAES, DOM
POEMS
   Being Married   93   250
   Kanheri Caves

BOOKS REVIEWED
   Poems 1955-1965   109   411

MORAUD, PAUL
ARTICLES ABOUT
   Correspondence
     from Jean Catel   16   343

MORE, PAUL ELMER
BOOKS REVIEWED
   Shelburne Essays
    on American Literature
    (Ed. by Daniel Aaron)   104   369

ARTICLES ABOUT
   An American Critic,
    by Morton Dauwen Zabel   50   330

MOREHOUSE, MARIAN
BOOKS REVIEWED
   Adventures in Value
    (With E. E. Cummings)   102   341

MORELAND, JANE P.
POEMS
   The Argument   134   268
   Prunings   140   141
   With Nan in My Garden
   Watching for Signs
   The Catastrophic Thing   170   75

MORELAND, JOHN RICHARD
BOOKS REVIEWED
   The Sea and April   33   229

MORELAND, PATRICK DACUS
BOOKS REVIEWED
   Seven Song   49   291

MORENO, FERNANDEZ
POEMS
   On Certain Things
    (Tr. by Muna Lee)   26   118

MORGAN, ANGELA
BOOKS REVIEWED
   Forward March!   14   220

MORGAN, EDWIN
POEMS
   Odd Moments   35   31
   Queer
   Interior
   An Old Print

   Carnival
   Birth
   The Turning Year   40   12
   Spring Circus
   Equinox
   Miracle   45   194
   Death of Hercules   52   14
   Fireworks   60   202
   Toro

ARTICLES
   Notes on the Metaphysics
    of Jules Laforgue   69   266

REVIEWS
   Rimbaud, by Wallace Fowlie   70   102
   The Lane Retrodden   75   178
    Life Is the Flesh,
     by Louise Townsend Nicholl
    The Hollow Vale, by James Turner
    Poetry Awards 1952
     (Ed. by Robert Thomas Moore, et al.)   82   363

BOOKS REVIEWED
   Flowers of Evil
    [Charles Baudelaire]   63   287
   Beowulf: A Verse Translation
    into Modern English   83   44
   Scottish Poetry, Number Two
    (Ed. with George Bruce
    and Maurice Lindsay)   113   35
   The Second Life: Selected Poems   114   266
   Penguin Modern Poets 15
    (With Alan Bold and
    Edward Brathwaite)   118   102
   From Glasgow to Saturn   124   45
   Rites of Passage: Selected Translations 131   225
   Collected Poems   159   157

MORGAN, ELIZABETH SEYDEL
POEMS
   "Willem DeKooning Declared Incompetent" 164   95
   At Epidaurus   168   335

MORGAN, EMANUEL
[Pseud. of BYNNER, WITTER]
ARTICLES
   Correspondence: A Spectral Ghost
    [Witter Bynner]   12   286

BOOKS REVIEWED
   Pins for Wings   18   52

ARTICLES ABOUT
   Baiting the Public,
    by Alice Corbin Henderson   12   169
   Rev. of *The Spectra Hoax*,
    by William Jay Smith   99   390

MORGAN, EVAN
  BOOKS REVIEWED
    The Eel and Other Poems   32   55

MORGAN, FREDERICK
  POEMS
    Primary Notion   94   32
    Epitaph ("What was unimportant...")
    Epitaph ("Here where he lies...")
    Poem ("Duck, riding the reservoir...")
    Canandaigua   134   136
    The Christmas Tree   143   162

  ARTICLES
    Correspondence
      [William Van O'Connor]   76   304

  BOOKS REVIEWED
    A Book of Change   122   237
    Northbook   143   39

MORGAN, JOHN
  POEMS
    The Twenty-Six Years War   117   156
    Keeping Up with the Dead
    USS Argonaut
    The Wildness of Wild Animals   133   220
    Listen
    Her Ecstasy   136   282

MORGAN, PETE
  POEMS
    *My Enemies
      Have Sweet Voices*   115   261

MORGAN, ROBERT
  POEMS
    Chant Royal   132   63
    Pigeon Loft   133   63
    Shucking Stick
    Ship Burial
    Snow Beside the Shed
    Cane Mill
    Lost Flower
    Fish-Top Falls
    Secret Pleasures
    Lost Colony
    Spirit Level   135   1
    Horace Kephart
    Lake Summit
    Earth Closet
    Zircon Pit
    Wedding Party
    White Autumn   138   311
    Mowing
    Purple Asters
    Harrow   144   11
    Rearview Mirror

    Oranges   145   146
    School Ground   146   289
    Rockpile
    Nail Bag
    Vietnam War Memorial
    The Charge   148   71
    Visitors
    Hayfield   150   12
    Moving the Bees
    π   161   204
    Music of the Spheres   163   16

  BOOKS REVIEWED
    Land Diving   133   45
    At the Edge of the Orchard Country   151   360
    Sigodlin   158   342
    *Green River:
      New and Selected Poems*   160   219

MORGAN, ROBIN
  BOOKS REVIEWED
    Monster   123   173
    Lady of the Beasts   130   293

MORGENSTERN, CHRISTIAN
  POEMS
    Gull Song   98   365
    The Underpants
    Margaret, ii
    The Servant Girl's Dream
    The Midnightmouse
    The Werwolf
      (Tr. by W. D. Snodgrass
      and Lore Groszmann)

  BOOKS REVIEWED
    Gallows Songs
      (Tr. by W. D. Snodgrass
      and Lore Segal)   112   418

MORLAND, HAROLD
  ARTICLES
    Correspondence   87   58

MORLEY, CHRISTOPHER
  BOOKS REVIEWED
    The Middle Kingdom   65   278

  ARTICLES ABOUT
    Jorge Guillén, Marianne Moore,
      T. S. Eliot: Some Recollections,
      by Wallace Fowlie   90   103

MORLEY, F. V.
  ARTICLES
    Poet, Publisher,
      and the Tribal Chant   75   40

MORLEY, HELENA   [Pseud.]
BOOKS REVIEWED
  The Diary of...
    (Tr. and ed. by Elizabeth Bishop)   94   247

MORLEY, HILDA
POEMS
  The Whiteness   146   I
  Egrets, Antigua
  Song of the Terrible   151   104

BOOKS REVIEWED
  To Hold in My Hand:
    Selected Poems, 1955-1983   146   293

MORLEY, S. GRISWOLD
BOOKS REVIEWED
  Sonnets and Poems,
    by Anthero de Quental (Tr.)   23   225

MORRELL, EDITH DOROTHEA
POEMS
  Of Trees   38   20
    The Year Has Made No Promises
    Inheritance

MORRILL, JANE
POEMS
  Tide-Worn   26   253

MORRIS, HARRISON S.
POEMS
  Contrast   2   96

MORRIS, HERBERT
POEMS
  The Color That Is Loss   74   325
  Graves   82   256
  The North of Wales   85   220
  Terrain
  Les Parapluies: Renoir
  The Rocks
  For That Unjourneyed Man
    and Visioned Sea   87   274
  A Walker in the Country of July
  Workmen
  Bone   88   212
  Blood
  Breath
  The Brahms
  A Shirt-Silk from Havana   90   18
  Prothalamium
  The Cyclist   91   187
  The Medium
  The Task
  The Clown's Heart   93   158
  Soleil
  Myself and Thou from Theatres of the Night 94   389

  Hotel de Dieu
  The Idea of a Capital for Brasil   97   294
  For the Other
  Submissions   102   221
  In Winter, the Magician
  Coming to the End of the Past   122   141
  Circus   143   217
  Early Views of Rio, Passion, Night   144   276
  Latin   147   135
  French   149   315
  The Map to Freud's House   154   193
  Duesenberg, 1929   165   74

BOOKS REVIEWED
  Peru   143   228
  Dream Palace   149   168
  The Little Voices of the Pears   156   36

MORRIS, JOHN N.
POEMS
  Nikko Kekko, Beautiful Nikko   87   203
  Over Grave Flowers
  For Captain Walter Phillips, U.S.M.C.
  The Quiet Life   118   336
  The Life Beside This One
  That Summer
  For Whiskey   122   33
  Comparing the Literature
  Three
  Mystery Story   122   329
  The Companion
  Out of England   124   91
  For the Children, About Their Deaths
  The Mirror
  The Hours You Keep   129   265
  Halloween
  Map Problems
  The Christmas Letter
  Archaeology   132   263
  The End of the Rental
  Man and Boy
  All He Knows
  At the Death of Gulliver
  Grandfather's Picture   138   39
  The Grand Birthday
  Boxtrap
  The Cure
  A Schedule of Benefits
  Reading Myself Asleep   144   260
  A Word from the Examiners
  Reading the Writing
  The Museum Shop Catalogue

BOOKS REVIEWED
  Green Business   119   34
  The Life Beside This One   129   233
  The Glass Houses   138   170
  A Schedule of Benefits   154   151

MORRIS, WILLIAM
ARTICLES ABOUT
Two Versions of the Nineteenth Century,
   by Morton Dauwen Zabel   44   270

MORRIS, WILLIAM L.
POEMS
Every Poem Is Perfect   138   337

MORRISON, BLAKE
ARTICLES ABOUT
A Letter from Britain,
   by William Logan   157   222

MORRISON, FRANCES
POEMS
Last Song   21   129
Promises   22   139
In April I Will Give My Heart

MORRISON, JULIA (MARIA)
POEMS
Alone, Will Does Not   95   222
Strawberry Tasters
After Seasons
Prothalamion   101   244

REVIEWS
A Run of Three   101   279
   Letters from Exile and Other Poems,
     by Lawrence P. Spingarn
   Poems 1951-1961,
     by Robert Hazel
   A Run of Jacks, by Richard F. Hugo
Americans and Others   104   115
   The Small Rain,
     by Raymond Roseliep
   Selected Poems,
     by Alain Bosquet
     (Tr. by Samuel Beckett,
     Charles Guenther, Edouard Roditi,
     and Ruth Whitman)
   Selected Poems,
     by Chairil Anwar
     (Tr. by Burton Raffel
     and Nurdin Salam)
   Elks, Mooses, Lions and Other Escapes,
     by David Cornel DeJong
   New Poems and Translations,
     by Richard O'Connell
   Confessions of a Non-Conformist,
     by Paul Petrie

MORRISON, LILLIAN
BOOKS REVIEWED
   Sprints and Distances:
   Sports in Poetry and the Poetry
     in Sport (Ed.)   108   343

MORRISON, MADISON
POEMS
Yesterday   127   333
The Blinding of Homer
I Was Thinking

MORRISON, THEODORE
BOOKS REVIEWED
   The Serpent in the Cloud   38   342
   The Devious Way   65   338
   The Dream of Alcestis
     [Euripides]   78   49

MORRISSEAU-LEROY, FELIX
ARTICLES ABOUT
Letter From Haiti, by Wallace Fowlie   94   398

MORRISSETTE, PAT
POEMS
A Lonely Road   28   140
Where Grey Madonnas Walk
University Portraits   30   145
   Evening Song of a Young Scholar
   Student at Lunch
On Turning a Page in a University Library   35   319
Under the Hemlock Is the Grass

ARTICLES
Notes on Mid-Western Oblivion
   [Thomas Pierce, Julia L. Dumont,
   M. Louisa Chitwood, Sarah Bolton,
   Luella Clark, James Hall, Micah Flint,
   Otway Curry, William D. Gallagher]   34   346

MORROW, ELIZABETH
POEMS
Quatrain   32   315

BOOKS REVIEWED
Quatrains for My Daughter   41   105

MORSE, KATHARINE D(UNCAN)
POEMS
Habitations   31   72
   The Room
   Shanty
Out of the Past   33   129
   Frère Pierre in the Choir Stalls
   The Assyrian Sword
   The Bedspread
The Nativity   37   126

BOOKS REVIEWED
A Gate of Cedar   23   224

MORSE, ROBERT
POEMS
Two Gardens   50   313

The Choice
A Flower Piece
New Year   117   193
Noche Triste   120   268

MORSE, SAMUEL FRENCH

POEMS

Hepaticas   46   141
Fracture of Light   48   146
   Song in the Cold Season
   Vision of a Woman
   Message Found in a Skull
Rehearsal Against Time   50   121
   Meteorology
   Helios: Parhelion
   Beyond Medusa
   Signals Before Storm
From The Seasonal Man   54   141
   Luke as Introspective
   Scene for Further Drama
   Allegory: The Wall
Sonnet ("How can he answer grief?")   57   177
The Source   65   291
Return
Schizothymia: Anonymous
Siste, Viator
Going for the Mail   68   140
The Toys
The Dinosaur: Essay for Gayety
The Circus
Variations: For Hope   70   81
The Days Towards Summer Solstice   74   144
The Summer Light
The Immobile World
The Words   87   335
The Enemy
Elegy in a Dream
Edgar, Solus
Footnote to a Revolution   90   205
Coming Down
In the Line Storm
A Kind of View
Two Voices in a Cave   92   73
The Peaceable Kingdom
Then, Now, Hereafter
Composer to the King   96   150
A Soldier   102   308
The Islands in Summer   104   357
Down the Penobscot   112   87

ARTICLES

A Note on the "Adagia"   90   45

REVIEWS

Works in Progress   50   291
   More than Bread,
     by Joseph Auslander
   Spell Against Time, by David Morton

The Disappearing Castle,
   by Charles Madge   50   342
Out of the Picture,
   by Louis MacNeice   51   104
Tomorrow's Phoenix,
   by Ruth Lechlitner   51   157
Selected Poems, by Allen Tate   51   262
Poems, by Rex Warner   52   36
Trial of a Judge,
   by Stephen Spender   52   292
The Carnival,
   by Frederic Prokosch   53   89
The Earth Complete,
   by Louis MacNeice   53   280
One Part Love,
   by Babette Deutsch   55   332
A Letter from Li Po and Other Poems,
   by Conrad Aiken   88   179
Five Young English Poets   89   193
   My Many-Coated Man,
     by Laurie Lee
   A Way of Looking,
     by Elizabeth Jennings
   The Less Deceived,
     by Philip Larkin
   A Word Carved on a Sill,
     by John Wain
   Song at the Year's Turning,
     by R. S. Thomas
In the Rose of Time: Poems 1931-1956,
   by Robert Fitzgerald   90   110
A Transatlantic View   92   318
   Collected Poems, 1930-1955,
     by George Barker
   The Collected Poems
     of Norman Cameron (1905-1953)
   Visitations, by Louis MacNeice
   Not Waving but Drowning,
     by Stevie Smith
   The Stones of Troy,
     by C. A. Trypanis
   The Sense of Movement,
     by Thom Gunn
O To Be a Dragon,
   by Marianne Moore   96   112
Present Tense   98   319
   The Screens and Other Poems,
     by I. A. Richards
   The Collected Poems of Weldon Kees
     (Ed. by Donald Justice)
   New Poems 1960,
     by Witter Bynner
   The Maximus Poems,
     by Charles Olson
   In the Arriving, by Vincent Ferrini
   Rocky Mountain Poems
     and Rivers Among Rocks,
     by Ralph Gustafson

Poetry and Experience,
  by Archibald MacLeish
  [Lu Chi]   99   191
Early and Late   99   320
  The Astronomy of Love,
    by Jon Stallworthy
  High Sun over Yram,
    by Mary Owings Miller
  Outside the Four Walls of Everything,
    by David Cornel DeJong
  Fact of Crystal,
    by Abbie Huston Evans
The Spectra Hoax,
  by William Jay Smith   99   390
Veterans and Recruits   102   330
  Collected Poems, by Roy Fuller
  Song for a Birth or a Death,
    by Elizabeth Jennings
  A Common Grace,
    by Norman MacCaig
  Poems, 1947-1961,
    by Elizabeth Sewell
  Water, Rock and Sand, by Peter Levi
  The Re-Ordering of the Stones,
    by Jon Silkin
  With Love Somehow, by Tony Connor
  Later Poems, by Austin Clarke
A Beginning   104   253
  The Letters of Robert Frost
    to Louis Untermeyer
    (Ed. by Louis Untermeyer)
  Robert Frost and John Bartlett:
    The Record of a Friendship,
    by Margaret Bartlett Anderson
  Robert Frost: Farm-Poultryman
    (Ed. by Edward Connery Lathem
    and Lawrance Thompson)
  The Poetry of Robert Frost:
    Constellations of Intention,
    by Reuben A. Brower
  The Major Themes of Robert Frost,
    by Radcliffe Squires
Ends and Means   105   404
  The Mad Islands and
    The Administrator: Two Radio Plays,
    by Louis MacNeice
  The Son of Learning:
    A Comedy in Three Acts,
    by Austin Clarke
  Selected Poems, by Stevie Smith
  Visions and Ruins, by Peter Russell
  An Irish Gathering, by Robin Skelton
  In a Blue Smoke, by James Liddy
  Half a Loaf, by Geoffrey Sutton
Four Occasions, Four Anthologies   111   410
  Where Is Vietnam?
    American Poets Respond
    (Ed. by Walter Lowenfels
    and Nan Braymer)

The New Modern Poetry:
    British and American Poetry
    Since World War II
    (Ed. by M. L. Rosenthal)
  The Oxford Book of Scottish Verse
    (Ed. by John MacQueen
    and Tom Scott)
  The Dark Tower:
    Nineteenth Century Narrative Poems
    (Ed. by Dairine Coffey)
Four Generations   112   131
  Collected Poems of Hugh MacDiarmid
    (Ed. by John C. Weston)
  Old-Fashioned Pilgrimage
    and Other Poems,
    by Austin Clarke
  Selected Poems, by C. Day Lewis
  The Solitaries, by Ted Walker
  Life Supports: New and Collected Poems,
    by William Bronk   141   105

BOOKS REVIEWED
  Time of Year   64   337
  The Scattered Causes   89   110
  Opus Posthumous—Poems, Plays, Prose,
    by Wallace Stevens (Ed.)   92   52
  The Changes   107   125

MORTIMER, ANTHONY
POEMS
  Paraclausithyron   138   331
  Grace After Pears

MORTON, DAVID
POEMS
  In the Cemetery   15   256
  The Convict
  Summer   16   196
  Symbols
  These Fields at Evening   20   125
  Out of the Dust   39   187
  As It Was in the Beginning   55   241
  Chorus for Our Play   57   186
  How Then...?
  Name and Address   61   540
  Sanctuary
  Man of Earth   63   79
  Stripped Identity   65   63
  ...Seeing the Changing Leaf
  Tapestry with Figures
  Weather Report
  The Word Will Listen   66   139
  Save Against Winter   69   19

BOOKS REVIEWED
  Ships in Harbor   19   44
  Harvest: A Book of Sonnets   25   283
  Nocturnes and Autumnals   32   227

Shorter Modern Poems, 1900-1931 (Ed.)   41   284
Earth's Processional
Spell Against Time   50   291
Angle of Earth and Sky   59   167
Poems, 1920-1945   67   270

ARTICLES ABOUT
Comment by John Ashbery   151   203

MORWITZ, ERNST
BOOKS REVIEWED
Poems, by Stefan George
   (Tr. with Carol North Valhope)   62   334

MOSBY, KATHERINE
POEMS
Three Readings of Catullus XI   134   326
Correspondents
Watercolor

MOSCOSO, GONZALO ESCUDERO
[See ESCUDERO MOSCOSO,
GONZALO]

MOSER, ALICE
BOOKS REVIEWED
Three Lyric Poets
   (Ed. by Alan Swallow)
   (With Tom H. McNeal
   and Byron Herbert Reece)   61   629

MOSES, W(ILLIAM) R(OBERT)
POEMS
Shore-Line Records   44   128
   Wilson's Terns
   Logical Man and the Evening Sky
Perch in the Water   45   257
The Bluejay and the Linden Tree
Wrecked Automobiles   58   82
Of Pride
Poem in Condemnation
A Trip in a Boat
Sentimental Reflection   67   242
Poem ("Man may be cold...")   68   301
Point of View   71   72
Mummies from Alaska   78   254
Big Dam   91   166
Grackle Days
Battle Report   97   11
Loon-Link

BOOKS REVIEWED
Identities   107   258
Passage   130   167

ARTICLES ABOUT
Poetry as a Jackdaw's Nest,
   by Sherman Conrad   58   90

MOSS, HOWARD
POEMS
The Year   61   370
The Arrow
A Game of Chance   63   1
Rider, Rider
The Shore Remembered
A Love Poem
The Fox Hunt
The Twenty-First Summer
Turning and Turning   64   119
Hudson Passage
Song ("As sunlight's fever...")
Club Death
Snow
Two Views of the Same Sea
A Wreath for Wednesday   67   177
The Fourth Wall
Death of a Grandmother
A Portrait
A Dream Dissolved
The Trial
Air   72   144
Storm
Mariner's Song
The City Lion   73   71
By the Stream   84   145
Those Who Cannot Are Forced
The Peacock
A Swimmer in the Air   89   9
A Song To Be Set to Music
A Marriage
King Midas   90   67
The Silences   101   80
Going Dutch   112   36
Great Spaces
The Love Songs of Horatio Alger, Jr.
Magic Affinities   118   74
The Cardinal   151   105

ARTICLES
Disorder as Myth:
   Hart Crane's The Bridge   62   32

REVIEWS
New Road 1943
   (Ed. by Alex Comfort
   and John Bayliss)   64   46
Short Is the Time, by C. Day Lewis   67   96
Borderline Ballads, by William Plomer   88   396

BOOKS REVIEWED
The Wound and the Weather   72   276
The Toy Fair   85   242
A Swimmer in the Air   91   41
A Winter Come, a Summer Gone:
   Poems 1946-1960   102   260
Finding Them Lost and Other Poems   107   394

Second Nature   114   331
Selected Poems   123   350
A Swim Off the Rocks   132   288
Rules of Sleep   145   348
New Selected Poems   147   291

MOSS, STANLEY
POEMS
Sestina: The Ships Go Nowhere   74   210
And Now There Is No Place to Look
Sailing from the United States   83   203
The Hangman   85   204
A Spanish Landscape   86   324
Grave Song   101   250
Song for Concertina
A Dead Nun's Complaint After the Dance   105   179
Work Song   149   226
Exchange of Gifts
To Ariel Bloch, My Arabist Friend
Songs of the Imaginary Arabs
Following the Saints
Lullaby
Elegy for Myself   151   105
April, Beijing   152   28
A Gambler's Story
The Decadent Poets of Kyoto   153   25
The Lace Makers
Lines for a Stammering Turkish Poet   155   257
New Moon   157   71
Stations   159   151
Swimmer   167   203

REVIEWS
A Poet of Absences   105   198
  Juan de Mairena: Epigrams, Maxims,
    Memoranda, and Memoirs
    of an Apocryphal Professor,
    by Antonio Machado
    (Tr. and ed. by Ben Belitt)
  Castilian Ilexes:
    Versions from Antonio Machado
    (Tr. by Charles Tomlinson
    and Henry Gifford)

BOOKS REVIEWED
The Wrong Angel   109   189
Antiworlds, by Andrei Voznesensky
    (Tr. with others)   110   40
The Intelligence of Clouds   154   283

MOTE, F. W.
BOOKS REVIEWED
The Poet Kao Ch'i: 1336-1374   104   264
The Poet Kao Ch'i: 1336-1374   107   196

MOTION, ANDREW
ARTICLES ABOUT
A Letter from Britain, by William Logan   157   222

MOTOKIYO, (KANZE SABURO)
[See also SEAMI]
POEMS
Nishikigi, A Play
    (Tr. by Ernest Fenollosa)   4   35

MOTOYAZU, KOMPARU ZEMBO
POEMS
Early Snow—a No Play
    (Tr. by Arthur Waley)   15   317

MOTT, MICHAEL
POEMS
Islanders, Inlanders   116   28
The Danaides
Pastoral
From A Personal Alphabet   120   1
Circe and Her Lovers   123   22
The Dice
Light-Year   125   125
Juniper   129   314
Crossing the Line
Meadow Grass   134   15

REVIEWS
A Skull in Salop and Other Poems
    and Poems & Poets,
    by Geoffrey Grigson   116   46
Recent Developments in British Poetry   118   102
    The Tribune's Visitation,
      by David Jones
    The Way of a World,
      by Charles Tomlinson
    Selected Poems, by Dannie Abse
    Travelling, by Michael Hamburger
    Islands, by Edward Brathwaite
    Work in Progress,
      by Peter Redgrove
    Arias from a Love Opera
      and Other Poems,
      by Robert Conquest
    The Animals' Arrival,
      by Elizabeth Jennings
    A Violent Country,
      by David Harsent
    Darker Ends, by Robert Nye
    To See the Matter Clearly,
      by Ruth Fainlight
    Notes to the Hurrying Man,
      by Brian Patten
    The White Room and Landscapes,
      by Lee Harwood
    The Grim Wayfarer,
      by Alan Jackson
    Two Voices, by D. M. Thomas
    The Powers That Be,
      by J. S. Cunningham
    The Blue Winged Bee,
      by Peter Whigham

Penguin Modern Poets 15:
  Alan Bold, Edward Brathwaite,
  Edwin Morgan
Strong Voices   127   159
  Shrapnel and *A Poet's Year,*
    by George MacBeth
  The Principle of Water,
    by Jon Silkin
Rituals Among Formal Ruins   127   352
  Sphere: The Form of a Motion,
    by A. R. Ammons
  Jan. 31, by Albert Goldbarth
  Mysteries of the Horizon,
    by Lawrence Raab
  Looking for Holes in the Ceiling,
    by Stephen Dunn
  [William Wordsworth, René Magritte]
  Collected Poems, by Austin Clarke
    [W. B. Yeats]   128   46

BOOKS REVIEWED
  Absence of Unicorns, Presence of Lions   129   170

MOTTRAM, ERIC
  POEMS
    The Cat Sat on the Mat   93   306

MOULT, THOMAS
  POEMS
    Here for a Time   16   188

  BOOKS REVIEWED
    The Best Poems of 1924 (Ed.)   27   343
    The Best Poems of 1943 (Ed.)   66   111

MOURE, MANUEL MAGALLANES
  [See MAGALLANES MOURE,
  MANUEL]

MOWRER, PAUL SCOTT
  ARTICLES ABOUT
    A Perfect Return,
      by Alice Corbin Henderson   1   87

MOYER, DONALD
  POEMS
    Devil's Relic   110   93
    The Coronation and the Funeral
    The Basin

MOYNAHAN, JULIAN
  POEMS
    White Nights   94   236
    The Graduation Exercise Recollected

  REVIEWS
    Collected Poems: 1940-1978,
      by Karl Shapiro   133   235

Gaudete; Cave Birds:
  An Alchemical Cave Drama;
  and *Moortown,*
  by Ted Hughes
  [Emily Brontë]   138   297

MUCKLEY, HELEN
  POEMS
    Changes   14   69
    The Deceiver

MUELLER, LISEL
  POEMS
    In Memory of Anton Webern,
      Dead September 15, 1945   92   20
    Nine Months Making
    Sunlight and Shadow
    In the Thriving Season   94   293
    The Bride's Complaint
    Afterthoughts on the Lovers
    The Mermaid   96   286
    Bach Transcribing Vivaldi
    The Siege   100   22
    A Long Way from Hell
    A Prayer for Rain   103   355
    The Blind Leading the Blind
    Cicadas
    The Poem of Love
    A Nude by Edward Hopper   110   226
    Names
    Civilizing the Child
    The Gift of Fire
    On Reading an Anthology
      of Postwar German Poetry
    Sleepless   115   108
    Life of a Queen   115   324
    A Poem About the Hounds
      and the Hares
    The Web
    For Richer, for Poorer
    Historical Museum, Manitoulin Island   120   96
    The Artist's Model, ca. 1912   132   71
    Why We Tell Stories   132   203
    The Story
    Found in the Cabbage Patch
    Fugitive   139   127
    What Is Left To Say
    Before the Credits Appear on the Screen
    Full Moon
    Stalking the Poem
    When I Am Asked   151   106
    Missing the Dead   151   453
    Writing in the Eighties
    Poem for My Birthday
    Cavalleria Rusticana
    Public Service Announcement
    Immortality   161   97
    Heartland   163   79

TRANSLATIONS
  Poems by Marie Luise Kaschnitz   136   343

ARTICLES
  Comment
    [Henry Rago]   151   215

REVIEWS
  "To Love the Enigma"   97   323
    Selected Works of Rainer Maria Rilke,
      Vol. I, Prose
      (Tr. by G. Craig Houston)
    Selected Works of Rainer Maria Rilke,
      Vol. II, Poetry
      (Tr. by J. B. Leishman)
  Four German Poets   101   287
    Goethe's Faust
      [Portions]
      (Tr. and ed. by Walter Kaufmann)
    Hölderlin
      (Tr. and ed. by Michael Hamburger)
    Hugo von Hofmannsthal:
      Poems and Verse Plays
      (Ed. by Michael Hamburger)
    Selected Letters of Rainer Maria Rilke
      (Ed. by Harry T. Moore)
  Poetry Chronicle   107   258
    The Last Hero, by Louis Coxe
    Identities, by W. R. Moses
    Dream Barker, by Jean Valentine
    The Pripet Marshes,
      by Irving Feldman
    Half Tame, by Roger Shattuck
    A Planting of Chives, by Gena Ford
    Questions of Travel,
      by Elizabeth Bishop   108   335
  Four Poets   109   48
    The History of the World as Pictures,
      by Nancy Sullivan
    Notes for a Guidebook,
      by Lucien Stryk
    Intent on Earth,
      by Marcia Lee Masters
    Stones from the Rubble,
      by Marion Montgomery
  A Range of Poems, by Gary Snyder   111   254
  German Chronicle   111   336
    Contemporary German Poetry,
      An Anthology
      (Tr. and ed. by Gertrude
      Clorius Schwebell)
      [Gottfried Benn]
    Selected Poems,
      by Günter Grass
      (Tr. by Michael Hamburger
      and Christopher Middleton)
    Manual of Piety (Die Hauspostille),
      by Bertolt Brecht
      (Tr. by Eric Bentley)

Versions of Reality   117   322
  Locations, by Jim Harrison
  Firstborn, by Louise Glück
  Breaking Camp, by Marge Piercy
  The Dream Animal,
    by Charles Wright
  Last Train to Prophetstown,
    by Dave Etter
  Once, by Alice Walker
  Bone Planet, by Louis Hammer
  In the Financial District,
    by Ralph Pomeroy
Five   122   293
  The Charges, by Albert Cook
  History Is Your Own Heartbeat,
    by Michael S. Harper
  Kali Yuga and Flesh:Dream:Book,
    by Robert Kelly
  Luna, by David Meltzer
  The Step, by Ron Loewinsohn
Three Poets   138   170
  The Glass Houses,
    by John N. Morris
  Satan Says, by Sharon Olds
  In the Fourth World,
    by Sandra M. Gilbert

BOOKS REVIEWED
  Dependencies   108   272
  The Private Life   130   342
  Second Language   151   360

ARTICLES ABOUT
  [Note on misprint]   104   124

MUIR, EDWIN
POEMS
  Poem ("O I have seen the heaven...")   49   196
  Then...   56   311
  The Recurrence   58   320
  The Grove
  The Finder Found
  The Trophy   63   146
  To the Old Gods

BOOKS REVIEWED
  First Poems   27   50
  Variations on a Time Theme   45   337
  The Labyrinth   75   239
  Collected Poems, 1921-1951   84   27
  An Autobiography   87   50
  One Foot in Eden   88   393
  The Estate of Poetry   101   272
  Stephen Vincent Benét
    and Edwin Muir
    [Recording]   101   275
  Collected Poems   108   399
  Essays on Literature & Society

ARTICLES ABOUT
"To Fashion the Transitory,"
   by Hayden Carruth   88   389
Edwin Muir, by David Galler   94   330
Rev. of *Four Poets on Poetry:*
   Essays by R. P. Blackmur,
   Yvor Winters, Marianne Moore,
   and Mark Van Doren
   (Ed. by Don Cameron Allen)   96   382
Rev. of *Barbarous Knowledge:*
   Myth in the Poetry of Yeats,
   Graves, and Muir,
   by Daniel Hoffman   112   52
Rev. of *Edwin Muir: Man and Poet,*
   by P. H. Butter   112   206
Rev. of *Defending Ancient Springs,*
   by Kathleen Raine   114   113

MUIR, KENNETH
BOOKS REVIEWED
   The Nettle and the Flower   45   106

MUKERJI, DHAN GOPAL
POEMS
   Old Courtesan's Lament   21   27

MULCAHY, GLORIA ALVERNAZ
BOOKS REVIEWED
   Songs That Untune the Sky   144   297

MULDOON, PAUL
POEMS
   The Throwback   167   75

TRANSLATIONS
   Poem by Nuala Ní Dhomhnaill   167   77

BOOKS REVIEWED
   Madoc: A Mystery   160   94
   Selected Poems: 1968-1987   165   97
   The Annals of Chile   170   37
   The Prince of the Quotidian

ARTICLES ABOUT
   A Letter from Britain,
      by William Logan   157   222
   A Map of Contemporary Irish Poetry,
      by Dennis O'Driscoll   167   94

MULHAUSER, F. L.
BOOKS REVIEWED
   The Poems of Arthur Hugh Clough
   (Ed. with H. F. Lowry
      and A. L. P. Norrington)   82   27

MULHERN, MAUREEN
POEMS
   Lava   162   90

MULKEY, DELISA
POEMS
   A History of Silk   170   222

MULLER, HERBERT J.
ARTICLES
   Speaking of Bookishness
      [J. Donald Adams, Kenneth Burke] 68   283

REVIEWS
   Poets at Work,
      by W. H. Auden, Karl Shapiro,
      Rudolf Arnheim,
      and Donald A. Stauffer
      [Charles D. Abbott]   72   311

MULLINS, HELENE
BOOKS REVIEWED
   Balm in Gilead   36   288

MULLOWNEY, ESTHER C.
POEMS
   Rising Moon   58   199
   Song for a Skip and a Hop

MUMFORD, ERIKA
POEMS
   Pierre Loti Visits
      the Maharaja of Travancore 143   280

MUMFORD, LEWIS
BOOKS REVIEWED
   The American Caravan
   (Ed. with Alfred Kreymborg
      and Paul Rosenfeld)   38   156

MUNDELL, WILLIAM
POEMS
   Butchering the Pig   84   326
   Hill Journey

MUNDORF, FRANK G.
POEMS
   Big Anna   72   23
   Saturday Night in the Accident Ward
   Mrs. Minnie Byers

MUNN, CAROL
POEMS
   View of the Dead   164   144

MUÑOZ MARIN, LUIS
POEMS
   Queries   25   136
   Umbrella
   Voices
   A Death
   At the Stake
   Mercenary

ARTICLES
    A Glance at Spanish-American Poetry   26 158

MUNSON, GORHAM (B.)
ARTICLES
  Correspondence
    [Ezra Pound, J. V. Healy]   57 399

BOOKS REVIEWED
  Robert Frost: A Study
    in Sensibility and Good Sense   31 292

MÜNSTERBERG, MARGARETE
ARTICLES
  Correspondence: Two Poems by Rilke   6 263

BOOKS REVIEWED
  A Harvest of German Verse (Tr.)   14 281

MURANO, SHIRO
POEMS
  Pole Vault
    (Tr. by Satoru Satu
    and Constance Urdang)   88 78

MURASAKI, [(LADY) SHIKIBU]
ARTICLES ABOUT
  Rev. of *The Pillow-Book of Sei Shonagon*
    (Tr. by Arthur Waley)   88 113

MURO, SAISEI
POEMS
  Winter Grass
    (Tr. by Satoru Satu
    and Constance Urdang)   88 95

MURPHY, BRUCE
REVIEWS
  Spirit and Substance   161 339
    At Last We Enter Paradise,
      by Richard Jones
    Hands of the Saddlemaker,
      by Nicholas Samaras
    The Restorers, by W. S. DiPiero
    The Burnt Pages, by John Ash
    Black Eagle Child,
      by Ray A. Young Bear
  Taking Chances   163 97
    Autobiographies, by Alfred Corn
    Concrete Music, by F. D. Reeve
    Night Vision, by Neal Bowers
    A Gilded Lapse of Time,
      by Gjertrud Schnackenberg
    After Russia,
      by Marina Tsvetaeva
      (Tr. by Michael Naydan)
  Modes   164 285
    Greed, by Ai
    Mr. Cogito, by Zbigniew Herbert

    Otherwise, by Eleanor Wilner
    Adversaria, by Timothy Russell
    Voices Over Water, by D. Nurkse
    Velocities, by Stephen Dobyns
  Brief Reviews   166 166
    Graphic Scenes, by Randy Blasing
    Inventing Angels, by Gary Fincke
    Worshipful Company of Fletchers,
      by James Tate
    Thinking the World Visible,
      by Valerie Wohlfeld
    Hinge & Sign, by Heather McHugh
  The State of the World   167 156
    The Simple Truth, by Philip Levine
    New and Selected Poems, by Gary Soto
    The Book of the Dead Man,
      by Marvin Bell
    Odd Mercy, by Gerald Stern
    5° and Other Poems,
      by Nicholas Christopher
    Afterworld, by Christine Garren
  Short Reviews   168 160
    The Neighbor, by Michael Collier
    Kyrie, by Ellen Bryant Voigt
    Red Sauce, Whiskey and Snow,
      by August Kleinzahler
    Time & Money, by William Matthews
    New and Selected Poems,
      by Donald Justice
  The Big Poem   170 90
    The Throne of the Third Heaven of the
      Nations Millennium General Assembly,
      by Denis Johnson
    Dark Fields of the Republic,
      by Adrienne Rich
    Selected Poems, by C. K. Williams
    On the Great Atlantic Rainway,
      Selected Poems 1950-1988,
      by Kenneth Koch

MURPHY, CHARLES R.
POEMS
  The Corn-Field   17 13
  Growth   18 235
    Advent
    Sown
    To Earth
    Winter
    Spring
    Humility
    Mid-May
  The Night of the Soul   45 84

MURPHY, DENNIS
POEMS
  Petal-Fall   40 137

BOOKS REVIEWED
  Boy with a Silver Plow   40 232

MURPHY, KAY A.
POEMS
   Christmas Card   145   145

MURPHY, RICHARD
POEMS
   The Poet on the Island   98   224
   Saint Gormgall's Well   118   333
   Little Hunger
   Corncrake
   Gallows Riddle
   Mangoes   167   88

ARTICLES
   Correspondence:
     Irish Bards and American Reviewers
     [Hayden Carruth, Patrick Kavanagh]   102   61

BOOKS REVIEWED
   The Battle of Aughrim   114   335

ARTICLES ABOUT
   A Map of Contemporary Irish Poetry,
     by Dennis O'Driscoll   167   94

MURPHY, WILLIAM J.
POEMS
   The Deeper Mine   76   137

MURRAY, ALBERT
ARTICLES ABOUT
   Rev. of *The Venus Hottentot*,
     by Elizabeth Alexander   158   214

MURRAY, AMY
BOOKS REVIEWED
   November Hereabout   57   395

MURRAY, CATHERINE
POEMS
   A Short Poem   109   21

MURRAY, DONALD M.
POEMS
   Waiting for a Poem   153   331
   At 64, Talking Without Words   155   407

MURRAY, G. E.
POEMS
   Northern Exposures   148   79
   Flying Low, Near France, Among Birds

MURRAY, GILBERT
BOOKS REVIEWED
   The Classical Tradition in Poetry   32   289

MURRAY, JOAN
BOOKS REVIEWED
   Poems (Ed. by Grant Code)   70   335

MURRAY, LES (A.)
POEMS
   The Head-Spider   169   64

BOOKS REVIEWED
   The Vernacular Republic   143   163
   The Daylight Moon   156   158
   The Rabbiter's Bounty: Collected Poems   160   157
   The Boys Who Stole the Funeral:
     A Novel Sequence

ARTICLES ABOUT
   Towards a Contemporary
   Australian Poetics,
     by John Kinsella   169   94

MURRAY, PHILIP
POEMS
   Still Life   71   180
   The Corinthian   73   24
   Rockabye Baby
   The Finches   76   77
   The Hex Sign   77   202
   Harmony
   The Christening
   De Arte Illuminandi   82   80
   Spider Poem   84   324
   Firefly: A Japanese Romance   85   208
   Song Against Sorrow   89   289
   L'Ogre a l'Estime   92   16
   Charm for the Tooth-Ache
   A Song of Love-Longing
   Weeds   97   83
   The Captive   104   159
   The Three Blind Mice at Acapulco
   Fu on the Owl   114   314
   T'ang   118   125
   Confessions of Philosopher Ting
   The Dean of St. Hilary   120   224
   Lourdes
   Fantasia on a Theme by Mrs. Gaskell
   The Moselle   123   73
   A Secret Life of E. A. Poe:
     Notes for a New Cryptology   124   335
   Eros as the Genius of Death   128   204
   Hebi-Gami: The Serpent Bridegroom   130   12
   On the Death of Steele's Father   135   264

REVIEWS
   Dominations:
     Rational, Romantic, Ironic   120   230
     The School for Wives, by Molière
     (Tr. by Richard Wilbur)
     The Collected Poetry of Aldous Huxley
     (Ed. by Donald Watt)
     Edwin Arlington Robinson,
     by Yvor Winters
     Perilous Arcady   120   304

The Eclogues of Virgil,
   by David R. Slavitt
Sappho to Valéry:
   Poems in Translation,
   by John Frederick Nims
Twenty Love Poems
   and a Song of Despair,
   by Pablo Neruda
   (Tr. by W. S. Merwin)
Neruda and Vallejo:
   Selected Poems
   (Ed. by Robert Bly)
   (Tr. by Robert Bly,
   John Knoepfle,
   and James Wright)

BOOKS REVIEWED
Poems After Martial (Tr.)   113   188

MURRY, J(OHN) MIDDLETON
BOOKS REVIEWED
Poems,
   by Anne, Countess
   of Winchelsea (Ed.)   34   111
Leaves of Grass
   One Hundred Years After
   (Ed. by Milton Hindus)
   [Contrib.]   87   183
Keats   92   121
William Blake   107   65

MURTON, JESSIE WILMORE
POEMS
Street Lights at Dusk   55   181

MUS, DAVID [Pseud.]
POEMS
"Rain..."   109   299
Blake's Seasons   111   226
Four Last Poems   114   107
   ("The poor soil around here...")
   ("'I see nothing,' she said...")
   ("You've been waiting...")
   ("I go back, dream shapes out...")
Journey of the Magi   115   175
Wall   117   251
An Evening Walk,
   Some Years Later   118   270
Alfoxton Park   122   283
From *The Joy of Cooking*   124   22
   Recipe
   Cooked Goose
   Temperatures
   La Cuisine Française
   Conserves
The Window   128   1
Crust and Key   128   330
December   129   125

REVIEWS
The Waste Land: A Facsimile
   and Transcript of the Original Drafts
   Including the Annotations of Ezra Pound,
   by T. S. Eliot (Ed. by Valerie Eliot)   121   156
Dans le leurre du seuil, by Yves Bonnefoy
   [Paul Cézanne]   128   163

MUSELLI, VINCENT
ARTICLES ABOUT
   Correspondence from Jean Catel   16   343

MUSGROVE, CHARLES HAMILTON
POEMS
The Scarlet Thread   7   17

MUSKE, CAROL
POEMS
The Separator   145   66
Sounding
Little L. A. Villanelle   161   133
Kenya   161   334

BOOKS REVIEWED
Wyndmere   147   156
Red Trousseau   164   39

MUSSER, BENJAMIN
POEMS
A Girl Is Singing   38   21

BOOKS REVIEWED
Untamed   31   228
How to Profit from That Impulse
   (Ed. with Lucia Trent
   and Ralph Cheyney)   34   56
Bucolics and Caviar   41   165

MYERS, E. LUCAS
POEMS
Journey in the Tessellated Corn   91   181
Ballade of the Early Seas

MYERS, GARY
POEMS
Invitation from a Deceased Spanish Poet   148   215
Ode to Sleep

MYERS, JACK
POEMS
Wing to Root   119   148
We Never Talk
The Trap
The Invention of Mushrooms
Visitation Rites   152   145
Bread, Meat, Greens, and Soap   162   78
The Stripper
It's Not My Cup of Tea   168   330

"N. A. C."
  [See CRAWFORD,
  NELSON ANTRIM]

NABOKOV, VLADIMIR
  BOOKS REVIEWED
  Three Russian Poets, Selections from
    Pushkin, Lermontov, and Tyutchev (Tr.)   66   289
  Poems   95   373
  Eugene Onegin, A Novel in Verse
    by Alexander Pushkin (Tr.)   106   236

NAHILL, ART
  POEMS
  Sarajevo   168   280

NAIDEN, JAMES
  POEMS
  The Face   118   29

  REVIEWS
  Quickly Aging Here:
    Some Poets of the 1970's
    (Ed. by Geof Hewitt)   118   46
  Six Variations   120   115
    Against Emptiness, by Paul Zweig
    The Gallery Goers,
      by Raymond DiPalma
    Leaving by the Closet Door,
      by Stephen Shrader
    Collected Poems 1968: My Life by Water,
      by Lorine Niedecker
    The Intricate Land, by John Knoepfle
    Argument for Love,
      by James Humphrey

NAIDU, SAROJINI
  BOOKS REVIEWED
  The Golden Threshold   10   47
  The Sceptered Flute: Songs of India   35   169

NAKANO, SHIGEHARU
  POEMS
  Good-By Before Dawn
    (Tr. by Satoru Satu
    and Constance Urdang)   88   80

NAPIER, JOHN T.
  POEMS
  A Letter to V. R. Lang   90   155

  BOOKS REVIEWED
  I Walk Through the Valley   102   335

NAPIER, MARGARET
  BOOKS REVIEWED
  Songs of the Dead   17   276

NARASIMHASWAMY, K. R.
  POEMS
  Wasn't It You?
    (Tr. by K. Raghavendra Rao)   93   266

NARDI, MARCIA
  POEMS
  They Said It Is All Clear Now   75   331
  Was It the Honey-Hearted Vowel?   84   212

  ARTICLES ABOUT
  Rev. of Paterson (Book Two),
    by William Carlos Williams   74   37

NASH, OGDEN
  ARTICLES ABOUT
  Poetry on Records,
    by Harry T. Moore   57   338

NASSAR, EUGENE
  BOOKS REVIEWED
  Wallace Stevens:
    An Anatomy of Figuration   109   201

NASSAUER, RUDOLF
  BOOKS REVIEWED
  Poems   74   48

NATHAN, LEONARD E.
  POEMS
  The Sky Hung Idiot Blue   87   223
  Between Town and City   89   19
  Figure in the Distance   90   78
  A Mexican in Passing
  Winter Obsessed Them   91   373

Children Defy the Winter King
Homage to The King's Choir
  We Did the Best   93   377
Looking Down
Seated Lovers Quarreling
  at the River's Edge
Winter of Possibles   95   347
Lydia, You Old Whore   97   89
To One Who Lost Her Son
Distance Calls
Wisdom of the Talmud
Cain
War Games
Fathers and Sons   101   339
The Moods of a Matchmaker
Remember To Close the Door
  As You Go Out   104   224
The Signs
Winter Tune
Translation from the Wind of Guadalajara   106   395
Thoughts Like Hawks
I Would Write More
In Disheartening Rain Before the Parthenon   109   14
Annunciation
"No Guide, No Sight"   111   301
Translating an Ancient Fragment

REVIEWS
  Three American Poets   90   325
    Covenant with Earth, by Lew Sarett
    New and Selected Poems,
      by Kenneth Fearing
    The Shadow on the Hour,
      by Ruth Lechlitner

BOOKS REVIEWED
  Western Reaches   93   399
  Glad and Sorry Seasons   104   108
  The Day the Perfect Speakers Left   117   261
  Returning Your Call   130   221

NATHAN, ROBERT
BOOKS REVIEWED
  A Cedar Box   35   170
  A Winter Tide   58   103
  Dunkirk   60   152
  Morning in Iowa   64   231
  The Darkening Meadows   67   170
  The Green Leaf   77   215

NATHANIEL, ISABEL
POEMS
  Sick at the Gulf   156   286

NAYDAN, MICHAEL
BOOKS REVIEWED
  After Russia,
    by Marina Tsvetaeva (Tr.)   163   97

NEAME, ALAN
POEMS
  Thursday Afternoon   91   311
  Medical College: Levant
  Conversation Piece, 1957
  The Riposte
  Night Scene
  An Academic Occasion   93   351
  Correcting
  Meeting

REVIEWS
  London Chronicle I   94   124
    The Skylark and Other Poems,
      by Ralph Hodgson
    Collected Poems,
      by John Betjeman
  London Chronicle II   94   196
    The Next Word,
      by Thomas Blackburn
    The Cocks of Hades,
      by C. A. Trypanis
    Poems, by Rex Taylor
  Aware or Disregarding   94   405
    Songs, by Christopher Logue
    Possible Laughter,
      by James Michie
    Domestic Interior,
      by Laurence Lerner
    The Loss of the Magyar,
      by Patricia Beer

NEDDERMANN, EMMY
ARTICLES ABOUT
  Juan Ramón Jiménez:
    The Landscape of the Soul,
      by Rachel Frank   82   224

NEESER, ROBERT W.
BOOKS REVIEWED
  American Naval Songs and Ballads (Ed.)   52   299

NEIHARDT, JOHN G.
POEMS
  The Death of Agrippina
    [Drama]   2   33

BOOKS REVIEWED
  The Song of Hugh Glass   7   264
  The Quest   9   324
  The Song of Three Friends   17   94
  Two Mothers
    (*Eight Hundred Rubles* and *Agrippina*)   19   51
  The Song of the Indian Wars   27   328
  Poetic Values:
    Their Reality and Our Need of Them   28   350
  Collected Poems of...   30   99
  The Song of Jed Smith   59   164

ARTICLES ABOUT
  The P.S.A. Prizes and Ours,
    by Harriet Monroe 17 88
  The Nebraska Laureate,
    by Harriet Monroe 18 212

NEILSON, JOHN SHAW
  BOOKS REVIEWED
    Ballad and Lyrical Poems 25 284

NEIMAN, GILBERT
  POEMS
    The Anarchic Architecht 60 143
    The Furious Hero
    Keen

  ARTICLES
    To Write Poetry Nowadays You Have
      to Have One Foot in the Grave
      [Paul Eluard, T. S. Eliot,
      Paul Valéry, Stephen Spender] .. 74 30

  BOOKS REVIEWED
    Blood Wedding,
      by Federico García Lorca (Tr.) .. 56 343

NELSON, ALZIRE
  POEMS
    A Negation 23 256
    Sequoias

NELSON, ERIC
  POEMS
    Thanksgiving 153 102
    Miscarriage
    Pleasures of the Flesh 156 151
    A Mind of Summer 158 259
    Estate Sale 168 93
    The Remains

NELSON, ERNEST W.
  ARTICLES
    Correspondence:
      Notes on German Poetry
      [Reginald Wilenski] 6 208
    Correspondence: About Emerson .. 11 166

NELSON, PAUL
  POEMS
    Rhodos 145 329

NELSON, PETER
  POEMS
    California: Late Afternoon 114 97

NELSON-DEIGHAN, SHANNON
  POEMS
    Victorian Hummingbird Case .. 164 281
    For the Imagists at the British Museum .. 164 319

NEMEROV, HOWARD
  POEMS
    Sigmund Freud 62 261
    Moralities 80 199
    Sunderland 87 35
    Cloud-Seeding 88 382
    A Clock with No Hands
    A Speckled Stone Mirror
    The Battenkill in Winter
    A Mobile of Carved Wooden Fish
    The Wheel King
    Political Reflection
    Art Song
    A Day on the Big Branch 91 71
    Holding the Mirror Up to Nature
    Steps for a Dancer
    The Dancer's Reply
    Sarabande
    Painting a Mountain Stream
    Runes 93 281
    Death and the Maiden 94 396
    The End of Summer School .. 99 81
    To the Mannequins
    The Dragonfly
    The Private Eye
    De Anima 100 141
    Vermeer
    Prometheus at Radio City
    These Words Also
    Idea 101 84
    Being of Three Minds 117 149
    Embarrassment Lives! On TV, Anyhow
    Solipsism & Solecism
    Item
    Prism
    Behavior
    Quaerendo Invenietis
    Beginner's Guide 119 6
    Druidic Rimes
    The Poet as Eagle Scout
    Threshold
    Snowflakes
    A Memory of My Friend
    Creation Myth on a Moebius Strip
    The Puzzle 120 216
    To the Poets
    Analogue
    Hide & Seek
    A Riddle the Sphinx Forgot
    30th Anniversary Report of the Class of '41
    On Getting Out of Vietnam
    Knowledge
    To D—, Dead by Her Own Hand
    Epitaph
    Sigmund Freud 121 23
    The Western Approaches 126 249
    Boy with Book of Knowledge
    Du rêve, de la mathématique, et de la mort

The Backward Look
Aftermath
Late Summer
Equations of a Villanelle
Figures of Thought
Amnesty
Novelists
Fugue
Cosmic Comics
The Spy
The Metaphysical Automobile
Hero with Girl and Gorgon
The Four Ages
The Weather of the World
Near the Old People's Home
Walking Down Westgate in the Fall
A Common Saw
Flower Arrangements
Learning the Trees
Seeing Things
TV
Reflexion of a Novelist
Exasperations of a Novelist
Fiction
Waiting Rooms
There
Conversing with Paradise
Playing the Inventions
Origin
Casting
Plane
Watching Football on TV
Translation
An Ending
The Revenants (After a Movie)   134   7
Remembering Ford Madox Ford
  and Parade's End
Pomp
Monet
Coming Home to New York
  When It Was Said To Be
  Going Down the Drain
A Moon Eclipsed   141   18
A Sprig of Dill
Learning
Adam and Eve in Later Life
Disseverings, Divorces
Poetics

ARTICLES
Correspondence   120   365
Thirteen Ways of Looking at a Skylark
  [W. B. Yeats]   126   294

REVIEWS
Sleep in a Nest of Flames,
  by Charles Henri Ford   76   234
Poems: North & South—A Cold Spring,
  by Elizabeth Bishop   87   179

Naked Poetry:
  Recent American Poetry in Open Forms
  (Ed. by Stephen Berg
  and Robert Mezey)   116   35

BOOKS REVIEWED
The Image and the Law   71   94
Guide to the Ruins   76   365
The Salt Garden   86   168
Mirrors and Windows: Poems   93   178
The Next Room of the Dream   102   389
Poetry and Fiction   105   397
Journal of the Fictive Life   109   332
Poets on Poetry (Ed.)   110   119
The Blue Swallows   112   418
Gnomes & Occasions   123   165
The Western Approaches: Poems 1973-75   129   164
Collected Poems   132   351
Figures of Thought: Speculations
  on the Meaning of Poetry & Other Essays
Sentences   138   344
War Stories:
  Poems About the Long Ago and Now   151   419
A Howard Nemerov Reader   159   346

ARTICLES ABOUT
"Sacred Beings":
  Writers in Recorded Conversation,
  by Michael Milburn   146   101
[Note]   153   50

NEMSER, PAUL
POEMS
Who Hungers for a Face that Fades Away
  (With Mark Rudman)   122   28

NERBER, JOHN
POEMS
Go, Lovely Rose   53   124
The Trench
The Nightingale
Sanctus
The Brook   57   140
A Poem ("How would this house...")
The Paradox
Ghosts   61   433
The Bridge
Preface for a Friend's Book
Grendel
O Doom What of Our Dream   64   141
Shipwreck
Blood Wedding
The Egoist
The Factory
The Spectre Image   66   260
Family Reunion
Yorick
Hamlet

Four Saints	67	303
Sebastian		
Teresa		
Augustine		
Cecilia		
The Captive Heart	68	185
Castaway		
Subway Station		
Sleep Poem		
The Grandmother	72	130
Above Me Perched in Air		

REVIEWS

The Poem of Bunker Hill,		
by Harry Brown	59	283
A Man in the Divided Sea,		
by Thomas Merton	69	165
The Faultless Shore,		
by Edward Weismiller	70	52

BOOKS REVIEWED

The Spectre Image	70	155

NERI, GIAMPIERO

POEMS

Sovrapposizioni / Overlappings		
(Tr. by Rebecca Messbarger)	155	74

NERUDA, PABLO
[Pseud. of RICARDO REYES,
NEFTALI]

POEMS

Fantom of the Freighter		
(Tr. by H. R. Hays)	62	62
Discoverers		
(Tr. by Angel Flores)	69	13
Widower's Tango		
(Tr. by Dudley Fitts)	70	124
"White thighs, hillocks of whiteness..."	74	315
"'Tis the morrow full of storm..."		
(Tr. by J. B. Donne)		
From the Canto General	79	204
The Poet		
Leviathan		
The Dictators		
Hunger in the South		
Open Sea		
Horseman in Rain		
(Tr. by Ben Belitt)		
Sexual Water		
(Tr. by James Wright)	96	152
Soldier Asleep	98	359
Old Ladies by the Sea		
Alberto Rojas Jiménez		
Comes Flying		
(Tr. by Ben Belitt)		
Party's End		
(Tr. by Ben Belitt)	112	183

BOOKS REVIEWED

3 Spanish American Poets		
(With Carlos Pellicer		
and Jorge Carrera Andrade)		
(Tr. by Joseph Leonard Grucci)	62	111
Selected Poems by...		
(Tr. by Angel Flores)	65	225
Residence on Earth		
(Tr. by Angel Flores)	70	150
Canto General	80	116
Selected Poems of...		
(Tr. and ed. by Ben Belitt)	101	349
The Elementary Odes of...		
(Tr. by Carlos Lozano)		
Bestiary		
(With Antonio Frasconi)		
(Tr. by Elsa Neuberger)	111	46
The Heights of Macchu Picchu		
(Tr. by Nathaniel Tarn)	112	191
Twenty Poems		
(Tr. by Robert Bly		
and James Wright)	113	338
Twenty Love Poems and		
a Song of Despair		
(Tr. by W. S. Merwin)	120	304
Neruda and Vallejo: Selected Poems		
(Ed. by Robert Bly)		
(Tr. by Robert Bly, John Knoepfle,		
and James Wright)		

ARTICLES ABOUT

The New American and		
His Point of View Toward Poetry,		
by Jorge Carrera Andrade		
(Tr. by H. R. Hays)	62	88

NETHERCOT, ARTHUR H.

POEMS

Triad	20	316

NETO, JOÃO CABRAL DE MELO
[See DE MELO NETO, JOÃO]

NEUBERG, VICTOR B.

ARTICLES ABOUT

London Letter,		
by D. S. Savage	51	277

NEUBERGER, ELSA

BOOKS REVIEWED

Bestiary,		
by Pablo Neruda (Tr.)	111	46

NEUGASS, JAMES

POEMS

Earthen Terror	44	14
A Landscape of Negatives		

NEVILLE, HELEN
POEMS
   As We Are   38   312
      The Problem
      A Prophecy
   Song ("Bury it in the wind...")   41   123
   Sea Tribute   47   317
   Time's Embrace   52   191

NEVILLE, MARIE
REVIEWS
   The Oxford Dictionary of Nursery Rhymes
      (Ed. by Iona and Peter Opie)
      [J. O. Halliwell]   84   167

NEWBERRY, JOHN STRONG
TRANSLATIONS
   Poems by Paul Fort   18   293

BOOKS REVIEWED
   Selected Poems and Ballads
      of Paul Fort (Tr.)   21   161

NEWBOLT, HENRY
BOOKS REVIEWED
   A New Study of English Poetry 16   288
   Poems New and Old   20   282

NEWCOMB, RICHARD
POEMS
   Pressing and Mending   143   289
   People Get the Faces

NEWLOVE, JOHN
BOOKS REVIEWED
   Elephants, Mothers & Others 108   45
   Moving in Alone
   What They Say   115   353
   Black Night Window

**NEWMAN, C(HARLES) H(ENRY)
[Pseud.]**
POEMS
   The Last Superstition   48   82
   When the Earth Is Cold

NEWMAN, ISRAEL
POEMS
   The Rubins   40   140
      Baileh Rubin
      Sam Rubin
      Irving Rubin
   Torah   46   84
   Dynamo   48   313
   Paper in Wind   54   305
   Strangers   63   252
   The Man with the Plough
   Walkers at Night   66   304

   Garrets
   Homecoming
   Silent Things

ARTICLES
   The Physiology of Consciousness
     and Its Relation to Poetry
     [Karl Shapiro]   73   96
   The Physiology of Consciousness
     and Its Relation to Poetry
     [Karl Shapiro]   73   162

NEWMAN, MICHAEL
POEMS
   Negative Passage   119   221

NEWMAN, P(AUL) B.
POEMS
   Making a Poem   65   298
   Notes on the African Campaign
   Parchman, Mississippi   73   82

NEWMAN, PRESTON
POEMS
   The Man Who Ran Away from a Bomb 61   542
   Galileo Goes to War   63   184
   The Indians in the Movies Say "Ugh!" 65   128

NEWMAN, STANLEY S.
POEMS
   Specimens   36   26
      Motorcar
      Double Sight
      Among Skyscrapers

NEWMANN, JOAN
POEMS
   Rounders   167   86
   Rice

NEWTON, DAVID
POEMS
   Central Park   64   67

NEWTON, (BREAN) DOUGLAS
POEMS
   The Cherubs of Venus   68   130
   Night Piece
   Bishop and Naturalist
   Gaity of Descendants
   Archaic Art
   Onionskin Man   70   243

NEWTON, KATHERINE
POEMS
   New Year's Day   27   196
   Gipsy
   Epitaph

The Philosopher	28	199
Six O'Clock	30	266
Inarticulate	32	25
To the Turning of Wheels	34	72

NEWTON, MARY LESLIE
POEMS

Two Fields	54	83

NICHOL, B P [B. P. NICHOLS]
BOOKS REVIEWED

Journeying & The Returns	112	276
The Cosmic Chef:		
An Evening of Concrete (Ed.)	119	356

NICHOLL, LOUISE TOWNSEND
POEMS

Waves	17	18
Beauty		
Timelessness	18	249
Hymn	24	141
July Moon	46	188
The Past Is a Foreign Port	58	248

BOOKS REVIEWED

Dawn in Snow	61	637
Life Is the Flesh	75	178
Collected Poems	84	175
The World's One Clock	95	248

NICHOLS, B. P.
[See NICHOL, B P]

NICHOLS, LEONORA
POEMS

Nocturne	32	251

NICHOLS, ROBERT
POEMS

Two Songs of the Enigma	14	184
Modern Love Song		
A Wandering Thing		
The Flower of Flame	15	63

BOOKS REVIEWED

Ardors and Endurances	12	274
Aurelia and Other Poems	19	162

NICHOLS, ROSS
BOOKS REVIEWED

Prose Chants and Proems	63	172

NICHOLSON, JOHN
ARTICLES ABOUT

Rev. of *Nikal Seyn and Decoration Day*,		
by Louis Coxe	111	43

NICHOLSON, NORMAN
POEMS

Song for 7 P.M.	51	303

Sonnet for an Introvert	53	179
The Crocus	66	256

BOOKS REVIEWED

Five Rivers	67	274

ARTICLES ABOUT

Criticism and Orthodoxy,		
by D. S. Savage	64	279

NICKLAUS, FREDERICK
POEMS

Old Woman Setting Silver	103	370
The Hands Are First to Believe		

BOOKS REVIEWED

The Man Who Bit the Sun	106	370

NICOLAS BLANCO, ANTONIO
POEMS

Intimate Prayer (Tr. by Muna Lee)	26	143

NICOLL, ALLARDYCE
BOOKS REVIEWED

Chapman's Homer:		
The Iliad (I) and The Odyssey (II) (Ed.)	91	60

NICOLL, W. ROBERTSON
BOOKS REVIEWED

The Complete Works of Emily Brontë,		
Vol. I—Poetry		
(Ed. with Clement Shorter)	9	259

NICOLSON, HAROLD
BOOKS REVIEWED

Paul Verlaine	20	223

NICOLSON, J. N.
BOOKS REVIEWED

King of the Black Isles	24	105
The Sainted Courtesan	27	216
The Drums of Yle		

NÍ DHOMHNAILL, NUALA
POEMS

Mo Mháistir Dorcha/My Dark Master		
(Tr. by Paul Muldoon)	167	76

ARTICLES ABOUT

A Map of Contemporary Irish Poetry,		
by Dennis O'Driscoll	167	94

NIEDECKER, LORINE
POEMS

Spirals	42	308
Promise of Brilliant Funeral		
When Ecstasy Is Inconvenient		
Three Poems	102	302
("River-marsh-drowse...")		

("Prosperity is poverty...")
("Now in one year...")
Five Poems   106   341
  ("(To my pres-/sure pump...)")
  ("Consider at the outset...")
  March
  ("Spring/stood there...")
  ("(The park/'a darling walk...')")
Four Poems   111   159
  ("Young in Fall I said...")
  ("We are what the seas...")
  ("Fall...")
  ("Smile/to see the lake...")

BOOKS REVIEWED
  New Goose   70   108
  My Friend Tree   102   42
  North Central   117   261
  Collected Poems 1968:
    My Life by Water   120   115

NIENABER, ALLISON
POEMS
  The Just Man   25   21

NIFLIS, MICHAEL
POEMS
  Movement   121   315

NIKOLAIDIS, ARISTOTLE
POEMS
  Word   139   84
  A Brief Code for Poets
  Views of an Ascetic
    (Tr. by Kimon Friar)

ARTICLES ABOUT
  Post-War Greek Poets,
    by Kimon Friar   139   99

NIMS, JOHN FREDERICK
POEMS
  Parting: 1940   56   307
  Prayer   59   184
  To Lovers
  Ventriloquism
  Love
  Mozart
  Apocalypse   60   175
  The Golden Age
  Elegy ("We saw you last...")
  From the Greek Anthology
  Seamusic
  In Our Time   61   525
    Slums
    Penny Arcade
    Ode: Chamber and Soul
    To Friends of Other Summers

  Seashore
  Colt Automatic
  Elevated   62   297
  Tennis Trophy
  Dollar Bill
  Movie
  Shot Down at Night
  The Blonde Sonata
  Clock Symphony   64   1
  The Woolen Bug
  Cradlesong
  Pigskin Abbey   67   82
  The Midnight Special
  Sign of Fever
  Nachtlied
  The Iron Pastoral   69   262
    All-Nite Lunchroom
    Love Poem
    Queen Street West
    Dimension
  Fairy Tale   75   18
  The Magical View of Nature
  The Masque of Blackness   75   249
  Ishtar   78   125
  Conclusion
  Parallax at Djebel-Muta
  Decline and Fall   83   323
  Etruscan Tomb
  The Young Ionia
  Florence   89   83
  Old River Road   95   263
  Parting: 1940   121   24
  Censorship   122   77
  A Scholar Wonders
  Near the Airport
  Clock Without Hands
  Worldly Success
  Verse Translator
  Phryne
  Cardiological   129   256
  Dropping the Names   151   107
  The Six-Cornered Snowflake   155   191

TRANSLATIONS
  Poems by St. John of the Cross   80   144
  Poems of St. John of the Cross   92   304
  Poem by Alfredo Rizzardi   94   321
  Poem by Ausias March   98   354
  Poems by Antonio Machado   98   384
  Poems by Goethe   116   345
  Poems by Mario Santagostini   155   149

ARTICLES
  In Honor of Allen Tate,
    by John Frederick Nims   135   63
  John Ciardi:
    The Many Lives of Poetry   148   283

REVIEWS

Opiate, Not Scalpel   60   155
> Tumultuous Shore,
>> by Arthur Davison Ficke
> There Will Be Bread and Love,
>> by Robert P. Tristram Coffin

Two Intellectual Poets   61   505
> Eleven Poems on the Same Theme,
>> by Robert Penn Warren
> The Second World,
>> by R. P. Blackmur
> The Lincoln Lyrics and
> The Garden Is Political,
>> by John Malcolm Brinnin   61   622

Dinner Party, by Jessica Nelson North   62   167

Two Catholic Poets   65   264
> Thirty Poems, by Thomas Merton
> Land of Unlikeness, by Robert Lowell

Poems, by A. M. Klein   66   104

Unit of Five,
> by Louis Dudek, Ronald Hambleton,
> P. K. Page, Raymond Souster,
> and James Wreford   66   334

The Poems of St. John of the Cross
> (Tr. by Roy Campbell)   80   153

BOOKS REVIEWED

Five Young American Poets:
> Third Series, 1944
>> (With Eve Merriam, Jean Garrigue,
>> Tennessee Williams, and
>> Alejandro Carrión)   66   95

The Iron Pastoral   71   149

A Fountain in Kentucky and Other Poems   77   105

Andromache (Tr.),
> in The Complete Greek Tragedies:
> Euripides III
> (Ed. by David Grene
> and Richmond Lattimore)   95   190

The Poems of St. John of the Cross (Tr.)   95   379

The Poem Itself
> (Ed. with Stanley Burnshaw,
> Dudley Fitts, and Henri Peyre)   98   56

Of Flesh and Bone   112   337

The Poems of St. John of the Cross,
> English Versions Newly Revised
> and Rewritten (Tr.)   113   262

Sappho to Valéry: Poems in Translation   120   304

The Six-Cornered Snowflake
> and Other Poems   159   32

The Six-Cornered Snowflake

Zany in Denim

ARTICLES ABOUT

For the Record, by George Dillon   73   28

[Note]   144   117

Comments by Carole Oles
> and Wesley McNair   151   222

NIRALA
[SURJAKUMAR TRIPATHI]

POEMS

The Stone-Breaker
> (Tr. by Romila Thapar)   93   255

NISHIWAKI, JUNZABURO

POEMS

Rain   88   75

The Sun
> (Tr. by Satoru Satu
> and Constance Urdang)

Dry Sedge   103   160

Parabola

NIST, JOHN

BOOKS REVIEWED

Modern Brazilian Poetry (Ed.)   103   261

In the Middle of the Road,
> Selected Poems of Carlos Drummond
> de Andrade (Ed. and tr.)   111   46

NITCHIE, ELIZABETH

BOOKS REVIEWED

The Criticism of Literature   34   161

NOGUCHI, YONE

POEMS

The Poet   2   71

Hokku   15   67
> ("Bits of song...")
> ("Full of faults...")
> ("But the march to life...")
> ("Song of sea in rain...")

The Keepsake   28   243

BOOKS REVIEWED

The Spirit of Japanese Poetry   7   89

Seen and Unseen:
> or Monologues of a Homeless Snail   20   162

Selected Poems

The Ukiyoye Primitives   43   92

ARTICLES ABOUT

Poetic Prose and Vers Libre,
> by Alice Corbin Henderson   2   70

Yone Noguchi, by Eunice Tietjens   15   96

NOGUERE, SUZANNE

POEMS

Pervigilium Veneris   121   324

Turbo Marmoratus Linné

With Their Heads   125   339

The Means

NOLAN, JAMES

POEMS

The Widow   134   99

Mr. Rock

BOOKS REVIEWED
Why I Live in the Forest   130   167
What Moves Is Not the Wind   138   231

NOLL, BINK
POEMS
The Blank Room   118   338
Gathering Watercress
Walls   123   13

BOOKS REVIEWED
The Center of the Circle   102   182
The House   147   227

NOLTE, JULIUS M.
POEMS
Man and Woman   32   318

NOON, WILLIAM T.
BOOKS REVIEWED
Poetry and Prayer   112   356

NORBERG, P. G.
[See NORDEN, PETER]

NORCROSS, ELLINOR L.
POEMS
In Life's Attic   24   305

NORDEN, HEINZ
TRANSLATIONS
Rilke: Letters to Benvenuta   77   276

NORDEN, PETER
[P. G. NORBERG]
POEMS
Good Morning   8   185

NORDFORS, MARGARET
POEMS
A Shape in Water   103   301

NORDHAUS, JEAN
POEMS
From a Window in Jerusalem   163   33
Silk
The Weekly Loaf
The Stammer
The Natural Sonneteer   164   69
Yiddish   165   322
Moses Mendelssohn Enters Berlin
   Through the Rosenthal Gate   168   278
Anniversary   169   265

NORMAN, CHARLES
POEMS
Ring Out, Ring In   57   187
Palimpsest   68   256
When Soldiers Sing

ARTICLES
Dr. Johnson and A Shropshire Lad   60   264

BOOKS REVIEWED
Poems   35   170
The Savage Century   60   344
Selected Poems   100   395

NORMAN,
HENDERSON DAINGERFIELD
BOOKS REVIEWED
Plays of Edmond Rostand (Tr.)   20   51

NORRINGTON, A. L. P.
BOOKS REVIEWED
The Poems of Arthur Hugh Clough
   (Ed. with H. F. Lowry
   and F. L. Mulhauser)   82   27

NORRIS, KATHLEEN
POEMS
Mrs. Adam   156   12
Ascension

NORRIS, LESLIE
BOOKS REVIEWED
Ransoms   120   107

NORRIS, WILLIAM A.
POEMS
O Changing One   18   201

NORSE, HAROLD
POEMS
Key West   63   80
Blue Monday   65   190
Within This Park
The Pride of Atreus   74   320
What the Birds Know
Suddenly All the Continents
The Voyage Home   79   331
The Eye Is Everywhere   80   196
The Statue in the Snow
Form   82   328
Parable
Three Voyages   84   19
Florence   89   92
Was It Florence or Venice   94   98
Color & Sound   95   345
Winter Scene
Night Piece

ARTICLES
Excerpts from notes and letters   89   177

BOOKS REVIEWED
The Undersea Mountain   83   335

The Roman Sonnets
   of Giuseppi Gioacchino Belli (Tr.)   98   403
The Dancing Beasts   100   310

NORTH, CHARLES
POEMS
  For You   119   20
  Poem ("Now that I am seeing...")
  Variation (Overheard)   121   141
  Another Nice Day for the Race
  Elegiacal Study   127   77

NORTH, JESSICA NELSON
["J. N. N.", "J. N."]
POEMS
  The Wages of Sin   19   76
  At Night   20   242
    The Sleeper
    First Autumn
    Dreams
    Suddenly
    Bogie
    Boatman
    To the Man Who Loves Twilight
  A Young Boy   22   11
    The Decision
    The Other Wind
  Sonnet ("Who would have thought...")   22   312
  Grist   25   254
    Hibernalia
    The Problem
    To Duncan
  Legerdemain   29   141
  Hensel
  Deity
  Impersonal
  Greeting Without Voice
  Bouquet   32   188
    Mathematical
    Creation
    Truth
    To Betsy
    The Mother
  About Women   37   61
    Rainy Morning
    The Burden
    Lady
    I Fear the Weak
    There Was One Taken
    Alarm
    Symbol
    Advice to a Girl Child
    Girls on an Island
  Winds of Spring   40   8
    Easter
    White Queen
    Origin
  A Rehearsal   44   119

    Reveille
    For Priapus
    Garden Theme
    Ancestral
    Homeless
    Afflicted
    Gray
    Night Fires
  Second Sight   47   237
    Confession
    Lake Cycle
    Chalk
    Grief
    This in Remembrance
    The Real Princess
    Bed-Time
    Stature
    Gardener
  No Compromise   49   136
  Four-Power Conference   55   80
  June Death
  Dinner Party
  Dragon Teeth
  Choreartium
  In Praise of Hands
  Arctic Voyage   59   252
  X-Ray   63   265
  Bird Haven, Morning
  Political Argument
  Stereopticon   69   61
  This Generation
  The Very Old
  The Glass House   80   261

ARTICLES
  The Late Rebellion   22   153
  Factors and Formulae   31   268
  Visual Poetry
    [E. E. Cummings]   31   334
  Eastward Bound   32   92
  Office Amenities   33   38
  Christmas
    (With Harriet Monroe)   33   148
  A Censorship for Critics
    [William Troy]   34   32
  The Hungry Generations
    [Thomas Carlyle]   34   90
  The Wrong-Headed Poets
    [William McFee]   34   156
  Convention and Revolt
    [Yvor Winters, Janet Lewis,
    Howard Baker]   34   212
  Quality in Madness
    [Gerard Manley Hopkins]   34   270
  Toward Posthumous Fame
    [Walter Ralegh, Agnes M. C. Latham]   34   335
  An Adventure Story
    [Harriet Monroe]   41   50

AE   46   334
[Tribute to Harriet Monroe]   49   146
A Forward Look   51   34
An Announcement   53   54
"A Torch in the Wind"
    [Lola Ridge]   58   209
The Magazine Today   61   384
Eunice Tietjens: A Memorial   65   104
Marion Strobel Mitchell   108   264

REVIEWS
New Poems, by John Drinkwater   27   158
Tiger Joy, by Stephen Vincent Benét   27   279
High Passage,
    by Thomas Hornsby Ferril   30   165
Gray Songs, by Mercy Baldwin   30   232
Collected Poems and A Poetry Recital,
    by James Stephens   31   41
Copper Sun, by Countée Cullen   31   284
Him, by E. E. Cummings   31   345
Man Possessed, by William Rose Benét   32   159
Burning Bush, by Louis Untermeyer   32   224
Animula Vagula and
    Guinea-Fowl and Other Poultry,
    by Leonard Bacon   32   282
Kanaka Moon,
    by Clifford Franklin Gessler   33   46
Trivial Breath, by Elinor Wylie   33   96
The Children Sing in the Far West,
    by Mary Austin   33   163
Funnybone Alley, by Alfred Kreymborg   33   164
The Hamlet of A. MacLeish,
    by Archibald MacLeish   33   219
Time Importuned,
    by Sylvia Townsend Warner   34   47
The Devil Is a Woman,
    by Alice Mary Kimball   34   100
Cavender's House,
    by Edwin Arlington Robinson   34   233
Further Poems of Emily Dickinson   35   164
Hell in Harness and Letters to Ladies,
    by Joseph Auslander   35   346
Witch and Other Poems,
    by Grace Hazard Conkling   36   47
Song of the New Hercules,
    by Leigh Hanes   37   345
Near and Far, by Edmund Blunden   38   113
Epistle to Prometheus; Fire for the Night;
    and Potable Gold,
    by Babette Deutsch   38   166
Old Pastures, by Padraic Colum   38   224
Behind Dark Spaces, by Melville Cane   38   345
Sheaves and The Golden Boat,
    by Rabindranath Tagore   44   235
Basket for a Fair, by Laura Benét   45   103
Not Mine to Finish,
    by Genevieve Taggard   45   168

The Tragedy of Man,
    by Imre Madách
    (Tr. by Paul Vajda and
    Charles Henry Meltzer)   47   285
Time Has No Shadow,
    by Katherine Garrison Chapin   50   231
Prismatic Ground,
    by Marguerite Young   51   109
Workers in Fire, by Margery Mansfield   51   273
Year's End, by Josephine W. Johnson   52   233
Adonais: A Life of John Keats,
    by Dorothy Hewlett   53   159
After Eden, by Emma Gray Trigg   54   346
Lines at Intersection, by Josephine Miles   55   277
Goldboat, by Belle Turnbull   57   274
Make Bright the Arrows,
    by Edna St. Vincent Millay   57   389
Blood for a Stranger, by Randall Jarrell   61   626
The Shape of Memory,
    by Winifred Welles   64   168
Birth Is Farewell,
    by Dilys Bennett Laing   66   51
Poems, by Madeline Gleason   66   102
No Eclipse: War Poems,
    by Ray Smith   67   160
Tribute to the Angels, by H. D.   67   341
Only the Years, by Ruth Lechlitner   68   224
Powerful Long Ladder,
    by Owen Dodson   69   175
The White Centre,
    by Patrick Anderson   69   284
Brady's Bend and Other Ballads,
    by Martha Keller   70   226
Parade   72   281
    Parade of Doves, by Eve Triem
    Rococo Summer and Other Poems,
        by Lawrence P. Spingarn
    Things Visible and Invisible,
        by Martha Bacon
    Chinese Love Songs,
        by Mabel Lorenz Ives   76   357
    The Cowherd and the Sky Maiden,
        by Esther Shepard

BOOKS REVIEWED
A Prayer Rug   22   281
The Long Leash   33   340
Dinner Party   62   167

ARTICLES ABOUT
Correspondence
    from Philip Conrad   32   112

NORTH, STERLING
POEMS
    Round and Round   31   140
        Soliloquy
        At the Centre

Old Stage Coach
Feud
Lament
No Haven 34 12
Evening in Autumn
False Season
Faun
These Two
Mare and Colt
Deserted Farm
Wild Ducks on the Chicago River
Autumn Equinox 39 70
To the Poet
To the Unfortunate Lover
To the Classicist
To the Fisherman
To the Metaphysicist
Lanterns in the Wind 49 312
Advice to a Young Man
I Cleared the Hedgerow
I Found Wild Honey in a Skull
Late Abroad

REVIEWS
Sunset Gun, by Dorothy Parker 33 156
Ballyhoo for a Mendicant,
by Carlton Talbott 34 173

NORTON, ALLEN
BOOKS REVIEWED
Saloon Sonnets With Sunday Flutings 5 38

NORTON, BEATRICE
BOOKS REVIEWED
Negro Poetry in America 27 221

NORTON, DAN S.
POEMS
Poor Tom 62 202

NORTON, GRACE FALLOW
POEMS
Heart's Holiday 3 127
Iolé
Oh Hush, My Heart!
Allegra Agonistes
Fly On! 7 134
Make No Vows
Hark to the Wind of the World
If My Mother Knew
I Give Thanks
The Burned House 15 252
Or Did You Love Death?
I Shall Remember 19 190
Shy Perfect Flower
The Miller's Youngest Daughter 22 175
Contradictions 24 180
Misadventure

Domestic Harmony
The Fool
Hearing a Staff and a Bell 34 268
Occidental
Phoenix 43 76
Songs of Prayer 45 143
Bread of the Stars
If the Prayer Be Whole
For Him Who Breathes Such Air
Mood 50 133
Dear Wolf 54 129

BOOKS REVIEWED
The Sister of the Wind 5 87
Roads 11 164
What Is Your Legion?
The Miller's Youngest Daughter 24 217

ARTICLES ABOUT
A Few Women Poets,
by Harriet Monroe 26 326

NORTON, M. D. HERTER
[See HERTER NORTON, M. D.]

NORTON, ROBERT
BOOKS REVIEWED
Eternal Passion in English Poetry
(Ed. with Edith Wharton) 57 221

NOSS, MURRAY
BOOKS REVIEWED
Samurai and Serpent Poems 88 52

NOVAK, SONIA RUTHELE
POEMS
Tyro 37 321
Calendars 41 131

NOVEMBER, SHARYN
POEMS
Christmas 137 133
Travelling by Water 138 140
At the Eye Clinic

NOVOMESKY, LACO
POEMS
Danse Macabre
(Tr. by David Daiches) 55 179

NOWLAN, ALDEN
BOOKS REVIEWED
The Things Which Are 103 266
Playing the Jesus Game 119 356
I Might Not Tell Everybody This 144 297

NOYES, ALFRED
POEMS
"The Hill-Flowers" 1 192

ARTICLES ABOUT
Our Contemporaries 9 162

NURKSE, D.
POEMS
Introit & Fugue 156 281
First Grade Homework
Only Child 165 324
Final Separation
The Highest Hill of Hope 170 320
Riches of the Interior

BOOKS REVIEWED
Voices Over Water 164 285

NUTT, HOWARD
POEMS
The Whole Course 48 261
Special Laughter
Metropolis Pilgrim
Decadent Finale
Thoreau 60 66
The Hunter Man 61 362
Incident 69 137

REVIEWS
Two Brief Notices 48 49
Sea Pieces and Other Poems,
by Forrest Anderson
The Crag, by Carla Lanyon Lanyon

BOOKS REVIEWED
Special Laughter 58 162

NUTTALL, JEFF
BOOKS REVIEWED
Pig 117 331
Poems: 1962-69 120 107

NYE, NAOMI SHIHAB
POEMS
Catalogue Army 140 74
The Man Who Hated Trees

BOOKS REVIEWED
Red Suitcase 168 281

NYE, ROBERT
BOOKS REVIEWED
Darker Ends 118 102
First Awakenings:
The Early Poems
of Laura Riding
(Ed. with Elizabeth Friedmann
and Alan J. Clark) 164 39

NYEGOSH, PETAR PETROVICH
ARTICLES ABOUT
Serbian Poetry,
by F. C. Weiskopf 61 438

NYHART, NINA
POEMS
Two Poems After Paul Klee 152 141
The Runner
Captive Pierrot
Diplomacy 168 158

OAKS, GLADYS
POEMS
Judas Meditates About the Christ   29   138
A Study in Frustrations

BOOKS REVIEWED
Nursery Rhymes
    for Children of Darkness   33   225

OATES, JOYCE CAROL
POEMS
Night   142   255
Ancient Snapshots
Love Anecdote
Weedy Logic   149   92
Burning Oak, November
Waiting on Elvis, 1956   151   109
Motive, Metaphor
Late December, New Jersey   153   159

ARTICLES
Comment   151   207

BOOKS REVIEWED
Anonymous Sins and Other Poems   117   195
The Fabulous Beasts   130   102

OBATA, SHIGEYOSHI
BOOKS REVIEWED
The Works of Li Po (Tr.)   22   334

OBERG, ARTHUR
POEMS
Voting in Favor of Happy Endings   127   79
On the Random Brightness
    of Letters and Numbers   128   205
Tempering the End of Summer's Fall
Fable for the Sad and the Beautiful   129   18
Distraction After a Night Storm
Obstructed View of the Arbitrary
    and the Profane
Bittersweet
Finding a Language for Beatrice

REVIEWS
Collected Poems 1956-1976,
    by David Wagoner   130   162

OBOLENSKY, DIMITRI
BOOKS REVIEWED
The Penguin Book of Russian Verse (Ed.)   100   124

O'BOLGER, T. D.
POEMS
The Counsels of O'Riordan, the Rannmaker   9   136

O'BRIEN, EDWARD J.
POEMS
Veni Creator   37   121
Chill and Furrowed Air   43   246

ARTICLES
The Younger Bards
    [Donald Turner, Donald Wakeling,
    H. Caldwell Cook, Adrian Tuffield,
    Douglas Simmonds]   6   188
Correspondence: August Stramm   8   213

O'BRIEN, JEAN
POEMS
Praise of Love   8   227
Prayer

O'BRIEN, LAURIE
POEMS
L'Art de Toucher le Clavecin   162   6
Rogues' Codes
Inventing the Piano   165   211

O'BRIEN, ROBERT DAVID
POEMS
Dryden's Cecilia   57   17
Promises to Keep   64   127

O'BYRNE, CATHAL
TRANSLATIONS
Poems by Anthony Raftery   24   256

BOOKS REVIEWED
The Grey Feet of the Wind   33   229

OCAMPO, SILVINA
POEMS
Sleepless Palinurus
    (Tr. by Dudley Fitts)   68   245

ARTICLES ABOUT
   [Contributors' notes]   68   296

O'CASEY, SEAN
ARTICLES ABOUT
   Poetry for the Theatre,
      by M. D. Zabel   45   152
   Rev. of *The Story*
   of the Abbey Theatre,
      by Peter Kavanagh   79   216

OCHESTER, ED
POEMS
   The Relatives   147   130
   Having Built the Coop   148   159
   New Day   150   224

O'CONNELL, RICHARD
TRANSLATIONS
   Poem by Gabriela Mistral
      (Tr. with James Graham Lujan)   63   204

BOOKS REVIEWED
   Three Tragedies,
      by Federico García Lorca
      (Tr. with James Graham-Luján)   75   114
   From an Interior Silence   102   49
   Cries of Flesh and Stone
   New Poems and Translations   104   115

O'CONNOR, DEIRDRE
POEMS
   My Grandfather's Cronies   157   31
   Almost Nothing
   Liminal   166   194
   My Mother Sells Her Mother's House
   at 8 Edith Place

O'CONNOR, FRANK
ARTICLES ABOUT
   A Letter from Ireland,
      by Joseph M. Hone   44   215

O'CONNOR, MARK
POEMS
   Pompeii   142   29
   The Source of Lake Ochrid

O'CONNOR, WILLIAM VAN
POEMS
   Manila   67   240

ARTICLES
   Correspondence:
      A Reply to David Daiches   62   291
   Correspondence
      [David Daiches]   63   55
   Shapiro's Southwest Pacific Poems   64   326

The Isolation of the Poet
   [Delmore Schwartz]   70   28
New Magazines, Here and Abroad   71   104
New Critical Journals in England   71   223
The Direction of the Little Magazine
   [Marianne Moore]   71   281
Mannequin Mythology:
   The Fashion Journals   72   284
The Little Magazine
   as a Cultural Journal
   [F. R. Leavis]   72   339
Little Magazines
   in the Third Generation   73   367
The Sounds that Little Magazines Make   74   179
Recent Magazines:
   The Expense of Conventions   76   118
Keats-Shelley Memorials   84   366
Joseph Warren Beach   91   192

REVIEWS
   André Gide, by Klaus Mann   63   276
   The Use of Color in the Verse
   of the English Romantic Poets,
      by A. E. Pratt   69   88
   Science and English Poetry:
   A Historical Sketch, 1590-1950,
      by Douglas Bush   76   352
   The Auroras of Autumn,
      by Wallace Stevens   77   109
   Poetry Explication
      (Ed. by George Arms
      and Joseph M. Kuntz)   77   289
   The Harvard Advocate
      (Ed. by Donald Hall)   78   241
   Vaudeville for a Princess,
      by Delmore Schwartz   79   55
   Modern Poetry: American and British
      (Ed. by Kimon Friar and
      John Malcolm Brinnin)   79   289
   Poems in Process, by Phyllis Bartlett   79   295
   The Man with the Blue Guitar,
   Including Ideas of Order,
      by Wallace Stevens   81   139
   Ode to the Sea, and Other Poems,
      by Howard Baker   109   187

BOOKS REVIEWED
   Climates of Tragedy   62   344
   Sense and Sensibility
   in Modern Poetry   74   353
   The Shaping Spirit:
   A Study of Wallace Stevens   76   355
   Poems for Study
      (With Leonard Unger)   84   43
   Obsessive Images, Symbolism
   in Poetry of the 1930's and 1940's,
      by Joseph Warren Beach (Ed.)   98   332

ARTICLES ABOUT
Correspondence from David Daiches   62   292
[Note]   72   289
Correspondence
from Frederick Morgan   76   304

O'CONOR, NORREYS JEPHSON
REVIEWS
The Principles of English Versification,
by Paull Franklin Baum   22   218

BOOKS REVIEWED
Songs of the Celtic Past   14   341

O'DOHERTY, BRIAN
POEMS
Poems from a Hospital   87   224
Katie
Poem ("Restless on whose bosom...")

O'DONNELL, CHARLES L.
POEMS
Forgiveness   8   72
Martin of Tours   9   116
A Road of France   14   197
On Indian Lake   14   249
Resolution   29   129
Beatitude
In the Upper Room   30   8
On Meeting a Lady   31   135
The Uncreated Beauty   35   119

BOOKS REVIEWED
Cloister and Other Poems   22   95
A Rime of the Rood, and Other Poems   34   170

O'DONNELL, GEORGE MARION
POEMS
Ancestral   47   190
Letter for the Confederates
For My Grandmother
Descent of Leaf   48   322
Talk of Friends   52   76
Commencement Oration   54   126

REVIEWS
In Dreams Begin Responsibilities,
by Delmore Schwartz   54   105

O'DONNELL, JOHN L.
POEMS
Sea Language   170   259

O'DONOGHUE, BERNARD
POEMS
Reassurance   167   15
Child Language Acquisition
Kilmacow

O'DRISCOLL, DENNIS
POEMS
Time Sharing   146   212
Normally Speaking
Reading Primo Levi on the Train   157   138
Customs   169   194

ARTICLES
A Map of Contemporary Irish Poetry
[W. B. Yeats, Seamus Heaney,
Patrick Kavanagh, Louis MacNeice,
Austin Clarke, Thomas Kinsella,
John Montague, Paul Durcan,
Paul Muldoon, Derek Mahon,
Michael Longley, Eavan Boland, Nuala
Ní Dhomhnaill, Biddy Jenkinson,
Richard Murphy, Denis Devlin,
Medbh McGuckian, Michael Hartnett]   167   94

OERKE, ANDREW
POEMS
The Sun   119   22
The Divine Comedy   120   149
Three Songs of the Southwest   126   196
("There is no one present...")
("Mount-and-rider zigzag...")
("The sun settles...")

OFFEN, RON
POEMS
Unknown, So Unnamed   102   85
Elliott Carter
Donn:

BOOKS REVIEWED
Poet as Bad Guy   104   258

OGA, TAKU
POEMS
Soldiers
(Tr. by Satoru Satu
and Constance Urdang)   88   98

O'GORMAN, NED
POEMS
This Will Be the Song   85   130
A Poem About a Prince   86   344
The Rose and the Body of the Rose
Childhood   88   162
The Resurrection of Animals
The Sunbathers   89   281
To My Father
L'Annunciazione; from Bellini   90   299
To a Monk Who Found
He Could Not Write Poetry
After He Had Recovered from a Long Illness
Easter Among Four Children   92   1
A Dirge

Because Noni Trespassed in the Night
In Memory of Sister Virgilia
   of the Sacred Heart
A Movement of Peoples
A Song for the Passionate
An Art of Poetry
A Description of the Sea for Lina Lenzi
   Who Has Never Seen It   93 167
An Afternoon with a Poet
The Blood
For Ezra Pound
The Complaint of a Young Priest
Two Poems on Larger Topics   95 81
Great Grandfather,
   Clamdiggers, and Homer
The Summer
The Spring
Johanna, the Big Cow   96 340
On Silence
To X
Toward a Language of the Ineffable
The Beginning of Jewels   97 285
Epithalamion
Oil   100 145
As It Was Then It Will Not Be Now
Beauty
The Burning Bush

REVIEWS
Three Poets   91 268
   The Boatman, by Jay Macpherson
   For Some Stringed Instrument,
     by Peter Kane Dufault
   The Sinai Sort, by Norman MacCaig
Language and Vision   93 329
   Selected Poems and New,
     by José Garcia Villa
   Life of a Man, by Giuseppe Ungaretti
     (Ed. by Allen Mandelbaum)
   A Poet Before the Cross,
     by Paul Claudel
     (Tr. by Wallace Fowlie)   95 50

BOOKS REVIEWED
The Night of the Hammer   95 304
Adam Before His Mirror   99 124
The Buzzard and the Peacock   105 201
The Harvesters' Vase   113 262

O'GRADY, DESMOND
TRANSLATIONS
Poem by Gabriel Rosenstock   167 47

O'GRADY, JENNIFER
POEMS
Moths   160 259
Illuminated Page   161 322
The Surrealist Learns To Fly

O'HARA, FRANK
POEMS
Ann Arbor Variations   79 136
Aus Einem April   85 63
Poem in January
Romanze, or The Music Students
Meditations in an Emergency
Chez Jane
The Eyelid Has Its Storms...   87 11
Now It Is Light...
For James Dean   87 339
On Seeing Larry Rivers'
   Washington Crossing the Delaware
   at the Museum of Modern Art
On Rachmaninoff's Birthday
Radio
For Janice and Kenneth to Voyage
Cambridge   90 90
Lisztiana
On a Mountain
Poem ("Instant coffee with...")
Variations on Pasternak's "Mein Liebchen,
   Was Willst Du Noch Mehr?"   96 81
In Favor of One's Time
Saint
Poem ("Hate is only one...")
To You
Walking to Work   113 332
Walking
Places for Oscar Salvador
Sudden Snow
The Tomb of Arnold Schoenberg   116 99
Unicorn
A Note to Harold Fondren
Dolce Colloquio
Dido
Homosexuality
Poem ("I am not sure...")
The Man Without a Country   130 63
Augustus
Princess Elizabeth of Bohemia, as Perdita
Intermezzo
Poem ("Green things are flowers...")
Maurice Ravel
The Mike Goldberg Variations
Noir Cacadou, or the Fatal Music of War
Room
Round Objects
A Wreath for John Wheelwright
Serenade

ARTICLES
Another Word
   on Kenneth Koch   85 349

REVIEWS
Rare Modern   89 307
   Storm at Castelfranco,
     by Chester Kallman

Some Trees, by John Ashbery
Mediterranean Cities, by Edwin Denby

BOOKS REVIEWED
Meditations in an Emergency   92   178
Lunch Poems   107   326
The Collected Poems of...
    (Ed. by Donald Allen)   122   40

ARTICLES ABOUT
On Kenneth Koch Again: A Rebuttal,
    by Harry Roskolenko   86   177
Rev. by David Lehman   119   224

Ó HEHIR, DIANA
POEMS
Lost Objects   134   68
Wind
Accuser
When You Die   136   199
Seasonal Change
Recognition
Private Song   139   23
Body
Snow
The Dead Pull Us Toward Winter
The Fisherman's Widow   142   195
How To Murder Your Best Friend
Apple   144   134
My Father Owns This City

BOOKS REVIEWED
The Power to Change Geography   135   229
Home Free   154   151

O'KEEFFE, GEORGIA
ARTICLES ABOUT
Rev. of Blossoms and Bones: On the Life
    and Work of Georgia O'Keeffe,
    by Christopher Buckley   154   283

OKIGBO, CHRISTOPHER
BOOKS REVIEWED
Heavensgate   103   394

OLDKNOW, ANTONY
POEMS
The Chosen Pass Over   121   204
Spring Comes to Buffalo River
Nude Under Pine Tree
Fishing   123   328
Curtain Call   124   330
The Scars of Waves

OLDS, SHARON
POEMS
Ideographs   133   34
The Guild

The Fear of Oneself   136   209
Armor
The Signal   139   30
The Quest
Cambridge Elegy
Burn Center
He Comes for the Jewish Family, 1942 141   263
Prayer During a Time
    My Son Is Having Seizures   142   316
The Month of June: 13 1/2
The Legless Fighter Pilot
The Cast   146   278
The Planned Child
May 1968   150   80
After Making Love in Winter
The Day They Tied Me Up   151   110
Znamenskaya Square, Leningrad, 1941 153   207
Earliest Memory
The Pull   158   316
His Terror
Beyond Harm
Sleep Suite   169   150
Her Last August   170   20

BOOKS REVIEWED
Satan Says   138   170
The Dead and the Living   145   36
The Gold Cell   149   231
The Father   164   39
The Wellspring   170   288

OLES, CAROLE
POEMS
Rain the Rememberer   132   96
Francestown Suite   133   82
One Page in
    The American Heritage Dictionary
On an Airplane, Considering Night
A Collage: The National Standard   136   276
I Will Draw You Three Lines
In Nashville
Like Musical Chairs   138   225
Better Vision
Preparing for Weather   143   29
Stitches   146   280
High Heels
On Greyhound, Boston to New York   151   111
How He Celebrated Daily Mass   151   466
The Interpretation of Baseball   152   133
For Evelyn   153   194
The Gambler   153   288
Day Ten After Heart Surgery,
    Signing a Check   157   17
Fugit Amor   157   287

ARTICLES
Comment
    [John Frederick Nims]   151   222

BOOKS REVIEWED
The Loneliness Factor   139   35
Quarry   144   40

OLESON, HELMER OREN
POEMS
Portraits and Observations   34   326
    Chin-Wagger's Epitaph
    Inferiority Complex
    Lines Written on a Hot Day
    I Fought Valiantly Today
    This Day
    The Subway-Rider

OLIVER, MARY
POEMS
The Son   143   214
The Moths
The Shark   146   6
Banyan
Every Morning   147   328
The Mango
Death at Wind River
The Hermit Crab   151   112
Death at a Great Distance   152   191
Singapore
The Kingfisher
Spring   156   1
What Is It?
The Waterfall   157   191
This Morning Again It Was
    in the Dusty Pines
Rain   159   7
Hummingbirds   160   209
In Malaysia
August   162   249
Beside the Waterfall
Fall   165   1
Morning Glories
Forty Years   167   328
Pilot Snake   168   258

BOOKS REVIEWED
American Primitive   145   36
Dream Work   150   102
House of Light   158   342
New and Selected Poems   162   224
White Pine   166   289

OLIVER, WADE
POEMS
Vigil   17   246
Requiem
Sons of Adam   21   196
Who'll Ride with Me?
What Suns? What Moons?
Patter
Black Water

At the Shaking of the Dawn
Sky-Rider   25   134
More Softly Silence
Banqueters   30   202
Shadow Song
Strange Pilgrimage   35   245
Jungfrau   38   131
Peking Dusk   40   317

BOOKS REVIEWED
Sky-Rider   32   284

O'LOUGHLIN, MICHAEL
POEMS
Birth Certificate: Amsterdam, 22 June 1988   167   40
At the Grave of Father Hopkins
Displacements

OLSEN, CHARLES OLUF
POEMS
"Applesauce"   30   84
A Tribute
Grain of the Wood   33   246
    In the City
    Kinship
    Rehabilitation
    Consider Two Cats
    Goal
    Temporal
    Rebuked
Around the Ring   37   147
    Last Courage
    Potent Circle
    Father John
    Stony Faith
    Life Be Kind!
To the Heart   44   316
    Hemlock Draught

OLSON, CHARLES
POEMS
The Red Fish-of-Bones   100   5
The Gulf of Maine   101   85
Poem ("Gravelly hill...")   103   78
The Grandfather-Father Poem   106   90
Cole's Island
Maximus, in Gloucester Sunday, LXV 108 185

BOOKS REVIEWED
The Maximus Poems/11-22   90   386
The Maximus Poems   98   319
Maximus from Dogtown   100   329
The Distances
Human Universe and Other Essays 109   40
Proprioception
A Bibliography on America for Ed Dorn
Selected Writings
    (Ed. by Robert Creeley)   111   413

O'Ryan   113   188
Causal Mythology   116   110
Maximus Poems IV, V, VI
Muthologos:
    The Collected Lectures & Interviews, Vol. I
    (Ed. by George F. Butterick)   136   219

ARTICLES ABOUT
Rev. of *The New American Poetry: 1945-1960*
    (Ed. by Donald M. Allen)   98   242
Rev. of *Olson/Melville:*
    A Study in Affinity,
    by Ann Charters   116   110
Rev. of *A Guide to the Maximus Poems*
    of Charles Olson,
    by George F. Butterick;
    Charles Olson: Call Him Ishmael,
    by Paul Christensen;
    Olson's Push: Origin, Black Mountain
    and Recent American Poetry,
    by Sherman Paul;
    and *Charles Olson: The Scholar's Art*,
    by Robert von Hallberg   136   219
Rev. of *A History of Modern Poetry*,
    Volume II: Modernism and After,
    by David Perkins   151   296

OLSON, ELDER (JAMES)
[E. JAMES OLSON]
POEMS
Soft Music   32   81
    Last Night
    Towers of Sleep
Waters   36   175
The Quarry
Body of Man Compared to a Tree
Garden-Piece
Dirge for the White Bird
The Gift
Angleworms
Lazarus
Thus Revealed   39   1
    Last Night
    Essay on Deity
Talisman of Words   41   23
Prelude to Despair
The Ghostly Spring
To Music
Song ("When shall this weight...")
Novel in Pictures   42   181
Preludes and Impromptus   44   26
    Wishes for His Poem
    Legend
    Prologue to His Book
    Madrigal
    Sonnet ("This is the thing...")
The Angel of the Annunciation   48   239
Soul's Journey

The Cock of Heaven
The Assumption
Number Ten Blucher Street
A Clock Striking at Midnight
Devil in Crystal   56   1
    Episode
    Abailard Sleeps at His Book
    Liber de Causis
    Encounter of Travelers
    The History
    Sonnet ("I have served Thee...")
The Rebellion   73   144
Ice-Age
Pavane for the New Year
Childe Roland, Etc.   81   59
Ballad of the Scarecrow Christ   82   1
"Plot Improbable, Character Unsympathetic"
The Fountain
The Night There Was Dancing in the Streets
Jack-in-the-Box
The Last Entries in the Journal   91   343
A Valentine for Marianne Moore
The Voice
The Exegesis
For the Demolition of a Theater
Ice-Skaters   97   63
Conversation Between a Mirror and the Sea
The Graveyard by the Sea
Exhibition of Modern Art   101   89
Exposition of the Quarrel of the Birds   102   317
Old Story, New Hero
Taxco
Volcán de Agua   136   211
Shark and Cockroach   151   114

ARTICLES
Is Theory Possible?
    [Karl Shapiro]   71   257
Comment
    [Harriet Monroe]   151   200

REVIEWS
The Achievement of T. S. Eliot,
    by F. O. Matthiessen   50   54
A Little Treasury of World Poetry
    (Ed. by Hubert Creekmore)   82   281
The Collected Poems of Dylan Thomas   83   213
The Fields Were Green,
    by George Arms   84   98

BOOKS REVIEWED
Thing of Sorrow   45   279
The Cock of Heaven   57   214
The Scarecrow Christ and Other Poems   86   168
The Poetry of Dylan Thomas   87   118
Plays and Poems   94   339
Tragedy and the Theory of Drama   102   198
Collected Poems   104   181

American Lyric Poems (Ed.)   106   429
Olson's Penny Arcade   129   170

ARTICLES ABOUT
Rev. of Critics and Criticism,
Ancient and Modern
(Ed. by R. S. Crane)   82   98
The Chicago Critics:
Yes and Perhaps,
by Martin J. Svaglic   82   157

OLSON, LAWRENCE
POEMS
Great Abaco   65   242
Landscape with Figure
Leda
Sonnet 26   68   189
The Patience of the Beast
10 A. M.
Song ("Stay with me now...")   69   76
Approaching Balboa
The Sea Fair   72   189
The Funeral   74   14
When I See Pictures of the Dead

BOOKS REVIEWED
The Cranes on Dying River   72   51

OLSON, LILY
POEMS
Dark Lines   27   256
Poverty
Civilization
Useless People

OLSON, TED
POEMS
Laughter   29   72
Hypothesis
Trinity   30   259
Blizzard   31   304
Heritage   36   141
Salute to Norway
March Plowing
Blood and Water
Pied Piper
Tailor of Earth
Against the Cold   39   304
Winter Night
Travelogue
Dirge for a Dark Age   48   20
Words Said for Comfort   54   133
Duologue   61   417
Once in Norway
Malediction on the Mind

BOOKS REVIEWED
A Stranger and Afraid   34   167

O'MALLEY, ERNEST
POEMS
From Two Islands   45   192
Deirdre
Poem ("We have not sought...")
Desert Buildings: Navajo Country
Mountjoy Hanged, 1921
Zuni Rocks   47   304
Indian
Shalako

Ó MUIRTHILE, LIAM
POEMS
An Luascán/The Swing
(Tr. by Ciaran Carson)   167   68

ONDAATJE, MICHAEL
BOOKS REVIEWED
The Dainty Monsters   115   353
The Man with Seven Toes   119   356
The Collected Works of Billy the Kid 144   297

O'NEIL, DAVID
POEMS
Moods and Moments   11   74
Child Eyes
Freedom
Human Chords
Enslaved
The Peasants
The Beach
Reaches of the Desert
The Ascent
Feather Shafts   28   260
Venice
Political Annunciation
Second Avenue Shylock
Soul States
The Nature of the Beast
Times Square

BOOKS REVIEWED
A Cabinet of Jade   12   225

O'NEIL, GEORGE
POEMS
Wings of Spring   14   74
The Marvel
Margot
Sparrow
Crone   27   137
No Shelter   32   15
Soporific
Huntsman's Rouse
Homage

BOOKS REVIEWED
The Cobbler in Willow Street
and Other Poems   17   276

The White Rooster and Other Poems	30	159
God Beguiled	36	40

O'NEILL, EUGENE
ARTICLES ABOUT
New York Plays,
　by Florence Kiper Frank　25　327
New York Plays,
　by Florence Kiper Frank　28　95
Again New York, by Harriet Monroe　32　150

O'NEILL, ROSE
BOOKS REVIEWED
The Master-Mistress　21　219

ONG, WALTER J.
REVIEWS
*To Criticize the Critic: Eight Essays
on Literature and Education,*
　by T. S. Eliot　108　265

OOSTERHUIS, HUUB
ARTICLES ABOUT
Rev. of *Ordinary Things,*
　by Jean Valentine
　[Judith Herzberg]　127　44

OPDYCKE, MARY ELLIS
POEMS
Pietà　25　142

OPIE, IONA
BOOKS REVIEWED
The Oxford Dictionary of Nursery Rhymes
　(Ed. with Peter Opie)　84　167

OPIE, PETER
BOOKS REVIEWED
The Oxford Dictionary of Nursery Rhymes
　(Ed. with Iona Opie)　84　167

OPPEN, GEORGE (A.)
POEMS
1930's　37　256
Discrete Series　39　198
Birthplace: New Rochelle　95　237
Myself I Sing
The Biblical Tree
Part of the Forest
The Source
Population　97　77
The Hills
Product
Stranger's Child
From a Photograph　99　371
Squall
Travelogue
Philai Te Kou Philai　102　224
Psalm

The Forms of Love　104　73
Street
Primitive
*Giovanni's "Rape of the Sabine Women"
at Wildenstein's*
Guest Room　105　387
The People, the People
Ballad ("Astrolabes and lexicons...")　111　171
A Preface
A Theological Definition
Historic Pun

REVIEWS
Three Poets　100　329
　Kaddish and Other Poems, 1958-1960,
　　by Allen Ginsberg
　*Maximus from Dogtown
　and The Distances,*
　　by Charles Olson
　Dark Brown, by Michael McClure

BOOKS REVIEWED
Discrete Series　44　220
The Materials　102　266
This in Which　108　339
Of Being Numerous　114　40
Seascape: Needle's Eye　126　172
Collected Poems　129　164

OPPENHEIM, EDWIN
BOOKS REVIEWED
The Reverberate Hills　5　140

OPPENHEIM, GARRETT
POEMS
Oil of Dada: First Look　51　319
The Olympian in Autumn　53　15
Epithalamion and Callithump　54　235

OPPENHEIM, JAMES
BOOKS REVIEWED
Songs for the New Age　5　88
The Book of Self　11　219
The Solitary　16　49
The Mystic Warrior　19　216
The Sea　25　333

ARTICLES ABOUT
The Seven Arts,
　by Alice Corbin Henderson　9　214

OPPENHEIMER, JOEL
POEMS
The Innocent Breasts　113　310

BOOKS REVIEWED
The Love Bit　102　335
The Woman Poems　127　234

ORAGE, ALFRED RICHARD
ARTICLES ABOUT
  Obituary   45   235

ORAS, ANTS
REVIEWS
  Anthology of Modern Estonian Poetry
    (Ed. and tr. by W. K. Matthews)
    [Gustav Suits, Marie Under,
    Betti Alver]   84   236

OREAN, THOMAS
POEMS
  Broken Terzine   39   140
  You and I
  Two Metaphors
  The Parting

OREL, HAROLD
REVIEWS
  A Poet's Notebook,
    by Edith Sitwell   77   292

ORGEL, STEPHEN
TRANSLATIONS
  Poems by Virgil
    and Giraut de Bornelh   116   353

ORIGO, IRIS
BOOKS REVIEWED
  Leopardi: A Study in Solitude   85   55

ORIOLI, GIUSEPPE
BOOKS REVIEWED
  Last Poems,
    by D. H. Lawrence
    (Ed. with Richard Aldington)   42   163

ORLEN, STEVEN
[STEVE ORLEN]
POEMS
  The New World,
    Requesting Nothing But Peace   114   373
  November   116   19
  Keeping Watch   117   165
  Sleeping on Doors   119   71
  The Deserted Husband
  To a Child Courting Death
  Country House   122   20
  Beauty and the Beast
  Abandoned Places   127   326
  Shame   154   323
  Celebrity   157   85

ORLOVITZ, GIL
POEMS
  Art of the Sonnet: XXIX   88   375
  Art of the Sonnet: IX   90   21

  Art of the Sonnet: VI, LV, LVI   91   94
  Art of the Sonnet: C   96   91

BOOKS REVIEWED
  The Diary of Dr. Eric Zeno   86   287
  The Diary of Alexander Patience   94   408
  The Papers of Professor Bold
  Something to Tell Mother
  Selected Poems   99   247

ORMOND, JOHN
POEMS
  Boundaries   125   9

BOOKS REVIEWED
  Requiem and Celebration   117   108

O'ROURKE, C.
[See KOENIG, ELEANOR]

ORR, BETTY
POEMS
  The Forfeit   10   200

ORR, GREGORY
POEMS
  After the Guest   135   142
  Two Songs of the River
  Then
  Available Now:
    Archaic Torsos of Both Sexes   150   285
  Father's Song   160   152
  Glukupikron   163   85
  Orpheus and Eurydice
  The Talk   170   258

BOOKS REVIEWED
  Burning the Empty Nests   123   173
  Gathering the Bones Together   129   102

ORR, PATRICK [Pseud.]
POEMS
  Annie Shore and Johnnie Doon   5   160
  In the Mohave

ARTICLES ABOUT
  They Come and Go,
    by Harriet Monroe   36   326

ORTIZ-VARGAS, A.
BOOKS REVIEWED
  The Towers of Manhattan   66   350

ORWELL, GEORGE
[Pseud. of BLAIR, ERIC]
ARTICLES ABOUT
  Rev. of Early Auden,
    by Edward Mendelson   139   292

OSBORN, E. B.
  BOOKS REVIEWED
    The Muse in Arms (Ed.)   12   285

OSBORNE, HAROLD
  BOOKS REVIEWED
    Aesthetics and Criticism   88   339

Ó SEARCAIGH, CATHAL
  POEMS
    Oíche/Night
      (Tr. by Frankie Sewell)   167   66

O'SEASNAIN, BRIAN PADRAIC
  BOOKS REVIEWED
    Star-Drift   18   223

O'SHAUGHNESSY, ARTHUR
  BOOKS REVIEWED
    Poems of…
      (Ed. by William Alexander Percy)   24   160

O'SHEA, EDWARD
  ARTICLES
    A Note on "The Watch-Fire,"
      by W. B. Yeats
      (With Christina Hunt Mahony)   135   224

O'SHEEL, SHAEMAS
  BOOKS REVIEWED
    Jealous of Dead Leaves   34   51

OSTENSO, MARTHA
  POEMS
    Waste-Land   24   128
    Solitude

OSTRIKER, ALICIA (SUSKIN)
  POEMS
    The End of the Line   134   196
    Fisherman
    After the Shipwreck
    Anxiety About Dying
    The Change   136   261
    In the Dust
    Message from the Sleeper at Hell's Mouth   139   189
    Poem Beginning with a Line by Dickinson   141   189
    Taking the Shuttle with Franz
    Moth in April
    Contest
    Single Woman Speaking   144   327
    A Clearing by a Stream
    The Woman Who Ran Away   147   19
    Sex
    Encountering the Dead
    A Young Woman, A Tree   150   331
    Stream   151   115
    I Can't Speak   154   225

Helium
  What I Want   159   203
  Metaphor   162   189
  The Orange Cat
  REVIEWS
    The Tune of Crisis   149   231
      Your Native Land, Your Life,
        by Adrienne Rich
      Sin, by Ai
      The Gold Cell, by Sharon Olds
      A Fish To Feed All Hunger,
        by Sandra Alcosser
  BOOKS REVIEWED
    A Woman Under the Surface:
      Poems and Prose Poems   141   349
    Stealing the Language: The Emergence
      of Women's Poetry in America   149   294
    Green Age   156   224
    The Crack in Everything   170   162

OSTROFF, ANTHONY
  POEMS
    Genesis   80   194
    Portrait of a Latter Day Refugee   82   21
    Folk Song   84   272
    Letter from Berkeley   85   322
    Lake Alan: Summer, 1954
    Elegy ("This hot, acacia…")   89   151
    Dirge   92   300
    Announcement   100   300
  BOOKS REVIEWED
    Imperatives   102   42
  ARTICLES ABOUT
    [Note]   83   305

O'SULLIVAN, SEUMAS
  POEMS
    My Sorrow   5   107
    Splendid and Terrible
    The Others
  BOOKS REVIEWED
    The Poems of…   25   52
    Dublin Poems   70   98

OTE, TAKUJI
  POEMS
    Blue Fox
      (Tr. by Satoru Satu
        and Constance Urdang)   88   96

O'TOOLE, KATHLEEN
  POEMS
    County Antrim Archeology   162   28

OUTRAM, RICHARD
POEMS
"...So in a Shapelesse Flame," — 95 350
Starlight Has Entered the Giant's Eye... — 101 255
The Hunter Delirious
  with an Infected Wound — 105 300
In Her Mirror Sinister
Wineglass and Candelabra

BOOKS REVIEWED
Exsultate, Jubilate — 112 201
Turns — 131 225

OU YANG HSIU
POEMS
Ming Fei
  (Tr. by Elizabeth K. Gilbert
  and Su Kai Ming) — 50 136

OVID
BOOKS REVIEWED
The Metamorphoses
  (Tr. by A. E. Watts) — 85 225
The Metamorphoses
  (Tr. by Rolfe Humphries) — 86 303
The Metamorphoses
  (Tr. by Horace Gregory) — 95 185
The Metamorphoses
  (Tr. by Horace Gregory) — 96 247

OWEN, EVAN
REVIEWS
Stone and Flower; Living in Time;
  and The Pythoness,
  by Kathleen Raine — 80 32
Tradition in the Making of Modern Poetry,
  by Howard Sergeant — 83 41

OWEN, GUY
POEMS
The White Horse — 98 226

OWEN, HAROLD
BOOKS REVIEWED
Journey from Obscurity, 1893-1918:
  Memoirs of the Owen Family — 104 41

OWEN, SUE
POEMS
The White Rabbit — 145 149
Written in Blood — 155 204

Total Darkness
Fire and Brimstone — 160 31
These Fireflies — 162 281

BOOKS REVIEWED
The Book of Winter — 156 224

OWEN, WILFRED
BOOKS REVIEWED
Poems — 18 276
The Poems of... — 40 159
The Collected Poems of...
  (Ed. by C. Day Lewis) — 104 41

ARTICLES ABOUT
The Winter's Publishing in England,
  by R. Hughes — 18 172
Poetry in the First World War,
  by David Daiches — 56 323
The Isolation of Isaac Rosenberg,
  by Horace Gregory — 68 30
Rev. of Journey from Obscurity,
  1893-1918: Memoirs
  of the Owen Family,
  by Harold Owen — 104 41
Waking Up
Over the Aeneid,
  by Paul Breslin — 143 347

OWENS, EVERETT
POEMS
Candles Against Darkness — 44 254
Strength from a Mountain
Laid Off
Old Woman
Admonition

OWENS, ROCHELLE
BOOKS REVIEWED
Salt & Core — 114 251

OXENHAM, JOHN
BOOKS REVIEWED
All's Well — 10 271

OZSVATH, ZSUZSANNA
TRANSLATIONS
Poems by Miklós Radnóti
  (Tr. with Frederick Turner) — 151 490

P

"P. C."
[See COLUM, PADRAIC]

"P. D."
[See also DE VRIES, PETER]
REVIEWS
Afternoons in April,
by Grace Hazard Conkling ... 7 152

"P. R."
[See REID, PHYLLIS]

"P. T. R."
POEMS
Plums ... 12 193

PACH, WALTER
ARTICLES
La Voce and Its Poets
[Giuseppe Prezzolini,
Ardengo Soffici] ... 10 50

PACHECO, C.
[See PESSOA, FERNANDO]

PACIFICI, SERGIO
REVIEWS
Three Translations ... 98 403
The Complete Poems
of Michelangelo
(Tr. by Joseph Tusiani)
The Roman Sonnets
of Giuseppi Gioacchino Belli
(Tr. by Harold Norse)
The Selected Writings
of Salvatore Quasimodo
(Tr. by Allen Mandelbaum)

BOOKS REVIEWED
The Promised Land, and Other Poems:
An Anthology of Four Contemporary
Italian Poets (Ed.)
[Umberto Saba, Giuseppe Ungaretti,
Eugenio Montale,
Salvatore Quasimodo] ... 94 350

PACK, ROBERT
POEMS
Father ... 96 291
To the Muse ... 109 97
Locked
Together We Lay Down ... 115 25
The Meeting ... 132 102
Rules ... 132 281
Looking at a Mountain Range—While
Listening to a Mozart Piano Concerto ... 135 317
The Kiss
Making Her Will ... 138 223
Clayfeld's Microscope ... 144 281
Big Bang ... 151 337
The Dead King ... 156 88
Late Summer Purple ... 170 323

BOOKS REVIEWED
Poets of Today II
(With Norma Farber
and Louis Simpson) ... 88 329
Guarded by Women ... 102 402
Poems of Doubt and Belief
(Ed. with Tom F. Driver) ... 106 429
Home from the Cemetery ... 116 120
Nothing But Light ... 123 241
Keeping Watch ... 130 342
Waking to My Name:
New and Selected Poems ... 140 102
Fathering the Map:
New and Selected Later Poems ... 165 289

PACKARD, WILLIAM
BOOKS REVIEWED
The Condition for All Poetry ... 92 384
Genius Is Desire ... 97 114
To Peel an Apple ... 104 47

PACKER, RICHARD
BOOKS REVIEWED
Prince of the Plague Country ... 110 195

PADEL, RUTH
POEMS
History of a Therapist ... 160 6

PADGAONKAR, MANGESH
Poems
   The Rock
     (Tr. by P. Machwe)   93   238

PADGETT, RON
Poems
   Travel   105   372

Books Reviewed
   Bean Spasms
     (With Ted Berrigan)   113   188
   Great Balls of Fire   119   224
   The Complete Poems,
     by Edwin Denby (Ed.)   150   36

PADHI, BIBHU (PRASAD)
Poems
   Rains in Cuttack   128   28
   Sea Breeze   129   270
   Midnight Consolings   155   219
   A Glass of Clear Water   161   194

PAGE, FLORENCE S.
Poems
   Gossamers   28   196
    Through Dry Plains
    Bounty
    A Knowledge
    Rainy Afternoon

PAGE, GEOFF
Poems
   The Waltz   169   65
   The Fundamentalists in Heaven
   Two Signatures

Articles About
   Towards a Contemporary
    Australian Poetics,
    by John Kinsella   169   94

PAGE, P. K.
Poems
   The Mole   60   197
   Failure at Tea   62   203
   Bank Strike—1942—Quebec
   Generation
   Some There Are Fearless
   Vacationists   64   239
   The Sick
   The Dreamer
   Quarrel
   Element
   The Condemned   66   235
   Children
   Contagion
   Stories of Snow
   Love Poem

   Young Girls   69   145
   Election Day
   Freak
   Blowing Boy
   Sisters
   After Rain   89   100
   Giovanni and the Indians
   Another Space   114   299
   Knitter's Prayer
   Fly: On Webs
   A Backwards Journey

Books Reviewed
   Unit of Five
    (With Louis Dudek, Ronald
    Hambleton, Raymond Souster,
    and James Wreford)   66   334
   As Ten As Twenty   70   208
   The Metal and the Flower   88   52
   Cry Ararat!, Poems New and Selected 113   35

PAIGE, D. D.
Books Reviewed
   The Letters of Ezra Pound,
    1907-1941 (Ed.)   79   150

PALACIO, DONNA WOLF
Poems
   Listening to Mozart   163   23

PALAMAS, KOSTES
Poems
   Who Knows in Other Stars
    (Tr. by Rae Dalven)   120   264
   Patrides
    (Tr. by Mary Gregory)   130   211

Books Reviewed
   Life Immovable
    (Tr. by A. E. Phoutrides)   17   48

PALAZZESCHI, ALDO
Articles About
   Five Years of Italian Poetry (1910-1915),
    by Emanuel Carnevali   13   209
   Contemporary Italian Poetry,
    by Edward Williamson   79   159

PALES MATOS, LUIS
Poems
   San Sabas
    (Tr. by Muna Lee)   26   144
   Lament
    (Tr. by H. R. Hays)   62   79

PALEY, GRACE
Books Reviewed
   Leaning Forward   148   36
   New and Collected Poems 164   39

PALGRAVE, FRANCIS TURNER
BOOKS REVIEWED
   The Golden Treasury (Ed.)   110   47

PALLAS, BRENT
POEMS
   Winter Flies   157   144
   Constance Wilde

PALLEN, CONDE BENOIST
BOOKS REVIEWED
   Collected Poems   9   152

PALLEY, JULIAN
BOOKS REVIEWED
   Affirmation:
     A Bilingual Anthology, 1919-1966,
     by Jorge Guillén (Tr.)   113   338

PALMA, MICHAEL
TRANSLATIONS
   Poems by Guido Gozzano   136   11
   Poems by Giorgio Caproni   155   30
   Poems by Tiziano Rossi   155   92
   Poems by Maurizio Cucchi   155   124

PALMER, ALICE FREEMAN
BOOKS REVIEWED
   A Marriage Cycle   9   151

PALMER, CHARLOTTE
POEMS
   A Large Silence   72   20
   Guide to Los Angeles
   Timbre

PALMER, DOUG
BOOKS REVIEWED
   Poems Read in the Spirit
    of Peace & Gladness (Ed.)   115   189

PALMER, GEORGE HERBERT
BOOKS REVIEWED
   Formative Types in English Poetry   16   288

PALMER, MICHAEL
BOOKS REVIEWED
   Sun   154   295

PALMER, SAMUEL
ARTICLES ABOUT
   Rev. of *Visionary and Dreamer,*
    by David Cecil   118   343

PALMER, [MRS.] WINTHROP
POEMS
   Leave Thy Desire   78   130
   Immaculate Conception   79   135

BOOKS REVIEWED
   The New Barbarian   79   347

PANGBORN, GEORGIA WOOD
POEMS
   The Walk on the Moor   6   121
   Morning on the Beach

**PANIGRAHI, KALANDI
CHARAN**
POEMS
   My Message
    (Tr. by Marendra Misra
    and Lila Ray)   93   243

PANKEY, ERIC
POEMS
   Work   152   319
   For Luck
   Memory of Heaven   155   226
   Clarity   156   204
   Bric-a-Brac   160   93
   The Resurrection of the Body   162   26
   June Vagaries   164   125
   The Language of Flowers

BOOKS REVIEWED
   Apocrypha   161   159

PAOLUCCI, ANNE
BOOKS REVIEWED
   Mandragola,
    by Niccolo Machiavelli
    (Tr. with Henry Paolucci)   94   350

PAOLUCCI, HENRY
BOOKS REVIEWED
   Mandragola,
    by Niccolo Machiavelli
    (Tr. with Anne Paolucci)   94   350

PAPADHITSAS, P. D.
POEMS
   Other Ways
    (Tr. by Kimon Friar)   139   83

ARTICLES ABOUT
   Post-War Greek Poets,
    by Kimon Friar   139   99

PAPADHOPOULOS, YANNIS
POEMS
   The Greek Colony in Alexandria
    (Tr. by Kimon Friar)   139   97

ARTICLES ABOUT
   Post-War Greek Poets,
    by Kimon Friar   139   99

PAPATZONIS, TAKIS

POEMS

The Dependence   78   164

Before the First Coming
(Tr. by Kimon Friar)

ARTICLES ABOUT

Contemporary Greek Poetry,
by Kimon Friar   78   145

PAPE, GREG

POEMS

Endless Nights of Rain   142   134

The Morning Horse,
Canyon de Chelly   151   348

Indian Ruins Along Rio de Flag

Morning of the First Birth   158   152

Image on a Sandstone Disc   169   138

BOOKS REVIEWED

Storm Pattern   162   37

Sunflower Facing the Sun

PAPINI, (GIOVANNI)

ARTICLES ABOUT

Five Years of Italian Poetry (1910-1915),
by Emanuel Carnevali   13   209

PAQUETTE, DONALD J.

POEMS

The Visitor   44   320

The Lone Traveler

Words for the Wind   47   196

PARADIS, PHILIP

POEMS

Comet Watch   149   338

**PARADISE, VIOLA I.
[VIOLA T. PARADISE]**

POEMS

Clothes   10   243

Weather Whims   12   66

Thoughts

Early Spring Night

Midnight Rain

Wind and Moonlight

Death

PARÉ, TERENCE P.

POEMS

Diminished Things   144   224

The Shape of Things   146   348

PARFITT, TUDOR

TRANSLATIONS

Poems by Yehuda Amichai
(Tr. with Glenda Abramson)   138   137

BOOKS REVIEWED

Great Tranquillity:
Questions and Answers,
by Yehuda Amichai
(Tr. with Glenda Abramson)   145   109

PARINI, JAY

POEMS

Anthracite Country   129   145

The Mariner   148   311

Town Life

Portrait of the Artist as a Young Lover   151   117

Swimming After Thoughts   156   222

The Lake House in Autumn   168   323

REVIEWS

The Small Valleys of Our Living   130   293

Moving Out,
by David Walker

Striking the Earth,
by John Woods

Open Doorways,
by Philip Appleman

The Names of the Lost,
by Philip Levine

Lady of the Beasts,
by Robin Morgan

PARISI, JOSEPH

ARTICLES

Foreword   151   ix

Some Notes on Post-War
Italian Poetry
(With Paolo Cherchi)
[Sandro Penna, Vittorio Sereni,
Mario Luzi, Giorgio Caproni,
Edoardo Sanguineti,
Andrea Zanzotto]   155   161

In Memory of James Merrill   166   311

REVIEWS

Coming to Terms   124   343

Good Morning,
by Mark Van Doren

Awakening,
by Lucien Stryk

The Uncorrected World,
by Kenneth O. Hanson

Emily Dickinson
in Southern California,
by X. J. Kennedy

Blood Lord,
by Hugh Seidman

The Beast & the Elders,
by Robert Siegel

Personae, Personalities   126   219

The Little That Is All,
by John Ciardi

The Mother's Breast
  & the Father's House,
  by Reed Whittemore
Quartered,
  by Samuel Hazo
Conversions, by Paul Smyth
The Other Hand,
  by Dabney Stuart
Noise in the Trees:
  Poems and a Memoir,
  by William Heyen
Blue Monday,
  by Calvin Forbes
Terry Street and *The Happier Life,*
  by Douglas Dunn
In the Temperate Zone,
  by Judith Kroll
Granite Lady,
  by Susan Fromberg Schaeffer
Harriet Monroe and the Poetry Renaissance:
  The First Ten Years of Poetry, *1912-22,*
  by Ellen Williams
  [Ezra Pound, Amy Lowell,
  W. B. Yeats, Alice Corbin Henderson]   131   39
Mirabell: Books of Number,
  by James Merrill
  [David Jackson]   135   161

PARK, CLYDE W.
ARTICLES
  A Note on Hermann Hesse's Verse   70   206

PARKER, DOROTHY
BOOKS REVIEWED
  Enough Rope   30   52
  Sunset Gun   33   156
  Death and Taxes   39   159

ARTICLES ABOUT
  Cattle in the Garden,
  by M. D. Zabel   38   268

PARKER, DOUGLASS
BOOKS REVIEWED
  Aristophanes:
   The Acharnians (Tr.)   102   56
  The Congresswomen
   of Aristophanes (Tr.)   113   188

PARKER, PHILIP
POEMS
  Cassiopoeia and the Poet   50   127
  Love's Fear
  In the Bodleian Library

PARKER, ROBERT W.
POEMS
  Another Kingdom   79   264

PARKINSON, THOMAS
REVIEWS
  Testimony and Function   93   117
   The Nature of Literature,
    by Herbert Read
   The Creative Experiment,
    by C. M. Bowra

BOOKS REVIEWED
  Men, Women, Vines   95   309

PARKS, LLOYD C.
TRANSLATIONS
  Poem by Jacques Prévert   74   138

PARODY, EDYTHE
POEMS
  For Saint Francis   65   304
  Prayersong
  Our Pastoral
  Circling a Slow Decline
  Gene
  The Dark Leaves

PARR, MICHAEL
BOOKS REVIEWED
  The Green Fig Tree   107   410

PARRA, NICAMOR
BOOKS REVIEWED
  Anti-Poems
   (Tr. by J. Elliott)   97   114
  Poems and Antipoems   112   418

PARSON, DONALD
BOOKS REVIEWED
  Portraits of Keats   85   55

PARSONS, GEOFFREY
BOOKS REVIEWED
  Peter's Progress   84   232

PARSONS, I. M.
BOOKS REVIEWED
  Men Who March Away:
   Poems of the First World War (Ed.)   108   343

PARSONS, JAMES
ARTICLES
  Myths, Emotions,
   and the Great Audience
   [Karl Shapiro]   77   52

ARTICLES ABOUT
  Reply from Karl Shapiro   77   56

PARSONS, ROBERT
[See GRAHAM, MARCUS]

PARTAIN, LEE
POEMS
  How the Son Thanks the Father   156 141

PARTRIDGE, PAULINE D.
POEMS
  Sacrament   12 187

PARVIN, BETTY
BOOKS REVIEWED
  The Bird with the Luck   117 261
  Sketchbook from Mercia

PASCHEN, ELISE
POEMS
  Voir Dire   162 85
  "I Will Leave You in Possession
    of the Field"
  Litany
  Salvage   165 265
  Angling

PASOLINI, PIER PAOLO
POEMS
  Frammento epistolare, al ragazzo Codignola/
    Part of a Letter to the Codignola Boy   155 46
  From Il pianto della scavatrice/
    (The Lament of the Excavator)
  The Fan
  Flesh and Sky
    (Tr. by David Stivender
    and J. D. McClatchy)

PASTAN, LINDA
POEMS
  Arithmetic Lesson: Infinity   129 211
  Egg
  On Hearing the Testimony
    of Those Revived After Cardiac Arrest   132 80
  Excursion   132 273
  Pain
  Blizzard   133 136
  My Achilles Son   135 148
  After Minor Surgery
  Dreams
  Ethics
  Widow's Walk, Somewhere Inland
  Hippolyte at Breakfast   137 76
  Helen Bids Farewell
    to Her Daughter Hermione
  I Am Learning To Abandon the World   138 329
  Extremities
  Lists   140 287
  Waking
  Crimes
  Water Wheel
  Lullaby for 17   142 271
  The Sonoran Desert, January
  Donatello's Magdalene   144 274

  Overture   145 1
  At My Desk
  Waiting Room
  Market Day   146 18
  The Seven Deadly Sins
  The Imperfect Paradise   147 343
  Grudnow   149 1
  Erosion
  Elegy ("Last night the moon...")
  At the Loom
  The Dogwoods   150 14
  Accidents
  Family Tree   151 119
  After an Absence   151 407
  Beauty Shop
  Subway   154 81
  The Hat Lady
  At the Equestrian Museum
  Waku
  The Way the Leaves Keep Falling   155 208
  The Myth of Perfectability
  Sometimes in Winter
  December 18: For M   157 142
  Sestina at 3 A.M.
  Angels   158 257
  All We Have To Go By
  Almost an Elegy   160 136
  Espaliered Pear Trees
  The Apple Shrine   162 63
  Wisteria Floribunda
  Gladiola
  Snow Showers, a Prothalamion   163 19
  In a Northern Country
  Poetry Reading   163 221
  Migraine   165 11
  Requiem   165 81
  The Lumberjacks
  Nocturnal   166 199
  Fame   168 194
  Le Sens de la Nuit
  Letter   169 146
  The Obligation To Be Happy
  The Invalid   169 212

ARTICLES
  Comment   151 221

BOOKS REVIEWED
  Waiting for My Life   140 346
  PM/AM: New and Selected Poems   143 228
  A Fraction of Darkness   148 36
  The Imperfect Paradise   154 340
  Heroes in Disguise   160 284
  An Early Afterlife   168 281

PASTERNAK, BORIS
POEMS
  "We're Few, Perhaps Three"   70 254

To a Friend
Out of Superstition
Improvisation
"We Were in Georgia"
Fresh Paint
Garden
    (Tr. by Babette Deutsch)
Summer Day   70   259
The Thrushes
    (Tr. by George Reavey)

BOOKS REVIEWED
Selected Writings
    (Tr. by C. M. Bowra, Babette Deutsch,
    Beatrice Scott, and Robert Payne)   76   238
The Poetry of...
    (Tr. and ed. by George Reavey)   96   108
Poems by...
    (Tr. by Eugene M. Kayden)

ARTICLES ABOUT
New Trends in Soviet Russian Poetry,
    by Vera Sandomirsky   58   324
Rev. of The Poets of Russia 1890-1930,
    by Renato Poggioli   97   320
The Farmer and the Poet,
    by Karl Shapiro   98   170
Rev. by James Martin   126   103

PASTORIUS, FRANCIS DANIEL
ARTICLES ABOUT
Francis Daniel Pastorius,
    by S. Foster Damon   44   37

PATCHEN, KENNETH
POEMS
Empty Dwelling Places   43   190
Tristanesque
Parting Coney Island
"So When She Lay Beside Me"   55   71
Egypt   61   667
But of Life?   81   61
Beautiful You Are   82   23
The Unanswering Correspondences
All Is Safe...
Under a Tree
Wide, Wide in the Rose's Side   86   71
The Great Birds
O She Is as Lovely-Often
First Came the Lion-Rider
O Now the Drenched Land Wakes
Poemscapes   89   31

BOOKS REVIEWED
Before the Brave   48   340
Before the Brave   56   32
First Will and Testament
The Dark Kingdom   60   160

The Teeth of the Lion   62   282
Cloth of the Tempest   63   278
An Astonished Eye Looks Out of the Air   70   108
Selected Poems   70   269
Red Wine and Yellow Hair   75   115
Hurrah for Anything   92   384
Selected Poems   92   389
When We Were Here Together
Poemscapes
Selected Poems   105   332
Hallelujah Anyway   111   189
The Collected Poems   114   40

ARTICLES ABOUT
Poetry of the Left, by Harriet Monroe   48   212
[Note]   94   134
[Note]   94   274

PATRICK, GEORGE Z.
BOOKS REVIEWED
Eugene Onegin,
    by Alexander Pushkin
    (Tr. with Dorothea Prall Radin)   50   294

PATTEN, BRIAN
BOOKS REVIEWED
Little Johnny's Confession   115   189
Notes to the Hurrying Man   118   102

PATTERSON,
ANTOINETTE DE COURSEY
POEMS
The Treasure Drawer   5   118
Sheila Eileen   8   69
Carnage
The Birches   12   307
Honors   13   15
Folk-Song—from the Danish   18   250
Lucrezia Borgia's Last Letter
The Seeker   21   19
A Dream-Poem   24   189

BOOKS REVIEWED
The Son of Merope and Other Poems   9   324
Old Swedish Fairy Tales,
    by Anna Wahlenberg (Tr.)   36   289

PATTERSON, REBECCA
BOOKS REVIEWED
The Riddle of Emily Dickinson   80   242

PATTERSON, SAMUEL WHITE
BOOKS REVIEWED
The Spirit of the American Revolution
    as Revealed in the Poetry of the Period   8   267
The Spirit of the American Revolution
    as Revealed in the Poetry of the Period   14   281

PATTERSON, WILLIAM MORRISON
ARTICLES
  A Later Word
    from Dr. Patterson   12 171

ARTICLES ABOUT
  Dr. Patterson on Rhythm,
    by Harriet Monroe   12 30

PAUKER, JOHN
BOOKS REVIEWED
  Yoked by Violence   76 302

PAUL, DAVID
BOOKS REVIEWED
  Paul Valéry, Plays
    (Tr. with Robert Fitzgerald) 97 121
  Idée Fixe,
    by Paul Valéry (Tr.)   107 267

PAUL, DOROTHY
POEMS
  Dark Mother   52 15

PAUL, JAMES
POEMS
  Feet, a Sermon   136 280
  The Water Tower

PAUL, SHERMAN
BOOKS REVIEWED
  Olson's Push:
    Origin, Black Mountain,
    and Recent American Poetry 136 219

PAULHAN, JEAN
BOOKS REVIEWED
  Les Cahiers de la Pléiade (Ed.)
    [St.-John Perse]   79 43

PAULIN, TOM
POEMS
  My Skelf   167 44

ARTICLES ABOUT
  A Letter from Britain,
    by William Logan   157 222

PAULSON, CHRISTINA
BOOKS REVIEWED
  I Do Best Alone at Night,
    by Gunnar Ekelöf
    (Tr. and ed. with Robert Bly) 113 188

PAUSCH, EMILY
POEMS
  Stop-Shorts   78 81
  Morning   93 68

PAVESE, CESARE
POEMS
  Untitled
    (Tr. by Brian Swann
    and Ruth Feldman)   116 302
  The Peace that Reigns 161 13
  Street Song
    (Tr. by Scott Davison)

PAVLICH, WALTER
POEMS
  On a Run Near the Water Project 158 79
  Running Near the End of the World
  Road with Five Waterfalls 160 252
  Awareness
  Street Pile   161 94
  Bad Nerves   165 12

PAXTON, JOSEPH FRANCIS
BOOKS REVIEWED
  University Anthology (Ed.)
    [University of Oklahoma] 24 162

PAYNE, ANNE BLACKWELL
POEMS
  While Prudence Weighs 35 202

BOOKS REVIEWED
  Released   41 165

PAYNE, ROBERT
BOOKS REVIEWED
  Selected Writings, by Boris Pasternak
    (Tr. with C. M. Bowra,
    Babette Deutsch, and Beatrice Scott) 76 238

PAYSON, MAHDAH
POEMS
  To My Mountain   8 295

PAZ, OCTAVIO
POEMS
  In Her Splendor Islanded
    (Tr. by Muriel Rukeyser) 92 171

BOOKS REVIEWED
  Entre la Piedra y la Flor 61 680
  An Anthology of Mexican Poetry (Ed.)
    (Tr. by Samuel Beckett) 95 379
  Sun Stone
    (Tr. by Peter Miller) 103 266
  Selected Poems of...
    (Tr. by Muriel Rukeyser) 104 382
  Sun Stone
    (Tr. by Muriel Rukeyser)
  The Collected Poems of... 1957-1987
    (Ed. by Eliot Weinberger)
    (Tr. by Eliot Weinberger et. al.) 154 29

PEABODY, JOSEPHINE PRESTON
BOOKS REVIEWED
The Wolf of Gubbio　　　　　　　　3　184
Harvest Moon　　　　　　　　　　9　269

ARTICLES ABOUT
Of Two Poets, by Harriet Monroe　　21　262

PEACHY, FREDERIC
REVIEWS
Recovering the Tragic Art　　　　95　190
The Poetry of Greek Tragedy,
　　by Richmond Lattimore
The Complete Greek Tragedies:
Euripides III, IV
　　(Ed. by David Grene
　　and Richmond Lattimore)
The Oedipus Plays of Sophocles
　　(Tr. by Paul Roche)
　　[Aeschylus]

PEACOCK, MOLLY
POEMS
The Choice　　　　　　　　　　147　266
Prayer
Commands of Love
The Spell　　　　　　　　　　149　189
A Simple Purchase
When I Love You　　　　　　　151　121
The Dark　　　　　　　　　　152　274

BOOKS REVIEWED
Raw Heaven　　　　　　　　　147　102
Take Heart　　　　　　　　　156　36

PEARCE, DONALD R.
BOOKS REVIEWED
The Senate Speeches
of W. B. Yeats (Ed.)　　　　98　253

PEARCE, HELEN
POEMS
Emily Bronte　　　　　　　　32　136
Sonnet ("Thou mad'st the swan...")
Wild Roofs of Kings　　　　　38　127

PEARCE, ROY HARVEY
BOOKS REVIEWED
The Continuity of American Poetry　102　269

PEARSE, PADRAIC
ARTICLES ABOUT
Correspondence
　　from Joseph Campbell　　　8　272

PEARSON, LU EMILY
BOOKS REVIEWED
Elizabethans at Home　　　　92　189

PEARSON, NORMAN HALL
BOOKS REVIEWED
Poets of the English Language
　　(Ed. with W. H. Auden)　　77　179

PEARSON, NORMAN HOLMES
ARTICLES ABOUT
The Forging of H. D.,
　　by Gloria G. Fromm　　　153　160

PEASE, JOSEPHINE VAN DOLZEN
POEMS
City Paces　　　　　　　　　31　318
Young Men Fly
Skyline
Late Frost
Night-Cap

PEATTIE, LOUISE REDFIELD
POEMS
Susan Lou　　　　　　　　　24　190

PECK, JOHN
POEMS
Apple　　　　　　　　　　119　276

REVIEWS
Poems of R. P. Blackmur
　　[Denis Donoghue, Yvor Winters]　133　290

BOOKS REVIEWED
Shagbark　　　　　　　　　123　353

PEDRICK, JEAN
POEMS
The Long Season　　　　　　100　164

PEEL, MARIE
BOOKS REVIEWED
Sons of My Skin: Selected Poems 1954-1974,
　　by Peter Redgrove (Ed.)　　131　292

PEEPLES, LUCIA
POEMS
Mine　　　　　　　　　　　11　197

PÉGUY, CHARLES
BOOKS REVIEWED
Basic Verities
　　(Tr. by Ann and Julian Green)　62　208
Men and Saints
　　(Tr. by Ann and Julian Green)　66　42

ARTICLES ABOUT
Correspondence
　　from Richard Aldington　　　5　144
Voice in Babel,
　　by Peter de Vries　　　　62　208

POETRY

French Poetry and
the Revival of Mysticism,
by Eugene Jolas 56 264
French Chronicle: Recent Publications,
by Wallace Fowlie 91 36

PELL, JAY
BOOKS REVIEWED
Spectre in the Fantastic Laboratory 90 114

PELLICER, CARLOS
BOOKS REVIEWED
Exágonos 61 680
3 Spanish American Poets
(With Pablo Neruda
and Jorge Carrera Andrade)
(Tr. by Mary and C. V. Wicker) 62 111

PENDLETON, CONRAD
[Pseud. of KIDD, WALTER E.]
POEMS
West Pasture 61 602
Staked
Riding Fence

PENNA, SANDRO
POEMS
La vita... è ricordarsi di un risveglio/
Life... Is Remembering Having Wakened 155 14
Interno/Interior
La veneta piazzetta/
The Little Venetian Square
Nuotatore/Swimmer
Laggiù, Dove una storia/Down There
(Tr. by William Jay Smith)

ARTICLES ABOUT
Some Notes on Post-War Italian Poetry,
by Paolo Cherchi and Joseph Parisi 155 161

PENNELL, ELIZABETH HART
POEMS
Youth and Age 18 85

PENNELL, JOSEPH STANLEY
POEMS
Poems of Silence 39 132
Noon-Day Bones
Towns
Transciency 43 13

PENNINGTON, ANNE
BOOKS REVIEWED
Vasko Popa: Collected Poems (Tr.) 136 40

PERCHIK, SIMON
POEMS
Five Poems 112 90

("Weeklight...")
("With one hand, the world...")
("Your breasts, little sister...")
("Across the Urals...")
("This leaf had eyes...")
Poem ("Without their Spring...") 117 164

BOOKS REVIEWED
I Counted Only April 105 336
Twenty Years of Hands 111 195

PERCY, WILLIAM ALEXANDER
POEMS
Sonnet ("Ignorant, in a world...") 40 63

BOOKS REVIEWED
Sappho in Levkas and Other Poems 10 213
Poems of Arthur O'Shaughnessy (Ed.) 24 160

PEREIRA, SAM
POEMS
Something About Sailing 144 104

PERELLA, NICOLAS J.
REVIEWS
A Great Poet, a Continuing Task 107 333
Giacomo Leopardi: Poems
(Tr. by Jean-Pierre Barricelli)
Leopardi and the Theory of Poetry,
by G. Singh

PERGAMENT, LOLA
POEMS
The Arrogant Leaf 45 264
The Trackless Way 47 86
Mute Testimony
Frail Tempest
Elegy on the Wind
Green Capture
All But the Brave
The Inheritors
The Pastoral
For Love Later 49 259
Slow Invasion 50 85
Escape into April
First Frost
Winter Love
Brief Refuge
For Survival
One Not Loved
My So Much Loved Variety 52 204

PERKINS, DAVID
REVIEWS
Collected Poems and *Figures of Thought:*
Speculations on the Meaning of Poetry
& Other Essays,
by Howard Nemerov 132 351

BOOKS REVIEWED
   A History of Modern Poetry, Volume II:
      Modernism and After   151   296

PERKINS, WILLIAM D.
POEMS
   Early Autumn: 1945   66   315

PERLBERG, MARK
POEMS
   The Dead Fox   122   75
   When at Night   134   216
   "Garden Vision"   153   13

REVIEWS
   Shorthand   126   172
      Seascape: Needle's Eye,
         by George Oppen
      Selected Poems,
         by Larry Eigner
         (Ed. by Samuel Charters
         and Andrea Wyatt)
      Song: I Want a Witness,
         by Michael S. Harper
      Helmet of the Wind,
         by Nancy Cardozo
      Midwatch,
         by Keith Wilson

PERLZWEIG, JUDITH
POEMS
   "Pretty Things"   26   266
   The Dreamboat
   Cloud Water
   Dancing ("Leaves fly away...")
   Flower Names
   Marbles
   Blocks
   Xylophone
   Autumn Songs
   Pretty Things   28   266
   Climbing
   First Snow
   Frozen Lake
   Tree
   Dancing ("Water dances...")
   Fountain
   Dancing Dust
   Eyes of the Dark
   Wind
   Love

PERRAULT, CHARLES
ARTICLES ABOUT
   Rev. of *Puss in Boots,*
      The Sleeping Beauty, & Cinderella:
      A Retelling of Three Classic Fairy Tales
      Based on the French of Charles Perrault,
      by Marianne Moore   105   190

PERREAULT, JOHN
BOOKS REVIEWED
   Camouflage   109   407

PERREAU-SAUSSINE, RICHARD
POEMS
   For Helen Keller   90   219
   Swimmer Emerging   93   26

PERRET, CHRISTOPHER
POEMS
   One Kind of Spring   95   288
   Rebirth You Say
   Set of Four Winds
   Not Ronald Perry's
      Chinese Horse   97   298

PERRINE, LAURENCE
POEMS
   Janus   144   133
   Limerick
   The Creation   157   323
   Justice and Mercy Reconciled
   A Question (For Robert Frost)
   The Testaments   163   129
   Genesis Reconsidered

PERRY, MARGARET E.
POEMS
   The River Pigs   74   26

PERRY, RONALD (LEE)
POEMS
   The Giraffe   87   210
   Pigeon Key
   Pavane
   The Elephant   89   295
   Cat Cay   91   20
   Adagio for Jazz
   Chaconne   92   155
   Landscape: Ragged Key
   The Shellpicker   93   295
   From *Letter to J.M.*
   Vientiane Journal
   Winter Stanzas for Norma   95   169
   The Chinese Horse
   Sonnet XI ("Begins to emerge...")
   Suite for Wind Instruments
   Sonnet XIII ("I write as one...")
   Le Quattro Stagioni   98   90
   Lines for a Crucifix
   A Warning to the Reader   102   238
   Aria & Variations   105   170
   The Mirror Walk   138   276
   The Hollow White   139   165
   Portrait of a Tree
   In the Smoke

BOOKS REVIEWED
  The Rock Harbor   96   314
  Voyages from Troy   102   402
  Denizens   140   35

PERSE, ST.-JOHN
[Pseud. of SAINT-LÉGER LÉGER, ALEXIS]
POEMS
  Exil   59   295
  Et Vous, Mers...
    (Tr. by Wallace Fowlie)   79   1
  Mer de Baal, Mer de Mammon...
    (Tr. by Wallace Fowlie)   86   187

ARTICLES
  Correspondence   86   124
  Correspondence
    (Tr. by Wallace Fowlie)   86   179

BOOKS REVIEWED
  Exile and Other Poems
    (Tr. by Denis Devlin)   74   343
  Les Cahiers de la Pléiade
    (Ed. by Jean Paulhan)   79   43
  Winds
    (Tr. by Hugh Chisholm)   82   345
  Seamarks
    (Tr. by Wallace Fowlie)   93   332
  Chronique
    (Tr. by Robert Fitzgerald)   99   194
  Birds
    (Tr. by Robert Fitzgerald)   110   184

ARTICLES ABOUT
  The Poetry of Unrest,
    by M. D. Zabel
    [*Anabasis*]   50   90
  A Note on Alexis Saint Léger Léger,
    by Archibald MacLeish   59   330
  St.-John Perse: Bibliography   59   336
  Homage to St.-John Perse,
    by Allen Tate   75   213
  St.-John Perse, by Wallace Fowlie   79   31
  Rev. of *Les Cahiers de la Pléiade*
    (Ed. by Jean Paulhan)   79   43
  Paris Letter, by Wallace Fowlie   96   371
  In Tribute to St.-John Perse,
    by Wallace Fowlie   97   255
  Letters from the Midi,
    by Wallace Fowlie   100   258
  Rev. of *St.-John Perse:
    A Study of His Poetry*,
    by Arthur Knodel   110   254
  Rev. of *The Limits of Symbolism:
    Studies of Five Modern French Poets*,
    by Bernard Weinberg   112   41

PERSIA SOCIETY OF LONDON
BOOKS REVIEWED
  Selections from the Rubiyat of Hafiz
    (Tr. by a member of
     the Persia Society of London)   20   346

PERSIUS
BOOKS REVIEWED
  The Satires of...
    (Tr. by W. S. Merwin)   101   353

PERSOV, ANNE
BOOKS REVIEWED
  Whatever You Reap   42   223

PESSOA, FERNANDO
[ALBERTO CAIERO, RICARDO REIS, ALVARO DE CAMPOS, BERNARDO SOARES, C. PACHECO, ANTONIO-MORA, pseuds.]
POEMS
  Autopsychography   87   26
  Odes
    ("Of the gardens of Adonis...")
    ("To be great, be whole...")
  Discontinuous Poems
  The Herdsman
    (Tr. by Edouard Roditi)

ARTICLES ABOUT
  The Several Names
    of Fernando Pessoa,
    by Edouard Roditi   87   40

PETERKIEWICZ, JERZY
BOOKS REVIEWED
  Five Centuries of Polish Poetry
    (With Burns Singer)   100   104
  Easter Vigil & Other Poems,
    by Karol Wojtyla (Tr.)
    [Pope John Paul II]   136   40

PETERKIN, JULIA M.
POEMS
  Venner's Sayings   23   59
    Green Thursday
    The Wind
    Gifts
    Two Kinds of Love
    Boy-Chillen
    Men
    Warning
    Greed of the Ground
    Advice
    Prayer from Lang Syne Plantation
  Vinner's Sayings   25   240

REVIEWS
  Fine Clothes for the Jew,
    by Langston Hughes   31   44

ARTICLES ABOUT
  [Note]   23   114
  Poets as Prosers, by Harriet Monroe   28   328

PETERS, H. F.
  BOOKS REVIEWED
  Rainer Maria Rilke:
    Masks and the Man   97   387

PETERS, MARGEDANT
  ARTICLES
  The Poet and Pedant Symposium
    [Allen Tate, Wright Thomas,
    Joe Horrell, Lionel Trilling]   57   194

  REVIEWS
  New Poetry Recordings   61   519
    Contemporary Poets Series
      [W. R. Benét, E. E. Cummings,
      Archibald MacLeish, Marianne Moore,
      Allen Tate, W. C. Williams]
    Great Themes in Poetry
      (Read by Basil Rathbone)

  ARTICLES ABOUT
  For the Record,
    by George Dillon   73   28

PETERS, W. A. M.
  BOOKS REVIEWED
  Gerard Manley Hopkins   .74   292

PETERSEN, DONALD
  POEMS
  The Stages of Narcissus   83   141

  BOOKS REVIEWED
  The Spectral Boy   105   336

PETERSEN, PAULANN
  POEMS
  Lullaby   164   273
  When I Walk
  Handwriting   168   128

PETERSON, EDWIN L(EWIS)
  POEMS
  To a Poet Long Dead   31   261
  Songs for My Soul   37   138

PETERSON, HOUSTON
  BOOKS REVIEWED
  Book of Sonnet Sequences (Ed.)   37   164
  The Melody of Chaos   39   163

Poet to Poet, a Treasury
  of Golden Criticism
  (Ed. with William S. Lynch)   66   345

PETERSON, JIM
  POEMS
  The Pretender   152   316
  The Other   154   10

PETERSON, KAREN
  POEMS
  Second Sight   168   204

PETERSON, ROBERT
  POEMS
  Evening Poem   110   21
  Two Sonnets
    ("When you look one way...")
    ("Mazatlan—an unenclosed system...")

  BOOKS REVIEWED
  The Binnacle   113   188

PETGEN, DOROTHY
  POEMS
  Vox Matris   22   142

PETRARCH
  BOOKS REVIEWED
  Some Love Songs of...
    (Tr. by William Dudley Foulke)   7   207
  Petrarch at Vaucluse:
    Letters in Verse and Prose
    (Tr. by Ernest Hatch Wilkins)   94   350

PETRI, GYÖRGY
  POEMS
  Horace Has a Bad Day
    (Tr. by Mária Körösy
    and Bruce Berlind)   164   85

PETRI, LORI
  POEMS
  Gardener   52   137

PETRIE, PAUL
  POEMS
  The Lover as a Beggar as a Dog   85   9
  Superseded Love Letters   88   19
  Fathers and Sons
  In Defense of Colds   90   296
  Snow
  Elegy for an Unrelated Cousin   93   27
  Mother Into Child
  Rites in October   95   153
  The Sceptic Speaks to St. Simeon
  Departure
  Renoir   97   17

Hill Top
On Looking at a Vermeer
After Seeing the Ballet "Job"
Pieces of a Round World   100   152
Pictures of Departure   104   15
Diana the Huntress
Kindertoten   112   21
In Praise of Old Stoves   114   313
Manhood   120   342
Three O'Clock Moon   127   258
The Explorers   129   32
The Superannuated Couple   144   149
The Onset of Senility

REVIEWS
Three Critics   95   122
    Cobras and Cockle Shells,
        by Frederick Eckman
    The Chequer'd Shade, by John Press
    Stewards of Excellence, by A. Alvarez
A Poetry Chronicle   102   49
    The Equal Tribunals,
        by Byron Vazakas
    Breakfast in Mycenae, by Lee Hatfield
    All the Time in the Dark,
        by John W. Clark
    The Living Seed, by John Moffitt
    A Touch of Recognition,
        by Maxine Cassin
    From an Interior Silence
        and Cries of Flesh and Stone,
        by Richard O'Connell

BOOKS REVIEWED
    Confessions of a Non-Conformist   104   115
    The Race with Time and the Devil   108   57
    From Under the Hill of Night: Poems   118   290

PETRONIUS, (GAIUS)
BOOKS REVIEWED
    The Satyricon
        (Tr. by William Arrowsmith)   96   247
    The Satyricon of...
        (Tr. by William Arrowsmith)   107   264

PETROSKI, HENRY
POEMS
    From the Observation Deck   125   33=
    Professor Z Introduces Professor A   133   278

PETROSKY, ANTHONY
BOOKS REVIEWED
    Jurgis Petraskas   144   40

PETRUNKEVITCH, WANDA
POEMS
    Death and the Aviator   6   236
    Inconsistency

PETTINGELL, PHOEBE
POEMS
    Ode on Zero   117   183
    Transport to Patmos
    Graven Images   119   23
    Labyrinths
    Frog Prince   120   138
    Fat Tuesday

REVIEWS
    Plurality of Worlds   119   234
        This World, by Harvey Shapiro
        The Only World There Is,
            by Miller Williams
        The Wife of Winter,
            by Michael Dennis Browne
        The Yellow Room, by Donald Hall
        Topography and Other Poems,
            by Ruth Stone
        Wallace Stevens: The Poems of Our Climate,
            by Harold Bloom   131   165
        Local Assays:
            On Contemporary American Poetry
            and The Roundhouse Voices:
            Selected and New Poems,
            by Dave Smith   147   346

PETTITT, KENNETH
POEMS
    Extra Objective   78   71

PEVEAR, RICHARD
BOOKS REVIEWED
    Night Talk and Other Poems   133   45

PEYRE, HENRI
BOOKS REVIEWED
    Pensées de Baudelaire (Ed.)   82   86
    Connaissance de Baudelaire
    The Poem Itself
        (Ed. with Stanley Burnshaw,
        Dudley Fitts, and John Frederick Nims) 98   56

PEYTON, JOHN R. C.
POEMS
    The Censor   14   198
    Geyser   19   77

PFAFFMANN, LOUISE
POEMS
    Elegy ("If her portrait refuses...")   100   166
    To the Unburned Daughter

PFEIFFER, ERIC
POEMS
    The Clearing   103   163
    For a Pregnant Lady
    For N.
    Drowning in September

BOOKS REVIEWED
Take With Me Now That Enormous Step   105   270

PFUND, HELEN LEDYARD
POEMS
Magazine Cover   40   191

PHELPS, ARTHUR L.
POEMS
There Was a Rose   12   190
An Old Man's Weariness
You Died for Dreams   14   185

PHELPS, LYON
POEMS
From "In Praise of Pilgrims"   104   82
Song from a Play
November at Bridgehampton Beach

PHELPS, MARY
BOOKS REVIEWED
A Bed of Strawberries   95   116

PHELPS, WILLIAM LYON
BOOKS REVIEWED
*The Advance of English Poetry
in the Twentieth Century*   14   159

ARTICLES ABOUT
Correspondence from Jean Catel   18   232

PHEMISTER, BRUCE
POEMS
Letter   74   86

PHILBERT, JULIEN
ARTICLES ABOUT
Verse Drama on the Paris Stage,
by Ruby Haykin   82   294

PHILBRICK, CHARLES H.
BOOKS REVIEWED
Wonderstrand Revisited   99   178

PHILIP, JOHN
POEMS
Poem ("Pamphleteering autumn...")   74   89

PHILIPS, KATHERINE
ARTICLES ABOUT
Correspondence from Edouard Roditi   67   173

PHILLIPS, BETTY
POEMS
Prospects   48   136
Perspective
Change
Sonnet to the Sea

PHILLIPS, LOUIS
REVIEWS
Anon and Various Time Machine Poems,
by Dick Allen   121   303

PHILLIPS, ROBERT
POEMS
The Tenant   121   286
Wish You Were Here   150   278
Letter from the Country
Suburban Interior   151   122

REVIEWS
Another Look, by Horace Gregory   128   300
Short Reviews   145   348
*Overnight in the Guest House
of the Mystic,*
by Dick Allen
*Drawn by Stones, by Earth, by Things
that Have Been in the Fire,*
by Marvin Bell
*Maximum Security Ward
and Other Poems,*
by Ramon Guthrie
(Ed. by Sally M. Gall)
Yin, by Carolyn Kizer
Rules of Sleep, by Howard Moss
Works and Days,
by David Schubert
(Ed. by T. and R. Weiss)

BOOKS REVIEWED
The Pregnant Man   135   348
Running on Empty   143   228
*Personal Accounts:
New & Selected Poems, 1966-1986*   149   94

PHILLIPS, STEPHEN
ARTICLES ABOUT
In Danger,
by Harriet Monroe   2   68
The Death of Stephen Phillips,
by Harriet Monroe   7   260

PHILLIPS, WILLIAM
ARTICLES
Private Experience
and Public Philosophy
(With Philip Rahv)   48   98

PHILPOTTS, EDEN
BOOKS REVIEWED
The Iscariot   1   94
As the Wind Blows   19   53

PHIPPS, BETTY
POEMS
Sky   28   197

PHLEGAR, THELMA
POEMS
   Octogenarian   52   69

PHOUTRIDES, A. E.
BOOKS REVIEWED
   Life Immovable,
     by Kostes Palamas (Tr.)   17   48

PICASSO, PABLO
ARTICLES ABOUT
   Rev. of *Selected Poems,*
     by John Masefield   53   144
   Homage to Max Jacob,
     by Wallace Fowlie   75   352

PICCOLO, LUCIO
[(BARON) LUCIO PICCOLO
DI CALANOVELLA]
POEMS
   Scirocco   98   386
   Mobile Universo di Folate
   From *Veneris Venefica Agrestis*
   The Sundial
     (Tr. by Sonia Raiziss
     and Alfredo de Palchi)
   The Days
     (Tr. by Brian Swann
     and Ruth Feldman)   116   303

ARTICLES ABOUT
   Rev. of *Canti Barocchi,*
     by Eugenio Montale
     (Tr. by Sonia Raiziss
     and Alfredo de Palchi)   98   392

PICHETTE, HENRI
ARTICLES ABOUT
   Verse Drama on the Paris Stage,
     by Ruby Haykin   82   294

PICK, JOHN
BOOKS REVIEWED
   Gerard Manley Hopkins, Priest and Poet   62   347

ARTICLES ABOUT
   Rev. of *Gerard Manley Hopkins,*
     by Eleanor Ruggles   65   142

PICKARD, CYNTHIA
POEMS
   The Slap   75   202
   Elements
   Primary
   Bird Dream   79   273

BOOKS REVIEWED
   Woman in Apartment   93   399

PICKARD, DEANNA
POEMS
   Her Lips   165   272

PICKARD, TOM
POEMS
   The Street Cleaner
     with His 18th Cent. Muck Cart   105   374
   Poem ("sitting/in firelight...")
   Poem ("fingers/of a hand...")

PICKERILL, EDWARD
POEMS
   Sixteen   21   72

PICKTHALL, MARJORIE
ARTICLES ABOUT
   The Development
     of Poetry in Canada, 1880–1940,
     by E. K. Brown   58   34

PICON, GAETAN
ARTICLES ABOUT
   Letters from the Midi, by Wallace Fowlie   100   258

PIDAL, RAMON MENENDEZ
[See MENENDEZ PIDAL, RAMON]

PIERCE, EDITH LOVEJOY
POEMS
   Winter Night   55   309
   Manifesto   59   191
   The Tongue of the Snake   66   316

BOOKS REVIEWED
   In This Our Day   65   278
   Therefore Choose Life   74   50

PIERCE, FRED E.
BOOKS REVIEWED
   Selections from the Symbolical Poems
     of William Blake (Ed.)   9   315

PIERCE, LORNE
BOOKS REVIEWED
   Canadian Poetry in English
     (Ed. with Bliss Carman
     and V. B. Rhodenhizer)   86   111

PIERCE, RAY
POEMS
   Exhortation   51   180
   Formula

PIERCE, THOMAS
ARTICLES ABOUT
   Notes on Mid-Western Oblivion,
     by Pat Morrissette   34   346

PIERCY, MARGE
BOOKS REVIEWED
Breaking Camp 117 322
Hard Loving 117 392
To Be of Use 125 229
Stone, Paper, Knife 143 295
My Mother's Body 147 156
Mars and Her Children 164   39

PIERSANTI, UMBERTO
POEMS
Quando l'ottobre lento trascolora/
    When Slow October Changes Color
    (Tr. by Stephen Sartarelli) 155 118

PIERSON, PHILIP
POEMS
The Monster's Photo Album 133 323

PIERSON, RUTH BALDWIN
POEMS
Extremity 37 199
Cloakless 40   7

PILKINGTON, KEVIN
POEMS
Fairfield Beach 140 148
The Reincarnation of Montana
Directions Through a Changing Scene 142 332
Jogging on the Beach
A Spruce in Vermont

PILLIN, WILLIAM
POEMS
Walking Through Daylight 49   81
    The Ancient Dead
    Wild Boys of the Road
    Bronzed Men
Note 51 130
Speech 52 182
In Autumn's Wake 53   59
O'Brien's Viewpoint
Endless Dark
Two Lives
Signature
Uncertain Clues 61 376
Shut the Door
Totalitarian Skeleton
Form Was a Classic Mirror
He 62 307
Song ("The crows in windward...")
Song ("How frugal was the mind...") 66 124
Ceramic Symbols
A Priori 67 254
That Which Is Good Is Simply Done 69   80
The Wanderer
Abel's Lament
If You Say Thou to Anything 85   93

Berceuse 86 335
Nocturne with Ghosts
On Hearing Frederick Play the Appassionata
In a Dream I Spoke 91 103
The Ascensions
Holy Beggars

BOOKS REVIEWED
Poems 57 278
Theory of Silence 76 365
Passage After Midnight 94 117

PINCKNEY, JOSEPHINE
POEMS
In the Barn 18 194
Strange
The Outcast
Swamp Lilies
Spring Makes Me Wonder 20   21
Japonica Bush 26   18
Hag! 30 310
A Recollection 40   67
A Fig for Selene

BOOKS REVIEWED
Sea-Drinking Cities 32 162

PINDAR
BOOKS REVIEWED
Some Odes of...
    (Tr. by Richmond Lattimore) 62 282
The Odes of...
    (Tr. by Richmond Lattimore) 70 340

PINDER, FRANCES DICKENSON
POEMS
Marsh Sketches 20   22
Sea Marsh
    Marsh Pools
    Shallows
Frost 21 253
Inland from Jupiter 48   28

PINKERFELD-'AMIR, ANDA
POEMS
Hagar
    (Tr. by Batyah Greenberg) 92 232

PINKNEY, DOROTHY COWLES
POEMS
Out of the Homely Light 61 655
Scene from a Common Tragedy, Unnamed 63 192
Tribunal for a Nine-Year-Old 65   78
Delicate Stop Watch
Personality: Split
Repeat the Bird in Spring
Windward of Voice and Feeling 78 131
Tenements: Train's Eye View

PINSKY, ROBERT
POEMS
Summoning the Personal Devil   114   381
Embassy Architecture
Catatonic   118   316
The View from the Road
The Destruction of Long Branch, N. J.
A Classic Moment
Waiting   121   288
Discretions of Alcibiades   124   82
From Essay on Psychiatrists   125   212
    XIV: Their Speech,
        Compared with Wisdom and Poetry
From An Explanation of America   132   125
Dying   136   206
History of My Heart   141   251
Voyage to the Moon   151   123

TRANSLATIONS
From Dante's Inferno   162   143
    Canto XVI
    Canto XVII

REVIEWS
Said, and Unsaid   122   168
    Instructions for Viewing a Solar Eclipse,
        by Dave Kelly
    Rooted in Silence,
        by Richard Schramm
    Turning To Look Back,
        by John Woods
    Once for the Last Bandit,
        by Samuel Hazo
Far from Prose   123   241
    Sleek for the Long Flight,
        by William Matthews
    Amputations,
        by Cynthia Macdonald
    In the Heart or Our City,
        by Raphael Rudnik
    Nothing But Light,
        by Robert Pack
The Late Hour, by Mark Strand   132   298
Signs and Wonders, by Carl Dennis   137   102

BOOKS REVIEWED
Sadness and Happiness   129   226
An Explanation of America   136   295
History of My Heart   147   227
Poetry and the World   156   297
The Want Bone   157   33
The Figured Wheel:
    New and Collected Poems 1966-1996   170   226

PINTO, VIVIAN DE SOLA
BOOKS REVIEWED
John Skelton,
    A Selection from His Poems (Ed.)   82   95

The Common Muse: An Anthology
    of Popular British Ballad Poetry,
    XVth-XXth Century
    (Ed. with Allan Edwin Rodway)   91   400
The Complete Poems
    of D. H. Lawrence
    (Ed. with F. Warren Roberts)   106   218

PIONTEK, HEINZ
ARTICLES ABOUT
German Lyric Poetry Since 1945,
    by Hans Egon Holthusen
    (Tr. by Herman Salinger)   88   257

PIPER, EDWIN FORD
POEMS
Ballads   15   175
    Bindlestiff
    Whoa, Zebe, Whoa
    Sweetgrass Range
March Wind   17   318
Whispering Often
Home
The Line Fence   21   20
Paintrock Road   25   237
    Chimney-Talk
    Obiter Dicta
    Indian Counsel
    Trail-Talk
    Six Yoke
Two Saddle Songs   29   310
    Riding Men
    Rustlers

BOOKS REVIEWED
Barbed Wire and Other Poems   12   276
Barbed Wire and Wayfarers   25   42
Paintrock Road   31   91

PIPER, H. W.
BOOKS REVIEWED
The Active Universe   102   341

PIPER, JANET (PRESSLEY)
POEMS
Before Wisdom   36   252
    Elementary Logic
    Pursuit of the Muse
    Ingrate
    Introvert

PIPES, JAMES
BOOKS REVIEWED
Ziba   64   41

PIPPIN, R. GENE
POEMS
In Herculaneum   130   17

PITCHFORD, KENNETH
POEMS
Lobotomy 82 266
Heraklion 96 300
Balcony Scene 130 311

BOOKS REVIEWED
A Suite of Angels 112 276
Color Photos of the Atrocities 124 167

PITKIN, ANNE
POEMS
Winter Ghazals 161 132

PITTER, RUTH
BOOKS REVIEWED
A Mad Lady's Garland 47 103
A Trophy of Arms. Poems: 1926-1935 51 43
The Spirit Watches 56 334
The Bridge: Poems 1939-1944 68 103

PITT-KETHLEY, FIONA
ARTICLES ABOUT
A Letter from Britain [II],
by William Logan 157 290

PIZER, LAURETTE
POEMS
Poem ("I wish that I might...") 59 197

PLACOTARI, ALEXANDRA
POEMS
Platytera
(Tr. by Rae Dalven) 145 335

PLANZ, ALLEN
POEMS
Pan-American 103 302

BOOKS REVIEWED
A Night for Rioting 117 204

PLARR, VICTOR
BOOKS REVIEWED
Ernest Dowson 6 43

PLATH, SYLVIA
POEMS
Wreath for a Bridal 89 231
Dream with Clam-Diggers
Strumpet Song
Metamorphosis
Two Sisters of Persephone
Epitaph for Fire and Flower
The Snowman on the Moor 90 229
Sow
Ella Mason and Her Eleven Cats
On the Difficulty of Conjuring up a Dryad

On the Decline of Oracles 94 368
The Death of Myth-Making
A Lesson in Vengeance
Stars over the Dordogne 99 346
Widow
Face Lift
Heavy Women
Love Letter
Fever 103 102 292
Purdah
Eavesdropper
Metamorphosis 121 25

BOOKS REVIEWED
The Colossus and Other Poems 101 412
Ariel 109 260
The Colossus and Other Poems 121 54
The Collected Poems
(Ed. by Ted Hughes) 142 170

ARTICLES ABOUT
Creative Glut,
by Karl Shapiro 135 36
Poets Aloud, by Donald Hall 139 297
Rev. of The Psycho-Political Muse:
American Poetry Since the Fifties,
by Paul Breslin 152 229

PLATT, DONALD
POEMS
Aria for this Listening Area 156 29
Kore

PLEYNET, MARCELIN
BOOKS REVIEWED
Lautréamont par lui-même 112 41

PLISETSKY, GERMAN
POEMS
Station 124 214
Rooms
Quiet Time
(Tr. by Daniel Weissbort)

PLOMER, WILLIAM
POEMS
The Half-Recluse 101 94

BOOKS REVIEWED
Visiting the Caves 49 223
Borderline Ballads 88 396
Collected Poems 97 260

PLOTZ, HELEN
BOOKS REVIEWED
The Earth Is the Lord's:
Poems of the Spirit (Ed.) 108 343
Poems from the German (Ed.) 113 188

PLUMLY, STANLEY
POEMS
Posthumous Keats   142   167
My Mother's Feet

BOOKS REVIEWED
Giraffe   126   103
Summer Celestial   145   161
Boy on the Step   158   41
The Marriage in the Trees   170   288

PLUNKETT, EUGENIA
POEMS
Sky-View Drive-In:
Memory of Psychotherapy   117   241

PLUNKETT, JOSEPH (MARY)
ARTICLES ABOUT
Correspondence
from Padraic Colum   8   268

PLUTZIK, HYAM
POEMS
Time and the Poem   97   158
The Lecture
On the Last Survivor
of Our War, 1861-1865
The Marriage

BOOKS REVIEWED
Aspects of Proteus   75   118
Apples From Shinar   96   185

PLYMELL, CHARLES
POEMS
December   110   90

BOOKS REVIEWED
Apocalypse Rose   112   274

PO CHU-I
POEMS
On Barbarous Modern Instruments
(Tr. by Arthur Waley)   11   254

POE, EDGAR ALLAN
ARTICLES ABOUT
Correspondence
from Willard Wattles   12   230
Poetry South,
by Hervey Allen
and DuBose Heyward   20   35
Poe in South Carolina,
by Hervey Allen   20   48
[Note on The Raven]   25   227
Rev. of Israfel, by Hervey Allen   29   266
Rev. of Edgar Allan Poe,
by Edward Shanks   50   353

Rev. of The Oxford Book of American Verse
(Ed. by F. O. Matthiessen)   79   36
Rev. of Baudelaire on Poe: Critical Papers
(Tr. and ed. by Lois
and Francis E. Hyslop, Jr.)   81   247
Rev. of The Forlorn Demon, by Allen Tate   83   220
Rev. of The Haunted Man,
by Philip Lindsay   86   118
"The Principle of Composition,"
by Kenneth Burke   99   46

POETRY SOCIETY OF GEORGIA
BOOKS REVIEWED
Anthology of Verse   37   164

**POETRY SOCIETY
OF SOUTH CAROLINA**
BOOKS REVIEWED
Yearbook of...   21   276

POGGIOLI, RENATO
REVIEWS
The Oxford Book of Italian Verse
(Ed. by St. John Lucas)
[2nd ed. by C. Dionisotti]   82   277

BOOKS REVIEWED
The Poets of Russia 1890-1930   97   320

POIRIER, RICHARD
BOOKS REVIEWED
Robert Frost   132   226
Collected Poems, Prose, & Plays,
by Robert Frost
(Ed. with Mark Richardson)   168   232

POLITE, FRANK
POEMS
Letter from Duluth   106   279
The Manservant   109   23
Image at Thirty
Small Craft Warnings   114   91
From The Puritan Cookbook

POLLENS, DAVID
POEMS
View, from Valéry   122   81
It's My Last Guess in City
In Situ   124   313
Tristi Fummo   128   29
House Plants
Shivah
Riddle

POLLET, ELIZABETH
ARTICLES
Correspondence
[Edward Dahlberg, Conrad Aiken]   82   176

POLLITT, JOSEPHINE
POEMS
President Emeritus   23   195
Jennie   23   310

POLLITT, KATHA
POEMS
Alcestis   128   212
Eggplant   132   154
Tomato   134   12
A Screen Depicting the Fifty-Four Episodes
    of the Tale of Genji on a Background
    of Gold Leaf
Pygmalion
Riverside Drive, November Fifth   135   91
Sea Grasses   137   38
A Poet of Our Climate
An Anthology of Socialist Verse   151   126
Fishbowl

BOOKS REVIEWED
Antarctic Traveller   141   170

POLLOCK, ESTILL
POEMS
Oz Verbatim   122   267
The American Book of the Dead   124   269
Letters to a Chosen Woman   126   64
Captain Blood Returns   129   5

POLLOCK, THOMAS CLARK
BOOKS REVIEWED
The Nature of Literature   60   86

POMEROY, RALPH
POEMS
Broom Season   72   69
Myself Above the Piazza Frescobaldi   84   338
The King of the Wild Beasts
Silence   89   287
Islands
Lakes Learn from the Season   91   89
In the Days When
    Purple Was New
Out of the Window
    into Moonlight
The Novelist at Home in New Jersey
Love Poem II
Patrol   93   301
Kite Flying
Resolutions
From "Diary of a Moveable"   96   302
Sentry Seurat   99   230
Letter to Pasternak
Confession   103   161
To Words
Overwhelmed by the Moon
    at the Wrong but Imperative Moment   110   243

REVIEWS
Seven Poets   96   375
    Poems, by John Tagliabue
    Ways of Happening,
        by Bruce Berlind
    Unit and Universe, by I. L. Salomon
    Nine by Three,
        by Robert Beum, Maxine Cassin,
        and Felix Stefanile
    The Clever Body,
        by Melvin Walker LaFollette

BOOKS REVIEWED
Stills & Movies   99   313
The Canaries As They Are   108   121
In the Financial District   117   322

ARTICLES ABOUT
[Note on misprint]   110   432

POND, MARGARET
[See CHURCH, PEGGY POND]

PONGE, FRANCIS
POEMS
L'Allumette   80   316
L'Appareil du Telephone
La Grenouille
Grand Nu Sous Bois
    (Tr. by Wallace Fowlie)

ARTICLES ABOUT
Foreword, by Wallace Fowlie   80   311

PONSOT, MARIE
POEMS
Berceuse   90   132
For a Still-Born Child
Ritournelle, Paris 1948
Private and Profane
Anniversary
For Elizabeth Bleecker Averell,
    D. 20 June 1957   91   352
Anti-Romantic
A Visit
Wedding Song
For My Brother:
    "Other Systems Must Exist"
Cassation for Good Friday, III   96   202
Hommages à Charles Perrault
Paeonia "Souvenir de Maxime Cornu",
    Incidentally   104   149

REVIEWS
The Antiphon, by Djuna Barnes   95   47
The Irreducible   95   304
    Helen in Egypt, and Other Plays,
        by John Heath-Stubbs

Certain Poems,
   by John Edward Hardy
A Suit of Nettles, by James Reaney
The Night of the Hammer,
   by Ned O'Gorman
Poems for Children   101   208
   The Man Who Sang the Sillies,
      by John Ciardi
   The Penny Fiddle: Poems for Children,
      by Robert Graves
   The Wind and the Rain:
      An Anthology of Poems
      for Young People
      (Ed. by John Hollander
      and Harold Bloom)

BOOKS REVIEWED
True Minds   94   333

POOLE, JOHN M(ORTON)
POEMS
Prothalamion   63   250
I Think the Sea Has No Heart   65   246
Death of U-Boat
Pattern of Fear
This Vegetable World   73   264

POPA, VASKO
BOOKS REVIEWED
Collected Poems
   (Tr. by Anne Pennington)   136   40
Homage to the Lame Wolf
   (Tr. by Charles Simic)

POPE, ALEXANDER
BOOKS REVIEWED
The Pleasures of Pope
   (Ed. by Peter Quennell)   77   340

ARTICLES ABOUT
   Rev. of *Poetry and Criticism*,
      by Edith Sitwell   29   41
   Poetry and Nature,
      by D. S. Savage   61   496
   Rev. of *Pope's Dunciad,*
      a Study of Its Meaning,
      by Aubrey Williams   88   277
   The Poetry of Charles Churchill: Part I,
      by Yvor Winters   98   44

POPE, DEBORAH
POEMS
Picture on the River Cherwell 162   187
Forecast   163   24
Hotel, River View
Resolution   165   257
In Dark Weather
Getting Through

PÖPPEL, ERNST
ARTICLES
   The Neural Lyre: Poetic Meter,
      the Brain, and Time
      (With Frederick Turner)
      [Jerre Levy, Barbara Lex]   142   277

PORCHE, FRANÇOIS
ARTICLES ABOUT
   Looking Backward,
      by Harriet Monroe   33   32

PORCHIA, ANTONIO
BOOKS REVIEWED
Voices
   (Tr. by W. S. Merwin)   120   113

PORTER, ALAN
BOOKS REVIEWED
Oxford Poetry, 1921
   (Ed. with Richard Hughes
      and Robert Graves)   24   162
The Signature of Pain   39   342

PORTER, ANNE
ARTICLES ABOUT
   Rev. of *Collected Poems*,
      by James Schuyler   163   225

PORTER, FAIRFIELD
POEMS
   The Pyromaniac   85   325
   The Island in the Evening
   Great Spruce Head Island

ARTICLES ABOUT
   Rev. of *Collected Poems*,
      by James Schuyler   163   225

PORTER, KATHERINE ANNE
BOOKS REVIEWED
   Katherine Anne Porter's
   French Song-Book   43   290

PORTER, KENNETH (W.)
POEMS
   Salut Aux Condamnés   38   142
   In Kansas   46   260
      Hawk and Junco
      Coyote
      Sunflowers over the Corn
   Hill Fort: Carradale Point 58   258
   Song of John Horse
   East Texas   62   317

ARTICLES
   [Note about *Song of John Horse*] 58   290

BOOKS REVIEWED
Christ in the Breadlines:
A Book of Poems
for Christmas and Lent
(With Seymour Gordon Link
and Harry Elmore Hurd)   42   168
The High Plains   54   342
No Rain from These Clouds   69   171

PORTER, PETER
POEMS
Susannah and the Elders   146   209
To Be on the Safe Side
Pontormo's Sister   151   127
Sun King Sulking   153   335
Browning Meets Wagner
at the Schlesingers'   169   68
A Walking Bass

ARTICLES
Comment   151   216

BOOKS REVIEWED
The Last of England   119   291
The Last of England   120   170
Preaching to the Converted   123   113
Living in a Calm Country   129   340

PORTOGALO, JOSÉ
[Pseud. of ANANIA, JOSÉ]
POEMS
Poem About a Little Girl
Who Owns a City and a River
(Tr. by Lloyd Mallan)   62   77

POSNER, DAVID (LOUIS)
POEMS
By Saint Callixtus' Tomb   90   274
Lesson in Anatomy
The Mirror
The Garden
Suburban Sunday
Song for Music
Doctor Johnson
Mount Athos   104   23
Algerian Summer   106   100
Dialogue with Norman Douglas   110   367
Dionysiou   132   155
Weasel

BOOKS REVIEWED
The Deserted Altar   94   333

POST, MARY BRINKER
POEMS
Windy Monday   30   204
Summer in the Garden   32   324
Ranch Girl at Evening   35   144

POSTER, WILLIAM
POEMS
Song of Crosscurrents and Counteractions   71   251
Song of Suppressed Rebellion

REVIEWS
A Private History, by John Hay   71   334
Forbid Thy Ravens, by Rolfe Humphries   72   219
Poems (1940-1947),
by Theodore Spencer   72   273
Phases of Development   73   355
The Seafaring, by Louis O. Coxe
Go to Sleep, World,
by Raymond Souster
Canada and New England   75   105
The Rocking Chair and Other Poems,
by A. M. Klein
Mr. Whittier and Other Poems,
by Winfield Townley Scott

POSTGATE, MARGARET I.
POEMS
The Veteran   12   241

POTTS, CHARLES
BOOKS REVIEWED
Burning Snake   112   274

POULET, GEORGES
BOOKS REVIEWED
The Classic Anthology Defined
by Confucius (Tr.)   85   159
The Interior Distance
(Tr. by Elliott Coleman)   95   379
The Metamorphoses of the Circle
(Tr. by Carley Dawson
and Elliott Coleman)   112   41

ARTICLES ABOUT
French Chronicle: Recent Publications,
by Wallace Fowlie   88   408

POULIN, A., JR.
BOOKS REVIEWED
Duino Elegies and The Sonnets to Orpheus,
by Rainer Maria Rilke (Tr.)   131   345
The Collected Poems, by John Logan
(Ed. with Jerome Mazzaro)   160   34

POUND, EZRA ["E. P."]
POEMS
To Whistler, American   1   7
Middle-Aged
Contemporania   2   1
Tenzone
The Condolence
The Garret
The Garden

Ortus		
Dance Figure		
Salutation		
Salutation the Second		
Pax Saturni		
Commission		
A Pact		
In a Station of the Metro		
Ancora	3	53
Surgit Fama		
The Choice		
April		
Gentildonna		
Lustra		
Xenia		
To Καλον	4	169
The Study in Aesthetics		
The Bellaires		
Salvationists		
Amitiés		
Ladies		
The Seeing Eye		
Abu Salammamm—A Song of Empire		
Provincia Deserta	5	251
Image from D'Orleans		
The Spring		
The Coming of War: Actaeon		
The Gipsy		
Dogmatic Statement Concerning the Game		
of Chess: Theme for a Series of Pictures		
Near Perigord	7	111
Villanelle: The Psychological Hour		
The Fish and the Shadow	8	275
O Atthis		
The Three Poets		
Pagani's		
The Lake Isle		
Impressions of Francois-Marie Arouet		
(De Voltaire)		
Homage to Quintus Septimius		
Florentis Christianus		
Dans Un Omnibus de Londres		
Three Cantos I ("Hang it all...")	10	113
Three Cantos II ("Leave Casella...")	10	180
Three Cantos III		
("Another's a half-cracked fellow...")	10	248
Poems from the Propertius Series	13	291
("Shades of Callimachus...")		
("I had been seen in the shade...")		
("Midnight, and a letter comes...")		
("When, when, and whenever...")		
Canto XXXIV	42	1
"Thou Shalt Not,"		
Said Martin Van Buren		
(Canto XXXVII)	43	297
From Canto LXXX	68	310
From Canto CXIII	101	95
Leviora	129	63

Statement of Being		
For the Triumph of the Arts		
Jacques Chardinel of the Albigenses		
Fragmenti		
Fragment to W. C. W.'s Romance		
In That Country		
I Wait		
Fragment		

ARTICLES

Tagore's Poems	1	92
Status Rerum		
[W. B. Yeats, Padraic Colum,		
Ford Madox Hueffer]	1	123
A Few Don'ts by an Imagiste	1	200
Paris		
[Henri-Martin Barzun]	3	26
The Tradition	3	137
Homage to Wilfrid Blunt	3	220
The Audience: I	5	29
The Renaissance: I—The Palette	5	227
Renaissance—II	5	283
The Renaissance—III	6	84
Hark to Sturge Moore	6	139
Correspondence: A Rejoinder		
[Leroy Titus Weeks]	6	157
Robert Bridges' New Book	7	40
On "Near Perigord"	7	143
Remy de Gourmont	7	197
Literary Prizes	7	304
Correspondence	7	321
Status Rerum—The Second	8	38
This Constant Preaching to the Mob	8	144
Emile Verhaeren	9	256
Things To Be Done	9	312
Irony, Laforgue, and Some Satire	11	93
The Hard and the Soft in French Poetry		
[Théophile Gautier, Jules Romains]	11	264
Thames Morasses	17	325
Correspondence:		
From the Editor of "The Exile"	30	174
Mr. Pound on Prizes	31	155
Practical Suggestions	33	327
Correspondence:		
A Possibly Impractical Suggestion	34	178
This Subsidy Business	35	212
Honor and the United States Senate	36	150
The Situation	38	95
Correspondence: Our English Number	40	52
Manifesto	41	40
Correspondence: Reply to Mr. Tate	41	231
The European in America	41	273
Cambridge Left	42	353
Correspondence:		
An Open Letter		
to John Gould Fletcher	43	292

Correspondence
  [Poem]   45   234
Correspondence:
  A Word from Mr. Pound
  [Horace Gregory]   47   55
Lucrum Tuum Damnum Publicum Est   48   273
Correspondence:
  The Printing Press Was Invented   49   55
Vale
  [Tribute to Harriet Monroe]   49   137
Another Chance   52   344
Letters to a Young Poet
  [Iris Barry]   76   342
Tagore's Poems   121   40

REVIEWS
An Anthology of Modern Bohemian Poetry
  (Tr. by P. Selver)   1   57
Présences, by P. J. Jouve   1   165
A Boy's Will, by Robert Frost   2   72
Helen Redeemed and Other Poems,
  by Maurice Hewlett
Love Poems and Others,
  by D. H. Lawrence   2   149
Odes et Prières, by Jules Romains   2   187
Art and Swadeshi,
  by Ananda K. Coomaraswamy   2   226
Poems and Songs,
  by Richard Middleton   3   33
Fire and Wine and The Dominant City,
  by John Gould Fletcher   3   111
Responsibilities, by W. B. Yeats   4   64
Collected Poems, by Ford Madox Hueffer   4   111
North of Boston, by Robert Frost   5   127
Ernest Dowson, by Victor Plarr   6   43
Poems, by E. Scotton Huelin   6   257
Sounds from Another Valley,
  by H. F. Sampson
The Song of the Five, by Cecil Garth
The Poetical Works of Lionel Johnson   7   313
Literature in Ireland,
  by Thomas MacDonagh   8   309
Responsibilities and Other Poems,
  by W. B. Yeats   9   150
Wheels, An Anthology of Verse
  [Wyndham Tennant, Nancy Cunard]   10   41
Tablettes de Cire, by A. de Brimont   10   160
Prufrock and Other Observations,
  by T. S. Eliot   10   264
Collected Poems, by William H. Davies   11   99
Passages from the Letters
  of John Butler Yeats
  (Ed. by Ezra Pound)   11   223
The Life of Algernon Charles Swinburne,
  by Edmund Gosse   11   322
The Four Winds,
  by Ralph Cheever Dunning   26   339

BOOKS REVIEWED
Passages from the Letters
  of John Butler Yeats (Ed.)   11   223
Lustra   11   330
Pavannes and Divisions   15   211
Quia Pauper Amavi   16   213
Poems 1918-21   21   95
Personae: The Collected Poems of...   30   216
A Draft of XXX Cantos   39   37
How To Read   41   107
Profile: An Anthology
  Collected in MCMXXXI
Guido Cavalcanti: Rime (Ed.)   41   336
Active Anthology (Ed.)   44   276
How To Read   46   279
The ABC of Reading
Make It New
The ABC of Economics
Social Credit: An Impact
Eleven New Cantos (XXXI-XLI)
The Fifth Decad of Cantos   51   324
Cantos LII-LXXI   57   200
Ezra Pound's ABC of Economics
Polite Essays
Culture
The Pisan Cantos   73   108
The Letters of Ezra Pound, 1907-1941
  (Ed. by D. D. Paige)   79   150
An Introduction to the Economic Nature
  of the United States
What Is Money For?
Social Credit: An Impact
Confucius:
  Great Digest & Unwobbling Pivot (Tr.)   81   127
The Spirit of Romance   83   29
Guide to Kulchur
The Translations of...   83   233
Dichtung und Prosa
  (Tr. by Eva Hesse)   83   357
Women of Trachis, by Sophocles (Tr.)
The Classic Anthology Defined
  by Confucius (Tr.)   85   159
Section: Rock Drill;
  85-95 de los Cantares   90   237
Sophokles' Women of Trachis (Tr.)
Selected Poems   91   389
Translations   106   361
"Ezra Pound Speaking":
  Radio Speeches of World War II
  (Ed. by Leonard W. Doob)   134   292

ARTICLES ABOUT
"That Mass of Dolts"   1   168
Correspondence from John Reed   2   112
Correspondence
  from William Butler Yeats   3   149
Review of Des Imagistes: An Anthology   5   38

Our Contemporaries
   [*Blast*]   5   42
Correspondence
   from Leroy Titus Weeks   6   48
[Note on misprint]   6   159
Correspondence
   from Robert A. Sanborn   7   158
The Work of Ezra Pound,
   by Carl Sandburg   7   249
Rev. of *Catholic Anthology—1914-1915*   8   94
These Five Years, by Harriet Monroe   11   33
Back to China, by Harriet Monroe   11   271
A Modern French Anthology, by S. W.   12   54
Correspondence
   from John Gould Fletcher   12   111
Sara Teasdale's Prize,
   by Harriet Monroe   12   264
An International Episode,
   by Harriet Monroe   13   94
Correspondence
   from William Gardner Hale   14   52
New International Magazines   19   224
The Editor in France,
   by Harriet Monroe   23   90
Ezra Pound, by Harriet Monroe   26   90
Poeta Nascitur, by Ford Madox Ford   29   326
Program: "Objectivists" 1931,
   by Louis Zukofsky   37   268
[Note on "Objectivists" issue]   37   295
[Note]   38   291
Recent Magazines, by M. D. Zabel   39   166
Rev. of *How to Teach Reading*,
   by F. R. Leavis   44   53
Poetry's Old Letters,
   by Harriet Monroe   47   30
Correspondence
   from John Drummond   52   302
Correspondence
   from Gorham Munson
   [J. V. Healy]   57   399
The End of Ezra Pound,
   by Eunice Tietjens   60   38
Contemporary Poetry Criticism,
   by J. V. Healy   61   672
Form in Modern Poetry,
   by D. S. Savage   65   30
A Note on the Obvious,
   by George Dillon   68   322
Ezra Pound, by T. S. Eliot   68   326
An Adjunct to the Muses' Diadem:
   A Note on E. P.,
   by R. P. Blackmur   68   338
Addendum, by J. V. Healy   68   347
Rev. of *A History
   of American Poetry, 1900-1940*,
   by Horace Gregory
   and Marya Zaturenska   69   210

The Background of the Pisan Cantos,
   by David Park Williams   73   216
Notes Towards an Autobiography:
   The Childish Background (III),
   by William Carlos Williams   74   94
The Bollingen Award: What Is It?
   by Hayden Carruth   74   154
The Anti-Poet All Told,
   by Hayden Carruth
   [Robert Hillyer]   74   274
Rev. of *An Examination of Ezra Pound*
   (Ed. by Peter Russell)   79   150
Poets and Psychologists,
   by Karl Shapiro   80   166
Rev. of *Ezra Pound and the Cantos*,
   by Harold H. Watts   81   127
Apprenticed in Provence,
   by Leonard Casper   81   203
Rev. of *A Preliminary Checklist
   of the Writings of...*
   (Ed. by John Edwards)   83   29
Rev. of *The Little Review Anthology*
   (Ed. by Margaret Anderson)   83   290
Rev. by Hugh Kenner   84   112
Rev. of *Canto 85*   86   41
Rev. of *The No Plays of Japan*
   (Tr. by Arthur Waley)   88   113
Correspondence
   from John R. Hendrickson
   and Hugh Kenner   91   209
Correspondence
   from William Burford
   and Robert Duncan
   [Louis Coxe]   92   193
Oliver St. John Gogarty,
   by Vivian Mercier   93   35
H. M.: In Memory,
   by Morton Dauwen Zabel   97   241
Rev. of *Myths and Texts*,
   by Gary Snyder   97   316
Rev. of *A Primer of Ezra Pound*,
   by M. L. Rosenthal   100   50
[Note on misprint]   101   297
Rev. of *A Bibliography of Ezra Pound*,
   by Donald Gallup;
   Ezra Pound: Poet as Sculptor,
   by Donald Davie;
   Poet in Exile: Ezra Pound,
   by Noel Stock;
   *The Cantos of Ezra Pound:
   A Critical Study*, by George Dekker;
   and *The Confucian Odes of Ezra Pound:
   A Critical Appraisal*, by L. S. Dembo   106   361
On a Picture of Ezra Pound,
   by Hayden Carruth   110   103
Rev. of *The Spoils*, by Basil Bunting   110   195
The Vocation of Poetry,
   by Henry Rago   110   328

Rev. of *"A" 1-12*,
   by Louis Zukofsky   111   112
Rev. of *The Earliest English Poems*
   (Tr. by Michael Alexander)   111   395
Review by Leila Laughlin
   [Rabindranath Tagore]   111   407
Ghosts and Benedictions,
   by Hugh Kenner   113   109
Correspondence: Pound's Text,
   by Hugh Kenner   113   285
Poeta Nascitur,
   by Ford Madox Ford   121   41
Program: "Objectivists" 1931,
   by Louis Zukofsky   121   45
Rev. of *The Waste Land:
   A Facsimile and Transcript of
   the Original Drafts Including
   the Annotations of Ezra Pound*,
   by T. S. Eliot
   (Ed. by Valerie Eliot)   121   156
Rev. of *Harriet Monroe
   and the Poetry Renaissance*,
   by Ellen Williams   131   39
Creative Glut, by Karl Shapiro   135   36
Allen Tate: A Poet
   on Poetry, 1924-1944,
   by Ashley Brown   135   103
Gists and Piths: From the Letters
   of Pound and Williams,
   by J. Laughlin   139   229
Poets Aloud, by Donald Hall   139   297
Setting the Hard Tasks,
   by J. D. McClatchy   141   39
Rev. of *Selected Poems*,
   by James Laughlin   149   94
Comment by Raymond Carver   151   204
Rev. of *The Owl of Minerva*,
   by James Laughlin   152   98
Rev. of *Collected Poems
   and The Man in the Wall*,
   by James Laughlin   165   289

POUND, LOUISE
BOOKS REVIEWED
   Poetic Origins and the Ballad   18   227
   American Ballads and Songs (Ed.)   22   105

POVEDA, JOSÉ MANUEL
   [See MANUEL POVEDA, JOSÉ]

POWELL, CLARENCE ALVA
BOOKS REVIEWED
   Industrial Sonnets   77   114

POWELL, DANNYE ROMINE
POEMS
   She Never Thought of Vegetables   166   95

POWELL, JIM
POEMS
   The Crooked House   153   205
   Napoleon Reviendra

BOOKS REVIEWED
   It Was Fever that Made the World   154   151

POWELL, JOSEPH
POEMS
   Something Visible   146   335
   Winter's Insomnia   149   74
   Ode to Sleep
   Tucquala Lake   152   209
   The Great Horned Owl   153   96
   Pioneer Square: Spare Change   165   66

POWELL, LYNN
POEMS
   Preparation for an Elegy   166   140

POWER, EILEEN
BOOKS REVIEWED
   Medieval People   85   55

POWER, W. L.
ARTICLES
   Correspondence   44   57

**POWERS, JESSICA
[(SISTER) MIRIAM
OF THE HOLY SPIRIT]**
POEMS
   The Great Poet   31   75
   Like Kildeers Crying   32   139
   Celestial Bird   33   124
   The Soul to the Body
   White Beauty   37   136
      The Kingdom of God
      The Mystic Face
   Church of Our Lady of Sorrows, Chicago   47   132
   Out of a Cloud: Farewell   97   174
   Siesta in Color   115   385

POWYS, JOHN COWPER
POEMS
   The Hope   13   16
   The Riddle   16   138

BOOKS REVIEWED
   Visions and Revisions   6   205
   Samphire   22   229

PRABHU, ALLAMA
POEMS
   Losing a World
   (Tr. by A. K. Ramanujan)   98   383

PRAED, WINTHROP MACKWORTH
ARTICLES ABOUT
Robinson and Praed,
by Hoyt H. Hudson   61   612

PRASAD, JAYSHANKAR
POEMS
Aubade ("Awake for the night...")
(Tr. by Romila Thapar)   93   257

PRATT, A. E.
BOOKS REVIEWED
The Use of Color in the Verse
of the English Romantic Poets   69   88

PRATT, C. W.
POEMS
Tracks   140   339
October

PRATT, CHARLES W.
POEMS
Experiment with a Birth in Nature   123   327
May 15   168   105

PRATT, E. J.
POEMS
The Invaded Field   58   1
Come Away Death
From Dunkirk   59   10
The Crew
The Multipedes on the Roads
In the Skies
The Unromantic Moon   82   143

BOOKS REVIEWED
Brébeuf and His Brethren   58   48
Dunkirk   60   152
Collected Poems   66   329
Toward the Last Spike   82   350
The Collected Poems   95   248

ARTICLES ABOUT
The Development
of Poetry in Canada, 1880-1940,
by E. K. Brown   58   34
Review by James Reaney   94   186

PRATT, WILLIAM
BOOKS REVIEWED
The Fugitive Poets (Ed.)   110   47

ARTICLES ABOUT
[Note about Laura Riding]   110   270

PRESCOTT, F. C.
BOOKS REVIEWED
The Poetic Mind   22   342

PRESS, JOHN
BOOKS REVIEWED
The Chequer'd Shade   95   122
The Golden Treasury
(Ed. of Vol. 5)   110   47

PRESTON, JOHN HYDE
POEMS
Psalm   31   258

PRESTON, KEITH
BOOKS REVIEWED
Types of Pan   17   100
Column Poets (Ed.)   27   343

ARTICLES ABOUT
"In Lighter Vein,"
by Harriet Monroe   30   330

PREUSS, WOLFGANG
POEMS
Resignation   38   133

PRÉVERT, JACQUES
POEMS
Rue de Seine
(Tr. by Lloyd C. Parks)   74   138

PREZZOLINI, GIUSEPPE
ARTICLES ABOUT
La Voce and Its Poets,
by Walter Pach   10   50

PRICE, MARTIN
BOOKS REVIEWED
To the Palace of Wisdom:
Studies in Order and Energy
from Dryden to Blake   104   369

PRICE, REYNOLDS
POEMS
The Annual Heron   135   154
Rescue   138   144
Pictures of the Dead   140   258
Ambrosia   143   90
A Heaven for Elizabeth Rodwell,
My Mother   144   144
Rincón   147   97
Lighthouse, Mosquito Inlet
Hawk Hill
Three Secrets   148   29
Unbeaten Play   151   129
31 December 1985   151   293
Near a Milestone
Good Friday   152   25
Easter Sunday
Back
Juncture   152   332

The Resident Heron	155	224
A Heron, a Deer—A Single Day		
An Afterlife: 1953-1988	156	215
An Actual Temple	166	69
On the Road	167	273
Napalm, L. B.		
After an AIDS Benefit With L. B.		
The Closing, the Ecstasy	169	280

BOOKS REVIEWED
Vital Provisions	143	228
The Laws of Ice	150	226
The Use of Fire	158	280

PRICE, ROBERT
BOOKS REVIEWED
The Hidden Airdrome		
and Uncollected Poems	90	114

PRIEST, GEORGE MADISON
BOOKS REVIEWED
Faust: Parts One and Two,		
by Goethe (Tr. and ed.)	61	406

PRIEST, GEORGE W.
POEMS
Song of the Mechanics	2	207

PRINCE, F. T.
POEMS
Strambotti	100	99

BOOKS REVIEWED
Poems	60	225
Memoirs in Oxford	119	291
Collected Poems	137	105

PRING-MILL, ROBERT
ARTICLES ABOUT
Rev. of *The Heights*		
of Macchu Picchu,		
by Pablo Neruda		
(Tr. by Nathaniel Tarn)	112	191

PRIOR, MOODY E.
ARTICLES ABOUT
Rev. of *English Institute Essays, 1949*		
(Ed. by Alan S. Downer)	77	48

PRITAM, AMRITA
POEMS
Pledge		
(Tr. by Harbans Singh)	93	226

PRITCHARD, SHEILA
POEMS
To the Land of My Inquiry	81	230

PRITCHARD, WILLIAM H.
ARTICLES
MacLeish Revisited		
[Ernest Hemingway, Robert Frost,		
Edmund Wilson]	141	291

REVIEWS
Positives	119	159
Blue Mountain, by James Liddy		
The Sad Mountain, by Tom Earley		
From Bourgeois Land,		
by Iain Crichton Smith		
The Loiners, by Tony Harrison		
Maximum Security Ward,		
by Ramon Guthrie		
Farming: A Hand Book,		
by Wendell Berry		
New & Selected Poems,		
by William Jay Smith		
Magic Papers, by Irving Feldman		
Notebook, by Robert Lowell		
Collected Poems 1950-1970,		
by Donald Davie	122	289
Despairing at Styles	127	292
A Mote in Heaven's Eye,		
by Donald Finkel		
Nails, by Gary Gildner		
The Terrible Shears,		
by D. J. Enright		
What Thou Lovest Well,		
Remains American,		
by Richard Hugo		
You Are Happy,		
by Margaret Atwood		
The House on Marshland,		
by Louise Glück		
Virtuoso Literature for Two		
and Four Hands,		
by Diane Wakoski		
Poems: Selected and New,		
by Adrienne Rich		
Expressing the Difference	132	230
Reservations, by James Richardson		
Collected Poems 1948-1976,		
by Dannie Abse		
Stories That Could Be True:		
New and Collected Poems,		
by William Stafford		
The Selected Poems 1951-1977		
and *The Snow Poems,*		
by A. R. Ammons		
Play's the Thing	136	295
Riven Doggeries, by James Tate		
The Messenger, by Jean Valentine		
New & Selected Poems,		
by Irving Feldman		
Blue Wine and Other Poems,		
by John Hollander		

An Explanation of America,
  by Robert Pinsky
[Robert Frost]
Weighing the Verse   138   107
  Being There: Poetry 1977-1980,
    by Robert Penn Warren
  Selected Poems 1950-1975,
    by Thom Gunn
  The Traveler's Tree: New
    and Selected Poems,
    by William Jay Smith
  Collected Poems 1944-1979,
    by Kingsley Amis
Early Auden, by Edward Mendelson
[George Orwell]   139   292
Poetry Chronicle   143   228
  The Hawk's Dream and Other Poems,
    by Donald Everett Axinn
  Vital Provisions,
    by Reynolds Price
  Heart of the Garfish,
    by Kathy Callaway
  Running on Empty,
    by Robert Phillips
  One Long Poem,
    by William Harmon
  The Students of Snow,
    by Jane Flanders
  PM/AM: New and Selected Poems,
    by Linda Pastan
  New and Selected Poems,
    by Tony Connor
  Peru, by Herbert Morris
  Whomp and Moonshiver,
    by Thomas Whitbread
  [Richard Wilbur]
  [Brad Leithauser]

BOOKS REVIEWED
  Randall Jarrell: A Literary Life   158   100
  Selected Poems,
    by Randall Jarrell (Ed.)

PROBST, LEETHA JOURNEY
POEMS
  Her Man   47   72

PROBSTFIELD, EDRIS MARY
POEMS
  A Wisp of Smoke   33   311

BOOKS REVIEWED
  Open Windows   46   53

PROKOSCH, FREDERIC
POEMS
  Red Fox   36   259
  Chorus   46   200

The Gothic Dusk   48   10
("Hesperus, the gentlest star...")   52   16
("Living and dying...")
("O the vines were golden...")
("Let the beast be chained...")
("Atlantic and Caribbean crawl...")   55   194
("I feel that life and death draw...")
("Tornado, thundering tongue...")
("Death, though not death only...")
Elegy ("Living and dying...")   57   115
The Athlete
The Victims
Snow Song   81   180

REVIEWS
  Last Poems and Two Plays,
    by William Butler Yeats   54   338

BOOKS REVIEWED
  The Assassins   49   337
  The Carnival   53   89
  Death at Sea   57   327
  Some Poems
    of Friedrich Hölderlin (Tr.)   63   169
  Sonnets by Louise Labé (Tr.)   73   364

PROSPERE, SUSAN
POEMS
  Affinities   142   96
  Oxford, on an Ancient Crossroads
    Beside the Thames
  Ministering Angels

PROTHERO, MATTHEW
BOOKS REVIEWED
  Love and Laughter (Ed.)   27   343

PROUDFOOT, ANDREA HOFER
POEMS
  The Ship's Prow   14   61

PROUST, ANTONIN
POEMS
  Modern Greek Popular Songs   17   68
    Rigi
    Song ("O my sweet dove...")
    Spring
    The Red Fish
    (Tr. by Eunice Tietjens)

PROVINES, ELOISE ELIZABETH
POEMS
  Siberian Sketches   25   201
    A Siberian Station
    Despair
    Executions
    Siberian Soldiers—1920

PROVOST, SARAH
POEMS
Sometimes a Woman Wants
    a Love Without Landscapes   139   327
Mercurochrome   145   10
Pastoral
The Lonely Man Plans a Picnic

PRUSSING, M. JEAN
POEMS
These Angles Sharp   54   86
September 2, 1939   55   67

REVIEWS
Four Poets   56   220
   This, My Letter,
     by Sara Henderson Hay
   Man in the Shadows,
     by Elias Lieberman
   San Joaquin, by William Everson
   Broken Crescendo,
     by Anne Hamilton

PRUTKOV, KOZMA [Pseud.]
POEMS
Love of Honor   104   203
The Heron and the Racing Rig
Romanza
A Poet's Will
Remembrance of Things Past
Junker Schmidt
The Worm and the Deaconess
Forget-Me-Nots and Footboards
My Portrait
   (Tr. by W. D. Snodgrass
   and Tonya Tolstoy)

ARTICLES ABOUT
Note on "Kozma Prutkov"   104   270

PRYCE, MARION
BOOKS REVIEWED
Linnets in the Slums   15   55

PRYCHODKO, MARINA
TRANSLATIONS
Poem by Vladimir Mayakovsky
   (Tr. with Ruth Herschberger)   102   100

PRYOR, RUTH
BOOKS REVIEWED
I That Was Born in Wales,
   by Vernon Watkins
   (Ed. with Gwen Watkins)   131   292

PUDNEY, JOHN
POEMS
The Children   39   76
Orchard

Vision   41   136
Heirs
Other Horizons

ARTICLES
Poets in Uniform   63   108

BOOKS REVIEWED
Spring Encounter   44   343
Open the Sky   46   51
Flight Above Cloud   65   51

PULITZER, JOSEPH
ARTICLES ABOUT
Editorial Amenities, by Harriet Monroe   14   262

PULSE, HELENE S(EARCY)
[HELEN S. PULS]
POEMS
In Ukraine   40   200
   The Steppe
   The Village Girl
   The Grandmother
Peeling Apples   56   134

PULSIFER, HAROLD TROWBRIDGE
BOOKS REVIEWED
Harvest of Time   41   283
First Symphony: A Sonnet Sequence   47   283

PURDY, ALFRED (WELLINGTON)
[A. W. PURDY]
BOOKS REVIEWED
North of Summer   114   202
Wild Grape Wine

PURNELL, IDELLA
POEMS
Biography   22   264
Samples   23   260
   Eve
   Tonala Besieged
   Closed Doors
   Life
   This Day
   The Wall
Post-Revolutionary   28   190
   He Is a Fairy Prince
   The Jarabe
   A Shot at Night
   Troops Come to Town
   Baby Boy
Toltec Gods   40   307
Now-A-Days   42   318
   Martha at Thirty
   A Thought for Contemporary Writers
Departure   46   136
Maxim   47   69

PUSHKIN, ALEXANDER SERGEYEVITCH

POEMS
Echo
(Tr. by Michael Mesic) 116 343

BOOKS REVIEWED
Eugene Onegin
(Tr. by Dorothea Prall Radin
and George Z. Patrick) 50 294
Three Russian Poets
(With Mikhail Lermontov
and Fyodor Tyutchev)
(Tr. by Vladimir Nabokov) 66 289
Eugene Onegin:
A Novel in Verse by...
(Tr. by Vladimir Nabokov) 106 236

ARTICLES ABOUT
Pushkin: 1837-1937,
by John Cournos 49 328

PUTNAM, F. S. [Pseud.]
POEMS
Presage 17 193

PUTNAM, (H.) PHELPS
BOOKS REVIEWED
The Five Seasons 40 335
The Collected Poems of...
(Ed. by Charles R. Walker) 121 229

ARTICLES ABOUT
Allen Tate:
A Poet on Poetry, 1924-1944,
by Ashley Brown 135 103

PUTNAM, SAMUEL
POEMS
The Horses of Her Hair 37 288

PYM, JOHN
POEMS
The Ice Age 103 368

QUASHA, GEORGE
POEMS
 The Lover's Request to His Beloved   110   382
 Hieroglyph for a Gull
 Look There! Mac's at the Mike!

QUASIMODO, SALVATORE
POEMS
 The Scrawny Flower Already Flies   84   187
 Lament for the South
 The Rain's Already with Us
 The Magpie Laughs,
  Black upon the Orange-Trees
 The Gentle Hill
 O My Sweet Animals
 Perhaps the Heart
 Elegos for the Dancer Cumani
 Colors of Rain and Iron
 Thanatos Athanatos
 To Pilgrim Me
  (Tr. by Allen Mandelbaum)

BOOKS REVIEWED
 The Selected Writings of...
  (Tr. by Allen Mandelbaum)   98   403

ARTICLES ABOUT
 Contemporary Italian Poetry,
  by Edward Williamson   79   233

QUENNELL, PETER
BOOKS REVIEWED
 Oxford Poetry: 1924
  (Ed. with Harold Acton)   26   47
 The Pleasures of Pope (Ed.)   77   340
 Shakespeare: A Biography   104   264

QUIN, ANN
BOOKS REVIEWED
 Three   112   353

QUINN, BERNETTA
 [(SISTER) BERNETTA QUINN,
 (O.S.F.)]
REVIEWS
 Relearning the Alphabet,
  by Denise Levertov   118   97

 Symbolic Landscapes   118   288
  Allegiances, by William Stafford
  No Continuing City,
   by Michael Longley
 Two Signatures   119   301
  The Gulf, by Derek Walcott
  Collected Poems,
   by Alan Dugan

QUINN, JOHN ROBERT
POEMS
 Walls and Open Gates   47   184
  No More I Ask
  These Are the Hills
  Processional
  Beyond This Wall
 Abundance   53   132
 Shoes   59   141
 White Goose in Snow   73   143

BOOKS REVIEWED
 Beyond This Wall   60   344

QUINN, KERKER
POEMS
 Gautier Visited Spain   52   68

REVIEWS
 The Crystal World,
  by Richard Aldington   52   160
 Further Letters
  of Gerard Manley Hopkins
  (Ed. by Claude Colleer Abbott)   53   150
 The Bright North,
  by Abbie Huston Evans   53   339
 German on the Left Page   55   96
  Translations from the Poetry
   of Rainer Maria Rilke
   (Tr. by M. D. Herter-Norton)
  Duino Elegies,
   by Rainer Maria Rilke
   (Tr. by J. B. Leishman
   and Stephen Spender)
 Meaning and Motive   55   340
  Poetry and the Ordinary Reader,
   by M. R. Ridley

R

"R. A."
[See ALDINGTON, RICHARD]

RAAB, LAWRENCE
POEMS
Sunday | 113 | 322
Walking Alone
Eight Landscapes
  from the Tarot Deck | 117 | 300
The Night of the Statues | 125 | 21
Disappointment | 133 | 265
You Would Know
The Rest
The Room
The Window
Familiar Landscapes
This Day | 137 | 292
Being Gone
Coming Home
Afterwards
For You
Other Children | 142 | 125
Looking at Pictures | 148 | 138
At Evening
Cloud, Castle, Lake
Stories in Which the Past Is Made | 151 | 133
Minor Painter, Paris, 1954 | 153 | 14
A Crow
The Secret Life | 154 | 5
Marriage | 157 | 87
The Peonies on My Desk | 160 | 143
The Lost Things
What He Thought About the Party | 160 | 270

BOOKS REVIEWED
Mysteries of the Horizon | 122 | 344
Mysteries of the Horizon | 127 | 352
The Collector of Cold Weather | 130 | 41
Other Children | 152 | 161
What We Don't Know
  About Each Other | 163 | 285

RABBITT, THOMAS
POEMS
The Dogs of War | 128 | 199

RABEARIVELO, JEAN-JOSEPH
BOOKS REVIEWED
24 Poems | 103 | 394

RABONI, GIOVANNI
POEMS
Città dall'alto/City from Above | 155 | 88
Figures in the Park
My Daughter's Birthday 1966
  (Tr. by David Stivender
  and J. D. McClatchy)

RACHEL (BLAUSTEIN)
POEMS
Let the Judgment Be
  (Tr. by Sholom J. Kahn) | 92 | 214

RACINE, JEAN
POEMS
From Andromaque
  (Tr. by Richard Wilbur) | 136 | 30

BOOKS REVIEWED
Phedre
  (Tr. by Robert Lowell)
  in Phaedra and Figaro | 100 | 41
Three Plays of...:
  Phaedra, Britannicus, Andromache
  (Tr. by George Dillon) | 100 | 47

ARTICLES ABOUT
Rev. of The Art of Jean Racine,
  by Bernard Weinberg | 104 | 187

RADHUBER, STANLEY
POEMS
Song in a Car | 114 | 96

RADIN, DOROTHEA PRALL
BOOKS REVIEWED
Eugene Onegin, by Alexander Pushkin
  (Tr. with George Z. Patrick) | 50 | 294

RADLOW, JAMES
POEMS
News of the Mysteries | 116 | 24

RADNÓTI, MIKLÓS
POEMS
   Letter to My Wife   151   490
   Foamy Sky
     (Tr. by Zsuzsanna Ozsvath
     and Frederick Turner)

RAFFEL, BURTON
BOOKS REVIEWED
   Selected Poems,
     by Chairil Anwar
     (Tr. with Nurdin Salam)   104   115
   Mia Poems   116   193

RAFTERY, ANTHONY
POEMS
   Curse on the Bush   24   256
   Prayer Before Death
     (Tr. by Cathal O'Byrne)

RAGO, HENRY (W.)
POEMS
   I Live   39   124
   Cypress Leaves   42   198
     Cemetery
     She, Nameless
     Lullaby for a Dead Boy
   Something There Is   44   20
     Heritage
     Episode
     Song Before Adventure
     Lucine
     Sonnet for God
   Shadows Under the Wind   46   195
     The Path
     Talisman
     The Bride
   Sanctuary   49   265
   Invocation for a Book   52   21
   Autumnal   55   79
   Meeting of a Poetry Society   56   186
   The Newsreel
   National Hook-Up
   Four Poems: A Memorial   60   320
   The Metaphor: Five Poems   71   309
   The Quarrel   77   138
   Departures
   Via Della Croce
   The Monster
   Promise Your Hand
   The Temple   78   197
   The Summer Countries
   How the Bright Earth Spun Like a Jewel
   The House   81   62
   Two Poems   82   73
     ("Translucent green on the wall...")
     ("Unchristened time came...")
   Presence of Statues   85   8

   The Letter: Morning
   A Sky of Late Summer   87   164
   The Knowledge of Light   91   1
   The Attending
   The Distances   99   101
   Poem for an Anniversary
   The Net
   Inscriptions
   The Promising   101   97
   Praise of Comedy: A Discourse   103   82
   Four Fragments   115   79
     ("Lifted to my eyes...")
     Some Letters About a Book
     ("Haven: the time done...")
     ("You,/Fair presence...")

ARTICLES
   Religion and Sensibility
     [I. A. Richards, Herbert Read,
     T. S. Eliot, Martin Turnell]   57   314
   "To Keep Our Metaphysics Warm"
     [David Daiches]   58   108
   Gertrude Stein
     [George W. John]   69   93
   A Statement by the New Editor   87   39
   Why We're Still Here
     [Robert Frost]   87   360
   [Letter to Lawrence Ferlinghetti]   90   260
   A Note on This Issue
     [Israeli Poets]   92   202
   A Further Note
     [Poets of India, Frederick Bock]   93   272
   Goodbye for a Year   96   370
   To Begin Our Fiftieth Year   99   45
   Foreword   101   i
   Foreword   103   xi
   T. S. Eliot: A Memoir and a Tribute   105   392
   Foreword   106   xi
   An Announcement by the Editor
     [Robert Mueller]   107   69
   The Vocation of Poetry
     [W. B. Yeats, Marianne Moore,
     T. S. Eliot, Ezra Pound]   110   328
   A Year's Leave, A Visiting Editor
     [Daryl Hine]   113   60
   The Poet in His Poem   113   413

REVIEWS
   Seven Song,
     by Patrick Dacus Moreland   49   291
   The Cock of Heaven,
     by Elder Olson   57   214
   Slow Music, by Genevieve Taggard   69   289
   The Judge Is Fury,
     by J. V. Cunningham   71   50
   The Grasshopper's Man and Other Poems,
     by Rosalie Moore   75   98

A Garland About Me, by George John   81   243
Three Poets   84   173
   The Human Climate,
     by Josephine Jacobsen
   Various Jangling Keys,
     by Edgar Bogardus
   A Glass Darkly, by Elliott Coleman

BOOKS REVIEWED
  The Travelers   75   229

ARTICLES ABOUT
  Poetry and the Post-Medieval Mind,
    by David Daiches   57   374
  Preview, by Barbara Gibbs   71   341
  For the Word, for the Silence,
    by Ralph J. Mills, Jr.   115   127
  "Islands Waited, Wait Still..."
    by Hayden Carruth   115   130
  Comments by Wallace Fowlie,
    Lisel Mueller, X. J. Kennedy,
    Maria Flook, and M. L. Rosenthal   151   208

RAGSDALE, WILMOTT
POEMS
  Summer Storm   78   204
  The World's Words
  Mouse to Mouth

RAHA, ASOKE VIJAY
POEMS
  A Winter Night
    (Tr. by Lila Ray)   93   212

RAHV, PHILIP
ARTICLES
  Private Experience
  and Public Philosophy
    (With William Phillips)   48   98

RAINE, CRAIG
POEMS
  The Explorers   146   193

ARTICLES ABOUT
  A Letter from Britain [II],
    by William Logan   157   290

RAINE, KATHLEEN
POEMS
  An End of the World   69   314
  The Instrument   80   1
  Rock
  The Locked Gates
  The Company
  La Recherche de l'Absolu   97   302
  Eudaimon
  Consort of Viols
  Childhood

Kore in Hades
Rose
Nocturn   101   102
The Hollow Hill   102   1

REVIEWS
  The Estate of Poetry,
    by Edwin Muir   101   272
  In Parenthesis,
    by David Jones   101   426

BOOKS REVIEWED
  Stone and Flower   80   32
  Living in Time
  The Pythoness
  The Year One   83   106
  Collected Poems   91   41
  Defending Ancient Springs   114   113
  Blake and Tradition   117   45

ARTICLES ABOUT
  London Letter: Some New Figures,
    by John McCormick   83   269

RAIZISS, SONIA
POEMS
  Signal Hill   57   132
  Fathers   88   361
  Marine Mood
  A Strangeness of Love   97   164
  Cocktail Aquarium   159   214

TRANSLATIONS
  Poems by Eugenio Montale   92   97
  Poems by Lucio Piccolo
    (With Alfredo de Palchi)   98   387
  Article by Eugenio Montale
    (With Alfredo de Palchi)
    [Lucio Piccolo]   98   392

BOOKS REVIEWED
  The Metaphysical Passion   81   328

RAJAN, B.
POEMS
  Statement for Adonis   73   263
  Damayanti   93   246

RAJU, P. T.
TRANSLATIONS
  Poem by Nanduri Subbarao   93   223

RAKOSI, CARL
[Pseud. of RAWLEY, CALLMAN]
POEMS
  Orphean Lost   37   237
  Fluteplayers from Finmarken
  Unswerving Marine

ARTICLES ABOUT
 Juan Ramón Jiménez:
  The Landscape of the Soul,
   by Rachel Frank   82   224
 [Notes]   82   239

RAMSAY, JANET
 POEMS
  To a Girl Dreaming of Marriage   39   194
  Charmed Region

RAMSEY, FREDA
 POEMS
  Payment   37   201

RAMSEY, PAUL
 POEMS
  A Mill   114   175
  Voyagings   116   12
  Suppose a Country Gave a Holiday and
   Then Suppose that the Tears Were True   122   90
  A Meditation on Number and on Definition

RAMSEY, WARREN
 POEMS
  Poem ("The farmers sit with cats...")   55   190

 BOOKS REVIEWED
  Jules Laforgue and the Ironic Inheritance 83   331

RAMSEY, WILLIAM LITTLE
 POEMS
  He Catches Hell   167   268

RAND, E. K.
 ARTICLES ABOUT
  Poetry on Records,
   by Harry T. Moore   57   52

RAND, ROBERT
 POEMS
  Graves of Dreams   14   84

RANDALL, BELLE
 POEMS
  A Child's Garden of Gods   98   231
  San Quentin and Two Kinds of Conscience
  Appropriate Postures
  Attention Please   119   69
  Afterward

 BOOKS REVIEWED
  101 Different Ways of Playing Solitaire
   and Other Poems   127   164

RANDALL, HUBERTA
 TRANSLATIONS
  Poems by Emile Verhaeren   85   125

RANDALL, JULIA
 POEMS
  Two Rhymes for Anne Williams   74   88
  Prothalamium   74   261
  Bloodroot   76   259
  Question: Of the Effects of Love
  Appalachian
  The Coast   100   160
  The Company

 REVIEWS
  The Wind of Time,
   by Rolfe Humphries   75   364
  Walk Through Two Landscapes,
   by Dilys Bennett Laing   76   231
  Horn in the Dust,
   by Selwyn S. Schwartz

 BOOKS REVIEWED
  The Solstice Tree
   (Ed. by Mary Owings Miller)   85   366
  The Puritan Carpenter   108   272
  Adam's Dream   118   35

RANDALL, MARGARET
 POEMS
  For Gregory   102   93
  The Marriage   109   325
  From So Many Rooms Has a House
   But One Roof   111   243
  Sad Poem   115   24

 REVIEWS
  The Good and the Useful   115   47
   Exercises for Ear,
    by Stephen Jonas
   After the Assassination,
    by R. A. Simpson
   Little Odes & The Raptors,
    by Michael McClure
   Valley of the Many-Colored Grasses,
    by Ronald Johnson
   [Guy Davenport]
   Uranium Poems,
    by Judith Johnson Sherwin
   The Metaphysical Giraffe,
    by Alvin Greenberg
   The Last Benedetta Poems,
    by Gerard Malanga
   Origins, by Morton Marcus

 BOOKS REVIEWED
  October   110   186
  Water I Slip Into at Night   113   188
  25 Stages of My Spine
  So Many Rooms Has a House
   But One Roof   114   251

RANDALL-MILLS, ELIZABETH
POEMS
  Host to the Great   55   240
  The Day
  An Alien Speaks   68   307

RANDOLPH, ROBERT M.
POEMS
  R. Cory in Winter   161   151

RANNIT, ALEKSIS
POEMS
  On the Island of Ogygia
    (Tr. by Henry Lyman)   131   321

RANSOM, JOHN CROWE
REVIEWS
  The Family Reunion, by T. S. Eliot   54   264

BOOKS REVIEWED
  Poems About God   16   51
  Two Gentlemen in Bonds   30   162
  Fugitives: An Anthology of Verse   32   102
  The World's Body:
    Foundations for Literary Criticism   55   51
  The New Criticism   61   575
  Selected Poems   67   212
  Selected Poems, Third Edition   117   275

ARTICLES ABOUT
  A Note on Three Southern Poets,
    by Robert Penn Warren   40   103
  Present-Day Tendencies,
    by Harriet Monroe   40   152
  A Glossary of the New Criticism,
    by William Elton   73   153
  A Glossary of the New Criticism,
    by William Elton   73   232
  A Glossary of the New Criticism,
    by William Elton   73   296
  Rev. of *Lectures in Criticism*
    [Johns Hopkins University]   74   353
  The Defense of Poetry,
    by Richard Eberhart   77   89
  Rev. of *Donne's Poetry and Modern Criticism*,
    by Leonard Unger   77   175
  Falling Asleep over Grillparzer:
    An Interview with Robert Lowell,
    by John McCormick   81   269
  Rev. of *Critics and Criticism,*
    Ancient and Modern
    (Ed. by R. S. Crane)   82   98
  Rev. of *John Crowe Ransom,*
    by John L. Stewart   102   269
  [Note]   103   403
  Rev. of *The Equilibrist: A Study of*
    John Crowe Ransom's Poems, 1916-1963,
    by Robert Buffington   113   338

RAO, K. RAGHAVENDRA
POEMS
  The Journey to Golgotha   93   252

TRANSLATIONS
  Poems by D. R. Bendre
    and K. R. Narasimhaswamy   93   265

RAPHAEL, FREDERIC
BOOKS REVIEWED
  The Poems of Catullus
    (Tr. with Kenneth McLeish)   136   40

RASCOE, BURTON
ARTICLES ABOUT
  Titans, Tea-Hounds,
    Rasslers, and Reviewers,
    by M. D. Zabel   41   326

RATCLIFF, CARTER
BOOKS REVIEWED
  Fever Coast   124   292

RATCLIFFE, DOROTHY UNA
POEMS
  Saint Bridget's Lullaby   23   128
  Grassington Road
  Star-Debt   26   316
  Song for Music   30   189
  Three Poems of Yorkshire   31   130
    Mass of the Moorlands
    The View-Point
    The Gypsy Bride
  Of Gipsies   37   81
    Return to the Isle of Skye
    Wild Flowers
    Wind at Midnight
  The Last Lover   44   71

BOOKS REVIEWED
  The Shoeing of Jerry-Go-Nimble
    and Other Dialect Poems   29   286
  Dale Lyrics
  Nightlights   36   289

RATCLIFFE, STEPHEN
POEMS
  Blood   127   211
  Domestic
  Logging
  Waterfall   129   207
  Summer Rain
  The View from Mono Pass
  Pause, Pico Blanco
  Readings from John Muir's Journal   131   272
  Rustic Diversions
  Postscript, On a Name   133   321
  Air

TRANSLATIONS
Poems by Thomas Campion   130   90

RATHBONE, BASIL
BOOKS REVIEWED
Great Themes in Poetry
[Recording]   61   519

RATHNER, EUGENE
POEMS
Midnight and History   60   134

RATTI, JOHN
POEMS
Women by the Sea   103   372
The Fire   108   19

BOOKS REVIEWED
A Remembered Darkness   118   41

RAU, A. V. RAJESWARA
BOOKS REVIEWED
Modern Indian Poetry: An Anthology (Ed.)   95   314

RAVENEL, BEATRICE
POEMS
The Gypsy   17   16
Tidewater   20   26
   Harbor Water
   White Azaleas in Magnolia Gardens
   Dew
   The Only Child
   Lill' Angels
Two Poems of Old Age   28   310
   Embers
   The Old Fisherman

BOOKS REVIEWED
The Arrow of Lightning   30   288

RAWLEY, CALLMAN
[See RAKOSI, CARL]

RAWORTH, TOM
POEMS
Provence   113   402

BOOKS REVIEWED
Haiku
   (With John Esam
   and Anselm Hollo)   114   251

RAY, DAVID
POEMS
This Life   102   235
Greece   115   241
A Midnight Diner by Edward Hopper
Twigs   152   349

BOOKS REVIEWED
From the Hungarian Revolution:
   A Collection of Poems (Ed.)   109   345
A Poetry Reading
   Against the Vietnam War
   (Ed. with Robert Bly)
Dragging the Main   118   169
Gathering Firewood:
   New Poems and Selected   127   164

RAY, LILA
TRANSLATIONS
Poems by Asoke Vijay Raha,
   Karuna Nidhan Bandypadhyay,
   and Naresh Guha   93   212
Poem by Kalandi Charan Panigrahi
   (Tr. with Marendra Misra)   93   243

RAY, MAN
BOOKS REVIEWED
Thorns of Thunder,
   by Paul Eluard
   (Ed. by George Reavey)
   (Tr. with Samuel Beckett,
   Denis Devlin, David Gascoyne,
   Eugene Jolas, George Reavey,
   and Ruthven Todd)   48   347

RAY, ROBERT BEVERLEY
POEMS
June 21   134   158
Pachelbel's Canon in D Major
On My 35th Birthday
The Logic of August   136   249
Morning Music
Pronunciamientos
   from the Guest House
Translations from an Imaginary Poet
The Aesthetics of Annotation   138   318
Les Cahiers du Chemin   139   313
A Passacaglia in Winter
The Meaning of Coincidence
   in the Old Stories

RAY, SHREELA
POEMS
Remembering Michelangelo's David   107   378
A Manner of Attachment

RAYAPROL, SRINIVAS
POEMS
The Man Who Died of a Fever   79   198
Legend
Three Love Poems   93   224
   ("And a lost road...")
   ("Child, she said...")
   ("Remember when as children...")

RAYFORD, JULIAN LEE
POEMS
  Thumb Tourist   42   78

RAYMUND, BERNARD
POEMS
  Listener   17   140
  Feet Are No Lovers   31   73
  Epistle to Kansas City   66   244
  Marine

REVIEWS
  A Time to Mourn,
    by D. S. Savage   65   274
  A Winter's Journey,
    by Richard Hart   66   343

BOOKS REVIEWED
  Hidden Waters   24   280

RAYNAUD, ERNEST
BOOKS REVIEWED
  La Mêlée Symboliste   18   113

RAYNOR, OWEN
POEMS
  Baltimore Summer   87   230

READ, BILL
BOOKS REVIEWED
  The Modern Poets:
    An American-British Anthology
    (Ed. with John Malcolm Brinnin)   104   245
  The Modern Poets:
    An American-British Anthology
    (Ed. with John Malcolm Brinnin)   119   169

READ, HERBERT
POEMS
  The Death of Kropotkin   77   21

ARTICLES
  [Note]   59   170

REVIEWS
  The Poem Itself
    (Ed. by Stanley Burnshaw,
    Dudley Fitts, Henri Peyre,
    and John Frederick Nims)   98   56

BOOKS REVIEWED
  A World Within a War   66   220
  Collected Poems   71   271
  Phases of English Poetry   77   362
  A Coat of Many Colors   89   322
  Moon's Farm and Other Poems
  The Nature of Literature   93   117
  Collected Poems   110   45

ARTICLES ABOUT
  Religion and Sensibility,
    by Henry Rago   57   314
  Rev. of *New Poems: 1943*
    (Ed. by Oscar Williams)   64   86
  Correspondence
    from John Theobald and H. R. Hays   67   114

READ, ROBERT B.
POEMS
  Fated Steps   48   24
  Wohin?
  Impregnable Summer
  The Quick
  As if Gods Were, for Surely Doom Is

READING, PETER
ARTICLES ABOUT
  A Letter from Britain [II],
    by William Logan   157   290

REANEY, JAMES
POEMS
  A Cellar Song   94   380
  The Windyard
  Four Emblem Poems   115   149
    Egypt
    The Farm
    Within Within
    The Tree

REVIEWS
  The Canadian Imagination   94   186
    The Penguin Book of Canadian Verse
    (Ed. by Ralph Gustafson)
    Winds of Unreason,
    by George Ellenbogen
    A Lattice for Momos,
    by R. G. Everson
    The Quality of Halves,
    by Marya Fiamengo
    A Laughter in the Mind,
    by Irving Layton
    Meditation at Noon, by Peter Miller
    Jupiter C for the Missile Age, 4 Poems,
    by Kenneth McRobbie
    Dazzle, by Dorothy Roberts
    The Season's Lovers,
    by Miriam Waddington
    [E. J. Pratt, Northrop Frye]

BOOKS REVIEWED
  A Suit of Nettles   95   304
  Twelve Letters to a Small Town   103   266

ARTICLES ABOUT
  Poets in Canada,
    by Margaret Avison   94   182

REAVEY, GEORGE
POEMS
   O Luce Eterna   41   197

TRANSLATIONS
   Poems by Boris Pasternak   70   259

BOOKS REVIEWED
   Thorns of Thunder,
      by Paul Eluard (Ed.)
      (Tr. with Samuel Beckett,
      Denis Devlin, David Gascoyne,
      Eugene Jolas, Man Ray,
      and Ruthven Todd)   48   347
   The Colours of Memory   87   299
   The Poetry of Boris Pasternak
      (Ed. and tr.)   96   108

REDFIELD, JAMES
REVIEWS
   Carmina Archilochi:
      The Fragments of Archilochos
      (Tr. by Guy Davenport) 105   329

REDFIELD, LOUISE
POEMS
   After Fever   16   17
   A Shy Child
   After Storm   21   135

REDFIELD, ROBERT, JR.
POEMS
   War Sketches   12   242
      Return to the Front
      On the Ambulance
      In Moulins Wood

REDGROVE, PETER
POEMS
   Dead Bird   90   153
   Old House
   Woman in a Flowered Dress 94   372
   From *Feeding-Pieces*
   One-Eyed Monster   100   95
   The Patient Successor
   A Silent Man
   Small Dirge   111   293
   Water-Witch, Wood-Witch,
      Wine-Witch
   More Than Meets the Eye 146   197
   Eden's Medicine

BOOKS REVIEWED
   The Nature of Cold Weather 100   104
   Work in Progress   118   102
   Sons of My Skin:
      Selected Poems 1954-1974
      (Ed. by Marie Peel)   131   292

RED HAWK
POEMS
   How I Love You   140   92
   Master, Master, Lord of the Dance

REDMAN, BEN RAY
BOOKS REVIEWED
   Edwin Arlington Robinson 29   229

REDPATH, THEODORE
BOOKS REVIEWED
   The Songs and Sonets
      of John Donne (Ed.)   104   120

REECE, BYRON HERBERT
BOOKS REVIEWED
   Three Lyric Poets
      (Ed. by Alan Swallow)
      (With Alice Moser
      and Tom H. McNeal)   61   629
   Ballad of the Bones and Other Poems 67   282

REED, AMY LOUISE
BOOKS REVIEWED
   The Background of Gray's Elegy 27   283

REED, HENRY
BOOKS REVIEWED
   A Map of Verona
      and Other Poems   72   165
   Three Plays by Ugo Betti (Tr.) 94   350

REED, ISHMAEL
BOOKS REVIEWED
   Conjure: Selected Poems, 1963-1970 122   237

REED, JEREMY
POEMS
   Life Expectations   153   320

REED, JOHN
POEMS
   Sangar   1   71
   The Night Sky   4   14
   Hospital Notes   10   240
      Coming Out of Ether
      Clinic
      Operating Room
   Proud New York   14   18

ARTICLES
   Correspondence:
      A Word to Mr. Pound   2   112

ARTICLES ABOUT
   Two Poets Have Died,
      by Harriet Monroe   17   208
   Announcement of Awards 25   102

REED, JOHN R(ICHARD)

POEMS

A Gallery of Spiders   118   192
Entropy   140   216
Strays
Transported   152   262
Treatment
Two for Roethke   163   269
Leaves from a Partbook
Second Coming   164   74
Pentimento   170   159
Blue Tattoo

REVIEWS

Magicians and Others   122   47
   The Typewriter Revolution
    & Other Poems,
    by D. J. Enright
   High Tide in the Garden,
    by Fleur Adcock
   Acting Immortal, by R. P. Dickey
   Bucyrus, by John Matthias
   The Daughters,
    by Stephen Berg
   Severance Pay, by Philip Whalen
   Riverbed, by David Wagoner
   More Under Saturn,
    by William Dickey

REEDY, WILLIAM MARION

ARTICLES ABOUT

The Death of Mr. Reedy,
  by Harriet Monroe   16   328

REES, ARTHUR D.

POEMS

Volunteers   13   125
  Tears, Idle Tears!
  Cares that Infest the Day
  Longings for Home
  Unseeing the Seen
  The Melancholy Plaint
   of the Russian Song

REESE, LIZETTE WOODWORTH

POEMS

Pastures   40   62

BOOKS REVIEWED

Wild Cherry   23   341
Little Henrietta   31   283
Pastures and Other Poems   44   40
The Old House in the Country   49   97

ARTICLES ABOUT

Going East,
  by Harriet Monroe   30   90
Honor to Lizette Reese,
  by Harriet Monroe   47   277

REEVE, F. D.

POEMS

A Seaside Crucifix   115   34
Hands
Verse Chronicle   115   61
Hope   116   164
The Long Trail
Opus Aestivus
Last Game for the New Life   118   218
Life-Size   124   155
3 Sunsets at Hammonasset   156   293
Red Square   158   338
Autumn Song
Full Moon in May   162   91
Twilight
Ragged Island   162   264
On Appledore   164   7
A Sonnet for Christmas   165   132
Longings   168   76
Telephone   170   85

REVIEWS

Verse Chronicle   115   61
   Tonight at Noon, by Adrian Henri
   To Make Me Grieve,
    by Molly Holden
   A Sense of Being, by John Horder
   Towards Silence,
    by Edward Lucie-Smith
   The Boy from the Green Cabaret
    Tells of His Mother,
    by Barry MacSweeney
   Selected Poems, by Ruth Miller
The Fire Screen, by James Merrill   117   388
Faces at the Bottom   118   234
   Face at the Bottom of the World,
    by Hagiwara Sakutaro
    (Tr. by Graeme Wilson)
   Running Lucky, by R. P. Dickey
   Say Yes, by Miriam Waddington
   Ruining the New Road,
    by William Matthews
Fresh Airs   119   39
   The World Anthology,
    Poems from St. Mark's Poetry Project
    (Ed. by Anne Waldman)
   The Poets of the New York School
    (Ed. by John Bernard Myers)
Veterum Sapientia   121   234
   Selected Poems, by Arthur Gregor
   By Daylight and In Dream,
    New and Collected Poems, 1904-1970,
    by John Hall Wheelock
   The Convex Mirror. Collected Poems,
    by Samuel Yellen
In My Father's House...   121   348
   Theseus and Other Poems,
    by Frederick Buell

The Family Goldschmitt,
  by Henri Coulette
Voice Unaccompanied,
  by Philip Martin
A Program for Survival,
  by Gibbons Ruark
A Grain of Mustard Seed,
  by May Sarton
White Lights & Whale Hearts,
  by Stephen Vincent
Christmas in Las Vegas,
  by Robert Watson
Carnival Cantata,
  by Henry Weinfield
Riding the Earthboy 40,
  by James Welch
Hermetic Definition and *Trilogy:*
  The Walls Do Not Fall,
  Tribute to the Angels,
  The Flowering of the Rod,
  by H. D.   124   162
Selected Poems,
  by Joseph Brodsky
  (Tr. by George L. Kline)   127   42
Of Shoemakers and Snails   170   37
  About Distance,
    by Gregory Djanikian
  In the Crevice of Time,
    by Josephine Jacobsen
  The Country Road,
    by James Laughlin
  The Vixen,
    by W. S. Merwin
  The Annals of Chile and
    The Prince of the Quotidian,
    by Paul Muldoon
  Late Empire, by David Wojahn
  Most Way Home,
    by Kevin Young

BOOKS REVIEWED
  The Blue Cat   122   344
  Concrete Music   163   97

REEVE, PAUL EATON
POEMS
  The Works   39   203
    Saga of Sealed Hero
    Tabloid Nucleus
  Myopic Fly, Esq.   41   142
  For R. D. R.
  Night Litany   44   249
  The Possessed
  The Unerring Flower   50   241
    Pardon for Weeds
    Summer Is a Child in a Glass Tower
    Poem ("It was otherwise...")
    Man into Beast
    Outgoing

REEVES, JAMES
POEMS
  A Matter of Discipline   49   205
  Christmas

BOOKS REVIEWED
  The Cassell Book of English Poetry (Ed.)   108   343
  A New Canon of English Poetry
    (Ed. with Martin Seymour-Smith)   114   113

REGIER, G. TRAVIS
POEMS
  Sleeping in Public   165   67

REHAN, ADA
ARTICLES ABOUT
  The Death of Stephen Phillips,
    by Harriet Monroe   7   260

REIBETANZ, JOHN
POEMS
  Sam Appleby, Horseman   133   218

REID, ALASTAIR
POEMS
  Living in Time   93   291
  Who Am I?
  Cat-Faith

BOOKS REVIEWED
  To Lighten My House   84   96
  Oddments Inklings Omens Moments   95   107

REID, DOROTHY E.
POEMS
  Miss Winnie   26   248
  History
  She Says   29   304
    Behind a Coffee Urn
    Kings
    Fig Leaf for a Stone Memorial
    Men
  Via Rosinante   31   198
  The Woman Who Was Marble   33   316
  Lean Armor   35   66
  To a Great Man   38   190
  Double Life   40   195

BOOKS REVIEWED
  Coach into Pumpkin   29   101

REID, FREDERICK W.
POEMS
  The Sea Is Sorrow's Seed   59   255

REID, PHYLLIS ["P. R."]
POEMS
  Prometheus   21   305
  Epitaph ("Poetry laid hands...")

Like a Roseleaf
Reproach 27 200

REID-HEYMAN, S.
BOOKS REVIEWED
A Vagabond's Wallet 10 44

REINERT, NANCY HORMEL
POEMS
Gopher Snake 136 96

REINSTEIN, HERMAN
POEMS
Infinitives 24 16
Lilliputian
Summer Gales 40 312
Grass in the Wind
Rena

REIS, RICARDO
[See PESSOA, FERNANDO]

REISS, JAMES
POEMS
On Learning the People's Republic
of China Has Lifted Its Ban on Beethoven 134 322
Guatemalan Worry Dolls 153 219

REISSIG, JULIO HERRERA
[See HERRERA REISSIG, JULIO]

REITER, JENDI
POEMS
The Miniaturist 157 197

REITER, THOMAS
POEMS
Class Bully 151 461

RENARD, JEAN-CLAUDE
POEMS
Poèmes [Extracts] 104 310
("Que mes taureaux...")
("Les bancs d'algues...")
("Tes soleils sont de houx...")
("Viennent les iles!...")
("Mes lievres, dans l'herbe...")
("Ce sang perdu...")
("Le cerf qui franchira...")
("Une odeur d'or...")
("O fourrage enrichi...")
(Tr. by Wallace Fowlie)

RENAUD, FLORIA
POEMS
Laughter 26 249

RENDALL, E(LIZABETH)
BOOKS REVIEWED
Thursday's Child 10 44

RENSSELAER, [MRS.] SCHUYLER VAN
[See VAN RENSSELAER,
(MRS.) SCHUYLER]

REPLANSKY, NAOMI
POEMS
Against Death 44 188
This Ae Nighte
The Piteous Lady
Amulet
Discovery of the World 67 247
The Mistress Addresses the Wife 83 259

TRANSLATIONS
Poem by Bertolt Brecht 71 128

BOOKS REVIEWED
Ring Song 81 321

REPS, PAUL
BOOKS REVIEWED
Zen Telegrams 95 248
Gold/Fish Signatures 102 335
Picture-Poem Primer 105 270

RESOR, ROBERT
POEMS
Goose Bay, Labrador: October, 1944 67 251
To Persephone, at a Railway Station 69 247

REVELL, DONALD
POEMS
Rodeo Aesthetique 129 195
Animaux
Motel View
Theriot Cove 133 91
Car Radio 147 211
To Penelope 149 6
St. Lucy's Day 151 267
Psalmist 153 154
The Night Orchard 154 211
An Episode of the Great Awakening
in New England 156 25

BOOKS REVIEWED
The Gaza of Winter 154 99
Erasures 164 223

REVERE, JONATHAN
POEMS
Gull Skeleton 118 22

REXROTH, KENNETH
POEMS
Last Page of a Manuscript 37 254
From The Crisis 52 200
Seven Poems for Marthe, My Wife 89 1
("In my childhood when I first...")

Marthe Away
Marthe Lonely
Quietly
A Dialogue of Watching
Marthe Growing
The Old Song and Dance
Air and Angels   101   103
Dimanche Bleu   109   172
Parity
Education
Confusion of the Senses
The Spark in the Tinder of Knowing   113   83

ARTICLES
Correspondence
[Objectivists]   38   51

REVIEWS
Here and Now,
by Denise Levertov   91   120

BOOKS REVIEWED
In What Hour   57   158
The Phoenix and the Tortoise   65   260
New British Poets (Ed.)   75   237
The Art of Worldly Wisdom   76   156
The Signature of All Things   76   159
Beyond the Mountains   78   356
One Hundred Poems from the Japanese   88   116
In Defense of the Earth   90   180
One Hundred Poems from the Chinese
Bird in the Bush: Obvious Essays   96   382
Assays   102   269
The Homestead Called Damascus   104   179
Natural Numbers:
New and Selected Poems
Poems from the Greek Anthology (Tr.)   107   264
The Collected Shorter Poems   111   184
The Heart's Garden The Garden's Heart   114   40

ARTICLES ABOUT
Rev. of New Directions 1944
(Ed. by James Laughlin)   66   161
Correspondence:
Letter from Harvard,
by John Ciardi   74   112
The Poetry of Kenneth Rexroth,
by Lawrence Lipton   90   168
[Note]   91   339

REYES, ALFONSO
BOOKS REVIEWED
Algunos Poemas   61   680

REYES, CARLOS
BOOKS REVIEWED
The Windows   111   323

REYNOLDS, CHARLES
POEMS
On Ancient Death   98   234

REYNOLDS, JULIA R.
POEMS
To Sappho   19   191

REYNOLDS, TIM
POEMS
What It Is Is   93   97
The Stone-Mason   97   81
The Revolutionists
Poem for Hermann Hesse   101   395
For Sharon & Don   110   370
Going Home
Catfish Goodbye

BOOKS REVIEWED
Ryoanji   105   336

REZNIKOFF, CHARLES
POEMS
A Group of Verse   37   252
Winter Sketches   41   192
("Now that black ground...")
Subway
("From the middle of the pool...")
("Along the flat roofs...")
("The squads, platoons...")

BOOKS REVIEWED
Poems   17   276
Jerusalem the Golden   44   338
Testimony
In Memoriam, 1933   46   230
Inscriptions: 1944-1956   96   52
By the Waters of Manhattan:
Selected Verse   102   266
Testimony:
The United States (1885-1890)   107   396
Holocaust   128   37

ARTICLES ABOUT
Sincerity and Objectification,
by Louis Zukofsky   37   272

RHODEN, KERNEY
POEMS
The Scenario   120   21
Platforms
Primavera   122   133

RHODENHIZER, V. B.
BOOKS REVIEWED
Canadian Poetry in English
(Ed. with Bliss Carman
and Lorne Pierce)   86   111

RHU, LAWRENCE
POEMS
   Lenten Confessional   125   254

RHYS, ERNEST
POEMS
   A Song of Happiness   1   114
   The Hunting-Song of Them
      That Did Not Hunt   2   204
   Dagonet's Canzonet
   April Romance   8   1
   A Breton Night
   Sonnetina: Punch and Judy
   The Woman of Sorrows
   Nesta's Morning Song
   Death and the Jester

RHYS, KEIDRYCH
POEMS
   Poem on Being   53   186
   Nonconformity
   Garn Goch
   Treasury
   Tragic Guilt   59   175

ARTICLES
   [Note]   59   169
   Correspondence   62   57

ARTICLES ABOUT
   London Letter, by D. S. Savage   51   277

RIBEMONT-DESSAIGNES, G(EORGES)
ARTICLES ABOUT
   The Disciples of Gertrude Stein,
      by Richard Aldington   17   35

RICCIO, OTTONE M.
BOOKS REVIEWED
   On Pain of Discovery   116   125

RICE, CALE YOUNG
POEMS
   The Malay to His Master   3   93

BOOKS REVIEWED
   High Perils   42   342

RICE, JOHN PIERREPONT
TRANSLATIONS
   Poems by José Santos Chocano   11   229

ARTICLES
   José Santos Chocano
      [Rubén Darío]   11   260

RICE, OLIVER
POEMS
   Poem ("Wahai, Grandfather...")   102   233

RICE, PAUL
POEMS
   Timber Rattler   157   149

RICE, PHILIP BLAIR
POEMS
   Agenbite of Inwit   65   1
   Calligrammes

REVIEWS
   Essays Ancient and Modern,
      by T. S. Eliot   50   51
   Realization: A Philosophy of Poetry,
      by Hugh McCarron   51   227
   The Rimbaud Mystery Clarified 56   95
      Arthur Rimbaud, by Enid Starkie
      Some Poems of Rimbaud
        (Tr. by Lionel Abel)
      A Season in Hell,
        by Arthur Rimbaud
        (Tr. by Delmore Schwartz)

RICE, RUTH MASON
POEMS
   Trailing Arbutus   18   83

RICH, ADRIENNE (CECILE)
POEMS
   The Rain of Blood   77   200
   Mathilde in Normandy
   David's Boyhood   90   302
   A Ball Is for Throwing
   A Mark of Resistance
   "Travail et Joie"
   In the North   101   233
   Sisters
   Peeling Onions
   Well in Ruined Courtyard
   Apology
   Peace
   Like This Together   106   109
   Night in the Kitchen   112   79
   Implosions
   5:30 A.M.
   For a Russian Poet
   The Break
   Dreamwood   151   136
   For a Friend in Travail   158   311
   Two Arts
   Final Notations

REVIEWS
   Found Objects, by Louis Zukofsky 105   128
   The Complete Poems of D. H. Lawrence
      (Ed. by Vivian De Sola Pinto
      and F. Warren Roberts)   106   218
   Six Anthologies   108   343
      The Cassell Book of English Poetry
        (Ed. by James Reeves)

The Earth Is the Lord's: Poems of the Spirit
  (Ed. by Helen Plotz)
Sprints and Distances:
  Sports in Poetry and the Poetry in Sport
  (Ed. by Lillian Morrison)
Men Who March Away:
  Poems of the First World War
  (Ed. by I. M. Parsons)
The Golden Journey:
  Poems for Young People
  (Ed. by Louise Bogan
  and William Jay Smith)
Medieval Welsh Lyrics
  (Tr. by Joseph P. Clancy)

BOOKS REVIEWED
  The Diamond Cutters   87   299
  Snapshots of a Daughter-in-Law   102   250
  Necessities of Life   109   267
  Leaflets   115   430
  Poems: Selected and New   127   292
  The Dream of a Common Language   133   227
  Your Native Land, Your Life   149   231
  Time's Power: Poems 1985-1988   156   158
  An Atlas of the Difficult World:
    Poems 1988-1991   160   284
  Dark Fields of the Republic   170   90

ARTICLES ABOUT
  "Sacred Beings": Writers
    in Recorded Conversation,
    by Michael Milburn   146   101
  [Note]   148   239

RICH, DANIEL CATTON
  POEMS
  Underneath   33   255
  The Fabric of This Dream   55   185
  On a Baroque Screen:
    Four Poems from South America   63   246

RICH, H. THOMPSON
  POEMS
  Desire   8   136
  The Drinker
  You Came and Went
  I Come Singing   11   67
  Afterwards
  Song ("Hills are all aflower...")   18   25
  Noises   30   19
  Courage

BOOKS REVIEWED
  I Come Singing: Rhythms and Songs   30   171

RICH, LILA
  POEMS
  Petals   10   201

The Snowstorm
Frozen Heart
War
Praise

RICHARDS, DORA
  POEMS
  Acquiescent   33   187

RICHARDS, E(DWARD) A.
  POEMS
  Under the Mountain   35   248
  Crazy Pete
  Her House
  Closing In
  Burning   53   134
  The Birds
  Prayer for A.D. 1941   57   294
  The Future Has Not Ended
  The Cycle
  Wintersong   59   200

BOOKS REVIEWED
  Time Strikes   55   220

RICHARDS, I(VOR) A(RMSTRONG)
  POEMS
  Alas Extra   98   155
  From Tomorrow Morning, Faustus!   100   341
  For Marianne Moore
    on Her Seventy-Fifth Birthday   101   410

BOOKS REVIEWED
  On Imagination:
    Coleridge's Critical Theory   47   52
  Playbook: Five Plays
    for a New Theater
    (With Lionel Abel, Robert Hivnor,
    Junjo Kinoshita, and James Merrill)   89   253
  Goodbye Earth and Other Poems   93   392
  The Screens and Other Poems   98   319
  I. A. Richards and Oscar Williams
    [Recording]   101   275
  New and Selected Poems   134   49

ARTICLES ABOUT
  Religion and Sensibility,
    by Henry Rago   57   314
  A Glossary of the New Criticism,
    by William Elton   73   153
  A Glossary of the New Criticism,
    by William Elton   73   232
  A Glossary of the New Criticism,
    by William Elton   73   296
  Rev. of Critics and Criticism,
    Ancient and Modern
    (Ed. by R. S. Crane)   82   98
  [Note on misprint]   101   227

RICHARDS, LAURA E.
BOOKS REVIEWED
  E. A. R.
    [Edwin Arlington Robinson]   50   150

RICHARDS, M. C.
BOOKS REVIEWED
  Centering   106   306

RICHARDS, TAD
POEMS
  Support Mental Health—Or I'll Kill You   103   298
  P. I.
  In Reply

RICHARDS, [MRS.] WALDO
BOOKS REVIEWED
  High Tide: Songs of Joy and Vision
    and Melody of Earth:
    Garden and Nature Poems (Ed.)   14   281
  The Magic Carpet: Poems for Travellers (Ed.)   27   343
  Love's High Way (Ed.)   32   96

RICHARDSON, DOROTHY LEE
POEMS
  Modern Grimm   73   275
  Essence
  Child on a Height   75   13
  Skull
  This Dust, Your Land   75   281

RICHARDSON, DOROTHY (M.)
POEMS
  Waiting   24   142
  Buns for Tea
  Sussex   27   67
  Discovery
  Barbara
  Message   30   256

RICHARDSON, JAMES
POEMS
  Post-Romantic   159   337

REVIEWS
  Collected Poems, by Philip Larkin
    (Ed. by Anthony Thwaite)   155   408
  Becoming a Poet: Elizabeth Bishop
    with Marianne Moore and Robert Lowell,
    by David Kalstone
    (Ed. by Robert Hemenway)   157   159
  Selected Poems 1946-1985 and
    The Changing Light at Sandover,
    by James Merrill   162   282

BOOKS REVIEWED
  Reservations   132   230
  Second Guesses   146   167
  As If   161   223

RICHARDSON, MABEL KINGSLEY
POEMS
  Stricken   48   254
  Telegram
  Hunter

RICHARDSON, MARK
BOOKS REVIEWED
  Collected Poems, Prose, & Plays,
    by Robert Frost
    (Ed. with Richard Poirier)   168   232

RICHARDSON, PETER
POEMS
  Daydreams   163   330
  Addendum   164   156

RICHART, BETTE
POEMS
  The Gift   73   207

RICHMAN, ROBERT
POEMS
  The Hunt of the Unicorn   76   27
  Possession   159   257

REVIEWS
  A Donald Justice Reader:
    Selected Poetry and Prose
    [Henri Coulette]   162   160

RICHTER, FRITZ
[(MRS.) NAT EINHORN]
POEMS
  Elegy ("Four seasons have had...")   43   133

RICKABY, FRANZ
BOOKS REVIEWED
  Ballads and Songs
    of the Shanty Boy (Ed.)   28   348

RICKEL, BOYER
POEMS
  From Where It's Dark   145   199
  Elegy ("The town all day awaited...")   147   74

BOOKS REVIEWED
  Arreboles   161   99

RICKS, DAVID
POEMS
  Genius Loci   162   5
  "Ethnic Cleansing"   162   139
  The Discovery of the Mind   165   63
  Revoked
  Shreds and Patches
  Variation on a Theme
    of Baudelaire   169   279

RICKWORD, EDGELL
ARTICLES ABOUT
London Note,
    by Benjamin Gilbert Brooks   35   214
English Poetry Today,
    by Basil Bunting   39   264
The Poet's Perspectives,
    by D. S. Savage   64   148

RIDDEL, JOSEPH N.
BOOKS REVIEWED
The Clairvoyant Eye:
    The Poetry and Poetics
    of Wallace Stevens   109   201

RIDEOUT, WALTER B.
BOOKS REVIEWED
American Poetry
    (Ed. with Gay Wilson Allen
    and James K. Robinson)   109   345

RIDGE, LOLA
POEMS
Chromatics   13   26
    The Song
    Iron Wine
    The Fiddler
    Dawn-Wind
    The Edge
Wild Duck   16   293
Altitude
After Storm
Cactus Seed
The Dream
In Russia   20   201
    The Spilling of the Wine
    Snow Dance for the Dead
    The White Bird
Back Yards   21   317
    The Fifth-Floor Window
    Lainyappe
    Saint's Bridge
    Marie
Chicago   23   311

REVIEWS
Precipitations, by Evelyn Scott   17   334
Willow Pollen,
    by Jeannette Marks   20   99
The King with Three Faces,
    by Marjorie Allen Seiffert   36   165

BOOKS REVIEWED
The Ghetto and Other Poems   13   335
Sun-Up   17   332
Red Flag   30   154
Firehead   36   36
Dance of Fire   47   40

ARTICLES ABOUT
Correspondence
    from Maxwell Bodenheim   14   170
A Few Women Poets, by Harriet Monroe   26   326
"A Torch in the Wind,"
    by Jessica Nelson North   58   209

RIDING, LAURA
[LAURA RIDING GOTTSCHALK,
LAURA RIDING JACKSON]
POEMS
The City of Cold Women   23   188
    The Sky
    The Wind
    The Lovers
    Voices
    Houses
    Gardens
    Interlude
Body's Head   27   59
    Hair
    Head Itself
    Forehead
    Eyes
    Nose
    Ears
    Mouth

BOOKS REVIEWED
Fugitives: An Anthology of Verse   32   102
A Joking Word   40   288
Laura and Francisca
Collected Poems of...   54   101
Selected Poems: In Five Sets   125   295
First Awakenings: The Early Poems of...
    (Ed. by Elizabeth Friedmann,
    Alan J. Clark, and Robert Nye)   164   39

ARTICLES ABOUT
Rev. of The Fugitive Poets
    (Ed. by William Pratt)   110   47
[Note about William Pratt]   110   270

RIDL, JACK
POEMS
American Suite for a Lost Daughter   152   152

RIDLAND, JOHN (M.)
POEMS
Bless Our Home   99   298
A Bucket of Water
Listening Booth
Painter with Child
Swimming for Jeni   143   276

BOOKS REVIEWED
Fires of Home:
    Poems, in Poets of Today VIII   99   379

RIDLER, ANNE
POEMS
Views of the North Coast   69   320
Poem   70   186
  ("The coffin's typical shape...")
  ("The specialty of time...")
  ("But O these dead...")
Poem ("Terminate torment...")   74   141
Mare Nostrum   78   11
On a Picture by Michele da Verona,
  of Arion as a Boy Riding
  Upon a Dolphin
Choosing a Name   81   110
A Matter of Life & Death   83   84
Leaving Ringshall: A Quodlibet   85   283
News of the World   90   286

BOOKS REVIEWED
A Dream Observed
  and Other Poems   59   98
The Trial of Thomas Cranmer   89   378
Selected Poems   101   424

RIDLEY, M. R.
BOOKS REVIEWED
Poetry and the Ordinary Reader   55   340

RIEU, E. V.
BOOKS REVIEWED
Homer: The Odyssey:
  A New Translation (Tr.)   72   28

RIGGS, KATHARINE
POEMS
Mockery   17   141

RIGGS, LYNN
POEMS
Rhythm of Rain   22   252
Dawn—Late Summer   26   255
Gilded Cavern   32   260
  Hour After Dawn
  Charger
  Bastinado
  The Wolves
  The Golden Cockerel
  Portrait of a Peer
  Statement
  The Fountain
The Room   61   533
Morning: Wartime   62   259

ARTICLES
Correspondence   61   698

BOOKS REVIEWED
The Iron Dish   37   347

RIGSBEE, DAVID
POEMS
White   149   270
The Mermaid

RIHAKU
[See LI PO]

RILEY, JAMES WHITCOMB
ARTICLES ABOUT
"The Music of the Human Heart,"
  by Edith Wyatt   1   59
James Whitcomb Riley,
  by Harriet Monroe   8   305

RILEY, MICHAEL D.
POEMS
Snow Man   161   145
Regret   162   218

RILKE, RAINER MARIA
POEMS
Growing Blind   6   263
People at Night
  (Tr. by Margarete Munsterberg)
Charles the Twelfth
  of Sweden Rides in the Ukraine
  (Tr. by Jessie Lemont)   18   319
What Will You Do?
  (Tr. by Babette Deutsch
  and Avrahm Yarmolinsky)   21   142
Pietà
  (Tr. by Jessie Lemont)   66   84
The Rose-Window
  (Tr. by Jessie Lemont)   68   195

ARTICLES
Letters to Benvenuta
  (Tr. by Heinz Norden)   77   276

BOOKS REVIEWED
Poems of...
  (Tr. by Jessie Lemont)   14   168
Rainer Maria Rilke: Poems
  (Tr. by J. B. Leishman)   45   344
Translations from the Poetry of...
  (Tr. by M. D. Herter-Norton)   55   96
Duino Elegies
  (Tr. by J. B. Leishman
  and Stephen Spender)
Wartime Letters of..., 1914-1921
  (Tr. by M. D. Herter-Norton)   56   271
Rainer Maria Rilke: Fifty Selected Poems
  (Tr. by C. F. MacIntyre)   61   441
Poems from the Book of Hours
  (Tr. by Babette Deutsch)
Sonnets to Orpheus
  (Tr. by M. D. Herter Norton)

Poems
  (Tr. by Jessie Lemont)   63   169
Letters of…, 1892-1910
  (Tr. by Jane Bannard Green
  and M. D. Herter-Norton)   67   221
Sonnets to Orpheus, Duino Elegies
  (Tr. by Jessie Lemont)   68   100
Thirty-One Poems
  (Tr. by Ludwig Lewisohn)   69   103
The Notebooks of Malte Laurids Brigge
  (Tr. by M. D. Herter-Norton)   76   92
Poems 1906-26
  (Tr. by J. B. Leishman)   93   192
Gedichte 1906 bis 1926
  (Ed. by Ernest Zinn)
The Letters of Rainer Maria Rilke and
  Princess Marie von Thurn und Taxis
  (Tr. by Nora Wydenbruck)   94   59
The Lay of the Love and Death
  of Cornet Christopher Rilke
  (Tr. by M. D. Herter-Norton)   95   373
Selected Works, vol. I, Prose
  (Tr. by G. Craig Houston)   97   323
Selected Works, vol. II, Poetry
  (Tr. by J. B. Leishman)
Selected Letters of…
  (Ed. by Harry T. Moore)   101   287
Visions of Christ
  (Ed. by Siegfried Mandel)
  (Tr. by Aaron Kramer)   113   188
Duino Elegies and
  The Sonnets to Orpheus
  (Tr. by A. Poulin, Jr.)   131   345
Duino Elegies
  (Tr. by David Young)   134   234
The Selected Poetry of…
  (Ed. and tr. by Stephen Mitchell)   145   229

ARTICLES ABOUT
  Modern German Poetry II,
    by Reginald H. Wilenski   5   234
  Correspondence
    from Margarete Munsterberg   6   263
  A Note on Modern German Poetry,
    by Babette Deutsch   21   149
  The New Poets of Germany,
    by Morton Dauwen Zabel   34   94
  A Lesson from Rilke,
    by Stanley J. Kunitz   45   328
  Rilke in His Age,
    by Louise Bogan   50   34
  Rev. of *Rainer Maria Rilke,*
    by E. M. Butler   61   441
  The Still Voice of German Poetry,
    by Edouard Roditi   68   208
  Correspondence from Jessie Lemont
    [Francis Golffing]   69   57

  Rev. of *William Blake:*
    The Politics of Vision,
    by Mark Schorer   69   223
  Comment by E. E. Cummings
    [*Letters to a Young Poet*]   74   91
  Rev. of *Rilke and Benvenuta,*
    by Magda von Hattingberg
    (Tr. by Cyrus Brooks)   76   92
  Rev. of *Rainer Maria Rilke:*
    A Study of His Later Poetry,
    by Hans Egon Holthusen
    (Tr. by J. P. Stern)   82   342
  Pages from an Italian Journal,
    by Charles Tomlinson   89   183
  Rev. of *Rainer Maria Rilke:*
    Masks and the Man,
    by H. F. Peters   97   387

RIMBAUD, ARTHUR
POEMS
  Wakes—III   37   262
  To One Reason
    (Tr. by Emanuel Carnevali)
  When Rimbaud Came to Charleroi
    (Tr. by J. E. Scruggs)   54   125

BOOKS REVIEWED
  Some Poems of…
    (Tr. by Lionel Abel)   56   95
  A Season in Hell
    (Tr. by Delmore Schwartz)
  Selected Verse Poems of…
    (Tr. by Norman Cameron)   63   96
  Prose Poems from "The Illuminations"
    (Tr. by Helen Rootham)   64   44
  A Season in Hell
    (Tr. by Louise Varèse)   67   278
  Prose Poems from "The Illuminations"
    (Tr. by Louise Varèse)   69   286
  Baudelaire, Rimbaud, Verlaine
    (Ed. by Joseph M. Bernstein)   72   105

ARTICLES ABOUT
  Rev. of *Paul Verlaine,*
    by Harold Nicolson   20   223
  Rimbaud in Our Time,
    by Delmore Schwartz   55   148
  Rev. of *Arthur Rimbaud,*
    by Enid Starkie   56   95
  Rev. of *William Blake:*
    The Politics of Vision,
    by Mark Schorer   69   223
  Rev. of *Rimbaud,*
    by Wallace Fowlie   70   102
  Rimbaud in 1949,
    by Wallace Fowlie
    [Akakia Viala, Nicolas Bataille, André
    Breton, Henry de Bouillane de Lacoste]   75   166

Rev. of *100 Modern Poems*
(Ed. by Selden Rodman)   76   167
French Chronicle: Recent Publications,
by Wallace Fowlie   88   408
Rev. of *Hart Crane:*
The Life of an American Poet,
by Philip Horton   91   117
Letter From Haiti, by Wallace Fowlie   94   398
Rev. of *The Design*
of Rimbaud's Poetry,
by John Porter Houston   104   187
Rev. of *The Limits of Symbolism:*
Studies of Five Modern French Poets,
by Bernard Weinberg   112   41

RIO, ANGEL DEL
[See DEL RIO, ANGEL]

RÍOS, ALBERTO
BOOKS REVIEWED
Teodoro Luna's Two Kisses   162   224

RIOS, FRANCESCA
[Pseud. of RIPPLY, INEZ]
POEMS
Autumn   21   79

ARTICLES ABOUT
[Note on name]   24   171

RIOSECO, ARTURO TORRES
[See TORRES RIOSECO, ARTURO]

RIPLEY, SHERMAN
BOOKS REVIEWED
Moon Shadows   30   353
Beyond: An Anthology
of Immortality (Ed.)   37   164

RIPPLY, INEZ
[See RIOS, FRANCESCA, pseud.]

RITCHIE, ELISAVIETTA
POEMS
Sorting Laundry   153   274

RITSOS, YANNIS
POEMS
The Night of a Solitary   103   306
Immobility of the Voyage
The Surpassing of Danger
Rainy
Ultimate Landing
Honest Confrontation
The Heard and the Unheard
Estrangement
Recollection
Moment

The Architect
(Tr. by Rae Dalven)
The Meaning of Simplicity   116   292
In the Barracks
Absence
Suspicious Sleep
Not Unsuspecting
Achievement
A Minimum Delay
(Tr. by Rae Dalven)
Injustice   120   260
Without Position
Security
(Tr. by Rae Dalven)
Twelve Poems for Cavafy
(Tr. by Bernard Mathieu)   125   1
Attenuation   158   204
Pro Forma
(Tr. by Martin McKinsey)

BOOKS REVIEWED
Ritsos in Parentheses
(Tr. by Edmund Keeley)   137   220

ARTICLES ABOUT
A Note on Yannis Ritsos,
by Rae Dalven   103   334

RITTENHOUSE, JESSIE (B.)
ARTICLES
The Poetry Society of America   1   166
Correspondence:
Miss Rittenhouse Explains
[Edgar Lee Masters]   17   227

BOOKS REVIEWED
The Little Book of Modern Verse (Ed.)   3   144
The Little Book of American Poets (Ed.) 7   318
The Lifted Cup   19   344
The Little Book
of Modern British Verse (Ed.)   27   343
Selected Poems
of Edith M. Thomas (Ed.)   29   229
Third Book of Modern Verse (Ed.)   32   96
The Bird-Lovers' Anthology
(Ed. with Clinton Scollard)   37   164
The Secret Bird   38   112
The Rollins Book of Verse 1929 (Ed.)   38   282
The Moving Tide:
New and Selected Lyrics   59   288

RITTER, MARGARET TOD
POEMS
Resurgence   27   141
Storm Chant   36   28

BOOKS REVIEWED
Wind Out of Betelgeuse   32   286

RITZ, JEAN-GEORGES
BOOKS REVIEWED
Robert Bridges and Gerard Hopkins,
1863-1889: A Literary Friendship   100   50

RIVARD, DAVID
POEMS
C'è Un'Altra Possibilità   156   265

RIVAS, HUMBERTO
BOOKS REVIEWED
A Cry in the Dark
(With German Horacio)   66   350

RIVERA, DIEGO
ARTICLES ABOUT
Mexico, by Harriet Monroe   42   92

RIVERS, J. W.
POEMS
Illinois: At Night,
Black Hawk's Statue Broods   148   73
April in a Mountain Cabin:
Swiss Pine Lake, North Carolina   151   137
Hiking with the Old Acorn Lady   152   211
Reconciliation
Respite   154   137
King Muza Recounts Details
of Event at Roncesvalles   170   327
The Sword of Saladin: A Moral Fable
Tolui's Son Kublai Prepares
To Take the Sung State
of Southern China

BOOKS REVIEWED
Proud and On My Feet   144   107

RIVIER, JEAN
POEMS
Poems from France   59   29
("Now poverty with its tired eyes...")
("Unhappiness to the women...")
La Femme en Lambeaux
(Tr. by George Dillon)

ARTICLES
Marseille Letter
[Patrice de la Tour du Pin, Jean Cayrol,
Pierre Emmanuel, Loys Masson,
Jean Dutrait, Léon-Gabriel Gros,
Toursky, Jean Tortel, Ilarie Voronca,
Lanza del Vasto, Luc Decaunes,
André Gaillard]   60   269

RIVOIRE, ANDRÉ
ARTICLES ABOUT
As It Is in Paris,
by Harriet Monroe   27   266

RIVOLA, FLORA SHUFELT
POEMS
Kinship   12   78
Question   20   77
The First King Who Found Out   25   138
Automaton
Fuel
Plowman on Horseback
Untrammelled   36   22
Peddlers
If Prairies Dream

RIZZARDI, ALFREDO
POEMS
Viali in Autunno
(Tr. by Robert Fitzgerald)   94   318
Costellazioni
(Tr. by John Frederick Nims)
Portovenere
Via Senzanome
(Tr. by Robert Fitzgerald)

ROACH, ELOISE
BOOKS REVIEWED
Platero and I,
by Juan Ramón Jiménez (Tr.)   92   184

ROBBINS, RUSSELL HOPE
BOOKS REVIEWED
Secular Lyrics of the XIVth
and XVth Centuries   81   258

ROBERSON, ED
BOOKS REVIEWED
When Thy King Is a Boy   119   342

ROBERTS, CECIL
BOOKS REVIEWED
Poems   16   336

ROBERTS, CHARLES G. D.
ARTICLES ABOUT
The Development of Poetry
in Canada, 1880-1940,
by E. K. Brown   58   34

ROBERTS, DOROTHY
BOOKS REVIEWED
Dazzle   94   186
Extended   112   201

ROBERTS, ELIZABETH MADOX
POEMS
Under the Tree   18   185
The Cornfield
The Pilaster
The Star
Water Noises

Crescent Moon		
Strange Tree		
A Child Asleep		
My Heart		
Talk from the Dust	20	257
The Sky		
Numbers		
Autumn		
The People		
A Beautiful Lady		
August Night		
Orpheus	24	201
Cinderella's Song		
A Ballet Song of Mary	31	127
Sailing for America	41	119
From *Song in a Meadow*	54	20
The Meeting		
A Word and a Tree		
Song for a Girl Sent to Drive Cows		
I, Adam		
Evening Song		
Moonlight in Summer		

ARTICLES
[Note]	41	351

BOOKS REVIEWED
Under the Tree	22	45
Under the Tree	38	227
Song in the Meadow	57	43

ARTICLES ABOUT
Some Recollections of the Poetry Club at the University of Chicago, by Gladys Campbell	107	110

ROBERTS, F. WARREN
BOOKS REVIEWED
The Complete Poems of D. H. Lawrence (Ed. with Vivian De Sola Pinto)	106	218

ROBERTS, LEN
POEMS
The Moment	148	333
Nights on Olmstead Street		
Learning on Olmstead Street	152	143
The Seven Steps		

BOOKS REVIEWED
Black Wings	156	100

ROBERTS, LYNETTE
POEMS
The Hypnotist	81	164
Love Is an Outlaw		
These Words I Write on Crinkled Tin		
Two Wine Glasses	82	321
Spring		

Tygwyn		
Winter Walk	85	11

ROBERTS, MARTHA
POEMS
Bed-Time	54	310

ROBERTS, MARY
BOOKS REVIEWED
Platero and I, by Juan Ramón Jiménez (Tr. with William Roberts)	92	184

ROBERTS, MARY ELEANOR
POEMS
Moon in the Morning	8	132

ROBERTS, MICHAEL ["M. R."]
POEMS
Nicholas Flanel the Alchemist	36	66
Darkness in Stony Places		
Siesta	39	246
Kangchenjunga		
Conditions of Men	49	190
All on a Summer Day		
The Mi-Go		
Erwin		
Under	51	71
Rondo and Gigue		
St. Ursanne	52	8
Bonneval		
Voices of Earth and Air		
Mediterranean	52	327
The Death	55	18
Rockall		
The Red Tower	58	70
The Images of Death		

ARTICLES
Notes on English Poets [T. S. Eliot, Gerard Manley Hopkins, W. H. Auden, Cecil Day Lewis, Julian Bell, William Empson]	39	271
Aspects of English Poetry: 1932-1937 [Dylan Thomas, George Barker]	49	210
A Check-List of Recent English Books of Verse 1931-1936	49	231
Recent Anthologies	49	233
Recent Critical Works on Modern Poetry	49	235

BOOKS REVIEWED
These Our Matins	38	229
New Signatures (Ed.)	44	46
New Country (Ed.)		
Poems	48	343
The Modern Mind	52	106
Orion Marches	55	335

ARTICLES ABOUT
"Obstinate Isles," by M. D. Zabel   41   214

ROBERTS, PHILIP
BOOKS REVIEWED
Will's Dream   131   225

ROBERTS, WILLIAM
BOOKS REVIEWED
Platero and I,
   by Juan Ramón Jiménez
   (Tr. with Mary Roberts)   92   184

ROBIN, RALPH
POEMS
Directions   136   97

ROBINS, NATALIE S.
POEMS
Shell   115   240
Abandoned Boat   127   17

BOOKS REVIEWED
Wild Lace   99   313

ROBINSON, DONALD FAY
POEMS
Portrait   33   144
Sons of Man   44   251

ROBINSON, EDWARD R.
POEMS
Hymn for Soldiers
   Who Have Lain in the Snow   129   284

ROBINSON, EDWIN ARLINGTON
POEMS
Eros Turannos   3   206
Bokardo   6   292
Avenel Gray   21   1
Thomas Hood   22   248

BOOKS REVIEWED
The Man Against the Sky   8   43
Merlin   10   211
Lancelot   16   217
The Three Taverns   18   273
Avon's Harvest
Collected Poems of...   19   278
Roman Bartholow   24   96
Dionysus in Doubt   27   40
Tristram   31   160
Sonnets   34   111
Cavender's House   34   233
Collected Poems of...   37   216
The Glory of the Nightingales
Matthias at the Door   39   212

Nicodemus   41   158
Talifer   43   221
Amaranth   45   158
Collected Poems of...   50   150
Tilbury Town: Selected Poems of...
   (Ed. by Lawrance Thompson)   84   108
Selected Poems of...
   (Ed. by Morton Dauwen Zabel)   108   187

ARTICLES ABOUT
Mr. Robinson's Jubilee,
   by Harriet Monroe   15   265
A New Pulitzer Prize,
   by Harriet Monroe   20   215
Edwin Arlington Robinson,
   by Harriet Monroe   25   206
Rev. of Edwin Arlington Robinson,
   by Ben Ray Redman   29   229
Obituary   46   114
Robinson as Man and Poet,
   by Harriet Monroe   46   150
Robinson in America, by M. D. Zabel   46   157
Rev. of E. A. R.,
   by Laura E. Richards,
   Next Door to a Poet,
   by Rollo Walter Brown,
   and A Bibliography
   of Edwin Arlington Robinson,
   by Charles Beecher Hogan   50   150
Rev. of Edwin Arlington Robinson,
   by Hermann Hagedorn   54   92
Robinson and Praed, by Hoyt H. Hudson
   [Winthrop Mackworth Praed]   61   612
Rev. of Edwin Arlington Robinson
   and His Manuscripts,
   by Esther Willard Bates   65   209
Rev. of A History
   of American Poetry, 1900-1940,
   by Horace Gregory
   and Marya Zaturenska   69   210
Rev. of Edwin Arlington Robinson,
   by Yvor Winters   70   94
From the Introduction to
   The Oxford Book of American Verse,
   by F. O. Matthiessen   77   31
Rev. of Edwin Arlington Robinson:
   A Critical Study,
   by Ellsworth Barnard   81   187
Rev. of More Clinical Sonnets,
   by Merrill Moore   84   32
Rev. of Edwin Arlington Robinson,
   by Edwin S. Fussell   92   121
Rev. of Edwin Arlington Robinson,
   by Yvor Winters   120   230
Rev. of The New Oxford Book
   of American Verse
   (Ed. by Richard Ellmann)   131   236

ROBINSON, ELOISE
POEMS
War 10 57
The Trees 12 188
Fatherland 13 1

ARTICLES
Correspondence:
Letter from France 13 55

ROBINSON, HENRY MORTON
BOOKS REVIEWED
Buck Fever 36 107

ROBINSON, JAMES K.
BOOKS REVIEWED
American Poetry
(Ed. with Gay Wilson Allen
and Walter B. Rideout) 109 345

ROBINSON, JANICE
ARTICLES ABOUT
The Forging of H. D.,
by Gloria G. Fromm 153 160

ROBINSON, LENNOX
BOOKS REVIEWED
The Golden Treasury of Irish Verse (Ed.) 27 343
The Oxford Book of Irish Verse:
XVII Century—XX Century
(Ed. with Donagh McDonagh) 94 260

ROBINSON, SELMA
BOOKS REVIEWED
City Child 41 105

ROBSON, W. W.
BOOKS REVIEWED
The Signs Among Us 118 41

ROCHE, JOHN PIERRE
POEMS
Pierrot Sings 7 285

ROCHE, LORETTA
POEMS
Spirit 26 26

ROCHE, PAUL
BOOKS REVIEWED
The Oedipus Plays of Sophocles (Tr.) 95 190

ROCKWELL, LILLIAN
BOOKS REVIEWED
Impatient Lover 82 34

RODGER, SARAH-ELIZABETH
POEMS
Long Ago 26 256

The Bread-Winner
The Twisted Pine
Songs on the Way 29 311
Hoof-Beats
Quest
History 36 72
Threshold
Burden
Borderland

RODGERS, W. R.
POEMS
Song for War 65 316

BOOKS REVIEWED
Awake! and Other Wartime Poems 60 94
Europa and the Bull 82 358
Collected Poems 122 40

RODIER, KATHARINE
POEMS
Atlantic City 145 81

RODITI, EDOUARD
POEMS
("No hour can darker be...") 41 194
("Elder and hemlock bathe...")
Lament 54 8
The Political Prisoner 56 121
John Lack-Land
London by Moonlight
Amare Est Amarum
Avenue des Champs Elysées 58 68
From Cassandra's Dream 61 656
The Plots
The Nature of Knowledge 65 10
A Parisian in Kansas City
A Private Life 77 333
A Private World 94 177

TRANSLATIONS
Poems by Fernando Pessoa 87 26
Poems by Hans Magnus Enzensberger
and Alexander Koval 88 250

ARTICLES
The Poetics of Translation
[John Dryden] 60 32
Public and Private Poetics 63 268
Correspondence 63 352
Poetry Is News
[The Silence of the Sea] 64 51
Correspondence
[Sherna Shalett Vinograd] 64 175
Correspondence
[Anne Killigrew] 67 173
Oscar Wilde's Poetry
as Art History 67 322

The Still Voice of German Poetry
[Josef Weinheber, Rainer Maria Rilke,
Hans Bergengruen]   68   208
Correspondence
[German Poetry]   69   56
Cafavis and the Permanence
of Greek History   81   389
The Several Names
of Fernando Pessoa   87   40

REVIEWS
Poetry, Mysticism, and Magic   53   218
L'Expérience poétique,
by Rolland de Renéville
Situation de la Poésie,
by Jacques and Raissa Maritain
The Writing on the Wall   54   284
The Autumn World,
by D. S. Savage
Confusions About X,
by Julian Symons
Poems and Songs, by Gavin Ewart
Anthologie des Poètes de la N.R.F.
[Paul Valéry]   56   225
Anthology of the Provencal Troubadors
(Ed. by Raymond Thompson Hill
and Thomas Goddard Bergin)   58   278
In a Silver Sea   60   225
Poems, by F. T. Prince
The Buried Stream,
Collected Poems 1908-1940,
by Geoffrey Faber
A Faust-Fight   61   406
Goethe's Faust,
A New American Translation,
by C. F. MacIntyre
Faust: Parts One and Two
(Tr. and ed.
by George Madison Priest)
An Anthology of Contemporary
Latin American Poetry
(Ed. by Dudley Fitts)   62   231
New Poems, by Dylan Thomas   63   48
Translations of Rimbaud and Lorca   63   96
Selected Verse Poems of Arthur Rimbaud
(Tr. by Norman Cameron)
Selected Poems of Federico García Lorca
(Tr. by Stephen Spender
and J. L. Gili)
Baudelaire, A Criticism,
by Joseph D. Bennett   66   48
A Season in Hell,
by Arthur Rimbaud
(Tr. by Louise Varèse)   67   278
Surrealism Serves the State   68   54
Ode to Bombed London,
by Philippe Soupault
(Tr. by Norman Cameron)

Three Prayers for Pilots,
by Jules Roy
(Tr. by George Ellidge)
100 Modern Poems
(Ed. by Selden Rodman)
[Arthur Rimbaud]   76   167
Baudelaire, by Jean-Paul Sartre   77   100
The Flea of Sodom,
by Edward Dahlberg   77   236

BOOKS REVIEWED
Prison Within Prison:
Three Elegies on Hebrew Themes   60   282
Poems 1928-1948   75   243
Selected Poems,
by Alain Bosquet
(Tr. with Samuel Beckett,
Charles Guenther, and Ruth Whitman)   104   115
Young Cherry Trees Secured Against Hares,
by André Breton (Tr.)   117   261

ARTICLES ABOUT
[Note on typo]   62   354
How Do You Spell Fool?
by Edward Dahlberg   78   54

RODKER, JOHN
POEMS
London Night   5   119
Under the Trees   7   182
Dead Queens   10   133
Because Some Lover
In a Garden
The Searchlight   15   26
To a Renault in the Country   30   262
Lines to an Etruscan Tomb

ARTICLES
Bernard Gilbert   30   274

REVIEWS
Linnets in the Slums, by Marion Pryce   15   55
Requiem, by Humbert Wolfe   31   218

BOOKS REVIEWED
Poems   6   153
Hymns   17   44

ARTICLES ABOUT
Rev. of Catholic Anthology—1914-1915   8   94
Correspondence
from Maxwell Bodenheim
[Richard Aldington]   17   170

RODMAN, SELDEN
POEMS
Edges   38   316
Edge of the Forest

Edge of the Lake
Dark Corners
Time of Day   41   318

REVIEWS
    To Lighten My House,
        by Alastair Reid   84   96
    Hungerfield and Other Poems,
        by Robinson Jeffers   84   226

BOOKS REVIEWED
    Mortal Triumph and Other Poems   41   161
    Lawrence, the Last Crusade   50   285
    A New Anthology of Modern Poetry (Ed.)   53   46
    The Airmen   58   264
    The Revolutionists   61   511
    War and the Poet
        (Ed. with Richard Eberhart)   69   46
    The Amazing Year   72   161
    100 Modern Poems (Ed.)   76   167

ARTICLES ABOUT
    Correspondence
        from Kimball Flaccus   53   162

RODWAY, ALLAN EDWIN
BOOKS REVIEWED
    The Common Muse: An Anthology
        of Popular British Ballad Poetry
        XVth-XXth Century
        (Ed. with Vivian De Sola Pinto)   91   400

ROE, ROBERT
[ROBERT J. ROE,
ROBERT L. ROE]
POEMS
    A Sailor's Note-Book   20   142
        Typhoon
        Sea
        Wind
        Moon
        Cautious
        Apparition
        Sailor
        Barney
        Insight
        Jock
        Stars
        Meinself
    Interplanes   21   86
        Symphonie Pathétique
        Portrait of a Man
        Apprentice
        Cortege
        Death
    Songs for a Dark Endurance   27   70
        The Traveler
        After Many Years
        The Damned

A Light Song
Gypsy Song
Blacksmith's Song   32   27
Another Immoral Season
Receipt
Aesthete to His Love   32   309
Seas and Singing Country   38   1
    Across the Southwest by Bus
    Choppers
    Refuge
Speak Softly   43   26

ARTICLES
    [Notes on A Sailor's Note-Book]   20   173

BOOKS REVIEWED
    Here You Have Me   24   276

ROESKE, PAULETTE
POEMS
    Looking for You One Year Later   141   287
    Wintering at a Summer Resort
    7:00 A. M. Lakefront
    Refugees at Avila Beach

ROETHKE, THEODORE
[See also ROTHBERG,
WINTERSET, pseud.]
POEMS
    Bound   40   316
    Fugitive
    "Long Live the Weeds"   48   203
    Reply to Censure   51   80
    Prognosis   53   138
    The Reckoning
    The Signals
    Against Disaster
    The Pause
    The Bringer of Tidings
    The Summons
    The Auction   54   69
    Orders for the Day   56   75
    Sale   57   292
    Second Shadow
    The Gossips   63   68
    Summer School Marms
    Florist's Root Cellar
    Dolor
    The Return   68   250
    The Long Alley   70   198
    Four Children's Poems   76   331
        The Serpent
        The Cow
        The Chair
        The Ceiling
    Words in the Violent Ward   77   262
    To an Anthologist
    Sensibility! O La!   78   311

O Lull Me, Lull Me
O, Thou Opening, O   81   64
Pub Songs   98   283
Supper with Lindsay   103   85
Song ("Witch-me-tiddle-dee...")
A Wheeze for Wystan
Straw for the Fire:
    From His Notebooks
    [Version by David Wagoner]   105   113
The Stony Garden
    [Version by David Wagoner]   113   104

ARTICLES
The Teaching Poet   79   250
Some Remarks on Rhythm   97   35

REVIEWS
And Spain Sings:
    Fifty Loyalist Ballads
    (Ed. by M. J. Benardete
    and Rolfe Humphries)   52   43
The Five-Fold Mesh,
    by Ben Belitt   53   214
Concerning the Young,
    by Willard Maas   53   336
Obiter Dicta   60   109
    The Alert, by Wilfrid Gibson
    Gautama the Enlightened,
        by John Masefield
A Lost Season, by Roy Fuller   67   218
The Earth-Bound,
    by Janet Lewis   69   220

BOOKS REVIEWED
Open House   58   222
The Lost Son and Other Poems   73   222
Words for the Wind   94   203
I Am! Says the Lamb   100   54
Sequence, Sometimes Metaphysical   105   119
The Far Field   105   122
On the Poet and His Craft:
    Selected Prose of...
    (Ed. by Ralph J. Mills, Jr.)   107   400
Collected Poems   109   262
Selected Letters of...
    (Ed. by Ralph J. Mills, Jr.)   113   338
Straw for the Fire: From the Notebooks
    of Theodore Roethke, 1943-63
    (Ed. by David Wagoner)   121   341

ARTICLES ABOUT
[Note on pseudonym]   103   139
Rev. of Theodore Roethke,
    Essays on the Poetry
    (Ed. by Arnold Stein)   109   198
Rev. of Theodore Roethke:
    An Introduction to the Poetry,
    by Karl Malkoff   112   52

Rev. of The Glass House:
    The Life of Theodore Roethke,
    by Allan Seager   114   327
Rev. of Summers of Vietnam
    and Other Poems,
    by Mary Kinzie   158   41

ROFFEY, HALL
POEMS
    Qualche Cosa Veduta   5   167

ROGERS, PATTIANN
POEMS
    The Literary Adventure   132   331
    Portrait
    Synthesizing the Word   134   206
    A Giant Has Swallowed the Earth for a Pill
    Concepts and Their Bodies
        (The Boy in the Field Alone)   136   330
    Achieving Perspective
    The Determinations of the Scene
    Discovering Your Subject   138   28
    The Last Blessing
    Exposing the Future with Conviction
    The Possible Advantages
        of the Expendable Multitudes
    The Possible Suffering
        of a God During Creation   140   30
    The Abandonment
    Eulogy for a Hermit Crab
    Trinity
    The Doctrine   141   22
    The Form of the Message   141   132
    The Origin of Order
    Being What We Are
    Finding the Cat
        in a Spring Field at Midnight
    The Delight of Being Lost
    The Verification of Vulnerability:
        Bog Turtle   143   1
    Statement Preliminary
        to the Invention of Solace
    The Body as Window
    Nude Standing Alone in the Forest:
        A Study of Place
    The Limitations of Death   144   339
    Investigative Logic in a Study of Love
    The Elegance of the Dichotomous Experience
    The Thing in Itself   147   215
    The Answering of Prayers
    The Laying-On of Hands   151   138
    A Common Sight   151   355
    How the Old See Death
    Amen   158   94
    Rapture of the Deep:
        The Pattern of Poseidon's Love Song   164   268
    Design of Gongs   166   96
    Calling to Measure
    Nearing Autobiography   168   28

BOOKS REVIEWED
The Expectations of Light   143   163
The Tattooed Lady in the Garden   151   360
Legendary Performance   152   161
Splitting and Binding   156   224
Firekeeper: New and Selected Poems   169   156

ROGERS, PRESTON
POEMS
Old Man in Summer   99   368
All Islands

ROGERS, VIRGINIA HORTON
BOOKS REVIEWED
Bathsheba   60   285

ROHDE, BARBARA
POEMS
Living Quarters   75   6

ROJO, ENRIQUE GONZALEZ
[See GONZALEZ ROJO,
ENRIQUE]

ROKEAH, DAVID
POEMS
Zealots of Yearning
    (Tr. by Ruth Finer Mintz)   92   245

ROLFE, EDWIN
POEMS
Lanes of Death and Birth   41   266
Before the Hour   48   61
    The Ship
    Night-World
Casualty   66   12
To Thine Own Self
Survival Is of the Essence
Recruit
Song ("Through all the cowering...")   67   134
About Eyes
Theodore Dreiser   68   134
A Poem to Delight My Friends
    Who Laugh at Science-Fiction   82   141

REVIEWS
Contemporary Spanish Poetry
    (Tr. by Eleanor L. Turnbull,
    with Pedro Salinas)   67   265

BOOKS REVIEWED
We Gather Strength
    (With Herman Spector, Joseph Kalar,
    and S. Funaroff)   44   50
Permit Me Refuge   89   118

ARTICLES ABOUT
Poetry of the Left,
    by Harriet Monroe   48   212

ROLLINGS, ALANE
BOOKS REVIEWED
The Struggle To Adore   165   219

ROLLINS, HYDER EDWARD
BOOKS REVIEWED
The Pack of Autolycus (Ed.)   30   352

ROMAINS, JULES
BOOKS REVIEWED
Odes et Prières   2   187
Europe   15   42

ARTICLES ABOUT
The Hard and the Soft
    in French Poetry,
    by Ezra Pound   11   264

ROMIG, EDNA DAVIS
POEMS
Speculation   48   138
Annunciation   50   260

RONALD, T. [Pseud.]
POEMS
The People's Army   72   138

RONAN, GEORGIA
POEMS
Immunity   74   83

RONSARD
[See DE RONSARD, PIERRE]

RONSLEY, JOSEPH
BOOKS REVIEWED
Yeats' Autobiography   113   338

ROOF, SIMONS
POEMS
Song for a Ship   66   190
Spring of Home
The Islanders
Laloma

ROOK, ALAN
POEMS
London, 1941   58   249

ROOT, E(DWARD) MERRILL
POEMS
Night on the River   16   197

BOOKS REVIEWED
Lost Eden   30   229
Dawn Is Forever   54   225
Shoulder the Sky   100   404

ROOT, JUDITH
POEMS
Waiting Room in Missouri   147   335
First Anniversary
  of an Accidental Shooting

ROOT, WILLIAM PITT
POEMS
Five Poems   116   167
  ("Dark woods...")
  ("Suddenly your skull shocks...")
  ("Dew: for a moment...")
  ("Sometimes fading in the valley...")
  ("The last hours of the year...")
Steelhead   124   319
Leopard Lost in High Snow
Half Shift   137   39
Dancers on an Island with No Roads
Song ("O/the slender brilliance...")
For the Better Maker   144   284
Remembering the Sea Elephant

REVIEWS
Anything But Over   123   34
  Campfires of the Resistance:
    Poetry from the Movement
    (Ed. by Todd Gitlin)
  Modern Greek Poetry
    (Tr. and ed. by Rae Dalven)
  The Sea and the Honeycomb:
    A Book of Tiny Poems
    (Ed. by Robert Bly)
  Twenty Poems of Tomas Tranströmer
    (Tr. by Robert Bly)
  Our Poets Speak
    (Ed. by D. St. John-Parsons)
  Classic Black African Poems
    (Ed. by Willard R. Trask)
  It's a New Day, by Sonia Sanchez
  Transformations, by Anne Sexton
  Fat Man Poems, by Peter Wild
  Not Every Year, by John Haislip
  Crying in the Cheap Seats,
    by Bill Tremblay

BOOKS REVIEWED
  The Storm   115   281

ROOTHAM, HELEN
BOOKS REVIEWED
Prose Poems from
  "The Illuminations,"
  by Arthur Rimbaud (Tr.)   64   44

RORTY, JAMES
POEMS
  The Conqueror   14   306
  The Broken of Heart   24   252
  Almost Eureka!   30   86

Boy and Gull
The Innocents
Domingo Day   39   9
  The Saint
  Dance Invocation
  The Coming of the Rain
Ezekiel's Casket   41   261

ARTICLES
Correspondence
  [Derrick Lehmer]   39   228

REVIEWS
  Lonesome Water, by Roy Helton   39   221

BOOKS REVIEWED
  Continent's End, an Anthology
    of Contemporary California Poets
    (Ed. with George Sterling
    and Genevieve Taggard)   27   217
  Children of the Sun   29   343

ARTICLES ABOUT
Correspondence
  from Derrick N. Lehmer   39   165
  [Note]   40   295

ROSADO VEGA, LUIS
POEMS
  To the Unknown Goddess
    (Tr. by Muna Lee)   26   132

ROSE, DAN
POEMS
  Direct Dialing the Abyss
    from a Payphone: Father   112   95

ROSE, JENNIFER
POEMS
  Valedictory   166   165

ROSE, MILTON S.
BOOKS REVIEWED
  Poems   33   168

ROSE, PETER
POEMS
  Perfect Pitch   169   71
  Shaft
  White Telephone

ARTICLES ABOUT
  Towards a Contemporary
    Australian Poetics,
    by John Kinsella   169   94

ROSE, W. K.
BOOKS REVIEWED
  The Letters of Wyndham Lewis (Ed.)   105   397

ROSE, WILLIAM
BOOKS REVIEWED
   A Book of Modern German
    Lyric Verse 1890-1955 (Ed.)   97 393

ROSELIEP, RAYMOND
POEMS
  Where Roots Tangle   95 287
  A Is for Apollo   97 80
  Wish for Paolo   101 398
  The Smoke Smell of Spring   104 91
  Canticle
  The Singing Lesson
  My Father's Trunk   106 199
  Riverman
  Kodachrome: Katherine Anne Porter
  Four Haiku
    Afternoon Walk
    Visitor, Fireside
    Feud
    Priest, to Inquirer
  In the Dry Light   108 294
  Tar Roof
  Eight Haiku
    To Students...
    Coleridge
    The Boy Tennyson
    Drinking Hymn
    New Year's Eve
    "Crucifixion": National Gallery
    When I Was Thirteen
    Eschatology
    In Extremis
  After Reading the Letters of Wallace Stevens   111 297
  Nun, in Coffin
  Song Sparrow
  Late Spring Poem
  Eve
  With Red Plums and Her Poems
  Two Haiku   112 388
    ("Cemetery owl...")
    ("Beauty, be patient...")

REVIEWS
  From Woodcarver to Wordcarver   107 326
    Lunch Poems, by Frank O'Hara
    The Astronomers,
      by Edgar Bowers
    Visions from the Ramble,
      by John Hollander
    A Woman Unashamed and Other Poems,
      by Paul Engle
    The Wreck of the Thresher
      and Other Poems,
      by William Meredith
    Finding Them Lost and Other Poems,
      by Howard Moss   107 394
  Tree, Lake, Moon: And Man   108 54
    The Greening Tree, by Ray Smith

  A View of Water, by Gene Baro
  Charades and Celebrations,
    by Constance Urdang
  Our Land & Our Sea & Hallelujah   111 189
  The Tracks of Babylon
    and Other Poems,
    by Edith L. Tiempo
  Civil Poems, by Josephine Miles
  Tidings, by James Broughton
  A Geography, by Thom Gunn
  Still Lives and Other Lives,
    by Saul Touster
  Poems for Nathan and Saul and
    Things We Dreamt We Died For,
    by Marvin Bell
  Hallelujah Anyway,
    by Kenneth Patchen

BOOKS REVIEWED
  The Linen Bands   99 384
  The Small Rain   104 115
  Love Makes the Air Light   108 272

ROSEN, KENNETH
POEMS
  Salmon   127 88
  Redwing   136 158
  Peeping Tom   141 274
  After the Race

ARTICLE
  Explaining a Poem
    [*Redwing*]   136 162

ROSEN, MALVINA (LEVINE)
POEMS
  Swift Glimpses   44 80
    City Angle
    Experience
    Reaction
    No Comfort

ROSEN, STANLEY
POEMS
  On My Grandmother's Funeral   76 79
  At Milton's Imagined Grave   86 154

ROSENBAUM, BENJAMIN
POEMS
  Songs of Youth   17 194
    Seeking Love
    Gone
    Glimpses of Her
    My Purple Gown from Tyre
  If You Come   22 265
  He
  Songs in Passing   23 68
    Change
    Niagara

Prayer
You
Night Talk
Day Piece
Faring Forth   26   20
I Come
These Are
For Janett
Memento
Oxford   29   134

BOOKS REVIEWED
Hill Solitudes   24   275
Green Nakedness   36 . 51

ROSENBERG, HAROLD
POEMS
Fragment from Abraham: An Oratorio   40   207
Shadow of Turning
Stage-Note for a Sunset
Air Formations
Brain of Happy Fable   41   264
Riding the Blinds
Ode ("As rain drops dye...")
New Meanings   44   1
    Address on Love as a Science
    Recollections in Mid-Afternoon
    The Men on the Wall
    Rural Movie Comedy
The Aeroplane Eye   45   325
    Voyage to the End of the Night
    A Matter of Manners
    Epos
1776   48   80
Household Lyrics 1934   48   246
    Décor for Nights Without Poetry
    Woman's Song
    The Alien of the World
The Man in Medals Blows a Horn   50   197
The End of the World   52   206
Yesterday, to Us   54   74
Snow on the Aerials
Ode ("Every imitation is an act...")   58   139

ARTICLES
The American Writers' Congress   46   222
The God in the Car
    [Archibald MacLeish]   52   334

REVIEWS
Death and Taxes,
    by Dorothy Parker   39   159
The Melody of Chaos,
    by Houston Peterson   39   163
Nicodemus,
    by Edwin Arlington Robinson   41   158
Pattern and Variation in Poetry,
    by Chard Powers Smith   42   54

4 Essais Indifférents
    pour une esthétique
    de l'inspiration,
    by René Taupin   42   175
Gilgamesh
    (Tr. by William Ellery Leonard)   44   289
The Shrouding,
    by Leo Kennedy   44   345
Elegies and Songs,
    by John Mavrogordato   45   231
Permanence and Change,
    by Kenneth Burke   47   347
Theory of Flight,
    by Muriel Rukeyser   48   107
Saint Peter Relates an Incident,
    Selected Poems,
    by James Weldon Johnson   49   49
The Hero of Arabia   50   285
    Lawrence, the Last Crusade,
        by Selden Rodman
    Ornament of Honor,
        by E. H. R. Altounyan
Two Tales   51   213
    The New World,
        by Edgar Lee Masters
    The Story of Lowry Maen,
        by Padraic Colum
Eleven Verse Plays,
    by Maxwell Anderson   57   258
Ringing the Changes   58   266
    A Letter from the Country
        and Other Poems,
        by Howard Baker
    The Paradox in the Circle,
        by Theodore Spencer

BOOKS REVIEWED
Trance Above the Streets   62   342
The Tradition of the New
    [John Cage]   102   341

ARTICLES ABOUT
Correspondence
    from Archibald MacLeish   52   342
Surrealist Influence
    in Contemporary English
    and American Poetry,
    by H. R. Hays   54   202

ROSENBERG, ISAAC
POEMS
Trench Poems   9   128
    Marching
    Break of Day in the Trenches

BOOKS REVIEWED
Collected Poems
    (Ed. by Gordon Bottomley
    and Denys Harding)   80   101

ARTICLES ABOUT
English Letter, by F. R. Leavis   46   274
The Isolation of Isaac Rosenberg,
   by Horace Gregory   68   30

ROSENBERG, LISA
POEMS
Candle Lighting   169   204
Introduction to Methods
   of Mathematical Physics   170   31

ROSENBERG, LIZ
POEMS
Where Were You?   150   97
My Husband Takes
   Some Photographs of Me
Fathers and Sons
Between Men and Women
All Those Hours Alone in the Dark   156   157
The Common Life
Dying   160   87

ROSENBERGER,
(FRANCIS) COLEMAN
POEMS
The Settlement of Virginia   66   181
Are You Just Back for a Visit
   Or Are You Going To Stay?   135   197

ARTICLES
Poets and Politicians
   [Archibald MacLeish,
   Bennett Champ Clark]   63   322
Correspondence
   [Selwyn Schwartz]   66   229

REVIEWS
Declaration and Discourse   55   103
Last Parade,
   by Herbert Bruncken
The Friends,
   by James Norman Hall
Two Midwesterners   59   164
The Song of Jed Smith,
   by John G. Neihardt
Illinois Poems,
   by Edgar Lee Masters
Two War Poems   60   152
Dunkirk, by E. J. Pratt
Dunkirk, by Robert Nathan
Experience and Exposition   61   690
Time Is Our House,
   by Louise McNeill
Lament for the Chieftains,
   by Martha Bacon
On Canadian Poetry   63   281
The Book of Canadian Poetry
   (Ed. by A. J. M. Smith)

A Little Anthology of Canadian Poets
   (Ed. by Ralph Gustafson)
On Canadian Poetry, by E. K. Brown
Day of Deliverance,
   by William Rose Benét   65   101
New Poems 1944
   (Ed. by Oscar Williams)   65   269
Tahl, by Jeremy Ingalls   67   106
Two Conspiracies:
   MacNeice and Aragon   68   44
   Aragon: Poet of the French Resistance
   (Ed. by Hannah Josephson
   and Malcolm Cowley)
   Springboard: Poems, 1941-1944,
   by Louis MacNeice

BOOKS REVIEWED
The Virginia Poems   63   228
XII Poems   70   108
American Sampler.
   A Selection of New Poetry (Ed.)   80   159

ROSENBLATT, JOE
BOOKS REVIEWED
Winter of the Luna Moth   115   353

ROSENFELD, PAUL
REVIEWS
Huntsman, What Quarry?
   by Edna St. Vincent Millay   55   47

BOOKS REVIEWED
The American Caravan
   (Ed. with Alfred Kreymborg
   and Lewis Mumford)   38   156

ROSENHEIM, NED
REVIEWS
The Double Axe,
   by Robinson Jeffers   73   351
The Forever Young,
   by Pauline Hanson   74   357

ROSENSTOCK, GABRIEL
POEMS
Mustanbih
   (Tr. by Desmond O'Grady)   167   46

ROSENTHAL, A. A.
POEMS
Fantasy   17   15
Syncrasy   20   197

ROSENTHAL, DAVID
POEMS
Remembering Dilys Laing   102   94
Overbrook Sanatorium
Chicago: The Mac Man   111   232

REVIEWS

Concretist Poets and Poetry   112 125
 Flowers in Concrete,
   by Mary Ellen Solt
 Ocean Stripe Series 4;
   6 Small Songs in 3's; 4 Sails;
   Glasgow Beasts, an a Burd Haw,
   an aw, a Fush; 6 Small Pears for Eugen
   Gomringer; and Autumn Poem,
   by Ian Hamilton Finlay

ROSENTHAL, M. L.

POEMS

 Father's Day (Orthodox)   99   10
 Message
 Two Elegiac Poems   104   25
   A Song of Dead Friends
   Psalm
 "To Think of Time"   107 308
 Winter Without Danny
 Love Song
 Reality, the Void Abandoned
   by Imagination   111 161
 Farewell
 At the Last   151 140

ARTICLES

 Delmore Schwartz   109 181
 Comment
   [Henry Rago]   151 218

REVIEWS

 New Works on Pound   106 361
   Translations, by Ezra Pound
   A Bibliography of Ezra Pound,
     by Donald Gallup
   Ezra Pound: Poet as Sculptor,
     by Donald Davie
   Poet in Exile: Ezra Pound,
     by Noel Stock
   The Cantos of Ezra Pound:
     A Critical Study,
     by George Dekker
   The Confucian Odes of Ezra Pound:
     A Critical Appraisal,
     by L. S. Dembo
 Voznesensky in Translation   110   40
   Antiworlds, by Andrei Voznesensky
     (Tr. by W. H. Auden, Jean Garrigue,
     Max Hayward, Stanley Kunitz,
     Stanley Moss, William Jay Smith,
     and Richard Wilbur)
     (Ed. by Patricia Blake
     and Max Hayward)
   Selected Poems,
     by Andrei Voznesensky
     (Tr. and ed. by Herbert Marshall)
 Poets & Critics & Poet-Critics   114 113

 From Zero to the Absolute,
   by Reed Whittemore
 The Poetry of Hart Crane:
   A Critical Study,
   by R. W. B. Lewis
 Forms of Discovery,
   by Yvor Winters
 Defending Ancient Springs,
   by Kathleen Raine
 A New Canon of English Poetry
   (Ed. by James Reeves
   and Martin Seymour-Smith)
 Two Centuries of Russian Verse
   (Ed. by Avrahm Yarmolinsky
   and Babette Deutsch)
 Modern Russian Poetry
   (Ed. by Vladimir Markov
   and Merrill Sparks)
 The Odyssey of Homer
   (Tr. by Richmond Lattimore)
 Collected Poems 1924-1955,
   by George Seferis
   (Tr. by Edmund Keeley
   and Philip Sherrard)
 The Complete Poems of Marianne Moore
 Collected Shorter Poems 1927-1957,
   by W. H. Auden
 The Cities, by Paul Blackburn
 Prepositions: The Collected Critical Essays,
   by Louis Zukofsky
 The Play and Place of Criticism,
   by Murray Krieger
 [J. V. Cunningham, Edwin Muir,
   David Gascoyne]
Plastic Possibilities   119   99
 Tragedy & Comedy: Four Cubist Plays,
   by Paul Goodman
 The Garbage Wars,
   by Donald Finkel
 Testament for My Students,
   by Kay Boyle
 Lies, by C. K. Williams
 Fifty Poems Fifty,
   by Reed Whittemore
 A Quick Graph:
   Collected Notes and Essays,
   by Robert Creeley
   (Ed. by Donald Allen)
 The Truth of Poetry:
   Tensions in Modern Poetry
   from Baudelaire to the Nineteen-Sixties,
   by Michael Hamburger

BOOKS REVIEWED

 The Modern Poets:
   A Critical Introduction   99 259
 A Primer of Ezra Pound   100   50
 Blue Boy on Skates   105 336
 The William Carlos Williams Reader (Ed.) 111   41

The New Modern Poetry:
  British and American Poetry
  Since World War II (Ed.)   111   410
The New Poets: American
  and British Poetry
  Since World War II   112   52
100 Postwar Poems (Ed.)   113   262
Beyond Power   115   426
The View from the Peacock's Tail 122   344

ROSENTHAL, MACHA
ARTICLES
  The Meaning
    of Kenneth Fearing's Poetry   64   208

REVIEWS
  New Directions 1944
    (Ed. by James Laughlin)   66   161
  Simple, Sensuous and Mild   67   270
    Poems, 1920-1945,
      by David Morton
    The Constant Mistress,
      by Tom Boggs
  Hard Cores and Soft   68   106
    An Anthology of Famous English
      and American Poetry
      (Ed. by William Rose Benét
      and Conrad Aiken)
    American Writing: 1944
      (Ed. by Helen Ferguson Caukin
      and Alan Swallow)
    Bred in the Bone
      (Ed. by Henry Fischer
      and Bruce Berlind)
    The Music Makers
      (Ed. by Stanton A. Coblentz)
    What Cheer
      (Ed. by David McCord)
  The Cranes on Dying River,
    by Lawrence Olson   72   51
  The Amazing Year,
    by Selden Rodman   72   161

ROSKOLENKIER, HARRY
[See ROSKOLENKO, HARRY]

ROSKOLENKO, HARRY
[HARRY ROSKOLENKIER]
POEMS
  Supper in an Alms-House   37   257
  Grocery Store Radio Concert   40   24
  Metaphysical Chant   42   310
  Fife and Drum   44   138
  Travels   44   318
    Freight-Car Minuet
    Journey
  Infants of Spring   46   311
  Martial Music   47   195

Sea-Weed   51   17
Sea and Land   52   199
To Rimbaud   56   74
Refugees   57   301
Ballad ("O yes, he died...")   59   243
Poems from the 14th Arrondissement 76   276
The Brutal Lyric   80   26
Analogy   84   73
I Stole the Mad Woman's Love,
  the Mad Woman Said   89   30

ARTICLES
  On Kenneth Koch Again: A Rebuttal
    [Frank O'Hara]   86   177
  A Letter from Australia   89   187

REVIEWS
  More People,
    by Edgar Lee Masters   55   211
  Mirrors of Venus: A Novel in Sonnets
    and *Political Self-Portrait,*
    by John Wheelwright   56   278
  The Anthology as an Art   77   179
    Poets of the English Language
      (Ed. by W. H. Auden
      and Norman Hall Pearson)
    A Little Treasury of Love Poems
      (Ed. by John Holmes)
  The Word of Love, by Paul Engle 79   111
  A Variety of Poets   82   34
    A Mask for Janus, by W. S. Merwin
    Impatient Lover,
      by Lillian Rockwell
    The Suburb by the Sea,
      by Robert Hillyer
  The Shadow Is Not the Rose   83   176
    The Plane and the Shadow,
      by Norman Rosten
    The Monument Rose,
      by Jean Garrigue
  Satire, Nonsense, and Worship   84   232
    Peter's Progress,
      by Geoffrey Parsons
    Poems, by Kenneth Koch
    The Sacred Seasons,
      by Carl Bode
  A Question of Governance   89   118
    Red Jacket, by Paul Goodman
    Permit Me Refuge, by Edwin Rolfe

BOOKS REVIEWED
  Sequence on Violence   56   164
  I Went into the Country   59   220
  Paris Poems   77   359

ROSS, ALAN
BOOKS REVIEWED
  Something of the Sea: Poems 1942-52   88   267

ROSS, CARY
POEMS
("Pegasus—")   44   82
("Although to say nothing...")

ROSS, DAVID
POEMS
Morning's Not in Our Time   55   15
Pleiades   102   88
Primavera
On a Blue Afternoon

BOOKS REVIEWED
Three Ages of Lake Light   103   256

ROSS, ELEANOR
[See also TAYLOR,
ELEANOR ROSS]
POEMS
The Bine Adkins Rose   77   27
Sister

ROSS, ROBERT
POEMS
Reproach   45   142

ROSS, W. W. E(USTACE)
["E. R."]
POEMS
Irrealistic Verses   44   179
    Love's Silver Bells
    The Old Song
    Reciprocal
    If Ice
    The Flower
    The Diver
    A Death

BOOKS REVIEWED
Laconics   38   280
Sonnets   42   114

ROSSELLI, AMELIA
POEMS
[I fiori vengono in dono e poi si dilatano]/
    [The flowers come as gifts]   155   84
[There's something like pain in the room]
[In ancient China]
    (Tr. by Beverly Allen)

ROSSER, J(ILL) ALLYN
POEMS
In the (Subjunctive) Mood   150   83
The Dropping of a Name
My Father's Palette   152   227
Clippings   153   222
Remains
Advice for the Unadvisable   153   282
Timeline

Soundtrack of a Desert Documentary   155   275
Much Later   157   95
The Sum Contradiction of Our Shades   157   253
Buffalo Bayou   161   16
Deep Pond at Dusk
    in Heavy Rain Against Pines
Raven
Coming Your Way   163   253
Late Letter   165   152
Before the Sickness Is Official   166   148
Sea and Rain   168   196
Lover Release Agreement

BOOKS REVIEWED
Bright Moves   159   32

ROSSETTI, CHRISTINA
BOOKS REVIEWED
Poems of...
    (Ed. by Kathleen Jarvis)   89   385

ARTICLES ABOUT
Christina Rossetti and Emily Dickinson,
    by M. D. Zabel   37   213

ROSSETTI, DANTE GABRIEL
ARTICLES ABOUT
Rossetti, by Harriet Monroe   32   270
Rev. of Thanks Before Going,
    by John Masefield   70   333
Rev. of Rossetti and the Fair Lady,
    by David Sonstroem   118   343

ROSSI, JOSEPH
BOOKS REVIEWED
De Sanctis on Dante
    (Tr. and ed. with Alfred Galpin)   96   323

ROSSI, M. M.
ARTICLES ABOUT
Letter from Ireland, by Joseph M. Hone   43   274

ROSSI, TIZIANO
POEMS
Giovani/Youth   155   92
Inviolate
    (Tr. by Michael Palma)

ROSSINI, CLARE
POEMS
Ideology   155   211
Valediction   167   286

ROSTAND, EDMOND
BOOKS REVIEWED
Plays of...
    (Tr. by Henderson
    Daingerfield Norman)   20   51

ARTICLES ABOUT
  Correspondence from Jean Catel   18   232

ROSTEN, NORMAN
POEMS
  Improvisations   51   134
    Sunrise
    Another Morning
    Fantasy
    I Witness a Death
    For Hedda
    Centrifugal
    Let One Spark Fall
    Aesthetic

ARTICLES
  Correspondence: Mr. Savage,
    Mr. Friar and the Social Poets   65   346

BOOKS REVIEWED
  Return Again, Traveler   58   156
  Seven Poets in Search of an Answer
    (With Maxwell Bodenheim,
    Joy Davidman, Langston Hughes,
    Aaron Kramer, Alfred Kreymborg,
    and Martha Millet)
    (Ed. by Thomas Yoseloff)   64   289
  The Fourth Decade   68   49
  The Big Road   69   101
  The Plane and the Shadow   83   176

ROSTREVOR, GEORGE
BOOKS REVIEWED
  Escape and Fantasy   17   276

ROSU, DONA
TRANSLATIONS
  Poems by Marin Sorescu
    (Tr. with W. D. Snodgrass
    and Luciana Costea)   159   191

ROTH, MARTIN
POEMS
  Weekend at Sea   115   389

ROTH, SAMUEL
POEMS
  Kol Nidre   12   126
  Human Speech
  Black London   21   76

BOOKS REVIEWED
  First Offerings: Sonnets and Lyrics   12   279
  Europe: A Book for America   17   341

ROTHBERG, WINTERSET
[Pseud. of ROETHKE, THEODORE]
REVIEWS
  In Country Sleep and Other Poems,
    by Dylan Thomas   81   184

ARTICLES ABOUT
  [Note on name]   103   139

ROTHENBERG, ALAN BAER
BOOKS REVIEWED
  Mass Chants
    and Other Poems   66   348

ROTHENBERG, JEROME
POEMS
  A Slower Music   103   367

BOOKS REVIEWED
  New Young German Poets (Tr.)   97   51
  White Sun Black Sun   99   178
  Sightings
    (With *Lunes*, by Robert Kelly)   108   191
  The Gorky Poems   109   195
  Poems for People
    Who Don't Read Poems,
    by Hans Magnus Enzensberger
    (Tr. with Michael Hamburger
    and the author)   113   188
  Poems 1964-67   114   251
  Poems for the Game
    of Silence 1960-1970   120   164

ROTHMAN, DAVID J.
POEMS
  One of the Lords of Life   163   320

ROUGHTON, BECKE
POEMS
  The Other   142   101

ROUGHTON, ROGER
POEMS
  Tomorrow Will Be Difficult   49   19
  Sliding Scale   49   204

ROUMAIN, JACQUES
POEMS
  When the Tom-Tom Beats
    (Tr. by L. C. Kaplan)   62   61

ROUMER, EMILE
ARTICLES ABOUT
  Letter From Haiti,
    by Wallace Fowlie   94   398

ROUSE, ANNE
POEMS
  Testament   167   207

ROUSSELOT, JEAN
POEMS
  Daniel
    (Tr. by Wallace Fowlie)   80   351

ROUX, SAINT-POL
ARTICLES ABOUT
  The Conspiracy of the Poets,
    by Pierre Seghers
    (Tr. by William Jay Smith)   67   25

ROWLEY, RICHARD
BOOKS REVIEWED
  Selected Poems   38   231

ROY, JULES
BOOKS REVIEWED
  Three Prayers for Pilots
    (Tr. by George Ellidge)   68   54

ROZHDESTVENSKY, ROBERT
POEMS
  A Distant Memory
    (Tr. by Daniel Weissbort)   124   217

RUARK, GIBBONS
POEMS
  For My Wife in Her Great Good Time   108   376
  The Muse's Answer
  Letter to Odysseus   110   391
  1965
  A Blind Wish for Randall Jarrell
  American Elegy   112   240
  The Visitor
  A Program for Survival   114   164
  The Goods She Can Carry:
    Canticle of Her Basket Made of Reeds   133   26
  Postscript to an Elegy   149   135

REVIEWS
  Yevtushenko and Voznesensky   111   121
    Yevtushenko Poems
      (Tr. by Herbert Marshall)
    Bratsk Station and Other New Poems,
      by Yevgeny Yevtushenko
      (Tr. by Tina Tupinika-Glaessner
      and Geoffrey Dutton)
    Selected Poems of Andrei Voznesensky
      (Tr. by Anselm Hollo)

BOOKS REVIEWED
  A Program for Survival   121   348
  Keeping Company   144   345

RUBENSTEIN, ELAINE
POEMS
  Deborah's Lament   145   267
  Aubade

RUBIA BARCIA, JOSÉ
BOOKS REVIEWED
  César Vallejo:
    The Complete Posthumous Poetry
    (Tr. with Clayton Eshleman)   137   220

RUBIN, DAVID LEE
POEMS
  Lines From a Madwoman's Diary   95   286

RUBIN, LARRY
POEMS
  The Visitant   98   235
  The Accident   102   20
  For a Poet-Athlete
  Curtains of the Sea   119   338
  Cain   129   155

BOOKS REVIEWED
  The World's Old Way   103   324
  Lanced in Light, Poems   113   35

RUBLE, ESTHER LOUISE
POEMS
  First Snow   19   186

RUDMAN, MARK
POEMS
  Who Hungers for a Face that Fades Away
    (With Paul Nemser)   122   28

RUDNIK, RAPHAEL
POEMS
  Broken Ballad   121   249
  Seasons and Stars   123   95
  You Are Something Shining   124   309
  Still Life
  In a Garden
  The Lovers
  Psalmist   129   87
  The Devils
  Dream   131   337
  Now That Your Body

BOOKS REVIEWED
  A Lesson from the Cyclops   117   108
  In the Heart or Our City   123   241

RUDOLF, ANTHONY
BOOKS REVIEWED
  Tyorkin & The Stovemakers:
    Poetry and Prose by Alexander Tvardovsky
    (Ed. and tr.)   129   102

RUFFILLI, PAOLO
POEMS
  Malaria
    (Tr. by Felix Stefanile)   155   138

RUGGLES, ELEANOR
BOOKS REVIEWED
  Gerard Manley Hopkins   65   142
  The West-Going Heart:
    A Life of Vachel Lindsay   98   59

RUGGLES, EUGENE
POEMS
   The White Goddess   110 241
   Poem at Sea on My Thirtieth Birthday

RUGGLES, KIRK
BOOKS REVIEWED
   Nothing You've Done   116 125

RUKEYSER, MURIEL
POEMS
   New York   42 16
      O City
      College Special
      Empire State Tower
   Scenes with Moving Figures   47 25
      Sand-Quarry
      Song for Dead Children
      Breathing Landscape
      The Surrounded
      Study in a Late Subway
   Time Exposures   48 86
   The Child Asleep
   Adventure at Midnight
   Night-Music
   Elegy ("As I went down...") 55 25
   The Soul and Body of John Brown 56 115
   The Child in the Great Wood 59 1
   Full Moon
   Waltz
   Sea Mercy
   A Leg in a Plaster Cast
   Suicide Blues
   Long Past Moncada
   Song ("The world is full...")
   The Children's Elegy   63 179
   Mrs. Walpurga   69 239
   Foghorn in Horror
   A Charm for Cantinflas
   A Certain Music
   Motive
   Nine Poems (for the Unborn Child) 71 190
   Pieces of Orpheus   74 327
   Tree of Meanings   79 187
      A Birth
      The Return
      Unborn Song
      Phaneron
      Asleep and Awake
      The Place at Alert Bay
   Poem from The Willkie Mysteries
     ("The sea has opened...")   81 68
   Body of Waking   86 1
      Song ("Make and be eaten...")
      Children, the Sandbar, That Summer
      After the Death of Her Mother
      King's Mountain
      Mother Garden's Round
   Hero Speech   91 292

   Waterlily Fire   99 335
   Song ("A voice flew out...") 101 107
   The Outer Banks   106 381
   Delta Poems   111 251
   From *Breaking Open*   122 311
     (18: "How we live...")
     (26: "In the night...")

TRANSLATIONS
   Poem by Octavio Paz   92 171

ARTICLES
   The Usable Truth   58 206
   Note to *Waterlily Fire*   99 342

REVIEWS
   Collected Poems of Robert Frost: 1939 54 218
   Heavenly City, Earthly City,
     by Robert Duncan   72 48
   Jewel of Our Longing,
     by Charlotte Marletto   74 236

BOOKS REVIEWED
   Theory of Flight   48 107
   U. S. 1   52 101
   A Turning Wind   55 214
   The Green Wave   73 173
   Orpheus   77 234
   Selected Poems   80 52
   Waterlily Fire: Poems 1935-1962 101 358
   Selected Poems of Octavio Paz (Tr.) 104 382
   Sun Stone, by Octavio Paz (Tr.)
   The Speed of Darkness   114 40
   Breaking Open   125 44
   A Muriel Rukeyser Reader
     (Ed. by Jan Heller Levi) 167 287

ARTICLES ABOUT
   Poetry of the Left,
     by Harriet Monroe   48 212
   Muriel Rukeyser:
     The Social Poet and the Problem of
     Communication,
     by John Malcolm Brinnin 61 554
   Rev. of *New Poems: 1943*
     (Ed. by Oscar Williams)   64 86
   "Sacred Beings":
     Writers in Recorded Conversation,
     by Michael Milburn   146 101

RUMENS, CAROL
POEMS
   Camouflage   146 208

RUMMONS, HELEN L.
POEMS
   Flight   36 241

RUNBECK, MARGIE-LEE
POEMS
  Emptiness   24   15

RUNNER, OLIVE
POEMS
  Freedom   12   302

RUSKIN, JOHN
ARTICLES ABOUT
Finishes: Notes
  on Ambition and Survival,
  by Christian Wiman   169   217

RUSS, PENELOPE
[Pseud. of KENNEDY,
KATHARINE]
POEMS
  Before Passion   22   263
  Secret Windows   25   80
  Your Eyes Are Old
  After Marriage
  Portrait
  On a Book of Poems

RUSSELL, A. J.
POEMS
  The House of Takumi   4   18

RUSSELL, FRANK
POEMS
  Have You Ever or Are You Now?   143   77

RUSSELL, GEORGE
[See "AE," pseud.]

RUSSELL, MARY
POEMS
  Still   31   257
  In Order   33   20
  After Winter
  Eurhythmy

RUSSELL, PETER
POEMS
  In Memoriam—Wyndham Lewis   91   255
  A Mountain Stream   92   349
  Mots Justes

BOOKS REVIEWED
  An Examination of Ezra Pound (Ed.)   79   150
  Three Elegies of Quintilius   86   41
  Visions and Ruins   105   404

RUSSELL, SYDNEY KING
POEMS
  Nocturne   35   200
  Women   43   192

BOOKS REVIEWED
  Lost Warrior   41   281
  Proud Universe   58   226
  Songs for America   62   285

RUSSELL, TIMOTHY
POEMS
  In Disiecta Membra   163   137
  In Ultima Thule
  Jade Plant   163   257

BOOKS REVIEWED
  Adversaria   164   285

RUSSELL, URSULA KIMBALL
POEMS
  First Year   38   78

RUSSMANN, HELEN C.
POEMS
  Fantasy   20   136

RUTHENBURG,
GRACE H(UTCHINSON)
POEMS
  Resort   26   76
  Prospect
  Fragilities   28   250
  Legacy
  Genii
  On a Stem
  Preparation   31   13
  Shah Jahan Built a Sepulchre

RUTHENBURG, GRACE DORCAS
POEMS
  Interior   44   125
  So They Say   47   322
  The Miracle
  Missionary

RUTHVEN, GREY
[See GOWRIE, GREY]

RUTHVEN, MADELEINE
POEMS
  The Mountain Road   49   18
  Chrysler Building   50   77

RUTLEDGE, ARCHIBALD
POEMS
  John Everyman   27   192

RUTSALA, VERN
POEMS
  In the Middle   114   242
  Unlocking the Door   117   162
  A Secret Army   119   192

Boxing Day
Mesh
Like the Poets of Ancient China   122   29
Paths
Quest
Drinking Late   125   133
The World   127   139
Moving West
Going to War
Time   134   150
The Death Committee
Less Is More...
East Wind
Skaters   137   127
Prospectus for Visitors
The Fears of the Poor
What We Have   141   75
Driving Around: A Memoir
Lela and Others   143   201
Uncle
An American Morning   145   196
Coming Home
Shelter   149   70
White Water
The Muses of Rooms   155   278
Becoming American   160   131
Listening to a Russian Choir   164   79

BOOKS REVIEWED
The Window   107   183
Walking Home from the Icehouse   140   293

RYAN, AGNES
BOOKS REVIEWED
A Whisper of Fire   17   276

RYAN, ANNE
BOOKS REVIEWED
Lost Hills   30   293

RYAN, JAMES J.
POEMS
Grey Leaves and Gold   33   235
In a Crystal Bowl
Change
Peace
Wild Duck
The Swan
The Rain
Rameses
Bell-Ringer
Her Heart Is Water
Obiit
Vis-à-Vis
"The Suns Are Dead"
Avowal   36   117
Autobiography
Interval

Because—
The Theme
Pass By Me, Life
To Die
Domine, Deus
Spring
Hazel
Petersen
Barbaric
Epilogue
The Shell
Dirge ("There is no counsel kept...")
Snow
Reflections   40   263
  To His Soul
  In Perpetuum
  I Urge My Soul
  Think Not
  Fatality
  Tabby
  Confession
  Quiet
  Towers
  In Spring
  Song ("Sweetheart, you steal...")
  Beauty
  Nympholept
I Do Not Ask   44   25
Octaves   48   187
  June
  Where!
  A Protest
  A Pity
  Young Suicide
  Israel
  Death Song
  Phantasus

RYAN, KATHRYN WHITE
POEMS
Fog   19   76
Moonlight   20   137
Convent
Song After Travel   24   21
High Noon   34   75

BOOKS REVIEWED
Golden Pheasant   28   110

RYAN, KAY
POEMS
Marianne Moore Announces Lunch   144   87
The Egyptians
The New Kabbalists   147   225
Renaissance
Don't Look Back   170   219

BOOKS REVIEWED
Elephant Rocks   170   101

RYAN, MARGARET
POEMS
   Bernini: Bacchanal:
     Faun Teased by Children   165   277

RYAN, MICHAEL
POEMS
   A Posthumous Poetics   122   332
   Stones   128   8
   The Black Hole
   To Tell You the Truth
   After
   Hopeless
   An Old Story
   The Great Dark
   When I Was Conceived   132   78
   The Past   133   88
   Waking at Night
   A Shape for It   135   273
   Larkinesque   143   266
   Tanglewood
   Winter Drought
   County Fair   154   205

ARTICLES
   A Talk on Wallace Stevens
     [Pitts Sanborn, Holly Stevens]   134   353

BOOKS REVIEWED
   Threats Instead of Trees   125   295
   God Hunger   156   36

RYAN, RICHARD
POEMS
   Helix   167   29
   Deafness

RYAN, TRACY
POEMS
   Noli Me Tangere   169   74

ARTICLES ABOUT
   Towards a Contemporary
     Australian Poetics,
     by John Kinsella   169   94

RYDER, ARTHUR WILLIAM
BOOKS REVIEWED
   Women's Eyes (Tr.)
     [Hindu poems]   9   274

RYLAND, GEORGE H.
ARTICLES ABOUT
   The Aristocrats,
     by Morton Dauwen Zabel   34   37

S

"S. D."
ARTICLES
Correspondence   7   324

"S. W."
ARTICLES
A Modern French Anthology
[Ezra Pound]   12   54

REVIEWS
Old Christmas and Other
Kentucky Tales in Verse,
by William Aspenwall Bradley   12   46

SABA, UMBERTO
ARTICLES ABOUT
Five Years of Italian Poetry (1910-1915),
by Emanuel Carnevali   13   209
Contemporary Italian Poetry,
by Edward Williamson   79   233

SABALALA, SANTIE
POEMS
The Raid   30   252

SABEL, MARX G.
POEMS
Appearances   15   22
Annotations   18   146
Jeremiad
No Good Thing
The Strange Load
Recordition   20   16
The Core
The Wise Man   25   137

SACHS, DAVID
POEMS
Heard from Spain   51   200
First Summary   53   180
Poem ("Sleep's long felicity...")
Sonnet ("True agony's not...")
Poem ("No Minerva was I...")
Snow Settles on the Town
Theogony   73   202
Villanelle for Christians   73   334

To Oedipus, Before His Disappearance
Exclamation for Sally   75   74

REVIEWS
Sequence on Violence,
by Harry Roskolenko   56   164
Aspects of Proteus, by Hyam Plutzik   75   118
The Beast in His Hunger, by Harry Brown   75   366
A Rhetoric of Motives, by Kenneth Burke   77   295

SACHS, NELLY
BOOKS REVIEWED
O the Chimneys: Selected Poems,
Including the Verse Play "Eli"   112   418

SACKLER, HOWARD (O.)
POEMS
Dream Between Tropic Roads   80   191

BOOKS REVIEWED
Want My Shepherd   87   53

SACKS, PETER
BOOKS REVIEWED
Promised Lands   158   280

SACKVILLE, MARGARET
POEMS
The Coming of Hippolytus   3   40

BOOKS REVIEWED
Selected Poems   19   158

SACKVILLE-WEST, VITA
BOOKS REVIEWED
The Land   31   228
Collected Poems   46   346

SADLER, AELDRYN
POEMS
The Pensioners of Beauty   23   245

SADOFF, IRA
POEMS
Four Variations on the History of Speech   123   154
Revision   127   12

Migration
Process
Remembrance of a Fall Walk   129   149
The Transcendentalist
Meditation
Reflection of a Young Woman
    by a Lake
Palm Reading in Winter
Nathaniel Hawthorne   132   72
The McCarthy Hearings   132   260
While Watching "Young and Innocent"
    I Think of My Mother
My Wife's Upstairs   135   26
Bleak House
The Subject Matter
Checks and Balances   140   197
A Solitary Walk
    Through Oakland, Maine

BOOKS REVIEWED
Settling Down   128   37

SAFARIK, ALLAN
  BOOKS REVIEWED
    God Loves Us
        Like Earthworms Love Wood   144   297

SAFFORD, MURIEL
  POEMS
    God-Lover   18   135

SAGE, JOAN
  [Pseud. of CALDWELL,
  DORIS PACKARD]
  POEMS
    Mirage   32   135

SAGMASTER, WALTER
  POEMS
    Song of Nations   28   144
    India
    China
    Scandinavia

SAHL, HANS
  BOOKS REVIEWED
    Die Hellen Naechte:
        Gedichte aus Frankreich   60   228

SAHTOURIS, MILTOS
  POEMS
    He Is Not Oedipus
        (Tr. by Kimon Friar)   78   180

  ARTICLES ABOUT
    Contemporary Greek Poetry,
        by Kimon Friar   78   145
    Post-War Greek Poets,
        by Kimon Friar   139   99

SAINTE-BEUVE,
    (CHARLES-AUGUSTIN)
  BOOKS REVIEWED
    Sainte-Beuve: Selected Essays
        (Tr. by Francis Steegmuller
        and Norbert Guterman)   103   183

SAINT GERAUD
    [Pseud. of KNOTT, BILL]
  BOOKS REVIEWED
    The Naomi Poems: Corpse and Beans   113   262

ST. JOHN, DAVID
  POEMS
    Elegy ("Who keeps the owl's breath?")   132   13
    The Avenues   134   203
    The Boathouse
    Woman and Leopard   142   138
    No Heaven   145   154
    From a Daybook   151   142
    The Doors   151   290

  BOOKS REVIEWED
    Hush   130   342
    The Shore   138   231
    No Heaven   147   291
    Study for the World's Body   166   289

ST. JOHN, EMILY PORTER
  POEMS
    Differentia   58   140

ST. JOHN, JESSIE
  POEMS
    A War Bride   33   65
    My House Companions Me   35   25
    Now Is the Winter Gone   38   15

  BOOKS REVIEWED
    Fruit of the Tree   43   290

ST. JOHN OF THE CROSS
  POEMS
    The Spiritual Canticle
        (Tr. by John Frederick Nims)   80   144
    Madrigal   92   304
    Of Falconry
    Ballad IV ("Amen, the father...")
        (Tr. by John Frederick Nims)

  Books Reviewed
    The Poems of...
        (Tr. by Roy Campbell)   80   153
    The Poems of...
        (Tr. by John Frederick Nims)   95   379
    The Poems of..., English Versions Newly
        Revised and Rewritten
        (Tr. by John Frederick Nims)   113   262

ST. JOHN-PARSONS, D.
Books Reviewed
  Our Poets Speak (Ed.)   123   34

ST. LEDGER-ROTY, LEE
Poems
  From the Vegetable Kingdom   72   182

ST. LÉGER LÉGER, ALEXIS
  [See PERSE, ST.-JOHN]

ST. MARK'S POETRY PROJECT
Books Reviewed
  The World Anthology, Poems from...
    (Ed. by Anne Waldman)   119   39

ST. MARTIN, HARDIE
Poems
  The Wall   95   94
  Snow
  That Night, Those Nights,
    If You'll Remember   100   295

Reviews
  Eighty Poems of Antonio Machado
    (Tr. by Willis Barnstone)   101   343

Books Reviewed
  Twenty Poems
    of Blas de Otero (Tr.)   107   338

SAINTSBURY, GEORGE
Articles About
  Robinson and Praed,
    by Hoyt H. Hudson   61   612

SAIT, ELIZABETH
Poems
  Casuistry   55   78
  Arcanum
  The House   59   25
  Narcissa   72   142
  La Venta Fantasy

SAJE, NATASHA
Poems
  A Short History of the Sybarites   162   66

SAKUTARO, HAGIWARA
Poems
  Zoo   116   370
  Shadow of My Former Self
  Hagitei Inn
  Early Summer
    (Tr. by Graeme Wilson)

Books Reviewed
  Face at the Bottom of the World
    (Tr. by Graeme Wilson)   118   234

SALAM, NURDIN
Books Reviewed
  Selected Poems,
    by Chairil Anwar
    (Tr. with Burton Raffel)   104   115

SALAMUN, TOMAZ
Poems
  The North
    (Tr. with Anselm Hollo)   122   197

SALE, WILLIAM M., JR.
Reviews
  Heinrich Heine: Paradox and Poet
    (The Life and The Poems),
    by Louis Untermeyer   52   46
  Aspects of Craft   56   222
    The Poet's Work, by John Holmes
    Lyrics in Brief
      (Ed. by Tom Boggs)
  The Protean Rilke   61   441
    Rainer Maria Rilke,
      by E. M. Butler
    Rainer Maria Rilke:
      Fifty Selected Poems
      (Tr. by C. F. MacIntyre)
    Poems from the Book of Hours
      (Tr. by Babette Deutsch)
    Sonnets to Orpheus
      (Tr. by M. D. Herter Norton)
  Gerard Manley Hopkins,
    by Eleanor Ruggles   65   142

SALEH, DENNIS
Poems
  Abuse, Abuse   113   404
  Crabs   116   172
  The Unconscious
  The Meadow   118   327
  Sexuality
  The Trout
  For Light
  White Apple
  Snake
  Desert   120   162
  Avocado   121   215
  Chameleon Ending
  Landscapes
  Decline   123   9
  Lazy   128   315
  Chameleon Errant   135   14
  Prodigal Sun

Books Reviewed
  100 Chameleons   133   346

SALEMSON, HAROLD J.
Articles
  The Poetry of Paul Valéry   32   36

REVIEWS
   Anthologie de la Nouvelle Poèsie Américaine
     (Ed. by Eugene Jolas)   33 165
   Windfalls,
     by Ralph Cheever Dunning   34 292

SALINAS, PEDRO
  BOOKS REVIEWED
   Contemporary Spanish Poetry
     (Tr. by Eleanor L. Turnbull)   67 265
   Zero
     (Tr. by Eleanor Turnbull)   74 48

SALINGER, HERMAN
  POEMS
   Vine   47 254
   Mississippi   56 246
   Lines in Bivouac   65 14
   Vulgar Word
   Simple Dialogue
   Army of Occupation   67 190
     Soliloquy at Verdun
     Germany 1945
   Army of Occupation II   68 79
     Roses for Defeat
     Abstinence
     Sunday
     Nocturne by the Rhine
   Requiem for Pan   70 21
   Morning Visit
   Self-Portrait   72 254
   Sultry Morning: Rural   75 14
   Souvenir of Dresden   77 74
   "There Was a Crooked Man"
   The Knee   80 22
   Mortal Melodies, No. 1
   Mortal Melodies, No. 2
   Mortal Melodies, No. 3
   Paternal Ashes   81 226
   Spectator   84 216
   Nursery Ceiling
   Three Deaths   85 27

  TRANSLATIONS
   Poems by Karl Krolow,
     Wolfgang Cordan,
     and Rudolf Hagelstange   88 253
   German Lyric Poetry Since 1945,
     by Hans Egon Holthusen (Tr.)
     [Oskar Loerke, Wilhelm Lehmann,
     Elizabeth Langgasser, Gunter Eich,
     Karl Krolow, Heinz Piontek,
     Walter Hollerer, Gottfried Benn,
     Ingeborg Bachmann, Paul Celan]   88 257

  ARTICLES
   Hans Egon Holthusen:
     The Panther and the Prophet   82 335

REVIEWS
   Rainer Maria Rilke: Poems
     (Tr. by J. B. Leishman)   45 344

BOOKS REVIEWED
   Germany—A Winter's Tale,
     by Heinrich Heine (Tr.)   66 56
   The Angel of Our Thirst   79 298
   A Sigh Is the Sword   104 47

SALINGER, WENDY
  BOOKS REVIEWED
   Folly River   140 35

SALISBURY, RALPH J.
  POEMS
   Indirection   95 213
   After Shakespeare
   Jefferson, Iowa: A Synopsis
     for My Son Jeff's Sake
   Girl and September Wind
   After Whitman's
     "There Was a Child Went Forth"
   Ariadne and the Beast
   Eugene, Oregon, U.S.A.:
     My Side Yard and Something
     from an Old Travel Book   110 173

SALKELD, BLANAID
  POEMS
   One in Dublin   45 202

SALKIN, CELIA
  ARTICLES ABOUT
   [Note]   33 232

SALMON, ANDRÉ
  ARTICLES ABOUT
   Three Poems by André Salmon,
     by René Taupin
     (Tr. by Louis Zukofsky)   37 289
   Three Poems by André Salmon, II,
     by René Taupin
     (Tr. by Louis Zukofsky)   37 333

SALMON, ARTHUR L.
  POEMS
   Dawn   38 192

SALOM, DIWALDO
  POEMS
   I Know Not
     (Tr. by Muna Lee)   26 129

SALOMON, I. L.
  REVIEWS
   Selected Poems,
     by Muriel Rukeyser   80 52

Dry Sun, Dry Wind, by David Wagoner   83   232
Ten Burnt Offerings, by Louis MacNeice   84   101

BOOKS REVIEWED
  Unit and Universe   96   375

SALT, SYDNEY S.
[SYD S. SALT]
POEMS
  Flowers on the Moon   38   198
    About Stones
    The Sword
    She — In Still Light
    To Death
  Endor   40   204
  Your Still Body
  About Gestures   49   253
  Illogical Days   51   78
    A Short Story
    The Demon
    Toy-Shop
    A Love Poem
  The Ancient Course Is Here   52   80

BOOKS REVIEWED
  Thirty Pieces   46   166
  Christopher Columbus and Other Poems   52   236
  New Journey   58   226

SALTER, MARY JO
POEMS
  Japanese Characters   142   202

BOOKS REVIEWED
  Henry Purcell in Japan   147   102
  Unfinished Painting   156   36
  Sunday Skaters   166   104

SAMARAS, NICHOLAS
POEMS
  Amnesiac   156   67
  Translation   157   332
  The Answers   160   82
  The Mansion of Forgetting   162   323

BOOKS REVIEWED
  Hands of the Saddlemaker   161   339

SAMMONS, JEFFREY L.
BOOKS REVIEWED
  Marx, Engels, and the Poets:
    Origins of Marxist Literary Criticism,
    by Peter Demetz (Tr.)   112   206

SAMPERI, FRANK
POEMS
  ("on/a/bridge...")   109   380
  ("lie/down/angel...")

BOOKS REVIEWED
  Crystals   112   56

SAMPSON, ASHLEY
POEMS
  Behold the Man   59   125
  Enemy in the Gates   66   311

SAMPSON, GEORGE
BOOKS REVIEWED
  Coleridge's Biographia Literaria
    (With Wordsworth's Preface
    and Essays on Poetry) (Ed.)   18   167

SAMPSON, H. F.
BOOKS REVIEWED
  Sounds from Another Valley   6   257

SAMPSON, HARRIET
POEMS
  Venice   32   134

SANBORN, PITTS
ARTICLES ABOUT
  A Talk on Wallace Stevens,
    by Michael Ryan   134   353

SANBORN, ROBERT ALDEN
POEMS
  To Walden   10   192
  The Island

ARTICLES
  Correspondence: A Recantation
    [Ezra Pound]   7   158

BOOKS REVIEWED
  Horizons   9   324

SANCHEZ, LUIS ANIBAL
[See ANIBAL SANCHEZ, LUIS]

SANCHEZ, SONIA
BOOKS REVIEWED
  It's a New Day   123   34

SANCHEZ LEON, ABELARDO
POEMS
  Poem ("Why did that have to be?")
    (Tr. by David Tipton)   116   368

SANDBURG, CARL
POEMS
  Chicago   3   191
  Jan Kubelik
  The Harbor
  The Hammer
  At a Window
  Lost

Who Am I?		
Momus		
The Road and the End		
Iron	4	95
Among the Red Guns	5	64
Sketch	7	1
Nocturne in a Deserted Brickyard		
Alone		
Monotone		
Under the Harvest Moon		
Joy		
The Great Hunt		
Days		
Handfuls		
They Will Say		
A Fence		
The Poor		
Killers		
Choose		
Kin		
Places		
Our Prayer of Thanks		
My People	10	1
Loam		
The Year		
Chicago Poet		
Street Window		
Adelaide Crapsey		
Repetitions		
Throw Roses		
Fire-Logs		
Baby Face		
Early Moon		
Alix		
Gargoyle		
Prairie Waters by Night		
Moonset		
Garden Wireless		
In Tall Grass		
Bringers		
Old Timers	10	298
The Four Brothers	11	59
Prairie	12	175
Redhaw Winds	13	22
Falltime		
Autumn Movement		
Valley Song		
"Old-Fashioned Requited Love"		
The Next Child Waits		
Assyrian Tablets		
Ashurnatsirpal the Third		
Bilbea		
Smoke Nights	15	233
Smoke and Steel		
Tangibles		
Night Movement—New York		
Losers		
Accomplished Facts		
People Who Must		

Bas-Relief		
The Law Says		
Calls		
Evening Waterfall		
Sea-Wash		
Moon-Riders	19	295
Feather Lights		
The Naked Stranger		
Medley		
Gypsy Mother		
Casuals	41	1
Broken Sonnet		
Our Hells		
Chromo		
Impossible Iambics		
Soapsuds		
Swell People		
Yessir Mister		
Heavy Folio		
Broom		
Be Ready	51	7
Night Bells		
Number Man	71	1
Harmonica Humdrums		
On a Flimmering Floom		
You Shall Ride		
Alice Corbin Is Gone	95	201

ARTICLES
The Work of Ezra Pound	7	249
Correspondence		
[Percy Hammond, Carmen Cerelli]	9	218
Aboriginal Poetry II		
[Frances Densmore]	9	234
Correspondence: Good-bye		
to Eunice Tietjens		
[Poem]	11	56
Correspondence:		
The Question of State Laureates	24	226
[Tribute to Harriet Monroe]	49	154

REVIEWS
Red Earth: Poems		
of New Mexico,		
by Alice Corbin	18	157
Ballads and Sea Songs		
from Nova Scotia		
(Ed. by W. Roy Mackenzie)	33	166

BOOKS REVIEWED
Chicago Poems	8	90
Cornhuskers	13	155
Smoke and Steel	17	266
Slabs of the Sun-Burnt West	20	332
Selected Poems of...		
(Ed. by Rebecca West)	31	53
Good Morning America	33	214
Complete Poems	78	345
Honey and Salt	102	388

ARTICLES ABOUT
The Poetry of War, by Harriet Monroe
  [Poem]   4   237
Rev. of *Catholic Anthology—1914-1915*   8   94
What May War Do,
  by Harriet Monroe   10   142
The Sandburg-Sarett Recital,
  by Emanuel Carnevali   15   271
Discovered in Paris,
  by Harriet Monroe   16   148
Correspondence from Dorothy Dudley   20   53
Kinaesthetic Verse,
  by Baker Brownell   22   36
Correspondence from Ernest Walsh   24   112
Carl Sandburg,
  by Harriet Monroe   24   320
Rev. of *From Whitman to Sandburg
  in American Poetry*,
  by Bruce Weirick   25   167
Poets as Prosers, by Harriet Monroe   28   328
Sandburg's Testament,
  by M. D. Zabel   49   33
Rev. of *Carl Sandburg's American Songbag*
  [Recording]   58   105

SANDBURG, HELGA
BOOKS REVIEWED
  To a New Husband   119   107

SANDEEN, ERNEST
POEMS
  Etherized Intelligentsia   61   592
  Lore of the Real
  Survey on the State of the Union
  The Chase   67   252
  The Unhappy Warrior
  Communion   72   192
  New Age
  At the Mercy Seat   75   73
  Anecdote of the Wind
  The Hurt of the Second Death   79   320
  Standard Time, Ithaca   80   134
  The Word and the Fish   83   135
  The Improvement of Prayer   85   260
  Death of a Maker
  Toy Windmill
  On the Adoption of Sons: An Anniversary
  Pater Noster in Winter   89   142
  L'Apres-Midi d'un Homme
  Last Things: I ("The blow...")   95   97
  Last Things: II ("There came...")
  *News Item: Chimpanzee Escapes
    from Zoo in Antwerp*
  Bus to Marienlund
  Surgery Ward, December 8
  Day in June   106   112
  Growing into Light   111   374

*Those Elders of the Great
  Tradition & the Rest of Us*
Rosary in Bed
Survival Against the Poem   126   152
The Poem as Baby-Sitter
Her Poem
How Time Is Kept   132   268
In the Cage
Predicting the Past   139   156
Interrogation   143   193
Seventy-Fourth Birthday
Translating the Latin
A Journey of the Mental Traveller   149   165
Dialogue at the Door
The Prowler
My Two Lives
A Late Twentieth-Century Prayer   151   143
Soon After Nightfall   159   141

REVIEWS
The Flung World   88   267
  As If: Poems New and Selected,
    by John Ciardi
  The Second Man and Other Poems,
    by Louis O. Coxe
  The Pauses of the Eye, by Ernest Kroll
  Something of the Sea: Poems 1942-52,
    by Alan Ross
  Poems, by Robert Conquest
  Light and Dark, by Barbara Howes   96   114
Facing the Muse   97   380
  Homage to Clio, by W. H. Auden
  The Play of Daniel
    (Ed. by Noah Greenberg)
  Collected Poems, by Robert Graves   100   305
  Person to Person, by John Ciardi   106   231
  Herakles: A Play in Verse,
    by Archibald MacLeish
    [Robert Lowell]   112   199
Recent Criticism   112   356
  A Primer of Ignorance,
    by R. P. Blackmur
    (Ed. by Joseph Frank)
  The Play and Place of Criticism,
    by Murray Krieger
  Poetry and Prayer,
    by William T. Noon
  Dryden's Poetry, by Earl Miner
  The Poetry of Vision,
    by Patricia Meyer Spacks
  *Six Metaphysical Poets:
    A Reader's Guide*,
    by George Williamson

BOOKS REVIEWED
  Antennas of Silence   89   110
  Children and Older Strangers   101   209
  Collected Poems, 1953-1977   133   45

SANDERS, ED
BOOKS REVIEWED
    King Lord/Queen Freak   108   125
    Peace Eye   108   191

SANDERS, EMMY VERONICA
POEMS
    Challenge   17   248
    The Companion
    Adelaide Crapsey
    Forty-Second Street
    Driftwood
    Hill-Top Duet
    Antagonisms   20   300
      Laughter
      Into These Things
      Passing
      Hill Speech
    You Are the Road   22   78

SANDERS, OTTYS
POEMS
    Two Texas Legends   26   59
      A Nest of Gold
      Indian Blue-Bonnets
    Far Countries   29   145
      A Minstrel from the Island of the Moon
      Beggars of the Sea
      Oblivion

SANDERS, RUTH MANNING
  [See MANNING–SANDERS, RUTH]

SANDOE, JAMES
ARTICLES
  Dagger of the Mind
  [Sheridan Le Fanu, Freeman Wills
  Crofts, Patrick Hamilton, Eric Ambler,
  Margaret Millar, Cornell Woolrich,
  Graham Greene]   68   146

SANDOMIRSKY, VERA
  [VERA SANDOMIRSKY DUNHAM]
ARTICLES
  New Trends in Soviet Russian Poetry
  [Alexander Blok, Sergei Essenin,
  Vladimir Maiakovsky, Boris Pasternak,
  Alexander Tvardovsky, Ilja Selvinsky,
  Michail Svetlov, Semjen Kirsanov]   58   324
  A Note on the Poetry
    of Anna Akhmatova   76   114

REVIEWS
  Soviet Poets and Poetry,
    by Alexander Kaun   63   343
  Three Poets of Modern Russia,
    by Leonid I. Strakhovsky
    [Nikolai Gumilyov, Anna Akhmatova,
    Osip Mandelstam]   76   112

SANDOZ, PAUL
BOOKS REVIEWED
    Legend   29   56

SANDQUIST, BARBARA
POEMS
    After Images   44   308
    De Mortuis
    Macabre
    The Waiting
    Sanctuary
    If I
    Last Communion

SANDY, STEPHEN
POEMS
    Home from the Range   109   317
    A Dissolve
    Work   116   174
    Roofs
    Post Card, Moss Garden
    Suburb
    Declension   122   73
    Winter Mountain
    End of the Picaro   124   27
    Lecture   126   198
    Hong Kong
    Claudel's Grave
    Balance   135   30
    Sterling Mountain
    A Little Yard
    Survivor, Walking   137   197
    Landscape with the Body of Judas   141   204
    Man in the Open Air   144   222
    Figure on a Wooded Path
    Bingham Hill   150   326
    Words for Dr. Richards   151   144

REVIEWS
  Experienced Bards   140   293
    Goshawk, Antelope
      and *Dream Flights*,
      by Dave Smith
    God's Measurements,
      by Laurence Lieberman
    Walking Home from the Icehouse,
      by Vern Rutsala
    Distractions, by Miller Williams
    Barn Fever and Other Poems,
      by Peter Davison
    The Bridge of Change,
      by John Logan
    The Red Coal, by Gerald Stern
    The Dollmaker's Ghost,
      by Larry Levis

BOOKS REVIEWED
    Stresses in the Peaceable Kingdom   112   48
    Riding to Greylock   144   345

SANER, REG

POEMS

Camping the Divide: Indian Peaks Colorado	123	227
How the Laws of Physics Love Chocolate	125	341
The Body		
Cony Creek		
Death		
Milking the Snowbank	131	73
Stitchwork		
Neither Lions Ravens Nor White Toads		
Clear Night, Small Fire, No Wind		
In the Iron Trough of the Year	133	128
Eastward from Somewhere:		
San Vitale, Ravenna		
Ghiberti's Baptistery Doors Revisited		
Mountain of the Holy Cross:		
San Juan Range		
The Man-in-the-Moon	139	152
Guidelines	145	159
Headwaters	149	278
Reaching Keet Seel		
Meanwhile	155	206
How		
Evening	156	296
Keen Edges		
Postcards from Italy	158	190
North Rim Esplanade Sundown	160	249
Spring Song		
The Red Poppy		
What Wilderness Tells You		
Forest Mornings I Can't Ask To Happen	163	318
North of Wupatki		
Four Short Poems	169	249
Winter Apple		
Next Table		
King Lear: *Cordelia's Nothing*		
Poetry		

BOOKS REVIEWED

Climbing into the Roots	128	355
So This Is the Map	140	346

SAN GEMIGNANO, FOLGORE DA
[See DA SAN GEMIGNANO,
FOLGORE]

SANGUINETI, EDOARDO

POEMS

Da *Erotopaegnia*/From *Erotopaegnia*	155	78
[*In te dormiva come un fibroma asciutto...*]/		
[*He slept in you like a dry fibroma...*]		
From *Hell's Purgatory*		
[*Through Hebecrevon, Lessay, Portbail...*]		
(Tr. by Charles Tomlinson)		

ARTICLES ABOUT

Some Notes on Post-War Italian Poetry,		
by Paolo Cherchi and Joseph Parisi	155	161

SANT, ANDREW

POEMS

Mussolini's Umbrella	169	78

SANTAGOSTINI, MARIO

POEMS

Da *Il Sogno di Agostino*/		
From *The Dream of Augustine*	155	148
Sei ormai l'unica bestia.../		
Now You Are the Only Beast		
Carla		
(Tr. by John Frederick Nims)		

SANTAYANA, GEORGE

BOOKS REVIEWED

Poems	23	338

ARTICLES ABOUT

Rev. of *The New Oxford Book*		
of American Verse		
(Ed. by Richard Ellmann)	131	236
The Things of the Eye,		
by Robert Fitzgerald	132	107

SANTOS, SHEROD

POEMS

Melancholy Divorcée	134	26
Begin, Distance		
Country Landscape		
An Unknown Man		
Begins Writing His Autobiography		
On the Last Day of the World	137	12
Three Fragments		
After a Long Illness		
The Breakdown	138	285
The Evening Light Along the Sound		
View from the Hotel Lobby		
Waiting for the Storm		
The Coming of Fall		
The Dream of Nothing	141	345
Evening Refrain		
The Harvest Season		
Eurydice		
The Unsleeping Genius		
of Misfortune	147	22
All Souls	150	341
Inspiration	151	146
Dalai Lama	161	214

BOOKS REVIEWED

Accidental Weather	143	163
The City of Women	165	97

SANTOS CHOCANO, JOSÉ

POEMS

Oda Salvaje	11	229
A Song of the Road		
El Charro		

The Magnolia
    (Tr. by John Pierrepont Rice)
Horses of the Conquistadores
    (Tr. by Muna Lee)   26   139

ARTICLES ABOUT
    José Santos Chocano,
        by John Pierrepont Rice
        [Rubén Darío]   11   260

SAPER, SARA
    POEMS
        Two Poems for F.   41   76
            ("I have grown stronger...")
            ("Now at the end...")

SAPHIER, WILLIAM
    POEMS
        Praise   10   26
        To...

    ARTICLES
        Correspondence:
            Back to the Machine-Shop   12   346

SAPINKOPF, LISA
    TRANSLATIONS
        Poems by Georgi Belev
            (Tr. with the author)   159   20

SAPIR, EDWARD
    POEMS
        The Soul of Summer   14   248
        Mary, Mary My Love
        Backwater   18   76
            A Childish Tale
            The Old Town
            Overlooked
            She Sits Vacant-Eyed
        A Walking Poem   20   317
        Foam-Waves   27   175
            Signal
            Three Hags Come Visiting
            Zuni
            Messengers
            Young Grief
            Come with the Wind
            Charon
            She Went to Sleep Below
        Feathered Songs   30   194
            Blowing Winds
            He Implores His Beloved
            The Tribune Tower
            When Long in His Eye
        Autumn Raindrops   39   80
        Levels
        God Blows a Message

    TRANSLATIONS
        French-Canadian Folk Songs   16   175

The Prince of Orange
The King of Spain's Daughter and the Diver
White as the Snow
The Dumb Shepherdess

ARTICLES
    Correspondence:
        Concerning Hilda Conkling   14   344
    Note on French-Canadian Folk-Songs
        [C. M. Barbeau]   16   210

REVIEWS
    Poems of Gerard Manley Hopkins
        (Ed. by Robert Bridges)   18   330
    Emily Dickinson, a Primitive   26   97
        The Complete Poems of Emily Dickinson
        The Life and Letters of Emily Dickinson,
            by Martha Dickinson Bianchi
    Those Not Elect, by Léonie Adams   27   275

BOOKS REVIEWED
    Dreams and Gibes   15   169
    Folk Songs of French Canada
        (Ed. with Marius Barbeau)   28   348

SAPPHO
    POEMS
        Fragment 105(a)   164   140
        Fragment 105(c)
            (Tr. by Anita George)

    BOOKS REVIEWED
        Sappho (Tr. by Henry Thornton Wharton)   18   284
        The Poems of...
            (Tr. by P. Maurice Hill)   86   303
        Sappho (Tr. by Mary Barnard)   95   185
        Sappho: Lyrics in the Original Greek
            with Translations, by Willis Barnstone 108   416

SARABHAI, BHARATI
    POEMS
        No Time for Remorse   93   248

SARETT, LEW (R.)
    POEMS
        The Blue Duck—A Chippewa Medicine Dance   13   59
        Chippewa Flute Song
        Council Talks   15   83
            Chief Bear's-Heart Makes Talk
            Little Caribou Makes Big Talk
        The Box of God   18   1
            Broken Bird
            Whistling Wings
            Talking Waters
        Requiem for a Croesus   25   85
        Tamarack Blue   26   295
        Tinder and Flint   33   175
            Mountain Hamlet
            Angus McGregor
            Mountain Goat

Broken Drake
Wailing Lynx
Feather
Lonely as a Bird
Split Rock   38   61
   Granite
   To an Ugly Whelp in a Litter of Wolves
   Scalp Dance
   Coyote Brood
   Clipped Wings
   Familiar Wings
   Cattle Bells

ARTICLES
  Correspondence   13   106
  Correspondence: About *Council Talks*   15   98
  [Note]   33   288
  [Tribute to Harriet Monroe]   49   149

BOOKS REVIEWED
  Many Many Moons   17   158
  The Box of God   21   325
  Wings Against the Moon   39   155
  The Collected Poems of...   59   154
  Covenant with Earth   90   325

ARTICLES ABOUT
  The Sandburg-Sarett Recital,
    by Emanuel Carnevali   15   271
  Their Wide Range,
    by Harriet Monroe   17   322
  Ten Years Old, by Harriet Monroe   21   32
  Lew Sarett and Our
    Aboriginal Inheritance,
    by Harriet Monroe   27   88

SARGENT, DANIEL
BOOKS REVIEWED
  The Road to Welles-Perennes:
    A Story in Verse   27   160

SARGENT, E. N.
BOOKS REVIEWED
  The African Boy   104   104

SARGENT, ROBERT
POEMS
  The Things of the World   157   217

SARGENT, SAMUEL M., JR.
POEMS
  Rain Etching   29   202

SAROYAN, ARAM
POEMS
  ("I have spent a year...")   104   20
  ("Bad dreams/come often...")
  At a Bus Stop

("My friends one by one...")
("Talking to you...")
Facts
From *Sled Hill Voices*   108   380
  ("sky...")   110   374
  ("a dish...")
  ("I crazy...")
  ("room now...")
  ("cham/pagne...")
  ("j;u;n;g;l;e;...")
  ("car swerves...")
  ("seek/air...")
  ("wind/oil...")
Poem ("night night night...")   112   162
Life Is No Arrival   124   332
Life Is a Dream

REVIEWS
  The Island, by Robert Creeley   104   45
  A 13-21, A Poem of a Life,
    by Louis Zukofsky   117   118

BOOKS REVIEWED
  Works   110   186
  Sled Hill Voices   113   188

SAROYAN, WILLIAM
POEMS
  The Beautiful People   58   79
  From *To Write a Poem*   73   22

ARTICLES ABOUT
  [Note]   58   114

SARTARELLI, STEPHEN
TRANSLATIONS
  Poems by Mario Luzi   155   27
  Poems by Stefano D'Arrigo   155   43
  Poems by Rodolfo di Biasio
    and Fabio Doplicher   155   95
  Poem by Umberto Piersanti   155   119

SARTON, MAY
POEMS
  Words on the Wind   37   144
    First Love
    Let No Wind Come
    They Also
    Fruit of Loneliness
  Encounter in April   40   14
  Antelope   43   27
  What the Old Man Said   57   176
  American Notebook   59   235
    Where the Grasses
    Boulder Dam
    Ohio Country
    A Northerner Sees the Cottonfields
    for the First Time

Of the Seasons
Sestina   65   231
Homage to Flanders
To the Living
Theme and Variations:
    Santa Fe, New Mexico   68   74
Meditation in Sunlight
The Window
Difficult Scene
The Lion and the Rose
Two Songs   74   271
    ("Lose the pain in the snow...")
    ("Silence is never cruel...")
Humpty Dumpty
The Sacred Wood   81   232
The Walled Garden at Clondalkin   85   344
A Country Incident   99   98
The Invocation to Kali   117   314
Prisoner at a Desk   119   269
August Third   151   147
The Phoenix Again   151   272
Wilderness Lost
Christmas Light
The O's of November   161   125
Lunch in the Garden
The Teacher
After the Long Enduring
A Handful of Thyme
Bliss

TRANSLATIONS
Poems by Paul Valéry
    (With Louise Bogan)   94   I

BOOKS REVIEWED
Encounter in April   50   229
The Lion and the Rose   73   292
In Time Like Air   94   339
Cloud, Stone, Sun, Vine   101   209
A Private Mythology   109   189
Mrs. Stevens Hears
    the Mermaids Singing   109   332
A Private Mythology   112   44
A Grain of Mustard Seed   121   348
Collected Poems: 1930-1973   126   103
Sarton Selected:
    An Anthology of the Journals,
    Novels and Poems of...
    (Ed. by Bradford Dudley Daziel)   160   284
Coming into Eighty   166   289

SARTRE, JEAN-PAUL
BOOKS REVIEWED
Baudelaire   77   100

ARTICLES ABOUT
"Existentialisme, Drôle de Mot,"
    by Paul Bordry   69   152

SASSOON, SIEGFRIED
BOOKS REVIEWED
The Old Huntsman   13   283
Counter-Attack and Other Poems   14   216
Picture-Show   16   159
The Heart's Journey   34   288
Memoirs of a Fox-Hunting Man
Prehistoric Burials   43   225
Vigils   48   292
Rhymed Ruminations   58   100
Collected Poems   74   41

ARTICLES ABOUT
Visitors from the Other Side,
    by Harriet Monroe   15   93
Poetry in the First World War,
    by David Daiches   56   323

SATIE, ERIK
ARTICLES ABOUT
The Editor in France,
    by Harriet Monroe   23   90

SATO, SATORU
POEMS
On the Bridge   88   105
Japan that Sank Under the Sea
Susuki and Dragonflies   105   165

TRANSLATIONS
Poems by Fuyuji Tanaka, Baku
    Yamanoguchi, Katsuhiko Kogure,
    Sannosuke Iwai, Mitsuharu Kaneko,
    Toson Shimazaki, Junzaburo Nishiwaki,
    Motomaro Senge, Iku Takenaka,
    Shiro Murano, Tatsuji Miyoshi,
    Shigeharu Nakano, Azuma Kondo,
    Fuyuhiko Kitagawa, Kyojiro Hagiwara,
    Shinkichi Takahashi, Kaoru Maruyama,
    Sonosuke Sato, Kotaro Takamura,
    Saisei Muro, Takuji Ote, Fuyue Anzai,
    Taku Oga, and Hakushu Kitahara
    (Tr. with Constance Urdang)   88   63

ARTICLES
A Note on These Poems
    (With Constance Urdang)   88   108

SATO, SONOSUKE
POEMS
The Moon   88   92
Our Maidservant
    (Tr. by Satoru Satu
    and Constance Urdang)

SATYARTHI, DEVENDRA
POEMS
The Earth Is Not an Old Woman
    (Tr. by P. Machwe)   93   228

SAUL, GEORGE BRANDON
BOOKS REVIEWED
The Cup of Sand   24   283

SAUL, HENRY
[See ZOLINSKI, HENRY SAUL]

SAUL, MILTON
ARTICLES
Poet, Publisher, and the Tribal Chant
(With Claude Fredericks)   75   24

SAUNDERS, JOSEPHINE
POEMS
The Circle and the Question   114   380
The Undersides of Words   116   97
With Hands Wide Open   151   148

SAUNDERS, WILLIAM
POEMS
Crescendo   85   71
Bold Dare
The Deal

SAVAGE, D. S.
POEMS
The Wild Swan   48   132
Factory
Fall of Leaves
Song ("Take the leaf falling...")   51   65
Phoenix   51   175
Rhapsody
Winter Offering
Song ("Wretched cold...")

ARTICLES
London Letter
[Victor B. Neuberg, David Gascoyne,
Dylan Thomas, George Barker,
Gavin Ewart, Keidrich Rhys]   51   277
Poetry Politics in London
[W. H. Auden, Geoffrey Grigson]   53   200
Avant-Garde and Camp Followers
[Laurence Whistler, Fear No More]   59   32
Harold Monro: A Study in Integration   60   324
Poetry and Nature
[John Donne, Alexander Pope,
Andrew Marvell]   61   496
The Poet's Perspectives
[W. H. Auden, Louis MacNeice,
Stephen Spender, Edgell Rickword,
George Woodcock]   64   148
Criticism and Orthodoxy
[Norman Nicholson, S. L. Bethell]   64   279
Form in Modern Poetry
[Stephen Spender, Marianne Moore,
Sacheverell Sitwell, Ezra Pound,
Thomas Hardy]   65   30

BOOKS REVIEWED
The Autumn World   54   284
A Time to Mourn: Poems 1933-1943   65   274

ARTICLES ABOUT
Correspondence from Geoffrey Grigson   54   52
Correspondence from Julian Symons   54   54
Correspondence from H. B. Mallalieu   54   55
Contemporary Poetry in Britain,
by David Daiches   62   150
Correspondence from Norman Rosten   65   346

SAVAGE, HUGH
POEMS
Moving House   162   27
Borzoi   163   74

SAVIDIS, GEORGE
TRANSLATIONS
Poem by Odysseus Elytis
(Tr. with Edmund Keeley)   105   1
Poems by Takis Sinopoulos
(Tr. with Edmund Keeley)   105   36

ARTICLES
A Note on Takis Sinopoulos   105   43

SAVOIE, TERRY
[TERRENCE SAVOIE]
POEMS
An Unconscious History   139   195
Letter to a Lost Friend
Father-Milk   149   287
Hairbrush   159   153
School for Missionaries

SAVORY, TEO
TRANSLATIONS
Poems by Eugène Guillevic
and Gunter Eich   116   358

BOOKS REVIEWED
Traveler's Palm   112   276

SAWITZKY, SUSAN CLAY
POEMS
Mariner   57   306

SAYERS, DOROTHY
BOOKS REVIEWED
Further Papers on Dante   96   323

ARTICLES ABOUT
Recent French Publications,
by Wallace Fowlie   93   40

SAYRES, DOROTHY
BOOKS REVIEWED
Op. 1   10   44

SCALISE, GREGORIO

POEMS

[*La mente e il corpo sono angeli*]/
  [*The mind and body are angels*]   155   104
[*Ora riapre un testo*]/
  [*Now to reopen a text*]
[*Authority has played*]
[*Saying again that flowers*]
  (Tr. by Adria Bernardi)

SCALLON, ANGUS VICTOR

POEMS

Wintersmead   43   323

SCAMMELL, WILLIAM

POEMS

Above Thirlmere   133   272
St Bees in Winter
High Summer
Night Piece
Aunt Jenny
A Letter from Cumbria   140   193

SCANNELL, VERNON

POEMS

Love Among the Tumblers   70   194
Pain   73   266
Song ("Slowly, now my lovely...")   74   266

SCARBOROUGH, DOROTHY

BOOKS REVIEWED

On the Trail of Negro Folk-Songs   27   221

SCARBROUGH, GEORGE (A.)

POEMS

Lines for an Aunt   72   7
Portrait Mostly in Black and White   78   135
Sunday Shopping   169   283
The Hummingbird   170   212
The Garden
Friendship Cemetery in Summer   170   322

SCARFE, FRANCIS

POEMS

The Grotto   69   310

BOOKS REVIEWED

Inscapes   58   159

ARTICLES ABOUT

Contemporary Poetry in Britain,
  by David Daiches   62   150

SCHACHT, MARSHALL

POEMS

Word and Wind Talk   34   73
Measureless
Gull Lesson

A Crow's Feather
A Way to Speak
Envy Under the "L"   39   197
News Reel   51   64
Review and Pre-View: North by East   51   201
  Motor Landscape
  R. F. D., Vermont
  "The New Yorker"
  Winter Feeding
  Not to Forget Miss Dickinson
  Buy a Plane, Mr. Hemingway
  Two Winds on Nova Scotia
The Sounding Vision   53   18
  Fiddle Practice
  The Fancy People
  The Further Goal
  Oration for My Nazi Cousins
  "Our Town"
"As Through a Glass Darkly"   56   314
Sewing Circle   62   190
The Children
The Only Noise
Breakfast Symphony, Station WQXR   68   10
Wave to the World   68   252
Vacation Postponed   70   8

REVIEWS

Cold Morning Sky,
  by Marya Zaturenska   51   266
Two Regions   53   92
  Maine Ballads,
    by Robert P. Tristram Coffin
  7 Men, by Boris Todrin
Wind the Clock,
  by Winfield Townley Scott   60   46
New England Earth,
  by Don Stanford   60   107

BOOKS REVIEWED

Fingerboard   76   361

SCHAEFFER, SUSAN FROMBERG

POEMS

Proverbs   120   6
Suicide
Backyard   125   256

BOOKS REVIEWED

Granite Lady   126   219

SCHAER, HANS

BOOKS REVIEWED

Religion and the Cure of Souls   77   168

SCHAPPES, MORRIS U.

ARTICLES

Correspondence
  [Objectivists, Louis Zukofsky]   42   117

REVIEWS
An "Objectivists" Anthology
   (Ed. by Louis Zukofsky)   41   340
Emily Dickinson Face to Face,
   by Martha Dickinson Bianchi   42   345
A Green Bough,
   by William Faulkner   43   48
André Spire and His Poetry,
   by Stanley Burnshaw   44   347

ARTICLES ABOUT
Correspondence
   from Louis Zukofsky   42   117

SCHAUFFLER, GOODRICH C.
POEMS
Chalandry   14   183

SCHAUFFLER, ROBERT HAVEN
BOOKS REVIEWED
Hobnails in Eden   34   111

SCHAUKAL, RICHARD
POEMS
Rococo
   (Tr. by Babette Deutsch
   and Avrahm Yarmolinsky)   21   145

ARTICLES ABOUT
Modern German Poetry II,
   by Reginald H. Wilenski   5   234

SCHAUMANN, HERBERT
POEMS
Among Those Notified   69   20
We, Too
Aphrodite and Ares   69   252

SCHEALER, JOHN M.
ARTICLES
Correspondence:
   On Relegating Masefield
   [Stanley Edgar Hyman]   71   112

SCHEELE, ROY
POEMS
Rock Openings   123   230
Nebraska Wine   161   328
Apology   165   83
Eohippus
Red Poppy   170   78

SCHEFFAUER, ETHEL TALBOT
POEMS
The Lost Kingdom   5   162
Adam the Dreamer   30   14
Herds at Evening

SCHEFFAUER, HERMAN (GEORGE)
ARTICLES ABOUT
Our Contemporaries,
   by Alice Corbin Henderson   3   187
Frugality and Deprecation,
   by Harriet Monroe   17   30

SCHEFFER, JOHN
POEMS
Affirmation   38   86
This Youth Bewildered

SCHENKER, DONALD
POEMS
A Picture of Mathew Brady   107   95

ARTICLES
[Note]   107   136

SCHERMERHORN, RUTH F.
BOOKS REVIEWED
Testament   46   53

SCHEVILL, JAMES (E.)
POEMS
Face, Face   62   23
Man Alone   62   255
Portrait of My Mother   64   12
A Winter Ode
Leave of Absence   65   178
The Siege of Leningrad
Photograph of a French Child   67   199
Landscape for a Prisoner of War Camp
Elegy in New York
Barber Shop   71   132
Divorce
A Guilty Father to His Daughter   84   260
The Old Blind Man in Spring   86   320

REVIEWS
Two Poets   66   226
   I, Jones, Soldier, by Joseph Schull
   Poems, by Jon Beck Shank
Like the Root, by George Zabriskie   66   290
At the End of the War   67   274
   Five Rivers, by Norman Nicholson
   The Cloth of Flesh, by Séan Jennett

BOOKS REVIEWED
Tensions   72   226
Selected Poems: 1945-49   99   247
Private Dooms & Public Destinations   102   182
The Stalingrad Elegies   105   264
The Black President and Other Plays   108   408
Release   117   261
Violence and Glory, Poems: 1962-1968   118   166
The Buddhist Car and Other Characters   125   166

SCHJELDAHL, PETER
POEMS
Whippoorwill   115   36
The New Life
The Course of Empire   125   251
A Younger Poet
Death in 1974

REVIEWS
Around the Corner   117   261
  Young Cherry Trees Secured
    Against Hares,
    by André Breton
    (Tr. by Edouard Roditi)
  The Coherences, by Anselm Hollo
  Moving Through Air,
    by Lewis Warsh
  The Parade of the Caterpillars,
    by Larry Fagin
  North Central,
    by Lorine Niedecker
  Smith Going Backward,
    by Steve Carey
  The Day the Perfect Speakers Left,
    by Leonard Nathan
  There's a Little Ambiguity Over There
    Among the Bluebells,
    by Ruth Krauss
  Release, by James Schevill
  The Rainbow-Walker,
    by Gene Frumkin
  Train Rides, by Andrew Crozier
  Acetylene Flowers, by Jerry Burns
  The Bird with the Luck and
    Sketchbook from Mercia,
    by Betty Parvin

BOOKS REVIEWED
White Country   113   428

SCHLOSS, DAVID
POEMS
Notes from the Interior   120   140
Fall   124   85
The Poem ("I had never heard...")
The Myth   127   271
Portrait of a Man
"Pleasant Room with View"
The Betting Machine
  Which Threw the Big Game
To Someone Somewhere in Canada
The Explorer
Envoi
To a Winter's Child
The Sleepwalkers
Views of the Burning   129   146
The Cloak   162   2
In a Blue Light   162   210
The Mind/Body Problem

SCHMIDT, ALEXANDER R.
[ALEX R. SCHMIDT]
POEMS
This Song-Shot Hour   48   139
Leeuwenhoek   63   22

SCHMIDT, MICHAEL
POEMS
The Well at Balankanche   118   147
Alone, and in a Lonely Place
Underwater
Trap   119   266
Scorpion
Cave Pool   120   154
The Winter Bird
Thrush Stone
The Spring   123   92

REVIEWS
A Defence   120   170
  Mercian Hymns, by Geoffrey Hill
  Amana Grass, by Jon Silkin
  The Last of England, by Peter Porter
  Collected Poems 1958-1970,
    by George MacBeth
  [Louis Simpson]

BOOKS REVIEWED
Desert of the Lions   123   113
My Brother Gloucester   130   230

SCHMITT, CARL
ARTICLES ABOUT
Correspondence from Brom Weber
  [Hart Crane]   84   245

SCHMITT, GLADYS L.
POEMS
Progeny   34   317

SCHMITT, PETER
POEMS
Tin Ear   153   341
Breakfast of Runnersup   162   216

SCHMITZ, DENNIS
BOOKS REVIEWED
We Weep for Our Strangeness   118   169
Goodwill, Inc.   132   31
Singing   147   291

SCHNACKENBERG, GJERTRUD
[GJERTRUD SCHNACKENBERG
SMYTH]
POEMS
The Boboli Gardens   124   125
Signs
Kandinsky's Night
From Laughing with One Eye   132   161

BOOKS REVIEWED
  Portraits and Elegies   145   36
  The Lamplit Answer   147   156
  A Gilded Lapse of Time   163   97

SCHNEIDER, ELIZABETH
BOOKS REVIEWED
  Aesthetic Motive   55   340
  Coleridge, Opium, and Kubla Khan   84   179

SCHNEIDER, ISIDOR
POEMS
  America—1919   17   24
    A Hymn for the Lynchers
    A Memory
    The Heroes
  Conversation   20   117
  The Mist
  The Dancer Instructs the Audience   26   82
  Fire! Fire!
  Jacob
  Angelus
  Anthology of Oom
  Skyscapes
  Morning Walks in the City
  A History of the Jews   35   324

REVIEWS
  Leda, by Aldous Huxley   17   217
  Caius Gracchus, by Odin Gregory   17   337
  One Poet   18   39
    Advice, by Maxwell Bodenheim
    The Forerunner, by Kahlil Gibran
    Neighbors, by Wilfrid Wilson Gibson
    The Birds and Other Poems,
      by J. C. Squire
    Songs While Wandering,
      by A. Newberry Choyce
  Ships in Harbor, by David Morton   19   44
  Minor Chords   19   158
    Bluestone, by Marguerite Wilkinson
    Selected Poems,
      by Lady Margaret Sackville
  Hidden Path, by Ned Hungerford   19   167
  Slavic Poetry   20   228
    Modern Russian Poetry
      (Ed. and tr. by Babette Deutsch
      and Avrahm Yarmolinsky)
    Anthology of Modern Slavonic Literature
      and *Modern Czech Poetry*
      (Tr. by P. Selver)
    An Anthology of Jugoslav Poetry
      (Ed. by Dr. B. S. Stanoyevich)

BOOKS REVIEWED
  The Temptation of Anthony   33   276

ARTICLES ABOUT
  [Note]   60   169

SCHNITTKIND, HENRY T.
BOOKS REVIEWED
  The Poets of the Future (Ed.)   14   281

SCHOENBAUM, SAMUEL
BOOKS REVIEWED
  Middleton's Tragedies   92   121

SCHOENBERGER, NANCY
POEMS
  Train to Seattle, Christmas Morning   137   143
  A Small Thing

SCHOLEM, GERSHOM
ARTICLES ABOUT
  Rev. of *A Map of Misreading*,
    by Harold Bloom   127   222

SCHOLES, KENNETH
POEMS
  Season's Greetings   65   134
  Crossroads
  A Marriage   69   192
  Dead Letter

SCHOONMAKER, EDWIN DAVIES
BOOKS REVIEWED
  The Americans   3   184

SCHOONMAKER, FRANK M.
POEMS
  Crystals   10   199
    O Poet
    To a Sparkling Piece of Crystal
    The Bubble
    The Brook

SCHORER, MARK
BOOKS REVIEWED
  William Blake: The Politics of Vision   69   223

SCHRAMM, RICHARD
POEMS
  The Return   118   206
  Escape   120   89
  Penitence
  The Calamity
  Messageries Maritimes
  The Inheritors

BOOKS REVIEWED
  Rooted in Silence   122   168

SCHREINER, STEVEN
POEMS
  The Diver   126   159

SCHROEDER, BETHANY
POEMS
  Blackberry Winter   145   70
  Spooner's Cove

SCHUBERT, DAVID
POEMS
Kind Valentine   48   198
Here Is the Street   50   1
    Crooked Road, Crooked Year
    The Lake
    When Apples on the Lilac
Crow on the Husk   50   81
Peter and Mother   51   187
Dissertation on the Detroit Free Press   62   198

ARTICLES
Correspondence
[Congress of American Writers]   50   357

BOOKS REVIEWED
Five Young American Poets,
    Second Series 1941
    (With Paul Goodman,
    Jeanne McGahey, Clark Mills,
    and Karl Shapiro)   60   215
Initial A
    (Ed. by Theodore Weiss
    and Judith E. Kranes)   99   379
Works and Days
    (Ed. by T. and R. Weiss)   145   348

SCHULL, JOSEPH
BOOKS REVIEWED
I, Jones, Soldier   66   226

SCHULMAN, GRACE
POEMS
The Examination:
    Remembrance of Words Lost   113   319
Tree of Life   129   3
That Maple
Blessed Is the Light   132   140
Flight Commands   138   261
Port of Many Names   142   151
New Year
After the Division   149   276
"Straight Talk, Straight as the Greek"   151   149
The Wedding   158   125

REVIEWS
Brief Reviews   147   102
    YIN: New Poems,
        by Carolyn Kizer
    Henry Purcell in Japan,
        by Mary Jo Salter
    Navigable Waterways,
        by Pamela Alexander
    Raw Heaven, by Molly Peacock
    Taking to Water,
        by Roberta Spear
    Hotel Fiesta,
        by Lynn Emanuel

BOOKS REVIEWED
Songs of Cifar and the Sweet Sea: Selections
    from "Songs of Cifar, 1967-1977,"
    by Pablo Antonio Cuadra
    (Tr. and ed. with
    Ann McCarthy de Zavala)   137   220
Hemispheres   147   156
For That Day Only   166   104

SCHULTZ, PHILIP
POEMS
Darwin, Tortoises, Galapagos
    Archipelago & New Hampshire   132   318
Savage Feelings
For My Father
Lines to a Jewish Cossack:
    For Isaac Babel   141   281
The Garden of Honor
The Eight-Mile Bike Ride   151   150
The Answering Machine   151   414
A Woman's Touch   167   258
Change
My Friend Is Making Himself   168   9
City Dogs
Stories   169   215

BOOKS REVIEWED
Deep Within the Ravine   146   38

SCHUTZE, MARTIN
ARTICLES ABOUT
A Bull in the China Shop,
    by Harriet Monroe   42 212

SCHUYLER, JAMES
POEMS
A White City   105   371
Seeking   111   320
Now and Then   113   1
May, 1972   120   327
Poem ("This beauty that I see...")   121   150
Deep Winter
In Wiry Winter
So Good
Hymn to Life   122   1
Feeling No Pain   127   249
Dec. 28, 1974
Korean Mums
"Can I Tempt You to a Pond Walk?"
Let's All Hear It for Mildred Bailey!   151   151

BOOKS REVIEWED
Alfred and Guinevere   93   321
Freely Espousing   117   54
A Nest of Ninnies
    (With John Ashbery)
The Crystal Lithium   122   235
The Morning of the Poem   137   297

A Few Days	149	31
Selected Poems	155	351
Collected Poems	163	225

ARTICLES ABOUT
Rev. of *The Poets*		
of the New York School		
(Ed. by John Bernard Myers)	119	39

SCHUYLER, MARGARETTA
BOOKS REVIEWED
Poems	21	222

SCHWABSKY, BARRY
POEMS
Now I'm Feeling Blue	134	79
Arthur: Perdido		
Fragment of a Pastoral		

SCHWARTZ, DELMORE
POEMS
Poem ("You, my photographer...")	49	252
Poem ("Old man...")		
("In the naked bed...")	51	198
("The heart, a black grape...")		
Hope Like the Phoenix Breast Rises Again	76	1
"My Love, My Love, My Love,		
Why Have You Left Me Alone?"		
"The Desperanto of Willynully"		
The Self Unsatisfied Runs Everywhere		
Chaplin upon the Cliff, Dining Alone		
The Rumor and the Whir		
of Unborn Wings		
The Heart Flies Up, Erratic as a Kite		
Why Do You Write an Endless History?		
The Self-Betrayal Which Is Nothing New		
Twelfth Night, Next Year,		
A Week-End in Eternity		
True Recognition Is Often Refused		
The Kingdom of Poetry	92	63
The Mounting Summer,		
Brilliant and Ominous	94	104
Swift		
The River Was the Emblem		
of All Beauty; All		
Summer Knowledge		
Apollo Musagete, Poetry,		
and the Leader of the Muses	101	108

ARTICLES
The Critical Method		
of R. P. Blackmur	53	28
Rimbaud in Our Time	55	148
The Vocation of the Poet		
in the Modern World		
[T. S. Eliot, James Joyce]	78	223
T. S. Eliot's Voice and His Voices	85	170
T. S. Eliot's Voice and His Voices	85	232

REVIEWS
Poems, by Louis MacNeice	48	115
Straight or Curly?		
by Clifford Dyment	50	233
The Fifth Decad of Cantos,		
by Ezra Pound	51	324
The Selected Poetry of Robinson Jeffers	55	30
Words for the Wind,		
by Theodore Roethke		
[W. B. Yeats]	94	203

BOOKS REVIEWED
In Dreams Begin Responsibilities	54	105
A Season in Hell,		
by Arthur Rimbaud (Tr.)	56	95
Vaudeville for a Princess	79	50
Vaudeville for a Princess	79	55
Summer Knowledge:		
New and Selected Poems	95	300
Selected Poems: Summer Knowledge	112	418

ARTICLES ABOUT
The New *Theatrum Poetarum*,		
by Alan S. Downer	60	206
The Isolation of the Poet,		
by William Van O'Connor	70	28
Rev. of *Poems of a Jew*,		
by Karl Shapiro	96	171
Delmore Schwartz,		
by M. L. Rosenthal	109	181

SCHWARTZ, IRWIN
POEMS
For Those Who Govern	85	137

SCHWARTZ, LLOYD
POEMS
Love	144	125

ARTICLES
Correspondence		
[Greg Kuzma, Martha Collins]	149	181

SCHWARTZ, SELWYN S.
POEMS
Judgment	60	26
Soldier Boy	62	129
Mother Earth	64	264
Sermon of October	67	65
Hampshire House	73	333
Nobility	79	26
Yahrzeit		
Tradition		
Ancestral Processions		
Tomb of Granite		
Marc Chagall	83	16
Birth	89	82

BOOKS REVIEWED
   The Poet in Blue Minor   62   173
   Passages of Refuge
   Preface to Maturity   66   106
   Horn in the Dust   76   231

ARTICLES ABOUT
   Correspondence
      from Coleman Rosenberger   66   229

SCHWEBELL, GERTRUDE CLORIUS
BOOKS REVIEWED
   Contemporary German Poetry, An Anthology
     (Tr. and ed.)   111   336

SCHWERNER, ARMAND
BOOKS REVIEWED
   The Lightfall   105   270

SCOLLARD, CLINTON
POEMS
   A Day for Wandering   3   126
   An Intimate of Night   17   253

BOOKS REVIEWED
   The Poems
     of Frank Dempster Sherman (Ed.)   12   109
   Elegy in Autumn   12   282
   The Bird-Lovers' Anthology
     (Ed. with Jessie B. Rittenhouse)   37   164

SCOLLARD, ELISABETH
BOOKS REVIEWED
   Candle and Cross   27   228

SCOTT, ALEXANDER
ARTICLES ABOUT
   Some Poets of the Scottish Renaissance,
     by Tom Scott   88   43

SCOTT, BEATRICE
BOOKS REVIEWED
   Selected Writings,
     by Boris Pasternak
     (Tr. with C. M. Bowra,
     Babette Deutsch, and Robert Payne)   76   238

SCOTT, DUNCAN CAMPBELL
POEMS
   Power   58   5

BOOKS REVIEWED
   Lundy's Lane and Other Poems   10   49

ARTICLES ABOUT
   Canadian Poetry Today,
     by Florence Randal Livesay   27   36
   The Development of Poetry
     in Canada, 1880-1940,
     by E. K. Brown   58   34

SCOTT, EVELYN
POEMS
   Tropical Life   15   70
     Twenty-Four Hours
     The Storm
     Rainy Season
     The Year
     Tropical Flowers
     Mail on the Ranch
     The City at Midnight
     Ship Masts
     The Silly Ewe
     Conservatism
     The Vampire Bat
     Fear
     Little Pigs

ARTICLES
   Correspondence:
     From Brazil to the U. S.   15   100
     Emilio de Menezes   16   40
     Brazilian Dance Songs   18   267

REVIEWS
   Three Plays of the Argentine
     (Ed. by Edward Bierstadt)
     (Tr. by Jacob S. Fassett, Jr.)   17   52
   Landscape West of Eden,
     by Conrad Aiken   46   162
   Poems, 1909-1936,
     by John Hall Wheelock   50   100
   The Golden Fleece of California,
     by Edgar Lee Masters   50   215

BOOKS REVIEWED
   Precipitations   17   334
   The Winter Alone   36   338

SCOTT, F. R.
POEMS
   ("When I see the falling bombs...")   58   12
   ("From those condemned to labor...")
   Dialogue   59   87
   To Certain Friends
   Resurrection   63   313
   Examiner
   For R.A.S.
   War News
   Villanelle for Our Time

BOOKS REVIEWED
   Events and Signals   88   52
   Selected Poems   111   323

SCOTT, FRANK
ARTICLES ABOUT
   The Development of Poetry
     in Canada, 1880-1940,
     by E. K. Brown   58   34

SCOTT, HERBERT
POEMS
   Late Fall, Setting Traps   115   174

SCOTT, MARGRETTA
POEMS
   Side-Lights on War   14   194
   Dolly Parker
   Mrs. John Wright
   Mrs. Finnigan
   David

SCOTT, MARK
POEMS
   The Cave of AIDS   158   23

SCOTT, PETER DALE
POEMS
   Cathedral Creche   85   142
   Les Bouffons d'Aprés-Guerre   98   26
   Parole

REVIEWS
   A Canadian Chronicle   115   353
   Memory No Servant, by Earle Birney
   The Shattered Plinths,
     by Irving Layton
   As Is, by Raymond Souster
   Collected Poems, by Red Lane
   21 x 3,
     by Dorothy Farmiloe,
     Len Gasparini,
     and Eugene McNamara
   If There Are Any Noahs,
     by Jim Brown
   Kingdom of Absence and Civil Elegies,
     by Dennis Lee
   Total War, by Harry Howith
   Winter of the Luna Moth,
     by Joe Rosenblatt
   What They Say and
     Black Night Window,
     by John Newlove
   Pointing, by Lionel Kearns
   Fireweed, by Ken Belford
   Lebanon Voices, by Bill Bissett
   The Dainty Monsters,
     by Michael Ondaatje

BOOKS REVIEWED
   Zbigniew Herbert: Selected Poems
     (Tr. with Czeslaw Milosz)   114   40

SCOTT, TOM
POEMS
   The Troops Talk O Wine and Wemen...   85   88
   Orpheus   86   94
   Telemachos
   Ithaka   89   302

   The Real Muse
   A Dream o the Rude   97   98
   On Hearing a Certain Pub
     Is Not Proper for Academics   99   14
   The Twins
   In Handsel o Poetry's Fifty Light Years   101   112

ARTICLES
   Some Poets of the Scottish Renaissance
     [Hugh MacDiarmid, Helen
     Cruickshank, William Jeffrey,
     William Soutar, Albert D. Mackie,
     Robert Garioch, Douglas Young,
     George Campbell Hay, Sydney
     Goodsir Smith, Alexander Scott]   88   43

REVIEWS
   The Russet Coat,
     by Christina Keith
     [Robert Burns]   89   382

BOOKS REVIEWED
   The Oxford Book of Scottish Verse
     (Ed. with John MacQueen)   111   410
   Late Mediaeval Scots Poetry (Ed.)   113   35

ARTICLES ABOUT
   Contemporary Poetry in Britain,
     by David Daiches   62   150
   London Letter: Some New Figures,
     by John McCormick   83   269

SCOTT, WINFIELD TOWNLEY
[W. T. SCOTT, WINFIELD SCOTT]
POEMS
   The Enchanted Lady   40   322
   Pennies for an Old Cup   42   11
   One Commandment
   Pause in a Sequence
   And If the Crystal Globe
   Last Suppers
   Light of Morning   44   131
   My Dear Time
   The First Reader
   Biography for Traman   46   179
   Sunday Night
   He Remembers His Childhood
   Passing a Steeple
   Backdrop for This Particular Stage
   Midway
   Blood and Seashell   50   188
   At Least One Spring
   Annual Legend   52   24
   Notes for a Future Ballet   52   57
   Morning Song   55   124
   All Our Answers
   The Game
   1925-1938
   Swedish Angel   58   141

Direction
Natural Causes
Fine Morning
We Who Could Not Be Pious   59   318
I Flatted that Rhyme?
Head Back, the Sunlight
Jack Spratt et Ux
Much Has Been Said
"Grandeur Is Gone, Gogarty..."
To All Objectivists   61   487
Mr. Whittier   63   65
("The hour is late...")   64   204
("And yet there's love...")
("These words may be a dress...")
("Your hair, for the first time...")
("Then, as seventeenth-century...")
("The hour is short...")
My Grandmother Townley's Funeral   68   84
North Light
May 1506
Identities
Blue Fish in a Blue Sky   72   81
Communication Established
Pvt. John Hogg
Bermuda Suite   74   249
Blue Sleigh   76   16
Numbered Summer
The Ghost   85   275
Two Lives and Others
Love and a Season
Questions for Us and Coronado   87   268
Merrill's Brook
The Blue Tree
Between Ironwood and the Sea   89   226
For the Reason of Juana de Asbaje   96   305
Dreamed Rain   101   163
Ancestors
Peterborough
Another Return
Penang
Confidential
Who's Been Here Before Me?
Dedication
Roethke   108   287
For an Old Sunday Painter
Gudhjem on Bornholm
Orchard Burial
Sprague Smith Studio
Once off England...
At Jaffrey Center
Uses of Poetry   111   36
North Easter
Bring
Poem ("The girl young enough...")   113   373
I Held a Hummingbird in My Hand
Restless at Midnight
That Woman of Lachaise
Seven Haiku

Multiple Venus
Once in Mexico
Weather-Wise
The Beautiful Girl
Time
Late
Love
Centenary for Private John Hogg
The Claiming of Private John Hogg

ARTICLES
The New Intellectualism:
    The Dry Reaction
    [Yvor Winters, Lincoln Fitzell,
    Randall Jarrell, John Berryman]   58   86

REVIEWS
Avalanche of April, by Kimball Flaccus   45   342
Golden Fleece, by William Rose Benét   47   223
The Island Called Pharos,
    by Archibald Fleming   48   111
Winged Child,
    by Jean Starr Untermeyer   48   288
A Letter from Pontus,
    by John Masefield   48   338
Unselected Poems   49   340
    Stand with Me Here,
        by Robert Francis
    Splendor in the Grass,
        by Audrey Wurdemann
    "The Unaccredited Profession"   50   150
    E. A. R., by Laura E. Richards
    Next Door to a Poet,
        by Rollo Walter Brown
    Collected Poems
        of Edwin Arlington Robinson
    A Bibliography
        of Edwin Arlington Robinson,
        by Charles Beecher Hogan
Poems, by C. F. MacIntyre   50   289
The Early World, by Robert Hunt   51   226
The Fifth Decad of Cantos,
    by Ezra Pound   51   324
New Poems, by W. B. Yeats   53   84
Edwin Arlington Robinson,
    by Hermann Hagedorn   54   92
Poems, by Alvin Foote   56   106
New Michigan Verse
    (Ed. by Carl Edwin Burklund)   58   344
West of Midnight, by Paul Engle   60   102
A Witness Tree, by Robert Frost   60   146
Collected Lyrics
    of Edna St. Vincent Millay   63   334
A Wreath for the Sea,
    by Robert Fitzgerald   64   111
Edwin Arlington Robinson
    and His Manuscripts,
    by Esther Willard Bates   65   209

The Summer Landscape,
   by Rolfe Humphries   65   330
Collected Poems, by E. J. Pratt   66   329
A Tent for April, by Patrick Anderson   67   224
A Man Against Time,
   by William Ellery Leonard   67   260
Selected Poems, by John Manifold   69   43
A History of American Poetry, 1900-1940,
   by Horace Gregory and
   Marya Zaturenska
   [Edwin Arlington Robinson,
   Ezra Pound, Robert Frost, T. S. Eliot,
   Harriet Monroe, Amy Lowell]   69   210
Edwin Arlington Robinson,
   by Yvor Winters   70   94
Collected Poems, by Siegfried Sassoon   74   41
Intentions and Commitments   87   53
   Selected Poems, by Lincoln Fitzell
   Person in the World, by Edith Henrich
   To the Loud Wind and Other Poems,
      by Donald Hall
   The Moral Circus, by Edwin Honig
   Riding Lights, by Norman MacCaig
   The Gentle Weight Lifter,
      by David Ignatow
   Want My Shepherd,
      by Howard O. Sackler
   The Precisions, by Cid Corman

BOOKS REVIEWED
Biography for Traman   50   224
Wind the Clock   60   46
The Sword on the Table   61   454
To Marry Strangers   67   157
Mr. Whittier, and Other Poems   75   105
The Dark Sister   93   46
Scrimshaw   96   230
Collected Poems   102   115
Change of Weather   106   309
New and Selected Poems
   (Ed. by George P. Elliott)   112   418
A Dirty Hand:
   The Literary Notebooks of...   115   345

ARTICLES ABOUT
Correspondence
   from John Gould Fletcher   58   230
Correspondence from Yvor Winters   70   285
Correspondence: Letter from Harvard,
   by John Ciardi   74   112
[Note]   83   305
[Note]   96   329

SCOTUS, SEDULIUS
ARTICLES ABOUT
Rev. of *Mediaeval Irish Lyrics*
   (Ed. and tr. by James Carney)   113   35

SCOVELL, E. J.
ARTICLES ABOUT
A Letter from Britain [II],
   by William Logan   157   290

SCRIMGEOUR, J. D.
POEMS
Two Lies About My Family   153   87

SCRIPPS, ROBERT PAINE
POEMS
Island Song   12   185

SCRUGGS, ANDERSON M.
POEMS
Sonnets of a Battlefield   41   78
   Missionary Ridge
   Chickamauga Park

BOOKS REVIEWED
Glory of Earth   44   286
Ritual for Myself   61   637

SCRUGGS, J. E.
POEMS
The Screech Owl   12   191
Albatross   36   18
From a Train at Dusk
Two Tongues   48   12
   My Bohemia
   Blotted Out

TRANSLATIONS
Poem by Arthur Rimbaud   54   125

SCRUTON, JAMES
POEMS
In the Age of the Radio Telescope   163   18
Charon   165   4
A Map of the Known World   166   218
The Diviner
Ordinary Plenty   168   147
Thrift
Crow's Nest

SCUDDER, ANTOINETTE
BOOKS REVIEWED
Indian Summer   28   56

SCULLY, JAMES
POEMS
The Change of Life   99   155
Lullaby
"Conception Is a Blessing"

BOOKS REVIEWED
The Marches   113   188

SCUPHAM, PETER
POEMS
  A Box of Ghosts   146   216
  Observer Corps: 1940

  BOOKS REVIEWED
  Prehistories   130   230
  Summer Palaces   138   231

SEAGER, ALLAN
POEMS
  Epilogue   46   86

  BOOKS REVIEWED
  The Glass House:
    The Life of Theodore Roethke   114   327

SEAMI [ZEAMI]
[See also MOTOKIYO,
(KANZE SABURO)]
ARTICLES ABOUT
  Rev. of *The No Plays of Japan*
    (Tr. by Arthur Waley)   88   113

SEARLE, LEROY
POEMS
  Turkey Shooting on Mount Monadnoc   121   274
  Sheep
  Riding in the Elevator   123   140
  Preparing for the Earth

  REVIEWS
  Craft and Vision: Six Poets   123   353
    Funland and Other Poems,
      by Dannie Abse
    48 Small Poems, by Marc Weber
    Between Two Lives,
      by Frederick Turner
    Child's Play, by David R. Slavitt
    Shagbark, by John Peck
    Half-Lives, by Erica Jong

SEATON, MAUREEN
POEMS
  Romancing Debussy   162   3

SEAY, JAMES
BOOKS REVIEWED
  Let Not Your Hart   118   166

SEBBA, GREGOR
REVIEWS
  German Chronicle   97   387
    An Anthology of German Poetry
      from Hölderlin to Rilke
      (Ed. by Angel Flores)
    Rainer Maria Rilke:
      Masks and the Man,
      by H. F. Peters

  Primal Vision: Selected Writings
    of Gottfried Benn
    (Ed. by E. B. Ashton)

SEBREE-SMITH, AMY
POEMS
  Branded   8   232

SECOND, LOUIS
[Pseud. of SHAW,
LOUIS AGASSIZ, II]
POEMS
  Embraced by Holy Arms   51   246
  Thackeray, Etc.   73   7

SEEGER, ALAN
BOOKS REVIEWED
  Poems   10   38

  ARTICLES ABOUT
  In Memoriam,
    by Harriet Monroe   7   98
  [Note]   7   214

SEFERIS, GEORGE
[GEORGE SEFERIADES]
POEMS
  A Word for Summer   78   158
  The Last Station
    (Tr. by Kimon Friar)
  Santorini   105   44
  Salamis in Cyprus
  Three Mules
    (Tr. by Edmund Keeley
    and Philip Sherrard)

  ARTICLES
  Letter to a Foreign Friend
    (Tr. by Nanos Valaorites)
    [T. S. Eliot, Dionysios Solomos]   105   50

  BOOKS REVIEWED
  Poems
    (Tr. by Rex Warner)   101   283
  Collected Poems 1924-1955
    (Tr. by Edmund Keeley
    and Philip Sherrard)   114   113

  ARTICLES ABOUT
  Contemporary Greek Poetry,
    by Kimon Friar   78   145
  Letter from Athens,
    by Vassilis Vassilikos   105   60

SEGAL, GEORGE
ARTICLES ABOUT
  Rev. of *All of Us Here,*
    by Irving Feldman   149   168

SEGAL, LORE
BOOKS REVIEWED
Gallows Songs,
   by Christian Morgenstern
   (Tr. with W. D. Snodgrass)   112   418

SEGALL, SALLY BENNETT
POEMS
Finding the Lion   150   75

SEGHERS, PIERRE
POEMS
Mort dans la Vie,
   les Jours Qui Ne Sont Plus   80   322
L'Echo
   (Tr. by Wallace Fowlie)

ARTICLES
The Conspiracy of the Poets
   (Tr. by William Jay Smith)
   [Louis Aragon, Saint-Pol Roux,
   Pierre Emmanuel, Loys Masson]   67   25

SEIDEL, FREDERICK
POEMS
The Young Reporter   108   85
Black Sappho

REVIEWS
77 Dream Songs,
   by John Berryman   105   257

BOOKS REVIEWED
Final Solutions   103   316
My Tokyo   163   336

SEIDEN, HENRY M.
POEMS
Tinnitus   164   147
Unknown Soldiers   170   269

SEIDEN, MORTON IRVING
BOOKS REVIEWED
William Butler Yeats:
   The Poet as a Mythmaker   103   185

SEIDMAN, HUGH
POEMS
Bookstore   113   250
Surreal Poem
Demonstration
Beginnings   120   204
Eurydice   136   290
The Ill   139   201

BOOKS REVIEWED
Collecting Evidence   118   295
Blood Lord   124   343
People Live, They Have Lives   163   336

SEIF, MORTON
POEMS
Bombos   73   272
In the Movies

SEIFFERT, ALLEN
POEMS
Desert Moonlight   41   198

SEIFFERT, HELEN STEPHENS
POEMS
This Fragile Chain   48   140
The Mole

SEIFFERT, MARJORIE ALLEN
["M. A. S." See also HAY,
ELIJAH, pseud.]
POEMS
Maternity   9   130
Epitaphs
November   11   69
When I Am Old   12   17
To a Child
To a Poet
Mountain Trails   12   300
The Old Woman—A Morality Play
   in Two Parts   13   204
Maura   15   27
Two Designs
   A Japanese Vase Wrought
     in Metals
   Lorenzo's Bas-Relief
     for a Florentine Chest
Cythaera and the Leaves   16   131
Cythaera and the Song
Cythaera and the Worm
Gallery of Paintings   18   177
   The Shop
   Dingy Street
   Interior
   Cubist Portrait
   Two Women
   Portrait of a Lady
   Dream-Kiss
   Shadow
   As You Are Now
   Nocturne
A Sequence   21   240
   At Certain Challenges
   The Ogre
   Stranger
   If Loving Me
   Portrait
   Where Beauty Walks Alone
   The Dark Hour
Red Leaves   22   134
Three Sonnets Concerning
   the Knowledge of Good and Evil   22   306

The New Eden
The Horse-Leech's Daughter
Youth Visits Our Inferno
Reverberations   24   115
  The Singing Bowl
  Grey Moth
  Riding
  Affaire Cérébrale
  The Screen
  She Once Thought Love
Things Unseen   27   1
  Black Kitchen
  The Sinking House
  Chang-Fu
  The City of Mirth
  Design for a Ring
  The Wistful Lady
  The Man-Made Woman
Ballad of a Queen   29   235
Ballad of the Dolphin's Daughter
Noah's Ark   32   1
To Certain Contemporaries   32   309
Bread Out of Iron   34   190
  Iron Fare
  Her Very Tree
  Game of Three
  The Secret Prayer
  The Crickets
  Berceuse
  These Very Stones
("Go find you love...")   37   324
("A new love is trying...")
("Celebrate the May...")
("Cool is your cheek...")
("I touch this bed...")
("This is for one...")
Whispered Lament   40   184
  All the Bright Courage
  The Eyes Know Hunger
  This Fruit
  The Pattern of This Leaf
  Truth Has So Strange a Flavor
  Night Song
  Epitaph ("I think the dead...")
  Now in the Frosty Springtime
Today You Waken   45   260
  Derelict
  From Winter's Tree
A Stone Is Hidden in the Peach   61   490
Time Is a Ripple's Ring
Autumn

ARTICLES
  Kreymborg's Plays for Poem-Mimes   13   224

REVIEWS
  War and Love, by Richard Aldington   14   338
  The Earth Turns South,
    by Clement Wood   15   51

Trackless Regions and The Sword,
  by G. O. Warren   15   221
Pictures of the Floating World,
  by Amy Lowell   15   332
Young Adventure,
  by Stephen Vincent Benét   16   53
Starved Rock, by Edgar Lee Masters   16   151
Harmonium, by Wallace Stevens   23   154
The Prophet, by Kahlil Gibran   23   216
Streets and Shadows,
  by Mercedes de Acosta   23   222
Spring and All,
  by William Carlos Williams   24   45
Heliodora and Other Poems, by H. D.   25   160
Caravan, by Witter Bynner   27   331
Leaves in Windy Weather,
  by Eunice Tietjens   35   220

BOOKS REVIEWED
  A Woman of Thirty   16   219
  Ballads of the Singing Bowl   30   338
  The King with Three Faces   36   165
  The Name of Life   53   283

ARTICLES ABOUT
  Baiting the Public,
    by Alice Corbin Henderson   12   169
  [Note on pseudonym]   12   347
  Marjorie Allen Seiffert,
    by Harriet Monroe   26   32

SEITZ, DON C.
  BOOKS REVIEWED
    Farm Voices   17   100

SELDOMRIDGE, CLARICE
  ARTICLES ABOUT
    When Children Write Verse,
      by Maude Sumner Smith   56   154

SELIG, RICHARD
  BOOKS REVIEWED
    Poems
      (Ed. by Peter Levi)   105   336

SELINSKY, PEARL S.
  POEMS
    Pyramid   168   31

SELLIN, ERIC
  BOOKS REVIEWED
    Night Voyage   107   183

SELVER, P.
  BOOKS REVIEWED
    Anthology of Modern
      Slavonic Literature (Tr.)   20   228
    Modern Czech Poetry (Tr.)

SELVINSKY, ILJA
ARTICLES ABOUT
New Trends
in Soviet Russian Poetry,
by Vera Sandomirsky   58   324

SENG-CH'I, T'ANG
[See T'ANG SENG-CH'I]

SENG DJI-NAN
POEMS
An Old Man's Song of Spring
(Tr. by Louise S. Hammond)   20   252

SENGE, MOTOMARO
POEMS
Secret
(Tr. by Satoru Satu
and Constance Urdang)   88   76

SENGHOR, LÉOPOLD SÉDAR
POEMS
From Midnight Elegy   103   179
For Kora
(Tr. by Charles Guenther)

ARTICLES ABOUT
A Note on Léopold Sédar Senghor,
by Charles Guenther   103   199

SERCHUK, PETER
POEMS
Them   157   86

SEREBROVSKAYA, E.
POEMS
Mines
(Tr. by Babette Deutsch)   70   253

SERENI, VITTORIO
POEMS
La spiaggia/The Beach   155   18
Sarà la noia/It's Perhaps the Boredom
Paura prima/First Fear
Paura seconda/Second Fear
(Tr. by William Jay Smith)

ARTICLES ABOUT
Some Notes on Post-War Italian Poetry,
by Paolo Cherchi and Joseph Parisi 155   161

SERGEANT, ELIZABETH SHEPLEY
BOOKS REVIEWED
Robert Frost, the Trial by Existence 100   50

SERGEANT, HOWARD
POEMS
The Inarticulate   67   316
The Islands   78   134

BOOKS REVIEWED
Tradition in the Making
of Modern Poetry   83   41
The Headlands   86   295
Mavericks
(Ed. with Dannie Abse)   91   124

SERGEL, ROGER L.
POEMS
The Gift of Death   14   21

SERVICE, ROBERT W.
BOOKS REVIEWED
Rhymes of a Red Cross Man   10   271

SEWELL, ELIZABETH
BOOKS REVIEWED
The Orphic Voice   99   387
Poems, 1947-1961   102   330
Signs and Cities   113   262

SEWELL, FRANKIE
TRANSLATIONS
Poem by Cathal Ó Searcaigh   167   67

SEXTON, ANNE
POEMS
The House   99   160
The Black Art   100   271
Water
Old
From the Garden
Woman with Girdle
For Eleanor Boylan Talking with God
Wallflower
Somewhere in Africa   101   113
Sylvia's Death   103   224
The Wedding Night   106   116
KE 6-8018

BOOKS REVIEWED
To Bedlam and Part Way Back   97   316
All My Pretty Ones   101   412
Live or Die   110   125
Love Poems   115   430
All My Pretty Ones   121   54
Transformations   123   34
The Book of Folly   127   286
The Death Notebooks
The Awful Rowing Toward God
45 Mercy Street
(Ed. by Linda Gray Sexton)   129   170
Words for Dr. Y
(Ed. by Linda Gray Sexton)   133   227
The Complete Poems   142   170
Selected Poems of...
(Ed. by Diane Wood Middlebrook
and Diana Hume George)   154   151

SEXTON, LINDA GRAY
BOOKS REVIEWED
45 Mercy Street, by Anne Sexton (Ed.)   129   170
Words for Dr. Y, by Anne Sexton (Ed.)   133   227

SEYFRIED, ROBIN
POEMS
The National Anthem   142   102
The Wives of the Poets   147   9
Poem with Questions Following   153   326

SEYMOUR, GEORGE STEELE
POEMS
Song for These Times   40   129

SEYMOUR, W. KEAN
BOOKS REVIEWED
A Miscellany of British Poetry (1919) (Ed.)   16   108

SEYMOUR-SMITH, MARTIN
BOOKS REVIEWED
All Devils Fading   89   45
A New Canon of English Poetry
(Ed. with James Reeves)   114   113

SHABO, GARY
POEMS
From the Scraps of Blank Paper   132   317

SHAFER, J(ACQUELINE) SINCLAIR
POEMS
Life Happening   45   8
Hurricane
Clumsy
Dismissal
When Desire Is Only a Word
Still Life   47   255

SHAFER, MARGARET
POEMS
Photograph: Nina   137   278

SHAFFER, ANN
POEMS
Disturbing the Season   164   142
From Here   167   262
Under the Crab Nebula   168   15
First Bite   168   226

SHAH, RAJENDRA
POEMS
Last Day
(Tr. by P. Machwe)   93   231

SHAKESPEARE, WILLIAM
BOOKS REVIEWED
The Sonnets of Shakespeare, Variorum Edition
(Ed. by Raymond M. Alden)   9   156

The Shakespeare Songs
(Ed. by Tucker Brooke)   35   337

ARTICLES ABOUT
The Shakespearean Motive,
by Harriet Monroe   6   29
Shakespeare, by Harriet Monroe   8   32
The 16th-Century Lyric
in England: Part III,
by Yvor Winters   54   35
Poetry on Records,
by Harry T. Moore   57   338
Rev. of The Well Wrought Urn,
by Cleanth Brooks   71   318
Rev. of By Avon River, by H. D.   75   223
Conversation on Cornelia Street:
A Dialogue with W. H. Auden,
by Howard Griffin   83   96
Rev. of Shakespeare:
From "Richard II" to "Henry V,"
by Derek Traversi;
Shakespearean Tragedy & the
Elizabethan Compromise,
by Paul N. Siegel;
Shakespeare: Modern Essays in Criticism
(Ed. by Leonard F. Dean)   92   189
Rev. of Shakespeare: A Biography,
by Peter Quennell   104   264

SHALEV, YITZHAK
ARTICLES ABOUT
Postscript: The Younger Poets,
by Simon Halkin   92   259

SHALOM, SHIN
POEMS
The Stoker   92   230
Not All Is So Simple
(Tr. by Ruth Finer Mintz)

SHANAFELT, CLARA
POEMS
To Thee   3   16
Caprice
Invocation   6   68
A Vivid Girl
Provincial
In Summer   8   122
Device
Jeune Fille
Pastel
A Gallant Woman
Scherzo
Ends   46   307
Lament   50   16

ARTICLES ABOUT
They Come and Go, by Harriet Monroe   36   326

SHANK, JON BECK
POEMS
   Chorus for Ants   66   18
   Ante Meridian
   The Dome and Our Lives

BOOKS REVIEWED
   Poems   66 226

SHANKS, EDWARD
BOOKS REVIEWED
   Songs   6 252
   The Queen of China and Other Poems   16 331
   Edgar Allan Poe   50 353

SHANTIRIS, KITA
POEMS
   The Good Guy   138   73
   No Te Preocupes, Blanca   140   18

SHAPCOTT, THOMAS
REVIEWS
   Two Tombstones   122   40
      The Collected Poems of Frank O'Hara
        (Ed. by Donald Allen)
      Collected Poems,
        by W. R. Rodgers

BOOKS REVIEWED
   Shabbytown Calendar   131 225

SHAPIRO, ALAN (b. 1952)
POEMS
   Randolf Routh to Charles Trevelyan 134 334
   The Dublin Evening Mail
   Captain Wynne to Randolf Routh
   Underground   154   18
   Virgil's Descent
   Sisters   161 265
   Soul

BOOKS REVIEWED
   Covenant   160 219

SHAPIRO, ALAN (b. 1926)
POEMS
   A Double Dying   168   29
   Against Poets   168 138

SHAPIRO, DAVID
POEMS
   Poems from Deal   108 167
   Ode ("Permit me to take...")   112 101
   About This Course   121 101
   The Music-Stand   121 278
   The Night Sky   123 159
   Princess Summer Fall Winter Spring
   From *The Devil's Trill Sonata* 126 331

REVIEWS
   The Crystal Lithium, by James Schuyler 122 235
   Into the Gloom   128 226
      Celebrations After the Death
        of John Brennan,
        by X. J. Kennedy
      The Buffalo Shoot, by Greg Kuzma
      The Bloomingdale Papers,
        by Hayden Carruth
      To All Appearances:
        Poems New and Selected,
        by Josephine Miles
   Brief Reviews   149 341
      Shadow Shadow, by Roger Weingarten
      Sapphics Against Anger
        and Other Poems,
        by Timothy Steele
      Anxious Latitudes, by Ralph Angel
      Cracking the Code,
        by David Bergman
      The Flying Change: Poems,
        by Henry Taylor
   Short Reviews   150   36
      The Happy Man, by Donald Hall
      Arts & Sciences, by Albert Goldbarth
      The Complete Poems,
        by Edwin Denby
        (Ed. by Ron Padgett)

BOOKS REVIEWED
   January   108 130
   Poems from Deal   117   54
   A Man Holding an Acoustic Panel 121 229
   The Page-Turner   125   44
   Lateness: A Book of Poems   134 226
   John Ashbery:
      An Introduction to the Poetry 137   42

SHAPIRO, EVALYN
REVIEWS
   Erotic Poems, by Philip Lamantia   70   47
   Poems by Samuel Greenberg
      (Ed. by Harold Holden
      and Jack McManis)   71 158

SHAPIRO, HARVEY
POEMS
   Provincetown, Mass.   75 137
   Walker Under Water   77 197
   On Some Words of Ben Azzai 102   22
   Modern Poetry and the Tradition
   A Writer   105 183
   Beyond the Demonic Element
   Purities
   Distances
   For WCW   110 159
   For Delmore Schwartz
   Days and Nights

Blue Max
Sister
A Jerusalem Notebook   136   214

TRANSLATIONS
Poem by Max Jacob   76   85

BOOKS REVIEWED
The Eye   86   56
The Book   88   273
Mountain, Fire, Thornbush   99   313
Battle Report   109   395
This World   119   234

SHAPIRO, KARL (JAY)
POEMS
University   57   24
Midnight Show
Love Poem
Necropolis
Hospital   58   175
Pharmacy
Snob
Mongolian Idiot
Scyros
The Contraband
My Grandmother
Conscription Camp   59   66
A Robbery
October 1
Terminal   60   57
Newsboy
Waitress
Travelogue for Exiles
Going to the War
Ballade of the Second-Best Bed   61   411
The Twins
A Cut Flower
Nostalgia
Paris   62   237
Nigger
Poem ("Lord, I have seen...")
Movie Actress
Jew
Red Indian
Jefferson
Christmas Tree   63   148
The Puritan   63   299
The Interlude
Ballet Mécanique
Shylock
The Leg
From Essay on Rime   66   197
Recapitulations   69   121
Attentions of Hymen   70   233
The Dirty Word
The Cross-Tree
Eden Retold   78   187

An Anniversary for F. O. Matthiessen   81   69
The Alphabet   83   315
Poems of a Jew   90   265
   Teasing the Nuns
   The First Time
   The Crucifix in the Filing Cabinet
   The Olive Tree
   151st Psalm
A Garden in Chicago   98   1
Emily Dickinson and Katherine Anne Porter
Americans Are Afraid of Lizards
Surrounded
A Modest Funeral
Waiting for the Pope
From The Bourgeois Poet   101   115
End Paper   103   90
From White-Haired Lover   111   1
Moving In   115   123
Philomela. Procne. Tereus.   123   319
Retirement   151   153
On Being Yanked from a Favorite Anthology
"A Room in Rome"   152   30

ARTICLES
A Note on American Poetry   69   273
A Farewell to Criticism   71   196
Prosody as the Meaning
   [E. E. Cummings, W. B. Yeats]   73   336
What Is Anti-Criticism?
   [Alfred, Lord Tennyson]   75   339
The Persistence of Poetry   76   89
Reply to James Parsons   77   56
Editorial Note   79   249
Poets and Psychologists
   [Ezra Pound]   80   166
Does Poetry Have a "Policy"?
   [Edward Dahlberg]   82   178
Dylan Thomas   87   100
The Unemployed Magician
   [D. H. Lawrence]   91   194
A Letter to American Poets and Libraries   92   330
The Farmer and the Poet
   [Reed Whittemore, Charles Baudelaire,
   Boris Pasternak]   98   170
Creative Glut
   [Allen Ginsberg, Sylvia Plath,
   Ezra Pound]   135   36

REVIEWS
Two Veterans   58   100
   Poems 1930-1940,
      by Edmund Blunden
   Rhymed Ruminations,
      by Siegfried Sassoon
The Airmen, by Selden Rodman   58   264
De Imitatione   58   340
   The End of a Decade, by Harry Brown

Shadow on the Sun, by Robert Friend
The Metaphor in the Jungle,
   by Parker Tyler

BOOKS REVIEWED
Five Young American Poets,
   Second Series 1941
   (With Paul Goodman,
   Jeanne McGahey, Clark Mills,
   and David Schubert)   60   215
Person, Place and Thing   61   620
Essay on Rime   68   39
Trial of a Poet   71   314
Poets at Work: Essays
   (With W. H. Auden, Rudolf Arnheim,
   and Donald A. Stauffer)   72   311
English Prosody and Modern Poetry   72   332
Poems of a Jew   96   171
In Defense of Ignorance   98   168
The Bourgeois Poet   106   225
Selected Poems   114   40
White-Haired Lover   114   335
To Abolish Children and Other Essays   115   346
Collected Poems: 1940-1978   133   235
Love & War, Art & God   146   167

ARTICLES ABOUT
Shapiro's Southwest Pacific Poems,
   by William Van O'Connor   64   326
[Note]   66   173
The Poetry of Karl Shapiro,
   by David Daiches   66   266
Is Theory Possible? by Elder Olson   71   257
History, Criticism, and the Audience,
   by John Gould Fletcher   72   110
The Physiology of Consciousness
   and Its Relation to Poetry,
   by Israel Newman   73   96
The Physiology of Consciousness
   and Its Relation to Poetry,
   by Israel Newman   73   162
Myths, Emotions,
   and the Great Audience,
   by James Parsons   77   52
Postscript, by Reed Whittemore   98   185
Allen Tate: A Poet on Poetry, 1924-1944,
   by Ashley Brown   135   103
Comment by Wallace Fowlie   151   208

SHAPIRO, LEO
ARTICLES
The Medievalism of T. S. Eliot
   [Dante]   56   202

REVIEWS
Richard Crashaw:
   A Study in Baroque Sensibility,
   by Austin Warren   57   160

The Collected Poems of Lew Sarett   59   154
American Renaissance,
   by F. O. Matthiessen   60   334
The Poet in Blue Minor
   and *Passages of Refuge*,
   by Selwyn S. Schwartz   62   173
Control Versus Passion   63   101
   The Bright Plain,
      by Charles Edward Eaton
   This Is My Beloved, by Walter Benton

SHARAT CHANDRA, G. S.
   [See CHANDRA, G. S. SHARAT]

SHARE, DON
POEMS
For Laura   164   258

SHARMAN, LYON
POEMS
Designs in Chinese Color   10   177
   The City
   Cloud-Loved
   Magicians and the Gods
   A Swallow
   Fish
   Porcelains

BOOKS REVIEWED
The Sea-Wall   27   282

SHARP, CECIL J.
BOOKS REVIEWED
English Folk Songs
   from the Southern Appalachians
   (Ed. by Maud Karpeles)   83   37

ARTICLES ABOUT
Rev. of *Songs of the Cattle Trail*
   and Cow Camp,
   by John A. Lomax   16   273

SHARP, DAVID JOSHUA
POEMS
Voyage Off and Out   129   317
Self-Definitions   131   130
Transformations
I Will Take Me Away
Casting Off   132   22

SHATTUCK, KATHARINE
POEMS
Jungle Piece   53   23

SHATTUCK, ROGER
POEMS
Rue Durock   74   317
Palimpsest   138   320
Street Scene

BOOKS REVIEWED
Selected Writings
  of Guillaume Apollinaire (Tr.)   77   162
Half Tame   107   258
Selected Works of Alfred Jarry
  (Ed. with Simon Watson Taylor)   107   267
Selected Works of Alfred Jarry
  (Ed. and tr.
  with Simon Watson Taylor)   111   124

SHAW, ANGELA
POEMS
Miscarriage   165   316
Crepuscule

SHAW, CARLETON FORD
POEMS
"Lost at Sea"   42   77
Prelude to War   59   28
Enemy

SHAW, DOROTHY STOTT
POEMS
Silversmith   36   256

SHAW, ELIZABETH
  [ELIZABETH SHAW
  MONTGOMERY]
POEMS
Against the Barren Years   33   81

SHAW, FRANCES
POEMS
Who Loves the Rain   3   202
The Child's Quest
Cologne Cathedral
Skeletons
Star Thought
Little Pagan Rain Song
The Ragpicker   6   166
The Beckoning Moon
The City Lights from a Skyscraper
The Harp of the Wind
The Organ Angels
Silent Ones
Three Voices
The Birds of God   10   79
The Dream Gift
Little Lonesome Soul
Grandmother   13   312
World Lullaby
Unfailing   17   254
Rain
Tapestry   21   302
Good Friday Song
Contentment
Renewal
Soldier's Night

Autumn Road-Song   23   10
Sailor's Polka   26   70
The Whisper
Rain
The Black Cat
In Winchilsea Churchyard
The Velvet Cloak
For a Hymn-Tune
By My Fire   29   14
  Plymouth Hoe in the Rain
  I Taught Three Babes
  The Garden of No-Delight
  The Trick
To Death   50   138
To an Architect   51   146

ARTICLES
Correspondence:
  A Tribute to Mr. Michelson
  [Poem]   13   107

REVIEWS
Carducci: A Selection of His Poems,
  by G. L. Bickersteth   4   198

BOOKS REVIEWED
Songs of a Baby's Day   10   216
Songs of a Baby's Day   33   164
Who Loves the Rain and Other Poems   63   351

SHAW, HOWARD VAN DOREN
ARTICLES ABOUT
Obituary   28   232

SHAW, LOUIS AGASSIZ, II
  [See SECOND, LOUIS, pseud.]

SHAW, ROBERT B.
POEMS
Aubade, Inside and Out   115   244
Burning Abortive Poems
Janus   117   227
Not Answering Letters
There
Another Day   119   339
Tagalong
Grass Widows
In the Attic   122   138
Heat Wave
Jack O'Lantern
Birth of a Critical Spirit   124   135
Climb and Cloudburst
Simile
A Man and His Watch   128   207
Renovations
Watching the Street
Partial Draft   135   19
Moss

Early Natural History   138   278
Chronometrics   142   215
Things We Will Never Know   145   278
Family Album
Narcissus
Echo
Safe Harbor   148   218
Spring's Awakening   150   1
To His Pulse   151   155
The Bookmark   155   395
Still Life: Belt on Bureau
Shut In
Last Days in Camden   159   325
A Pair of Bookends   161   211
Florilegium
Halfway   162   346
Man with Metal Detector   164   276
Proscenium Masks
The Porch Swing
First Bird
Another Orpheus   167   282
A Paper Cut   169   271
An Exhumation

REVIEWS
Two Old Pros   115   277
   The Collected Poems of Babette Deutsch
   Selected Letters of E. E. Cummings
      (Ed. by F. W. Dupee
      and George Stade)
Both Sides of the Water   117   108˙
   Sandgrains on a Tray,
      by Alan Brownjohn
   The Night of Stones,
      by George Macbeth
   Requiem and Celebration,
      by John Ormond
   Door into the Dark,
      by Seamus Heaney
   Findings, by Wendell Berry
   A Bed by the Sea, by Arthur Gregor
   A Lesson from the Cyclops,
      by Raphael Rudnik
   Collected and New Poems: 1924-1963,
      by Mark Van Doren
Poets in Midstream   118   228
   Poems 1934-1969, by David Ignatow
   Pretending To Be Asleep,
      by Peter Davison
   The Eye-Beaters, Blood, Victory,
      Madness, Buckhead and Mercy,
      by James Dickey
   Malcolm Mooney's Land,
      by W. S. Graham
   Broken Laws, by Daniel Hoffman
   Earth Walk: New and Selected Poems,
      by William Meredith
As He Is   118   349

A Reader's Guide to W. H. Auden,
   by John Fuller
A Certain World: A Commonplace Book,
   by W. H. Auden
The Swimmers and Other Selected Poems,
   by Allen Tate   119   222
The Long and the Short of It   119   342
   There Are Men Too Gentle
      To Live Among Wolves,
      by James Kavanaugh
   Treasury Holiday,
      by William Harmon
   Country of the Minotaur,
      by Brewster Ghiselin
   Skin Diving in the Virgins
      and Other Poems,
      by John Malcolm Brinnin
   The Whispering Roots and Other Poems,
      by C. Day-Lewis
   Poems from an Island,
      by Michael Shayer
   When Thy King Is a Boy,
      by Ed Roberson
   Some Deaths in the Delta,
      by Rosellen Brown
   Articles, by Andrew Hoyem
   Assays of Bias, by Arthur Freeman
   Dismantling the Silence,
      by Charles Simic
   Findings, by Richard Howard
   Selected Poems,
      by Sándor Weöres
      and Ferenc Juhász
The Trouble with Francis
   (An Autobiography),
   by Robert Francis   121   102
Straw for the Fire: From the Notebooks
   of Theodore Roethke, 1943-63
   (Ed. by David Wagoner)   121   341
No Strokes of Lightning   122   344
   Epistle to a Godson and Other Poems,
      by W. H. Auden
   Lugging Vegetables to Nantucket,
      by Peter Klappert
   Mysteries of the Horizon,
      by Lawrence Raab
   The View from the Peacock's Tail,
      by M. L. Rosenthal
   The Blue Cat, by F. D. Reeve
   The Blue Garden, by Barbara Howes
   In the Terrified Radiance,
      by Stanley Burnshaw
   Collected Poems: 1951-1971,
      by A. R. Ammons   123   109
   Selected Poems and Montreal,
      by John Glassco   126   50
   The Hidden Waterfall,
      by Marya Zaturenska   126   100
   Godine's Chapbooks   126   352

Letters for the New England Dead,
  by Mary Baron
Sunbelly, by Kenneth Fields
To the Air, by Thom Gunn
The Head of the Bed,
  by John Hollander
Angle of Geese and Other Poems,
  by N. Scott Momaday
High Notes and Low   129   233
  Collected Poems 1951-1975,
    by Charles Causley
  Turns, by John Matthias
  The Life Beside This One,
    by John N. Morris
  North, by Seamus Heaney
Collected Poems, 1936-1976,
  by Robert Francis
  [Robert Frost]   131   106
Quartet   139   171
  Caviare at the Funeral,
    by Louis Simpson
  The Cheer, by William Meredith
  Night Blooming Cactus,
    by Robert Watson
  Selected Poems, by Mark Strand
Fireflies and Other Animals   141   170
  What Manner of Beast,
    by Donald Finkel
  Work and Love, by Stephen Dunn
  Scenes from Another Life,
    by J. D. McClatchy
  The Ruined Motel,
    by Reginald Gibbons
  Gardens of the World,
    by Radcliffe Squires
  The Rainbow Grocery and
    The Sacrifice Consenting,
    by William Dickey
  Antarctic Traveller, by Katha Pollitt
  Hundreds of Fireflies,
    by Brad Leithauser
Brief Reviews   148   36
  The Long Approach,
    by Maxine Kumin
  Leaning Forward, by Grace Paley
  A Fraction of Darkness,
    by Linda Pastan
  Saints & Strangers,
    by Andrew Hudgins
  The Triumph of Achilles,
    by Louise Glück
  Alternate Means of Transport,
    by Cynthia Macdonald
  Orrery, by Richard Kenney
  The New World: An Epic Poem,
    by Frederick Turner
Brief Reviews   149   94
  Blue Juniata: A Life,
    by Malcolm Cowley

Selected Poems: 1935-1985,
  by James Laughlin
The Selected Poetry of Hayden Carruth
New and Collected Poems: 1970-1985,
  by David Ignatow
Relations: Selected Poems, 1950-1985,
  by Philip Booth
Personal Accounts:
  New & Selected Poems, 1966-1986,
    by Robert Phillips
Collected Poems: 1917-1982,
  by Archibald MacLeish
  [Ezra Pound, Robert Frost]
Short Reviews   150   226
  Imperfect Love, by Miller Williams
  Unending Blues, by Charles Simic
  Ultramarine, by Raymond Carver
  The Laws of Ice, by Reynolds Price
  Foreseeable Futures,
    by William Matthews
  Dust Light, Leaves,
    by Christopher Buckley
  Cemetery Nights,
    by Stephen Dobyns
  Glassworks, by David Wojahn
Short Reviews   152   35
  New and Selected Poems,
    by Marvin Bell
  Collected Poems, 1957-1982 and *Sabbaths*,
    by Wendell Berry
  Selected Shorter Poems,
    by Donald Finkel
  The Sisters: New and Selected Poems,
    by Josephine Jacobsen
  Selected Poems, 1956-1986,
    by Anne Stevenson
  From Princeton One Autumn Afternoon:
    Collected Poems of Theodore Weiss,
    1950-1986
  Selected Poems of Jay Wright
Short Reviews   154   283
  Desperate Characters,
    by Nicholas Christopher
  The Intelligence of Clouds,
    by Stanley Moss
  Blossoms and Bones:
    On the Life and Work
    of Georgia O'Keeffe,
    by Christopher Buckley
  Frameless Windows, Squares of Light,
    by Cathy Song
  A Guide to Forgetting,
    by Jeffrey Skinner
  Shores and Headlands,
    by Emily Grosholz
Short Reviews   156   158
  The Folded Heart,
    by Michael Collier
  Pass It On, by Rachel Hadas

Blues If You Want,
  by William Matthews
The Daylight Moon, by Les A. Murray
Time's Power: Poems 1985-1988,
  by Adrienne Rich
Collected Poems: 1937-1971,
  by John Berryman
  (Ed. by Charles Thornbury)
Rereading Randall Jarrell   158   100
  Randall Jarrell: A Literary Life,
    William H. Pritchard
  Selected Poems,
    by Randall Jarrell
    (Ed. by William H. Pritchard)
  [Robert Lowell]
A Howard Nemerov Reader   159   346
Elizabeth Bishop and the Critics   161   34
  Elizabeth Bishop:
    The Biography of a Poetry,
    by Lorrie Goldensohn
  Elizabeth Bishop: Questions of Mastery,
    by Bonnie Costello
  [Robert Lowell]
Seers and Skeptics   163   39
  Late Fire, Late Snow:
    New and Uncollected Poems,
    by Robert Francis
  Dark Horses, by X. J. Kennedy
  The World Book,
    by Steven Cramer
  Sudden Harbor,
    by Richard Foerster
From A to Y   164   97
  Garbage, by A. R. Ammons
  Mirrors of Astonishment,
    by Rachel Hadas
  Stained Glass, by Rosanna Warren
  The Fire in All Things,
    by Stephen Yenser
High Reachers   165   158
  Earthly Measures,
    by Edward Hirsch
  A Silence Opens, by Amy Clampitt
  New and Collected Poems, 1952-1992,
    by Geoffrey Hill
Spectrum   166   104
  For That Day Only,
    by Grace Schulman
  Green Notebook, Winter Road,
    by Jane Cooper
  Sunday Skaters, by Mary Jo Salter
  The Color Wheel,
    by Timothy Steele
Juvenilia: Poems, 1922-1928,
  by W. H. Auden
  (Ed. by Katherine Bucknell)
  [Thomas Hardy]   166   226
A Scattering of Salts,
  by James Merrill   166   354

Collected Poems, Prose & Plays,
  by Robert Frost
  (Ed. by Richard Poirier and
  Mark Richardson)
  [Edward Connery Lathem]   168   232

BOOKS REVIEWED
  Comforting the Wilderness   134   226
  The Wonder of Seeing Double   153   229
  The Post Office Murals Restored   167   223

SHAW, THEODORE L.
  BOOKS REVIEWED
    Precious Rubbish   92   121

SHAYER, MICHAEL
  BOOKS REVIEWED
    Poems from an Island   119   342

SHECK, LAURIE
  POEMS
    The Deer   134   83
    Love Poem
    Untitled   140   131
    Undressing
    The Soul Revisiting the Body   144   337

  BOOKS REVIEWED
    Io at Night   158   41

SHECTMAN, ROBIN
  POEMS
    Venus, or Maybe Mercury   168   17

SHEEHAN, DONALD
  REVIEWS
    Alone with America:
    Essays on the Art of Poetry
    in the United States Since 1950,
    by Richard Howard   117   258

SHELLEY, MELVIN G(EER)
  POEMS
    Blond Cat   52   205
    Pierrot   55   308

SHELLEY, PERCY BYSSHE
  BOOKS REVIEWED
    The Letters of...
    (Ed. by Roger Ingpen)   8   204

  ARTICLES ABOUT
    Shelley, by Harriet Monroe   20   206
    Poetic Parallels, by Harriet Monroe   35   328
    Rev. of *Shelley,*
      by Newman Ivey White   57   386
    Correspondence from William Van
      O'Connor: Keats-Shelley Memorials   84   366

SHELLEY, ROBERT
POEMS
   Harvest   79   283

SHELLY, PERCY V. D.
BOOKS REVIEWED
   The Living Chaucer   59   226

SHELTON, RICHARD
POEMS
   Rendezvous   115   395
   Saturday Night at the Elks' Club
   October
   The White Hotel
   Report of the Unsatisfied Lover
   The Fourteenth Anniversary   121   90
   The Little Dogs   124   87
   Survival   126   323
   How To Amuse a Stone 134   262
   The Ship in a Bottle
   Point of View

BOOKS REVIEWED
   The Tattooed Desert   120   235
   Of All the Dirty Words 122   237
   You Can't Have Everything 132   31
   The Bus to Veracruz   135   348

SHEPARD, ESTHER
BOOKS REVIEWED
   The Cowherd and the Sky Maiden 76   357

SHEPARD, ODELL
POEMS
   A Nun   9   292

SHEPARD, ROY
POEMS
   Inside the Concord Museum 167   338

SHEPHERD, ERIC
BOOKS REVIEWED
   Pilgrimage   11   108

SHEPHERD, GAIL
POEMS
   For a Lost Child   145   336

SHEPHERD, HARRIS B.
POEMS
   Dicky   34   198

SHEPHERD, REGINALD
POEMS
   Kindertotenlieder   161   79
   The Friend
   A Brief Manual for Swimmers 164   266
   Phenomenology

SHERBO, ARTHUR
BOOKS REVIEWED
   Christopher Smart,
     Scholar of the University 115   196

SHERBY, J. M.
POEMS
   Escape to Sonora   42   22
   Balcony in Mexico
   Emilio a Beggar
   Daughter of Nagal
   To Mountain Peons

SHERMAN, FRANK DEMPSTER
BOOKS REVIEWED
   The Poems of...
     (Ed. by Clinton Scollard) 12   109

SHERMAN, G(EORGE) W(ITTER)
POEMS
   Epoch   70   15
   From *The Chemists*   73   75
   Relic from Okinawa
   Ubi Sunt
   Spring of the Embargo 79   142
   "The Spec"

SHERMAN, SUSAN
POEMS
   The Palace of the Lowest Moon 105   85

SHERRARD, PHILIP
TRANSLATIONS
   Poems by George Seferis
     (With Edmund Keeley) 105   44
   Poems by C. P. Cavafy
     (With Edmund Keeley) 120   266

BOOKS REVIEWED
   Six Poets of Modern Greece
     (Tr. with Edmund Keeley) 101   283
   Collected Poems 1924-1955,
     by George Seferis
     (Tr. with Edmund Keeley) 114   113
   Angelos Sikelianos: Selected Poems
     (Tr. with Edmund Keeley) 137   220

SHERRY, LAURA
POEMS
   A Town on the River   17   6
   My Town
   On Our Farm
   The Hunter
   A Woodsman
   Jean Joseph Rolette
   Louis des Chiens
   Bohemian Town
   Ridge People   20   293
   My Country

A Native
Nothin'—Somethin'
Howard Bently
Grand-Dad's Bluff
In Mist
Light Magic
Late Autumn in the Hills
The Season
Old Prairie du Chien   25   59
In Old Day Eighteen-Thirty
Courting in Campbell's Coulee
Jean Lessar's Wife
I'm Good Cath'lic
Me and My Man
Little Rosie of the Picadee
Get Fiddle and Bow

REVIEWS
Poems, by Haniel Long   18   101
Plays for Merry Andrews,
    by Alfred Kreymborg   18   218
Pageantry and Rhetoric   19   51
Rip Van Winkle,
    by Percy Mackaye
Two Mothers
    (Eight Hundred Rubles
    and Agrippina),
    by John G. Neihardt
Pawns; Mary Stuart; and Poems,
    by John Drinkwater   19   94
Breakers and Granite,
    by John Gould Fletcher   19   155

BOOKS REVIEWED
Old Prairie du Chien   40   348

SHERRY, PEARL (ANDELSON)
POEMS
From a Bay-Window   19   133
Autumn Rain
Steeples
Portrait of an Old Lady
To a Dead Love
To Felix
April Snow
Solace
Beach Song
Song on Death
Out of a Cavalcade of Dust
Philosophic Dialogue   21   136
Worker in Marble
Chapter
Thin Refuge
Out of a Weariness
A Trivial Day in Early Autumn
Sea-Girl
Slow Songs   28   128
My Mind
Song ("The sky is yellow...")

Boat Song
The Lovers
Motoring
Abstract Moment
Identity
Observations   33   82
Enlarged Dominion
Late-Summer Day
Waiting
Sea-Walk
The Lion
Alligator
Musical Afternoon
In the Dance
Messiah
To a Child of Nine Months
Progression
Finality   44   252
An Instant in Time
The Walk
The Weight of Time   55   304
Skaters
Migration and Return
The Moon at Full
Fermi Lab: Sisyphus of Quarks   165   143

REVIEWS
Curtains, by Hazel Hall   19   100
Heavens and Earth,
    by Stephen Vincent Benét   19   340
We, the Musk Chasers,
    by Loureine Aber   20   96
The Golden Darkness
    and In Gossamer Grey,
    by Oscar Williams   20   157
Dreams Out of Darkness,
    by Jean Starr Untermeyer   20   220
Poems: Second Series,
    by J. C. Squire   20   274
The Magpie's Shadow,
    by Yvor Winters   20   342
Igdrasil, by Royall Snow   21   45
The Shepherd,
    by Edmund Blunden   21   104
Verse, by Adelaide Crapsey   21   333
The Wheel in Midsummer,
    by Janet Lewis   32   222
Blue Harvest, by Frances M. Frost   39   161
Skipping Along Alone,
    by Winifred Welles   40   51

BOOKS REVIEWED
Fringe   23   218

ARTICLES ABOUT
A Symposium
    on Marianne Moore,
    by Harriet Monroe   19   208

SHERWIN, JUDITH (JOHNSON)
POEMS
Watersong   112   94
The Grasses   118   20
The Spoilers and the Spoils   132   10

BOOKS REVIEWED
Uranium Poems   115   47
Impossible Buildings   124   103

SHERWOOD, CHARLES L.
POEMS
My Ten Buckeyes   13   74

SHETLEY, VERNON
REVIEWS
A Babel of Tongues   134   226
    A Full Heart, by Edward Field
    Kicking the Leaves, by Donald Hall
    Room for Error, by Charles Martin
    Comforting the Wilderness,
        by Robert Shaw
    Bad Boats, by Laura Jensen
    Lateness: A Book of Poems,
        by David Shapiro
Take But Degree Away   137   297
    The Venetian Vespers,
        by Anthony Hecht
    Mortal Acts, Mortal Words,
        by Galway Kinnell
    The Morning of the Poem,
        by James Schuyler
    Scripts for the Pageant,
        by James Merrill
    Shadow Train,
        by John Ashbery
    [George Meredith]   140   236
This World and the Other   143   101
    From the First Nine: Poems 1946-1976
        and The Changing Light at Sandover,
        by James Merrill
    James Merrill: Essays in Criticism
        (Ed. by David Lehman
        and Charles Berger)
Brief Reviews   146   38
    Talking Soft Dutch,
        by Linda McCarriston
    Jacklight, by Louise Erdrich
    The Swimmer, by Susan Ludvigson
    Deep Within the Ravine,
        by Philip Schultz
    Emily's Bread,
        by Sandra M. Gilbert
    The Idiot Princess of the Last Dynasty,
        by Peter Klappert
Short Reviews   147   291
    Singing, by Dennis Schmitz
    Other Lives, by Christopher Buckley
    The Near World, by Carl Dennis

    No Heaven, by David St. John
    Facing Nature, by John Updike
    New Selected Poems,
        by Howard Moss
    Late Settings, by James Merrill
Short Reviews   152   98
    The Owl of Minerva,
        by James Laughlin
    [Ezra Pound]
    Under the Vulture-Tree,
        by David Bottoms
    The West Door, by Alfred Corn
    Skating with Heather Grace,
        by Thomas Lynch
    The Arkansas Testament,
        by Derek Walcott
    [James Merrill]
    An Oregon Message,
        by William Stafford
    April Galleons, by John Ashbery

SHIDELER, ROSS
POEMS
The Audience   127   36

SHIH, HU
[See HU SHIH]

SHIH, SU
[See SU SHIH]

SHIH, YEH
[See YEH SHIH]

SHIH-AN, LIU
[See LIU SHIH-AN]

SHIH SHUN LIU
BOOKS REVIEWED
One Hundred and One
    Chinese Poems (Tr.)   114   196

SHILLITO, EDWARD
BOOKS REVIEWED
The Omega and Other Poems   15   169

SHIMAZAKI, TOSON
POEMS
First Love   88   73
By the Ancient Castle at Komoro
    (Tr. by Satoru Satu
    and Constance Urdang)

SHIMONI, DAVID
POEMS
The Flower Pot   92   206
Gleanings
And It Happens That Spirit
    (Tr. by Ruth Finer Mintz)

SHINN, SHARON
POEMS
   Student Union   137   334

SHIPLEY, JOSEPH T.
BOOKS REVIEWED
   Dictionary of World Literature (Ed.)   83   35

SHIRLEY, ALEDA
POEMS
   The Feel of Not To Feel It   142   264
   One of a Number of Good Intentions
   Tertium Quid   145   283
   The Wandering Year   147   341
   Finding the Room   148   152
   Sunset Grand Couturier
   L'Ivresse des Grandes Profondeurs
   Aubade ("Though the room's...")   149   63
   Cant   150   191
   The Garden at Giverny
   The Glass Lotus   152   338
   The Last Dusk of August

BOOKS REVIEWED
   Chinese Architecture   150   162

SHLONSKY, AVRAHAM
POEMS
   Yizrael   92   221
   From *Toil*
   Jerusalem Is a Hill City
     (Tr. by Ruth Finer Mintz)

SHNEUR, ZALMAN
POEMS
   The Fruited Month   92   211
   Poppies
     (Tr. by Ruth Finer Mintz)

ARTICLES ABOUT
   [Note]   94   206

SHOMER, ENID
POEMS
   Wild Plum   150   28
   For Those Who Are No Longer Young   152   271
   Villa Maria
   Romantic, at Horseshoe Key   156   137
   The Last Father Poem
   Reading a Violent Love Poem
     to the Deaf   157   214
   The Suit Too Small, the Words   158   3
   Pope Joan   159   340
   In the Viennese Style   161   284
   Elegy and Rant for My Father   162   30
   Passive Resistance   166   25
   Black Drum   166   136
   Letter Home from Brooklyn   170   1

ARTICLES ABOUT
   [Note on misprint]   160   174

SHONAGON, SEI
[Pseud. of KIYOWARA
NO NAGIKO]
POEMS
   Who's There?
     (Tr. by Graeme Wilson)   153   298

BOOKS REVIEWED
   The Pillow-Book of...
     (Tr. by Arthur Waley)   88   113

SHORE, JANE
POEMS
   The Princess and the Pea   121   190
   The Sniper as Axis Mundi
   Landing Off Season
   Ararat
   November
   Landscape with Trees   123   143
   The Sleeper Watched:
     Three Studies
   The Anniversary
   A Letter Sent to Summer
   The Glass Paperweight   125   206
   Animals That Die in Our Houses
   An Astronomer's Journal
   This World Without Miracles   126   326
   Literature   137   321
   Tender Acre
   Sleeping Beauty
   Young Woman
     on the Flying Trapeze

BOOKS REVIEWED
   Eye Level   133   169
   The Minute Hand   151   419

SHOREY, PAUL
ARTICLES ABOUT
   Dr. Chubb on the Platform,
     by Harriet Monroe   16   205

SHORT, GARY
POEMS
   Breath   168   94
   I Lay My Brother Down

SHORT, JOHN
POEMS
   Memorabilia   71   75

SHORT, ROBERT
BOOKS REVIEWED
   Thirteen Moons   144   297

SHORTER, CLEMENT
BOOKS REVIEWED
The Complete Works of Emily Brontë,
Vol. I—Poetry
(Ed. with W. Robertson Nicoll)　9　259

SHRADER, STEPHEN
BOOKS REVIEWED
Leaving by the Closet Door　120　115

SHREIBER, DAVID
POEMS
Marching to Georgia　48　70

SHSCHIPACHEV, STEPAN
POEMS
"Here Sorrow Had No Limit"　70　249
Duel
(Tr. by Babette Deutsch)

SHUEY, MARY WILLIS
POEMS
Quilts　12　313

SHULENBERGER, ARVID
POEMS
Incident　73　200
Device
Night Fighter Kill
Museum　74　149
Recurrent Figure
Evening Walk
Airmen and Scholars
Art and the Lady

REVIEWS
After Every Green Thing,
by Dannie Abse　75　102
The Divine Pilgrim and *Skylight One,*
by Conrad Aiken　76　162
The White Bird, by Ann Stanford　76　365
Theory of Silence, by William Pillin
Guide to the Ruins,
by Howard Nemerov

SHULMAN, SUSIE
POEMS
The Going-Part　142　330
An Everyday Integrity

SHUMAN, MARIAN
POEMS
Sonnet ("If we have anything...")　45　77
The Sage　46　143

SHUMWAY, MARY
BOOKS REVIEWED
Song of the Archer　105　410

SHU TING
POEMS
Missing　149　253
To the Oak
(Tr. by Carolyn Kizer,
with Y. H. Zhao)

SHUTTLE, PENELOPE
POEMS
The Knife Knows How　146　201
The Hell-Bender

SIBLEY, GRACE
POEMS
Moments　28　259
Impression
Rebellion

SIDGWICK, J. B.
BOOKS REVIEWED
The Shorter Poems
of Walter Savage Landor (Ed.)　72　336

SIDNEY, [SIR] PHILIP
ARTICLES ABOUT
The Sixteenth to the Twentieth,
by Alfred Kreymborg　12　330
The 16th-Century Lyric
in England: Part II,
by Yvor Winters　53　320
The 16th-Century Lyric
in England: Part III,
by Yvor Winters　54　35

SIEBEL, JULIA
POEMS
At Seventy-Five　107　93

SIEBURTH, RICHARD
REVIEWS
"Ezra Pound Speaking":
Radio Speeches of World War II
(Ed. by Leonard W. Doob)
[Mary de Rachewiltz]　134　292

SIEGEL, ELI
POEMS
With Noble Amount　80　265
The Lord Has Stolen Her Whims　85　155
This Is True

BOOKS REVIEWED
Preface to Nice Deity,
by Martha Baird　89　64
Hot Afternoons Have Been in Montana:
Poems by...　91　266
James and the Children　113　109

ARTICLES ABOUT
   Correspondence from Nat Herz   80   303
   Ghosts and Benedictions,
      by Hugh Kenner   113   109

SIEGEL, PAUL N.
   BOOKS REVIEWED
   Shakespearean Tragedy & the
      Elizabethan Compromise   92   189

SIEGEL, ROBERT
   POEMS
   A Bear   117   371
   A Visit to the Farm   119   319
   Ego
   A Lady Who Lov'd a Swine   124   89
   Bull   130   96
   Them
   Hog Heaven
   TV Documentary
   Knave of Hearts

   REVIEWS
   Emerson's Smile   130   102
      New and Collected Poems, 1917-1976,
         by Archibald MacLeish
      The Fabulous Beasts,
         by Joyce Carol Oates
      Geography of the Near Past,
         by Al Young
      Your Name Is You,
         by Edwin Fussell
      Available Light, by Philip Booth
      [Hyatt Waggoner, Robert Frost]

   BOOKS REVIEWED
   The Beasts & the Elders   124   343
   In a Pig's Eye   140   102

SIEGELBAUM, HAROLD
   POEMS
   The Theft   69   142

SIEGRIST, MARY
   BOOKS REVIEWED
   You That Come After   30   230

SIEVEKING, LANCE
   BOOKS REVIEWED
   Bats in the Belfry   32   114

SIFTON, PAUL F.
   POEMS
   Wolverine Winter   11   190

SIGERSON, DORA
   BOOKS REVIEWED
   The Sad Years   14   219

SIGMUND, JAY G.
   POEMS
   Taxidermist   29   86

   BOOKS REVIEWED
   Drowsy Ones   30   233
   The Ridge Road   44   55

SIGNORELLI-PAPPAS, RITA
   POEMS
   Beautiful Girl Cafe   157   283
   Hunger Artist

SIGURDSSON, OLAFUR JOHANN
   POEMS
   Autumnal Equinox   128   148
   The Lake's Flight
   Old Nightsong
      (Tr. by George Johnston)

SIKELIANOS, ANGHELOS
[ANGELOS SIKELIANUS]
   POEMS
   Sparta   78   154
   The Virgin of Sparta
   The Mother of Dante
   [Αγραφον]
      (Tr. by Kimon Friar)
   Free Dodecanese   120   261
   Supper
      (Tr. by Rae Dalven)

   BOOKS REVIEWED
   Selected Poems
      (Tr. by Edmund Keeley
      and Philip Sherrard)   137   220

   ARTICLES ABOUT
   Contemporary Greek Poetry,
      by Kimon Friar   78   145

SILCOCK, ARNOLD
   BOOKS REVIEWED
   Verse and Worse: A Private Collection (Ed.)   86   118

SILKIN, JON
   POEMS
   White   88   22
   To Michael Riviere,
      for His Second Son, Thomas   91   81
   For a Deaf Girl
   Air that Pricks Earth with Life and Turns   119   249
   Poem ("As each of you sits...")   120   349
   Persisting   123   80

   REVIEWS
   One Foot in Eden,
      by Edwin Muir   88   393

Polarities   130   230
   Laboratories of the Spirit,
     by R. S. Thomas
   Other Exiles,
     by Edward Brathwaite
   Prehistories, by Peter Scupham
   My Brother Gloucester,
     by Michael Schmidt

BOOKS REVIEWED
   The Two Freedoms   94   189
   The Re-Ordering of the Stones   102   330
   Nature with Man   107   410
   Poems Selected and New   109   114
   Flower Poems   110   112
   Amana Grass   120   170
   The Principle of Water   127   159
   The Little Time-Keeper   131   292

ARTICLES ABOUT
   Rev. of *Somewhere*
    Is Such a Kingdom,
     by Geoffrey Hill   128   232

SILL, LOUISE MORGAN
BOOKS REVIEWED
   The Tidings Brought to Mary,
    by Paul Claudel (Tr.)   9   321

SILLARS, ROBERTSON
POEMS
   Didactic Poem   51   247

SILLIMAN, RONALD
POEMS
   He Was a Visitor   113   255

SILLITOE, ALAN
BOOKS REVIEWED
   Love in the Environs of Voronezh 117   204

SILVA, JOSÉ ASUNCION
[See ASUNCION SILVA, JOSÉ]

SILVAY, CHALLISS
POEMS
   White Music   25   200

SILVERMAN, KENNETH
BOOKS REVIEWED
   Colonial American Poetry (Ed.)   113   262

SIMIC, CHARLES
POEMS
   House   115   257
   Explorers
   The Body   118   187
   The Grass

The Pillow
The Flies
Suffering
Green Lampshade   135   129
Furniture Mover
Crepuscular
Henri Rousseau's Bed   147   199
The Immortal   151   156
Back at the Chicken Shack
Evening Walk   156   295
Romantic Landscape   163   7
Tattooed City
Late Arrival
My Friend Someone   170   66
All These Mirrors

BOOKS REVIEWED
   What the Grass Says   113   188
   Somewhere Among Us a Stone
    Is Taking Notes   118   355
   Dismantling the Silence   119   342
   Return to a Place Lit
    by a Glass of Milk   125   295
   Charon's Cosmology   133   100
   Homage to the Lame Wolf,
    by Vasko Popa (Tr.)   136   40
   Classic Ballroom Dances   138   231
   Austerities   143   39
   Unending Blues   150   226
   Selected Poems 1963-1983   159   223
   The Book of Gods and Devils
   A Wedding in Hell   168   33
   Walking the Black Cat: Poems   170   226

SIMMERMAN, JIM
POEMS
   Almost Dancing   145   287
   Finally
   Fetch   146   137
   Lighthouse
   The Gulls
   Moon Go Away,
    I Don't Love You No More   152   314
   Just To Love the Dog
   Kite   154   227
   Distance
   Take a Hike   157   194
   The Glass Park
   The Monastic   170   145

BOOKS REVIEWED
   Once Out of Nature   156   100

SIMMONDS, DOUGLAS
ARTICLES ABOUT
   The Younger Bards,
    by Edward J. O'Brien   6   188

SIMON, CHARLIE MAY
BOOKS REVIEWED
Johnswood
    [John Gould Fletcher]   84   284

SIMON, JOHN
REVIEWS
Traduttore, Traditore or
    The Tradition of Traducing   136   40
A Longing for the Light:
    Selected Poems of Vicente Aleixandre
    (Tr. by Lewis Hyde)
Hours in the Garden
    and Other Poems,
    by Hermann Hesse
    (Tr. by Rika Lesser)
The Storm & Other Poems,
    by Eugenio Montale
    (Tr. by Charles Wright)
The Face Behind the Face,
    by Yevgeny Yevtushenko
    (Tr. by Arthur Boyars
    and Simon Franklin)
Nostalgia for the Present,
    by Andrei Voznesensky
    (Ed. by Vera Dunham
    and Max Hayward)
Easter Vigil & Other Poems,
    by Karol Wojtyla
    (Pope John Paul II)
    (Tr. by Jerzy Peterkiewicz)
Bells in Winter,
    by Czeslaw Milosz
    (Tr. by the author
    and Lillian Vallee)
The Poems of Catullus
    (Tr. by Frederic Raphael
    and Kenneth McLeish)
Poems of Pierre de Ronsard
    (Tr. and ed. by Nicholas Kilmer)
The First Encounter,
    by Andrey Bely
    (Tr. by Gerald Janecek)
Vasko Popa: Collected Poems
    (Tr. by Anne Pennington)
Homage to the Lame Wolf,
    by Vasko Popa
    (Tr. by Charles Simic)
Traduttore, Traditore or
    The Tradition of Traducing, II   137   220
César Vallejo:
    The Complete Posthumous Poetry
    (Tr. by Clayton Eshleman
    and José Rubia Barcia)
Songs of Cifar and the Sweet Sea: Selections
    from "Songs of Cifar, 1967-1977,"
    by Pablo Antonio Cuadra
    (Tr. and ed. by Grace Schulman
    and Ann McCarthy de Zavala)

A World Rich in Anniversaries,
    by Jean Follain
    (Tr. by Mary Feeney
    and William Matthews)
Salamander: Selected Poems
    of Robert Marteau
    (Tr. by Ann Winters)
Bertolt Brecht: Poems 1913-56
    (Ed. by John Willett
    and Ralph L. Mannheim)
The Oresteia of Aeschylus
    (Tr. by Robert Lowell)
Angelos Sikelianos: Selected Poems
    (Tr. by Edmund Keeley
    and Philip Sherrard)
Ritsos in Parentheses
    (Tr. by Edmund Keeley)

SIMON, MAURYA
POEMS
    Return to Dresden, 1945   143   315
    The Way We Are   147   27
    A Door in the Wind
    The Sadness of Rivers   150   2
    The View from Here   153   251
    Post Meridien
    Theme and Variations
    Last Words   161   338
    Maya   164   202
    Taj Mahal
    Russell Market

BOOKS REVIEWED
    The Enchanted Room   150   162
    Days of Awe   156   224

SIMON, ROBERT
ARTICLES ABOUT
    Verse Drama and the Radio,
    by Amy Bonner   58   280

SIMONS, HI
[H. AUSTIN SIMONS]
POEMS
    Incidentals   19   258
    Dust in the Road
    Taps
    The Star
    Portrait of an Old Roué

REVIEWS
    Parts of a World, by Wallace Stevens   61   448

BOOKS REVIEWED
    Orioles and Blackbirds   22   156

SIMPSON, LOUIS
POEMS
    O What Can Ail Thee, Knight at Arms?   149   332

Friends
  The People Next Door   152   63

BOOKS REVIEWED
  Poets of Today II
    (With Norma Farber
    and Robert Pack)   88   329
  A Dream of Governors   96   47
  Riverside Drive   102   269
  At the End of the Open Road   104   104
  Selected Poems   108   269
  Caviare at the Funeral   139   171
  People Live Here:
    Selected Poems, 1949-1983   144   107
  The Best Hour of the Night   145   161
  In the Room We Share   157   96

ARTICLES ABOUT
  Rev. by Michael Schmidt   120   170

SIMPSON, MABEL
  POEMS
    To a Poet   26   254
    Vesper
    The Dew Upon   .   28   307
    Lament
    Passage
    I Saw a Door
    Lend Me Your Wings
    As in Some Dream   31   76
      The Swan
      This Golden Tree
      Now Far
      Pursuit
    In the Hour   37   196
    In Quietness   41   134
      Silent
      Distance Comes
      Here the Page
      Some Day
    To Meet the Rose   44   24
      Now
      Loss
      Sometime to Find
    Slow Clouds   46   198
      The Field Beyond
      Night
      This Life
    The Village in the Moonlight   51   139
    Only Death   55   247

  BOOKS REVIEWED
    Poems   27   334

SIMPSON, R. A.
  POEMS
    Civil War House: England   95   96
    The Tall Grass   169   79

BOOKS REVIEWED
  After the Assassination   115   47

ARTICLES ABOUT
  Rev. of *The Penguin Book*
    of Australian Verse
    (Ed. by John Thompson,
    Kenneth Slessor, and R. G. Howarth)   94   44

SIMPSON, WILLIAM H(ASKELL)
  POEMS
    Maytime   14   81
    In Hopi-Land and Other Lands   15   197
      Ghosts
      Burdens
      Hopi Maiden
      Homesick Song
      Hopi-Tuh
      Dance of the Dust Witches
      Grand Canyon
      The New Day
      The North Woods
      The Fog Ghost
      Shadow Faces
      Deserted
      November
      Pity Not
    Along Old Trails   20   59
      Los Llanos
      Hopi Song of the Desert
      Yucca Is Yellowing
      Bareback
      Rain in the Hills
      Navajo
      Tewa Song
      Desert Night
      Mañana
      Burro Loads
      Landscape
      Trees
      Country Night
      Inarticulate
      So Little You Are
      De Noche
      The Trail Up-Sky
      Campo Santo
    Desert Trails   27   27
      Sun-Down-Shining
      Dias Pasados
      Winds of March
      Grand Canyon
      Telegraph Poles
      Vaquero
      Song of Lo-Mn-Kwa
    New Mexico and Beyond   40   299
      Oraibi—Afterwards
      Santo Domingo Spring Dance
      El Poco Tiempo
      It Was Yesterday

Desert Marvel
Earth Ways—Star Ways

BOOKS REVIEWED
Along Old Trails:
  Poems of New Mexico and Arizona   35   226

SINCLAIR, MAY
BOOKS REVIEWED
The Dark Night   25   99

SINCLAIR, SHAN
POEMS
Sidelong Glances   44   18
  Meglio Tardi Che Mai!
  Return
  Conclusion

SINGER, BURNS
BOOKS REVIEWED
Still and All   91   45
Five Centuries of Polish Poetry
  (With Jerzy Peterkiewicz)   100   104

SINGER, HELEN
POEMS
Old Rome   87   291
Graubunden: Cape Ann
Painting of a Courtesan
  on a Roof, at Venice
The Presence of Their Honor
A Good Man's Dying   94   281
From an Exotic Country
The View at San Thomé
The Brave Names
To the Todas
The Villa
Blast Off
To Stella, Who Would Be 77
The Year of Zhivago
At Higginbotham's Doorway, Madras   102   359
Boom and Bust Beneath the Bo Tree
Of H. J., Asking Directions at Windsor
To Calif., a Concession
The Neighbor Boy Diving
If I Believe My Eyes
The Unkept, Unweeded Garden:
  Animism Undermined
Taking the Dust
Across This Landscape
The Unguarded Rooms   113   231
A Delhi Lawn and Its Dew
Mr. Mohan Pal's Plant
Retread
The Old Salt
In the Ending, the Word Is Not
The Most Distant Future
Those Without Metaphor

SINGH, G.
BOOKS REVIEWED
Leopardi and the Theory
  of Poetry   107   333

SINGH, HARBANS
TRANSLATIONS
Poem by Amrita Pritam   93   226

SINGLETON, ALICE [Pseud.]
POEMS
Toy Balloons   28   245

SINGLETON, ANNE [Pseud.]
POEMS
Intimacies   31   192
  For My Mother
  Earth-Born
  For the Hour After Love
  I Shall Not Call
  Lift Up Your Heart
Countermand   35   304
  Unshadowed Pool
  Unicorns at Sunrise
  Love That Is Water
  Dead Star
  November Burning

SINISGALLI, LEONARDO
ARTICLES ABOUT
Contemporary Italian Poetry,
  by Edward Williamson   79   233

SINK, SUSAN
POEMS
Coda: Summer on the Dig   160   189

SINOPOULOS, TAKIS
POEMS
Magda   105   36
  Sophia Etc.
  Sight and Vision
  Ioanna's Invitation
  One of Constantine's Nights
  The Beheading
    (Tr. by Edmund Keeley
    and George Savidis)

ARTICLES ABOUT
A Note on Takis Sinopoulos,
  by George Savidis   105   43
Post-War Greek Poets,
  by Kimon Friar   139   99

SIRR, PETER
POEMS
Arrivals   167   9

SISSMAN, L. E.
BOOKS REVIEWED
Scattered Returns   116   40
Hello Darkness: The Collected Poems of...
   (Ed. by Peter Davison)   133   100

ARTICLES ABOUT
Bringing Poems to Medical School
   Teaching: A Memoir,
   by Robert Coles   152   294

SISSON, C. H.
POEMS
Et in Arcadia Ego   158   340
The Wind

BOOKS REVIEWED
The London Zoo   100   191

SISSON, JONATHAN
POEMS
The Crows of St. Thomas   139   139

SITWELL, EDITH
POEMS
Elegy for Dylan Thomas   87   63

ARTICLES
Correspondence   86   62
Roy Campbell   92   42

BOOKS REVIEWED
Wheels, 1919 (Tourth Cycle) (Ed.) 16   108
Clowns' Houses   17   161
Bucolic Comedies   23   281
The Sleeping Beauty   29   41
Troy Park
Poetry and Criticism
Rustic Elegies   31   224
Gold Coast Customs and Other Poems 36   101
The Collected Poems of...   37   339
Selected Poems, with an Essay
   on Her Own Poetry   50   161
Street Songs   61   684
The Song of the Cold   74   239
A Poet's Notebook   77   292
Poor Men's Music   79   106
The Collected Poems of...   87   48
The Atlantic Book of British
   and American Poetry (Ed.)   95   182
Swinburne: A Selection (Ed.) 100   324

ARTICLES ABOUT
The Editor in England,
   by Harriet Monroe   23   32
A Word from London,
   by Benjamin Gilbert Brooks   28   40

London Note,
   by Benjamin Gilbert Brooks   35   214
Mr. MacNeice and Miss Sitwell,
   by Richard Crowder   63   218
Rev. of *New Poems: 1943*
   (Ed. by Oscar Williams)   64   86
The "Vita Nuova" of Baroque Art in the
   Recent Poetry of Edith Sitwell,
   by Horace Gregory   66   148
London Letter,
   by Waldemar Hansen   73   280
Poetry on Records,
   by Harry T. Moore   79   353
Rev. of *Union Street*,
   by Charles Causley   95   248
Rev. of *Four Poets on Poetry:*
   Essays by R. P. Blackmur, Yvor Winters,
   Marianne Moore, and Mark Van Doren
   (Ed. by Don Cameron Allen) 96   382

SITWELL, OSBERT
POEMS
Mrs. Freudenthal Consults
   the Witch of Endor   17   130
Dead Man's Wood
Maxixe   20   126

BOOKS REVIEWED
Argonaut and Juggernaut   17   161
Out of the Flame   28   274

SITWELL, SACHEVERELL
BOOKS REVIEWED
The People's Palace   17   161
The Hundred and One Harlequins 24   331
The Thirteenth Caesar   28   274
The Cyder Feast and Other Poems 31   347
Doctor Donne and Gargantua:
   The First Six Cantos   38   162
Selected Poems   74   304

ARTICLES ABOUT
A Word from London,
   by Benjamin Gilbert Brooks   28   40
Poems and Pictures,
   by Morton Dauwen Zabel   34   217
Form in Modern Poetry,
   by D. S. Savage   65   30
Rococo: The Poetry
   of Sacheverell Sitwell,
   by Joseph Warren Beach   74   217

SIUE TAO-HENG
POEMS
("Westward, the cascade dissolves...")
   (Tr. by George Margulies
   and Willard R. Trask)   46   7

SJÖBERG, LEIF
BOOKS REVIEWED
Markings,
   by Dag Hammarskjöld
   (Tr. with W. H. Auden)   106   356

SKALING, WILLIAM H.
ARTICLES
Correspondence: That Cowboy Poet
   [Charles Badger Clark]   11   56

SKAVLAN, MARGARET
POEMS
Up North   36   77
   A Corner on Eggs
   Skagway Was a Wolf
   A Toast

SKEEN, RUTH LOOMIS
POEMS
March   15   301

SKELTON, JOHN
BOOKS REVIEWED
John Skelton, A Selection from His Poems
   (Ed. by Vivian De Sola Pinto)   82   95

SKELTON, ROBIN
POEMS
Three Poems for Ireland   102   231
   The Queens
   Parnell, Eighteen-Ninety
   Spring Race Meeting
Two Memorials   104   31
   A Chain of Daisies
   Big Field
The Voices   110   33
Toad   115   162
Spider
Fly
Landmarks   131   148
The Short Cut   137   213
Triptych

REVIEWS
Self Portrait; Come Dance with Kitty Stobling,
   and Other Poems; and *Collected Poems,*
   by Patrick Kavanagh   106   234
Canadian Chronicle   109   53
   For the Record, by Luella Booth
   A Breakfast for Barbarians,
      by Gwendolyn MacEwen
   Ten Elephants on Yonge Street,
      by Raymond Souster
   Wrestle with an Angel,
      by R. G. Everson
   A Divided Voice,
      by Francis Sparshott

The Wooden Horse, by Daryl Hine
Five Poets and Their Stances   114   397
   New Poems, by Roy Fuller
   King Log, by Geoffrey Hill
   Selected Poems, by Patric Dickinson
   Night-Crossing, by Derek Mahon
   Stephen's Green Revisited,
      by Richard Weber
Recent Canadian Poetry   144   297
   The Contemporary Canadian
      Poem Anthology
      (Ed. by George Bowering)
   Murder in the Dark,
      by Margaret Atwood
   Singing the Stars,
      by Toby MacLennan
   Beyond Labels, by Robert Zend
   Collected Poems,
      by Raymond Souster
   I Might Not Tell Everybody This,
      by Alden Nowlan
   The Way Home and *Digging In,*
      by Elizabeth Brewster
   The Secret Life of Railroaders,
      by Jim McLean
   Going for Coffee,
      by Tom Wayman
   The Men They Were,
      by Howard White
   Beyond Here, by Jim Green
   Aggressive Transport,
      by Brian Fawcett
   Good Housekeeping,
      by David Walter-Toews
   Feet in the Earth,
      by Rosemary Hollingshead
   Journal of Susanna Moodie,
      by Margaret Atwood
   The Collected Works of Billy the Kid,
      by Michael Ondaatje
   The Overlanders,
      by Florence McNeil
   What Place Is This,
      by Rosalind McPhee
   Kissing the Body of My Lord,
      by Doug Beardsley
   To Kill a White Dog,
      by John B. Lee
   Thirteen Moons, by Robert Short
   The Mossback Canon,
      by E. F. Dyck
   The Black Bird, by David Halliday
   As Close As We Came,
      by Barry Callaghan
   Selected Poems 1972-1982,
      by Robert Bringhurst
   A Steady Hand, by Mike Doyle
   Giving Back Diamonds,
      by Marilyn Bowering

God Loves Us Like
   Earthworms Love Wood,
    by Allan Safarik
No Birds or Flowers,
   by Diane Keating
Songs That Untune the Sky,
   by Gloria Alvernaz Mulcahy
False Shuffles,
   by Jane Urquhart
Matinee Light, by Diana Hartog
Flying Dutchman,
   by James Harrison
Night Letters, by Bill Furey
Something Still Hard to Find,
   by Douglas LePan
Poems 1940-1966,
   by Margaret Avison
A Wild Peculiar Joy,
   by Irving Layton
Half a Life's Story, by Robert Sward
The Rain Falls Like Rain,
   by David Helwig
The Vision Tree:
   The Selected Poems of Phyllis Webb
The Inner Ear
   (Ed. by Gary Geddes)
Writing Right
   (Ed. by Douglas Barbour
   and Marni L. Stanley)
New Oxford Book
   of Canadian Verse in English
   (Ed. by Margaret Atwood)

BOOKS REVIEWED
  The Dark Window   102   193
  An Irish Gathering   105   404
  Five Poets of the Pacific Northwest (Ed.)
   [Kenneth Hanson, Richard Hugo,
   Carolyn Kizer, William Stafford,
   David Wagoner]   111   258
  Selected Poems   114   335
  An Irish Album   119   356
  The Collected Shorter Poems 1947-1977   140   170
  Samhain   168   107

SKILLMAN, JUDITH
POEMS
  The Librarian Decides on Cryonics   148   258
  Written on Learning of Arrhythmia in the
   Unborn Child   148   338
  The Worship of the Visible Spectrum

SKILLMAN, MAUDE
POEMS
  The Hussy   27   187

SKINNER, CONSTANCE LINDSAY
POEMS
  Songs of the Coast-Dwellers   5   1

The Chief's Prayer
   After the Salmon Catch
Song of the Search
Song of the Conqueror of Women
Song of the Full Catch
The Change-Song
Song of the Little Son
Song of Whip-Plaiting
Song of the Young Mother
  No Answer Is Given
Summer Dawn   7   169
Kan-Il-Lak the Singer
  To Nak-Ku
  Nak-Ku Answers
Spring to the Earth-Witch   9   242
Chief Capilano Greets
  His Namesake at Dawn
Winter Dawn   19   248
Dawn Song   25   246

ARTICLES
  The Aztec Poets   26   166

BOOKS REVIEWED
  Songs of the Coast Dwellers   36   278

ARTICLES ABOUT
  [Note on Indian songs]   5   46

SKINNER, JEFFREY
POEMS
  His Side   136   79
  Her Side
  Hey, Nineteen   146   330
  The Company of Heaven   152   344
  Those Who Insist They've Returned   154   16
  Like Water
  The Dangerous Teaching   154   311
  Living Poets
  John Ashbery   169   324

BOOKS REVIEWED
  Late Stars   147   227
  A Guide to Forgetting   154   283

SKINNER, OTIS
ARTICLES ABOUT
  Poetry on Records,
   by Harry T. Moore   57   338

SKLAREW, MYRA
POEMS
  The Messiah Reconsidered   151   287

SKLOOT, FLOYD
POEMS
  Solstice   159   131

SLACK, CHARLES
POEMS
   A Short Unidentified Man...   74   195

SLATAPER, SCIPIO
ARTICLES ABOUT
   Five Years of Italian Poetry (1910-1915),
      by Emanuel Carnevali   13   209

SLATER, MARY WHITE
POEMS
   Barefoot Sandals   11   72

SLAUGHTER, WILLIAM
POEMS
   Climbing Tai Shan   153   28

SLAVITT, DAVID R.
POEMS
   Poison   131   90
   Night Thoughts
   Poster   132   196
   Museum Piece   141   159
   Last Days at Delphi

BOOKS REVIEWED
   Suits for the Dead:
      Poems, in Poets of Today VIII   99   379
   The Eclogues of Virgil (Tr.)   120   304
   Child's Play   123   353
   Vital Signs: New and Selected Poems   129   285
   Rounding the Horn   135   229

SLEIGH, TOM
POEMS
   The Very End   143   30
   Seventh Floor: Cancer Ward   147   269
   M. on Her Thirtieth Birthday
   Animus   150   22
   The Seal
   First Love

BOOKS REVIEWED
   The Chain   170   101

SLESSOR, KENNETH
BOOKS REVIEWED
   The Penguin Book of Australian Verse
      (Ed. with John Thompson
      and R. G. Howarth)   94   44

SLIM, SUNDOWN [Pseud.]
POEMS
   Fools   27   316

SLOAN, JACOB
BOOKS REVIEWED
   Generation of Journey   66   340

SLOAN, JOCELYN
POEMS
   In at the Death   99   228

SLOMAN, JOEL
POEMS
   Insecta Anonymous   106   331
   Ate
   The Astronaut of Waste

BOOKS REVIEWED
   Virgil's Machines   109   195

SLOSS, HENRY
POEMS
   The Cat Songs   123   339
   The Wedding at Vernazzano   131   21
   The Parthenon   161   217

SMALL, FLORENCE S.
[See EDSALL, FLORENCE S.]

SMART, CHRISTOPHER
BOOKS REVIEWED
   The Collected Poems of...
      (Ed. by Norman Callan)   76   218

ARTICLES ABOUT
   Rev. of *Poor Kit Smart,*
      by Christopher Devlin   99   375
   Rev. of *Christopher Smart,*
      Scholar of the University,
      by Arthur Sherbo   115   196

SMITH, A. J. M.
POEMS
   Emblems of Air   44   197
      To a Young Poet
      The Crows
      A Soldier's Ghost
   Good Friday   46   82
   Surrealism in the Service of Christ   58   9
   The Mermaid
   The Cry
   Calvary   62   20
   To the Christian Doctors   62   200
   On Reading an Anthology
      of Popular Poems
   A Portrait, and a Prophecy
   Lines Written on the Occasion
      of President Nixon's Address
      to the Nation, May 8, 1972   120   335

REVIEWS
   Foretaste, by Peggy Pond Church   44   340
   The Nettle and the Flower,
      by Kenneth Muir   45   106
   The Women of Lissadell   45   214

Selected Poems,
  by Eva Gore-Booth
Prison Letters of Countess Markievicz
  (With Poems by Eva Gore-Booth)
Poems, by W. H. Auden   47   43
American Primitives   48   169
  Fightery Dick and Other Poems,
    by Derrick Norman Lehmer
  Turkey in the Straw,
    by MacKinley Kantor
  Westering,
    by Thomas Hornsby Ferril
Passport to the War, by Stanley Kunitz   64   165
The Golden Mirror,
  by Marya Zaturenska   65   150
Five Young American Poets:
  Third Series, 1944
  [Eve Merriam, John Frederick Nims,
  Jean Garrigue, Tennessee Williams,
  Alejandro Carrión]   66   95
The Spectre Image, by John Nerber   70   155

BOOKS REVIEWED
  The Book of Canadian Poetry (Ed.)   63   281
  News of the Phoenix   65   157
  The Oxford Book of Canadian Verse (Ed.)   99   324
  Collected Poems   103   266
  The Collected Poems of Anne Wilkinson
    and a Prose Memoir (Ed.)   114   335

ARTICLES ABOUT
  The Development of Poetry
  in Canada, 1880–1940,
    by E. K. Brown   58   34

SMITH, ALICE GUSTAVA
  [See also STELLA, (SISTER) MARIS]
POEMS
  In the Upper Air   46   80
  Flight
  Seasonal
  The Season Turns   49   258
  Late Autumn
  Snow

SMITH, ART
POEMS
  Wisps of the Street   24   312
  Polk Street Nocturne
  Halsted Midnight
  Adams Street Bridge
  Illusion
  Dawn
  Old Toys
  Streets and Dunes   28   202
  Early Boul Mich
  Skin-Deep
  Dune Path

Temple
Wood-Cut
Boul Mich 4 A.M.
Hull House Window
Old Woman
Lightly
Regeneration   39   28

SMITH, ARTHUR
POEMS
  Western Roll   145   338
  Winter Annuals   155   264

SMITH, BARBARA HERRNSTEIN
BOOKS REVIEWED
  Poetic Closure:
    A Study of How Poems End   115   346

SMITH, BILL
POEMS
  Windy Bank   146   214

SMITH, BRUCE
POEMS
  Winter and Spring. Things I Forgot To Tell
    Thean Logan Before She Left   135   270
  Snow on the Ocean   145   73
  The Child We Didn't Have   169   259

BOOKS REVIEWED
  The Common Wages   144   231

SMITH, CHARD POWERS
POEMS
  Songs of Silence   25   198
  A Grave in Winter
  Waiting
  Silence
  Her Dawn
  One-Hundred-Per-Cent French   27   20
  Dead March for a Roman General   29   196
  Threnody
  Synchrony   33   19

BOOKS REVIEWED
  Along the Wind   29   289
  Lost Address   33   44
  Hamilton: A Poetic Drama in Three Acts   37   53
  Pattern and Variation in Poetry   42   54

SMITH, CHARLIE
POEMS
  The Miniature City   163   208
  Conceit
  The Essential Story
  Ruffians
  Beds   168   153
  Poems Without Words

Visitation	168	322
Desolation Your Inheritance	170	147

BOOKS REVIEWED
| *The Palms* | 163 | 285 |

SMITH, CLARA WILLIAMS
POEMS
This Single Hour	50	320
By a Nameless Lake		
Scrub Growth		
"Vats of Golden Soup"		

SMITH, CLARK ASHTON
POEMS
Remembered Light	1	78
Sorrowing of Winds		
Fire of Snow	6	178
In the Wind		
December	33	123
The Old Water-Wheel	61	492

BOOKS REVIEWED
| *The Star-Treader and Other Poems* | 2 | 26 |

SMITH, DAVE
POEMS
Dome Poem	125	325
Apples in Early October	131	24
Willows, Pond Glitter		
Dreams in Sunlit Rooms		
Tide Pools	135	311
The Soft Belly of the World		
A Place in the Forest		
Rainy Day: Last Run	140	226
Waking in the Endless Mountains		
Runaway	142	345
The Purpose of the Chesapeake & Ohio Canal		
Squirrel Season		
Careless Love	147	257
Driving Lesson		
Championship Fight		
Palmetto Special	151	158
Sugar	152	223
The Virginian		
Writing Spider		
Clay		
Mighty Joe Turner's Blues	164	11
A Boy with Ringworm		

REVIEWS
New and Selected Things Taking Place, by May Swenson	135	291
The Zodiac and *The Strength of Fields,* by James Dickey [Vincent Lombardi]	137	349
Short Reviews	147	35

Station Island, by Seamus Heaney
The Mural of Wakeful Sleep, by Laurence Lieberman
Where Water Comes Together with Other Water, by Raymond Carver
Collected Poems: 1957-1982, by Wendell Berry
Selected Poems and *Sweet Will,* by Philip Levine
New and Selected Poems: 1923-1985, by Robert Penn Warren

BOOKS REVIEWED
Cumberland Station	133	45
Goshawk, Antelope	140	293
Dream Flights		
In the House of the Judge	143	295
Local Assays: On Contemporary American Poetry	147	346
The Roundhouse Voices: Selected and New Poems		
Fate's Kite: Poems, 1991-1995	170	347

SMITH, DORIS LISBETH
POEMS
| *The Lonely* | 37 | 302 |

SMITH, EDNA LOUISE
POEMS
| *Her Story* | 26 | 192 |

SMITH, GARY
POEMS
Mourning Doves	129	318
Swelter		
A Small Boy, Once Lost and Found		

SMITH, GEORGE SMEDLEY
BOOKS REVIEWED
| *Lines for the Canonization of Pedro Domecq* | 63 | 52 |

SMITH, GERALD A.
REVIEWS
| *The Selected Letters of William Cowper* (Ed. by Mark Van Doren) | 80 | 297 |

SMITH, GRANVILLE PAUL
BOOKS REVIEWED
| *Trajectory* | 77 | 215 |

SMITH, IAIN CRICHTON
BOOKS REVIEWED
| *From Bourgeois Land* | 119 | 159 |

SMITH, ISRAEL
POEMS
| *Advertisement* | 45 | 253 |

My Only Gift	46	137
Sojourn in Vermont	58	315
Memory of an Evening Fox	63	139

SMITH, JAMES STEEL
POEMS

Shore Gun	64	77
The Young Dead		
On a Persian Painting	65	241
Campanile		
Night Piece	66	130
Physical Fitness		
Train Wreck		
Railroad Agent		

SMITH, JORDAN
POEMS

Days of 1974	143	293
Audiophile	155	274
Tristan	164	22

BOOKS REVIEWED

An Apology for Loving the Old Hymns		
[William Johnson]	143	163

SMITH, KEN
BOOKS REVIEWED

Eleven Poems	110	112

SMITH, LE ROY
BOOKS REVIEWED

A Character Invented	88	52

SMITH, LE ROY, JR.
BOOKS REVIEWED

The Opulent Citizen	94	333

SMITH, LEWIS WORTHINGTON
POEMS

Aglavaine	6	282
Driftwood		

BOOKS REVIEWED

Ships in Port	12	279

SMITH, MAUDE SUMNER
ARTICLES

When Children Write Verse		
[Darrell J. Beckley, Clarice Seldomridge,		
Tom Baird, Ward Baxter]	56	154

SMITH, MAURINE
POEMS

Joy	19	14
Ceremony		
First Comer		
Wind		
Swallows Brush a Pool		

BOOKS REVIEWED

The Keen Edge	21	335

SMITH, MAY RILEY
ARTICLES ABOUT

Obituary	29	352

SMITH, R. T.
POEMS

Rushlight	152	329
Self as Trout		
Brieves from The Book of Kells	155	259
Gristle and Heron	158	72
St. Gristle Nocturne		
Gristlewolf		
Sect	161	136
The Magdalene	164	328
Boy, Recollected	168	83
Manicure		
Reading Groups		
Horse	169	335
Illumination		

REVIEWS

Selected Poems,		
by Eavan Boland	156	236

SMITH, RAY
POEMS

This Is the Country, Yes	63	260
Listen, for I Have Kept a Fanatic Heart		
Embarkation	64	248
The Dear Dark Head		
Tonight		
They		
Stonehenge		
The Breathless Aisle		
Octaves in Wartime	66	61
The Sign		
The Dance		
German Dead		
The Edge of Cold		
Machado, Poet of Spain		
The Beaches		
To Love a Changing Shape		
The Brink		
Men Grow the Gods They Create		
Rain in the City	68	61
The War Dead		
Born 1915		
Violence Upon the Roads		
The Tree		
Greek Head		
It Was But Little Time		
Drive to the Rhine		
Channel Port, 1944	69	205
Channel Crossing		
Brittany		

Joy of Flesh
Earthstorm
The Long Legend   71   129
My Grandfather Framed
    by an Autumn Day
Painting by Rousseau
The Apple   84   261
Mexican Desert   85   28
Orozco in Guadalajara   109   22
Unpoem for M   113   167

ARTICLES
Correspondence   65   163

REVIEWS
American Child, by Paul Engle   67   215
Poets Betrayed by Didacticism   68   168
    Green World, by Miriam Waddington
    Ho! Watchman of the Night Ho!
        by Lee ver Duft
Two Kinds of Myth   70   165
    Nothing Is a Wonderful Thing,
        by Helen Wolfert
    How God Fix Jonah,
        by Lorenz Graham
The Lion and the Rose, by May Sarton   73   292
The Seeming Real,
    by Frederick Mortimer Clapp   73   360
The Careless Clock, by Mark Van Doren   74   177
The Lion & the Lady, by Emma Swan   76   363

BOOKS REVIEWED
No Eclipse: War Poems   67   160
The Greening Tree   108   54

SMITH, SIDNEY GOODSIR
[See SMITH, SYDNEY GOODSIR]

SMITH, STEVIE
POEMS
Lord Say and Seal   105   109
Here Lies…
Miss Snooks, Poetess
Northumberland House
The Grange

BOOKS REVIEWED
Not Waving but Drowning   92   309
Not Waving but Drowning   92   318
Selected Poems   105   404
The Best Beast   117   195
Collected Poems   129   170

SMITH, SYDNEY GOODSIR
[SIDNEY GOODSIR SMITH]
POEMS
The Muse in Rose Street   88   28
Mareeld
Granton
Cokkils
The Jungfrau in Season Bricht wi Eternal
    Whiteness is Natheless Raped by the Buits
    o a Cloud o Witness
The Grace o God and the Meth Drinker
Tu Fu's View of Fife   101   122
Aurora Sluggart

BOOKS REVIEWED
So Late into the Night,
    Fifty Lyrics 1944-1948   86   52
Figs and Thistles   96   320
The Wallace   102   393
Collected Poems: 1941-1975   131   292

ARTICLES ABOUT
Some Poets of the Scottish Renaissance,
    by Tom Scott   88   43

SMITH, WILLIAM JAY
POEMS
The Panther from Its Dark and Hidden Lair   60   138
Penates in Peril
Portrait for a Lapidary   61   475
Academic Procession
Polynesian in Khaki
All Earth's Divided
Elegy   62   256
A Plaque for Forest Park
Of Islands   63   321
Poem Near Pearl Harbor
Epithalamium
Au Tombeau du Maréchal Pet-de-Nain
3 for 25
Columbus Circle Swing
"Abruptly All the Palm Trees"
Dark Valentine   65   70
    Neo-Classical Poem
    Hotel Continental
    Today I Have Touched the Earth
    Convoy
    The Waves Which Come Down
        from the Edge of the Sky
At the Terminal   68   237
How Like that Gallery You Are
Your Eyes, My Harlequins
O Love, O Love, These Oceans Vast
When All the Wild Valley Recovers the Leaf
The Vision
The Massacre of the Innocents
African Sequence
Evening at Grandpont   73   63
The Inhabitants of Atlantis
The Girl in Glass
The Farm
On Parting
Persian Miniature   74   326
The Piazza   75   199

For a Deaf Angora Cat
The Lady in Orange County
Marine   76   74
London
Song ("The sunlight is Spanish...")   81   71
Autumn   81   302
Nightwood
Tulip   83   187
Movies for the Troops
Natural History
Vision at Twilight   87   6
A Parable
A Green Place   90   35
Interior
In Memoriam Wallace Stevens
Letter
The World Below the Window
The Dressmaker's Workroom   91   7
At the Tombs of the House of Savoy
Love Birds
Ballad of the Lady Quid Pro Quo   99   141
Riddles
Quail in Autumn
A Tune for the Teletype
Northern Lights   101   123
The Tin Can   102   351
Fishing for Albacore   113   295
Journey to the Interior   151   160

TRANSLATIONS
Poems by Louis Aragon   67   16
Article by Pierre Seghers   67   25
Article by Jean-Richard Bloch   67   52
Poems by Jules Laforgue   78   210
Poems by Valery Larbaud   85   249
Poems by Sandro Penna
   and Vittorio Sereni   155   15
Poems by Alain Bosquet   166   159

ARTICLES
A Note on American Youth   69   275
Figures on a Frieze
   [Fiction]   89   188
Master of Silences:
   Walter de la Mare 1873-1956   91   112

REVIEWS
The Song of Lazarus,
   by Alex Comfort   68   116
Patchen's Province
   and Other Landscapes   70   108
An Astonished Eye
   Looks Out of the Air,
   by Kenneth Patchen
Anew, by Louis Zukofsky
XII Poems,
   by Francis Coleman Rosenberger
New Goose, by Lorine Niedecker

The Landscape Has Voices,
   by Scott Greer
Journey to the Coastal Marsh,
   by James Feibleman
Asiatic Station, by Cloyd Mann Criswell
Jules Laforgue and the Ironic Inheritance,
   by Warren Ramsey   83   331
A Letter from Li Po and Other Poems,
   by Conrad Aiken   88   175

BOOKS REVIEWED
Poems   73   116
Celebration at Dark   78   237
Poems 1947-1957   94   250
The Spectra Hoax   99   390
The Golden Journey: Poems for Young People
   (Ed. with Louise Bogan)   108   343
The Tin Can   109   184
Antiworlds, by Andrei Voznesensky
   (Tr. with others)   110   40
Poems from France (Ed.)   113   188
New & Selected Poems   119   159
The Traveler's Tree:
   New and Selected Poems   138   107

ARTICLES ABOUT
French Chronicle: Recent Publications,
   by Wallace Fowlie   88   408

SMITHYMAN, KENDRICK
BOOKS REVIEWED
The Night Shift
   (With James K. Baxter, Charles Doyle,
   and Louis Johnson)   94   44

SMOCK, FREDERICK
POEMS
Angels   160   28

SMYTH, FLORIDA WATTS
POEMS
Wind   33   125
They Sign for Peace   35   75
A Tall Tree   38   256
Edge of the Park
An Old House
Turn Wheel, Turn   42   140
Reality   62   309

SMYTH, GJERTRUD
SCHNACKENBERG
[See SCHNACKENBERG,
GJERTRUD]

SMYTH, MARY WINSLOW
BOOKS REVIEWED
Minstrelsy of Maine
   (Ed. with Fannie Hardy Eckstrom)   32   96

SMYTH, PAUL
POEMS
From *Thistles and Thorns:*
   Lyrics of Abraham and Sarah   118   249
Of His Affliction   120   28
Ave, Vale   122   69
Desert Watch   127   195
A Gift
A Box Turtle   130   337
An Elm Leaf
They
A Paperweight
Timing   132   219
Of Scholarship, Divorce, and Lunch
Day Moon
Poetics   134   208
After the Windstorm   137   283

REVIEWS
Less Tit than Tat   123   165
   Gnomes & Occasions,
     by Howard Nemerov
   Legion: Civic Choruses,
     by William Harmon
   Inscriptions, by Anthony Thwaite
   Runes, by James K. Baxter
   Another Life, by Derek Walcott

BOOKS REVIEWED
Native Grass   122   351
Conversions   126   219

SMYTHE, DANIEL (W.)
POEMS
Power   42   130
Sky Lines   46   264
   Introduction to Earth
   The Vaunting Hand
   Storm Setting
   Shore Birds
   Light with Drums
Rock and Pavement   51   74
   Storm over New York
   Aquarium
   On the Maine Rocks
The Pheasant   58   245
Desk   72   80

BOOKS REVIEWED
Steep Acres   61   696

SNAITH, STANLEY
BOOKS REVIEWED
The Common Festival   79   106

SNELLING, FLORENCE D.
POEMS
March in Tryon   13   314

SNIVELY, SUSAN
POEMS
For a Painting of a Winter Barn   122   323
Landing

SNODGRASS, W. D.
POEMS
Autumn Variations   157   63
As a Child, Sleepless

TRANSLATIONS
Poems by Christian Morgenstern
   (With Lore Groszmann)   98   365
Versions of Kozma Prutkov
   (With Tanya Tolstoy)   104   203
Poems by Orlando di Lasso
   and Federico García Lorca   157   270
Poems by Marin Sorescu
   (Tr. with Luciana Costea
   and Dona Rosu)   159   191

BOOKS REVIEWED
Heart's Needle   95   116
John Ciardi and W. D. Snodgrass
   [Recording]   101   275
Gallows Songs,
   by Christian Morgenstern
   (Tr. with Lore Segal)   112   418
After Experience, Poems   113   35
Each in His Season   165   97

ARTICLES ABOUT
"Sacred Beings": Writers
   in Recorded Conversation,
   by Michael Milburn   146   101
[Note]   157   301

SNOW, KAREN
BOOKS REVIEWED
Wonders   140   35

SNOW, ROYALL (H.)
ARTICLES
Correspondence:
   A Word of Protest   14   56

REVIEWS
From the Nineties to the Present   20   282
   A Shropshire Lad,
     by A. E. Housman
   Poems New and Old,
     by Henry Newbolt
   Poems, with Fables in Prose,
     by Herbert Trench
   Later Poems, by Bliss Carman
   The Collected Poems
     of James Elroy Flecker
   Bucolic Comedies, by Edith Sitwell   23   281

Oxford Poetry: 1924
  (Ed. by Harold Acton
    and Peter Quennell)   26   47
Oxford: Thick Smoke
    and Thin Fire   28   112
An Indian Ass,
  by Harold Acton
Babbling April,
  by Graham Greene

BOOKS REVIEWED
  Igdrasil   21   45
  Thomas Lovell Beddoes,
    Eccentric and Poet   34   111

SNOW, WILBERT
POEMS
  Long Lives   25   83
    Aged Ninety Years
    Postlude
  Spruces   34   80
  Etching   37   319

BOOKS REVIEWED
  Maine Coast   23   45
  The Inner Harbor   30   170
  Maine Tides   58   103

SNYDER, FRANKLYN B.
REVIEWS
  Selected Letters of Robert Burns
    (Ed. by DeLancey Ferguson)   84   41

SNYDER, GARY
POEMS
  Four from Six Years   103   97
  Through the Smoke Hole   106   120
  Three Worlds::Three Realms::Six Roads   109   147
  Eight Songs of Clouds and Water   111   353
  The Hudsonian Curlew   115   119

BOOKS REVIEWED
  Riprap   96   238
  Myths and Texts   97   316
  A Range of Poems   111   254
  Earth House Hold   118   174
  Regarding Wave   120   164
  Turtle Island   126   346
  Axe Handles   144   345
  No Nature   164   157

SOARES, BERNARDO
[See PESSOA, FERNANDO]

SOBILOFF, HY
[HI SOBILOFF, H. J. SOBILOFF]
POEMS
  The Clock Heart   92   164

A Notice to My Emotions
Blind Boy in Nassau   100   370
A Jamaican Child
Horse Language
You Cannot Paint Nature
The Famous Kitchen
Walking Flashes
  in Eleuthera Bahamas
To Millicent Smith,
  Whom I Didn't Know   105   318
Outside My Autumn Morning
To My Doctor
Three Ladies with Their Hats
  On Having Lunch
My Windblown Poem
Tom Jones My Tom Cat
As the Conversation Goes
My Wild Flowers Anonymous
Waiting
The Cut   107   386
Shall I Tell You How I Feel
Drying a Memory
The Hummingbird
Never Having Been a Lizard
An Ant Without a Hill
Shapeless Folds
A True Storm
Elegy for Twelve   110   155
Poem ("My tear-ducts flood...")   112   389
Thought's Feeling
Introspection
Baudelaire's Cats
Victim
Lost City Cat
Road Under Repair
A Woman Knitting
Stuffed Owl
Echo
For Henry Rago   115   112
Across the Storm   115   334
The Journey Underneath
Shells

BOOKS REVIEWED
  Dinosaurs and Violins   86   295
  Breathing of First Things   104   108

SOBIN, A(NTHONY) G.
[ANTHONY SOBIN]
POEMS
  Why I Am Sad   124   97
  The January Sky
  Wilderness Area
  Eating the Bowfin   134   147
  The Stinkhorn
  Revolutions   153   141

SOBIN, ANTHONY
[See SOBIN, A(NTHONY) G.]

SOCRATES
ARTICLES ABOUT
Notes on Language
and Its Deconstruction,
by Erich Heller   145   229

SOFFICI, ARDENGO
ARTICLES ABOUT
La Voce and Its Poets,
by Walter Pach   10   50

SOFIELD, DAVID
POEMS
No   124   29
Clearing Your Desk

SOLES, MARY
POEMS
Two Poems   94   78
("I've gone a morning...")
("Hunger/wind/worn...")

SOLHEIM, JAMES
POEMS
Faith of Our Fathers   143   153
*My Father After a Day's Work
at Otto Steel*
*Variations: Couple Seen
Through a Window*   146   336
Existence One Thursday   147   25
Echocardiogram   152   264
Roughing-In a House
*Blessed by Meteors and
by the Benevolent Men of Space*   156   27

SOLMI, SERGIO
ARTICLES ABOUT
Contemporary Italian Poetry,
by Edward Williamson   79   233

SOLOMON, MARVIN
POEMS
The Amusing Muse   72   125
Mass Execution
Animal
The Rutting Season
Early Rising
The Park   76   274
Hollyhocks   80   20
Lines to Some Crystallized Violets   80   204
"Oiseaux Tristes"   83   125
The Pigeons
The Animal
Shutters
"Alborada del Gracioso"   84   131
The Art Museums
The Promised Land   85   14
The Mondrian   86   10

The White Rabbit
Jays in the Wood   88   313
A Winter's Tale
The Poodle
The Chinese Kite   89   357
Children and Leaves   91   98
Last One In
The Fourth of July   94   166
The Persimmon Tree
A Beautiful Day at Jerusalem's Mills
Wind Gongs   96   295
*Landscape with Yellow Birds:
By Paul Klee*
Orisons
Two Druid Hill Sonnets
The Natchez Trace   100   286
Answering   158   37
Sympathy Note
Math
Emily's Room   159   136
*The Headache that Wasn't There,
Isn't There*   159   318
Some Things My Father Liked   161   271
The Divine Sarah   162   21
Nijinsky's Solo
AIDS
The Razor   165   193

BOOKS REVIEWED
First Poems   83   227
The Royal Tiger's Face   99   379
A View from Africa   104   47

SOLOMON, ROBERT J.
POEMS
Don Quixote in the Desert   128   213

SOLOMOS, DIONYSIOS
ARTICLES ABOUT
Letter to a Foreign Friend,
by George Seferis
(Tr. by Nanos Valaorites)   105   50

SOLT, MARY ELLEN
POEMS
Flowers in Concrete
[With note]   107   380

BOOKS REVIEWED
Flowers in Concrete   112   125

SOLUM, SJANNA
BOOKS REVIEWED
Lodestone   77   215

SOMOZA, JOSEPH
BOOKS REVIEWED
Greyhound: A Poem Sequence   116   193

681

SONG, CATHY
POEMS
The Tree House   148   12
The Window and the Field
Litany
The Age of Reptiles
Points of Reference   153   134
School Figures
The Grammar of Silk   157   5
Mother on River Street
Out of Our Hands   157   199
Eat   159   132
Christmas Eve
The Hotel by the Lake   160   322
Adagio
Square Mile
Sunworshippers   162   331

BOOKS REVIEWED
Picture Bride   144   40
Frameless Windows, Squares of Light   154   283

SONIAT, KATHERINE
POEMS
Missing   142   28
Primary Motif   144   4
Notes of Departure
Necktie, and So Forth   146   249
Lighthouse Telephone   148   219
Daughter   148   335
Desire   151   161
Secrets About Nothing   152   217
Rose Cloth Tattering from the Barbed Wire 155 405

SONSTROEM, DAVID
BOOKS REVIEWED
Rossetti and the Fair Lady   118   343

SOPHOCLES
BOOKS REVIEWED
Electra
(Tr. by Francis Fergusson)   53   96
Oedipus Rex
(Tr. by Dudley Fitts
and Robert Fitzgerald)   76   299
Women of Trachis
(Tr. by Ezra Pound)   83   357
Three Tragedies (Oedipus the King,
tr. by David Grene; Oedipus at Colonus,
tr. by Robert Fitzgerald; Antigone,
tr. by Elizabeth Wyckoff)   85   225
Women of Trachis
(Tr. by Ezra Pound)   90   237
The Oedipus Plays of Sophocles
(Tr. by Paul Roche)   95   190

ARTICLES ABOUT
Rev. of The Idea of a Theatre,
by Francis Fergusson   77   227

SORESCU, MARIN
POEMS
Otravuri   136   24
Poisons
Carbon Paper
Shakespeare
Seneca
Question
(Tr. by Michael Hamburger)
Creation   159   191
Solemnly
Thieves
I Bound Up the Trees' Eyes
(Tr. by W. D. Snodgrass
with Dona Rosu and Luciana Costea)

SORKIN, ADAM J.
TRANSLATIONS
Poems by Daniela Crăsnaru
(Tr. with Sergiu Celac)   159   18

SORRENTINO, GILBERT
POEMS
From Shapes of Winter   100   162
Silences   102   299
Two for Franz Kline
Old Soldiers Never Die   104   360
From The Perfect Fiction   107   369
Football Poem I   110   174
Land of Cotton
Long Gone Blues
Some Bright Paintings
Brooklyn-Newark Blue Poem   111   367
Poem ("Living friends live...")   113   409
Handbook of Versification   115   161

REVIEWS
The Homestead Called Damascus
and Natural Numbers:
New and Selected Poems,
by Kenneth Rexroth   104   179
World and Self: Instances   106   306
The World, the Worldless,
by William Bronk
Some Deaths, by Walter Lowenfels
Centering, by M. C. Richards
Language, by Jack Spicer   108   134
Ten Pamphlets   112   56
State of the Union,
by Aimé Césaire
(Tr. by Clayton Eshleman
and Denis Kelly)
Lachrymae Mateo,
by Clayton Eshleman
Sing-Song, by Paul Blackburn
Crystals, by Frank Samperi
Definitions, by David Antin
The Galilee Hitch-Hiker,
by Richard Brautigan

Voyages, by Robin Magowan
Living with Chris,
   by Ted Berrigan
Identikit, by Jim Brodey
Aloud, by Bill Dodd
Black Mountaineering   116   110
  The Black Mountain Review, 1-8
  Numbers, by Robert Indiana
    and Robert Creeley
  The First Decade:
    Selected Poems, 1940-1950;
    Derivations: Selected Poems, 1950-1956;
    and *Roots and Branches*,
    by Robert Duncan
  Olson/Melville: A Study in Affinity,
    by Ann Charters
  Causal Mythology and
    Maximus Poems IV, V, VI,
    by Charles Olson
  [William Carlos Williams]

BOOKS REVIEWED
  Black and White   107   121
  The Sky Changes   112   353
  The Perfect Fiction   113   338

SOSNORA, VIKTOR
  POEMS
  Crocodile Tears   124   226
  The Summer Garden
  From *The Last Songs of Boyan*
  Pushkin in Mikhailovskoye
    (Tr. by Daniel Weissbort)

SOTHEBY, WILLIAM
  ARTICLES ABOUT
  Rev. of *Keats and the Daemon King*,
    by Werner W. Beyer   70   168

SOTO, GARY
  POEMS
  From *Elements of San Joaquin*   124   94
  October   127   83
  Manuel Zaragoza's Tale of Sunlight
  Avocado Lake
  Moving
  The Cellar   129   254
  Mitla   130   149
  The First
  Tampamachoco
  The Drought
  Antigua
  The Starlings
  Salt   132   139
  Chiapas   133   213
  La Familia de Lopez, 1901
  The Ashes   135   331
  The Widow Perez

Sueño   136   340
Towards It
Hitchhiking with a Friend and a Book
  That Explains the Pacific Ocean   138   218
Walking with Jackie, Sitting with a Dog
Her
Hunger Among Crabs   139   334
Failing in the Presence of Ants
Getting Serious   141   220
The Estonian Comes to Dinner
Oranges   142   161
Saturday Under the Sky
Envying the Children of San Francisco
Looking Around, Believing   143   189
When We Wake
Between Words
Finding a Lucky Number   144   187
Desire
The Plum's Heart
Morning on This Street
Ambition
The Jungle Cafe
Sorrow in French   147   93
Small Town with One Road
That Girl
The Seventieth Year   148   167
Heaven
Ars Poetica, or Mazatlan, On a Day
  When Bodies Wash to the Shore   150   144
Rough Translation of a Sabines Poem
Who Will Know Us?   151   162
Worry at the End of the Month   152   74
Elegy ("The mountain, snow-covered...")
The Dictionaries   154   74
The Box Fan   158   7
Not Moving
Making Up Time   160   198
Summer Marriage   162   203
Sizing Up a Marriage
Water Wheel   163   197
The Old House in My 40th Year
The History of Science   165   203
Some History
The Skeptics   166   267
Getting Ahead
Pagan Life
Inheritance   170   148
Devising Your Own Time

ARTICLES
  Comment   151   220

BOOKS REVIEWED
  The Tale of Sunlight   135   348
  Black Hair   146   167
  Home Course in Religion   160   34
  New and Selected Poems   167   156

SOULE, GEORGE
ARTICLES ABOUT
  A Word to the Carping Critic,
    by Harriet Monroe   11   89

SOUPAULT, PHILIPPE
BOOKS REVIEWED
  Ode to Bombed London
    (Tr. by Norman Cameron)   68   54

SOUSTER, RAYMOND
POEMS
  Just in from the Cold   94   301
  November, Early
  One A.M.: Bleury and Mayor
  Michele Lalonde, Reading   97   221
  The Last Mile
  Riel, 16 Novembre, 1885
  Man with the Mouth-Organ
  Winter Valley   102   372
  Eddie Condon at the New Colonial
  The Change
  The Hunting of the Deer   105   238
  My Nighthawk
  Church Street Pawnshop
  Thaw   108   17
  The Bed from Holland
  Night Raider

BOOKS REVIEWED
  Unit of Five
    (With Louis Dudek,
    Ronald Hambleton, P. K. Page,
    and James Wreford)   66   334
  When We Are Young   69   349
  Go to Sleep, World   73   355
  A Local Pride   102   42
  The Colour of the Times   108   45
  Ten Elephants on Yonge Street   109   53
  As Is   115   353
  Lost and Found   116   51
  Made in Canada:
    New Poems of the Seventies
    (Ed. with Douglas Lochhead)   119   356
  So Far, So Good
  Collected Poems   144   297

SOUTAR, WILLIAM
BOOKS REVIEWED
  Poems in Scots and English   100   104

ARTICLES ABOUT
  Some Poets of the Scottish Renaissance,
    by Tom Scott   88   43

SOUTHWICK, MARCIA
POEMS
  Landscape   132   12

  Winter Gulls   133   196
  Owning a Dead Man
  The Night Won't Save Anyone   135   267

SOUTHWORTH, JAMES G.
BOOKS REVIEWED
  More Modern American Poets   85   55

SPAAR, LISA RUSS
POEMS
  A Doubt   164   217

SPACKS, BARRY
POEMS
  Narcissus at Seventeen   95   221
  Botticelli in Atlantic City
  October   108   98
  Recommendations
  Robert's Song   109   367
  Child Adam   117   186
  The Rising   118   325
  To a Computer Writing Verses
  Malediction   120   82
  A Quiet Day
  The Slow Year
  Local Messages   123   152
  Before a Statue of Kuan Yin
  The Rodin at Wellesley College   126   321
  Imagining a Unicorn   130   276
  The Summer Weight of Lemons   134   253
  Spanish Traffic
  The Assimilation
  The Poetry Bug   136   328
  Judges in Summer
  Living Simply   139   150
  What's Fine
  Brief Sparrow   149   30
  Bachelard on Art   153   311
  The Practice   160   283
  Zen Pace   162   349
  Precious Disasters   169   252
  Innerbird   170   139
  What's-Her-Name

REVIEWS
  Collected Poems of Rolfe Humphries   108   337
  Four Poets   112   48
    Hunt in an Unmapped Interior
      and Other Poems and
      Canticle for Electronic Music,
      by J. Michael Yates
    The Darkest Continent,
      by Jack Marshall
    Stresses in the Peaceable Kingdom,
      by Stephen Sandy
    Cold Water, by Lou Lipsitz
    Poems 3, by Alan Dugan   112   270

BOOKS REVIEWED
  The Company of Children   115   281
  Something Human   121   292

SPACKS, PATRICIA MEYER
  BOOKS REVIEWED
    The Poetry of Vision   112   356

SPAETH, J. DUNCAN
  BOOKS REVIEWED
    Old English Poetry: Translations into
      Alliterative Verse (Tr.)   21   53

SPAIN, RICHARD LEON
  POEMS
    Arkansas Poems   46   67
      A Hill Mother
      Planting
      Wind
    Casual Bloom   48   252
    Bequest
    Interim
    Unconsenting   50   315
    Night Journey   52   11

  BOOKS REVIEWED
    Rock and Cumulus   61   696

SPANOS, WILLIAM V.
  BOOKS REVIEWED
    The Christian Tradition
      in Modern British Verse Drama   115   196

SPARE, AUSTIN O.
  ARTICLES ABOUT
    A New Quarterly
      [*Form*, Francis Marsden]   8   323

SPARK, MURIEL
  POEMS
    The Pearl-Miners   82   318

SPARKS, MERRILL
  BOOKS REVIEWED
    Modern Russian Poetry
      (Ed. with Vladimir Markov)   114   113

SPARROW, JOHN
  BOOKS REVIEWED
    Sense and Poetry   44   291

SPARSHOTT, FRANCIS
  POEMS
    Seasalter   92   161

  BOOKS REVIEWED
    A Divided Voice   109   53

SPAULDING, JOHN
  POEMS
    Nineteenth-Century Photographs   158   336

SPAZIANI, MARIA LUISA
  POEMS
    [*Se fosse un mare questo vento immenso*]/
      [*If it were a sea, this immense wind*] 155   66
    [*Your life is a baby not yet born*]
    [*Sunday in the provinces*]
      (Tr. by Beverly Allen)

SPEAKES, RICHARD
  POEMS
    Heartbreak Hotel Piano-Bar   147   212
    Patsy Cline
    Embodied
    Mama Loves Janis Joplin   150   86
    Code of Ethics — Coin Laundry Association
    I Beseech Thee, and Thy Mercy   160   91
    Red Lilies   165   144
    A Rose that Remembers Itself

SPEAR, ROBERTA
  POEMS
    Oi-dle-doi-dle-doi   142   136
    Ice   144   199
    Cinque Terre:
      The Land of Five Noises
    Just South   147   29
    In the Moon   149   146
    The Uncles   151   163
    The Old Ones at Dawn   153   67

  BOOKS REVIEWED
    Silks   140   35
    Taking to Water   147   102
    The Pilgrim Among Us   161   99

SPEARE, M. E.
  BOOKS REVIEWED
    The Pocket Book of Verse (Ed.)   57   221

SPEARS, MONROE K.
  ARTICLES
    Christopher Fry
      and the Redemption of Joy   78   28

  REVIEWS
    Paterson (Book Three),
      by William Carlos Williams   76   39
    The Enchafed Flood,
      by W. H. Auden   76   291

  BOOKS REVIEWED
    The Poetry of W. H. Auden:
      The Disenchanted Island   104   264

SPEARS, WOODRIDGE
POEMS
  Among These Pines   65   192
  St. Luke's Summer
  Of an Engraving at a School   72   8

SPECTOR, HERMAN
POEMS
  Sunday on Third Avenue   55   238

BOOKS REVIEWED
  We Gather Strength
    (With Joseph Kalar, Edwin Rolfe,
    and S. Funaroff)   44   50

SPEIRS, JOHN
BOOKS REVIEWED
  Medieval English Poetry:
    The Non-Chaucerian Tradition 97   195

SPENCE, MICHAEL
POEMS
  First Love in Two Dimensions 146 329
  Adam Chooses   149 192
  The Hollow Bargain
  Card Game
  Saudade   168   75

SPENCER, BERNARD
BOOKS REVIEWED
  Aegean Islands and Other Poems 73 357
  Collected Poems   110 195

SPENCER, LILIAN WHITE
POEMS
  Finale   25 196
  Anno Domini   35 131
  Arrowheads
    Hopi Woman
    Pueblo Pastoral
    Plumed Serpent
    Upside-Down God
    For Swiftness
    Arapahoe Wealth
    Call of the Mountain Lions
    Red Prayer
  Amerindian   39 125
    Shoes of Death
    Navajo Hunt
    Hemisphere Peaks   48   9

BOOKS REVIEWED
  Arrowheads   36 109

SPENCER, THEODORE
POEMS
  Return   60 246

BOOKS REVIEWED
  The Paradox in the Circle   58 266
  The World in Your Hand   62 277
  An Act of Life   64 229
  Poems (1940-1947)   72 273

ARTICLES ABOUT
  Rev. of Theodore Spencer
    [Recording]   58 105
  Rev. of Contemporary Poetry, Volume Ten
    (Ed. by Mary Owings Miller) 79 116

SPENDER, STEPHEN
POEMS
  Speech   49 184
  The Human Condition   53   8
  The Houses Fronting Railway Lines 54   1
  Poem ("After the wrestling...")
  The Marginal Field
  A Footnote to Marx's Chapter, "The Working
    Day"
  ("Doing anything and everything...") 57 122
  ("As I sit staring...")
  The Fates   59 309
  Tom's A-Cold   73   1
  Journal Leaves   101 126
  Farewell to My Student   151 165

ARTICLES
  Moods and Reactions
    [W. B. Yeats, T. S. Eliot,
    D. H. Lawrence, W. H. Auden] 67   88
  A Note on Seriousness in Poetry
    [T. S. Eliot]   72   92
  Correspondence   85 186

REVIEWS
  Trial of a Poet, by Karl Shapiro 71 314
  Nones, by W. H. Auden   78 352

BOOKS REVIEWED
  Poems   42 225
  The Destructive Element   50 280
  Forward from Liberalism
  Trial of a Judge   52 292
  Duino Elegies,
    by Rainer Maria Rilke
    (Tr. with J. B. Leishman)   55   96
  Poems of F. García Lorca
    (Tr. with J. L. Gili)   56 343
  The Still Centre   57   46
  Ruins and Visions   61 386
  Selected Poems of Federico García Lorca
    (Tr. with J. L. Gili)   63   96
  Poems of Dedication   71 153
  The Edge of Being   74 348
  Collected Poems   86 237

The Making of a Poem   102   341
Selected Poems   106   294
Collected Poems: 1928-1985   149   31

ARTICLES ABOUT
    Correspondence from John A. Holmes   42   355
    The Purposes of Stephen Spender,
        by M. D. Zabel   45   208
    English Letter, by F. R. Leavis   46   274
    Poetry of the Left, by Harriet Monroe   48   212
    Poetry in the Making,
        by Charles David Abbott   55   258
    The New Theatrum Poetarum,
        by Alan S. Downer   60   206
    Rev. of New Poems: 1943
        (Ed. by Oscar Williams)   64   86
    The Poet's Perspectives,
        by D. S. Savage   64   148
    Form in Modern Poetry,
        by D. S. Savage   65   30
    A New Engagement? by George Dillon   72   89
    Correspondence from Ebria Feinblatt
        and Marshall N. Levin   72   342
    To Write Poetry Nowadays You Have
        to Have One Foot in the Grave,
        by Gilbert Neiman   74   30
    The Defense of Poetry,
        by Richard Eberhart   77   89
    Rev. by Frank MacShane   118   295
    [Note]   145   52

SPENSER, EDMUND
ARTICLES ABOUT
    The 16th-Century Lyric
        in England: Part II,
        by Yvor Winters   53   320
    Rev. of A Map of Misreading,
        by Harold Bloom   127   222

SPERA, GABRIEL
POEMS
    My Ex-Husband   159   260
    Mr. Daly   160   5
    Balkan   162   138

SPEYER, LEONORA
POEMS
    Three Summer Poems   16   192
        The Squall
        The Locust
        Crickets at Dawn
    In Praise of Abrigada   19   242
    Reflections   20   308
        Duet
        At the Hospital for the Insane
        Song Overheard
        Kind Fate

    The Stronghold
    Looking On
    A Truth About a Lie
    Couplets
    Ballad of a Lost House   25   1
    Fiddler's Farewell   27   201
    Monk and Lady   31   117
    The Voice   52   74
    Star-Fear
    Poets' Party   58   76
    Snow in April
    The Weeper

BOOKS REVIEWED
    A Canopic Jar   19   47
    Fiddler's Farewell   28   218
    Naked Heel   41   100
    Slow Wall   56   217

ARTICLES ABOUT
    The Pulitzer Award System,
        by Harriet Monroe   30   210

SPICEHANDLER, EZRA
BOOKS REVIEWED
    The Modern Hebrew Poem Itself
        (Ed. with Stanley Burnshaw
        and T. Carmi)   111   258

SPICER, ANNE HIGGINSON
POEMS
    Three Griefs   21   200

TRANSLATIONS
    Poem by Hélène Vacaresco   26   81

SPICER, JACK
BOOKS REVIEWED
    After Lorca   93   182
    The Heads of the Town Up to the Aether 102   182
    Language   108   134

SPIDEL, LIANNE
POEMS
    Sins of the Mothers   168   264
    My Twenty-Eighth Grade Book   168   316

SPINGARN, LAWRENCE P(ERRY)
POEMS
    Portrait by Bachrach   68   303
    Cold Comfort
    West   73   206
    The Slave Coast   85   84
    Dirge for a Landing

BOOKS REVIEWED
    Rococo Summer and Other Poems   72   281
    Letters from Exile and Other Poems   101   279

SPIRE, ANDRÉ
POEMS
Outrecuidance 35 120
Honeymoon Trip 59 192
The Blue Bird
Paris
   (Tr. by Clark Mills)

BOOKS REVIEWED
Le Secret 15 42
Poèmes d'ici et de là-bas 65 342

ARTICLES ABOUT
Vers-Libre in Full Bloom, I,
   by Stanley Burnshaw 32 277
Vers-Libre in Full Bloom, II,
   by Stanley Burnshaw 32 334
Rev. of André Spire
   and His Poetry,
   by Stanley Burnshaw 44 347

SPIRES, ELIZABETH
POEMS
Death Dress 133 38
Globe
At the Bambi Motel 134 194
Boardwalk 136 321
Catchpenny Road
The Playground 143 33
My Daughter
Angel 145 153
Profil Perdu 150 156
Fabergé's Egg 153 72
Black Fairy Tale
Letter in July 160 218

BOOKS REVIEWED
Swan's Island 148 99
Annonciade 158 214
Worldling 169 286

SPIVACK, KATHLEEN
POEMS
Mythmaking 109 163
High 111 234
The Water Gives Up Its Counsel 114 84
Drifting
Night Terror
The Tank 116 86
Snapping Turtle
Rain 117 361
Dido: Swarming 120 195
Crystal Night: Berlin 1938 .... 138 280
He Doesn't Move
Outboard Engines 139 217
The Young Wife Who Went Deaf 141 228
Windows

REVIEWS
The Sorrow Dance, by Denise Levertov . 112 123
Notebook 1967-68, by Robert Lowell ... 116 191

BOOKS REVIEWED
Flying Inland 125 229
The Jane Poems 127 44
Swimmer in the Spreading Dawn 140 346

SPURR, DAVID
REVIEWS
Selected Poems, by John Ashbery 148 228
The News of Life and Death 165 289
   Collected Poems, by Thom Gunn
   Fathering the Map:
      New and Selected Later Poems,
      by Robert Pack
   Collected Poems and
      The Man in the Wall,
      by James Laughlin
   [Ezra Pound, Catullus]

SQUIRE, J. C.
BOOKS REVIEWED
Poems: First Series 16 331
The Birds and Other Poems 18 39
Poems: Second Series 20 274
Collected Poems 97 260

SQUIRES, (J.) RADCLIFFE
[J. R. SQUIRES]
POEMS
Casualty 70 129
Journey to Pompeii 72 183
Marblehead 75 328
Poor Old Bruckner
Day-Love 80 27
The Red Flower 83 190
The Moment
Clara Bodfish 90 93
The Forms of Blindness
Self as an Eye
The Graiae 95 24
Sunday in the Laboratory
The Visible Moments

REVIEWS
The Art of Worldly Wisdom,
   by Kenneth Rexroth 76 156
Yoked by Violence, by John Pauker ... 76 302
No Moat No Castle,
   by Donald F. Drummond
The Broken Landscape,
   by John Williams

BOOKS REVIEWED
Where the Compass Spins 79 349
The Loyalties of Robinson Jeffers ... 90 254

The Major Themes of Robert Frost   104   253
The Loyalties of Robinson Jeffers   104   264
The Light Under Islands, Poems   113   35
Gardens of the World   141   170

SSU WEN-MING
POEMS
    Passing by Pao-Ch'ing Temple
    (Tr. by Helen Burwell Chapin)   46   11

STABLER, JORDAN HERBERT
BOOKS REVIEWED
    The Jargon of Master Francois Villon   14   287

STADE, GEORGE
BOOKS REVIEWED
    Selected Letters of E. E. Cummings
    (Ed. with F. W. Dupee)   115   277

STAFFORD, WILLIAM (E.)
POEMS
    A Posy   71   70
    Footnote
    Meditation
    Faint Message
    Super Market   73   19
    Sunday Avenue
    Juke Joint   75   259
    Boom Town   79   274
    A Survey   81   166
    Near
    Watching the Jet Planes Dive   84   343
    Two Evenings
    Weather Report
    Following
    Sayings from the Northern Ice   88   363
    The Bravery of Love
    The Move to California   90   14
    The Farm on the Great Plain   91   248
    Shepherd
    Chickens the Weasel Killed
    As Pippa Lilted
    At the Old Place
    Augustine
    Things We Did That Meant Something
    On Penitencia Creek
    Our City Is Guarded by Automatic Rockets
    In Dear Detail, by Ideal Light   94   227
    At Earle Birney's School
    In Medias Res   96   226
    Communion at Lunch
    Subsistence
    By the Escalator
    Thought, the Pacifist
    After Plotinus
    In Response to a Question:
    "What Does the Earth Say?"   98   146
    Found in a Storm

The Museum at Tillamook
Return to Single-Shot
One Day in August
The Thought Machine
On an Island in the San Juans   99   343
Vocation
Even Now
The Day I Got the Good Idea   102   174
The Collector
A Human Condition
Across Kansas
The Rescued Year   104   238
Growing Up: Mother
A Family Turn
How I Escaped
Following the "Markings" of Dag
    Hammarskjöld: A Gathering in the Spirit
    of His Life and Writings   106   319
Portrait of a Refugee Musician   109   250
Priest Lake
In Fur
Brother
In Fog
That Weather
Monuments for a Friendly Girl
    at a Tenth Grade Party
In Sublette's Barn
Reaching Out To Turn On a Light   111   389
What I Heard Whispered
    at the Edge of Liberal, Kansas
On Winter Ridge
Uncle Bill Visits
An Introduction to Literature
The Girl Engaged to the Boy Who Died
The Guitar by the Chair
In a Time of Need   119   127
Oak
Stories To Live in the World With
Walking Away an Undeclared War   120   323
The Day You Are Reading This   124   100
Twelve Threads
Lines To Stop Talking By
This Room When Winter Comes
This Town: Winter Morning
Resolutions   132   76
Gasoline   132   262
One of the Fathers   135   87
Sending These Messages   135   187
Looking Across the River
With Neighbors One Afternoon
Watching Her Go
Learning a Word While Climbing
A Tentative Welcome to Readers
Stone, Paper, Scissors   140   214
How To Regain Your Soul
The Day Millicent Found the World   150   330
Presenting These Pieces   151   166
Noticing

Your Life

Coming Back   152   27

Third Street   160   319

Annals of T'ai Chi: "Push Hands"

The Magic Mountain

ARTICLES

Comment   151   203

REVIEWS

Several Tongues   95   248

  Union Street, by Charles Causley

  Of the Festivity, by William Dickey

  First and Second Love,

    by Eleanor Farjeon

  The Collected Poems of E. J. Pratt

  The Stone and the Shell,

    by Sara Henderson Hay

  The World's One Clock,

    by Louise Townsend Nicholl

  Zen Telegrams, by Paul Reps

    [Edith Sitwell, W. H. Auden,

    Edward Thomas, Northrop Frye]

Breath in Cold Air   97   192

  Back to Life

    (Ed. by Robert Conquest)

  Anerca: Eskimo Poems and Drawings

    (Ed. by Edmund Carpenter)

  Facing North,

    by Terence Heywood

    and Edward Lowbury

    [Margarita Aliger]

Confrontations   99   381

  Beasts in Clothes, by Harold Witt

  The Linen Bands,

    by Raymond Roseliep

  The Outdoor Labyrinth,

    by Myron H. Broomell

  Companions to Your Doom,

    by Richard Emil Braun

  Changes, by Michael Benedikt

In Praise of Adam,

    by Reuel Denney   101   203

Touching Sacred Objects   102   115

  Collected Poems,

    by Winfield Townley Scott

  Collected Verse Plays,

    by Richard Eberhart

  16 Once Published,

    by Louis Zukofsky

The Norfolk Poems of Hayden Carruth   102   323

Honey and Salt, by Carl Sandburg   102   388

Terminations, Revelations   104   104

  At the End of the Open Road,

    by Louis Simpson

  Between Matter and Principle,

    by Alan Stephens

  My Bones Being Wiser,

    by Vassar Miller

The African Boy, by E. N. Sargent

Interpreter's House,

  by William Dickey

The Journal of John Cardan and

  To What Strangers, What Welcome,

  by J. V. Cunningham   105   262

Losses, Engagements, Privacies   106   294

  The Whitsun Weddings,

    by Philip Larkin

  Selected Poems, by Stephen Spender

  Man Does, Woman Is,

    by Robert Graves

  Markings,

    by Dag Hammarskjöld

    (Tr. by Leif Sjöberg

    and W. H. Auden)   106   356

Weighed and Found Wanted   106   429

  Roofs of Gold

    (Ed. by Padraic Colum)

  Poems of Doubt and Belief

    (Ed. by Tom F. Driver

    and Robert Pack)

  American Lyric Poems

    (Ed. by Elder Olson)

  Poets of Today

    (Ed. by Walter Lowenfels)

  American Poems

    (Ed. by Jascha Kessler)

  New Negro Poets: U.S.A.

    (Ed. by Langston Hughes)

  Dylan Thomas's Choice

    (Ed. by Ralph Maud

    and Aneirin Talfan Davies)

  A New Directions Reader

    (Ed. by Hayden Carruth

    and J. Laughlin)

Selected Poems of Edwin Arlington Robinson

  (Ed. by Morton Dauwen Zabel)

  [James Dickey]   108   187

Looking Up at Leaves,

  by Barbara Howes   109   270

A Five-Book Shelf   111   184

  Half Sun Half Sleep,

    by May Swenson

  Excursions: New and Selected Poems,

    by Katherine Hoskins

  Buckshee, by Ford Madox Ford

  This Strangest Everything,

    by John Ciardi

  The Collected Shorter Poems,

    by Kenneth Rexroth

  [Ingemar Gustafson, Karin Boye]

Selected Writings by Charles Olson

  (Ed. by Robert Creeley)   111   413

Books That Look Out,

  Books That Look In   113   421

  Openings, by Wendell Berry

  The Unblinding,

    by Laurence Lieberman

Awaken, Bells Falling,
    by Lewis Turco
In the Mecca, by Gwendolyn Brooks
The Talking Girl,
    by John Thompson
Selected Poems of Rosemary Thomas

BOOKS REVIEWED
Traveling Through the Dark   102   42
The Rescued Year   110   42
Allegiances   118   288
Stories That Could Be True:
    New and Collected Poems   132   230
Smoke's Way   144   231
An Oregon Message   152   98
Passwords   160   34
My Name is William Tell   162   96
Even in Quiet Places   170   162

ARTICLES ABOUT
Review by Peter Stitt   138   46

STAGEBERG, N. C.
BOOKS REVIEWED
Poetry as Experience
    (With W. L. Anderson)   84   43

STAINTON, ALBERT
POEMS
The Pigeon Entablature   127   35

STALLINGS, A. E.
POEMS
Eurydice's Footnote   165   253
A Lament for the Dead Pets
    of Our Childhood   167   215
A Postcard from Greece   168   19
Lemur Comes from the Latin for Ghosts
Persephone Writes a Letter to Her Mother   169   269
The Dogdom of the Dead   170   128

STALLMAN, ROBERT W(OOSTER)
POEMS
The Windmill   75   12
The Kettle   76   197

REVIEWS
The Little Magazine:
    A History and a Bibliography,
    by Frederick J. Hoffman,
    Charles Allen, and Carolyn F. Ulrich   70   274

BOOKS REVIEWED
Critiques and Essays in Criticism,
    1920-1948 (Ed.)   77   239

ARTICLES ABOUT
[Note]   84   119

STALLWORTHY, JON
BOOKS REVIEWED
The Astronomy of Love   99   320
Root and Branch   118   169
The Twelve and Other Poems,
    by Alexander Blok
    (Tr. with Peter France)   119   45
The Apple Barrel   127   98
Hand in Hand
A Familiar Tree   137   105

STAMBLER, BERNARD
BOOKS REVIEWED
Dante's Other World   96   323

STANFORD, ANN
POEMS
Lost Objects   87   206
The Measure
Person and Place   96   212
Motion Toward Noon   102   378
The Messenger
The Burning of Ilium   120   357
The Old Couple   127   30
The Spy   129   26
The Chase
The Turn
After Exile
Listening to Color

BOOKS REVIEWED
The White Bird   76   365
Magellan   93   399
The Weathercock   110   258

STANFORD, DEREK
POEMS
Private Autumn   73   86

STANFORD, DON
POEMS
The Lizard King Here   42   263

REVIEWS
Poems, by Anna Maria Armi   59   340
The Function of Criticism,
    by Yvor Winters   91   393

BOOKS REVIEWED
New England Earth   60   107
The Traveler   88   273

STANGE, G. ROBERT
REVIEWS
The Little Review Anthology
    (Ed. by Margaret Anderson)   83   290
Thomas Hardy: A Critical Biography,
    by Evelyn Hardy   85   356

STANLEY, MARION EDWARD
POEMS
The Old Men   33   308
Bargain

STANLEY, MARNI L.
BOOKS REVIEWED
Writing Right
(Ed. with Douglas Barbour)   144   297

STANLEY-WRENCH, MARGARET
POEMS
The New Swallows   60   63
For the Bombed Cities

STANOYEVICH, B. S.
BOOKS REVIEWED
An Anthology of Jugoslav Poetry (Ed.)   20   228

STANTON, ANTOINETTE
POEMS
Poem ("They whisper the sea...")   79   261

STANTON, JOSEPH
POEMS
Edward Hopper's New York Movie   154   200

STANTON, MAURA
POEMS
The Sled   122   195
The Dreams
Childhood   140   279
Biography
The Wilderness
Modern Lives   146   25
Twelve Below
Spring
Pole Vaulting   149   214
Wander Indiana
Living Apart   151   167
Mis-Diagnosis   158   29

BOOKS REVIEWED
Tales of the Supernatural   154   99

STANTON, THEODORE
ARTICLES
Correspondence:
Fifty Years Since Baudelaire   11   168

STAP, DON
POEMS
Trying To Write   142   344

STAPLES, HUGH B.
BOOKS REVIEWED
Robert Lowell:
The First Twenty Years   102   269

STAPLETON, LAURENCE
BOOKS REVIEWED
Marianne Moore: The Poet's Advance   139   340

STARBUCK, GEORGE
POEMS
Three Dreams on a Warm Sabbath   95   218
Elegy ("Mosaic. Let there be...")   106   289
For an American Burial
From Baudelaire: Spleen et Idéal
Pro Forma
Poem Issued by Me to Congressmen...   109   30
Of Late
The Sad Ballad
of the Fifteen Consecutive Rhymes   115   269
Sonnet in the Shape
of a Potted Christmas Tree   133   168
The Universe Is Closed and Has REMS   140   249
On Gozzoli's Painted Room
in the Medici Palace
Catalogue Raisonné of My Refrigerator Door   151   168
Reading the Facts about Frost
in The Norton Anthology   152   9
Gastarbeiter
Dame Edith's Hundredth
Session
Fifty Years of No George Gershwin Rag
Fifty Years of No George Gershwin Rag
Part Two
Pilgrim Tale
Dogs' Golfballs
Magnificat. Brave Cat at Snifter Fishbowl.

TRANSLATIONS
Poems from Baudelaire   106   291

BOOKS REVIEWED
Bone Thoughts   97   316
The Argot Merchant Disaster:
Poems New and Selected   142   350

STARBUCK, VICTOR
POEMS
The Idler   5   212
The Poet
Night for Adventures   8   234
The Freeholder   16   310

STARK, ELVA JUNE
POEMS
A Kind of Peace   67   76

STARK, INEZ CUNNINGHAM
[See also BOULTON, INEZ]
POEMS
The Body   54   134
Julia Gibbs
Leonardo Meets His Mother
The Angel of the Lord   57   181
Ether   60   69

REVIEWS
   Kings and the Moon,
     by James Stephens   55   160
   The Native Scene   58   103
     Pattern of a Day,
       by Robert Hillyer
     The Tomb of Thomas Jefferson,
       by Lawrence Lee
     A Winter Tide, by Robert Nathan
     Maine Tides, by Wilbert Snow

STARKIE, ENID
  BOOKS REVIEWED
   Arthur Rimbaud   56   95

  ARTICLES ABOUT
   Baudelaire, by M. D. Zabel   42   38
   Recent French Publications,
     by Wallace Fowlie   93   40

STARRETT, VINCENT
  POEMS
   Hell, Said the Duchess   52   262
   To Wicky: My Wire
   Quest   57   363
   Oracle of the Dog   62   12
   Rain Before Seven

  BOOKS REVIEWED
   Ebony Flame   22   284
   Autolycus in Limbo   62   350

STAUFFER, DONALD A.
  BOOKS REVIEWED
   The Nature of Poetry   68   290
   Poets at Work: Essays
     (With W. H. Auden, Karl Shapiro,
     and Rudolf Arnheim)   72   311

STAVER, FREDERICK
  BOOKS REVIEWED
   The Penalty of Adam   99   313

STEAD, W. F.
  ARTICLES ABOUT
   [Note]   84   119

STEARN, NOEL H.
  POEMS
   Airs Overhead   30   80
   Song ("Sky blue, mist gray...")
   Michigamme

STEARNS, FLORENCE DICKINSON
  POEMS
   If in the Language of the Polished Leaves   52   77
   The Tie that Separates   53   305
   Answer in Green   56   26

BOOKS REVIEWED
  Strange Dimension   56   48

STEARNS, HAROLD C(RAWFORD)
  POEMS
   Reuben Roy   13   76

  BOOKS REVIEWED
   The Little Book of Society Verse
     (Ed. with Claude M. Fuess)   22   168

STEARNS, MARSHALL W.
  REVIEWS
   The Wedge,
     by William Carlos Williams   66   35

STEDMAN, EDMUND CLARENCE
  ARTICLES ABOUT
   Stedman's Centenary,
     by Harriet Monroe   43   268

STEEGMULLER, FRANCIS
  BOOKS REVIEWED
   Sainte-Beuve: Selected Essays
     (Tr. with Norbert Guterman)   103   183
   Apollinaire: Poet Among the Painters   104   187

STEELE, TIMOTHY
  POEMS
   Wait   119   329
   Homecoming in Late March
   Three Notes Toward Definitions   130   218
   On the Eve of a Birthday   141   69
   The Chorus   142   259
   Chanson Philosophique
   Angel   143   127
   The Library
   Eros   145   262
   Ethics
   December in Los Angeles   161   134
   Hortulus

  BOOKS REVIEWED
   Sapphics Against Anger and Other Poems   149   341
   The Color Wheel   166   104

STEFAN, MARINA
  POEMS
   Going to Egypt   155   260

STEFANILE, FELIX (N.)
  POEMS
   The Marionettes   79   326
   That Underground Sun
   In the Sea's Alchemies   82   324
   An Old Reunion   84   10
   Winter Year
   Spoiled by All My Tyrants   85   339

A Late Elegy for a Baseball Player   87   15
An Old Bootblack in the Cafeteria
The Afternoon as an Aria
Brown, All of the Autumn
A Poem for S—   91   233
Sea Gulls
Services   94   382
That Miser, Fear
On My Day Off a Grouchy Poem   99   217
Lullaby for a Dark Night
From *Some Songs for Billie Holiday*
   Rory
   Love Song
A Fig-Tree in America
An Ode for Pindar
   for William Carlos Williams   102   147
The Fortune Hunter
A Cartoon for Aristotle
My Long Lost Brother
Years   108   110
Atlantis   111   376

TRANSLATIONS
  Poem by Paolo Ruffilli   155   138

REVIEWS
  The Angels of Discombooberation   96   179
    The Constipated Owl and *A Legionere*,
     by Mason Jordan Mason
    Answers, by E. V. Griffith
    Ragas, by David Meltzer
    Watermelons,
     by Ron Loewinsohn
    Odd Pieces, by Richard Culter
    Machines & Illusions,
     by David Gallatin
  A Catalogue of Nine   103   324
    Breakfast Rum, by David Cohen
    Two Sides of an Island,
     by Martin Halpern
    The Destruction of Cathedrals,
     by Daisy Aldan
    Selected Poems, by Loring Williams
    Voyage Noir,
     by Robin Magowan
    Ups & Downs of a Third Baseman,
     by R. R. Cuscaden
    Sorrow's Spy, by James L. Weil
    The World's Old Way,
     by Larry Rubin
    The Hungry Lions,
     by Joanne de Longchamps
  Profiles and Presences   109   198
    American Poetry since 1945,
     by Stephen Stepanchev
    Contemporary American Poetry,
     by Ralph J. Mills, Jr.
    The Poetic Themes of Robert Lowell,
     by Jerome Mazzaro

Theodore Roethke, Essays on the Poetry
   (Ed. by Arnold Stein)

BOOKS REVIEWED
  River Full of Craft   90   386
  Nine by Three
    (With Robert Beum
    and Maxine Cassin)   96   375

ARTICLES ABOUT
  [Note on misprint]   96   327

STEIG, ARTHUR EBEL
POEMS
  They Pass   45   82
    La Passada Folor
    Lamentation
  Poems Because of Phyllis   47   314
    Poem at the River's Edge
    Hosanna
    Nocturne
    October

STEIN, ARNOLD
POEMS
  Our Ancient Sires   69   22

BOOKS REVIEWED
  Perilous Balance   68   227
  Heroic Knowledge: An Interpretation
    of *Paradise Regained*
    and *Samson Agonistes*   93   404
  Theodore Roethke, Essays on the Poetry (Ed.)   109   198
  George Herbert's Lyrics   115   196

STEIN, CHARLES
BOOKS REVIEWED
  Provisional Measures   110   105

STEIN, GERTRUDE
POEMS
  Stanzas in Meditation   55   229
  Stanzas in Meditation   121   26

BOOKS REVIEWED
  Stanzas in Meditation   90   250

ARTICLES ABOUT
  The Disciples of Gertrude Stein,
    by Richard Aldington   17   35
  Why Not Laugh? by Harriet Monroe   33   206
  A Note on Stein and Abstraction,
    by Wendell Wilcox   55   254
  Rev. of *Collected Poems*, by E. J. Pratt 66   329
  Gertrude Stein, by Henry Rago   69   93
  Rev. of *The Third Rose:*
    Gertrude Stein and Her World,
    by John Malcolm Brinnin   98   59

STEIN, KEVIN
POEMS
   Terms   149   288
   Birds in a Circle
   Cheating   153   217
   Whose Tracks Those Are   155   333
   Authorial Distance   163   77

STEINER, GEORGE
[FRANCIS GEORGE STEINER]
POEMS
   Lyric of Desire   75   267

BOOKS REVIEWED
   The Penguin Book of Modern Verse
     in Translation (Ed.)   113   188

STEINER, JACQUELINE
POEMS
   Arrival in Cambridge   65   251

STEINER, STAN
POEMS
   Unearth the Man   88   145
   With Muted Passions
   Wearing the Odd Clothes of Exile
   a Puerto Rican Youth Arrives
   in New York City and Is Laughed At   90   224

STEINGASS, DAVID
POEMS
   Getting Crazy in the Garden   123   232
   The First Twilight Nail of Spring   156   4
   The Night Everything Waits for Us

BOOKS REVIEWED
   Body Compass   118   41
   American Handbook   127   98

STEINMANN, MARTIN
BOOKS REVIEWED
   The Permanence of Yeats
     (Ed. with James Hall)   76   227

STEINMETZ, CHARLES P.
ARTICLES ABOUT
   A Scientist's Challenge,
     by Harriet Monroe   15   149
   Science and Art Again I,
     by Alice Corbin Henderson   15   204
   Science and Art Again II,
     by Harriet Monroe   15   208

STELLA, (SISTER) MARIS
[(SISTER) MAXIS STELLA]
[See also SMITH, ALICE GUSTAVA]
POEMS
   Resurrection   62   24
   To a Young Flier Returned to College   69   200

BOOKS REVIEWED
   Here Only a Dove   58   275

STELLA, [SISTER] MAXIS
[See STELLA, (SISTER) MARIS]

STEPANCHEV, STEPHEN
POEMS
   Facing the Day   49   249
     Drouth
     The Laughing God
     Cactus
     This Sister Ever
   Words To Fix Time   52   125
     Approach
     Program: Arranged
     Apocalypse
     Hear Now the Gates
   Strength to War   62   258
   End of a War   68   82
   The Red Lily   79   134
   Crows over the Wheatfield
   Three Priests in April   81   235
   Say That   83   78
   Triangle   85   128
   The Gambler
   Desiring Other Selves   88   155
   Waiting
   A Flirting Hat
   The Artist and the Nude   90   88
   Unmelodious Song
   The Stone Statesman   97   23
   Awaking to Fire   101   185
   A Slow Wife
   Conventional Dialogue
   Beside a Lake
   A Visit to Mokrin, Yugoslavia   140   192
   Inspiration   153   349
   Seven Horizons   156   292
   November   159   87
   Homeless   161   96
   Thinking About Tu Fu   161   147
   Born in December   165   125
   A Wound that Never Heals
   Darkness Snowing

ARTICLES
   Correspondence   61   639
   Commentaries   74   44

REVIEWS
   Two Poets and the War   63   50
     Forty Poems,
      by John Lehmann
     The Middle of a War,
      by Roy Fuller
     Come Back to Earth,
      by Roy Helton   68   163

Commentaries   74   44
   Long Island Triptych and Other Poems,
     by Lindley Williams Hubbell
   Poems, by Robert Finch

BOOKS REVIEWED
   Three Priests in April   89   244
   American Poetry since 1945   109   198
   Mining the Darkness   129   102

STEPHAN, RUTH (DART)
POEMS
   Eyelet   57   188
   Sea Sprout
   Hiatus
   To God
   On a Chinese Waterfall   59   74
   Moment After Rain
   Weariness
   Crevasse
   It Is by Thought
   Directional
   Moment of Glory
   Night Comes to Bear Mountain   63   18
   Socratic
   Rendezvous
   Talkers
   Daitokuji Poems   101   175
   Sky-Time
   A Plump Song
   Song for Death's Mountain

REVIEWS
   Arcadia Borealis: Selected Poems
     of Erik Axel Karlfeldt
     (Tr. by Charles Wharton Stork)   56   284
   The Mind's Geography,
     by George Zabriskie   61   452
   Two Religious Poets   61   637
     Dawn in Snow,
      by Louise Townsend Nicholl
     Ritual for Myself,
      by Anderson M. Scruggs
   Icelandic Poems and Stories
     (Ed. by Richard Beck)   62   228
   Afternoon of a Pawnbroker,
     by Kenneth Fearing   63   163
   The Big Time, by Alfred Hayes   64   292
   Day and Night,
     by Dorothy Livesay   65   220
   Selected Poems,
     by Rafael Alberti
     (Tr. by Lloyd Mallan)   67   166
   Travelers in a Secret Country   70   159
     Secret Country,
      by Jorge Carrera Andrade
      (Tr. by Muna Lee)
     The Northern Stranger,
      by Lysander Kemp

ARTICLES ABOUT
   [Note]   72   289
   [Note]   102   134

STEPHENS, ALAN
POEMS
   My Friend the Motorcyclist   102   80
   A Side-Gallery for Some Insects

REVIEWS
   Pictures from Breughel and Other Poems,
     by William Carlos Williams   101   360

BOOKS REVIEWED
   The Sum   94   117
   Between Matter and Principle   104   104

STEPHENS, JAMES
POEMS
   The Waste Places   4   189
   Hawks
   The Liar
   Dark Wings

BOOKS REVIEWED
   Songs from the Clay   6   93
   The Rocky Road to Dublin   9   98
   Green Branches   13   161
   Reincarnations
   Irish Fairy Tales   18   49
   Collected Poems of...   31   41
   A Poetry Recital
   Strict Joy and Other Poems   40   229
   Kings and the Moon   55   160
   Collected Poems   86   287
   A James Stephens Reader
     (Ed. by Lloyd Frankenberg)   102   324

STEPHENS, WILLIAM
POEMS
   Classic Myth   47   144
     Proem
     Odysseus
     Artemis
     Theseus
     Epilogue
   In Memory of Vachel Lindsay   49   322
   Louisiana   50   196
   Substratum   51   126
   The Winning of the West   52   72
   Strange Nature
   The Old Men   53   17
   Topical Poem   60   80
   Dark Earth   61   480
   Temporal Dialogue

STERLING, GEORGE
POEMS
   A Legend of the Dove   1   75

At the Grand Cañon
Kindred

ARTICLES
Correspondence to *Reedy's Mirror*   13   105

BOOKS REVIEWED
Beyond the Breakers and Other Poems   7   307
Selected Poems   22   330
Continent's End, an Anthology of
  Contemporary California Poets
  (Ed. with Genevieve Taggard
  and James Rorty)   27   217

ARTICLES ABOUT
Two Poets Say Farewell,
  by Harriet Monroe
  [Allen Upward]   29   208

STERN, BERT
POEMS
A Little Poem   169   320
Steerage   170   136

STERN, GERALD
POEMS
I Remember Galileo   134   221
Potpourri
Magritte Dancing
Waving Goodbye
Little Did the Junco Know   135   125
Thinking About Shelley   136   144
June Fourth
Acacia
Picking the Roses   140   326
Song ("There's nothing in this...")
Steve Dunn's Spider
Of Blessed Name   144   289
One Bird To Love Forever
Another Insane Devotion   150   349
It Was in Houston
Brain of My Heart   151   169
The Bull-Roarer   151   480
Mimi   164   127
Light
Did I Say
One of the Smallest   169   195
Visiting My Own House in Iowa City
Someone To Watch Over Me
Big Annie Rooney
This Time
Both of Them Were Sixty-Five

BOOKS REVIEWED
The Red Coal   140   293
Rejoicings: Poems 1966-1972   146   293
Paradise Poems
Lovesick   155   229

Leaving Another Kingdom: Selected Poems   157   96
Bread Without Sugar   161   99
Odd Mercy   167   156

ARTICLES ABOUT
[Note]   168   175

STERN, J. P.
BOOKS REVIEWED
Rainer Maria Rilke:
  A Study of His Later Poetry,
  by Hans Egon Holthusen (Tr.)   82   342

STERN, RICHARD (G.)
POEMS
The Hole   167   331

REVIEWS
Rainer Maria Rilke:
  A Study of His Later Poetry,
  by Hans Egon Holthusen
  (Tr. by J. P. Stern)   82   342

STERNBERG, RICARDO
POEMS
Exigencies of the Poem   133   73
Ana Louca
Francis's Barn

STERNLIEB, BARRY
POEMS
First Lesson   146   86
Tea Garden   150   130
Pine Judgment   163   96
Water Route   167   340
Ikebana

STEVENS, ALEX
POEMS
Trust This Recipe   129   16
The Plain-Speech Symposium   141   331
A Midwest Mezzotint
Western Nocturne   143   138

STEVENS, BEATRICE
POEMS
Hay   12   256

STEVENS, FRANCES
POEMS
Earth   32   313

STEVENS, HOLLY
[HOLLY STEVENS STEPHENSON]
BOOKS REVIEWED
Letters of Wallace Stevens (Ed.)   111   39
The Palm at the End of the Mind:
  Selected Poems and a Play
  by Wallace Stevens (Ed.)   119   171

Souvenirs and Prophecies:
  The Young Wallace Stevens   132   166

ARTICLES ABOUT
A Talk on Wallace Stevens,
  by Michael Ryan   134   353

STEVENS, THOMAS WOOD
POEMS
  In the Laboratory   5   20
  The Pageant   12   82
  The Cactus   56   173

STEVENS, WALLACE
POEMS
  Phases   5   70
  Sunday Morning   7   81
  Three Travelers Watch a Sunrise   8   163
  Carlos Among the Candles   11   115
  "Lettres d'un Soldat"   12   59
    ("The spirit wakes in the night...")
    Anecdotal Revery
    Morale
    Comme Dieu Dispense de Graces
    The Surprises of the Superhuman
    ("There is another mother...")
    Negation
    ("John Smith and his son...")
    ("Life contracts and death...")
  Pecksniffiana   15   1
    Fabliau of Florida
    Homunculus et La Belle Etoile
    The Weeping Burgher
    Peter Parasol
    Exposition of the Contents of a Cab
    Ploughing on Sunday
    Banal Sojourn
    The Indigo Glass in the Grass
    Anecdote of the Jar
    Of the Surface of Things
    The Curtains in the House
      of the Metaphysician
    The Place of the Solitaires
    The Paltry Nude Starts
      on a Spring Voyage
    Colloquy with a Polish Aunt
  Sur Ma Guzzla Gracile   19   1
    Palace of the Babies
    From the Misery of Don Joost
    The Doctor of Geneva
    Gubbinal
    The Snow Man
    Tea at the Palaz of Hoon
    The Cuban Doctor
    Another Weeping Woman
    Of the Manner of Addressing Clouds
    Of Heaven Considered as a Tomb
    The Load of Sugar-Cane
    Hibiscus on the Sleeping Shores

  Good Man, Bad Woman   41   6
  Like Decorations in a Nigger Cemetery   45   239
  The Man with the Blue Guitar   50   61
  A Rabbit as King of the Ghosts   51   1
  Illustrations of the Poetic as a Sense   54   177
    The Common Life
    The Sense of the Sleight-of-Hand Man
    The Candle a Saint
    A Dish of Peaches in Russia
    Arcades of Philadelphia the Past
    Of Hartford in a Purple Light
  Certain Phenomena of Sound   61   358
  The Ultimate Poem Is Abstract   71   10
  Bouquet of Roses in Sunlight
  Things of August   75   125
  St. Armorer's Church
    from the Outside   81   72
  Phases   121   31

ARTICLES
  [Tribute to Harriet Monroe]   49   154
  From the "Adagia"   90   40

BOOKS REVIEWED
  Harmonium   23   154
  Harmonium [New ed.]   39   148
  Ideas of Order   47   153
  Owl's Clover   49   268
  Ideas of Order
  The Man with the Blue Guitar
    and Other Poems   51   153
  Parts of a World   61   448
  Notes Toward a Supreme Fiction   62   48
  Esthétique du Mal   68   97
  Transport to Summer   71   271
  Three Academic Pieces   72   270
  The Auroras of Autumn   77   109
  The Man with the Blue Guitar,
    Including Ideas of Order   81   139
  Collected Poems   85   288
  Opus Posthumous—Poems, Plays, Prose
    (Ed. by Samuel French Morse)   92   52
  Letters
    (Ed. by Holly Stevens)   111   39
  The Palm at the End of the Mind:
    Selected Poems and a Play by...
    (Ed. by Holly Stevens)   119   171

ARTICLES ABOUT
  Mr. Yeats and the Poetic Drama,
    by Harriet Monroe   16   32
  Rev. of Others for 1919
    (Ed. by Alfred Kreymborg)   17   150
  A Cavalier of Beauty,
    by Harriet Monroe   23   322
  Rev. of New Poems: 1943
    (Ed. by Oscar Williams)   64   86

Rev. of *The Use of Color in the Verse*
  of the English Romantic Poets,
  by A. E. Pratt   69   88
Rev. of *The Image and the Law,*
  by Howard Nemerov   71   94
The Poetry of Wallace Stevens,
  by J. V. C(unningham)   75   149
Rev. of *The Shaping Spirit,*
  by William Van O'Connor   76   355
Wallace Stevens,
  by William Carlos Williams   87   234
A Note on the "Adagia,"
  by Samuel French Morse   90   45
French Chronicle: Recent Publications,
  by Wallace Fowlie   91   36
Rev. of *The Achievement of...*
  (Ed. by Ashley Brown
  and Robert Haller)   102   269
Rev. of *Wallace Stevens:*
  An Anatomy of Figuration,
  by Eugene Nassar;
  The Clairvoyant Eye,
  by Joseph N. Riddel;
  and *Introduction to...*
  by Henry W. Wells   109   201
Rev. of *Poets of Reality:*
  Six Twentieth-Century Writers,
  by J. Hillis Miller   110   254
Rev. of *The Gaiety of Language:*
  An Essay on the Radical Poetics
  of W. B. Yeats and Wallace Stevens,
  by Frank Lentricchia   115   346
Rev. of *Wallace Stevens:*
  The Poems of Our Climate,
  by Harold Bloom   131   165
Rev. of *The New Oxford Book*
  of American Verse
  (Ed. by Richard Ellmann)   131   236
Rev. of *Souvenirs and Prophecies:*
  The Young Wallace Stevens,
  by Holly Stevens   132   166
A Talk on Wallace Stevens,
  by Michael Ryan   134   353
Allen Tate: A Poet on Poetry, 1924-1944,
  by Ashley Brown   135   103
Rev. of *No Traveller,* by Richard Howard   155   283
Rev. of *The Collected Poems*
  of Henri Coulette
  (Ed. by Donald Justice
  and Robert Mezey)   158   214

STEVENSON, ANNE
POEMS
  In the Tunnel of Summers   146   204
  Calendar
  The Ballad of the Made Maid
  Nightmares, Daymoths   151   171
  Icon

BOOKS REVIEWED
  Living in America   109   340
  Reversals   117   331
  Correspondences   127   98
  Selected Poems, 1956-1986   152   35

STEVENSON, BURTON E(GBERT)
BOOKS REVIEWED
  The Home Book of Verse (Ed.)   14   281
  The Home Book
  of Modern Verse (Ed.)   27   343

STEVENSON, DIANE
POEMS
  Family Album   150   188
  Lullaby
  Matins
  Sources of Light
  Descartes   154   189

STEVENSON, ELLEN
[ELLEN BORDEN]
POEMS
  Songs   32   320
    ("The golden arms of dawn...")
    ("I have walked alone by day...")
    ("I hold the mirrors...")
    ("I have felt grief...")
  Night Flight   59   65

STEVENSON, FANNY OSBOURNE
ARTICLES ABOUT
  Rev. of *Mermaids in the Basement,*
  by Carolyn Kizer   151   360

STEVENSON, QUENTIN
BOOKS REVIEWED
  The Succession   92   309

STEVENSON, ROBERT LOUIS
ARTICLES ABOUT
  Rev. of *Winged Chariot*
  and Other Poems,
  by Walter de la Mare   80   213

STEWART, DESMOND
POEMS
  Dawn over a Waste City   72   241
  Italian Cemetery
  Return from Babylon
  Vi Connolly's Spring Song   93   98

REVIEWS
  The Oxford Book of Irish Verse:
  XVII Century-XX Century
  (Ed. by Donagh MacDonagh
  and Lennox Robinson)
  [Oliver Goldsmith, W. B. Yeats]   94   260

STEWART, DOUGLAS
BOOKS REVIEWED
Poetry in Australia
(Ed. with T. Inglis Moore)   110   47

STEWART, H. W.
POEMS
Tasmanian Sketches   17   76
Supplicants
Gum-Trees
Sky
Dawn   21   130
Reverie

ARTICLES
Correspondence: Australian
and U. S. Copyrights   17   348
Aboriginal Tasmanian Poetry   18   271

STEWART, IRENE
POEMS
The Little Queen's Sleep   27   310
A Fountain Sealed   30   244
Transition
Dirge

STEWART, JACK
POEMS
Fishing   158   95
Bluepoints
At Home with Angels   164   75

STEWART, JOHN L.
BOOKS REVIEWED
John Crowe Ransom   102   269

STEWART, LUELLA
POEMS
Desire   15   21

STEWART, PAMELA
POEMS
Sonnet of God   126   160
Consent

BOOKS REVIEWED
Half-Tones   133   346

STEWART, SUSAN
POEMS
Roads   124   314
Consecration   142   33
Fire Ceremony
Man Dancing with a Baby   144   152
*Budapest, March 1928: The Genius of
Friendship*

BOOKS REVIEWED
Yellow Stars and Ice   140   346

STICKNEY, JOSEPH TRUMBULL
ARTICLES ABOUT
Stickney's Poetry,
by R. P. Blackmur   42   158

STILL, JAMES
POEMS
Autumnal   47   12
Mountain Fox Hunt
Mountain Infare
When the Dulcimers Are Gone
Brought Back   50   70
White Highways
Earth-Bread

BOOKS REVIEWED
Hounds on the Mountain   51   347

STILL, JOHN
BOOKS REVIEWED
Poems in Captivity   16   336

STILLMAN, E. CLARK
POEMS
Crows   32   138
Ground
The Hills Between   42   71

STILLMAN, FRANCES JENNINGS
POEMS
The Scars   59   196
Martyrs' Blood

STILLMAN, MILDRED WHITNEY
POEMS
April Poems   34   18
Easter Eve
First Supper
Discovery

BOOKS REVIEWED
Queens and Crickets   33   168

STITT, PETER
REVIEWS
Summer Birds and Haunch of Winter   135   229
The Vermont Suicides,
by Roger Weingarten
Rounding the Horn,
by David Slavitt
Designing Women,
by Pamela White Hadas
Riversongs, by Michael Anania
The Power To Change Geography,
by Diana Ó Hehir
Praise, by Robert Hass
The Star-Apple Kingdom,
by Derek Walcott
The Poems of Stanley Kunitz 1928-1978 136 347

West of Your City   138   46
  In Broken Country,
    by David Wagoner
  The Triggering Town and *Selected Poems*,
    by Richard Hugo
  [William Stafford]
Imagination in the Ascendant   143   39
  The Wheel, by Wendell Berry
  Magpie on the Gallows,
    by Madeline DeFrees
  Candles in Babylon,
    by Denise Levertov
  Northbook, by Frederick Morgan
  Letters from a Father and Other Poems,
    by Mona Van Duyn
  Austerities, by Charles Simic
  The Balthus Poems,
    by Stephen Dobyns
The Poetry of Realism   144   231
  Smoke's Way, by William Stafford
  Family Reunion:
    Selected and New Poems,
    by Paul Zimmer
  Alliance, Illinois, by Dave Etter
  The Gymnast of Inertia,
    by William Hathaway
  The Common Wages,
    by Bruce Smith
Blessings and Rain   148   99
  Blessing,
    by Christopher Jane Corkery
  Driving the Body Back,
    by Mary Swander
  Swan's Island,
    by Elizabeth Spires
  Any Given Day, by Ralph Burns
  Winter Stars, by Larry Levis
  Wild Gratitude,
    by Edward Hirsch
  Rain, by William Carpenter
Aestheticians and the Pit of the Self   152   161
  The Exact Place,
    by Mary Ann Waters
  Other Children, by Lawrence Raab
  Kingdoms of the Ordinary,
    by Robley Wilson, Jr.
  Legendary Performance,
    by Pattiann Rogers
  The Lotus Flowers,
    by Ellen Bryant Voigt
  The Flying Dutchman and
    After the Noise of Saigon,
    by Walter McDonald
  Against Romance,
    by Michael Blumenthal

BOOKS REVIEWED
  James Wright: The Heart of the Light
    (Ed. with Frank Graziano)   157   343

STIVENDER, DAVID
  TRANSLATIONS
    Poems by Pier Paolo Pasolini
      (Tr. with J. D. McClatchy)   155   47
    Poems by Giovanni Raboni
      (Tr. with J. D. McClatchy)   155   89

STOCK, NOEL
  BOOKS REVIEWED
    Poet in Exile: Ezra Pound   106   361

STOCK, ROBERT
  POEMS
    That the Sestina Is What It Is
      Despite What It Is Not   90   25
    Revelation According to the Beloved   92   13
    Ballade To Be Read
      in the Medici Gardens
    The Irritated Office
    Moses on Pisgah   96   218
    After Troy   104   227
    Tight-Rope Construction Surrounded
      by a Thousand Sonnets   122   312
    Wrestling with Angels   126   197

  REVIEWS
    Selected Poems,
      by Lawrence Durrell   91   396

  BOOKS REVIEWED
    Covenants   113   188

STOCKETT, M. LETITIA
  POEMS
    Free   22   20

STODDARD, CHARLES WARREN
  BOOKS REVIEWED
    Poems of...
      (Ed. by Ina Coolbrith)   12   279

STODDARD, HOPE
  POEMS
    Grisette   31   317

STOEHR, TAYLOR
  BOOKS REVIEWED
    Collected Poems,
      by Paul Goodman (Ed.)   128   100

STOKES, TERRY
  BOOKS REVIEWED
    Boning the Dreamer   129   226

STOLOFF, CAROLYN
  BOOKS REVIEWED
    Dying To Survive   124   167

STONE, ALISON
POEMS
Foggy Notion   149   262
Rocket to Russia
Spofford Hall   150   78
Brandeis Senior Year
Not Seeking New Worlds   151   457
Starving for God   154   220
Beneath the Beautiful
What the Spirit Seeks   156   94
Heritage   160   154
The Body's Small Pleasures
Not Finding Tranquility by the Lake   160   338
Persephone's First Season in Hell   161   22
Persephone Returning   164   134
Not Cure, Not Denial   166   146

STONE, BRIAN
BOOKS REVIEWED
Sir Gawain and the Green Knight (Tr.)   97   195

STONE, JOHN
POEMS
You Round the Bend   140   267
Three for the Mona Lisa

STONE, LUELLA
POEMS
Priez Pour Nous   33   136
I Saw a Fawn

STONE, MYRNA
POEMS
Penitential   165   318
From the Kitchen
Taraxacum Officinale
Simulacrum   168   191
My Mother's Room   168   265

STONE, RUTH
POEMS
The Pear   79   130
The Mother
Union
Siesta   82   63
The Wind Fire
Forecast
The Magnet
For a Post Card of My Mother at the Beach   84   138
Experience
The Fleet
Of Heroes   87   30
As Real as Life
Home Movie
Vernal Equinox   89   210
Confession
Orchard
Juveniles

Private Pantomime
In the Madness of Age

BOOKS REVIEWED
In an Iridescent Time   97   185
Topography and Other Poems   119   234
Cheap   129   296

STONE, WALTER
BOOKS REVIEWED
Poems, 1955-1958, in *Poets of Today VI*
(Ed. by John Hall Wheelock)   95   373

STORER, EDWARD
BOOKS REVIEWED
Terra Italica   18   103

ARTICLES ABOUT
Our Contemporaries:
Autumn Leaves from England   7   99

STOREY, EDWARD
BOOKS REVIEWED
North Bank Night   117   331

STOREY, VIOLET ALLEYN
POEMS
Analogy   24   310
Elfin
The Neat One   26   315

BOOKS REVIEWED
Green of the Year   33   168

STORK, CHARLES WHARTON
POEMS
The Rose and God   24   23
Song of a Ploughman   29   258

TRANSLATIONS
Poem by Georg Trakl   6   102
Poem by Ludwig Holstein   21   73
Poem by Erik Axel Karlfeldt   40   145
Poem by Erik Axel Karlfeldt   42   14

ARTICLES
Correspondence:
Death of a Young German Poet
[Georg Trakl]   6   102
Erik Axel Karlfeldt, Swedish Poet   40   152

BOOKS REVIEWED
Gustaf Froding—Selected Poems (Tr.)   12   52
Anthology of Swedish Lyrics (Tr.)   14   281
Contemporary Verse Anthology (Ed.)   18   106
*Arcadia Borealis: Selected Poems
of Erik Axel Karlfeldt* (Tr.)   56   284
Anthology of Norwegian Lyrics (Ed.)   62   54
A Second Book of Danish Verse (Tr.)   71   339

ARTICLES ABOUT
[Note on misprint]   62   175

STORK, GEORGE WHARTON
BOOKS REVIEWED
The Queen of Orplede   2   107

STORM, MARIAN
POEMS
Vigil at Candlemas   31   196
Dirge for Guitar
Catastrophe   41   83
Michoacán: Two Scenes   50   82
Cove on the Orilla
Coast Panther

STORNI, ALFONSINA
POEMS
Running Water
(Tr. by Muna Lee)   26   117

STOTT, LIBBY
POEMS
After the Heart Attack   164   218
Retired   168   103

STOUTENBURG, ADRIEN
POEMS
The Binge   74   72

ARTICLES
Correspondence
[Harry Strickhausen]   108   136

BOOKS REVIEWED
Heroes, Advise Us   107   183
Short History of the Fur Trade   114   401

STRAKHOVSKY, LEONID I.
BOOKS REVIEWED
Three Poets of Modern Russia
[Nikolai Gumilyov,
Anna Akhmatova,
Osip Mandelstam]   76   112

STRAMM, AUGUST
ARTICLES ABOUT
Correspondence
from Edward J. O'Brien   8   213

STRAND, MARK
POEMS
Black Maps   116   178
Seven Poems
("At the edge...")
("A scar remembers...")
("When we walk...")
("My body lies down...")
("The rock is pleasure...")
("When I talk...")
("I have a key...")
The Untelling   122   274
To Himself   151   173

BOOKS REVIEWED
Sleeping with One Eye Open   108   191
Darker   118   344
The Contemporary American Poets:
American Poetry Since 1940 (Ed.)   119   109
The Story of Our Lives   124   280
The Owl's Insomnia,
by Rafael Alberti
(Ed. and tr.)
The Late Hour   132   298
Selected Poems   139   171
The Continuous Life   158   41
Dark Harbor   166   289

ARTICLES ABOUT
Review by Linda Gregerson   167   287

STRANDBERG, VICTOR H.
BOOKS REVIEWED
A Colder Fire:
The Poetry of Robert Penn Warren   110   254

STRANGE, MICHAEL
BOOKS REVIEWED
Resurrecting Life   18   222
Clair de Lune

STRASSER, JUDITH
POEMS
On Reading Descartes' Error   166   152

STRAUB, PETER
POEMS
Thinking About America   116   93
The Desert Motion   117   243
The Bow
Using the Bow
The Sleepers
On Hampstead Heath with Women
Encantadas   119   91
("Spill out ashes...")
("Some of our exceptions...")
("Does enchantment pour...?'")

STRAUSS, JENNIFER
POEMS
Snaps from Patagonia   169   80

STRETTELL, ALMA
BOOKS REVIEWED
Poems of Emile Verhaeren (Tr.)   8   96

STRICKHAUSEN, HARRY
POEMS
The Frozen Lake   90   358
Gemini   95   20
Of the Real World   104   156
Shadow and Image

ARTICLES
Correspondence
[Adrien Stoutenburg]   108   136

REVIEWS
Summer Knowledge: New and Selected Poems,
    by Delmore Schwartz   95   300
The Branch Will Not Break,
    by James Wright   102   391
Recent Criticism   104   264
    The Loyalties of Robinson Jeffers,
        by Radcliffe Squires
    Swifter than Reason: The Poetry and
        Criticism of Robert Graves,
        by Douglas Day
    The Poetry of W. H. Auden:
        The Disenchanted Island,
        by Monroe K. Spears
    The Religious Sonnets of Dylan Thomas:
        A Study in Imagery and Meaning,
        by H. H. Kleinman
    Shakespeare: A Biography,
        by Peter Quennell
    The Poet Kao Ch'i, 1336-1374,
        by F. W. Mote
Seven Poets   107   183
    Preambles and Other Poems,
        by Alvin Feinman
    Figure for Scamander and Others,
        by Carol Johnson
    Ship on the Beach, by Theodore Holmes
    And In Him, Too; In Us,
        by Konstantinos Lardas
    Night Voyage, by Eric Sellin
    The Window, by Vern Rutsala
    Heroes, Advise Us,
        by Adrien Stoutenburg

STRINGER, ARTHUR
POEMS
A Woman at Dusk   2   153

BOOKS REVIEWED
Open Water   5   240
A Woman at Dusk   34   108

STROBEL, MARION
["M. S.", MARION STROBEL
MITCHELL]
POEMS
Perennials   15   312
    Anticipation

Spring Day
Ennui
Let Me Play Net
The Last Ritual
Hands
    ("Will you not stay away...")
    ("How can I offer you the dull...")
That Year   17   240
    Anodyne
    Little Things
    I Give Smiles
    Without Words
    High Dive
    Marriage-Caprice
    Miserere
    Kindness
Song Sketches   19   303
    We Have a Day
    Spring Morning
    Tonight
    The Silence Stirs Again
    The Night
    I Would Pretend
    Admonition
    Frightened Face
    Daily Prayer
    L'Envoi
Kaleidoscope   21   291
    Encounter
    I Talk with Myself
    Full-Blown
    The Gestures You Make
    A Bride
    Dialogue
    Pitiful in Your Bravery
    Boomerang
    After These Days
    Pastoral
People   24   59
    In the Tropics
    Two Liars
    Pretty Penny
    Growth
    Portrait of a Friend
    Story-Teller
    Penitent Wife
    The Tragic Few
    Tropical Pool
Songs for Sally   25   128
    Prescience
    What Have I Done?
    Eight Months Old
    A Dress for My Daughter
    A Song to Sally
    On Christmas
    My Offerings
    A God for You
In Passing   28   297
    Song of Summer

In This Room		
Gift from the Empty-Handed		
Too Well I Know		
Sand Picture		
Flirt		
Torch-Bearers		
For a Lady Pursued		
Still Life		
Captive		
Last Migration		
Protest		
Bridges		
Lost City	31	235
Discus-Thrower		
Surf-Boarding		
Fall of Rain		
August Child		
Flight of Feet		
Maternity		
Godiva		
Young Girl		
Bride		
Dog over Snow		
Still-Hunt		
Fable		
Belfry		
Man of Any Nation	35	72
Panorama	38	177
Encounter		
Through Autumn Arbors		
Shame		
Two Seasons Only		
Portrait Without Words		
Touch		
Lament		
Doubt		
Words to the Wise	40	239
Te Deum		
Invocation		
The Singing Ladder		
The Quail		
Hallelujah		
To My Children		
Crisis	44	246
This Living City		
For Barren Women		
From Out the Four Black Walls		
Man in Blue Shirt-Sleeves		
Coat of Arms		
The Dawn Is Here	48	121
Flight of Faith		
Forego the Flesh		
Musician		
Memory of Jackson Park		
Proud House		
So Does the Dream Go On		
Let Me Not		
Before Annihilation		
For Harriet Monroe	49	143
No Other Bell	50	246
For My Father		
Public Garden		
North East Wind		
Involuntary Spies	53	195
Curfew		
Snow		
Under What Flying Colors		
Ascent		
For Grief		
The Target Is the Same	56	300
In the Season of Good Will	59	134
Bon Voyage	60	124
Small Song		
First Letter		
Return to Sender: Died of Wounds		
Man and Bike		
Tribute	65	136
First Lesson: Relativity		
The Fruit Farm		
Concourse		
Bas Relief		
Tax Exempt		
After Ardennes	67	195
Round Trip	70	141
A Fantasy and Fact		
Tarpon: Strike and Getaway		
Prayers for One Person		
Catch	81	74

ARTICLES
Correspondence:		
Marion Strobel Resigns	27	54
The Romance of It		
[Harriet Monroe]	41	47
[Tribute to Harriet Monroe]	49	143
543 Cass Street	71	39
Intramural	74	93

REVIEWS
Poems, by T. S. Eliot	16	157
Black Branches, by Orrick Johns	16	162
A Flag of Truce	17	100
Something Else Again,		
by F. P. A.		
[Franklin P. Adams]		
Types of Pan, by Keith Preston		
Including Horace,		
by Louis Untermeyer		
Idylls of the Skillet Fork,		
by Payson S. Wild		
Farm Voices, by Don C. Seitz		
A Line-o'-Verse or Two,		
by Bert Leston Taylor		
The House of Dust,		
by Conrad Aiken	17	220
Resurrecting Life and *Clair de Lune*,		
by Michael Strange	18	222

Two English Poets   18   343
    The Waggoner,
      by Edmund Blunden
    The Kaleidoscope, by Sherard Vines
Second April,
    by Edna St. Vincent Millay   19   151
Saturday Market, by Charlotte Mew   20   152
The Blue Ship, by Herbert Jones   20   280
The Cockpit of Idols,
    by Muriel Stuart   20   338
Cross-Currents,
    by Margaret Widdemer   20   340
The Barcarole of James Smith
    and Other Poems,
    by Herbert S. Gorman   21   213
The Black Panther,
    by John Hall Wheelock   21   224
Delicate Sheaves   21   335
    The Indians in the Woods,
      by Janet Lewis
    The Keen Edge,
      by Maurine Smith
Manikin Number Two,
    by William Carlos Williams   23   103
Songs of Youth,
    by Mary Dixon Thayer   23   111
The Miller's Youngest Daughter,
    by Grace Fallow Norton   24   217
Sunrise Trumpets,
    by Joseph Auslander   24   219
Marriage Songs,
    by Mary Carolyn Davies   24   339
Atlas and Beyond,
    by Elizabeth Coatsworth   25   224
Spring Thunder and Other Poems,
    by Mark Van Doren   25   279
The Unknown Goddess,
    by Humbert Wolfe   28   108
This Waking Hour,
    by Leon Serabian Herald   28   167
Wild Plum: Lyrics, by Orrick Johns   29   221
The Selected Poems
    of Arthur Davison Ficke   29   275
The Guilty Sun, by James Daly   29   346
The Evergreen Tree,
    by Kathleen Millay   32   169
The Set-Up,
    by Joseph Moncure March   33   279
John Deth and Other Poems,
    by Conrad Aiken   38   107
Whatever You Reap, by Anne Persov   42   223
Glory of Earth,
    by Anderson M. Scruggs   44   286
Four Women   51   223
    Mirror to Mortality,
      by Martha Keller
    Road to America, by Frances Frost

    The Hills Grow Smaller,
      by Zoë Akins
    One More Manhattan,
      by Phyllis McGinley
    Memory, by Walter de la Mare   54   288
Old Possum and Others   55   221
    Old Possum's Book of Practical Cats,
      by T. S. Eliot
    Madeline, by Ludwig Bemelmans
    Before Things Happen,
      by Dorothy Aldis
    With Wings as Eagles,
      by William Rose Benét   57   220
    The Metaphysical Sword,
      by Jeremy Ingalls   59   218
New Poems 1942
    (Ed. by Oscar Williams)   60   288
Two War Anthologies   63   346
    The New Treasury of War Poetry,
      1939 to 1943
      (Ed. by George Herbert Clarke)
    War Poems of the United Nations
      (Ed. by Joy Davidman)
Dr. Johnson's Waterfall,
    by Helen Bevington   69   234

BOOKS REVIEWED
    Once in a Blue Moon   26   346
    Lost City   34   236

ARTICLES ABOUT
    A Symposium on Marianne Moore,
      by Harriet Monroe   19   208
    A Few Women Poets,
      by Harriet Monroe   26   326
    Marion Strobel Mitchell,
      by Jessica Nelson North   108   264

STRODE, HUDSON
  BOOKS REVIEWED
    Immortal Lyrics (Ed.)   57   221

STRODE, MURIEL
  BOOKS REVIEWED
    A Soul's Faring   22   168

STRONG, L. A. G.
  POEMS
    The Parson's Daughter   31   255
    Childless   34   325
    The Rebel   39   25

  BOOKS REVIEWED
    By Haunted Stream (Ed.)   27   343
    The Best Poems of 1924 (Ed.)
    Selected Poems   42   295
    Common Sense About Poetry

STRONGIN, LYNN

POEMS

Andromache	119	142
Dutch Painting		
Countdown	121	277

STRUTHERS, ANN

POEMS

Writing Moby-Dick	153	319

STRYK, LUCIEN

POEMS

Cherries	132	138
November	141	68
Rooms	146	14
Botanist	151	174
Dreaming to Music	152	313
Light	154	148

TRANSLATIONS

Poems by Shinkichi Takahashi		
(Tr. with Takashi Ikemoto)	116	364

BOOKS REVIEWED

The Trespasser	90	114
Notes for a Guidebook	109	48
The Pit and Other Poems	117	54
Awakening	124	343
Selected Poems	132	31

STUART, DABNEY

POEMS

Fair	103	169
I Love You	105	232
For the Birds		
Dry Leaves		
Building a Snow Man		
Home Room	107	243
Ties		
The Student	109	17
Anniversary	111	223
Sunburst		
Worldly Goods		
The Fool's Song	121	223
The Slut's Song		
The Fool and the Poet		
The Ballad of What Has Happened		
The Slut and the Poet		
The Ballad of the Frozen Field		
Plowing It Under	131	141
The Top of the Forest		
Listening	146	97

REVIEWS

Seven Poets and a Playwright	104	258
The New Handbook of Heaven,		
by Diane di Prima		

The Twenty-Third of Love,		
by Mason Jordan Mason		
Mirandum, by Vincent Ferrini		
Unfair Arguments with Existence:		
Seven Plays for a New Theater,		
by Lawrence Ferlinghetti		
The World of the Lie,		
by Ron Loewinsohn		
Hermes Past the Hour,		
by Judson Crews		
Poet as Bad Guy, by Ron Offen		
It Catches My Heart in Its Hands,		
by Charles Bukowski		

BOOKS REVIEWED

The Diving Bell	110	258
The Other Hand	126	219
Round and Round: A Triptych	132	288

STUART, FRANCIS

POEMS

The Trees in the Square	73	210

STUART, H(ARRY)

POEMS

Munich	22	1
Helen		
Bull-Fight		
Summer		
For a Dancer		
Fragment		
Remember		
At Dawn		
Love's Obscurity	25	87
Its Many Echoings		
Sonnet ("Far torrents fill...")		
Her Nature		
Four Poems to a Wave		
The Heart's Content	29	29
Summer		
By the Waterfall		
September		
Refuge		

BOOKS REVIEWED

We Have Kept the Faith	24	158

STUART, JESSE

POEMS

From Young Kentucky	44	61
Youth in Spring	48	130
Ridley Donnell	53	75
For Archie Wren: Traitor	54	186

BOOKS REVIEWED

Man with a Bull-Tongue Plow	45	217
Album of Destiny	66	168
Hold April	102	125

STUART, MURIEL
POEMS
   Bluebell Night   10   76
   In Their Image   21   68
   The Seed-Shop
   In the Orchard
   Dialogues   27   24
      After Seven Years
      Colloquy
   Unknown Warrior   37   84

BOOKS REVIEWED
   The Cockpit of Idols   20 338
   New Poems and Old   29   45

ARTICLES ABOUT
   The Editor in England,
     by Harriet Monroe   23   32

STUART, RUTH MC ENERY
POEMS
   Sitting Blind by the Sea   4 144

BOOKS REVIEWED
   Plantation Songs and Other Verse   9   54

STULL, CHARLENE
POEMS
   Down This Hill   164   89

STULL, RICHARD
POEMS
   Changing Light   127 262
   Afterward
   The First Year   130   25
   Fame
   Content

STURGE MOORE, T.
POEMS
   Isaac and Rebekah   8 239

BOOKS REVIEWED
   The Sea Is Kind   5   84
   The Little School   18   50
   The Poems of...   39 280

ARTICLES ABOUT
   Hark to Sturge Moore,
     by Ezra Pound   6 139
   Rev. of *An Annual of New Poetry, 1917* 11 333
   Rev. of *W. B. Yeats and T. Sturge Moore,*
     Their Correspondence
     (Ed. by Ursula Bridge)   83 357

STURGES, LUCY H.
POEMS
   Orthodox   33   23

STUURMAN, EDITH
POEMS
   The Lamb   77   73
   The Fish   81 182
   The Cricket

SUBBARAO, NANDURI
POEMS
   Enki
     (Tr. by P. T. Raju)   93 223

SUBLETT, DYAN
POEMS
   The Women Who Teach Languages 145 328

SUCKLING, NORMAN
BOOKS REVIEWED
   Paul Valéry and the Civilized Mind 85 300

SUCKOW, RUTH
POEMS
   By Hill and Dale   18 142
   Prayer at Timber-Line
   Beauty
   The Odd Ones
   Grampa Schuler

SUERMONDT, TIM
POEMS
   Briefly Eavesdropping on Walt Whitman,
     Virginia, 1863   164 195

SUITS, GUSTAV
ARTICLES ABOUT
   Rev. of *Anthology*
     of Modern Estonian Poetry
     (Ed. and tr. by W. K. Matthews) 84 236

SUK, JULIE
POEMS
   Remembering the Plot   159 266
   Playing Against Sleep
   Beyond the Hill
   Quicksilver
   La Tempesta
   Leaving the World
     We've Loved Speechless 162 275
   Lamentation
   The Acres You Cross 166 220
   Rounds
   Today You Traverse the Mountain
   From Ruin   170 342

SU KAI MING
TRANSLATIONS
   Poems by Ou Yang Hsiu
     and Feng Yien Chi
     (Tr. with Elizabeth Y. Gilbert) 50 136

SULLIVAN, A. M.

POEMS
Computation	38	138
The Insatiable	41	187
Speculation		
Chronicle		
Huckster	44	143
Symbols for Deceit	53	304

BOOKS REVIEWED
A Day in Manhattan	60	163
Incident in Silver	77	215

SULLIVAN, ALAN

POEMS
The Book of Time	168	27

SULLIVAN, LOUIS H.

ARTICLES
Wherefore the Poet?	7	305

SULLIVAN, NANCY

POEMS
An Edward Hopper Poem	96	163
To My Body	114	19
At Yaddo, Thinking About the War	120	343

REVIEWS
Snap Judgments	116	120
Snaps, by Victor Hernandez Cruz		
Oases, by Marcus Cumberlege		
Home from the Cemetery,		
by Robert Pack		
Poems,		
by Yehuda Amichai		
(Tr. by Assia Gutmann)		
Iconodule and Iconoclast	119	107
Iconographs, by May Swenson		
The Wishing Animal,		
by Joanne de Longchamps		
Figure and Field, by Jean Farley		
To a New Husband,		
by Helga Sandburg		

BOOKS REVIEWED
The History of the World as Pictures	109	48

ARTICLES ABOUT
Correspondence		
from Kenneth Lillquist	120	59

SULLIVAN, SUZANNE

POEMS
Poem ("Ripening tall...")	78	83

SUMMERS, EVE BRODLIQUE

POEMS
Of Ruined Cities	14	193

SUMMERS, HOLLIS

POEMS
The Lawnmower	83	319
King's X	85	77
A Poem for Mother's Day	140	159
Hummer		
The Meek		

BOOKS REVIEWED
The Walks Near Athens	95	309

SUN, CHENG YU
[See CHENG YU SUN]

SUPERVIELLE, JULES

BOOKS REVIEWED
Selected Writings	113	338

ARTICLES ABOUT
Verse Drama on the Paris Stage,		
by Ruby Haykin	82	294

SU SHIH

POEMS
On the Birth of a Son		
(Tr. by Arthur Waley)	11	199

ARTICLES ABOUT
The Chinese Chanting of the Classics,		
by Eunice Tietjens	9	35
Rev. of *An Introduction to Sung Poetry*,		
by Kojiro Yoshikawa		
(Tr. by Burton Watson)	112	283

SUTHERLAND, JOHN

POEMS
In the Aquarium	68	137
The Double Man		
With Expert Tailoring		
Self-Sufficiency		
Convalescent	73	81

REVIEWS
Toward the Last Spike, by E. J. Pratt	82	350
Poems: Complete Edition with Recent Poems,		
by John Masefield	86	49

SUTHERLAND, MONICA

BOOKS REVIEWED
La Fontaine: The Man and His Work	85	55

SUTPHEN, JOYCE

POEMS
Death Becomes Me	164	209
The Temptation To Invent	165	254
Not for Burning	167	264
Resurrection #6		
Of Virtue		
Condition		

BOOKS REVIEWED
   Straight Out of View   169   156

SUTTER, BARTON
POEMS
   Shoe Shop   135   261
   Static

SUTTON, GEOFFREY
BOOKS REVIEWED
   Half a Loaf   105   404

SUTTON, H. L(EE)
POEMS
   History Lesson   66   8
   News Item   74   143

SUTTON, KATHLEEN
POEMS
   Who Would Be Valiant   51   77
   Southern Farm
   This Is the Season   52   20
   It Is Not All Beauty   59   261

SVAGLIC, MARTIN J.
ARTICLES
   The Chicago Critics: Yes and Perhaps
   [Rev. of *Critics and Criticism*, II.
   Elder Olson, Aristotle, R. S. Crane]   82   157

REVIEWS
   Critics and Criticism, Ancient and Modern
   (Ed. by R. S. Crane)
   [Eliseo Vivas, John Crowe Ransom,
   Richard P. McKeon, Elder Olson,
   William Empson, S. T. Coleridge,
   W. R. Keast, Robert Penn Warren,
   Cleanth Brooks, I. A. Richards]   82   98
   The Forlorn Demon, by Allen Tate
   [Edgar Allan Poe]   83   220

SVETLOV, MICHAIL
ARTICLES ABOUT
   New Trends in Soviet Russian Poetry,
   by Vera Sandomirsky   58   324

SVOBODA, TERESE
POEMS
   Prairie   127   76

SWAIN, Y. F.
POEMS
   At Midnight   29   318
   Plea for Free Verse

SWALLOW, ALAN
POEMS
   Road South: Wyoming to Louisiana   51   194
   Stone

   Ode to Russia   61   428
   For My Infant Daughter   63   64

ARTICLES
   Poet, Publisher, and the Tribal Chant   75   48

BOOKS REVIEWED
   Three Lyric Poets (Ed.)
   [Byron Herbert Reece, Alice Moser,
   Tom H. McNeal]   61   629
   American Writing 1942 (Ed.)   63   223
   XI Poems   63   228
   American Writing: 1944
   (Ed. with Helen Ferguson Caukin)   68   106
   The Remembered Land   69   52
   The War Poems of...   74   175

SWAMI, SHREE PUROHIT
BOOKS REVIEWED
   The Ten Principal Upanishads
   (Tr. with W. B. Yeats)   51   216

SWAN, EMMA
POEMS
   Mind on Paper   50   10
   Sea-Storm
   Winter Season
   Walking
   The Dictates of Right Reason
   The Search-Light
   The Lion & the Lady   74   262
   Promenade   81   114
   Joy   81   236

BOOKS REVIEWED
   The Lion & the Lady   76   363

SWAN, JON
BOOKS REVIEWED
   Journeys and Return:
   Poems, in *Poets of Today VII*   99   178

SWANDER, MARY
POEMS
   Dutton's Cave   127   11
   Letter   129   272
   In a Dream
   Song ("And each night...")

BOOKS REVIEWED
   Driving the Body Back   148   99

SWANN, BRIAN
POEMS
   Bandusian Spring   114   244
   Darkness and Deeper Dark
   Solitary Singer
   Unknowing   121   145

Hermetic Happenings   124   31
Prehistoric Music
Reaching   125   259
In Memory of Raymond Brown   154   230

TRANSLATIONS
Poem by Cesare Pavese
    (Tr. with Ruth Feldman)   116   302
Poem by Lucio Piccolo
    (Tr. with Ruth Feldman)   116   303

SWANSON, E. FLORENCE
POEMS
Windy Eucharist   40   320
Pity the Dead
Double Suicide

SWARD, ROBERT (S.)
POEMS
The House   89   290
Miss Elderli Dora
    Des Moines, — One March   91   185
Mr Middlegreens, etc.
Barbecue   94   85
A Letter to His Psychiatrist   96   140
Turnpike
A Walk in the Scenery
Beach Scenes, — and Other Scenes
Pet Shop
Kissing the Dancer   100   374
EL-101
Lost Umbrellas
Steeple
Marriage
An End to Doubt
My Father, with Wings   103   234
Terminal Theater
The Nazarucks
Ghosts
Italian Films   105   310
Historical Society
Old Postal Cards
Arrival
Pavane
There's No Way Out
Concert   108   35
In Mexico

REVIEWS
A Poetry Chronicle   96   238
    Ceremonies in Mind, by Tram Combs
    The Descent from Daimonji,
        by Cid Corman
    Guide to the City, by Michael Grieg
    The Flight of Mr. Sun,
        by John Barkley Hart
    Ekstasis, by Philip Lamantia
    Riprap, by Gary Snyder

Webster's Third New International Dictionary
    (Ed. by Philip B. Gove)   100   190
Signatures   102   335
    Gold/Fish Signatures, by Paul Reps
    I Walk Through the Valley,
        by John Napier
    Tall Tales from Far Corners,
        by Gena Ford
    The Love Bit, by Joel Oppenheimer
    The Little Love of Our Yearning,
        by William J. Margolis
    The Fascination of the Abomination,
        by Reed Whittemore   104   380
Landscape and Language   109   407
    Sketches for a New Mexico Hill Town,
        by Keith Wilson
    Games, by Richard Kolmar
    Camouflage, by John Perreault
    Flag Flutter & U. S. Electric,
        by Clark Coolidge
Poets at Novels   112   353
    The Sky Changes,
        by Gilbert Sorrentino
    Three, by Ann Quin
    You Didn't Even Try,
        by Philip Whalen
    Elizabeth Newt, by Harold Fleming

BOOKS REVIEWED
Uncle Dog   102   42
Kissing the Dancer and Other Poems   105   336
Thousand-Year-Old Fiancée
    and Other Poems   108   408
Half a Life's Story   144   297

SWARTZ, ROBERTA TEALE
POEMS
The Hawthorne Tree   22   260
March Incredulous   25   301
Whistle Wind
Not Like Your Folk
Preoccupation
Lord Juggler   38   128
Woven Hours
Caritas
Impressions of Divinity
Pro Archia   44   314
Unripe Falling   48   14
Latter-Day Moon   54   308
You, Peony
First Frost

REVIEWS
The Spirit Watches, by Ruth Pitter   56   334

BOOKS REVIEWED
Lilliput   30   285
Lord Juggler and Other Poems   41   279

SWEENEY, JAMES JOHNSON
POEMS
 Guernica   56 128

ARTICLES
 Little Gidding:
 Introductory to a Reading
 [T. S. Eliot]   62 214

SWEENEY, JOHN L.
POEMS
 Premonitory Memorial   98 23
 Projection for John Dee
 Loch Inchiquin
 Sunion

SWEENEY, MATTHEW
POEMS
 Cacti   158 144
 Writing to a Dead Man 166 154

SWEENY, MILDRED MC NEAL
BOOKS REVIEWED
 Men of No Land   4 166

SWEETKIND, M.
POEMS
 Honey Hives   36 86

SWENSON, KAREN
POEMS
 Tide Pools in Deception Pass 122 331
 The Chinese Laundryman 133 157

BOOKS REVIEWED
 An Attic of Ideals   127 44

SWENSON, MAY
POEMS
 Green Red Brown and White 77 198
 Boy in Canoe   82 267
 The Garden at St. John's
 Frontispiece   88 153
 A Lake Scene   91 301
 Snow in New York   95 343
 Instead of the Camargue (1) 98 299
 Japanese Breakfast 101 329
 Italian Sampler
 Gods. Children.   105 227
 His Suicide   109 330
 Earth Will Not Let Go 113 170
 The DNA Molecule
 My Face the Night   115 86
 I'll Be
 Fire Island
 The Beam
 July 4th   120 353
 Fashion in the 70's 132 94

Going to the Whitney
 and Walking on the Floor 132 207
Digging in the Garden of Age
 I Uncover a Live Root
Ending
A Day Like Rousseau's Dream 137 96
Blood Test
Dummy, 51, To Go to Museum
 Ventriloquist Dead at 75
Saguaros Above Tucson
Third Floor Walk-Up, 1984 151 175
Sleeping Alone   151 394
A Spring Morning
Unable to Write It
What Matters
The Rest of My Life
I'm One
The Most Important 163 63
[Statement]
In Progress
Under the Best of Circumstances
Beginning Ended
Overview
The Sea

REVIEWS
Four New Volumes   89 373
 The Greenhouse in the Garden,
  by Charles Edward Eaton
 New and Selected Poems,
  by Thomas Hornsby Ferril
 Unexpected Truce, by Don Geiger
 Twenty Poems, by Cecil Hemley
A Poetry Chronicle   102 118
 Movie-Going, by John Hollander
 A Paper Horse, by Robert Watson
 Original Child Bomb,
  by Thomas Merton
 Wilson's Night Thoughts,
  by Edmund Wilson
 The Drawbridge,
  by Donald F. Drummond
 Deaths for the Ladies,
  by Norman Mailer

BOOKS REVIEWED
 Another Animal: Poems 88 52
 A Cage of Spines   94 189
 To Mix with Time: New and Selected Poems 103 330
 Half Sun Half Sleep
  [Ingemar Gustafson, Karin Boye] 111 184
 Iconographs   119 107
 New and Selected Things Taking Place 135 291
 In Other Words   154 233
 The Love Poems of... 161 286

SWERIG, VIVIAN
POEMS
 Muted   24 129

SWETT, MARGERY
[See MANSFIELD,
MARGERY SWETT]

SWIFT, IVAN
  POEMS
    Descent   18   312

  BOOKS REVIEWED
    The Blue Crane   18   223

  ARTICLES ABOUT
    The Laureate They Deserve?
      by Margery Swett (Mansfield)   25   38

SWIFT, JOAN
  POEMS
    Chiton   154   276

SWIGART, ROB
  POEMS
    The Sin of Seven   121   212
    Still Lives   126   77
    Retroactive Debridement

SWINBURNE, ALGERNON CHARLES
  BOOKS REVIEWED
    The Springtide of Life: Poems of Childhood   13   344
    Swinburne: Poems
      (Ed. by Bonamy Dobrée)   100   324
    Swinburne: A Selection
      (Ed. by Edith Sitwell)

  ARTICLES ABOUT
    Rev. of *The Life of
      Algernon Charles Swinburne,*
      by Edmund Gosse   11   322
    Rev. of *Swinburne,* by Samuel C. Chew   34   294

SWING, BILL
  POEMS
    Alta Eager   70   128

SWINGLER, RANDALL
  POEMS
    Onrush of Darkness   46   254
    Man Like Sun

  BOOKS REVIEWED
    The God in the Cave   79   106

SYLVAY, CHALLISS
  BOOKS REVIEWED
    Pagan Fires   34   111

SYLVESTER, FREDERICK OAKES
  BOOKS REVIEWED
    The Great River, Poems and Pictures   2   107

SYLVESTER, WILLIAM (A.)
  POEMS
    Sestina at the Sea   92   362

  REVIEWS
    Good and Light   70   278
      The Blue Hen's Chickens,
        by Vincent McHugh
      A Wider Arc, by Melville Cane
    How I See Apocalypse, by Henry Treece   72   103
    Meaning and Truth in the Arts,
      by John Hospers   72   326

SYMANSKI, EDWARD ALAN
  POEMS
    Colors   31   316
    Immigrant
    She Goes   40   324

SYMINGTON, JOEL MICHAEL
[Pseud. of ASHBERY, JOHN]
  POEMS
    Poem ("Though we seek always...")   67   66
    Lost Cove

SYMONS, ARTHUR
  POEMS
    At the Three Fountains   10   84
    To a Grey Dress   12   252
    Dreams

SYMONS, JULIAN
  POEMS
    Poem ("Sitting in the garden...")   52   314
    Three War Poems   56   301
      End of a Year
      Pub
      Poem ("The imagery personal...")
    Hart Crane   59   248
    Spring Poem
    Eleven Meetings
    The Clock

  ARTICLES
    Correspondence: The Other Cheek
      [D. S. Savage]   54   54
    Louis MacNeice:
      The Artist as Everyman   56   86

  BOOKS REVIEWED
    Confusions About X   54   284
    The Second Man   65   51

SYNGE, JOHN MILLINGTON
  ARTICLES ABOUT
    Rev. of *John Millington Synge
      and the Irish Theatre,*
      by Maurice Bourgeois   4   239

Rev. of *John M. Synge*,
by John Masefield 7 96
Synge and the Irish,
by M. D. Zabel 42 101
Rev. of *The Story of the Abbey Theatre*,
by Peter Kavanagh 79 216

SYPHER, WYLIE
REVIEWS
The Idea of a Theatre,
by Francis Fergusson 77 227

SYRIAN, AJAN
POEMS
"I Sing of My Life While I Live It" 6 107
*The Syrian Lover in Exile Remembers
Thee, Light of My Land*
Alma Mater
After Vespers
From the Near East 12 233
Armenian Marching Song
Syrian Mother's Lullaby
The Prayer Rug of Islam

T

"T. C. L."
  [See LEA, THOMAS C.]

TAAFFE, JAMES G.
  BOOKS REVIEWED
  Poems on Poetry
    (Ed. with Robert Wallace)   110   47

TABOR, EITHNE
  BOOKS REVIEWED
  The Cliff's Edge:
    Songs of a Psychotic   78   243

TAGGARD, GENEVIEVE
  POEMS
  From the Frail Sea   16   142
  The Way Things Go   17   257
    Endless Circle
    Sea-Change
    Tropical Girl to Her Garden
    Moonrise Mockery
    Zenith
    Married
    Drouth
    Saturday Afternoon
    Lost
    Found
  Boys and Girls   18   119
  Three Mornings   26   14
  Gipsy Confession   27   244
  Picture
  Word to a Ripple
  Two in a Dark Tower   30   324
  The Still Search
  Dilemma of the Elm   32   256
  Affirmations   44   206
    The Four Songs
    Metaphysical Exercise
    Changes of the Soul
  Turn to the East   53   66
  To My Mother
  Coming and Going of Storms   56   243
  Gilfeather   57   366
  Songs for Musical Setting
  Range, Range the Words Around   58   305

  Hymn to the Sun with Imperative Refrain   60   10
  K. D.
  Invocation   68   25

  ARTICLES
  [Note on Katherine Garrison Chapin]   53   286

  BOOKS REVIEWED
  For Eager Lovers   22   43
  Hawaiian Hilltop   26   108
  Continent's End, an Anthology
    of Contemporary California Poets
    (Ed. with George Sterling
    and James Rorty)   27   217
  Words for the Chisel   28   221
  Traveling Standing Still   33   154
  Circumference: Varieties
    of Metaphysical Verse—1456-1928 (Ed.)   37   50
  Not Mine to Finish   45   168
  Ten Introductions:
    A Collection of Modern Verse
    (Ed. with Dudley Fitts)   46   112
  Calling Western Union   50   106
  Collected Poems, 1918-1938   54   280
  Long View   61   400
  Slow Music   69   289

  ARTICLES ABOUT
  A Few Women Poets,
    by Harriet Monroe   26   326
  Cattle in the Garden,
    by M. D. Zabel   38   268

TAGLIABUE, JOHN
  POEMS
  The Divine Dancers   86   82
  Three Poems   87   266
    ("The sea gulls...")
    ("Those abysses of silence...")
    ("These lovers have wandered...")
  Mexican Poems   89   349
  Some Poems   91   371
    ("In the morning...")
    One Morning As I Calmly
      Love My House

("When I think of...")
Some Poems from Japan   95   16
    ("Sleepy standing...")
    ("In various alleys...")
    ("'The fact is the sweetest...'")
    ("An old Chinese Zen traveller...")
Conquistador With the Flag
    of the Alphabet   96   274
A Noh Actor
Very Still Noh Dancers
    with the White Masks of Beauty
After the Galley Proofs
A Wide Dim Scene of Farmers...   99   288
A Boat with a Blue Canopy...
From A Shakespeare Notebook   102   166
From An Outdoor Blake Festival   104   222
Six Poems from a Greek Journey   108   20
Part of a Hindu Festival   110   83
Three Poems [On the Way
    to a Particular Person: France]   112   99
    Concerning Some Saints
    and Impressionist Painters
    With Sun Hats We Meet
        Out in the Country
    In Addition in the Distance the Eiffel
        Tower Imitates a Flowery Propagandist
The Gracious Heroine Helps the Dancer
    Become Free   114   22

REVIEWS
The Poetry of Juan Ramón Jiménez   92   184
    Platero and I,
        by Juan Ramón Jiménez
        (Tr. by William and Mary Roberts)
    Platero and I,
        by Juan Ramón Jiménez
        (Tr. by Eloise Roach)
    The Selected Writings
        of Juan Ramón Jiménez
        (Tr. by H. R. Hays)

BOOKS REVIEWED
Poems   96   375
A Japanese Journal   111   195
The Buddha Uproar   113   188

TAGORE, RABINDRANATH
    [RABINDRA NATH TAGORE]
POEMS
    ("Thou hast made me known...")   1   84
    ("No more noisy, loud words...")
    ("On the day when the lotus...")
    ("By all means they try to hold me...")
    ("I was not aware...")
    ("Thou art the sky...")
    ("Over the green and yellow...")   2   81
    ("Keep me fully glad...")
    ("My soul is alight...")

    ("O you mad, you superbly drunk!...")
    ("Leave off your works, bride...")
    ("Come as you are...")
    ("Sing the song of the moment...")
    ("Lest I should know you...")
    ("Amidst the rush and roar of life...")
    ("Tell me if this is all true...")
    ("I asked of Destiny...")
    ("With a glance of your eyes...")
    ("We both live in the same village...")
    ("I found a few old letters...")
    Narratives   3   75
        The Temple of Gold
        The Price
        Union
        The Gift
        The Tryst
    Epigrams   8   283
    "I Will Not Let You Go"
        (Tr. by Humayun Kabir)   93   203

BOOKS REVIEWED
    The King of the Dark Chamber   5   131
    Sheaves   44   235
    The Golden Boat
    One Hundred and One: Poems by...
        (Ed. by Humayun Kabir)   111   407
    Moon, For What Do You Wait?: Poems by...
        (Ed. by Richard Lewis)

ARTICLES ABOUT
    Tagore's Poems, by Ezra Pound   1   92
    Incarnations, by Harriet Monroe   2   101
    Rev. of Art and Swadeshi,
        by Ananda K. Coomaraswamy   2   226
    A Partisan Verdict,
        by Alice Corbin Henderson   7   50
    Obituary   58   348
    Remarks on the Occasion
        of the Tagore Centenary,
        by Robert Frost   99   106
    Tagore's Poems, by Ezra Pound   121   40

T'AI TA-MIEN
POEMS
    The Palace Blossoms
        (Tr. by Amy Lowell
        and Florence Ayscough)   13   236

TAKAHASHI, SHINKICHI
POEMS
    Birth
        (Tr. by Satoru Satu
        and Constance Urdang)   88   89
    Plovers
        (Tr. by Hisakazu Kaneko)   101   173
    A Spray of Hot Air   116   364
    Canna

Sun Through the Leaves
Ice
    (Tr. by Lucien Stryk
    and Takashi Ikemoto)

TAKAMURA, KOTARO
POEMS
   Winter Has Come
    (Tr. by Satoru Satu
    and Constance Urdang)   88   94

TAKENAKA, IKU
POEMS
   At Lyons
    (Tr. by Satoru Satu
    and Constance Urdang)   88   77

TALAL, MARILYNN
POEMS
   The Egyptian Museum of Antiquities   154   26
   The Blue Road   163   157
   Mrs. Shapanka's Embrace   170   343

TALARICO, ROSS
POEMS
   The Perfect Flaw   128   320

TALBOT, JOHN
POEMS
   Shavings   169   258

TALBOTT, CARLTON
POEMS
   Six Woodcuts   33   201
   Bygone Episodes   35   260
    Strange Legend in Mosaic
    Fiasco in Fresco
    Tapestry Panel:
     The Life and Death of Basil

BOOKS REVIEWED
   Ballyhoo for a Mendicant   34   173
   Droll Parade   36   112

TALISMAN
BOOKS REVIEWED
   A Western Sampler
    [Editors of Talisman]   104   245

TALL, DEBORAH
POEMS
   Interlude   135   21
   Yearning
   Bishop's Rock
   Scheherezade
   Anima   138   210
   Memorabilia
   Grounded   162   75

TALLMAN, ROBERT
POEMS
   Edge to Edge ("But there are...")   41   247
   From Beyond   42   74
    Edge to Edge ("But there are...")
   Stars et Cetera

TAMARKIN, MOLLY
POEMS
   The Common Robusta   166   262
   Pastry

TAMBIMUTTU, (M. J.)
TRANSLATIONS
   Poem by Jigar Morabadi
    (Tr. with Rahm Ali Alhashmi)   93   235
   Poem by Bewas
    (Tr. with Gobind L. Bhatia)   93   254

ARTICLES
   A Note on This Collection   93   268

ARTICLES ABOUT
   Contemporary Poetry in Britain,
    by David Daiches   62   150

TAMKUS, DANIEL
POEMS
   Coming of the Bridal Wind   87   353

TANAKA, FUYUJI
POEMS
   Native Village   88   63
   A Small Mountain Town
   Evening Landscape, One Day in Winter
   By the Marsh
   The Village
   The Cold Glass Door
   Woodcocks Returning Northward
    (Tr. by Satoru Satu
    and Constance Urdang)
   A Mountain Town   101   169
   An Autumn Village
    (Tr. by Hisakazu Kaneko)

TANAQUIL, PAUL [Pseud.]
POEMS
   Moondown   16   82
   Semper Eadem   19   138
   The Lover   19   261
   Avanti   26   77

TANASSO, ELDA
POEMS
   The Hunted Voice   50   26
   Snow and Holy Ghost
   Desires
   Storm at Dawn

Sea at Night
This Quiet-Time   54   254
Spring-Piece   58   188

TANDY, JENNETTE (REID)
POEMS
At Grandmother's   23   78
Sunday Afternoon
Planting
Machines
I Wish

T'ANG SENG-CH'I
POEMS
On Finding a Hairpin
in a Disused Well
(Tr. by Arthur Waley)   11   198

TANIKAWA, SHUNTARO
POEMS
Museum   88   70

T'AO CH'IEN
POEMS
On the Classic of the Hills and Sea
(Tr. by Amy Lowell
and Florence Ayscough)   13   238

ARTICLES ABOUT
Correspondence
from Arthur Waley   14   55

TARAFA
POEMS
The Bedouin Praises His Camel
(Tr. by Eunice Tietjens)   32   186

TARN, NATHANIEL
BOOKS REVIEWED
The Heights of Macchu Picchu,
by Pablo Neruda (Tr.)   112   191

TASSONI, ALESSANDRO
POEMS
Sonnet ("My kith and kin...")
(Tr. by Francis Golffing)   128   139

TATE, ALLEN
POEMS
The Rooftree   39   59
Sonnets of the Blood
Message from Paris
The Wolves
The Anabasis   40   74
Brief Message
From Sonnets of the Blood   121   34
VII ("The fire I praise...")
The Swimmers   135   67

ARTICLES
Correspondence: A Polite Protest
[Donald Davidson]   25   169
Editorial Note   40   90
Hart Crane and the American Mind   40   210
Homage to St.-John Perse
[Walt Whitman]   75   213
Preface to Libretto for the Republic of Liberia
[M. B. Tolson]   76   216
Correspondence   86   248
Mere Literature and the Lost Traveller   135   93

REVIEWS
The Cicadas and Other Poems,
by Aldous Huxley   39   285
Viva, by E. E. Cummings   39   332
How to Read and Profile: An Anthology
Collected in MCMXXXI,
by Ezra Pound   41   107
How to Teach Reading:
A Primer for Ezra Pound,
by F. R. Leavis   44   53
Hart Crane: The Life of an American Poet,
by Philip Horton   50   219
Whitman, by Edgar Lee Masters   50   350

BOOKS REVIEWED
Fugitives: An Anthology of Verse   32   102
Mr. Pope and Other Poems   33   281
Poems: 1928-1931   40   34
The Mediterranean, and Other Poems 50   96
Reactionary Essays on Poetry and Ideas
Selected Poems   51   262
Reason in Madness: Critical Essays 60   86
Contemporary Poets Series
[Recording]   61   519
The Vigil of Venus (Tr.)   64   30
The Winter Sea   66   324
A Southern Vanguard: The John Peale Bishop
Memorial Volume (Ed.)   72   222
On the Limits of Poetry   74   54
Two Conceits   77   114
The Forlorn Demon   83   220
Modern Verse in English, 1900-1950
(Ed. with Lord David Cecil)   96   122
Poems   99   120
Collected Essays   99   123
Selected Poems, by Denis Devlin
(Ed. with Robert Penn Warren) 103   191
Essays of Four Decades   116   43
The Swimmers and Other Selected Poems   119   222

ARTICLES ABOUT
[Note on misprint]   39   172
Correspondence from Ezra Pound   41   231
The Poet and Pedant Symposium,
by Margedant Peters   57   194

A Glossary of the New Criticism,
  by William Elton · 73 · 232
A Glossary of the New Criticism,
  by William Elton · 73 · 296
Rev. of *Lectures in Criticism*
  [Johns Hopkins University] · 74 · 353
Rev. of *Donne's Poetry
  and Modern Criticism*,
  by Leonard Unger · 77 · 175
Rev. of *Le Cahiers de la Pléiade*
  (Ed. by Jean Paulhan)
  [St.-John Perse] · 79 · 43
[Note] · 83 · 56
Correspondence
  from Brom Weber
  [Hart Crane] · 92 · 332
In Honor of Allen Tate,
  by John Frederick Nims · 135 · 63
*Allen Tate: A Poet
  on Poetry, 1924-1944*,
  by Ashley Brown · 135 · 103

TATE, JAMES
POEMS
  *The Whole World's
    Sadly Talking to Itself—W. B. Yeats* · 110 · 239
  Pity Ascending with the Fog
  Jim's All-Night Diner · 113 · 27
  Cryptozoa · 114 · 25
  The Square at Dawn
  The Blue Booby
  Pride's Crossing
  Saint John of the Cross in Prison · 117 · 185
  With a Child All Day · 132 · 275
  To Fuzzy · 138 · 267
  It Wasn't Me
  Red Bricks and Camphor Trees
  Nuisance · 151 · 177
  City at Night · 154 · 191
  No Spitting Up
  Trying To Help

BOOKS REVIEWED
  The Lost Pilot · 111 · 329
  Notes of Woe · 114 · 401
  The Torches · 117 · 392
  The Oblivion Ha-Ha · 119 · 45
  Viper Jazz · 130 · 221
  Riven Doggeries · 136 · 295
  Constant Defender · 145 · 99
  Worshipful Company of Fletchers · 166 · 166

TAUPIN, RENÉ
ARTICLES
  Three Poems by André Salmon
    (Tr. by Louis Zukofsky) · 37 · 289
  Three Poems by André Salmon, II
    (Tr. by Louis Zukofsky) · 37 · 333

BOOKS REVIEWED
  *L'Influence du Symbolisme Francais
    sur la Poésie Américaine
    (de 1910 à 1920)* · 37 · 44
  *4 Essais Indifférents
    pour une Esthetique de l'Inspiration* · 42 · 175

TAX, ERVIN
ARTICLES ABOUT
  Correspondence from Will Wharton
    [Decker Press] · 77 · 58

**TAXIS, MARIE
[See VON THURN UND TAXIS, MARIE]**

TAYLOR, BERT LESTON
BOOKS REVIEWED
  A Line-o'-Verse or Two · 17 · 100

ARTICLES ABOUT
  The Death of "B. L. T.,"
    by Harriet Monroe · 18 · 97
  "In Lighter Vein,"
    by Harriet Monroe · 30 · 330

TAYLOR, BRUCE
POEMS
  Calling It the Given · 165 · 21
  Like
  Arabesque
  Gray Drapes

TAYLOR, DAVIDSON
POEMS
  Night Letter · 60 · 140

ARTICLES ABOUT
  Verse Drama and the Radio,
    by Amy Bonner · 58 · 280

TAYLOR, EDWARD
BOOKS REVIEWED
  The Poetical Works of...
    (Ed. by Thomas H. Johnson) · 56 · 165

**TAYLOR, ELEANOR ROSS
[See also ROSS, ELEANOR]**
POEMS
  After Twenty Years · 109 · 241
  Bulletin
  Pause, in Flight
  Painting Remembered · 112 · 236
  Mother's Blessing
  Lemon Tree
  His Wishes
  Cemetery Statue
  The Skipped Page · 117 · 299
  Over a Stone · 138 · 15

ARTICLES
  Correspondence   120   364

REVIEWS
  Ariel, by Sylvia Plath   109   260

BOOKS REVIEWED
  Wilderness of Ladies   98   118

TAYLOR, FRAJAM
  ARTICLES
  The Hawk and the Stone
    [Robinson Jeffers]   55   39
  The Rebellious Will
    of Gerard Manley Hopkins   59   270

  REVIEWS
  Homeward to America, by John Ciardi   56   337
  Keats and the Daemon King,
    by Werner W. Beyer
    [C. M. Wieland,
    William Sotheby]   70   168
  Selected Poems,
    by Kenneth Patchen   70   269

TAYLOR, FRANCES BEATRICE
  POEMS
  The Spell   29   198
  Outlaw   33   243

TAYLOR, HENRY
  POEMS
  Taking to the Woods   145   33
  Master of None   151   178
  For William Stafford   166   150
  Another Postponement of Destruction   168   332

  TRANSLATIONS
  Poem by Vladmir Levchev
    (Tr. with the author)   168   32

  ARTICLES
  Comment   151   224

  REVIEWS
  Easy Listening (Part I)   162   37
    House of Mirrors,
      by Joseph Hutchison
    The Double Negatives of the Living,
      by Gary Fincke
    Rules of Engagement: Poems 1974-1991,
      by P. H. Liotta
    All These Lands You Call One Country,
      by Stephen Corey
    Storm Pattern and
      Sunflower Facing the Sun,
      by Greg Pape
  Easy Listening (Part II)   162   96

  The Wild Iris, by Louise Glück
  The Wages of Goodness,
    by Michael Blumenthal
  Dark Verses & Light, by Tom Disch
  Liquid Paper: New and Selected Poems,
    by Peter Meinke
  My Name Is William Tell,
    by William Stafford

BOOKS REVIEWED
  The Flying Change: Poems   149   341

TAYLOR, JOHN
  REVIEWS
  Short Reviews   169   286
    Armored Hearts:
      Selected & New Poems,
      by David Bottoms
    The Life and Letters,
      by Irving Feldman
    Passing Through: The Later Poems
      New and Selected,
      by Stanley Kunitz
    Facing the River,
      by Czeslaw Milosz
      (Tr. by the author and Robert Hass)
    Worldling, by Elizabeth Spires
    The Empty Bed,
      by Rachel Hadas
  Short Reviews   170   162
    Even in Quiet Places,
      by William Stafford
    The Education of Desire,
      by William Dickey
    Scrambled Eggs & Whiskey:
      Poems 1991-1995,
      by Hayden Carruth
    So Forth, by Joseph Brodsky
    Fight Among the Tombs,
      by Anthony Hecht
    The Crack in Everything,
      by Alicia Suskin Ostriker

TAYLOR, JUDITH
  POEMS
  Persephone   165   321

TAYLOR, K. P. A.
  POEMS
  The Road   89   27

TAYLOR, LES
  POEMS
  The Forest for the Trees   129   24
  Boxwood   131   142

TAYLOR, MARCELLA
  POEMS
  African Child   156   22

TAYLOR, MARILYN
POEMS
To a Young Diver   158   137
Golden Warriors End Year with Big Loss   162   222

TAYLOR, PAUL B.
BOOKS REVIEWED
The Elder Edda, A Selection
(Tr. with W. H. Auden)   117   341

TAYLOR, PETER
BOOKS REVIEWED
Randall Jarrell 1914-1965
(Ed. with Robert Lowell
and Robert Penn Warren)   112   118

TAYLOR, REX
BOOKS REVIEWED
Poems   94   196

TAYLOR, ROD
BOOKS REVIEWED
Florida East Coast Champion   121   239

TAYLOR, SIMON WATSON
BOOKS REVIEWED
Selected Works of Alfred Jarry
(Ed. with Roger Shattuck)   107   267
Selected Works of Alfred Jarry
(Ed. and tr. with Roger Shattuck)   111   124

TAYLOR, UNA
BOOKS REVIEWED
Maurice Maeterlinck, a Critical Study   8   96

TEAGUE, TONEY
POEMS
Assault on Second Avenue   138   221
Woman in White

TEASDALE, SARA
POEMS
Old Love and New   3   199
Over the Roofs
Debt
September Midnight
Leaves   7   12
Morning
The Answer
Songs Out of Stress   10   124
Barter
Spirit's House
Lessons
Refuge
Wood Song
Blue Squills   12   16
Memories   14   291
The Voice

The Long Hill
Spring Torrents
What Do I Care
My Heart Is Heavy
It Is Not a Word
Song ("Let it be forgotten...")
To Eleanora Duse   22   246
On the South Downs   24   1
The Flight
I Could Snatch a Day
Epitaph ("Serene descent...")
"She Who Could Bind You"
An End
The Tune
Berkshire Notes
February Twilight
In the Wood
Autumn Dusk
A December Day
Conflict   144   128
Nights Without Sleep
To a Loose Woman
Afterwards
In Florence   144   275

REVIEWS
Under the Tree,
by Elizabeth Madox Roberts   38   227

BOOKS REVIEWED
Rivers to the Sea   7   147
The Answering Voice—One Hundred
Love Lyrics by Women (Ed.)   11   278
Flame and Shadow   17   272
Rainbow Gold, Poems Old
and New Selected for Boys and Girls   22   279
Dark of the Moon   29   157
Strange Victory   43   96
A Country House   43   225
The Collected Poems of...   51   148

ARTICLES ABOUT
[Note on misprints]   10   222
Sara Teasdale's Prize,
by Harriet Monroe   12   264
[Note]   13   109
Sara Teasdale, by Harriet Monore   25   262
[Note on misprints]   25   345
Typographical Queries,
by Harriet Monroe   28   32
Sara Teasdale, by Harriet Monroe   42   30
Rev. of Sara Teasdale: A Biography,
by Margaret Haley Carpenter   97   392

TEDLOCK, E. W.
BOOKS REVIEWED
Dylan Thomas:
The Legend and the Poet (Ed.)   98   124

TEELE, ROY E.
REVIEWS
From the East   109   272
  Anthology of Chinese Literature:
    From Early Times to
    the Fourteenth Century
    (Ed. by Cyril Birch
    and Donald Keene)
  Anthology of Korean Poetry:
    From the Earliest Era to the Present
    (Tr. by Peter H. Lee)
  First Voices:
    Six Poets from Pakistan
    (Ed. by Shahid Hosain)
  Modern Hindi Poetry: An Anthology
    (Ed. by Vidya Niwas Misra)
Out of China   112   283
  An Introduction to Sung Poetry,
    by Kojiro Yoshikawa
    (Tr. by Burton Watson)
    [Su Shih]
  The Chinese Knight-Errant,
    by James J. Y. Liu
  A Little Primer of Tu Fu,
    by David Hawkes
  A Collection of Chinese Lyrics,
    by Alan Ayling
    (From trs. by Duncan Mackintosh)
Far Eastern Chronicle   112   347
  An Anthology of Chinese Verse:
    Han, Wei, Chin, and
    the Northern Southern Dynasties
    (Tr. by J. D. Frodsham
    and Ch'eng Hsi)
  The Narrow Road to the Deep North
    and Other Travel Sketches,
    by Bashō
    (Tr. by Nobuyuki Yuasa)
  Bhartrihari: Poems
    (Tr. by Barbara Stoler Miller)
  The Dhammapada
    (Tr. by P. Lal)
  The Manyoshu:
    A New and Complete Translation
    (Tr. by H. H. Honda)
Far Eastern Chronicle   114   196
  The Interior Landscape: Love Poems
    from a Classical Tamil Anthology
    (Tr. by A. K. Ramanujan)
  Sanskrit Poetry
    from Vidyakara's "Treasury"
    (Tr. by Daniel H. H. Ingalls)
  Superior Poems of Our Time,
    by Fujiwara Teika
    (Tr. by Robert H. Brower
    and Earl Miner)
  Tales of Ise: Lyrical Episodes
    from Tenth-Century Japan
    (Tr. by Helen Craig McCullough)

  The Murmuring Stream:
    The Life and Works
    of Hsieh Ling-Yun,
    by J. D. Frodsham
  One Hundred and One Chinese Poems
    (Tr. by Shih Shun Liu)
Two Poets and Japan   118   174
  Earth House Hold, by Gary Snyder
  Indiana, by Clayton Eshleman

TEIKA, FUJIWARA
BOOKS REVIEWED
  Superior Poems of Our Time
    (Tr. by Robert H. Brower
    and Earl Miner)   114   196

TELFAIR, NANCY
POEMS
  Sonnets for an Early Morning   38   134
  The Young Farmer
  A Woman Who Sells
  The Widow

TEMPLE, JEAN
POEMS
  Skeleton   37   307

TEMPLE, JOHN
BOOKS REVIEWED
  Rothschild's Lapwing   114   251

TEMPLIN, E. H.
POEMS
  Sierra Night   96   164

TEN HOOR, FREDERICK
POEMS
  A Word   37   137
  A Wish for My Brother   44   79
  Burning Brush   46   256
  Inquiries   49   65
    No One Knows
    Loud Enclosure
    No Gate
    The Caterpillar Leaf

TENNANT, WYNDHAM
BOOKS REVIEWED
  Wheels, An Anthology of Verse   10   41

TENNEY, RUTH
POEMS
  In China   21   128
    Lullaby of the Outcast
    Noon in the Temple
  From the Far East   30   257
    In a Peking Shop
    Flood Bride
    On a White Marble Head

TENNYSON, ALFRED [LORD]
BOOKS REVIEWED
   A Selection from the Poems of...
    (Ed. by W. H. Auden)   65   335

ARTICLES ABOUT
   What Is Anti-Criticism? by Karl Shapiro 75 339
   The Face Behind the Poem,
    by George Barker   97 310

TERADA, REI
POEMS
   On Painting   158 205
   Wordsworth After The Prelude
   Dino Campana   168 137

TERENCE, (PUBLIUS)
BOOKS REVIEWED
   The Comedies of...
    (Tr. by Laurence Echard)
    (Ed. by Robert Graves) 107 264

TERMAN, PHILIP
POEMS
   What We Pass On   158 323
   Yom Kippur
   G-d   161 267
   Eloquence
   My Father's Mother
   Attachments   169 206
   The House of Sages

TERRANOVA, ELAINE
BOOKS REVIEWED
   The Cult of the Right Hand 160 284

TERRELL, R(ACHAEL) MARSHALL
POEMS
   Los Angeles   32 132

TERRILL, KATHRYN
POEMS
   The Darker Side of Mary Worth 137 331

TERRONE, MARIA
POEMS
   Madame Curie   170 71
   Drifts

TERRY, ELLEN
ARTICLES ABOUT
   Should He Be Educated?
    by Harriet Monroe   37 90

TERRY, PATRICIA
ARTICLES ABOUT
   Recent French Publications,
    by Wallace Fowlie   93 40

TESSIMOND, A. S. J.
POEMS
   Lines   32 22
   What Is This Wind   35 259
   The Children Look at the Parents 42 194
   Cocoon for a Skeleton
   Portrait   47 199

BOOKS REVIEWED
   The Walls of Glass   44 343

TEWKESBURY, PAUL C.
POEMS
   A Bad Penny   27 293

THANHOUSER, MARIAN
POEMS
   At Night   18 313
   Lures   30 127
    Young Witches
    Home

THAPAR, ROMILA
TRANSLATIONS
   Poems by Nirala
    and Jayshankar Prasad 93 255

THATCHER, LUCY W.
BOOKS REVIEWED
   The Listening Child (Ed.) 28 114

THAYER, GEORGIANA
BOOKS REVIEWED
   Eve Passes   29 350

THAYER, HARRIET M.
POEMS
   Palm Sunday—France 38 18

THAYER, MARY DIXON
BOOKS REVIEWED
   Songs of Youth   23 111
   New York and Other Poems 28 290

THEOBALD, JOHN
POEMS
   Englishman in New York 45 11
   Find Great Men
   The Bird at Dawn   47 22
   The Law Above Pity
   Ballad for Lili Marlene 66 142
   The Two Rocks
   Sleeping Infant. New Year's Eve
   Stanzas from a Pastoral 67 317
   Saturday Night. Bourbon and Soda
   Sunday Afternoon: Cocktails 68 191
   From An Oxford Odyssey 72 197

ARTICLES
Correspondence
[H. R. Hays, Herbert Read]   67   114
The World in a Cross Word
[John Malcolm Brinnin]   71   82

REVIEWS
That Strain Again   71   327
The Prodigal Never Returns,
by Hugh Chisholm
Cry Cadence, by Howard Griffin
The Kid, by Conrad Aiken   72   224
Form and Sensibility   73   357
Aegean Islands and Other Poems,
by Bernard Spencer
A Way of Happening,
by Ruth Herschberger
Three and One   74   50
Therefore Choose Life,
by Edith Lovejoy Pierce
To Walk a Crooked Mile,
by Thomas McGrath
Poems Out of a Hat, by Walter Leuba
Never a Greater Need,
by Walter Benton

BOOKS REVIEWED
The Earthquake and Other Poems   74   241
An Oxford Odyssey   86   242

THEOCRITUS
POEMS
Idyll VII
(Tr. by Daryl Hine)   128   155

ARTICLES ABOUT
Rev. of The Penguin Book
of Homosexual Verse
(Ed. by Stephen Coote)   144   166

THERESE, [SISTER] M.
BOOKS REVIEWED
Give Joan a Sword   64   171

THIBAUDEAU, COLLEEN
POEMS
Poem ("There's a waterfall...")   115   169
My Granddaughters Are Combing
Out Their Long Hair   120   85

THIBAULT, FRANK
[See WEIBAULT, F. G.,
pseud. with WEISS,
HENRY GEORGE]

THIRLWALL, JOHN C.
BOOKS REVIEWED
The Selected Letters
of William Carlos Williams (Ed.)   92   174

THOM, ROBERT
BOOKS REVIEWED
Viaticum   76   229
Children of the Ladybug   89   378

THOMAS, CALVIN, JR.
POEMS
For a Girl Killed at Sea   87   14

THOMAS, D. M.
POEMS
The Sea-King to Kerenza   119   259
Kerenza on Sand-Dunes

BOOKS REVIEWED
Two Voices   118   102
Love and Other Deaths   129   340

THOMAS, DYLAN
POEMS
We Lying by Seasand   49   183
("When all my five and country...")   52   247
("O make me a mask and a wall...")
("Not from this anger...")
("The spire cranes...")
Poem ("Her tombstone told...")   55   66
Poem in October   65   257
A Winter's Tale   66   175
Out of a War of Wits   87   84
This Is Remembered
Shiloh's Seed
Before We Mothernaked Fall
The Almanac of Time
Poem on His Birthday
[Facs. drafts]   87   92
We Lying by Seasand   121   33

BOOKS REVIEWED
The World I Breathe   56   159
New Poems   63   48
In Country Sleep and Other Poems   81   184
The Collected Poems of...   83   213
Quite Early One Morning   87   114
Adventures in the Skin Trade
and Other Stories
The Doctor and the Devils   87   116
Under Milk Wood   87   119
The Collected Poems of...   94   111
Dylan Thomas: Letters to Vernon Watkins
(Ed. by Vernon Watkins)   94   114

ARTICLES ABOUT
Aspects of English Poetry: 1932-1937,
by Michael Roberts   49   210
London Letter, by D. S. Savage   51   277
Surrealist Influence in Contemporary
English and American Poetry,
by H. R. Hays   54   202

Contemporary Poetry in Britain,
   by David Daiches   62   150
The "Romantic" Heritage
   in the Writings of Dylan Thomas,
   by Horace Gregory   69   326
Rev. of *Dylan Thomas:*
   "Dog Among the Fairies,"
   by Henry Treece   75   357
Rev. of *The Sorrows of Cold Stone.*
   Poems 1940-1950,
   by John Malcolm Brinnin   80   159
Dylan Thomas (1914-1953)   83   244
Dylan Thomas
   on Visiting Lecturers
   [Note]   84   305
Dylan Thomas, by Karl Shapiro   87   100
Memories of Dylan Thomas
   at the B.B.C.,
   by Roy Campbell   87   111
Rev. of *The Poetry of Dylan Thomas,*
   by Elder Olson   87   118
Rev. of *Dylan Thomas:*
   The Legend and the Poet
   (Ed. by E. W. Tedlock)   98   124
Rev. of *The Religious Sonnets of Dylan*
   Thomas: A Study in Imagery and Meaning,
   by H. H. Kleinman   104   264
Rev. of *Dylan Thomas's Choice*
   (Ed. by Ralph Maud
   and Aneirin Talfan Davies)   106   429
Rev. of *Dylan Thomas*
   and Poetic Dissociation,
   by David Holbrook   108   65

THOMAS, EDITH M.
  Books Reviewed
   The Flower from the Ashes, and Other Verse   10   215
   The White Messenger, and Other War Poems
   Selected Poems of…
     (Ed. by Jessie B. Rittenhouse)   29   229

THOMAS, EDWARD
[See also EASTAWAY,
EDWARD, pseud.]
  Books Reviewed
   Poems   12   102
   Last Poems   14   103
   Collected Poems of…
     (Ed. by R. George Thomas)   135   342

  Articles About
   Rev. of *An Annual of New Poetry, 1917*   11   333
   [Note on pseudonym]   11   338
   Rev. of *Edward Thomas:*
     The Last Four Years,
     by Eleanor Farjeon;
     As It Was and *World Without End,*
     by Helen Thomas   95   52

   Rev. of *First and Second Love,*
     by Eleanor Farjeon   95   248
   Rev. of *Edward Thomas:*
     A Poet for His Country,
     by Jan Marsh   135   342

THOMAS, HELEN
  Books Reviewed
   As It Was
     [Edward Thomas]   95   52
   World Without End

THOMAS, HENRY C.
  Poems
   A Girl Dancing on the Shore   12   257

THOMAS, KEITH
  Poems
   The Mate   52   133
   After the Concert   61   481

THOMAS, MARTHA BANNING
  Poems
   I Am Afraid   25   309
   December Night   30   73

THOMAS, R. GEORGE
  Books Reviewed
   Collected Poems of Edward Thomas (Ed.)   135   342

THOMAS, R. S.
  Poems
   The Meeting   100   79
   Indoors
   This
   Strangers
   To Church
   No

  Books Reviewed
   Song at the Year's Turning   89   193
   Tares   100   104
   The Penguin Book of Religious Verse (Ed.)   104   245
   H'm   124   45
   Laboratories of the Spirit   130   230

THOMAS, RANDOLPH
  Poems
   The Course of the Telling   168   30

THOMAS, ROSEMARY
  Poems
   Sleeping Peacock   74   73
   Mark Van Doren   111   319

  Books Reviewed
   Immediate Sun   81   324
   Selected Poems of…   113   421

THOMAS, WRIGHT
BOOKS REVIEWED
Reading Poems:
  An Introduction to Critical Study
  (Ed. with Stuart Gerry Brown)   59   346
Reading Poems
  (With S. G. Brown)   84   43

ARTICLES ABOUT
The Poet and Pedant Symposium,
  by Margedant Peters   57   194

THOMPSON, [MRS.] ARTHUR
ARTICLES
Correspondence to Grace Heron
  [Harriet Monroe]   49   173

THOMPSON, BLANCHE
BOOKS REVIEWED
Silver Pennies:
  Modern Poems for Boys and Girls (Ed.)   28   114

THOMPSON, DAPHNE KIEFFER
POEMS
Indiana   8   70
An Old Song

THOMPSON, DOROTHY BROWN
POEMS
Winter Thaw   69   255

THOMPSON, DUNSTAN
POEMS
The Artifice of Eternity   55   72

BOOKS REVIEWED
Poems   65   47
Lament for the Sleepwalker   70   217

ARTICLES ABOUT
Rev. of *New Poems: 1943*
  (Ed. by Oscar Williams)   64   86

THOMPSON, EDWARD
BOOKS REVIEWED
100 Poems   66   170

THOMPSON, FRANCIS
POEMS
To My Friend   2   92
An Homage   47   127

BOOKS REVIEWED
The Works of...   3   179

THOMPSON, JOHN
REVIEWS
Articulate Energy,
  by Donald Davie   93   325

A Poetry Chronicle   95   107
  His Thought Made Pockets
  & The Plane Buckt,
    by John Berryman
  The Wilderness and Other Poems,
    by Louis O. Coxe
  Poems Written in Berlin,
    by Barbara Gibbs
  The Sense of Movement,
    by Thom Gunn
  A Sense of the World,
    by Elizabeth Jennings
  Oddments Inklings Omens Moments,
    by Alastair Reid
  Poems, by Allen Tate   99   120

BOOKS REVIEWED
The Penguin Book of Australian Verse
  (Ed. with Kenneth Slessor
  and R. G. Howarth)   94   44
The Talking Girl   113   421

THOMPSON, LAWRANCE
BOOKS REVIEWED
Young Longfellow   54   29
Tilbury Town: Selected Poems
  of Edwin Arlington Robinson (Ed.)   84   108
Robert Frost: Farm-Poultryman
  (Ed. with Edward Connery Lathem)   104   253
Selected Letters of Robert Frost (Ed.)   107   192
Robert Frost: The Early Years   110   425

THOMPSON, NORA B.
TRANSLATIONS
Poems by Flavio Herrera   74   194

THOMPSON, PAUL
POEMS
Oklahoma Poems   36   254
  Claremore Mound
  The Silver Stallion

THOMPSON, VANCE
BOOKS REVIEWED
The Night Watchman and Other Poems   6   93

THOMPSON, WILLIAM M., JR.
POEMS
60   166   158

THOMSON, DAVID CLEGHORN
POEMS
The Return   26   261

THOMSON, JAMES
BOOKS REVIEWED
Poems of James Thomson, "B.V."
  (Ed. by Gordon Hall Gerould)   32   229

ARTICLES ABOUT
Two Versions of the Nineteenth Century,
    by Morton Dauwen Zabel   44   270

THOMSON, ROSAMUND DARGAN
POEMS
    The Climber   62   185
    Where Fliers Fell
    Gates
    Solemn Traveling

THOMSON, SHARON
POEMS
    The Family Tree   135   321
    Meditation
    Boiling

THORE, KATHARINE PARKER
POEMS
    The Mohawk Trail   23   86

THORLEY, WILFRID
BOOKS REVIEWED
    Fleurs de Lys (Tr. and ed.)   18   111

THORN, MICHAL [Pseud.]
POEMS
    By an Aviary   50   198
    The Blackthorn
    Possessions

THORNBURY, CHARLES
BOOKS REVIEWED
    Collected Poems: 1937-1971,
    by John Berryman (Ed.)   156   158

**THORP, N. HOWARD
["JACK" THORP]**
POEMS
    Cowboy Songs   16   235
    Sky-High
    Old Hank
    The Little Cow-Girl
    Pecos Tom
    "'Light, Stranger, 'Light"
    Women Outlaws
    Old Paint
    What's Become of the Punchers

REVIEWS
    Right Royal, by John Masefield   18   279

BOOKS REVIEWED
    Songs of the Cowboys (Ed.)   22   105

THURBER, JAMES
ARTICLES ABOUT
    James Thurber: The Comic Prufrock,
    by Peter DeVries   63   150

THWAITE, ANTHONY
BOOKS REVIEWED
    Home Truths   92   378
    The Owl in the Tree   104   375

    Inscriptions   123   165
    Collected Poems,
    by Philip Larkin (Ed.)   155   408

THWAITES, MICHAEL
BOOKS REVIEWED
    The Jervis Bay and Other Poems   61   629

TICHY, SUSAN
BOOKS REVIEWED
    The Hands in Exile   145   36

TIEMPO, EDITH L.
POEMS
    Lament for the Littlest Fellow   79   275
    The Pestle   89   223
    Mid-Morning for Sheba
    The Tracks of Babylon   97   168

REVIEWS
    Selected Poems of Gabriela Mistral
    (Tr. by Langston Hughes)   92   106

BOOKS REVIEWED
    The Tracks of Babylon and Other Poems   111   189

TIETJENS, EUNICE ["E. T."]
POEMS
    The Steam Shovel   4   221
    Christmas at Saint Luke's Hospital   5   110
    The Bacchante to Her Babe   5   272
    Profiles from China   9   117
        The Story Teller
        Our Chinese Acquaintance
        A Scholar
        Chinese New Year
        The Most-Sacred Mountain
    Facets   14   243
        Completion
        On the Height
        Parting After a Quarrel
        Praise for Him
        At the Banquet
        Defeat
        The Tepid Hour
    Fire   19   262
    Neanderthal   22   198
    To a Picture of the Tired Siegmund   22   247
    Profiles from Home   25   175
        The Statue of Liberty
        The Skyscraper
        Afternoon at Vassar
        The Society Leader
        The Wall-Street Promoter
        The Follower of Kropotkin
        The Negro Church
    The Man Who Loved Mary   30   1
    Leaves in Windy Weather   34   140
        Requiem for a Faun
        Magic
        Your Face Remembered
        Query

The Return   37   14
Revolt
The Later Moment   41   14
  So Be It
  Even Beauty
  Desert
Welter   42   327
Compliment Macabre   46   305
A Sonnet of the Body
An Old Woman
Cycle
From the Florida Everglades   51   304
  Shell-Fish
  Nuptial Flight
  Flashes from the Glades
Horizon at Sea   55   318
Caribbean
Fire-Brick
Under the Caribbean: The Deeps   59   78

TRANSLATIONS
Poems adapted from Antonin Proust   17   68
Poem by Tarafa   32   186

ARTICLES
Correspondence: To Poetry
  [Poem]   6   157
Correspondence: Poetry
  and the Panama-Pacific Exposition   6   264
The Chinese Chanting of the Classics
  [Su Shih]   9   35
Appreciation   9   198
Correspondence: Lament
  of a Poetry Editor
  [Poem]   9   218
Broadsides   10   110
Yone Noguchi   15   96
A Postscript to the Foregoing   15   326
The Sub-Conscious Cliché   18   153
On Translating Chinese Poetry
  [Louise Hammond]   20   268
On Translating Chinese Poetry, II
  [Herbert A. Giles, James Legge,
  Helen Waddell, Amy Lowell]   20   328
[Note on Amy Lowell]   21   172
The Lyric in Poetry   22   148
Apologia
  [Amy Lowell]   22   267
A Plea for a Revaluation of the Trite   22   322
Microcosm
  [Harriet Monroe]   41   43
The Cuckoo School of Criticism
  [Edward Davison]   46   96
[Note on Edward Davison]   46   352
On Teaching the Writing of Poetry   47   92
[Tribute to Harriet Monroe]   49   138
The Attitude Toward the Poet   55   93
The End of Ezra Pound   60   38

REVIEWS
Unconditioned Songs, by Anonymous   4   166
Men of No Land,
  by Mildred McNeal Sweeny
The Foothills of Parnassus,
  by John Kendrick Bangs
Songs for the New Age,
  by James Oppenheim   5   88
The Falconer of God, and Other Poems,
  by William Rose Benét   5   91
Trees and Other Poems,
  by Joyce Kilmer   5   140
The Reverberate Hills,
  by Edwin Oppenheim
Processionals,
  by John Curtis Underwood   7   47
Plantation Songs and Other Verse,
  by Ruth McEnery Stuart   9   54
The Rocky Road to Dublin,
  by James Stephens   9   98
Turns and Movies and Other Tales in Verse,
  by Conrad Aiken
Songs of Armageddon and Other Poems,
  by George Sylvester Viereck
The Christmas Trail and Other Poems,
  by Shirley Harvey   9   155
Amores, by D. H. Lawrence   9   264
The Great White Wall,
  by William Rose Benét   9   322
The Golden Threshold,
  by Sarojini Naidu   10   47
An April Elegy,
  by Arthur Davison Ficke   10   323
Counter-Attack and Other Poems,
  by Siegfried Sassoon   14   216
Flame and Shadow, by Sara Teasdale   17   272
Punch, the Immortal Liar,
  by Conrad Aiken   18   160
Fox Footprints,
  by Elizabeth J. Coatsworth   22   163
April Twilights and Other Poems,
  by Willa Cather   22   221
A Prayer Rug,
  by Jessica Nelson North   22   281
Bids for Premature Judgment   22   330
  Collected Poems, by Vachel Lindsay
  Selected Poems,
    by John Masefield
  Selected Poems, by George Sterling
Poems About Birds
  (Ed. by H. J. Massingham)   23   111
Black Armor, by Elinor Wylie   23   276
The Winged Horse,
  by Joseph Auslander
  and Frank Ernest Hill   31   349
The Jade Mountain,
  by Kiang Kang-Hu
  (Tr. by Witter Bynner)   35   289

Chinese Poems in English Rhyme
   (Tr. by Admiral Ts'ai T'ing-Kan)   42   174
Song and Its Fountains, by AE   42   177
The Name of Life,
   by Marjorie Allen Seiffert   53   283
November Hereabout, by Amy Murray   57   395
Under One Roof, by Agnes Lee   58   269

BOOKS REVIEWED
   Profiles from China   10   326
   Body and Raiment   15   272
   Profiles from China
   Profiles from Home   26   227
   Poetry of the Orient (Ed.)   34   102
   Leaves in Windy Weather   35   220
   The World at My Shoulder   52   356

ARTICLES ABOUT
   Comments by Samuel Travers Clover   6   266
   [Poem by Carl Sandburg]   11   56
   Back to China, by Harriet Monroe   11   271
   Correspondence from Amy Lowell   21   167
   A Few Women Poets,
      by Harriet Monroe   26   326
   Poets as Prosers, by Harriet Monroe   28   328
   Correspondence from Edward Davison   46   352
   Eunice Tietjens: A Memorial,
      by Jessica Nelson North   65   104

TIETJENS, JANET
REVIEWS
   Rainbow Gold, Poems Old and New
   Selected for Boys and Girls,
      by Sara Teasdale   22   279

TIFFT, ELLEN
POEMS
   Ride Quickly Schuyler   76   142

TILDEN, ETHEL ARNOLD
POEMS
   Essence   24   19
   A Poem for Pat Who Builds Houses   26   314
   Acceptance
   Late Afternoon   41   203
   Nocturne   44   133

BOOKS REVIEWED
   Quest and Acceptance   28   174

TILLER, TERENCE
BOOKS REVIEWED
   Poems   59   98

TILLINGHAST, RICHARD
POEMS
   Angels and Ministers of Grace   107   375
   For a Teacher's Wife, Dying of Cancer

Winter Insomnia   110   394
Passage
A Letter   114   29

REVIEWS
   A Prizewinner, the Real Thing,
      and Two Others   109   118
      The War of the Secret Agents
      and Other Poems,
         by Henri Coulette
      Love Always, by Vi Gale
      Toward Montebello,
         by Warren Carrier
      Winter News, by John Haines
   Seven Poets   110   258
      Dry Summer in Provence,
         by Millen Brand
      The Grey Tower,
         by Donald F. Drummond
      The Diving Bell,
         by Dabney Stuart
      Estrangements,
         by Arthur Freeman
      The Weathercock, by Ann Stanford
      Single Source,
         by William Everson
      The Dumbfounding,
         by Margaret Avison
   Stars & Departures,
      Hummingbirds & Statues   166   289
      White Pine, by Mary Oliver
      Study for the World's Body,
         by David St. John
      Dark Harbor, by Mark Strand
      Pairs: New Poems, by Philip Booth
      Coming into Eighty, by May Sarton
      Off-Season at the Edge of the World,
         by Debora Greger

BOOKS REVIEWED
   Sleep Watch   117   204

ARTICLES ABOUT
   Correspondence from Edward Field
   [Millen Brand]   110   433

TILLYARD, E. M. W.
BOOKS REVIEWED
   The English Epic
   and Its Background   86   118

TINDALL, WILLIAM YORK
ARTICLES
   Joyce's Chambermade Music   80   105

BOOKS REVIEWED
   Forces in Modern
   British Literature 1885-1946   71   165
   James Joyce, Chamber Music (Ed.)   85   109

TIPTON, DAVID
POEMS
   Gunshots   114   391
   Plans
   Pachacamac

TRANSLATIONS
   Poem by Abelardo Sanchez Leon   116   368

TISERA, MARY
POEMS
   On Ash Wednesday   143   287

TITTERTON, L. H.
ARTICLES ABOUT
   Verse Drama and the Radio,
     by Amy Bonner   58   280

TITZELL, JOSIAH
BOOKS REVIEWED
   Galanty Show   60   163

TOBIN, DANIEL
POEMS
   Passages   159   88

TODD, MABEL LOOMIS
BOOKS REVIEWED
   Letters of Emily Dickinson (Ed.)   41   219
   Bolts of Melody, New Poems
     of Emily Dickinson
     (Ed. with Millicent Todd Bingham)   66   274

TODD, RUTHVEN
POEMS
   Easter in Essex   54   88
   Poem ("The child forseeing...")
   For Pablo Picasso
   Love Is No Ghost   57   20
   Tomorrow Will Come Soon
   Poem for Picasso's New Baby   72   85
   Rivers: On Living in Brooklyn
   Upon This Rock
   Croton-on-Hudson
   Love Is the Law   73   21
   An Upper, Left Central, Incisor 88   291
   Trout Flies
   Laugharne Churchyard in 1954

BOOKS REVIEWED
   Thorns of Thunder,
     by Paul Eluard
     (Ed. by George Reavey)
     (Tr. with Samuel Beckett,
     Denis Devlin, David Gascoyne,
     Eugene Jolas, Man Ray,
     and George Reavey)   48   347

Proems
   (With Patrick Evans, Rayner
   Heppenstall, Edgar Foxall, Lawrence
   Durrell, and Oswald Blakeston)   53   155
   A Mantelpiece of Shells   86   168
   Garland for the Winter Solstice 101   205

TODRIN, BORIS
POEMS
   The Flight   52   64
   Spanish Sowing: 1938
   Durutti   54   132

BOOKS REVIEWED
   7 Men   53   92
   At the Gates   65   160

TOLKIEN, J. R. R.
BOOKS REVIEWED
   The Adventures of Tom Bombadil 105   190
   Tree and Leaf   108   65

TOLSON, M(ELVIN) B.
POEMS
   From *Libretto for the Republic of Liberia* 76   208
   E. & O. E.   78   330
   The Man from Halicarnassus   81   75

ARTICLES
   [Notes to *E. & O. E.*]   78   369

REVIEWS
   Selected Poems of Claude McKay 83   287

BOOKS REVIEWED
   Libretto for the Republic of Liberia 86   174

ARTICLES ABOUT
   Preface to *Libretto*
     for the Republic of Liberia,
     by Allen Tate   76   216

TOLSTOY, TANYA
TRANSLATIONS
   Poems of Kozma Prutkov
     (Tr. with W. D. Snodgrass)   104   203

TOMLINSON, CHARLES
POEMS
   The Slag Heap: Alchemical Thoughts 77   79
   Poem of the Neighbours
   Nine Variations
     in a Chinese Winter Setting
   Beauty and the Beast   88   348
   Icos
   Reflections
   Reeds

Tramontana at Lerici
Ponte Veneziano
The Mausoleum
A Meditation on John Constable   90   6
More Foreign Cities
Glass Grain
Civilities of Lamplight
Antecedents   91   28
Cradock Newton   92   104
Chateau de Muzot
In Defence of Metaphysics
Autumn   94   8
Ode to Arnold Schoenberg   95   358
At Wells: Polyphony
Sea Poem
Maillol
Return to Hinton   98   133
Portrait of Mrs. Spaxton
The Hand at Callow Hill Farm
The Picture of J. T. in a Prospect of Stone
The Archer   99   273
Harvest Festival
Up at La Serra
Hill Walk   101   129
On a Theme of Pasternak
American Scenes   103   102
Arizona Desert   106   123
A Death in the Desert
On the Mountain
Arroyo Seco
Las Trampas U.S.A.
Old Man at Valdez
Weeper in Jalisco
News from Nowhere
In Winter Woods   107   159
The Door
Bone
The Hill
The Fox
The Way of a World   111   67
Clouds
Words for the Madrigalist
Logic
On the Principle of Blowclocks
The End
Rumour
The Beautiful Aeroplane
Eden   112   323
Adam
Prometheus
In the Fullness of Time
Music's Trinity
The Chances of Rhyme
Against Extremity
Movements   117   95
The Lighthouse   120   150
The Sea Is Open to the Light
On Water

North with Lawren Harris   151   180
Night Ferry
The Operation   155   379
Before the Concert
Fire   158   136

TRANSLATIONS
    Poems by Antonio Machado   101   303
    Versions of César Vallejo
        (Tr. with Henry Gifford)   109   229
    Poems by Edoardo Sanguineti   155   78

ARTICLES
    Pages from an Italian Journal
        [Rainer Maria Rilke]   89   183
    Comment   151   216

REVIEWS
    Poets of the 1950's:
        An Anthology of New English Verse
        (Ed. by D. J. Enright)
        [Philip Larkin, Kingsley Amis,
        Donald Davie, Robert Conquest]   89   260
    Poems of Christina Rossetti
        (Ed. by Kathleen Jarvis)   89   385
    Poet Without an Audience   90   321
        The Letters of William Blake
            (Ed. by Geoffrey Keynes)
        William Blake's Vala
            (Ed. by H. M. Margoliouth)
        William Blake:
            The Finger on the Furnace,
            by Laura DeWitt James
    The Common Muse:
        An Anthology of Popular British
        Ballad Poetry XVth-XXth Century
        (Ed. by Vivian De Sola Pinto
        and Allan Edwin Rodway)
        [William Wordsworth]   91   400
    Yuan Mei; The Nine Songs;
        and The Way and Its Power,
        by Arthur Waley
        [Lao Tzu, Martin Buber]   93   408
    Edward Thomas   95   52
        Edward Thomas:
            The Last Four Years,
            by Eleanor Farjeon
        As It Was and World Without End,
            by Helen Thomas
    Poetry and Silence   96   108
        The Poetry of Boris Pasternak
            (Tr. and ed. by George Reavey)
        Poems of Boris Pasternak
            (Tr. by Eugene M. Kayden)
            [Stéphane Mallarmé,
            Fyodor Tyutchev]
    Medieval Literature
        and the Common Reader   97   195

Medieval English Poetry:
   The Non-Chaucerian Tradition,
   by John Speirs
Lyrics of the Middle Ages
   (Ed. by Hubert Creekmore)
Sir Gawain and the Green Knight
   (Tr. by Brian Stone)
Collected Poems, by Lawrence Durrell   98   53
Essays and Introductions,
   by W. B. Yeats   98   263
Two Englands   99   54
   The Edge of Day, by Laurie Lee
   Bid Me to Live, by H. D.
The School of Donne, by A. Alvarez   99   261
Poor Kit Smart, by Christopher Devlin   99   375
Poets and Mushrooms: A Retrospect
   of British Poetry in 1961   100   104
   A Sequence for Francis Parkman
   and *New and Selected Poems,*
   by Donald Davie
   Poetry Today and *An Anthology*
   of Modern Verse 1940-60 (Ed.),
   by Elizabeth Jennings
   My Sad Captains,
   by Thom Gunn
   The Sun My Monument,
   by Laurie Lee
   The Nature of Cold Weather,
   by Peter Redgrove
   Poems and Translations,
   by Thomas Kinsella
   Tares, by R. S. Thomas
   Poems in Scots and English,
   by William Soutar
   Late Poems, by Austin Clarke
   Legends and Pastorals,
   by Graham Hough
   More Poems, by Robert Graves
   Five Centuries of Polish Poetry,
   by Jerzy Peterkiewicz
   and Burns Singer
   Versions from Fyodor Tyutchev
   (Tr. by Charles Tomlinson
   and Henry Gifford)
   Collected Poems, by Ronald Bottrall
   The Many Named Beloved,
   by Samuel Menashe
   Poems, by A. D. Hope
   [Norman MacCaig, Ted Hughes,
   Robert Graves]
A Miscellany   102   341
   Patriotic Gore, by Edmund Wilson
   The Tradition of the New,
   by Harold Rosenberg
   [John Cage]
   Poetry and the Physical Voice,
   by Francis Berry
   E. E. Cummings and the Critics
   (Ed. by S. V. Baum)

Adventures in Value,
   by Marion Morehouse
   and E. E. Cummings
The Active Universe, by H. W. Piper
The Making of a Poem,
   by Stephen Spender
Oxford Addresses on Poetry,
   by Robert Graves
The Yeats Country, by Sheelah Kirby
Wilfred Owen   104   41
   The Collected Poems of...
   (Ed. by C. Day Lewis)
   Journey from Obscurity, 1893-1918:
   Memoirs of the Owen Family,
   by Harold Owen
Certaines Choses Naturelles,
   by James Laughlin
   (Tr. by Alain Bosquet)   105   125
Poemas Humanos,
   by César Vallejo
   (Tr. by Clayton Eshleman)
   [Robert Duncan]   114   193

BOOKS REVIEWED
   The Necklace   88   324
   Seeing is Believing   93   335
   Versions from Fyodor Tyutchev
   (Tr. with Henry Gifford)   100   104
   Versions from Fyodor Tyutchev:
   1803- 1873 (Tr.)   101   418
   A Peopled Landscape   104   243
   Castilian Ilexes:
   Versions from Antonio Machado
   (Tr. with Henry Gifford)   105   198
   American Scenes   109   112
   The Way of a World   118   102
   Written on Water   123   113
   Selected Poems: 1951-1974   137   105
   The Shaft
   Collected Poems   150   286
   Collected Poems   154   29

TOMPKINS, EUFINA C.
POEMS
   Mirage   15   258

TONGUE, MARGARET
POEMS
   The Minnow   95   211
   Resurrection

BOOKS REVIEWED
   A Book of Kinds   94   117

TOOMER, JEAN
ARTICLES ABOUT
   Rev. of *Poetry and the World,*
   by Robert Pinsky   156   297

TORGOWNIK, WILLIAM
POEMS
   Observations   26   245
    In the Orchard
    I Love the Sea
    Mask
    Aspiration
    Champions

TORREGIAN, SOTÈRE
BOOKS REVIEWED
   The Wounded Mattress   120   164

TORRENCE, RIDGELEY
POEMS
   Santa Barbara Beach   1   180
   The Bird and the Tree   6   20
   Survivors   9   188
   This Light   55   59
   The Watcher
   Harvest Home
   Heard from a Dark Stage
   Adam's Dying

BOOKS REVIEWED
   Hesperides   26   286

TORRES, EMMANUEL
POEMS
   Woman with Child   88   378

TORRES, LUIS LLORENS
  [See LLORENS TORRES, LUIS]

TORRES BODET, JAIME
BOOKS REVIEWED
   Poemas   26   172
   Selected Poems of...
    (Tr. by Sonja Karsen)   107   338

TORRES RIOSECO, ARTURO
BOOKS REVIEWED
   The Epic of Latin American Literature   62   105

TORTEL, JEAN
ARTICLES ABOUT
   Marseille Letter,
    by Jean Rivier   60   269

TOSHIAKI, HONDA
ARTICLES ABOUT
   Rev. of *The Japanese*
    Discovery of Europe,
    by Donald Keene   88   109

TOURSKY
ARTICLES ABOUT
   Marseille Letter,
    by Jean Rivier   60   269

TOUSTER, SAUL
POEMS
   Charles Péguy (1873-1914)   89   238
   The Poet
   Listen to Your Body   99   360
   The Doorknob   105   180
   Green Apple: Still Life I
   Green Apple: Still Life II
   Green Apple: Still Life III

BOOKS REVIEWED
   Still Lives and Other Lives   111   189

TOWLE, ANDREW
POEMS
   Between Stations   152   197
   Nocturne
   The Dead Sea at Dinner   153   93
   Luna Moth   157   274
   Vanished   170   73

TOWLE, TONY
POEMS
   Works on Paper   125   311

BOOKS REVIEWED
   North   119   224

TOWNE, CHARLES HANSON
POEMS
   Beyond the Stars   1   35
   On First Looking
    into the Manuscript of Endymion   6   17

ARTICLES
   Edwin Markham 1852-1940   56   30

BOOKS REVIEWED
   Beyond the Stars and Other Poems   5   90
   Today and Tomorrow   8   264
   Selected Poems of...   27   170

TOWNE, NAPIER
POEMS
   Metempsychosis   44   139
   Dream Styles
   Moral   46   262

TOWNSEND, EMILY
POEMS
   Dactylo-Epitrites for Dudley Fitts   98   157

TOWNSEND, GERTRUDE
POEMS
   Deepening Night   25   303

TOYNBEE, PHILIP
BOOKS REVIEWED
   Pantaloon   102   393

733

TRACY, EDITH CHAPMAN
TRANSLATIONS
  Poems by Konstantin Balmont   12   258

TRACY, HENRY
TRANSLATIONS
  Poems from the Navajo
    (Tr. with Ina Sizer Cassidy)   43   119

TRACY, PAUL E.
POEMS
  The Plumber   35   30
  Cold   39   306
  Road Gang   42   18
  The Father

TRACY, ROBERT
TRANSLATIONS
  Poems by Osip Mandelstam   136   21

TRAKL, GEORG
POEMS
  Whispered in the Afternoon
    (Tr. by Charles Wharton Stork)   6   102
  Sebastian in Dream
    (Tr. by Michael Hamburger)   98   151

BOOKS REVIEWED
  Twenty Poems of…
    (Tr. by James Wright and Robert Bly)   100   319

ARTICLES ABOUT
  Correspondence
    from Charles Wharton Stork   6   102

TRANQUILLUS, GAIUS SUETONIUS
BOOKS REVIEWED
  The Twelve Caesars
    (Tr. by Robert Graves)   93   395

TRANSTRÖMER, TOMAS
BOOKS REVIEWED
  Twenty Poems
    (Tr. by Robert Bly)   123   34

TRANTER, JOHN
POEMS
  Respirating Buds   169   82

ARTICLES
  Australian Poetry 1940–1980:
    A Personal View
    [Judith Wright, James McAuley,
    Francis Webb]   169   86

ARTICLES ABOUT
  Towards a Contemporary
    Australian Poetics,
    by John Kinsella   169   94

TRAPP, JACOB
POEMS
  Slow Paces   48   134
  Lonely for One Forgotten
  Portrait
  Night Wish

TRASK, SHERWOOD
POEMS
  Levee Songs   30   249

TRASK, WILLARD R. ["W. R. T."]
TRANSLATIONS
  Poems by Yuan Chieh,
    the Emperor Yang, Lu Fu Li,
    Kao Ch'i, Siue Tao-Heng,
    Hong Tche-Kong, and K'ong
    Chao-Ngan
    (Tr. with George Margulies)   46   3
  Chinese Folk Songs   46   8
  Songs of the Fourth Century A.D.
  Songs of the Fifth Century A.D.
  Song of the Sixth Century A.D.
    (Tr. with George Margulies)

ARTICLES
  Three Chinese Poets of Long Ago
    (With George Margulies)
    [Yuan Chieh, the Emperor Yang,
    Kao Ch'i]   46   46

BOOKS REVIEWED
  European Literature
    and the Latin Middle Ages,
    by Ernst Robert Curtius (Tr.)   84   158
  The Unwritten Song, Vol. I (Ed.)   111   266
  The Unwritten Song, Vol. II (Ed. and tr.)   114   56
  Classic Black African Poems (Ed.)   123   34

TRAVERS, ELIZABETH
POEMS
  Death of the Explorer   69   143
  The Wirewalkers
  Elegy for a Pet Beagle   74   136

TRAVERSI, DEREK
BOOKS REVIEWED
  Shakespeare:
    From "Richard II" to "Henry V"   92   189

TRAWICK, LEONARD
POEMS
  Severed Parts   132   141
  Wood Fires
  The Underworld
  Psyches   136   155
  Feeling for Fish

TREE, IRIS
POEMS
   Afterwards   13   72
   The Frog   21   252
   Wintry Alley

BOOKS REVIEWED
   Poems   19   165
   The Traveller and Other Poems   30   290

TREECE, HENRY
POEMS
   Poem ("I wore a cloak of music...")   57   139
   The Lying Word   58   202
   City
   The Dyke-Builder
   Legend
   Rustic Metaphor
   There Is a Cause for Faith...   60   139
   Elegy ("O do you not hear them...")   69   299
   Bardic Poem   71   134
   Deep in the Forest
   Fickle as Tiger
   There Is an Ocean
   We, as Old as Two Wars

BOOKS REVIEWED
   38 Poems   56   274
   The Collected Poems of...   69   346
   How I See Apocalypse   72   103
   Dylan Thomas: "Dog Among the Fairies"   75   357

ARTICLES ABOUT
   Contemporary Poetry in Britain,
      by David Daiches   62   150

TREFETHEN, FLORENCE
POEMS
   Mid-Pacific   115   318

TREMBLAY, BILL
BOOKS REVIEWED
   Crying in the Cheap Seats   123   34

TRENCH, HERBERT
POEMS
   Song of the Vine, in England   12   249

ARTICLES
   Correspondence:
      An English Poet on "Poetry"   13   285

BOOKS REVIEWED
   Poems, with Fables in Prose   20   282

ARTICLES ABOUT
   Obituary
      [Excerpt from correspondence]   22   346

TREND, J. B.
ARTICLES ABOUT
   Juan Ramón Jiménez:
      The Landscape of the Soul,
      by Rachel Frank   82   224

TRENT, LUCIA
BOOKS REVIEWED
   How to Profit from That Impulse
      (Ed. with Ralph Cheyney
      and Benjamin Musser)   34   56

TRETHEWEY, ERIC
POEMS
   Luck   149   80
   In the Landscape of Opinion
   Where Were You Headed?
   Woods Talk   157   313
   Aubade ("Fortunate, those who...")
   Wait   162   208

TREVELYAN, R. C.
ARTICLES ABOUT
   Rev. of *An Annual*
      of New Poetry, 1917   11   333

TRIBBLE, JON
POEMS
   Fathers   154   149

TRIEM, EVE
[EVA TRIEM]
POEMS
   Flute Songs   54   248
   The Witness   59   262
   It Was Before the Dawn
   Premonition
   Concert, in Wartime   63   196
   Magic in the House
   Dubuque, Iowa   70   310
   The Lamp, and Heliodora   89   272
   Here Are Roses
   Not Yet the New Adam
   With a Branch of Acacia
   The New Man   96   357
   A Flame of Five Jays   101   396
   The Gull
   The Exile Tells His Friends   106   335
   The Hostage   108   241
   Trees, Near and Far

REVIEWS
   Three Poets   96   314
      These Islands Also,
         by Jeremy Ingalls
      The Rock Harbor, by Ronald Perry
      With Eyes at the Back of Our Heads,
         by Denise Levertov

BOOKS REVIEWED
Parade of Doves   72   281
Poems   108   121

TRIGG, EMMA GRAY
POEMS
To an Artist in the Machine Age   51   133
Hermes Intra Muros   54   78
"Poetry Is Fiddling"
Austrian Spring: 1939
Night Club   57   249

BOOKS REVIEWED
After Eden   54   346

TRILLING, LIONEL
BOOKS REVIEWED
Selected Letters of John Keats (Ed.)   84   296
The Experience of Literature (Ed.)   113   188

ARTICLES ABOUT
The Poet and Pedant Symposium,
    by Margedant Peters   57   194
Rev. of Wordsworth: Centenary Studies
    Presented at Cornell
    and Princeton Universities
    (Ed. by Gilbert T. Dunklin)   80   233
[Note]   83   56

TRIMBLE, MARY
POEMS
131 Views of Fuji by Hokusai   170   26

TRIMPI, (W.) WESLEY
POEMS
To El Greco   74   264
Adirondacks: Late Summer 1948

BOOKS REVIEWED
The Glass of Perseus   86   56

TRINE, GRACE HYDE
BOOKS REVIEWED
Dreams and Voices (Ed.)   18   106

TRIPLETT, PIMONE
POEMS
The Glass, 1778   168   139
The Annunciation

TRIVELPIECE, LAUREL
POEMS
Progress   145   202
Morning Mists
Unborn
Ink Blots
Ceres   152   323
Grazing

Outside the Garden   160   140
Bringing in the Cows
The Turkish Bee   160   260
Reaching for the Sun   166   16
Dailiness
In Remission

TROLLOPE, [MRS.]
ARTICLES ABOUT
Rev. of Collected Poems 1909-1962,
    by T. S. Eliot   106   239

TROMBLY, ALBERT EDMUND
POEMS
Rio Grande Valley   23   18
I Observe   48   258
    Acorns and Apples
    Fences
    Spectrum
    Enough To Be

TRANSLATIONS
Poem from the Old French   16   186

ARTICLES
Correspondence
    [Mona Van Duyn]   65   165

BOOKS REVIEWED
Grain of Sand, and Other Poems   64   339

TROWBRIDGE, WILLIAM
POEMS
Walking Back   148   315
Living with Solar Keratosis   154   271
Sometimes on the Porch in Summer

TROWER, PETER
POEMS
Grease for the Wheels of Winter   121   125
The Presumers   123   234
The Last Stand of Magic
Relearning Winter   126   204
Along Green Tunnels
The Reclaimed   129   250

TROY, WILLIAM
REVIEWS
Literature of the Will   51   206
    New Writing
        (Ed. by John Lehmann)
    New Letters in America
        (Ed. by Horace Gregory)
    Collected Poems of William Empson   74   234

BOOKS REVIEWED
Selected Essays
    (Ed. by Stanley Edgar Hyman)   112   116

ARTICLES ABOUT
  A Censorship for Critics,
    by Jessica Nelson North   34   32

TRUDELL, DENNIS
  POEMS
    Epilogue   115   233
    Hotel in Paris
    A Way
    Excursions

TRUEBLOOD, CHARLES K.
  REVIEWS
    Selected Poems,
      by Edith Sitwell   50   161
    The Note-Books and Papers
      of Gerard Manley Hopkins
      (Ed. by Humphry House)   50   274

TRUSSELL, DONNA
  POEMS
    On Sky-Vue Boulevard   153   276
    To Miss Candace Mayes,
      Lost on the Titanic

TRUSTMAN, DEBORAH
  POEMS
    Leviathan and Other Mysteries   124   34
    Very Rich Hours   127   152
    The Eclipse
    Watercolor   129   198
    The Fall
    Clearing
    Shelling

TRYPANIS, C. A.
  BOOKS REVIEWED
    The Stones of Troy   92   318
    The Cocks of Hades   94   196
    Grooves in the Wind   105   207
    Pompeian Dog   108   399

TS'AI T'ING-KAN, [ADMIRAL]
  BOOKS REVIEWED
    Chinese Poems in English Rhyme (Tr.)   42   174

TSVETAYEVA, MARINA
  [MARINA TSEVETAEVA]
  BOOKS REVIEWED
    Selected Poems
      (Tr. by Elaine Feinstein)   124   232
    After Russia
      (Tr. by Michael Naydan)   163   97

TUCKER, ALLEN
  BOOKS REVIEWED
    There and Here   16   336

TUCKER, IRWIN ST. JOHN
  BOOKS REVIEWED
    The Chosen Nation   14   220

TUCKERMAN,
  FREDERICK GODDARD
  BOOKS REVIEWED
    The Complete Poems of...
      (Ed. by N. Scott Momaday)   107   401

TUFFIELD, ADRIAN
  ARTICLES ABOUT
    The Younger Bards,
      by Edward J. O'Brien   6   188

TUFTS, CAROL
  POEMS
    Hades and Persephone   165   3

TU FU
  POEMS
    Pounding the Clothes   90   28
    Farewell to My Soldier-Friend
      (Tr. by Chao Tze-Chiang)
      [Version by Carolyn Kizer]   103   63
    Thwarted
      [Version by Carolyn Kizer]   105   163

  BOOKS REVIEWED
    Tu Fu, the Autobiography
      of a Chinese Poet
      (Tr. by Florence Ayscough)   47   219
    Travels of a Chinese Poet
      (Tr. by Florence Ayscough)

  ARTICLES ABOUT
    Rev. of Tu Fu, China's Greatest Poet,
      by William Hung   83   295
    Rev. of One Hundred Poems
      from the Chinese,
      by Kenneth Rexroth   90   180
    Rev. of A Little Primer of Tu Fu,
      by David Hawkes   112   283

TULL, JEWELL BOTHWELL
  POEMS
    October   21   22
    Gender
    Foolish Bird
    Gray River
    Sum
    God-Like
    Seven Ages   24   186
    Bits of Song   28   246
    The Dance
    Preparation
    To a Heartless Connoisseur
    Coquette

Transformation
Peace
To Socrates
Abracadabra   34   262
  The Charm
  The Rite
  The Sign
Contrarieties   38   259
  Immortality
  Tragedy

TUNSTALL, VIRGINIA LYNE
POEMS
  Traveler Forget   57   298
  Alien

TUPINIKA-GLAESSNER, TINA
BOOKS REVIEWED
  Bratsk Station and Other New Poems,
  by Yevgeny Yevtushenko
  (Tr. with Geoffrey Dutton)   III   121

TURBERVILE, GEORGE
ARTICLES ABOUT
  The 16th-Century Lyric
    in England: Part I,
    by Yvor Winters   53   258

TURBYFILL, MARK
POEMS
  Wind-Flowers   10   68
    Prayer for Sophistication
    Strangers
    Pulse of Spring
    Oh That Love Has Come at All!
    To a Cool Breeze
  A Song for Souls Under Fire   12   244
  My Heart, Like Hyacinth
  The Adventurer
  Mellow
  Without Chaperon
  The Forest of Dead Trees
  Benediction
  Journeys and Discoveries   15   14
    Chicago
    End of Summer
    A Song of Givers and Takers
    Words About Love
    Journey
  Voluntaries   18   136
    The Intangible Symphony
    The Power of Nothing
    Repletion
    The Sea Storm
    Things Not Seen
  Outlines   24   124
    Charm
    Weather Caprice
    Subject and Object

Phantasy
Velocity
Ballet Memories   27   247
  A Trophy of Battle
  Georgette Leblanc
  Ornamental Dissolution
  The Wave
A Marriage with Space   28   61
  Part One: The Builder
  Part Two: The Bridge of Days
  Part Three: The Edifice of Light
Absolutely and Sincerely   32   61
  Station J-A-Z-Z Broadcasting
  Like a Fish
  Our American Mercury
  The Incarnation of Romance
  Judas Jazz
Dance Poems   38   322
  Adagio Chiricoesque
  Apollo Alone Approves
  What Held You?
  Seeking the Feet
  Sand Storm
Invitation to the Dance   51   258
Dark Banquet
Portrait Impression
The Poet
Dance and Transfiguration
Hardy Perennials   52   190
Outside a Hothouse   61   546
A Lost Dancer

REVIEWS
  Images, by Richard Aldington
    [New ed.]   15   162

BOOKS REVIEWED
  The Living Frieze   19   337
  A Marriage with Space and Other Poems   31   211

ARTICLES ABOUT
  Mr. Turbyfill's Poem,
    by Harriet Monroe   28   92
  What to Think?
    by Harriet Monroe   28   215

TURCO, LEWIS
POEMS
  House and Shutter   96   159
  Some Food for Thought   99   364
  Awaken, Bells Falling   103   247
  November 22, 1963   105   84
  The Villagers   106   409
  From Pocoangelini   108   230
  An Arras Tapestry   III   166
  Home Thoughts   113   246
  The Kitchen   114   308
  The Bedroom

The Scythe
The Cell   117   356
The Children of Rome   118   262
A Song ("The ravages of the worm...")
Foxfire: Tarot Queen of Pentacles   120   208
The Lovers: Tarot Key VI
Death: Tarot Key XIII
The Devil: Tarot Key XV
The Tower: Tarot Key XVI
Epistles: The Tarot IX of Swords

REVIEWS
Inventing To Discover   106   369
    A Circle of Stone,
        by Miller Williams
    Arms of Light, by Claire McAllister
    The Common Ground, by John Galt
    Collected Poems 1916-1970,
        by Conrad Aiken   118   287

BOOKS REVIEWED
    First Poems   99   184
    The Sketches of...   102   402
    Awaken, Bells Falling   113   421
    The Inhabitant: Poems   121   343

TURGEON, GREGOIRE
POEMS
    At Home   130   79

TURNBULL, BELLE
POEMS
    Marginal Notes   24   198
    Incident of the Hawk-Watch
    Man Ponders His Problem
    One Man
    In a Restaurant
    To a Mountain Meadow
    In a Puritan's House   30   137
    At That Point Mr. Probus   51   128
    Time as a Wellspring
    Lunch Time in the Tunnel
    Lyric Mood
    Along That Range   53   240
    Preface to a Work
        on the Ten Mile District
    Hardrock Miner
    Summons to the Undertaker
    House   57   12

BOOKS REVIEWED
    Goldboat   57   274

TURNBULL, ELEANOR L.
BOOKS REVIEWED
    Contemporary Spanish Poetry
        (With Pedro Salinas) (Tr.)   67   265
    Zero, by Pedro Salinas (Tr.)   74   48

Ten Centuries of Spanish Poetry (Ed.)   87   303
Ten Centuries of Spanish Verse (Ed.)   93   188

TURNBULL, GAEL
POEMS
    Twenty Words: Twenty Days:
        A Sketchbook & A Morula   106   136

BOOKS REVIEWED
    A Very Particular Hill   105   270
    A Trampoline: Poems 1952-1964   117   331

TURNELL, MARTIN
BOOKS REVIEWED
    Poetry and Crisis   55   86
    Masters & Friends, by Paul Valéry (Tr.)
        (Ed. by Jackson Mathews)   113   338

ARTICLES ABOUT
    Religion and Sensibility, by Henry Rago   57   314

TURNER, ALBERTA
POEMS
    Stumping Wise   144   99

TURNER, ALVA N.
POEMS
    Old Age   20   138
    Our Sorrow
    Margarette
    Coming of June   22   76
    The Philosopher   23   198
    The Psychological Moment of Love   25   183
    Defeat   30   193
    Unmolested Beauty   90   29

TURNER, DONALD
ARTICLES ABOUT
    The Younger Bards,
        by Edward J. O'Brien   6   188

TURNER, ETHEL
POEMS
    Of Rupert Brooke   24   137

TURNER, FREDERICK
POEMS
    Dumbarton Oaks   142   273
    The Agape
    On Goya's "Saturn"   143   337
    Bone China Broken   147   69
    The Blessing
    The Distribution
    On Gibbs' Law   153   143

TRANSLATIONS
    Poems by Miklós Radnóti
        (Tr. with Zsuzsanna Ozsvath)   151   490

ARTICLES
The Neural Lyre:
  Poetic Meter, the Brain, and Time
  (With Ernst Pöppel)
  [Jerre Levy, Barbara Lex]   142   277

BOOKS REVIEWED
  Between Two Lives   123   353
  The New World: An Epic Poem   148   36

TURNER, JACK
POEMS
  Re-Creation   161   215
  TV Movie   166   273
  The Plan   168   146
  Identifying the Body   170   143
  Night Windows

TURNER, JAMES
BOOKS REVIEWED
  The Hollow Vale   75   178

TURNER, JUANITA
POEMS
  For Those Who Would Be Safe   32   319

TURNER, LEO C.
POEMS
  In Oklahoma   30   59
    Floaters
    Answer to Prayer
    A Boy's Trust
    Prairie Chickens
    First Call
    Three Crows
    Cloud Cast
    Seeking and Living
  Withering   43   136
    Earth Kept
    Oklahoma Trees
    Drouth

TURNER, LORENZO D.
REVIEWS
  Libretto for the Republic of Liberia,
    by Melvin B. Tolson   86   174

TURNER, NANCY BYRD
POEMS
  Though One Should Strive   12   315
  She Is Not Old   48   319

TURNER, W. J.
BOOKS REVIEWED
  The Dark Wind   17   276
  Fossils of a Future Time?   71   45

ARTICLES ABOUT
  Rev. of Georgian Poetry, 1916-1917   12   332

TURNER, W. PRICE
POEMS
  Conversations in Corners   99   38

BOOKS REVIEWED
  The Rudiment of an Eye   89   64
  The Flying Corset   102   193
  Fables from Life   110   112

TURNOY, BETTY
POEMS
  Two Poems   78   79
    ("I would elect to love you...")
    ("I would sit in this house...")
  Query   93   72
  The Possibility

TURQUET-MILNES, [MRS.] G.
ARTICLES ABOUT
  Paul Valéry, by M. D. Zabel   45   90

TUSIANI, JOSEPH
BOOKS REVIEWED
  The Complete Poems
    of Michelangelo (Tr.)   98   403

TUSSMAN, MALKA HAIFETZ
POEMS
  Spoil   102   381
  Play Without Words
  By an Abandoned House
    (Tr. by Jack Hirschman)

ARTICLES ABOUT
  A Note on Malka Tussman,
    by Jack Hirschman   102   406

TUTTLETON, JAMES
ARTICLES ABOUT
  Rev. of A History
    of Modern Poetry, Vol. II:
    Modernism and After,
    by David Perkins   151   296

TUVE, ROSEMOND
BOOKS REVIEWED
  Elizabethan and Metaphysical Imagery   72   156

TVARDOVSKY, ALEXANDER
TROFIMOVITCH
BOOKS REVIEWED
  Tyorkin & The Stovemakers:
    Poetry and Prose by...
    (Ed. and tr. by Anthony Rudolf)   129   102

ARTICLES ABOUT
  New Trends in Soviet Russian Poetry,
    by Vera Sandomirsky   58   324

TWAIN, MARK
[SAMUEL LANGHORNE CLEMENS]
ARTICLES ABOUT
On the Great River,
  by Harriet Monroe   46   268

TWICHELL, CHASE
POEMS
Blurry Cow   142   104
Abandoned House in Late Light
Lapses of Turquoise Sea   152   205

BOOKS REVIEWED
Northern Spy   140   346

TWITCHELL, ANNA SPENCER
POEMS
To a Mountain Pine   9   187
Compensation   13   313
Quatrain   17   255

TYLER, PARKER
POEMS
Hymn ("for one proud moment...")   37   285
Sight Complement   42   313
Anthology of Nouns   53   253
Ode for Reality
The Drowsy Mesmerist
The Process   57   234
The Heroes   60   82
The Sonnet of Rodin   79   82
A Ballad for Maldoror
Solitaire   80   192
Nijinsky
The Dandy and His Echo   83   210
To a Photograph   85   151
Advice to Lovers as Dancers   86   258
Chez Cythera
The Retreat   88   148
Prismatic Psyche
Baroque Epigram
Three Sonnets on Works of Art   91   246
  Leonardo's "Head of Our Saviour"
  Degas' "Woman with Chrysanthemums"
  Seurat's "La Grande Jatte"
From "A Summer Sequence"   93   155

ARTICLES
Note on Hymn and Left Instantly Designs
  (With Charles Henri Ford)   37   287

REVIEWS
The Literary Origins of Surrealism,
  by Anna Balakian   70   282

Jung's Emblems, the Poet's Enigmas
  [T. S. Eliot]   77   168
The Dream of Poliphilo,
  by Linda Fierz-David
The Hieroglyphics of Horapollo,
  by George Boas
Religion and the Cure of Souls,
  by Hans Schaer
Essays on a Science of Mythology,
  by C. G. Jung and C. Kerényi
The Seven-League Crutches,
  by Randall Jarrell   79   335
The Creative Process
  (Ed. by Brewster Ghiselin)
  [Paul Valéry]   81   133
Ring Song,
  by Naomi Replansky   81   321
Brother to Dragons,
  by Robert Penn Warren
  [Thomas Jefferson]   83   167
Pictures from an Institution,
  by Randall Jarrell   86   46
The Doctor and the Devils,
  by Dylan Thomas   87   116
Mr. Arcularis, by Conrad Aiken   91   333

BOOKS REVIEWED
The Metaphor in the Jungle   58   340
The Granite Butterfly   69   231

ARTICLES ABOUT
Correspondence
  from Waldemar Hansen   70   113
Correspondence
  from Anna Balakian   71   227

TYNGKWEI, LII
[See LII TYNGKWEI]

TYUTCHEV, FYODOR
BOOKS REVIEWED
Three Russian Poets
  (With Alexander Pushkin
  and Mikhail Lermontov)
  (Tr. by Vladimir Nabokov)   66   289
Versions from...
  (Tr. by Charles Tomlinson
  and Henry Gifford)   100   104
Versions from...: 1803-1873
  (Tr. by Charles Tomlinson)   101   418

ARTICLES ABOUT
Rev. of The Poetry of Boris Pasternak
  (Ed. and tr. by George Reavey)   96   108

UDELL, GERALDINE
ARTICLES
   [Tribute to Harriet Monroe]   49   151

UHLMAN, GEORGE
  [See MARIAN, GEORGE, pseud.]

ULLMAN, GEORGE
BOOKS REVIEWED
   Captive Balloons   24   341

ULLMAN, LESLIE
POEMS
   My Mother Is Not Watching   148   316
   Dawn Feeding   150   260
   Peace
   Mauve   153   267
   Amethyst
   Aquamarine   157   72
   French   157   205
   Running Horse   160   339
   The Mountain Outside My Window   163   17
   Estrogen   169   275
   Lent
   Museo de Oro
   Entropy   170   279

REVIEWS
   Short Reviews   169   156
     The Ghost Volcano,
      by Sandra M. Gilbert
     Straight Out of View,
      by Joyce Sutphen
     Firekeeper: New and Selected Poems,
      by Pattiann Rogers
     The Bank of Beautiful Sins,
      by Robert Wrigley
   Short Reviews   169   339
     Meadowlands, by Louise Glück
     Edge Effect: Trails and Portrayals
      and *The Spaces Between Birds,*
      by Sandra McPherson
     The Legend of Light, by Bob Hicok

BOOKS REVIEWED
   Natural Histories   140   35
   Dreams by No One's Daughter   153   106

ULMER, JAMES
POEMS
   Locked Room   139   283
   Rhododendrons
   From a Box of Old Photographs   142   207
   Before the Harvest

ULRICH, CAROLYN F.
BOOKS REVIEWED
   The Little Magazine:
    A History and a Bibliography
    (With Frederick J. Hoffman
    and Charles Allen)   70   274

UNDER, MARIE
ARTICLES ABOUT
   Rev. of *Anthology*
    of Modern Estonian Poetry
    (Ed. and tr. by W. K. Matthews)   84   236

UNDERWOOD, EDNA WORTHLEY
ARTICLES
   Correspondence: In South America   14   229

BOOKS REVIEWED
   Moons of Nippon   16   283

UNDERWOOD, JOHN CURTIS
POEMS
   War Times   12   117
    The Song of the Cheechas
    At Bethlehem
    The Red Coffins
    Down Fifth Avenue

BOOKS REVIEWED
   Processionals   7   47
   War Flames   10   271

ARTICLES ABOUT
   Correspondence
    from Paul Fortier Jones   13   228

UNGARETTI, GIUSEPPE
BOOKS REVIEWED
   Life of a Man
    (Ed. by Allen Mandelbaum)   93   329

ARTICLES ABOUT
Contemporary Italian Poetry,
    by Edward Williamson   79   159
Ungaretti's "La Terra Promessa":
    A Commentary and Some Examples,
    by Allen Mandelbaum   88   168

UNGER, HOWARD
POEMS
    We Who Have Lost   12   73

UNGER, LEONARD
REVIEWS
    The Collected Poems
        of William Butler Yeats   80   43
    The Finer Tone: Keats' Major Poems,
        by Earl Wasserman   84   37

BOOKS REVIEWED
    Donne's Poetry and Modern Criticism   77   175
    Poems for Study
        (With William Van O'Connor)   84   43
    T. S. Eliot: Moments and Patterns   112   52
    Seven Modern American Poets:
        An Introduction (Ed.)   112   206

UNNA, SARAH
POEMS
    The Victors   15   136
    Roads   19   316

UNTERECKER, JOHN
POEMS
    Photographs   115   330
    The Hero   119   26
    ...Within, Into, Inside, Under, Within...   129   311
    Hospital   130   134
    Arroyo: Flash Flood   154   269

BOOKS REVIEWED
    Voyager: A Life of Hart Crane   116   256

UNTERMEYER, JEAN STARR
POEMS
    A Man   9   184
    Rain
    Clay Hills   12   314
    Discover Me Again
    From the Day-Book of a Forgotten Prince   19   74
    Open Day   34   127
    After Flood
    Momentary Daniel
    Stony Water
    Time   40   250
    Relighted Torch
    Solution
    Kristin's Song   52   7
    The Realists   56   127

BOOKS REVIEWED
    Growing Pains   14   47
    Dreams Out of Darkness   20   220
    Steep Ascent   32   167
    Winged Child   48   288
    Love and Need:
        Collected Poems: 1918-1940   58   219

UNTERMEYER, LOUIS ["L. U."]
POEMS
    Magic   8   128
    Beauty
    Home   8   296
    The Beloved   14   72
    Conquest
    End of the Comedy
    Monologue from a Mattress   19   318
    Business of Ravens   31   306
    Prayer in Cornwall   37   76
    Due to Being Opposite

ARTICLES
    Correspondence
        [Heinrich Heine]   7   212
    Correspondence:
        The Retort Courteous
        [Poem]   9   109
    Correspondence
        [Yvor Winters]   20   168
    Correspondence:
        Mr. Untermeyer Protests   22   109

REVIEWS
    The Listeners, by Walter de la Mare   8   312
    The Espalier,
        by Sylvia Townsend Warner   28   224
    Three Notable Collections   103   382
        Collected and New Poems: 1924-1963,
            by Mark Van Doren
        Collected Poems: 1919-1962,
            by Babette Deutsch
        Caged in an Animal's Mind,
            by Stanley Burnshaw

BOOKS REVIEWED
    Challenge   4   201
    —And Other Poets   8   321
    These Times   11   157
    Poems of Heinrich Heine (Ed. and tr.)   11   279
    The New Era in American Poetry   14   159
    Including Horace   17   100
    The New Adam   17   212
    Modern British Poetry (Ed.)   18   106
    Modern American Poetry (Ed.)   27   343
    Modern British Poetry (Ed.)
    Burning Bush   32   224
    Modern American Poetry [3d ed.] (Ed.)   37   164

Modern British Poetry [3d ed.] (Ed.)
Heinrich Heine: Paradox and Poet
   [*The Life* and *The Poems*]   52   46
From Another World:
   The Autobiography of...   55   281
A Treasury of Great Poems (Ed.)   62   45
Early American Poets (Ed.)   81   261
Long Feud   102   125
Modern American Poetry and
   Modern British Poetry (Ed.)   103   261
The Letters of Robert Frost
   to Louis Untermeyer (Ed.)   104   253

ARTICLES ABOUT
  Correspondence from Clement Wood   5   141
  Rev. of *American Poetry 1922—A Miscellany*   22   50
  [Note]   97   327
  [Note on misprint]   104   124

UNTERMEYER, RICHARD
POEMS
  Dick   6   192
    As to Heaven
    As to God
    As to Truths

UPDEGRAFF, ALLAN
POEMS
  The Dance Before the Arch   4   182
  The Daily Round   15   259

UPDIKE, JOHN
POEMS
  To a Former Mistress, Now Dead   160   201
  Back from Vacation
  Elderly Sex
  Down Time   164   259
  Compliment
  Not Cancelled Yet
  61 and 2/3
  Venetian Candy   169   189
  Vero Beach Birthday
  One Tough Keratosis
  Subtropical Night
  Flight to Limbo

BOOKS REVIEWED
  Midpoint   115   426
  Facing Nature   147   291
  Collected Poems: 1953-1993   163   285

UPPER, JOSEPH
BOOKS REVIEWED
  Walking Shadow   41   165

UPTON, LEE
POEMS
  Paperweights   146   153
  Miniatures

UPWARD, ALLEN
POEMS
  Scented Leaves—From a Chinese Jar   2   191
  Baldur   8   55
  Holidays
  Finis

ARTICLES ABOUT
  Our Contemporaries
   [Poem]   6   317
  Two Poets Say Farewell,
   by Harriet Monroe   29   208

URBAN, WILBUR MARSHALL
BOOKS REVIEWED
  Language and Reality: The Philosophy of
   Language and the Principles of Symbolism   56   285

URBINA, LUIS G.
POEMS
  Clear Night
   (Tr. by Muna Lee)   26   132

URDANG, CONSTANCE
POEMS
  Birth of Venus   89   105
  Anecdote in the Parque España   91   96
  For Jonathan
  Four Unromantic Portraits   94   94
  Five Celebrations   97   20
  Editorials   102   17
  Pastorals
  To Pipe the Animals Aboard Noah's Ark   104   78
  In the Garden
  These Also Wait for Death   106   347
  Exhortation
  Song for Stones
  Her House   112   22
  Images   118   141
  Street Thief
  The Day the Houses Sank
  The Other Life   140   6
  Clouds
  Night Air
  The River   144   214
  Mexican Afternoons   158   202
  Transcendence   160   90

TRANSLATIONS
  Poems by Fuyuji Tanaka, Baku
   Yamanoguchi, Katsuhiko Kogure,
   Sannosuke Iwai, Mitsuharu Kaneko,
   Toson Shimazaki, Junzaburo Nishiwaki,
   Motomaro Senge, Iku Takenaka, Shiro
   Murano, Tatsuji Miyoshi, Shigeharu
   Nakano, Azuma Kondo, Fuyuhiko
   Kitagawa, Kyojiro Hagiwara, Shinkichi
   Takahashi, Kaoru Maruyama,

Sonosuke Sato, Kotaro Takamura,
Saisei Muro, Takuji Ote, Fuyue Anzai,
Taku Oga, and Hakushu Kitahara
(Tr. with Satoru Sato)   88   63

ARTICLES
A Note on These Poems
(With Satoru Sato)   88   108

REVIEWS
A Poetry Chronicle   105   336
    I Counted Only April,
        by Simon Perchik
    The Spectral Boy,
        by Donald Petersen
    Ryoanji, by Tim Reynolds
    Blue Boy on Skates,
        by M. L. Rosenthal
    Poems, by Richard Selig
        (Ed. by Peter Levi)
    Kissing the Dancer and Other Poems,
        by Robert Sward
Gregor, Sarton, Vazakas   112   44
    Basic Movements,
        by Arthur Gregor
    A Private Mythology, by May Sarton
    The Marble Manifesto,
        by Byron Vazakas

BOOKS REVIEWED
    Charades and Celebrations   108   54
    The Picnic in the Cemetery   130   221
    Only the World   144   40

URQUHART, JANE
BOOKS REVIEWED
    False Shuffles   144   297

URRUTIA, DIEGO DUBLE
    [See DUBLE URRUTIA, DIEGO]

USCHOLD, MAUD E(LFRID)
POEMS
    Whimsies   29   195
        Baroque
        Lines in Passing
    Oak   32   193
    In August   36   258
        Corn
        Dirge for Forests
    Words   40   315

USCHUK, PAMELA
POEMS
    Meditations Beside Kootenai Creek 144   74
    After Reading Louise Bogan's Journals 145   134
    Black Ice

VACARESCO, HELENE
POEMS
Black Sails
(Tr. by Anne Higginson Spicer)   26   81

VAIL, LAURENCE
POEMS
Grey Crust   19   136

VAJDA, PAUL
BOOKS REVIEWED
The Tragedy of Man,
by Imre Madách
(Tr. with Charles Henry Meltzer)   47   285

VAKALO, ELENI
POEMS
From *Planet Education, V*
(Tr. by Kimon Friar)   139   81

ARTICLES ABOUT
Post-War Greek Poets,
by Kimon Friar   139   99

VALAORITIS, NANOS
[NANOS VALAORITES]
POEMS
The Birds
(Tr. by Kimon Friar)   78   182

TRANSLATIONS
Correspondence
from George Seferis   105   50

ARTICLES ABOUT
Contemporary Greek Poetry,
by Kimon Friar   78   145

VALENCIA, GUILLERMO
POEMS
From *Anarchs*
(Tr. by Muna Lee)   26   125

VALENTINE, JEAN
POEMS
The Summer House   108   246

Orpheus and Eurydice   110   3
December
Separation   111   218
April
Du Musst Dein Leben Andern — Rilke
Broken-Down Girl   113   379
Archangel
Photograph of Delmore Schwartz
Dearest,

BOOKS REVIEWED
Dream Barker   107   258
Pilgrims   117   204
Ordinary Things
[Huub Oosterhuis, Judith Herzberg]   127   44
The Messenger   136   295
The River at Wolf   161   159

VALÉRY, PAUL
POEMS
A Juan Ramón Jiménez   82   215
Canticle of the Columns   94   1
The Spinner
To the Plane Tree
(Tr. by Louise Bogan
and May Sarton)

BOOKS REVIEWED
The Marine Cemetery
(Adapted by Sidney Alexander)   76   172
Plays
(Tr. by David Paul
and Robert Fitzgerald)   97   121
Aesthetics
(Tr. by Ralph Manheim)   106   366
Idée Fixe
(Tr. by David Paul)   107   267
Masters & Friends: Volume IX
of the Collected Works in English
(Tr. by Martin Turnell)
(Ed. by Jackson Matthews)   113   338

ARTICLES ABOUT
Paris Letter, by Jean Catel   18   168
Paris Letter, by Jean Catel   19   229

Paris Notes, by Jean Catel   20   287
Literature of Repose,
   by Jean Catel   23   96
As It Is in Paris, by Jean Catel   25   268
As It Is in Paris,
   by Harriet Monroe   27   266
The Poetry of Paul Valéry,
   by Harold J. Salemson   32   36
Valéry's Epigrams,
   by Harriet Monroe   35   208
The Soaring Scientific Mind,
   by Harriet Monroe   36   266
Paul Valéry, by M. D. Zabel   45   90
Rev. of *Anthologie des Poètes de la N.R.F.*   56   225
Correspondence from George Dillon   67   49
To Write Poetry Nowadays You Have
   to Have One Foot in the Grave,
   by Gilbert Neiman   74   30
Paul Valéry, by Wallace Fowlie   76   279
Rev. of *The Creative Process*
   (Ed. by Brewster Ghiselin)   81   133
Rev. of *Paul Valéry*
   and the Civilized Mind,
   by Norman Suckling   85   300
A Commemoration:
   "Les Fleurs du Mal" 1857-1957,
   by Wallace Fowlie   90   376
French Chronicle:
   Recent Publications,
   by Wallace Fowlie   91   36
Rev. of *The Limits of Symbolism:*
   Studies of Five Modern French Poets,
   by Bernard Weinberg   112   41

VALHOPE, CAROL NORTH
BOOKS REVIEWED
Poems, by Stefan George
   (Tr. with Ernst Morwitz)   62   334

VALLE, ROSAMEL DEL
[See DEL VALLE, ROSAMEL]

VALLEE, LILLIAN
BOOKS REVIEWED
Bells in Winter,
   by Czeslaw Milosz
   (Tr. with the author)   136   40

VALLE-INCLÁN
ARTICLES ABOUT
Rev. of *Modern Spanish Theatre*
   (Ed. by Michael Benedikt
   and George Wellwarth)   113   338

VALLEJO, CÉSAR
POEMS
The Big People
   (Tr. by James Wright)   98   352

Masses
   (Tr. by Robert Bly)   98   353
Trilce LII   109   229
Trilce LVIII
Trilce LXV
Trilce LXVI
   (Tr. by Henry Gifford
   and Charles Tomlinson)

BOOKS REVIEWED
Poemas Humanos
   (Tr. by Clayton Eshleman)   114   193
Neruda and Vallejo: Selected Poems
   (Ed. by Robert Bly)
   (Tr. by Robert Bly,
   John Knoepfle,
   and James Wright)   120   304
The Complete Posthumous Poetry
   (Tr. by Clayton Eshleman
   and José Rubia Barcia)   137   220

ARTICLES ABOUT
Rev. of *Vallejo,*
   by Xavier Abril
   and *Twenty Poems of...*
   (Tr. by John Knoepfle,
   James Wright, and Robert Bly)   105   196

VAN ALSTYNE, CHARLES
POEMS
Sonnet ("Old man feeding pigeons...")   46   201

VAN BUSKIRK, ALDEN
POEMS
Carol   105   250
Hate Poem

VANCE, THOMAS
POEMS
*The Prisoner of War Returns
   Through the Underground*   87   192
The Instant in the Eye
The Stroke of Noon   89   283
Woman in an Empty House
On the Difficulty of Justice
Theory of Tragedy   95   338
Pastoral Ballet
The End of Regret

TRANSLATIONS
Poems by Stig Dagerman
   (Tr. with Vera Vance)   103   231

ARTICLES
A Note on Stig Dagerman   103   255

BOOKS REVIEWED
Skeleton of Light   99   379

VANCE, VERA
TRANSLATIONS
Poems by Stig Dagerman
(Tr. with Thomas Vance)   103   231

VANDERPYL, FRITZ R.
ARTICLES
Art and Eiffel Towers   16   98

VANDERSEE, CHARLES
POEMS
Remembering the Present   142   340

VAN DER VEER, JULIA
POEMS
A Cow   38   258

VAN DOREN, MARK
POEMS
High Meadows   24   315
Apple Hell   29   85
The Liquid Heart   81   78
What Now?   111   213
Looking for Something Lost
King Wind
Will You, Won't You?
Wait Till Then
Slowly, Slowly Wisdom Gathers

BOOKS REVIEWED
Spring Thunder and Other Poems   25   279
7 P.M. and Other Poems   31   47
Now the Sky and Other Poems   36   50
Anthology of World Poetry (Ed.)   37   164
Jonathan Gentry   40   222
A Winter Diary and Other Poems   47   46
The Last Look and Other Poems   51   164
Collected Poems, 1922-1938   54   157
The Mayfield Deer   60   43
The Seven Sleepers   64   343
The Careless Clock   74   177
The Selected Letters
of William Cowper (Ed.)   80   297
Introduction to Poetry   84   43
Selected Letters of William Cowper (Ed.)   84   296
Mortal Summer   85   362
Selected Poems   86   287
Four Poets on Poetry: Essays by R. P.
Blackmur, Yvor Winters, Marianne Moore,
and Mark Van Doren
(Ed. by Don Cameron Allen)   96   382
Morning Worship   97   109
Collected and New Poems: 1924-1963   103   382
100 Poems   112   418
Introduction to Poetry:
Commentaries on Thirty Poems   115   346
Collected and New Poems: 1924-1963   117   108
Good Morning   124   343

VAN DRUTEN, JOHN
POEMS
Week-End Leave   30   201

VAN DUYM, HIDDE VAN AMEYDEN
TRANSLATIONS
Poems by Paul Van Ostaijen   104   171
Article by Paul Van Ostaijen   104   176

ARTICLES
Paul Van Ostaijen: An Introduction   104   177

VAN DUYN, MONA
POEMS
The Gentle Snorer   83   206
Death by Aesthetics
Three Valentines to the Wide World   88   207
A Kind of Music   93   139
A Serious Case
Recovery   97   72
Elementary Attitudes   100   8
The Gardener to His God   103   173
Open Letter, Personal
A Time of Bees
A Garland for Christopher Smart   104   4
The Good Man   107   100
What I Want to Say
"The Wish To Be Believed"
The Challenger
The Creation   112   375
Eros to Howard Nemerov
Advice to a God
Open Letter from a Constant Reader   114   80
Birthday Card for a Psychiatrist
Homework
A Small Excursion   120   103
Since You Asked Me...
The Case of The   128   321
The Ballad of Blossom   134   287
Photographs   138   151
In Bed with a Book   149   76
Near Changes
Views
A Bouquet of Zinnias   151   182
To a Friend Who Threw Away Hair Dyes   151   411
Falling in Love at Sixty-Five
Glad Heart at the Supermarket   155   326
Sonnet for Minimalists   155   377
The Burning of Yellowstone
For May Swenson   157   189
Long Stretch Minimalist Sonnet   160   63
Minimalist Sonnets
Closures
The Beginning
Insiders
Mr. and Mrs. Jack Sprat in the Kitchen
Passing Thought
Extra Time

ARTICLES
  Comment   151   214

REVIEWS
  Two Traditions   64   48
    The Stone Ants,
      by Hubert Creekmore
    Mortal Hunger,
      by Gustav Davidson
  Five Worlds   64   171
    Statement, by Don Gordon
    Give Joan a Sword, by M. Thérèse
    At the Long Sault,
      by Archibald Lampman
    Wonderings, by John Masefield
    Winter Solstice,
      by Gerald Bullett
  Wartime Attitudes and Platitudes   64   339
    The Long Nights,
      by Joseph Joel Keith
    Grain of Sand, and Other Poems,
      by Albert Edmund Trombly
    The Compass Eye,
      by Harold Vinal
  Conscience: Personal,
      Political, Philosophical   66   284
    War Elegies, by William Everson
    Blood of the Tenement,
      by Vincent Ferrini
    A Poet's Youth,
      by Allan Dowling
    That's All that Matters,
      by Oscar Williams   67   155
    The Fourth Decade,
      by Norman Rosten   68   49
    Against the Circle,
      by Brewster Ghiselin   69   162
  Two Young Poets   86   56
    The Glass of Perseus,
      by Wesley Trimpi
    The Eye, by Harvey Shapiro
  A Wide Range   88   329
    Europe, by Louis Dudek
    Two Sides of a Poem,
      by Katherine Bellamann
    Figures from a Double World,
      by Thomas McGrath
    Poets of Today II,
      by Norma Farber, Robert Pack,
      and Louis Simpson
    Sonnets of Love and Liberty,
      by Walter Lowenfels
    *The Country of a Thousand Years of Peace
      and Other Poems,*
      by James Merrill   94   199
  Ways to Meaning   100   390
    Fever & Chills, by George P. Elliott
    On the Morning of Color,
      by John Woods

    The Tennis Court Oath,
      by John Ashbery
    "Leaf by Leaf"   102   260
    Poems 1930-1960,
      by Josephine Miles
    Water Street, by James Merrill
    A Winter Come, a Summer Gone,
      by Howard Moss
  Vision, Celebration, and Testimony   105   264
    Flower Herding on Mount Monadnock,
      by Galway Kinnell
    A Local Storm,
      by Donald Justice
    The Stalingrad Elegies,
      by James Schevill
  The Poet as Novelist   109   332
    *Mrs. Stevens Hears
      the Mermaids Singing,*
      by May Sarton
    Journal of the Fictive Life,
      by Howard Nemerov
    The (Diblos) Notebook,
      by James Merrill
    The Escape Artist,
      by David Wagoner
    Black Light, by Galway Kinnell
    The System of Dante's Hell,
      by LeRoi Jones
  Seven Women   115   430
    Love Poems, by Anne Sexton
    The Animals in That Country,
      by Margaret Atwood
    Leaflets, by Adrienne Rich
    The Weather of Six Mornings,
      by Jane Cooper
    Latest Will, by Lenore Marshall
    A Bad Girl's Book of Animals,
      by Wong May
    The Marriage Wig and Other Poems,
      by Ruth Whitman

BOOKS REVIEWED
  Valentines to the Wide World   96   47
  A Time of Bees   106   296
  To See, To Take   118   166
  *Merciful Disguises:
    Published and Unpublished Poems*   126   167
  Letters from a Father and Other Poems   143   39
  Near Changes   157   33
  Firefall   163   158

ARTICLES ABOUT
  Correspondence
    from Albert Edmund Trombly   65   165
  [Note]   154   242

VAN GHENT, DOROTHY
  POEMS
    Depositions for the Fatherland   52   186

VAN KEUREN, W. G.
POEMS
To a Stranger in Passing   52   321
Inscriptions for the Quick   54   190

VAN LEEUWEN, JUDITH
POEMS
View   99   370
Urbanizational

VAN OSTAIJEN, PAUL
POEMS
Gedicht ("Een schoon gezicht...")   104   170
Berceuse voor Volwassenen
Avondgeluiden
Gedicht ("Zon brandt de rozelaar...")
De Oude Man
   (Tr. by Hidde van Ameyden
   van Duym)

ARTICLES
Autobiography
   (Tr. by Hidde van Ameyden
   van Duym)   104   176

ARTICLES ABOUT
Paul Van Ostaijen: An Introduction,
   by Hidde van Ameyden van Duym   104   177

VAN REIN, ANNE
POEMS
Cable   34   81

**VAN RENSSELAER,
[MRS.] SCHUYLER**
POEMS
Under Two Windows   1   44
Aubade ("The dawn is here...")
Nocturne ("My darling, come!....")

**VAN SLYKE, B(ERENICE) K.
[BEREN VAN SLYKE]**
POEMS
Orpheus in the Street   13   252
In Winter
First Snow   23   142
Je Viendrai au Jardin
To One Sleeping in Daytime   37   20
Advice in Spring
Paradox
Pursuit So Hidden   54   140

REVIEWS
Le Poète et l'Inspiration,
   by Francis Jammes   21   47
The Prophet in His Own Country   21   276
   Poems of Heroism in American Life
      (Ed. by John R. Howard)
   Ohio Valley Verse

   Yearbook of the Poetry Society
      of South Carolina
   Peoria Book of Verse
   Figs from California
      (Ed. by W. W. Lyman)
   Peabody High School Book of Verse
   Homework and Hobbyhorses
   Bulletin of University of Oklahoma
      Oxford Poetry, 1922
   Variations on a Theme,
      by Grace Hazard Conkling   22   93
   Lyric Forms from France,
      by Helen Louise Cohen   22   107
   Kinfolks, by Ann Cobb   22   160
   The Great Dream,
      by Marguerite Wilkinson   23   48
   A Book of Love, by Charles Vildrac
      (Tr. by Witter Bynner)   24   223
   The Song of the Indian Wars,
      by John G. Neihardt   27   328
   Dawn Boy: Blackfoot and Navajo Songs,
      by Eda Lou Walton   28   165

VAN STONE, MARY R.
BOOKS REVIEWED
Spanish Folk Songs of New Mexico (Ed.)   28   348

VAN WINCKEL, NANCE
POEMS
Goodnight   149   217
Counting Towards Sleep

**VAN WYK LOUW, N. P.
[See LOUW, N. P. VAN WYK]**

VARESE, LOUISE
BOOKS REVIEWED
A Season in Hell,
   by Arthur Rimbaud (Tr.)   67   278
Prose Poems from the Illuminations,
   by Arthur Rimbaud (Tr.)   69   286

**VARGAS, A. ORTIZ
[See ORTIZ-VARGAS, A.]**

VARVITSIOTIS, TAKIS
POEMS
Reposing Under the Cold Stone
   (Tr. by Kimon Friar)   139   76

ARTICLES ABOUT
Post-War Greek Poets,
   by Kimon Friar   139   99

VAS DIAS, ROBERT
POEMS
The Greenness of the Burma Jade World   107   306
Ceremony

REVIEWS
  Six Books by Seven Poets   110   186
    Transmutations, by Stephen Jonas
    Touch, by David Franks
    October, by Margaret Randall
    The Stones of Konarak,
      by Judson Crews
    Works, by Aram Saroyan
    Three on a Match,
      by Wendell B. Anderson,
      Cerise Farallon, and Judson Crews

VASILIADHIS, ARISTOTLE
  [See ALEXANDHROU, ARIS, pseud.]

VASSILIKOS, VASSILIS
  ARTICLES
    Letter from Athens
      (Tr. by Kriton Hourmousiades)
      [C. P. Cavafy, George Seferis,
      Odysseus Elytis, Nikos Engonopoulos,
      Nikos Gatsos]   105   60

  BOOKS REVIEWED
    The Plant, the Well, the Angel: A Trilogy
      (Tr. by Edmund and Mary Keeley)   105   65

VAUGHAN, HENRY
  ARTICLES ABOUT
    Rev. of *Six Metaphysical Poets:
    A Reader's Guide*,
      by George Williamson   112   356

VAUGHN, MALCOLM W.
  ARTICLES
    Correspondence:
      Letter from France   13   55

VAUGHN, ROBERT
  POEMS
    The Last Chance   102   90
    Judith

VAUX, [LORD] THOMAS
  BOOKS REVIEWED
    The Poems of Lord Vaux
      (Ed. by Larry P. Vonalt)   99   187

VAZAKAS, BYRON
  POEMS
    Skyscraper   64   256
    The Hotel in the Glen
    A Place in the World   73   329
    Downward   76   20
    The Letter
    The Orphans
    Night Fugue   79   140
    Kleptomane
    The Ballad of the Noble Stairs   81   79

    Winckelmann in Rome   82   69
    Try, Traveler   83   200
    Things Pass, Things Change
    The Pavilion on the Pier   85   132
    Epitaph for the Old Howard
    The Innocents   86   146

  REVIEWS
    Where the Compass Spins,
      by Radcliffe Squires   79   349
    Underhill, Poems 1946-1953,
      by Richard Eberhart   85   106

  BOOKS REVIEWED
    Transfigured Night   69   158
    The Equal Tribunals   102   49
    The Marble Manifesto   112   44

VEGA, LUIS ROSADO
  [See ROSADO VEGA, LUIS]

VEINBERG, JON
  POEMS
    Sparrows as Ghosts   148   7
    Martha
    Next to Tut
    Spirits of the Wind   150   218
    Refugee

VELARDE, RAMON LOPEZ
  [See LOPEZ VELARDE, RAMON]

VELDE, WILLIAM
  POEMS
    Terminal Masque with Pan   125   274

VELTON, WILLIAM
  POEMS
    Autumn and After   88   380

VENCLOVA, TOMAS
  POEMS
    The Eleventh Song   132   342
    A Poem About Memory
    In Memory of the Poet. Variant.
      (Tr. by Jonas Zdanys)

  ARTICLES ABOUT
    A Note on Tomas Venclova,
      by Jonas Zdanys   132   348

VENDLER, HELEN (HENNESSY)
  REVIEWS
    New and Selected Poems, by I. A. Richards 134   49
    Worldly Hopes,
      by A. R. Ammons
      [G. M. Hopkins,
      William Wordsworth]   141   26

BOOKS REVIEWED
    Yeats's Vision and the Later Plays   103   185

VENIT, JAMES
REVIEWS
    The American Poetry Anthology
      (Ed. by Daniel Halpern)
      [Peter Cooley, Paul Monette,
      Marvin Bell, Jon Anderson]   128   106

VENUTI, LAWRENCE
TRANSLATIONS
    Poems by Giuseppe Conte
      and Cesare Viviani   155   127
    Poems by Milo De Angelis   155   151

VERDER, D. H.
BOOKS REVIEWED
    A Book of Lyrics   34   111

VER DUFT, LEE
BOOKS REVIEWED
    Ho! Watchman of the Night Ho!   68   168

VERGIL
[See VIRGIL]

VERHAEREN, ÉMILE
POEMS
    Frost   85   125
    The Cow Girl
      (Tr. by Huberta Randall)

BOOKS REVIEWED
    Poems of...
      (Tr. by Alma Strettell)   8   96
    The Cloister, a Play in Four Acts
      (Tr. by Osman Edwards)

ARTICLES ABOUT
    Rev. of *Six French Poets*, by Amy Lowell   7   202
    Emile Verhaeren, by Ezra Pound   9   256

VERLAINE, PAUL
BOOKS REVIEWED
    Baudelaire, Rimbaud, Verlaine
      (Ed. by Joseph M. Bernstein)   72   105

ARTICLES ABOUT
    Rev. of *Paul Verlaine*,
      by Harold Nicolson   20   223
    Mallarmé, by Wallace Fowlie   80   37
    Recent French Publications,
      by Wallace Fowlie   93   40

VERNON, JOHN
POEMS
    Mud Man   140   79
    Bone Pit

    Planting and Variations
    Barns Collapsing

VERRY, ETHEL
POEMS
    A Lady   24   13
    The House-to-House Seamstress
    A Father

VERY, ALICE
BOOKS REVIEWED
    The Human Abstract   50   113

VERY, JONES
BOOKS REVIEWED
    Selected Poems
      (Ed. by Nathan Lyons)   111   333

VESTAL, STANLEY
[Pseud. of CAMPBELL,
WALTER STANLEY]
POEMS
    Sooner Songs and Ballads   26   177
      Saddle Songs
      Kit Carson's Mule
      Kit Carson of the U.S.N.
      The Lost Trail
    Prairie Pictographs   32   252
      Prairie Dog
      Rabbit
      Burrowing Owl
      Rattlesnake
      Spider
      Buffalo

ARTICLES
    [Note on "Sooner Songs"]   26   233

BOOKS REVIEWED
    Fandango: Ballads of the Old West   33   158

ARTICLES ABOUT
    In Texas and Oklahoma,
      by Harriet Monroe   26   215
    [Note on name]   26   233

VESTDIJK, SIMON
ARTICLES ABOUT
    Down There on a Visit:
      Poetry in the Netherlands,
      by Turner Cassity   102   38

VIALA, AKAKIA
ARTICLES ABOUT
    Rimbaud in 1949, by Wallace Fowlie   75   166

VICTOR, FLORENCE
POEMS
    Postcard   98   236
    People in Europe Were Starving   119   77

VIDAVER, DORIS
TRANSLATIONS
Poem by Jacob Glatstein   146   256

VIDYAKARA
BOOKS REVIEWED
Sanskrit Poetry
from Vidyakara's "Treasury"
(Tr. by Daniel H. H. Ingalls)   114   196

VIERECK, ALEXIS
POEMS
Accident   119   330

VIERECK, GEORGE SYLVESTER
ARTICLES
Correspondence
[Margery Swett Mansfield]   25   342

BOOKS REVIEWED
Songs of Armageddon and Other Poems   9   98
The Haunted House and Other Poems   25   221
The Three Sphinxes and Other Poems

ARTICLES ABOUT
The Viereck Incident,
by Harriet Monroe   13   265

VIERECK, PETER
POEMS
Graves Are Made to Waltz On   56   185
Sonnet for Servants of the Word   68   302
"Vale" from Carthage   70   182
Five Theological Cradle-Songs   71   115
Better Come Quietly
Why Can't I Live Forever?
Blindman's Buff
Game Called on Account of Darkness
Hide and Seek
A Sort of Redemption   72   238
Elegy to All Sainthood Everywhere
Love Song of Judas Smith   74   256
Again, Again!   80   6
Girl-Child Pastoral   81   80
Nostalgia   82   18
Benediction   85   255
A Walk on Moss   87   1
We Ran All the Way Home   96   265

BOOKS REVIEWED
Terror and Decorum   73   289
Strike Through the Mask!   76   99
The First Morning   84   89
Dream and Responsibility   84   93
The Persimmon Tree   89   316
The Tree Witch   100   404
New and Selected Poems   112   337

ARTICLES ABOUT
Correspondence
from John Hall Wheelock   76   306
The Defense of Poetry,
by Richard Eberhart   77   89

VIETOR, KARL
BOOKS REVIEWED
Goethe the Poet
(Tr. by Moses Hadas)   75   232

VIGÉE, CLAUDE
ARTICLES ABOUT
Recent French Publications,
by Wallace Fowlie   93   40

VIGNY
[See DE VIGNY, ALFRED VICTOR]

VIITA, LAURI
POEMS
To a Critic
(Tr. by Meri Lehtinen)   98   350

VILAR, JEAN
ARTICLES ABOUT
Verse Drama on the Paris Stage,
by Ruby Haykin   82   294

VILDRAC, CHARLES
POEMS
Gloire   2   168
The Farewell
(Tr. by Witter Bynner)   13   243

BOOKS REVIEWED
A Book of Love
(Tr. by Witter Bynner)   24   223

ARTICLES ABOUT
Paris Letter, by Jean Catel   19   229

VILLA, CARLO
POEMS
Cento di questi fogli/
One Hundred of These Pages   155   80
Donne/Women
(Tr. by Rebecca Messbarger)

VILLA, JOSÉ GARCIA
[See GARCIA VILLA, JOSÉ]

VILLAURRUTIA, XAVIER
BOOKS REVIEWED
Decima Muerte   61   680

VILLON, FRANÇOIS
POEMS
Ballade of the Ladies of Time Past
(Tr. by Richard Wilbur)   105   81

BOOKS REVIEWED
   The Poems
      (Tr. by Galway Kinnell)   111   124

ARTICLES ABOUT
   Rev. of *The Jargon of Master Francois Villon*,
      by Jordan Herbert Stabler   14   287
   Rev. of *The Poetry of Villon*, by John Fox   104   187

VINAL, HAROLD
POEMS
   Forgotten   18   197
   Two in a House   29   321
   They Endure   34   264
     Eternal
     The Dark River
     To a Pagan
     Covert
   Daybreak   44   78
   Valediction   46   253
   The Quest   54   313
   The Island
   Crag Above Water
   The Journey   60   81

BOOKS REVIEWED
   White April   22   168
   Voyage   24   221
   Nor Youth Nor Age   27   48
   A Stranger in Heaven   32   225
   The Compass Eye   64   339

ARTICLES ABOUT
   The Vinal Books, by Harriet Monroe   31   289

VINCENT, HOWARD P.
BOOKS REVIEWED
   Collected Poems of Herman Melville (Ed.)   72   167

VINCENT, STEPHEN
BOOKS REVIEWED
   White Lights & Whale Hearts   121   348

VINES, SHERARD
POEMS
   The Bull   16   82

BOOKS REVIEWED
   The Two Worlds   10   44
   The Kaleidoscope   18   343

VINOGRAD, SHERNA SHALETT
ARTICLES
   Correspondence   64   115

ARTICLES ABOUT
   Correspondence
     from Edouard Roditi   64   175

VINOKUROV, YEVGENY
POEMS
   Passer-By   124   187
   Trams
   Birds
   I Love the Statues in This Town
   When the Parachute Does Not Open
   The First Sentence
   Pain
     (Tr. by Daniel Weissbort)

VIRGIL [VERGIL]
[MARO, PUBLIUS VERGILIUS]
POEMS
   Eclogue II
     (Tr. by Stephen Orgel)   116   353
   Eclogue IX
     (Tr. by Paul Alpers)   128   143
   The Storm
     (Tr. by Robert Fitzgerald)   136   1

BOOKS REVIEWED
   The Georgics
     (Tr. by Cecil Day Lewis)   71   337
   The Eclogues of...
     (Tr. by David R. Slavitt)   120   304

ARTICLES ABOUT
   Bays for Virgil, by M. D. Zabel   37   37
   Waking Up Over the *Aeneid*,
     by Paul Breslin   143   347

VIVANTE, LEONE
BOOKS REVIEWED
   English Poetry and Its Contribution to the
     Knowledge of a Creative Principle   78   290

VIVAS, ELISEO
REVIEWS
   The Creative Experiment,
     by C. M. Bowra
     [T. S. Eliot, Federico García Lorca]   75   217
   Lorca, the Poet and His People,
     by Artur Barea
     (Tr. by Ilsa Barea)   76   46

BOOKS REVIEWED
   Creation and Discovery:
     Essays in Criticism and Aesthetics   88   339
   D. H. Lawrence, the Failure
     and Triumph of Art   100   50
   The Artistic Transaction and Essays
     on Theory of Literature   104   369

ARTICLES ABOUT
   Rev. of *Critics and Criticism*,
     Ancient and Modern
     (Ed. by R. S. Crane)   82   98

VIVIANI, CESARE
POEMS
[fera aderisce   come era caldo l'abito]/
[cruel fair adheres]   155   132
[Il cielo passava l'ultima luce e i fiori]/
[The sky overtook the fading light]
(Tr. by Lawrence Venuti)

VLIET, R. G.
POEMS
Mrs. McElroy   135   192
Jet Plane
Penny Ballad of Elvious Ricks

VLIET, R. WADE
POEMS
Tropical   44   136
Latin-American Idyll
This the Hunting Bee Has Found

VOEGTLEN, ANNE REYNOLDS
POEMS
Ste.-Chapelle   169   143
Firefly   170   161

VOIGT, ELLEN BRYANT
POEMS
The Starveling   132   79
Prey   133   90
Why She Says No   139   268
Pittsylvania County
Quarrel
The Lesson   146   135

BOOKS REVIEWED
The Forces of Plenty   143   295
The Lotus Flowers   152   161
Two Trees   162   224
Kyrie   168   160

VOLKMAN, KAREN
POEMS
Casanova in Love   162   221
From Shore   164   271

VONALT, LARRY P.
BOOKS REVIEWED
The Poems of Lord Vaux (Ed.)   99   187

**VON DER VOGELWEIDE,
  WALTHER**
POEMS
Under the Lime-Tree
(Tr. by Vernon Watkins)   73   26

VON HALLBERG, ROBERT
BOOKS REVIEWED
Charles Olson: The Scholar's Art   136   219

VON HATTINGBERG, MAGDA
[See also BENVENUTA]
BOOKS REVIEWED
Rilke and Benvenuta
(Tr. by Cyrus Brooks)   76   92

VON HEIDENSTAM, VERNER
BOOKS REVIEWED
The Soothsayer   17   48

ARTICLES ABOUT
Verner von Heidenstam,
by Svea Bernhard   10   35

VON HOFMANNSTHAL, HUGO
BOOKS REVIEWED
Madonna Dianora, a Play in Verse
(Tr. by Harriet Betty Boas)   9   159
Poems and Verse Plays
(Ed. by Michael Hamburger)   101   287

ARTICLES ABOUT
Modern German Poetry II,
by Reginald H. Wilenski   5   234
Obituary   35   174

**VON THURN UND TAXIS
  (HOHENLOHE), MARIE**
BOOKS REVIEWED
The Letters of Rainer Maria Rilke
and Princess...
(Tr. by Nora Wydenbruck)   94   59

VORONCA, ILARIE
ARTICLES ABOUT
Marseille Letter, by Jean Rivier   60   269

VOSIK, TOM
POEMS
To Someone Nameless   121   35
Sleep Song   124   329
Five Songs for Nicolas Roeg   127   69

VOZNESENSKY, ANDREI
BOOKS REVIEWED
Antiworlds
(Tr. by W. H. Auden, Jean Garrigue,
Max Hayward, Stanley Kunitz,
Stanley Moss, William Jay Smith,
and Richard Wilbur)
(Ed. by Patricia Blake
and Max Hayward)   110   40
Selected Poems
(Tr. and ed. by Herbert Marshall)
Selected Poems
(Tr. by Anselm Hollo)   111   121
Nostalgia for the Present
(Ed. by Vera Dunham
and Max Hayward)   136   40

VRETTAKOS, NIKIFOROS

POEMS

Elegy of Flowering Fire
(Tr. by Kimon Friar)   78   169

ARTICLES ABOUT

Contemporary Greek Poetry,
by Kimon Friar   78   145

VROMAN, L.

POEMS

Winter Comes Again   75   320
Old Miniatures
The Island of Ngusa Kembangan
Thunderstorm
Feathers
Misty Future

"W. L."
[See LOWENFELS, WALTER]

"W. R. T."
[See TRASK, WILLARD R.]

WADDELL, HELEN
ARTICLES ABOUT
On Translating Chinese Poetry, II,
by Eunice Tietjens 20   328
Correspondence
from Amy Lowell 21   167

WADDINGTON, MIRIAM
BOOKS REVIEWED
Green World 68   168
The Season's Lovers 94   186
The Glass Trumpet 111   323
Say Yes 118   234

WADE, CORY
POEMS
Knitting Litany 157   4
The Ambition Bird 165   214

WADE, JAMES PALMER
POEMS
Three Persons 38   310
Equinox
Apocalyptic
How One Man Died
Bergruine Englehaus 40   84
Norfolk Hills 43   249

WADE, SIDNEY
POEMS
Turkish Bath 168   135

WAGGONER, HYATT
BOOKS REVIEWED
*American Poets from the Puritans
to the Present* 113   262

ARTICLES ABOUT
Review by Robert Siegel 130   102

WAGNER, CHARLES A.
POEMS
The Unknown Soldier 35   61

BOOKS REVIEWED
Prize Poems 1913-1929 (Ed.) 37   164

WAGNER, GEOFFREY
REVIEWS
The Summer Dance, by J. C. Hall 81   254

BOOKS REVIEWED
Flowers of Evil,
by Charles Baudelaire (Tr.) 72   105

WAGONER, DAVID (R.)
POEMS
Beginning 73   140
Marsh Leaf
Mice in Halo 74   206
Vigil
Warning 75   138
Lawn Design
Afternoon of Sand
Finale
Sam the Aerialist 77   249
Edmond of New Hope
Erich the Printer—(b. 1883-d. 1938) 80   187
Max of Wolf Lake—(b. 1891-d. 1942)
An Anthem for Man 84   348
Credo Adoration
Lines for a Dangerous Day 88   137
The Crisis
Epitaph
The Coronation
Murder Mystery 89   276
Song at the End of Winter
The Migration 90   372
Elegy for a Distant Relative
The Man from the Top of the Mind
Words Above a Narrow Entrance 92   67
A Warning to My Love
*To My Friend
Whose Parachute Did Not Open*
The Recognition

The Emergency Maker	100	168
A Day in the City		
Once Upon a Picnic Ground		
Offertory		
The Nesting Ground		
On Seeing an X-Ray of My Head	102	27
Advice to the Orchestra		
The Breathing Lesson		
Water Music for the Progress of Love in a Life-Raft Down the Sammamish Slough	104	99
Stretching Canvases		
By the Orchard		
The Words		
Leaving Something Behind		
Straw for the Fire [By Theodore Roethke] (Ed.)	105	113
A Room with a View	106	350
Come Before His Countenance with a Joyful Leaping		
Talking to the Forest		
Running		
The March of Coxey's Army	110	211
Getting Above Ourselves on Sunday		
Getting Out of Jail on Monday		
Archeological Notes		
The Apotheosis of the Garbagemen	113	32
Note from Body to Soul		
Ceremony on Pier 40		
The Stony Garden [By Theodore Roethke] (Ed.)	113	104
Fortuna Imperatrix Mundi	114	181
Lost	118	219
Riverbed		
Old Man, Old Man		
Fog		
Muse	120	196
The Burning Bush		
Worms		
Dust Devil		
Prayer		
Litany	121	340
Elegy for Yards, Pounds, and Gallons	123	133
An Offering for Dungeness Bay	124	156
For a Winter Wren		
Moving Into the Garden		
The Boy of the House		
Living in the Ruins		
Travelling Light	125	219
Tracking		
Walking in a Swamp		
Breaking Camp		
Rôles	127	41
Walking at Night	127	155
Being Shot		
The Breaking Point		
The Death of the Moon	130	155
Thistledown		
The Gift		
Cutting Down a Tree		
Elegy for a Minor Romantic Poet		
Crossing a River	132	6
Seeing Things		
Burial Song		
After Reading Too Many Poems, I Watch a Robin Taking a Bath	133	187
Being Herded Past the Prison's Honor Farm		
To a Panhandler Who, for a Quarter, Said "God Bless You"		
Elegy While Pruning Roses		
Wading in a Marsh		
Under the Sign of Moth	135	218
Caterpillar Song		
Spider Song		
Moth Song		
The Last Laugh	137	87
My Father's Ghost		
My Physics Teacher		
Note with the Gift of a Bird's Nest		
Palindrome—Inside Out		
Poem About Breath	138	249
To a Farmer Who Hung Five Hawks on His Barbed Wire		
March for a One-Man Band		
The Old Raccoon		
Big Game		
Lifesaving		
The Horsemen	140	341
Under the Raven's Nest		
The Fire-Bringers		
Song After Midnight		
Their Bodies	141	24
A Guide to the Field	142	197
Our Blindness		
By Starlight		
The Waterlily		
Mockingbird	146	63
Our Model		
Our Father		
The Play		
Ode to Twelve Yards of Unscreened Fill Dirt	148	1
For a Third Anniversary		
The Astronomer's Apprentice		
For the Young Vine Maples	151	184
Dizzy	152	221
Come with Me		
On a Mountainside	163	1
On the Plains		
In a Field of Wildflowers		
On the Forest Floor		
Homecoming	163	212
For the Woman Who Phoned Poetry Northwest, Thinking It Was Poultry Northwest		
Taming a Bear	163	323

A Woman Photographing Holsteins
Clancy the Burro's First Day in Heaven
Let Us Put You in Your Dream Car   165   72
My Father Laughing
    in the Chicago Theater   166   138
The Pink Boy
The Padded Cell   166   278
At the Mouth of a Creek   167   276
A Summer Storm in Navarre, Ohio   170   187
In the House of the Dragon
Planting a Red Maple
For a Man Dancing
    by Himself in a Tavern
A Letter Home   170   264
Plainsong Against
    the Raising of the Dead   170   317

REVIEWS
    The Toy Fair, by Howard Moss   85   242
    Selected Poems 1928-1958,
        by Stanley Kunitz   93   174

BOOKS REVIEWED
    Dry Sun, Dry Wind   83   232
    A Place to Stand   93   46
    The Nesting Ground   103   330
    The Escape Artist   109   332
    Staying Alive   109   400
    New and Selected Poems   117   392
    Straw for the Fire: From the Notebooks of
        Theodore Roethke, 1943-63 (Ed.)   121   341
    Riverbed   122   47
    Sleeping in the Woods   126   346
    Collected Poems 1956-1976   130   162
    In Broken Country   138   46

ARTICLES ABOUT
    [Note]   158   244

WAHL, JEAN
POEMS
    On Reading The Four Quartets   73   317

WAHLENBERG, ANNA
BOOKS REVIEWED
    Old Swedish Fairy Tales
        (Tr. by Antoinette
        de Coursey Patterson)   36   289

WAIN, JOHN
POEMS
    Anecdote of 2 A.M.   92   163

BOOKS REVIEWED
    A Word Carved on a Sill   89   193
    Weep Before God   102   193
    Feng   131   292

ARTICLES ABOUT
    London Letter: Some New Figures,
        by John McCormick   83   269

WAINWRIGHT, JEFFREY
ARTICLES ABOUT
    A Letter from Britain [II],
        by William Logan   157   290

WAKEFIELD, KATHLEEN
POEMS
    Afterward   166   224
    "You Shall Be Weeping and Crying"   170   83

WAKELING, DONALD
ARTICLES ABOUT
    The Younger Bards,
        by Edward J. O'Brien   6   188

WAKEMAN, JOHN
POEMS
    Love in Brooklyn   135   266

WAKOSKI, DIANE
POEMS
    Apparitions Are Not Singular Occurrences   98   82
    Picture of a Girl Drawn in Black and White
    Smudging   117   351
    The Story of Richard Maxfield   122   206
    The Ring   130   125
    Tearing Up My Mother's Letters
    The Hitchhikers

REVIEWS
    Songs & Notes   118   355
        Songs, by Robert Kelly
        Somewhere Among Us
            a Stone Is Taking Notes,
            by Charles Simic

BOOKS REVIEWED
    Greed, Parts 3 and 4   118   98
    The Magellanic Clouds   120   164
    Smudging   124   167
    Virtuoso Literature
        for Two and Four Hands   127   292
    Dancing on the Grave
        of a Son of a Bitch   128   290

WALCOTT, DEREK
[DEREK WOLCOTT]
BOOKS REVIEWED
    Selected Poems   105   332
    The Gulf   119   301
    Another Life   123   165
    Sea Grapes   130   221
    The Star-Apple Kingdom   135   229
    The Fortunate Traveller   141   349

Midsummer   145   161
Collected Poems: 1948-1984   148   169
The Arkansas Testament   152   98

WALDMAN, ANNE
POEMS
Light & Shadow   122   317

BOOKS REVIEWED
The World Anthology, Poems
  from St. Mark's Poetry Project (Ed.)   119   39
Giant Night   119   224
Life Notes   123   236

WALDRON, WINIFRED
POEMS
Hoofs   12   138
Swallows
Arpeggio   19   138
Arpeggio—Spring   21   307

WALDROP, KEITH
POEMS
From The Ruins of Providence   133   194
  Lullaby in January
  Around the Block

BOOKS REVIEWED
A Windmill Near Calvary   113   428

WALEY, ARTHUR
TRANSLATIONS
Poems by Anonymous,
  T'ang Seng-ch'i, Wang Chi,
  Ch'en Tzu-ang, Su Shih,
  Lu Yu, and Wang Tzu-tuan   11   198
Poems by Anonymous, Hsu-ling,
  and Po Chu-i   11   252
A No Play by Komparu
  Zembo Motoyazu   15   317

ARTICLES
Correspondence: Mr. Waley
  on the T'ao Ch'ien Poem
  [Florence Ayscough]   14   55
Correspondence:
  A Word from Mr. Waley
  [Jun Fujita]   17   103

BOOKS REVIEWED
Chinese Poems (Tr.)   13   273
170 Chinese Poems (Tr.)   14   281
A Hundred and Seventy Chinese Poems (Tr.)   15   337
More Translations from the Chinese
Japanese Poetry: The "Uta"   16   283
The Pillow-Book of Sei Shonagon (Tr.)   88   113
The No Plays of Japan
Yuan Mei   93   408

The Nine Songs, A Study
  of Shammanism in Ancient China
The Way and Its Power, A Study
  of the Tao Te Ching and Its Place
  in Chinese Thought

ARTICLES ABOUT
Correspondence
  from Richard Aldington   15   226

WALKER, ALICE
BOOKS REVIEWED
Once   117   322
Good Night, Willie Lee,
  I'll See You in the Morning   135   348

WALKER, CHARLES R.
BOOKS REVIEWED
Iphigenia in Aulis (Tr.), in The Complete
  Greek Tragedies: Euripides IV
  (Ed. by David Grene
  and Richmond Lattimore)   95   190
The Collected Poems
  of H. Phelps Putnam (Ed.)   121   229

WALKER, DAVID
POEMS
The Farmer's Son   105   106
Homing
The Maker of Postcards   133   326
Message from a Grave
The Boy on the Waterville Bridge
Pigeons, Swallows, & Co.

BOOKS REVIEWED
Moving Out   130   293

WALKER, JEANNE MURRAY
POEMS
Ariadne   132   323
There Conveys Meaning
The B Movie
The Shawl   147   76
Seizure   148   331
Inspecting the Garden After Dark
Coming Into History   150   91
Invocation To Convince a Baby
  Already Twelve Days Overdue
  To Come Out of the Womb
Theater   151   185
Birth   153   189
I Won't Read the Alphabet Book Once More
Going Home
Poem for the Missing Beauty Operator   156   202
L. J. Sand in His Paint
  and General Store, 1959
Aunt Joe Learns To Keep Her Balance   158   198
Deciding Where To Stop

Keeping the Plane Up	162	70
Driving to My Son's Concert	168	317

WALKER, JOHN
BOOKS REVIEWED
| *Arma Virumque Cano* | 78 | 45 |

WALKER, MARGARET
POEMS
For My People	51	81
The Struggle Staggers Us	52	198
We Have Been Believers	53	302

REVIEWS
Time Strikes, by E. A. Richards	55	220
Each to the Other: A Novel in Verse,		
by Christopher La Farge	56	281

BOOKS REVIEWED
| *For My People* | 61 | 634 |

WALKER, MARY
POEMS
| *The Norther* | 28 | 22 |

WALKER, MARY FRASER
POEMS
The Liar's Stance	85	78
Mercy		
The Climate of a New Season		

WALKER, ROBERTS
ARTICLES
| Correspondence: Magenta | | |
| [Amy Lowell] | 21 | 284 |

WALKER, TED
BOOKS REVIEWED
Fox on a Barn Door	109	411
Those Other Growths	110	112
The Solitaries	112	131

WALLACE, J. W.
BOOKS REVIEWED
| *Visits to Walt Whitman in 1890-1891* | | |
| (With J. Johnston) | 14 | 106 |

WALLACE, ROBERT
POEMS
A Snapshot for Miss Bricka....	98	237
The Double-Play		
A Last Photograph, Being Divorced	106	190
Directions for Keeping a Muse		
For Lawson and Ann	110	249
From *A Strew of Tacks*		

REVIEWS
| *Down from the Forked Hill Unsullied* | 108 | 121 |

The Privilege, by Maxine Kumin		
Poems, by Eve Triem		
The Sunfish and the Partridge,		
by Donald Junkins		
The Canaries As They Are,		
by Ralph Pomeroy		

BOOKS REVIEWED
Views from a Ferris Wheel	108	269
Poems on Poetry		
(Ed. with James G. Taaffe)	110	47

WALLACE, RONALD
POEMS
In the Apiary	127	331
Installing the Bees		
Pastoral	129	23
Smoking	149	328
Apple Cider	152	321
The Fat of the Land		
Love and Sex	153	287
The Poetry Report	153	330
The Life Next at Hand	155	394
The Swing	158	1
February 14	159	281
The Furnace Men	161	152
Grandfather, His Book	161	197
Hardware	164	154
The Friday Night Fights	168	79

WALLACE-CRABBE, CHRIS
POEMS
Orpheus	130	10
Parthia		
The Dead Cartesian	156	91
Afternoon in the Central Nervous System	158	279
The Interval	169	84
Wittgenstein's Shade		

BOOKS REVIEWED
| *I'm Deadly Serious* | 154 | 151 |

WALLACH, IRA JAN
POEMS
Ephemera	42	321
Tidemarks		
Rejoinder		

WALLER, GARY
POEMS
European Vacation	142	223
Grave Meeting		
Of the 497 Kinds of Love, This Is #43	145	255

WALLER, JOHN
POEMS
| *The Palace of the Sleeping Princess* | 66 | 27 |
| *The Aquarium* | | |

Haunted Wood
Commando   66   193
Oscar Wilde and Aubrey Beardsley   68   243
Hyères les Palmiers   69   316

BOOKS REVIEWED
Crusade   68   349
The Collected Poems of Keith Douglas
  (Ed. with G. S. Fraser)   79   356

WALLERSTEIN, RUTH
BOOKS REVIEWED
Studies in Seventeenth-Century Poetic   80   163

WALLESER, JOSEPH
POEMS
Beside the Master   10   127

WALLIS, CHARLES GLENN
BOOKS REVIEWED
No Mortal Blow   67   288

WALLIS, KEENE
POEMS
Gospel with Banjo and Chorus   17   22

WALLOP, GERARD
POEMS
On the Trail   22   74
  Morning Song
  Acceptance
  The Singing Boy

WALMSLEY, LEWIS C.
BOOKS REVIEWED
Poems by Wang Wêi
  (Tr. with Chang Yin-Nan)   96   309

WALSH, CHAD
POEMS
Elysian Fields, Calif.   84   256

REVIEWS
The Region of the Summer Stars,
  by Charles Williams   79   103

BOOKS REVIEWED
Eden Two-Way   86   287
The Unknowing Dance   105   414
The End of Nature   126   44

WALSH, ERNEST
POEMS
I Ask for a Friend   19   194
Sonnet ("When Love unveiled...")
The Fickle Lover
Collapse
In Hospital   23   175

Greater than the Sun
White Spiders
The Song of the Hopeless Sick
Despair
The White Death
Introspection
Residual
To One Asking Questions
Thrones
Bridges
Brancusi   25   25
Tunisian
Scarecrow
Quarrel
Sonnet ("Why should I say...")
A Reply

ARTICLES
Correspondence
  [Carl Sandburg]   24   112

BOOKS REVIEWED
Poems and Sonnets   46   349

ARTICLES ABOUT
[Note]   23   344
Free Verse Again,
  by Margery Swett (Mansfield)   25   153
And Ernest Walsh,
  by Harriet Monroe   29   213
Ernest Walsh, by Harriet Monroe   41   208

WALSH, PETER B.
POEMS
I Dreamt the Negro,
  Beautiful as Night   85   193

WALSH, THOMAS
BOOKS REVIEWED
Gardens Overseas and Other Poems   12   279
The Catholic Anthology (Ed.)   32   96

WALSHE, JOHN D.
BOOKS REVIEWED
The Vision Beatific   22   284

WALTERS, L. D'O.
BOOKS REVIEWED
Irish Poets of Today (Ed.)   21   51

WALTER-TOEWS, DAVID
BOOKS REVIEWED
Good Housekeeping   144   297

WALTON, EDA LOU
POEMS
Hill Songs   16   86
  I Met Three Lovers

One Spring
From a Promontory
Indian Prayer
Strength
Morning and Night
Beyond Sorrow   18   260
So It Befell
Without Grief
I Would Be Free
Crisis
Despair
Now More Than Ever Divided
In Recompense
Preludes   24   72
A Hidden Rhythm
Portrait
Winter Roses
Without Figures
Bridal Sleep
Tunes in the Dark   27   142
The White Night
Enigma
What Is Love?
The Futile Seasons
Raison D'Etre
African Moon Song
The Nesting Mind   32   140
Indeterminate Road
The Path of Glory
Mea Culpa
The Black Swan
Moonrise
In Transit   36   29
Pyramidal Earth
Portrait of an Old Man
On a Lake
The Pool   51   12
Alternate, None
But On a Day   68   305
Childhood Memory
In the End as the Beginning
Those Whom Death Leaves   91   84
Golden Anniversary
An Old Song
Portrait
Now Must the Mind Write
Rock Wren
At Bay
Clock and Three Candles   94   89
Epitaph ("A lamb just born...")
In Passage Tropical
"From the Top Down"   99   304
To Render Harmless

ARTICLES
Navaho Verse Rhythms   24   40

REVIEWS
On the Trail of Negro Song   27   221

On the Trail of Negro Folk-Songs,
   by Dorothy Scarborough
The Book of American Negro Spirituals
   (Ed. by James Weldon Johnson)
Negro Poetry in America,
   by Beatrice Norton
American–Indian Studies   28   53
American Indian Love Lyrics
   (Ed. by Nellie Barnes)
Manito Masks,
   by Hartley Alexander
Aspen Leaves, by Elvira Foote   36   52
Such Counsels You Gave to Me,
   and Other Poems,
   by Robinson Jeffers   51   209
New Directions in Prose
   and Poetry, 1937
   (Ed. by James Laughlin IV)   51   344
Younger Voices   83   343
Of Love, by Tom Boggs
Survivor's Leave,
   by Charles Causley
Spring and Death,
   by Charles Higham
Humanity,
   by Gretchen Warren

BOOKS REVIEWED
Dawn Boy: Blackfoot and Navajo Songs   28   165
The City Day (Ed.)   37   164
Jane Matthew and Other Poems   40   165
So Many Daughters   85   114

ARTICLES ABOUT
Obituary   99   330

WAMSLEY, HOWARD
POEMS
The Archaist   107   303

REVIEWS
Rivers and Mountains,
   by John Ashbery   109   185

WANEK, CONNIE
POEMS
Abstract   158   200
Broom

WANG AN-SHIH
POEMS
Night-Time in Spring
   (Tr. by Louise S. Hammond)   20   253

WANG CHANG-LING
POEMS
A Recluse
   (Tr. by Amy Lowell
   and Florence Ayscough)   13   239

WANG CHI
POEMS
  What Should a Man Want?
    (Tr. by Arthur Waley)   11   199

WANG CHING-SENG
POEMS
  The Inn at the Western Lake
    (Tr. by Amy Lowell
    and Florence Ayscough)   13   242

WANG TZU-TUAN
POEMS
  On Seeing Swallows in His Prison-Cell
    (Tr. by Arthur Waley)   11   200

WANG WÊI
POEMS
  Lonely
    (Tr. by Moon Kwan)   18   130
  Answering Vice-Prefect Chang   19   235
  Bound Home to Mount Sung
  A Message to P'ai Ti
  On the Way to the Temple
  Mount Chung-Nan
  A View of the Han River
  *In My Lodge at Wang-Ch'uan
    After a Long Rain*
  My Retreat at Chung-Nan
  In a Retreat Among Bamboos
  Lines
  A Parting
  A Song at Wei-Ch'eng
  The Beautiful Hsi-Shih
  A Song of Young Girls from Lo-Yang
  *Harmonizing a Poem
    by Palace-Attendant Kuo*
  A Green Stream
    (Tr. by Witter Bynner
    and Kiang Kang-Hu)
  News from Home
    (Tr. by Henry H. Hart)   35   259

  BOOKS REVIEWED
  Poems
    (Tr. by Chang Yin-nan
    and Lewis C. Walmsley)   96   309

  ARTICLES ABOUT
  Translating Wang Wêi,
    by Witter Bynner   19   272

WAN KIN-LAU
POEMS
  Lion and Sand   120   75

WAPLES, DOROTHY
POEMS
  Homesteading in Wyoming   35   313

**WARBURTON, WILLIAM
[BISHOP OF GLOUCESTER]**
ARTICLES ABOUT
  The Poetry of Charles Churchill, Part II,
    by Yvor Winters   98   104

WARD, ADDISON
POEMS
  Sonnet ("Monsters in their...")   74   87

WARD, C. E.
BOOKS REVIEWED
  The Gaucho Martín Fierro,
    by José Hernández (Tr.)
    (Ed. by Frank G. Carrino
    and Alberto J. Carlos)   113   338

WARD, HAZEL
POEMS
  Dirge   37   71

WARD, J. P.
POEMS
  The Guards   131   286
  Calvin
  The Word-Hoard

WARD, KATHARINE L.
POEMS
  To Atalanta Wedded   30   141

WARD, LEO L.
POEMS
  Voices Out of the Land   33   350
  Butchering Day
  The Wabash
  Prairie

WARD, MAY WILLIAMS
POEMS
  My Little Sister   25   247
  The Proof   29   322
  Fellow Travelers
  The Optimist
  Clichés
  Let Us Sit Near
  Decrescendo
  Sleep Spell
  Tree Cut Down   44   193
  The Time of Delicate Petals   54   131
  Wet Summer   70   246

  BOOKS REVIEWED
  Seesaw   36   106

WARD, OLIVE
POEMS
  Aflare   29   252
  Bravado

The Feather
The Man of It
Portraits in Perspective   33   198
Makeshift
A Woman We Shunned
Macallister
Winged

WARD, THOMAS HUMPHREY
BOOKS REVIEWED
The English Poets, vol. V (Ed.)   14   281

WARDELL, BERTHA
POEMS
Sacrilege   26   25

ARTICLES
Correspondence: The Allied Arts Again   19   171

WAREHAM, LOUISE
POEMS
Some Wrong   165   255
Object
Compulsion

WARNER, R. E.
POEMS
Birds   49   199
Egyptian Kite
Long Tailed Tit
Mallard

WARNER, REX
BOOKS REVIEWED
Poems   52   36
The Medea (Tr.)   86   303
George Seferis: Poems (Tr.)   101   283

WARNER, SYLVIA TOWNSEND
BOOKS REVIEWED
The Espalier   28   224
Time Importuned   34   47
Rainbow   43   225
Opus 7   44   165
Whether a Dove or Seagull
(With Valentine Ackland)

WARREN, AUSTIN
REVIEWS
Lord Weary's Castle, by Robert Lowell   70   262
The Achievement of Some Recent Critics   77   239
The Importance of Scrutiny
(Ed. by Eric Bentley)
Critiques and Essays in Criticism
(Ed. by R. W. Stallman)

BOOKS REVIEWED
Richard Crashaw,
A Study in Baroque Sensibility   57   160

Rage for Order   72   318
Theory of Literature
(With René Wellek)   75   303
New England Saints   91   273
Richard Crashaw,
A Study in Baroque Sensibility
The New England Conscience   111   203

WARREN, G. O.
POEMS
Secrecy   13   311

BOOKS REVIEWED
Trackless Regions   15   221
The Sword

WARREN, GRETCHEN
POEMS
The Wild Bird   8   182

BOOKS REVIEWED
Humanity   83   343

WARREN, JAMES E., JR.
POEMS
Bather Sleeping   52   271

WARREN, LANSING
BOOKS REVIEWED
En Repos and Elsewhere Over There
(With Robert A. Donaldson)   14   220

WARREN, ROBERT PENN
POEMS
Kentucky Mountain Farm   40   59
The Owl
The Cardinal
Watershed
The Limited   41   200
So Frost Astounds   44   196
The Return: An Elegy   45   85
October Poems   47   9
The Garden
Man Coming of Age
Bearded Oaks   51   10
Terror   57   285
Question and Answer
Revelation   59   202
Mexico Is a Foreign Country:
Four Studies in Naturalism   62   121
Butterflies Over the Map
The World Comes Galloping: A True Story
Small Soldiers with Drum
in Large Landscape
The Mango on the Mango Tree
The Lie   82   125
Synonyms   135   76
The Moonlight's Dream
Aspen Leaf in Windless World

ARTICLES
A Note on Three Southern Poets
    [John Gould Fletcher, Donald Davidson,
    John Crowe Ransom]   40   103

REVIEWS
The Poems of Lascelles Abercrombie   40   47
Strict Joy and Other Poems,
    by James Stephens   40   229
Ships and Lovers,
    by Thomas Caldecot Chubb   42   292
High Perils, by Cale Young Rice   42   342
Halfway House, by Edmund Blunden   43   287
Now with His Love,
    by John Peale Bishop   43   342
Ballads of Square-Toed Americans
    and The Yoke of Thunder,
    by Robert P. Tristram Coffin   44   334
Atlantides, by Haniel Long   45   226
Collected Poems,
    by V. Sackville-West   46   346
Trial Balances
    (Ed. by Ann Winslow)   48   172
Solstice and Other Poems,
    by Robinson Jeffers   49   279

BOOKS REVIEWED
Fugitives: An Anthology of Verse   32   102
Thirty-Six Poems   48   37
Eleven Poems on the Same Theme   61   505
Selected Poems   65   94
Brother to Dragons
    [Thomas Jefferson]   03   167
Understanding Poetry
    (With Cleanth Brooks)   84   43
Promises, Poems 1954-1956   92   49
You, Emperors, and Others:
    Poems 1957-60   99   56
Selected Poems,
    by Denis Devlin
    (Ed. with Allen Tate)   103   191
Selected Poems, New and Old, 1923-1966   110   416
Randall Jarrell 1914-1965
    (Ed. with Robert Lowell
    and Peter Taylor)   112   118
Or Else—Poem/Poems 1968-1974   128   349
Selected Poems 1923-1975   131   169
Being There: Poetry 1977-1980   138   107
New and Selected Poems: 1923-1985   147   35

ARTICLES ABOUT
Rev. of The Rime of the Ancient Mariner,
    by Samuel Taylor Coleridge   70   42
A Glossary of the New Criticism,
    by William Elton   73   153
A Glossary of the New Criticism,
    by William Elton   73   232

A Glossary of the New Criticism,
    by William Elton   73   296
Poetry on Records, by Harry T. Moore   79   353
Rev. of Critics and Criticism,
    Ancient and Modern
    (Ed. by R. S. Crane)   82   98
Rev. of Robert Penn Warren:
    The Dark and Bloody Ground,
    by Leonard Casper   99   56
Rev. of A Colder Fire: The Poetry
    of Robert Penn Warren,
    by Victor H. Strandberg   110   254
Poets Aloud, by Donald Hall   139   297
"Sacred Beings":
    Writers in Recorded Conversation,
    by Michael Milburn   146   101

WARREN, ROSANNA
BOOKS REVIEWED
    Stained Glass   164   97

WARRISTON, R. B. N.
POEMS
    Sanctuary   42   203

WARSH, LEWIS
POEMS
    Always There   110   169
    In the Ocean Air
    Crystals
    A Continuum
    The California Poem   113   12
    Gout
    The Static
    The Eye   114   303
    Message   116   182
    Flashing
    Souffle

REVIEWS
Poetry Chronicle   112   276
    The Distance Anywhere,
        by Kenneth O. Hanson
    Variety Photoplays,
        by Edward Field
    Journeying & The Returns,
        by B. P. Nichols
    Young Man's Letter, by John Gill
    Traveler's Palm, by Teo Savory
    A Suite of Angels,
        by Kenneth Pitchford
    The Blossom, or Billy the Kid
        and The Beard,
        by Michael McClure
Out of Sight   115   440
    Stones, by Tom Clark
    The Pill Versus the Springfield Mine
        Disaster and In Watermelon Sugar,
        by Richard Brautigan

Instructions for Undressing the Human Race,
  by Fernando Alegria
  (Tr. by Matthew Zion
  and Lennart Bruce)

BOOKS REVIEWED
  Moving Through Air   117   261

WARWICK, IOANNA-VERONIKA
POEMS
  Factories in Lodz   163   191
  Holding the Python   163   322

WASKOW, HOWARD J.
BOOKS REVIEWED
  Whitman: Explorations in Form   111   333

WASSERBURG, CHARLES
POEMS
  Geode   155   384

WASSERMAN, EARL
BOOKS REVIEWED
  The Finer Tone: Keats' Major Poems   84   37

WATERHOUSE, ELIZABETH
POEMS
  Slim Pickings   141   163
  Weather Permitting
  It's Not that I'm Unfeeling, But

WATERS, JIM
POEMS
  Poems of a Toiler   26   262
    Reiteration
    Summer Rain
    Twilight Impressions
    Night
    Hunger
    Toil
    December Winds
    Weary
    A Prayer
  So-and-So   39   136

WATERS, MARY ANN
POEMS
  Seeking the Elements   143   323
  Airplane Conversation with an Engineer
    Who Designed Ammunition
  Taxi   145   5
  Although It Was Late in the Season
  Diver
  Snowstorm   147   189
  The Quarry: A Dialogue
    from Above and Below
  Home Cooking
  Cowboy

Travelling Highway 97:
  Biggs Junction to Weed   151   186
  Car   152   81
  Bath

BOOKS REVIEWED
  The Exact Place   152   161

WATERS, MICHAEL
POEMS
  Not Just Any Death   130   143
  If I Die
  Preserves
  The Mystery of the Caves   139   263
  Pollen   144   219
  Reading Dickens   146   71
  The Conversion of St. Paul   149   150
  Romance in the Old Folks' Home
  Homo Sapiens   151   344
  The Inarticulate   152   202
  Bountiful
  Scorpions
  Hummingbirds   153   293
  Paradys   154   281
  "Night in the Tropics" (1858-59?)   156   283
  Shhh
  Not Love   160   194

BOOKS REVIEWED
  Anniversary of the Air   147   227
  The Burden Lifters   156   100

WATHEN, R. J.
BOOKS REVIEWED
  Bricks   110   195

WATKINS, GWEN
BOOKS REVIEWED
  I That Was Born in Wales,
  by Vernon Watkins
  (Ed. with Ruth Pryor)   131   292

WATKINS, VERNON
POEMS
  Arakhova and the Daemon   69   312
  The Yew-Tree   71   122
  Time's Deathbed   71   289
  Music of Colours: The Blossom Scattered   75   142
  Three Harps   77   1
  A Bell Unrung
  The Three Friends
  Call It All Names, But Do Not Call It Rest   81   83
  Woodpecker and Lyre-Bird   81   305
  Ballad of the Trial of Sodom
  From The Childhood of Hölderlin   84   220
  Taliesin and the Mockers   87   75
  The Tributary Seasons

Erinna and the Waters	88	141
Camelot	89	338
The Forge of the Solstice	91	24
The Mask of Winter		
The Crane	92	144
Demands of the Muse		
Revisited Waters (Part 4, "Origins")		
Ballad of the Mermaid of Zennor	95	11
Zennor Cottages		
Semele	97	1
Ironies of the Self		
Music of Colours—Dragonfoil II		
Logos	98	280
Revisited Waters		
Triads	101	131
From "Ballad of the Outer Dark"	103	110
Englyn	103	288
Digging the Past	107	312
To a Shell		
Cwmrhydyceirw Elegiacs	111	247
Sea Chant		
Matrix of Morning		
Rhadamanthus and the New Soul	128	73

TRANSLATIONS
Poem by Walther von der Vogelweide	73	26
Poems by Heinrich Heine	74	257

ARTICLES
Correspondence	87	i

REVIEWS
Dylan Thomas: The Legend and the Poet		
(Ed. by E. W. Tedlock)	98	124

BOOKS REVIEWED
Selected Poems	73	170
The North Sea,		
by Heinrich Heine (Tr.)	81	149
Dylan Thomas:		
Letters to Vernon Watkins (Ed.)	94	114
Ballad of the Mari Lwyd	97	260
Cypress and Acacia		
Vernon Watkins Reads His Works		
[Recording]	101	275
Affinities	103	316
Selected Poems	113	338
Fidelities	115	426
I That Was Born in Wales		
(Ed. by Gwen Watkins		
and Ruth Pryor)	131	292

ARTICLES ABOUT
London Letter: The Publishing Season,		
by John McCormick	85	176
Rev. of Letters to Vernon Watkins,		
by David Jones	131	292

WATSON, BURTON
BOOKS REVIEWED
Cold Mountain:		
100 Poems by Han-Shan (Ed. and tr.)	107	196
An Introduction to Sung Poetry,		
by Kojiro Yoshikawa (Tr.)	112	283

WATSON, J. SIBLEY
[See BLUM, W. C., Pseud.]

WATSON, MINOR [Pseud.]
POEMS
To a Friend	3	131

WATSON, ROBERT (W.)
POEMS
A Paper Horse	96	95
A Woman's Question	105	244
Luxury Flight from New York		
to Los Angeles	115	224
The Radio Astronomer		
Christmas in Las Vegas	118	83
Divorcée		
The Glass Door		
God as Magician	135	287
Lost		
Repossessed		
Abandoned Husband		

REVIEWS
Two Books of Criticism	107	332
The Suspect in Poetry,		
by James Dickey		
Sound and Form in Modern Poetry,		
by Harvey Gross		
Five Sleepers	117	204
Sleep Watch,		
by Richard Tillinghast		
Pilgrims, by Jean Valentine		
Sweating Out the Winter,		
by David P. Young		
A Night for Rioting,		
by Allen Planz		
Love in the Environs of Voronezh,		
by Alan Sillitoe		

BOOKS REVIEWED
A Paper Horse	102	118
Advantages of Dark	109	395
Christmas in Las Vegas	121	348
Night Blooming Cactus	139	171

WATSON, ROSAMUND MARRIOTT
BOOKS REVIEWED
The Poems of…	1	94

WATSON, WILFRED
BOOKS REVIEWED
Friday's Child	89	110

WATSON, [SIR] WILLIAM
BOOKS REVIEWED
Retrogression and Other Poems   11   225
Pencraft: A Plea for the Older Ways
Ireland Unfreed: Poems of 1921   19   346

WATT, DONALD
BOOKS REVIEWED
The Collected Poetry of Aldous Huxley (Ed.)   120   230

WATT, WILLIAM
POEMS
Six Eclogs   99   221
  ("You, I, we have all seen...")
  ("Over a desert-floor...")
  Winter Solstice
  ("L'ápres-deux...")
  Altamira
  ("Running a comb through...")

WATTERSON, WILLIAM COLLINS
POEMS
Eine Kleine Nachtmusik   159   139
To a Young Museum Guard   159   222

WATTLES, WILLARD
POEMS
On the Road   11   20
  Hrolf's Thrall—His Song
  Difference
  A Song of No Consequence
  Heaven
  The Builder
  Ding Dong Bell
In Memory   15   80
Epitaph for the Unburied Dead
But I Have Lived
I Who Have Known Your Beauty

ARTICLES
Correspondence: On Reading the
  Braithwaite Anthology for 1916
  [Poem]   10   52
Correspondence: An Anthology of 1842
  [Edgar Allan Poe]   12   230

BOOKS REVIEWED
Sunflowers: A Book of Kansas Poems (Ed.)   12   337
Lanterns in Gethsemane   14   277
Sunflowers (Ed.)   14   281

WATTS, A. E.
BOOKS REVIEWED
The Metamorphoses of Ovid (Tr.)   85   225

ARTICLES ABOUT
Rev. of Ovid: The Metamorphoses
  (Tr. by Horace Gregory)   95   185

WATTS, HAROLD H.
BOOKS REVIEWED
Ezra Pound and the Cantos   81   127

WATTS, HARVEY MAITLAND
BOOKS REVIEWED
The Wife of Potiphar with Other Poems   2   26

WATTS-SMYTH, FLORIDA
[See SMYTH, FLORIDA WATTS]

WAYMAN, TOM
POEMS
Paper   141   156
Trial

BOOKS REVIEWED
Going for Coffee   144   297

WAYNE, JANE O.
POEMS
With Solitude   138   93
First Freeze
Braiding Your Hair
The Family Album   144   322
Autumnal Equinox
Isoptera   149   199
The Last Visit
Walking into the Wind
The Finishing Touches   154   94
Inheritance
Waiting Room   161   82
Intensive Care
On the Heart List
Waking Up
In the Runaway's House   165   9
In a Mood

WAYNE, PHILIP
BOOKS REVIEWED
Faust, Part One,
  by J. W. von Goethe (Tr.)   75   232

WEATHERHEAD, A. KINGSLEY
BOOKS REVIEWED
The Edge of the Image   113   262

WEATHERS, WINSTON
POEMS
Journey to Iona   141   84
Epitaph for the Children
  Drowned in the River   143   212
On Entering the Hospice   162   24
A Sacrament

WEAVER, EDITH
POEMS
Lost Cinderella   70   69

WEAVER, J(OHN)
V(AN) A(LSTYNE), JR.
POEMS
Northern Lights   12   72
The Sowing
Drug Store   15   262
Nocturne
"Picture Ahead"   21   80
Dilemma

BOOKS REVIEWED
In American   18   162
Finders: More Poems in American   22   48
Turning Point   37   230

WEAVER, RICHARD
POEMS
The Crusade   126   27

WEAVER, RICHARD M.
REVIEWS
Elizabethan and Metaphysical Imagery,
by Rosamond Tuve   72   156

WEAVER, ROBERT
BOOKS REVIEWED
The First Five Years: A Selection from
The Tamarack Review (Ed.)   103   266

WEAVER, WILLIAM FENSE
POEMS
Michelangelo   70   190

WEBB, FRANCIS
ARTICLES ABOUT
Australian Poetry 1940–1980:
A Personal View,
by John Tranter   169   86

WEBB, IGOR
POEMS
Teaching Poetry of the First World War   117   33

WEBB, J. RODERICK
POEMS
Loweswater   68   20
Music Recital
Elegy
Near Loweswater   69   311

WEBB, MARY
BOOKS REVIEWED
Fifty-One Poems   73   49

WEBB, PHYLLIS
REVIEWS
Canadian Chronicle   104   385
The Rising Fire,
by Gwendolyn MacEwen

A Friction of Lights,
by Eldon Grier
Jawbreakers, by Milton Acorn
Poetry 64—Poésie 64
(Ed. by Jacques Godbout
and John Robert Colombo)

BOOKS REVIEWED
The Sea Is Also a Garden   103   266
The Vision Tree: The Selected Poems   144   297

WEBB, TESSA SWEAZY
POEMS
Storm   44   141

WEBB, WINIFRED
POEMS
Farmer's Blood   2   202
The Heartening
Contentment
Quest
Enough   9   121

WEBER, BROM
ARTICLES
Correspondence
[Hart Crane, Babette Deutsch,
Carl Schmitt]   84   245
Correspondence
[Oscar Cargill, Hart Crane,
Allen Tate, Yvor Winters]   92   332

REVIEWS
The Verbal Icon,
by W. K. Wimsatt, Jr.
[A. C. Bradley]   87   312

BOOKS REVIEWED
The Letters of Hart Crane,
1916-1932 (Ed.)   83   353

WEBER, LEE ANDREW
POEMS
The Missouri   26   202
A Machinist   30   311
Undine   32   258

WEBER, MARC
BOOKS REVIEWED
48 Small Poems   123   353

WEBER, RICHARD
BOOKS REVIEWED
Stephen's Green Revisited   114   397

WEBER, ROLAND V.
ARTICLES
Correspondence:
Poetry on the Radio   36   227

WEBSTER, HARVEY CURTIS
POEMS
  Trainee   63   187

ARTICLES
  Humanism as the Father Face
    [John Ciardi]   70   146

REVIEWS
  Influence and Originality   63   99
    The Sun at Noon, by James Hearst
    Arenas, by Tom Boggs
    The Best Poems of 1943
      (Ed. by Thomas Moult)   66   111
  Two with Too Many   67   170
    The Darkening Meadows,
      by Robert Nathan
    Thirst of the Antelope,
      by Gustav Davidson
  Goodness, Substance, Eloquence   68   227
    Perilous Balance, by Arnold Stein
    Poems: mcmxlii,
      by William Everson
    Brief Enterprise,
      by Alice Monks Mears
    The Burning Mountain,
      by John Gould Fletcher   69   353
  On These I Stand, by Countée Cullen   70   222
  Poems of Dedication,
    by Stephen Spender   71   153
  Take Away the Darkness,
    by Witter Bynner   72   44
  One-Way Ticket,
    by Langston Hughes   75   300
  Five Poets   101   209
    The Looking Glass,
      by Isabella Gardner
    Children and Older Strangers,
      by Ernest Sandeen
    Cloud, Stone, Sun, Vine,
      by May Sarton
    Journey to a Known Place,
      by Hayden Carruth
    Poems from a Cage, by Dilys Laing
  Six Poets   133   227
    In the Stopping Train,
      by Donald Davie
    The Trash Dragon of Shensi,
      by Andrew Glaze
    A Voice in the Mountain,
      by Peter Davison
    Words for Dr. Y,
      by Anne Sexton
      (Ed. by Linda Gray Sexton)
    The Retrieval System,
      by Maxine Kumin
    The Dream of a Common Language,
      by Adrienne Rich

ARTICLES ABOUT
  Correspondence
    from Witter Bynner   72   344

WEBSTER, LOUISE
POEMS
  One Time at Salem   27   318

WEBSTER, MARY MORISON
BOOKS REVIEWED
  To-Morrow, A Book of Poems   22   344

WEBSTER, PAUL FRANCIS
POEMS
  Willow Woman   37   197

WEEKS, DONALD
POEMS
  Giraffe   69   261

WEEKS, DORIS CONE
POEMS
  Durer   72   77

WEEKS, HOWARD
POEMS
  What Furred Creature   37   246

WEEKS, LEROY TITUS
ARTICLES
  Correspondence: The New Beauty
    [Ezra Pound]   6   48

ARTICLES ABOUT
  Correspondence from Ezra Pound   6   157

WEHR, WESLEY
POEMS
  Liebeslied   79   264

WÊI, WANG
  [See WANG WÊI]

WEIBAULT, F. G.
  [Pseud. of WEISS,
  HENRY GEORGE,
  and THIBAULT, FRANK]
POEMS
  There's One Waiting for You   54   81

WEIL, ERIC
POEMS
  The Path of the Headlights   136   63
  Before Cooking an Eggplant

WEIL, JAMES L.
POEMS
  Runnymede: 14 May 1965   108   27
  About Roses

Like That
To Her Hand   109   376
Mr. Weil
Your Father
Mountain Pool   111   305

REVIEWS
For Sharing   109   195
    This Do (& The Talents),
        by Theodore Enslin
    The Gorky Poems, by Jerome Rothenberg
    Virgil's Machines, by Joel Sloman

BOOKS REVIEWED
    Sorrow's Spy   103   324
    The Thing Said and Other Poems   108   191
    The Correspondences: Poems 1965-1967 116   193

WEIMAN, ANDREW
POEMS
    Andy-Diana DNA Letter   137   94

WEINBERG, BERNARD
BOOKS REVIEWED
    A History of Literary Criticism
        in the Italian Renaissance   102   198
    The Art of Jean Racine   104   187
    The Limits of Symbolism: Studies of Five
        Modern French Poets
        [Baudelaire, Rimbaud, Mallarmé,
        Valéry, St.-John Perse]   112   41

WEINBERGER, ELIOT
BOOKS REVIEWED
    The Collected Poems
        of Octavio Paz 1957-1987 (Ed.)
        (Tr. with others)   154   29

WEINER, HANNAH
POEMS
    Code Poem   113   393

WEINER, REBECCA
POEMS
    Birds   138   214
    Driving Around

WEINFIELD, HENRY
POEMS
    The Fisherman and His Soul   119   261
    Adam and Eve   127   198

BOOKS REVIEWED
    Carnival Cantata   121   348

WEINGARTEN, ROGER
POEMS
    Memoir   133   199
    Under the Wine Tree at the Edge of Desire

Victorian Bacchanal
Tunnel Effect   135   257
Clay Tenements
Shadow Shadow   137   202
The Afterlife   138   208
For the Reader   141   265
New Year's, Montpelier, 1885   145   189
Not Quite a Love Poem
Apples
Premature Elegy by Firelight
My Brain Tumor   147   337
A Late Twentieth-Century Afternoon
    with the Dead
It's Like That
Barn Cat Summer   148   129
Then My Father's Insomnia Will Break
    Like the Wine Glass I Crushed Underfoot
    at My Wedding   149   153
Nightwatch   150   263
Persona Non Grata
Just Another Sunset   151   189
The Forever Bird   152   268

BOOKS REVIEWED
    The Vermont Suicides   135   229
    Shadow Shadow   149   341

WEINHEBER, JOSEF
POEMS
    At the Roots   85   35
    Mind and Life
    Sotto Voce
    Tree in the Frost
    Dandelion
    Blossoming Tree Before Nightfall
    On the Transitory
        (Tr. by Harry Bergholz)

ARTICLES ABOUT
    The Still Voice of German Poetry,
        by Edouard Roditi   68   208
    A Note on Josef Weinheber,
        by Harry Bergholz   85   42

WEINSTEIN, ARNOLD
POEMS
    Epithalamium   87   157

WEINSTEIN, EDWARD
POEMS
    The Cultural Skeleton   79   263

WEINSTOCK, CLARENCE
POEMS
    Romans   36   59
    Caesar
    Petronius
    Julian the Apostate Dying in Persia

Saint Augustine Meditates
The Foolish Lover   40   325
For Those Fighting   62   21

REVIEWS
The Romanesque Lyric,
  by Philip Schuyler Allen
  (Trs. by Howard Mumford Jones)   33   227
Circumference: Varieties
  of Metaphysical Verse—1456-1928
  (Ed. by Genevieve Taggard)   37   50

WEIRICK, BRUCE
BOOKS REVIEWED
Illini Poetry, 1918-23 (Ed.)   24   162
From Whitman to Sandburg
  in American Poetry   25   167

WEISENTHAL, MORRIS
POEMS
Trapeze   66   82
Darkness
Death in Jersey
Elegy for Friend
Release   68   309

WEISKOPF, F. C.
ARTICLES
The Spirit of Czech Poetry
  [Frantisek Ladislav Celakovsky]   55   200
On the Continent
  [Franz Werfel, Walter Hasenclever,
  Heinrich Keisch, Louis Aragon]   56   332
Serbian Poetry
  [Vuk Stefanovich Karadjich,
  Petar Petrovich Nyegosh]   61   438

REVIEWS
Gedichte aus Reigate,
  by Rudolph Fuchs   58   272

WEISMAN, RICHARD
POEMS
The Condition of Music   123   77
You Don't Know
Enough

WEISMILLER, EDWARD
POEMS
The Latched Gate   48   149
Kin
The Gleaners
Break of Dawn
Lament in Spring
The Weather of the Dawn   52   135
Shadow
The Shape of Mountains
We Walk in Water

The Question   61   596
Night Watch
Airplanes, 1938
Sea Floor   63   21
In a Sanitarium   102   306
Space of Time

REVIEWS
The Helmsman,
  by J. V. Cunningham   60   279
Long View, by Genevieve Taggard   61   400

BOOKS REVIEWED
The Deer Come Down   50   45
The Faultless Shore   70   52

WEISS, DAVID
POEMS
The Landlord   135   274
Closing Time   139   146
In an Orchard on Thanksgiving
After All   141   210
This World

WEISS, HENRY GEORGE
[See WEIBAULT, F. G.,
pseud. with THIBAULT, FRANK]

WEISS, NEIL
POEMS
Refrain   74   74
Perception of Rhythm   76   257
Song of Quiet
Late Reader   84   336
Lily   85   206
The Hike
Grief   88   316
The Hunt
The New Overcoat
The Ageing Athlete
Laocoön and the Bomb   92   302
From The Fantast in the City
Cuckoo Clock
Gulls   95   166
Friends
Letter Written Standing in a Train

BOOKS REVIEWED
Origin of a Design   100   404

WEISS, PENELOPE
REVIEWS
Three Poets   108   57
  The Race with Time and the Devil,
    by Paul Petrie
  Lines to the South and Other Poems,
    by John William Corrington
  Survivals, by Edwin Honig

WEISS, R(ENÉE)
BOOKS REVIEWED
Quarterly Review of Literature Poetry Series
   (Ed. with T. Weiss)   140   35
Works and Days, by David Schubert
   (Ed. with T. Weiss)   145   348

WEISS, SANFORD
POEMS
Poem ("One night in the lilting...")   86   232
Camera   111   303
In Praise of Him

WEISS, T(HEODORE)
POEMS
Central Standard Time   65   314
The Match   74   199
The Dance Called David
The Catch   75   63
   The Hook
   A Commonplace
   To Penny When She Comes
     of Reading Age
   A Ghost Story
Interview   77   207
The Face   79   201
Hayseed   81   85
Sonata Pathétique   82   146
Absolutely Roomy   87   162
The Giant Yea   89   14
The Little Winter Gardens
The Shield   91   170
So He Was Sung
The Fire at Alexandria   94   150
One Sundry Thing
The Telltale Moment
To Forget Me
The Web   99   354
In the Round
The Reapings
Through the Strings   106   160
The Last Day and the First   112   171
Between the Lines
Far Out, Far In
A Fitting Revenge   116   80
The Little Red Book
A Very Tokyo
In Defense of Dull Times   121   266
An Old Cart   151   190
Occupied   157   257
Satisfied

REVIEWS
Collected Poems, by Horace Gregory   105   134

BOOKS REVIEWED
The Catch   81   324
Outlanders   98   118

Initial A,
   by David Schubert
   (Ed. with Judith E. Kranes)   99   379
Gunsight   102   250
The Medium   108   269
The Last Day and the First   114   335
The World Before Us   120   49
Fireweeds   130   41
Quarterly Review of Literature Poetry Series
   (Ed. with R. Weiss)   140   35
Views and Spectacles:
   New and Selected Shorter Poems   140   102
Recoveries: A Poem   141   349
Works and Days,
   by David Schubert
   (Ed. with R. Weiss)   145   348
From Princeton One Autumn Afternoon:
   Collected Poems of..., 1950-1986   152   35

WEISSBORT, DANIEL
POEMS
Thwarted   142   329
My London

TRANSLATIONS
Poems by Yevgeny Vinokurov,
   Olga Berggolts, Nikolai Zabolotsky,
   Natalya Gorbanevskaya, Gleb
   Gorbovsky, German Plisetsky,
   Robert Rozhdestvensky, Aleksandr
   Kushner, and Viktor Sosnora   124   187
Poem by Joseph Brodsky   131   311

WEISSER, JEROME H.
POEMS
At the Window   63   202
Valediction   72   195
Sporting Print
Portrait of an Old Man   74   146

WEISSLITZ, E. F.
POEMS
Knowledge   101   179

WEISSMANN, DAVID
POEMS
Orchards   122   135
And Company
Little Violent Interlude
Static   124   149
Wind
Thinking at Night   127   67

WELCH, JAMES
POEMS
Dreaming Winter   112   16
Harlem, Montana:
   Just Off the Reservation

BOOKS REVIEWED
   Riding the Earthboy 40   121   348
   Riding the Earthboy 40   129   285

WELCH, LEW
POEMS
   From "The Hermit Songs"   104   228

BOOKS REVIEWED
   On Out   108   198
   Hermit Poems

WELCH, MARIE DE L.
POEMS
   Sky-Eaters   31   22
   Shadows of the Fruit   33   309
     Hill Quietness
     Weed
     Misty Orchard
     Sea City
     Starless Night
   The Single Name   52   124

BOOKS REVIEWED
   Poems   44   228
   This Is Our Own   56   104

WELLEK, RENÉ
BOOKS REVIEWED
   Theory of Literature
     (With Austin Warren)   75   303

WELLES, WINIFRED
POEMS
   Silver Fog   20   83
   The Edge of the Wilderness 34   206
   Boy
   Feast in the Forest
   Brown Bread
   A Dog Who Ate a Pond Lily
   A Child's Drawing of a Cobweb
   The Heart of Light
   Gossamer Urns   39   117
     Drawing of an Angel
     Invocation to Fancy
     The Body of the Roots
     Blossoming Antlers
     People into Sprites
     Spinster
     Clouds Over a Cottage
     Song Before Entering
      Paradise Forever
   People and Houses   47   119
     The Two Brothers
     Old House
     The Downstairs Bedroom
     White Valentine
     Scared Parson

REVIEWS
   Threshold and Hearth, by Marya Zaturenska   45   282

BOOKS REVIEWED
   The Hesitant Heart   17   276
   This Delicate Love   35   217
   Skipping Along Alone   40   51
   Blossoming Antlers   44   159
   A Spectacle for Scholars   48   285
   The Shape of Memory   64   168

ARTICLES ABOUT
   Obituary   55   225

WELLS, CAROLYN
BOOKS REVIEWED
   Carolyn Wells' Book
     of American Limericks (Ed.)   27   343

WELLS, CATHERINE
POEMS
   War   7   72

WELLS, HENRY W.
BOOKS REVIEWED
   New Poets from Old:
     A Study in Literary Genetics   59   102
   The American Way of Poetry   63   166
   Selected Poems,
     by Marsden Hartley (Ed.)   68   220
   Introduction to Wallace Stevens 109   201

WELLS, MARIE
POEMS
   Borrowed Time   78   86
   To Begin as the Riven   93   70

WELLS, OLIVER
BOOKS REVIEWED
   An Anthology of Younger Poets (Ed.) 41   284

WELLS, PETER
POEMS
   Poem ("The tethered beast...")   61   534

WELLS, SIMON
ARTICLES ABOUT
   [Note]   52   360

WELSH, ROBERT GILBERT
POEMS
   The Djinn   12   310
   Readers

WELLWARTH, GEORGE
BOOKS REVIEWED
   Modern Spanish Theatre:
     An Anthology of Plays
     (Ed. with Michael Benedikt)   113   338

WEN CHENG-MING
POEMS
The Emperor's Return
from a Journey to the South
(Tr. by Amy Lowell
and Florence Ayscough)   13   234

WENDT, INGRID
POEMS
Sestina ("The day you found him...")   144   139

WENIEWSKA, CELINA
BOOKS REVIEWED
Polish Writing Today (Ed.)   113   35

WENTHE, WILLIAM
POEMS
Trope   159   338

WEÖRES, SANDOR
BOOKS REVIEWED
Selected Poems
(With Ferenc Juhász)   119   342

WERFEL, FRANZ
POEMS
An Old Woman Passes
(Tr. by Babette Deutsch
and Avrahm Yarmolinsky)   21   142

ARTICLES ABOUT
A Note on Modern German Poetry,
by Babette Deutsch   21   149
New York Plays,
by Florence Kiper Frank   28   95
On the Continent, by F. C. Weiskopf   56   332

WERNER, MARGUERITE EDWARDS
POEMS
Before Words Come   21   313

WESCOTT, GLENWAY
POEMS
Still-Hunt   18   303
Ominous Concord
Without Sleep
The Chaste Lovers
To L. S.
The Poet at Night-Fall
The Hunter
Foresight   22   262
The Stone Valley   23   25
Evening Illusion
The Free and the Bound
Coyotes
Mountain
Gifts of the River
The Summer Ending   54   306

ARTICLES
Alexander Blok   19   149

REVIEWS
Classics in English   18   284
Sappho
(Tr. by Henry Thornton Wharton)
The Golden Treasury of the Greeks
(Tr. by Alexander Lothian)
Medallions in Clay
(Tr. by Richard Aldington)
The Poet's Translation Series: Second Set
(Tr. by H. D.)
[Choruses from *Iphigenia*
in Aulis and *Hippolytus*,
by Euripides]
A Canopic Jar, by Leonora Speyer   19   47
Poems, by Stewart Mitchell   20   49

BOOKS REVIEWED
The Bitterns   18   339

ARTICLES ABOUT
Poets as Prosers, by Harriet Monroe   28   328
Some Recollections of the Poetry Club
at the University of Chicago,
by Gladys Campbell   107   110

WESENBERG, ALICE BIDWELL
POEMS
When Bullfrogs Talk   28   201
Death's Time   53   137

WESLEY, FRANCES
POEMS
Pervigilium   45   259

WEST, JAY
POEMS
Litter   63   203

WEST, JESSICA
POEMS
Sympathy   40   254
Living Death

WEST, PAUL
BOOKS REVIEWED
The Snow Leopard   107   406

WEST, RAY B., JR.
REVIEWS
The Earthquake and Other Poems,
by John Theobald   74   241

WEST, REBECCA
BOOKS REVIEWED
Selected Poems of Carl Sandburg (Ed.)   31   53

ARTICLES ABOUT
    Joy in Great Art, by Harriet Monroe   47   208

WESTERN, HUGH
    BOOKS REVIEWED
      This Last Devotion   60   285

WESTON, JESSIE L.
    BOOKS REVIEWED
      Romance, Vision and Satire:
        English Alliterative Poems
        of the Fourteenth Century Newly
        Rendered in the Original Metres   2   145

WESTON, JOHN C.
    BOOKS REVIEWED
      Collected Poems of Hugh MacDiarmid (Ed.)   112   131

WESTON, MILDRED
    POEMS
      A Portrait   20   79

    BOOKS REVIEWED
      The Singing Hill   30   233

WETHERILL, J. K.
    POEMS
      The Heart on the Highroad   7   129
      Chinoiserie

WEVILL, DAVID
    POEMS
      The Elder Son   98   240

    BOOKS REVIEWED
      Birth of a Shark   108   45

WEXLER, IRVING
    POEMS
      Love Song: Carthage Beach   63   200
      Surgery: At Sea

WEYAND, NORMAN
    BOOKS REVIEWED
      Immortal Diamond (Ed.)
        [Gerard Manley Hopkins]   74   292

WHALEN, PHILIP
    POEMS
      Invocation and Theophany   106   166

    BOOKS REVIEWED
      Memoirs of an Interglacial Age   97   114
      You Didn't Even Try   112   353
      On Bear's Head   117   338
      Severance Pay   122   47
      The Kindness of Strangers: Poems 1969-1974   130   167
      Enough Said: Poems 1974-1979   140   346

WHALER, JAMES
    BOOKS REVIEWED
      Hale's Pond   32   47
      Green River: A Poem for Rafinesque   40   44

WHARTON, EDITH
    BOOKS REVIEWED
      Eternal Passion in English Poetry
        (Ed. with Robert Norton)   57   221

WHARTON, HENRY THORNTON
    BOOKS REVIEWED
      Sappho (Tr.)   18   284

WHARTON, WILL
    ARTICLES
    Correspondence
      [James Decker, Dorothy Decker,
      Ervin Tax, Decker Press]   77   58

    BOOKS REVIEWED
      Graphiti from Elsinore   76   170

WHEELER, W. REGINALD
    BOOKS REVIEWED
      A Book of Verse on the Great War (Ed.)   12   285

WHEELOCK, JOHN HALL
    POEMS
      Triumph of the Singer   2   164
      The Thunder-Shower
      Song ("All my love for my sweet...")
      Alone   7   76
      Song at Night
      Beethoven
      Holy Light   10   128
      The Moonlight Sonata   10   303
      The Sorrowful Masquerade   17   189
      In the Dark City   20   187
      Those Two   28   193
      Golgotha   30   10
      Night-Piece   95   206
      Summer Night
      Evening-Star
      Earth, Take Me Back   105   83
      The Prayer of the Cricket

    ARTICLES
    Correspondence
      [Paul Goodman, Peter Viereck]   76   306

    REVIEWS
      Chords from Albireo,
        by Danford Barney   16   340

    BOOKS REVIEWED
      The Human Fantasy   1   131
      The Beloved Adventure

Love and Liberation   4   163
Dust and Light   15   343
The Black Panther   21   224
The Bright Doom   31   280
Poems, 1909-1936   50   100
Poems Old and New   89   319
Poets of Today VI: Northwind and Other
    Poems, by Gene Baro; The Clothing's
    New Emperor and Other Poems,
    by Donald Finkel; Poems, 1955-1958,
    by Walter Stone (Ed.)   95   373
Poets of Today VII (Ed.)   99   178
Robert Hillyer and John Hall Wheelock
    [Recording]   101   275
What Is Poetry?   104   369
Dear Men and Women: New Poems   110   123
By Daylight and In Dream, New and
    Collected Poems, 1904-1970   121   234

ARTICLES ABOUT
Correspondence
    from Marguerite Wilkinson   21   339

WHEELWRIGHT, JOHN
POEMS
Slow Curtain   37   263
Questions and Answers   41   86
    Why Must You Know
    Would You Think
    Canal Street
    Mossy Marbles
The Lord's Prayer to the Poor   47   189
Two Tongues in a Tower   48   74
Sabotage   50   312
Two Sonnets from "Mirrors of Venus"   52   132
    Kin
    Link

REVIEWS
A Joking Word and Laura and Francisca,
    by Laura Riding   40   288
Finale of Seem and Apollinaire: An Elegy,
    by Walter Lowenfels   42   49
Christ in the Breadlines,
    by Kenneth W. Porter,
    Seymour Gordon Link,
    and Harry Elmore Hurd   42   168
The Poems of Richard Aldington   45   47
Hoxsie Sells His Acres,
    by Christopher LaFarge   45   228
No Apology for Poetrie, by Sherry Mangan   45   339
Poems and Sonnets, by Ernest Walsh   46   349
Invisible Landscapes, by Edgar Lee Masters 48   41
A Further Range, by Robert Frost   49   45
The Human Abstract, by Alice Very   50   113
Poet as Funny Man   50   210
    Hellements of Hickonomics,
        by Stephen Leacock

The Melancholy Lute,
    by Franklin P. Adams
Death and General Putnam
    and Gaily the Troubador,
    by Arthur Guiterman
The Goose on the Capitol
    and Rhyme and Punishment,
    by Leonard Bacon
Lament for the Death of a Bullfighter
    and Other Poems,
    by Federico García Lorca
    (Tr. by A. L. Lloyd)   51   167
Bullinger Bound and Other Poems,
    by Leonard Bacon   52   229
Toward the Recovery of Speech   54   164
    Air Raid: A Verse Play for Radio,
        by Archibald MacLeish
    The Planets: A Modern Allegory,
        by Alfred Kreymborg

BOOKS REVIEWED
Rock and Shell   44   282
Mirrors of Venus: A Novel in Sonnets   56   278
Political Self-Portrait
Selected Poems   59   45
Collected Poems of...   122   351

ARTICLES ABOUT
Obituary   57   223

WHEELWRIGHT, PHILIP
BOOKS REVIEWED
Metaphor and Reality   102   198

WHICHER, GEORGE FRISBIE
BOOKS REVIEWED
This Was a Poet: A Critical Biography
    of Emily Dickinson   53   312

WHIGHAM, PETER
BOOKS REVIEWED
The Blue Winged Bee   118   102

WHISTLER, LAURENCE
BOOKS REVIEWED
Four Walls   50   347
The Emperor Heart

ARTICLES ABOUT
Avant-Garde and Camp Followers,
    by D. S. Savage   59   32

WHITAKER, THOMAS R.
BOOKS REVIEWED
Swan and Shadow:
    Yeats's Dialogue with History   107   192

WHITALL, JAMES
BOOKS REVIEWED
Chinese Lyrics from the Book of Jade (Tr.) 14   281

WHITBREAD, THOMAS
BOOKS REVIEWED
Whomp and Moonshiver   143   228

WHITBY, CHARLES
BOOKS REVIEWED
Concerto in A Minor   29   56

WHITCOMB, SELDEN LINCOLN
POEMS
The Path-Makers   24   242

WHITE, ALISON GENEVIEVE
REVIEWS
Sensibility, Naturalism, Etc.:
    Old Canons Extended   74   353
Lectures in Criticism
    [Johns Hopkins University,
    John Crowe Ransom, Allen Tate]
The Limits of Art, an Anthology
    (Ed. by Huntington Cairns)
Sense and Sensibility in Modern Poetry,
    by William Van O'Connor

WHITE, E. B.
BOOKS REVIEWED
The Lady Is Cold   35   170

WHITE, EDMUND
REVIEWS
Selected Poems, by Howard Moss   123   350

WHITE, EMILY
POEMS
Criticism   60   136
Prayer of the Traveler   78   76
Entourage
The Story of Motion
The Last Spinning

WHITE, GRACE HOFFMAN
POEMS
Silence   30   139
April   32   17
Silverpoint   35   251
Silences of Love
Her Eyes
Aftermath

BOOKS REVIEWED
Wings to Dare   27   348

WHITE, HAL SAUNDERS
POEMS
Middle Moments   34   88
God Perfects Pear Trees
Sunday Morning
Winter Wife
Puzzle No More

WHITE, HERVEY
BOOKS REVIEWED
The Adventures of Young Maverick   1   94

WHITE, HOWARD
BOOKS REVIEWED
The Men They Were   144   297

WHITE, J. P.
POEMS
Why I Can't Live
    in Cheyenne, Anymore   140   99
Vermont Gray, a Train, a Boat
One Morning Another Good Man Is Gone
The Arctic Balloonists Talk to
    the Ones They Left Behind   145   157
Su Tung P'o Awakens in Moonlight
    To Write a Letter to His Wife   146   140
We Who Set Out for the New World
In a Rowboat on a Lake in Minnesota
On the Return of Halley's Comet   147   221
Walking Pound's Canals
Walking to the Theatre, I Tell You
    a Story About a Runaway   149   83
Thanksgiving Night, Old Town,
    Portland, Oregon
To Confucius   150   257
Playing for the Pickerel One August Night
In Ecclesiastes I Read   151   191
The Son of a Sailor   154   128
Living Among Women   155   271
Degas   159   216

REVIEWS
Short Reviews   149   168
    Unattainable Earth,
        by Czeslaw Milosz
        (Tr. by Robert Hass)
    Dream Palace, by Herbert Morris
    Local Time, by Stephen Dunn
    Hurricane Lamp, by Turner Cassity
    Stars Principal, by J. D. McClatchy
    A Short History of the Island of Butterflies,
        by Nicholas Christopher
    All of Us Here,
        by Irving Feldman
    [George Segal]

WHITE, JOAN
POEMS
The Favorite Child   85   146

WHITE, MILES
POEMS
Precipice   74   86
At the Centennial of a City   76   69
Elegy (For B?)
A Stone's Throw

WHITE, MIMI
POEMS
A Simple Love Story   162   89
Zaydee's Short Career
   in the Russian Army   163   192

WHITE, NEWMAN IVEY
BOOKS REVIEWED
Shelley   57   386

WHITE, PATRICK
POEMS
The Gesture   129   133
Mars
The Legend in Andromeda

WHITE, WILLIAM ALLEN
ARTICLES
Correspondence: To the Rejected   22   170

WHITEHALL, HAROLD
ARTICLES ABOUT
Reading Sprung Rhythms,
  by Brewster Ghiselin
  [Gerard Manley Hopkins]   70   86

WHITEHOUSE, H. REMSEN
BOOKS REVIEWED
The Life of Lamartine   14   108

WHITELEY, MARY N. S.
POEMS
Negro Singing   40   318
Irregular Eulogy
Question Without Answer
Memory   44   315
Salt Etching   46   259
Garment Workers' Strike   49   264
No Horns Blowing
No Word   54   318
Transiency
New Rhythmed Strides   59   189
Silence
Mind's Return
Shells of Exile   66   75

REVIEWS
Anthropos: The Future of Art,
  by E. E. Cummings   70   211

WHITFORD, ROBERT CALVIN
POEMS
Bathsheba   10   83

WHITMAN, CEDRIC
POEMS
Dissonance   134   85
Snowman   143   145

WHITMAN, RUTH
POEMS
Birth Day   98   156
The Lost Steps   100   379
A Spider on My Poem   106   336
Three Letters

TRANSLATIONS
Poems by Odysseus Elytis   105   21

REVIEWS
A Treasury of Yiddish Poetry
  (Ed. by Irving Howe
  and Eliezer Greenberg)   118   354

BOOKS REVIEWED
Blood and Milk Poems   104   108
Selected Poems, by Alain Bosquet
  (Tr. with Samuel Beckett,
  Charles Guenther,
  and Edouard Roditi)   104   115
An Anthology of Modern Yiddish Poetry
  (Ed. and tr.)   113   35
The Marriage Wig and Other Poems   115   430

WHITMAN, WALT
BOOKS REVIEWED
The Letters of Anne Gilchrist
  and Walt Whitman
  (Ed. by Thomas B. Harned)   14   106
Patriotic Poems of...
Leaves of Grass   86   118
Leaves of Grass
  (Ed. by Harold W. Blodgett
  and Scully Bradley)   107   397

ARTICLES ABOUT
A Perfect Return,
  by Alice Corbin Henderson   1   87
Our Contemporaries:
  Whitman Amended   6   261
Walt Whitman, by Harriet Monroe   14   89
Rev. of Visits to Walt Whitman
  in 1890-1891,
  by J. Johnston
  and J. W. Wallace   14   106
Rev. of From Whitman to Sandburg
  in American Poetry,
  by Bruce Weirick   25   167
Rev. of Whitman,
  by Edgar Lee Masters   50   350
Rev. of Whitman,
  by Newton Arvin and Walt Whitman
  and the Springs of Courage,
  by Haniel Long   53   273
Hopkins' Ancestry: Part I,
  by Terence Heywood   54   209

Rev. of *American Renaissance*,
  by F. O. Matthiessen   60   334
Rev. of *Walt Whitman:*
  Poet of Democracy,
  by Hugh l'Anson Fausset   61   687
Homage to St.-John Perse,
  by Allen Tate   75   213
From the Introduction to
  The Oxford Book of American Verse,
  by F. O. Matthiessen   77   31
Rev. of *The Oxford Book of American Verse*
  (Ed. by F. O. Matthiessen)   79   36
Commemoration
  [Note]   84   305
Rev. of *Leaves of Grass*
  One Hundred Years After
  (Ed. by Milton Hindus);
  The Solitary Singer,
  by Gay Wilson Allen;
  Walt Whitman Abroad
  (Ed. by Gay Wilson Allen);
  Whitman's Manuscripts:
  Leaves of Grass, 1860
  (Ed. by Fredson Bowers);
  Walt Whitman's Concept of the
  American Common Man,
  by Leadie M. Clark;
  and *Walt Whitman: A Selection*
  of the Manuscripts, Books
  and Association Items
  (Ed. by Charles E. Feinberg)   87   183
Rev. of *A Critical Guide*
  to Leaves of Grass,
  by James E. Miller, Jr.   92   116
Rev. of *Whitman: Explorations in Form*,
  by Howard J. Waskow   111   333
Rev. of *The Penguin Book*
  of Homosexual Verse
  (Ed. by Stephen Coote)   144   166
Review by Paul Breslin   153   30
Review by Sandra M. Gilbert   160   284
Rev. of *American Poetry:*
  The Nineteenth Century
  (Ed. by John Hollander)   165   340
Review by David Baker   168   33

WHITMARSH, ESTHER A.
POEMS
  Life Everlasting   17   17

WHITTEMORE, REED
POEMS
  The Primitives   71   18
  The Siege
  A Closet Drama   73   187
  Variations on Being Thirty   75   9
  Ladders   84   268
  On the Unimportance of Words

Thoughts of the California Desert
Fathers and Sons   86   311
An English Teacher
Another Teacher
God's Acres
The Walk Home   89   106
The Weather This Spring
The World Around Us
A Tale of a Poem and a Squash   92   346
The Palms
A Winter Scene
Three Sonnets to Time   94   303
  ("When a man dies...")
  ("In books, and in sealed...")
  ("Again and again we deceive...")
Three Poems to Jackson

ARTICLES
  Correspondence
    [William Elton]   73   370
  Correspondence
    [Edna St. Vincent Millay]   90   259
  Postscript
    [Karl Shapiro]   98   185

REVIEWS
  The Pisan Cantos, by Ezra Pound   73   108
  Sense and/or Sensibility   86   295
    The Middle Voice,
      by Constance Carrier
    Brief Oasis, by Wilson Clough
    33 Night Sonnets,
      by Elliott Coleman
    The Nightfishing, by W. S. Graham
    In the Cold Country,
      by Barbara Howes
    The Headlands,
      by Howard Sergeant
    Dinosaurs and Violins,
      by Hy Sobiloff
    Poems, by Diana Witherby
  His Very Self and Voice
    (Ed. by Ernest J. Lovell, Jr.)
    [Lord Byron]   87   372
  Collected Poems of Edna St. Vincent Millay
    (Ed. by Norma Millay)   90   52
  Shakespeare Yet   92   189
    Shakespeare: From "Richard II"
      to "Henry V,"
      by Derek Traversi
    Shakespearean Tragedy
      & The Elizabethan Compromise,
      by Paul N. Siegel
    Elizabethans at Home,
      by Lu Emily Pearson
    Shakespeare: Modern Essays in Criticism
      (Ed. by Leonard F. Dean)
  In Defense of Ignorance, by Karl Shapiro   98   168

BOOKS REVIEWED
    Heroes and Heroines   71   97
    An American Takes a Walk   89   110
    The Self-Made Man   96   230
    The Boy from Iowa   101   356
    The Fascination of the Abomination   104   380
    Poems: New and Selected   112   194
    From Zero to the Absolute   114   113
    Fifty Poems Fifty   119   99
    The Mother's Breast & The Father's House   126   219

ARTICLES ABOUT
    The Farmer and the Poet,
      by Karl Shapiro   98   170

WHITTIER, JOHN GREENLEAF
ARTICLES ABOUT
    Rev. of *The Fields Were Green*,
      by George Arms   84   98
    [Note]   91   140

WHITTINGTON, ROBERT
POEMS
    The Squirrels   53   16
    The Vacation   60   198
    The Poet Becomes One
      of the Shovels   72   76

WHITWORTH, JOHN
ARTICLES ABOUT
    A Letter from Britain [II],
      by William Logan   157   290

WICHMAN, JULIET RICE
POEMS
    Revelation   38   137

WICKER, C. V.
BOOKS REVIEWED
    3 Spanish American Poets
      (Tr. with Mary Wicker)
      [Carlos Pellicer]   62   111

WICKER, MARY
BOOKS REVIEWED
    3 Spanish American Poets
      (Tr. with C. V. Wicker)
      [Carlos Pellicer]   62   111

WICKERS, BRIAN
POEMS
    Account   170   283

WICKERT, MAX
POEMS
    Nocturne ("When night falls...")   119   218
    Aubade ("When at night...")   137   19
    From *The Pat Sonnets*

    (1. "Shakespeare in vain...")
    (2. "The urgent Cleopatra...")
    (4. "No one will hint...")
    (5. "By love possessed?...")
    (6. "They cry 'Forever!'...")
    (7. "O these experimental...")
    (8. "That I love you...")
    (9. "The hero heaves a happy...")
    From *The Pat Sonnets*   140   8
    (III, 7: "When in my kitchen...")
    (IV, 8: "There is a darkness...")
    (V, 1: "Each time we meet...")
    (V, 2: "You almost say to me...")
    (V, 3: "This is my rescue...")
    (V, 10: "A common story...")

WICKHAM, ANNA
POEMS
    My Lady Surrenders   9   182
    The Silence
    Sentiments
    Completion
    After Annunciation
    King Alfred and the Peasant Woman   20   198
    A Poet Advises a Change of Clothes

BOOKS REVIEWED
    The Contemplative Quarry   6   252
    The Contemplative Quarry
      and the Man with a Hammer   20   93

WICKHAM, GRACE
POEMS
    One Moment   36   19

WICKLESS, HARRISON
POEMS
    Rejection Slip   144   106

WIDDEMER, MARGARET
POEMS
    The Jester   1   51
    The Beggars
    Teresina's Face   2   167
    The Wakened God   5   73
    Voices of Women   5   215
      A Lost Friend
      The Net
      The Singer at the Gate
      The Last Song of Bilitis
    Youth-Song   11   26
    Vain Hiding
    I Did Not Know
    Prescience
    Romantique   22   21
    Jade Carving   36   137
    Willow   74   147

BOOKS REVIEWED

The Factories with Other Lyrics	7	147
The Old Road to Paradise	14	273
Cross-Currents	20	340
Collected Poems	33	284

WIECK, FRED D.
REVIEWS

The North Sea, by Heinrich Heine		
(Tr. by Vernon Watkins)	81	149

WIEDER, LAURANCE
POEMS

A Gift, for Some Reason	115	393

WIELAND, C. M.
ARTICLES ABOUT

Rev. of Keats and the Daemon King,		
by Werner W. Beyer	70	168

WIENERS, JOHN
BOOKS REVIEWED

The Hotel Wentley Poems	94	408
Ace of Pentacles	105	326

WIGGAM, LIONEL
POEMS

Child of Grass	43	310
The High Hill		
In Spite of This		
For His Father		
Struggle		
Nebulae	46	127
Child of Grass		
Men and Stars		
Mathematics		
Perseus Slew the Monster	60	315
Encounter	62	316
In Praise of Delay		

REVIEWS

Elephants at War, by Thomas W. Duncan	50	57

BOOKS REVIEWED

Landscape with Figures	50	110

WIGGIN, KATE DOUGLAS
BOOKS REVIEWED

To Mother [Intro.]	14	281

WILBORN, WILLIAM
POEMS

The Disconsolate Cowboy	137	332
For Aunt Lizzie		
On the Uncompleted Madonna		
of Michelangelo in the National Gallery	157	125
Of Arms	161	276

WILBUR, RICHARD
POEMS

Ceremony	71	231
A Simile for Her Smile		
The Death of a Toad		
Five Women Bathing in Moonlight		
Wellfleet: The House		
Conjuration		
Museum Piece		
Driftwood	73	125
We		
To an American Poet Just Dead		
Weather Bird		
Castles and Distances	76	311
A Courtyard Thaw		
"A World Without Objects		
Is a Sensible Emptiness"		
Part of a Letter		
A Chronic Condition	81	87
Marginalia	83	265
Lamarck Elaborated		
A Plain Song for Comadre		
Gemini	98	275
To Ishtar		
Hamlen Brook	141	25
Trolling for Blues	151	192
Three Riddles from Symphosius	152	1
Under a Tree		
Worlds		

TRANSLATIONS

Poems by René Char	87	316
From Tartuffe, by Molière [I: ii-v]	98	369
From Tartuffe, by Molière		
[From Act III]	101	133
Villon: Ballade of the Ladies of Time Past	105	81
From Andromache, Act II,		
by Jean Racine	136	31

REVIEWS

Poems 1943-1947, by C. Day Lewis	74	114
A Fountain in Kentucky,		
by John Frederick Nims	77	105
Collected Poems 1955, by Robert Graves	87	175

BOOKS REVIEWED

The Beautiful Changes	71	221
Ceremony and Other Poems	82	37
Things of This World	88	398
The Misanthrope (Tr.)		
Advice to a Prophet and Other Poems	100	37
Advice to a Prophet and Other Poems	100	40
Antiworlds, by Andrei Voznesensky		
(Tr. with others)	110	40
Walking to Sleep	115	422
The School for Wives, by Molière (Tr.)	120	230
The Mind-Reader	130	41
New and Collected Poems	154	99

ARTICLES ABOUT

Rev. of Whomp and Moonshiver,		
by Thomas Whitbread	143	228

WILCOX, ELLA WHEELER
ARTICLES ABOUT
The Enemies We Have Made,
by Harriet Monroe
[*The Dial*]   4   61

WILCOX, WENDELL
ARTICLES
A Note on Stein and Abstraction   55   254

WILD, PAYSON S.
BOOKS REVIEWED
Idylls of the Skillet Fork   17   100

WILD, PETER
POEMS
Campers   115   171
Granite Mtns.
A Day Lined with Cork
Poem ("There are no medals...")   120   201
The Buffalo
The Turkoman   124   312

BOOKS REVIEWED
Terms and Renewals   121   343
Fat Man Poems   123   34
Cochise   125   166

WILDE, IRENE
POEMS
The Magic Flute   55   239

WILDE, OSCAR
ARTICLES ABOUT
Oscar Wilde's Poetry as Art History,
by Edouard Roditi   67   322

WILDER, AMOS N.
POEMS
A Hard Death   107   168

REVIEWS
Before the Brave and
First Will and Testament,
by Kenneth Patchen   56   32
A Street in Bronzeville,
by Gwendolyn Brooks   67   164

BOOKS REVIEWED
The Spiritual Aspects of the New Poetry   57   49
Modern Poetry and the Christian Tradition   86   108

WILDER, CHARLOTTE (ELIZABETH)
POEMS
The Last Hour   24   200
Of Persons Not Alive   39   303
City Streets   47   198
To Beauty
Sanctuary   52   202

BOOKS REVIEWED
Mortal Sequence   55   217

WILDER, DORIS (ROSALIND)
POEMS
Street at Night   37   315

WILDER, REX
POEMS
René Underground   160   29
Still Life   163   275
Screened Porch, Druid Hills   168   104

WILDER, THORNTON
ARTICLES
James Joyce (1882-1941)   57   370

WILENSKI, REGINALD H.
ARTICLES
Modern German Poetry—I
[Ferdinand Hardekopf]   5   178
Modern German Poetry—II
[Hugo von Hofmannsthal,
Richard Schaukal, Rainer Maria Rilke]   5   234

ARTICLES ABOUT
Correspondence
from Ernest W. Nelson   6   208

WILHELM, RICHARD
ARTICLES ABOUT
Rev. of *The I Ching
or Books of Changes*
(Tr. by Cary F. Baynes)   83   205

WILJER, ROBERT
POEMS
Moose   136   72
Cheerio   139   20
Quick Dip   150   26
Afterward
Esthetic Surgery   153   297

WILK, MELVIN
POEMS
Mornings on the Air at Ten   162   206

WILKES, JOHN
ARTICLES ABOUT
The Poetry of Charles Churchill: Part I,
by Yvor Winters   98   44
The Poetry of Charles Churchill: Part II,
by Yvor Winters   98   104

WILKINS, ERNEST HATCH
BOOKS REVIEWED
*Petrarch at Vaucluse:
Letters in Verse and Prose* (Tr.)   94   350

WILKINSON, ANNE
BOOKS REVIEWED
The Hangman Ties the Holly — 89 — 64
The Collected Poems of...
and a Prose Memoir
(Ed. by A. J. M. Smith) — 114 — 335

WILKINSON, FLORENCE
POEMS
Our Lady of Idleness — 3 — 82
Latin Quarter Ways — 7 — 187
Students
The Little Cafe
Blanche of the Quarter
Her Death — 16 — 22
The Hope of Heaven
Speech
Don Juan in Portugal — 19 — 78

WILKINSON, MARGUERITE
[See also GRAVES, HARLEY, pseud.]
POEMS
The Charwoman — 7 — 79
Birth
Summer in Coronado — 8 — 229

ARTICLES
Correspondence: A Confession — 12 — 56
Correspondence: Poems in
"The Touchstone" — 17 — 229
Correspondence: Mr. Wheelock's Book — 21 — 339

BOOKS REVIEWED
In Vivid Gardens — 2 — 26
Golden Songs of the Golden State (Ed.) — 14 — 281
New Voices—An Introduction
to Contemporary Poetry — 15 — 224
Bluestone — 19 — 158
The Great Dream — 23 — 48
Citadels — 29 — 223

ARTICLES ABOUT
Marguerite Wilkinson, by Harriet Monroe — 31 — 332

WILL, FREDERIC
POEMS
Subaquatic — 107 — 85
In Time of Tapping
After Keats
In Memorium
Né en Illinois
For a Childhood
Three from China — 109 — 77
The Scholar
Lo-Fu
Intercult Talk
For Mike Quill — 111 — 229
Circe — 115 — 6

REVIEWS
Roots and Branches and *As Testimony:*
The Poem and the Scene,
by Robert Duncan — 106 — 427
Words, by Robert Creeley — 111 — 256

BOOKS REVIEWED
A Wedge of Words — 102 — 42
Metaphrasis: An Anthology
from the University of Iowa
Translation Workshop 1964-1965 (Ed.) — 109 — 345
Planets — 111 — 43
Literature Inside Out:
Ten Speculative Essays — 111 — 203

WILLETT, JOHN
BOOKS REVIEWED
Bertolt Brecht: Poems 1913-56
(Ed. with Ralph L. Manheim) — 137 — 220

WILLETTS, RONALD FREDERICK
BOOKS REVIEWED
Ion (Tr.), in *The Complete Greek Tragedies:*
Euripides III (Ed. by David Grene
and Richmond Lattimore) — 95 — 190

WILLEY, ROSEMARY
POEMS
All the Needs — 161 — 221

WILLIAMS, AUBREY
BOOKS REVIEWED
Pope's Dunciad,
A Study of Its Meaning — 88 — 277

WILLIAMS, B. Y.
POEMS
Inscription for the West Gate — 55 — 70

WILLIAMS, BERTHA
POEMS
Song ("I would kneel...") — 46 — 191

WILLIAMS, C. K.
POEMS
Sleeping Over — 103 — 364
Innings — 118 — 78
The Undead
Clay Out of Silence
The Rampage
Claws — 120 — 354

BOOKS REVIEWED
Lies — 119 — 99
I Am the Bitter Name — 121 — 292
Tar — 144 — 345
Flesh and Blood — 151 — 419
Poems 1963-1983 — 154 — 29

A Dream of Mind   163   158
Selected Poems   170   90

WILLIAMS, CHARLES
BOOKS REVIEWED
    Poetry at Present   36   350
    The Region of the Summer Stars   79   103

WILLIAMS, CLINTON
POEMS
    Christmas: 1945   67   130
    Utah West
    Double Canfield
    Chicago Style
    U.S.O.
    Birds Everywhere
    Oysters Have Private Lives
    The Quest   68   251
    Trolley Stop

WILLIAMS, DAVID PARK
ARTICLES
    The Background of The Pisan Cantos   73   216

WILLIAMS, ED
ARTICLES ABOUT
    Towards an Autobiography:
        The Childish Background (I),
        by William Carlos Williams   72   147
    Towards an Autobiography:
        The Childish Background (II),
        by William Carlos Williams   72   264
    Notes Towards an Autobiography:
        The Childish Background (III),
        by William Carlos Williams   74   94

WILLIAMS, ELLEN
BOOKS REVIEWED
    Harriet Monroe and the Poetry Renaissance:
        The First Ten Years of Poetry, 1912-22   131   39

WILLIAMS, ELVA
POEMS
    Introversion   78   87
    Poem ("Try not trying...")
    After Lautréamont

WILLIAMS, FRANCIS HOWARD
POEMS
    I Walked in the Open   5   113

WILLIAMS, GWYN
BOOKS REVIEWED
    The Rent That's Due to Love (Tr.)   77   351

WILLIAMS, HUGO
POEMS
    Waiting To Go On   146   219
    Unfinished Poem

BOOKS REVIEWED
    Symptoms of Loss   109   126

WILLIAMS, JAMES
POEMS
    Arrival   166   103

WILLIAMS, JOHN
POEMS
    The Wall   74   319

BOOKS REVIEWED
    The Broken Landscape   76   302

WILLIAMS, JONATHAN
BOOKS REVIEWED
    The Empire Finals at Verona   97   114
    In England's Green &   102   182
    An Ear in Bartram's Tree:
        Selected Poems 1957-1967   117   331

WILLIAMS, LEW
BOOKS REVIEWED
    The Nameless   61   516

WILLIAMS, LORING
BOOKS REVIEWED
    Selected Poems   103   324

WILLIAMS, MILLER
POEMS
    The Girl   100   16
    On the Reburial of a Second Lieutenant
    For J W, on His Marriage in the Faith 102   376
    For Rebecca, For Whom Nothing Has Been
        Written Page After Page   132   276
    Style
    The Woman in the Room
    Love and How It Becomes Important
        in Our Day to Day Lives
    Evening: A Studio in Rome
    Logos   139   286
    A Short Play
    Trying
    Rebecca at Play
    Birth of the Blues
    A Poem for Emily   145   219
    The Aging Actress Sees Herself a Starlet
        on the Late Show   148   156
    Tearing Down the Hotel
    On a Trailways Bus a Man Who Holds
        His Head Strangely Speaks to
        the Seat Beside Him

TRANSLATIONS
    Poems by Giuseppe Gioachino Belli   136   5

BOOKS REVIEWED
    A Circle of Stone   106   369

So Long at the Fair   113   188
The Only World There Is   119   234
Distractions   140   293
Imperfect Love   150   226

WILLIAMS, NORMAN
BOOKS REVIEWED
The Unlovely Child   149   31

WILLIAMS, OSCAR [Pseud.]
POEMS
Under the Sun   16   300
  To One Unknown
  O My Love
  My Greatness
  Mood
  Chiaroscuros
  Revenge
Golden Darkness   18   202
  There Was a Time
  Clouds and Waves
  Cobwebs
  Grey
  Rains
  The Golden Fleece
  Because
  Motes
  The Subway Is Lit
  The Bubble
  The Return
A Morning in the 20th Century   51   312
The Past Is Dragging Statues   52   328
  The Spritely Dead
  Independence Day
  The Dream
  "Why the Sea Is Salt"
  Portrait of Reality
  Man and Squirrel
  Summer Day
Song for December 24th   53   128
Movie   54   250
On the Summer Sky the Airship Hangs
Wooden Horse of Myth
Three Men Around a Golden Coin
Purely Personal Poem   55   300
The Gaze
Man, Frightening Animal
As I Lie Both Awake and Asleep   60   242
The Bali Stone Bicycle
Lines at Night
The Final Stand
The Accountable   61   583
Man and Storm
The Shuttle
War Poem
Written in Stone
The Hub
The Red Sea Crossing   63   188
On Rising in the Morning

Chant   64   317
The First Born
Ballad of the Loser
I See the Garden
The Paper in the Meadow
On the Roof
The Hunter
Poem ("This is what we...")
The Catch
Poet   81   88

REVIEWS
The Silver Stallion   18   223
  Young Girl and Other Poems,
    by Hildegarde Flanner
  Poems for Men, by John Austin
  Star-Drift,
    by Brian Padraic O'Seasnain
  Poems and Essays, by Alfred Hitch
  Moods of Manhattan,
    by Louise Mallinckrodt Kueffner
  The Blue Crane, by Ivan Swift
  High Company, by Harry Lee
  A Music-Teacher's Note-Book,
    by Henry Bellamann
Letter to a Comrade, by Joy Davidman   54   33
New Directions, 1942
  (Ed. by James Laughlin)   61   693

BOOKS REVIEWED
The Golden Darkness   20   157
In Gossamer Grey
The Man Coming Toward You   56   214
New Poems: 1940 (Ed.)   58   215
New Poems 1942 (Ed.)   60   288
New Poems: 1943 (Ed.)   64   86
New Poems 1944: An Anthology
  of American and British Verse
  with a Selection of Poems
  from the Armed Forces (Ed.)   65   269
Workshop: A Little Anthology
  of Student Verse Together with Excerpts
  from Lectures on Poetry   65   283
That's All That Matters   67   155
The War Poets, an Anthology of the
  War Poetry of the 20th Century (Ed.)   67   344
A Little Treasury of Modern Poetry (Ed.)   69   109
A Little Treasury of Great Poetry (Ed.)   72   336
A Little Treasury of British Poetry (Ed.)   81   191
The Silver Treasury of Light Verse (Ed.)   91   124
I. A. Richards and Oscar Williams
  [Recording]   101   275
The Mentor Book of Major American Poets
  (Ed. with Edwin Honig)   103   261
The Mentor Book of Major British Poets
  from William Blake
  to Dylan Thomas (Ed.)   104   245
Master Poems of the English Language (Ed.)   109   345

WILLIAMS, PHILIP LEE
POEMS
Cinnamon Toast 166   264

WILLIAMS, TENNESSEE
[THOMAS LANIER WILLIAMS]
POEMS
The Shuttle 50   142
  This Hour
    My Love Was Light
We Have Not Long To Love 157   289

BOOKS REVIEWED
Five Young American Poets: Third Series, 1944
  (With Eve Merriam, John Frederick Nims,
  Jean Garrigue, and Alejandro Carrión)   66   95
In the Winter of Cities 90   256
Orpheus Descending, with Battle of Angels   93   402
Suddenly Last Summer

WILLIAMS, THOMAS LANIER
[See WILLIAMS, TENNESSEE]

WILLIAMS, WIGHTMAN
BOOKS REVIEWED
A Blear Ball 68   166
My Country Dreams 77   114

WILLIAMS, WILLIAM CARLOS
POEMS
Peace on Earth 2   93
Sicilian Emigrant's Song:
Postlude
Proof of Immortality
Root Buds 6   62
  The Shadow
  Metric Figure
  Sub Terra
  Slow Movement
  A Confidence
Love-Song 9   81
Naked
Marriage
Apology
Summer Song
The Old Worshipper
History 10   194
Smell!
Le Médécin Malgré Lui 12   192
Broken Windows 13   300
  Berket and the Stars
  The Young Laundryman
  Time the Hangman
  Complete Destruction
  The Poor
  A Friend of Mine
  The Gentle Man
  To Be Closely Written...
  The Soughing Wind

Epitaph ("An old willow...")
Spring
Stroller
Memory of April
Play
Lines
The Dark Day
Thursday
Man in a Room
A Goodnight 17   182
Wild Orchard 19   200
The Lonely Street
Spouts
The Widow's Lament in Springtime
The Unfrocked Priest 36   194
Poem ("As the cat...")
The Botticellian Trees 37   266
"That's the American Style" 43   I
  The Flowers Alone
  The Locust Tree in Flower
  Tree and Sky
  The Centenarian
  4th of July
  Sea-Trout and Butterfish
  An Old Song
  A Foot-Note
An Elegy for D. H. Lawrence 45   311
Item 46   134
To an Elder Poet 49   69
Autumn 51   4
Africa
Weasel Snout
Illegitimate Things 54   295
The Poet and His Poems
Defiance to Cupid
A Cold Front
The Forgotten City
In Chains
Raleigh Was Right 56   69
The Observer 57   125
From a Window
River Rhyme
The World Narrowed to a Point
A Fond Farewell
Fertile
The Unknown
Burning the Christmas Greens 63   207
From Paterson: Book II 71   30
Lear 72   59
The Three Graces 75   88
Paterson, Book V: The River of Heaven   81   89
The Orchestra 81   159
For Eleanor and Bill Monohan 82   82
Of Asphodel: Coda 84   249
Of Asphodel (Book 2) 86   99
From Paterson V 92   341
Some Simple Measures in the American Idiom
  and the Variable Foot 93   386

3 Stances   95   325
  ("Elaine")
  ("Erica")
  ("Emily")
Stormy   101   141
Cézanne   103   253
The Moral
Proof of Immortality   121   38

ARTICLES
  Correspondence:
    On First Opening The Lyric Year
    [Poem]   2   114
  Notes from a Talk on Poetry   14   211
  Correspondence: Riddles and Runes
    [Poem]   16   173
  Correspondence: Dr. Williams
    and the English Attitude
    [F. R. Leavis]   44   174
  Correspondence:
    A Warm Word for Daiches   58   112
  Towards an Autobiography:
    The Childish Background (I)
    [Ed Williams]   72   147
  Towards an Autobiography:
    The Childish Background (II)
    [Ed Williams]   72   264
  Notes Towards an Autobiography:
    The Childish Background (III)
    [Arlo Bates, Ezra Pound,
    W. B. Yeats, Ed Williams]   74   94
  A Letter
    [Activist Poets,
    Luis de Gongora y Argote]   78   107
  Wallace Stevens   87   234
  [Note]   93   416

REVIEWS
  Discrete Series, by George Oppen   44   220
  Red Renaissance; Thinking of Russia;
    Salvation; and Road to Utterly,
    by H. H. Lewis   47   227
  55 Poems, by Louis Zukofsky   60   338
  A Mask of Mercy, by Robert Frost   72   38
  Complete Poems, by Carl Sandburg   78   345
  In Defense of the Earth and
    One Hundred Poems from the Chinese,
    by Kenneth Rexroth
    [Tu Fu]   90   180
  Chapman's Homer: The Iliad (I) and
    The Odyssey (II)
    (Ed. by Allardyce Nicoll)   91   60

BOOKS REVIEWED
  Al Que Quiere!   12   38
  Kora in Hell: Improvisations   17   329
  Sour Grapes   20   216

Manikin Number Two   23   103
Spring and All   24   45
Imagist Anthology 1930
  (With Richard Aldington,
  John Cournos, H. D., John Gould
  Fletcher, F. S. Flint, Ford Madox Ford,
  James Joyce, and D. H. Lawrence)   36   213
The Cod Head   43   225
Collected Poems 1921-1931   44   103
An Early Martyr and Other Poems   48   105
Adam & Eve & the City   49   94
The Complete
  Collected Poems (1906- 1938)   54   326
Contemporary Poets Series
  [Recording]   61   519
The Wedge   66   35
Paterson (Book I)   69   277
Paterson (Book II)   74   37
The Clouds, Aigeltinger, Russia, Etc.
Paterson (Book III)   76   39
The Autobiography of...   80   89
Paterson, Parts I-IV   80   276
The Desert Music and Other Poems   85   351
Leaves of Grass One Hundred Years After
  (Ed. by Milton Hindus)
  [Contributor]   87   183
Journey to Love   87   366
In the American Grain   90   315
The Selected Letters of...
  (Ed. by John C. Thirlwall)   92   174
Paterson, Book Five   94   127
I Wanted to Write a Poem
Intro. to "A" 1-12,
  by Louis Zukofsky   97   102
Pictures from Breughel and Other Poems 101   360
The Collected Later Poems by...   103   316
The William Carlos Williams Reader
  (Ed. by M. L. Rosenthal)   111   41
The Collected Poems: Volume I, 1909-1939
  (Ed. by A. Walton Litz
  and Christopher MacGowan)   150   286

ARTICLES ABOUT
  The Glittering Metropolis,
    by Harriet Monroe   14   30
  Correspondence
    from Robert McAlmon   18   54
  Rev. of New Directions 1942
    (Ed. by James Laughlin)   61   693
  Rev. of New Directions 1944
    (Ed. by James Laughlin)   66   161
  Rev. of The Selected Poems 1912-1944,
    by Alfred Kreymborg   66   215
  Rev. of Transfigured Night,
    by Byron Vazakas   69   158
  [Note]   73   55

Rev. of *William Carlos Williams,*
   by Vivienne Koch   76   177
Poetry on Records,
   by Harry T. Moore   79   353
Rev. of *William Carlos Williams,*
   by Vivienne Koch   80   291
Williams and His Muse,
   by Frederick J. Hoffman   84   23
Rev. of *"A" 1-12,* by Louis Zukofsky   97   102
Rev. of *All: The Collected Short Poems,*
   by Louis Zukofsky   107   52
Rev. of *Poets of Reality:*
   Six Twentieth-Century Writers,
   by J. Hillis Miller   110   254
Ghosts and Benedictions,
   by Hugh Kenner   113   109
Review by Gilbert Sorrentino   116   110
Rev. of *Duino Elegies,*
   by Rainer Maria Rilke
   (Tr. by David Young)   134   234
Gists and Piths: From the Letters
   of Pound and Williams,
   by J. Laughlin   139   229
Poets Aloud, by Donald Hall   139   297
Rev. of *Poetry and the World,*
   by Robert Pinsky   156   297

WILLIAMS-ELLIS, A.
BOOKS REVIEWED
   An Anatomy of Poetry   27   283

WILLIAMSON, ALAN
POEMS
   April 5, 1968   115   259
   Aubade, Reconstructed in Tranquility
   The First Spring Nights   119   252
   Temporary Earth
   Customs of the Barbarians   123   324
   Childless Couple   132   148
   Sandy
   Old Toys Come Back   139   19
   The Chair   145   275
   Puccini Dying   170   87

REVIEWS
   Beginners and Renewers   115   281
   Prometheus Bound, by Robert Lowell
   The Company of Children,
      by Barry Spacks
   The Storm, by William Pitt Root
   Speech, for Instance,
      by Sidney Goldfarb
   Five Poets   118   169
   Odes, by Paul Carroll
   The Invention of New Jersey,
      by Jack Anderson
   Dragging the Main, by David Ray
   Root and Branch, by Jon Stallworthy

We Weep for Our Strangeness,
   by Dennis Schmitz
Pity for the Clear Word   119   296
   Collected Poems, by James Wright
   Spring Shade: Poems 1931-1970,
      by Robert Fitzgerald
   Trying To Come Apart,
      by James Den Boer
   Fruits & Vegetables, by Erica Jong
"'Fool,' Said My Muse to Me..."   133   100
   Hello, Darkness: The Collected Poems
      of L. E. Sissman
      (Ed. by Peter Davison)
   Selected Poems, by Margaret Atwood
   Charon's Cosmology,
      by Charles Simic
   A Call in the Midst of the Crowd,
      by Alfred Corn
In a Middle Style   135   348
   The Pregnant Man,
      by Robert Phillips
   The Bus to Veracruz,
      by Richard Shelton
   The Tale of Sunlight,
      by Gary Soto
   Good Night, Willie Lee,
      I'll See You in the Morning,
      by Alice Walker
Dim Human Avenues   137   169
   Ashes: Poems New and Old and
      Seven Years from Somewhere,
      by Philip Levine
   The Woman on the Bridge
      Over the Chicago River,
      by Allen Grossman
   The Everlastings, by Norman Dubie
   Crossing, by John Matthias
Confession and Tragedy   142   170
   The Collected Poems,
      by Sylvia Plath
      (Ed. by Ted Hughes)
   The Complete Poems,
      by Anne Sexton
      [Maxine Kumin]

BOOKS REVIEWED
   Presence   143   163
   The Muse of Distance   153   30

WILLIAMSON, EDWARD
ARTICLES
   Contemporary Italian Poetry
      [Aldo Palazzeschi, Corrado Govoni,
      Guido Gozzano, Dino Campana,
      Giuseppe Ungaretti, Eugenio Montale]   79   159
   Contemporary Italian Poetry
      [Umberto Saba, Sergio Solmi,
      Libero de Libero, Salvatore Quasimodo,
      Leonardo Sinisgalli, Aldo Capasso]   79   233

WILLIAMSON, GEORGE
POEMS
The Nameless One 24 81

REVIEWS
T. S. Eliot: The Design of His Poetry,
by Elizabeth Drew 75 112

BOOKS REVIEWED
A Reader's Guide to T. S. Eliot 82 287
Six Metaphysical Poets: A Reader's Guide
[John Donne, George Herbert,
Richard Crashaw, Abraham Cowley,
Henry Vaughan, Andrew Marvell] 112 356

WILLIAMSON, GREG
POEMS
Picnic in the Park 158 270
Drawing Hands
Taxidermy 164 282
The Mysterious Stranger 165 194
The Counterfeiter

WILLIAMSON, HUGH ROSS
BOOKS REVIEWED
The Poetry of T. S. Eliot 42 44

WILMER, CLIVE
ARTICLES ABOUT
A Letter from Britain [II],
by William Logan 157 290

WILNER, ELEANOR
POEMS
Epitaph ("Though only a girl...") 126 162
Unstrung
For a Poet of Nature
Water Lace and White Eyes

BOOKS REVIEWED
Sarah's Choice 156 224
Otherwise 164 285

WILSON, ADELAIDE
POEMS
A Song of Death 25 86

WILSON, ALBERT FREDERICK
POEMS
Woodrow Wilson 16 314
On Clyburn Hill a Lectern Is 25 125

BOOKS REVIEWED
The Township Line 17 343

WILSON, ANNE ELIZABETH
POEMS
Recompense 18 145
The Sweet Lady

BOOKS REVIEWED
Eager Footsteps 27 226

WILSON, CALVIN DILL
POEMS
The Old Gods 12 124
Phantom Hoofs 36 133

**WILSON, CHARLOTTE [Pseud.]
[See BAKER, KARLE WILSON]**

WILSON, CHARLOTTE A.
POEMS
Poem ("Adrift on a high...") 94 238

WILSON, DAVID HAWXHURST
REVIEWS
Language and Reality,
by Wilbur Marshall Urban 56 285

WILSON, EDMUND, JR.
POEMS
G. H. Q., January, 1919 17 78
Not Here
Sleeping and Waking 47 243
Land's Edge 50 186
Provincetown, 1936
Past Midnight
Morning
Three Women 55 182

BOOKS REVIEWED
Poets, Farewell! 35 222
The Triple Thinkers 52 144
Wilson's Night Thoughts 102 118
Patriotic Gore 102 341

ARTICLES ABOUT
[Note on misprint] 50 360
MacLeish Revisited,
by William Pritchard 141 291

WILSON, EDWARD
POEMS
The Living Corpse 132 256
That Weekend Our Team Won
Fingers 133 332
Dogwoods 137 8

WILSON, GRAEME
TRANSLATIONS
Poems by Hagiwara Sakutaro 116 370
Poem by Sei Shonagon 153 298

BOOKS REVIEWED
Face at the Bottom of the World,
by Hagiwara Sakutaro (Tr.) 118 234

WILSON, JOHN
POEMS
Southern California Snow   145   144

WILSON, JOHN MINNICH
POEMS
Black Astronomy   36   316

WILSON, KEITH
POEMS
From *Graves Registry*   109   302
Note to a Sister
Classes
A Wedding Poem   113   23
The Near Miss
Sacred Fire Mountain

BOOKS REVIEWED
Sketches for a New Mexico Hill Town   109   407
Midwatch   126   172

WILSON, LO VERNE
POEMS
Epitaph ("Let it be written...")   42   257

WILSON, MARGARET ADELAIDE
POEMS
Light Years   29   312

WILSON, MILES
POEMS
Body   160   8
Stripper   162   82

WILSON, PAT
BOOKS REVIEWED
The Bright Sea   81   335

WILSON, ROB
POEMS
Ananda Air, III   138   322
Nothing

WILSON, ROBERT BURNS
ARTICLES ABOUT
Correspondence from "A Kentuckian"   20   171

WILSON, ROBLEY, JR.
POEMS
The Islands   132   23
On Not Knowing the Names
  of the Flowers in Montana   134   260
The Suspense of Meeting
The Opera   136   207
Porcupines
A Literary Lesson   137   279
Endsong   139   27
Desire

Three Dreams   140   20
Recluse
The Mozart Broadcast
In Early Morning Traffic   142   25
A Lady in Charcoal
Keys
The Mornings I Oversleep   144   228
The Summer Place
Hanging Curtains   148   142
Sunday at the Shore
What You See   151   193
Company Cafeteria   151   401
Vanities   155   273

BOOKS REVIEWED
Kingdoms of the Ordinary   152   161

WILSON, ROMER
POEMS
From *A May Pastoral*   38   74

WILSON, RONALD
POEMS
Greek Torso   158   193
An Old Woman Gives Away Her Things   158   254
Fall
Guide to Homes   166   197

WILSON, STANLEY KIDDER
BOOKS REVIEWED
Blind Dawn   62   50

WILSON, T. C.
POEMS
The Flower   41   141
Gettysburg   42   266
When the Light Is Gone
Spring Morning
In 1934   46   194
To Rimbaud   47   313
There Comes an End   48   72
  Tear Down the Walls
  Poem ("To sing a song...")
When the Time Is Up   55   122
Song ("The nuptial fetes...")

REVIEWS
The Dark Land,
  by Kathleen Tankersley Young   42   50
Selected Poems and
  Common Sense About Poetry,
  by L. A. G. Strong   42   295
The Pamphlet Poets   43   225
  Two Poems, by Dudley Fitts
  Two Stories, by John Kemmerer
  A Statement, by Kay Boyle
  The Pepper Trees,
    by Kathleen Tankersley Young

Wherefore: Peace,
  by Raymond Ellsworth Larson
Chicago Side-Show, by Albert Halper
Before March,
  by Archibald MacLeish
A Country House, by Sara Teasdale
Rainbow,
  by Sylvia Townsend Warner
Prehistoric Burials,
  by Siegfried Sassoon
The Cod Head,
  by William Carlos Williams
Frescoes for Mr. Rockefeller's City,
  by Archibald MacLeish
Hellenic, by Martha Champion
In Praise of Mara,
  by Kimball Flaccus
The Brimming Cup,
  by Carlyle MacIntyre
Jerusalem the Golden and *Testimony,*
  by Charles Reznikoff   44   338
Two English Poets   44   343
  The Walls of Glass,
    by A. S. J. Tessimond
  Spring Encounter, by John Pudney
Guest Book, by Witter Bynner   47   101
An Early Martyr and Other Poems,
  by William Carlos Williams   48   105
Calling Western Union,
  by Genevieve Taggard   50   106
Biography for Traman,
  by Winfield Townley Scott   50   224
Poems 1929-1936, by Dudley Fitts   51   107
Poems, by Louis MacNeice   51   339
Letters from Iceland,
  by W. H. Auden
  and Louis MacNeice   52   39
The Triple Thinkers,
  by Edmund Wilson   52   144
A New Anthology of Modern Poetry
  (Ed. by Selden Rodman)   53   46
Dead Reckoning, by Kenneth Fearing   54   26
A Turning Wind, by Muriel Rukeyser   55   214

ARTICLES ABOUT
Correspondence
  from Kimball Flaccus   53   162

WIMAN, CHRISTIAN
POEMS
  Elsewhere   166   192
  Living Room

ARTICLES
Finishes: Notes
  on Ambition and Survival
  [John Berryman, Robert Lowell,
  Seamus Heaney, John Ruskin,
  John Keats, Ivor Gurney]   169   217

WIMSATT, W. K., JR.
REVIEWS
  Gay in the Mystery   87   308
    Creative Intuition in Art and Poetry,
      by Jacques Maritain
    The Situation of Poetry,
      by Jacques and Raissa Maritain

BOOKS REVIEWED
  The Verbal Icon   87   312
  Literary Criticism: A Short History
    (Ed. with Cleanth Brooks)   91   320

**WINCHELSEA, ANNE
[COUNTESS OF]**
BOOKS REVIEWED
  Poems (Ed. by John Middleton Murry)   34   111

WING, KLEBER
POEMS
  Hawaiian Love Song   69   196

ARTICLES ABOUT
  [Note]   69   236

WING TEK LUM
POEMS
  To the Old Masters   140   85

WINSLOW, ANN
BOOKS REVIEWED
  Trial Balances (Ed.)   48   172

WINSLOW, WALKER
POEMS
  Pacific Blooms   46   314
  Flower Girl
  Three Leis for a Parting

WINSTON, CARLETON
POEMS
  From Without the Fence   51   255

WINTERS, ANNE
POEMS
  Paolo Uccello   118   8
  Alternate Lives   122   71
  Pregnant Woman Reading Letter   126   88
  Suburban Hours
  Demolition Crane   130   280
  The Hall of Armor
  Still Life with Pots
  Readings in the Navigators

TRANSLATIONS
  Poem by Robert Marteau   134   35

ARTICLES
  The Poetry of Robert Marteau
    [Marc Chagall]   134   46

BOOKS REVIEWED
  Salamander: Selected Poems
    of Robert Marteau (Tr.)   137 220
  The Key to the City   149 31

WINTERS, (A.) YVOR
[A. Y. WINTERS]
POEMS
  Monodies   14 301
    Montezuma
    Wild Horses
    On the Mesa
    Concerning Blake
    The Old Weep Gently
    Little Rabbit
  Two Songs of Advent   17 142
  Hawks' Eyes
  The Far Voice
  The Walker
  Ballad ("I sat alone...")
  The Immobile Wind
  Song for a Small Boy Who Herds Goats
  Ballad of Men
  The Priesthood
  Where My Sight Goes
  Death Goes Before Me
  The Little Deity Alone in the Desert   20 318
  Late Winter
  A Requiem for the Memory of Bees
  Chicago Spring
  Old Spring
  The Silent Days
  Lament, Beside an Acequia,
    for the Wife of Awa-Tsireh
  "The Fragile Season"
  The Schoolmaster at Spring   22 84
  The Schoolmaster and the Queres of the Mines
  The Dry Year
  The Schoolmaster Writes to a Poet
  Static Autumn
  The Solitude of Glass   25 186
  The Upper Meadows
  A Nocturne for October 31st   51 320
  A Summer Commentary
  In Praise of California Wines
  On the Portrait of a Scholar
    of the Italian Renaissance
  Defense of Empire   65 59
  An Epitaph for the American Dead
  Moonlight Alert
  "Aere Caliginoso"
  At the Site of the Murphy Cabin
  To the Holy Spirit   69 138
  Night of Battle
  A Song ("These walls are brown...")
  An Ode ("This was our heritage...")   71 12

TRANSLATIONS
  Poems by Pero Meogo
    and an anonymous Spanish poet   29 302

ARTICLES
  Correspondence: A Poet's Handbook   14 346
  The 16th-Century Lyric
    in England: Part I
    [Barnabe Googe, George Turbervile,
    George Gascoigne]   53 258
  The 16th-Century Lyric
    in England: Part II
    [Thomas Wyatt, Jasper Heywood,
    Philip Sidney, Edmund Spenser,
    Michael Drayton, Fulke Greville]   53 320
  The 16th-Century Lyric
    in England: Part III
    [Thomas Campion, Philip Sidney,
    Ben Jonson, John Donne,
    William Shakespeare]   54 35
  Agnes Lee   54 335
  Correspondence
    [Thomas Howells]   63 291
  Correspondence
    [Winfield Townley Scott]   70 285
  The Poet and the University: A Reply   75 170
  The Poetry of Charles Churchill: Part I
    [John Wilkes, John Milton,
    John Dryden, Alexander Pope,
    William Hogarth]   98 44
  The Poetry of Charles Churchill: Part II
    [William Warburton, John Wilkes]   98 104

REVIEWS
  The Solitary,
    by James Oppenheim   16 49
  Collected Poems
    of Edwin Arlington Robinson   19 278
  The Living Frieze, by Mark Turbyfill   19 337
  The Contemplative Quarry
    and the Man with a Hammer,
    by Anna Wickham   20 93
  Sour Grapes,
    by William Carlos Williams   20 216
  Under the Tree,
    by Elizabeth Madox Roberts   22 45
  Fringe, by Pearl Andelson (Sherry)   23 218
  Observations, by Marianne Moore   26 39
  Streets in the Moon,
    by Archibald MacLeish   29 278
  White Buildings, by Hart Crane   30 47
  Fugitives: An Anthology of Verse
    [T. S. Eliot]   32 102
  Dear Judas, by Robinson Jeffers   35 279
  Tilted Moons, by S. Foster Damon   35 340
  The Noise that Time Makes,
    by Merrill Moore   36 104
  The Bridge, by Hart Crane   36 153

BOOKS REVIEWED
  The Immobile Wind   18 339
  The Magpie's Shadow   20 342

Diadems and Fagots,
  by Olavo Bilac
  and Pierre de Ronsard
  (Tr. with John Meem)   23   113
The Bare Hills   32   41
The Proof   37   225
The Journey and Other Poems   40   163
Before Disaster   45   288
Primitivism and Decadence, a Study of
  American Experimental Poetry   50   173
Twelve Poets of the Pacific (Ed.)   51   48
The Anatomy of Nonsense   63   86
The Giant Weapon   65   43
Edwin Arlington Robinson   70   94
Poets of the Pacific, Second Series (Ed.)   76   104
Three Poems   77   114
Collected Poems   82   151
The Function of Criticism   91   393
Four Poets on Poetry: Essays by R. P.
  Blackmur, Yvor Winters, Marianne Moore,
  and Mark Van Doren
  (Ed. by Don Cameron Allen)   96   382
Collected Poems   98   40
Forms of Discovery   114   113
Edwin Arlington Robinson   120   230

ARTICLES ABOUT
Correspondence from Baker Brownell   19   347
Correspondence
  from Louis Untermeyer   20   168
Convention and Revolt,
  by Jessica Nelson North   34   212
A Note on Yvor Winters,
  by R. P. Blackmur   57   144
The New Intellectualism:
  The Dry Reaction,
  by W. T. Scott   58   86
Correspondence
  from Thomas Howells   63   293
A Glossary of the New Criticism,
  by William Elton   73   232
A Glossary of the New Criticism,
  by William Elton   73   296
The University and the Poet,
  by Hayden Carruth   75   89
Correspondence from Brom Weber
  [Hart Crane]   92   332
Rev. of The Exclusions of a Rhyme,
  by J. V. Cunningham   97   181
Rev. of The Complete Poems
  of Frederick Goddard Tuckerman
  (Ed. by N. Scott Momaday)   107   401
Rev. of Able Was I Ere I Saw Elba,
  by Daniel Hoffman   132   170
Rev. of Poems of R. P. Blackmur   133   290
Allen Tate: A Poet on Poetry, 1924-1944,
  by Ashley Brown   135   103

WIRTSHAFTER, REITZA DINE
[REITZA DINE]
POEMS
  The Shadow and the Sun   43   264
  Envoi
  Ilya   46   140
  The Atom's Range
  Notes of a Naturalist   50   17
    The Inner Zone
    Lost Trails
    Dry Spell
    Night Change

BOOKS REVIEWED
  Fence of Fire   62   50

WIRTZ, DOROTHY
POEMS
  Reflections in the Louvre   73   262

WISTRAND, ROBERT
POEMS
  Poem ("Time will tell...")   55   313
  Marginal Note   62   128
  Report
  Field Hospital   64   138
  Reply
  Asylum
  Footnote to Remorse
  Interval   65   182
  Newsreel

WITEK, TERRI
POEMS
  I Tell You Another Story   154   204

WITHEFORD, HUBERT
BOOKS REVIEWED
  The Falcon Mask   81   335

WITHERBY, DIANA
POEMS
  Institution Child   74   75
  St James' Park

BOOKS REVIEWED
  Poems   86   295

WITT, HAROLD
POEMS
  Photograph of Ghosts   83   13
  The Lately Mockingbird   85   268
  Beasts   86   334
  Notre Dame Perfected by Reflection   88   373
  The Platonist Sees Snakes
    at an Ideal Moment
  Back   90   11
  Botanical Garden

West   91   178
Daphnis
Of Various Errors
Spontaneous Bottle   93   156
Theseus   96   89
Blurred Leaves in the Foreground   115   160

REVIEWS
Givers   118   41
   Body Compass,
      by David Steingass
   A Remembered Darkness,
      by John Ratti
   The Signs Among Us,
      by W. W. Robson
   Nature & Love Poems,
      by Ruth Herschberger
   Givers & Takers, by Jane Mayhall

BOOKS REVIEWED
   Family in the Forest   89   64
   Superman Unbound   90   386
   The Death of Venus   94   117
   Beasts in Clothes   99   384
   Pop. By 1940: 40,000   120   107

WITTE, GEORGE
POEMS
   Gully   155   386
   Thaw
   Totenwald
   Narcissus

WUBBER, DON
POEMS
   Four Poems   78   72
      ("Above the Gates...")
      ("What seeds the mind rolls...")
      ("Never dead, never hung...")
      ("I am the stranger...")

WOESSNER, WARREN
POEMS
   Return from Absolute Zero   118   10
   Operation
   Black Crow
   Laos in the Air
   Getting the Laundry

WOFFORD, PHILIP
POEMS
   Clear Hill to Running Ditch   126   16

WOHLFELD, VALERIE
POEMS
   Thinking the World Visible   158   76

BOOKS REVIEWED
   Thinking the World Visible   166   166

WOJAHN, DAVID
POEMS
   Elegy for James Wright   138   79
   Miracles
   Matins
   Glassworks at Saratoga   145   25
   This Moment
   Pentecost   148   94
   A Fifteenth Anniversary: John Berryman 151   194
   The Novelist   153   321
   The Naming
   White Lanterns   157   20
   Tribute and Ash   163   280
   Homage to Ryszard Kapuściński   164   187
   Zola the Hobbyist: 1895   168   216

REVIEWS
   Short Reviews   146   167
      Love & War, Art & God,
         by Karl Shapiro
      Selected Poems, by John Ciardi
      Black Hair, by Gary Soto
      Second Guesses, by James Richardson
      Days We Would
         Rather Know and Laps,
         by Michael Blumenthal
      Good Trembling, by Baron Wormser
      A Happy Childhood,
         by William Matthews
   Short Reviews   165   219
      Against the Evidence:
         Selected Poems 1934-1994,
         by David Ignatow
      New and Selected Poems: 1971-1994,
         by Stephen Dunn
      My Brother Running and Other Poems,
         by Wesley McNair
      The Glass Hammer: A Southern Childhood,
         by Andrew Hudgins
      Rhapsodies of a Repeat Offender,
         by Wayne Koestenbaum
      The Misunderstanding of Desire,
         by Sophie Cabot Black
      The Struggle to Adore,
         by Alane Rollings
      [Dorothy Bradford]

BOOKS REVIEWED
   Icehouse Lights   143   163
   Glassworks   150   226
   Mystery Train   158   158
   Late Empire   170   37

WOJTYLA, KAROL
[(POPE) JOHN PAUL II]
BOOKS REVIEWED
   Easter Vigil & Other Poems
      (Tr. by Jerzy Peterkiewicz)   136   40

WOLCOTT, DEREK
  [See WALCOTT, DEREK]

WOLF, LEONARD
  POEMS
    The Wild Goose Comes   78   249
    Stood the Arabian Arab Up To Sing
    Cleveland, O.
    Sempiternal Evensong
    Archimago
    The Peacock in the Desert   80   201
    Florentine Sunday Song   82   75
    The Garden
    Classics
    The Yewberry   88   21
    For Mrs. Cadwallader   92   151
    A Praise for the Sun

WOLF, MICHELE
  POEMS
    Man with Picture Frame   163   149
    "The Sleeping Gypsy"   166   255

WOLF, ROBERT (L.)
  POEMS
    Prologue for the Modern Male   23   141
    The Ninth Hour   28   134
    Monastery

  REVIEWS
    Body of This Death, by Louise Bogan   23   335

  BOOKS REVIEWED
    After Disillusion   23   343

  ARTICLES ABOUT
    Once More the Revolution,
      by Harriet Monroe   24   266

WOLFE, HUMBERT
  BOOKS REVIEWED
    The Unknown Goddess   28   108
    Kensington Gardens   30   222
    Lampoons
    Requiem   31   218
    This Blind Rose   34   111
    Cursory Rhymes
    The Uncelestial City   39   54

WOLFERT, HELEN
  POEMS
    They Sleep   42   265

  BOOKS REVIEWED
    Nothing Is a Wonderful Thing   70   165

WOLFF, ADOLF
  POEMS
    Fireflies   8   291

WOLFF, DAVID [Pseud.]
  POEMS
    On Signing Up   48   71
    The City   55   169
    While We Slept   56   316

WOLKER, JIRI
  POEMS
    The Face at the Window
      (Tr. by David Daiches)   55   177

WONG MAY
  POEMS
    Silence   114   365
    Going
    Waiting for God   118   14
    Landscape

  ARTICLES
    Correspondence   120   364

  BOOKS REVIEWED
    A Bad Girl's Book of Animals   115   430

WOOD, CHARLES ERSKINE SCOTT
  POEMS
    The Buddha   14   85
    Kitty
    Songs from "The Adventurer"
    Fuchsias and Geraniums
    A Fallen Pine   23   246
    A Fragment
    A Song ("Life is so short...")
    To His Mare
    The Water-Hole
    Lay Me on the Hill-Top

  BOOKS REVIEWED
    The Poet in the Desert   6   308
    The Poet in the Desert   18   283
    Maia—A Sonnet Sequence

WOOD, CLEMENT
  POEMS
    Spring-Piece   8   15
    The Link
    Seedtime   9   179
    O Dear Brown Lands   11   125
    Coin of the Year
    Berkshires in April   12   14

  ARTICLES
    Correspondence: A Lyrical Challenge
      [Louis Untermeyer]   5   141

  BOOKS REVIEWED
    Glad of Earth   11   281
    The Earth Turns South   15   51

Jehovah   17   167
The Tide Comes In   24   51
Poets of America   27   287
The Craft of Poetry   34   161

WOOD, EVE
POEMS
  Arranged Marriage, China, 1921   164   138

WOOD, FRANK
POEMS
  Chalfont St. Giles   68   253

REVIEWS
  Words and the Man   69   103
    Thirty-One Poems,
      by Rainer Maria Rilke
      (Tr. by Ludwig Lewisohn)
    Wanderpoem, or Angelic Mythamorphosis
      of the City of London,
      by Eugene Jolas
  Rilke and Benvenuta   76.   92
    Rilke and Benvenuta,
      by Madga von Hattingberg
      (Tr. by Cyrus Brooks)
    The Notebooks of Malte Laurids Brigge
      (Tr. by M. D. Herter Norton)

WOOD, JOHN A.
POEMS
  Elegiac Stanza on a Photograph
    of Ethel Rosenberg in Her Kitchen   132   200
  Afternoon with an Aesthete

WOOD, MILDRED CUMMER
POEMS
  Easy Parting   12   259

WOOD, NARCISSE
POEMS
  Praising Her Hands   23   135

WOOD, SALLY
TRANSLATIONS
  Poem by Louis Aragon   67   14

WOOD, SUSAN
POEMS
  Late-Bloomers   148   321
  Eggs
  Distances
  Sunday Nights   150   200
  On Fire

WOODBERRY, GEORGE EDWARD
BOOKS REVIEWED
  The Kingdom of All-Souls,
    and Two Other Poems   3   69

Ideal Passion—Sonnets   11   103
The Roamer and Other Poems   18   44

ARTICLES ABOUT
  Rev. of George Edward Woodberry
    —A Study of His Poetry,
    by Louis V. Ledoux   11   103

WOODCOCK, GEORGE
BOOKS REVIEWED
  The White Island   58   159
  Imagine the South   74   48

ARTICLES ABOUT
  The Poet's Perspectives,
    by D. S. Savage   64   148

WOODS, JOHN
POEMS
  Shape of the Wood   80   200
  The Visits of My Aunt   83   14
  The Old Quarry   83   79
  The Downfall Plot   84   316
  Near Carter's Mill
  The Map of Water   89   215
  Poem by Water
  Poem at Thirty   91   176
  How So Lovely Walks the Wind
  Poem ("Lie closed, my lately...")   94   234
  Two Songs for Lute
  Outcome and Downfall   96   165
  Happily Because April
  Wheel of Saturday   103   292
  Scale
  Terrible Is the Child
  Too Early for Dinner at Donald Hall's
  Animal
  Going to the Field   106   411
  Trying to Keep Out of Trouble   109   369
  What the Organist Knows
  The Dead Soldier
  Now the Singing Is Over
  The Day Shall Be Known for Foxes
  Coming to the Saltlick   113   80
  In the Full of Love
  Looking Up and Down

REVIEWS
  American Child, by Paul Engle   89   122
  In the Winter of Cities,
    by Tennessee Williams   90   256
  The Teeming Catalogue   96   47
    The Cruising Auk,
      by George Johnston
    A Dream of Governors,
      by Louis Simpson
    Valentines to the Wide World,
      by Mona Van Duyn

A Poetry Chronicle   100   404
  Collected Poems, by George Abbe
  A Little Geste, and Other Poems,
    by Daniel G. Hoffman
  The Fortune Teller, by John Holmes
  The New Book/A Book of Torture,
    by Michael McClure
  The Lovemaker, by Robert Mezey
  Shoulder the Sky,
    by E. Merrill Root
  The Tree Witch, by Peter Viereck
  Origin of a Design, by Neil Weiss
Six Poets   104   108
  Absent and Present,
    by Chester Kallman
  Manhattan Pastures,
    by Sandra Hochman
  Glad and Sorry Seasons,
    by Leonard E. Nathan
  Blood and Milk Poems,
    by Ruth Whitman
  Sand Verbena, by Suzanne Gross
  Breathing of First Things,
    by Hy Sobiloff

BOOKS REVIEWED
  The Deaths at Paragon, Indiana   88   183
  On the Morning of Color   100   390
  The Cutting Edge   109   395
  Turning To Look Back   122   168
  Striking the Earth   130   293

WOOL, SANDRA
POEMS
  To a Suitor Rejected:
    Invitation Not To Call   79   200
  For A.H.L.   82   133
  Moses Among the Daughters of Jeraboam
  A Small Boy Thinks About a Contemporary
    with Pigtails and Inhibitions

WOOLF, ROSEMARY
BOOKS REVIEWED
  English Religious Lyric
    in the Middle Ages   115   196

WOOLF, VIRGINIA
ARTICLES ABOUT
  Poems and Pictures,
    by Morton Dauwen Zabel   34   217

WOOLRICH, CORNELL
ARTICLES ABOUT
  Dagger of the Mind, by James Sandoe   68   146

WORDSWORTH, DOROTHY
BOOKS REVIEWED
  The Poetry of...
    (Ed. by Hyman Eigerman)   57   280

ARTICLES ABOUT
  Rev. of Rebels and Conservatives:
    Dorothy and William Wordsworth
    and Their Circle,
    by Amanda M. Ellis   113   262

WORDSWORTH, WILLIAM
BOOKS REVIEWED
  Coleridge's Biographia Literaria
    (With Wordsworth's Preface
    and Essays on Poetry)
    (Ed. by George Sampson)   18   167

ARTICLES ABOUT
  Rev. of Wordsworth and Milton,
    Poets and Prophets. A Study
    of Their Reactions to Political Events,
    by Herbert J. C. Grierson   51   37
  Rev. of Wordsworth: Centenary Studies
    Presented at Cornell
    and Princeton Universities
    (Ed. by Gilbert T. Dunklin)   80   233
  Rev. of The Common Muse
    (Ed. by Vivian De Sola Pinto
    and Allan Edwin Rodway)   91   400
  Rev. of Rebels and Conservatives:
    Dorothy and William Wordsworth
    and Their Circle,
    by Amanda M. Ellis   113   262
  Rev. of Sphere,
    by A. R. Ammons   127   352
  Rev. of Worldly Hopes,
    by A. R. Ammons   141   26
  Rev. of A History of Modern Poetry,
    Vol. II: Modernism and After,
    by David Perkins   151   296
  Rev. of Blue Autumn,
    by Christopher Buckley   159   101

WORMHOUDT, ROBERT
POEMS
  To Her Father   46   71

WORMSER, BARON
POEMS
  Of Small Towns   138   63
  Bureaucrats Investigated
  Numerous Questions
  Servants
  A History of Photography
  "The Spirit that Speaks"
  The Lesser God   139   271
  Letter from New England
  Passing Significance
  A Report on the Victorians
  Shards   141   232
  An Inclusive Letter
  Some Happiness

I Try To Explain to My Children
 a Newspaper Article Which Says
 that According to a Computer
 a Nuclear War Is Likely To Occur
 in the Next Twenty Years   143   342
For My Brother Who Died Before
 I Was Born   144   161
In Baseball
Annuals
An Advent of Paganism   146   267
Married Sex
Lament Upon the Closing of the Northern
 Conservatory in Bangor, Maine
In a Cab
A Reply to the Journalist Who Informed
 the Russian People in Izvestia
 That There Was No Santa Claus   149   149
American Poem of the Senior Citizenry 151 196
The Poverty of Theory   162   202

BOOKS REVIEWED
The White Words   143   295
Good Trembling   146   167

WOROZBYT, THEODORE, JR.
POEMS
Neighborhood Light   153   260
Chess
A Unified Theory of Light   156   272
Northern Lights
Mollusk   158   97
Surviving Tongue   158   148
Visitors
A Particle Physicist Picks Up the Muse
 in Mel's Deli   160   13
Horoscope   161   156
The Guitar   164   255

WORTH, KATHRYN
POEMS
Poems for a Child   43   10
 Mater Filae
 Annus Quartus
 Child in the Seasons
 To a Child Plucking Fruit
Hidden Land   45   20
 New-Born
 Birth
 Annus Primus
 Daintily Now
 Immaculate with Silence
The Dynasty   47   76
 Child in the Centuries
 Genetrix
 Infant and Gravity
 Death of the Ascendants
Medio in Amore   50   316
Celestial Science   55   16

Lunar Eclipse
Thy Sun for Orbit
In the Observatory
BOOKS REVIEWED
Sign of Capricornus   51   270

WREFORD, JAMES
BOOKS REVIEWED
Unit of Five
 (With Louis Dudek,
 Ronald Hambleton, P. K. Page,
 and Raymond Souster)   66   334

WREN, PAUL
POEMS
Gravity   43   248
Journey the Long Way Round   45   266

WRENCH, MARGARET STANLEY
[See STANLEY-WRENCH,
MARGARET]

WRIGHT, C D
BOOKS REVIEWED
Translations of the Gospel
 Back into Tongues   144   40
String Light   160   284

WRIGHT, CAROLYNE
POEMS
Choosing My Name   132   340
Celebration for the Cold Snap   139   154
Logos of the Sentimentalist   145   220
The Ship in the Bottle
Post-Revolutionary Letter   148   208
Love Affair in a Small Town
Return to Seattle: Bastille Day
Victor Jara (1938-1973)
A Change of Maps   156   270

WRIGHT, CELESTE TURNER
POEMS
Noblesse Oblige   62   315
Buffo   100   24
Armory

WRIGHT, CHARLES
POEMS
Addendum   114   353
The Killing
The Offering
Half-Moon
In the Midnight Hour
Eye
Self-Portrait
Illumination
The Grave of the Right Hand

Nightletter   116   186
Epithalamion
Entries
Salt
Night Piece
Blackwater Mountain   119   215
Nouns
Portrait of the Poet in Abraham
    von Werdt's Dream
Dog Creek Mainline   120   212
Negatives
The Fever Toy
Victory Garden   120   360
The Grave of the Right Hand   121   39
Congenital   122   249
Nightdream
Clinchfield Station
Northhanger Ridge
Chinoiserie
Skins   125   152
Vesper Journal   153   16
Bicoastal Journal
Mid-Winter Snowfall in the Piazza Dante   155   253
Reading Lao Tzu Again in the New Year
Chickamauga   157   219
Black and Blue
Miles Davis and Elizabeth Bishop
    Fake the Break   160   311
Peccatology
Apologia Pro Vita Sua   166   1
Lives of the Saints   167   125
In the Kingdom of the Past,
    the Brown-Eyed Man Is King   169   187
Venetian Dog
Thinking About the Poet Larry Levis
    One Afternoon in Late May   170   24
In the Valley of the Magra   170   125
Returned to the Yaak Cabin,
    I Overhear an Old Greek Song

TRANSLATIONS
Poems by Luciano Erba   155   63
Poems by Giovanni Giudici   155   71

BOOKS REVIEWED
The Dream Animal   117   322
Hard Freight   125   166
China Trace   133   169
The Storm & Other Poems,
    by Eugenio Montale (Tr.)   136   40
The Southern Cross   141   349
Zone Journals   155   229
The World of the Ten Thousand Things:
    Poems 1980-1990   158   280
Chickamauga   168   33

ARTICLES ABOUT
[Note]   162   246

WRIGHT, DAVID
POEMS
    A Note to the Choreographer Walter Gore   87   161
    At the Death of Roy Campbell   92   25
    A House of Friends
    At the Kaiser's Villa   95   86
    A Death in Johannesburg   101   188
    Rhapsody of a Middle-Aged Man
    Five Songs   119   130
        Stream
        Moon
        Valley
        River
        Mountain
    A Peripatetic Letter to Isabella Fey   127   90

REVIEWS
    Six British Poets   92   309
        Night Thoughts, by David Gascoyne
        Not Waving but Drowning,
            by Stevie Smith
        Pegasus and Other Poems,
            by Cecil Day Lewis
        Heart of Grace, by Patrick Galvin
        A Dead Sparrow, by Brian Giles
        The Succession,
            by Quentin Stevenson
        Poets in South Africa: An Anthology
            (Ed. by Roy Macnab)
            [Roy Campbell, Guy Butler,
            Anthony Delius]   95   244

BOOKS REVIEWED
    Adam at Evening   110   195

WRIGHT, HAROLD HOLSTON
POEMS
    Days   16   27
    Kinship
    Pastel
    A Letter

WRIGHT, JAMES
POEMS
    The Resurrected   84   207
    Elegy in a Firelit Room
    A Presentation of Two Birds to My Son   85   198
    Morning Hymn to a Dark Girl   86   347
    Erinna to Sappho
    Sappho's Child
    For Her Who Carried My Child   88   1
    A Little Girl on Her Way to School
    A Gesture by a Lady
        with an Assumed Name
    Where the Plump Spider Sways to Rest
    Aubade at the Zama Replacement Depot   89   353
    Directions out of a Dream
    The Morality of Poetry   90   360
    Nightpiece

At the Executed Murderer's Grave   92   277
To My Older Brother
The Farmer
The Alarm
The Blessing   97   343
Near Mansfield, Ohio
A Lazy Poem on a Saturday Evening
Miners
Just Before a Thunder Shower
Sitting in a Small Screen-House
    on a Summer Morning   101   142
Listening to the Mourners   111   283
The Life
The Lights in the Hallway
Old Age Compensation
Outside Fargo, North Dakota
Your Name in Arezzo   133   286
Sheep in the Rain
A Flower Passage
Between Wars   136   125
Venice
Against Surrealism   139   72
May Morning

TRANSLATIONS
Poem by Federico García Lorca   96   151
Poem by Pablo Neruda   96   152
Poem by César Vallejo   98   352

REVIEWS
Four New Volumes   93   46
    I Marry You, by John Ciardi
    The Dark Sister,
        by Winfield Townley Scott
    Summer Unbound, by E. L. Mayo
    A Place to Stand, by David Wagoner
A Poetry Chronicle   95   373
    Poets of Today VI: Northwind
        and Other Poems, by Gene Baro;
    The Clothing's New Emperor
        and Other Poems, by Donald Finkel;
    Poems, 1955-1958, by Walter Stone
        (Ed. by John Hall Wheelock)
    The Lay of the Love and Death
        of Cornet Christopher Rilke,
        by Rainer Maria Rilke
        (Tr. by M. D. Herter Norton)
    Poems, by Vladimir Nabokov
A Shelf of New Poets   99   178
    Poets of Today VII: Into the Stone
        and Other Poems, by James Dickey;
    Views of the Oxford Colleges
        and Other Poems, by Paris Leary;
    Journeys and Return: Poems,
        by Jon Swan
    On the Way to the Island,
        by David Ferry
    Nags Head and Other Poems,
        by Lee Anderson

White Sun Black Sun,
    by Jerome Rothenberg
Wonderstrand Revisited,
    by Charles H. Philbrick
Wage War on Silence, by Vassar Miller
The Heights of Macchu Picchu,
    by Pablo Neruda
    (Tr. by Nathaniel Tarn)
    [Robert Pring-Mill]   112   191

BOOKS REVIEWED
The Green Wall   94   333
Saint Judas   96   185
Twenty Poems of Georg Trakl
    (Tr. with Robert Bly)   100   319
The Branch Will Not Break   102   391
Twenty Poems of César Vallejo
    (Tr. with John Knoepfle
    and Robert Bly)   105   196
Twenty Poems, by Pablo Neruda
    (Tr. with Robert Bly)   113   338
Shall We Gather at the River   114   40
Collected Poems   119   296
Neruda and Vallejo: Selected Poems
    (Ed. by Robert Bly)
    (Tr. with Robert Bly
    and John Knoepfle)   120   304
Two Citizens   124   292
To a Blossoming Pear Tree   136   164
Above the River: The Complete Poems 157   343

ARTICLES ABOUT
"Sacred Beings":
    Writers In Recorded Conversation,
    by Michael Milburn   146   101
Rev. of James Wright: The Heart of the Light
    (Ed. by Peter Stitt and Frank Graziano) 157   343

WRIGHT, JAY
BOOKS REVIEWED
Selected Poems of...   152   35

WRIGHT, JUDITH
BOOKS REVIEWED
Birds   105   201

ARTICLES ABOUT
Australian Poetry 1940-1980:
    A Personal View,
    by John Tranter   169   86
Towards a Contemporary
    Australian Poetics,
    by John Kinsella   169   94

WRIGHT, MARGARETTA W.
ARTICLES
Correspondence:
    A Bad Time with a Freudian
    [John Gould Fletcher, Martha Keller] 70   54

WRIGHT, WILLIAM HEERMANS
POEMS
   At the Furrier's   36   136

WRIGLEY, ROBERT
POEMS
   American Manhood   152   155
   The Emblem
   What My Father Believed
   Camping
   Creel   152   195
   For the Last Summer
   My Father's Fingernails   154   134
   C.O.
   Little Deaths   162   33
   Homage   162   255

BOOKS REVIEWED
   What My Father Believed   161   159
   The Bank of Beautiful Sins   169   156

WRINN, MARY J. J.
POEMS
   Spoken at Yuletide   51   127
   Grecian Lamp Unearthed Near Sparta 53   133
   Omen

WRYNN, ANTHONY
POEMS
   The Spotted Birds   31   136
   Medallion
   With Wings   37   22
     Not as the Wind
     The Bird Starting
   The Bright Prey   52   25
   An Abandoned Settlement
   The Last Swimmer
   Forest Woman's Explanation
     to a Wanderer
   Saint John in the Wilderness
   A Woman Reviews Paradise   60   24
   The Printed Visions

WUNDERLICH, MARK
POEMS
   In the Winter of This Climate 167   136
   To Sleep in a New City
   On Opening
   Aubade   167   261

WURDEMANN, AUDREY
POEMS
   Earth Grows Old   31   260
   The Weavers   35   143
   Spring Song   38   70
   Arabesque
   Tartary
   Shadow

   Feathered Flute
   As Liquid Snow
   Two for Eros   41   250

BOOKS REVIEWED
   The House of Silk   31   226
   Bright Ambush   45   220
   Splendor in the Grass   49   340

WURM, ROSS
REVIEWS
   Murder in the Cathedral,
     by T. S. Eliot
     [Recording]   85   113

WYATT, ANDREA
BOOKS REVIEWED
   Selected Poems,
     by Larry Eigner
     (Ed. with Samuel Charters) 126   172

WYATT, EDITH (FRANKLIN)
["E. W."]
POEMS
   Sympathy   1   112
   Clover   5   152
   April Weather
   Summer Hail
   To F. W.
   On the Great Plateau
   Sleep   9   111
   City Whistles
   Of Shakespeare's Sonnets   38   19
   Translations   52   131
   Valentine   53   250
   On the Air
   Stream of Consciousness—1816 56   190
   Perugino's World
   Mexican Exhibit   60   254
   To My Mother and My Father

ARTICLES
   "The Music of the Human Heart"
     [James Whitcomb Riley]   1   59
   Poetry and Criticism   4   234
   [Tribute to Harriet Monroe]   49   142
   Correspondence:
     A Review for Reviewers   68   171

REVIEWS
   The Story of a Round House
     and Other Poems,
     by John Masefield   1   160
   The Man on the Hill-Top,
     by Arthur Davison Ficke   6   247
   Poems, by G. K. Chesterton   7   267
   The Letters of Percy Bysshe Shelley
     (Ed. by Roger Ingpen)   8   204

Those Brontes   9   259
  Bronte Poems
    (Ed. by A. C. Benson)
  The Complete Works of Emily Bronte,
    Vol. I—Poetry
    (Ed. by W. Robertson Nicoll
    and Clement Shorter)
  The Years Between, by Rudyard Kipling   15   277
  Wind Out of Betelgeuse,
    by Margaret Tod Ritter   32   286
  Who Loves the Rain and Other Poems,
    by Frances Shaw   63   351

BOOKS REVIEWED
  The Wind in the Corn
    and Other Poems   11   218

ARTICLES ABOUT
  Poets as Prosers,
    by Harriet Monroe   28   328

WYATT, THOMAS
ARTICLES ABOUT
  The 16th-Century Lyric
    in England: Part II,
    by Yvor Winters   53   320

WYCKOFF, ELIZABETH
BOOKS REVIEWED
  Antigone (Tr.)   85   225

WYDENBRUCK, NORA
BOOKS REVIEWED
  The Letters of Rainer Maria Rilke and
    Princess Marie von Thurn und Taxis (Tr.) 94   59

WYETH, JOHN ALLAN
BOOKS REVIEWED
  This Man's Army:
    A War in Fifty-Odd Sonnets   41   165

WYLDE, V. N.
POEMS
  A Day Alone   43   9

WYLIE, ELINOR
POEMS
  Still Colors   18   18
    Velvet Shoes
    "Fire and Sleet and Candle-Light"
    Silver Filagree
    Atavism
  The Persian Kitten   22   121
  Address to My Soul   32   78
  The Heart Upon the Sleeve
  Lament for Glasgerion   32   128
  Last Supper
BOOKS REVIEWED
  Nets To Catch the Wind   19   220
  Black Armor   23   276
  Trivial Breath   33   96
  Angels and Earthly Creatures   34   230
  The Collected Poems of...   40   273
  Last Poems of...   62   164

ARTICLES ABOUT
  A Few Women Poets,
    by Harriet Monroe   26   326
  Poets as Prosers,
    by Harriet Monroe   28   328
  Elinor Wylie, by Harriet Monroe   33   266
  The Mechanism of Sensibility,
    by Morton Dauwen Zabel   34   150
  Correspondence
    from William Rose Benét
    [John Gould Fletcher]   59   350

WYLIE, MAX
ARTICLES ABOUT
  Verse Drama and the Radio,
    by Amy Bonner   58   280

WYNAND, DERK
TRANSLATIONS
  Poems by Jean Chatard   116 375

WYNNE, MADELINE YALE
POEMS
  Cotton Fields   6   179

(X)

YAGI, JUKICHI
POEMS
Pure in Heart
(Tr. by Hisakazu Kaneko)　　101　172

YAMAMOTO, TARO
POEMS
At a Barber Shop
(Tr. by Hisakazu Kaneko)　　101　171

YAMANOGUCHI, BAKU
POEMS
Marriage　　88　67
Tatami Floor
(Tr. by Satoru Satu
and Constance Urdang)

YANG
　[THE EMPEROR YANG OF SUI]
POEMS
Festival in the Eastern Hall　　46　4
Spring Night
Autumn Sadness
Late Spring
(Tr. by George Margulies
and Willard R. Trask)

ARTICLES ABOUT
Three Chinese Poets of Long Ago,
by George Margulies
and Willard R. Trask　　46　46

YARALIAN, SEVAG
POEMS
The Card Players　　147　196
Winter Rain

Y ARGOTE, LUIS DE GONGORA
　[See DE GONGORA Y ARGOTE,
　LUIS]

YARMOLINSKY, AVRAHM
　[ABRAHAM YARMOLINSKY]
TRANSLATIONS
Poem by Valery Bryusov　　14　79

Poems by Wilhelm Klemm,
Rainer Maria Rilke, Franz Werfel,
Georg Heym, Albert Ehrenstein,
Richard Schaukal, and Arno Holz
(Tr. with Babette Deutsch)　　21　141

BOOKS REVIEWED
Modern Russian Poetry
(Ed. and tr. with Babette Deutsch)　　20　228
Contemporary German Poetry
(Ed. and tr. with Babette Deutsch)　　24　52
A Treasury of Russian Verse (Ed.)
(Tr. by Babette Deutsch)　　80　95
Two Centuries of Russian Verse
(Ed. with Babette Deutsch)　　114　113

YARROW, P. J.
BOOKS REVIEWED
Corneille　　104　187

YATES, J. MICHAEL
POEMS
The Ice Rider　　105　246
Scorpion　　106　403
It Hardly Matters

BOOKS REVIEWED
*Hunt in an Unmapped
Interior and Other Poems*　　112　48
Canticle for Electronic Music
The Great Bear Lake Meditations　　119　356
*Contemporary Poetry
of British Columbia* (Ed.)

YEATS, JACK B.
BOOKS REVIEWED
A Broadside　　6　252

YEATS, JOHN BUTLER
BOOKS REVIEWED
Passages from the Letters of...
(Ed. by Ezra Pound)　　11　223
*J. B. Yeats: Letters to His Son,
W. B. Yeats, and Others, 1869-1922*
(Ed. by Joseph Hone)　　69　291

YEATS, W(ILLIAM) B(UTLER)

POEMS

The Mountain Tomb	1	67
To a Child Dancing Upon the Shore		
Fallen Majesty		
Love and the Bird		
The Realists		
The Grey Rock	2	17
The Two Kings	3	1
To a Friend Whose Work		
Has Come to Nothing	4	52
Paudeen		
To a Shade		
When Helen Lived		
Beggar to Beggar Cried		
The Witch		
The Peacock		
Running to Paradise		
The Player Queen		
To a Child Dancing in the Wind		
The Magi		
A Coat		
The Dawn	7	217
On Woman		
The Fisherman		
The Hawk		
Memory		
The Thorn Tree		
The Phoenix		
There Is a Queen in China		
The Scholars		
Ego Dominus Tuus	11	29
The Only Jealousy of Emer	13	175
A Prayer for My Daughter	13	59
Poems and Commentaries: Supernatural	45	121
Supernatural Songs		
Ribh at the Tomb of Baile and Aillinn		
Ribh Prefers an Older Theology		
Ribh Considers Christian Love		
Insufficient		
He and She		
The Four Ages of Man		
Conjunctions		
A Needle's Eye		
Meru		
Three Songs to the Same Tune		
A Full Moon in March	45	299
The Watch-Fire	135	223

ARTICLES

Correspondence		
[Ezra Pound]	3	149
Commentary on the Three Songs	45	130

BOOKS REVIEWED

Responsibilities	4	64
Responsibilities and Other Poems	9	150
Reveries Over Childhood and Youth	11	51

The Wild Swans at Coole,		
Other Verses and a Play in Verse	13	42
Visions and Beliefs in the West of Ireland		
(Ed. by Lady Gregory)		
[Notes]	18	49
Four Plays for Dancers	19	288
Autobiographies: Reveries		
Over Childhood and Youth	30	279
The Trembling of the Veil		
Poetical Works of...	30	346
Vol. I, Lyrical Poems		
Vol. II, Dramatic Poems		
The Tower	33	41
The Winding Stair	42	40
Words for Music Perhaps and Other Poems		
Collected Poems of...	43	279
The Winding Stair		
Wheels and Butterflies	46	100
The King of the Great Clock Tower:		
Commentaries and Poems	46	104
Collected Plays	48	221
The Ten Principal Upanishads		
(Tr. with Shree Purohit Swami)	51	216
New Poems	53	84
Last Poems and Two Plays	54	338
The Collected Poems of...	80	43
The Autobiography of...	84	153
The Senate Speeches of...		
(Ed. by Donald R. Pearce)	98	253
Essays and Introductions	98	263

ARTICLES ABOUT

Status Rerum, by Ezra Pound	1	123
Poetry's Banquet	4	25
"Too Far from Paris,"		
by Alice Corbin Henderson	4	105
The Later Yeats, by Mary M. Colum	7	258
The Hawk's Well,		
by Alice Corbin Henderson	10	163
Visitors from the Other Side,		
by Harriet Monroe	15	93
The Later Yeats	15	288
Mr. Yeats and the Poetic Drama,		
by Harriet Monroe	16	32
Honors and Prizes,		
by Harriet Monroe	29	92
Synge and the Irish, by M. D. Zabel	42	101
[Note on error]	42	179
[Note on version of Three Songs]	45	177
Yeats at Thirty and Seventy,		
by M. D. Zabel	47	268
Poet as Anthologist, by M. D. Zabel	49	273
A Letter from Ireland,		
by Joseph Hone		
[Oxford Anthology]	49	332
Rev. of The Life of W. B. Yeats,		
by Joseph M. Hone	62	223

The "Vita Nuova" of Baroque Art
  in the Recent Poetry
  of Edith Sitwell,
  by Horace Gregory   65   148
Rev. of *The Winter Sea*,
  by Allen Tate   66   324
Moods and Reactions,
  by Stephen Spender   67   88
Rev. of *J. B. Yeats: Letters to His Son,
  W. B. Yeats, and Others, 1869-1922*
  (Ed. by Joseph Hone)   69   291
Prosody as the Meaning,
  by Karl Shapiro   73   336
Notes Towards an Autobiography:
  The Childish Background (III),
  by William Carlos Williams   74   94
Rev. of *Yeats: The Man and the Masks*,
  by Richard Ellmann   74   244
Rev. of *The Permanence of Yeats*
  (Ed. by James Hall
  and Martin Steinmann)   76   227
Rev. of *The Story of the Abbey Theatre*,
  by Peter Kavanagh   79   216
Rev. of *The Interpretation of the Cuchulain
  Legend in the Works of W. B. Yeats*,
  by Birgit Bjersby   81   331
Rev. of *W. B. Yeats: The Tragic Phase*,
  by Vivienne Koch
[Note on *The Only Jealousy of Emer*]   82   242
Rev. of *W. B. Yeats and T. Sturge Moore,
  Their Correspondence*
  (Ed. by Ursula Bridge)   83   357
Rev. by Donald Davie   91   56
Oliver St. John Gogarty,
  by Vivian Mercier   93   35
Rev. of *Words for the Wind*,
  by Theodore Roethke   94   203
Rev. of *The Oxford Book of Irish Verse*
  (Ed. by Donagh MacDonagh
  and Lennox Robinson)   94   260
Rev. of *The Masterpiece and the Man:
  Yeats as I Knew Him*,
  by Monk Gibbon   98   59
Rev. of *The Yeats Country*,
  by Sheelah Kirby   102   341
Rev. of *William Butler Yeats:
  The Poet as a Mythmaker*,
  by Morton Irving Seiden;
  Yeats's Vision and the Later Plays,
  by Helen Hennessy Vendler   103   185
Rev. of *Swan and Shadow:
  Yeats's Dialogue with History*,
  by Thomas R. Whitaker   107   192
The Vocation of Poetry,
  by Henry Rago   110   328
Review by Leila Laughlin
  [R. Tagore]   111   407

Rev. of *Barbarous Knowledge: Myth
  in the Poetry of Yeats, Graves, and Muir*,
  by Daniel Hoffman;
  W. B. Yeats: Man and Poet,
  by Norman Jeffares   112   52
Rev. of *Yeats' Autobiography*,
  by Joseph Ronsley   113   338
Rev. of *The Gaiety of Language:
  An Essay on the Radical Poetics
  of W. B. Yeats and Wallace Stevens*,
  by Frank Lentricchia   115   346
Rev. of *Yeats*, by Harold Bloom   117   43
Rev. of *The Anxiety of Influence*,
  by Harold Bloom   122   298
Thirteen Ways of Looking at a Skylark,
  by Howard Nemerov   126   294
Rev. of *The Apple Barrel*,
  by Jon Stallworthy   127   98
Rev. of *Collected Poems*, by Austin Clarke   128   46
Rev. of *Harriet Monroe
  and the Poetry Renaissance*,
  by Ellen Williams   131   39
A Note on "The Watch-Fire,"
  by Christina Hunt Mahony
  and Edward O'Shea   135   224
Contemporary British Poetry:
  A Romantic Persistence?
  by John Bayley   146   227
Rev. of *A History of Modern Poetry,
  Vol. II: Modernism and After*,
  by David Perkins   151   296
A Map of Contemporary Irish Poetry,
  by Dennis O'Driscoll   167   94

YEH SHIH
POEMS
  *On Being Denied Admittance
    to a Friend's Garden*
    (Tr. by Louise S. Hammond)   20   252

YELLEN, SAMUEL
BOOKS REVIEWED
  The Convex Mirror. Collected Poems   121   234

YENSER, STEPHEN
POEMS
  Moving Again   118   255
  The Racket
  Calypso on Tinos
  Common Property   125   15
  Intensive Care
  Valentine   163   249
  A Day in the Life   168   63

ARTICLES
  Metamorphoses
    [James Merrill]   166   331

REVIEWS
   Braving the Elements,
     by James Merrill   122 163
   History; The Dolphin; and
     For Lizzie and Harriet,
     by Robert Lowell   123 304
   Merciful Disguises: Published
     and Unpublished Poems,
     by Mona Van Duyn   126 167
   Or Else—Poem/Poems 1968-1974,
     by Robert Penn Warren   128 349
   Sun, by Michael Palmer   154 295
   Necessary Measures   158 214
     The Collected Poems
       of Henri Coulette
       (Ed. by Donald Justice
       and Robert Mezey)
       [Wallace Stevens]
     When One Has Lived
       a Long Time Alone,
       by Galway Kinnell
     Going Back to the River,
       by Marilyn Hacker
     Annonciade, by Elizabeth Spires
     On Ballycastle Beach,
       by Medbh McGuckian
     The Venus Hottentot,
       by Elizabeth Alexander
       [Albert Murray]
     For Louis Pasteur,
       by Edgar Bowers

BOOKS REVIEWED
   The Fire in All Things   164   97

ARTICLES ABOUT
   Four Letters to Stephen Yenser,
     by James Merrill   166 324

YESENIN, SERGEY
   [See ESSENIN, SERGEI]

YEVTUSHENKO, YEVGENY
  BOOKS REVIEWED
   Selected Poems
     (Tr. by Robin Milner-Gulland
     and Peter Levi)   102 400
   Yevtushenko Poems
     (Tr. by Herbert Marshall)   111 121
   Bratsk Station and Other New Poems
     (Tr. by Tina Tupinika-Glaessner
     and Geoffrey Dutton)
   The Face Behind the Face
     (Tr. by Arthur Boyars
     and Simon Franklin)   136   40

YIN-NAN, CHANG
   [See CHANG YIN-NAN]

YORK, FRANCES
  POEMS
   Ignorance   30 314
   Acquittal
   The Toiler

YOSELOFF, THOMAS
  BOOKS REVIEWED
   Seven Poets in Search of an Answer (Ed.)
     [Maxwell Bodenheim, Joy Davidman,
     Langston Hughes, Aaron Kramer,
     Alfred Kreymborg, Martha Millet,
     and Norman Rosten]   64 289

YOSHIHARA, SACHIKO
  POEMS
   Air Raid
     (Tr. by Naoshi Koriyama
     and Edward Lueders)   143 320

YOSHIKAWA, KOJIRO
  BOOKS REVIEWED
   An Introduction to Sung Poetry
     (Tr. by Burton Watson)   112 283

YOUNG, AL
  BOOKS REVIEWED
   Geography of the Near Past 130 102

YOUNG, ANNE
  POEMS
   Ghostly Sight   47 130
    Brides
    "To a Green Thought in a Green Shade"
   The Willow Tree   52   12
   Pastoral   55 132

YOUNG, DAVID (P.)
  POEMS
   After My Death   128 273
   Four About Metaphysics
   Two Views of the Cathedral
   The Names of a Hare in English 131   78

  BOOKS REVIEWED
   Sweating Out the Winter   117 204
   Boxcars   127 164
   Duino Elegies,
     by Rainer Maria Rilke (Tr.) 134 234
   The Names of a Hare in English 139   35

YOUNG, DEAN
  POEMS
   Interference & Delivery   151 340
   Age of Discovery

YOUNG, DOUGLAS
  ARTICLES ABOUT
   Some Poets of the Scottish Renaissance,
     by Tom Scott   88   43

YOUNG, ELLA
POEMS
Fiametta | 10 | 129
Greeting
Rain | 33 | 18
Chrysede
Sunset | 38 | 257
Northland Spring | 40 | 13

YOUNG, FERN
POEMS
Spirit of Research | 42 | 146

YOUNG, GARY
POEMS
Winter Drought | 131 | 144
Winter Solstice
Prayer | 135 | 323
To an Estranged Wife
Monday | 137 | 335
Tornado Watch, Bloomington, Indiana
Loch Lomond

YOUNG, IAN
BOOKS REVIEWED
Year of the Quiet Sun | 119 | 356

YOUNG, JAMES P.
POEMS
Discoveries | 28 | 252
Gnats
Soul
Not So

YOUNG, KARL
BOOKS REVIEWED
The Note-Books of Matthew Arnold
(Ed. with Howard Foster Lowry
and Waldo Hilary Dunn) | 81 | 196

YOUNG, KATHLEEN TANKERSLEY
POEMS
Question for Your Question | 40 | 310

BOOKS REVIEWED
Ten Poems | 38 | 339
The Dark Land | 42 | 50
The Pepper Trees | 43 | 225

ARTICLES ABOUT
Obituary | 42 | 298

YOUNG, KEVIN
POEMS
The Living | 162 | 343

BOOKS REVIEWED
Most Way Home | 170 | 37

YOUNG, MARGUERITE (V.)
POEMS
Condiments | 36 | 260
Lot's Wife
Ballad-Loving
A Girl's Song
Recurring
Biography | 41 | 133
Delicate Meshes | 44 | 192
Woodlands Far Removed
Minnows and a Monster
Heavy Gift | 46 | 324
Song's Preface
Spring
Archer in a World
Heart Who Stays
Anthology Piece
Elegy for the Body
The Tree
Gulliver | 49 | 315
Sequence
Milton's Wife
Awakening
Death in Lilliput
Heroics
Ventriloquist: The Coffee Hour | 56 | 132
The Home-Coming | 60 | 17
Farewell at the Station | 61 | 551
Figures of Space
The Raven

REVIEWS
Lower than the Angels,
by Rosalie Dunlap Hickler | 46 | 232
Intrepid Bird, by Mary Britton Miller | 47 | 99
Cobwebs of Cable,
by Florence Ripley Mastin | 48 | 345

BOOKS REVIEWED
Prismatic Ground | 51 | 109
Moderate Fable | 65 | 215

YOUNG, MURRAY
POEMS
A Leaf for John Ford | 36 | 318
The End of Labor

YOUNG, PEARCE
POEMS
Upon a Poem by Ben Jonson | 75 | 16

YOUNG, STANLEY
BOOKS REVIEWED
Robin Landing | 52 | 164

YOUNG BEAR, RAY A.
BOOKS REVIEWED
Black Eagle Child | 161 | 339

YOURGRAU, BARRY
POEMS
Apocrypha   140   204

YOWS, KRISTINA
POEMS
From the Terrace of the Temple   154   216
Le Pont Neuf: A Night Photograph
To Anne
Red Dust

YUAN CHIEH
POEMS
Song-Poems of Inmost Thoughts   46   3
    ("Autumn begins...")
    ("Now it is day...")
        (Tr. by George Margulies
        and Willard R. Trask)

ARTICLES ABOUT
    Three Chinese Poets of Long Ago,
        by George Margulies
        and Willard R. Trask   46   46

YUAN MEI
ARTICLES ABOUT
    Rev. of *Yuan Mei*,
        by Arthur Waley   93   408

YUASA, NOBUYUKI
BOOKS REVIEWED
    *Bashō: The Narrow Road to the Deep North
    and Other Travel Sketches* (Tr.)   112   347

YU WU-LING
POEMS
Roads in Loyang
        (Tr. by Helen Burwell Chapin)   46   13

Z

ZABEL, MORTON DAUWEN ["M. D. Z."]

POEMS

Things and Venus — 31 200
  Teufelsdrockh Minor
  The Celibate
  Mixed Marriage
  Journal to Stella
  Culture and Anarchy
  Scène à Faire
  Hoar Frost
Figures in a Winter Landscape — 35 177
  Legend
  Herakles Archer
  Written on Wind
  Arrotino
  Two Fables of Lovers
  White Advent
The Speediest Ash — 41 59
  The Storm at Nightfall
  Codex Exoniensis
  The Traitors
  The Wall at Ilmenau
  The Nettle, the Flower
  Song from a Tragedy
  Homage to Murren

ARTICLES

The Aristocrats
  [George H. Ryland, Owen Barfield] — 34 37
The New Poets of Germany
  [Heinrich Eduard Jacob,
  Rainer Maria Rilke] — 34 94
The Mechanism of Sensibility
  [T. S. Eliot, Elinor Wylie,
  John Donne] — 34 150
Poems and Pictures
  [Virginia Woolf, James Joyce,
  Sacheverell Sitwell] — 34 217
The Mighty Line — 34 274
The Way of Periodicals
  [The Dial, The Little Review] — 34 330
Cities or Scenery — 35 152
Beautiful Reprints and Editions — 35 231
The Trail of Consciousness — 35 266
The Lyrics of James Joyce — 36 206

Bays for Virgil — 37 37
Eric Gill — 37 41
Gerard Manley Hopkins — 37 152
Christina Rossetti and Emily Dickinson — 37 213
Recent Magazines — 38 170
Cattle in the Garden — 38 268
Recent Magazines
  [Eugene Jolas] — 38 348
Recent Magazines
  [Iris Barry, Ezra Pound,
  H. L. Mencken, Percy Hutchison] — 39 166
Recent Magazines — 39 345
Recent Magazines — 40 169
Recent Magazines — 40 350
An Aside — 41 54
Recent Magazines — 41 168
"Obstinate Isles"
  [Michael Roberts] — 41 214
Titans, Tea-Hounds, Rasslers,
  and Reviewers
  [Q. D. Leavis, Burton Rascoe] — 41 326
Recent Magazines — 41 343
The Book of Hart Crane
  [William Blake] — 42 33
Synge and the Irish
  [W. B. Yeats] — 42 101
Recent Magazines — 42 346
Baudelaire
  [Enid Starkie] — 43 38
Recent Magazines — 43 168
Stefan George 1868-1933 — 43 333
Recent Magazines — 43 348
Cinema of Hamlet
  [Archibald MacLeish] — 44 150
Recent Magazines — 44 168
Two Versions of the Nineteenth Century
  [William Morris, James Thomson] — 44 270
Toward Standards of Criticism
  [F. R. Leavis] — 45 40
Paul Valéry
  [Theodora Bosanquet,
  Mrs. G. Turquet-Milnes] — 45 90
Poetry for the Theatre
  [Sean O'Casey, T. S. Eliot] — 45 152

Recent Magazines 45 170
The Purposes of Stephen Spender
  [Rupert Brooke] 45 208
The Poetics of Henry James 45 270
Recent Magazines 45 350
Robinson in America 46 157
Recent Magazines 46 171
Hopkins in His Letters
  [Claude Colleer Abbott,
  Robert Bridges, Richard Watson Dixon] 46 210
Yeats at Thirty and Seventy 47 268
A Literalist of the Imagination
  [Marianne Moore] 47 326
Recent Magazines 48 51
Recent Magazines
  [Eugene Jolas] 48 351
Sandburg's Testament 49 33
Harriet Monroe: December 23, 1860–
  September 26, 1936 49 85
A Statement
  [Harriet Monroe] 49 161
Poet as Anthologist
  [W. B. Yeats] 49 273
Volume Fifty 50 30
The Poetry of Unrest
  [St.-John Perse] 50 90
The Use of Prizes 50 154
The Century of Leopardi 50 270
An American Critic
  [Paul Elmer More] 50 330
Poetry's Quarter-Century
  [Harriet Monroe] 51 28
H. M.: In Memory
  [Harriet Monroe, Ezra Pound] 97 241

REVIEWS
Astrolabe, by S. Foster Damon 31 167
A Marriage with Space,
  by Mark Turbyfill 31 211
The Bright Doom,
  by John Hall Wheelock 31 280
The Cyder Feast and Other Poems,
  by Sacheverell Sitwell 31 347
Creatures, by Padraic Colum 32 53
Anthologies 32 96
  Oxford Book of American Verse
    (Ed. by Bliss Carman)
  The Book of Poetry
    (Ed. by Edwin Markham)
  The Catholic Anthology
    (Ed. by Thomas Walsh)
  Lotus and Chrysanthemum
    (Ed. by Joseph Lewis French)
  A Persian Anthology
    (Ed. by Edward Granville Browne)
  Caroling Dusk
    (Ed. by Countée Cullen)

  Minstrelsy of Maine
    (Ed. by Fannie Hardy Eckstrom
    and Mary Winslow Smyth)
  The Spirit of St. Louis
  The Sacco-Vanzetti Anthology of Verse
  Love's High Way
    (Ed. by Mrs. Waldo Richards)
  Third Book of Modern Verse
    (Ed. by Jessie Rittenhouse)
  200 Best and Second Best Poems
    (Ed. by C. Lewis Hind)
  The Grub Street Book of Verse
  Saplings, Second Series, 1927
Tristan and Isolt,
  by John Masefield 32 109
Steep Ascent,
  by Jean Starr Untermeyer 32 167
Floodgate, by David McCord 32 171
Nocturnes and Autumnals,
  by David Morton 32 227
Poems of James Thomson, "B.V."
  (Ed. by Gordon Hall Gerould) 32 229
Sky-Rider, by Wade Oliver 32 284
The City, by Ruth Manning Sanders 32 348
The Gobbler of God,
  by Percy Mackaye 32 352
Traveling Standing Still,
  by Genevieve Taggard 33 154
The Black Rock, by John Gould Fletcher 33 222
Mr. Pope and Other Poems,
  by Allen Tate 33 281
Cawdor and Other Poems,
  by Robinson Jeffers 33 336
Collected Poems, by A. E. Coppard 34 48
Retreat, by Edmund Blunden 34 54
Dedication, by Viola Gerard Garvin 34 106
A Rime of the Rood,
  by Charles L. O'Donnell 34 170
Lost City, by Marion Strobel 34 236
The Heart's Journey and Memoirs
  of a Fox-Hunting Man,
  by Siegfried Sassoon 34 288
Golden Falcon,
  by Robert P. Tristram Coffin 34 356
Noah's Dove, by Laura Benét 35 49
Dark Summer, by Louise Bogan 35 158
Manhattan Men,
  by Alfred Kreymborg 35 168
The Sceptered Flute,
  by Sarojini Naidu 35 169
Poets, Farewell! by Edmund Wilson 35 222
Be Still,
  by William Closson Emory 35 229
High Falcon, by Léonie Adams 35 332
Alice Meynell: A Memoir,
  by Viola Meynell 35 349
God Beguiled, by George O'Neil 36 40

Now the Sky and Other Poems,
   by Mark Van Doren   36   50
The Testament of Beauty,
   by Robert Bridges   36   96
Intellectual Things,
   by Stanley J. Kunitz   36   218
New Found Land,
   by Archibald MacLeish   36   270
Europa and Other Poems and Sonnets,
   by Rolfe Humphries   36   286
Ash Wednesday; Journey of the Magi;
   A Song for Simeon; Animula; and *Dante,*
   by T. S. Eliot   36   330
Poetry at Present, by Charles Williams   36   350
The Proof, by Yvor Winters   37   225
Wild Apples and *An Offering of Swans,*
   by Oliver Gogarty   37   349
A Dawn in Britain I   38   35
   The Ecliptic,
      by Joseph Gordon Macleod
   Poems, by W. H. Auden
A Dawn in Britain II   38   101
   The Ecliptic,
      by Joseph Gordon Macleod
   Poems, by W. H. Auden
The American Caravan
   (Ed. by Alfred Kreymborg,
   Lewis Mumford and Paul Rosenfeld)   38   156
Imagism and the Imagists,
   by Glenn Hughes   38   169
New Lyrics and a Few Old Ones,
   by Agnes Lee   38   221
Harmonium [New ed.],
   by Wallace Stevens   39   148
Panama, by Blaise Cendrars
   (Tr. by John Dos Passos)   39   224
Two English Classicists   39   280
   The Shorter Poems of Robert Bridges
   The Poems of T. Sturge Moore
Poems: 1928-1931, by Allen Tate   40   34
The Collected Poems of Elinor Wylie   40   273
The Five Seasons, by Phelps Putnam   40   335
Triumphal March and
   Difficulties of a Statesman,
   by T. S. Eliot   41   152
Three Anthologies   41   284
   An Anthology of Younger Poets
      (Ed. by Oliver Wells)
   Shorter Modern Poems, 1900-1931
      (Ed. by David Morton)
   Earth's Processional,
      by David Morton
   Silk of the Corn,
      by Members of the Iowa
      Federation of Women's Clubs
Collected Poems and
   The Winding Stair and Other Poems,
   by William Butler Yeats   43   279

The Use of Poetry and the Use of Criticism,
   by T. S. Eliot   44   32
The King of the Great Clock Tower:
   Commentaries and Poems,
   by William Butler Yeats   46   104
Thirty-Six Poems,
   by Robert Penn Warren   48   37
Break the Heart's Anger, by Paul Engle   48   228
Burning City,
   by Stephen Vincent Benét   48   276
Thorns of Thunder,
   by Paul Eluard
   (Ed. by George Reavey)
   (Tr. by Samuel Beckett, Denis Devlin,
   David Gascoyne, Eugene Jolas,
   Man Ray, George Reavey,
   and Ruthven Todd)   48   347
Poems, by Stéphane Mallarmé
   (Tr. by Roger Fry)
   (Commentaries by Charles Mauron)   49   350

BOOKS REVIEWED
Selected Poems
   of Edwin Arlington Robinson (Ed.)   108   187

ARTICLES ABOUT
   [Note]   97   272
   Comment by Wallace Fowlie   151   208

ZABOLOTSKY, NIKOLAI
POEMS
   All That Was in the Soul   124   200
   Yesterday Reflecting Upon Death
   Metamorphoses
   A Woodland Lake
   In This Birch Grove
   A Dream
   Swallow
   I Touched the Leaves of the Eucalyptus
      (Tr. by Daniel Weissbort)

ZABRISKIE, GEORGE
BOOKS REVIEWED
   The Mind's Geography   61   452
   Like the Root   66   290

ZACHARY, R. Y.
ARTICLES ABOUT
   Rev. of *New Directions 1944*
      (Ed. by James Laughlin)   66   161

ZADE, WAYNE
POEMS
   The Lover on Trial   117   188
   A Conclusion of Love
   The Hunter   121   147
   Trade Expectations
   The Flying Dutchman

ZAISS, DAVID
POEMS
  The Pleasure of Filling Space   113   400
  Too Many Ducks   116   6
  The Wong's Short Visit
  In the White Giant's Mouth
  The Special Delivery of Celebrants

REVIEWS
  Perfect Circles   116   51
    Collected Poems 1968, by Roy Fisher
    Lost and Found,
      by Raymond Souster
    The Odes, by Charles Boer
    A Choice in Attitudes, by Gray Burr

ZANZOTTO, ANDREA
POEMS
  L'elegia in petèl/The Baby-Talk Elegy
    (Tr. by Beverly Allen)   155   56

ARTICLES ABOUT
  Some Notes on Post-War Italian Poetry,
    by Paolo Cherchi and Joseph Parisi   155   161

ZARANKA, WILLIAM
POEMS
  Twenty-Two Motels   146   151
  Diorama

ZARIN, CYNTHIA
POEMS
  Charlottesville, August   134   272

ZARZYSKI, PAUL
POEMS
  Measuring   149   285
  The Antler Tree   153   226
  Angelina, My Noni's Name,
    Means Messenger   157   28

ZATURENSKA, MARYA
[MARYA ZATURENSKY, MARYA
ZATURENSKA GREGORY]
POEMS
  A Russian Easter   16   24
  Russian Peasants
  Spinners   18   314
    She Longs for the Country
    The Spinners at Willowsleigh
    Song of a Factory Girl
    A Song for Vanished Beauty
    An Old Tale
    Memories
    "The Girl Takes Her Place
    Among the Mothers"   22   256
  Elegies Over John Reed   23   319
    They Bury Him in the Kremlin

    Song of the Scarlet Banners
    The Elegy of the Kremlin Bells
  Dream Places   32   83
    The Secret Garden
    Nostalgia
  Hither and Yon   36   202
    Love Song
    Fulfilment
    The Quiet House
    Chorale for Autumn
    The Empress Marie Louise
  They Pass   39   129
    Clock-Beat, Heart-Beat
    Symbol
    Oath on an Altar
  Beyond the Mountains   43   237
    Fruits Unharvested
    Strange Captivity
    Chains of Filigree
    Landscapes
    Reflections of a Centaur
  Everlasting Morning   48   299
    Cold Morning Sky
    The Flower, the Universe
    Renewal of Fountains
    The Fountain
    Inviolate Infancy
    The Daisy
    Miranda in Hesperides
  The Tide   50   301
  In Song, the Countersign
  The Messenger
  Unveil the Autumn
  Song of the Girl in the Red Cloak   70   244
  The Black Sibyl
  Inscription on a Mountain   81   91
  The Emblem   81   348
  The Fountains of Rome   84   63
  Four Ghosts   95   103
  Voices Heard in the Air
  The Waiting
  Sentimental Colloquy   122   338
  The Vision of Dido
  Prospero's Soliloquy
  Bird and the Muse

ARTICLES
  [Tribute to Harriet Monroe]
    (With Horace Gregory)   49   157
  Correspondence   120   364

REVIEWS
  For Eager Lovers,
    by Genevieve Taggard   22   43
  Cloister and Other Poems,
    by Charles L. O'Donnell   22   95
  Bright Ambush,
    by Audrey Wurdemann   45   220

Journey Taken by a Woman,
  by Susanna Valentine Mitchell   47   164
Tradition Isn't Convention   73   177
  Poems for Music, 1917-1947,
    by Robert Hillyer
  Collected Lyrical Poems,
    by Vivian Locke Ellis
A Poetry Chronicle   100   191
  Poems and Translations,
    by Thomas Kinsella
  Apollonian Poems, by Arthur Freeman
  The Many Islands,
    by William Goodreau
  The Only Need, by Brian Higgins
  Sunday Is a Day of Incest,
    by Michael Bullock
  The Devil's Picture Book,
    by Daryl Hine
  Any Day, by K. W. Gransden
  The London Zoo, by C. H. Sisson

BOOKS REVIEWED
  Threshold and Hearth   45   282
  Cold Morning Sky   51   266
  The Listening Landscape   58   337
  The Golden Mirror   65   150
  A History of American Poetry, 1900-1940
    (With Horace Gregory)   69   210
  The Mentor Book of Religious Verse
    (Ed. with Horace Gregory)   91   124
  Terraces of Light   98   186
  The Crystal Cabinet
    (Ed. with Horace Gregory)   103   261
  The Hidden Waterfall   126   100

ZAUSMER, EMANUEL
  POEMS
    Lyric ("On the coast of stars...")   23   82

ZDANYS, JONAS
  TRANSLATIONS
    Poems by Tomas Venclova   132   342

  ARTICLES
    A Note on Tomas Venclova   132   348

ZEAMI [See SEAMI]

ZEIDNER, LISA
  POEMS
    What Really Happens
      When the Plane Goes Down   144   80
    Safety in Numbers
    A Bomb   150   101

ZEND, ROBERT
  BOOKS REVIEWED
    Beyond Labels   144   297

ZERDEN, D. L.
  POEMS
    Riverside Drive   157   156
    Spring Market on Canal Street   164   9

ZHAO, Y. H.
  TRANSLATIONS
    Poems by Shu Ting
      (Tr. with Carolyn Kizer)   149   253

ZIMMER, PAUL
  BOOKS REVIEWED
    The Republic of Many Voices   118   35
    Family Reunion: Selected and New Poems   144   231

ZIMROTH, EVAN
  POEMS
    Eutrophication   134   74
    Another Trashy Aubade   135   276
    Unfinished Portraits
    On Hearing that Childbirth
      Is Like Orgasm
    Lilly's Song
    Playground   140   224
    Postcard from Idyllic Isle la Motte
    The Drama Critic Warns of Clichés   144   7

  BOOKS REVIEWED
    Giselle Considers Her Future   139   35

ZINN, ERNEST
  BOOKS REVIEWED
    Gedichte 1906 bis 1926,
      by Rainer Maria Rilke (Ed.)   93   192

ZINNES, HARRIET
  REVIEWS
    Onward to Solipsism   72   222
    A Southern Vanguard
      (Ed. by Allen Tate)
    New Road: Directions
      in European Art and Letters, #4
      (Ed. by Fred Marnau)
    Theory of Literature,
      by René Wellek
      and Austin Warren   75   303
    Studies in Seventeenth-Century Poetic,
      by Ruth Wallerstein   80   163
    Animal Vegetable Mineral,
      by Babette Deutsch   86   48
    Locations for the Critic   88   339
      Creation and Discovery,
      by Eliseo Vivas
      Aesthetics and Criticism,
      by Harold Osborne

  BOOKS REVIEWED
    An Eye for an I   109   401

ZION, MATTHEW
BOOKS REVIEWED
Instructions for Undressing the Human Race,
   by Fernando Alegria
   (Tr. with Lennart Bruce)   115   440

ZITNER, S. P.
POEMS
Light Bulb: Lares   90   220

REVIEWS
Tell Me, Tell Me, by Marianne Moore   110   423
The William Carlos Williams Reader
   (Ed. by M. L. Rosenthal)   111   41

ZIZIK, JOEL
POEMS
A Third Kind of Moment   158   145

ZOLINSKY, HENRY (SAUL)
[HENRY SAUL]
POEMS
Will Power   19   137
Pain
Feeling   23   134
Sorrow and Joy
Horatio   37   259

ZORACH, MARGUERITE
POEMS
The Moon Rose   12   308

ZORACH, WILLIAM
POEMS
The Abandoned Farm   10   75
Look, the Sea!   12   309

ZUBER, ISABEL
POEMS
Croning   157   25
Bane and Simples   165   14
Missing the Milky Way

ZUKOFSKY, CELIA
POEMS
Peliaco Quondam
   (With Louis Zukofsky)   114   219

TRANSLATIONS
Poems from Gaius Valerius Catullus
   (Tr. with Louis Zukofsky)   94   148
Versions of Catullus
   (Tr. with Louis Zukofsky)   105   155

BOOKS REVIEWED
Bottom: On Shakespeare,
   by Louis Zukofsky
   (Music by Celia Zukofsky)   107   60

ZUKOFSKY, LOUIS
POEMS
Of Dying Beauty   23   197
Siren and Signal   34   146
"A"—Seventh Movement   37   242
"A"—Second Movement   40   26
29   42   312
"Mantis"   45   320
"A"-9   58   128
1892-1941   60   314
The Judge and the Bird   85   74
The Guests   87   346
Two from Barely and Widely   92   133
   Stratford-on-Avon 1957
   ("This year/that Valentine is...")
Jaunt   95   296
From Bottom: On Shakespeare   97   141
Atque in Perpetuum A. W.   101   143
The Old Poet Moves to
   a New Apartment 14 Times   101   373
"A"-17: A Coronal   103   124
"A"-14   107   1
"A"-15   108   357
"A"-18   110   281
"A"-19   111   82
"A"-21: Rudens (Acts I and II)   112   297
"A"-21: Rudens (Act III)   112   402
Peliaco Quondam (With Celia Zukofsky)   114   219
"A"-22 ("AN ERA/ANY TIME...")   122   215
"A"-22, Part II ("Centuries...")   124   35

TRANSLATIONS
Three Poems by André Salmon,
   by René Taupin (Tr.)   37   289
Three Poems by André Salmon, II,
   by René Taupin (Tr.)   37   333
Poems from Gaius Valerius Catullus
   (Tr. with Celia Zukofsky)   94   148
Versions of Catullus
   (Tr. with Celia Zukofsky)   105   155

ARTICLES
Program: "Objectivists" 1931
   [Ezra Pound, Ernest Hemingway]   37   268
Sincerity and Objectification
   [Charles Reznikoff]   37   272
[Note on *Hymn,* by Parker Tyler,
   and *Left Instantly Designs,*
   by Charles Henri Ford]   37   287
Correspondence
   [Objectivists, Stanley Burnshaw]   38   51
Correspondence
   [Objectivists, M. U. Schappes]   42   117
Program: "Objectivists" 1931
   [Ezra Pound, Ernest Hemingway]   121   45

REVIEWS
Redimiculum Matellarum,
    by Basil Bunting   38   160
William Carlos Williams,
    by Vivienne Koch   76   177
The Whip, by Robert Creeley   92   110
Pronounced Golgonoozà?   107   65
    William Blake: A Reading
        of the Shorter Poems,
        by Hazard Adams
    Blake's Apocalypse:
        A Study in Poetic Argument,
        by Harold Bloom
    A Study of the Illuminated Books
        of William Blake,
        by Sir Geoffrey Keynes
    William Blake,
        by John Middleton Murry

BOOKS REVIEWED
An "Objectivists" Anthology (Ed.)   41   340
55 Poems   60   338
Anew   70   108
Some Time   91   266
"A" 1-12   97   102
16 Once Published   102   115
Found Objects   105   128
All: The Collected Short Poems, 1923-1958 107   52
All: The Collected Short Poems, 1923-1958 107   55
Bottom: On Shakespeare
    (Music by Celia Zukofsky)   107   60
After I's
All, the Collected Short Poems, 1956-1964 110 420
"A" 1-12   111   112
Prepositions: The Collected Critical Essays 114 113
"A" 13-21, A Poem of a Life   117   118
"A" 22 & 23   130   285

ARTICLES ABOUT
The Arrogance of Youth,
    by Harriet Monroe   37   328
Correspondence from Horace Gregory
    and Stanley Burnshaw   38   51
Correspondence from Walter Lowenfels   38   289
Correspondence from M. U. Schappes   42   117
[Note]   103   140
Correspondence
    from David Federman   107   271

ZWEIG, MARTHA (MAC NEAL)
POEMS
Michael, Some Work Finished   111   241
Charm Before Sleeping
On Stannard Mountain   163   71

ZWEIG, PAUL
POEMS
The Bells   105   373
Gifts for the Silent Boy   109   12
Walking Over Brooklyn
The Marriage   110   386
Anger
There Are Women
Voyage to Tasmania   112   243
The Faces
Listening to Gregorian Chant
    in San Marco, Venice
Night Song   120   152
The Homecoming   122   143
The Black Stone
The Failure of Narcissus

REVIEWS
French Chronicle   111   124
    Selected Works of Alfred Jarry
        (Ed. and tr. by Roger Shattuck
        and Simon Watson Taylor)
    Alcools, by Guillaume Apollinaire
        (Tr. by Anne Hyde Greet)
    Blaise Cendrars, Selected Writings
        (Ed. by Walter Albert)
    Flowers of Evil,
        by Charles Baudelaire
        (Tr. by Florence Louie Friedman)
    The Poems of Francois Villon
        (Tr. by Galway Kinnell)
    The Years as Catches; The Sweetness and
        Greatness of Dante's Divine Comedy;
        Of the War: Passages 22-27; and Medea
        at Kolchis, The Maiden Head,
        by Robert Duncan   111   402

BOOKS REVIEWED
Yvan Goll: Selected Poems (Ed.)   114   40
Against Emptiness   120   115
The Dark Side of the Earth   127   164
Eternity's Woods   147   227

ZWINGER, SUSAN
POEMS
Driving It West   119   323
Deckers
Quarrel with Intimacy   122   79
Heitman's, Solon, Iowa   127   15
Prehistoric Miscarriages

ZYDEK, FREDRICK
POEMS
A Few Words for My Mortician   170   315

KEY TO ISSUES
By Volume, Number, Date, and Page Numbers

Vol. 1	#1	October	1912	1- 32
	#2	November	1912	33- 66
	#3	December	1912	67-100
	#4	January	1913	101-136
	#5	February	1913	137-172
	#6	March	1913	173-210
Vol. 2	#1	April	1913	1- 32
	#2	May	1913	33- 80
	#3	June	1913	81-118
	#4	July	1913	119-152
	#5	August	1913	153-190
	#6	September	1913	191-230
Vol. 3	#1	October	1913	1- 36
	#2	November	1913	37- 74
	#3	December	1913	75-114
	#4	January	1914	115-152
	#5	February	1914	153-190
	#6	March	1914	191-226
Vol. 4	#1	April	1914	1- 34
	#2	May	1914	35- 74
	#3	June	1914	75-122
	#4	July	1914	123-168
	#5	August	1914	169-206
	#6	September	1914	207-250
Vol. 5	#1	October	1914	1- 48
	#2	November	1914	49- 98
	#3	December	1914	99-148
	#4	January	1915	149-198
	#5	February	1915	199-250
	#6	March	1915	251-302
Vol. 6	#1	April	1915	1- 52
	#2	May	1915	53-106
	#3	June	1915	107-160
	#4	July	1915	161-214
	#5	August	1915	215-268
	#6	September	1915	269-322
Vol. 7	#1	October	1915	1- 54
	#2	November	1915	55-110
	#3	December	1915	111-162
	#4	January	1916	163-216
	#5	February	1916	217-270
	#6	March	1916	271-326
Vol. 8	#1	April	1916	1- 54
	#2	May	1916	55-108
	#3	June	1916	109-162
	#4	July	1916	163-218
	#5	August	1916	219-274
	#6	September	1916	275-330
Vol. 9	#1	October	1916	1- 56
	#2	November	1916	57-110
	#3	December	1916	111-164
	#4	January	1917	165-220
	#5	February	1917	221-276
	#6	March	1917	277-332
Vol. 10	#1	April	1917	1- 56
	#2	May	1917	57-112
	#3	June	1917	113-168
	#4	July	1917	169-224
	#5	August	1917	225-280
	#6	September	1917	281-336
Vol. 11	#1	October	1917	1- 58
	#2	November	1917	59-114
	#3	December	1917	115-170
	#4	January	1918	171-228
	#5	February	1918	229-286
	#6	March	1918	287-344
Vol. 12	#1	April	1918	1- 58
	#2	May	1918	59-116
	#3	June	1918	117-174
	#4	July	1918	175-232
	#5	August	1918	233-290
	#6	September	1918	291-348
Vol. 13	#1	October	1918	1- 58
	#2	November	1918	59-116
	#3	December	1918	117-174
	#4	January	1919	175-232
	#5	February	1919	233-290
	#6	March	1919	291-348
Vol. 14	#1	April	1919	1- 58
	#2	May	1919	59-116
	#3	June	1919	117-174
	#4	July	1919	175-232
	#5	August	1919	233-290
	#6	September	1919	291-348
Vol. 15	#1	October	1919	1- 58
	#2	November	1919	59-116
	#3	December	1919	117-174
	#4	January	1920	175-232
	#5	February	1920	233-290
	#6	March	1920	291-348
Vol. 16	#1	April	1920	1- 58
	#2	May	1920	59-116
	#3	June	1920	117-174
	#4	July	1920	175-234
	#5	August	1920	235-292
	#6	September	1920	293-350
Vol. 17	#1	October	1920	1- 58
	#2	November	1920	59-116
	#3	December	1920	117-174
	#4	January	1921	175-232
	#5	February	1921	233-290
	#6	March	1921	291-350

Vol. 18	#1	April	1921	1- 60			#4	July	1925	177–234
	#2	May	1921	61–118			#5	August	1925	234–294
	#3	June	1921	119–176			#6	September	1925	295–354
	#4	July	1921	177–234						
	#5	August	1921	235–292		Vol. 27	#1	October	1925	1- 58
	#6	September	1921	293–350			#2	November	1925	59–116
							#3	December	1925	117–174
Vol. 19	#1	October	1921	1- 58			#4	January	1926	175–232
	#2	November	1921	59–116			#5	February	1926	233–292
	#3	December	1921	117–174			#6	March	1926	293–352
	#4	January	1922	175–234						
	#5	February	1922	235–294		Vol. 28	#1	April	1926	1- 60
	#6	March	1922	295–352			#2	May	1926	61–118
							#3	June	1926	119–178
Vol. 20	#1	April	1922	1- 58			#4	July	1926	179–236
	#2	May	1922	59–116			#5	August	1926	237–296
	#3	June	1922	117–174			#6	September	1926	297–356
	#4	July	1922	175–234						
	#5	August	1922	235–292		Vol. 29	#1	October	1926	1- 60
	#6	September	1922	293–350			#2	November	1926	61–118
							#3	December	1926	119–176
Vol. 21	#1	October	1922	1- 58			#4	January	1927	177–234
	#2	November	1922	59–116			#5	February	1927	235–294
	#3	December	1922	117–174			#6	March	1927	295–354
	#4	January	1923	175–232						
	#5	February	1923	233–290		Vol. 30	#1	April	1927	1- 58
	#6	March	1923	291–348			#2	May	1927	59–118
							#3	June	1927	119–178
Vol. 22	#1	April	1923	1- 58			#4	July	1927	179–238
	#2	May	1923	59–116			#5	August	1927	239–298
	#3	June	1923	117–174			#6	September	1927	299–358
	#4	July	1923	175–232						
	#5	August	1923	233–290		Vol. 31	#1	October	1927	1- 58
	#6	September	1923	291–348			#2	November	1927	59–116
							#3	December	1927	117–174
Vol. 23	#1	October	1923	1- 58			#4	January	1928	175–234
	#2	November	1923	59–116			#5	February	1928	235–294
	#3	December	1923	117–174			#6	March	1928	295–354
	#4	January	1924	175–232						
	#5	February	1924	233–290		Vol. 32	#1	April	1928	1- 60
	#6	March	1924	291–348			#2	May	1928	61–118
							#3	June	1928	119–178
Vol. 24	#1	April	1924	1- 58			#4	July	1928	179–238
	#2	May	1924	59–114			#5	August	1928	239–298
	#3	June	1924	115–172			#6	September	1928	299–358
	#4	July	1924	173–230						
	#5	August	1924	231–288		Vol. 33	#1	October	1928	1- 58
	#6	September	1924	289–346			#2	November	1928	59–116
							#3	December	1928	117–174
Vol. 25	#1	October	1924	1- 58			#4	January	1929	175–234
	#2	November	1924	59–116			#5	February	1929	235–292
	#3	December	1924	117–174			#6	March	1929	293–352
	#4	January	1925	175–230						
	#5	February	1925	231–288		Vol. 34	#1	April	1929	1- 60
	#6	March	1925	289–346			#2	May	1929	61–120
							#3	June	1929	121–180
Vol. 26	#1	April	1925	1- 58			#4	July	1929	181–240
	#2	May	1925	59–116			#5	August	1929	241–300
	#3	June	1925	117–176			#6	September	1929	301–360

Vol. 35	#1	October	1929	1- 60
	#2	November	1929	61-118
	#3	December	1929	119-176
	#4	January	1930	177-236
	#5	February	1930	237-296
	#6	March	1930	297-354
Vol. 36	#1	April	1930	1- 58
	#2	May	1930	59-116
	#3	June	1930	117-174
	#4	July	1930	175-234
	#5	August	1930	235-294
	#6	September	1930	295-354
Vol. 37	#1	October	1930	1- 60
	#2	November	1930	61-120
	#3	December	1930	121-176
	#4	January	1931	177-236
	#5	February	1931	237-296
	#6	March	1931	297-356
Vol. 38	#1	April	1931	1- 60
	#2	May	1931	61-118
	#3	June	1931	119-176
	#4	July	1931	177-236
	#5	August	1931	237-294
	#6	September	1931	295-354
Vol. 39	#1	October	1931	1- 58
	#2	November	1931	59-116
	#3	December	1931	117-174
	#4	January	1932	175-232
	#5	February	1932	233-292
	#6	March	1932	293-352
Vol. 40	#1	April	1932	1- 58
	#2	May	1932	59-118
	#3	June	1932	119-178
	#4	July	1932	179-238
	#5	August	1932	239-298
	#6	September	1932	299-358
Vol. 41	#1	October	1932	1- 58
	#2	November	1932	59-118
	#3	December	1932	119-176
	#4	January	1933	177-236
	#5	February	1933	237-294
	#6	March	1933	295-354
Vol. 42	#1	April	1933	1- 60
	#2	May	1933	61-120
	#3	June	1933	121-180
	#4	July	1933	181-240
	#5	August	1933	241-300
	#6	September	1933	301-360
Vol. 43	#1	October	1933	1- 58
	#2	November	1933	59-118
	#3	December	1933	119-176

	#4	January	1934	177-236
	#5	February	1934	237-296
	#6	March	1934	297-356
Vol. 44	#1	April	1934	1- 60
	#2	May	1934	61-118
	#3	June	1934	119-178
	#4	July	1934	179-238
	#5	August	1934	239-298
	#6	September	1934	299-358
Vol. 45	#1	October	1934	1- 60
	#2	November	1934	61-120
	#3	December	1934	121-178
	#4	January	1935	179-238
	#5	February	1935	239-298
	#6	March	1935	299-358
Vol. 46	#1	April	1935	1- 60
	#2	May	1935	61-118
	#3	June	1935	119-178
	#4	July	1935	179-236
	#5	August	1935	237-296
	#6	September	1935	297-356
Vol. 47	#1	October	1935	1- 60
	#2	November	1935	61-118
	#3	December	1935	119-176
	#4	January	1936	177-236
	#5	February	1936	237-294
	#6	March	1936	295-352
Vol. 48	#1	April	1936	1- 60
	#2	May	1936	61-120
	#3	June	1936	121-180
	#4	July	1936	181-238
	#5	August	1936	239-298
	#6	September	1936	299-358
Vol. 49	#1	October	1936	1- 58
	#2	November	1936	59-118
	#3	December	1936	119-178
	#4	January	1937	179-238
	#5	February	1937	239-298
	#6	March	1937	299-358
Vol. 50	#1	April	1937	1- 60
	#2	May	1937	61-120
	#3	June	1937	121-180
	#4	July	1937	181-240
	#5	August	1937	241-300
	#6	September	1937	301-360
Vol. 51	#1	October	1937	1- 58
	#2	November	1937	59-116
	#3	December	1937	117-174
	#4	January	1938	175-234
	#5	February	1938	235-294
	#6	March	1938	295-354

Vol. 52	#1	April	1938	1- 56	
	#2	May	1938	57-114	
	#3	June	1938	115-172	
	#4	July	1938	173-246	
	#5	August	1938	247-306	
	#6	September	1938	307-364	
Vol. 53	#1	October	1938	1- 58	
	#2	November	1938	59-114	
	#3	December	1938	115-168	
	#4	January	1939	169-228	
	#5	February	1939	229-288	
	#6	March	1939	289-346	
Vol. 54	#1	April	1939	1- 60	
	#2	May	1939	61-118	
	#3	June	1939	119-176	
	#4	July	1939	177-234	
	#5	August	1939	235-294	
	#6	September	1939	295-352	
Vol. 55	#1	October	1939	1- 58	
	#2	November	1939	59-114	
	#3	December	1939	115-168	
	#4	January	1940	169-228	
	#5	February	1940	229-288	
	#6	March	1940	289-348	
Vol. 56	#1	April	1940	1- 58	
	#2	May	1940	59-114	
	#3	June	1940	115-172	
	#4	July	1940	173-232	
	#5	August	1940	233-292	
	#6	September	1940	293-350	
Vol. 57	#1	October	1940	1- 58	
	#2	November	1940	115-170	
	#3	December	1940	171-226	
	#4	January	1941	227-284	
	#5	February	1941	285-344	
	#6	March	1941	345-402	
Vol. 58	#1	April	1941	1- 58	
	#2	May	1941	59-116	
	#3	June	1941	117-174	
	#4	July	1941	175-232	
	#5	August	1941	233-292	
	#6	September	1941	293-352	
Vol. 59	#1	October	1941	1- 58	
	#2	November	1941	59-114	
	#3	December	1941	115-174	
	#4	January	1942	175-234	
	#5	February	1942	235-294	
	#6	March	1942	295-354	
Vol. 60	#1	April	1942	1- 56	
	#2	May	1942	57-114	
	#3	June	1942	115-174	
	#4	July	1942	175-234	
	#5	August	1942	235-294	
	#6	September	1942	295-352	
Vol. 61	#1	October	1942	353-410	
	#2	November	1942	411-466	
	#3	December	1942	467-524	
	#4	January	1943	525-582	
	#5	February	1943	583-642	
	#6	March	1943	643-700	
Vol. 62	#1	April	1943	1- 60	
	#2	May	1943	61-120	
	#3	June	1943	121-178	
	#4	July	1943	179-236	
	#5	August	1943	237-296	
	#6	September	1943	297-356	
Vol. 63	#1	October	1943	1- 58	
	#2	November	1943	59-118	
	#3	December	1943	119-178	
	#4	January	1944	179-238	
	#5	February	1944	239-298	
	#6	March	1944	299-356	
Vol. 64	#1	April	1944	1- 58	
	#2	May	1944	59-118	
	#3	June	1944	119-178	
	#4	July	1944	179-238	
	#5	August	1944	239-296	
	#6	September	1944	297-354	
Vol. 65	#1	October	1944	1- 58	
	#2	November	1944	59-114	
	#3	December	1944	115-170	
	#4	January	1945	171-230	
	#5	February	1945	231-290	
	#6	March	1945	291-350	
Vol. 66	#1	April	1945	1- 60	
	#2	May	1945	61-116	
	#3	June	1945	117-174	
	#4	July	1945	175-234	
	#5	August	1945	235-294	
	#6	September	1945	295-354	
Vol. 67	#1	October	1945	1- 58	
	#2	November	1945	59-118	
	#3	December	1945	119-176	
	#4	January	1946	177-232	
	#5	February	1946	233-292	
	#6	March	1946	293-352	
Vol. 68	#1	April	1946	1- 60	
	#2	May	1946	61-120	
	#3	June	1946	121-178	
	#4	July	1946	179-236	
	#5	August	1946	237-296	
	#6	September	1946	297-356	

Vol. 69	#1 October	1946	1- 60
	#2 November	1946	61-120
	#3 December	1946	121-178
	#4 January	1947	179-238
	#5 February	1947	239-298
	#6 March	1947	299-358
Vol. 70	#1 April	1947	1- 58
	#2 May	1947	59-116
	#3 June	1947	117-174
	#4 July	1947	175-232
	#5 August	1947	233-292
	#6 September	1947	293-350
Vol. 71	#1 October	1947	1- 60
	#2 November	1947	61-114
	#3 December	1947	115-172
	#4 January	1948	173-230
	#5 February	1948	231-288
	#6 March	1948	289-346
Vol. 72	#1 April	1948	1- 58
	#2 May	1948	59-116
	#3 June	1948	117-174
	#4 July	1948	175-232
	#5 August	1948	233-290
	#6 September	1948	291-348
Vol. 73	#1 October	1948	1- 62
	#2 November	1948	63-124
	#3 December	1948	125-186
	#4 January	1949	187-248
	#5 February	1949	249-310
	#6 March	1949	311-372
Vol. 74	#1 April	1949	1- 62
	#2 May	1949	63-124
	#3 June	1949	125-186
	#4 July	1949	187-248
	#5 August	1949	249-310
	#6 September	1949	311-372
Vol. 75	#1 October	1949	1- 62
	#2 November	1949	63-124
	#3 December	1949	125-186
	#4 January	1950	187-248
	#5 February	1950	249-310
	#6 March	1950	311-372
Vol. 76	#1 April	1950	1- 62
	#2 May	1950	63-124
	#3 June	1950	125-186
	#4 July	1950	187-248
	#5 August	1950	249-310
	#6 September	1950	311-372
Vol. 77	#1 October	1950	1- 62
	#2 November	1950	63-124
	#3 December	1950	125-186

	#4 January	1951	187-248
	#5 February	1951	249-310
	#6 March	1951	311-372
Vol. 78	#1 April	1951	1- 62
	#2 May	1951	63-124
	#3 June	1951	125-186
	#4 July	1951	187-248
	#5 August	1951	249-310
	#6 September	1951	311-372
Vol. 79	#1 October	1951	1- 62
	#2 November	1951	63-124
	#3 December	1951	125-186
	#4 January	1952	187-248
	#5 February	1952	249-310
	#6 March	1952	311-372
Vol. 80	#1 April	1952	1- 62
	#2 May	1952	63-124
	#3 June	1952	125-186
	#4 July	1952	187-248
	#5 August	1952	249-310
	#6 September	1952	311-372
Vol. 81	#1 October	1952	1- 96
	#2 November	1952	97-158
	#3 December	1952	159-220
	#4 January	1953	221-282
	#5 February	1953	283-344
	#6 March	1953	345-406
Vol. 82	#1 April	1953	1- 62
	#2 May	1953	63-124
	#3 June	1953	125-186
	#4 July	1953	187-248
	#5 August	1953	249-310
	#6 September	1953	311-372
Vol. 83	#1 October	1953	1- 62
	#2 November	1953	63-124
	#3 December	1953	125-186
	#4 January	1954	187-248
	#5 February	1954	249-310
	#6 March	1954	311-372
Vol. 84	#1 April	1954	1- 62
	#2 May	1954	63-124
	#3 June	1954	125-186
	#4 July	1954	187-248
	#5 August	1954	249-310
	#6 September	1954	311-374
Vol. 85	#1 October	1954	1- 62
	#2 November	1954	63-122
	#3 December	1954	125-184
	#4 January	1955	187-248
	#5 February	1955	249-310
	#6 March	1955	311-372

Vol. 86	#1	April	1955	1- 59			#4	July	1959	211–280
	#2	May	1955	63–124			#5	August	1959	281–358
	#3	June	1955	125–186			#6	September	1959	359–424
	#4	July	1955	187–248						
	#5	August	1955	249–310		Vol. 95	#1	October	1959	1- 66
	#6	September	1955	311–374			#2	November	1959	69–138
							#3	December	1959	139–200
Vol. 87	#1	October	1955	1- 62			#4	January	1960	201–262
	#2	November	1955	63–130			#5	February	1960	263–324
	#3	December	1955	130–195			#6	March	1960	325–390
	#4	January	1956	192–253						
	#5	February	1956	254–315		Vol. 96	#1	April	1960	1- 70
	#6	March	1956	316–382			#2	May	1960	71–132
							#3	June	1960	133–194
Vol. 88	#1	April	1956	1- 62			#4	July	1960	195–264
	#2	May	1956	63–124			#5	August	1960	265–334
	#3	June	1956	125–203			#6	September	1960	335–400
	#4	July	1956	207–285						
	#5	August	1956	287–349		Vol. 97	#1	October	1960	1- 62
	#6	September	1956	348–415			#2	November	1960	63–140
							#3	December	1960	141–202
Vol. 89	#1	October	1956	1- 73			#4	January	1961	203–272
	#2	November	1956	74–135			#5	February	1961	273–334
	#3	December	1956	136–204			#6	March	1961	335–400
	#4	January	1957	205–266						
	#5	February	1957	267–332		Vol. 98	#1	April	1961	1- 70
	#6	March	1957	333–403			#2	May	1961	71–132
							#3	June	1961	133–202
Vol. 90	#1	April	1957	1- 65			#4	July	1961	203–272
	#2	May	1957	67–127			#5	August	1961	273–342
	#3	June	1957	129–197			#6	September	1961	343–408
	#4	July	1957	199–264						
	#5	August	1957	265–333		Vol. 99	#1	October	1961	1- 70
	#6	September	1957	335–403			#2	November	1961	71–140
							#3	December	1961	141–202
Vol. 91	#1	October	1957	1- 70			#4	January	1962	203–272
	#2	November	1957	71–148			#5	February	1962	273–334
	#3	December	1957	149–218			#6	March	1962	335–400
	#4	January	1958	219–280						
	#5	February	1958	281–342		Vol. 100	#1	April	1962	1- 70
	#6	March	1958	343–416			#2	May	1962	70–140
							#3	June	1962	141–210
Vol. 92	#1	April	1958	1- 61			#4	July	1962	211–270
	#2	May	1958	63–132			#5	August	1962	271–340
	#3	June	1958	133–202			#6	September	1962	341–420
	#4	July	1958	203–270						
	#5	August	1958	271–340		Vol. 101	#1-2	(Double Issue)		
	#6	September	1958	341–406				Oct.-Nov.	1962	1–162
							#3	December	1962	163–232
Vol. 93	#1	October	1958	1- 62			#4	January	1963	233–302
	#2	November	1958	63–132			#5	February	1963	303–372
	#3	December	1958	133–202			#6	March	1963	373–438
	#4	January	1959	203–280						
	#5	February	1959	281–350		Vol. 102	#1	April	1963	1- 70
	#6	March	1959	350–416			#2	May	1963	71–140
							#3	June	1963	141–210
Vol. 94	#1	April	1959	1- 70			#4	July	1963	211–280
	#2	May	1959	70–140			#5	August	1963	281–350
	#3	June	1959	141–210			#6	September	1963	351–414

Vol. 103	#1-2 (Double Issue)					#4	January	1968	213-282
		OctNov.	1963	1-148		#5	February	1968	283-352
	#3	December	1963	149-218		#6	March	1968	353-432
	#4	January	1964	219-280					
	#5	February	1964	281-342	Vol. 112	#1	April	1968	1- 78
	#6	March	1964	343-408		#2	May	1968	79-148
						#3	June	1968	149-226
Vol. 104	#1	April	1964	1- 62		#4	July	1968	227-296
	#2	May	1964	63-132		#5	August	1968	297-374
	#3	June	1964	133-202		#6	September	1968	375-440
	#4	July	1964	203-272					
	#5	August	1964	273-334	Vol. 113	#1	October	1968	1- 68
	#6	September	1964	335-400		#2	November	1968	69-146
						#3	December	1968	147-224
Vol. 105	#1	October	1964	1- 74		#4	January	1969	225-294
	#2	November	1964	81-154		#5	February	1969	295-372
	#3	December	1964	155-224		#6	March	1969	373-438
	#4	January	1965	225-286					
	#5	February	1965	287-348	Vol. 114	#1	April	1969	1- 70
	#6	March	1965	349-432		#2	May	1969	71-148
						#3	June	1969	149-218
Vol. 106	#1-2 (Double Issue)					#4	July	1969	219-288
		April-May	1965	1-180		#5	August	1969	289-350
	#3	June	1965	181-256		#6	September	1969	353-418
	#4	July	1965	257-318					
	#5	August	1965	319-380	Vol. 115	#1	October	1969	1- 78
	#6	September	1965	381-442		#2	November	1969	79-148
						#3	December	1969	149-218
Vol. 107	#1	October	1965	1- 74		#4	January	1970	219-296
	#2	November	1965	75-142		#5	February	1970	297-374
	#3	December	1965	143-212		#6	March	1970	375-456
	#4	January	1966	213-282					
	#5	February	1966	283-352	Vol. 116	#1	April	1970	1- 70
	#6	March	1966	353-420		#2	May	1970	71-140
						#3	June	1970	141-210
Vol. 108	#1	April	1966	1- 78		#4	July	1970	211-272
	#2	May	1966	79-148		#5-6 (Double Issue)			
	#3	June	1966	149-216			Aug.-Sep.	1970	273-404
	#4	July	1966	217-286					
	#5	August	1966	287-356	Vol. 117	#1	October	1970	1- 70
	#6	September	1966	357-438		#2	November	1970	71-148
						#3	December	1970	149-226
Vol. 109	#1	October	1966	1- 68		#4	January	1971	227-288
	#2	November	1966	69-146		#5	February	1971	289-350
	#3	December	1966	147-216		#6	March	1971	351-410
	#4	January	1967	217-286					
	#5	February	1967	287-356	Vol. 118	#1	April	1971	1- 62
	#6	March	1967	357-422		#2	May	1971	63-124
						#3	June	1971	125-186
Vol. 110	#1	April	1967	1- 70		#4	July	1971	187-248
	#2	May	1967	71-140		#5	August	1971	249-310
	#3	June	1967	141-210		#6	September	1971	311-370
	#4	July	1967	211-280					
	#5	August	1967	281-358	Vol. 119	#1	October	1971	1- 62
	#6	September	1967	359-442		#2	November	1971	63-124
						#3	December	1971	125-186
Vol. 111	#1	October	1967	1- 70		#4	January	1972	187-248
	#2	November	1967	67-142		#5	February	1972	249-310
	#3	December	1967	143-212		#6	March	1972	311-370

Vol. 120	#1	April	1972	1- 70	
	#2	May	1972	71-132	
	#3	June	1972	133-194	
	#4	July	1972	195-256	
	#5	August	1972	257-318	
	#6	September	1972	319-370	
Vol. 121	#1	October	1972	1- 62	
	#2	November	1972	63-124	
	#3	December	1972	125-186	
	#4	January	1973	187-248	
	#5	February	1973	249-310	
	#6	March	1973	311-370	
Vol. 122	#1	April	1973	1- 62	
	#2	May	1973	63-124	
	#3	June	1973	125-186	
	#4	July	1973	187-248	
	#5	August	1973	249-310	
	#6	September	1973	311-364	
Vol. 123	#1	October	1973	1- 62	
	#2	November	1973	63-132	
	#3	December	1973	133-194	
	#4	January	1974	195-256	
	#5	February	1974	257-318	
	#6	March	1974	319-372	
Vol. 124	#1	April	1974	1- 62	
	#2	May	1974	63-124	
	#3	June	1974	125-186	
	#4	July	1974	187-246	
	#5	August	1974	247-308	
	#6	September	1974	309-362	
Vol. 125	#1	October	1974	1- 62	
	#2	November	1974	63-124	
	#3	December	1974	125-186	
	#4	January	1975	187-248	
	#5	February	1975	249-310	
	#6	March	1975	311-364	
Vol. 126	#1	April	1975	1- 62	
	#2	May	1975	63-124	
	#3	June	1975	125-186	
	#4	July	1975	187-248	
	#5	August	1975	249-310	
	#6	September	1975	311-364	
Vol. 127	#1	October	1975	1- 62	
	#2	November	1975	63-124	
	#3	December	1975	125-186	
	#4	January	1976	187-248	
	#5	February	1976	249-310	
	#6	March	1976	311-364	
Vol. 128	#1	April	1976	1- 62	
	#2	May	1976	63-124	
	#3	June	1976	125-186	
	#4	July	1976	187-248	
	#5	August	1976	249-310	
	#6	September	1976	311-364	
Vol. 129	#1	October	1976	1- 62	
	#2	November	1976	63-124	
	#3	December	1976	125-186	
	#4	January	1977	187-248	
	#5	February	1977	249-310	
	#6	March	1977	311-366	
Vol. 130	#1	April	1977	1- 62	
	#2	May	1977	63-124	
	#3	June	1977	125-186	
	#4	July	1977	187-248	
	#5	August	1977	249-310	
	#6	September	1977	311-362	
Vol. 131	#1	October	1977	1- 62	
	#2	November	1977	63-124	
	#3	December	1977	125-186	
	#4	January	1978	187-248	
	#5	February	1978	249-310	
	#6	March	1978	311-364	
Vol. 132	#1	April	1978	1- 62	
	#2	May	1978	63-124	
	#3	June	1978	125-186	
	#4	July	1978	187-248	
	#5	August	1978	249-310	
	#6	September	1978	311-362	
Vol. 133	#1	October	1978	1- 62	
	#2	November	1978	63-124	
	#3	December	1978	125-186	
	#4	January	1979	187-248	
	#5	February	1979	249-310	
	#6	March	1979	311-362	
Vol. 134	#1	April	1979	1- 62	
	#2	May	1979	63-124	
	#3	June	1979	125-186	
	#4	July	1979	187-248	
	#5	August	1979	249-310	
	#6	September	1979	311-362	
Vol. 135	#1	October	1979	1- 62	
	#2	November	1979	63-124	
	#3	December	1979	125-186	
	#4	January	1980	187-248	
	#5	February	1980	249-310	
	#6	March	1980	311-362	
Vol. 136	#1	April	1980	1- 62	
	#2	May	1980	63-124	
	#3	June	1980	125-186	
	#4	July	1980	187-248	
	#5	August	1980	249-310	
	#6	September	1980	311-364	

Vol. 137	#1	October	1980	1– 62
	#2	November	1980	63–126
	#3	December	1980	127–188
	#4	January	1981	189–250
	#5	February	1981	251–312
	#6	March	1981	313–366
Vol. 138	#1	April	1981	1– 62
	#2	May	1981	63–122
	#3	June	1981	125–186
	#4	July	1981	187–248
	#5	August	1981	249–310
	#6	September	1981	311–362
Vol. 139	#1	October	1981	1– 62
	#2	November	1981	63–124
	#3	December	1981	127–188
	#4	January	1982	189–250
	#5	February	1982	251–312
	#6	March	1982	313–362
Vol. 140	#1	April	1982	1– 62
	#2	May	1982	63–124
	#3	June	1982	125–186
	#4	July	1982	187–248
	#5	August	1982	249–310
	#6	September	1982	311–362
Vol. 141	#1	October	1982	1– 62
	#2	November	1982	63–124
	#3	December	1982	127–188
	#4	January	1983	189–250
	#5	February	1983	251–312
	#6	March	1983	313–362
Vol. 142	#1	April	1983	1– 62
	#2	May	1983	63–124
	#3	June	1983	125–186
	#4	July	1983	187–248
	#5	August	1983	249–310
	#6	September	1983	311–362
Vol. 143	#1	October	1983	1– 62
	#2	November	1983	63–124
	#3	December	1983	127–188
	#4	January	1984	189–250
	#5	February	1984	251–312
	#6	March	1984	313–362
Vol. 144	#1	April	1984	1– 62
	#2	May	1984	63–124
	#3	June	1984	125–186
	#4	July	1984	187–248
	#5	August	1984	249–310
	#6	September	1984	311–360
Vol. 145	#1	October	1984	1– 62
	#2	November	1984	63–124
	#3	December	1984	127–188
	#4	January	1985	189–250
	#5	February	1985	251–312
	#6	March	1985	313–362
Vol. 146	#1	April	1985	1– 62
	#2	May	1985	63–124
	#3	June	1985	125–186
	#4	July	1985	187–248
	#5	August	1985	249–310
	#6	September	1985	311–360
Vol. 147	#1	October	1985	1– 62
	#2	November	1985	63–124
	#3	December	1985	127–188
	#4	January	1986	189–250
	#5	February	1986	251–312
	#6	March	1986	313–362
Vol. 148	#1	April	1986	1– 62
	#2	May	1986	63–124
	#3	June	1986	125–186
	#4	July	1986	187–248
	#5	August	1986	249–310
	#6	September	1986	311–360
Vol. 149	#1	October	1986	1– 62
	#2	November	1986	63–124
	#3	December	1986	127–188
	#4	January	1987	189–250
	#5	February	1987	251–312
	#6	March	1987	313–362
Vol. 150	#1	April	1987	1– 62
	#2	May	1987	63–124
	#3	June	1987	125–186
	#4	July	1987	187–248
	#5	August	1987	249–310
	#6	September	1987	311–358
Vol. 151	#1–2	(Double Issue)		
		Oct.–Nov.	1987	1–266
	#3	December	1987	267–328
	#4	January	1988	329–390
	#5	February	1988	391–452
	#6	March	1988	453–498
Vol. 152	#1	April	1988	1– 62
	#2	May	1988	63–124
	#3	June	1988	125–186
	#4	July	1988	187–248
	#5	August	1988	249–310
	#6	September	1988	311–358
Vol. 153	#1	October	1988	1– 62
	#2	November	1988	63–124
	#3	December	1988	127–188
	#4	January	1989	189–250
	#5	February	1989	251–312
	#6	March	1989	311–358

Vol. 154	#1	April	1989	1- 62	
	#2	May	1989	63-124	
	#3	June	1989	125-186	
	#4	July	1989	187-248	
	#5	August	1989	249-310	
	#6	September	1989	311-358	
Vol. 155	#1-2 (Double Issue)				
		Oct.-Nov.	1989	1-190	
	#3	December	1989	191-252	
	#4	January	1990	253-314	
	#5	February	1990	315-376	
	#6	March	1990	377-424	
Vol. 156	#1	April	1990	1- 62	
	#2	May	1990	63-124	
	#3	June	1990	125-186	
	#4	July	1990	187-248	
	#5	August	1990	249-310	
	#6	September	1990	311-358	
Vol. 157	#1	October	1990	1- 62	
	#2	November	1990	63-124	
	#3	December	1990	125-186	
	#4	January	1991	189-250	
	#5	February	1991	251-312	
	#6	March	1991	313-362	
Vol. 158	#1	April	1991	1- 62	
	#2	May	1991	63-124	
	#3	June	1991	125-186	
	#4	July	1991	187-248	
	#5	August	1991	249-310	
	#6	September	1991	311-360	
Vol. 159	#1	October	1991	1- 62	
	#2	November	1991	63-124	
	#3	December	1991	125-186	
	#4	January	1992	189-250	
	#5	February	1992	251-312	
	#6	March	1992	313-362	
Vol. 160	#1	April	1992	1- 62	
	#2	May	1992	63-124	
	#3	June	1992	125-186	
	#4	July	1992	187-248	
	#5	August	1992	249-310	
	#6	September	1992	311-360	
Vol. 161	#1	October	1992	1- 62	
	#2	November	1992	63-124	
	#3	December	1992	125-186	
	#4	January	1993	189-250	
	#5	February	1993	251-312	
	#6	March	1993	313-362	
Vol. 162	#1	April	1993	1- 62	
	#2	May	1993	63-124	
	#3	June	1993	125-186	
	#4	July	1993	187-248	
	#5	August	1993	249-310	
	#6	September	1993	311-358	
Vol. 163	#1	October	1993	1- 62	
	#2	November	1993	63-124	
	#3	December	1993	125-186	
	#4	January	1994	189-250	
	#5	February	1994	251-310	
	#6	March	1994	311-358	
Vol. 164	#1	April	1994	1- 62	
	#2	May	1994	63-124	
	#3	June	1994	125-186	
	#4	July	1994	187-248	
	#5	August	1994	249-310	
	#6	September	1994	311-358	
Vol. 165	#1	October	1994	1- 62	
	#2	November	1994	63-124	
	#3	December	1994	125-186	
	#4	January	1995	187-248	
	#5	February	1995	249-310	
	#6	March	1995	311-360	
Vol. 166	#1	April	1995	1- 62	
	#2	May	1995	63-124	
	#3	June	1995	125-186	
	#4	July	1995	187-248	
	#5	August	1995	249-310	
	#6	September	1995	311-364	
Vol. 167	#1-2 (Double Issue)				
		Oct.-Nov.	1995	1-128	
	#3	December	1995	125-186	
	#4	January	1996	187-248	
	#5	February	1996	249-310	
	#6	March	1996	311-358	
Vol. 168	#1	April	1996	1- 62	
	#2	May	1996	63-124	
	#3	June	1996	125-186	
	#4	July	1996	187-248	
	#5	August	1996	249-310	
	#6	September	1996	311-358	
Vol. 169	#1 (Double Issue)				
		Oct.-Nov.	1996	1-124	
	#2	December	1996	125-186	
	#3	January	1997	187-248	
	#4	February	1997	249-310	
	#5	March	1997	311-360	
Vol. 170	#1	April	1997	1- 62	
	#2	May	1997	63-124	
	#3	June	1997	125-186	
	#4	July	1997	187-248	
	#5	August	1997	249-310	
	#6	September	1997	311-358	

should have these parts identified: inside address, salutation, body, complimentary close, and signature.

A challenging task for all students would be to make a list of salutations and complimentary closings. How would one greet the Queen of England, the archbishop of a church, a senator, a delegate to the United Nations, or a firm of lawyers? The following standards may be placed on a chart and used to evaluate letters:

1. Did I tell something interesting? Was I thinking of the receiver and not of myself?
2. Do I have five parts to my letter?
   A heading.
   A greeting.
   A message.
   A closing.
   A name.
3. Did I write neatly so that the person who receives my letter can read it easily?
4. Did I indent the first word of each paragraph?
5. Did I align the margins on each part of my letter?

Reports

Reports can evolve from scientific observations and experiments, surveys, and interviews. They can be based on research that provides additional information for the class in content areas, such as science, social studies, math, art, or physical education. Book reports can take many forms, one of which involves students designing book jackets with summaries for classroom display.

The teacher should develop, with the class, standards for checking the form and neatness of a written report. This checking method is often called proofreading, editing, or correcting. The standards might be as follows:

STANDARDS FOR EDITING A REPORT

1. Write the title of the report in the center of the line. Leave a space between the top of the paper and the title. Skip a line after the title.
2. Begin the first word of the title with a capital letter. Capitalize each important word of the title. Do not capitalize *a, an, and, at, as the, of, to, in, from,* and *with,* because they are not considered important words.
3. Have good margins at the top, bottom, left, and right.
4. Use clear writing.
5. Use correct spelling and punctuation.
6. Have "sentence sense." Do not use incomplete, run-on, or choppy sentences.
7. Indent all paragraphs.
8. Sign your name at the bottom of the last page.

The teacher and the class might develop an editing code using those signs familiar to the newspaper office, as well as other signs which might prove helpful. While the editing signs in Figure 11–1 can be used in your classroom, a more complete list can be obtained from any standard English grammar book.

= space should be left

One of the most valuable activities associated with working on a school newspaper is the development of a "style sheet," which summarizes the major rules of punctuation, capitalization, and spelling. The local newspaper will usually give a school a copy of the style sheet that guides their writers.

JOURNALISTIC WRITING. Newspapers contain a variety of writing types and styles, including editorials

SP	=	spelling
C	=	capital letter
INC	=	incomplete sentence
ℓ	=	take out
∪	=	transpose, or turn about
¢	=	small letter (lower case letter)
⌣	=	join sentences
PUNC	=	punctuation wrong or omitted
¶	=	indent paragraph
ℒ	=	something should be omitted
(?)	=	material not clear

Figure 11–1. Editing signs.

(opinions), news stories, feature stories, advertisements, recipes, "how-to" essays, advice columns, weather reports, and interviews. Classroom newspapers can evolve from field trips, everyday classroom activities, and even books and stories read. Students in a fifth-grade classroom read the book *Johnny Tremaine* as a class project. Then small groups of students wrote a newspaper that reflected the times and lives of the people during the Revolutionary War. These newspapers were then circulated around the room for all to read. In a midwestern sixth-grade class, students wrote a newspaper every grading period. Their writings centered on activities and work that had been done during that period. These newspapers then went home to parents, who were delighted to be informed of classroom happenings.

3. **As early as third grade, teachers should introduce students to concepts of editing and revising.** With the exception of short, personal writings, such as notes, messages, and journals, most writing activities should span a period of several days. Students can use this time to follow the steps of the writing process.

Children need ample opportunity to think, organize, and write. During the prewriting and writing phases of the process, they need to spend little time attending to form. Instead, they should focus on formulating and refining ideas and thoughts and getting them on paper.

This is the point at which having a clear purpose and specific audience begin to pay off. Students with a heightened awareness of these elements will be motivated to turn their attention to the form of their written work in order to communicate effectively.

The teacher can use various systems of editing.

Teachers must devise instances of writing that address issues of audience and purpose. Journals containing stories, poems, jokes, and personal narratives can be prepared using handwriting or word processing. (Photo by Linda Lungren)

These include self-editing, peer editing in pairs, peer editing in small groups, and teacher conferences. (These are discussed in detail in Chapter 12.) Teachers can best approach this stage of the writing process from a diagnostic/prescriptive point of view. No matter which editing system is used, teachers should always be aware of their pupils' strengths and weaknesses in mechanics and usage.

Students' progress and development in writing can be monitored in several ways. The least effective involves the teacher as judge and audience of students' works that have been written only for a score or grade. Aside from this too frequently used methodology, teachers can simply walk around the room, looking at students' papers and talking to them as they write, thereby noticing which problems occur most often. Then it is within the context of these postwriting phases of editing and revising that skill in using the formal conventions of English can most logically be taught. When the teacher deems it necessary to reinforce or clarify certain grammatical concepts, the following types of activities have proven useful.

1. Slot and filler activities—used by structural linguists,/slot and filler/activities allow students to generate grammatical elements within the context of sentences. The teacher can give students a sentence like,

> *The child loved to eat chocolate-covered peanuts.*

Then, a noun (if this is the concept being studied) is removed and students fill the slot with words of their own choosing.

> *The _____ loved . . .*

Young children can be given large cards with various parts of speech on them. The teacher directs several of them to line up in front of the room to form a sentence. Then one child can drop out, leaving an open slot for a child with a similar grammatical element (noun, verb, other) on his or her card to fill.

2. Sentence expansion—activities based on the transformational linguists' concept of the *kernel sentence*, the smallest sentence unit. Teachers can provide kernel sentences to their students. An example would be,

> *The puppy ran.*

Classroom discussion can center on several grammatical elements (adjectives, adverbs, prepositions in phrases) that will expand the *meaning* of the sentence. For example, the teacher can ask students to rewrite the preceding sentence, adding a word that tells *how* the puppy ran. The children might add the words *fast, yesterday,* or *away,* telling, respectively, *how, when,* and *where* the puppy ran. Through this active practice students are much more likely to internalize the function of adverbs within sentences rather than just learning the definition of an adverb.

3. Sentence combining—provides students with an opportunity to practice varying the structure of sentences that they write. Give students simple sentences:

> The child fell down.
> He hurt his arm.
> Mark was happy.
> His sister was sad.
> The child could choose to have chocolate cake.
> He could choose banana cake for his birthday.

Then, ask them to rewrite the sentences, joining them with the conjunctions *and, but, or, nor, for, yet,* and *so.* (With younger students, the first three would be the easiest at the beginning.) This would also be a good opportunity to discuss *conjunctions* as *joining* words. (*Con-* is the Latin prefix meaning "with," and *junction* is from the Latin root *jungere* meaning "to join.")

A less controlled method of using sentence combining involves providing students with two or more sentences to combine without setting any specific method for combining. For example,

> The child ran to school.
> He was excited.
> Today is his birthday.

can be combined in several ways:

The child was excited as she ran to school because today is her birthday.

Because today is her birthday, the child was excited as she ran to school.

Today is her birthday, so the child ran excitedly to school.

Even more combinations can be made than these. One important concept for children to see and understand is that there is not just one *correct* way of combining these sentences. Students will enjoy sharing their combinations orally with their classmates. Through this oral sharing of written work, students in a classroom are honing not only their writing and speaking skills, but also their reading and listening skills—as they read their own sentences and then, in turn, listen critically to others read theirs. Here, the word *critical* should be distinguished from the word *criticism* and instead associated with the notion of being an astute and attentive listener, one who is listening for the varying sentence structures that his/her classmates are composing.

Students do not have to view the study of grammar and mechanics as Medieval instruments of torture devised by demented academicians, namely, their teachers. They will not constantly be asking "Why are we doing this?" or thinking, "We don't need to know this *stuff*." Why? The answer is that they will see an immediate need for this information in order to apply it to their own writing. After all, rote memorization of any body of information is the most elementary form of learning and the least likely to be transferred and applied, and application of skills in the use of Standard English is certainly the goal of every language arts teacher. Thus, it seems evident that any work done in the areas of grammar and mechanics should be viewed as an intermediate, rather than a final step, in this area of curriculum. The final step should be the direct application of knowledge of English conventions to the language skills of speaking and writing.

Summary

Issues that are embedded in the processes of teaching writing as a process and ensuring that students learn grammar, usage, and punctuation have been the central focus of this chapter. The history of instruction in grammar and punctuation and specifics regarding what, when, and how to teach grammar and punctuation, were also explored.

Suggested Classroom Projects and Questions for Discussion

Projects

1. Many schools have publications for children's poems, short stories, fables, and illustrations. Your principal gives you the task of organizing a publication for outstanding reports, letters, and other materials. Devise a system whereby you would set up such a program, including notification of teachers, a system for collecting papers, and procedures for publishing.
2. Problems stimulate the able child. Create some folders that present a series of problems and the suggested means whereby the answers may be found to use with such students.
3. Evaluate ten films or filmstrips that might be used to stimulate imaginative writing. *The Hunter in the Forest* is suggested in many school courses of study.
4. Evaluate a specific suggestion with respect to creative writing. Such suggestions as the following may be used: Ask children to write the story of a comic book episode or write a summary of a television show; encourage children to experiment with flannelboard characters or puppets as they develop a story or play before writing.
5. Make a study of worthy free materials that may be secured through letters written by children. Use the following sources as a guide:

Byrn, L., *Where to Get Free and Inexpensive Materials.* San Francisco: Fearon Publishers, 2263 Union St.
Educators' Progress Service. *Elementary Teachers Guide to Free Curriculum Materials.* Randolph, Wisc. (Published Annually)
Peabody College for Teachers. *Free and Inexpensive Learning Materials,* 9th ed. Nashville, Tenn.
Miller, B. *So You Want to Start a Picture File.* Riverside, Calif.
———. *Sources of Free and Inexpensive Pictures for the Classroom.*
———. *Sources of Free Travel Posters and Geographic Aids.*

Field Enterprises. *Sources of Free and Inexpensive Educational Materials*. Chicago, Merchandise Mart Plaza.

6. Imagine that a class you are teaching has a basic understanding of grammatical terminology concerning parts of speech, but many students are having difficulty with subject-verb agreement. Adhering to a *functional* point of view, devise a series of lessons wherein you address this issue.

7. A parent of one of your students is concerned because his child is not learning grammar as an isolated content area. This parent was taught in school that grammar study, including sentence diagramming, has intrinsic value. Outline the points that you would present to the parent on this issue.

8. Plan a unit for third-grade students that will help them understand the concept of "level of usage." (See Project 12.)

9. Outline a lesson plan that addresses a particular issue(s) of grammar and/or mechanics as a part of the writing process.

10. The principal walks into your second-grade classroom and notices that many of the students' papers that are displayed around the room contain spelling errors. He/she asks you why you would display incorrect work. What would you tell him/her?

11. Make a bulletin board display that highlights the role of standard usage and mechanics in effective written communication.

12. Make a bulletin board display that shows and clarifies the concept of levels of usage.

Questions

1. Is it better to recognize a situation for which a child will want to write or to use a device to motivate him to write? Explain which is better and provide an example.

2. Do you consider that children can be as creative in a task such as letter writing as in story writing?

3. To what extent is it true that the skills of language are the skills of conformity?

4. Few children will ever become authors or even reporters. Should a greater effort be made in the area of practical writing than in the area of personal or imaginative writing?

5. To what extent is punctuation a personal matter?

6. The newspapers frequently carry stories about errors caused by punctuation. At one time a tariff law was passed to admit fruit trees free of duty. A comma between fruit and trees cost the government a great deal of revenue before it was corrected. Do you know of other examples?

7. Why is it possible for two people to punctuate a paper in different ways and both be correct?

8. Do the following three rules cover most situations?
    a. A comma may be used to prevent a possible misreading.
    b. A nonessential part of a sentence should be set off with one comma if it comes first or last in the sentence and with two commas if it comes anywhere else.
    c. When two or more words or groups of words are similar in form or function, they should be separated by commas.

9. In addition to letter writing and reports, there are other functional language situations when a child needs to write. When would a child need to write a description, an advertisement, a notice, an invitation, a biography, a joke?

10. Students are always questioning the relevance of certain activities, particularly in the areas of grammar and mechanics. How would you rationalize the teaching of these content areas to your students?

11. What is the best time to begin addressing issues of grammar and mechanics in the classroom, and how should this be approached with the primary grades?

12. Teaching the conventions of grammar and mechanics as isolated subject areas has not been effective in improving students' use of their language. How can these conventions be taught in order to affect improvement in language use?

13. How does the study of levels of usage help students understand the need to learn to use Standard English?

14. Distinguish between the teaching of grammar and the teaching of usage.

Chapter 12

The Writing Process

(Photo by Linda Lungren)

OBJECTIVES

After reading this chapter, the student should be able to:
1. understand writing as a process.
2. implement the writing process instructionally.
3. understand the developmental nature of writing skills.
4. understand the classroom time commitment necessary for effective writing instruction.
5. utilize effective ways to handle the paperwork generated by a writing program.
6. utilize modern technology in the writing program.

302

What Is the Writing Process?

A common myth that dominated writing instruction in America for over two hundred years is slowly being dispelled. It is the myth embodied in the instructional plan of "assign-write-correct," wherein the teacher assigns a composition topic, the student writes the prescribed product, and the teacher, as all-knowing evaluator, provides a grade. Of course, the assumption underlying this plan is that the student can write a perfect composition given certain "basic skills," usually defined as the study of traditional grammar and topics of discourse, time, and a clearly stated topic.

Educators now know that this lock-step instructional design is far from being a complete picture of composition. In fact, it represents only small components of a dynamic process in which thoughts, or what Moffett (1979) refers to as *inner speech,* are processed to become explicit, concrete, written products.

In the writing process, the writer invents, refines, selects, and eliminates ideas in order to generate information for composing. This is, however, only the beginning of the process. The writer continually adjusts and revises ideas both before and after they are manifest as print. In addition to being part of the act of composing, these adjustments and revisions of thought become proofreading, editing, and revising of text.

Actually, what has emerged from study and research is the view that there is no one distinctive writing process. More accurately, writing is many processes (Emig, 1971) which are dynamic and recursive. The linear scheme of assign-write-correct has been replaced by a model that emphasizes what Murray (1968) calls the *cycle of craft.*

Depending on the labels being used, this cycle has been represented as having anywhere from three to, as Murray suggests, seven compartments.

Three-Stage Process	*Seven-Stage Process*
Prewriting	Discovering a subject
	Sensing an audience
Writing	Searching for information
	Creating a design
	Writing
Postwriting	Evaluating critically
	Rewriting

One representation of the writing process divides the third stage of the three-stage model into two distinct functions: editing and revising; for editing and revising are, indeed, separate and equally critical to the writing process.

> Prewriting
> > Writing
> > > Editing
> > > > Revising

The *prewriting* phase is the period during which the writer invents, selects, and organizes ideas. This is the time for brainstorming, drawing semantic maps, and outlining, a time for thinking, researching, and planning.

It is also the period during which audience and purpose for the writing task are set. Outside the classroom, very little, if anything, is written without the writer's being directed by clear purpose. That purpose may be to express personal feelings, inform, describe, persuade, or clarify ideas for the writer or someone else. This motivating purpose is, unfortunately, often lacking in the classroom. Most children find it difficult to sustain the level of interest and attention required to compose when they are writing only for a teacher/evaluator, for children understand at a very young age that writing is a form of communication and that communication for the sole purpose of producing a paper to be graded is relatively meaningless.

The *writing* or composing phase of the process was, in years past, the writer's final task, for then the actual product was created. Once the composition was finished, the only task left was for the teacher to red-

pen the papers of earnest students whose efforts failed to meet prescribed standards of form and content.

Today, however, educators realize that the composing phase is only one more piece of the puzzle necessary to complete the writing process. It is a time for thinking and organizing *and* writing. It is also a time when the teacher can monitor, assist, and praise students' progress.

Graves (1973) emphasized the importance of teacher monitoring and assistance during the writing phase of the process. He reported that as early as grade one, effective writers can predict what they will write from four to ten sentences ahead. By observing and monitoring this phase of the process, teachers can identify children who cannot predict and provide on-the-spot help at a time when it is most needed. It is clear that the time of actual composition is not an end or final act; it is a time for writing, a time for learning, a time for skill development *as* a product is created.

The *editing* phase is a period during which the writer momentarily steps away from the composition to assess both content (ideas and organization) and form (grammar, punctuation, paragraphing) of what has been written. Editing can be done through oral or silent review of the composition. Feedback can come from teachers, fellow students, or parents.

This is the time for instruction in appropriate grammatical issues. After all, a sentence like the following could definitely mislead a trusting reader:

> *Sugar coffee and cookies were on the table for the luncheon.*

Of course, the writer understands the message, but additional punctuation is needed to clarify meaning for the reader. Probably "sugar coffee" was *not* on the luncheon menu.

Finally, in the *revising* stage of the process, elements of form and content are revised, expanded, clarified, or otherwise modified and then rewritten.

Problems in organization, punctuation, and usage have been addressed. Feedback from the editing stage has helped the writer to rethink and refashion the composition. No judgments concerning the writer's competency have been made. No red-pen assault has taken place. Just as in the real world of writers (the world outside the classroom), students are free, with effective instruction, to rethink, revise, and rewrite until they have a product that says *what* they want in the *way* they want it said. This certainly provides a sense of accomplishment.

Looking back at the description of each stage of the writing process (the four-stage process described here), several ideas consistently appear. One word in particular is consistent throughout: *thinking*. When Fearn (1983) discussed the writing process, he stated that the writer thinks *before* writing, *during* writing, and *after* writing. The process is not three or five or seven stages separated from one another by distinct boundaries. Rather, the stages function as an interactive set of processes guided by the writer's thoughts, and during each stage the writer can function alternatively as planner, writer, and editor. Editing and revising can, and often do, occur during the writing stage; planning, as described in the prewriting phase, can also occur during the actual composing; and, certainly, composing can take place during the revising stage of the process. In addition, one writer may start to write early in the process, planning and writing almost simultaneously and producing a very rough draft to be edited and revised, whereas another writer might not begin to write until thoughts and ideas have been well formulated and outlined.

It is clear that the writing process is not a sequential-stage model. The stages do not follow one another in a linear pattern of steps, and not all children approach the process in exactly the same way. Thinking and writing are dynamic, not static, processes. However, it is useful to understand the general characteristics of the process in order to skillfully guide students to an awareness of writing as much more than a completed product. Writing is a craft through which thoughts and ideas become tools for communicating and learning.

History of Writing Instruction in America

Writing instruction was introduced into schools in the midnineteenth century, about 150 years after English language teaching first began with alphabetic instruction in *The New England Primer* (Huey, 1908). At that time, instruction emphasized the written product, neglecting altogether the process that led to its production. Texts focused on differences among discourse types (narration, description, exposition, and so on), outlining, and paragraphing. *English Composition,* T. Whiting Bancroft's text published first in 1884, added to the curriculum the ideas of topic sentences and narrowing of the topic; however, like all texts of this era, Bancroft's emphasized *only* the completed written product as a grammatically correct, specific mode of discourse.

The potential for a broader look at writing instruction came in 1935 when the National Council of Teachers of English published *An Experience Curriculum.* This publication recommended an emphasis on the social relevance of writing as a vehicle of communication, thus focusing more than ever before on the writer. Unfortunately, World War II negated the effect of *An Experience Curriculum* by setting the tone for a highly technical and functional curriculum; it wasn't until the sixties that the concept of a student-centered curriculum again emerged, with an emphasis on maximum growth for each individual.

Focusing on the individual, Janet Emig (1971) and Donald Graves (1973) conducted research with a new emphasis. They looked not at the final product of the writing task, but at the writer and the processes involved *during* composing. This view of writing as a process, not simply a product, has been supported by such programs as the Bay Area Writing Project, which have greatly influenced writing instruction by helping teachers increase their levels of knowledge and proficiency in the process.

Current research provides expanding knowledge about the processes involved in the development of all language skill areas (reading, writing, speaking, and listening). Knowledge in each area has contributed to a deeper understanding of the others.

Yet Moffett (1979) reminds us that writing in American classrooms is still used primarily as an instrument to test reading comprehension (through book reports, essay tests, and research papers). The emphasis is on organizing available information into a formal structure with very little focus on what he terms *real authoring,* the organizing and transferring of the child's own thoughts into the medium of print. Our growing understanding of the writing process gives impetus to the need to look beyond the surface structure of a composition to children's abilities to invent, select, eliminate, adjust, and revise their thoughts and ideas. Educators are realizing the importance of focusing on the child's ability to generate thoughts and ideas before addressing the formal aspects of the final product.

Shirley Haley-James (1981) calls for future research to examine ever more closely not only the composing process of the student, but also the processes involved in the teaching of writing. This decade promises to provide valuable insight into writing instruction as educators learn more about the processes of language skill development, learning, and teaching. The emphasis has shifted from concern only for the form of a final product to a need to understand better the pathways that lead to that product.

How Does the Writing Process Become a Basis for Classroom Instruction?

A three-day sequence provides adequate time for most writing endeavors. The first period should be used for the stimulation of ideas, discussion of various words and skills needed to develop a topic, and the experimental first drafts of the material. The second period should be a true writing laboratory with each child writing and receiving help as needed. The third day should

be used to correct errors, reorganize material, and write the final copy if the child wishes to revise the material. Some projects take longer. This means that during the year less written composition may be done, but what is done will have purpose and merit.

The teaching sequence is that of motivation, skill development, refinement, and use. Motivation involves any experience that starts a flow of ideas. The discussion helps the students determine the thoughts they wish to develop in their writing. Skill development involves planned vocabulary materials, reviews of punctuation, writing and spelling skills, and help with the organization of ideas.

Refinement involves making corrections, proofreading, and writing to improve content, form, usage, spelling, and handwriting. Use is the recognition given the final product as it is read to the class, reproduced in a newspaper, placed on a bulletin board, or shared in a way appropriate to the content.

A teacher may plan a lesson in written composition in a six-step sequence. First, children are either motivated to write or helped to recognize that they have something to express in writing. Second, the vocabulary needed to express the writers' ideas is made available. Third, forms already taught are recalled, because we want the children to practice correct habits. Fourth, time is provided for the writing experience. Fifth, the written material is shared. Sixth, improvements are made in the composition appropriate to the writers' purposes.

You will notice that these six steps generally correspond to the stages of the writing process. Steps 1, 2, and 3 are essentially prewriting activities; step 4 is the composing phase of the process; and steps 5 and 6 represent the stages of editing and revision, the postwriting phase of the process.

This six-step procedure cannot always be completed in one language period. A letter may be started in the language class and completed during the spelling or social studies time. A story or poem may be started on one day, completed on the second, and, if necessary, revised on a third. The amount of writing will depend on the interest and purpose of those involved. Writing

should never become busy work or a time-filling activity. A limited amount of writing that has a purpose and is carefully guided to prevent the repetition of error will produce the most satisfying results.

The following classroom procedures have been suggested by teachers for each of these six steps.

MOTIVATION

Preprimer Stories. Children are encouraged to make their own preprimers. These may be a compilation of the stories of several students or the work of one. Topics may concern cowboys, our town, my family, our pets, our school.

Diary or Daily News. At first the children will dictate a report to the teacher on "what we did today." Later they will write their own reports. This may be a rotating activity. One group may be sharing orally for the day or week, another working on a project, and a third keeping the diary. "Our Friday News" is an excellent way to summarize the work of the week for parents and the principal.

Wishes, Fears, Troubles. Feelings stimulate a great deal of creative thought. Expression of such feelings helps the teacher understand the child as well as helping the child to get problems out in the open. Making pictures, and then talking or writing about these topics, illustrates this suggestion.

> "If I could have my wish"
> "I do not like _____"
> "Things that scare me"
> "If I could be something else, I would be a _____"

Reports. Most adult writing is done to tell what happened, what a person learned, or what a person did. Simple encyclopedias make it possible for students to share interesting information through written reports. Some even call these term papers, with sources appropriately indicated.

Seasons, Holidays, and Nature. The environment is a natural stimulant for writing. Windy days, storms,

and rain are things to tell about. A Halloween, Thanksgiving, or February Hero book, made of a compilation of writing, is a rewarding project. In the second grade and beyond, children can print directly on ditto masters so that a book can be assembled for each.

Titles. All that some children need to start the flow of ideas and the desire to write is a title:

Witches' Brew   Vacation Fun
My Pet   My Toys
Adventures of a Penny   Dear Santa
Chimpanzee Tells All   When I Was Sick
My Old School   Danger
The Old House   Fire! Fire!

First Lines. Getting started is difficult for many. These first lines reproduced on writing paper will often help:

1. Dear Santa, Please _____.
2. My name is _____. I live at _____.
3. Once there was a monkey _____.
4. I am _____. I have _____. I can _____.

"If" Stories: Suggested Plots

1. If you were a circus pony, what adventures might you have?
2. If you were a lost dog, what might happen to you?
3. If you were a calf that liked to run away, what might happen to you?
4. If you were a dog that saw a turtle in the road, what might happen?
5. If you could go anywhere in the world, where would you go?
6. If you had ten dollars to spend for Christmas, what would you buy?

Tell a Story About These Facts

1. I am a crow named Chicago. Tell the story of how I hid some silver and what happened to it.

Suggested words: thief, chased, claws, dogs, barked, fireman, ladder, afraid, tired.

2. I am a fireman named Jim. One day there was a big fire. Tell what happened.
3. I am a monkey named Bimbo. I love to tease my master. Tell how this got me in trouble.
4. I am a baby brother. I got lost one day. Tell what happened to me.

Post Office. Establish a mail box for each child. At any time, any child may write a letter to any other child in the class. The teacher may write a letter as well. Letters may be mailed only at noon and picked up only in the morning before school. To maintain standards it must be understood that no letter will be put into the receiver's box unless it is correctly written.

Outer Space Stories. Discuss the following: Today we are going to write a space story. Should we take a trip to Venus or stop at the moon? Will it be a dream, or an original story, or a news account in the *Venus Morning News?* Maybe it will be a colony of pilgrims on the moon or the diary of one who stayed at home. Perhaps the trip was not planned at all but the result of an accident.

Picture Stimulators. Picture stimulators are among the best means of motivating a child to write. A picture of a clown cut from a magazine is glued to an idea card. Below it are some stimulating questions: Have you been to the circus? Why is the clown so happy? On the back are words the child might wish to use as he writes a story. Appropriate words might be *clown, circus, tent, laughing, trick, joke, music.* These pictures are equally good as stimulators for oral stories prior to writing.

A Writer's Corner. A technique used by many teachers to stimulate writing is a writer's corner in the classroom. The corner consists of a table and chairs placed below a bulletin board. Questions, pictures, and ideas for word usage can be attractively displayed on the bulletin board for motivation. These are changed frequently. Writing paper, pencils, a dictionary, and needed lists of words are kept on the table, as are folders of pictures with words describing the

pictures. Large sheets of paper with a mimeographed picture in the corner have been successfully used by some teachers to obtain a variety of stories about one picture.

The materials on the writer's table must be introduced to the children so that they know how to use them correctly. The pictures should be used by the class as a regular writing activity before the materials are placed on the writer's table. This does not mean that every new game or picture placed on the writer's table must be introduced to the group first. It does mean that any different type of material that the teacher places on this table should be explained so that the child knows exactly how to use it.

Periodically some recognition should be given to children who are using the writer's desk. Putting up "The Story of the Week," which can be selected by the teacher or the class, and making a booklet of the best stories are two ways to help stimulate more creative work. Written material may be put in a box and later read aloud by the teacher. The children guess the name of the author in the manner of a television quiz program.

One device for the writer's table is a threefold stand made of cardboard. Each fold is about 9 × 11. The center fold has a stimulating picture that is slipped behind a sheet of acetate. On the right is a group of words appropriate to the picture also in an acetate envelope. On the left are reminders to the writer. The teacher can change the pictures and vocabulary as she wishes. The reminders might be "Every story has a title," "All sentences begin with capitals," or "All names start with capitals."

There can be envelopes for letters, a calendar, a usable dictionary, a telephone book (for addresses), extra pencils, special paper (stationery), erasers, and other items to make writing attractive.

The writer's desk can be used by children when they have finished other assigned work. It is desirable to have only one child using the desk at a time. However, if the teacher wishes, children may take certain materials to their desks.

In developing language material for this individual activity, teachers should remember that "above-average" or "gifted" children are more likely to use them at first, and teachers should plan activities that will be challenging to them.

VOCABULARY DEVELOPMENT

When students write they sometimes wish to use words from their listening vocabulary. One student may ask, "What do you call the signs in the newspaper that tell what people have to sell?" He is seeking the word *advertisement*. The same is true of such words as *alfalfa* (what do cows eat?) or *infinity* (space). At such times the teacher provides the word desired.

In other situations the teacher anticipates that writing and spelling certain words will be necessary and provides convenient references. Interesting words in stories read should be noticed so that they will be available to future authors. Simple picture dictionaries of the names of things may be consulted or created.

Word Cards. Because seasonal words will be needed every year, a packet of cards for Halloween, Thanksgiving, and Christmas or Hanukkah can be constructed by older children or the teacher. At the appropriate time these words are spread along the chalkboard to help writers. Pictures on each card, such as a picture of a pumpkin beside the word, will help those still having reading problems.

Word Lists. A folder for each child that contains the words most often used will prevent errors and make writing easier for the child. This is a combination of a spelling and reading list:

The Words We Use Most Often

These are the words we use most often.
We use them when we write.
We use them when we read.
We can use this as a dictionary.
We can check the spelling of words here.
Check yourself to see how many you know.
Learn the ones you do not know.
Learn to say them very quickly.

a	been	days	from	men	or	snow	think	way
about	before	dear	fun	money	other	so	this	we
after	best	did	gave	more	our	some	thought	week
again	better	didn't	get	morning	out	something	three	well
all	big	do	getting	most	over	soon	through	went
along	book	dog	girl	mother	people	started	time	were
also	boy	don't	girls	much	place	stay	to	what
always	boys	door	give	my	play	still	today	when
am	brother	down	go	name	pretty	summer	told	where
an	but	each	going	never	put	sure	too	which
and	by	eat	good	new	ran	take	took	while
another	called	enough	great	next	read	teacher	town	white
any	came	ever	had	nice	ready	tell	tree	who
are	can	every	happy	night	right	than	two	winter
around	car	father	hard	no	room	that	until	with
as	children	few	has	not	said	the	up	work
asked	Christmas	find	have	now	saw	their	us	would
at	city	fire	he	of	say	them	use	write
away	cold	first	heard	off	school	then	used	year
back	come	five	help	old	see	there	very	years
be	comes	for	her	on	she	these	want	you
beautiful	coming	found	here	once	should	they	wanted	your
because	could	four	may	one	side	thing	was	
bed	country	friend	me	only	small	things	water	

Other Words That Will Help Us

ask	fall	own	stop
ate	far	please	ten
black	fast	pull	thank
blue	fly	red	those
both	full	ride	together
bring	funny	right	try
brown	goes	round	under
buy	green	run	upon
call	grow	seven	walk
carry	hat	shall	warm
clean	hold	show	wash
cut	hurt	sing	why
does	its	sit	wish
done	jump	six	yellow
draw	myself	sleep	yes
drink	open	start	

The following word book or a card file of frequently used words is suggested as a handy reference for words that are used in certain situations. These are usually created by the teacher after discussion with the children. Contents might include some of the following:

Days of the Week

Sunday	Thursday
Monday	Friday
Tuesday	Saturday
Wednesday	

Months of the Year

January	March	May
February	April	June

July	September	November
August	October	December

Sounds That Animals Make

quack	bow wow
mew	oink oink
cluck	whinny
moo	neigh
coo	

Kinds of Weather

foggy	rainy
cloudy	windy
sunny	hot
clear	cold

Places We Go on Trips

beach	zoo
mountains	harbor
museum	country
desert	farm

Special Words for

tastes	feelings
colors	actions
smells	sights

Students may also generate word lists on particular topics suggested by the teacher. For example, the teacher could ask small groups to "brainstorm" all of the words they can think of to describe food, clothes, feelings, and so forth. The teacher can then paste these word lists on the classroom walls for the children to use in their writings.

Training the Five Senses. Play games that emphasize sensory response. Ask a student to perform an action while the others listen. Then tell how it sounded. Such actions as tapping on the desk, tapping on the window, dropping a book, drumming with two pencils, opening a window, and so on, are appropriate.

Next imagine that you are a bird that could fly anywhere. Tell what you hear and ask the class to guess where the bird is.

Close your eyes and picture something you saw at home this morning or on the way to school. See whether your words will help others see the same thing. The teacher or a student may ask questions until the complete image is visualized.

Match the beginning and ending of sentences such as these:

The door bell	tiptoed softly.
The clock	screamed.
Mother	hummed.
The whistle	clanged.
The fire alarm	whimpered.
The baby	blew.

STANDARDS

Standards are designed to assist expression of ideas, not to interfere with them. Yet we do not value a language anarchy. Security built on a knowledge of proper form will aid any writer.

Reminder Charts. Prior to writing, attention is called to certain skills previously used. These can be reviewed rapidly, then posted as a reminder while writing.

Capital Letters. Names start with capital letters.

Nancy, Ken, Jay, Erin

Sentences start with capital letters.

See the cat.
Where are you going?

Because all writing involves handwriting skills, the quality practiced is important. Prior to a writing lesson, a five-minute review of the formation of certain letters is valuable. This may involve chalkboard demon-

strations by the pupils, an examination of small hand-writing reference cards at each student's writing place, or a review of the letter forms usually posted over the blackboard. Second-grade children should know all the letter forms. Primary-grade children should be helped with letters as needed, especially the capital letter forms.

A major use of standards is to direct proofreading of material. Children should not be expected to proof-read for all errors, but they should check for certain specifics. The following would be appropriate:

Did I capitalize the words in my title?
Did I keep a margin?
Did I use my best writing?
Did I put only one line through words I wanted to change? (Prevents erasing or scribbling over a word.)

LABORATORY WRITING EXERCISES

Such activities as the writer's table are individual devices that free the children from classroom pressures. At other times the guidance of the teacher is desirable as certain skills and concepts are practiced.

Group Composition. Working on composition as a group helps to establish security among members of the class, gives the teacher an opportunity to prevent errors in spelling and usage, and builds good human relationships. Some children need this experience before they are able to organize their thoughts and express themselves independently. Subjects for group composition can develop from a common experience or from ideas derived from social studies curriculum. The children contribute ideas that the teacher writes

Working on composition as a group helps to establish security among members of the class, gives the teacher an opportunity to prevent errors in spelling and usage, and builds good human relationships. (Photo by Linda Lungren)

on the chalkboard. Later those who wish may copy the product. Letters to a sick classmate, notes sent home about a program, or letters to another class are examples of group composition topics.

Staggered Writing Assignment. Although writing will frequently be done by the entire class, a variation is to ask only one group to write. This makes it possible for the teacher to give more personal help; evaluate with greater care (because there are fewer papers); and provide for the individual differences in a group. There is a competitive element in writing as well as in reading. Those operating at approximately the same levels profit most by group instruction.

Classroom Helpers. At times it will give recognition to a few and help others to appoint one student in each group who may give help with spelling, punctuation, or other problems. Upper-grade children may be given recognition by permitting them to be "human dictionaries" in a lower grade during a writing period.

Prevention of Error Practice. Practicing an error tends to fix it as a habit. With experience, teachers learn to anticipate problems that the class or individuals will have. To prevent spelling errors and to encourage the use of vocabulary, word cards with illustrations of meaning might be made for the seasons. Halloween words that children want to use would include *gate, witch, ghost, haunted, screamed.* These words might be reviewed, then placed on the chalkboard. A child who wants to use a word has a clue to identify it with the picture. After selecting the word he wants, he takes it to his desk, copies it, then returns it to the chalkboard. Review of handwriting and punctuation standards may be carried out before the writing period. The children should be given time to proofread, with questions to guide them. The teacher should never ask a child to do something which is known to be beyond the ability of that child. If some write a dramatic sketch, it does not follow that all should. It might be well to have some writing with a partner

as a group activity either at the planning level or at presentation time.

SHARING THE WRITTEN COMPOSITIONS

Use the sharing time at the beginning of the day to read some of the compositions.
Post compositions on the bulletin board.
Make a booklet such as "Our Halloween Stories."

Some educators strongly recommend that the teacher or a parent type stories written by children and correct the major errors. This enhances the children's confidence that he can write and has something to say. There is much testimony that with confidence thus established the children improve in error reduction and clarity of expression.

Collect the written efforts in a folder and send it home after the parent conference.

Publish in a school newspaper compositions that have special merit.

Exchange compositions with another class at the same level or a different appropriate one at the end of a year.

IMPROVING COMPOSITION SKILLS

The teacher finds something to praise in each composition: "I like the way you used (*a word*)." "The ending is good."

Errors are noted as revealing instructional needs of children. The teacher then composes a story that reflects these errors or, with the permission of a child, uses one of the papers submitted. The problem is presented to the class as "How can we make this interesting paper better?"

The story is written on the board:

Spooky

Spooky was a ghost. He was a friendly ghost. He could do everything. But he could not float. He could not moan. He was a funny ghost. He was a happy ghost too.

After the story is read aloud, the class discusses the sentences and the possibility of joining some of them to make the story sound more interesting and flow more easily.

Making Our Sentences Sound More Interesting

Make one sentence from these two short sentences:

1. Spooky was a ghost. He was a friendly ghost.

   _____

2. I have a ball. It is a red ball.

   _____

3. Lynne has a pencil. It is green.

   _____

4. Mary is my friend. She is my best friend.

   _____

5. Kelly threw the ball. She threw it to me.

   _____

6. This is my wagon. It is big.

   _____

7. I have a doll. He is handsome.

   _____

8. They have the blocks. There are six.

   _____

9. I like your story. It is a good story.

   _____

10. It is on the table. The table is large.

    _____

The class may practice on a written drill of the type shown below (the term *transform* may be used if the students are familiar with the new grammar).

The children then look over their previous stories and change sentences. Other drills of the following nature may be used:

Sentence Drill

Make a sentence by drawing a line from a group of words in List A to a group of words in List B. Be sure they belong together.

A	B
1. The dog	me his book.
2. The little boy	see the game.
3. Brian gave	bought some ice cream.
4. We went to	barked at the cat.
5. I like	to read.

Write the words you need to finish each sentence. Choose them from the group of words below.

the red ball	ice cream and cake
We have	splashing down
I wish	three blocks to school
She went	four new dresses

1. I like _____ .
2. _____ three new girls now.
3. Every day I walk _____ .
4. _____ I had three dollars.
5. The rain came _____ .
6. Denise has _____ .
7. _____ to the skating party.
8. We are going to have _____ .

Paragraph Drill

Copy these sentences so they tell a story. When you decide which sentences to use first, be sure to indent the sentence. These sentences should make a one-paragraph story.

She ate their porridge and sat in their chairs.
They lived in the woods.
Once there were three bears.
A little girl came to their house.

Is There a Developmental Sequence for Writing Instruction?

For anyone who has spent more than fifteen minutes with a child between the ages of eighteen months and two and a half years, it is obvious that the child's early talk is a gross approximation of adult language. For example, *"Mama, cookie please"* (probably pro-

nounced more like *pwease*) is very effective communication between that mother and child. The child engages in functional oral language use long before applying correct form of the language.

The same developmental phenomenon occurs with print forms of language. A child who reads *cereal* on the Cheerios box shows understanding of the intent of what is printed on the package. Through experience, the child clearly has internalized the function of print; however, understanding the way the formal structure of the language works (the letter and sound correspondence) has not yet been mastered. Likewise, the first grader who writes on a Father's Day card

in sid you will finb sum thing speshl

is communicating a clear message. There is no doubt that this child realizes the function of writing. Again, however, it is only through experience (including guided instruction) and maturation that the child gains increasing control over conventional form.

Because thinking and composing are closely aligned, the development of a child's writing abilities closely parallels developing mental capabilities. Britton (1975) notes that early writing tends to be very egocentric and self-expressive, "speech written down." It is only as the child gains proficiency in dealing with abstract concepts that *transactional writing*—writing that involves reasoning, problem solving, and explanation—and *poetic writing*—figurative and symbolic—take place.

Using the Writing Process Developmentally in the Primary Grades

There are several key ideas that should form a basis for writing instruction in the primary grades.

1. Fluency precedes form. This simply means that children should be encouraged to write often in a supportive and risk-free environment. Before teachers can focus on form and quality of writing, children must first be able to express their ideas and thoughts. After all, it is impossible to correct writing that the child cannot produce. In addition, it is important to realize that emphasis on the mechanics of writing (spelling, punctuation, grammar) will only stifle the young child's desire to experiment with and explore the world of words.

    Bennett (1981) looked at distinctly different compositions by two first graders. One was a perfectly punctuated, perfectly spelled two-word title. The other was a page of written expression with several spelling and punctuation errors. Clearly, the second composition exemplified an attitude of experimentation, of confident expression. The second and more fluent child, through practice and development, eventually had much more original material to edit and revise than the first, whose writing may have already been perfect but who was definitely inhibited by fear of making mistakes.

2. A child's writing should flow from personal experience. First writing behaviors may involve copying letters and words. For some children, the first classroom writing may be an entirely alien experience, and this type of activity can reinforce reading and spelling as well as motor skills. However, we have seen that at a very early age children understand that writing is communication; if we are to foster children's desire to communicate; we must allow them to draw upon their repertoire of personal experiences, whether they are dictating ideas for someone else to transcribe or composing their own work.

3. A prime motivator for writing is not, ultimately, a gold star or sticker; it is the motivation that accompanies achievement, defined as a sense of accomplishment through learning and growth. Children often complain that they don't like to write. It would be wonderful if teachers could persuade all children to love writing, but a more realistic and more important goal is to make them like *what* they write. That

goal can be accomplished in a classroom where writing is purposeful, where children write often, and where pupils are guided developmentally through the writing process—beginning where they can succeed (one- or two-word labels for pictures, single sentences, and so on) and moving to more complex tasks (short paragraphs, stories, and so on) only when they are ready.

When teachers honor the developmental nature of the writing task, they design instruction for the beginning writer that addresses the concepts of fluency, self-expression, and motivation. Because children enter school with highly developed oral vocabularies, oral work is an important component of writing instruction.

Young children can express themselves orally, through a dramatic skit, or by creating pictures. As a child relates personal experiences and ideas or tells about a picture or an object, the teacher can ask questions and make suggestions about the words, ideas, or manner of speaking. At other times the child makes the picture first, then tells what is happening in the picture. This provides a focus for children in determining which of his ideas are important and which are subordinate.

"What would be a good name for Harold's story?" the teacher asks. After several suggestions have been made, the teacher turns to Harold. "Which one do you like best?" After he has decided, the teacher writes the name for all to see. With this beginning, children will soon be dictating stories that the teacher writes and the child reads. As the teacher writes, she points out where she begins and how each sentence ends: "I'll put the first word here, then go to the right. This is the end of the sentence so I will put a period here." A "book" of these stories is placed on the reading table so that children can read and reread the stories they have written. Writing can be a classwide experience, the efforts of a small group, or an individual's working alone with the teacher. Such experience usu-

The young child can express herself orally, through a dramatic skit, or by creating a picture. As she relates personal experiences and ideas, the teacher can ask questions and make suggestions to her about her words, ideas, or manner of speaking. (Photo by Linda Lungren)

ally follows a discussion period during which children think together and express themselves freely. In the small-group method, the members work faster, and the interest factors and feelings of success are high. The teacher is immediately able to supply needed words or correct spelling, to stimulate thinking, and to stimulate curiosity. In turn, other groups will work with the teacher. Writing experiences of the entire class now involve a common topic, such as "Thanksgiv-

ing." During the discussion period, words that may be used are placed on the chalkboard. Specific aspects suitable for writing may be listed, such as "My Favorite Thanksgiving," "A Turkey's Ideas About Thanksgiving," "Why I Am Thankful." Thus the individual compositions will vary, although using a similar vocabulary.

The first efforts usually contain misspelled words, incomplete sentences, and some meager punctuation and capitalization attempts. These first stories are not corrected, but as the child reads the story to the teacher, his voice indicates beginnings and endings. He then adds, with the teacher's help, his own periods, question marks, and capitals. After children have written many stories and write with ease, the teacher and child correct the first rough draft. Children now take the initiative in finding his errors or in completing the spelling of a word where only the initial letter is given. The students may copy their stories and share them with their classmates. Sometimes the story is placed with others in a bound volume. Children frequently offer stories without a title, probably because a title or name inhibits their ease of writing. The teacher or other children may suggest a title when a child shares an unnamed story with them.

EXAMPLES OF CHILDREN'S WRITING. The following is an early effort of a San Diego boy in the first grade that was published in a classroom book titled *Our Writing:*

The Dome Bird
(as written by Richard, Grade 1)

One day dome bird thote two + two was twente. One day men buill schools up. and it was time for dome bird to come to school. One day the teacher put up some arethmatik. then dome bird sat down to rite. The dom bird saw two + two on the board. He put twente on the paper. the teacher saw dome Bird arethmatick so she put an X on the paper so the dome bird saw the X so dom bird Learnd how much two + two was.

The Dumb Bird
(as read by Richard)

One day dumb bird thought two plus two was twenty. One day some men built schools and it was time for dumb bird to come to school. One day the teacher put up some arithmetic. Then dumb bird sat down to write. The dumb bird saw two plus two on the board. He put twenty on the paper. The teacher saw dumb bird's arithmetic, so she put an X on the paper. The dumb bird saw the X, so dumb bird learned how much two plus two was.

As soon as print script has been mastered, the students follow the pattern established by the teacher and write their own story. These will show a great range of *interest* and *expression,* both of which are important to the writer.

One will laboriously write "The House" with many smudges and add his/her name. Others will cover pages as they write stories like this:

Chu   Jan. 22, 1987

wonts there was a 1 and a half year old girl. her name was tiny because she was so little. One day she saw a dog. she wanted to bathe him because he was so dirty. she asked her mother but she said no get that dirty thing out of here. but tiny brahgt a tub in the yard, then she brahgt some waters and put in it. she bathed him. she got wet and dirty. but the dog was not dirty any more. he went away and he did not come back again because he did not like the water. I love to make storys.

the end

The only capital letters Chu knew were those in his name, but that did not stop him. He probably asked for help on *brahgt* and having spelled it wrong once was loyal to his first spelling when the word was repeated. Most revealing of all is a little note in one corner of the page: "I love to make storys."

In encouraging students to write, an expanded writing program that allows for ungraded written exchanges among pupils is a must. Topics that traditionally have been used to elicit composition from students

include holidays, classroom events, pets, hobbies, weather, siblings, family events, and birthdays. The following are examples of students' writing about such topics.

> Mrs. Cunningham likes music. Donald brought in a record for Mrs. Cunningham. It was country and western. I like to sing.
>
> by Bart

> A car hit a teacher's parked automobile. It even hit a house It almost poured rain too.
>
> by Linda

> Today was a happy day. Today Miss Bovee [student teacher] came. She will stay until school closes.
>
> Sharon

Holidays receive special notice:

Easter Day

April 5, 1988

> On Easter Day we had an egg hunt. I found more eggs than my brother. One egg was under the abalone shell. I found an egg in both vases. I had fun on Easter. Most of the eggs were in the living room. But some were in the dining room. The eggs were all different colors. They are very pretty. I helped dye the eggs. I had fun on Easter.
>
> Carly

As a prewriting activity, certain words determined by the class to be necessary for the topic were written on the board. Among these were *dye, Easter, colors.* The words *different* and *dining* were corrected before the story was posted. In this class all children wrote on the same topic.

A favorite writing experience at the beginning of second grade is to write "What I Want to Be" stories. These can be reproduced in a little book for parents' night. If the children use a ditto pencil or write on ditto masters, this also provides an example of the child's writing. These are typical examples:

A Jet Pilot

> I want to be a Jet pilot. You have to learn many things before you can be a Jet pilot. You must know how to fly your plane are you might crash. If the plane runs out of gas i will parachute out.
>
> by Nancy

A Fire Man

> I want to be a fire person and put out fires and help people out of fires. I want to be a good fire person I want to slide down the poles. I want to help people to be good and not cause fires.
>
> by Dihn

A School Teacher

> I want to be a school teacher and teach children how to spell and do numbers. I want to teach them how to tell time and many other things I want children who do good work and not spend their time talking.
>
> by Jaime

Second-grade children advance rapidly. By the end of the year some will write this well. The literary pattern now follows that of favorite books.

Flicka the Filly

> Dick's father was at the Johnsons' farm getting a colt. Dick was going to train it. When his father came home Dick ran to the truck. The colt was beautiful. It was pure white with a black mane and tail and right on its forehead was a gold star. "What will you name her, son?" asked his father.
>
> "I'll call her Flicka," said Dick.
>
> The next day Dick got up early. He ate his breakfast and went to the stable.
>
> "Come on, Flicka," said Dick. "I'm going to train you." Flicka went with Dick to the pasture.
>
> "First you must learn to obey your master," said Dick. Dick walked away and said "Stay."
>
> Flicka did as he said. Flicka obeyed him with the

other tricks, too. And they had lots of fun for the rest of their lives.

by Anita

How Can the Writing Process Be Implemented in the Intermediate Grades?

NARRATION. Just as *storytelling* pictures are used in the primary grades, so they may be used at the intermediate level. Those with great human interest, such as the illustrations of Norman Rockwell, are especially good. Pictures expressing beauty, mood, and action are equally motivating. Class members may select a picture from the group presented by the teacher or all write about the same one. Because children sometimes are impressed by the ideas of other children and thus limit their creativity, it is a challenge to be original and see a story in a picture that no one else imagines. As a prewriting activity, the class discusses two or three before making a choice to use one as the basis for a story. The characters are discussed. The children are asked to imagine what is happening now, what happened previously, and what is likely to happen next. Words that describe the action, beauty, or feeling are selected. Possible titles are suggested and first lines written. During a second period the stories are written. Later, children may select pictures from magazines for the writing table or for additional stories.

After the imagination of children has been aroused, it sometimes takes only a title to start them thinking of a story. Such titles as these may be put in a box on the writer's table to help some get started:

The Midnight Visitor
The Falling Star
The Hidden Valley
Lost in a Storm
An Animal Friend
A Secret
My Ambition
Flying at Night
Faster than Sound

In a similar way, opening-paragraph starters help writers get on their way:

"She's gone! Now I am going to find her diary," muttered Daryl to himself as he crept up the stairs noiselessly.

Andrea stood stock still. Her legs refused to go. The sweat broke out on her forehead.

Denny walked to the window to let in a little air. As he began to raise it, something outside caught his eye. He stood with his mouth open. There on the lawn below the window was the strangest thing he had ever seen.

At first the noise was very faint and seemed far away. It was an odd noise, one that the children didn't recognize. As it moved closer they went out to see what it might be.

Mildred knew that if her mother found out, she wouldn't be able to sit for days, but she was determined to carry out her plan in spite of this.

The children were playing on the beach when they found the strange footprints in the sand. Their curiosity got the best of them and they decided to follow them along the shore.

"Quick, come here," called Trevor, "I want to show you what I've found!" As the others ran to join him, they stopped short, staring in surprise.

When Father came home that evening, he was whistling happily. The children knew what that meant. He had another of his wonderful surprises.

There was a strange silence about the forest that night. It had an air of waiting for something to happen.

These may be put on cards and placed in an "idea box" to help those who seek topics. Some children need only a word or phrase to start a series of thoughts that lead to writing:

ghost	mud
fog	some luck
gravy	pride
my worst scare	rolling along
nightmare	long journey
rolling waves	longest day of my life

little old lady   face like a lion
a bright idea   time to think
late again

Agado (1984) suggests a highly motivational story-writing activity that involves dividing the class into groups of five or six students each. Each student receives a mimeographed sheet with a story starter written at the top. For example:

> The teacher could tell from the look in Tammy's eyes that she was daydreaming again.

Each child is directed to read the story starter and to add no more than two sentences to the story. Papers are then passed to the left around the group. The children each read the story that has been passed to them, and they add one or two sentences to continue the story. This sequence continues until the story returns to the first writer.

Because responsibility for the story rests with not one, but all, of the children in the group, no one is intimidated by the fear of sounding silly or making a mistake. Children will enjoy sharing their stories and hearing their ideas prompt story ideas from their peers. The oral reading and sharing of written products such as this one not only are fun, but also provide reinforcement of story elements (character, setting, plot, and so on).

The object of writing does not need to be a story. Frequently the purpose is to help children write with vividness and insight. The actual plotting of a story, with beginning, characterization, episodes, climax, and ending, may be too complex for many in the elementary grades. It does not matter whether the material is a story, report, autobiography, dramatic play, or sketch. It *does* matter that the child is learning to express ideas effectively in writing.

Painting word pictures will interest students, yet not demand the time that storywriting involves. Ask the children what pictures the word makes them see. Then ask them to write a word picture. These are examples:

snow   Snow, soft and cold and white, drifted lazily through the air, rested fluffily upon the boughs of the evergreen trees, and in time covered the earth with quiet beauty.

waves   Waves rolled endlessly toward the shore, crashing thunderously against the gray rocks and sending countless sprays of foam skyward.

airplane   Airplanes roared down the runways, then effortlessly left the ground and soared majestically into the sky, soon becoming mere specks in the distance.

Objects will start a child's imagination working. One teacher brought in a bag of old shoes that included a football shoe, a tennis slipper, and a satin pump. She presented such questions as "Who wore this shoe?" "Where has it been?" "Why was it thrown away?" The class was motivated, and writing of a highly imaginative nature resulted.

Variations on old themes will help some get started. What happened to Goldilocks on the next day? What did the three bears do at Christmas? What type of queen was Cinderella? Social studies may motivate historical writing in the form of a news account of such events as the discovery by Columbus of the New World or the discovery of gold in California.

A "story formula" will challenge some. A good story has five parts: a beginning, a problem, a high point or climax, a following action or solution, and a satisfactory ending. This chart may be used to check the formula:

1. Does your story have a good beginning? Tell the four *W*'s: who, when, where, and what's the problem?
2. Did you make the reader aware of the problem?
3. Does your story reach a high point or climax?
4. Is there an adequate explanation of the way that the problem was solved?
5. Do all the parts fit together at the end in a way that satisfies the reader?

Five-sentence stories may outline the plot of a story:

1. Mother and I were sitting in the kitchen after dinner one quiet evening.

2. Suddenly we heard a scratching noise at the back door.
3. Mother screamed and jumped up on a chair as a gray mouse darted across the floor.
4. I stood there and laughed at the funny sight, while Mother recovered from terror.
5. I imagine the mouse was more frightened than Mother was.

Charts of this nature may be used as guides:

Stories Can Begin

1. with conversation to set the stage for action.
2. with the end of the story, then going back to the beginning.
3. with the middle of the story, then to the actual beginning.
4. with a characterization of the chief character or characters.
5. with a summary paragraph to tell the point of the story.
6. with description.
7. with the time, place, or circumstance.
8. with a question.

Stories Can Be Described

1. by a simple statement of fact: Bob is lazy.
2. by describing the way Bob does things.
3. by recounting an episode to prove that Bob is lazy.
4. by using synonyms of the word.
7. by reporting what others say.
8. by telling what he is not.
9. by repeating his own characterization of himself.

Self-characterization is easier than describing another. A "Who Am I?" paper that may be read by the teacher while the class identifies the writer may be the beginning of character study.

Some children, by virtue of personality, home, or early school training, are alert to the details of the world in which they live; others need help in the development of all five senses. These children must be encouraged to find pleasure in observation and in the discussion of what they see.

It is easy to start an enthusiastic discussion concerning the flavor of certain foods. It is fun, too, to put into words the taste of cod liver oil, an uncured olive, or a mouthful of the Pacific Ocean. Children soon discover that following one's nose may be an interesting experience leading to the earthy smell of recently turned sod, the tang of the sea, the fragrance of clean linen just off the line, or the musty odor of old newspapers stored in the garage.

Vocabulary is increased and the power of expression heightened when pupils are helped to *see the importance of contrasting words and ideas*. They will enjoy trying it too.

quietness of the forest
vs. *clang of the city streets*
smooth as the snow-covered lawn
vs. *rough and jagged as the ice on the pond*

Students are easily helped to understand that whole sentences can be built to reflect contrasting ideas that will best express their own feelings:

The forest was dim. Bart thought of the meadow near his home where a sparkling brook with little minnows rushed down mossy rocks in warm sunshine.

Students enjoy the *euphony* of a sentence or line in which the same first letter or sound in a group of words is repeated a number of times. Alliteration can become stilted when it is used as a mechanical exercise. With older children it should be encouraged not as a game but rather as a technique to enhance the meaning of words.

soft slumber summer
lonely leaf
nodding noon
whispering wind
weird white world

Young children use similes naturally and easily. Although they may not label them as such, older children

use metaphors in the same manner. Comparison is a natural method of description for young and old alike. Children enjoy completing these phrases:

as soft as	as easy as
as loud as	as hot as
as happy as	as muffled as
as sad as	as slippery as
as stern as	as long as
as drowsy as	as short as
as bright as	as pointed as
as cold as	as flat as

They become conscious of the use of similes in writing about things that "looked like" or were "as gentle as." One class found that the wind today "was as gentle as"

a lamb
my mother's voice
a soft, furry cloud
a rose opening
when night falls

Tactile perception can be used to enrich children's writing. Various objects can be passed among the children and their reactions written on the board. One teacher passed a bowl of ice cubes. In seeking to express their reaction, the children sought and found many words to describe what they had touched. Ice is

cold	hard
slippery	sharp
smooth	shivery

The teacher can use a small figurine, holding it up and asking the class to look at it closely, then putting the figurine behind something. The teacher now asks the class to describe what was seen. The teacher can pretend she has never seen the object, so that she can be very curious about the responses, encouraging accurate, descriptive analysis. After the first attempt, the class tries again, looks at the object once more, develops vocabulary to explain, and goes through the entire object—all responses being verbal. On the third try, using a new object, the class can try writing a description.

After preliminary work on developing "word pictures," the teacher can put three sentences on the board, such as

An airplane went up.
It flew.
It came down.

The class can be encouraged to develop a more interesting and exciting picture of the situation. Action words and descriptive words can be included orally. As a real picture begins to form, children can appreciate the power of such words as *soared, skimmed,* and *floated.*

As a written work experience, children can take another set of three sentences and see how well they can paint another word picture:

The wind blew.
The windows shook.
The storm came.

Ask the children what pictures a word makes them see. Then let them write a word picture.

Rain

Rain splashed upon the earth, forming puddles on the ground, pelting against the windows, and dripping endlessly from the eaves of the buildings.

Waves

Waves rolled shoreward in long unbroken lines, each crest forming for an instant a magic crown of transparent green before toppling over into a churning mass of yellow-white foam.

Children are amused by their first encounter with figurative language. Their practical minds create laugh-provoking pictures when they read such statements as "His eyes dropped," "She turned green with envy," "He put his foot in his mouth," "The doctor was tied up," "Someone spilled the beans." Cartoons can be made to accompany metaphors.

Teach shades of meaning by mounting pictures of increasing size on deepening shades of colored paper.

Blow "word bubbles" to get synonyms. Start each row with a word, such as *happy, pretty, small,* or *old.* Let children blow their bubbles larger by giving synonyms for each word.

Although use of a thesaurus is beyond the ability of most primary children, it does help to make a "classroom thesaurus" of words to use instead of *sad, funny, beautiful,* and other overused words. The study of words separated from the situation in which children would use them is an isolated and usually ineffective learning situation. Meaningful exercises of this nature, however, are helpful after the need for adequate vocabulary is felt by a writer. Consider the following activities for independent student work.

Activity 1—Synonyms

To the Pupil:

Life would be pretty dull if we ate the same foods at every meal or played the same game every day. Life would be equally dull if we said and heard the same words all the time. We need to know enough words so that we don't wear out the same old, tired ones. We can give words a rest by using synonyms. *Synonyms* are words that have almost the same meaning, like *little, small,* and *tiny.*

1. Do you know a word to use in place of *big*? _____
2. Do you know another word that is a synonym for *big*? _____
3. Use your dictionary to help you find three more synonyms for *big.* _____ _____ _____
4. In the exercise below, *circle* the three words that have meanings somewhat alike. Also, choose the best word to *fill the space* in each sentence. Use your dictionary to help you.

space	distance	New York is a long _____ from here.
place	install	San Diego is a fun _____ to visit.
deposit	plan	I will _____ my money in the bank.
crack	split	There was a _____ in the plaster.
break	build	Be careful not to _____ the glass.

5. *Write* the correct synonym on the line beside each word. *Check by using your dictionary.*

pair _____	doze _____
jammed _____	funny _____
coast _____	pretty _____
coarse _____	strange _____

nap	lovely	amusing	odd
crowded	shore	couple	rough

Activity 2—Antonyms

To the Pupil:

One day during sharing period Andy told the class this story about his trip to the circus:

"The girl did stunts. Everything she did, the clown tried to do, too. The girl was graceful, but the clown—well, the clown wasn't graceful."

Andy needed a word to describe the opposite of *graceful*. He could have used *awkward* or *clumsy* but he just couldn't think of these words. Words that are opposite in meaning to other words are called *antonyms*. To speak and write better we need to know many antonyms.

Circle the word that means the opposite, or almost the opposite, of the first word in each line:

leave	play	sleep	stay
attach	detach	try	wish
powerful	different	homeless	weak
great	small	large	buff
scarce	plentiful	first	thin
most	least	soft	sweet
expensive	late	next	cheap
damp	clean	strong	dry
good	right	bad	ready
give	grow	take	go

Activity 3—Descriptive Words

To the Pupil:

Think of the word *apple*. Does this word do something to you? Now think of *the juicy, red apple*. These added words that tell about the apple make us think about the delicious taste of this fruit. When we describe or tell about

something, we can make it much more interesting by using words that make our listeners or readers see, hear, touch, taste, or smell.

Write a word in the blank in front of each word that will help to describe that word. Use the words in parentheses to help you.

1. the _____ car (see)
2. the _____ motor (sound)
3. the _____ flowers (smell)
4. the _____ pie (taste)
5. the _____ satin cloth (touch)

Use these describing words to write in the following sentences:
howling   rough   sour   pungent   glittering

1. The _____ floor scratched his feet.
2. The sky was sprinkled with _____ stars.
3. Pine needles have a _____ odor.
4. The _____ dog kept some people awake.
5. She had a _____ pickle in her lunch box.

Activity 4—Word Pictures

To the Pupil:

When we write or speak, we paint word pictures in the minds of readers and listeners. These word pictures can be simple black-and-white drawings or they can be wide-screen, 3-D, technicolor, action movies. Compare these two sentences:

1. The fire engine stopped in front of the burning house.
2. Siren screaming and tires screeching, the bright red fire engine braked to a halt in front of the blazing building.

Which sentence painted a better word picture for you? Now try to rewrite the following sentences. Make them paint better pictures.

1. Sharon was doing tricks on her bicycle.
   _____
   _____

2. Susan and Ricky were playing with paper dolls.
   _____
   _____

3. Mike hit a home run.

_____

_____

4. Irene was wearing a red hat.

_____

_____

5. The horse jumped over the fence.

_____

_____

EXPOSITION. Expository writing is explanatory writing, in which a writer explains something to a reader. Exposition may contain facts as well as ideas and opinions, and its success depends upon the clarity and thoroughness with which the ideas and information are presented.

Students use the skills of exposition every day. They explain why one teacher is better than another or why one class is more fun and interesting than another. They provide creative and sometimes lengthy explanations of why homework assignments are not completed. They explain over the phone to a friend how to do a complex algebra problem. They explain how to; they define; they analyze; they persuade; they compare and contrast. On a daily basis students display the interest, knowledge, organization, and sense of audience needed to write exposition successfully.

In the classroom, exposition is widely used in all content areas. Whatever the subject, students need to understand the importance of clarity, content, and organization in expository writing.

Students can choose a simple geometric shape, a familiar object, or a letter of the alphabet and explain in a five- to seven-sentence paragraph how to draw that object without naming it. Students then form pairs, exchange papers, and attempt to follow their partners' directions. They will quickly be aware of the effectiveness of this written communication. If their partner is easily able to draw the object, the feedback is immediate and positive. If the partner/reader is having difficulty, the writer can revise and refine the content and let the reader try again.

In another practice activity, students write directions telling how to get from one place in the classroom (or school) to another and see how successfully another person can follow them. Students not only gain insight into the requirements of exposition, but also enjoy the interactive nature of the activity.

Games can provide the basis for expository writing. Students can choose a simple, yet unfamiliar, game to explain to a classmate. The classmate can take notes and then write the instructions in clear, organized writing. The students then play the game according to the instructions. They will receive immediate feedback concerning the content, clarity, and organization of the exposition.

Most students find themselves intuitively using transitions as signals and devices to make their meaning clear to a reader. The following are among the commonly used transitions. Class discussion of their usefulness makes their importance even more evident to writers and provides students who may not be intuitively using them aware of their value. The teacher can read the paper of a student who has effectively used transitions. This same paper can then be read without the transitions. Students can easily recognize the help that these signal words supply to the reader.

Transitions to Show Order

first	a third reason
first of all	third
in the first place	last
to begin with	lastly
second	
secondly	

Transitions to Show Time

before	soon	meanwhile
before that	earlier	while
since	last	until
since then	after, after that	finally
next	later	
formerly	afterward	
now	immediately	

Signal Words

also	above all	in other words
again	for example	
as well as	to be specific	
in addition to	for instance	
others	such as	

Ending Transitions

in conclusion	in summary
to conclude	last of all
to sum up	lastly
for these reasons	

Abstract words and ideas are often difficult for students to explain. However, these concepts are often concretely applied in students' own lives. The school motto in San Marcos Junior High, San Marcos, California, is "I am responsible for myself." After brainstorming ideas about the meaning of *responsibility,* students can write five- to seven-sentence paragraphs defining responsibility as it applies to the school. These papers can be shared with the school principal, printed in the school newspaper, placed on the classroom Best Effort Board, or highlighted by placement on the wall in the school's main entrance hallway.

Classrooms can adopt mottos. Perhaps a class views itself as the most successful, the most enthusiastic, or the most loyal. Classroom brainstorming sessions can provide forums for discussion of these concepts. Students can then write expository papers to be printed in a classroom booklet that is shared with all class members.

Abstract concepts are also often exemplified in literary figures. Students can respond to a literary work by explaining traits of characters. For example, a student who reads *Call of the Wild* can explain the concept of bravery as exemplified in the character of Buck. In *Farewell to Manzanar,* the concept of prejudice can be defined through the lives of the Wakatsuki family.

Comparison and contrast ideas can also be found in literature. Winnie in Babbitt's *Tuck Everlasting* and Margaret in Blume's *Are You There God? It's Me Margaret,* are similar in their feelings of loneliness and alienation and yet are very different.

Social studies and science readily lend themselves to expository writing. Students gain better understanding of the workings of American government by comparing and contrasting the House of Representatives and the Senate. In science, the workings of veins and arteries can be compared and contrasted.

Journals, course content, and learning logs can provide content for exposition. The possibilities are endless. Teachers can provide writing experiences through which the writers/students gain new insights, but also through which students as readers are provided with new information. This latter element is just as important as the writing process itself, for the writer without an audience or purpose for writing is being cheated of a significant impetus for communication.

It is important that teachers clearly explain the structure of the expository writing task. A sample paragraph or essay can be modeled by the class's producing composite writing that the teacher puts on the chalkboard or overhead projector. Students can write rough drafts and evaluate their peers' work, providing immediate feedback and ample opportunity for practice.

Clear rubrics provide frameworks for students to work within. A skill-specific rubric for exposition might look something like the following with holistic scores (see p. 327) being assigned by a point scale of 1 (low) to 4 (high).

Holistic Scoring Scale

Very Inadequate Response = (1)

Organization: Paper has very little sense of organization. It has no clear beginning and ending. The reader has major difficulties following the explanation.

Clarity: Most of information is difficult to understand.

Content: Information does not explain the topic. Much irrelevant information is included.

Mechanics: Numerous grammatical and mechanical errors make the information difficult to understand.

Less than Adequate Response = (2)

Organization: Paper is not organized. It may lack a clear beginning and ending. The reader has difficulty moving from one idea to another.

Clarity: Parts of paper are difficult to understand.

Content: Information is insufficient to provide a clear explanation, and some unnecessary information is included.

Mechanics: Grammatical and mechanical errors are frequent enough to create problems for the reader.

Adequate Response = (3)

Organization: Paper is organized with a beginning and ending. The structure is logical, and there are no major problems in reading.

Clarity: Most information is clearly explained.

Content: There is sufficient information to explain the subject.

Mechanics: Some grammatical and mechanical errors exist but do not detract from the explanation.

More than Adequate Response = (4)

Organization: Well-organized paper with a clear beginning and end. Transitions are smooth and clear. Content is logically structured.

Clarity: All information clearly explained.

Content: Information is thorough enough to provide a clear explanation.

Mechanics: Grammatical or mechanical errors are slight and hardly noticeable.

How Much Classroom Time Should Be Devoted to Writing?

Time on task is a phrase often found in current research literature. As with most terminology that becomes clichélike with overuse, some clever and innovative jargon will eventually take its place; but regardless of the professional terminology used, research supports the notion that excellence and growth cannot occur in any academic area without a time commitment.

Students and teachers all understand that reading and math are important. Their importance is reinforced by time spent engaged in reading and math activities. In a year-long study for the Ford Foundation, Graves (1973) found that virtually no composition was taking place in the classroom. He observed that writing was used almost exclusively as a testing instrument, wherein students wrote short answers and incomplete sentences in response to questions. The message appears to be that writing is less important than math and reading.

Fortunately, up-to-date research suggests that this view of the world is changing; and with the realization of the need to commit time to all language skill areas, the issue of *how much time should be spent on writing* arises. Certainly, there is no magic number. Fearn (1983) suggests that 10 percent of instructional time be devoted to writing. In an elementary school day of approximately 250 instructional minutes, it is thus reasonable to devote 20 to 30 minutes to writing. The message then becomes clear to children that this, too, is an important skill worthy of their energy and attention.

However, the concept of time on task is somewhat misleading. Although engaged time is a crucial variable for development, it is not only the time spent but *the way* it is spent that is significant.

For the young writer, time and a supportive environment are all that is necessary to promote fluency in writing. In young children particularly, fluency must precede growth and development in writing. Caroselli (1981) suggests giving pencils, paper, and crayons to first graders on the first day of school and directing them to write anything they like. The teacher will see varying degrees of maturity and development in the children's letters, drawings, and attention spans. Each paper should be dated and saved as a measure of future learning. Children will enjoy seeing their writings displayed in the room. It works well to reserve one portion of a bulletin board or wall space as a Best Effort Board where students know they can go to see their own and their peers' writings.

Uninterrupted sustained silent writing (USSW) encourages fluency. Journal writing is a form of USSW. Just as lessons in reading and math usually take place at a predetermined time every day, journal writing can take place daily at a prescribed time. During this five- to fifteen-minute period, perhaps at the beginning of writing instruction or the first few minutes of the school day, the teacher directs students to write continuously for the set period of time on anything they wish. A special composition booklet or portion of a notebook should be reserved for journal entries. The goal is to encourage a free flow of uninterrupted ideas.

The time allowed for this activity will vary according to the capabilities of the students. Generally, beginning writers can sustain continuous writing for approximately five minutes. The teacher can adjust this level after becoming familiar with students' attention spans.

Occasionally, journal ideas can be assigned to students. For example, if they are working on an oceanography unit in science, the teacher might assign a journal topic that would complement the unit, such as "What sea creature would you most like or not like to be and why."

In his *Developmental Writing* program, Fearn (1983) utilizes a short, intense, and highly motivational variation on USSW. Called *Power Writing*, this activity requires that students write for one minute on an assigned prompt (tests, music, beach). The objective is for students to write as fast as they can *and* as well as they can.

Each Power Writing session consists of three one-minute rounds. After each round, students count the number of words they have produced and record that number on a chart like the following:

POWER WRITING

Day 1– Date	Round 1	Round 2	Round 3
Day 2			
3			
4			
5			
6			
7			
8			

At first, Power Writing can be done biweekly or weekly. After students have shown growth in fluency, as shown by increasing number counts, this activity can be continued on an alternate-week or even monthly basis.

Students can see growth in their classmates' fluency levels by the teacher's recording all students' number counts after each round by Power Writing. Teachers must be sensitive not to expose less successful writers.

"How many of you wrote zero to five words . . . six to ten words . . ." and so on.

Besides its value for promoting fluency, *effective* time on task requires direct instruction in writing. Time spent writing does not automatically result in increased proficiency. Composing must be preceded by input from prewriting activities and followed by feedback on what was written (the editing and revising stages of the writing process).

Words	Round 1	Round 2	Round 3
36–40			
31–35			
26–30			
21–25			
16–20			
11–15			
6–10			
0–5			

The teacher simply writes a chart like the preceding one on the blackboard. After counting the words written after each one-minute writing, students respond as the teacher asks for a show of hands by saying,

For revision in the writing process, students select the second or third round of their Power Writing effort and respond to the teacher's direction, "Fix it so you could turn it in for a grade. You have three

minutes." Now, students have a real draft with which to work.

After three minutes, the teacher inquires, "What did you do?" and as students respond ("Changed spelling. Fixed a sentence. Put in an ending sentence. Put two sentences together."), the teacher writes the list on the board. When the list includes perhaps six to eight items, the teacher announces, "Those are revision skills. When I ask you to revise, those are the kinds of things you should do."

Interestingly, when Power Writing and revision occur again, the list changes. Students learn, thereby, that revision is piece-specific, not generic. And they revise, for they have a real draft. Power Writing is a whole process activity, one of the few available in the natural state.

How Does a Teacher Handle the Paperwork in a Writing Program?

Many teachers see themselves as evaluators. They feel it is their duty to evaluate in some way all of the work children do. In a daily writing program, thirty children might generate sixty to ninety pieces of writing a week. Even if teachers spend only one and a-half minutes per paper (most would probably spend two to three minutes), they would have to find approximately two more hours per week to grade written work.

The problem with this view of the teacher's role is that it resurrects the notion that the final product is the only goal of the writing program. It ignores the fact that writing is a skill to be nurtured and developed; it is a *process,* not just a single product.

Therefore, the writing teacher must step outside the role of evaluator and into the role of facilitator. Does the band teacher formally evaluate every practice session and the physical education teacher grade the student's first attempt at a back handspring in a gymnastics unit? Of course not! They provide classroom environments in which students are free to practice and interact with their peers, concurrently receiving encouragement and feedback.

Not unlike band students and the gymnasts, writers must practice to develop their skill in writing. They must do so in a risk-free environment where there is continuous encouragement and feedback. In other words, the young writer must regularly be engaged in the writing process. Throughout this process (prewriting, writing, editing, and revising), the teacher encourages students' efforts and monitors progress. With direction, students are also capable of monitoring their own work and that of their peers. The last two stages of the writing process are specific times for students to receive further instruction and feedback as part of the composing process.

Editing or proofreading and rewriting are aspects of idea refinement. The fact that the first effort to write is a rough drafting of ideas or an experiment with ideas must be established as early as the fourth grade. Because rewriting a long selection can be a burden at this level, the short episode, the humorous incident, the descriptive paragraph, or the news item should be the writing objective.

Standards for proofreading should be established one at a time. Many children need freedom to write without the threat of proofreading or editing all their efforts. Each student can keep a writing folder in the classroom with a bank of rough drafts. Once a week students can choose one draft to take through the entire writing process for evaluation. The goals of the learner and the teacher will determine the extent to which material should be examined. These will reflect the language skills being taught at the grade level. For example, if students have been working on capitalization of proper nouns, the teacher can utilize the concept of *primary trait scoring,* which is the evaluation of specified elements—periods, main idea, capitalization—and on a particular writing activity evaluate only capitalization, for instance. If the written work is short, a five- to seven-sentence paragraph or a fifty-word story, actual teacher time spent on evaluation is kept to a minimum. If errors are indicated by a check (√)

in the margin beside the line containing the error, the onus is on the student to reread what was written critically and to make corrections.

This technique shifts responsibility for correction from the teacher to the student, where it belongs. These checks (√'s) serve as markers indicating where more extensive editing is needed. After a final editing and revision, students feel a great sense of accomplishment at producing an error-free piece of writing.

The following items would be appropriate for fourth-grade editing:

Proofreading My Story

1. Is my paper headed correctly?
2. Did I skip a line after my heading?
3. Did I capitalize the important words in the title?
4. Did I skip a line before I began to write my story?
5. Did I indent for each paragraph?
6. Do I have a margin?
7. Is each word spelled correctly?
8. Is each sentence complete? Did I omit words?
9. Have I a period or question mark after each sentence?
10. Did I include the important points in my story? Did I tell my story in sequence?

A class may be organized so that each writer has an editing partner. This partner then edits the paper. This report is submitted with the original and rewritten paper.

Proofreading

1. Did this person indent?
2. Did this person watch his margin?
3. Has he checked his spelling?
4. Did he use capitals when they are needed?
5. Is his paper neat?
6. Does this person know when to end a sentence and begin a new one?

7. Has this person used too many *ands?*
8. Do you feel this person checked his paper when it was finished?

I checked _____ paper.
My name is _____ .

Lessons in proofreading should be included in the language period. Exercises of this nature emphasize the skills of proofreading.

Proofread the following story:

1. Does each sentence start with a capital letter? (There should be twelve sentences.)
2. Are all the words correctly spelled? (There are five misspelled words.)
3. Do all the sentences tell about the topic? (There is one that does not belong.)
4. Are the paragraphs indented?

Once upon a time there lived a boy named Billy he lived with his mother and father. Once when his father was outside getting water the Indians came along and burned the house. Only Billy was alive and then he ran to the mountains and stayed there for five days. Billy and his family came from Warren, Ohio.

On the fifth day he saw a nest on a rockey cliffth. In the nest he saw a baby eagle. The mother eagle had been shot with an arrow. He took the baby eagle for a pet. Billy and the eagle grew up in the forest. They ate together and slept together. They had no family but they were not alone.

Displays of work "Before Proofreading" and "After Proofreading" will emphasize the improvement possible. A committee of proofreaders can serve the class. Three students are assigned the task of proofreading stories placed in a box at the reading table. When their work is completed, the work is placed in a rewrite box. After a visit to a newspaper, the role of editor can be dramatized in this way.

A variation on the classroom editing committee is for individual students to be given tasks of editing papers for only one of the following: spelling, punctuation, organization, and so on. Students with a particular strength can function as experts in that area.

Classroom recognition can be given to children's writing in several ways. This recognition provides strong motivation for students to polish their work during the editing and revising stages of the writing process. One school makes a scrapbook of "Our Very Best Writing." When the class feels that something is worthy of this collection, the material is added. At the end of the year this is presented to the principal. Scrapbooks made in former years are available on certain occasions.

Children enjoy reading something written by an older brother or sister. Upper-grade students are impressed with material they wrote while in a lower grade. Eventually it may be possible for a student to read material written by one of his parents when the parent was in the fifth grade. The teacher must plan so that the best product of each individual is included and so that no one is left out. During the year a child might substitute a new selection for one previously selected.

Bulletin boards of children's writing provide recognition and encouragement. Some schools have strict rules about the display of imperfect papers. In light of the objectives of a particular writing assignment, it seems that a paper with a few errors checked is still worthy of display. Few children are going to find pleasure in rewriting an entire paper just to have it placed on the bulletin board.

Publication in a school paper or magazine is the ultimate recognition for many. Creative writing is not news writing and as such must have a special place in any publication. Many school systems now publish an annual magazine of creative writing. When a selection is considered worthy, it is sent to an editing committee. This committee acknowledges the selection with a letter of recognition explaining that the work will be considered but that not all material submitted will be used. The letter is adequate recognition for many children. If a child's material is selected for the magazine, he receives three copies of the publication and another letter. The existence of such a publication influences many teachers who ordinarily would be more secure stressing drill on the mechanics of language to attempt projects involving creative writing.

Perhaps the most important idea that those who work with children in the area of creative or imaginative writing have found to be true is one of the utmost simplicity: You cannot teach children to write creatively; you can only help them express the original ideas within them. Behind the story, poem, or letter; behind the clear, concise sentence or the stumbling search for words are the children and all that they can become. Creative writing is one more way to understand them.

One of the acknowledged tasks of the elementary school years is to further the pupil's self-concept. Few experiences in school can so effectively destroy a positive self-image as the teaching of composition. Excessive correction has thwarted the pencil of many a beginner. In other cases, no correction at all has been offered for fear of cramping self-expression. When to correct and when not to correct children's writing has been a dilemma for many teachers.

Solutions arrived at in both England and America reveal surprising agreement. Correction is applied to children's practical writings—letters, reports, records, and other forms of factual prose in which the written paper itself is seen by an audience.

Pride in achieving correct form is developed in these more objective examples. On the other hand, imaginative expression is for enjoyment. Story and verse are to be read aloud to one's class, either by the author or by the teacher, and need not be corrected or rewritten. After being enjoyed by an audience, they are filed privately; their physical form is relatively unimportant. They have already served their purpose in oral communication. Here again the oral basis for learning to write operates with real efficiency. Only when stories or verse are to be made public in a class newspaper or school publication must they be edited and rewritten. When they are made public, they must be put into good form, as an obligation to others as well as a mark of self-respect.

Correction of any writing is best done orally by

teacher and pupil in an editing conference, taking turns reading aloud. Thus they apply the oral-auditory facility established long before the more recently acquired skills of writing and reading.

When writing is an opportunity to reveal one's own feelings and imagination without fear of criticism and with the assurance of respectful listeners, the pupil's self-image is enhanced. Not being on the defensive, one can appreciate the good writing of others, both peers and professionals. One can enjoy what is worthy in the teacher's eyes because he or she too is worthy as a writer. Both the listening audience and those who see the corrected public writing fortify one's pleasure and pride in writing and in oneself.

Another suggestion to lighten teachers' workload of grading is only to evaluate or grade five papers per assignment. Over a span of six assignments that thirty students have taken through the entire writing process, each student will have a grade. Instead of actually grading 180 papers, the teacher will grade only 30. Meanwhile, all students are writing, editing, and revising. They are all practicing their craft. In each of the six assignments, the twenty-five students who are not being graded will receive a check in the gradebook indicating that each child has honored the time on task requirement of each assignment.

Scoring Alternatives

Grades and learning have become almost synonymous in today's educational system. Every teacher is familiar with "grade card time," when letters (or numbers) that have been recorded in grade books are tallied. The resulting grade (which is generally perceived as having a capital *G*) represents to most people degrees of progress and achievement. Essentially, it tends somehow to represent the amount of learning that has taken place concretely.

In spite of this phenomenon, most teachers really grade students' papers for two much more specific and informative reasons. They realize that through a grading system that is well planned and clearly presented to students, they can

1. provide instructive feedback to students concerning work they have done and
2. gain valuable insights for themselves concerning their students' understanding of content and the success of their instructional program.

In the area of writing, extensive research has provided teachers with scoring (or grading) systems that are both evaluative and informative for them and their students. Two systems in particular have been used widely for directed writing assignments. They are *holistic* and *primary trait* scoring. The choice to use one or the other should be made before writing takes place and the purpose and method for evaluation clearly presented to students.

HOLISTIC SCORING. *Evaluating Writing,* Cooper (1983) refers to holistic scoring as "general impression scoring." The objective of this scoring system is to look at a piece of writing as a total product, not as a group of separate parts which, added together, make up the whole. In holistic scoring, parts are not separated. The assumption is that all factors of writing are intertwined and equally important and thus are not to be isolated for individual scrutiny.

Although holistic scores come from the evaluator's general impression, they do not materialize from an unfocused judgment based on whim. Instead, specific scoring guides, called *rubrics*, are devised and individualized for each writing assignment being evaluated. These rubrics are the standard by which each paper is evaluated.

Scoring guides are based on three scales. Evaluators can choose between nine-point, six-point, and four-point scales. These numbers are used in rubrics because they steer the reader/evaluator away from the option of judging any paper as average, for this evaluation provides very little information for either the teacher/evaluator or the student/writer. After all, what is an *average* paper? Neither teacher nor student is left with

a clear idea of whether the guidelines were addressed either adequately or inadequately. If the evaluator's objective is to present a clear message through the scoring system, then the concept of *average* is rightly avoided.

The choice of scale depends primarily on the teacher's objective. The nine-point scale offers the widest range of score and the finest distinction in quality. The six-point scale also offers a wide range of scores through which to delineate writing quality. The four-point scale is used to make broader distinctions among papers. This latter scale quickly becomes a very broad, pass-fail evaluation of a paper.

The following are general examples of nine-, six-, and four-point rubrics:

9-Point Scale

9–8 Excellent paper. A 9 is reserved for papers that are nearly perfect in content, organization, mechanics, and language use. Both 8 and 9 are excellent papers in areas of form and content, with 9's being definitely of higher quality.

7 Still an excellent paper, but not quite so well organized, creative, and articulate.

6–5 An adequate paper, but deficient in its organization, use of content, style, and/or mechanics.

4–3 A lower-half paper that is weak in organization, content, style, and/or mechanics.

2 A very weak paper that addresses the topic but is only loosely organized, with serious faults in organization, content, language use, style, and mechanics.

1 A paper that addresses the topic but that is disorganized, inarticulate, and full of errors.

6-Point Scale

6–5 Excellent paper. A 6 is reserved for papers that are nearly perfect in content, organization, mechanics, and language use. Both 5 and 6 are excellent papers in area of form and content, with 6's being definitely of higher quality.

4 A passing paper judged adequate in terms of content, organization, mechanics, and style. It may lack imagination and creativity.

3 A lower-half paper that is weak in content, organization, style, and/or mechanics.

2 A very weak paper that addresses the topic but is only loosely organized, with serious faults in organization, content, language use, style, and mechanics.

1 A paper that addresses the topic but that is disorganized, inarticulate, and full of errors.

4-Point Scale

4 An excellent paper that is well organized and displays facile uses of language, content, and mechanics.

3 A paper that demonstrates adequate organization, content, language use, and handling of mechanics. It may lack imagination and creativity.

2 A lower-half paper that is deficient in organization, content, language use, and/or mechanics.

1 An unacceptable paper that addresses the topic but that is weak in organization, content, and language use and is full of errors in mechanics.

In each rubric, the scale encourages the reader to think beyond the indecisive *average* judgment of a work. Before fine distinctions are made, the evaluator must decide whether a paper is *above* or *below* average. The reader must ask, "Is the paper a *lower-* or *upper-*half paper?" From there, the evaluator can more specifically define the quality of writing.

Upper half/Lower half

9–8	7	6–5	/	4	3	2	1	Here the 5 is considered a lower-half paper.
6–5	4		/	3	2	1		
4	3		/	2	1			

Teachers can tailor the general rubric to specific assignments made. For example, the following is a

sample 4-point rubric for a conventional narrative paragraph.

4 Excellent paper. It is well-organized. The topic sentence clearly states the main idea. The body presents information in logical sequence. The conclusion clearly restates the main idea. Vocabulary is precise, sentences are varied, and there are few errors in mechanics.

3 An adequate paragraph. Organization is clear. Language use and content are mundane. There are a few mechanical errors.

2 A paragraph that addresses the topic but that is deficient in organization, content, language use, and mechanics.

1 An unacceptable paragraph that has no clearly articulated main idea and is full of mechanical errors.

If the holistic scoring system is to be meaningful to students as well as teachers, students need to understand the characteristics of, for example on a 4-point scale, a *4* paper, a *3* paper, a *2* paper and a *1* paper. Teachers can duplicate and share with students papers that represent each score on the scale. These papers can be used for practice grading and classroom discussions so that students clearly understand how the evaluation system works.

PRIMARY TRAIT SCORING. The primary trait scoring system was developed through extensive research by the National Assessment of Educational Progress (NAEP). It is a quick and efficient method of scoring based on the objectives of individual writing assignments. The question asked in primary trait scoring is "Does the writing fulfill the objectives of a particular writing task?"

Before this scoring system can be used, students, as well as teachers, must understand that writing is a purposeful activity and that its primary objective (primary trait) is to communicate effectively regarding that purpose. Once clear criteria for meeting the primary trait are stated, this method of scoring provides a clear message to both writers and evaluators (that is, writers either have or have not, to some degree, met the goals of the writing task). Reasons for this can then be explored. If many writers are unsuccessful, perhaps the instruction, the writing prompt, or the scoring guide needs reevaluation.

Purposes for writing are related closely to the definition of writing as a means of expression and communication. Mullis (1985) presents three major areas of writing purpose that have formed a basis for primary trait scoring: informational or explanatory writing, persuasive writing, and literary or imaginative writing.

Specific steps lead to successful implementation of a primary trait scoring system. First, the writing task must be clearly defined, for example, persuading the junior high principal that end-of-the-year parties should be allowed in classrooms. After establishing the purpose, in this case persuasion, the means for fulfilling that purpose must be clearly stated (providing reasons and rationale that would appeal to the principal in order to most effectively fulfill the purpose). Thus, the primary trait could be stated as follows:

Presenting thoughts and reasons with logical appeal as a means of persuasion.

Then, what remains is the actual writing of a scoring guide.

Typically, a primary trait scoring guide includes four levels of skill. Level 1 indicates a paper that would provide little or no evidence. A Level 2 paper would provide very few appropriate reasons. Level 3 would show some thought as evidenced by some appropriate reasons. Level 4 represents a well-organized paper with convincing reasons and evidence supporting the case.

As in holistic scoring, the rubrics or scoring guides are criterion-referenced and, as such, need to be adjusted for the purpose of each writing task. Before writing takes place, classroom discussions should center on the primary trait and the elements of the scoring guides. Students can be instrumental in helping to articulate these elements and thus have an even better understanding of how to fulfill the objectives of the writing task.

Sample Scoring Guide

1. Position statement unclearly or inappropriately stated. Evidence is illogical and/or emotional or nonexistent. Paper lacks any clear organizational scheme.
2. Position statement is clear but paper offers minimal evidence for support. The paper attempts to provide logical organization but falls short of unifying arguments presented.
3. Position statement is both clearly stated and supported with several lines of argument. The lines of evidence and support are moderately well developed.
4. Position statement is clearly stated. Lines of argument and evidence are presented in a systematic and convincing fashion.

Implementing Primary Trait and Holistic Scoring Practices

Let's look at the holistic and primary trait scoring systems in practice. Both methods have been designed with two groups in mind, readers *and* writers. Readers may be either teachers already faced with mounds of paperwork or students with a finite amount of class time to spend on scoring papers. Regardless of *who* is doing the reading, scoring systems that require only 30 seconds per paper (true for papers of approximately one page) are valuable writing process tools. In addition, writers benefit from receiving immediate and clear feedback based on preestablished guidelines.

PRIMARY TRAIT

The first task in using the primary trait scoring system is to have a specific purpose for writing that is articulated clearly for both writer and scorer. Is the purpose to inform, persuade, or share an experience? Whatever the purpose for writing, it must present a clear and specific focus for the work. This focus is embodied in the prompt.

To better understand how this system works, let's examine two narrative writing samples. The prompt was used by students in the seventh grade.

Prompt: Write a narrative paragraph about a frightening experience you have had. Arrange the details in order so that the sequence can easily be visualized by a reader.

Now, according to this prompt, the primary trait of this narrative paragraph about a frightening experience is the presentation of events in clear, sequential order. Therefore, the rubric for scoring would be to judge presentation of narrative events as:

4—highly skilled
3—competent

2—minimal
1—inadequate

WRITING SAMPLE 1

The most frightning experience I ever had was when I was riding down the hill we live on on my bike. It started out like any other school day. First, I got on my bike and started down the hill. Then I accidentally turned my handle bars too sharp, and I went flying. My bike fell right on top of me. Then my friend got my mom, and she said I was all right. Finally, I was up and went off to school. That was one of the most frightning experiances I've had.

This first narrative paragraph definitely relates the events of this experience in a sequential order. Because the friend does not appear until near the end, and we aren't sure from where, the scorer rated this narrative a "3," which was competent in the presentation of narrative events.

This same scorer rated writing sample 2 a "4," which was highly competent in the presentation of narrative events. Although this student has a few more errors in the paragraph, the scorer judged the presentation of the primary trait to be highly skilled because of the more detailed and complete telling of the narrative event.

WRITING SAMPLE 2

My most frightening experience as a child was when I lay silently in my bed, my eyes were wide open. I could not sleep because I heard many strange, freaky noises. I couldn't stand it any longer. I got up to go to my parents bedroom when I noticed a long, white figure in my door way. I felt goose bumps go up my spine. Suddenly I had a surge of energy to punch this shadowy figure out of my way. I made a fist with my hand punched it and ran to my parents room. Finally with a comfortable nights sleep in my parents room I woke up. I remembered my terrible time I had last night. I reluctlantly went back to my room to find my white bathrobe laying on the floor under my doorway, the ghost. That was my most frightening experience as a child.

You'll notice that neither of the writers of samples 1 or 2 presented information in an illogical or confusing manner. Likewise, no crucial events were ignored. Paragraphs which might be rated a 2—minimal presentation of events—or a 1—inadequate presentation of events—would have had one or both of these characteristics.

HOLISTIC

When we use holistic scoring, the first and most crucial issue is having a rubric that is clear to both scorer and writer. This has been said before, but it is important enough to reemphasize. It is also important that writers and scorers examine sample papers that are representative of the various points on the

scoring scale, for only by doing this will everyone feel secure in knowing the expectations set forth by the rubric.

In writing samples 3 and 4 the students are writing to the prompt: describe a place where you like to go to relax. Both chose the beach as their favorite place. On a four-point scoring guide, sample 3 was judged as a "3." It demonstrates adequate handling of the topic and adequate use of the conventions of English usage. Misuse of the word *fragrant* and misspelling of the word *against* (agianst) do not significantly detract from the content of the paragraph.

WRITING SAMPLE 3

The beach is my favorite place to relax. I always feel peaceful at the beach. I like to watch the waves come to shore and smell the salty fragrant in the air. It feels nice when I see how playful the seagulls are as they fly over the ocean. I like the feeling of the cold water when it goes between my toes and the sound of the waves as they crash agianst the rocks. That is why I like to relax at the beach.

WRITING SAMPLE 4

I believe that the most relaxing place, I can think of is, the beach. Where else could you lie on soft, warn, sand, as the sun turns to a bright, orange, ball. The sound of silky waves, as they come ashore, and dance at your feet. Prehaps; the mild taste of salt on the tip of your tongue. While you breathe in the cool air, which lingeres of its origin; over the sea. These are some reasons why I believe the beach is so relaxing.

Comparison of Holistic and Primary Trait Scoring

	Holistic	*Primary Trait*
Purpose	To provide an overall or general impression of the quality of written work as a coherent whole.	To provide an analysis that focuses on a specific primary trait that is integral to the success of a given type of writing.
Value	To provide general feedback to student/writers and teacher/evaluators concerning success of a writing task and of the writing instruction.	To provide specific feedback to student/writers and teacher/evaluators concerning the success of writing as it addresses the purpose of a given type of writing task.
Scoring Time	One to two minutes per paper.	One to two minutes per paper.

The same scorer rated sample 4 a "2." It appears that this student has attempted to be creative in her use of description (i.e., "while you breathe in the cool air, which lingeres of its origin") and sophisticated in her use of conventions (i.e., semicolons). However, her success with both is deficient and detracts somewhat from the sense of the paragraph.

When determining the type of scoring to be used, it is essential to understand the purpose and values of each.

What Is the Place of Modern Technology in the Writing Program?

Imagine thirty students eager to produce and polish their compositions. Imagine a classroom of students who comment, "Oh, no! Do we have to stop now?" at the end of a writing session. These are not idealized situations fit only for a too-good-to-be-true work of fiction. They are, in fact, realistic responses of students who use the word processing capabilities of the microcomputer.

At a very basic level, the physical act of writing represents tedium for many students. The tedium that children may feel when writing, rewriting, and attending to neatness is eliminated by the word processor. Although knowledge of a typewriter keyboard is an asset, it is not necessary for effective use of the computer. Children quickly become adept at using the hunt-and-peck method of typing on the computer keyboard.

Using the process approach to composing, students' computer time is most efficiently used if the prewriting activities are completed *before* sitting down at the computer. The prewriting phase may include organizing their ideas into an outline or even a very rough first draft of what will be written.

Even the youngest student can, with guidance, use simple editing commands. The following commands would be sufficient for most student editing:

Insert a letter, word, space, or line.
Delete a letter, word, space, or line.
Indent a letter, word, space, or line.
Move up and down lines within the composition.

As students compose and as their text is on the monitor, the teacher has an excellent opportunity to talk to them about their work. Students, of course, relish positive comments about their compositions; however, while on the computer they seem more open to constructive criticism. They can revise as they are composing without fear of starting over or of messing up what they have already accomplished.

If each student has his or her own disk, there is freedom at any point in the process to print a copy of what has been composed. Writers need time to think about what they have written, to contemplate ideas and the way they have been stated. Intermediate-grade students are more capable of engaging in this aspect of the process than are primary age children. It is sometimes advantageous to allow students to print a copy of their work to take home with them or to bring to class the next day to discuss. They can make notes on this copy and take it with them back to the computer to complete the writing process.

Peer editing is an effective evaluation tool on the computer. Again, students seem less intimidated by comments and suggestions when they have control of the editing process. Peer editors also seem more willing to make concrete suggestions when they are evaluating work done on the word processor. Editing can be done as it is in regular classroom composition. Editors can evaluate for one item (spelling, capitalization, punctuation, organization of ideas) or for a list of prescribed items that correspond to the objectives of the assignment.

Many computer programs have been written for language arts. Many that are designed for the writing program involve the more mechanical aspects of composing. They may require students to read a paragraph on the monitor and then pick the topic sentence from a multiple choice list. When the teacher feels that drill and practice on certain aspects of composition are warranted, this type of program has value for writing instruction. However, primary emphasis in a writing program should be on the students' generating their own material and not on drill-and-practice activities.

A typical schedule in the intermediate grades for composing a piece on the word processor might look like the following:

Writing Fables

Prewriting

Days 1 and 2: *In class*   Read fables.
Discuss characteristics of fables.
Decide on fable idea.
Write very rough first draft.

Writing

Day 3: *At computer*   Spend 20 minutes putting first draft on computer.

Print hard copy.

Editing/Revising

Day 4: *In class*   Bring fables to the classroom.
Read them aloud.
Class makes comments and suggestions.
Students reread and evaluate own work.

Editing/Revising (continued)

Day 5: *At computer*   Students call up fable on disk.
Students form pairs and carefully edit one another's fables.
Final editing.
Print final hard copy.

Day 6: *In class*   Display finished products.

Teacher evaluates finished products as desired.

Summary

The development of writing as a process that can be interwoven throughout all dimensions of the curriculum has been the theme of this chapter. Holistic and primary trait scoring techniques, evaluation strategies to manage the paperwork load caused by additional writing assignments, and uses of the computer in writing were also highlighted.

Suggested Classroom Projects and Questions for Discussion

Projects

1. Choose one grade level and design a six-week writing program, beginning on day one of the school year. This program will continue during the school year, but you will plan specifically only for the first six weeks.
2. Design one writing assignment and explain the process by which students would take this activity through all stages of the writing process. Include appropriate prewriting activities and editing techniques.
3. Investigate procedures used with respect to publication of a collection of creative writing. How are the materials selected; who pays for the publication; how is the material distributed?
4. Design one writing activity that follows the assign-write-correct format. Then, analyze that assignment in light of what you know about the writing process.
5. Outline a one-day seminar on the writing process that you would present to elementary school teachers who are unfamiliar with it. Include at least one hands-on experience for the teachers.
6. Design a highly motivational writing activity appropriate for third-grade level. Write lesson plans for this activity and explain its motivational aspects.
7. Choose one particular grade level and design a writing activity to use with the microcomputer. Write lesson plans detailing procedures involved in the activity.
8. A parent of one of your students is concerned because you are not grading all of the written work her child is producing in your classroom. Write to that parent, presenting a clear rationale for your methodology of only occasionally grading students' writings.
9. Investigate use of the writing process model in at least five elementary language arts textbooks currently used by schools. From this perspective, write a paper containing a comparative analysis of the textbooks.
10. Write a presentation to the school board convincing them of the benefits of implementing a new writing program in your entire district. Address components of the program and procedures for implementation.
11. Make a bulletin board display of the writing process. Devise a way to highlight or exemplify each component of the process.

Questions

1. How does the assign-write-correct model of writing instruction differ from the writing process model?
2. What is the primary goal of writing instruction for very young writers, and why is it important?
3. How has writing instruction changed over the past hundred years?
4. Explain the developmental view of writing instruction.
5. What is the relationship between oral language development and the development of written language?
6. How can you apply the saying, "Nothing succeeds like success" to writing instruction?
7. Discuss the various roles of the teacher in a writing program.
8. Explain the idea that the steps in the writing process are not carried out in a linear fashion.
9. Discuss the significance of errors in writings of young children. Give specific examples to support issues in your discussion.
10. Discuss the purposes of each stage in the writing process: prewriting, writing, postwriting.

Chapter 13

The Reading/Writing Connection

(Photo by Linda Lungren)

OBJECTIVES

At the end of this chapter, the student should be able to:

1. understand the differences and similarities between reading and writing.
2. understand the rationale for integrating reading and writing within the curriculum.
3. employ instructional methods for integrating reading and writing throughout the curriculum.

What Is Writing?

What happens in your mind when you sit down and involve yourself in a writing activity? Do you think about each letter you are going to write? Do you think about only the word you are writing? Does the spelling of the words seem to occur automatically? Does your mind race ahead of your pencil, pen, or keyboard? Is your hand movement (spelling and handwriting) dissociated from whatever your mind is thinking about? Is your mind engaged in composing instead? Is it producing what you want to say? As we attempt to answer these questions, we begin to realize that the act of composing involves the *integration* of many language arts processes.

Flood and Salus (1984, p. 123) describe writing as "a sophisticated cognitive process in which the writer acquires, organizes, and produces information." Britton (1970, p. 7) ties language to thought by stating that "we use language as a means of organizing a representation of the world." Vygotsky (1962) suggests that the child has a "sense of word" that includes all of the association with it. These associations become inner speech, classified as thought. Both Vygotsky (1962) and Piaget (1952) support the construct that an individual's language usage is closely related to concept development and formation. Moffett (1979, p. 278) presents a hierarchical definition of writing, beginning with the simple drawing of letters to what he refers to as "revision of inner speech." This last, and in Moffett's hierarchy the highest definition of writing, suggests that writing is a manifestation of thinking. If this is what writing is, how can it be fostered in the classroom?

Theory and research of the past two decades, of which the preceding definitions are only a few, highlight the notion that writing is both a thinking and learning process. Children's ability to express themselves in writing is dependent upon their ability to develop and relate ideas. In addition, children's learning capabilities are heightened when they write. They select, eliminate, and arrange thoughts and ideas, which become new insights and associations and thus new learning.

Athey (1983, p. 197) affirms the cognitive base upon which all language skills rest. She offers the cognitive psychologist's view of thought and language when she states,

> Knowledge is not a simple reproduction of what is experienced, but an active construction embodying elements of what is previously known, what is believed, and what is expected. The constructive nature of experience carries over into our dealing with language, both oral and written. Language has a cognitive base, which is the same whether the activity be listening, speaking, reading or writing.

The role of the teacher is to provide an environment that encourages such expression and to acquaint our students with the processes that enable them to become proficient writers.

What Is Reading?

You can ask yourself many questions about how you are processing the print on this page. Did you look at each letter? Each word? Were you thinking about the names of the letters or only about the meaning you were extracting from the print? Yes, just as you are thinking, reading is a complex process that places demands on an individual's (1) perceptual, (2) linguistic, (3) cognitive, (4) experimental, and (5) affective systems. The following tasks are related to these five components:

1. Visual and auditory perception of printed materials.
2. An understanding of relationship between letters and sounds and of the structure of languages.
3. Analysis and synthesis of printed information that leads to concept formation.
4. Past experience that allows the reader to react to and assimilate information.

5. Interest and motivation that facilitate understanding of concepts.

Basically, reading is "a process of *perceiving, interpreting,* and *evaluating* printed material" (Lapp and Flood, 1986). The desired result of this process is *comprehension,* the understanding of concepts that have been presented in print. Although there are various ways in which reading has in the past been defined, most linguists, educators, and psychologists would agree that without comprehension, reading does not take place.

Since reading is essentially comprehension of information from print, it is logical next to address the question of the way the reading process actually takes place. During the 1970s several explanations of this process were postulated. They were categorized as *bottom-up, top-down,* and *interactive* models of reading.

Proponents of the bottom-up view suggested that reading involves, first, the decoding of words and, second, comprehension of printed material as each word is decoded and understood. Top-down theorists suggest that higher-order, cognitive processing of concepts facilitates comprehension of letters and words and their attendant sounds. A third group of theorists supported an interactive view of reading, whereby decoding and comprehension neither preceded nor succeeded one another. Rather, through his or her knowledge of language along with prior experiences, the reader uses letter-sound correspondence, language structure, and concept formations in parallel fashion to arrive at meaning. This last view most accurately represents the complexity of reading, for even beginning readers must bring simultaneously to the act of reading an understanding of letters and words, a notion of syntax or structure of language, and prior knowledge in order for comprehension to take place.

When we examine reading and writing more closely, we see that both are skills through which we engage in the construction of meaning (Photo by Linda Lungren)

What Are the Differences and Similarities Between the Language Skills of Reading and Writing?

Among curriculum developers and language arts specialists, the terms *reading* and *writing* are quite often mentioned in the same breath—like ham and eggs or peanut butter and jelly. Why are reading and writing becoming so closely linked in conversation and practice? The answer lies in their similarities.

The word *similarities* here is carefully chosen, for reading and writing are clearly not identical acts. One deals with the printed page upon which words have already been written and the other with the production of these words. In addition, the reader can only infer the writer's intent from prearranged words and sen-

CHILD 1: LEVEL 2.2

This lady has just boght some tomatos

CHILD 2: LEVEL 2.2

she might make a Salad or eat them ragh.

she might make a Salad
or eat them raw.

CHILD 3: LEVEL 2.2

When she gets home she mite give some of them to her friends

Figure 13–3. Complex verbs from Basal A children's writing.

read two distinctively different basal readers.* In Basal A, sentences frequently contained subordinate clauses, participial phrases, and complex verbs. In Basal B, sentences were most often simple and shorter and tended to be written one to a line. As shown in Figures 13–1, 13–2, 13–3, and 13–4, her analysis of students' writing revealed a striking similarity between what they read and what they wrote.

Several other findings reinforce the view of the complementary nature of reading and writing (Stotsky, 1983).

1. Better writers not only tend to be better readers, but tend to read more.

* Figures 13–1, 13–2, 13–3, and 13–4 from B. Eckhoff, "How reading affects children's writing." In *Language Arts.* Urbana, Ill.: National Council of Teachers of English, 1983. Copyright © 1983 by The National Council of Teachers of English. Reprinted by permission.

CHILD 1: LEVEL 2.2

She is looking very happy to see tomatoes growing in her garen.

CHILD 2: LEVEL 2.2

She probbly is going to pick up the other tomatoes in back of her and put them were they go.

CHILD 3: LEVEL 2.2

And when she got home she made a big salad for a party her son was having.

Figure 13–4. Elaborate structures used by Basal A children.

2. Reading strategies designed to improve writing are at least as successful as grammar and additional writing activities.

3. Writing exercises designed to improve reading comprehension have a significant level of success.

In essence, each language skill is a form of rehearsal for the other. When students write, they are structuring their thoughts so they can be represented in print. As readers, they grow to understand the writer's representations, an act that is, by definition, reading comprehension.

What Are Effective Instructional Methods for Integrating Reading and Writing?

Previous sections in this chapter have examined *what* (the differences and similarities between reading and writing) and *why* (reasons to capitalize on their similarities). Now let's look at *how:* how can classroom strategies and practices be structured to emphasize the complementary nature of reading and writing and their relationship as mutually enhancing language skills?

Primary

Most primary-level students overwhelmingly share a lively and uninhibited desire to learn. Their openness and willingness to dive into learning experiences are virtually unmatched at any other educational level. Primary-grade teachers have the unique opportunity to capitalize on this enthusiasm and to develop their students' language skills through natural language activities, and one of the best ways to do this is through the integration of reading and writing activities.

Students develop their oral language skills naturally. To them it simply makes sense to practice and refine their speech over the first few years of their lives. They do not view speech development as boring drill and practice. It isn't. It's a purposeful, meaningful activity. Children are motivated to communicate their wants, needs, and ideas in the most effective way possible. By structuring natural language activities through the *language experience approach* (LEA), we can help students maintain these feelings of motivation and purpose concerning the development of their reading and writing skills.

LANGUAGE EXPERIENCE APPROACH. Before children become fervent writers, particularly in kindergarten and first grade, we can take advantage of the vast language experience that they bring to the classroom. First, we can use various cues to encourage children to talk and to share their ideas through that talk. For example, we might ask a kindergarten child to tell what he did this morning before coming to school. As the child shares ideas, we transcribe his speech. Children in second and third grades enjoy the experience of talking into a recorder and then transcribing their own talk.

The teacher who has transcribed the children's oral language can then do the following:

1. Provide the children with a sheet of lined paper and a copy of the transcription.
2. Direct the children to recopy the transcriptions and then illustrate what they have written.
3. Encourage the children to read and reread what they have written.

If the children have been asked to talk about a particular subject or theme, the work of each child can be bound with that of the other students into a thematic book and thus be available for all to read. This is a great opportunity for students to feel that they have had their work immortalized in print, and parents enjoy reading their children's books during open house and classroom visitations.

If the classroom has a computer and printer available, the children's oral language can be transcribed on the computer. It is thrilling for children to see what they have said being printed from the computer. They will thoroughly enjoy illustrating and reading their creations. By encouraging them to share with their peers, everyone will have much interesting material to read. Before long, students will be clamoring to do their own transcribing on the computer, thus eagerly beginning independent composing.

Kindergarten students can create their own little books simply by using their own name and two other words, such as *will* and *go*. They can write

Linda will go

on one page and illustrate the sentence. On a second page they can write

Will Linda go?

and illustrate that. Again, students can work with various combinations of words to create these minibooks, which they can reread and their classmates can read also. When children read their own writing, they wear the shoes of both reader and author and begin to understand the dynamic connection between reading and writing, comprehension and production.

NARRATIVE WRITING. Many primary-grade teachers recognize that children come to school well versed in narration. Storytelling abounds in Mother Goose stories, cartoons, and movies. However, having this background knowledge does not guarantee that students will be able to generate complete stories with well-developed characterizations, setting, plot, conflict, and theme. In order to enhance their concept of story, teachers can encourage active comprehension of the various story components through reading. For example, they can better help students understand characterization by discussing their *first* impressions of characters, the way the author creates these impressions, the characters' changes throughout the book, and students' final impressions of the characters.

After reading a story and during class discussion of parts of the story, students next write questions that call for further analysis of the components discussed. For example, from the story *Alexander and the Terrible, Horrible, No Good, Very Bad Day* by Judith Viorst, students might ask questions such as

Who is Alexander?
Where does the story take place?
Why is he having a bad day?
What makes him feel better?

Did any part of the story sound like something that has happened to you? Students can take turns asking a partner their questions.

Another technique that helps younger students understand story patterns is the cut-apart story. Teachers write story parts on tagboard strips. Students then reconstruct the narrative by placing the strips in a logical sequence. Once they have restructured the

story, they can rewrite it on their own paper and share it orally with the class.

Before children actually write their own stories, they can work in another way with story parts that have been prefabricated. For primary age children, the concept of the story should be kept simple. Instead of using technical terms such as *characterization, setting, plot, theme, conflict,* and *resolution,* terms like *who, what, where,* and *when* are easier for youngsters to understand. Place examples of each of these story components on slips of paper in separate boxes and allow children to choose one slip from each box. For example,

Who	*What*
a doctor	a party
an eight-year-old boy	a storm
a horse	a wrong turn
a puppy	a bad day
a six-year-old girl	a race
a magician	an accident

Where	*When*
castle	morning
beach	afternoon
farm	evening
ice cream store	12:00 noon
school	midnight
forest	

Once students have chosen their story parts, they can write short (no more than one page) stories. Brevity should be encouraged. Limiting students' writing does not limit their creativity. On the contrary, it encourages creative thinking because it focuses students' attention on the value of saying what they want to convey clearly and concisely. In addition, students' writing can be evaluated just as effectively from a one-page work as from a three-page work, for any writing problems that a student has will show up in the first

fifty words and tend simply to be repeated thereafter throughout the rest of the work.

EXPOSITORY WRITING. Most children can begin to understand the patterns of informational or expository writing as early as the third grade. By using the steps

1. *predict*
2. *listen/read*
3. *summarize*
4. *share*

teachers can actively involve students in comprehension, sharpen their critical listening skills, provide practice in analyzing and synthesizing information, and encourage rereading and rethinking of information. This technique works well in all content areas. However, to illustrate it, let us look at a science lesson on the black widow spider, which follows this plan.

1. **Predict**—Students bring to the classroom a wide range of prior knowledge. By encouraging them to use what they already know, we encourage them to become actively involved in their own learning. We can stimulate this prior knowledge by asking them to predict what they will learn about the black widow spider. Their predictions can be catalogued on a semantic map for further use.

If the subject matter permits, this is a good opportunity for students to illustrate what their subject might look like.

The semantic map of students' predictions might look like the first black widow spider map.

2. **Listen**—This step may be either a listening or silent reading activity. Whichever is used, the skill of being critical listeners/readers is an important one for children to develop. By engaging in the prereading activity in Step 1, we help students focus more on major points and less on minor details.

3. **Summarize**—This step involves two parts. First, after listening to or reading the information, students make their own semantic maps, comparing their predictions with what they actually found. This can be

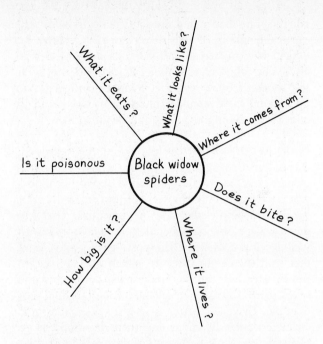

done on the board at first and later individually. Their findings should first be placed on a semantic map.

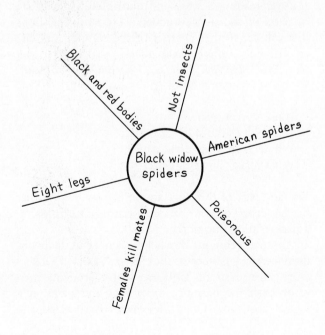

During this portion of the activity, teachers can help students differentiate main points from details in the information. For example, the idea that "black widow spiders are dangerous" would be the main idea of this map.

After formulating the main idea, students next complete their text by listing details that prove and expand their main idea.

Combining Main Idea and Supporting Details

Theme of main idea: *A black widow spider is very dangerous.*

Supporting details
1. *It is poisonous.*
2. *Females are the most deadly.*
3. *Females devour their mates.*
4. *Black widow spiders are not insects.*
5. *They have eight legs.*

Next, students transfer the main points on their maps to a three- to five-sentence summary. For example:

Black widow spiders are dangerous.
They originated in the United States.
Black widow spiders have eight legs.
Females kill their mates.
Black widow spiders are very poisonous.

Finally, they write their main idea statement and relevant information as a short expository paragraph. After composing their texts, students will want to complete the writing process by following the steps of (1) receiving feedback, (2) rewriting, and (3) editing.

4. **Share**—By reading their summaries aloud, either to a partner or to the class, students are able to hear and discuss the various ways in which different students have synthesized and organized their information.

Another strategy for enabling students to write expository paragraphs involves (1) selecting a topic, (2) developing the main idea, and (3) presenting supporting details related to the main idea. As suggested by Flood, Lapp, and Farnan (1985) students can complete the following five-part form, thereby clarifying and organizing their thoughts before actually writing.

Procedures for Writing Expository Passages

Step 1. Prewriting:
Topic: _____

Part A: Facts I already knew about the topic
1. _____
2. _____
3. _____
4. _____

Part B: Facts I have learned about the topic

	Source	Fact
1.	Reference material (e.g., encyclopedia)	1.

2. Reference material	2.
3. Teacher	3.
4. Other adult authority	4.
5. Miscellaneous	5.

Step 2. Composing
Theme or main idea _____
_____

Supporting details
1. _____
2. _____
3. _____
4. _____
5. _____

Step 3. Feedback
Teacher
Students
Others

Step 4. Rewriting

Step 5. Editing (polishing)

Step 1. Prewriting

The goal of this initial stage of the strategy is for students to generate a topic for their writing. This is accomplished through an oral and written interview. The teacher first asks the student to choose a topic he or she wants to write about. The student might respond, for example, that he or she wants to write about *pets*. The teacher would continue the dialogue by asking, "What is your favorite kind of pet? What makes that a good pet to have? Do you have a pet? Does your pet take lots of care? What kind of things should you consider when choosing a pet?"

After this prewriting session, during which students have generated some information about their topic, the teacher will direct them to fill in the first part (Part A) of the interview form.

Part B of the prewriting stage involves students' gathering additional information about their topics. This information can come from reference materials, teachers, librarians, parents, or other knowledgeable adults/children.

Step 2. Composing

After students have gathered additional information on their topic, they can begin the composing process by selecting the most important information they have acquired. After they have chosen pieces of information, they generate one main idea statement that could relate to all of the information they have selected.

After formulating the main idea, students next complete their text by listing details that prove and expand their main idea.

Finally, they write their main idea statement and relevant information as a short expository paragraph that might look similar to the one about black widow spiders.

Steps 3–5. Feedback, Rewriting, Editing

After composing their paragraphs, ask the students to turn their papers over and on the back write a statement expressing the paragraph's main idea. Then ask each student to select a partner with whom to exchange papers. Looking only at the front of the paper, ask students to read their partner's paragraph. Next students should formulate what they believe is the main idea of the paragraph and write a statement expressing that idea on the front of the paper, underneath the paragraph.

If one student had written the sample paragraph about *black widow spiders* he or she would write the main idea, "Black widow spiders are dangerous," on the paper as the main idea of the paragraph. Then this student and another student might want to discuss whether (1) the writer needs to present his or her idea more clearly or (2) the reader needs help in understanding the way expository text conveys and supports a main idea. Finally, students would rewrite their paragraphs, making modifications in their rough drafts based on the peer discussions.

Intermediate

LITERATURE AND COMPOSITION. In recent years there has been a return to an old practice of using examples from literature to encourage writing by students. At one time students imitated the sentences of Sir Walter Scott or Charles Dickens. Such exercises do influence students who identify with authors and who wish to acquire the disciplines of authorship. Like a knowledge of grammar, the knowledge of plot structure or technique of description and characterization can be useful to some young writers. Understand-ing what is read is tied to the reader's prior knowledge. Students understand best what they can in some way relate to their own lives. To help your students understand complex literature, you may wish to devise an activity in which they produce a written personal response to literature. This response must go beyond simple tastes and preference.

We do not know whether children grow in ability more from writing a fable than from "writing a story." We do not know whether an awareness of story line helps the young writer any more than the intuitive

354 • COMPONENTS OF THE LANGUAGE ARTS PROGRAM

imitation of favorite story patterns. Teachers who are trained in the discipline of English and who believe that simple elements of the discipline should be taught to children frequently gain good results with a planned formal series of lessons on specific writing techniques. Other teachers equally well trained gain impressive results through programs that encourage the student to write creatively without starting with an analysis of specific forms. In order to contrast the practices, it is necessary to consider the extremes.

Literature is evidence of the success that some individuals have achieved through written composition. As a child identifies with the authors of fine books, the knowledge of technique used will influence reading and writing efforts. It is possible that overemphasis on literary form and analysis could block effective writing and reading; the student might become so involved with analyzing the way the task is done that the content would become secondary. With this caution in mind many teachers will find that children's interest in great writing can motivate their desire to grow in written communication.

As suggested throughout this chapter prose excerpts can be used to help teach writing. Begin by having the students read several excerpts about a particular theme. The following are about autumn.

Farmer Boy

By Laura Ingalls Wilder

Now the harvest moon shone round and yellow over the fields at night, and there was a frosty chill in the air. All the corn was cut and stood in tall shocks. The moon cast their black shadows on the ground where pumpkins lay naked above their withered leaves.

In the beech grove all the yellow leaves had fallen. They lay thick on the ground beneath the slim trunks and delicate bare limbs of the beeches. The beechnuts had fallen after the leaves and lay on top of them. Father and Royal lifted the matted leaves carefully on their pitchforks and put them, nuts and all, into the wagon. And Alice and Almanzo ran up and down in the wagon, trampling down the rustling leaves to make room for more.

When the wagon was full, Royal drove away with Father to the barns, but Almanzo and Alice stayed to play till the wagon came back.

A chill wind was blowing and the sunlight was hazy. Squirrels frisked about, storing away nuts for the winter. High in the sky the wild ducks were honking, hurrying south. It was a wonderful day for playing wild indian, all among the trees.

In *My Side of the Mountain*, Jean George expresses her view of the changing seasons.

September blazed a trail into the mountains. First she burned the grasses. The grasses seeded and were harvested by the mice and the winds.

Then she sent the squirrels and chipmunks running boldly through the forest, collecting and hiding nuts.

Then she gathered birds together in flocks, and the mountain top was full of songs and twittering and flashing wings. The birds were ready to move to the south.

How have Jean George and Laura Ingalls Wilder differed in their descriptions of squirrels gathering nuts and birds flying south? Which is more appealing to you? Why?

Notice how Marjorie Kinnan Rawlings pays particular attention to the changing weather in her description of fall from *The Yearling*.

The first heavy frost came at the end of November. The leaves of the big hickory at the north end of the clearing turned as yellow as butter. The sweet gums were yellow and red and the blackjack thicket across the road from the house flamed with a red as bright as a campfire. The grapevines were golden and the sumac was like oak embers. The October blooming of dog-fennel and sea-myrtle had turned to a feathery fluff. The days came in, cool and crisp, warmed to a pleasant slowness, and chilled again. The Baxters sat in the evening in the front room before the first hearthfire.

Pay close attention to the way that Virginia Sorensen describes the colors of the trees in this selection from *Miracles on Maple Hill*.

You would think Maple Mountain was on fire.

In every direction the trees were red and yellow. When the sun struck them suddenly, flying through windy clouds, the brightness was almost more than Marley could bear. The redness seemed to come from inside each tree in a wonderful way; it was the red she saw through her hand when she held it against the sun. The yellowness glistened like golden hair, and the wind shook it, and bits of gold spun down upon the grass.

What a lovely world! Every morning on Maple Hill, Marley woke in the very middle of a scarlet and golden miracle.

Read the descriptions again to look for techniques the authors have used to present their observations about autumn.

1. To which senses do the four writers appeal?
2. Which sensory words and phrases do you especially like?
3. Take your senses to an imaginary spring picnic or a summer barbecue. Use pantomine to show what you see, hear, smell, taste, and touch.
4. How does fall come to the city? Think of images that will re-create the sights, sounds, taste, smells, and feel of a city autumn. Build these images into a descriptive paragraph.

Children can be encouraged to analyze an author's writing purposefully and critically in order to read as writers.

The Reading Log. Cooper (1985) suggests the reading log as a way to help students attend to literature and evaluate writings from a variety of perspectives; *reading logs* are journals in which students write regularly in response to what they read. When reading a work of literature, our goal is for students to think, reflect, and respond to it in a personal way. The reading log is designed to accomplish those objectives. The emphasis is on quantity, that is, regular and thoughtful writings, rather than on polished, formal essays. Reading log entries can include the following:

1. Personal responses to a character, plot, setting, particular passage, and so on.
2. Summaries.
3. Comments that compare early predictions with the actual reading.

Reading logs capitalize on the complementary nature of reading and writing. They help students gain an appreciation for literature and to develop, through analysis and reflection, an understanding of a literary work from the author's point of view. These regular entries can be kept simply as records of students' thoughts or as references for further discussions and analyses of literary pieces. In addition, they provide opportunities for students to consider and to express personal reactions to a written work.

FABLES ENHANCE THE WRITING PROCESS. Any literary genre can provide models for students' own writings. Because of their unique characteristics, fables lend themselves to use as models for students to read, discuss, and write. The following steps will help you introduce students to fable reading and writing.

1. Expose students to a variety of fables. They are great for oral as well as silent reading.
2. Discuss the characteristics of fables.
3. Provide opportunities for the students to go through the steps of the writing process to develop their own fables.

Frazier (1967) suggested using the following procedure with respect to a fable.

May Hill Arbuthnot equates writing an original fable to a mathematical procedure. She suggests selecting some animal character and a moral such as, "Pride goeth before a fall." If a rabbit is chosen, he cannot be a well-rounded individual with only one weakness; rather, he must be all weakness—and in this case the weakness is pride. So the mathematical equation becomes: Proud Rabbit $+ X$ (single episode) $=$ Pride goeth before a fall. The writer must solve for X by finding an episode to explain the moral.

Teachers who wish to experiment with fables in their classrooms will find these seven steps for presentation and writing of fables helpful:

1. Scatter the reading of many fables throughout several months.
2. Review the easier fables and those liked by the children. Write the lesson or moral on the chalkboard.
3. List other lessons that could appear in a fable on the board.
4. Select one lesson from either group of morals and write a fable together in class.
5. Let pupils select a lesson or moral and tell how a story or fable could present the idea.
6. Let pupils work in groups or committees and write fables with one of the group acting as secretary or scribe. Go over the fables together in class.
7. Let pupils write their own fables after selecting a moral.

These steps should not be compressed into a tight time pattern but should be extended over a period of time since learning to write fables requires both experience with that type of literature and the development of the intellectual discipline to stay within the form.

The following fable illustrates the first type of fable plot pattern. The characters are flat and impersonal, and no one regrets the fate of the lazy chicken. Like most simple fables, this composition by a fourth-grade pupil is brief, involving a single incident, and the ending is expected and justifiable. The originality found in other types of writing is not often found in a fable because the form is restricting and the content is prescribed by the moral.

Lazy Chicken

Once there was a chicken who, even though chickens get up early, this chicken did not. She liked to sleep late in the morning. But her friends who got up early, got the best food. And one day the farmer who owned this chicken was discouraged with this chicken. "She never gets up early, or lays good eggs, or eats good food," said the farmer very discouraged. So the next Sunday that little chicken was on the farmer's plate.
Moral: Laziness does not pay off.

The second fable was also written by a fourth-grade boy after a number of fables had been studied in class. Note that the young writer has developed a clear, concise plot and has concluded with a moral.

The Woodsman and the Hawk

There was once a woodsman who lived alone in a little hut. One day he was out in front of his hut when all of a sudden he heard two things at once, a hawk screaming and gunfire. He looked around. All of a sudden he happened to hear some flapping of wings. He looked down. There beside him was a panting hawk. The hawk said breathlessly, "Please kind sir, could you help me; a couple of dogs and a hunter are chasing me. Do you have a place to hide me?" "Why of course I do. Go into the hut and eat as much meat from my dog's bowl as you want. But come out when I tell you." In a few minutes the hunter and his two dogs came by the hut. The hunter asked, "Have you seen a hawk in the sky or on the ground around here?" "No, I haven't," he said, but as the woodsman said these words he winked his eye and pointed towards the hut. Anyhow the hunter did not see these signs, and so went on. When the hunter was out of sight the woodsman told the hawk to come out. The hawk went on its way without saying a word. The woodsman asked, "Why do you go without thanking me for what I have done?" The hawk turned around and said, "I saw what you did as you said those words." Adding to that, he said, "The tongue can be as sly as the hand."

STORIES ENHANCE THE WRITING PROCESS. In addition to using a fable to teach various aspects of the writing process, the following exercises may be used after reading a story.

Exercise A: Steps in Your Story (Organization). When writing a story it is important to keep the events

in order. If you have to reduce your steps, the reader may become confused or, worse yet, uninterested.

The following events from *Tales of the Arabian Nights* by Charlotte Dixon are not *in sequence*. Read the story and then put the events in a step-by-step order.

The ship landed on a deserted island.

His escape from the island was effected by tying himself to the foot of a huge bird.

Sinbad grew restless in Baghdad and decided to set out on a second journey.

He hid in a cave where he remained all night, too frightened to sleep.

Sinbad decided to picnic on the island and do some investigating of the land.

The bird dropped him in a valley of snakes.

Then he discovered a means of escape from the valley.

He fell asleep and on wakening, found the ship had pulled out without him.

Finally, he arrived back in Baghdad.

He found and collected many diamonds in the valley.

Exercise B: Developing a Sense of Metaphor. In the same story we read *comparisons* such as "feet as thick as tree-trunks," "snakes as long as trees," and the globe "felt like soft silk." When you use comparison in your writing, it helps the reader get a clear picture of what you are saying. The following comparisons are used in everyday language. Can you think of a new way to say:

1. Dead as a doornail?
2. Sick as a dog?
3. Pretty as a picture?
4. Clear as a bell?
5. Smart as a whip?
6. Cool as a cucumber?

Using Exaggeration for Effect. Effective use of exaggeration makes a story more interesting. It is important not to use such extreme exaggerations that it becomes ridiculous. The following statements or word groups came from the story. Would you accept them as facts or exaggerations? Explain your answer.

1. The egg "had a circumference of about fifty feet."
2. "I found myself in a hollow surrounded by huge mountains."

Exercise D: Interpretation of Colloquial Expressions. In the story you found the expression "out of the frying pan into the fire." You know its meaning: jump from one troublesome situation into an even worse one. Write a sentence in which you express each of the following in a straightforward way:

1. Get down to brass tacks.
2. Chip off the old block.
3. Snake in the grass.
4. Calm before the storm.
5. Hit the nail on the head.

Exercise E: Writing Your Story. Use the following form to get your students started writing a story. Although this form can be used independently or in group work, it may be helpful initially to work through it together sharing ideas. It can be used similarly to the "Procedures for Writing Expository Passages."

Procedures for Writing a Story

Step 1.   Prewriting

	Name	Description (Age, Height, etc.)	Relationships among Characters
Who is in the story? (Characters)	1. ____	_____	_____
	2. ____	_____	_____

Where and when does the story take place? (Setting)

Place   Time (Hour, Day, Month, Year)

What happens in the story? (Events)

1. _____
2. _____
3. _____
4. _____
5. _____

Step 2.   Composing
       (Climax of conflict)
       (Resolution)

Step 3.   Feedback
       Teacher
       Students
       Others

Step 4.   Rewriting

Step 5.   Editing (polishing)

As you work with the students in the editing of their work, the following form may be helpful as an example of a useful self-evaluation format.

Example: Student Self-Evaluation Checklist

Name _____ Date _____
Draft _____ Type of Writing _____

Procedure:
1. Examine your text for each of the following.
2. Expand it until you feel you are finished.
3. Check any areas where you need help.

Purpose
____ My text has a definite purpose.
____ I have used language that clearly conveys my purpose.

Audience
____ I have addressed certain readers as I wrote.
____ I composed my opening sentence to catch the attention of my audience.

Setting (optional for story writing)
____ I have provided a clear description of when and where this is taking place.
____ I have included imagery appropriate to this setting.

Response
____ Every fact or detail I gave relates to the response I am trying to obtain.
____ I provided the reader with the information needed to obtain the intended response.

Format
____ I have used the appropriate format for this type of writing.
____ I have checked each sentence to be sure that the subject and verb agreed.
____ I began and ended each sentence with the appropriate punctuation.

Sager (1982) suggests a four-part program, "Reading, Writing, and Rating Stories," which encompasses many techniques to encourage children to improve the clarity and style of their writing. Students are provided with stories that they rate according to vocabulary, elaboration, organization, and structure. They are given the criteria for rating each factor, and in the process of assigning values to the stories in their lessons they develop an understanding of the need for *rewriting* in the achievement of a good written product. Thus children return to their own compositions and apply the same judgments they used in the lessons; they rework and rewrite their own stories. Two examples of Sager writing scales are given below.

After hearing several of the *Just So Stories* by Rudyard Kipling, one boy wrote this original story and was then encouraged to use the following Sager Scales to evaluate it.

The Story of the Elephant That Had No Trunk

Once upon a time there lived an elephant. This elephant was very sad because he had no trunk. The way this elephant lost his trunk was.

He was walking along just minding his own business, when out of the blue came a rhinoceros. This rhinoceros was the biggest, fattest rhinoceros you have ever seen. And the elephant crouched down of fright. The rhinoceros stepped on the trunk and off it came. That's the way the elephant lost his trunk.

Writing Scale for Vocabulary

Definition: Vocabulary is the use of words to express a particular thought or idea.

Rate 3: A variety of new and interesting words and comparisons that create vivid impressions
Words that help the reader use his senses
Synonyms that provide variety and interest
Exact words that paint vivid pictures
Unusual expressions, word combinations and comparisons that add zest and color to the story

Rate 2: Words that are adequately descriptive and exact, but lack overall excellence
Some words that are descriptive and exact
Some use of new and interesting words
Some variety of word choice
Some vivid words and comparisons

Rate 1: A few interesting words, but little variety of word choice
Vague, general words more often than exact words
Few descriptive or picture words or phrases

Rate 0: Only common, overworked words with no variety or word choice
Dull, uninteresting words

Quoted verbatim from C. Sager, *Reading, Writing and Rating Stories*. N. Billerica, MA.: Curriculum Associates, 1982, p. 67. Permission granted to reprint.

Writing Scale for Elaboration

Definition: Elaboration is an abundance of related ideas which flow smoothly from one idea to the next.

Rate 3: A variety of related ideas that helps the reader see, hear and feel what the author intends
Details that make people, places and/or events come alive
Details that make the reader feel what the characters feel
Details and ideas that create an impression on the reader
All ideas fully developed
Ideas that follow each other easily and naturally

Rate 2: Ideas that are clear, but fail to make an impression on the reader
Ideas that follow each other easily and naturally, but lack punch
Some details that help the reader use his feelings
Some ideas that are fully developed
Some details that are either inadequate or overdone

Rate 1: Much more detail needed to help the reader see, hear and feel what the author intends
Ideas that are sometimes confusing and hard to follow
Details that are often inadequate
Important questions that are left unanswered

Rate 0: Ideas that are not clear or easy to follow
No details
Ideas that are suggested, but never carried out
Ideas that are jumbled and/or unconnected

Quoted verbatim from C. Sager, *Reading, Writing and Rating Stories.* N. Billerica, MA.: Curriculum Associates, 1982, p. 68. Permission granted to reprint.

POETRY ENHANCES THE WRITING PROCESS. A teacher is an artist at releasing the creativity in others. Truly creative writing cannot be taught; it can only be released and guided. If we see our task as releasing and guiding poetic expression, certain conditions must be established. First, there must be a climate in which creative effort is fostered. The teacher should point out that certain expressions used by children are imaginative and contain poetic ideas. One day a child mentioned that the sun seemed to be playing peek-a-boo as it hid behind a cloud, then shone again. A comment that this would make a good poem may be enough to get him to write. A quiet place to write, away from the group, is another aspect of climate. Then when such expressions emerge the teacher might ask, "Would you like to go to the writing table and write a poem now while the idea is fresh?" A part of the climate in a room is represented by things valued. The fact that the teacher uses a poem as a central theme for a bulletin board, reads poems to the class

with personal enjoyment, or sends a notice home in verse form makes poetry have significance. Second, the teacher provides stimulations that motivate the writer to get started. Sometimes these dramatize a feeling. One student teacher played a recording of a choir singing "The Battle Hymn of the Republic," then asked, "How would you express your thoughts if asked what the United States means to you?" One verse written under these conditions won a national award. Holidays act as punctuation marks in the humdrum repetition of living. Someone has said that one trouble with life was that it is "so doggone daily." When we make some days have special feeling in them it provides all of us with a bit of variety. Halloween, Thanksgiving, Valentine's Day, Mother's Day, and birthdays have emotional associations that stimulate writing.

In addition to a classroom climate that enhances poetry appreciation and personal motivation, the teacher releases creative talents by providing specific writing aids. These include help with the mechanics of writing and spelling, the development of a vocabulary that expresses the right shade of meaning, and the understanding of poetic form. Before the children write Halloween poetry the class might discuss possible words to use. These would include *ghost, witch, haunting, creeping, scare, afraid*. With older children a rhyming dictionary is a great help. Occasionally after a poem has been enjoyed by the group, take time to look at it as one craftsman admires the work of another. The poem "Trees" can be studied in this way without diminishing its beauty. Notice the rhyme pattern. Then discuss the use of words. Why is "lovely" better than "pretty" in the second line? What image did the writer create by using the words "a nest of robins in her hair" and "lifts her leafy arms to pray"? Ask the group to think of similar images, such as "finger chimneys pointing toward the sky" or "little cars pouting in the parking lot."

A combination of words and ideas must be brought together in order to create a poem. Some children are more talented with words and ideas than others, but all children should be able to achieve this combina-

tion to a degree. The greater command a child has over words and the more original or varied his ideas, the better will be the quality of the poetry he can create.

The temptation, then, would be to set up a series of lessons designed to build vocabulary and extend ideas. Before doing so it is well to consider the influence of patterns on creativity. Suppose we set up a series of exercises like this:

1. See the cat
   It wears a _____.
2. I have a bill
   It is from the _____.
3. This boy is tall
   He must be _____.
4. This girl is late
   She must be _____.

It would appear that the child *completed* a rhyme, but did he *create* one? At best he learned a small element of the poet's craft concerning words that rhyme.

Another type of exercise provides an idea in the form of a picture, usually of a nursery rhyme. One might be of "Jack and Jill," another of "Jack Be Nimble" or "Mistress Mary." Here again the emphasis is not on creativity, but on the pleasure of repeating familiar rhyme forms. Still another exercise provides lists of words that rhyme:

day	wall	nice	pail
hay	all	spice	whale
old	kitten	mice	tree
told	mitten	ice	see
ball	bitten	sail	free
tall	written	mail	bee

A suggested verse is given:

I threw a ball
High over the wall
And a boy named Jack
Threw it right back.

Although this is patterned, there is the possibility for a bit of original thinking and the satisfaction of

completing a verse. Certainly the rhyme words influenced the idea. Instead of starting with a feeling or something to say, the child was assigned the task of manipulating the words of others. The results have little more emotional appeal than the original list of rhyming words.

Creativity from a child's point of view might be thought of as a personal interpretation of experience. The child might ask, "What do certain sounds or sights mean to me? How do I feel when I see or do something? What words can I use that will help others re-create my feelings?"

One group of first-grade children was asked to think of favorite sounds. The following responses were typical:

> The sound of nice music.
> The sound of the recess bell.

But there were others more personal and possibly more creative, such as those that follow.

> The sounds my mother makes in the kitchen getting
> supper ready.
> The sound of the slamming of the car door when
> my daddy comes home from work.

From the beginning it would be well to share with children poetry both with and without rhyme patterns. Help them discover the beauty or fun of an idea or word picture in a verse as well as the song of rhyme. *Fog* by Carl Sandburg is a good illustration of a poem without rhyme.

The following patterns, free from emphasis in rhyme, may induce students to express themselves in free verse as well as rhymed.

Spring Music

> Spring is a singing time,
> Birds sing in the trees.
> . . . .
> . . . . . .
> And I sing too.

The Feel of Things

> I like the feel of things.
> The softness of pussy willows.
> The smoothness of velvet.
> . . . . .
> . . . . .
> I like the feel of things.

Children sense the meter of poetry and eventually will want to write with this in mind. The teacher might put a line on the board and have the class count the beats one would hear if each syllable had equal emphasis.

> The man in the moon looked down
> — — — — — — —

Then the class experiments with lines like the following and decides which sounds best:

> Upon the sleeping little town.
> Upon the laughing happy clown.
> To see the children gay and brown.
> To see that snow had fallen over hill and town.

Then they take some words they know and note how these words have similar points of emphasis:

altogether	player
manufacture	remember
tangerine	suggestion
doorkeeper	happiness
pleasant	

This can be changed with the usual markings for accented and unaccented syllables in poetry:

altogether becomes __ __ __ ´ __
remember becomes __ __ ´ __

Then note that in certain poems some words appear as unaccented syllables. If you say the words *ta* for unaccented and *tum* for the accented syllable you can note the meter of a poem.

> Then the little Hiawatha (or *tum ta tum ta tum ta
> tum ta*)
> Said unto the old Nakomis
> All the hills are edged with valleys

Writing words for songs emphasizes meter. One student teacher interested a group of sixth-grade children in writing by using Calypso music. After learning that the singer made up his song as he went along, the class tried to write "songs." The following is an example of their songs.

I got a donkey he's big and fat.
He sits on a pillow and the pillow goes flat.
My donkey, he's a good for nothing beast
Cause he takes all my food for his Sunday feast.

Maxine

One class listened to a recorded reading of translations of famous Japanese haiku. The ideas of suggestion, emphasized in the last line, and imagery were captured by the children who wrote these lines at the Hunter School in Fairbanks, Alaska.

The boy turned to me
And he smiled with a cute grin.
I did the same thing.

Big Indian Chief
You are brave but very dumb.
Let people rule too!

I hate dogs a lot.
They bark when someone walks by,
Especially me.

I left Alaska, but on the way
I saw purple mountains
And turned back.

A cry is heard. All is still
A pack of wolves
Has made its kill . . . Silence.

The morning sun
Chasing night shadows
Across the awakening world.

The pattern of a haiku poem consists of three lines, the first line having five syllables, the second line seven, and the third line five. Because the English syllable differs from the Japanese it is not always possible to follow this pattern.

Cinquains have much of the same effect in English. The first line has five words and each succeeding line one less:

The white waves bite at
the sandy ocean shore
like a hungry
child eating
cookies.

Or starting with only four words, one gets this result:

The empty house stands
among dead grass
lonely and
still

A second type of cinquain may be developed by initiating a purpose for each line.

First line—one word giving the title.
Second line—two words describing the title.
Third line—three words expressing an action.
Fourth line—four words expressing a feeling.
Fifth line—another word for the title.

Rather than have children start with such a complex task as writing verses about how they feel or things they have seen, some teachers prefer to start with group composition.

The following poem is based on an experience of Eileen Birch, a second-grade teacher who once asked her children to think of quiet things. As each child made a suggestion she wrote it on the chalkboard.

As quiet as snow falling
As quiet as butter melting
As quiet as a cloud in the sky
As quiet as a kitten
As soap bubbles
A tree growing
Santa Claus coming
As quiet as you and I

The children knew that they had created a mood because of the hush in the room. Such experiences can be a step toward individual effort.

A method of writing that will give everyone a sense of participation is the word-stimulus method. The teacher asks the pupils to get ready for a surprise, assuring them that this is not a test and that the papers will be ungraded.

"I am going to tell you a word," the teacher continues, "and you are to write the picture that comes to your mind. You may tell what you see, hear, feel, or imagine. Just tell me the picture that you see in your imagination. Spell as well as you can; we will get the exact spelling later." Then she gives a word like *rain, sunshine, baby, wind, spring,* or *night.*

After the children have finished writing, the papers are collected. Now these individual efforts are assembled into a group poem. This is called a mosaic poem, or cumulative composition, because, like a mosaic painting, it is made from many parts. First the closely related ideas are grouped. One stanza might contain those about gentle rain, another about violent storms, another about the blessings of rain. These are put together with some rearrangement of word order but with no effort to rhyme. Then the class usually has to add several lines at the bottom that create a conclusion.

Meanings experienced through poetry call for personal and individual responses. The deep feeling that one person senses in a sentence may be missed by another. We do not seek to have children write a verse in order to please the teacher, to get a good grade, or to participate in a program. Our purpose is to help children discover in poetry some inner satisfaction that is an intimate personal experience. Deserved praise is an important aspect of encouraging children to write. Expect them to present a tremendous range of quality, but encourage each child as he creates at his appropriate level.

An equally important aspect is time to write. Providing a quiet time during the course of the week when children may choose to write or read will reward the teacher with worthy contributions. Occasionally this time has to be scheduled, but often it will have to be taken from some other activity. Sometimes the weather is a deciding factor. During a winter snow when the flakes are sinking slowly to earth or just after a spring rain when every object appears clean-washed would be an excellent occasion for such work. The teacher might say, "Let's have a quiet period now. You may read or write. We will tune in on thirty minutes of silence."

Children like to write poetry in areas that have emotional appeal. Here are some examples:

1. Gripes and Protests

To the Boy That Sits in Front of Me

You think that you are funny
You think that you're the best
You think that you're a honey
While you're really just a pest.

In arithmetic you're terrible
In reading you're a dunce
And when you talk the teacher must
Remind you more than once!

Merry Lee Tash, GRADE 5

2. Personal Experiences

After School

I'm staying after school again.
This is an awful mess;
I might as well get down to work
'Til I can leave I guess.
Let's see, arithmetic's all done.
And so is reading work,
(Just think ME staying after school!
I sure feel like a jerk.)
I could improve my writing.
Oh no, I'd just hate that.
If I could just get out of here
I'd gladly eat my hat,
I guess it's just what I deserve
For acting like a fool,
But you won't catch me here again
Staying after school!

Silas, GRADE 6

Cookies

Measure
   Sift
      Beat
Cut
   Cook
      Eat.

Vernon, GRADE 1 (Dictated)

3. *Wonders*

Grass

Green and soft and sweet,
Grass is glistening

Lying on warm grass
I feel relaxed and lazy

With an ant's small size
Grass is probably a kind of jungle.

Jane, AGE 10

4. *"If I Were" Poems or Flights of Imagination*

If I were a star on the top of the tree,
On Christmas night, here's what I'd see:

Angels and candles, tinsel and balls,
Bright lights and bells and Santa Claus;
Popcorn and long red cranberry string,
Chains of paper—both red and green.
And if I look closely—I'll take my chances—
I see tiny packages tied to the branches.

Around the tree, all over the floor
Are lots of packages—and there's more—
A train, a bike, a doll, a bat,
A DOG? A puppy—imagine that!!

As we accept as our responsibility of releasing the talents and abilities of the students, there are some teaching practices that should be considered.

Praise is powerful if it causes continuous growth. Point out the strength of a creative effort. At first teachers are so pleased to get any completed work that a low level of expectancy can be established by excessive praise. The expressions "Your first line is especially good" and "The words *lonely lullaby* create a good sound and feeling" give praise to the points of best quality.

Two major faults of children's poetry call for special attention. A child may start with a good idea, then come to a dull thump of an ending just to get something that rhymes.

As I looked up at the sky
I saw some planes go flying by
And as I walked home to rest
There came a plane from the west.

After children have achieved some security in the writing of verse it is well to discuss this problem. Encourage them to write nonrhyming poetry until they have discovered how to use many of the aids available such as rhyming dictionaries and a thesaurus.

The second fault is that of writing parodies on familiar verse. It is fun to write parodies when this is the purpose of writing, but the following is questionable as creative poetry. Call it a parody. Then help the child use his idea in a more original form.

I think that I shall never see
An airplane tiny as a bee
A plane that may in summer fly
Into a piece of apple pie.

Closely related to this problem is that of the child who hands in something not his own. Little children sometimes get the idea that the task is to write any poem, rather than one of their own creation. Some misguided older person helps them and they show up with "Roses are red, violets are blue," etc. When this happens, remember that there is no moral issue involved. The child wanted to please. You might say, "That is a cute verse but it has been written before. I think you can write one that no one has ever heard." Or the teacher might suggest, "Maybe instead of writing a poem you could draw a picture or cartoon of your idea." And the teacher might ask herself if she had made poetry writing a bit too important for the present time if children feel pressured to do this type of thing to gain approbation.

Nearly all children and many adults write rhymes and doggerel that have few poetic qualities. As they listen to great poetry with growing appreciation, their writing will reflect the appreciation they have developed. Consumers of poetry are needed as well as writers. Crude efforts produced by experimentation with rhyme may increase a person's awareness of the skills of other poets.

Releasing poetic expression for some who have little inherent talent should not become a challenging burden to the teacher. The object is to release the talent in those so endowed so that all may be enriched by sharing their contributions. Our task is done if we help all to develop this talent to some degree and those gifted in this area to achieve expression in quality that is worthy of them.

CONTENT AREA WRITING ACTIVITIES. In all content areas, writing about what has been read provides support for the learning process. Writing about content requires thought and response and virtually precludes passivity and inattention. For example, reading and writing about math highlight the process of problem solving rather than only emphasizing the product, as do most drill and practice exercises.

Developing Word Problems. A problem such as $2 + 2 = \underline{\hspace{1cm}}$ can be approached in a couple of ways. Students can simply practice $2 + 2 = 4$, or they can reflect on the process involved. Given the task of writing *what* they were thinking about as they solved $2 + 2 = 4$, students begin to focus on the thought processes that they used to arrive at the solution. This technique works well when students are working on word problems, for without an already formatted problem statement, the process needed for the solution becomes even more important.

Much of an understanding of the practical application of math occurs through word problems. Students can gain an even better understanding of word problems by writing their own. They can be helped in their writing of word problems by knowing that only

six outcomes are possible. These outcomes are in the form of the following six phrases:

is equal to   is greater than or equal to
is greater than   is less than or equal to
is less than   is not equal to

The Learning Log. The *learning log* is a journallike activity similar to the reading log. Instead of focusing on personal response, the teacher asks students to write summary statements of main ideas from their readings. By following these simple steps, students can enhance their retention of content area concepts.

1. Students first engage in directed-reading activities. These include examining chapter headings and subheadings and predicting what information will be gleaned from the readings.
2. Students read the text section by section. Sections may be individual paragraphs or the text following each major heading and subheading.

After reading each section, students close the text and summarize main points from the reading in their own words. The process of summarizing causes students to analyze and synthesize material as they select certain ideas, reject others, and refashion them into a new structure, the summary. These summaries, written daily, can serve as future readings for discussion and review.

In an activity that is a variation on summary writing, students read content area materials and write small books that illustrate major concepts. These books can actually be bound and kept in the classroom as reference materials for all students.

Creating Dialogue. Through dialogue writing, students can articulate and clarify subject matter concepts. In two-character dialogues, students use novel figures to discuss content area concepts and issues. For example, a dialogue between a plant and an ant based on a science lesson on photosynthesis can be written. In this dialogue these two novel characters would discuss and thereby explain photosynthesis. Students will en-

joy sharing their dialogues with their classmates. This class sharing can be as simple as a reading by the author to two students' role playing the parts with props.

In a physical education class, the subtleties of foul shot techniques can be written in a dialogue between a basketball and a backboard.

In a health class, the dangers of drugs, including alcohol and nicotine, can be discussed in a dialogue between a liver and a heart.

Summary

This chapter began with a discussion of the cognitive processes the learner engages during reading or writing. An examination of the differences and similarities of these language processes was included. A rationale for the integration of these processes and instructional procedures for accomplishing such an integration were also presented. Thinking as the process that unifies reading and writing was examined.

Suggested Classroom Projects and Questions for Discussion

Projects

1. Design a chart that illustrates the similarities and differences between reading and writing. Include as many variables as possible.
2. Choose a specific content area and develop a lesson for a second-grade class. The lesson should address the four language skills of reading, writing, speaking, and listening.
3. Look at two or more intermediate-level language arts textbooks. Investigate and report on the percentage of activities that incorporate both reading and writing. Compare and contrast the texts on this issue.
4. Choose a primary- or intermediate-level content area textbook and report on the types of activities that you find. Discuss the extent to which reading and writing are integrated to enhance students' learning.
5. Write a letter that you might send to the director of curriculum in your district. The letter should explain briefly by which criteria a new intermediate social studies text should be chosen. Also include a brief rationale to support your reasoning.
6. Design a specific LEA activity for a kindergarten class based on information in this chapter. Include the rationale for the activity and ways you would implement it.
7. Choose an activity from a content area text that does *not* integrate the skills of reading and writing. Rewrite the activity so that it adheres to the concepts presented in this chapter.
8. Outline a short inservice talk concerning the use of reading and writing in content areas to share with other teachers. The scope of your inservice presentation should include information on your rationale for specific activity suggestions.
9. Develop a primary-grade lesson on short story writing. Objectives of the lesson are twofold: to enhance children's understanding of short story components and to utilize the language skills of reading, writing, speaking, and listening.
10. Design an activity that helps children learn a literary concept (main idea, sequencing, figure of speech, and so on) through reading and writing. Be specific about the concept and literary materials used.

Questions

1. Explain the expression "Writing is thinking."
2. How does the LEA capitalize on children's natural language development?
3. Discuss the view of reading and writing as mutually enhancing language skills.
4. What is meant by the statement that reading, writing, and speaking are natural language functions?
5. Discuss the reading log as a vehicle for students' response to literature and its validity.
6. How can literature be used to help children develop their writing skills?
7. Discuss various ways of defining reading. Formulate a short definition that best explains the reading process.
8. How can writing be used to increase the understanding of math concepts?
9. What are the most significant similarities between the language skills of reading and writing?
10. Why are most good writers also good readers? What is the value of using a computer in a language arts program?

Chapter 14

Extending Language Arts Skills Through Multiple Resources

(Photo by Linda Lungren)

OBJECTIVES

After reading this chapter, the student should be able to:

1. understand what forms of print and nonprint media are available for use in the classroom.
2. understand the power and influence of the media and how to capitalize on related techniques such as Reader's Theater.
3. understand the critical thinking skills as well as the reference skills elementary students should know.
4. understand how to use the newspaper and how to integrate the computer into the regular elementary classroom.

369

Why Use Various Forms of Print and Nonprint Media in the Classroom?

In today's world, information is gathered and disseminated to the public faster than ever before. Students are exposed to many forms of electronic communication daily, and it is estimated that the average American child spends 28 hours per week interacting with electronic media (Olson, 1983). In this age of information, children need to develop the skills required to locate, interpret, and critically respond to information in various forms of print and nonprint media. This chapter will focus on the effective use of the media in the classroom to enhance the language arts curriculum.

The forms of nonprint media discussed in this chapter include records, cassette recordings, slides, filmstrips, films, videocassette recordings, television, and computers. Also included is the newspaper, a very useful and valuable form of print medium. As our technical advances continue, these forms of media are becoming less expensive and more available for use by the classroom teacher, and they can be used in a multitude of ways to enhance the language arts curriculum. Often students are motivated to read a book by viewing a literature film. The use of recordings is effective in improving students' listening skills, and it provides an opportunity for the beginning reader to improve reading skills by reading along with the recording. Viewing a film may provide the stimulus for creative writing or other forms of creative expression. In addition to enhancing the language arts skills directly, newspapers, films, and television provide the opportunity for students to develop critical thinking skills, which underlie reading, writing, speaking, and listening.

Rasinski (1984) suggests that there are basically two ways to use media in the classroom: as the "initiating experience," which will be followed by reading, writing, or speaking, or as the experience itself. In the first case, a student may view a literature filmstrip and respond to it by writing a poem, dramatizing a scene from the filmstrip, or reading a portion of the script in Reader's Theater style. The medium serves as the stimulus for a response. In the second case, a student may read a book and respond to it by making a filmstrip, recording a choral reading of a portion of the book, or composing a written response on the word processor. Now the medium is the vehicle for expressing a response, which may be used as an initiating experience for other students.

Teachers should become familiar with the media collection in the school library. They should also be aware of the new literature films, filmstrips, recordings, and educational programs as they become available. *The Booklist* (American Library Association) and *School Library Journal* are two excellent monthly periodicals that provide reviews of many new releases.

Using Audio Recordings

Records and cassette recordings are inexpensive and provide many opportunities to enhance language arts skills. Literary recordings are excellent tools for improving listening skills and imagery. Students enjoy hearing an author read his own work and are held captive when listening to a skilled and professional narrator. Recordings often include background music and sound effects that enhance the work. Read-along recordings, in which the oral reading is paced more slowly and an aural signal is given to indicate page turns, are very useful for beginning readers. Older students may enjoy making read-along tapes for younger, less skilled readers.

Recordings can also enhance a story or a particular area of study in the content areas. Musical recordings of songs popular during the 1920s can bring a study of that era to life. A recording of Appalachian folk songs enlivens the experience of reading a book set in that area of the country. Students may also produce their own recordings when reading passages from a favorite book, reciting poetry, or participating in Reader's Theater. Attention to the mood created by a poem or story can be attained by asking students to select

recordings appropriate for background music when the literature is read aloud. See Appendix C for a list of records and cassette tapes.

Why Use Student-Made Slides?

Slides are an excellent means of motivation for a class discussion in any content area. They can be shown as an introduction to a unit of study or a piece of literature to be read, providing necessary background information. Slides are easy to make and therefore are an excellent way for students to express a response to literature. A slide can be made to illustrate a poem, accompany an oral book report or storytelling session, or accompany reports in the content areas.

Handmade slides may be produced in the following manner. Provide students with a two- by two-inch box drawn on a blank piece of paper. Students draw their illustration inside the box, using a lead pencil. With young children who experience difficulty with the small space, use a four- by four-inch box and make a 50 percent reduction of their illustration using a photocopier. When the illustrations are finished, copy them onto a transparency, using a thermofax machine. The students may then color the picture with permanent markers. Cut the transparency to size and mount it in cardboard slide mounts. Commercial slide mounts may be purchased, or they may be obtained from libraries that discard outdated materials or from parents who may dispose of old or unsuccessful slides.

How Does the Use of Filmstrips Enhance the Language Arts Curriculum?

There are numerous literature filmstrips available that are appropriate for the elementary classroom. Most of them include a cassette tape or record of the narration. Children delight in seeing their favorite picture book on a filmstrip, enhanced by professional narration

and musical background or sound effects. Older students are interested in comparing their visual images for a book with those presented by the filmstrip illustrator and those by other students. Literature filmstrips are often used to motivate students to read more books by the same author or on a similar topic. When literature is presented through an audiovisual medium, the less skilled reader can experience a book that he would be unable to read himself.

Filmstrips are also good sources of background information. A well-made filmstrip can be both informative and entertaining. For example, before beginning a study of folktales, children can learn about the oral tradition of stories by viewing the sound filmstrip *All About Folktales* (Pied Piper). When continuing the unit, viewing several folktales on filmstrip will provide contrast to the reading of tales by the teacher and will enable the students to compare a filmstrip version with the book. Many distributors have sound filmstrips of a wide variety of folktales. Because they were originally transferred orally from generation to generation and from country to country, folktales make an excellent source for storytelling. Students are interested to hear folktales from different countries that are variations of the same theme. After listening to many folktales and after viewing several on film, they will be ready to prepare a tale for their classmates.

Commercial filmstrips are also available for direct teaching of specific language arts skills. The teacher should preview these materials to ensure that the objectives of the filmstrips are appropriate for the level of the students, and that the content reinforces or enhances the current curriculum. See Appendix C for a list of commercial filmstrips for teaching language arts skills and a list of commercial filmstrips of children's literature.

Like slides, filmstrips are also easy for students to make. A student-made strip is a good way to illustrate a book report. It can also provide a background for oral reading or a report in a content area. One first-grade teacher used a class filmstrip as the culminating project for a unit on safety. The class spent time learning to identify traffic signs and to tell what they mean.

Each student made a picture of one traffic sign on a frame for the filmstrip and then dictated a sentence explaining the meaning of the sign into a tape recorder. The product was a class filmstrip, narrated and drawn by each member of the class. This type of oral expression was especially good for those students who were uneasy speaking in front of the group. With the opportunity to practice in the nonthreatening privacy of the recording corner, they were able to express themselves.

In order for students to make their own filmstrips, the teacher must acquire the appropriate blank filmstrip acetate for them. This can be purchased at a film supply store or can be made by immersing an old, discarded filmstrip in bleach to remove the color. The teacher then can draw a replica of the acetate on a blank sheet of paper, marking off every four notches as one frame.

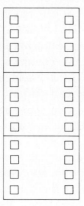

Students first draw their pictures on the paper. Then they lay the acetate over the picture and trace and color the pictures with permanent markers. Make sure they leave five to ten blank frames at the beginning and end to get the filmstrip in and out of the projector. If narration is appropriate, they can dictate their prepared script into a tape recorder. An audible sound, recorded after their narration is complete, will be an indication to advance to the next frame.

Using Films and Videocassettes

Teachers use films in the classroom for many of the same reasons they use filmstrips. They are good motivational devices to use in the literature class and can be shown before or after reading the story in a book. They encourage discussion of the work itself, and of the artist's interpretation of it. Art films are a good stimulus for oral or dramatic interpretation and can inspire creative writing and oral discussion. Films can also provide background information for a book or area of study in the content areas.

Teachers have often used videotaping in the classroom for students' self-evaluation of oral presentations. Students can gauge their progress by viewing themselves over a period of time. They may also choose videotaping as a means of preserving creative drama, pantomime, or role playing. Tapes can be shared with other classrooms. Students studying propaganda techniques used by advertisers on television will find the video camera useful for taping and evaluating the effectiveness of their own propaganda presentations. Videotaping in the classroom, however, can be time-consuming. The teacher must prepare specific objectives for using the video camera and then must weigh the value of the experience against the time it will involve.

Videocassette recorders have recently become very popular. Schools may now purchase or rent many literature films and educational programs on videocassette tapes.

Using Reader's Theater

Reader's Theater is one way students may wish to respond to what they see and hear in films and recordings, and it enables them to improve their oral interpretation and listening skills. It is nonthreatening to many students, because they do not act, but merely suggest characterizations in their oral reading. Reader's theater is a practical activity for the classroom because the

Teachers have often used video taping in the classroom for students' self-evaluation of oral presentations. (Photo by Linda Lungren)

entire class can be involved. Scripts often include parts that differ in difficulty, allowing students with different reading abilities to participate together. Those students who are not reading participate as the audience. This is not a passive role in Reader's Theater, since the audience is required to draw on their listening skills and imaginations to visualize the setting and the action.

For Reader's Theater, an area of the classroom becomes the stage. Readers may sit on stools or they may stand, and they read directly from the script. No costumes are used, although background music and a few minor props may enhance the presentation. Exits and entrances may be indicated by the narrator or by asking the readers to sit or stand, step forward or backward, or turn away from or face the audience. Readers may need to be reminded that they are interpreters, not actors, and that no action should be shown.

Although Reader's Theater is not meant to be a polished performance, attention to the following factors suggested by Sebesta (1985) will enhance the experience:

1. Prior to reading the script, ask students to perform some creative drama for characterization. They should move the way they think the character would move and talk the way the character would talk.
2. Then the students can discuss the way the characters contrast with each other and methods in which they can show this contrast as they read the characters' parts.
3. Finally, practice reading to establish the pace. Overlapping (one reader says his first word at nearly the same time as the previous reader

says his last word) eliminates pauses and provides the opportunity for a dramatic pause at a critical time in the reading.

Reader's Theater scrips are available commercially. Catalogues can be ordered from the following:

Reader's Theatre News. P.O. Box 15847, San Diego, Calif. 92115.
Contemporary Drama Service. Box 457-PL, Downers Grove, Ill. 60515.

The Economy Company has assembled two kits with scripts to supplement its *Keys to Reading* series; however, they can also be used independently. Kit A is appropriate for grades one to three, and Kit B for grades four to six. The teacher's guide indicates the level of difficulty of each reader's part and specifies the comprehension skills reinforced by each play. These kits are available from

The Economy Company, Educational Publishers. 1901 North Walnut, Oklahoma City, Okla. 73125.

Teachers who do not have access to commercially prepared scripts will find that it is easy to create their own. For best results, select stories with a lot of dialogue. The narration should be kept to a minimum, giving the part to two narrators if necessary. Students can also make their favorite stories or poems into script form. Appendix C contains examples of scripts students will enjoy.

The following scripts were prepared by Ramon Ross, a national authority on the role of Reader's Theater as a means to expand the language arts.

The Zax

N 1: One day, making tracks in the prairie of Prax, came a North-Going Zax and a South-Going Zax.
N 2: And it happened that both of them came to a place where they bumped. There they stood. Foot to foot. Face to face.
NGZ: Look here, now!

N 1: the North-Going Zax said.
NGZ: I say! You are blocking my path. You are right in my way. I'm a North-Going Zax and I always go north. Get out of my way, and let me go forth!
SGZ: Who's in whose way?
N 2: snapped the South-Going Zax.
SGZ: I always go south, making south-going tracks. So you're in MY way! And I ask you to move and let me go south in my south-going groove.
N 1: Then the North-Going Zax puffed his chest up with his pride.
NGZ: I never,
N 1: he said.
NGZ: take a step to one side. And I'll prove to you that I won't change my ways if I have to keep standing here fifty-nine days!
SGZ: And I'll prove to YOU,
N 2: yelled the South-Going Zax.
SGZ: That I can stand here in the prairie of Prax for fifty-nine years! For I live by a rule that I learned as a boy back in South-Going School. Never budge! That's my rule. Never budge in the least! Not an inch to the west! Not an inch to the east! I'll stay here, not budging! I can and I will if it makes you and me and the whole world stand still!
N 1: Well . . . Of course the world didn't stand still. The world grew. In a couple of years, the new highway came through.
N 2: And they built it right over those two stubborn Zax and left them there, standing upbudged in their tracks.

How to Tell Bad News

from McGuffey's Fifth Eclectic Reader, American Book Company, New York

Mr. H: Ha! Steward, how are you, my old boy? How do things go on at home?

Steward: Bad enough, your honor; the magpie's dead.

Mr. H.: Poor Mag! So he's gone. How came he to die?

Steward: Overeat himself, sir.

Mr. H.: Did he? A greedy dog: why what did he get he liked so well?

Steward: Horseflesh, sir; he died of eating horseflesh.

Mr. H.: How came he to get so much horseflesh?

Steward: All your father's horses, sir.

Mr. H.: What! are they dead, too?

Steward: Ay, sir; they died of overwork.

Mr. H.: And why were they overworked, pray?

Steward: To carry water, sir.

Mr. H.: To carry water! and what were they carrying water for?

Steward: Sure, sir, to put out the fire.

Mr. H.: Fire! what fire?

Steward: O, sir, your father's house is burned to the ground.

Mr. H.: My father's house burned down! and how came it set on fire?

Steward: I think, sir, it must have been the torches.

Mr. H.: Torches! what torches?

Steward: At your mother's funeral.

Mr. H.: My mother dead!

Steward: Ah, poor lady! she never looked up, after it.

Mr. H.: After what?

Steward: The loss of your father.

Mr. H.: My father gone, too?

Steward: Yes poor gentleman! he took to his bed as soon as he heard of it.

Mr. H.: Heard of what?

Steward: The bad news, sir, and please your honor.

Mr. H.: What! more miseries! more bad news!

Steward: Yes sir; your bank has failed, and your credit is lost, and you are not worth a shilling in the world. I made bold, sir, to wait on you about it, for I thought you would like to hear the news.

What Night Would It Be?

by John Ciardi

Group I: If the moon shines
   On the black pines
Group II: And an owl flies
   And a ghost cries
Group I: And the hairs rise
   On the back
Group II: On the back
All: On the back of your neck—
Group I: If you look quick
   At the moon-slick
   On the black air
Group II: And what goes there
   Rides a broomstick
Group I: And if things pick
   At the back
Group II: At the back
All: At the back of your neck—
Group I: Would you know then
   By the small men
Group II: With the lit grins
   And with no chins
Group I: By the owl's hoo,
Group II: And the ghost's boo,
Group I: By the Tom Cat,
Group II: And the Black Bat
Group I: On the night air,
Group II: And the thing there,
Group I: By the thing,
Group II: By the thing,
All: By the dark thing there
Group I: (Yes you do,
Group II: yes, you do
All: know the thing I mean)
Group I: It's now,
Group II: It's now,
All: It's—Halloween!

What Influences Does the Television Have on Children?

Television has been criticized as being the major barrier against developing a love for reading (Johnson, 1979). It is estimated that by the time the average American child finishes high school, he will have spent 10,000 to 15,000 hours watching television, more time than he spent in the classroom (Wirth, 1983). The child must be taught to understand the power of the medium of television and to develop the skills required to view it critically. Foster (1979) suggests that a person's spontaneous response to a film or television movie is emotional, not intellectual. He maintains that an intellectual response is made after the film is over, and only if it is discussed and analyzed. It is through discussion that children are asked to interpret and criticize what they have seen consciously. Teachers who use television in the classroom are able to follow up the viewing with discussion or activities to ensure that students do make an intellectual response. However, students must learn some critical viewing techniques that will be able to apply when watching television at home. Young children perceive what they see on television as reality. Television characters often find easy solutions to problems or choose violence as a solution. Television commercials stress attractive looks, and advertisers create needs and desires for their products. Children must be taught how to protect themselves from being manipulated by these behaviors and values.

Using the Newspaper in the Classroom

The newspaper is a valuable tool for teaching language arts skills. Its content is current and relevant to the students' lives. It can be used with all grade levels and provides the student with many opportunities to practice language arts skills in different content areas. The newspaper has many sections, which should enable every student to find something of interest. The vocabulary words found in the newspaper are practical; they are often words that the students will hear and use many times in their lives. Teachers can help students to develop a habit of reading the paper daily, a habit that will stay with them later in life.

Older students benefit from studying various writing styles and applying critical reading skills. Instruction in the differences in the form and content of editorials, news stories, and news features can improve their reading and writing skills. Study of the newspaper is often used as an introduction to a class-written paper. Students can learn the organization of the newspaper, understanding the purpose for each of its sections. Writing their own paper will give them many opportunities to practice writing and editing skills.

The newspaper can also be used by younger students. Pictures provide opportunities for story telling and language experience stories. Students can use the comics to predict story outcomes. The newspaper can also be used for locating pictures or words beginning with a specific sound or letter, or locating capital letters and end punctuation marks. Many newspapers include a children's page with articles written at younger children's reading and interest levels.

Appendix C contains examples of newspaper activities that you may choose to use with your students.

How Can the Use of Media Help Teach Children Critical Thinking Strategies?

Whether the media with which children are involved are films, television shows, radio broadcasts, or the newspaper, the critical thinking skills that will enable children to make rational judgments about what they have seen or heard must be taught. Students need practice making judgments, distinguishing fact from opinion, determining the validity of information presented as fact, and judging the adequacy of the information source. They need to be able to make inferences

Newspapers and magazines can be used with all grade levels and provide the student with many opportunities to practice language arts skills in different content areas. Older students will benefit from studying various writing styles and applying critical reading skills. (Photo by Linda Lungren)

about implied information and to draw thoughtful conclusions. The following questions for consideration when reading a newspaper article are offered by Cheyney (1984, pp. 16–17), but they apply to other media forms as well.

The Writer's Competency and Integrity
  Is the writer an authority?
  How does this writer know?
  Does the writer make sense?

The Writer's Use of Sources and Evidence
  What evidence is presented to document the assertions?
  Is this fact or opinion?
  Is anything missing?
  What is the writer's purpose?
The Reader's Ability to Form, Revise, and Test Opinions
  Are the premises valid?
  Why are these facts important to me?
  Do the conclusions necessarily follow?
  What have others said about this topic?
  Who stands to gain if I accept this without question?
  Does my lack of knowledge keep me from accepting this?
  Does my background make me intolerant of this point of view?
  Is the information as true today as when it was written?
  What more do I need to know before I come to my own conclusions?

Radio, television, and the newspaper all use advertising. Good advertising is necessary to promote competition, ensuring the prevalence of good-quality products and keeping prices down. Newspapers receive 70 percent of their revenue from advertising (Greenup, 1983). Advertising thus allows the availability of a valuable medium at a very low cost to the consumer. However, many advertisers use propaganda techniques to influence the public. Although these techniques often distort reality, young children may view this distortion as reality. Consequently their values and desires may reflect those promoted by advertisements. With an awareness of these propaganda techniques, students will be able to view advertisements more objectively. The following techniques may be found in both oral and written form.

Name Calling: Creating a negative association with a person or product by identifying it with something undesirable.
Glittering Generalities: Using words that are vague

but that appeal to people's emotions and to what they think is good, like the phrase "the American way."

Plain Folks: Associating the person or product with ordinary people; often used by politicians.

Snob Appeal: Creating an association with the elite if you use this product or vote for this person.

Transfer: Associating a person or product with a symbol that already creates a negative or positive impression. The feeling for the symbol transfers to the person or product.

Testimonial: Giving of an endorsement by a celebrity.

Bandwagon: Suggesting that one should follow the crowd and buy a product or endorse a person because everyone else does.

Repetition: Using words or phrases so often that they become accepted as true.

Card Stacking: Presenting only one side of an issue, hiding or omitting some facts, or mixing fact and opinion.

Using the Computer Effectively in the Language Arts Classroom

The microcomputer has and will continue to have a profound impact on our schools and the manner in which students receive instruction. The field of educational computing is rapidly changing, therefore making it difficult to predict the future in hardware and software.

When computers were first introduced into the elementary and secondary classrooms, the primary focus was to teach the students general computer literacy and programming in various computer languages such as Basic and Pascal. By necessity their primary application was in the fields of mathematics and science. To accommodate this thrust, college courses were designed to provide instruction in *programming* in the various computer languages.

As the computer gained in popularity in general education, more curriculum areas became interested in computer applications, thus broadening the focus to include computer-assisted instruction and word processing as well as computer programming. It is with this change of focus that the language arts area has been able to capitalize on computer applications.

Useful Computer Terminology

Before we continue further it may be helpful to provide a glossary of terms related to the computer.

Courseware: Computer programs written especially for educational purposes.

Disk: Can be either floppy or hard. A disk is used to store computer programs. A *floppy disk* is small and inexpensive and made of flexible material. It is the one used most often in the computer-assisted instruction in the classroom. A *hard disk* contains more information and accesses that information faster than does a floppy disk.

Disk Drive: The record player of the computer. The disk drive transfers information from the disk to the memory of the computer.

Memory: The amount of characters of information that can be stored by the computer. *Read-only memory* (ROM)—permanent memory of computer; *random access memory* (RAM)—temporary memory of the computer.

Microcomputer: Small, self-contained desktop computers such as Apple, IBM, Commodore, TRS-80, and Kaypro.

Modem: Device for communicating to a computer via a telephone line.

Program: A set of instructions or commands composed of letters, symbols, or words for directing computers to perform desired operations.

Software: Programs (set of instructions) that govern the operation of a computer. (*Hardware* is the computer itself.)

Teacher's Utility: A utility program that assists the teacher in producing customized materials used in teaching, such as

crossword puzzles, multiple-choice tests, parent reports, and grade books.

Word Processing Program: Software that turns the computer into a typewriter. It allows correcting, editing, rearranging, and storing information before printing.

Computer Applications in the Language Arts

Perhaps the three most prevalent uses of the computer in the language arts classroom today are computer-assisted instruction (CAI), word processing, and teacher utility programs.

COMPUTER-ASSISTED INSTRUCTION (CAI). There is a wide variety of commercially produced software designed to instruct the students in various aspects of language arts and reading. Common uses of microcomputer software include drill and practice, tutorials, instructional games, and simulations. Although these categories on the surface appear to be clear-cut, it becomes obvious when exploring the literature that many programs overlap several categories and others fail to fit into any category.

1. Drill and practice: These programs are designed to be used after the student has gained an initial proficiency or understanding of the tasks. They provide the student with needed additional practice for mastery of the new skills or information. Many of these drill and practice programs are designed so that the teacher can customize the word lists to address skills being taught in that particular classroom. In this way the same piece of software can be used in several different grade levels.

2. Tutorial: These programs present self-paced lessons that teach new information in a step-by-step manner by using explanations, examples, questions, and branching.

3. Instructional games: Through these programs the students develop reasoning or problem-solving skills through inductive and deductive thinking processes. In these programs it is important that students apply information to a new setting, think logically, and follow directions. Programs teach skills applicable to a variety of content areas.

4. Simulations: These programs imitate a real or imaginary system based on the theory of the way that system operates. The students apply principles, discover relationships, and test assumptions in a realistic context.

WORD PROCESSING. Word processing software transforms the computer into a sophisticated electronic typewriter and, therefore, enhances the writing program. Some of the extensions of word processing into the classroom might include student stories, class newspapers, recipes, letters and messages, lists, diaries, reports, journals, and keyboarding skills.

Some of the word processing programs have added an interactive dimension to the software program. The students are led by various clues or writing aids on the computer screen to compose a story. This alleviates the frustration of looking at a blank computer screen, wondering how to begin and what to say. A more detailed discussion of word processing applications is presented in Chapter 12.

TEACHER UTILITY PROGRAMS. Teachers can use the computer in a great variety of ways to enhance instruction. Graphics software enables them to produce professional-looking charts, graphs, and posters. Authoring programs make it possible for teachers to produce computer-assisted instruction without learning a programming language. Teachers are then able to customize computer materials to the particular levels or abilities of a group of students. They can also produce a variety of worksheets that are tailor-made for the students through some teacher utility programs.

The computer can also assist the teacher in manag-

ing classroom instruction. This can be done through various programs: readability analysis, record keeping, grade book, calculator, and so on. In many cases the program can help teachers sort through the information they have on students, then analyze it, draw conclusions, and write reports based on the information. Some programs can also diagnose student problems or needs on the basis of a test and then direct the student to do certain assignments or lessons. This information is then stored on disk for future reference.

Software Evaluation

With the rising popularity of the computer in the classroom, there has been an increased number of software programs developed for the classroom. As with any type of educational material, there is a wide range of quality and applicability of software, and all software should be evaluated before purchase.

SOURCES OF EVALUATIONS. There are several sources of software evaluations with inherent limitations and biases. Any or all of these will aid in selecting software that will serve educational goals: word of mouth from colleagues, distributor or publisher, retail stores, journals and computer magazines, and commercial evaluation services. However, while pursuing these sources, please consider the following potential problems:

1. Some reviews are written from the perspective of a computer expert, with technical aspects being paramount.
2. Some reviews are written from the perspective of a language arts educator, with the curriculum aspect paramount and technical aspects secondary.
3. Evaluations can be like movie reviews with differing opinions. Which one do you believe and trust?
4. The field is continually changing so some reviews are outdated quickly.

ASPECTS TO CONSIDER. There are numerous articles written on software evaluation, and we would recommend that you examine some of the texts listed in the bibliography for an in-depth discussion. Briefly, some aspects to consider in evaluating software are creativity, instructional objectives, content, screen formatting, instructions, student response, program response, motivational devices, technical quality, documentation, and teacher utility.

LUNGREN QUICK SOFTWARE REVIEW. There are numerous software evaluation forms available for your use. Whichever one you decide to use, we would recommend that you develop a systematic procedure for all software that you review and ultimately use. This will provide assistance to you and your colleagues at various times in the year should funds become available for purchase.

One such form that we have found invaluable as a source for review and future software purchases is the *Lungren Quick Software Review* (see Figure 14–1). It provides the user with pertinent information, can be filled out quickly, lends itself to a developing notebook collection, and provides important information for future use.

Suggestions for Maximum Computer Usage

The computer has been integrated increasingly into the classroom in terms of time used as well as types of applications. As teachers are being trained in computer usage, as publishers are becoming more aware of educational needs and applications, and as more curriculum developers are becoming more involved, our knowledge of using the computer as a classroom aid is expanding.

In the beginning, the novelty of having the computer in the classroom was enough for most teachers. However, as they become more knowledgeable about computer applications and software, they are becoming more involved in using the computer to reinforce and supplement the existing curriculum.

LUNGREN QUICK SOFTWARE REVIEW

Program name: _____ Publisher address: _____

_____

Price: _____ No. of disks: _____ Backup Disks? _____

Computer brand/model: _____

Peripherals:

_____ paddles/joystick   _____ voice digitizer   _____ color monitor

_____ disk drive(s)   _____ cassette   _____ printer

_____ other

Type of work:

_____ Independent   _____ Team   _____ Teacher Directed

Ease or difficulty of use (i.e., documentation: code words, etc.) _____

_____

Instructional system–drill/practice tutorial _____

simulation game word processing _____

teacher utility etc.: _____

Management system/record keeping:

_____ on disk/long term   _____ short term/on screen   _____ provided in manual/paper

_____ aid/hindrance

Grade level:

Concept _____ Actual format _____

Objectives (skills): _____

_____

General reaction: _____

_____

Anticipated student reaction to program: _____

_____

Subject area:

How can this be used in *my* classroom? _____

_____

Where does it fit into *my* curricular design? _____

_____

Can I modify this program to suit my needs? (words lists, etc.)

_____ yes   _____ no

Would I purchase this software (why/why not)? _____

_____

Figure 14–1. Lungren Quick Software Review. (Used by permission of Linda Lungren, San Diego, Calif.)

Realizing that many of you may be limited in the amount of time the computer is in your classrooms, we are suggesting the following guidelines to aid you in achieving maximum use of the computer in your classroom.

1. Use the computer only for those activities that would best be served by the computer rather than by nonelectronic teaching methods.
2. Use the computer in conjunction with more traditional teaching methods and materials.
3. Make use of the computer for whole-group or small-group instruction when appropriate. Introducing a new piece of software to an entire group may alleviate the necessity to repeat the directions to each new student at the computer.
4. Since each piece of software may have a different set of instructions, prepare your students before they go to the computer.
5. Arrange a user schedule for the computer. Students should be told what they are to do at the computer and at what time.
6. Use microcomputer activities for peer tutoring experiences. Student-to-student instruction on the computer is really very successful in many instances.
7. Above all, make a commitment to use the computer. Teachers must be careful not to restrict groups, time, and individuals.

There are many advantages to using the computer in the classroom. Some of these are taking the drudgery out of routine activities, freeing the teacher for more time on teaching and reteaching, giving students immediate feedback, providing a very patient computer tutor, and allowing the student to study at his own pace. Clement (1981) has reported many positive student attitudes toward the computer and its educational uses, as well as its ability to motivate and maintain high interest.

There is no reason for educators to be concerned about the computer's replacing the teacher. The computer is merely a tool that challenges educators to tap its full potential.

Using the Library and Media Center

Using the library or media center requires knowledge of specific reference skills. To the student who has mastered these skills, the library is a source of information and recreation. The ability to locate information quickly and efficiently increases one's desire to read and use books. The student lacking in these skills, however, may be left feeling overwhelmed and frustrated. Many school libraries contain both print and nonprint media, and students need to develop confidence in the selection and use of all available types of media.

Primary grade students may begin to develop an understanding of the way in which books and materials are classified and organized by establishing a classroom library. By making a card catalogue for books in the classroom, students can learn the skills of classification and alphabetization. They also learn the importance of organizing library materials for quick and easy reference. Books used in a classroom library may be donated by parents or by other community members. Individual or class language experience stories, student-authored poems or narratives, and content area reports may also be bound and catalogued. Oral presentations of Reader's Theater or choral reading can be taped and filed in the class listening center for others to enjoy.

To enable students to locate materials and information quickly and efficiently, knowledge of reference skills is essential. These skills must be taught directly. Some feel that reference skills instruction is most successful when integrated with subject area content (Eisenberg, 1984). This involves considerable cooperation between the school librarian and the classroom

Many school libraries contain both print and nonprint media, and the student will need to develop confidence in the selection and use of all available types of media. (Photo by Linda Lungren)

teacher, and a thorough knowledge of both the library skills curriculum and the elementary content area curriculum. Although it is unlikely that a teacher would have the time to devote to the development of such an integrated curriculum, the teacher can include skills instruction in an activity that enhances the content areas taught in the classroom. Students can thus see a practical application for the skills they are learning.

Care and Knowledge of Books

Primary school students should be taught the proper way to handle and carry books and to care for them at home. They should be introduced to the terms *spine* and *cover* and be able to identify these parts of a book. Young students should also be able to locate a book's title, author, and illustrator and should use them in referring to specific books. An introduction to the table of contents allows students to locate general sections by using chapter titles and subheadings.

Intermediate students should be able to locate a book's publisher, copyright date, index, appendices, and glossary and should know the information contained in each. Students should be able to judge whether the information contained in a book is current by looking at the copyright date. It is helpful to teach the function of an index by contrasting it to the table of contents. Indices are alphabetized by topic, and many books contain both subject and author indices. Intermediate grade students should know that a glossary contains words that are related to the book's content, and that a definition and explanation are given for each word. They should also be taught that an appendix contains supplementary information, often in the form of charts or graphs.

Locating Reference Materials

Primary students should be able to locate picture books; easy-to-read books, magazines and newspapers; picture dictionaries; the card catalogue; and records and tapes. They should be taught how to check out books and how to demonstrate proper behavior in the library. Primary students should have many opportunities to identify books by the title, author, and illustrator.

Intermediate grade students should be able to locate fiction and nonfiction collections, encyclopedias and dictionaries, the vertical file, microfilm and the microfilm reader, atlases, almanacs, and specialized encyclopedias and dictionaries. They should know what type of information is included in each reference book or area of the library, and when it is necessary to obtain that type of information. They should also be able to select reference materials of appropriate difficulty.

Reference Skills

DICTIONARY SKILLS. Primary grade students should have many opportunities to practice alphabetizing by first, and later by second, letters. They should also be able to use a picture dictionary to locate words and to determine their correct spelling.

Intermediate grade students should be able to alphabetize words to their third, fourth, fifth, and sixth letters. Practice should be given in using guide words to locate words quickly. Intermediate grade students also need practice selecting the appropriate word meaning from several given meanings. Instruction should also be given in locating synonyms and antonyms, referring to syllabication when hyphenating words, using diacritical markings for correct pronunciation, and determining correct accents.

USING THE CARD CATALOGUE. Primary school students should understand that title, author, and subject cards all contain the same information and should know how to recognize each type. Intermediate grade students should be taught to read the abbreviations used in the card catalogue, to use the card catalogue to locate books on the shelf by call numbers, and to use cross-reference cards. Students need opportunities to practice categorizing books or information by topic when preparing to use the subject card.

USING THE ENCYCLOPEDIA. Primary grade students should understand the type of information contained in encyclopedias. Intermediate school students should be able to locate an encyclopedia written at their reading level. They should be taught to use the index to locate the correct volume, use cross-references and guide words, check the copyright date to determine whether the information is current, and use more than one encyclopedia to compare information.

USING PERIODICALS. Primary school students should be able to locate the magazine section in the library and to select magazines of interest. Intermediate grade students should understand that periodicals contain the most recent information on many subjects. Skills necessary to use periodicals efficiently include identifying subject headings that may lead to a useful reference, understanding the abbreviations used in the *Reader's Guide to Periodical Literature* or other journal indexes, and locating articles in the periodical from the reference given in the journal index.

Understanding Library Organization

Intermediate-grade students should have an understanding of the way books are classified and arranged. The fiction collection is usually arranged alphabetically by the author's last name. Nonfiction is classified by the Dewey Decimal System or the Library of Congress system. Biographies are usually alphabetized by the last name of the person about whom the book is written, and periodicals are alphabetized by title. Although it is not necessary to require students to memorize the Dewey Decimal or Library of Congress systems, they should become familiar enough with them that they can locate the books they need. Refer to Appendix C for activities for teaching library and reference skills.

Summary

Instructional procedures for extending language arts skills through media resources have been the general focus of this chapter. Specific strategies for expanding language learning through print and nonprint media, such as libraries, newspapers, audio recordings, filmstrips, films and videocassettes, reader's theater, television, and computers, were also presented. Evaluation and organizational concerns often voiced by teachers attempting such an integration were also examined.

Suggested Classroom Projects and Questions for Discussion

Projects
1. Prepare a lesson in which a musical recording is used to stimulate creative writing.
2. Select a film or filmstrip for use with children. Specify

an objective and the way you would use the film/filmstrip to meet the objective.

3. Prepare a series of slides to teach a specific language arts skill.
4. Rewrite a children's story or chapter of a book in Reader's Theater script form.
5. Locate examples of the propaganda techniques described in this chapter. Prepare a lesson plan for using them to teach critical thinking skills.
6. Prepare a bulletin board for teaching the four purposes of editorials.
7. Prepare objectives and a lesson plan for teaching one area of language arts by using the newspaper.
8. Develop a lesson plan to teach a reference skill at the primary or intermediate level.
9. Develop and use a checklist to evaluate students' ability to use reference skills.
10. Select a type of language arts software. Prepare a lesson plan that involves *introducing* the piece of software, *implementing* it in the lesson, and *extending* the learning activity beyond the software.

Questions

1. What are some reasons for using different forms of print and nonprint media in the classroom?
2. Do you feel it is necessary for teachers to preview the films and filmstrips used in the classroom?
3. How do student-made slides and filmstrips improve the students' language arts skills?
4. What are the benefits of using Reader's Theater?
5. How would you reply to a statement that films and filmstrips are more entertaining than instructional?
6. Why is television a more controversial medium than the radio or newspaper?
7. How can teachers make parents aware of the need to view and discuss television programs with their children?
8. Why is it important for students to learn to identify and recognize propaganda techniques?
9. How would you convince your principal that your class should receive a newspaper subscription?
10. What skills in language arts would best be taught by using the computer? Why?

Chapter 15

Classroom Organization of Curriculum and Instructional Procedures

(Photo by Linda Lungren)

OBJECTIVES

At the end of this chapter students should be able to:
1. discuss the factors that contribute to effective classroom management.
2. analyze the components of successful grouping practices.
3. write behavioral objectives.

Why Do You Need a Plan for Effective Classroom Operation?

There is no one best way for all students to learn. As a classroom teacher you will need to design an operational plan with multiple means to ensure learning for individuals, who will be working independently, in small groups, and also in whole class instruction.

1. As a teacher you are responsible for the individual development of each student. Your professional expertise must be conveyed in a variety of ways if each is to grow intellectually and emotionally from the encounter. You cannot teach students only today's body of literal facts and expect them to be critical decision makers tomorrow. Your curriculum must encourage this growth by being custom-tailored to each learner. It can be individualized through the development of a well-planned design.

2. Students are not on their own in learning. The degree of decision-making responsibility the student shares must be commensurate with his or her experience and ability. It is the teacher's responsibility to plan the program and thus guide each student's independence and initiative in the individualized programs.

3. The degree of program personalization must depend on the task to be accomplished, the readiness exposures of the student for the given task, and the abilities to manage multiple methods for accomplishing a given task. You may be more successful in your attempts to personalize through management of your program if you start with only one content area. Once you are successful with initial attempts, you may want to expand the program. You are the program manager. Be careful not to design a program that you are unable to manage.

4. Use the materials you currently have to personalize your program. Do not use a lack of materials as an excuse for not attempting to personal-ize your curriculum. Your *incentive* is the prime factor in the success of these initial attempts.

Organizing and managing the learning environment are complex tasks that can be accomplished through continuous, careful planning and evaluation. When attempting to accomplish this task several key questions must be addressed. Where is the classroom located? What is the school building like? How involved are the parents? What are the students like? What existing curricular and societal structures predetermine classroom interactions?

These questions may be effectively addressed through a personalized system of classroom management. Figure 15.1 is one model of such management. Study it and then adapt or modify it for the personalized operation of your classroom and curriculum.

Planning for Effective Classroom Operation

Identify Structures and Individuals

Consideration must focus on the existing structures and individuals that directly affect the happenings within your classroom. Although some of these structures may be governed by you (philosophy and psychology), others (societal influence, budget allocations) may be outside your range of authority, and still others (curricular requirements, time schedules) may have been established before your arrival but be subject to change.

You must be familiar with all the structures in your environment and the extent of your decision-making power regarding each. You may gain initial insights into this area through social and professional interactions with colleagues and administrators. A review of existing school policies, as well as curriculum guides, will offer you some insights into the parametric structure of the existing curriculum. Individuals in the school community who may directly affect events within your classroom include the administration, col-

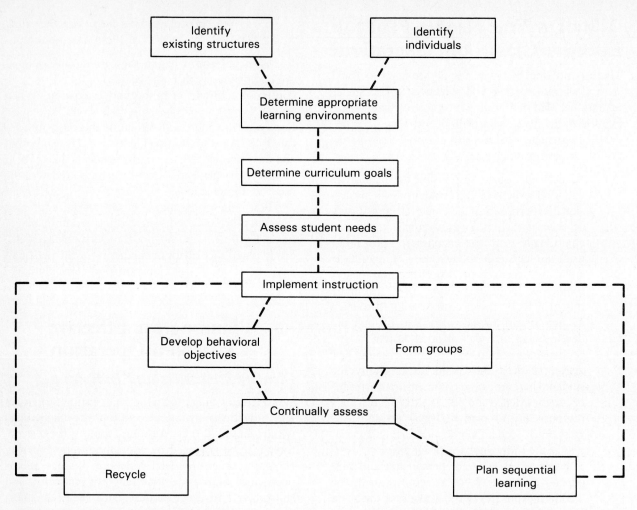

Figure 15-1. Classroom management model.

leagues, parents, community, and students. By asking yourself questions like the following you will gain the necessary insights to plan a successful learning environment for *all* your students.

Administration

1. What is the administration's view of the relationship between classroom organization and learning?

2. Are their views similar to mine?
3. What decisions are made by whom?

Resources

1. What funds are available for my classroom?
2. What types of media are available?
3. Are there computer resources?
4. What resources are shared?
5. How are classroom materials selected?

6. What portion of each school day is devoted to classroom instruction?
7. Are professional aids available to me?

Parents

1. What is the socioeconomic stratification of the parents of my students?
2. Are any of the parents of my students members of the school board?
3. Will the parents support me in class practices (homework, disciplines)?
4. Are parents available to work as classroom volunteers?
5. What educational goals for their children are held by parents of my students?

Colleagues

1. Who are my colleagues?
2. What types of learning environments do they believe foster effective teaching?
3. Do there appear to be any major educational beliefs shared by the majority of the faculty?
4. What should be my role as a member of this educational community?
5. How can I accomplish my goals and maintain a strong working relationship with my colleagues?

Community

1. Which portion of the community controls school board decision making?
2. Is the surrounding community well represented (economically, socially) by the family makeup of the students in my classroom?

Students

1. Who are my students?
2. What have been their life exposures?

3. What may be their projected educational/life goals?
4. Are my students first-language English speakers?
5. What portion of my students are gifted?
6. How many of my students have been diagnosed as learning-handicapped?

Self

1. What do I believe is the relationship between learning and classroom environment?
2. Do I harbor any prejudice or fears with regard to my students, parents, administration, colleagues?
3. Are there any obvious barriers that may hinder my performance as a teacher?

Determine an Appropriate Learning Environment

After you have attempted to answer questions of the type outlined you will need to focus on the relationships among learning, instruction, and environment. Students learn very effectively when they are placed in cooperative learning situations. Such situations occur when competition among classroom members is at a minimum. A resource that can provide you with excellent insights into cooperative learning is *Using Student Team Learning* by Robert Slavin. This resource may be ordered from Johns Hopkins University, Center for Social Organization of Schools, 3505 N. Charles St., Baltimore, Maryland 21218.

Within your classroom do you plan to present your instruction through whole-group presentation? This method will be effective for the initial lessons of a topic, unit, or concept. However, since most of your students will have varying degrees of knowledge and ability on any given topic, you may have to provide small-group input to ensure mastery for all. Successful teachers use individual small groups and whole-group techniques as needed.

Determine Curriculum Goals

Once you have planned the environment, you will need to plan the goals of your curriculum. What can be accomplished given your materials, students, and time constraints? Many school systems provide curriculum guides that indicate the curriculum goals for subject area instruction by grade level. For example:

Curriculum Area: Science, Grade 5

Topic: Life Cycles
General Objectives

1. Define a life cycle.
2. Develop an understanding of the life cycle of plants.
3. Develop an understanding of the biological life cycle of animals.
4. Promote an awareness of emotional and psychological cycles in humans.
5. Establish an appreciation for each stage of life from birth to death.
6. Develop a personal awareness of one's own physical and emotional place in the cycle.
7. Evaluate personal and societal feelings about life and death.

Curriculum Area: Social Studies, Grade 3

Topic: Exploring Your Environment
General Objectives

1. Develop an awareness of self.
2. Identify significant others.
3. Identify geographic boundaries.
4. Identify cultural boundaries.
5. Compare strengths and weaknesses of boundary limitations.
6. Evaluate social change you can effect.

It is also possible to plan curriculum goals from the topics presented in the grade-level textbook. As you design the curricular goals of your program, you will want concurrently to assess the needs of the existing program. In making this program assessment, you should ask the following questions:

1. What previous topics have been explored at this grade level?
2. Do these topics apply to the objectives of the system?
3. Am I infringing on material that my colleagues may cover?
4. What resources are available to me?
5. How much in-class time do I have to accomplish each goal?

Assess Student Needs

To determine individual needs, the teacher must begin the process of diagnosing student competencies. Through *formal* measures, such as standardized reading tests, and *informal* measures, such as informal reading inventories, observation scales, teacher-made checklists, interest inventories, and textbook placement exams, you can assess each student's competencies as compared to knowledge needed to accomplish each stated goal. By making a comparison of this type you are able to determine the type of instruction needed.

Instructional Implementation

Once you have assessed the knowledge readiness levels of your students you will be ready to plan more specific instruction. Such instruction may be classified through behavioral statements. After you specify the behavior to be accomplished you will be ready to group for instruction.

DEVELOP BEHAVIORAL OBJECTIVES. As Lapp and Flood (1986) suggest, a behavioral objective states an instructional goal in terms of measurable student performance. If objectives are well formulated, they will enable the teacher to move smoothly into the actual development and use of instructional materials. A behavioral objective has three basic components:

(1) the operational *conditions* to be present when the behavior occurs, (2) the terminal *behavior* the student should exhibit upon completing instruction, and (3) the level of *performance* needed to determine mastery.

Operational conditions are the circumstances or restraints under which the behavior is to be performed. If, for example, it is necessary for the student to be in a particular environment or to have specific tools/resources when performing the behavior, such conditions must be stated.

Acceptable

1. Given a short article containing numerous grammatical errors.
2. Given a list of ten prefixes.
3. Given six pictures showing poor water conservation practices.

Unacceptable

1. Given a lesson on grammar.
2. After instruction on prefixes.
3. After reading a brochure on water conservation methods.

(Note that although the unacceptable condition statements relate closely to the acceptable conditions, they do not specify the precise resources/tools the student will have available to him or her when actually performing the desired behavior.)

An acceptable statement of terminal *behavior* describes the student's behavior with such specificity that it cannot be misinterpreted. It answers the question "What will the student be doing to demonstrate that the goal has been met?" Let us look at the following examples:

Acceptable

1. The student will be able to write . . .
2. The student will be able to identify (verbally, visually) . . .
3. The student will be able to read . . .

Unacceptable

1. The student knows . . .
2. The student will enjoy . . .
3. The student will acquire an appreciation of . . .

An acceptable statement of *performance* level describes how well the student must perform to meet the objective. It must be *specific,* as these examples show:

Acceptable

1. . . . at least six of the following professions.
2. . . . with at least 75 percent accuracy.
3. . . . with no more than three errors.

Unacceptable

1. . . . show marked improvement over previous scores.
2. . . . with greater accuracy than before the lesson.
3. . . . better than last week.

Sometimes a general objective is conceived first and is then designed into a behavioral objective. For example, a classroom objective may be to introduce students to the theme of space-age careers. The following is a behavioral objective derived from such a broad objective:

Given a question about space-age career options, the student will be able to name at least three such careers and describe two ways in which the careers benefit society.

Behavioral objectives will help you to determine the following:

1. If the accomplishment of the stated objective has any value to the total development of the student.
2. If the student has accomplished the objective:
   a. Whether there are related objectives within the theme that are to be designed and utilized at this time.
   b. Methods of instruction and performance

Grouping allows for personalization of instruction and provides for economy of teacher effort to instruct a group of students with similar needs, interests, and purposes. (Photo by Linda Lungren)

level needed for implementation of related objectives.

3. If the student has not accomplished the objective:
   a. Whether the objective can be accomplished by this student at this time.
   b. Whether the performance level of the objective was too difficult.
   c. What new methods of instruction are needed to enable the student to accomplish the objective.

FORMING GROUPS AND DETERMINING MANNER OF INSTRUCTION. After instructional levels have been determined through informal and standard-

ized testing, students can be grouped according to their skill development needs, achievement, interests, purposes for learning, and attitudes toward a topic. Grouping allows for personalization of instruction and provides for economy of teacher effort to instruct a group of students with similar needs, interests, and purposes rather than to work with a total classroom of heterogeneous individuals. Materials can be matched to the learner more effectively than would be possible if instruction were geared to a whole class. Grouping is beneficial to the learner because the instruction is matched with interests, needs, purposes, and skills. The information on team learning that is suggested throughout this book will offer you much assistance in planning effective grouping techniques.

Assessment and Record Keeping

Lapp and Flood (1986) suggest that it is important to remember that you will be constantly evaluating each student's progress against your curricular goals and behavioral objectives. This assessment will help you to determine the effectiveness of your instructional program, and it will be a red flag to you if a particular student is having undue difficulty or needs to have his or her learning prescription reevaluated.

Students who are successfully meeting objectives will be given *new challenges* as your various groups change, both in content and in the student composition. Students who have evidenced difficulty may be *recycled* though the learning experience with new instructional examples and assignments designed for their needs. Well-managed sequential learning activities are at the core of a successful instructional program.

With the help of an educational management system, you can survey, plan, implement, recycle, or sequence an integrated theme. Continuous evaluation is the prime ingredient for success in a program of this type. A system of management enables you, as a teacher, to state clearly desired terminal behaviors, evaluate instructional effectiveness, and determine sequential learning. Mastery of instruction may be affected by the amount of instructional time utilized for topical presentation, complexity of material, and student interest.

As you review the effectiveness of your classroom organizational plan, we encourage you to consider the following points.

1. Sequencing instruction through the aid of a managed organizational system enables you to avoid a hit-or-miss, ineffectual type of teaching.
2. Sequencing instruction through the use of a managed organizational system enables students to proceed according to their developing competencies.
3. Sequencing instruction through the aid of a managed organizational system enables you to manage complex skills better by presenting them in smaller, subordinate parts.
4. Sequencing instruction through the aid of a managed organizational system enables you to develop a clearer understanding of how students learn.

Summary

Every classroom teacher attempts to develop an effective plan for managing his or her classroom. One model, designed to provide teachers with strategies to aid them with classroom organization and management, was presented in the chapter. Specifics regarding student assessment, through informal and standardized measures; the role of the parent; development of objectives; formation of groups; and record keeping were examined.

Suggested Classroom Projects and Questions for Discussion

Projects

1. Design a management plan that reflects the operation of your classroom. If you are not yet teaching, design the plan for your intended classroom.
2. From the library select several texts that deal with the topic of *instruction*. Prepare a list of the factors that constitute effective instruction. Discuss ways that these factors will be part of your classroom organizational plan.
3. Select from the library several books that discuss *learning*. Prepare a statement describing the relationship between long-term learning and effective instruction.
4. Develop an initial lesson in social studies for a fifth-grade class. Design sequential and recycling activities.
5. Discuss the ways you could redirect a student who is off-task or is not working on an in-class assignment.
6. Describe ways to keep your classroom atmosphere positive and supportive and to use rewards and penalties to motivate students.
7. Design a list of rewards/incentives and penalties that you plan to use in your classroom. Describe ways that they encourage personal student growth.
8. Select several texts from the library that discuss grading practices. After reading these selections think of ways

in which you can account for individual work within a group while encouraging cooperative learning.

9. Discuss the strengths and weaknesses of grouping for instruction.
10. Develop a card file of resources that explain how to construct teacher-made resources.

Questions

1. How is personalized instruction facilitated through continuous evaluation?
2. Of what value are behavioral objectives in program planning?
3. How can your colleagues affect the workings of your classroom?
4. On what basis should groups be formed and how should they best be used?
5. Why is cooperative learning an effective method of instructional grouping?
6. Why is it important to understand the educational goals held for your students by their parents?
7. How will your philosophy of learning affect the organization of your classroom?
8. Why is it necessary to reteach information to some of your students?
9. What segment of the management model presented in this chapter encourages reteaching?
10. How do sequential teaching and reteaching/recycling differ? How are they similar?

Appendix A

Literary Resources for Classroom Use

Poetry Without Rhyme

Quiet Giants

The swaying palm trees,
See them whisper amongst themselves,
Like children in rows.

Brandon Barker

Good Night

Many ways to spell good night.
Fireworks at a pier on the Fouth of July spell it with
    red
        wheels and yellow spokes.
They fizz in the air, touch the water and quit.
Rockets make a trajectory and gold-and-blue and then
    go
        out.
Railroad trains at night spell with a smokestack
        mushrooming a white pillar.
Steamboats turn a curve in the Mississippi crying in
        a baritone that crosses lowland cottonfields to
        a razorback hill.
It is easy to spell good night.
        Many ways to spell good night.

Carl Sandburg

Poetry That Provides Example

Three Cheers for Peter

When Peter eats a lollypop
He doesn't walk or run or hop
He sits upon the bottom stair
Or in the kitchen on a chair
He doesn't try to chew or bite
Or swallow chunks; he just sits tight
And sucks. And he is careful not
To let it make a sticky spot
On furniture. Three cheers for Peter
He's a good safe candy eater.

Alice Hartich

Recommended Books for Oral Reading

The following books are recommended for oral reading.

Kindergarten

Bedtime for Frances, by Russell Hoban. Harper, 1960. A
        badger child tries to delay bedtime just as other chil-
        dren do.

The Biggest Bear, by Lynd Ward. Houghton, 1952. A Caldecott Medal Book about a boy's pet bear cub that becomes overwhelming when he grows up. *Nic of the Woods,* by the same author, is equally successful as a dog story.

Blueberries for Sal, by Robert McCloskey. Viking, 1948. Anticipation is strong in this story about Sal and her mother, and little bear and his mother, getting all mixed up while gathering blueberries.

Contrary Woodrow, by Sue Felt. Doubleday, 1958. About kindergarten and Valentine's Day.

The Country Bunny and the Little Gold Shoes, by DuBose Heyward. Houghton, 1939. A favorite Easter story.

Curious George, by H. A. Rey. Houghton, 1941. Only one of many monkey stories: *Curious George Flies a Kite, Curious George Learns the Alphabet, Curious George Goes to the Hospital,* and others.

Edith and Mr. Bear, by Darr Wright. Doubleday, 1964. All the Darr Wright books are highly recommended.

George and the Cherry Tree, by Aliki. Dial, 1964. One of the few simple picture books available for seasonal demand.

Grandfather Twilight, by Barbara Berger. Philomel, 1984. Twilight is personified in this delicate tale.

Happy Birthday from Carolyn Haywood, by Carolyn Haywood. William Morrow, 1984. Nine warm but humorous stories about Betsy and her friends.

The Happy Lion, by Louise Fatio. McGraw-Hill, 1934. All the people who visited the zoo were the lion's friends until he got out of the cage. More titles in this series.

Happy Mother's Day, by Steven Kroll. Holiday, 1985. Mom receives one Mother's Day surprise after another from her family.

The Magic Tree, by Gerald McDermott. Landmark Productions, 1973. A story of twins, one ugly, one handsome, and their lives in the African heartland.

Make Way for Ducklings, by Robert McCloskey. Viking, 1941. A family of mallard ducks makes their home in the middle of Boston. Outstanding Caldecott Award book.

Maude and Claude Go Abroad, by Susan Meddaugh. Houghton Mifflin, 1980. The humorous adventures of two fox children as they sail to France on the *S. S. Reynard.*

May I Bring a Friend? by Beatrice S. De Regniers. Atheneum, 1964. Children are carried away as each successive caller at the queen's tea party is more ridiculous. Rare illustrations and delightful rhymes.

Nobody Stole the Pie, by Sonia Levitin. Harcourt, 1980. The villagers bake a giant pie, learning the value of cooperation.

No More Baths, by Brock Cole. Doubleday, 1980. After running away to avoid taking a bath, Jessie lives with Mrs. Chicken, Mrs. Pig, and Mrs. Duck but decides home is best.

No Roses for Harry, by Gene Zion. Harper, 1958. Indomitable Harry knows that no self-respecting dog would wear a sweater with roses, even one knitted by Grandma.

Old MacDonald Had a Farm, by Pam Adams. Grosset & Dunlop, 1976. A mildly amusing version of this familiar rhyme. Each new animal appears in a cutout.

The Red Balloon, by Albert Lamorisse. Doubleday, 1957. An imaginative picture book that leads to discussion.

Rosebud, by Ed Emberly. Little, 1966. Delightful turtle story.

Swimmy, by Leo Lionni. Pantheon, 1963. Like *Rosebud,* a book for sharp eyes. *Inch by Inch,* by the same author-illustrator, uses the concept of size.

The Train, by David McPhail. Little, Brown, 1977. A boy and his train play in the middle of the night.

Willy Bear, by Mildred Kantrowitz. Parent's Magazine Press, 1976. A well-done story about the anxieties a small boy faces on his first day at school.

First Grade

Babar and Father Christmas, by Jean deBrunhoff. Random House, 1949. A fine introduction to the Babar books. Children squeal when Babar falls through the roof.

Beat the Story-Drum, Pum-Pum, retold by Ashley Bryan, Atheneum, 1980. The animals in these five African tales have small problems that get them into big trouble.

East of the Sun and West of the Moon, by Mercer Mayer. Four Winds Press, 1980. A magnificent retelling of the classic fairy tale.

Giants, Indeed! by Virginia Kahl. Scribner's, 1974. A humorous story about a boy who assumes giants are his size and what happens when he meets a family of giants.

Hailstones and Halibut Bones, by Mary O'Neill. Doubleday, 1961. Intriguing book of verse that invites creativity with color.

Hattie Be Quiet, Hattie Be Good, by Dick Gackenbach. Harper & Row, 1977. The story of Hattie, a helpful rabbit.

It Wasn't My Fault, by Helen Lester. Houghton, 1985. Murdley Gurdson has more than his share of problems when he sets out to find the culprit who laid an egg on his head.

Jeanne-Marie Counts Her Sheep, by Françoise. Scribner's, 1951. A simple story, picture, counting book.

Miss Nelson Is Missing, by Harry Allard. Houghton, 1977. A well-illustrated fun book in which the lenient Miss Nelson teaches her misbehaving class a lesson by becoming a strict teacher.

Nine Days to Christmas, by Marie Hall Ets. Viking, 1959. A Caldecott book about a Mexican Christmas, introducing the piñata.

A Pocketful of Cricket, by Rebecca Caudill. Holt, 1964. A quiet story about a boy's affection for his pet cricket and the first day of school.

Red Is Never a Mouse, by Eth Clifford. Bobbs, 1960. A book of color.

Regards to the Man in the Moon, by Ezra Jack Keats. Four Winds Press, 1981. Louie and his friend use their imaginations to hurtle through space in their homemade spaceship.

Ski Pup, by Don Freeman. Viking, 1963. Hugo, a Saint Bernard rescue dog, accidentally becomes a ski dog.

The Snowy Day, by Ezra Jack Keats. Viking, 1962. An experience in visual perception. A little boy tries out the snow.

Ten Tall Tales, by E. V. Bird. Carolrhode, 1984. Collection of ten humorous stories about the Old West.

Time of Wonder, by Robert McCloskey. Viking, 1957. One can feel the fog and the other sensations of beach life at the ocean.

Wash Day on Noah's Ark, by Glen Rounds. Holiday, 1985. The hilarious story of Mrs. Noah when she decides to do the wash.

Where the Wild Things Are, by Maurice Sendak. Harper, 1964. A very imaginative monster book about a little boy who gets even after being sent to his room.

Whistle for Willie, by Ezra Jack Keats. Viking, 1964. Willie's day is full of the small discoveries of all children.

Second Grade

And to Think That I Saw It on Mulberry Street, by Dr. Seuss. Vanguard, 1937. Nonsense rhyme about a street where the ordinary becomes the extraordinary.

The Bears on Hemlock Mountain, by Alice Dalgleish. Scribner's, 1952. Everyone told Jonathan there were no bears on the mountain. Suspense mounts as Jonathan crosses the mountain.

Brighty of the Grand Canyon, by Marguerite Henry. Rand, 1953. Highly recommended, this story of a lone burro found by an old prospector has magnificient drawings of the Grand Canyon.

The Cat's Purr, by Ashley Bryan. Atheneum, 1985. This African folk tale tells how the cat got its purr.

Charlotte's Web, by E. B. White. Harper, 1952. The gentle friendship of a pig, a spider, and a little girl who could talk to animals.

Clown Dog, by Lavinia Davis. Doubleday, 1961. A boy defends his dog in a new neighborhood until his pet becomes a hero by discovering an orphaned fawn.

Down, Down the Mountain, by Ellis Credle. Nelson, 1961. Two Blue Ridge Mountain children want creaky-squeaky shoes more than anything else in the world.

Easter in November, by Lilo Hess. Crowell, 1964. A surprise Easter story about an ususual breed of chickens that hatches colored eggs.

Fanny's Sister, by Penelope Lively. E. P. Dutton & Co., 1980. Fanny, the eldest of eight, wishes the new baby would go away and panics when her wish seems to come true.

The Girl and the Moon Man, retold by Jeanette Winter. Pantheon, 1984. This Siberian folk tale explains why the moon lights up the sky.

Good-bye Ruby Red, by Geraldine Kaye. Children's Publishers, 1976. A fantasy in which a paper doll comes to life.

Jumanji, by Chris Van Allsburg. Houghton Mifflin, 1981. Strange things happen when two children begin to play a jungle adventure board game. Caldecott Award winner.

King Orville and the Bullfrogs, by Kathleen Abell. Little, Brown, 1974. A fairy tale with humorously detailed drawings.

Lentil, by Robert McCloskey. Viking, 1940. Lentil's harmonica saves the day. Illustrations large enough to be seen by the class.

Lilly, Willy and the Mail-Order Witch, by Othello Bach. Caedmon, 1983. The children in this story have many adventures when they order a witch through the mail.

Little Orphan Annie, by James Whitcomb Riley. G. P. Putnam's Sons, 1983. New illustrated edition of the classic poem.

Little Runner of the Longhouse, by Betty Baker. Harper, 1962. A much needed easy treatment of Iroquois life.

Marshmallow, by Clare T. Newberry. Harper, 1942. A pet cat cannot understand when a little white bunny comes to live at his home. Exceptional illustrations, fine story.

Mike's House, by Julia Sauer. Viking, 1954. Most second graders have been introduced to *Mike Mulligan and His Steam Shovel*, by Virginia Burton, and will chuckle at this story of a boy who will not make a compromise.

Millions of Cats, by Wanda Gag. Coward, 1928. How does a little old woman choose one from millions of cats?

Mouse Soup, by Arnold Lobel. Harper & Row, 1977. A mouse tale in which a mouse and a weasel put stories into soup.

Prince of the Dolomites, by Tomie de Paola. Harcourt, 1980. An Italian folk tale of a young prince who falls in love with a princess of the moon.

Reindeer Trail, by Berta and Elmer Hader. Macmillan, 1959. How the fleet-footed reindeer brought to Alaska by the friendly Lapps saved the Eskimos from starving.

The Story of Helen Keller, by Lorena Hickel. Grosset & Dunlop, 1958. This version of a great lady's life is simple enough to be enjoyed by second and third grades.

Tom Tit Tot, illus. by Evaline Ness. Scribner's, 1965. The comic illustrations fit the "gatless" girl in this refreshing variation of Rumplestiltskin.

Two Is Company, Three's a Crowd, by Berta and Elmer Hader. Macmillan, 1965. Fine to use when the geese are migrating. The story of how Big John and his wife feed a few and soon have more than they can handle.

Third Grade

The Barrel in the Basement, by Barbara Brooks Wallace. Atheneum, 1985. A timid elf proves himself in the tradition of great elf heroes.

The Borrowers, by Mary Norton. Harcourt, 1953. If you can't find your stamps or thimbles, the Borrowers are probably using them for pictures or footstools. One third grade constructed a home for the little people.

The Courage of Sarah Noble, by Alice Dalgleish. Scribner's 1954. The true story of a brave little girl who, in 1707, went with her father into Indian territory.

Dancing Cloud, the Navajo Boy, by Mary Buff. Viking, 1957. Excellent story of Navajo life with striking full-spread illustrations.

The Day the Hurricane Happened, by Lonzo Anderson. Scribner's, 1974. An adventure story of two young people in a Virgin Island hurricane.

The Enormous Egg, by Oliver Butterworth. Little, Brown, 1956. Young Nate Twitchell finds an oversized egg in his chicken nest that hatches into a baby dinosaur and complications.

Fables, by Arnold Lobel. Harper, 1980. A Caldecott Award–winning collection of twenty short fables.

Henry Huggins, by Beverly Cleary. William Morrow, 1950. All the Henry books are enthusiastically recommended.

Homer Price, by Robert McCloskey. Viking, 1943. Each chapter is its own story. *The Doughnuts* and *Super Duper* are samples of the humor.

The Hundred Penny Box, by Sharon Mathis. Viking, 1975. The story of an old woman and a young boy and the love they share.

The Indian and the Buffalo, by Robert Hofsinde. William Morrow, 1961. This author has given us much authentic Indian material.

In the Dinosaur's Paw, by Patricia Reilly Giff. Dell, 1985. Richard Best is convinced that the initials on the ruler he found are those of a dinosaur. Once he has the ruler, all his wishes come true.

Just the Thing for Geraldine, by Ellen Conford. Little, Brown, 1974. Story of Geraldine and her attempts at various pasttimes.

The Limerick Trick, by Scott Corbett. Little, Brown, 1960. Kerby needs to write a limerick to win a contest.

The Light at Tern Rock, by Julia Sauer. Viking, 1951. Excellent Christmas reading. A boy learns patience the hard way when he is forced to spend Christmas tending the lighthouse beacon.

Little House in the Big Woods, by Laura Ingalls Wilder. Harper, 1953. Very scenic and descriptive language.

Little Navajo Bluebird, by A. N. Clark. Viking, 1943. A fine picture of present-day Navajo life.

Mary Poppins, by P. L. Travers. Harcourt, 1962. Remarkable things happen when Miss Poppins blows in as the new nanny.

The Matchlock Gun, by Walter Edmonds. Dodd, 1941. Historical fiction set in the Mohawk Valley during the French and Indian War. A boy is left to protect the family when the father answers the call for help from a settlement under attack.

The Missing Piece, by Shel Silverstein. Harper & Row, 1976. An "it" looks for the missing piece to "it."

The Mousewife, by Rumer Godden. Viking, 1982. A tale of unselfish friendship between a mousewife and a dove.

The Nightingale, by Hans C. Andersen; illus. by Harold Berson. Lippincott, 1963. A fine retelling of a favorite story.

The Nutcacker, trans. by Warren Chappell. Knopf, 1958. An excellent selection for Christmas. May be used with the music.

The Otter's Story, by Emil Liers. Viking, 1953. Like *The Beaver's Story*, recommended as an absorbing, unsentimental animal story.

Paddle-to-the-Sea, by Holling C. Holling. Houghton, 1941. An Indian boy carves a toy canoe and launches it in the waters of northern Canada. The story traces its journey through the Great Lakes, over the Falls, into the Atlantic. Striking illustrations showing landscape and industry native to the area.

Tatsinda, by Elizabeth Enright. Harcourt, 1963. A fantasy with weird creatures, strange names, and a little girl pursued because she is different.

A Weed Is a Flower: The Life of George Washington Carver, by Aliki. Prentice, 1965. Fine introduction to biography.

Fourth Grade

Away Goes Sally, by Elizabeth Coatsworth. Macmillan, 1934. Sally moves from New England to the Maine wilderness in the original house trailer—a log cabin on runners.

The Bee Man of Orn, by Frank Stockton. Holt, 1964. A man wishes to live his life over. The surprise ending delights the children.

The Beetle Bush, by Beverly Keller. Coward, 1976. About a born loser who finally achieves success.

Behind the Attic Wall, by Sylvia Cassedy. Crowell, 1983. When the twelve-year-old orphan is taken in by a mysterious uncle, she creates a reality of her own.

The Bluejay Boarders, by Harold Keith. Crowell, 1972. Three children take over the care of a nest of newborn bluejays.

The Children of Green Knowe, by L. M. Boston. Harcourt, 1955. A beautifully written fantasy. Children will differ about what is real and what is imagined.

Chitty-Chitty-Bang-Bang, by Ian Fleming. Random House, 1964. A magic car becomes a boat or airplane when the family escapes from gangsters. Highly recommended.

Families Are Like That, by the Child Study Association of America. Crowell, 1975. A book of short stories concerning children and the problems they face in family life.

The Fledgling, by Jane Langton. Harper & Row, 1980. A fantasy story of a young boy who wants to fly.

The Half-A-Moon Inn, by Paul Fleischman. Harper, 1980. A mute boy is separated from his mother by a blizzard and is later kidnapped in this adventure story.

Ice King, by Ernestine Byrd. Scribner's, 1965. Sensitive story of a friendship between an Eskimo boy and a bear orphaned by hunters.

The Magic Bed-Knob, by Mary Norton, in *Bed-Knobs and Broomsticks*. Harcourt, 1957. Sheer fantasy about English children and their magician friend who gets the book off to a fine start when she falls off her broomstick and sprains her ankle.

Mama Hattie's Girl, by Lois Lenski. Lippincott, 1953. This regional book gives meaning to the place of black people in the North and South and is also excellent for the relationship between child and grandmother.

Matilda Investigates, by Mary Anderson. Atheneum, 1973. The story of an eleven-year-old girl who tries to become New York's first woman detective.

Misty of Chincoteague, by Marguerite Henry. Rand, 1947. A captivating horse story that begins with Pony Penning Dat, still held on Chincoteague Island.

The Moffats, by Eleanor Estes. Harcourt, 1941. A family story full of humorous incidents. The Halloween chapter is hilarious.

Pippi Longstocking, by Astrid Lindgren. Viking, 1950. A story about an uninhibited little Swedish girl who lives by herself and does only what she pleases in very unusual ways.

The Shy Stegosaurus of Cricket Creek, by Evelyn Lampman. Doubleday, 1955. George is the dinosaur who escaped extinction.

Stone Fox, by John R. Gardiner. Crowell, 1980. An active story based on a Rocky Mountain legend in which a young boy enters a bobsled race in an attempt to save his grandfather's farm.

Strawberry Girl, by Lois Lenski. Lippincott, 1945. A realistic

story about a family of Florida "crackers"; strong regional background.

Stuart Little, by E. B. White. Harper, 1945. The mouseman has been a "smash" in one fourth grade. Good for the first day of school.

Wind in the Willows, by Kenneth Grahame. Scribner's, 1961. A classic that few children will enjoy unless it is first shared aloud.

The Witch of Blackbird Pond, by Elizabeth Speare. Houghton, 1958. Excellent background of Puritan America and the witchcraft movement. A Newbery Medal winner.

Young Mark Twain and the Mississippi, by Kane Harnett. Random House, 1966. One of the excellent Landmark Series.

Fifth Grade

The Alfred Summer, by Jan Slepian. Macmillan, 1980. A handicapped boy begins to build lasting friendships, rising above his physical limitations.

And Now Miguel, by Joseph Krumgold. Crowell, 1958. Authentic picture of sheep raising in New Mexico and a boy who longs to become a man.

The Animal Family, by Randall Jarrell. Pantheon, 1965. A mystic story of a woodsman, a mermaid, and the animals. Like *The Children of Green Knowe*, children will puzzle over the story.

Apricots at Midnight: and Other Stories from a Patchwork Quilt, by Adele Geras. Atheneum, 1982. The patches of a wonderful quilt give rise to the ten stories in this collection.

The Complete Peterkin Papers, by Lucretia Hale. Houghton, 1960. The uninhibited Peterkin family finds solutions peculiar to them. Ridiculous humor.

*F*T*C* Superstar!* by Mary Anderson. Atheneum, 1976. Story of an actor-cat who succeeds in his profession with help from a pigeon friend. Clever caricatures.

Farmer Boy, by Laura Ingalls Wilder. Harper, 1933. Good to show how people lived before modern conveniences. Early New York State.

The Island of the Blue Dolphins, by Scott O'Dell. Houghton, 1960. Based on the actual life of the sole inhabitant of the island, this Newbery winner has had great appeal for intermediate grades.

Miss Pickerell Goes to Mars, by Ellen MacGregor. McGraw, 1951. Miss Pickerell shuddered at the thought of a ferris wheel or stepladder. Her jaunt on a spaceship is a complete surprise. One of many in a series.

Prune, by Ramon Royal Ross. Atheneum, 1984. The story of the friendship and adventure that are shared by a prune, a magpie, and a muskrat.

Shadow of a Bull, by Maia Wojciechowska. Atheneum, 1964. The future is decided for the nine-year-old son of a famous bullfighter when he is born. A fine treatment of a child's reaction to public pressure in a setting rare to children's literature. A Newbery Award winner.

Susy's Scoundrel, by Harold Keith. Crowell, 1974. Story of Susy's pet coyote, who outwits hunters who think that he is killing sheep.

Twenty and Ten, by Claire Bishop. Viking, 1952. Twenty school children in France befriend ten Jewish children fleeing from the Gestapo during World War II.

Sixth Grade

Anastasia Again! by Lois Lowry. Houghton Mifflin, 1981. When Anastasia moves to the suburbs with her family the hilarious adventures begin.

Aunt America, by Marie Halun Block. Atheneum, 1963. Life behind the Iron Curtain. Children need to understand the concepts of freedom.

The Bronze Bow, by Elizabeth Speare. Houghton, 1961. An unusual setting portraying the hatred of the Jews for their Roman conquerors during the time of Christ. Used before Easter each year by one fifth-grade teacher. A Newbery Medal book.

The Christmas Carol, by Charles Dickens. Many editions. The descriptive flavor of Dickens' words is not heard in the television versions.

The Disappearing Man, and other mysteries, by Isaac Asimov. Walker, 1985. Three short stories about Larry, whose father is a detective on the city police force, and how he solves the mysteries ahead of his dad.

Emma's Dilemma, by Gen Leroy. Harper, 1975. The story of Emma, whose problems grow when she finds her dog must go because grandma, who comes to live with them, is allergic to the dog.

Follow My Leader, by James Garfield. Viking, 1975. A boy adjusts to blindness at the age of eleven.

The Incredible Journey, by Sheila Burnford. Little, Brown, 1961. Fascinating adventure of a motley group of animals traveling together.

It's Like This, Cat, by Emily Neville. Harper, 1963. Sophisti-

cated sixth graders will enjoy this story of New York City and a boy who never quite understands his parents, and vice versa. A Newbery book.

Last Night I Saw Andromeda, by Charlotte Anker. Walck Co., 1975. Determined to find a scientific interest to please her father, Jenny starts collecting fossils.

The Loner, by Ester Wier. McKay, 1963. Excellent character study of a boy who travels with migrants until he meets "Boss" and desperately wants to please her. Fine picture of sheep raising.

Martin Rides the Moor, by Vian Smith. Doubleday, 1965. A wild pony is the salvation of a boy deafened by an accident.

My Name Is Pablo, by Alice Sommerfelt. Criterion, 1966. Youth problems in Mexico City.

Onion John, by Joseph Krumgold. Crowell, 1959. A close friendship develops between the boy and the town junkman. Excellent human relations; humorous but realistic.

Second Hand Family, by Richard Parker. Bobbs, 1965. An up-to-date treatment of teenage interests. Concerns a group that plays rock and roll. Enjoyed by preteens.

Story for a Black Night, by Clayton Bess. Parnassus Press, 1982. In this West African story, a woman defies custom in an act of charity and suffers the consequences.

The White Panther, by Theodore Waldeck. Viking, 1941. A fast-moving story about a panther stalked by man and beast because he was born white.

A Wrinkle in Time, by Madeline L'Engle. Farrar, 1962. Science fiction at its best.

Flannelboard Story

Peculiar Company

A little old woman lived all alone in a little old house in the woods. One Halloween she sat in the corner, and as she sat she spun.

Still she sat and
Still she spun and
Still she wished for company.

Then she saw her door open a little way, and in came

A pair of big, big feet
And sat down by the fireside

"That is very strange," thought the little old woman, but—

Still she sat and
Still she spun and
Still she wished for company.

Then in came

A pair of small, small legs,
And sat down on the big, big feet
"Now that is very strange," thought the old woman, but—

Still she sat and
Still she spun and
Still she wished for company.

Then in came

A wee, wee waist
And sat down on the small, small legs.
"Now that is very strange," thought the old woman, but—

Still she sat and
Still she spun and
Still she wished for company.

Then in came

A pair of broad, broad shoulders,
And sat down on the wee, wee waist.
But—

Still she sat and
Still she spun and
Still she wished for company.

Then in through the door came

A pair of long, long arms
And sat down on the broad, broad shoulders.
"Now that is very strange," thought the old woman, but—

Still she sat and
Still she spun and
Still she wished for company.

Then in came

A pair of fat, fat hands,
And sat down on the long, long arms.
But—

Still she sat and
Still she spun and
Still she wished for company.

Then in came

A round, round head
And sat down on top of all
That sat by the fireside.

The little old woman stopped her spinning and asked

"Where did you get such big feet?"
"By much tramping, by much tramping," said
   Somebody.

"Where did you get such small, small legs?"
"By much running, by much running," said
   Somebody.

"Where did you get such a wee, wee waist?"
"Nobody knows, nobody knows," said Somebody.

"Where did you get such broad, broad shoulders?"
"From carrying brooms," said Somebody.

"Where did you get such long, long arms?"
"Swinging the scythe, swinging the scythe," said
   Somebody.

"Where did you get such fat, fat hands?"
"By working, by working," said Somebody.

"How did you get such a huge, huge head?"
"Of a pumpkin I made it," said Somebody.

Then said the little old woman,
"What did you come for?"

"You!" said Somebody.

Paul Anderson

Poetry for Classroom Use

Choral Readings

Funny the Way Different Cars Start

Solo 1:   Funny the way different cars start.
Row 1:   Some with a plunk and a jerk,

Row 2:   Some with a cough and a puff of smoke—
         Out of the back,
Row 3:   Some with only a little click—
         With hardly any noise.
Solo 2:   Funny the way different cars run.
Row 4:   Some rattle and bang,
Row 5:   Some whirrr,
Row 6:   Some knock and knock,
Girls: Some purr
Boys: And hummmmm
All: Smoothly on with hardly any noise.

Dorothy Baruch

The Giant Shoes

Solo 1: There once was a Giant who needed new
     shoes,
Refrain: Left! Right! Tie them up tight!
Solo 2: Said he, "I'll go to the shoestore and choose."
Refrain: Left! Right! Tie them up tight!
Solo 3: "High ones, and low ones, and black one
     and brown."
Refrain: Left! Right! Tie them up tight!
Solo 4: "Give me the biggest you have in the town."
Refrain: Left! Right! Tie them up tight!
Solo 5: The shoeman said, "These are the biggest
     I've got."
Refrain: Left! Right! Tie them up tight!
Solo 6: "Take them and try them and keep them or
     not."
Refrain: Left! Right! Tie them up tight!
Solo 7: "They fit," said the Giant, "and squeak, I'll
     buy them."
Refrain: Left! Right! Tie them up tight!
Solo 8: He wore them all year 'cause he couldn't
     untie them,
Refrain: Untie them! Untie them!
Solo or Group: He wore them all year 'cause he
     couldn't untie them.

Edwina Fallis

Choral Readings Involving a Group

Bundles

Good for stressing enunciation.

A bundle is a funny thing
It always sets me wondering;
For whether it is thin or wide,
You never know just what's inside.
Especially on Christmas week,
Temptation is so great to peek;
Now wouldn't it be much more fun
If shoppers carried things undone?

John Farrar

The American Flag

Solo:	There's a flag that floats above us,
	Wrought in red and white and blue—
	A spangled flag of stars and stripes
	Protecting me and you.
Unison:	Sacrifices helped to make it
	As men fought the long months through—
Boys:	Nights of marching
Girls:	Days of fighting
Unison:	For the red and white and blue.
Girls:	There is beauty in that emblem
Boys:	There is courage in it, too;
Girls:	There is loyalty
Boys:	There is valor
Unison:	In the red and white and blue.
Solo:	In that flag which floats unconquered
	Over land and sea
	There's equality and freedom
Unison:	There is true democracy.
Solo:	There is glory in that emblem
	Wrought in red and white and blue—
Unison:	It's the stars and stripes forever
	Guarding me and guarding you.

Louise Abney

Little Echo

All:	Little Echo is an elf		
	Who plays at hide and seek.		
	You never, never find him.		
	But you can hear him speak:		
Low:	Hello	High:	Hello
Low:	Hello	High:	Hello
Low:	I'm here	High:	I'm here
Low	Come near	High:	Come near
All:	I'm here.		

Los Angeles City Schools

Locomotive

Unison:	Mobs of people
	Lots of noise
	Rattling baggage.
	Porter boys.
	Grinding brakes.
	Shifting gears
	Merry laughter,
	Parting tears!
Solo:	All ab-o-o-ard! All ab-o-o-ard!
Dark:	Slowly
	Slowly
	Turning,
	Massive engine moving on.
Medium:	Smoking
	Smoking
	Higher
	Higher
	Smokestacks hurl the smoke anon.
Light:	Fuel
	Fuel
	Fire
	Fire
	Faster
	Faster
	Speed
	Speed!
Unison:	Got to reach my destination.
	Got no time for hesitation.
	Have to please the population.
	I am working for the nation.
	Hurry, hurry to my station.

Medium: Past the valleys, past the hilltops,
Past the river, past the pond,
Past the farmhouse or the city
Quickly covering the ground.
High: I'm racing the sun
I'm racing the moon
I'm racing the stars
I'm faster than time
Low: The mountains clear away for me.
They build a bridge across the sea.
The iron weight above my wheel
Medium: Trembles even rails of steel
Dark: Through tunnels, black, a sooty black
With dusty smoke and grime,
Light: Faster, faster, night's descending
All: I must reach my place on time!

Rodney Bennett

Poems Involving Finger Play

Little Jack Horner

Little Jack Horner sat in a corner
(Sit straight in chair; left hand held in lap in the pie.)
Eating his Christmas pie.
(Pretend to eat pie with right hand.)
He put in his thumb and pulled out a plum
(Stick thumb of right hand into pie; pull out the plum.)
And said, "What a good boy am I!"
(Hold hands high in air.)

Flag Salute

This salute to the flag may be used the first semester in school; then gradually introduce our national salute.

The work of my hands
(Cup both hands in front of you.)
The thoughts of my head
(Both hands on top of head.)
The love of my heart
(Hands folded over chest.)

I give to my flag.
(Extend hands and arms toward flag.)

Two Dickey Birds

Two little dickey birds sitting on a wall;
(Fists clenched, thumbs erect.)
One named Peter, the other named Paul.
(Nod one thumb, then the other.)
Fly away, Peter; fly away, Paul.
(One hand, then other moved to behind back.)
Come back, Peter; come back, Paul.
(One hand, then the other reappears.)

Five Little Squirrels

Five little squirrels
Sitting in a tree,
The first one said,
"What do I see?"
The second one said,
"I smell a gun."
The third one said,
"Quick, let's run!"
The fourth one said,
"Let's hide in the shade."
The fifth one said,
"Oh, I'm not afraid."
But—bang! went the gun
Away they did run!

Little Turtle

There was a little turtle.
(Upper right index finger.)
He lived in a box.
(Place in cupped left hand.)
He swam in a puddle
(Move finger in circle.)
He climbed on the rocks.
(Move up on left fingers.)
He snapped at a mosquito.
(Snap right hand in air.)
He snapped at a flea.
He snapped at a minnow.
He snapped at me.
(Snap toward self.)

He caught the mosquito.
  (Close right fist in air.)
He caught the flea.
He caught the minnow.
But he didn't catch me.
  (Point toward self, shake head.)

Two Telegraph Poles

Two tall telegraph poles
  (Pointer fingers erect.)
Across them a wire is strung.
  (Middle fingers outstretched to touch pointer
  fingers.)
Two little birds hopped on.
  (Thumbs to position against "wire.")
And swung, and swung, and swung.
  (Sway arms back and forth from body.)

Caterpillar

Roly-poly caterpillar
Into a corner crept,
Spun around himself a blanket,
Then for a long time slept.
Roly-poly caterpillar
Wakening by and by—
Found himself with beautiful wings,
Changed to a butterfly.

Itsy, Bitsy Spider

Itsy, bitsy spider went up the water spout.
  (Hands make a climbing motion; or thumbs on
  index fingers of opposite hands, one after the
  other.)
Down came the rain and washed the spider out.
  (Drop hands.)
Out came the sun and dried up all the rain.
  (Arms circled overhead.)
Itsy, bitsy spider went up the spout again.
  (Make "spider" motion again.)

Grandmother

Here are grandmother's glasses,
  (Circle thumb and finger, each hand, over eyes.)
Here is grandmother's hat.
  (Fingertips together on head.)

This is the way she folds her hands
And puts them in her lap.

Ready for Bed

This little boy is ready for bed.
  (Hold up forefinger.)
Down on the pillow he lays his head.
  (Place finger in palm of opposite hand.)
Covers himself all up tight.
  (Fold fingers over forefinger.)
Falls fast asleep for the night.
  (Cock head toward shoulder, close eyes.)
Morning comes, he opens his eyes,
  (Quickly lift head, open eyes.)
Throws back the covers with great surprise,
  (Open palm to uncover forefinger.)
Up he jumps and gets all dressed.
  (Quickly raise forefinger off palm.)
To hurry to school to play with the rest.
  (Move finger off to the side.)

Five Little Soldiers

Five little soldiers standing in a row
Three stood straight and two stood so,
Along came the captain, and what do you think
They all stood up straight just as quick as a wink.

Five Little Pumpkins

Five little pumpkins sitting on a gate.
The first one said, "My it's getting late!"
The second one said, "There are witches in the air."
The third one said, "But we don't care."
The fourth one said, "Let's run, let's run!"
The fifth one said, "Isn't Halloween fun?"
"Woo-oo-oo" went the wind, out went the light.
Those five little pumpkins ran fast out of sight.

Poems Counteracting Sex Stereotyping

Books that might be provided are

What Can She Be? A Veterinarian? by Gloria and Esther
  Goldreich.

What Can She Be? A Lawyer? by Gloria and Esther Goldreich.
What Can She Be? A Farmer? by Gloria and Esther Goldreich.
What Can She Be? A Police Officer? by Gloria and Esther Goldreich.
What Can She Be? A Musician? by Gloria and Esther Goldreich.
Challenge to Become a Doctor: The Story of Elizabeth Blackwell by Leah Lurie Heyn.
Johnny Learns to Type by Mabel Crain.
William's Doll by Charlotte Zolotow.
Henry Reed's Baby-Sitting Service by Keith Robertson.

Poems Counteracting Racial Stereotyping

The following books, which depict Blacks in a positive way and reflect the social and cultural traditions that are part of being Black and American, are recommended.

Evan's Corner, by Elizabeth Starr Hill.
What Mary Jo Shared, by Janice M. Udry.
The Snowy Day, Whistle for Willie, and *Peter's Chair* by Ezra Jack Keats.
Hooray for Jasper, by Betty Horvath.
Cornrows, by Camille Yarbrough.
The Lucky Stone, by Lucille Clifton.
Mr. Kelso's Lion, by Arna Bontemps.
Fly, Jimmy, Fly, by Walter Dean Myers.
Stevie, by John Steptoe.
The Hundred Penny Box, by Sharon Bell Mathis.
Ben's Trumpet, by Rachel Isadora.
Song of the Empty Bottles, by Osmond Molarsky.
A Quiet Place, by Rose Blue.

Books That Deal with Old Age and Death in a Sensitive Way

Grandmother Told Me, by Jan Wahl.
Could Be Worse, by James Stevenson.
Grandpa and Me, by Patricia Lee Gauch.
The Sneaky Machine, by Marguerita Rudolph.
A Little at a Time, by David A. Adler.
Watch Out for Chicken Feet in Your Soup, by Tomie de Paola.

Bibliotherapy Suggestions

Tuck Everlasting, by Natalie Babbitt.
The Pinballs, by Betsy Byars.
My Brother Stevie, by Eleanor Cymer.
The Cat Ate My Gymsuit, by Paula Danziger.
Harriet the Spy, by Louise Fitzhugh.
Island of the Blue Dolphins, by Scott O'Dell.
The Great Gilly Hopkins, by Katherine Paterson.

Poems to Develop Empathy for the Handicapped

He's My Brother, by Joe Lasker.
Kelly's Creek, by Doris Buchanan Smith.
Me and Einstein: Breaking Through the Reading Barrier, by Rose Blue.
Home Is Where Your Feet Are Standing, by Patricia Windsor.
Do Bananas Chew Gum? by Jamie Gilson.
"Inviting Jason" in *Altogether One at a Time*, by E. L. Konigsburg.

As suggested in Chapter 8, the following books are useful for developing empathy for cognitively disabled children:

Summer of the Swans, by Betsy Byars.
Welcome Home, Jellybean, by Marlene Fanta Shyer.
The Alfred Summer, by Jan Slepian.
The Hayburners, by Gene Smith.

As noted in Chapter 8, Radencich (1985) suggests the following books for promoting positive attitudes toward children for whom English is a second language:

The Christmas Cookie Tree, by Ruth Irion.
Candita's Choice, by Mina Lewiton.
I Am Here Yo Estoy Aqui, by Rose Blue.
A Feast of Light, by Gunhilla Norris.
The Shy One, by Dorothy Nathan.
El Gran Cesar, by Jesse Ruiz.
Maria Luisa and *Call Me Danica*, by Winifred Madison.
Lupita Mañana, by Patricia Beatty.

Poems Related to Curriculum Content

Post Office

A Letter Is a Gypsy Elf

A letter is a gypsy elf
It goes where I would go myself;
East or West or North it goes;
Or South, past pretty bungalows,
Over mountain, over hill,
Any place it must and will,
It finds good friends that live so far
You cannot travel where they are.

Annette Wynne

Science

Clouds

Over the hill the clouds race by
Playing tag in a blue, blue sky;
Some are fat and some are thin.
And one cloud has a double chin.
One is a girl with a turned up nose
And one wears slippers with pointed toes;
There's a puppy dog too, with a bumpity tail,
And a farmer boy with his milking pail.

Sometimes they jumble all in a mass
And get tangled up with others that pass.
And over the hill they go racing by
Playing tag in a blue, blue sky.

Helen Wing

Cloud Names

Cumulus clouds
Drift over the sky,
Fluffy as soapsuds
Billowing by.

Along the horizon
In layers of light

The stratus clouds glow
In the sunset bright.

Cirrus clouds hang
So loosely together
Their cottony film
Means a change of weather.

Nimbus clouds threaten
With blackness of storm
Shut the door, light the fire
Be cozy and warm.

Los Angeles City Schools

Arithmetic

Counting

Today I'll remember forever and ever
Because I can count to ten.
It isn't an accident any more either,
I've done it over and over again.

I used to leave out five and three
And sometimes eight and four;
And once in a while I'd mix up nine
As seven or two, but not any more.

I count my fingers on one hand first,
And this little pig is one,
And when old thumb goes off to market
That's fine, and one of my hands is done.

So when I open my other hand
And start in counting again
From pick up sticks to big fat hen,
Five, six, seven, eight, nine and ten.

Harry Behn

The effect of reading a poem like *I Wish* by Nancy Byrd Turner or *A Mortifying Mistake* by Maria Pratt after a dull arithmetic period will justify all your efforts to create a poetry file.

A Mortifying Mistake

I studied my tables over and over,
  and backward and forward, too;
But I couldn't remember six times nine,
  and I didn't know what to do,
Till sister told me to play with my doll,
  and not to bother my head.
"If you call her 'Fifty-four' for a while,
  you'll learn it by heart," she said.

So I took my favorite, Mary Ann
  (though I thought 'twas a dreadful shame
To give such a perfectly lovely child
  such a perfectly horrid name),
And I called her my dear little "fifty-four"
  a hundred times, till I knew
The answer of six times nine as well as
  the answer of two times two.

Next day Elizabeth Wigglesworth,
  who always acts so proud,
Said "Six times nine is fifty-two,"
  and I nearly laughed aloud!
But I wished I hadn't when teacher said,
  "Now Dorothy, tell if you can."
For I thought of my doll—and sakes alive!
  —I answered, "Mary Ann!"

Maria Pratt

Cultural Examples

Senegalase

Forefathers

Listen more often to things rather than beings.
Hear the fire's voice,
Hear the voice of water,
In the wind hear the sobbing of the trees,
It is our forefathers breathing.

The dead are not gone forever.
They are in the paling shadows
And in the darkening shadows.
The dead are not beneath the ground,

They are in the rustling tree,
In the murmuring woods,
In the still water,
In the flowing water,
In the lonely place, in the crowd;
The dead are not dead.

Listen more often to things rather than beings.
Hear the fire's voice.
Hear the voice of water.
In the wind hear the sobbing of the trees.
It is the breathing of our forefathers
Who are not gone, not beneath the ground,
Not dead.

Author unknown

Korean

Song of Five Friends

How many friends have I? Count them.
Water and stone, pine and bamboo—
The rising moon on the east mountain,
Welcome, it too is my friend.
What need is there, I say,
To have more friends than five?

They say clouds are fine; I mean the color.
But, alas, they often darken.
They say winds are clear; I mean the sound.
But, alas, they often cease to blow.
It is only the water, then,
That is perpetual and good.

Why do flowers fade so soon
Once they are in their glory?
Why do grasses yellow so soon
Once they have grown tall?
Perhaps it is the stone, then,
That is constant and good.

Flowers bloom when it is warm;
Leaves fall when days are cool.
But O pine, how is it
That you scorn frost, ignore snow?
I know now your towering self,
Straight even among the Nine Springs.

You're not a tree, no,
Nor a plant, not even that.
Who let you shoot so straight;
What makes you empty within?
You are green in all seasons,
Welcome, bamboo, my friend.

Small but floating high,
You shed light on all creation.
And what can match your brightness
In the coal dark of the night?
You look at me but with no words:
That's why, O moon, you are my friend.

Author unknown

Choral Reading Program Sample

The following poems, lessons, and activities are samples of an excellent choral reading program that has been designed to aid teachers in developing the language of all learners. The program was written by Maurice Poe and Barbara Schmidt and published and reprinted here with the permission of Curriculum Associates, Inc., 800 Worcester Rd., Wellesley, Massachusetts 02181. Included here are two choral readings that can be read together with your students. The final selection is a choral reading lesson which provides excellent examples of the integrated language arts.

Bocca-Wacca-Wattamus

They took Ryan O'Brien to breakfast
  and asked what he wanted to eat.
His mother looked very nervous
  as he wiggled around in his seat.
    "I want bocca-wacca-wattamus and salamander stew,
      Riggle-raggle ragamuffins, rutabagas, too.
      I want diffy-daffy dandelions and then, for my dessert,
      a dish of loony lingaberries smothered with fried dirt."

    "Ryan!" squealed his mother.
    "Wow!" said his sister.
    "Yuck!" said his brother.
    "We're all out," said the waiter.

They took Ryan O'Brien to lunch
  at the best restaurant in the town.
His mother looked very nervous
  as the family began to sit down.

    "I want bocca-wacca-wattamus and salamander stew,
      Riggle-raggle ragamuffins, rutabagas, too.
      I want diffy-daffy dandelions and then, for my dessert,
      a dish of loony lingaberries smothered with fried dirt."

    "Ryan!" squealed his mother.
    "Wow!" said his sister.
    "Yuck!" said his brother.
    "Not in season," said the waitress.

They took Ryan O'Brien to dinner
  "And what will you have today?"
His mother looked very nervous
  As Ryan began to say,

    "I want bocca-wacca-wattamus and salamander stew,
      Riggle-raggle ragamuffins, rutabagas, too.
      I want diffy-daffy dandelions and then, for my dessert,
      a dish of loony lingaberries smothered with fried dirt."

    "Ryan!" squealed his mother.
    "Wow!" said his sister.
    "Yuck!" said his brother.
    "Medium or rare?" said the waiter.

Barbara Schmidt

Have You Met . . . Katy Cassandra Kadidilly Klup???

I-OPENER: Make a picture in your head of the way your bedroom looks when it's a real mess! List five things that make it messy.

(CHORUS)
Katy Cassandra
Ka-di-dilly Klup
Would never ever
Pick things up.

She'd toss her things
Into the air.
And where they landed
She didn't care.

She'd throw her clothes
Down on the floor
And under a bed
Or over a door.

    AND. . .
(CHORUS)
Katy Cassandra
Ka-di-dilly Klup
Would never ever
Pick things up.

Her room was filled
From bottom to top
With papers and books
And bottles of pop.

T-shirts and sneakers
Were piled in a mound;
Games and stuffed animals
Lay all around.
    AND . . .
(CHORUS)
Katy Cassandra
Ka-di-dilly Klup
Would never ever
Pick things up.

No one has seen Katy
Since way back last May.
Somebody told someone
That she moved away.

But I'm not so sure
And here is my guess . . .
Katy is buried somewhere
In that mess!
    ALL BECAUSE . . .
(CHORUS)
Katy Cassandra
Ka-di-dilly Klup
Would never ever
Pick things up.

Sample Lesson for "Poor Old Lady"

Teacher Guide

Students will:

—participate in practicing predicting skills.
—enjoy and identify the nonsense in the poem.
—extend vocabulary.
—participate in story theater dramatization.
—identify the sequence of events in the poem.
—reinforce the concept of comparative size.

Materials: Student book
                Yarn and name tag cards
Preparation: Print the names of the eight characters in the poem on the
                name tags. String name tags with yarn.

Prereading Warm-Up

Teacher:

Imagine that you are going to take a big bite of your very most favorite food. What would that food be? Mine would be . . . (Teacher shares his or her favorite and elicits favorites from students. Teacher writes their responses on the chalkboard.)

Show me how you would look chewing and swallowing that food. Now, imagine that you are about to swallow something bigger! Maybe something as big as a cow or a horse. How would that look? Do you think anyone could really swallow something that large in one gulp? Well, look who's visiting our class today . . . a poor old lady with a tremendous appetite. She starts out with a fly, but she gets hungrier and hungrier.

Find the poem in your rhyme-along book. Find the picture of the cat. Now find the picture of the spider . . . (Teacher focuses student attention on the various pictured characters.)

As I read this poem about this silly old lady, see whether you can point to each of the things she swallows as I read.

Sharing the Poem

First, teacher reads the poem aloud. Teacher asks students to point to the appropriate characters as they follow along. Then, the poem is read aloud a second time with the students' joining in. Teacher again asks students to point to the appropriate characters as they read together.

Poor Old Lady

Poor old lady, she swallowed a fly.
I don't know why she swallowed a fly.
Poor old lady, I think she'll die.

Poor old lady, she swallowed a spider.
It squirmed and wriggled and turned inside her.
She swallowed the spider to catch the fly.
I don't know why she swallowed a fly.
Poor old lady, I think she'll die.

Poor old lady, she swallowed a bird.
How absurd! She swallowed a bird.
She swallowed the bird to catch the spider,
She swallowed the spider to catch the fly.
I don't know why she swallowed a fly.
Poor old lady, I think she'll die.

Poor old lady, she swallowed a cat.
Think of that! She swallowed a cat.
She swallowed the cat to catch the bird,
She swallowed the bird to catch the spider,
She swallowed the spider to catch the fly.
I don't know why she swallowed a fly.
Poor old lady, I think she'll die.

Poor old lady, she swallowed a dog.
She went the whole hog when she swallowed the dog.
She swallowed the dog to catch the cat,
She swallowed the cat to catch the bird,
She swallowed the bird to catch the spider,
She swallowed the spider to catch the fly.
I don't know why she swallowed a fly.
Poor old lady, I think she'll die.

Poor old lady, she swallowed a cow.
I don't know how she swallowed a cow.
She swallowed the cow to catch the dog,
She swallowed the dog to catch the cat,
She swallowed the cat to catch the bird,
She swallowed the bird to catch the spider,
She swallowed the spider to catch the fly.
I don't know why she swallowed a fly.
Poor old lady, I think she'll die.

Poor old lady, she swallowed a horse.
She died, of course.

TEACHER:

I bet that poor old lady had an awful stomachache. Can you remember all the things she ate? Tell me the first thing . . . the second . . . (Teacher elicits sequence. He or she writes the answers on the chalkboard as the students respond.)

Now tell me the largest thing she ate. And which is the smallest? (Teacher again writes student responses on the chalkboard.)

How many parts/sections does the poem have? (Teacher should explain that the white spaces divide the parts of the poem.)

Let's divide into seven groups: flies, spiders, birds, cats, dogs, cows, and horses. When we get to the part of the poem that matches your picture, your group will read. (Teacher divides the class into groups and leads them in a group reading.)

Putting Ideas to Work

TEACHER:

What good expression you've been putting in your voices to read this sad story! This seems like a good poem to share with another class so let's turn it into a play. Our play will have seven readers and eight actor-outers. Everyone will get a turn. Here are some name tags for the characters in our play.

A name tag strung with yarn is placed around the neck of each performer. Name tags identify "old lady," "spider," "fly," and so on.

Teacher should encourage "narrators" to read their parts dramatically. As the performers pantomime the action, they are encouraged to exaggerate their actions. The "old lady" may be wearing an old sheet that grows bigger and bigger as each mouthful is swallowed.

For a variation on the story theater, students create paper headdresses representing the characters for their dramatization (cow horns, dog ears, fly antennae and wings, and so forth).

Extending Language and Thinking

This poem lends itself to direct instruction on *-ed* endings, with a discussion on how words change to indicate something that has already happened. Write *swallow* in one column on the chalkboard and *swallowed* in a second column. Ask students to suggest sentences using each word and write their sentences in the appropriate columns on the chalkboard. Then compare the sentences, emphasizing the element of time.

Have students identify the words in the selection that mean *to move* (*squirmed, wriggled, turned*) and those that mean *to eat* (*chewing, biting, swallowing*). Draw two columns on the chalkboard, one with the heading *to move* and the other with the heading *to eat*. Write the appropriate words in the columns. When the columns are complete, ask the students to make up sentences using words from the *to move* and *to eat* categories. Then ask some students to read their sentences aloud and to write these sentences on the chalkboard.

Strengthening Language for Second-Language Learners

Ask students to draw a picture of their favorite animal. The picture can be labeled with the animal's name in the student's native language and in English. Students can tell one thing they know about their animal as they share their pictures with others.

Ask students to cut out, trace, or copy pictures of animals from magazines, animal books, and so on. Play a "name-the-animal" game to determine their

knowledge of animal names in English. (Teacher holds up each of the students' pictures for identification and response.)

Print the names of animals on cards. Students can match the names with the pictures in subsequent exercises. (Using yarn, the words can be matched to the pictures on a bulletin board.)

Across the Curriculum

ART

Ask students to trace or copy animals illustrated in the text. They then color, cut out, and paste the animal to an ice cream stick. The stick puppets can be used with future choral readings and dramatizations of the poem.

CREATIVE WRITING

Students can use their own words and ideas to complete "I don't know why . . ." statements. Encourage them to write several lines and emphasize that the lines *do not have to rhyme*.

SCIENCE

Ask students to identify all the animals in this poem. List the animals on the chalkboard. Invite students to suggest the names of other animals to add to the list. Once the list has ten to fifteen animals, copy the names of the animals on cards. Ask a student to select an animal from the stack of cards. Members of the class ask questions of the card holder (Does your animal fly? Does it eat hay? Does it live in the mountains?). The person correctly identifying the animal is allowed to select a card from the stack and the game continues.

SOCIAL STUDIES

To develop the concept of cause and effect, explain to students that for every *action* there is a *reaction*. When you get thirsty, what do you do? (Drink water.) In the poem there are several examples of *cause and effect relationships*. Take the students through these relationships by asking, "Why did she swallow the spider?" (to catch the fly), "the bird?" (to catch the spider), and so on.

Word Origin Resource Books

ADELSON, L. (1972). *Dandelions Don't Bite*. New York: Pantheon Books.

EPSTEIN, S. & B. EPSTEIN. (1954). *The First Book of Words*. New York: Franklin Watts.

ERNST, M. (1954). *Words*. New York: Knopf.

FUNK, C. E. (1955). *Heavens to Betsy*. New York: Harper & Row.

——— (1950). *Thereby Hangs a Tale*. New York: Harper & Row.

GARRISON, W. B. (1950). *Why You Say It*. Nashville: Abingdon.

LAIRD, H. & C. LAIRD. (1957). *Tree of Language*. Cleveland: World.

Books for Children: Word Books and Books of Word Origins

ALEXANDER, A. (1962). *The Magic of Words*. Englewood Cliffs, N.J.: Prentice-Hall.

BRANDRETH, G. (1980). *The Joy of Lex*. New York: William Morrow.

CHRIST, H. I. (1963). *Winning Words*. Boston: D. C. Heath.

DALY, K. N. (1982). *The Macmillan Picture Wordbook*. New York: Macmillan.

FUNK, C. E. *A Hog on Ice and Other Curious Expressions*.

FUNK, C. E. *Thereby Hangs a Tale: Stories of Curious Word Origins*.

FUNK, C. E. *Heavens to Betsy! and Other Curious Sayings*.

FUNK, C. E. & C. E. FUNK, JR. (1958). *Horsefeathers and Other Curious Words*. New York: Harper & Row.

HOBAN, T. (1981). *More than One*. New York: Greenwillow Books.

———. (1973). *Over, Under, and Through and Other Spatial Concepts*. New York: Macmillan.

HYMES, L. & J. HYMES, JR. (1964). *Oodles of Noodles and Other Hymes' Rhymes*. New York: Young Scott Books.

LIONNI, L. (1968). *The Alphabet Tree*. New York: Pantheon.

LONGMAN, H. (1968). *Would You Put Your Money in a Sand Bank?* Chicago: Rand McNally.

McLENIGHAN, V. (1982). *Stop-Go, Fast-Slow*. Chicago: Children's Press.

MERRIAM, E. (1960). *A Gaggle of Geese*. New York: Knopf.

ROSSNER, J. (1963). *What Kind of Feet Does a Bear Have?* Indianapolis: Bobbs-Merrill.

SAXON, G. (1964). *Secrets in Animal Names*. Englewood Cliffs, N.J.: Prentice-Hall.

SCARRY, R. (1980). *Richard Scarry's Best Word Book Ever*. New York: Golden Press.

WILBUR, R. (1973). *Opposites*. New York: Harcourt Brace Jovanovich.

Appendix B

Language Arts Games and Activities

Dictionary Games and Activities

Although the dictionary is usually not introduced for the student's use until fourth grade, there are several good practices that will familiarize the students with dictionary procedure prior to the fourth year of school.

1. In the second and third grades children should be encouraged to keep their own file of words they have learned in reading. A brightly painted shoe box makes an excellent file of this sort. Each divider cut from cardboard should be labeled with a letter of the alphabet in both small letters and capitals. Children write the words they want to keep on file on cards or construction paper, or they find words in magazines to cut out and paste on the cards. Then the words are filed behind the proper letter of the alphabet.

2. Another device is to make picture dictionaries for either individual or class use. Children choose a big scrapbook, label the pages with each letter of the alphabet, and write the words on the scrapbook pages, complete with accompanying pictures.

After the dictionary is introduced in either the third or fourth grade, the following exercise may be used to facilitate its use:

1. A dictionary is placed on the first desk of each row. The teacher writes any ten words on the board. At a given signal, the first pupil in each row looks up the first word. When he finds it, he jots down the page number and passes the dictionary to the person behind him, who does the same for the second word, and so on. The first row finished is the winner. If a mistake is made in a page number, the second row finished is the winner.

2. The same game is played with definitions or pronunciations.

3. The same game may be played with names of mythological characters.

4. Each student brings to class a sentence containing a difficult word. A dictionary is placed on each student's desk and the class is divided into two teams. A pupil reads his sentences and states the word he wants defined. The opposing team is given approximately half a minute to look up the word in the dictionary. At a signal from the teacher, dictionaries are closed and the one who presented the sentence calls a pupil from the opposing team to define the word. If the pupil misses, he is eliminated and another is called. The game is continued until all of one team has been eliminated.

Worksheets like the following are sometimes used to practice dictionary skills:

Worksheet Activities

Worksheet activities are individual projects. Each individual has a dictionary, paper, pencil. Questions for the contest have been put on the board and covered with a map or newspaper.

1. *Omitted letters:* What letter or letters if any have been omitted?

   pro _ _ dure   picni _ _ ing
   dorm _ tory   hosp _ _ able
   vac _ um   cartil _ age
   super _ ede   indel _ ble
   reform _ tory   privil _ ge

2. *Plurals:* Give the plurals of

alumnus	stratum
bandit	court-martial
basis	bacillus
index	teaspoon
mother-in-law	spoonful

3. *Alphabetical order:* Write in alphabetical order

Denver	St. Louis
Milwaukee	Chicago
Nashville	San Francisco
New York	St. Paul
New Orleans	Los Angeles
Miami	Seattle
Warren	Bloomington

4. *Comparative and superlative:* Give the comparative and superlative degrees of *silly, polite, tidy, wet, sad, old, good, little, many.*

5. *Prefix:* The children find the meaning of the following prefixes or bound morphemes, then write words that use them. Example: prefix *re-* means "again," "back," or "down" (*retreat, return, relate*).

   Use these prefixes: *re-, in-, sub-, ex-, inter-, intra-, de-, con-, pre-, dis-, ante-, bi-, contra-, extra-, post-, trans-, dia-, hemi-, semi-, demi-, poly-, peri-, syn-, mis-, pro-, over-, be-, un-, mal-, ultra-, super-, medi-, tri-.*

6. *Words of all nations:* The following English words have been adapted or borrowed from other languages. Look up the word and list the country from which it comes.

ski	canoe	fiesta
coffee	circus	rodeo
kimono	sky	assembly
sonata	radio	waltz
garage	dachshund	cafeteria
kindergarten	piano	sauerkraut
tobacco	menu	ranch

7. *Where are they found?* After each word in the following, write on the blank line the place where each is found; that is, in the air, on the land, or in water.

   1. sturgeon _____
   2. tripod _____
   3. amoeba _____
   4. dromedary _____
   5. octopus _____
   6. linnet _____
   7. prawn _____
   8. eglantine _____
   9. oracle _____
   10. obelisk _____

8. *Who uses what?* In this group a word is given, such as *plane.* Opposite the word is listed the worker or profession, such as *lawyer, carpenter, taxi driver.* You are to underline the one who uses the tool or item named. In the example it is the *carpenter* who uses the *plane* in his work.

1. splice	aviator, tea taster, sailor
2. snaffle	jockey, Marine, auctioneer
3. palette	miner, artist, keypunch operator
4. girder	knight, builder, gardener

5. font   minister, librarian, horticulturist

6. harpsichord   undertaker, druggist, musician

7. foil   teacher, fencer, cyclist

8. awl   cobbler, grocer, sculptor

9. pestle   judge, jeweler, druggist

10. creel   student, angler, mail carrier

9. *Alphabetizing*

bewitch	sum	understood
suspect	wag	pedal
hog	task	tank
custom	hook	tan
summer	cartridge	penny
cattle	simmer	understand
real	offend	plea
home	peanut	suit
cult	under	wall
sit	please	plot
boiler	reach	underneath
scrape	you	pleasure
cart	piano	wander

10. *Synonyms:* A *synonym* is a word that has the same meaning as another word. Write a synonym for each of the following:

craven	aspect
lucid	wrath
irksome	adept
fickle	soothe
robust	rebuke

11. *Abbreviations:* Write down the meanings of the following abbreviations:

bbls.	A.D.	bldg.	no.	dept.
cong.	gal.	Rev.	St.	vol.
P.M.	doz.	ans.	Capt.	S.W.
inc.	Gen.	Hon.	Gov.	riv.
P.O.	M.D.	R.F.D.	B.C.	pp.
supt.	Y.M.C.A.	mfg.	wk.	U.S.N.

R.R.	P.S.	etc.	i.e.	S.S.
A.M.	vs.	O.K.	Pvt.	viz.
D.D.	Fem.	adv.	Apr.	I.O.U.

12. *Syllabication:* Words divided at the ends of lines in printing, typing, and handwriting should be divided between syllables. Copy from your dictionary the following words, showing their proper division into syllables. Spell them correctly and omit the diacritical marks.

nicety	miraculous	geranium
phraseology	locomotive	European
suburban	statistics	democracy
burglar	originate	armistice
comparable	dirigible	finale
lamentable	heroine	despicable
seizure	syllable	

13. *Identification exercises*

a. Tell whether the following are bird, fish, or tree:

tanager, barnacle, almond, vulture, cardinal, anchovy, gannet, yew, warbler, verio, sumac, toucan, acacia, tarpon, avocado, sucker, bittern, cinnamon, sycamore, sole, chestnut, ebony, starling, rock, auk, flicker

b. Tell whether the following are flower, animal, or vegetable:

anemone, gherkin, hyena, syringa, kohlrabi, yak, gibbon, jasmine, mammoth, gentian, okra, lemur, rhubarb, poinsettia, arbutus, sloth, puma

c. Tell who uses the following:

trowel, platinum, rifle, scissors, snaffle, kilt, accordion, adze, splice, anvil, kayak, davits, lute, calumet, palette, mosque, girder, auger, font, percolator, brig, puck, discus, strop, calk, doily, epaulet, hoop, canister, creel, awl, scepter, lasso, mangle, metronome, easel

d. Tell where the following are found:

> sturgeon, autogiro, bison, tripod, cobra, weevil, amoeba, dromedary, chalet, brougham, veranda, dolphin, constellation, corral, caisson, cheetah, squid, sloop, mollusk, phoebe, ketch, manatee, osprey, obelisk, ferret, coot, ermine, merganser, scrole, elevator, eglantine, phaeton, grebe

14. *Matching:* Match the ending in the right-hand column with the correct beginning in the left-hand column, and write it in the blank space:

acci	ize	_____
sever	fy	_____
special	ance	_____
tick	pose	_____
uni	dox	_____
veri	dent	_____
trans	et	_____
wheth	fy	_____
para	er	_____

15. *Homonyms:* In our language we have a number of words that are pronounced alike but that have different meanings. The words *to, too, two* are homonyms. Try to find a homonym for each of the following and write it on the line after the word given:

bear _____	days _____	ball _____
pair _____	there _____	sun _____
him _____	whole _____	be _____
way _____	tacked _____	rode _____
ewe _____	right _____	air _____
feet _____	meet _____	sea _____
here _____	blue _____	sew _____
peace _____	our _____	cent _____
ate _____	rain _____	deer _____
would _____	won _____	steak _____

16. *Word analysis:* Use a dictionary to do these exercises. Write the words in the blanks provided.

Find a word beginning with the indicated prefix and having the indicated meaning.

Prefix	Definition	Word
ab-	to take a person away by force	_____
ab-	to go away hurriedly and secretly	_____
ab-	to free a person from debt or a duty	_____
ad-	to stick fast	_____
ad-	to be next to	_____
ad-	to warn	_____
ad-	to move forward	_____
ad-	to give notice of something	_____
anti-	to be against society	_____
anti-	a remedy that prevents poison from taking effect	_____

The following exercise is done in the same manner as the preceding one.

Prefix	Definition	Word
com-	to fight with someone	_____
com-	to speak of something with approval	_____
com-	to find fault with something	_____
com-	to mix with	_____
de-	to keep from entering	_____
de-	to grow less in size	_____
de-	to protect from danger	_____
dis-	to not be honest	_____
post-	afternoon	_____

Spelling Games and Activities

Games for Primary Grades

1. *Puzzle Elements:*
   a. I am in *see, sing,* and *say.* What sound am I?
   b. I am in *took,* but I am in *look.* I am __.
   c. *Baby, book, ball.* The *b* is at the __.

2. *Making New Words by Changing a Vowel:*

pen	pot	bat	cat	bug	for	ham
pan	pat	bet	cot	big	fur	hum
pin	pit	bit	cut	beg	far	him
pun	pet	but		bag	fir	
	put					

3. *Writing Alliterative Sentences:*

> Bob bought big blue balloons.

This might be a team affair with two or three working together to produce the sentence. Older children like to make advertising slogans:

> Peter Piper's purple pepper pot, please!
> Can Charlie's canaries comfort Charlie's comrades?

4. *Treasure Box:* Words are written on separate slips of paper that are then folded and put into a box called the treasure box. Each child in turn draws out a slip, which he hands to the teacher without opening. The teacher pronounces the word and the child attempts to spell it. Any misspelled words are handed back to the children who had difficulty with them. The object is for the pupil to end the game with no slips of paper. Those who do have slips learn to spell the words that are on them. This exercise can be performed by two children in a quiet corner.

5. *Turn Up Letters:* The players are seated at a table. Before them on the table face down are a number of alphabet cards. The players decide on some category for the game—animals, birds, cities, flowers, and so on. Then each player in turn picks up a card and exhibits the letter. The first child to write a word beginning with that letter, belonging to the category decided on and spelled correctly, gets the card. The spelling of the word may be challenged. If it is incorrect, the challenger gets the card. When all the cards have been turned up, the player having the most cards wins.

6. *Alphabet Jumble:* Two sets of the alphabet are placed in a long chalk tray. Two children compete to see which one can be first to arrange one set in correct alphabetical order.

7. *Find It:* Words are listed on the chalkboard. The teacher or a student gives the definition of the word and the children in turn spell the word defined.

8. *Hear It:* The words are listed on the board. The leader says, "I am thinking of a word that starts with the same sound as one hears at the beginning of ____" or "one that rhymes with ____." The children write the words indicated and gain a point for their own score for each correct selection.

9. *Guess and Spell:* "It" selects an object that is in plain sight in the room. The other children start guessing the first letter of that object. When the first letter is guessed, they start working on the second, then the third, until the word is spelled. The correct letters may be put on the chalkboard as they are spelled by the one who is "it." When any student thinks that he may be able to spell the total word after the first few letters have been guessed, he may challenge the leader and complete the word. He then becomes "it."

10. *Novelty Spelling:* Instead of calling words from a spelling list, the teacher asks questions such as "Can you spell a word that rhymes with *joint*?" "Can you spell a word contining *ph* which sounds like *f*?" "Can you spell a word that means ____?" Ask members of the class in turn to read their lists. The variety adds interest and influences vocabulary.

11. *Chalkboard Spelling:* Primary-grade children feel that it is a privilege to write on the chalkboard. Reserve a place at the board where a child may go during his free time just as he might go to the library corner. Put a different exercise on the board for each child, such as:

What children in our room have names that start with *B*?

What do you want for Christmas?

What do you like to eat?

Where would you like to visit?

How many words do you know that start with *wh*?

12. *Use the Word:* The words of the spelling lesson are placed on the board and left during the day. Each time one of the words is used in a child's writing during the day counts one point for his side. This can be row-against-row competition. The word does not count unless the one who writes it reports it for the count.

13. *Pear Tree:* How many pear (pair) trees can you develop with your class? Synonyms and antonyms? But how about such pears (pairs) as *horse, colt; cow, calf*? Or *hands, gloves; feet, shoes*? Or *swimming, swimmer; archer, archery*? Divide your class into committees to develop these trees. Each committee draws a large tree and puts pairs of words on yellow or light green pears. Add leaves for effect.

Games for Upper Grades

1. *Dictionary Games:* One child opens the dictionary at random, saying, "I have opened the dictionary to an *sp-* page." Each child then writes as many words starting with *sp-* as he can. Two teams may compete, each child in turn adding a word. To prevent careless or poor writing, each team may have a "recorder" who writes the words suggested by the team. Have three to five on a team. The winning team may be challenged by another team.

2. *Memory Game:* Several picture cards, each portraying a single object, are shown to pupils (or they may be the objects themselves). The pictures or objects are then concealed and the children are asked to write the names of all the objects they remember. To vary this game, expose a list of words and then ask pupils to write as many as they can recall. It is more difficult if the words must be written in alphabetical order. For some children a test of listening is valuable. Start by asking them to listen to three words, then write them. Keep increasing the number of words.

3. *Baseball:* One form uses word cards and is especially good for practice on words frequently misspelled. Each card contains a word; a value such as one base hit, home run, and so on; and the position of the player who is to catch the ball if it is misspelled. The cards would look like this:

all right 2-base hit 3rd baseman	separate home run pitcher	February 3-base hit right field

Sometimes children take positions in the classroom as if it were a baseball diamond. It is equally interesting to use a chalkboard diagram with players remaining at their seats while the team captain indicates their movement on the diagram.

In another form, four diamonds are drawn on the chalkboard. The first member of the team at bat goes to the first diamond. The first word is given by the pitcher. The pitcher may be the teacher or a member of the opposing team. The child at the board writes the word. Those at their seats write the word for practice. If the word is spelled successfully by the batter, he moves to the second diamond (first base), and a new player goes to the first diamond. Again the teacher pronounces a word to be spelled. Both players at the board write the word. If both spell the word correctly, each player moves to another diamond and a third player goes to the first diamond. If either player misspells the word, he is out. Thus it is possible for two or more players to be put out by one word. When a player advances through all four diamonds, a score is made for the team he represents.

4. *The Maiden and the Dragon:* At one chalkboard area a "maiden" is drawn, tied to a rock by five

ropes. On the other side a dragon is drawn, facing five waves. (Flannelboard figures make this easier.)

One group represents the maiden, the other the dragon. The waves are protecting the maiden from the dragon. The game proceeds in the manner of a traditional spelldown. Each time a member of the team of the maiden misspells a word, one of the waves is erased. Each time a member of the team of the dragon misspells a word, one of the maiden's ropes is cut. If all the waves are erased first, the dragon is released to devour the maiden. But, if all the maiden's ropes are cut first, the maiden is freed and the dragon dies. Suspense develops although no player leaves the game.

5. *Roots and Branches:* This game is intended to develop awareness of parts of words. Make four cards for each of several root words, for example, *march, marched, marching, marcher; fear, feared, fearing, fearful;* and so on.

   Make enough copies of each set of words for four "books." Shuffle the cards and deal six cards at a time to each player. Players sort their cards as in playing "Authors." If a player holds four cards of words from the same root, he can make a book. Each player in turn may call for a card by naming the card he holds and may continue to call as long as other players hold wanted cards. When there are no more available cards of the kind he calls, he discards, and the next player takes his turn. The objective is to get as many books as possible. Care should be taken in preparing the cards for this game not to introduce different elements too fast for slow readers, for example, doubling the final consonant of a root or changing the sound, as *lose* and *lost.*

6. *Word Addition:* To facilitate the use of word endings and prefixes, words are listed on the board. Each child uses that list of words to see how many new words can be made by adding beginnings and endings. Plural forms and *-ing, -er, -ed, -r, pre-,* and *im-* may be used. Words that may be used are *run, occupy, view, prove, write, large, build, hear, stand, call, part, play.*

7. *Ghost:* One child starts with a letter that is also a word, as *I* or *a*. The next child adds another letter to make still another word, as *in.* The next child might spell *tin,* the next *into.* The letters may be rearranged, but each previous letter must be included and just one letter added. The child who cannot make a new word in this way is a "ghost," the object of the game being to avoid becoming one. This is a good game for a large number of players.

8. *Spelling Jingles:* When the children come across a new word, they can help establish its spelling in their minds by writing jingles using the word in rhyme. The children enjoy composing the jingles and, at the same time, learn to spell the new word and other similar words.

Night	*Rain*
When it is night.	I know it will rain,
We need a light.	My toe is in pain.

9. *What's My Word?* Each child has a different word. One stands in front of the group. Each student in turn may ask one question, then spell the word he thinks is the word of the one in front. The questions may concern the meaning, the beginning sound, a rhyming word, or the word root. The student who identifies the word takes the leader's position.

10. *Travel:* Ticket salespeople are appointed for various points, such as "airplane ride to New York," "bus ride to Los Angeles," and so on. Each has a group of words. Students in turn apply for tickets and are given them after spelling all the words on the salesperson's list. A variation might be a county fair or a circus, with the ticket admitting the speller to special events.

11. *Smoked Bacon:* Make two or more sets of cardboard letters with the letters of *smoked bacon.* Teams face each other with each child holding one letter. The teacher calls out a word that can be spelled by these letters. The first team to get in correct positions gets a point. These letters form at least a hundred words.

    This can be a chalkboard game. Write *smoked bacon* on the board. Let each team write a word in turn. The winner is the one who writes the longest list of words in a certain time limit. As a flannelboard game, this may be a group or individual activity.

12. *New Spelldown:* The fifteen to sixteen words of the week's lessons are put on the board. Each child is assigned one word, which becomes his "name." (Two or more may have the same word.) The leader goes to the front of the room and calls on one of the students. This child faces the rear of the room (because the words are still on the chalkboard) and is asked to spell the leader's word. If he is incorrect, he sits down; if correct, he asks the leader to spell his word. The class, looking at the words on the chalkboard, acts as judge. When the leader misses, the challenger takes his place.

13. *Fourth-Grade Scramble:* Take any week's lesson and scramble the letters in each word. The teacher scrambles the letters of a word on the board and the children write the word correctly on their papers. If each letter of the word is on a separate card, they may be placed on the chalk rail. One child unscrambles the word, writes it on the chalkboard, and uses it in a sentence. The class watching this may write the words as each one is unscrambled. A true scramble avoids placing the letters in a horizontal sequence but writes all over the board. Letter cards may be so scrambled on a flannelboard.

14. *You Can't Catch Me:* As the teacher gives the first word, each child writes it on his paper. Then the papers are passed in a predetermined order (to the left, for example). The child receiving the paper checks the last word and writes the word correctly if necessary. Then the teacher gives the second word and the papers are passed. Every paper should be perfect if all errors are caught. While this may not always happen, those words needing review will have received attention in a different way.

Fun for All Ages

1. *Spelldowns:* Traditional spelldowns involve one team that competes with another. If a child misspells a word and the person whose turn it is to spell on the opposite team spells it correctly, that child is "spelled down" and takes his seat. He can be saved if the opponents misspell the word and the next person on his team spells it successfully. A good PTA feature is to have a group of girls spell against their fathers. Ordinarily, "boys versus girls" is not encouraged, but sometimes a fifth-grade team will challenge a sixth-grade team. (The National Education Association has a clever play available that uses a spelldown dramatically. Write for "Command Performance," by Tom Erhard.) Rather than using oral spelling alone it adds to the educational value to have the words written neatly on the chalkboard by the contestants.

2. *Checkers:* Checkers is a spelldown in which the student who spells a word correctly "jumps" two persons in the direction of the end of the line. When he reaches the end, he goes to his seat. The advantage of such procedure is that those who need practice remain, whereas those who know the words have time for independent work. This may be called a spell-up, and the students may move from the end of the line to the top when they drop from the line.

3. *Spellups:* Spellups are the same as the traditional spelling bee with one exception: instead of the teams lining up, each team member remains seated until he misses a word; then he stands. When a player misses a word, the person standing is given a chance to spell the word correctly. If he succeeds, he sits down. Remember this is a game. If errors are embarrassing to any individual, it would be wise to avoid such direct comparison.

Appendix C

◆━━◆

Media Resources and Activities

Commercial Recordings

The following records and cassette tapes are a few of the high-quality recordings that are available.

Alexander and the Terrible, No Good, Very Bad Day Caedmon, 1984, disk, grades 1–5. Side A includes six stories by Judith Viorst: *Alexander Who Used to Be Rich Last Sunday; Rosie and Michael; My Mama Says There Aren't Any Zombies; Ghosts, Vampires . . .; The Tenth Good Thing About Barney.* Side B contains poetry readings from *If I Were in Charge of the World.*

Amazing Grace: Youthful Thunder Children's Radio Theatre, 1984, cassette, grades 6–9. Includes issues of censorship and freedom. Good stimulus for discussion.

Arnold Adoff Reads Four Complete Books Earworks Rocking Horse Winners, 1983, cassette, grades K–5. Readings: *Eats, Outside/Inside, Birds,* and *Black Is Brown.*

Billy and Blaze Stories Caedmon, 1984, disk, grades K–3. Stories taken from seven different books by C. W. Anderson, read by David Cassidy.

The Blue Sword Random House, 1983, cassettes, grades 4–6. The Newbery Honor Book by Robin McKinley.

Brer Rabbit Stories Weston Woods, 1984, cassette, grades 2–6.

Children's Playhouse 15: The Sixth Annual Henny Penny Play-writing Contest Children's Radio Theatre, 1984, cassette, grades 3–6. Four award-winning plays written and enacted by students ages 11–16. Useful for children's writing workshops.

Close Your Eyes (Series) Jubelieve Prods., 1984, cassettes, grades K–4. Includes eight stories by Daghmar Frahme, told by Joyce Reed Taylor and Jo Diotalevi. The adventure stories include fantasy characters who use cooperation to solve problems.

Doctor DeSoto and Other Stories Caedmon, 1984, record, grades K–6. Includes William Stieg's 1982 Honor Book, *Doctor DeSoto,* and *Caleb and Kate,* and chapters 8–11 of *Dominic* (chapters 1–7 available on another tape).

Dominic Caedmon, 1984, disk, grades 4–6. Chapters 1–7 of the novel by William Stieg.

A Gentle Wind (Series) Gentle Wind, 1983, cassettes, Grades 1–5. Includes *All Together, Are We Almost There?* and *Elsie Piddock Skips in Her Sleep.*

Grimm's Fairy Tales (set) Listen for Pleasure, 1984, cassettes, grades 2–5. Includes *Snow White and the Seven Dwarfs, Hansel and Gretel, Rapunzel, The Frog Prince, Cinderella, Rumpelstiltskin, Tom Thumb, Sleeping Beauty,* and *The Brave Little Tailor.*

Honey, I Love Caedmon, 1984, record, grades K–6. Jazz music accompanies the reading of poems by Eloise Greenfield.

Howliday Inn Caedmon, 1984, disk or cassette, grades 3–6. A radio mystery theater adaptation of the book by James Howe.

The Hundred and One Dalmatians (set) Listen for Pleasure, 1984, cassettes, grades 2–6. An abridged version of the novel by Dodie Smith.

I Wrote a Poem Quadrangle Music, 1984, disk, grades 4–8. Lyrics written by children ages 7–15 are sung by Mike Glick and the New Song Trio.

Incognito Mosquito, Private Insective Caedmon, 1984, disk or cassette, grades 4–6. Don Adams reads four mini-mysteries from the book by E. A. Hass.

Just So Stories Musical Heritage Society, 1984, record, grades 3 and up. Includes *How the Whale Got His Throat* and *How the Camel Got His Hump.*

Lilly, Willy and the Mail-Order Witch Caedmon, 1983, record or cassette, grades 2–5. Lilly and her brother have many adventures when they order a witch through the mail.

Listening Lab: Levels 1–9 Troll. 1981, cassettes, duplicating

masters, grades K–9. Students listen to short stories and answer questions. Includes the following skills for each level:

1–2: Discovering the main idea.
Alike and different.
Learning to follow directions.
3–4: Recalling details.
Comparing and contrasting.
Discovering similes and metaphors.
5–6: Working with sequence.
Understanding characterization.
Identifying word moods.
7–9: Understanding outlines.
Understanding flashbacks.
Drawing conclusions.

Lullaby River Produced by Danly Prods. Distributed by American Distribution Centers, 1984, cassette, grades K–3. Includes a story about Tucker the Turtle, soothing sounds of the river, and nine songs accompanied by woodwinds and strings.

Mainly Mother Goose: Songs and Rhymes for Merry Young Souls Elephant Records, 1984, record, grades preschool–6. The 61 selections include Mother Goose songs and rhymes, American songs and fingerplays, and French nursery rhymes.

Reading Rainbow Songs Caedmon, 1984, disk or cassette, preschool–3. Includes the theme song from the PBS *Reading Rainbow* show and 19 themes from children's books. Some are songs with vocals, and others are instrumental arrangements.

Santa Claus Caedmon, 1984, disk or cassette, grades K–8. Seventeen stories and poems about Santa Claus narrated by Sandy Duncan.

Strega Nona's Magic Lessons and Other Stories by Tomie de Paola Caedmon, 1983, 1984, disk or cassette, grades 1–6. Includes *Strega Nona, Big Anthony and the Magic Ring, Strega Nona's Magic Lessons, Oliver Button Is a Sissy, Nana Upstairs and Nana Downstairs, Now One Foot and the Other*, and *Helga's Dowry*.

Super Sampler and *The Second Sampler* A Gentle Wind, 1983, cassettes, grades 3 and up. Provides a sample of stories and songs recorded by A Gentle Wind in 1981 and 1982.

Tales of the Southwest (The Storytelling Circle Series) Weston Woods, 1984, grades 1–6. Includes three Hispanic and three Native American stories.

The Velveteen Rabbit Caedmon, 1984, disk or cassette, grades 1–6. A warm, sensitive rendition of the story by Margery Williams.

Where the Sidewalk Ends Harper & Row Jr. Books Group, 1984, cassette, grades 4–6. Shel Silverstein recites 39 of his poems, accompanied with appropriate background music and sound effects.

We've Got to Come Full Circle Folkways, 1984, disk, grades K–5. Folk songs and stories about the Chesapeake Bay and the Potomac River basin encourage discussions about ecology and use of our natural resources.

Whoever Heard of a Fird? Caedmon, 1984, disk or cassette, grades 1–5. Fanciful story-song by Othello Bach in which the main character is part fish and part bird. An entertaining tale of friendship.

Winnie-the-Pooh and Eeyore Caedmon, 1984, disk or cassette, preschool–3. Four chapters from *The House at Pooh Corner* and *Winnie the Pooh* are told and sung by Carol Channing.

Read-Alongs

Arthur Goes to Camp (Holiday and Seasons Series) Random House, 1983, cassette and book, grades K–3.

The Balloon That Ran Away (Read Along . . . for Fun Series) January Prods., 1985, cassette, books, grades 1–3. Story by Michele Spirn.

Blubber (Soundways to Reading Series) Listening Library, 1983, cassette, books, grades 3–5. Includes chapters 1–4 of the book by Judy Blume and questions for discussion; encourages students to read the remainder on their own.

The Book of Pigericks (Read-Along Series) Random House, 1983, 1984, cassette and book, preschool–2. Includes 38 pig limericks by Arnold Lobel.

The Cats' Burglar Random House, 1984, cassette, book, grades K–3. Side one contains word-for-word reading of book by Peggy Parish; side two includes music and sound effects for listening.

Cupid's Valentine (Holidays Are Fun Sound Readers Series) January Prods, 1985, cassette, books, preschool–2. Phyllis Dolgin's story about Cupid, a Persian cat, who is in love with Valentine, the new cat across the hall.

Dawn (Read-Along House Series) Random House, 1984,

cassette/book, grades K–4. Molly Bang's new adaptation of an old Japanese legend, *The Crane Maiden*.

Goodnight Moon Live Oak Media, 1984, cassette, book, preschool–1. Pleasant recording of the book by Margaret Wise Brown.

The Great Big Especially Beautiful Easter Egg Random House, 1984, cassette, book, grades K–3. Excellent recording of the book by James Stevenson.

Ira Sleeps Over Live Oak Media, 1984, cassette, book, preschool–4. Book by Bernard Waber.

Just So Stories, The Jungle Book, and *The Second Jungle Book,* ABC, 1983, cassettes, grades 3–6. Kipling's classic tales are read word for word and provide pleasant listening as well as a read-along.

Little Rabbit's Loose Tooth Pied Piper, 1984, sound filmstrip, cassette, book, grades K–2. Story by Lucy Bate.

A Medieval Feast (Read-Along House Series) Random House, 1983, cassette, book, grades 2–5. Book by Aliki.

Ox-Cart Man Live Oak Media, 1984, cassette, book, preschool–4. Narrated by author Donald Hall.

Red Fox and His Canoe Pied Piper, 1984, sound filmstrip, cassette, book, grades K–2. Book by Nathaniel Benchley.

Something Special for Me (Read-Along House Series) Random House, 1983, cassette, book, grades K–6. Story by Vera Williams.

Wally the Wordworm Stemmer House, 1984, cassette, book, grades 2–6. Those who love the sounds of language and challenging words will enjoy the puns, riddles, and words with interesting sounds.

Commercial Filmstrips for Teaching Language Arts Skills

The following sound filmstrips are a sampling of those available for teaching specific language arts skills.

Building Better Sentences: A Unit of Study (Series) United Learning, 1984, four filmstrips, four cassettes, grades 3–4. Story format is used to present basic information about sentences.

Developing Reading Skills (Series) Random House, 1983. Four units, each including six filmstrips and six cassettes. Units include Word Perception; Phonics: Vowel Sounds, Phonics: Consonants B–M; Phonics: Consonants N–Z.

Learn Along Filmstrip Library Starring Shari Lewis and Lamb-chop (Series) SVE, 1984, preschool–3. Includes six filmstrips, six cassettes, and skill sheets. Teaches concepts of left and right, color identification, memorization of personal information, naming of body parts, and vocabulary. Musical scores and song lyrics are included.

Q*Bert Starts Thinking (Series) SVE, 1984, grades K–3. Includes three filmstrips and three cassettes. Provides problem-solving situations involving observation, comparison, classification, and decision making using the Q*Bert arcade game character. Optional stop frames allow for discussion.

Sesame Street: Word Families (Series) Guidance Associates, 1985. Five filmstrips and five cassettes teach the *-at, -en, -et, -an, -ar, -ig, -onk, -op, -un,* and *-us* families, using familiar Muppet characters. Activities and follow-up worksheets are included.

Steps to Better Writing: Writing a Report Nystrom, 1980, grades 4–8. Six filmstrips and six cassettes include Choosing a Subject, Gathering Information, Preparing a Bibliography, Outlining and Note-Taking, Writing the First Draft, Doing the Final Paper. Emphasizes use of *Reader's Guide to Periodical Literature* and the card catalog and use of the encyclopedia for broad background information.

Steps to Better Writing: Writing to Explain Nystrom, 1980, grades 5–8. Six filmstrips and six cassettes include Using Examples, Giving the Meaning, Making Comparisions, Dividing Into Groups, Showing How, and Explaining Why. Activities are included for practicing what is learned.

Commercial Filmstrips of Children's Literature

The following is a list of sound filmstrips of children's literature.

Annie's Mystery Adventure (Series) SVE 1984, grades 4–6. Little Orphan Annie solves four mysteries involving situations that provide opportunities for critical thinking.

Adventures of Tom Sawyer Filmstrip Library (Series) Troll Associates, 1984, grades 3–6. Includes *Tom Sawyer: Danger in the Graveyard, Tom Sawyer Becomes a Pirate,*

Tom Sawyer and Buried Treasure, and *Tom Sawyer Lost in a Cave.*

A Closer Look at Peter Rabbit (Signature Collection Series) Weston Woods, 1984, grade 6 and up. A literary analysis of the story of Peter Rabbit by Beatrix Potter.

Arthur's Thanksgiving (Holidays and Seasons Series) Random House, 1983, grades K–5. The story of Arthur the aardvark, based on the book by Marc Brown.

Aunt Nina and Her Nephews and Nieces Weston Woods, 1984, grades K–2. An adaptation of the book by Franz Brandenberg, in which Aunt Nina and her nieces and nephews celebrate the birthday of her cat.

Blubber (First Choice Authors and Books Series, Unit 22) Pied Piper, 1984, grades 4–7. An adaptation of the book by Judy Blume.

Bugg Adventure (Series) SVE 1983, grades 1–3. Six stories about Buggville, each designed to teach a moral.

The Butter Battle Book Random House, 1984, grades K–3. Ed Asner narrates this adaptation of the book by Dr. Seuss.

Christmastime Treasures Encyclopaedia Britannica Ed., 1982, grades K–6. Includes *The Twelve Days of Christmas, The Gift of the Little Juggler, The Story of Silent Night,* and *The Little Match Girl.* Presents each story with a historical perspective.

Come Away from the Water, Shirley Weston Woods, 1984, grades K–3. Based on the picture book by John Burningham.

Freckle Juice (First Choice Authors and Books Series) Pied Piper, 1984, grades 2–6. Verbatim recording of the book by Judy Blume. Can be used as a read-along.

Ghosts of the Sea Pomfret House, 1981, available from *Encyclopaedia Britannica,* Ed., grades 4–8. Includes *The Ghosts of Georges Bank, The White Stallion Ghosts, Ocean-Born Mary,* and *The Flying Dutchman.* Student activities are included with these legends of the sea.

The Glorious Flight Live Oak Media, 1984, grades K–3. An adaptation of Alice and Martin Provensen's Caldecott Award book.

Goodnight Moon Weston Woods, 1984, Preschool–1. Based on the book by Margaret Wise Brown.

Graven Images (Newbery Series) Random House, 1983, grades 4–8. Three stories based on Paul Fleischman's Newbery Honor Book.

Here Comes the Strikeout (First Choice Authors and Books Series) Pied Piper, 1984, grades K–3. An adaptation of the book by Leonard Kessler. One cassette is for read-along, the other for listening and/or viewing.

Ira Sleep Over Live Oak Media, 1984, grades K–3. Based on the book by Bernard Waber. Ira is invited to sleep over with his friend for the first time and can't decide whether or not to take his teddy bear along.

I Will Not Go to Market Today Random House, 1984, grades K–3, Based on the book by Harry Allard.

Jim Meets the Thing (System 5 Filmstrips for 1983–1984 Series) Random House, 1984, grades K–2. Based on the book by Miriam Cohen.

King of the Cats Weston Woods, 1984, grades K–3. An American folktale based on the book by Paul Galdone.

Literature for Children Series 7C—Introduction to Picture Books (Series) Pied Piper, 1984, grades 1–3. Includes *Scary Stories, Yummy Stories About Food, Nature Stories and Poems, Stories About Pets,* and *By the Sea.* Includes narrations of story selections and dialogue about using picture books and locating them in the library.

The Littlest Angel SVE, 1983, 1984, grades 1–6. Based on the book by Charles Tazewell.

Little Rabbit's Loose Tooth Pied Piper, 1984, grades K–2. Faithful version of the book by Lucy Bates.

Maud Hart Lovelace: A Minnesota Childhood Heritage Prods., 1983, 1984, grades 3 and up. Focuses on the life of Maud Hart and the influence it had on the Betsy-Tacy books she wrote and illustrated.

Miss Nelson Is Missing Weston Woods, 1984, grades K–4. Based on the book by Harry Allard.

Mouse Soup Random House, 1983, grades K–3. Adapted from the book by Arnold Lobel.

Mr. and Mrs. Pig's Evening Out Weston Woods, 1984, preschool–3. Based on the book by Mary Rayner.

The Nature of Gnomes (Series) Spoken Arts, 1984, grades K–6. Includes *Gnomes and Their Homes, Gnomes and Their Animal Friends, Gnomes and Their Enemies,* and *Gnomes and Us.* Based on *Gnomes* and *Secrets of the Gnomes* by Wil Huygen. Useful for creative writing or art projects.

The Nightgown of the Sullen Moon (For Young Imaginations Series) Random House, 1984, preschool–3. In this adaptation of the book by Nancy Willard, the moon wishes for a nightgown to wear. She comes to earth and searches until she finds just the right one.

Paddington on Top (Series) Learning Tree Filmstrips, 1984, grades 2–5. Includes *Paddington in Court, Keeping*

Fit, Paddington in Tough, and *Comings and Goings at No. 32.* Based on the book by Michael Bond.

Peter Spier's Christmas Spoken Arts, 1984, grades K–5. Based on the book by Peter Spier.

Reading the Classics (Series) SVE 1983, Includes *Tom Sawyer, Little Women, Journey to the Center of the Earth, Kidnapped, Frankenstein,* and *The Red-Headed League.*

Red Riding Hood Weston Woods, 1984, grades K–2. Follows Beatrice de Regnier's verse rendition of the Grimm fairy tale.

A Ring of Endless Light (Newbery Award Series) Random House 1984, grades 6–10. An adaptation of the book by Madeleine L'Engle.

Sammy the Seal (First Choice Authors and Books, Unit 27) Pied Piper, 1984, grades K–3. Verbatim recording of the book by Syd Hoff. Can be used as a read-along.

The Snowman Weston Woods, 1984, grades K–3. Nonnarrated story of a young boy who builds a snowman and later dreams it comes to life. Illustrations are from the book by Raymond Brigg. Useful for storytelling and creative writing.

Superfudge Pied Piper, 1984, grades 2–6. Based on the book by Judy Blume.

Sweet Whispers, Brother Rush (Set) Random House, 1983, grades 5–8. Based on the Newbery Honor Book by Virginia Hamilton.

Tales from the Odyssey (Series) Troll Associates, 1984, grades 4–8. Includes *The Wooden Horse, The Voyage of Odysseus, Odysseus and the Cyclops, Odysseus and the Saints, Odysseus and the Magic of Circe, Odysseus and the Great Challenge,* and *The Return of Odysseus.*

Ten, Nine, Eight (Caldecott Series) Random House, 1984, grades K–3. Based on 1984 Caldecott Honor Book by Molly Bang. Read-along cassette included.

Wanda Gag: A Minnesota Childhood Heritage Prods., 1984, grades 3 and up. Explores the life of Wanda Gag, author and illustrator of *Millions of Cats.*

What's under My Bed Weston Woods, 1984, grades K–3. Adapted from the book by James Stevenson.

Commercial Films and Video Recordings

American Storytelling Second Story Television, 1982, 1983, videocassette, grades 5 and up. Useful for storytime for upper elementary students or for studying the art of storytelling.

Angus Lost Phoenix, 1982, film, grades K–3. Nonverbal adaptation of the book by Marjorie Flack.

The Ant and the Grasshopper Phoenix, 1980, film, grades K–4. An animated version of the fable by Aesop.

A Boy, a Dog, and a Frog Phoenix, 1981, film, grades K–3. Adaptation of the book by Mercer Mayer.

By Word of Mouth . . . Storytelling in America Steven Kostant, 1984, videocassette, grades 4 and up. Includes excerpts from nearly twenty tales, with comments on the art of storytelling.

Cannonball Phoenix, 1984, film or videocassette, preschool–grade 6. Adapted from the book *Cannonball Simp* by John Burningham, this film uses circus music and live-action photography to tell the story of Hugo the Clown.

Curious George Churchill Films, 1984, film or videocassette, grades 1–4. Three-dimensional animation is used to tell the story by H. A. Rey.

Doctor Desoto Weston Woods, 1984, film, grades K–6. Follows the book by William Steig.

Dr. Seuss (Series) Phoenix, film, grades K–6. Includes *The Cat in the Hat,* 1972; *Dr. Seuss On the Loose: The Sneetches, The Zax,* 1974; *The Hoober-Bloob Highway,* 1975; and *The Lorax,* 1972. Produced by CBS, Inc.

Everybody Knows That Phoenix, 1984, film or videocassette, preschool–grade 4. Based on the book by Susan Pearson, this film is useful for discussing stereotyping.

Folk Tales Barr Films, 1984, film or videocassette, grades 3–8. The traditional animated Fat Albert gang visits with Bill Cosby as he introduces the concept of tall tales. Characters included are Paul Bunyan, Babe the Blue Ox, and Brimstone Bill. Use as an introduction to folktales and storytelling.

In Search of Father Christmas Wombat Prods., 1984, film or videocassette, grades 4 and up. Use as an introduction to folklore, tradition, or the customs of Christmas.

Jack and the Dentist's Daughter (From the Brothers Grimm Series) Davenport Films, 1984, film or videocassette, grades 5 and up. Adapted from Grimms's *The Master Thief,* this film has the classic theme of using wit to outwit others.

The Goose Girl (from the Brothers Grimm Series) Davenport Films, 1983, film or videocassette, grades 5 and up.

Sound effects and background music enhance this version of the story by the Grimm brothers.

King of the Cats Weston Woods, 1984, film, grades K–3. A gravedigger encounters a funeral procession of cats and is surprised at the reaction of his own cat. Based on Paul Galdone's book.

Mole in Town Phoenix, 1984, film, grades 1–6. Mole, porcupine, and rabbit rid themselves of their grief over the fact that the city is taking away their woodlands.

The Snake Prince Wombat Prods., 1982, 1983, film or videocassette, grades K–4. Puppets are used in this wordless production of the fairy tale.

The Velveteen Rabbit Random House, 1984, videocassette, grades one–4. Film adaptation of Margery Williams' classic 1922 tale.

Vowel Combinations: What Are Letters For BFA Educational Media, 1984, film, grades 1–3. Bertha the Barn Bug and Tumbleweed Tom introduce children to vowel combinations. Includes basic rules for vowel combinations, examples, and exceptions to the rules.

Why Mosquitoes Buzz in People's Ears Weston Woods, 1984, film, preschool–grade 3. Based on the book by Verna Aardema, this animated version draws successfully on the original illustrations by Leo and Diane Dillon.

William's Doll Phoenix, 1981, film, grades K–6. Based on Charlotte Zolotow's story of a little boy who longs for a doll.

Distributors

ABC-Audio Book Contractors
Box 40115
Washington, D.C. 20016

American Distribution Centers
7609 W. Industrial Dr.
Forest Park, IL 60130

BFA Educational Media
468 Park Avenue South
New York, NY 10016

Caedmon
1995 Broadway
New York, NY 10023

Children's Radio Theater
1314 14th St. N. W.
Washington, D.C. 20005

Churchill Films
662 N. Robertson Blvd.
Los Angeles, CA 90069

Davenport Films
Rt. 1, Box 527
Delaplane, VA 22025

Earworks Rocking Horse Winners
Box 293
Yellow Springs, OH 45382

EBEC–Encyclopaedia Britannica
  Educational Corp.
425 N. Michigan Ave.
Chicago, IL 60611

Elephant Records
77 Berkeley St.
Toronto, Canada
M5A 2W5

Folkways Records
632 Broadway
New York, NY 10012

Gentle Wind
Box 3103
Albany, NY 12203

Guidance Associates
Communications Park
Box 3000
Mt. Kisco, NY 10549

Harper & Row Junior Book Group
10 E. 53d St.
New York, NY 10022

Heritage Productions
10255 Scarborough Rd.
Minneapolis, MN 55437

January Productions
249 Goffle Rd.
Hawthorne, NJ 07507

Jubelieve Productions
Box 2138
Kamuela, HI 96743

Steven Kostant
11 Eastman Rd.
Somerville, MA 02143

Learning Tree Filmstrips
Box 4116
Englewood, CO 80155

Listen for Pleasure
417 Center St.
Lewiston, NJ 14092

Listening Library
One Park Avenue
Old Greenwich, CT 06870

Live Oak Media
Box 34
Ancramdale, NY 12503

Musical Heritage Society
1710 Highway 35
Ocean, NJ 01712

Nystrom
3333 Elston Ave.
Chicago, IL 60618

Phoenix Films and Video
468 Park Ave. S.
New York, NY 10016

Pied Piper Productions
Box 320
Verdugo City, CA 91046

Quadrangle Music
Box 1322
New Haven, CT 06505

Random House School Division
400 Hahn Rd.
Westminster, MD 21157

Second Story Television
118 E. 11th St.
New York, NY 10003

Spoken Arts
310 North Ave.
New Rochelle, NY 10801

Stemmer House Publishing
2627 Cave Rd.
Owings Mills, MD 21117

SVE–Society for Visual Education
1345 Diversey Pkwy.
Chicago, IL 60614

Troll Associates
320 Rt. 17
Mahwah, NJ 07430

Weston Woods Studios
Weston, CT 06883

Wombat Productions
250 West 57th St.
New York, NY 10019

Activities to Improve Word Recognition

1. Purpose: To reinforce knowledge of letter sounds.

Procedure: Write individual alphabet letters on note cards. Clip several pictures from the newspaper, making sure to have at least one picture for each letter. Then ask students to match each letter with a picture beginning with that sound. Letters may be written on the back of the pictures for self-correction.

2. Purpose: To reinforce identification of upper- and lowercase letters.

Procedure: Clip several lowercase letters from the paper, mounting them on a piece of construction paper. Students then locate the corresponding uppercase letters, pasting them next to the appropriate lowercase letters.

3. Purpose: To improve sight word recognition.

Procedure: Mount and number several pictures that represent words which are in the students' sight word vocabularies. Clip articles from the paper that include the words. Students look through the articles to locate the sight words, writing them next to the number of the picture that they identify or describe.

4. Purpose: To improve structural analysis skills.

Procedure: Make a copy of an article, deleting all *-ed* and *-ing* suffixes. Students write in the proper suffix, checking results with the original.

5. Purpose: To improve structural analysis skills.

Procedure: After studying a particular word family (*ake, ide, op,* etc.) students locate ten words from that word family, writing down the page on which they are found.

Activities to Improve Vocabulary Skills

1. Purpose: To expand vocabulary with synonyms.

Procedure: Cut and mount a picture from the paper. Students write three adjectives that describe the picture. Then they look in a thesaurus for two synonyms for each of the three words. Students then write three sentences describing the picture, using as many of the descriptive words as they can.

2. Purpose: To identify words conveying emotions.

Procedure: Clip five pictures of people who show various emotions. The comics are a good source for this. Clip from the paper words that describe the emotions, such as anger, fear, happiness, or sorrow. Students then match the words to the appropriate pictures. Variation: The students may locate and clip the words themselves or, given the words, may be asked to locate the pictures.

3. Purpose: To learn the vocabulary used by journalists.

Procedure: Instruct students in the meanings of the following terms used by journalists: *balloon, banner, byline, cutline, dateline, editor, headline, index, lead, nameplate.* Students locate an example of each.

4. Purpose: To expand vocabulary with synonyms.

  Procedure: Students read the sports page to find how many ways journalists say *win* and *lose*.

5. Purpose: To identify words with multiple meanings.

  Procedure: Select words from the sports page that have multiple meanings, such as *play, star, pitcher, date, field, meet,* and *match*. Provide students with several definitions for each word. Students read articles containing those words and select the definitions appropriate for the context. (idea from Hamrick, 1981).

6. Purpose: To identify a word from clues about its meaning.

  Procedure: Select a word from the newspaper. Write it on a card. One student holds it over another student's head. The student who cannot see the word asks questions about it, trying to determine what it is. Questions may be asked about spelling, grammatical function, or meaning.

7. Purpose: Using context clues to determine meaning.

  Procedure: Identify words that may be unfamiliar to students. They determine the meaning from the context. Select examples in which the writer included definitions, examples, or synonyms in the article.

8. Purpose: To determine connotations of synonyms.

  Procedure: Select an adjective from an advertisement in the paper. The class brainstorms synonyms, using a thesaurus if necessary. Decide which words have a positive connotation and which have a negative conno-

tation. Students select those words advertisers would be most likely to use.

9. Purpose: To reinforce word meanings.

  Procedure: Keep a list of the vocabulary words discussed in class. Select twenty to thirty words that are related to a certain content area. Given graph paper, one student creates a crossword puzzle, planning first how the words will intersect, and then writing appropriate definitions for clues. Make copies for the rest of the class. Students may work on constructing puzzles in small groups, and then exchange puzzles with another group.

Activities to Improve Comprehension

1. Purpose: To improve comprehension of main idea.

  Procedure: Clip several short articles from the paper. Separate the headlines from the articles. Students are then asked to match the articles with the appropriate headlines.

2. Purpose: To improve comprehension of main idea.

  Procedure: Students select a favorite comic strip and create a headline for it, summarizing the main idea.

3. Purpose: To improve comprehension of main idea.

  Procedure: Give students several articles with accompanying pictures. They select the correct picture for each article.

4. Purpose: To improve comprehension of main idea.

  Procedure: Students read an article whose title

has been removed. They write an appropriate title, stating the main idea of the article, and then compare it to the original title.

5. Purpose: To improve comprehension of details.

Procedure: Provide students with questions asking the *who, what, when, where,* and *why* about an article. Students read the article to answer the questions.

6. Purpose: To improve comprehension of details.

Procedure: Provide students with an outline of an article in which some details have been omitted. They read the article, filling in the missing information.

7. Purpose: To improve comprehension of details.

Procedure: Provide students with questions that will require them to make an inference from details stated in the article. They read the article and answer the questions, indicating which details support their answers.

8. Purpose: To improve sequencing skills.

Procedure: Cut apart the frames of a comic strip. Students put the frames in the correct sequence. They can self-correct if frames are mounted on construction paper and are numbered in the correct sequence on the back.

9. Purpose: To improve sequencing skills.

Procedure: Cut several sentences from the newspaper. Cut the words apart, keeping the words for each sentence in a separate envelope. Students put the sentences back in the correct order.

10. Purpose: To improve sequencing skills.

Procedure: Select an article describing a definite sequence of events. After the students read the article, they tell what happened in the correct sequence.

11. Purpose: To improve sequencing skills.

Procedure: Separate the paragraphs of a newspaper article. Students place them in the correct sequence. Variation: Include one or two paragraphs from a different article, telling the students how many "extra" paragraphs there are. Students take out those that do not belong.

12. Purpose: To improve skills of prediction.

Procedure: Cut out and mount the middle frame of a comic strip. Students tell what they think happened before and after that frame, checking predictions with the original frames.

13. Purpose: To improve skills of prediction.

Procedure: Remove the last frame from a comic strip. Students predict how the strip ends, comparing their predictions with the original. Variation: Students write one frame beyond the last frame in the comic strip.

14. Purpose: To improve critical thinking skills.

Procedure: Students locate words in the editorial section that are used to indicate opinion (*think, imply, suggest, probably, suppose, best, prettiest*). Then they identify five people or comic strip characters who give their opinions on a topic.

15. Purpose: To improve critical thinking skills.

Procedure: After discussing propaganda techniques, students locate an example of each technique as it is used in the paper's advertisements. Examples may also be found in editorials

or in a news story's account of the actions of a politician.

16. Purpose: To improve critical thinking skills.
Procedure: After discussing the purposes of editorials (to inform, to explain, to influence, and to entertain), students classify several editorials into these four categories.

17. Purpose: To improve critical thinking skills.
Procedure: Clip several pictures from advertisements. Students sort them into predetermined categories (closed sort), or make their own categories and ask other students to guess the criteria they used (open sort). Variation: Students may classify vocabulary words instead of pictures.

18. Purpose: To improve critical thinking skills.
Procedure: Students compare the information in a news story with that of a news feature on the same topic. They may also compare one newspaper's coverage of an event with that of another paper or a news magazine.

19. Purpose: To improve critical thinking skills.
Procedure: Students listen to radio and television broadcasts of a news incident and compare it with the coverage by the newspaper. Then they identify bias in the various media or in different networks of the same media. Discuss how various media differ, and how that difference influences the way they report the news.

20. Purpose: To improve critical thinking skills.
Procedure: Discuss some of the symbols often used in editorial cartoons (donkey, elephant, Uncle Sam). Students locate symbols and determine their meaning and what the cartoonist is trying to say. Ask students to identify what recent event inspired

the drawing of the cartoon and to locate editorials that agree and disagree with the cartoonist's point of view (idea from Cheyney, 1984).

Activities to Improve Writing Skills

1. Purpose: To improve spelling skills.
Procedure: Provide students with several scrambled words and their definitions. They unscramble the words, cutting the letters from the paper and pasting them in the correct sequence.

2. Purpose: To improve spelling skills.
Procedure: Students cut letters from the newspaper to spell words on their weekly spelling list. Encourage them to locate words with similar vowel or consonant combinations, clipping the portions of the word that are the same.

3. Purpose: To improve punctuation skills.
Procedure: Duplicate an article, removing all end punctuation. Students can insert the appropriate punctuation while the article is read orally by the teacher or while reading it silently. Check answers with the original. Variation: Omit capital letters or quotation marks.

4. Purpose: To reinforce correct sentence structure.
Procedure: Provide students with several headlines. Compare them with sentences, discussing what is missing in the headlines. Students rewrite the headlines in complete sentences.

5. Purpose: To provide opportunities for creative writing.

   Procedure: White-out the balloons in a comic strip. Students write their own words in the empty balloons.

6. Purpose: To provide opportunities for creative writing.

   Procedure: After studying various propaganda techniques, students write an advertisement, using one of the techniques.

7. Purpose: To provide opportunities for creative writing.

   Procedure: After reading and discussing an editorial, students write one with the opposing point of view.

8. Purpose: To provide opportunities for creative writing.

   Procedure: After reading and discussing the comics for several weeks, students write a paper describing the impressions they would have about the earth and its inhabitants if they were aliens who had only been exposed to the comics section of the paper (idea from Guenther, 1983).

9. Purpose: To provide opportunities for creative writing.

   Procedure: Students develop a series of New Year's resolutions for their favorite comic strip character (idea from Guenther, 1983).

10. Purpose: To provide opportunities for creative writing.

    Procedure: After reading and discussing the book and movie review sections of the paper, students write their own reviews for the class newspaper, sharing them with the other classes. This activity could be used as an alternative to the traditional book report.

11. Purpose: To provide opportunities for creative writing.

    Procedure: Students write an ad for an object or a service without naming it. They they read the ad aloud, giving the other students a chance to guess what it is they are advertising.

12. Purpose: To provide opportunities for creative writing.

    Procedure: Call the students' attention to the lead in several news articles. Tell them that the format of a news article is called an inverted pyramid because the most important information is found in the lead or first statement of the article, followed by explanations and details (Cheyney, 1984).

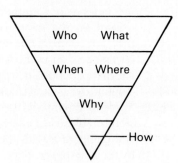

After discussing the format, students rewrite folk tales or fairy tales in news story style. Some students may enjoy rewriting passages of their history text in this fashion.

13. Purpose: To provide opportunities for creative writing.

    Procedure: Students write a comic strip as a narrative giving the necessary background information and indicating dialogue correctly.

14. Purpose: To provide opportunities for creative writing.

Procedure: Provided with an action-filled picture, students write what could have happened before and after the picture was taken.

15. Purpose: To provide opportunities for creative writing.

Procedure: Students write descriptive passages about a favorite comic strip character. Then they read them aloud, giving the other students a chance to guess which character is being described.

16. Purpose: To provide opportunities for creative writing.

Procedure: Students create an invention for each of five comic strip characters that would help them with their problems or weaknesses, including a description of the invention and an explanation of the way it works. (idea from Guenther, 1983).

17. Purpose: To provide opportunities for creative writing.

Procedure: Students write their own answers to the questions from an advice column, comparing them with the answers provided by the columnist.

18. Purpose: To provide opportunities for creative writing.

Procedure: Students create a new character for their favorite comic strip, write a description of the new character and ways it would add to the strip, and write one strip including the new character (idea from Guenther, 1983).

19. Purpose: To provide opportunities for creative writing.

Procedure: Instruct students to write a headline and news story about what happened in one comic strip. Be sure they include information that answers the questions *who, what, when, where, why,* and *how.*

20. Purpose: To provide opportunities for creative writing.

Procedure: Instruct students to imagine what would happen if a character from one comic strip suddenly appeared in a different strip. Then they choose a character and write it into one episode of another comic strip (idea from Guenther, 1983).

Activities to Improve Speaking Skills

1. Purpose: To provide opportunities for storytelling.

Procedure: Young children create their own stories about the pictures in the comic strips.

2. Purpose: To provide opportunities for oral reading.

Procedure: Students make finger puppets by cutting out the heads and shoulders of comic characters. They move the puppets to coincide with the reading of the dialogue (idea from Cheyney, 1984).

3. Purpose: To provide opportunities for extemporaneous speaking.

Procedure: Cut short excerpts from the paper, mix them in a box, and ask students to draw an item, read it, and give a short talk on the basis of the newspaper clipping (idea from Cheyney, 1984).

4. Purpose: To provide opportunities for oral interpretation.

Procedure: Students read the comics in Reader's Theater style.

5. Purpose: To improve oral reading skills.

Procedure: Students select key news, weather,

and sports articles; practice reading them orally; and present them to the rest of the class as if they were radio broadcasters.

6. Purpose: To improve public speaking skills.

Procedure: Students write and present their own television commercials, using one or more forms of propaganda. Class members in the audience try to determine which techniques they used.

7. Purpose: To improve public speaking skills.

Procedure: Assign students to various topics or news stories that will continue for several days. They give short daily summaries of the articles relevant to their topics.

8. Purpose: To provide opportunities for improvisational drama.

Procedure: Put several newspaper headlines in a box. Students draw a title and perform an impromptu skit based on the topic drawn.

9. Purpose: To provide opportunities for persuasive speaking.

Procedure: Students prepare to debate a controversial issue, using editorials and news stories as background for each side.

Activities to Improve Listening Skills

1. Purpose: To improve listening skills.

Procedure: Prepare a modified oral cloze activity by deleting key words from a newspaper article. List those deleted words on the board. Read the article to the class, pausing when a word is deleted. Students identify the missing word.

2. Purpose: To improve listening skills.

Procedure: After reading an article to the class, give an oral description of a person in the article. Students must guess who the person is.

3. Purpose: To improve listening skills.

Procedure: Read an article to the class, omitting one important fact. Students read the article silently to locate the missing information.

4. Purpose: To improve listening skills.

Procedure: Send three or four students from the room. Read a short newspaper article and then ask one person at a time to return to the room to hear a summary of the article from a class member. The first student asks another student back and tells his understanding of the summary, and so on, until all the students have returned. Reread the article to determine whether and where accuracy in listening broke down (Cheyney, 1984).

5. Purpose: To improve listening for details.

Procedure: Read articles to the class periodically, asking them to answer the questions *who, what, when, where, why,* and *how.*

Activities to Improve Reference Skills

1. Purpose: To improve skills of alphabetizing.

Procedure: Clip several classified ads from the paper. Students arrange them in alphabetical order. Begin using ads that require alphabetizing by the first letter only, gradually including second, third, and fourth letters.

2. Purpose: To improve students' ability to read charts and tables.

Procedure: Prepare a series of questions that require students to use the television schedule, weather charts, or sports tables.

3. Purpose: To improve students' ability to use an index.

   Procedure: Prepare a series of questions requiring students to use the newspaper index to locate the appropriate articles quickly.

4. Purpose: To improve students' ability to scan.

   Procedure: Prepare a list of items for a newspaper scavenger hunt. Instruct students to scan for items such as the index, a byline, a name of a state, an acronym, or a compound word. Be sure the items listed are in the paper given to the students.

5. Purpose: To improve students' ability to skim.

   Procedure: Instruct students to skim the want ads for jobs that did not exist twenty years ago.

Activities for Teaching Reference Skills

1. Purpose: To teach alphabetizing.

   Procedure: With words from their personal word banks, students practice alphabetizing, using the first letter only, increasing to using second, third, and fourth letters.

2. Purpose: To teach alphabetizing and reinforce word meanings.

   Procedure: Students construct a picture dictionary by selecting words from a particular category or unit of instruction or by using words from reading groups. Words are alphabetized, and students may draw illustrations or use pictures from magazines.

3. Purpose: To teach alphabetizing.

   Procedure: Students assemble a class telephone directory, placing appropriate guide words on each page.

4. Purpose: To teach alphabetizing.

   Procedure: Construct three containers, labeled as follows: A–I, J–Q, and R–Z. Students sort letter cards into the appropriate containers.

5. Purpose: To reinforce alphabetical order.

   Procedure: Prepare a maze so at every decision point there are two words. Students must choose the path indicated by the word that would come first alphabetically in order to finish the maze.

6. Purpose: To practice using guide words.

   Procedure: Given two guide words, students select from a list of words those that would be found on that page

Gate	Group
gum	
gain	
grin	
friends	
ginger	
goat	
grump	

7. Purpose: To practice locating the correct word meaning.

   Procedure: Given several words used in sentences, students locate the number of the appropriate definition.

   _____ He *ran* away.
   _____ She *ran* through the mail.
   _____ Her stocking *ran*.
   _____ Days *ran* into weeks.
   _____ We *ran* into debt.

8. Purpose: To practice locating words by using guide words.

 Procedure: Given a word written on the board, teams or individuals have races to locate the word and give the guide words and page number on which it was found.

9. Purpose: To practice using the encyclopedia index.

 Procedure: Given a list of topics, students use the index to locate the correct volume of the encyclopedia.

10. Purpose: To teach the type of information found in various reference books.

 Procedure: Design a crossword puzzle using types of references, such as dictionary, encyclopedia, card catalog, periodicals, thesaurus, atlas, almanac, index, glossary, table of contents, appendix, and *Reader's Guide to Periodical Literature*. Write clues that specify the type of information to be located. Students may create crossword puzzles for their classmates.

11. Purpose: To teach the use of a book's index.

 Procedure: Given a list of questions that can be answered in the book's content, students determine the topic to use to find the information under and the pages to check.

12. Purpose: To teach the way to read phonetic spellings.

 Procedure: Prepare two sets of cards for each of several words. On one set, write the words with their correct spellings. On the other set, write the phonetic spellings of the words. Students play Concentration, matching the phonetic spellings to the correct word.

13. Purpose: To review phonetic pronunciation markings.

 Procedure: Given words written phonetically, students write the correct spelling. Include some homonyms and indicate to the students the number of spellings possible.

(sŭm) some
       sum
(wā)   way
       weigh
(frĕnd) friend

14. Purpose: To practice locating words in the dictionary.

 Procedure: Write several nonsense sentences, underlining the one word in each sentence that does not make sense. Students look up the underlined word and locate a word on the same page that would make the sentence make sense. Write sentences specifically for the dictionary the students will use, as dictionaries vary.

 We were stranded on an isomer. The house was said to be haunted by a gherkin.

 A beautiful pugilist flew overhead.

Bibliography

Chapter 1

AINSWORTH, S. (1970). Report and commentary. In *Conditioning in stuttering therapy: Application and limitations,* Vol. 7. Memphis: Speech Foundation of America.

ALEXANDER, K. L., & PALLAS, A. M. (1984). Curriculum reform and school performance: An evaluation of the new basics. *American Journal of Education, 92,* 391–420.

ARCHER, A. (1985). *Teachers made a difference! Critical variables in teaching basic skills to low-performing students.* Paper presented at the Ninth Annual State Conference of California Association of Program Specialists.

ARNOLD, D. G. & SWABY, B. (1984). Neurolinguistic applications for remediation of reading problems. *The Reading Teacher, 37* (*9*), 831–34.

Associated Press Editorial. (1984, April 16). U.S. Hispanic population soars to 15.9 million. *The San Diego Union.*

BATES, G. W. (1984). Developing reading strategies for the gifted: A research-based approach. *Journal of Reading, 27* (*7*), 590–93.

BIGGE, J. L., & O'DONNELL, J. (1977). *Teaching individuals with physical and multiple disabilities.* Columbus, OH: Charles E. Merrill Publishing Company.

BLOODSTEIN, O. (1969). *A handbook on stuttering.* Chicago: National Easter Seal Society for Crippled Children and Adults.

BRANSFORD, J. D., VYE, N. J., & STEIN, B. S. (1984). A comparison of successful and less successful learners: Can we enhance comprehension and mastery skills? In J. Flood (Ed.), *Promoting reading comprehension* (pp. 216–31). Newark, DEL: International Reading Association.

BURKE, J. (1978). *Connections.* Boston: Little, Brown and Company.

CAIN, E. J., JR. (1984). The challenge of technology: Educating the exceptional child for the world of tommorrow. *Teaching Exceptional Children, 16* (*4*), 238–241.

CARDENAS, J. & FIRST, J. M. (1985, September). Children at risk. *Educational Leadership, 43* (*1*), 4–9.

CEGELKA, P. T., & LEWIS, R. B. (1983). The once and future world: Portents for the handicapped. *The Journal for Special Educators, 19* (*4*), 61–73.

CUMMINS, J. (1981). The role of primary language development in promoting educational success for language minority students. In *Schooling and language minority students: A theoretical framework.* Los Angeles: Evaluation, Dissemination and Assessment Center, California State University.

DEGLER, L. S., & RISKO, V. J. (1979, May). Teaching reading to mainstreamed sensory impaired children. *The Reading Teacher, 32,* 921–25.

EDSON, C. H. (1983). Risking the nation: Historical dimensions on survival and educational reform. *Issues in Education, 1,* 171–184.

FENSTERMACHER, G. D. & GOODLAD, J. I. (1983), In G. D. Fenstermacher & J. I. Goodlad (Eds.), *Individual differences and common curriculum.* Eighty-Second

Yearbook of the National Society for the Study of Education, Part 1. Chicago: National Society for the Study of Education.

GEARHART, B. R., & WEISHAHN, M. W. (1976). *The handicapped child in the regular classroom.* St. Louis: The C. V. Mosby Company.

GENENSKY, S. M. (1970). *A functional classification system of the visually impaired to replace the legal definition of blindness.* Santa Monica, CA: The Rand Corporation.

GILLET J. W. & GENTRY. J. R. (1983, January). Bridges between nonstandard and standard English with extensions of dictated stories. *The Reading Teacher, 36* (4), 360–365.

GITELMAN, H. (1984, March). Motivating accelerated learners to read. *The Reading Teacher, 37,* 678–679.

GONDELMAN, J. (1982, June 10). Bilingual education an emotional issue. San Diego, CA: *San Diego Union,* pp. A1, A2.

———. (1984, June 11). Does bilingual education work? San Diego, CA: *San Diego Union,* pp. A1, A6.

———. (1984, June 12). Proposed changes in the law. San Diego, CA: *San Diego Union,* p. A1.

HALLAHAN, D. P., & KAUFFMAN, J. M. (1975). Research on the education of distractible and hyperactive children. In W. M. Cruickshank and D. P. Hallahan (Eds.), *Perceptual and learning disabilities in children. Research and Theory,* 2. Syracuse, NY: Syracuse Univeristy Press.

HARLEY, R., SPOLLEN, J., & LONG, S. (1973, May). A study of reliability and validity of the visual efficiency scale with preschool children. *Education of the Visually Handicapped, 5,* 38–42.

HULL, F. M., MIEKLE, P. W., TIMMONS, R. J., & WILLEFORD, J. A. (1969). *National speech and hearing survey report.* Project No. 50978. Washington, DC: U.S. Office of Education, Bureau of Education for the Handicapped.

KIRK, S. A. (1958). *Early education of the mentally retarded: An experimental study.* Urbana, IL: University of Illinois Press.

KRASHEN, S. D. (1981). Bilingual education and second language acquisition theory. In *Schooling and language minority students: A theoretical framework.* Los Angeles: Evaluation, Dissemination and Assessment Center, California State University.

LADO, R. (1976). *Linguistics across cultures* (pp. 747–751). Ann Arbor: University of Michigan Press.

LAPP, D. & FLOOD, J. (1983). *Teaching reading to every child* (2nd ed.). New York: Macmillan Publishing Company.

———. (1986). *Teaching students to read.* New York: Macmillan Publishing Company.

LEWIS, R. & DOORLAG, D. H. (1983). *Teaching special students in the mainstream.* Columbus, OH: Charles E. Merrill Publishing Company.

LONG, R. (1984, February). Soviet children's books: Expanding children's view of the Soviet Union. *Journal of Reading, 27* (5), 418–423.

LOWENBRAUN, S., AFFLECK, J. & ARCHER A. (1981). *Teaching the mildly handicapped in the regular class* (2d ed.). Columbus, OH: Charles E. Merril Publishing Company.

LUKASEVICH, A. (1983, February). Three dozen useful information sources on reading for the gifted. *The Reading Teacher, 36,* 542–548.

MACE-MATLUCK, B. J. (1983). *Literacy instruction in bilingual settings: A synthesis of current research,* ERIC Document ED 222 079. Los Alamitos, CA: National Center for Bilingual Research.

MARLAND, S. (1972). *Education of the gifted and talented.* (Report to the Congress of the United States by the U.S. Commissioner of Education.) Washington, DC: U.S. Government Printing Office.

MOLLER, B. (1984). An instructional model for gifted advanced readers. *Journal of Reading, 27,* 4, 324–27.

MYKLEBUST, H. R. (1968). Learning disabilities: Definition and overview. In H. R. Myklebust (Ed.), *Progress in learning disabilities,* Vol. 1 (pp. 1–15). New York: Grune & Stratton.

NELSON-HERBER, J. & HERBER, H. (1984). A positive approach to assessment and correction of reading difficulties in middle and secondary schools. In J. Flood (Ed.), *Promoting reading comprehension* (pp. 232–234). Newark, DEL: International Reading Association.

NGUYEN, L. & HENKIN, A. (1981). *Fundamental vietnamese vocabulary.* Iowa City, IA: National Center for Materials and Curriculum Development, The University of Iowa.

———. (1985, December). A second generation readability formula for Vietnamese. *Journal of Reading, 29, 3,* 219–225.

PARNES, S., NOLLER R., & BIONDI, A. (1977). *Guide to creative action.* New York: Charles Scribner's Sons.

PAST, K. & PAST, A. (1980, May). A bilingual kindergarten

immersed in print. *The Reading Teacher, 50,* 907–913.

PERKINS, W. H. (1971). *Speech pathology: An applied behavioral science.* St. Louis: The C. V. Mosby Company.

PIAGET, J. (1963). *The origins of intelligence in children.* New York: W. W. Norton and Co., Inc.

Report to Ad Hoc Committee to Define Deaf and Hard of Hearing. (1975). *American Annals of the Deaf, 120,* 590–12.

ROTHROCK, D. (1982). The rise and decline of individualized instruction. *Educational Leadership, 39,* 528–531.

SANTIAGO, R. L. (1985, September). Understanding bilingual education, or the sheep in wolf's clothing. *Educational Leadership, 43, 1,* 79–82.

SCHIEFELBUSCH, R. L. & LLOYD, L. L. (1974). In R. L. Schiefelbusch & L. L. Lloyd (Eds.) *Language perspectives—acquisition, retardation and intervention.* Baltimore: University Park Press.

SCHON, I. (1985, December). Poetry for Spanish-speaking adolescents. *Journal of Reading, 29, 3,* 243–245.

SHANNON, P. (1985, October). Reading instructions and social class. *Language Arts, 62, 6,* 604–613.

SLAVIN, R. E. (1980). *Using student team learning.* Baltimore: The Johns Hopkins University Press.

SLOANE, H. N. & MACAULAY, B. D. (1968). In H. N. Sloane & B. D. MacAulay (Eds.), *Operant procedures in remedial speech and language training.* Boston: Houghton Mifflin Company.

SPAULDING, S. (1956, December). A Spanish readability formula. *Modern Language Journal, 40,* 435.

STEINBERG, L., BLINDE, P. L. & CHAN, K. S. (1984, Spring). Dropping out among language minority youth. *Review of Educational Research, 54, 1,* 113–132.

STIHE, E. L. & BOHANNON, J. N. (1983). Imitations, Interactions, and Language Acquisition. *J Child Lang, 10,* 589–603.

TREFFINGER, D. (1980). *Encouraging creative learning for the gifted and talented.* Los Angeles: National/State Leadership Training Institute of the Gifted and Talented.

TURNBULL, A. P. & SCHULZ, J. B. (1979). *Mainstreaming handicapped students: A guide for the classroom teacher.* Boston: Allyn & Bacon.

U.S. Department of Education. (1984). *The nation responds: Recent efforts to improve education.* Washington, D.C.: U.S. Government Printing Office.

VAN RIPER, C. (1972). *Speech correction: Principles and methods* (5th ed.). Englewood Cliffs, NJ: Prentice-Hall, Inc.

VARNHAGEN, C. & GOLDMAN, S. (1986, May). Improving comprehension: Casual relations instruction for learning handicapped learners. *The Reading Teacher, 39* (9), 896–904.

VORHAUS, R. (1984, February). Strategies for reading in a second language. *Journal of Reading, 27* (5), 412–417.

WANG, M. C. & LINDVALL, C. M. (1984). Individual differences and school learning environments: Theory, research, and design. In E. W. Gordon (Ed.), *Review of Research in Education,* Vol. 2. Washington, D.C.: American Educational Research Association.

———. & WALBERG, H. J. (1985). In M. C. Wang & H. J. Walberg (Eds.), *Adapting instruction to individual differences.* Berkeley, Calif.: McCutchan.

WANG, M., RUBENSTEIN, J. & REYNOLDS, M. (1985, September). Clearing the road to success for students with special needs. *Educational Leadership, 43, 1,* 62–67.

WAXMAN, H. C., WANG, M. C., ANDERSON, K. A. & WALBERG, H. J. (1985, September). Synthesis of research on the effects of adaptive education. *Educational Leadership, 43,* 26–29.

WHITE, N. J. (1937). I've taught them all. *The Clearinghouse, 12* (3), 151, 192.

ZIVIAN, M. & SAMUELS, M. (1986, Spring). Performance on a word-likeness task by normal readers and reading-disabled children. *Reading Research Quarterly, 21* (2), 150–160.

Chapter 2

ABELMAN, R. (1984, January–February). Children and TV: The ABC's of TV literacy. *Childhood Education, 60, 3,* 200–205.

ALLEN, E. G. & LAMINACK, L. L. (1982, March). Language experience reading—It's a natural. *Reading Teacher, 35, 6,* 708–715.

BECK, I. L. (1973) A longitudinal study of the reading achievement effects of formal reading instruction in the kindergarten: A summative and formative evaluation. Unpublished doctoral dissertation, University of Pittsburgh.

BERRY, K. S. (1985, January). Talking to learn subject matter/learning subject matter talk. *Language Arts, 62 (1),* 708–715.

BERNSTEIN, B. (1967). Elaborated and restricted codes: Their social origin and some consequences. In B. Gumperz & D. Mymes (Eds.), *The ethnography of communication.* American Anthropologist Publication.

BOIKO, C. (1967). *Children's plays for creative actors.* Boston: Plays, Inc.

BUCKLEY, M. (1986, April). When teachers decide to integrate the language arts. *Language Arts, 63 (4),* 369–377.

CLAY, M. (1986, April). Constructive processes: Talking, reading, writing, art, and craft. *The Reading Teacher, 39 (8),* 764–770.

COOPER, M. (1984, Spring). Televised books and their effects on children's reading. *Use of English, 35 (2),* 41–49.

DURKIN, D. (1974). *Teaching them to read.* Boston: Allyn and Bacon, Inc.

DYSON, A. H. (1982, November/December). Reading, writing, and language: Young children solving the written language puzzle. *Language Arts, 59 (8),* 829–839.

FAKOURI, M. E. (1984, Summer). Television and the young viewer. *Contemporary Education, 55 (4),* 216–219.

GIROUX, H. A. (1984, January). Rethinking the language of schooling. *Language Arts, 61 (1),* 33–40.

LOBAN, W. (1976). *Language Development: Kindergarten through Grade Twelve.* Urbana, IL: National Council of Teachers of English.

MARTINEZ, M. & ROSER, N. (1985, April). Read it again: The value of repeated readings during storytime. *The Reading Teacher, 38 (8),* 782–786.

NEUMAN, S. B. (1980, April). Television: Its effects on reading and school achievement. *The Reading Teacher, 33,* 801–805.

PEZDEK, K. & STEVENS, E. (1984, March). Children's memory for auditory and visual information on television. *Developmental Psychology, 20 (2),* 212–218.

PIAGET, J. (1963). *The Origins of Intelligence in Children.* New York: Norton.

RAFFA, J. B. (1985, Winter). Television and values: Implications for education. *Educational Forum, 49 (2),* 189–198.

RHODES, L. K. & HILL, M. W. (1985, March). Supporting reading in the home—naturally: Selected materials for parents. *The Reading Teacher, 38 (7),* 619–623.

ROSER, N. L. (1974, April). Electric company critque: Can great be good enough? *The Reading Teacher, 27 (7),* 680–684.

SEARLS, D. T., MEAD, N. A., & WARD B. (1985, November). The relationship of students' reading skills to TV watching, leisure time reading, and homework. *Journal of Reading, 29 (2),* 158–163.

SEMINOFF, N. (1986, May). Children's periodicals throughout the world: An overlooked educational resource. *The Reading Teacher, 39 (9),* 889–895.

WHIMBEY, A. (1985, November). Reading, writing, reasoning linked in testing and training. *Journal of Reading, 29 (2),* 118–123.

Chapter 3

BAMBAS, R. C. (1980). *The English language: Its origin and history.* Norman, OK: University of Oklahoma Press.

BARON, D. E. (1982). *Going Native: The regeneration of Saxon English.* University, AL: University of Alabama Press, American Dialect Society.

CLAIBORNE, R. (1983). *Our marvelous native tongue: The life and times of the English language.* New York: New York Times Books.

DILLARD, J. L. (1976). *American talk: Where Our Words Come From.* New York: Random House, Inc.

GILBERT, A. J. (1979). *Literary language from Chaucer to Johnson.* New York: Barnes & Noble Books.

HOWATT, A. P. R. (1984). *A history of English language teaching.* Oxford: Oxford University Press.

KELLY, P. (1986, Summer). Gender differences in male/female reading choices. *Journal of Reading Behavior, 18 (3),* 243–256.

KEY, M. R. (1975). *Male/female language.* Metuchen, NJ: Scarecrow Press.

LAKOFF, R. (1975). *Language and woman's place.* New York: Harper & Row, Publishers, Inc.

LAPP, D. & FLOOD, J. (1983). *Teaching reading to every child,* 2d ed. New York: Macmillan Publishing Company.

———. (1986). *Teaching students to read.* New York: Macmillan Publishing Company.

PEI, M. (1965). *The story of language.* New York: New American Library.

PINNELL, G. S. & GREEN, J. L. (1986, April). Research currents: Learning from language research to talk about education. *Language Arts, 63 (4),* 384–389.

PYLES, T. & ALGEO, J. (1982). *The origins and development of the English language.* New York: Harcourt Brace Jovanovich, Inc.

STEWART, G. R. (1979). *American given names: Their origin and history in the context of the English language.* New York: Oxford University Press.

TRAPP, J. B. (1973). *The Oxford anthology of English literature: Medieval English literature.* London: Oxford University Press.

Chapter 4

ALYESHMERNI, M. & TAUBER, P. (1975). *Working with aspects of language.* New York: Harcourt Brace Jovanovich, Inc.

BERKO-GLEASON, J. (1958). The child's learning of English morphology. *Word, 14,* 150–177.

———. (1973). Language and social context: Selected readings. *Contemporary Psychology, 18 (4),* 178–179.

BERMAN, R. A. (1983). On the study of first language acquisition. *Language Learning, 33 (5),* 221–245

BLACHOWICZ, C. (1984, spring). Children's linguistic insight: What we think we know. *Reading Horizons, 24 (3),* 202–207.

BROWN, R. & BELLUGI, U. (1964). Three processes in the child's acquisition of syntax. In E. H. Lenneberg (Ed.), *New directions in the study of language.* Cambridge, MA: MIT Press.

BROWN, R. & FRASER, C. (1963). The acquisition of syntax. In C. N. Cofer & B. S. Musgrave (Eds.), *Verbal behavior and learning: Problems and processes,* pp. 158–197. New York: McGraw-Hill Book Co.

BUSS, K. (1984). Melody: Importance in learning oral and book language. *Reading Psychology, 5 (3–4),* 298–301.

CAHIR, S. R. & SHUY, R. W. (1981, March). Classroom language learning: What do the researchers know? *Language Arts, 58 (3)* 370.

CAZDEN, C. B. (1981). *Language in early childhood education.* Washington, DC: National Association for the Education of Young Children.

CHOMSKY, C. S. (1969). *The acquisition of syntax in children from 5 to 10.* Cambridge, MA: MIT Press.

CHOMSKY, N. (1957). *Syntactic structures.* The Hague: Mouton.

———. (1965). *Aspects of the theory of syntax.* Cambridge, MA: MIT Press.

———. (1972). *Language and mind.* New York: Harcourt Brace Jovanovich, Inc.

CLARK, E. V. (1971). On acquisition of the meaning of "before" and "after." *Journal of Verbal Learning and Verbal Behavior, 10,* 266–275.

———. (1970). The primitive nature of children's relational concepts. In J. R. Hayes (Ed.), *Cognition and the development of language.* New York: John Wiley & Sons, Inc.

CURTISS, S., ET AL. (1974). The linguistic development of genie. *Language, 50 (3),* 528–554.

DE VILLIERS, P. A. & DE VILLIERS, J. G. (1979). *Early Language.* Cambridge, MA: Harvard University Press.

DONALDSON, M. (1978). *Children's minds.* New York: W. W. Norton & Company.

EIMAS, P. D. & CORBIT, J. D. (1973). Selective adaptations of linguistic feature detectors. *Cognitive Psychology, 4 (1),* 99–109.

ELLIOTT, N. (1984, Spring). Communicative development from birth. *Western Journal of Speech Communication, 48 (2),* 184–196.

FLEGG, J. (1980, Fall). Mother–child interaction studied. *Communication Quarterly.*

FROMKIN, V. & ROBMAN, R. (1974). *An introduction to language.* New York: Holt, Rinehart and Winston, 1974.

FURROW, D. & NELSON, K. (1984, October). Environmental correlates of individual differences in language acquisition. *Journal of Child Language, 11 (3),* 523–534.

GREANEY, V. (1986, April). Parental influence on reading. *The Reading Teacher, 39 (8),* 813–818.

HALLIDAY, M. A. (1973). *Explorations in the functions of language.* London: Edward Arnold & Co.

HOHMANN, M., ET AL. (1979). *Young children in action: A manual for preschool educators.* Ypsilanti, MI: High/Scope Press.

IRWIN, O. C. (1947). Infant speech: Consonantal sounds according to place of articulation. *Journal of Speech and Hearing Disorders, 12,* 397–401.

———. (1947). Infant speech: variability and the problem of diagnosis. *Journal of Speech and Hearing Disorders, 12,* 287–289.

JAKOBSON, R. (1968). *Child language, aphasia and general sounds.* The Hague: Mouton.

KINSBOURNE, M. & WHITE, W. L. (1974). *Hemispheric Disconnection and Cerebral Function.* Springfield, IL: Charles C. Thomas, Publisher.

KUCZAJ, S. A. (1977). The acquisition of regular and irregular past tense forms. *Journal of Verbal Learning and Verbal Behavior, 16,* 589–600.

LARRICK, N. (1959). *Your child and his reading: How parents can help.* New York: Public Affairs Committee.

LENNEBERG, E. H. (1964). A biological perspective of language. In E. H. Lenneberg (Ed.), *New directions in the study of Language.* Cambridge, MA: MIT Press.

———. (1966). The natural history of language. In F. Smith & G. Miller (Eds.), *The genesis of language. Cambridge, MA: MIT Press.*

———. (1967). *Biological foundations of language.* New York: John Wiley and Sons.

LINDHOLM, K. J. (1980). Bilingual children: Some interpretations of cognitive and linguistic development. In K. E. Nelson (Ed.), *Child Language, 2.* New York: Gardner Press.

LOBAN, W. (1976). *Language development: Kindergarten through Grade Twelve.* Urbana, IL: National Council of Teachers of English.

LORENZE, K. Z. (1970, October). On killing members of one's own species. *Bulletin of the Atomic Scientists, 26,* 2–5.

MALSTROM, J. (1977). *Understanding Language.* New York: St. Martin's Press.

McCARTHY, D. (1934). Language development in children. In L. Carmichael (Ed.), *Manual of Child Psychology,* (2d ed.), 492–630. New York: John Wiley and Sons.

MENYUK, P. (1963). Syntactic structures in the language of children. *Journal of Child Development, 32,* 407–422.

———. (1969). *Sentences children use.* Cambridge, MA: MIT Press.

MOSKOWITZ, B. A. (1978, November). The acquisition of language. *Scientific American, 239 (5),* 92–108.

PEI, M. (1956). *Language for everybody.* New York: Devin-Adair.

PIAGET, J. (1963). *The origins of intelligence in children.* New York: W. W. Norton & Company.

RAPHAEL, M. L. (1981) *Chassidic tales adapted.* Columbus, OH: Department of Jewish Studies, Ohio State University.

ROSENBERG, R. (1984, Spring). Wordplay magic. *Exercise Exchange, 29 (2)* 24–30.

ROSS, G. (1986, February). Acquisition and generalization of novel object concepts by young language learners. *Journal of Child Language, 13,* 67–83.

ROSS, R. R. (1980). *Storyteller.* Columbus, OH: Charles E. Merrill Publishing Company.

ROTH, R. (1986, February). Practical use of language in school. *Language Arts, 63 (2),* 134–142.

SHIRLEY, M. M. (1933). *The first two years: A study of twenty-five babies.* Minneapolis: University of Minnesota Press.

SIMMONS, B. AND LAWRENCE, P. S. (1981, January/February). Beginning reading: Welcome parents. *Childhood Education,* 156–160.

STIBBS, A. (1980). *Assessing children's language: Guidelines for teachers.* London: Ward Lock Educational and National Association for the Teaching of English.

TAYLOR, N. E., BLUM, I. H., & LOGSDON, D. M. (1986). The development of written language awareness: Environmental aspects and program characteristics. *Reading Research Quarterly, 21 (2),* 132–149.

WEBER-OLSEN, M. (1984, Spring). Motherese: The language of parent and child. *Texas Tech Journal of Education, 11 (2),* 123–141.

WELLS, G. (1980). Apprenticeship in meaning. In K. E. Nelson (Ed.), *Child Language, 2.* New York: Gardner Press.

WELLS, G. & WELLS, J. (1984, Summer). Learning to talk and talking to learn. *Theory into Practice, 23 (3),* 190–197.

Chapter 5

ARMSTRONG, L. (1985, February). Is anybody listening? *Learning, 13 (6),* 33

BROWN, D. (1954). *Auding as the primary language ability.* Unpublished dissertation, Stanford University.

DiSIBIO, R. A. (1982, Fall). Listening . . . the neglected art? *Reading Improvement, 19 (3),* 217–218.

DUKER, S. (1969). Listening. In R. L. Ebel (Ed.), *Encyclopedia of educational research,* pp. 747–751. New York: Macmillan Publishing Company.

GIANNANGELO, D. M. & FRAZER, B. M. (1975, December). Listening: A critical skill that must be taught. *Kappa Delta Research, 12 (2),* 42–43.

GOLD, Y. (Winter, 1981). Teaching attentive listening. *Reading Improvement, 8 (4),* 319–320.

HEILMAN, A. W. (1985). *Phonics in proper perspective* (5th ed.). Columbus, OH: Charles E. Merrill Publishing Company.

HOBBS, C. (1986, April). Helping your students to listen better. *Learning, 14,* 66–67.

HOFFMAN, S. M. (1978). *The effect of a listening skills program on the reading comprehension of fourth grade students.* Unpublished doctoral dissertation, Walden University.

JOLLY, T. (1980, February). Listen my children and you shall read. *Language Arts, 57 (2),* 214–217

LEMONS, R. L. & MOORE, S. C. (1982, Fall). The effects of training in listening on the development of reading skills. *Reading Improvement, 19 (3),* 212–216.

LUNDSTEEN, S. (1979). *Listening: Its impact at all levels on reading and other language arts.* Urbana, IL: National Council of Teachers of English.

OTTO, W. & SMITH, R. (1980). *Corrective and remedial teaching.* Boston: Houghton Mifflin Company.

PEARSON, P. D. & FIELDING, L. (1982, September). Research update: Listening comprehension. *Language Arts, 59,* 617–629.

RANKIN, P. T. (1926). The measurement of the ability to understand spoken language. Unpublished dissertation. Ann Arbor, MI: University of Michigan.

ROBINSON, S. & SMITH, D. D. (1981, April). Listening skills: Teaching learning disabled students to be better listeners. *Focus on Exceptional Children, 18 (8).*

RUSSELL, D. & RUSSELL, E. F. (1959). *Listening aids through the grades.* New York: Teachers College, Columbia University, Bureau of Publications.

SHOOP, M. (1986, March). Inquest: A listening and reading comprehension strategy. *The Reading Teacher, 39 (7),* 670–674.

STEWIG, J. W. (1983). *Exploring language arts in the elementary classroom.* New York: Holt, Rinehart and Winston.

WEPMAN, J. W. (1960). Auditory discrimination, speech and reading. *Elementary School Journal, 60,* 326.

WILT, M. (1959). *Creativity in the elementary school.* New York: Appleton-Century-Crofts.

Chapter 6

BARNES, D. (1976). *From Communication to Curriculum.* New York: Penguin books.

BENNETT, S. G. (1984, April). *Do junior high school reading/language arts teachers use oral communication to improve reading comprehension? A study of two teachers.* Paper presented at the annual meeting of the NCTE Spring Conference, Columbus, OH.

CAMARATA, S. & LEONARD, L. B. (1986, February). Young children pronounce object words more accurately than action words. *Journal of Child Language, 13,* 51–65.

CHAFE, W. L. (1982). Integration and involvement in speaking, writing, and oral literature. In D. Tannen (Ed.), *Spoken and Written Language.* Norwood, NJ: Ablex.

———. (1985). Linguistic differences produced by differences between speaking and writing. In D. R. Olson, N. Torrance & A. Hildyard (Eds.), *Literacy, language and learning.* Cambridge: Cambridge University Press.

CHAPMAN, K. L. ET AL. (1986, February). The effects of feedback on young children's inappropriate word usage. *Journal of Child Language, 13,* 101–117.

DURRELL, D. & CROSSLEY, A. (1957). *Thirty plays for classroom reading.* Boston: Plays, Inc.

FRYE, A. (1969). *Syllabus for speech.* [Mimeograph]. Sacramento, CA: California State Department of Instruction.

KANG-NING, C. (1981, Winter). Education for Chinese and Indochinese. *Theory into practice, 20,* 35–44.

KIEFER, B. Z., & DESTEFANO, J. S. (1985). Cultures together in the classroom: "What you sayin?" In A. Jaggar & M. T. Smith-Burke (Eds.), *Observing the language learner.* Newark, DEL: International Reading Association, and Urbana, IL.: National Council of Teachers of English.

LAPP, D. & FLOOD, J. (1983). *Teaching Reading to Every Child* 2d ed. New York: Macmillan Publishing Company.

———. (1986). *Teaching Students to Read.* New York: Macmillan Publishing Company.

LENNEBERG, E. H. (1970). On explaining language. In E. V. Gunderson (Ed.). *Language and reading—An interdisciplinary approach.* Washington, D.C.: Center for Applied Linguistics.

MEAD, N. A. (1980, September). *Developing oral communication skills: Implications of theory and research for instruction and training.* Paper presented at the National Basic Skills Orientation Conference, Arlington, VA.

MEHAN, H. (1979). *Learning lessons: Social organization in the classroom.* Cambridge, MA: Harvard University Press.

MICHAELS, S. (1981, December). Sharing time: Children's narrative style and differential access to literacy. *Language in Society, 10,* 423–442.

MICHAELS, S. & FOSTER, M. (1985). Peer–peer learning: Evidence from a student-run sharing time. In A. Jaggar & M. T. Smith-Burke (Eds.), *Observing the language learner.* Newark, DEL: International Reading Association, and Urbana, IL.: National Council of Teachers of English.

NCTE (1983, February). Forum: Essentials of English. *Language Arts, 60* (*2*), 244–248.

NEW, C. (1982, March). *Sharing time as a teacher-led speech event.* Paper presented at University of Pennsylvania Ethnography in Education Research Forum, Philadelphia, PA.

PATIN, H. (1964). Class and caste in urban education. *Chicago School Journal, 45,* 305–310.

PHILIPS, S. (1982). *The Invisible Culture: Communication in the classroom on the Warm Springs Indian Reservation.* New York: Longman, Inc.

PIAGET, J. (1962). *Plays, Dreams, and Imitation in Childhood.* New York: W. W. Norton & Company, Inc.

POOLE, I. (1934). *The genetic development of the articulation of consonant sounds.* Doctoral dissertation, University of Michigan.

POOLEY, R. C. (1968). *English language arts in Wisconsin.* Madison, WI.: Madison Department of Public Instruction.

———. (1974). *Teaching of English usage.* Urbana, IL.: National Council of Teachers of English.

RASMUSSEN, C. (1949). *Speech methods in the elementary school.* New York: Ronald Press.

SHAFTEL, G., & SCHAFTEL, F. (1952). *Role playing: The problem story.* New York: National Conference of Christians and Jews.

SKINNER, B. F. (1972). *Beyond freedom and dignity.* New York: Alfred A. Knopf, Inc.

SMITH, M. (1963). *Listening Habits and Speech Sound Discrimination.* Haywood, CA: Alameda County School Department.

STRICKLAND, D. & CULLINAN, B. (1986, March). Literature and language. *Language Arts, 63* (*3*), 221–225.

TABA, H., LEVINE, S., & ELZEY, F. F. (1964). *Thinking in elementary school children: Cooperative research project number 1574.* Washington, D.C.: Research Program of the Office of Education, U.S. Department of Health, Education and Welfare.

VAN RIPER, C. (1971). *Nature of stuttering.* Englewood Cliffs, NJ: Prentice-Hall, Inc.

———. (1972). *Speech correction: Principles and Methods.* Englewood Cliffs, NJ: Prentice-Hall, Inc.

———. (1973). *Treatment of stuttering.* Englewood Cliffs, NJ: Prentice-Hall, Inc.

VAN RIPER, C., & BUTLER, K. (1955). *Speech in the elementary Classroom.* New York: Harper & Row, Publishers, Inc.

WANAT, S. F. (1971, November). Language acquisition: Basic issues. *The Reading Teacher, 25,* 142–147.

WATSON, K. & YOUNG B. (1986, February). Discourse for learning in the classroom. *Language Arts, 63* (*2*), 126–133.

WILCOX, K. (1982). Differential socialization in the classroom: Implications for equal opportunity. In G. Spindler (Ed.), *Doing the ethnography of schooling: Educational anthropology in action.* New York: Holt, Rinehart & Winston.

Chapter 7

ALVERMANN, D., DILLON, D., O'BRIEN, D. & SMITH, L. (1985, October). The role of the textbook in discussion. *Journal of Reading, 29* (*1*), 50–57.

BECK, I., MCKEOWN, M., & MCCASLIN, E. (1983). Vocabulary development: All contexts are not created equal. *The Elementary School Journal, 83* (*3*), 177–181.

BLACHOWICZ, C. L. Z. (1985, May). Vocabulary development and reading: From research to instruction. *The Reading Teacher, 38* (*9*), 876–881.

BLACKBURN, E. (1984, April). Common ground: Developing relationships between reading and writing. *Language Arts, 61* (*4*), 367–375.

BOOTHBY, P. R., & ALVERMANN, D. (1982, November/December). What are we proud of in the teaching of reading? *Language Arts, 59* (*8*), 840–843

DAVEY, B. (1986, March). Using textbook activity guides to help students learn from textbooks. *Journal of Reading, 29* (*6*), 489–494.

DAVIS, C. A. (1985, April). Cloze and comprehension: A qualitative analysis and critique. *Journal of Reading, 28* (*7*), 585–589.

ELDRIDGE, B. (1985, October). Reading in context: An

alternative approach for the adolescent disabled reader. *Journal of Reading, 29 (1),* 9–17.

FLOOD, J. (ED.). (1984). *Promoting reading comprehension.* Newark, DEL: International Reading Association.

———. (Ed.). (1984). *Understanding reading comprehension.* Newark, DEL: International Reading Association.

FLOOD, J. (1986, April). The text, the student and the teacher: Learning from exposition in middle schools. *The Reading Teacher, 39 (8),* 784–791.

FLOOD J., & LAPP, D. (1977). *Prose Analysis and the Effects of Staging on Prose Comprehension.* Paper presented at the Second Annual Reading Association of Ireland Conference, Dublin, Ireland.

GAUS, P. J. (1983, December), The indispensable reading teacher. *The Reading Teacher, 37 (3),* 269–272.

HORN, C. C., & MANIS, F. R., (1985). Normal and disabled readers' use of orthographic structure in processing print. *Journal of Reading Behavior, 17 (2),* 143–161.

JOHNSON, D., & PEARSON, P. D. (1984). *Teaching Reading Vocabulary* (2d ed.). New York: Holt, Rinehart and Winston.

KIMMEL, S., & MACGINITIE, W. (1985, April). Helping students revise hypotheses while reading. *The Reading Teacher, 38 (8),* 768–771.

LAPP, D., & FLOOD, J. (1983). *Teaching reading to every child* (2d ed.). New York: Macmillan Publishing Company.

———. (1986). *Teaching every student to read.* New York: Macmillan Publishing Company.

MALLON, B., & BERGLUND, R. (1984, May). The language experience approach to reading: Recurring questions and their answers. *The Reading Teacher, 37 (9),* 867–873.

MANNING, M. M. & MANNING, G. L. (1984, October). Early readers and nonreaders from low socioeconomic environments: What their parents report. *The Reading Teacher, 38 (1),* 32–35.

MARTINEZ, M. & ROSER, N. (1985, April). Read it again: The value of repeated readings during storytime. *The Reading Teacher, 38 (8),* 782–786.

PALINCSAR, A. & BROWN, A. (1986, April). Interactive teaching to promote independent learning from text. *The Reading Teacher, 39 (8),* 771–777.

ROSER, N., & MARTINEZ, M. (1985, September). Roles adults play in preschoolers' response to literature. *Language Arts, 62 (5),* 485–490.

TAFT, M. L., & LESLIE, L. (1985). The effects of prior knowledge and oral reading accuracy on miscues and comprehension. *Journal of Reading Behavior, 17 (2),* 163–179.

TAYLOR, B. M., & NOSBUSH, L. (1983, December). Oral reading for meaning: A technique for improving word identification skills. *The Reading Teacher, 37 (3)* 234–237.

THOMAS, K. (1985, September). Early reading as a social interaction process. *Language Arts, 62 (5),* 469–475.

THORNDIKE, E. L. (1917). Reading and reasoning: A study of mistakes in paragraph reading. *Journal of Educational Psychology, 8,* 323–332.

Chapter 8

ADAMS, K. I. (1981). *Multicultural representation in children's books.* (ERIC Document Reproduction Service No. ED 219 750).

APPLEBEE, A. N. (1978). *The child's concept of story: Ages 2 to 17.* Chicago: The University of Chicago Press.

BARTO, A. (1980). Children's responses to illustrations of poetry. In G. Fox & G. Hammon (Eds.), *Responses to children's literature: Proceedings of the Fourth Symposium of the International Research Society for Children's Literature* (pp. 81–87). New York: K. G. Saur.

BRENNAN, A. J. (1983). *Children and Death.* (ERIC Document Reproduction Service No. ED 246 995).

BUNBURY, R. (1980). Children's understanding of literature. In G. Fox & G. Hammond (Eds.), *Responses to children's literature: Proceedings of the Fourth Symposium of the International Research Society for Children's Literature* (pp. 92–101). New York: K. G. Saur.

CARTER, C. (CHAIR) (1984). *Literature—News that stays news.* Urbana, IL: National Council of Teachers of English.

COLLINS, L. J., INGOLDSBY, B. B., & DELLMANN, M. M. (1984). Sex-role sterotyping in children's literature: A change from the past. *Childhood Education, 60 (4),* 278–285.

CULLINAN, B. & STRICKLAND, D. (1986, April). The early years: Language, literature, and literacy in classroom research. *The Reading Teacher, 39 (8),* 798–806.

CULLINAN, B. E., HARWOOD, K., & GALDA, L. (1983). The reader and the story: Comprehension and response. *Journal of Research and Development in Education, 16 (3),* 29–38.

DOHERTY-HALE, D. (1984). Children's literature for the learning disabled. *Learning Disability Quarterly, 7 (4)*, 336–342.

FEIFEL, H. (1977). *New meanings of death.* New York: McGraw-Hill Book Company.

FILLMER, H. T. (1984). Children's descriptions of and attitudes toward the elderly. *Educational Gerontology, 10*, 1–2, 99–107.

GILLIS, R. J. (1978). *Children's books for times of stress.* Bloomington: Indiana University Press.

GOLDEN, J. M., (1978). *A schema for analyzing response to literature applied to the responses of fifth and eighth graders to realistic and fantasy short stories.* (ERIC Document Reproduction Service No. ED 192 306).

GRIFFIN, L. (1970). *Multi-ethnic books for young children.* National Association for the Education of Young Children.

HICKMAN, J. (1980). *Extending the dimensions of research in response to literature: Response in an elementary school setting.* Columbus, Ohio State University. (ERIC Document Reproduction Service No. ED 189 600).

———. (1983). Everything considered: Response to literature in an elementary school setting. *Journal of Research and Development in Education, 16*, (3), 8–13.

HILLMAN, J. S. (1976, September). Occupational roles in children's literature. *Elementary School Journal*, 1–4.

HUCK, C. S. (1979). *Children's Literature in the Elementary School, 3d ed.* New York: Holt, Rinehart and Winston.

JENNINGS, S. (1975, March). Effects of sex typing in children's stories on preference and recall. *Child Development*, 220–223.

KAZEMEK, F. (1986, March). Literature and moral development from a feminine perspective. *Language Arts, 63* (3), 264–272.

KELLY, P. (1983). Sex stereotypes of reading materials. Unpublished master's thesis, San Diego State University.

———. (1986, Summer). The influence of reading content on student's perceptions of the masculinity or femininity of reading. *Journal of Reading Behavior, 18* (3), 243–256.

KIMMEL, M. M. & SEGEL, E. (1983). *For reading out loud! A guide to sharing books with children.* New York: Delacorte Press.

LUCKING, R. A. (1976). A study of the effects of a hierarchically-ordered questioning technique on adolescents' response to short stories, *Research in the Teaching of English, 10*, 269–276.

MAVROGENES, N. A. (1982). Positive images of grandparents in children's picture books. *Reading Teacher, 35* (8), 896–901.

MURPHY, C. (1975, April). Sex stereotyping in literature during early childhood. *Counseling and Values*, 186–191.

ORDAL, C. C. (1983). Death as seen in books suitable for young children. *Omega: Journal of Death and Dying, 14* (3), 249–277.

PETROSKY, A. R. (1976). The effects of reality perception and fantasy on response to literature. *Research in the Teaching of English, 10*, 239–258.

POE, M. & SCHMIDT, B. (1987). *Willie MacGurkle and friends.* North Billerica, MA: Curriculum Associates.

PURVES, A. C. (1973). *Literature Education in Ten Countries.* New York: John Wiley & Sons, Inc.

———. (1979). That sunny dome: Those caves of ice: A model for research in reader response. *College English, 40* (7), 802–812.

PURVES, A. C. & MONSON, D. L. (1984). *Experiencing Children's Literature.* Glenview, IL: Scott, Foresman and Company.

RADENCICH, M. C. (1985). Books that promote positive attitudes toward second language learning. *Reading Teacher, 38* (6), 528–530.

RANDOLPH-ROBINSON, B. (1984). The depiction of South Africa in children's literature. *Interracial Books for Children Bulletin, 15*, 7–8, 14–22.

REID, M. A. (1983). *The Image of the Child in Contemporary Black Literature: The Child in Its Environment, North vs. South.* Paper presented at the Annual Meeting of the Conference on College Composition and Communication, Detroit: March 17–19, 1983. (ERIC Document Reproduction Service No. ED 234 425).

RICH, P. E., MYRICK, R. D., & CAMPBELL, C. (1983). Changing children's perceptions of the elderly. *Educational Gerontology, 9* (5–6), 483–491.

ROBINSON, D. J. (1985). Talking it out: The use of books in discussion for developmental bibliography with children. *Top of the News, 41* (2), 151–155.

ROSER, N. L., & FRITH, M. (Eds.) (1983). *Children's choices: Teaching with Books Children Like.* Newark, DEL: International Reading Association.

ROSS, R. (1980). *Storyteller, 2d ed..* Columbus, OH: Charles E. Merrill Publishing Company.

SADKER, D. (1976, March). Death—a fact of life in children's literature. *Instructor*, 75–84.

SALIND, S. J., & MOE, L. (1983). Modifying non-handicapped students' attitudes toward their peers through children's literature. *Journal for Special Educators, 19* (*3*), 22–28.

SANDBURG, C. (1930). *Early moon.* New York: Harcourt Brace Jovanovich, Inc.

SCHON, I. (1984). Recent outstanding and ordinary books about Mexico, Mexicans, and Mexican-Americans. *Top of the News, 41* (*1*), 60–64.

SERRA, J. K. & LAMB, P. (1984). The elderly in basal readers. *Reading Teacher, 38* (*3*), 277–281.

SIMS, R. (1982). *Shadow and substance: Afro-American experience in contemporary children's fiction.* Urbana, IL: National Council of Teachers of English.

SOMERS, A. B. & WORTHINGTON, J. E. (1979). *Response Guides for Teaching Children's Books.* Urbana, IL: National Council of Teachers of English.

SPEECE, M. W. & BRENT, S. B. (1984). Children's concept of death: A review of three components of a death concept. *Child Development, 55* (*5*), 1671–1686.

STONE, K. (developer) (1984). *Bibliography of Nonsexist Supplementary Books (K–12).* Phoenix: Oryx Press.

STUDIER, C. E. (1978). *A comparison of the responses of fifth grade students to modern fantasy and realistic fiction.* (Doctoral Dissertation, University of Georgia, 1978). *Dissertation Abstracts International, 39,* 7201A–7202A.

SWENSON, E. J. (1972, March). The treatment of death in children's literature. *Elementary English,* 401–404.

TOOTHAKER, R. E. (1976, March). Curiosities of children that literature can satisfy. *Childhood Education, 52,* 5, 262–267.

TRAVERS, D. M. (1984). The poetry teacher: Behavior and attitudes. *Research in the Teaching of English, 18* (*4*), 367–384.

TWAY, E. (1981). *Reading ladders for human relations.* Urbana, IL: National Council of Teachers of English.

VALENTINE, S. (1986, March). Beginning poets dig for poems. *Language Arts, 63,* (*3*), 246–252.

WAGNER, C. (1985). *Factors influencing young children's response to literature.* Unpublished master's thesis, San Diego State University.

WAGONER, S. A. (1984). The portrayal of the cognitively disabled in children's literature. *Reading Teacher, 37* (*6*), 502–508.

WEITZMAN, L. V., EIFLER, E. H., & ROSS, C. (1972). Sex-role socialization in picture books for preschool children. *American Journal of Sociology, 77,* 1125–1150.

WHITE, M. L. (Ed.) (1981). *Adventuring with books.* Urbana, IL: National Council of Teachers of English.

WOLF, L. C. (1975, May). Children's literature and the development of empathy in young children. *Elementary English, 49.*

Chapter 9

ANDERSON, P. S. (1958). *Resource Materials for Teachers of Spelling.* Minneapolis: Burgess Publishing Company.

ARCHER, A. (1982). *Basic skills curriculum/spelling program: User's manual.* San Diego, CA: San Diego City Schools.

———. (1986). *Teacher-directed handwriting instruction.* Technical paper. San Diego, CA: San Diego State University.

ASHTON-WARNER, S. (1963). *Teacher.* New York: Simon & Schuster, Inc.

BARROW, R. W. (1980). Visual and phonological strategies in reading and spelling. In U. Frith (Ed.), *Cognitive processes in spelling.* London: Academic Press.

BARROW, R. W. (1985). Interactions between spelling and sound in literacy. In D. R. Olson, N. Torrance, & A. Hildyard (Eds.), *Literacy, Language and Learning.* New York: Cambridge University Press.

BAUER, D. & STANOVICH, K. E. (1980). Lexical access and the spelling to sound regularity effect. *Memory and Cognition, 8,* 424–432.

BEERS, J. W. & HENDERSON, E. H. (1977, Fall). A study of developing orthographic concepts among first grade children. *Research in the Teaching of English, 11,* 133–148.

BETTS, E. A. (1940). *Spelling vocabulary study: Grade placement of words in seventeen spellers.* New York: American Book Company.

———. (1949). *Grade placement of words in eight recent spellers.* New York: New American Library.

BISSEX, G. L. (1980). *GNYS AT WRK: A Child Learns to Write and Read.* Cambridge, MA: Harvard University Press.

BLAKE, H. E., & R. EMANS. (1970, February). Some spelling facts. *Elementary English,* 241–249.

BLANCHARD, M. G. (1944). *An experimental comparison of*

the test-study and the study-test methods of teaching spelling in the eighth grade. Unpublished master's thesis, Fordham University.

BOARD OF EDUCATION OF THE CITY OF NEW YORK. (1953–1954). *Teaching Spelling.* Series No. 6. New York: Curriculum Bulletin.

CHOMSKY, C. (1970, May). Reading, writing and phonology. *Harvard Educational Review, 40,* 287–309.

_____. (1972). Write now, read later. In C. Cazden (Ed.), *Language in Early Childhood Education.* Washington, DC: National Association for the Education of Young Children.

_____. (1974, May). *Invented spelling in first grade.* Unpublished paper, Harvard Graduate School of Education.

CHOMSKY, N., and HALLE, M. (1968). *The sound patterns of English.* New York: Harper & Row, Publishers, Inc.

CITRON, A. F. (1981, Fall). Our spelling: Pride, prudery and waste. *Urban Review, 13 (3),* 181–188.

COTTON, K. (1982). *Effective practice for spelling instruction: Literature synthesis.* St. Louis, MO: CEMREL, Inc. and Portland, OR: Northwest Regional Educational Laboratory. (ERIC Document Reproduction Service No. ED 219 788.)

DISTEFANO, P., & HAGERTY, P. (1983, January–February). An analysis of high-frequency words found in commercial spelling series and misspelled in students' writing. *Journal of Educational Research, 76 (3),* 181–185.

ERHI, L. C. (1980). Do beginners learn to read function words better in sentences or in lists? *Reading Research Quarterly, 15 (4),* 451–476.

FERNALD, G. M. (1943). Remedial techniques in basic school subjects. New York: McGraw-Hill Book Co.

FITZGERALD, J. A. (1953, January). The teaching of spelling. *Elementary English, 30.*

FITZSIMMONS, R. J. & LOOMER, B. M. (1978). *Spelling: Learning and Instruction.* Des Moines, IA: Iowa State Department of Public Instruction. (ERIC Document Reproduction Service No. ED 176 285).

FRITH, V. (1980). Unexpected spelling problem. In U. Frith (Ed.), *Cognitive processes in spelling.* London: Academic Press.

GANSCHOW, L. (1981, March). Discovering children's learning strategies for spelling through error pattern analysis. *The Reading Teacher, 34 (6),* 676–680.

GATES, A. I. (1931, June). An experimental comparison of the study-test and test-study methods in spelling. *Journal of Educational Psychology, 22, 1.*

GEEDY, P. S. (1975, February). What research tells us about spelling. *Elementary English,* 233–236.

GENTRY, J. R. (1981, January). Learning to spell developmentally. *The Reading Teacher, 34 (4),* 378–381.

_____. (1982). An analysis of developmental spelling in GNYS AT WRK. *The Reading Teacher, 36,* 192–200.

GRAHAM, R. T., and RUDORF, E. H. (1970, March). Dialect and spelling. *Elementary English,* 363–375.

GRAHAM, S. & FREEMAN, S. (1986, Winter). Strategy training and teacher vs. student-controlled study conditions: Effects on LD students' spelling performance. *Learning Disabilities Quarterly, 9,* 15–22.

GRAVES, D. (1977, January). Research update of spelling texts and structural analysis methods. *Language Arts, 54 (1),* 86–90.

GREENE, H. A. (1977). *The new Iowa spelling scale.* (Revised by Bradley M. Loomer). Iowa City: University of Iowa, Division of Continuing Education.

GROFF, P. *The Syllable: Its Nature and Pedagogical Usefulness.* Portland, OR: Northwest Regional Educational Laboratory.

GROSSE POINT PUBLIC SCHOOLS. (1948). *Thinking About Spelling.* Grosse Pointe, MI.

GRUBGELD, E. (1986, February). Helping the problem speller without suppressing the writer. *English Journal, 75,* 58–61.

HALL, S., & HALL, C. (1984). It takes a lot of letters to spell "ERZ." *Language Arts, 61,* 822–827.

HANNA, P. R. & MOORE, J. T., JR. (1953, February). Spelling—from spoken word to written symbol. *Elementary School Journal, 13 (6),* 329–337. Boston: Houghton Mifflin Company.

HENDERSON, E. H., and BEERS, J. W. (Eds.) (1980). *Developmental and cognitive aspects of learning to spell: A reflection of word knowledge.* Newark, DEL: International Reading Association.

HILLERICH, R. L. (1977, March). Let's teach spelling—not phonetic misspelling. *Language Arts, 54,* 301–307.

_____. (1984, May–June). An effort toward improving the spelling pretest. *Journal of Educational Research, 77 (5),* 309–311.

HORN, E. (1919, February). Principles of methods in teaching spelling as derived from scientific investigation. In G. M. Whipple (Ed.) *Eighteenth Yearbook of Na-*

tional Society for the Study of Education, Part II. Bloomington, IL.

———. (1927). The basic writing vocabulary. Iowa City: University of Iowa.

———. (1954, May). Phonics and spelling. *Journal of Education*.

———. (1960). Spelling. *Encyclopedia of educational research* (3d ed.). New York: Macmillan Publishing Company.

———. (1962). Teaching spelling: What research says to the teacher. American Educational Research Association, *3*.

JAMES, M. C. (1986, May). Self-selected spelling. *Academic Therapy, 21*, 557–563.

JOHNSON, D. D. & MAJER, E. (1976, September). Johnson's basic vocabulary: Words for grades 1 and 2. *Elementary School Journal*, 74–82.

JOHNSON, T., LONGFORD, K., & QUORN, K. (1981, May). Characteristics of an effective spelling program. *Language Arts, 58*.

LOOMER, B. (1978). *Educator's Guide to Spelling Research and Practice*. Iowa State Department of Instruction and the University of Iowa.

MARTIN, M. (1983, March). Success! Teaching spelling with music. *Academic Therapy, 18 (4)*, 505–507.

McPHERSON, E. (1981, Fall). Spelling revisited. *Spelling Progress Quarterly, 1*.

McTEAGUE, F. (1980, Winter). Do teachers teach spelling? *TESL Talk, 11 (1)*, 33–35.

MEDWAY, P. (1976, May). Let down by spelling. (London) *Times Educational Supplement, 3182*, 19.

NOLEN, P. (1980, February). Sound reasoning in spelling. *The Reading Teacher, 33 (5)*, 538–543.

ORMROD, J. (1986, May). Learning to spell: Three studies at the university level. *Research in the Teaching of English, 20, 2*, 160–173.

PARKER, A. J. (1982). Phonological recoding in lexical decision: Effects of spelling-to-sound regularity depend upon how regularity is defined. *Memory and Cognition, 10*, 43–53.

PETTY, W. (1969, November). The teaching of spelling. *Bulletin of the School of Education, 45 (6)*. Bloomington: Indiana University.

READ, C. (1971, February). Pre-school children's knowledge of English phonology. *Harvard Educational Review, 41*, 1–34.

———. (1985). Effects of phonology on beginning spelling: Some cross-linguistic evidence. In D. R. Olson, N. Torrance, & A. Hildyard (Eds.), *Literacy, Language and Learning*. New York: Cambridge University Press.

RICE, J. M. (1897). The futility of the spelling grind. *Forum, 23*, 169–172.

RINSLAND, H. D. (1945). A basic writing vocabulary of elementary school children. New York: Macmillan Publishing Company.

SCHLAGAL, R. C. (1986, Winter). Informal and qualitative assessment of spelling. *Pointes, 30*, 37–41.

SEARS, N. C. & JOHNSON, D. M. (1986, March/April). The effects of visual imagery on spelling performance and retention among elementary students. *Journal of Educational Research, 79*, 230–233.

SEIDENBERG, M. S., WATERS, G. S., BARNES, M. A., & TANENHAUS, M. K. (1984). When does irregular spelling or pronunciation influence word recognition? *Journal of Verbal Learning and Verbal Behavior, 23*, 383–404.

SMITH, P. T. (1980a). In defense of conservatism in English orthography. *Visible Language, 14*, 122–136.

———. (1980b). Linguistic information in spelling. In U. Frith (Ed.), *Cognitive Processes in Spelling*. London: Academic Press.

STETSON, E. & LAURENT, C. (Eds.) (1984). *Training teachers to use research-based strategies improves student achievement in spelling*. Region V Education Service Center.

STETSON, E., TAYLOR, W., & BOUTIN, F. (1982). *Eight years of theory and practice in spelling: Those who wrote the programs forgot to read the literature*. Paper presented at the National Reading Conference, Clearwater, FL.

STETSON, E. G. & BOUTIN, F. (1980). Spelling instruction is diagnostic prescriptive minus the diagnostic. Research Report No. 143.

WILSON, M., & BOCK, R. D. (1985, Summer). Spellability: A linearly ordered content domain. *American Educational Research Journal, 22 (2)*, 297–307.

WOLFE, R., SR. (1952, April). A study of spelling errors. *Elementary School Journal, 12 (8)*, 458–466.

WOODRUFF, G. W., et al. (1986). *Working Words in Spelling*. North Billerica, MA: Curriculum Associates.

ZUTELL, J. (1979, February). Spelling strategies of primary school children and their relationship to Piaget's concept of decentration. *Research in the Teaching of English, 13*, 69–80.

Chapter 10

ACKOV, E. N., & GREFF, K. N. (1975). Handwriting: Copying vs. tracing as the most effective type of practice. *Journal of Educational Research, 69 (3)*, 6–8.

ADDY, P., & WYLIE, R. (1973). The "right" way to write. *Childhood Education, 49*, 253–254.

ANDERSON D. (1965). Handwriting research: Movement and quality. *Elementary English, 42*, 45–53.

ARCHER, A. L. (1986). *Teacher-directed handwriting instruction.* Technical Paper, San Diego State University.

BRACEY, S. A. & WARD, J. (1980, Summer). Dark, dark went the bog: Instructional interventions for remediating b and d reversals. *Reading Improvement, 17*, 104–112.

BURNHAM, J. A. (1986, May). Cutting down on embarrassing reversals. *Academic Therapy, 21*, 551–556.

CAWELTI, G. & ADKISON, J. (1985, April). ASCD reveals elementary school time allocations for subject areas; Other trends noted. *ASCD curriculum update.*

COLEMAN, E. B. (1970, August). Collecting a data base for a reading technology. *Journal of Educational Psychology* Monograph, *61 (4)*, 2.

D'ANGELO, K. (1982, January). Developing liability and uniqueness in handwriting with calligraphy. *Language Arts, 59 (1)*, 23–27.

GOODNOW, J. J., & LEVINE, R. (1973, January). The grammar of action: Sequence and syntax in children's copying. *Cognitive Psychology, 4*, 82–98.

GRAVES, D. (1978). Research update: Handwriting is for writing. *Language Arts, 55*, 393–399.

GROFF, P. (1975). Can pupils read what teachers write? *Elementary School Journal, 76 (1)*, 32–39.

HAGIN, R. A. (1983). Write right—or left: A practical approach to handwriting. *Journal of Learning Disabilities, 16 (5)*, 266–271.

HALPIN, G. (1976, September). Special paper for beginning handwriting: An unjustified practice? *Journal of Educational Research*, 668–669.

HANOVER, S. (1983, March). Handwriting comes naturally? *Academic Therapy, 18 (4)*, 407–412.

HARRISON, S. (1981, Spring). Open letter from a left-handed teacher: Some sinistral ideas on the teaching of handwriting. *Teaching Exceptional Children, 13 (3)*, 116–120.

HARTLEY, S. T. & SALZWEDEL, K. D. (1980, September). Behavioral writing for an autistic-like child. *Academic Therapy, 16 (1)*, 101–110.

HOFFMAN, S. (1982, April 26–30). *Parents' teaching strategies with children learning to read and write: Before and after classroom instruction.* Paper presented at the 27th Annual Meeting of the International Reading Association, Chicago, IL.

KIRK, V. (1978). *Rule-based instruction: A cognitive approach to beginning handwriting instruction.* Unpublished doctoral dissertation, Teachers' College, Columbia University.

KOSIEWICZ, M. M. (1982, Winter). Effects of self-instruction and self-correction procedures on handwriting performance. *Learning Disability Quarterly, 5 (1)*, 71–78.

LAMME, L. L. (1983, Fall). Is the handwriting of beginning writers influenced by writing tools? *Journal of Research and Development in Education, 17 (1)*, 32–38.

LIEBERMAN, A. & MILLER, L. (1984). *Teachers: Their world and Their work.* Alexandria, VA: Association for Supervision and Curriculum Development.

MANNING, M. L. (1986, January). Responding to renewed emphasis on handwriting. *Clearing House, 59*, 211–213.

McGARVEY, J. (1986, March). Is it time to boot out cursive writing? *Classroom Computer Learning, 6*, 36–37.

PECK, M., et al. (1980, May–June). Another decade of research in handwriting: Progress and prospect in the 1970's. *Journal of Educational Research, 73 (5)*, 283–298.

RAND, C. W. (1973, March). Copying in drawing: The importance of adequate visual analysis versus the ability to utilize drawing rules. *Child Development, 44*, 47–53.

ROSENHAUS, M. (1957, March). You can teach handwriting with only six rules. *The Instructor, 60*.

THURBER, D. N. (1981). *D'Nealian Handwriting.* Glenview, IL: Scott, Foresman and Company.

TOMPKINS, G. E. (1980, October). Let's go on a bear hunt: A fresh approach to penmanship drill. *Language Arts, 57 (7)*, 782–786.

Chapter 11

APPLEBY, B. C. (1984, October). Writing, reviewing, and revising. *English Journal, 73 (6)*, 89–93.

BURROWS, A. T. (1965). Children's language. *National Elementary School Principal, 45 (1)*, 16–21.

BURROWS, A. T., JACKSON, C., & SAUNDERS, D. O. (1964). *They all want to write.* New York: Holt, Rinehart and Winston.

CLAY, M. (1975). *What did I write?* Auckland, New Zealand: Heinemann Educational Books.

CLEGG, A. B. (1964). *The excitement of writing.* London: Chatto and Windus.

CONNORS, R. J. (1985, February). Mechanical correctness as a focus in composition instruction. *College Composition and Communication, 38 (1)*, 61–72.

DAVIS, F. (1984, October). In defense of grammar. *English Education, 16 (3)*, 151–164.

DUFFY, G. G. (1969). *Teaching Linguistics.* Dansville, NY: Instructor Publications.

EBEL, R. L. (Ed.) (1969). *Encyclopedia of educational research.* New York: Macmillan Publishing Company.

EVANS, W. H. (1981, October). Toward a wider concept of English education. *English Education, 13 (3)*, 131–137.

FINEGAN, E. (1980). *Attitudes toward English usage: The history of a war of words.* New York: Teachers College Press.

FLESH, R. (1954). *How to make sense.* New York: Harper & Row, Publishers, Inc.

FLOOD, J., & LAPP, D. (1985, May). The reading/language arts curriculum of secondary schools: What has been and what might be. *English Education, 17 (2)*, 79–90.

FLOOD, J. & SALUS, P. (1984). *Language and the Language Arts.* Englewood Cliffs, NJ: Prentice-Hall, Inc.

FRAZIER, A. S. et al. (1985, April). Facets: Grammatical devices in advertising. *English Journal, 74 (4)*, 18–21.

HANNAN, E. & HAMILTON, G. (1984, April). Writing: What to look for, what to do. *Language Arts, 61 (4)*, 364–366.

HARTWELL, P. (1985, February). Grammar, grammars, and the teaching of grammar. *College English, 47 (2)*, 105–127.

HIPPLE, T. & BARTHOLOMEW, B. (1982, May). What beginning teachers need to know about grading. *English Education, 14 (2)*, 95–98.

JOHNSON, K. (1985). Vernacular English and the language arts. *Ginn Occasional Papers: Writings in Reading and Language Arts, 9.* Lexington, MA: Ginn and Company.

KAUFER, D., JAYES, J. & FOWLER, L. (1986, May). Composing written sentences. *Research in the Teaching of English, 20 (2)*, 121–140.

KELLY, P. P. (1984, November). Teaching the process of writing. *English Journal, 73 (7)*, 94–95.

LASSO, G. A. (1981, December). My grammar and spelling are hurting my riting. *English Journal, 70 (8)*, 42–43.

LEIBERT, B. (1971). *Linguistics and the New English Teacher.* New York: Macmillan Publishing Company.

LENSKI, L. (1949, November). Helping children to create. *Childhood Education, 26*, 101–105.

MARRON, H. I. (1964). *A History of Education in Antiquity.* New York: New American Library of Literature.

McCLURE, E. F. & STEFFENSEN, M. S. (1985, October). A study of the use of conjunctions across grades and ethnic groups. *Research in the Teaching of English, 19 (3)*, 217–236.

PETERS, W. H. (1983, December). Future research in English education: Some modest proposals. *English Education, 15 (4)*, 204–216.

PFAFF, S. M. (1981, December). Grammar handbooks: Helpful references. *English Journal, 70 (8)*, 54–55.

POOLEY, R. C. (1960, March). Dare schools set a standard in English usage? *English Journal, 49*, 179–180.

RUTH, L., & MURPHY, S. (1984, December). Designing topics for writing assessment: Problems of meaning. *College Composition and Communication, 35 (4)*, 410–422.

SMALL, R. (1985, October). Why I'll never teach grammar again. *English Education, 17 (3)*, 174–178.

SOMMERS, N. (1982, May). Responding to students' writing. *College Composition and Communication, 33 (2)*, 148–156.

YATVIN, J. (1981). A functional writing program for the middle grades. In S. Haley-James (Ed.), *Perspectives on writing in grades 1–8.* Urbana, IL: National Council of Teachers of English.

Chapter 12

AGADO, G. A. (1984, June). Story starters and group writing motivate children to write. *Reading Teacher, 37 (4)*, 438–439.

ATHEY, I. (1983, March–April). Language development factors related to reading development. *Journal of Educational Research, 7,* 197–202.

BARNARD D. P., & KENDRICK, R. (1983). A new consciousness for integrating communicative arts instruction. *Ginn Occasional Papers: Writings in Reading and Language Arts, 6.* Lexington, MA: Ginn and Company.

BENNETT, S. G. (1983, May). What everyone should know (has known but done little to implement) about evaluating students' writing. *Position Paper 120.*

BRITTON, J. (1970). *Language and Learning.* Coral Gables, FL: University of Miami Press.

_____. (1975). Now that you go to school. In R. L. Larson (Ed.), *Children and Writing in the Elementary School: Theories and Techniques.* New York: Oxford University Press.

CAROSELLI, M. (1981). Romance precedes precision: Recommended teaching practices. In S. Haley-James (Ed.), *Perspectives on writing in grades 1–8.* Urbana, IL: National Council of Teachers of English.

COOPER, C. R. (1977). Holistic evaluation of writing. In *Evaluating Writing: Describing, measuring, judging.* Ed. by C. R. Cooper & L. Odell. Urbana, IL: National Council of Teachers of English.

EMIG, J. (1971). *Components of the Composing Process Among Twelfth Graders.* Urbana, IL: National Council of Teachers of English.

FEARN, L. (1983). *Developmental Writing.* San Diego, CA: Kabyn Books.

FLOOD, J. & SALUS, P. (1984). *Language and the Language Arts.* Englewood Cliffs, NJ: Prentice-Hall, Inc.

GRAVES, D. H. (1973). *Children's Writing: Research directions and hypotheses based upon an examination of the writing process of seven-year-olds.* Unpublished doctoral dissertation, State University of New York at Buffalo.

HALEY-JAMES, S. (Ed.) (1981). *Perspectives on writing in grades 1–8.* Urbana, IL: National Council of Teachers of English.

HARSTE, J., BURKE, C. L., & WOODWARD, V. A. (1979, March). *Children's Language and World: Initial Encounters with Print.* Unpublished manuscript, Indiana University, Bloomington.

HINK, K. E. (1985, March). Let's stop worrying about revision. *Language Arts, 62* (3), 249–254.

HULL, G. & BARTHOLOMAE, D. (1986, April). Teaching writing as learning process. *Educational Leadership, 43* (7), 44–53.

LAPP, D., & FLOOD, J. (1985, May). The reading/language arts curriculum of secondary schools: What has been and what might be. *English Education, 17,* 2.

MOFFETT, J. (1979). Integrity in the teaching of writing. *Phi Delta Kappan, 61,* 276–279.

MULLIS, I. V. (1985). NAEP perspectives on literacy: A preview of 1983–84 writing assessment results. Paper presented at annual meeting of the American Educational Research Association.

MURRAY, D. M. (1968). *A Teacher Teaches Writing: A Practical Method of Teaching Composition.* Boston: Houghton Mifflin Company.

NEUBERT, G. & McNELIS, S. (1986, April). Improving writing in the disciplines. *Educational Leadership, 43* (7), 54–60.

RYAN, S. (1986, March). Do prose models really teach writing? *Language Arts, 63* (3), 284–290.

SQUIRE, J. R. (1984). Instructional focus and the teaching of writing. *Ginn Occasional Papers: Writings in reading and language arts, No. 1.* Lexington, MA: Ginn and Company.

TANNEN, D. (1985). Relative focus on involvement in oral and written discourse. In D. Olson, N. Torrance, & A. Hildyard (Eds.), *Literacy, language, and learning,* pp. 124–147. New York: Cambridge University Press.

Chapter 13

ATHEY, I. (1983, March–April). Language development factors related to reading development. *Journal of Educational Research, 7,* 197–202.

BAGHBAN, M. (1984). *Our daughter learns to read and write.* Newark, DEL: International Reading Association.

BAUMANN, J. F. (1986). Effect of rewritten content textbook passages on middle grade students' comprehension of main ideas: Making the inconsiderate considerate. *Journal of Reading Behavior, 18* (1), 1–21.

BECK, I. (1986, April). Using research on reading. *Educational Leadership, 43* (7), 13–15.

BRITTON, J. (1970). *Language and Learning.* Coral Gables, FL: University of Miami Press.

CALFEE, R. C., & CURLEY, R. (1984). Structures of prose in content areas. In J. Flood (Ed.), *Promoting Reading Comprehension,* pp. 161–180. Newark, DEL: International Reading Association.

CLAY, M. (1975). *What did I write?* London: Heinemann Educational Books.

COLLINS, A., & GENTNER, D. (1980). A framework for a cognitive theory of writing. In Lee W. Gregg and Erwin Steinberg (Eds.), *Cognitive Processes in Writing*. Hillsdale, NJ: Lawrence Erlbaum Associates, Publishers.

COOPER, C. (1985). Writing about literature. *San Diego Writing Project Newsletter, 7 (3)*. San Diego, CA: University of California.

DEFORD, D. E. (1981, September). Literacy: reading, writing, and other essentials. *Language Arts, 58,* 652–658.

ECKHOFF, B. (1983, May). How reading affects children's writing. *Language Arts, 60,* 607–616.

FEARN, L., & GOLDMAN, E. (1983). *The Writing Kabyn.* San Diego, CA: Kabyn Books.

FLOOD, J. (1986, April). The text, the student and the teacher; Learning exposition in the middle school. *The Reading Teacher, 39 (78),* 784–791.

FLOOD, J., & LAPP, D. (1986). Reading and writing relations assumptions and direction. *Mid-Decade Seminar on Future Direction of Research.* Urbana, IL: National Conference on Research in English.

FLOOD, J., LAPP, D., & FARNAN, N. (1985, December). A reading-writing procedure that teaches expository paragraph structure. *The Reading Teacher.*

FLOOD, J., LAPP, D., & FLOOD, S. (1984). Types of writing included in basal reading programs: Preprimer through second grade readers. *National reading conference yearbook.*

FLOOD, J., & SALUS, P. (1984). *Language and the Language Arts.* Englewood Cliffs, NJ: Prentice-Hall, Inc.

FRAZIER, A. (1967). *New directions in elementary english,* pp. 216–217. Urbana, IL: National Council of Teachers of English.

GOODMAN, K., & GOODMAN, Y. (1983, May). Reading and writing relationships: pragmatic functions. *Language Arts, 60,* 590–599.

HARSTE, J., BURKE, C. L., & WOODWARD, V. A. (1979, March). *Children's Language and World: Initial Encounters with Print.* Unpublished manuscript, Indiana University, Bloomington.

HAYES, J. R., & FLOWER, L. S. (1980). Identifying the organization of the writing processes. In Lee W. Gregg & Erwin R. Steinberg (Eds.), *Cognitive processes in writing.* Hillsdale, NJ: Lawrence Erlbaum Associates.

HENNINGS, D. G. (1984). A writing approach to reading comprehension—schema theory in action. In J. Jenson (Ed.), *Composing and Comprehending,* pp. 191–200. Urbana, IL: National Conference on Research in English.

HENRY, G. H. (1974). *Teaching Reading as Concept Development: Emphasis on Affective Thinking.* Newark, DEL: International Reading Association.

INDRISANO, R. (1984). Reading and writing revisited. *Ginn Occasional Papers: Writings in reading and language arts, 18.* Lexington, MA: Ginn and Company.

JENSEN, J. (1984). Introduction to composing and comprehending. In J. Jenson (Ed.), *Composing and Comprehending,* p. 4. Urbana, IL: National Conference on Research in English.

LAPP, D., & FLOOD, J. (1983). *Teaching reading to every child,* 2d ed. New York: Macmillan Publishing Company.

———. (1986). *Teaching students to read.* New York: Macmillan Publishing Company.

LOBAN, W. (1963). *The Language of Elementary School Children.* Research Report 1. Urbana, IL: National Council of Teachers of English.

LUNSFORD, A. (1978, February). What we know—and don't know—about remedial writing. *College Composition and Communications, 29,* 47–52.

MATHEWSON, G. (1976). The function of attitude in the reading process. In H. Singer and R. Ruddel (Eds.), *Theoretical Models and Processes of Reading,* 2d ed. Newark, DEL: International Reading Association.

MEYER, B. (1984). Organizational aspects of texts: Effects of reading comprehension and applications for the classroom. In J. Flood (Ed.), *Promoting Reading Comprehension,* pp. 113–138. Newark, DEL: International Reading Association.

MOFFETT, J. (1979). Integrity in the teaching of writing. *Phi Delta Kappan, 61,* 276–279.

PIAGET, J. (1952). *The Origins of Intelligence in Children.* New York: W. W. Norton and Company.

POINDEXTER, C. & PRESCOTT, S. (1986, May). A technique for teaching students to draw inferences from text. *The Reading Teacher, 39 (9),* 908–911.

RICE, M. (1984, Spring). A cognition account of differences between children's comprehension and productions of language. *Western Journal of Speech Communication, 48,* 145–153.

SAGER, C. (1982). *Reading, Writing and Rating Stories*. North Billerica, MA: Curriculum Associates.

SILVATORI, M. (1983, November). Reading and writing a text: Correlations between reading and writing patterns. *College English, 45*, 657–676.

SPIVEY, N. (1983). *Discourse synthesis: Constructing texts in reading and writing*. Doctoral dissertation, University of Texas at Austin.

SQUIRE, J. R. (1983, May). Composing and comprehending: Two sides of the same basic process. *Language Arts, 60* (5), 581–589.

STOTSKY, S. (1982). The role of writing in developmental reading. *Journal of Reading, 25*, 330–339.

———. (1983, May). Research on reading/writing relationships: a synthesis and suggested direction. *Language Arts, 60* (5), 627–642.

TCHUDI, S. N., & TCHUDI, S. J. (1983). *Teaching writing in the content areas*. Urbana, IL: National Council of Teachers of English.

VYGOTSKY, L. S. (1962). Thought and language. Cambridge, MA: M.I.T. Press.

WEISS, M. J. (1986, April). Writers and readers: The literary connection. *The Reading Teacher, 39* (8), 758–763.

WILSON, M. J. (1981, May). A review of recent research on the integration of reading and writing. *The Reading Teacher, 34*, 896–901.

WITTROCK, M. C. (1983, May). Writing and the teaching of reading. *Language Arts, 60* (5), 600–606.

Chapter 14

BALAJTHY, E. (1986). *Microcomputers in reading and language arts*. Englewood Cliffs, NJ: Prentice-Hall, Inc.

CHEYNEY, A. B. (1984). *Teaching Reading Skills through the Newspaper*, 2d ed. Newark, DEL: International Reading Association.

CLEMENT, F. J. (1981, April). Affective considerations in computer-based education. *Educational Technology, 21* (4), 28–32.

DOG, P. F. (1985, September). Exciting effects of Logo in an urban public school system. *Educational Leadership, 43* (1), 45–47.

EISENBERG, M. (1984). Curriculum mapping and implementation of an elementary school library media skills curriculum. *School Library Media Quarterly, 12* (5), 411–418.

FOSTER, H. (1979). *The New Literacy: The Language of Film and Television*. Urbana, IL: National Council of Teachers of English.

GREENUP, T. (1983). Newspaper activities for young consumers. *Albuquerque Journal/Tribune*, New Mexico: Newspapers in Education Project. (ERIC Document Number 246 002.)

GUENTHER, J. (1983). Fun with the funnies: 50 motivating activities for language arts, writing, and social studies, grades 4–6. Glenview, IL: Scott, Foresman and Company. (ERIC Document Number 250 701.)

HAMRICK, L. (1981). *Newspaper in education activity book*. Temple, Texas: *Temple Daily Telegram*. (ERIC Document Number 250 703.)

JOHNSON, R. E. (1979). Using media to turn kids on to reading in the content areas. In D. L. Monson & D. K. McClenathan (Eds.), *Developing Active Readers: Ideas for Parents, Teachers, and Librarians*. Newark, DEL: International Reading Association.

MCBRIDE, J. R. (1985, October). Computerized adaptive testing. *Educational Leadership, 43* (2), 25–28.

OLSON, N. S. (Ed.) (1983). Using the new technologies in language communication education. *The Talking and Writing Series, K–12: Successful classroom practices*. Department of Education Basic Skills Improvement Program. Washington, DC: Dingle Associates, Inc. (ERIC Document Number 233 378.)

POE, M. & SCHMIDT, B. (1987). *Willie MacGurkle and friends: Choraling in the classroom*. North Billerica, MA: Curriculum Associates.

POGROW, S., & BUCHANAN, B. (1985, September). *Higher-order thinking for compensatory students*. *Educational Leadership, 43* (1), 40–43.

RASINSKI, T. V. (1984, May 6–10). *The role of media in encouraging thinking and language*. Paper presented at the Annual Meeting of the International Reading Association, Atlanta, GA: (ERIC Document Number 246 397.)

ROSS, R. (1980). *Storyteller*. Columbus, OH: Charles E. Merrill Publishing Company.

RUDE, R. T. (1986). *Teaching Reading Using Microcomputers*. Englewood Cliffs, NJ: Prentice-Hall, Inc.

SEBESTA, S. (1985, March 1–2). *Reading: Living through literature*. Speech presented at the Sixth Annual Lan-

guage/Reading Conference, San Diego State University.

WIRTH, T. E. (1983, October 5). *Potential of television in educating children.* Speech given at the Joint Hearing before the Subcommittee on Telecommunications, Consumer Protection, and Finance of the Committee on Energy and Commerce and the Subcommittee on Elementary, Secondary, and Vocational Education of the Committee on Education and Labor. H. R., 98th Cong., 1st Sess. (ERIC Document No. 245 672.)

Chapter 15

ABRAMS, J. D. (1985, September). Making outcome-based education work. *Educational Leadership, 43 (1),* 30–32.

COSTA, A. L. (1985). *Developing minds: A resource book for teaching thinking.* Alexandria, VA: Association for Supervision and Curriculum Development.

EMMER, E. T., et al. (1984). *Classroom management for secondary teachers.* Englewood Cliffs, NJ: Prentice-Hall, Inc.

EMMER, E. T., & EVERTSON, C. M. (1981). Synthesis of research on classroom management. *Educational Leadership, 38,* 342–347.

EMMER, E. T., EVERTSON, C. M., & ANDERSON, L. M. (1980). Effective classroom management at the beginning of the school year. *The Elementary School Journal, 80,* 219–231.

EVERTSON, C. M. & EMMER, E. T. (1982). Effective management at the beginning of the school year in junior high classes. *Journal of Educational Psychology, 74,* 485–498.

HANEY, W. (1985, October). Making testing more educational. *Educational Leadership, 43 (2),* 4–15.

HEIMAN, M. (1985, September). Learning to learn. *Educational Leadership, 43 (1),* 20–25.

LAPP, D. (1972, February). Behavioral objectives writing skills test. *Journal of Education, 154,* 13–24. (Test available from Educational Testing Services, Princeton, NJ.)

LAPP, D. (Ed.) (1980). *Making reading possible through effective classroom management.* Newark, DEL: International Reading Association.

LAPP, D. & FLOOD, J. (1986). *Teaching students to read.* New York: Macmillan Publishing Company.

MAGER, R. F. (1984). *Preparing instructional objectives.* Palo Alto, CA: Fearon Publishers.

ROBINSON, H. A. (1986, May). Behavior objectives vs. transactions. *English Education, 18 (2),* 85–91.

ROSENSHINE, B. (1986, April). Synthesis of research on explicit teaching. *Educational Leadership, 43 (7),* 60–69.

SANFORD, J. P. et al. (1983). Improving classroom management. *Educational Leadership, 40,* 56–61.

SCHALOCK, D. et al. (1985, October). Integrating teaching and testing with program management. *Educational Leadership, 43 (2),* 55–59.

SMARTSCHON, G. F. (1985, October). Final examinations as tools for instructional management. *Educational Leadership, 43 (2),* 77–78.

Index

Index

Abney, L., 171
Accent marks, 230
Accommodation, in developing child, 43
Activities. *See also* Games
  to correct language usage errors, 109–11
  creative-dramatic, 120–128
    reading-dependent, 122–28
    reading-independent, 120–22
  with dictionary, 227–31
  for gifted students, 22
  in handwriting instruction, 251–52, 254–55
  for listening, 97–99
    using reading, 91
  for oral communication skills, 109–28
  for phonics, 137–43
  in punctuation, 289–93
  for reading, to develop interest in book reports, 178–81
    to encourage, 135, 158–59
    practice and transfer, 148–50
  for speech, 114–20
  for spelling practice, 208–11, 220–22, 225
  storytelling, 183–86
  for very young, 6–7
  for writing, 306–308, 353–68
    using antonyms, 323
    in content area, 367–68
    using descriptive words, 323–24
    in expository writing, 325–26
    in improving composition skills, 312–13
    laboratory writing exercises, 311–12
    in revising writing, to reinforce concepts of, 299–300
    using synonyms, 322
    using word pictures, 324–25
Adaptation, in developing child, 43
Adaptive education, 29–30

Advertising in media, 377–78
  propaganda techniques, 378
Agado, G. A., 319
Age developmental stages, 9–10, 43–44
Alleman, E. C., 175
Alliteration, 320
Alphabet strip, 257
"American Speaking," 58
An Experience Curriculum, 305
Antonyms, activity using, 323
Archer, A., 205–206, 249–50
Articulation, 6, 17–19, 103
  positions of, 69–70, 69
Assessment tests, bilingual, 14–15
  to determine effectiveness of instructional program, 393
  role in reading program, 150–51
    formal, 150
    informal, 150–51
      cloze technique, 151
      IRI, 151
Assimilation, in developing child, 43
Athey, I., 143
Attention, in listening, 86
  to storyteller, 184
Auding, definition of, 82–83
  attention and code selection, 85–86
  comprehension, 87
  schema search and match, 86–87
Auditory acuity, 83
  symptoms of deficient, 83
Auditory analysis, 84
  blending and juncture, 84–85
  sequencing and memory, 85
Auditory discrimination, 84, 112, 113–14, 144
  games to develop, 112–13
  in phonics, 144
  Wepman, test, 84

Auditory perception. *See also* Hearing
  principles of, 83–84
  in spelling, 196
  teaching skills in, 97–98
Ayres, L. P., 257

Bancroft, T. W., 305
Basal reader, 138, 146–47
Bennett, S. G., 106, 314
Berko-Gleason, J., 70
Berman, R. A., 67
Bilingual child (student). *See also* Bilingual education
  appropriate instructional sequence for, 16–19
  identifying, 11–14
  planning a language arts program for, 14–20
Bilingual education, features of, 15
  linguistic influences on, 16–19
  materials selection for, 15–16
  model for instruction in, 16–19
Blachowicz, C., 67
Book reports, 177–81
  activities to develop interest in, 178–81
  inappropriate approaches of, 177
  in intermediate grades, 179
  oral, 178–79
    form for, 180
  personal reading notebook form for, 182
  in primary grades, 178
  purposes of, 178
  written forms of, 178–79
Books, awards for outstanding, 162–63
  care and knowledge of, 383
  for children, sources of information on, 161–64
  class, 296
  picture, nine suggestions for reading, 177
Britton, J., 314, 343

Brown, D., 82
Brown, R., 64
Burke, J., 21
Buss, K., 64

Cahir, S. R., 64
Caldecott Medal awards, 163
Callahan, C., 23
Capitalization, as cause of spelling confusion, 210
    chart of rules for, 210
    exercises for, 211, 289–90
Card catalogue, 384
Cardenas, J., 4
Caroselli, M., 328
Cassette recordings, 370–71
Caxton, W., 55
Cazden, C. B., 65
Chafe, W. L., 106–107
Chaucer, G., 55–56
Cheney, A. B., 377
Children. *See also* Students
    growth patterns of (Piaget), 8
    intermediate grade, 8–10
    primary school, characteristics, 8–9
    very young, working with, 5–7
Chomsky, C. S., 72–73
Chomsky, N., 66
Choral readings, 126–27, 170–72
Ciardi, J., 375
Cinquains, 364
Clark, E. V., 72–73
Clark, H. H., 72
Classroom organization, 386–93
    assessment of, 393
    instructional implementation of, 390
        developing behavioral objectives for, 390–92
        forming groups in, 389, 392
    management model of, 388
    need for, 387
    planning for effective, 387–93
        assessing needs in, 390
        determining goals in, 390
        individuals involved in, 388–89
Clement, F. J., 382
Cognitive growth, 8–10
Coleman, E. B., 246–47
Collins, L. J., 155
Colon, 288
Comma, 288

Communication, 35–46
    content of, 36
    language as art of, 36
    oral. *See* Oral communication
    personal, written, 296–97
    systems of, symbol and sign as, 51
Composing, as stage of writing, 353
Comprehension, definition, 87
    procedures to ensure reading, 147–50
    process, 85
    reading means, 131
Comprehensive instructional framework (CIF), 29
Computer, in classroom, 339–40, 378–82
    guidelines for maximum use of, 382
    software evaluation, 380
    terminology, 378–79
    uses of, 379–80, 339–40
        computer-assisted instruction (CAI), 379
        teacher utility programs, 380
        word processing, 379
        in writing program, 339–40
Concept development, by children, 42–43
    children's literature and, 157
Consonant(s). *See also* Consonant sounds.
    single, chart on, 145
Consonant sounds, blends of, 140–42, 145
    at first-reader level, 145
    in sequence of learning, 138–39
    teaching of, 139–42
        using substitution practice, 139–40
        using word-card devices, 141
Content area writing, 367–68
Cooper, C., 355
Cooper, C. R., 333
Cooperative learning, 389, 392
Courtesy, instruction in language arts program, 128
Creativity, in classroom dramatics, 120–28
    in writing, 286–87
Cultural aspects, 48–60
    of bilingual education, 12
    language influenced by, 48–50, 60, 102
    listening influenced by, 82
    reflected in history of English language, 51–58
Culture, definition, 48
Cummins, J., 12
Curriculum goals, 390

Cursive handwriting. *See* Handwriting, cursive

De Villiers, P. A., 66
Death, concept of in children's literature, 156–57
Decoding, 133
Developmental stages, 9–10, 43–44
Di Sibio, R. A., 94
Diacritical Marks, 230–31
Dialect(s), 58–60, 59
Dickinson, E., 36
Diction, 294
Dictionary(ies), American, 226
    of letter forms, 257
    made by children, in study of spelling, 225
    picture, for drill on consonants, 141, 145
        in primary grades, 226
    skills, 226–31, 384
    teaching use of, 225–31
        activities for, 227–31
        alphabetical sequence, 226–27
        definitions, 228–30
        guide words, 227–28
        pronunciation, 230–31
Dixon, C., 357
D'Nealian handwriting, 257, 259
Doherty-Hale, D., 156
Donaldson, M., 72
Dramatics. *See also* Plays
    creative, in classroom, 120–28
        formal, 125–26
        radio and television production, 126
        reading-dependent, 124–28
            choral readings, 126–27
            literature reading, 124–25
            play reading, 124
            Reader's Theater, 127–28
        reading-independent, 120–23
            group, 120–21
            pantomime, 120–21
            puppets, 121–23
            role playing, 120
            sociodrama, 121
Duff, A., 164
Duffy, G. G., 285

Eckhoff, B., 346–47
Editing, of report, standards for, 297
    on word processor, 339–40
    in writing, 353

Editing signs, 297
Education for All Handicapped Children Act, 23
Eimas, P. D., 65
Elderly, stereotyping in children's literature, 156
Emig, J., 305
English language. *See also* Language, Bilingual education
    cultural influences on, 48–50
    history of, 51–58
    Middle, 54–55
    Modern, 55–58
    Old, 53–54
    as second language (ESL), 11–13
    Shakespeare's, 56
    Standard, 102, 284–85, 300
Encyclopedia, using, 384
English-only instruction, 11–12
Environment, for gifted students, 23
    in hearing, 83, 94
    home, 44–45. *See also* Parents
    in language acquisition, importance in, 65–66, 103
    learning, 387–89
    for oral communication, 107–108
    in poetry appreciation, 362
    for spelling, enriching, 193–94
Evaluation, of comprehension, 148
    of handwriting, 259, 266–71
    self-, of writing, 359
    software, 380–81
        Lungren quick software review, 380–81
Expository writing, 325–27, 350–53
    early, 350–53
    lesson on, 350–51
    procedures for, form, 351–52
        composing, 353
        feedback, rewriting, editing, 353
        prewriting, 352
External learning stimulants, 44–45

Fables, and the writing process, 355–56
Farb, P., 48
Fearn, L., 304, 328
Fernard, G. M., 224–25
Film, 372
Filmstrips, 371–72
    student-made, 372
Finger plays, poems involving, 172–73

Fisher, A., 174
Flannelboard, in book reporting, 178
    construction of, 185
    for storytelling, 184–85
Flood, J., 11, 13, 14, 16, 24–27, 116, 135, 293, 343, 351, 390, 393
Foster, H., 376
Frazier, A., 355
Frierwood, E. H., 187
Furrow, D., 65

Games. *See also* Activities
    for public usage habits, establishing, 109–11
    for speech improvement, 111–14
    spelling, used for motivation in, 231–32
Geedy, P. S., 193, 197
Gentry, J. R., 193
George, J., 354
Giannangelo, D. M., 88
Gifted students, 20–23
    activities for, 22
    environment for, 23
    identification of, 20–21
    programs for, 21–22
Goal(s), attainable, 40–41
    curriculum, 390
    of handwriting instruction, 237–38
    of literature program, 154
Gold, Y., 95
Golds, S. A., 240
Grammar, 68, 73–75, 284–300
    definition of, 293
    nature of, 73–75
    necessity of teaching formal rules of, 284–85
    rule formation theory in, 75
    in second-language teaching, 285
    transformational, 74–75
Graphemes, 194–95
Graves, D. H., 304–305, 328
Greene, H. A., 199
Grouping, for instruction, 389, 392
Guide words, 227–28

Haiku, 364
Hall, S., 191
Halliday, M. A., 73
Handwriting, 237–82
    activities to correct, reversals, 281

Handwriting—*Continued*
    connected print script approach to, 255–56
    cursive, 239–240
        equipment for, 253
        Rosenhaus's guiding rules for, 272
        teaching of, 253–59, 271–76
        transfer from manuscript writing to, 252–56
    developmental sequence in acquisition of, by grade, 9–10, 243–44
    D'Nealian program of, 257, 259
    evaluation of student, 259, 266–71
    generating interest in instruction in, 251–52
    historical trends in instruction on, 238–40
    instruction for learning-handicapped students, 280–81
    left-handedness in, 278–80
    legibility of, improving, 276–78
    lessons on, 248, 253–55
    maturational factors in, 241–42
        in intermediate grades, 241–42
        in primary grades, 241
    objectives of instruction in, 237–38
    practice in, 251
    print script, 239–56
        cursive vs., 240
        equipment for, 244–45
        mechanics of, 244
        teaching of, 244–52
        transfer to cursive writing from, 252–56
    readiness for, 241–43
    samples, letter formation, 257–65
    scales, 257, 259–65
    time spent on, 241
    tips for good, five elements of, 267
    worksheets for lessons in, 251
Hanna, P. R., 194, 197
Hearing, 83. *See also* Auding; Listening
Heilman, A. W., 84
History, of English language, 51–58
Hobbs, V., 174
Holistic scoring, 326–27, 333–39
Horn, E., 195–98, 205, 207, 212–13
Huck, C. S., 161
Hyperactive child, 28
Hyperliteracy, 58
Hyphen, 289

Individualized educational program (IEP), 29
Individualized instruction, 10, 30, 41–42, 387
  for reading, 134
Integrating the language arts, 37, 39
Intermediate level students. *See* Students, middle level
It's and its, 209–10

Jacobs, L., 39–40
Jakobson, R., 68, 72
Jennings, S., 154
Johnson, D. D., 197
Johnson, K., 285
Johnson, S., 226
Journalistic writing, 297–98

Kelly, P., 155
Kernel sentence, 299
Kimmel, S., 175
Kindergarten, beginning language skills in, 7
  development of child in, 9
  understanding child in, 5–7
Kinsbourne, M., 65
Kirk, S. A., 28
Kirk, V., 248
Krashen, S. D., 12, 65

Lado, R., 12
Laird, S., 96–97
Lamb, P., 198t
Lamme, L. L., 241
Language. *See also* English; Communication
  acquisition of, 63–73
    critical period hypothesis in, 65
    maturation related to, 63–65
    neurophysiology, psychology and environment in, 65–66
    phonology and morphology in, 68–71
    second language, 66
    syntax and semantics in, 71–73
  characteristics of, 51
  as communication, 36–37
  cultural influences on, 48–50, 60, 102
  development of, 75–77
    metalinguistic, 76–77
    pragmatic, 75–76
    time in, 12

Language—*Continued*
  encouraging correct, 109–11
  expansion of, role of teacher in, 75–77, 108–128
  functional, 42
  functions of (Halliday), 73
  history of English, 51–58
  Indo-European, 52
  learning in the curriculum, 38–39
  principles to understand heritage of, 58–60
  private, 102–103
  proficiency, 14
  public, 102–103
    correct, 108–111
  second. *See* Bilingual education; English, as second language
  self-concept and, 105
  structure vs. function in, 51
  symbolic nature of, 37–38
  system, 50–51
  usage errors, 108–11
Language arts program, 38–45. *See also* Language
  using computer in, 378–82
  definition of, 38–39
  integrating of, 37, 39
  objectives of, 76, 106
  oral, suggestions for basis of, 115–19
  teaching of, 39–45
Language experience approach (LEA), 115
  as context for spelling instruction, 205
  puppet use in, 122
Language readiness, 6
  promotion of readiness, 6
Language skills, balanced, 12
  beginning, 7
  extending, 103, 108–28
Lapp, D., 11, 13, 14, 16, 24–27, 116, 135, 351, 390, 393
Larrick, N., 67, 164
Le Cron, H. C., 174
Learning, external stimulants to, 44–45
  personalized, 41–42
  principles of, 40–45
    developing concepts, 42–44
    retaining what has been learned, 44
    teacher–student interaction, 40–41
  situations for, simulated, 42
Learning disabled students, 28–29
Learning log, 367

Left-handed children, 278–80
  provisions for, 278–80
  writing difficulties of, 278
  writing instruction for, 279–80
Legibility, handwriting, 276–78
Lenneberg, E. H., 63, 65–66, 72–73, 102
Letter writing, 295–97, 307
Library, understanding organization of, 384
  using, 382–84
Limited-English proficient (LEP), 11
Listening, 81–100. *See also* Auding; Auditory discrimination
  analysis of, 83–87
  developmental skills in, 97–99
    classroom activities for, 97–99
    during sharing period, 99
    through questions, 98
  developmental stages in, by age and grade, 9–10
  differences in, 82
  habits in, good and bad, 88–90
  instruction in, 89–90, 95–99
  levels of, 87
  nonlistening and, 82, 94
  parental influence on, 82
  "planned," for young children, 7
  preparing for, 94
  reading and, relationship between, 90–92
  responsibility of teacher in, 89
  roadblocks, checklist of, 94
  skills, diagnosing, 92–93
    guidelines in teaching, 95–96
  strategies for effective, 91
  time spent in, 82
  types of, 87–88
Literacy, dual, 12–13. *See also* Bilingual child; Bilingual education
Literature, 153–86, 353–55
  analysis of children's, 157–59
  book reports on, 177–81
  composition and, 353–55
  concept development and children's, 157
  curiosities of children satisfied by, 157
  discussion of, 160–61
  goal of, program, 154, 158
  important issues in children's, 154–57
    death, 156–57
    elderly stereotyping, 156
    empathy, 156

Literature—*Continued*
  racial stereotyping, 155
  sex stereotyping, 154–55
  parent involvement in, 164–65
  poetry. *See* Poetry
  purpose of teaching, in elementary
      school, 154
  responses to, 159–60
  sources of, 161–64
  teachers as effective storytellers, 158,
      181, 183–86
Loban, W., 39, 64
Lundsteen, S., 86–87, 93–94
Lungren quick software review, 380–
      81

Main idea, in expository writing, 351
  in literature, 161
Manuscript writing. *See* Print script
Manuzio, A., 239
Marland, S., 20
Martin, M., 234
Mavrogenes, N. A., 156
McCarthy, D., 67
Mead, N. A., 106
Media, in classroom, use of, 370–85
  non-print, audio recordings, 370–71
      computer(s), 378–82
      films, 372
      filmstrips, 371–72
      library resources, 382–84
      Reader's Theater, 373–76
      slides, 371
      television, 376
      videocassettes, 372
  print, library resources, 382–84
      magazines, 377
      newspaper, 376
  in teaching critical thinking skills, 377–
      78
Media center, use of, 382–84
Memorization, in dramatics, 125
  of poetry, 165
Memory, auditory, 85, 97
Menyuk, P., 71
Metalinguistic development, 76–77
Metaphor(s), 321, 357
Michaels, S., 117
Mnemonics, as spelling aid, 211–12
Model, of classroom management, 388
Moffett, J., 303, 305, 343

Morphemes, 70–71
  grammatical, 70–71
  lexical, 70
Morphology, 70
Morris, W., 239
Motivation, 40–41
  in effective schools, 346
  games used for, in spelling, 231–32
  in oral reading, 124
  in written composition, 306–308
Murray, D. M., 303

Narrative writing, 318–25, 349–50
New Iowa Spelling Scale, 199
Newbery Medal awards, 162
Newspaper, in the classroom, 376–
      77
  school, 297–98, 332

Oral communication skills development,
      101–129. *See also* Language;
      Speech
  classroom methods for extending, 114–
      28
      creative dramatics, 120–28
      creative-imaginative situations, 119
      discussions, 115–117
      informal conversation, 115
      language experience approach (LEA),
          115
      oral reports, 117–119
  environmental factors in, 108–108
  objectives of, 106
Oral language, as base, in bilingual educa-
      tion, 11
  in family, 64–65
Oral reading, 124. *See also* Reading aloud
  preparation for, 176
  storytelling and, 158, 181
  in verse choir, 170–72
Ordal, C. C., 156
Orthography, 192
  English, 194–96
Orthopedically and other health-impaired
      students, 27–28
Otto, W., 94

Pantomime, 120–21
Parents. *See also* Environment, home
  importance of, in development of listen-
      ing skills, 82

Parents—*Continued*
  in planning for effective classroom man-
      agement, 389
  reading and talking to children by, 44,
      49, 64
Parnes, S., 22
Pearson, P. D., 82–83, 95
Pei, M., 36, 60
Period, 287
Periodicals, using, 384
Personalized learning, 41–42. *See also* Indi-
      vidualized instruction
Personalized program of classroom man-
      agement, 387
  model for, 388
Pestalozzi, J., 242
Phonemes, 69, 137, 194–95
Phonetics, in spelling, 194–96, 207,
      224
  consistencies in, 194–95
  inconsistencies in, 195–96
Phonics, 137–43
  generalizations about, 223–24
      consonant sounds, 139–42. *See also*
          Consonants
      vowel sounds, 142–43
  at preprimer level, 143–45
  at primary level, 145
  in reading program, 137–43
      in basal readers, 138
  sequence of learning in program using,
      138–39
  wrong teaching practices concerning,
      137–38
Phonology, 68–70
  principles of, 69
Piaget, J., 8, 43, 65, 102, 343
Picture book, nine suggestions for reading,
      177
Picture stories, in Orient, 186
Pitch, of voice, in listening, 84
Plays. *See also* Dramatics
  formal dramatic, 125–26
  reading of, 124
Poetry, 165–75
  to enhance writing, 361–67
  file, 173–75
  involving finger play, 172–73
  in modern curriculum, 165
      sample lesson plan for, 167–70
  mosaic, 365

Poetry—*Continued*
oral reading of, by teacher, 166
verse choir, 170–72
suggestions of, for appreciation, 169–70, 173–75
with verse choir, 170–72
Poole, I., 111–12
Pooley, R. C., 110
Power writing, 328–30
Practice and transfer activities, in reading, 148–50
Pragmatics, 75
Primary level students. *See* Students, primary level
Principles of teaching (six), 40–45
Print script, 240–71. *See also* Handwriting
connected, 355–56
definition of, 240
difference between cursive and, 240
mechanics of, 244
transferring to cursive writing from, 252–56
Private language, 102–103
Pronunciation, in choral readings, 126
as dictionary skill, 230–31
accent marks, 230
diacritical marks, 230–31
syllabication, 230
Proofreading, 297–300, 330–31. *See also* Editing
standards for, written report, 297, 311, 330–31
Public language, 102–103
correct, 108–111, 284–85
Punctuation, 287–93
charts and bulletin boards for teaching of, 290–91
classroom activities for, intermediate years, 291–93
primary years, 289, 291
types of, 287–89
apostrophe, 288
colon, 288
comma, 288
hyphen, 289
period, 287
question mark, 287–88
quotation marks, 288
semicolon, 288–89
uses of, 287–89

Puppets, 121–23
in storytelling, 186
Purves, A. C., 159

Question mark, 287–88
Questions, 67, 71–72
in literature appreciation, using, 160
two ways to form, 71
Quotation marks, 288

Racial stereotyping in children's literature, 155
Randolph-Robinson, B., 155
Rankin, P., 82
Rasinski, T. V., 370
Rawlings, M. K., 354
Reader-text interaction, 135–36
Reader's Theater, 127–28, 373–76
Readiness, handwriting, 242–43, 253
language, 6–7
listening, 94–96
reading, 136
teacher responsibility in, 136
Reading, 130–51, 343–49. *See also* Literature; Reading instruction; Reading/writing connection
choral, 170–72
involving group, 172
with refrains, 171–72
clues, part of child's word skills, 134–35
is comprehending, 133–36, 147–50
developmental stages in, by age and grade, 9–10
encouragement of, 158–59, 181
five components of, 343–44
instruction. *See* Reading instruction
link with writing, 344–47. *See also* Reading/writing connection
listening and, relationship between, 90–92
meanings of, 133–34, 343–44
parent involvement in, 44, 164–65
phonics in, 137–43
as process, 135–36, 343–44
silent, 145
summer program for, 164
teacher as most important variable, 131–34

Reading aloud to children. *See also* Oral reading
of picture books, 176–77
preparation for, 176
by teacher, 175–77
of poetry, 166
Reading instruction, 143–47. *See also* Reading/writing connection
at intermediate level, 146–47
at primary level, 143–46
first-reader experiences, 145
preprimer exercises, 143–44
primer exercises, 144–45
second-reader level, 146
third-reader level, 146
Reading log, 355
Reading/writing connection, 342–68
in curriculum, 346–47
instructional methods in, 348–67
at intermediate level, 353–67
fables, using, 355
literature, using, 353–55
poetry, using, 361–67
reading logs, 355
stories, using, 356–57
at primary level, 348–53
expository writing, 350–53
language experience approach (LEA), 348–49
narrative writing, 349–50
similarities in, 344–46
affective domain, 346
cognitive components, 345–46
linguistic elements, 345
perceptual factors, 345
Records, 370–71
used in listening, 94
Reference skills, instruction in, 383–84
Referentiality, 293
Renzulli, J., 21t
Reports, book. *See* Book reports
oral, 117–19, 178–79
demonstrations and directions, 118–19
interviewing and surveying, 118
newstimes, 117
written, 297
proofreading of, 297–99
Rice, J. M., 199
Rich, P. E., 156
Richardson, M., 239
Rinsland, H. D., 196

Robinson, D. J., 156
Root word(s), definition, 214
    dictionary study of, 228–29
    in spelling, 213–16, 228–29
Rosenhaus, M., 272
Roser, N., 162
Ross, R., 374–75
Rossetti, C., 171
Rubrics, for expository writing, 326–27, 333–35

Sager, C., 359–61
Salind, S. J., 156
Scale(s), for scoring writing assignments, 326–27, 333–39. *See also* Scoring
    for elaboration, 361
    holistic, 326–27, 333–39
    New Iowa Spelling, 199
    primary trait, 333, 335–39
        comparison of holistic and, 338
    for vocabulary, 360
Schon, I., 155
Schwa, 196
Scope and sequence chart, bilingual learners, 16–19
Sebasta, S., 373
Second language. *See* Bilingual education; English, as second language
Self-concept, furthered, in teaching of written composition, 286, 332–33
    language and, 105
Self-evaluation checklist, in writing, 359
Semantic map(s), 98, 350
Semantics, 72–73
Semicolon, 288–89
Sequencing instruction, 393
Serra, J. K., 156
Shakespeare, William, 56, 76
Sharing period, 99, 117
    book report as part of, 178
Silent reading, 145
Simile(s), 321
Sims, R., 155
Simulated learning situations, 42
Skinner, B. F., 102
Slavin, R., 387
Slides, 371
    student-made, 371
Slot and filler activities, 299
Sociodrama, 121
Somers, A. B., 160

Sorensen, V., 354–55
Speaking, developmental stages in, by age and grade, 9–10
    writing and, relationship between, 106–107
Speech. *See also* Oral communication
    early development of, 63–65
    instructional activities for all grades, 114–19
    parental, in language acquisition, 64–65
    use of, 66–67
Speech defects, 103–105
    due to cleft palate, 104
    due to malocclusion, 104
    stuttering, 104–105
Speech impaired students, 24–26
Spelling, 188–234
    becoming better in, 225
    as developmental process, 190, 193–94
        stages of, 190–92
            correct, 192
            phonetic, 192
            precommunicative, 190
            semiphonetic, 190–91
            transitional, 192
    dictionary skills needed for, 225–31
        activities with, 227–31
        alphabetical sequence, 226–27
        definitions, 228–30
        guide words, 227–28
        pronunciation, 230–31
    electronic devices and, 233–34
    enriching program in, to challenge all students, 232–34
    environment for enriching, 193–94
    errors in, 207–12
        exercises to correct, 208–11
        frequent causes of, 208
    games for motivating teaching of, 231–32
    generalizations formed in, 212–25
        endings added to root words, 213–16
        most common, 222–24
        silent E, 216–20
    in modern English, 55
    one hundred most used, words, 196
    patterns recommended for elementary level, 197–98
    phonetic consistencies in, 194–95
    phonetic inconsistencies in, 195–96

Spelling—*Continued*
    silent letters in, 196
    skills in, building, 193–94
        major, 189
    teaching of, effective, 189, 199–207
        exercises in, 208–11, 220–22
        lesson plans in, 200–206, 213–22
        self-corrected test for, 205–206
        self-study method for, 207
        systematic instruction for, 205
        test-study plan for, 199–200
    testing, 224
    when to introduce, 198–99
    word knowledge skills in, 189–90
    words to be included in program in, 196–98
    writing approach to, 232–33
"Spelling demons," 234
Squire, J. R., 346
Standard English. *See* English, standard
Standards, writing, 310–11
Stereotyping, in children's literature, 154–57
    death, 156–57
    elderly, 156
    racial, 155
    sex, 154–55
"Story formula," 319–20
Storytelling, 158, 181–86
    of folk tales, 183–84
    teacher effectiveness in, 181, 183–86
        devices for, 184–86
        flannelboard, 184–85
        puppets, 186
Students, 3–29. *See also* Children
    bilingual, 11–20
    gifted, 20–23
    kindergarten, 5–7, 9
    meeting their needs, 29–30
    middle level, 8–10
    primary level, 7–9
    "regular," 4
    special needs, 23–29
        hearing impaired, 23–24
        learning disabled, 28–29
        orthopedically and other health impaired, 27–28
        speech impaired, 24–26
        visually impaired, 26–27
    who they are, 3–29
Study-test plan, for spelling, 200–201

Stuttering, 25
Subject–verb agreement, 293
Syllabication, 230
Syllables, key, of spelling consistencies, 224
Synonyms, activity using, 322
Syntax, in bilingual education, 17–19
  in questions, 71–72
  in relative clauses, 72
  use of, by young children, 64
System(s), of communication, symbol and
    sign, 58
  language as, 50–51, 58

Tape recorders, in spelling, 234
Taylor, L., 171
Teacher, activities for use by. *See* Activities
  listening by, 89
  reading to children by, 175–77
  role of, in grading writing assignments,
    330–38
    in language expansion, 40–44, 75–77,
      108–28
    in poetry writing, 361, 366–67
    in writing, 330, 343
  as storyteller, effective, 181, 183–86
  voice qualities of, 108
Teacher–student interaction, 40–41
Teaching. *See also* Teacher
  the language arts, 39–45
  six principles of, 40–45
  spelling, 199–207
Team learning, 392
Television, effect of, on children, 376
  in home environment, 44–45
  on listening, 82
  on speaking, 103
Test(s), to assess reading program, 150–
    51
  for auditory discrimination, 84, 92
  to determine language proficiency, 14–
    15
  self-corrected, for spelling, 205
Test-study plan, in spelling, 199–200
Thonis, E., 11–13
Thorndike, E. L., 135
To, Too, Two, 207–209
Toothaker, R. E., 157
Topic, in prewriting stage, 352
Trefflinger, D., 22
Typewriter, use of, in elementary grades,
  239

Uninterrupted sustained silent writing,
    329
  power writing, 328–30
Usage, word, definition, 293
  levels of, 284–85

Verse, for use with young children, 170–
    73
Verse choir, to encourage classroom use
    of poetry, 170–72
Videocassettes, 126, 372
Visualization, by the listener, 85–86
  activities for, 98
  in handwriting lesson, 248
Visually-impaired students, 26–27
Vocabulary, development of, 67–68
  of bilingual child, 16–17
  as part of writing process, 308–10
Vocal, language as, 58
Vocalizations, by age, 72
  by infants, 68
Voice, of teacher, qualities of, 108
  disorders, of speech impaired, 25
Vowel sounds, inconsistencies in, 195–96
  in sequence of learning, 138–39
  teaching of, 142–43
Vygotsky, L. S., 343

Wagner, C., 159
Wanat, S. F., 102
Weber-Olson, M., 64
Webster, Noah, 226
Weitzman, L. V., 155
Wells, G., 64
White, N. J., 5
Widdemer, M., 167–68
Wilder, L. I., 49, 354
Wilt, M., 82
Wise, M., 240
Wolf, L. C., 156
Wolfe, R., 207
Word(s). *See also* Spelling; Vocabulary
  Anglo-Saxon, 53–54
  definition, 50
  file of frequently used, 309–10
  foreign, added to English, 57–58
  Latin origin of, 53
  lists of, used most often, 308–309
  pictures, 319, 321, 324–25
  problems, 367
  recognition, 143–44, 146

Word processing, 379
  of compositions, 339–40
Word stimulus method, of writing, 365
Word usage, frequency of, 197
  standards of, 293
"Word wheel," 141
Worksheets, for lesson in handwriting, 251
Writing. *See also* Handwriting; Written
    composition
  for audience and purpose, 296–98, 303,
    335
  classroom time devoted to, 328–30
    USSW, 328–30
  content-area, activities, 367–68
  conventions of, grammar and mechanics
    in, 283–301
  developmental stages in, by age and
    grade, 9–10
  dialogue, 367
  functional approach to, 295–300
  history of, instruction, 305
  in intermediate grades, 318–27
    expository, 325–27
    narrative, 318–25
  journalistic, 297–98
  link with reading, 344–47. *See also* Read-
    ing/writing connection
  oral work important in, 315
  place of modern technology in, 339–40
  "practical" and "personal," 286–87, 295
  in primary grades, 314–18
    examples of children's writing, 316–
      18
  as process, 303–22
    activities to encourage, 353–68
    as basis for classroom instruction,
      305–14
      in groups, 311–12
    editing (revising) phase, 304, 330,
      353
    prewriting phase, 303, 352
    writing or composing phase, 303–
      304, 353
  role of teacher in, 330, 343
  scoring, for writing assignments, 326–
    27, 333–39
    holistic, 326–27, 333–39
    primary trait, 333, 335–39
    sample guide, 336
    samples, 336–39
  speaking and, relationship between,
    106–109

Writing—*Continued*
  spelling and, 232–33
  a story, procedures for, 358
  what is, 343
  word stimulus method of, 365
Written composition. *See also* Writing
  in groups, 311–12
  improving skills, 313

Written composition—*Continued*
  lesson plan for, in six-step sequence, 306
  letters as, 295–97
  motivation for, 306–308, 314–22
  punctuation for, 287–89
  qualities of good, 294
  recognition of, 332

Written composition—*Continued*
  sharing, 312
  syntax used in, in intermediate grades, 294
  vocabulary development in, 308–10

Yatvin, J., 295

DATE DUE

Demco, Inc. 38-293